HANDBOOK OF REGIONAL AND URBAN ECONOMICS
VOLUME 4

HANDBOOKS IN ECONOMICS

7

Series Editors

KENNETH J. ARROW
MICHAEL D. INTRILIGATOR

ELSEVIER
NORTH-HOLLAND
AMSTERDAM • BOSTON • HEIDELBERG • LONDON • NEW YORK • OXFORD
PARIS • SAN DIEGO • SAN FRANCISCO • SINGAPORE • SYDNEY • TOKYO

HANDBOOK OF REGIONAL AND URBAN ECONOMICS

VOLUME 4
CITIES AND GEOGRAPHY

Edited by

J. VERNON HENDERSON

Brown University, Providence, RI

and

JACQUES-FRANÇOIS THISSE

Université catholique de Louvain, Louvain-la-Neuve

2004

ELSEVIER

NORTH-HOLLAND

AMSTERDAM • BOSTON • HEIDELBERG • LONDON • NEW YORK • OXFORD
PARIS • SAN DIEGO • SAN FRANCISCO • SINGAPORE • SYDNEY • TOKYO

ELSEVIER B.V.
Sara Burgerhartstraat 25
P.O. Box 211
1000 AE Amsterdam
The Netherlands

ELSEVIER Inc.
525 B Street, Suite 1900
San Diego, CA 92101-4495
USA

ELSEVIER Ltd
The Boulevard
Langford Lane, Kidlington
Oxford OX5 1GB, UK

ELSEVIER Ltd
84 Theobalds Road
London WC1X 8RR
UK

First edition 2004

Library of Congress Cataloging in Publication Data
A catalog record is available from the Library of Congress.

British Library Cataloguing in Publication Data
A catalogue record is available from the British Library.

ISBN: 0-444-50967-4
ISSN: 0169-7218 (Series)

∞ The paper used in this publication meets the requirements of ANSI/NISO Z39.48-1992 (Permanence of Paper).

Printed in The Netherlands.

INTRODUCTION TO THE SERIES

The aim of the *Handbooks in Economics* series is to produce Handbooks for various branches of economics, each of which is a definitive source, reference, and teaching supplement for use by professional researchers and advanced graduate students. Each Handbook provides self-contained surveys of the current state of a branch of economics in the form of chapters prepared by leading specialists on various aspects of this branch of economics. These surveys summarize not only received results but also newer developments, from recent journal articles and discussion papers. Some original material is also included, but the main goal is to provide comprehensive and accessible surveys. The Handbooks are intended to provide not only useful reference volumes for professional collections but also possible supplementary readings for advanced courses for graduate students in economics.

KENNETH J. ARROW and MICHAEL D. INTRILIGATOR

PUBLISHER'S NOTE

For a complete overview of the Handbooks in Economics Series, please refer to the listing at the end of this volume.

CONTENTS OF THE HANDBOOK

VOLUME 1: REGIONAL ECONOMICS
P. NIJKAMP, Editor

PART 1 – LOCATIONAL ANALYSIS

PART 2 – SPECIFIC URBAN MARKETS

PART 4: THE LONG-RUN VIEW ON CITIES AND GEOGRAPHY

CONTENTS OF VOLUME 4

PART 2: THE DESIGN OF LOCAL GOVERNMENTS AND POLICIES

FOREWORD

A salient feature of the spatial economy is the extreme variation in land use intensity. This may be illustrated by contrasting rural areas and small towns in the American Plains with megalopolises, such as New York or Tokyo that accommodate a huge range of consumption and production activities. In the European Union, the top 38 cities cover 0.6% of its territory and, in 2000, accommodate about 25% of its population and about 30% of its GDP. In Japan, the economy is very much dominated by its core regions, formed by the five prefectures containing the three main metropolitan areas: Tokyo and Kanagawa prefectures, Aichi prefecture (containing Nagoya MA), and Osaka and Hyogo prefectures. In 1998, these regions account for only 5.2% of the area of Japan, but for 33% of its population and 42% of its GDP. In the United States, census data show that, in 1997, 53% of the American population lived in the top 40 MSAs, which accommodate 48% of the manufacturing employment. In 1992 paved and built land accounts for a mere 1.9% of the area of the United States. This volume provides a broad overview of the rapid progress made by economists during the last decade in developing a better understanding of

(a) why economic activities are so spatially concentrated, and
(b) what are the consequences of such an unequal distribution for economic agents and the efficiency of the space-economy.

In order to reach our objective, we focus on two different spatial units:

(i) *cities*, in which land consumption and spatial externalities are crucial, and
(ii) *multi-regional systems*, in which trade and factor mobility are the key elements.

This division has dictated the general organization of the Handbook.

While urban economics has grown rapidly as a field since the late 1960s and regional economics has a long tradition, one of the features of recent contributions that make them so exciting to the profession is their strong connection to other recent developments in modern economics. First of all, modern urban economics and economic geography start with firms and consumers/workers operating in either type of space mentioned above. The approach is, therefore, rooted in microeconomics. In economic geography à la Krugman, the equilibrium outcome is seldom unique. Even though this issue is not new in economic theory, it is fair to say that the implications of multiple equilibria are now far better understood and well illustrated in spatial modeling. Hence, the state of a spatial economy seems to be path-dependent and contingent. Second, while economic geography is closely related to trade theory, it is also very much connected to modern industrial organization. In particular, the economic geography of a territory is recognized now to be related to the way firms organize their production activities, management, and outsourcing, within and across firms. There are also strong links to recent intellectual developments such as the new growth theories, where many scholars see cities as the engine of growth, as well as theories on social networks and other forms of local interactions, the urban neighborhood being the place where many non-market relationships are developed. Last, another distinctive feature of the recent contributions to regional and urban economics is the growing number of empirical studies, which aim at testing theories, using modern econometric methods. Both types of studies are covered in this volume in almost equal shares. Note also that a few chapters deal with the geography as well as with the urban history of different areas in the world, in a attempt to make the scope of the field broader and richer in terms of perspectives for future research, as well as to point out how wide spread recent developments are in terms of touching scholars around the world.

In choosing authors, we have focused on recruiting people who are at the center of these new developments, both young and more mature scholars. Many of the co-author pairings are people who have not written together before and others exploit well-known teams. The authors have been wonderful in producing a set of chapters that we find absolutely outstanding, which of all truly focus on developments made over the last decade.

Editing a Handbook is somewhat of a collective adventure. In preparing this volume, we were given two great opportunities to have the chapters presented in two conferences. A first set of papers was presented at the 49th North American Meeting of the Regional Science Association International held in Porto Rico in November 2002. We thank Hesham Abdel-Rahman for turning over so many of the annual sessions which he organizes to us. The other chapters were presented in a workshop held in Paris in December 2002. This latter conference was co-organized by the *Centre for Economic Policy Research*, the Federation Jourdan in Paris and the Institut National de Recherche Agronomique (France), the financial support of which is gratefully acknowledged. These conferences allowed authors to get widespread and intensive feedback, before preparing final versions. Finally, the two editors have enjoyed the hospitality of the Sauder School of Business, University of British Columbia in July 2003 when preparing the final version of the Handbook. Given the scientific background of the editors, the fact that everything was organized in very attractive places should come as a surprise.

J. Vernon Henderson
Jacques-François Thisse[1]
Editors

[1] The second editor thanks the Ministère de l'éducation, de la recherche et de la formation (Communauté française de Belgique), Convention 00/05-262, for financial support.

PART 1

CITIES AND URBAN SYSTEMS: FROM THEORY TO FACTS

Chapter 48

MICRO-FOUNDATIONS OF URBAN AGGLOMERATION ECONOMIES

GILLES DURANTON[1]

Department of Geography and Environment, London School of Economics, Houghton Street, London WC2A 2AE, UK
e-mail: g.duranton@lse.ac.uk
url: http://cep.lse.ac.uk/~duranton

DIEGO PUGA[2]

Department of Economics, University of Toronto, 150 Saint George Street, Toronto, Ontario M5S 3G7, Canada
e-mail: d.puga@utoronto.ca
url: http://dpuga.economics.utoronto.ca

Contents

[1] Also affiliated with the Centre for Economic Policy Research and the Centre for Economic Performance at the London School of Economics.
[2] Also affiliated with the Canadian Institute for Advanced Research, the Centre for Economic Policy Research, and the National Bureau of Economic Research.

Handbook of Regional and Urban Economics, Volume 4. Edited by J.V. Henderson and J.F. Thisse

DOI: 10.1016/S0169-7218(04)07048-0

Abstract

This handbook chapter studies the theoretical micro-foundations of urban agglomeration economies. We distinguish three types of micro-foundations, based on sharing, matching, and learning mechanisms. For each of these three categories, we develop one or more core models in detail and discuss the literature in relation to those models. This allows us to give a precise characterisation of some of the main theoretical underpinnings of urban agglomeration economies, to discuss modelling issues that arise when working with these tools, and to compare different sources of agglomeration economies in terms of the aggregate urban outcomes they produce as well as in terms of their normative implications.

Keywords

cities, agglomeration, increasing returns, micro-foundations

JEL classification: R12, R13, R32

1. Introduction

Only 1.9% of the land area of the United States was built-up or paved by 1992. Yet, despite the wide availability of open space, almost all recent development is less than one kilometre away from earlier development. Not only does the proximity of earlier development matter, but so does its density. Places where about one-half of the land in the immediate vicinity is already built-up seem to be most attractive for new development [Burchfield et al. (2003)].

One cannot make sense of this sort of numbers, of the extent to which people cluster together in cities and towns, without considering some form of agglomeration economies or localised aggregate increasing returns. While space is not homogeneous, it is futile to try to justify the marked unevenness of development solely on the basis of space being naturally heterogeneous: the land on which Chicago has been built, for instance, is not all that different from other places on the shore of Lake Michigan that have been more sparsely developed [see Cronon (1991)]. And, once we abstract from the heterogeneity of the underlying space, without indivisibilities or increasing returns, any competitive equilibrium in the presence of transport costs will feature only fully autarchic locations [this result, due to Starrett (1978), is known as the spatial impossibility theorem].[1] People in each of these locations, like Robinson Crusoe, will produce all goods at a small scale for self-consumption. Re-stated, without some form of increasing returns we cannot reconcile cities with trade.

While increasing returns are essential to understand why there are cities, it is hard to think of any single activity or facility subject to large-enough indivisibilities to justify the existence of cities. Thus, one of the main challenges for urban economists is to uncover mechanisms by which small-scale indivisibilities (or any other small-scale non-convexities) aggregate up to localised aggregate increasing returns capable of sustaining cities. We can then regard cities as the outcome of a trade-off between agglomeration economies or localised aggregate increasing returns and the costs of urban congestion.

This is the object of this chapter: to study mechanisms that provide the microeconomic foundations of urban agglomeration economies. We focus on the theoretical underpinnings of urban agglomeration economies, while the chapter by Rosenthal and Strange (2004) in this volume discusses the corresponding empirical evidence.

By studying the micro-foundations of urban agglomeration economies, we are looking inside the black box that justifies the very existence of cities. We regard this as one of the fundamental quests in urban economics for three main reasons. First, it is only by studying what gives rise to urban agglomeration economies – rather than merely stating that they exist – that we gain any real insight into why there are cities. Second, alternative micro-foundations cannot be regarded as interchangeable contents for the black box. The micro-foundations of urban agglomeration economies interact with other building blocks of urban models in ways that we cannot recognise unless they are

[1] See Ottaviano and Thisse (2004) in this volume for a detailed discussion of Starrett's (1978) theorem.

explicitly stated. For instance, the composition of cities typically emerges as a consequence of the scope of different sources of agglomeration economies and their interaction with other aspects of individual behaviour. Third, different micro-foundations have very different welfare and policy implications. If we begin building an urban model by postulating an aggregate production function with increasing returns, we can only take this function as given. If instead we derive this aggregate production function from first principles, we may see that its efficiency can be improved upon. The means for achieving such an improvement will depend on the specifics of individual behaviour and technology. Thus, while different assumptions regarding individual behaviour and technology may support similar aggregate outcomes, the normative implications of alternative micro-foundations can differ substantially.

Urban agglomeration economies are commonly classified into those arising from labour-market interactions, from linkages between intermediate- and final-goods suppliers, and from knowledge spill-overs, loosely following the three main examples provided by Marshall (1890) in his discussion of the sources of agglomeration economies.[2] While this may be a sensible starting point for an empirical appraisal, we do not regard this as a particularly useful basis for a taxonomy of theoretical mechanisms. Consider, for instance, a model in which agglomeration facilitates the matching between firms and inputs. These inputs may be labelled workers, intermediates, or ideas. Depending on the label chosen, a matching model of urban agglomeration economies could be presented as a formalisation of either one of Marshall's three basic *sources* of agglomeration economies even though it captures a single *mechanism*. Since the focus of this chapter is on theory, we want to distinguish theories by the mechanism driving them rather than by the labels tagged to model components in particular papers. With this objective in mind, we distinguish three types of micro-foundations, based on *sharing*, *matching*, and *learning* mechanisms.[3]

Our discussion of micro-foundations of urban agglomeration economies based on sharing mechanisms deals with sharing indivisible facilities, sharing the gains from the wider variety of input suppliers that can be sustained by a larger final-goods industry, sharing the gains from the narrower specialisation that can be sustained with larger production, and sharing risks. In discussing micro-foundations based on matching, we study mechanisms by which agglomeration improves either the expected quality of matches or the probability of matching, and alleviates hold-up problems. Finally,

[2] Marshall is arguably the best known and most influent of the early analysts of agglomeration. However Smith (1776) can be credited with the first analysis of the benefits from agglomeration, albeit with a more narrow argument relying on the division of labour. Von Thünen (1826) pursued and extended his work. He also proposed original arguments building on the interaction between fixed costs and transport costs not far from some of those developed below as highlighted by Fujita (2000).

[3] Marshall (1890, IV.X.3) successively discusses knowledge spill-overs, linkages between input suppliers and final producers, and labour-market interactions. However, his discussion of each of these sources of agglomeration economies highlights a different mechanism. Spill-overs are discussed in relation to the acquisition of skills by workers and their learning about new technologies. The discussion of linkages explicitly mentions the benefits of sharing intermediate suppliers producing under increasing returns. Finally, the fist part of his labour-market argument points at a matching mechanism.

when we look at micro-foundations based on learning we discuss mechanisms based on the generation, the diffusion, and the accumulation of knowledge.[4]

For each of the three main categories of this taxonomy, sharing, matching, and learning, we develop one or more core models in detail and discuss the literature in relation to those models. This allows us to give a precise characterisation of some of the main theoretical underpinnings of urban agglomeration economies, to illustrate some important modelling issues that arise when working with these tools, and to compare different sources of agglomeration economies in terms of the aggregate urban outcomes they produce as well as in terms of their normative implications.

2. Sharing

2.1. *Sharing indivisible goods and facilities*

To justify the existence of cities, perhaps the simplest argument is to invoke the existence of indivisibilities in the provision of certain goods or facilities. Consider a simple example: an ice hockey rink. This is an expensive facility with substantial fixed costs: it needs to be of regulated dimensions, have a sophisticated refrigeration system to produce and maintain the ice, a Zamboni to resurface it, etc. Few individuals, if any, would hold a rink for themselves. And while having a community of 1000 people share a rink is feasible, building a rink for each of those people at 1/1000th of the usual scale is not. An ice hockey rink is therefore an indivisible facility that can be shared by many users. It is also an excludable good, in the sense that use of the rink can be limited to members of a club or a community. At the same time, as the size of the community using the rink grows, the facility will be subject to increasing crowding. Crowding will take two forms. First, there will be capacity constraints when too many people simultaneously try to use the facility. Second, and more interesting in an urban context, crowding will also occur because the facility needs to be located somewhere and, as the size of the community of users grows, some of those users will be located too far away from the facility.[5]

The problems associated with the provision of this type of facilities were first highlighted by Buchanan (1965). They are the subject of a voluminous literature referred to as club theory (or theory of local public goods when the spatial dimension is explicitly taken into account). The main focus of this very large literature is on equilibrium concepts (competitive, free mobility, Nash, core) and policy instruments. These issues are

[4] In this chapter, we discuss only models in which both the demand and supply of factors (mainly labour) are endogenous. In particular, we do not discuss the strategic location literature which takes the location of consumers as given. This literature is discussed in depth by Gabszewicz and Thisse (1992).

[5] Note that this example is representative of a wide class of shared facilities that are excludable and subject to indivisibilities and crowding. These range from parks, museums, opera houses, and schools, to airports, train stations, and even power plants.

well beyond the scope of this chapter and are thoroughly reviewed in Scotchmer (2002). Here we just describe briefly how one large indivisibility could provide a very simple formal motive for the existence of cities.

Consider then a shared indivisible facility. Once the large fixed cost associated with this facility has been incurred, it provides an essential good to consumers at a constant marginal cost. However, to enjoy this good consumers must commute between their residence and the facility. We can immediately see that there is a trade-off between the gains from sharing the fixed cost of the facility among a larger number of consumers and the costs of increasingly crowding the land around the facility (e.g., because of road congestion, small lot sizes, etc.). We may think of a city as the equilibrium outcome of such trade-off. In this context, cities would be no more than spatial clubs organised to share a common local public good or facility.[6]

This 'large indivisibility' argument motivates urban increasing returns by directly assuming increasing returns at the aggregate level. Large indivisibilities in the provision of some public good are just one possible motivation for this. A common alternative is to assume large indivisibilities in some production activity. This corresponds to the idea of a factory-town, where large fixed costs create internal increasing returns in a production activity that employs the workforce of an entire city whose size is bounded by crowding. There is in fact a long tradition of modelling cities as the outcome of large indivisibilities in production [Koopmans (1957), Mills (1967), Mirrlees (1972)]. And since they constitute such a simple modelling device, factory-towns are still used as the simplest possible prototype cities to study a variety of issues, including fiscal decentralisation [Henderson and Abdel-Rahman (1991)], urban production patterns [Abdel-Rahman and Fujita (1993)], and economic growth in a system of cities [Duranton (2000)]. However, it is fair to say that factory-towns are empirically the exception rather than the rule in most countries.

Finally, it has been suggested that this type of large indivisibilities could apply to the existence of market places [Wang (1990), Berliant and Wang (1993), Wang (1993), Berliant and Konishi (2000), Konishi (2000)].[7] Indeed, economic historians

6 We do not worry here about the financing of the shared facility. Let us simply note that under competitive facility provision financed by local capitalisation in the land market, the equilibrium is efficient. This result is known as the Henry George Theorem [Flatters, Henderson and Mieszkowski (1974), Stiglitz (1977), Arnott and Stiglitz (1979)] and is discussed at length in Fujita (1989) and in Fujita and Thisse (2002). An equivalent result applies to the case of a factory-town discussed below [Serck-Hanssen (1969), Starrett (1974), Vickrey (1977)].

7 These papers typically consider a small finite number of connected regions with differing endowments. Because of Ricardian comparative advantage, some marketplaces emerge and they are labelled cities. Wang (1990) establishes the existence and optimality of a competitive equilibrium with one endogenous marketplace in a pure exchange economy with exogenous consumer location. Berliant and Wang (1993) allow for endogenous location of consumers in a three-region economy. Wang (1993) also allows for endogenous location in a two-region economy with immobile goods. Berliant and Konishi (2000) revisit this problem in a production economy. Allowing for multiple marketplaces and differences in transport costs and marketplace set-up costs, they establish some existence and efficiency results. Finally, Konishi (2000) shows how asym-

[e.g., Bairoch (1988)] have long recognised the crucial role played by cities in market exchange. However, the hypothesis of large indivisibilities in marketplaces is once again at best a small part of the puzzle of why cities exist.

To summarise, given Starrett's (1978) result that without some form of increasing returns we cannot explain agglomeration within a homogeneous area, the easiest route to take in justifying the existence of cities is to assume increasing returns at the city level by means of a large indivisibility. While large indivisibilities are useful modelling devices when the main object of interest is not the foundations of urban agglomeration economies, they side-step the issue of what gives rise to increasing returns at the level of cities. Cities facilitate sharing many indivisible public goods, production facilities, and marketplaces. However, it would be unrealistic to justify cities on the basis of a single activity subject to extremely large indivisibilities. The challenge in urban modelling is to propose mechanisms whereby different activities subject to small non-convexities gather in the same location to form a city. Stated differently, *micro-founded models of cities need to reconcile plausible city-level increasing returns with non-degenerate market structures.*

2.2. *Sharing the gains from variety*

In this section, we first derive an aggregate production function that exhibits aggregate increasing returns due to input sharing despite constant returns to scale in perfectly competitive final production. This is based on Ethier's (1982) production-side version of Dixit and Stiglitz (1977). Aggregate increasing returns arise here from *the productive advantages of sharing a wider variety* of differentiated intermediate inputs produced by a monopolistically competitive industry à la Chamberlin (1933). We then embed this model in an urban framework following Abdel-Rahman and Fujita (1990). This allows us to derive equilibrium city sizes resulting from a trade-off between aggregate increasing returns and congestion costs as well as a basic result on urban specialisation due to Henderson (1974).

2.2.1. *From firm-level to aggregate increasing returns*

There are m sectors, super-indexed by $j = 1, \dots, m$. In each sector, perfectly competitive firms produce goods for final consumption under constant returns to scale. Final producers use intermediate inputs, which are specific to each sector and enter into plants' technology with a constant elasticity of substitution $(1 + \epsilon^j)/\epsilon^j$, where $\epsilon^j > 0$.

metries in transport costs can lead to the formation of hub-cities where workers employed in the transport sector agglomerate. The large indivisibilities assumed in these papers presumably reflect not so much fixed costs of market infrastructure but other considerations, such as the advantages of centralised quality assurance [see Cronon (1991), and the chapter by Kim and Margo (2004), in this volume for a discussion of how this sort of consideration helped Chicago become the main metropolis of the American Midwest].

Thus, aggregate final production in sector j is given by

$$Y^j = \left\{ \int_0^{n^j} \left[x^j(h)\right]^{1/(1+\epsilon^j)} \mathrm{d}h \right\}^{1+\epsilon^j}, \tag{1}$$

where $x^j(h)$ denotes the aggregate amount of intermediate h used and n^j is the 'number' (mass) of intermediate inputs produced in equilibrium, to be endogenously determined.

As in Ethier (1982), intermediate inputs are produced by monopolistically competitive firms à la Dixit and Stiglitz (1977). Each intermediate producer's technology is described by the production function

$$x^j(h) = \beta^j l^j(h) - \alpha^j, \tag{2}$$

where $l^j(h)$ denotes the firm's labour input, β^j is the marginal productivity of labour, and α^j is a fixed cost in sector j. Thus, there are increasing returns to scale in the production of each variety of intermediates.[8] This and the fact that there is an unlimited range of intermediate varieties that could be produced and no economies of scope imply that each intermediate firm produces just one variety and that no variety is produced by more than one firm.

Let us denote by $q^j(h)$ the price of sector j intermediate variety h. The minimisation of final production costs $\int_0^{n^j} q^j(h)x^j(h)\,\mathrm{d}h$ subject to the technological constraint of Equation (1) yields the following conditional intermediate input demand:

$$x^j(h) = \frac{[q^j(h)]^{-(1+\epsilon^j)/\epsilon^j} Y^j}{\{\int_0^{n^j} [q^j(h')]^{-1/\epsilon^j}\,\mathrm{d}h'\}^{1+\epsilon^j}}. \tag{3}$$

It is immediate from (3) that each intermediate firm faces an elasticity of demand with respect to its own price of $-(1+\epsilon^j)/\epsilon^j$. Hence, the profit-maximising price for each intermediate is a fixed relative markup over marginal cost:

$$q^j = \frac{1+\epsilon^j}{\beta^j} w^j, \tag{4}$$

where w^j denotes the wage in sector j. Note that we have dropped index h since all variables take identical values for all intermediate suppliers in the same sector.

There is free entry and exit of intermediate suppliers. This drives their maximised profits to zero: $q^j x^j - w^j l^j = 0$. Using Equations (2) and (4) to expand this expression and solving for x^j shows that the only level of output by an intermediate producer consistent with zero profits is

$$x^j = \frac{\alpha^j}{\epsilon^j}. \tag{5}$$

[8] Obviously, technology could also be described in terms of the labour required to produce any level of output, $l^j(h) = (x^j(h) - \alpha^j)/\beta^j$, as it is often done following Dixit and Stiglitz (1977).

This, together with (2), implies that each intermediate producer hires $l^j = \alpha^j(1+\epsilon^j)/(\beta^j\epsilon^j)$ workers. Hence, the equilibrium number of intermediate producers in sector j is

$$n^j = \frac{L^j}{l^j} = \frac{\beta^j\epsilon^j}{\alpha^j(1+\epsilon^j)}L^j, \tag{6}$$

where L^j denotes total labour supply in intermediate sector j.

By choice of units of intermediate output, we can set $\beta^j = (1+\epsilon^j)(\alpha^j/\epsilon^j)^{\epsilon^j/(1+\epsilon^j)}$. Substituting (6) and (5) into (1) yields aggregate production in sector j as

$$Y^j = \left[n^j\left(x^j\right)^{1/(1+\epsilon^j)}\right]^{1+\epsilon^j} = \left(L^j\right)^{1+\epsilon^j}. \tag{7}$$

This obviously exhibits aggregate increasing returns to scale at the sector level. The reason is that an increase in the labour input of sector j must be associated with more intermediate producers, as can be seen from (6); and, by (1), final producers become more productive when they have access to a wider range of varieties. Re-stated, *an increase in final production by virtue of sharing a wider variety of intermediate suppliers requires a less-than-proportional increase in primary factors.*[9]

2.2.2. *Urban structure*

Next, following Abdel-Rahman and Fujita (1990), let us place in an urban context the production structure we have just described. Consider an economy with a continuum of potential locations for cities, sub-indexed by i.[10]

Let us model the internal spatial structure of each city in a very simple fashion. Production in each city takes place at a single point, defined as the Central Business District

[9] Papageorgiou and Thisse (1985) propose an alternative approach in which agglomeration also relies on sharing the gains from variety. Their approach, which builds on a shopping framework, highlights well the importance of interactions between firms and households. While the shopping behaviour of individuals is exogenously imposed rather than derived from a well-specified preference structure, it has later been shown to be consistent with random utility maximisation [Anderson, de Palma and Thisse (1992)].

[10] Here we follow Abdel-Rahman and Fujita (1990) in embedding the production structure described above in a system of cities. In earlier papers, Abdel-Rahman (1988), Fujita (1988), and Rivera-Batiz (1988) embed similar production structures in an urban framework with a single city. The details of these pioneering papers differ slightly from those of our presentation. Instead of having the monopolistically competitive sector supplying differentiated intermediates, Abdel-Rahman (1988) has this sector producing differentiated final goods. They are aggregated with a constant elasticity of substitution into a sub-utility function, which enters as an argument into a Cobb–Douglas utility function together with land and a traded good produced under constant return. Also, our specification of the urban structure is a bit simpler than his, as we impose a fixed size for residences. Rivera-Batiz (1988) considers two sources of agglomeration economies, by assuming gains from variety both at the level of intermediates (like here) and of final goods. Finally, Fujita (1988) uses a different specification for the gains from variety, which bears resemblance with the entropy functions used in information theory. Another difference is that in his model both firms and households compete for urban land, whereas we only consider a residential land market. Also, he assumes that goods are imperfectly mobile within the city, which allows for non-monocentric urban structures.

(CBD).[11] Surrounding each city's CBD, there is a line with residences of unit length. Residents commute from their residence to the CBD and back at a cost. In practise, commuting costs include both the direct monetary cost of travelling and the opportunity cost of the time spent on the journey [Small (1992)]. However, let us simplify by assuming that the only cost of commuting is the opportunity cost of time.[12] Specifically, each worker loses in commuting a fraction of her unit of working time equal to 2τ times the distance travelled in going to the CBD and back home ($\tau > 0$).

Each worker chooses her place of residence so as to maximise utility given her income and the land rent function in the city. Because of fixed lot size, this is equivalent to choosing residence so as to maximise net income. Thus, a worker in sector j in city i maximises $w_i^j(1 - 4\tau s) - R_i(s)$ with respect to s, where s is the distance to the CBD and $R_i(s)$ is the differential land rent in city i for a residence located at distance s from the CBD.

The possibility of arbitrage across residential locations both within and across sectors ensures that at the residential equilibrium the sum of commuting cost and land rent expenditures is the same for all residents with the same wage; that workers sort themselves according to their wage, with higher-paid workers (who have a higher opportunity cost of commuting time) living closer to the CBD; that the city is symmetric and the city edges are at a distance $N_i/2$ of the CBD (where N_i is total population in city i); and that the land rent function [i.e., the upper envelope of all bid-rent functions, Alonso (1964)] is continuous, convex, and piece-wise linear.[13] Without loss of generality, the rent at the city edges is normalised to zero. Integrating land rent over the city yields total land rent:

$$R_i = \int_{-N_i/2}^{N_i/2} R_i(s)\,\mathrm{d}s. \tag{8}$$

The net amount of labour available to sector j at the CBD of city i, L_i^j, is equal to the number of workers employed in that sector minus their commuting time. Summing across sectors immediately implies the following expression relating labour supply net

[11] We take the existence of a CBD as given. For contributions that derive this endogenously, see Borukhov and Hochman (1977), Fujita and Ogawa (1982), and the additional references provided in Section 4.2.2.

[12] This allows us to solve for equilibrium city sizes without having to track output prices in a multiple-sector setting. In Section 3.1, we explore the opposite simplification of having only a monetary cost of commuting.

[13] Models with a richer internal urban structure often consider endogenous differences across residences in terms of their size and land intensity [see Brueckner (1987) for a review]. Then, residences closer to the CBD are not only more expensive but also smaller and more land-intensive. Matters are further complicated when one considers durable housing and the possibility of redevelopment [see Brueckner (2000) for a review]. There is also a large literature analysing the sorting of residents across neighbourhoods. It considers how income affects the valuation of land, that of leisure foregone in commuting, and that of access to amenities, all of which contribute to determining residential location [see Beckmann (1969), Brueckner (1987), and Brueckner, Thisse and Zenou (1999)].

of commuting costs, $\sum_{j=1}^{m} L_i^j$, to population, N_i:

$$\sum_{j=1}^{m} L_i^j = N_i(1 - \tau N_i). \tag{9}$$

Finally, workers can move at no cost across sectors as well as across cities. Income from land rents is equally distributed across all local residents.

2.2.3. *Urban specialisation*

One important difference between our presentation of this framework and the original contribution of Abdel-Rahman and Fujita (1990) is that we consider more than one sector. This allows us to derive Henderson's (1974) result on urban specialisation, which can be seen as a statement on the scope of urban agglomeration economies. This type of agglomeration economies based on the proximity to firms in the same sector is often labelled 'localisation economies'. For simplicity, assume that final goods can be freely traded across cities.[14] Intermediate goods, on the other hand, can only be used by local firms.[15]

We now prove that *in this simple set-up each city must be specialised in a single sector in equilibrium*. Suppose, on the contrary, that there is more than one active sector in some city. Zero profits in final production imply that $w_i^j L_i^j = P^j Y_i^j$, where P^j is the price of the final good in sector j. Substituting into this equation our expression for aggregate output (7), we can solve for the wage per unit of net labour paid by firms in sector j:

$$w_i^j = P^j \left(L_i^j\right)^{\epsilon^j}. \tag{10}$$

The possibility of arbitrage by workers across sectors and residences ensures the equalisation of this wage across all active sectors in all cities. Starting from a configuration where this equality holds, consider a small perturbation in the distribution of workers across sectors in some city. It follows immediately from (10) that sectors that have gained employment will now pay higher wages as a result of having more intermediate suppliers and thus a higher level of output per worker. Net income will be further enhanced by the advantage this higher wage provides in the residential housing market. That will allow firms in this enlarged sector to attract even more workers. Sectors that have lost employment will instead provide lower wages and income and, as a result, lose even more workers. Thus, in order to be stable with respect to small perturbations in the

[14] We discuss below the consequences of relaxing this assumption. Basically, introducing trade costs in final goods provides a static motivation for urban diversification.

[15] If intermediates are tradeable across cities final producers in each sector still benefit from having greater local employment and more local firms engaged in intermediate production, as long as the intermediates produced locally are available at a lower transport cost than those purchased from remote locations and represent a non-negligible share of the total set of intermediates.

distribution of workers, any equilibrium must be characterised by full specialisation of each and every city in a single sector.

2.2.4. *Equilibrium city sizes*

We now turn to calculating equilibrium city sizes. Consider how the utility of individual workers in a city varies with the city's population. With free trade in final goods and homothetic preferences, utility is an increasing function of consumption expenditure. In equilibrium, all workers receive the same consumption expenditure because the lengthier commuting for those living further away from the CBD is exactly offset by lower land rents. Substituting the expression for net labour of Equation (9) into the aggregate production function of Equation (7), dividing by N_i, and using the urban specialisation result yields consumption expenditure for each worker as

$$c_i^j = P^j (N_i^j)^{\epsilon^j} (1 - \tau N_i^j)^{1+\epsilon^j}. \tag{11}$$

Note that land rents do not appear in this expression because each worker receives an income from her share of local land rents equal to the rent of the average local worker. While individual land rents differ from the average, lower rents for those living further away from the CBD are exactly offset by lengthier commuting.

As shown in Figure 1, utility is a single-peaked function of city size which reaches its maximum for population

$$N^{j*} = \frac{\epsilon^j}{(1+2\epsilon^j)\tau}. \tag{12}$$

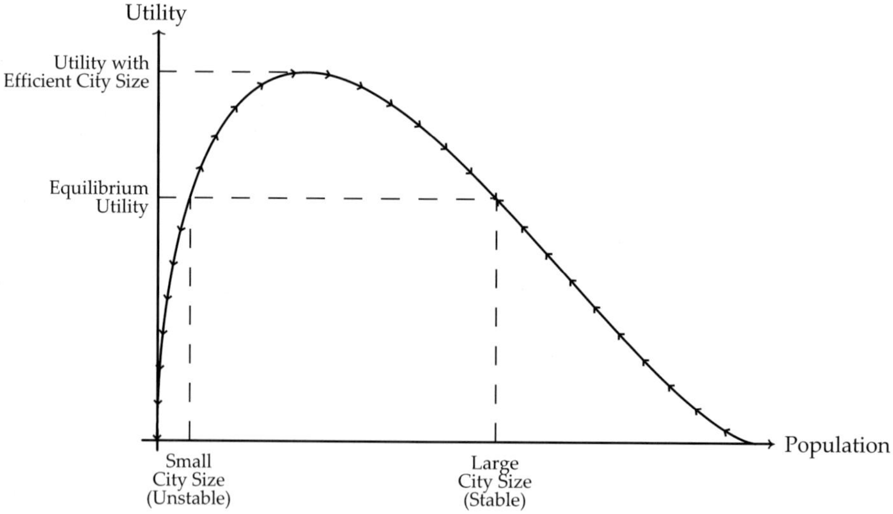

Figure 1. Utility as a function of city size.

The efficient size of a city is the result of a trade-off between urban agglomeration economies and urban crowding. Efficient city size N^{j*} decreases with commuting costs as measured by τ and increases with the extent of aggregate increasing returns as measured by ϵ^j.[16] An immediate corollary of this is that the efficient size is larger for cities specialised in sectors that exhibit greater aggregate increasing returns [as argued by Henderson (1974)].

In equilibrium, *all cities of the same specialisation are of equal size and this size is not smaller than the efficient size*. To see this, notice first that cities of a given specialisation are of at most two different sizes in equilibrium (one above and one below the efficient size). This follows from (11) and utility equalisation across cities. However, cities below the efficient size will not survive small perturbations in the distribution of workers – as illustrated by the arrows in Figure 1, those that gain population will get closer to the efficient size and attract even more workers while those that lose population will get further away from the efficient size and lose even more workers. The same does not apply to cities above the efficient size – in this case, those that gain population will get further away from the efficient size while those that lose population will get closer. The combination of free mobility with a stability requirement therefore implies the result that cities of the same specialisation are of equal size and too large.

The result that cities are too large is the consequence of a coordination failure with respect to city creation. Everyone would prefer, say, three cities of the efficient size to two cities 50% above the efficient size. But an individual worker is too small to create a city on her own and so far there is no mechanism for her to coordinate with other workers. Various mechanisms for city creation would achieve efficient city sizes. Two such mechanisms are competitive profit-maximising developers and active local governments [see Henderson (1985) and Becker and Henderson (2000)]. Once this coordination failure is resolved, the equilibrium is fully efficient.

Efficiency in this type of models depends on three sorts of assumptions: those about city formation, those about urban structure, and those about the micro-foundations of urban agglomeration economies. As just mentioned, the main issue with city formation is the ability to resolve a coordination failure. Regarding internal urban structure, the main issue in the literature is who collects land rents. If landlords are non-resident ('absentee') part of the benefits of local agglomeration are captured by agents who are unaffected by the costs of local crowding. The assumption of common land ownership used in this section resolves this source of inefficiency [Pines and Sadka (1986)].[17] An additional issue is whether congestion distorts individual choices [Oron, Pines and Sheshinski (1973), Solow (1973)]. Finally, what has received almost no attention in the literature is the fact that the source of urban agglomeration economies also matters for

[16] As ϵ^j increases, the elasticity of substitution across the varieties of intermediate inputs $(1+\epsilon^j)/\epsilon^j$ falls, so that there is a greater benefit from having access to a wider range of varieties.

[17] Under common land ownership the share of land rents received by each household is equal to the marginal externality arising from urban agglomeration economies. Thus, the redistributed land rents act as a Pigouvian subsidy.

the efficiency of equilibrium [a notable exception is the introduction to Chapter 8 of Fujita (1989)]. We have chosen to start with a model in which the micro-foundations of agglomeration economies create no inefficiencies – more accurately, the inefficiencies present exactly cancel out.[18] In Section 3.1, we will show that different micro-foundations have very different welfare implications.

2.2.5. *Cross-sector interactions and trade costs*

The urban specialisation result derived above relies crucially on two assumptions: that inputs are only shared within and not across sectors and that trade in final goods is costless while trade in intermediate inputs is infinitely costly. In order to make this type of model consistent with the empirical coexistence of diversified and specialised cities and to incorporate space in a more meaningful way, several contributions have extended it to allow for cross-sector interactions and for trade costs. Here we just mention some of these extensions. For a more detailed discussion, see Abdel-Rahman and Anas (2004) in this volume as well as Duranton and Puga (2000).

A first set of extensions to the basic input sharing framework allows for cross-sector interactions, either by incorporating non-tradeable goods produced in all cities [Abdel-Rahman (1990)], or by assuming economies of scope that result in cost savings when several sectors operate in the same city [Abdel-Rahman (1994)]. Both extensions provide a static motive for urban diversity. Another static motive for urban diversity arises in the presence of transport costs. These are incorporated in a version of the input-sharing framework with discrete space by Abdel-Rahman (1996). This extension highlights the trade-off between the gains from urban specialisation due to localisation economies and the transport costs incurred when other goods have to be shipped to a specialised city. This trade-off creates a tendency for cities to become more specialised by sector as transport costs decline.[19]

The next steps towards a better modelling of physical distance in urban systems have been taken in a series of papers that extend the approach developed by Krugman (1991a) for regional systems to continuous space [Krugman (1993a, 1993b), Fujita and Krugman (1995), Fujita and Mori (1996, 1997), Fujita, Krugman and Mori (1999), Fujita

[18] As shown by Spence (1976) and Dixit and Stiglitz (1977), in their now standard model of monopolistic competition with a constant elasticity of substitution across varieties, the private benefit to firms from entering and stealing some customers from incumbents exactly equals the social benefit from increased variety. Hence, the equilibrium number of firms is efficient. While intermediate firms price above marginal cost, relative input prices within each sector are unaffected by the common mark-up so that input choices are undistorted.

[19] The comparative statics of Abdel-Rahman (1996) provide a nice justification for the increasing sectoral specialisation of cities during the nineteenth century. However, despite a sustained decline in shipping costs over the last 50 years, cities have become less rather than more specialised by sector. Duranton and Puga (2001a) give evidence of a strong transformation of the urban structure of the United States from a mainly sectoral to a mainly functional specialisation. They provide an explanation for this transformation by extending the canonical input sharing model to incorporate a spatial friction motivated by the costs of remote management together with some cross-sector interactions arising from the sharing of business service suppliers by headquarters.

and Krugman (2000), Fujita and Hamaguchi (2001)].[20] These papers introduce continuous physical space and an agricultural sector that uses land and labour to supply food to cities whose number, population, composition, and location are endogenous. Two additional differences with respect to the standard input-sharing framework presented above are the lack of urban congestion costs and the different mechanism driving city formation (here cities are the aggregate outcome of uncoordinated decisions by firms and workers whereas in the framework above competitive profit-maximising land developers act as a coordinating device). When there is a single manufacturing sector, this framework quite naturally generates a system of cities, where cities may have different sizes and smaller cities are miniature replicas of the larger cities. When there are multiple manufacturing sectors and goods have different shipping costs, this type of framework can generate hierarchical systems of cities as in traditional central-place theory. Starting from an economy with a unique city, population growth expands the agricultural hinterland and leads sectors with higher shipping costs to spread out. The main city keeps all sectors, but new peripheral cities form, initially producing goods with high shipping costs and importing the remaining goods from the main city.

To conclude on this section, we note that Chamberlinian input sharing occupies a dominant position in the literature on urban agglomeration economies. This is partly because of the simplicity and intuitive appeal of this framework, but cumulative causation has probably played a role as well – this framework is well known by most authors in the field and using it facilitates comparisons with previous results. However, urban agglomeration economies cannot be reduced to this simple input sharing framework.

2.3. Sharing the gains from individual specialisation

The micro-economic foundations for urban agglomeration economies presented in the previous section capture a plausible motive for agglomeration. However, they have been subject to two main criticisms. First, they seem somewhat mechanical: a larger workforce leads to the production of more varieties of intermediates, and this increases final output more than proportionately because of the constant-elasticity-of-substitution aggregation by final producers. Second, any expansion in intermediate production takes the form of an increase in the number of intermediate suppliers and not in the scale

[20] Fujita and Krugman (2000) explore analytically a number of equilibrium configurations in this type of framework, while Fujita, Krugman and Mori (1999) deal with equilibrium selection issues. Krugman (1993a) proposes a much simpler framework where the number and location of cities is set exogenously. Krugman (1993b) analyses the location problem for a unique city in a bounded agricultural interval. Fujita and Krugman (1995) is a simpler version of Fujita and Krugman (2000) where only one equilibrium configuration is explored. Fujita and Mori (1996) extend this type of framework to a more complex geography with land and sea to show why large cities are often port cities. Fujita and Mori (1997) is a first dynamic treatment of equilibrium selection issues, which is then refined in Fujita, Krugman and Mori (1999). Finally, Fujita and Hamaguchi (2001) is an extension of Fujita and Krugman (2000) that explicitly considers intermediate goods.

of operation of each supplier.[21] That is, an increase in the workforce only shifts the *extensive* margin of production.

Adam Smith's (1776) original pin factory example points at another direction: the *intensive* margin instead of the extensive margin of production. In the pin factory example, *having more workers increases output more than proportionately not because extra workers can carry new tasks but because it allows existing workers to specialise on a narrower set of tasks*. In other words, the Smithian hypothesis is that there are productivity gains from an increase in specialisation when workers spend more time on each task.

To justify this hypothesis, Smith gives three main reasons. First, by performing the same task more often workers improve their dexterity at this particular task. Today we would call this 'learning by doing'. Second, not having workers switch tasks saves some fixed costs, such as those associated with changing tools, changing location within the factory, etc. Third, a greater division of labour fosters labour-saving innovations because simpler tasks can be mechanised more easily. Rosen (1983) also highlights that when acquiring skills entails fixed costs it is advantageous for each individual to specialise her investment in skills to a narrow band of skills and employ them as intensively as possible.[22]

In an urban context, these ideas have been taken up by a small number of authors [Baumgardner (1988), Becker and Murphy (1992), Duranton (1998), Becker and Henderson (2000), Henderson and Becker (2000)].[23] The exposition below follows Duranton (1998). The rest of the literature is discussed further below.

2.3.1. *From individual gains from specialisation to aggregate increasing returns*

Consider a perfectly competitive industry in which firms produce a final good by combining a variety of tasks that enter into their technology with a constant elasticity of substitution $(\epsilon + 1)/\epsilon$, just as intermediates entered into Equation (1) of Section 2.2.[24] The main difference with the previous framework is that only a given set of tasks may be produced. Specifically, with tasks indexed by h, we assume that $h \in [0, \bar{n}]$, where $\bar{n}$ is fixed. This assumption plays two roles. It formalises the idea that final goods are produced by performing a fixed collection of tasks. It also leaves aside the gains from

[21] See Holmes (1999) for a version of Dixit and Stiglitz (1977) that considers both.

[22] Stigler (1951) argues that the Smithian argument also applies to the division of labour between firms. However, to-date there is no complete formalisation of his argument.

[23] We deal here only with the papers that explicitly model the gains from an increase in specialisation following the intuitions given by Smith (1776). Some papers, despite heavy references to Smith (1776), model increasing returns in a different fashion. For instance, Kim (1989) actually develops a matching argument. It is thus discussed in Section 3.

[24] Note the change in terminology. To follow the literature, we now speak of tasks rather than intermediate goods. But formally, these concepts are equivalent. Note also that we have dropped super-index $j = 1, \ldots, m$ for sectors. All that would be achieved by considering more than one sector would be the chance to re-derive the urban specialisation result of Section 2.2.

variety explored earlier as a source of agglomeration economies. Thus, aggregate final production is given by

$$Y = \left\{ \int_0^{\bar{n}} \left[x(h)\right]^{1/(1+\epsilon)} \mathrm{d}h \right\}^{1+\epsilon}. \tag{13}$$

Each atomistic worker is endowed with one unit of labour. Any worker allocating an amount of time $l(h)$ to perform task h produces

$$x(h) = \beta\left[l(h)\right]^{1+\theta}, \tag{14}$$

units of this task, where β is a productivity parameter and θ measures the intensity of the individual gains from specialisation. Note that $l(h)$ can be interpreted as a measure of specialisation, since the more time that is allocated to task h the less time that is left for other tasks. This equation corresponds to (2) in the previous framework. As in Equation (2), there are increasing returns to scale in the production of each task. However, the source of the gains is different. Here the gains are internal to an individual worker rather than to an intermediate firm (to be consistent with the learning-by-doing justification given above) and they arise because a worker's marginal productivity in a given task increases with specialisation in that task.

Workers' decisions are modelled as a two-stage game.[25] In the first stage, workers choose which tasks to perform. In the second stage, workers set prices for the tasks they have decided to perform. We consider only the unique symmetric sub-game perfect equilibrium of this game. Whenever two or more workers choose to perform the same task in the first stage, they become Bertrand competitors in the second stage and receive no revenue from this task. If instead only one worker chooses to perform some task in the first stage, she will be able to obtain the following revenue from this task in the second stage:[26]

$$q(h)x(h) = Y^{\epsilon/(1+\epsilon)}\left[x(h)\right]^{1/(1+\epsilon)} = Y^{\epsilon/(1+\epsilon)}\beta^{1/(1+\epsilon)}\left[l(h)\right]^{(1+\theta)/(1+\epsilon)}. \tag{15}$$

This revenue is always positive. Thus, a sub-game perfect equilibrium must have the property that no task is performed by more than one worker. Furthermore, if $\theta < \epsilon$ (which we assume is the case), then marginal revenue is decreasing in $l(h)$. Thus, a sub-game perfect equilibrium must also have the property that every task is performed by some worker. Combining these two properties implies that there is a unique symmetric sub-game perfect equilibrium in which each and every task is performed by just one

[25] This differs from Duranton (1998), who uses a solution concept based on a conjectural variation argument in a one-stage game.

[26] To derive this expression, we first derive the conditional demand for task h, which is completely analogous to the conditional demand for intermediate input h of Equation (3). We can then use this to determine the unit cost of final output: $\int_0^{\bar{n}} q(h)x(h)\,\mathrm{d}h = \{\int_0^{\bar{n}} [q(h)]^{-1/\epsilon}\,\mathrm{d}h\}^{-\epsilon}$. This unit costs equals 1 since the final good is the numéraire. Using this result to simplify the expression for conditional demand, solving this for $q(h)$, and multiplying the result by $x(h)$ yields the first part of Equation (15). The second part results from replacing $x(h)$ by its value in Equation (13).

worker. Given that there are L workers and $\bar{n}$ tasks, this implies that each worker devotes $L/\bar{n}$ of her unit labour endowment to each of the $\bar{n}/L$ tasks she performs. Substituting $l(h) = L/\bar{n}$ into Equation (14), and this in turn into Equation (13), yields aggregate production as

$$Y = \beta \bar{n}^{\epsilon-\theta}(L)^{1+\theta}. \tag{16}$$

Like (7), this equation exhibits aggregate increasing returns to scale. However, note that the extent of increasing returns is driven by the gains from labour specialisation as measured by θ and not by ϵ, the elasticity of substitution across tasks as in equation Equation (7) (since $\bar{n}$ is fixed).[27] In this model, an increase in the size of the workforce leads to a deepening of the division of labour between workers, which makes each worker more productive. Put differently, *there are gains from the division of labour that are limited by the extent of the (labour) market.*

This aggregate production function can be embedded in the same urban framework as above. If we normalise $\bar{n} = 1$, efficient city size is now equal to $N^* = \theta/((2\theta + 1)\tau)$. Again, the efficient size of a city is the result of a trade-off between urban agglomeration economies (this time driven by the specialisation of labour) and urban crowding.

2.3.2. *Alternative specifications*

Baumgardner (1988), Becker and Murphy (1992), and Becker and Henderson (2000) propose alternative specifications to model the effects of the division of labour. Baumgardner (1988) uses a partial equilibrium framework with exogenous locations. In his model, tasks are interpreted as differentiated final goods for which demand may vary, like the different specialities performed by medical doctors. Interestingly, he considers three different equilibrium concepts: a monopoly worker, a co-operative coalition of workers, and Cournot competition between workers (instead of price competition as assumed above). Results are robust to these changes in the equilibrium concept, and very similar to those obtained above: there are gains to the division of labour and these are limited by the extent of the market. It is worth noting that with Cournot competition, workers may compete directly and produce similar tasks whereas efficiency requires a complete segmentation of tasks across workers.

Becker and Murphy (1992) consider a framework where tasks are produced according to a specification equivalent to (14). These tasks are then perfect complements to produce the final good. The aggregation of tasks in their model is not done through a market mechanism but rather in a co-operative fashion within production teams. In this setting, Becker and Murphy (1992) obtain a reduced form for the aggregate production function similar to that of Equation (16). Their main objective however is to argue against the existence of increasing returns at the city level. To sustain this conclusion,

[27] Note that the only result in this section that relies on the constant elasticity of substitution aggregation is that all tasks are produced in equilibrium.

they add some un-specified co-ordination costs to the production for final goods. These co-ordination costs put an upper bound to the division of labour. When the market is sufficiently large, the division of labour is then limited by co-ordination costs rather than by the extent of the market.

Becker and Henderson (2000) build on Becker and Murphy (1992) in a full-fledged urban model. They consider the role of entrepreneurs whose monitoring increases the marginal product of workers. Having entrepreneurs in charge of a smaller range of tasks allows them to monitor their workers better. As in Becker and Murphy (1992), the details of the market structure remain unspecified. In equilibrium, this alternative mechanism again yields increasing returns at the city level.

2.4. Sharing risk

An alternative sharing mechanism that has long been recognised as a source of agglomeration economies is labour pooling. The basic idea, to use Alfred Marshall's phrase, is that 'a localised industry gains a great advantage from the fact that it offers a constant market for skill' [Marshall (1890, p. 271)]. What follows is based on the formalisation of this argument by Krugman (1991b).

Consider an industry composed of a discrete number of firms n producing under decreasing returns to scale using workers drawn from a continuum a homogeneous good used as the numéraire.[28] Each firm's technology is described by the production function

$$y(h) = \left[\beta + \varepsilon(h)\right]l(h) - \frac{1}{2}\gamma\left[l(h)\right]^2, \tag{17}$$

where γ measures the intensity of decreasing returns and $\varepsilon(h)$ is a firm-specific productivity shock. Firm-specific shocks are identically and independently distributed over $[-\varepsilon, \varepsilon]$ with mean 0 and variance σ^2.

Firms decide how many workers to hire after experiencing their firm-specific productivity shock and taking market wages as given. Profit-maximising wage-taking firms pay workers their marginal value product which, by (17), implies

$$w = \beta + \varepsilon(h) - \gamma l(h). \tag{18}$$

Summing Equation (18) over the n firms, dividing the result by n, and using the labour market clearing condition $\sum_{h=1}^{n} l(h) = L$, yields

$$w = \beta - \gamma\frac{L}{n} + \frac{1}{n}\sum_{h=1}^{n}\varepsilon(h). \tag{19}$$

Hence the expected wage is

$$\mathrm{E}(w) = \beta - \gamma\frac{L}{n}. \tag{20}$$

[28] The argument generalises readily to differentiated firms. The assumption of a homogeneous good ensures that, unlike previously, product variety plays no role here.

This expected wage increases with the number of firms. This is because, with decreasing returns, a reduction of employment in each firm implies a higher marginal product of labour and thus higher wages. The expected wage also decreases with the size of the local labour force (L) and with the intensity of decreasing returns (γ).

In equilibrium, employment in all firms must be non-negative. This non-negativity constraint will not be binding for any realisation of the firm-specific productivity shocks if Equation (18) implies a positive employment for a firm whose idiosyncratic productivity shock is $-\varepsilon$ when all other firms experience a positive productivity shock equal to ε. In this case, using (18), $l(h) > 0$ requires $w < \beta - \varepsilon$. Substituting into this expression the wage given by (19) yields the condition:

$$\frac{\gamma}{\varepsilon} \geqslant \frac{2(n-1)}{L}. \tag{21}$$

We assume that this parameter restriction, which requires the support of the distribution of productivity shocks not to be too large relative to the intensity of decreasing returns, is satisfied (otherwise the computations that follow become intractable).

The profit of final producer h is given by $\pi(h) = y(h) - wl(h)$. Using Equations (17) and (18), this simplifies into

$$\pi(h) = \frac{[\beta + \varepsilon(h) - w]^2}{2\gamma}. \tag{22}$$

Note that this profit function is convex in the firm-specific productivity shock since the firm responds to the shock by adjusting its level of production. Similarly the profit function is convex in the wage.

Taking expectations of (22) yields a firm's expected profit. Since the expected value of the square of a random variable is equal to the square of its mean plus its variance, expected profits in location i are equal to

$$\mathrm{E}(\pi) = \frac{[\beta - \mathrm{E}(w)]^2 + \mathrm{var}[\varepsilon(h) - w]}{2\gamma}. \tag{23}$$

Note that

$$\mathrm{var}\big[\varepsilon(h) - w\big] \equiv \mathrm{var}\big[\varepsilon(h)\big] + \mathrm{var}(w) - 2\,\mathrm{cov}\big[\varepsilon(h), w\big]. \tag{24}$$

Thus, firms' expected profits increase with the variance of firm-specific productivity shocks and with the variance of wages, consistently with the convexity argument given above. However, they decrease with the covariance of firm-specific productivity shocks and wages: *if wages are higher when the firm wants to expand production in response to a positive shock and lower when the firm wants to contract production in response to a negative shock, profits become less convex in the shock and fall in expectation.* Using (19), it is easy to verify that $\mathrm{var}(w) = \mathrm{cov}[\varepsilon(h), w] = \sigma^2/n$. Substituting this and $\mathrm{var}[\varepsilon(h)] = \sigma^2$ into the previous expression yields $\mathrm{var}[\varepsilon(h) - w] = (n-1)\sigma^2/n$.

Using this and Equation (20) in (23) gives, after simplification:

$$\mathrm{E}(\pi) = \frac{\gamma}{2}\left(\frac{L}{n}\right)^2 + \frac{n-1}{n}\frac{\sigma^2}{2\gamma}. \tag{25}$$

This final expression for the expected profit of an individual firm contains the main result of this section.[29] The first term on the right-hand side of (25) is the value that individual firm profits would take in the absence of shocks (i.e., with $\sigma^2 = 0$). Because of decreasing returns, there is a positive wedge between the marginal product of labour paid to the workers and their average product received by the firm. Thus, this first term in (25) increases with the intensity of decreasing returns (γ) and with employment per firm (L/n).

The second term on the right-hand side of (25) captures a positive *labour pooling* effect. Each firm benefits from sharing its labour market with more firms in the face of idiosyncratic shocks. In addition to increasing with the number of firms, the benefits from labour pooling increase with the variance of the idiosyncratic shocks.[30] These benefits also decrease with the intensity of decreasing returns because labour demand by firms becomes less elastic with respect to the idiosyncratic shocks.

Suppose now that we consider two local labour markets, sub-indexed 1 and 2, with risk-neutral firms and workers choosing their location before the idiosyncratic productivity shocks are realised. Krugman (1991b) defines an interior equilibrium in this framework as an allocation of firms and workers across locations such that expected profits and expected wages are equalised across locations: $E(\pi_1) - E(\pi_2) = 0$ and $E(w_1) - E(w_2) = 0$.[31] The two indifference loci are represented in Figure 2, and labelled WW for workers and FF for firms. It is clear that the symmetric situation where $n_1 = n_2 = n/2$ and $L_1 = L_2 = L/2$ satisfies these two conditions. This symmetric equilibrium is represented by point A in Figure 2. Using Equation (20), the locus of worker indifference WW where $E(w_1) - E(w_2) = 0$ corresponds to the straight line $n_1 = nL_1/L$. Regarding the locus of firm indifference FF, using (25) one can show that the symmetric equilibrium is its only interior intersection with the WW locus. Furthermore, to the left of the symmetric equilibrium point A, FF is convex and lies below WW. To the right of A, FF is concave and lies above WW. The

[29] Equation (25) corrects a mistake in the corresponding Equation (C 10) in Krugman (1991b). The mistake is apparent by inspection: the expression for the expected profit of an individual firm in Krugman (1991b) implies that, in the absence of idiosyncratic shocks ($\sigma^2 = 0$), each firm makes a larger profit the *smaller* the extent of decreasing returns (as measured by γ).

[30] This is, of course, subject to Equation (21) being satisfied. If (21) is not satisfied, firms expect to be inactive when their idiosyncratic shock falls below a certain threshold. This will reduce the variance of the shocks for active firms and thus decrease the second term in the profit expression (25). Note that this non-negativity constraint for employment is absent from Krugman (1991b).

[31] Note that this is equivalent to assuming that individual firms and workers have zero mass, so that individual deviations do not affect expected profits nor expected wages. This is consistent with the assumption of a continuum of workers but inconsistent with the (necessary) assumption of a discrete number of firms. We return to this issue below.

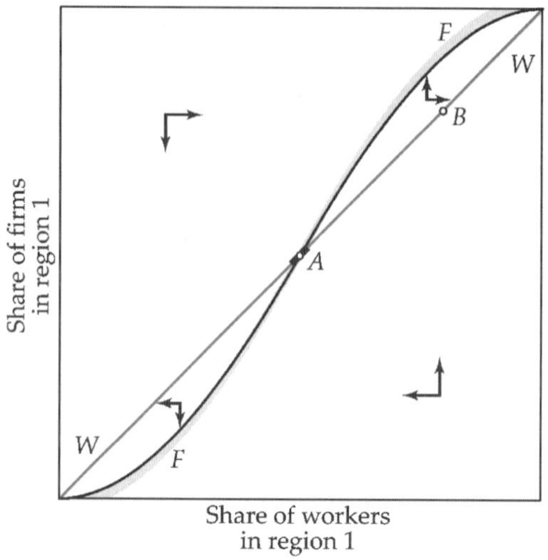

Figure 2. Phase diagram for the labour-market pooling equilibrium.

intuition can be seen graphically by considering point B on the WW locus. At this point, the ratio of firms to workers is the same in both location but location 1 has more of both. By Equation (25), profits are thus higher in location 1. As depicted by the arrows in the phase diagram (Figure 2), the symmetric equilibrium is saddle-path unstable with respect to small simultaneous perturbations in the number of firms and workers. Thus, firms and workers necessarily agglomerate in a single local labour market.

Ellison and Fudenberg (2003) point out that the equilibrium concept in Krugman (1991b) is not consistent with the assumption of a discrete number of firms needed to create the labour pooling effect. With a discrete number of firms, the equilibrium condition ensuring that firms have no incentive to deviate is not the equalisation of expected firm profits across locations but the condition that a firm does not increase its expected profits by changing location. This condition is represented in Figure 2 by the shaded area around the FF loci. Note that a firm deviating from the symmetric equilibrium raises the expected wage that all firms, including itself, have to pay so it cannot achieve higher expected profits by deviating. This means that the symmetric equilibrium is always a strict equilibrium. Furthermore, Ellison and Fudenberg (2003) show that the model in Krugman (1991b) is an example of a class of models characterised by a plateau of equilibria: any allocation with a fraction of firms and workers in one region in the range

$$\frac{n_1}{n} = \frac{L_1}{L} \in \left\{ \frac{\sigma^2}{2\gamma^2(L/n)^2 + \sigma^2}, 1 - \frac{\sigma^2}{2\gamma^2(L/n)^2 + \sigma^2} \right\} \tag{26}$$

is an equilibrium.[32] This plateau is represented in Figure 2 by the thick diagonal segment centred on the symmetric equilibrium. The size of this plateau is greater the greater the extent of firm-level decreasing returns (γ), the smaller the variance of productivity shocks (σ^2), and the larger the worker-to-firm ratio in the economy (L/n). This is because all of these make the benefit of the larger market due to labour pooling less important relative to the bidding-up of wages that the firm generates by moving to that larger market. At the same time, agglomeration of all firms and workers in one location is also an equilibrium.[33]

This model calls for a few additional comments. First, risk-aversion plays no role in the agglomeration process. Agglomeration only stems from there being efficiency gains from sharing resources among firms that do not know ex-ante how much of these resources they will need. Because the variance of the wage decreases with the number of firms, introducing risk-aversion would only reinforce the benefits from labour pooling on the workers' side.[34] Second, having sticky wages and allowing for unemployment instead of the current competitive wage setting would also reinforce the tendency for firms and workers to agglomerate. In this case, workers have a greater incentive to agglomerate to minimise the risk of being unemployed and thus receiving zero income, whereas firms have a greater incentive to agglomerate to avoid being constrained by a small workforce when they face a positive shock. Third, strategic (rather than competitive) behaviour by firms in the labour market would slightly complicate the results. In particular, allowing for some monopsony power would weaken the tendency of firms to agglomerate. This is because agglomeration would increase competition in the labour market and thus reduce monopsony rents. At the same time, strategic interactions in the labour market would reinforce the benefits of agglomeration for workers.[35] Finally, note that the result crucially relies on some small indivisibilities (firms are in finite number and cannot be active in more than one location). Without such indivisibilities, all firms could locate in all labour markets independently of their size and the location of labour would no longer matter.

This type of model has been recently extended by Stahl and Walz (2001) and Gerlach, Rønde and Stahl (2001). Stahl and Walz (2001) introduce sector-specific shocks together with firm-specific shocks. They also assume that workers can move across sectors at a cost. The benefits of pooling are larger between sectors than within sectors

[32] This result is a direct application of Theorem 1 in Ellison and Fudenberg (2003). See that paper for a statement and proof of the theorem as well as a discussion of its application to the labour pooling model of Krugman (1991b).

[33] Note that embedding this simple model in the same urban structure used in previous sections creates the usual trade-off between urban agglomeration economies and urban congestion costs.

[34] In Economides and Siow (1988), consumers face uncertain endowments of different goods and need to go to a market to trade. The variance of prices is lower in markets with more traders. When utility is concave in all its arguments, consumers gain from market agglomeration. At the same time, operating in a larger market is more expensive, so that there is a trade-off between liquidity and the costs of trade.

[35] In case the preferred location patterns for firms differ from those of workers, the exact timing of the location decisions becomes decisive to determine the final outcome.

because of the weaker correlation between shocks across different sectors. At the same time, the costs of pooling workers are also larger between sectors than within sectors because of the switching costs. In equilibrium, there is thus a trade-off between the agglomeration of firms in the same sector and the agglomeration of firms in different sectors. Gerlach, Rønde and Stahl (2001) relax the assumption of shocks being exogenous. Instead, they assume two firms making risky investments to increase their productivity. In line with the results above, the incentive for firms to agglomerate increases with the size of the expected asymmetry in outcome between firms. The incentive to agglomerate is strongest when the probability to have a successful investment is 50% (which maximises the probability of the two firms being ex-post in different states) and when innovations are drastic. In their framework, these benefits of agglomeration for firms are limited by the costs of labour-market competition.

3. Matching

3.1. *Improving the quality of matches*

In this section, we present a labour-market version of Salop's (1979) matching model and embed it in an urban framework. In this context, there are two sources of agglomeration economies. The first is a matching externality first highlighted by Helsley and Strange (1990), whereby *an increase in the number of agents trying to match improves the expected quality of each match.*[36] Extending their framework to allow for labour-market competition introduces a second source of agglomeration economies, whereby *stronger competition helps to save in fixed costs by making the number of firms increase less than proportionately with the labour force.*

3.1.1. *From firm-level to aggregate increasing returns*

Consider an industry with an endogenously determined number of firms.[37] Each firm has the same technology as the intermediate producers of Section 2.2, described by the production function $y(h) = \beta l(h) - \alpha$. However, in contrast to Section 2.2, these firms are now final producers of a homogeneous good (which we take as the numéraire) and have horizontally differentiated skill requirements.[38] There is a continuum of workers

[36] Kim (1990) considers a similar matching structure in the context of a closed local labour market, and in Kim (1991) he embeds this in an explicitly urban framework. The model in Kim (1990, 1991) and that in Helsley and Strange (1990) differ mainly in terms of the wage setting mechanism.

[37] This can easily be extended to m sectors. However, given that in Section 2.2 we already showed that having m sectors and increasing returns at the sector and city level results in equilibrium urban specialisation, there is little added value to considering more than one sector in this section as well.

[38] Electricity generation is an example of an industry producing a homogeneous output using very different techniques and workers.

with heterogeneous skills each supplying one unit of labour. When a firm hires a worker that is less than a perfect match for its skill requirement, there is a cost of mismatch borne by the worker (one may think of this as a training cost). Each firm posts a wage so as to maximise its profits and each worker gets a job with the firm that offers him the highest wage net of mismatch costs.

For simplicity, the skill space is taken to be the unit circle. Firms' skill requirements are evenly spaced around the unit circle.[39] Workers' skills are uniformly distributed on the unit circle with density equal to the labour force L. If a worker's skill differs from the skill requirement of her employer by a distance z then the cost of mismatch, expressed in units of the numéraire, is μz.

Suppose that n firms have entered the market. Because firms are symmetrically located in skill space it makes sense to look for a symmetric equilibrium in which they all offer the same wage w. Let us concentrate on the case in which there is full employment so that firms are competing for workers. In this case, each firm will effectively have only two competitors, whose skill requirements are at a distance $1/n$ to its left and to its right. A worker located at a distance z from firm h is indifferent between working for firm h posting wage $w(h)$ and working for h's closest competitor posting wage w, where z is defined by

$$w(h) - \mu z = w - \mu\left(\frac{1}{n} - z\right). \tag{27}$$

Firm h will thus hire any workers whose skill is within a distance z of its skill requirement and have employment

$$l(h) = 2Lz = \frac{L}{n} + \left[w(h) - w\right]\frac{L}{\mu}. \tag{28}$$

This equation shows that by offering a higher wage than its competitors a firm can increase its workforce above its proportionate labour-market share (L/n). For any given wage increase, the firm lures fewer workers away from its competitors the higher are mismatch costs (μ), which make the firm a worse substitute for workers' current employer, and the lower is the density of workers in skill space (L).

Substituting (28) into the expression for firm h's profits, $\pi(h) = [\beta - w(h)]l(h) - \alpha$, differentiating the resulting concave function with respect to $w(h)$, and then substituting $w(h) = w$ yields the equilibrium wage.[40] This is equal to

$$w = \beta - \frac{\mu}{n}. \tag{29}$$

[39] Maximal differentiation is usually imposed exogenously in this class of models. Evenly-spaced firm locations have only been derived as an equilibrium outcome in this class of models in very special cases because firm profits are in general not a continuous function of locations and wages. See Economides (1989) for a derivation of evenly spaced firm locations as a subgame perfect equilibrium in the product differentiation counterpart to this model with quadratic transportation costs.

[40] Note that a firm would be unable to make a profit by deviating from this symmetric equilibrium with a wage high enough to steal all workers from its closest competitors. Thus, profits are continuous in wages over the relevant range.

Wages differ from workers' marginal product (β) because firms have monopsony power. At the same time, firms compete for workers and are forced to pay higher wages the greater the number of competitors that they face (n). The intensity of labour-market competition decreases with mismatch costs (μ). Substituting (28) and (29) into individual firm profits yields

$$\pi = \frac{\mu}{n} \times \frac{L}{n} - \alpha. \tag{30}$$

By paying its L/n workers μ/n below their marginal product, each firm offsets its fixed cost α. Entry reduces individual firm profits for two reasons. First, workers get split between more firms – a market-crowding effect. Second, entry intensifies competition amongst firms for workers, forcing them to lower their wage margin – a competition effect.

Free entry drives profits down to zero, so the equilibrium number of firms is

$$n = \sqrt{\frac{\mu L}{\alpha}}. \tag{31}$$

Using this expression, and given that at the symmetric equilibrium each firm employs $l = L/n$ workers, we can write aggregate production as

$$Y = n(\beta l - \alpha) = \left(\beta - \sqrt{\frac{\alpha\mu}{L}}\right)L. \tag{32}$$

This obviously exhibits aggregate increasing returns to scale. What may be surprising is that *here the source of aggregate increasing returns is competition between firms*. The mechanism is simple and fairly general. As the workforce (L) grows, the number of firms increases less than proportionately due to greater labour-market competition – see (31). Consequently, each firm ends up hiring more workers. In the presence of fixed production costs, this increases output per worker.

3.1.2. *From output to income per worker*

The concept of urban agglomeration economies is wider than that of increasing returns to scale in the urban aggregate production function. The model in this section is a good illustration of this. Individual utility increases with the size of the (local) labour force not only because increased competition gives rise to aggregate increasing returns, but also because there is a matching externality that further enhances income per worker.

To go from output to income per worker, we need to incorporate mismatch costs. Output per worker is obtained by dividing total output as given in (32) by the workforce. The average worker has a skill that differs from its employer's requirement by $1/4n$, so the average mismatch costs is $\mu/4n$. Subtracting the average mismatch costs from output per worker yields average income per worker as

$$\mathrm{E}(\omega) = \beta - \frac{5}{4}\sqrt{\frac{\alpha\mu}{L}}. \tag{33}$$

Average income per worker increases with the size of the workforce not only because of the combination of labour-market competition with fixed production costs, but also because *there is a matching externality: as the workforce grows and the number of firms increases the average worker is able to find an employer that is a better match for its skill.*

The presence of this matching externality implies that firm entry is socially beneficial so long as the marginal reduction in mismatch costs offsets the extra fixed cost (i.e., so long as $\mu L/(4n^2) \geqslant \alpha$). The fact that firms do not factor this into their entry decision creates an inefficiency favouring too little entry. However, there is a second inefficiency associated with firm entry working in the opposite direction. This arises because firms enter so long as they can lure enough workers away from their competitors so as to recover the fixed cost (i.e., by (30), so long as $\mu L/n^2 \geqslant \alpha$). Since 'business stealing' per se is socially wasteful, this tends to produce excessive entry. In this particular specification, the business stealing inefficiency dominates so that in equilibrium there are too many firms (twice as many as is socially desirable). However, excessive firm entry is not a general outcome in this type of model. Instead, it depends delicately on the details of the specification.[41]

3.1.3. Urban structure

Next, to embed the production structure we have just described in an urban context, we keep our earlier specification of Section 2.2 except for the commuting technology. The only cost of commuting is now a monetary cost 2τ per unit of distance ($\tau > 0$), so that commuting costs for a worker living at a distance s from the CBD are $4\tau s$.[42] Now that commuting costs are not incurred in working time, urban population is equal to the local labour force ($N_i = L_i$).

Since lot size is fixed and commuting costs per unit of distance are independent of income, every worker is willing to pay the same rent $R_i(s)$ for a residence located at a distance s from the CBD. The possibility of arbitrage across residences implies that in equilibrium half of each city's population lives at either side of the CBD and that the sum of every dweller's rent and the corresponding commuting costs is equal to the commuting costs of someone living at the city edge: $4\tau s + R_i(s) = 4\tau(N_i/2)$. Thus, the rent function for any worker in city i is $R_i(s) = 2\tau(N_i - 2|s|)$, which in this simple specification increases linearly as one approaches the CBD. Integrating this over the city's extension yields total rents in each city as

$$R_i = \int_{-N_i/2}^{N_i/2} R_i(s)\,\mathrm{d}s = \tau N_i{}^2. \tag{34}$$

[41] These two inefficiencies associated with firm entry correspond to the benefits of increased variety versus business stealing in the model of Section 2.2. However, here the two corresponding inefficiencies do not cancel out. At the same time, there is still no pricing inefficiency. Although here wages differ from workers' marginal product, this does not create a distortion because labour supply is inelastic.

[42] Maintaining commuting costs incurred in labour time as in Section 2.2 now that labour is heterogeneous would require dealing with more complex interactions between the housing and the labour markets [Brueckner, Thisse and Zenou (2002)].

3.1.4. Equilibrium city sizes

Finally, we turn to the derivation of equilibrium city sizes. Let us assume that workers allocate themselves across cities before firms enter.[43] Further, let us require the equilibrium allocation of workers across cities to be such that no individual could achieve a higher expected utility by locating elsewhere, and also require it to be stable with respect to small perturbations. With free trade of the only final good and risk neutral agents, expected utility is an increasing function of expected consumption expenditure. Expected consumption expenditure is equal to the average gross income per worker, as given by (33), minus the sum of commuting cost and land rent expenditures (equal to $4\tau N_i/2$ for every worker) plus the income from the individual share of local land rents [R_i/N_i, where R_i is given by (34)], which simplifies into

$$c_i = \beta - \frac{5}{4}\sqrt{\frac{\alpha\mu}{N_i}} - \tau N_i. \tag{35}$$

From this we can see that individual consumption expenditure, and thus utility, is a concave function of city size which reaches a maximum for

$$N^* = \sqrt[3]{\left(\frac{5}{8\tau}\right)^2 \alpha\mu}. \tag{36}$$

This city size is constrained efficient, in the sense that it provides the highest level of expected utility conditional on the number of firms being determined by free entry (which we have shown above results in too many firms). *The constrained-efficient city size N^* is the result of a trade-off between urban agglomeration economies and urban crowding.* N^* decreases with commuting costs as measured by τ and increases with the extent of aggregate increasing returns as measured by $\alpha\mu$.[44] Once again, in equilibrium all cities are of the same size and this is not smaller than N^*.

However, unlike in the sharing model of Section 2.2, a coordinating mechanism such as competitive land developers is not enough to achieve efficiency, but only constrained efficiency. To achieve unconstrained efficiency, one would need an instrument to restrain firm entry.[45]

[43] This sequence of events ensures that workers can anticipate their expected mismatch but not the precise value of this when they choose their city of residence. Alternatively, we could assume that before choosing a city, workers know only the number of firms but not their exact location within each city.

[44] As the fixed cost (α) and the mismatch cost (μ) increase, the fixed cost savings from greater competition and the matching externality both become more pronounced.

[45] Since the efficient number of firms is $\sqrt{\mu L/\alpha}/2$, the unconstrained efficient city size is $\sqrt[3]{(1/2\tau)^2\alpha\mu} < N^*$. The result that the unconstrained-efficient city size is less than the constrained-efficient size and thus than the equilibrium city size is not a general result. For an example of another matching model of urban agglomeration economies where instead cities may be too small in equilibrium, see Berliant, Reed and Wang (2000), discussed in the following section.

3.1.5. Alternative specifications

Although less popular than the basic sharing model explored in Section 2.2, Helsley and Strange's (1990) urban version of Salop's (1979) matching model has been extended in a variety of directions and adapted to different situations. When commuting costs are paid in labour time, Brueckner, Thisse and Zenou (2002) show that complex interactions between the housing and the labour markets occur. In an interesting contribution, Kim (1989) allows workers to invest either in general human capital (which reduces the cost of mismatch) or in specific human capital (which increases their skill-specific productivity). He shows that as the size of the local market increases, the investment in specific human capital increases relative to that in general human capital. This can be interpreted as increased specialisation with city size. Tharakan and Tropeano (2001) and Amiti and Pissarides (2002) also use Salop's (1979) matching model but embed it in the regional framework proposed by Krugman (1991a) rather than in a standard urban framework.

Helsley and Strange (1991) consider a two-period model where immobile capital must be matched with entrepreneurs. When a project fails in the first period, the bank repossesses the asset. A larger city then makes it easier to re-allocate this asset to an alternative entrepreneur in the second period. This argument is further developed in Zhang (2002) who uses an infinite time horizon framework. As in Helsley and Strange (1991), more available machines and more idle entrepreneurs in a city give rise to a thick-market externality leading to better matches between entrepreneurs and machines. Over time, incumbent entrepreneurs go randomly out of business and are replaced by new entrepreneurs. Reallocating idle machines between new entrants is costly and this cost increases with time. Consequently, reallocation takes place only at certain times (in waves) rather than at each period. This bunching mechanism is the dynamic counterpart of spatial agglomeration. Furthermore, the two frictions interact together as larger markets find it worthwhile to have more frequent waves of reallocations. The main predictions is that waves of reallocations should be more frequent and yield better results in larger cities. In Helsley and Strange (2002), urban matching is explicitly adapted to an innovation context. They show how a dense network of suppliers in a city can facilitate innovation by lowering the cost of developing new products.

Ellison, Fudenberg and Mobius (2002) explore a related agglomeration mechanism in the context of competing auctions. They consider the simultaneous choice by buyers and sellers between two competing markets. Following this location choice, buyers learn their private valuations of the homogeneous good and a uniform-price auction is held at each location. They show that larger markets are more efficient for a given buyer-to-seller ratio. However, markets of different sizes may coexist in equilibrium if, as in Ellison and Fudenberg (2003), relocation to the larger market reduces its attractiveness sufficiently.

In a recent contribution, Venables (2002) also argues that cities improve the quality of matches. His core argument, however, is very different from that in Helsley and Strange (1990). In his model, workers (whose skills can be high or low) are randomly matched with a local partner to produce. Their income equals one-half of the pair's output. Both low-skilled and high-skilled workers are more productive when matched with a high-skilled partner than when matched with a low-skilled partner. However, the productive gains from having a high-skilled partner are greater for high-skilled workers.

While efficiency in this context requires assortative matching, low-skilled workers have no incentive to reveal their skill level. To induce them to do so, high-skilled workers may find it worthwhile to agglomerate in cities despite the additional costs that this entails. The reason is the following. When all high-skilled workers live in cities and all low-skilled workers live in the hinterland, a low-skilled worker who moved to the city would gain half of the difference in output between a low-and-low skilled pair and a high-and-low skilled pair. At the same time, she would have to incur the additional costs of living in the city. If these additional costs are sufficiently large, low-skilled workers are better-off staying in the hinterland. At the same time, if the complementarity between high-skilled workers is sufficiently strong, they find it advantageous to pay the costs of living in a city where they can be matched with other high-skilled workers rather than live in the hinterland and be matched with low-skilled workers. In other words, *the crowding costs associated with cities can act as a signalling device* as in Spence (1973).[46]

3.2. Improving the chances of matching

In the previous section, we have discussed models in which an increase in the number of agents trying to match improves the expected quality of each match. Another possible source of urban agglomeration economies based on a matching mechanism arises when *an increase in the number of agents trying to match improves the chances of matching*. Urban models exploring this second possibility incorporate elements from models of equilibrium unemployment in which job search and recruiting are subject to frictions [for recent reviews see Mortensen and Pissarides (1999), Petrongolo and Pissarides (2001)]. The core element of these models is an aggregate matching function that expresses the number of job matches as a function of the number of unemployed job seekers and the number of available job vacancies (or, more generally, matches as a function of the number of buyers and sellers in the market).

[46] In a very different signalling model, DeCoster and Strange (1993) show that agglomeration can be the result of a pooling rather than a separating equilibrium, unlike Venables (2002). In DeCoster and Strange (1993), good entrepreneurs receive correlated signals about a few good locations, whereas bad entrepreneurs receive uncorrelated signals that are not informative. Banks can use the location decision of an entrepreneur to infer information about her quality and decide whether to finance her. Under some parameter values, there is an equilibrium in which all entrepreneurs agglomerate at a focal point. This outcome is inefficient because the focal point is congested and likely to be a bad location. However, this is an equilibrium because banks expect good entrepreneurs to cluster in the good locations and bad entrepreneurs to be dispersed. Hence by agglomerating, bad entrepreneurs can avoid revealing their bad quality. Good entrepreneurs also locate at the focal point because they do not want to be left alone in a (good) location where banks would then infer that they are of bad quality. In this case, agglomeration is spurious.

It is common in the frictional search literature to present aggregate matching functions as constructs similar to aggregate production functions. Such a comparison is particularly helpful in the current context. Just like urban agglomeration economies can be related to a local aggregate production function that exhibits increasing returns to scale, they can also be related to a local aggregate matching function that exhibits increasing returns to scale. A matching function subject to increasing returns is such that a proportional increase in the number of job seekers and vacancies results in a more than proportional increase in the number of job matches. In this case, an increase in the number of agents in a city reduces search frictions and results in smaller proportions of unemployed workers and unfilled vacancies. More generally, an increase in all inputs ensures that a smaller proportion of these inputs remains idle. This results in a more than proportional increase in output even when production takes place under constant returns to scale.[47]

Starting from an aggregate production function or an aggregate matching function may be useful when the main objective is to explore some of the aggregate implications of increasing returns in aggregate production or in aggregate matching.[48] However, when the aim is to understand the microeconomic underpinnings of urban increasing returns, it is essential to understand how aggregate production or aggregate matching follow from individual behaviour. There are various approaches to providing micro-foundations for an aggregate matching function. However, most of them do not yield an aggregate matching function with increasing returns to scale.[49]

The first and most common approach relies on uncoordinated random matching by agents [early examples are Butters (1977), Hall (1979), Pissarides (1979), and Peters (1991)]. A typical motivation for this random-search approach is that workers need to apply for a single job knowing where vacancies are but not knowing which particular vacancies other workers will apply to fill. When workers use identical mixed strategies to choose where to apply, some vacancies receive applications from several workers and all applicants but one to each of those vacancies remain unemployed, while other vacancies receive no application and remain unfilled. Let V denote the stock of available vacancies and U denote the stock of unemployed workers. Suppose that all vacancies

[47] In a different vein and following Stahl (1982a, 1982b) and Wolinsky (1983), this type of argument has been used in the shopping literature to model shopping externalities and the clustering of retail outlets. The modelling options however are quite different from those used here. See Schulz and Stahl (1996) for a more recent contribution and a discussion of this literature.

[48] Aggregate matching functions have been widely used in urban economics to analyse the spatial mismatch hypothesis. According to this, adverse economic outcomes for minorities are caused by the mismatch between their residential location and the location of jobs. A possible explanation is that workers located far from jobs experience a higher cost of job search and a lower pay-off when finding a job. In equilibrium, they search less intensely and are thus less likely to find a job. See Gobillon, Selod and Zenou (2003) for a comprehensive survey on these issues.

[49] This is often seen as a desirable property in the labour literature. However, some contributions [e.g., Diamond (1982)] explore the macroeconomic implications of a matching function with increasing returns.

are equally attractive to every worker.[50] Then the probability that an unemployed worker applies to any given vacancy is $1/V$, so the probability that a vacancy receives no applications is $(1 - 1/V)^U$. Thus the aggregate matching function expressing the expected number of matches as a function of the stock of vacancies and unemployed workers is

$$M(U, V) = V\left[1 - (1 - 1/V)^U\right]. \tag{37}$$

This aggregate matching function exhibits decreasing returns to scale. The intensity of decreasing returns falls as the number of vacancies and unemployed workers increases, approaching constant returns to scale as a limiting case. The source of matching frictions in this case is the lack of coordination amongst workers in deciding where to send their application.

A second approach to providing micro-foundations for an aggregate matching function is that of Lagos (2000), who shows how search frictions can arise endogenously when agents choose their location to better target their search. However, once again the resulting matching function exhibits constant returns to scale.

A third approach, pioneered by Coles (1994) and Coles and Smith (1998), instead yields naturally a matching function with increasing returns to scale. Consider an unemployed worker who can simultaneously apply to all job vacancies that may suit her. In the first instance, the worker applies to the entire stock of available vacancies. Suppose that there is an exogenous probability ψ that a certain applicant-vacancy pairing is unacceptable. Then with probability ψ^V all of these initial applications get rejected, and from then on the worker applies only to new vacancies as they are opened. Similarly, a new vacancy receives applications from the entire stock of workers. With probability ψ^U none of these initial applications result in a suitable pairing, and from then on the vacancy only receives applications from newly unemployed workers. If new vacancies and unemployed workers arrive in continuous time, the total number of matches is then the sum of matches between the flow of vacancies v and the stock of unemployed workers U and of matches between the flow of unemployed workers u and the stock of vacancies V:

$$M(U, V) = v\left(1 - \psi^U\right) + u\left(1 - \psi^V\right). \tag{38}$$

This aggregate matching function exhibits increasing returns to scale in the stocks and the flows. The intuition is simple: *in a market with more job opportunities that can be explored simultaneously it is less likely that none of them work out.*

A matching function exhibiting increasing returns captures the idea that in a large city people have more options. However, an immediate implication of this is that they will

[50] In a fully specified model, this depends on the wages offered with each vacancy. Firms anticipate frictions when setting their wages by trading off ex-post profits against attracting at least one applicant [see Burdett, Shi and Wright (2001), and Coles and Eeckhout (2003), for discussions of price setting in these models].

also become more choosy.[51] Berliant, Reed and Wang (2000) provide a particularly insightful formalisation of this implication. They begin with an aggregate matching function subject to increasing returns, but reinterpret it as a 'meetings function' where meetings do not always result in a match. Agents are heterogeneous and become more productive when matched with someone that is neither too similar nor too different from them (if agents are too similar they have little to learn from each other, whereas if they are too different they have trouble understanding each other).

Urban agglomeration economies in Berliant, Reed and Wang (2000) arise from an appealing combination of the mechanism discussed in this section (an increase in the number of agents trying to match improves the chances of matching) and a mechanism related to the one discussed in the previous section (an increase in the number of agents trying to match improves the expected quality of each match).[52] Increasing returns in the aggregate meetings function implies that a rise in population raises the meeting rate. Knowing that the probability of finding other unmatched agents is higher in locations with a larger population, agents will be more selective when deciding whether or not to accept a match. Thus, an increase in population, by increasing the probability of finding a match, also allows agents to require a higher quality of matches. At the same time, agents are less selective than is socially efficient. This is because they do not take into account that by accepting pairings more readily they contribute to reducing the number of unmatched agents and make it more difficult for everyone else to find a suitable partner. Berliant, Reed and Wang (2000) show that when this inefficiency is large enough cities may be too small relative to the efficient size.[53] As usual, in-migrants do not consider the negative crowding effect that they inflict to the other residents. This causes cities to be too large. At the same time, the inefficiency that arises from agents not being selective enough works in the opposite direction by reducing the level of utility for a given city size, which tends to make utility in the city equal outside utility for a smaller city size. Depending on the relative magnitude of these two externalities, in equilibrium cities may be either too large or too small relative to what would be chosen by a city planner who could set both population and selectiveness in matching.

[51] In terms of Equation (38), this implies that the probability ψ that a given pairing does not result in a successful match ought to be endogenous and decreasing in the matching rate.

[52] See Sato (2001) for another recent contribution that combines a matching function with a quality story.

[53] In deriving this result, Berliant, Reed and Wang (2000) determine equilibrium city sizes using an 'open-city' approach rather than the 'systems-of-cities' approach discussed in Section 2.2. This open-city approach amounts to taking the prevailing utility level in the economy as given and looking at a single city in isolation. Instead of having migration take place across cities until utility is equalised, migration into or out of the single city being considered takes place until the local utility level equals the exogenous utility level in the rest of the economy. [See Abdel-Rahman and Anas (2004) in this volume for further discussion]. As in the systems-of-cities approach, in the open-city approach there is a tendency for cities to be too large relative to what is socially efficient. This can be seen by looking back at Figure 1. If the level marked 'equilibrium utility' is what can be achieved elsewhere and is below the level of utility that would be achieved with an efficient size of this city, migration into the city will continue after the utility of the representative agent tips over its maximum level and will only stop when the level of utility in the city falls to that attainable elsewhere.

3.3. Mitigating hold-up problems

Bilateral relationships between buyers and suppliers or between employers and employees are often plagued by hold-up problems that find their root in contractual incompleteness and relationship-specific investments. When contracts are incomplete and subject to ex-post renegotiation, and one or both parties of a bilateral relationship need to make an ex-ante relationship-specific investment, the investor may be held up at the renegotiation stage by the other party. Ex-ante, the prospect of being held-up ex-post discourages socially profitable investments [for discussions of the hold-up problem, see Klein, Crawford and Alchian (1978), Williamson (1985), Hart (1995)].

If the parties can switch to an alternative partner at the renegotiation stage and extract value from their ex-ante investments, hold-up problems are less of an issue. In an urban context, it may be argued that cities, by hosting a large number of potential partners, can help mitigate hold-up problems. Stated differently, *asset specificity is likely to be less of an issue in an environment where the number of potential partners is large*. This type of idea has been recently explored in an urban and regional setting [Rotemberg and Saloner (2000), Matouschek and Robert-Nicoud (2002)] as well as in an international trade context [McLaren (2000), Grossman and Helpman (2002a)]. See, in particular, McLaren (2000) for a lucid discussion of the issue. The formulation below is based on Matouschek and Robert-Nicoud (2002).

Consider an industry with two (discrete) firms and a continuum of workers of mass 2. Firms produce under decreasing returns to scale a homogeneous good according to a non-stochastic version of the production function of Equation (17):

$$y(h) = \beta l(h) - \frac{1}{2}\gamma\left[l(h)\right]^2, \tag{39}$$

where $l(h)$ is the effective labour supplied to firm h and γ measures the intensity of decreasing returns.

To supply labour, workers need to make a human capital investment. As usual in this literature, this investment is assumed to be observable but not verifiable by outsiders. That is, firms can see how much workers have invested but workers' investments cannot be contracted upon because no court could certify them in case of disagreement.

By investing to attain a level of human capital k at a cost $k/2$ per unit, a worker is able to supply $l = \phi k$ units of effective labour.[54] The consumption expenditure of a worker investing k and thus providing ϕk units of effective labour is given by

$$c(k) = wl - \frac{k^2}{2} = w\phi k - \frac{k^2}{2}, \tag{40}$$

[54] We consider here the particular case of an employee making a human capital investment. Using the same model, we could think instead of a supplier making an investment to raise quality. In addition, as in McLaren (2000) and Grossman and Helpman (2002b), it may be possible to argue that this investment could be made in-house by the buyer, albeit less efficiently than when out-sourced to a supplier. This type of additional assumption would allow us to derive results regarding the internal organisation of firms depending on their environment.

where w is the wage per unit of effective labour and $k^2/2$ is the cost of the investment.

The timing is as follows. First, each firm chooses its location. Then, each worker decides on her level of investment and also chooses a location. Finally, each firm makes a take-it-or-leave-it wage offer to each worker it wishes to employ at the same location.[55]

This model can be solved by a straightforward backward induction argument. When firms choose separate locations at the first stage, they can exploit their monopsony power at the third stage and offer workers their reservation wage (normalised to zero). Anticipating this, at the second stage workers are indifferent between locations and make no investment in human capital so that $k = 0$. As result, firms make no profit. This is the standard hold-up problem: firms cannot commit to reward workers when they invest. Workers are left at their outside option, which is independent of their skills. Consequently they do not invest and no surplus is created.

When instead firms choose the same location at the first stage, they compete in wages at the third stage. In this case, workers are paid at their marginal product in equilibrium. Using (39), the wage is given by

$$w(h) = \beta - \gamma l(h). \tag{41}$$

Inserting this equation into (40) and maximising consumption expenditure with respect to the investment made by each worker at the second stage, we find this to be

$$k = \phi w = \phi\bigl[\beta - \gamma l(h)\bigr]. \tag{42}$$

All workers choose the location where firms are located and in equilibrium the labour market clears, so that $l(h) = \phi k$ in each firm. Inserting this into (42) yields

$$k = \frac{\phi\beta}{1 + \gamma\phi^2}. \tag{43}$$

Wage competition forces firms to pay workers at their marginal product. Ex-ante, the prospect of higher rewards encourages workers to invest in human capital. More generally, competition between firms in the same location gives workers an outside option, which depends (unlike in the case where firms locate separately) positively on their skills and thus favours investment. In other words, *the decision by firms to agglomerate acts as device to credibly commit to pay their workers*. After replacement in (40) and the profit of firms, it can be verified that all parties make a positive surplus in equilibrium.

As made clear by this model, when non-contractible investments are undertaken by the long side of the market (workers in this specification), agglomeration mitigates the hold-up problem. However, Matouschek and Robert-Nicoud (2002) also show that *agglomeration can worsen the hold-up problem when non-contractible investments have to be made by the short side of the market* (firms in this specification). This is because

[55] Considering instead that any surplus is shared between worker and firm would make the results less stark but would not alter their nature.

agglomeration, by reducing the rents of firms, also reduces their marginal incentive to increase these rents.

The main weakness of the above model is that because of the extreme nature of wage competition, no more than two firms are needed to eliminate the hold-up problem. However, it is easy to imagine weaker forms of wage competition (as in the model of wage competition presented in Section 3.2) where the hold-up problem would diminish gradually with the number of firms.[56] It may also be interesting to enrich this model and consider that workers could choose the degree of specificity of their human capital investment, as in Kim (1989) or more recently Grossman and Helpman (2002b).

4. Learning

Learning in a broad sense (encompassing schooling, training, and research) is a very important activity both in terms of the resources devoted to it and in terms of its contribution to economic development. According to Jovanovic (1997), modern economies devote more than 20% of their resources to learning. A fundamental feature of learning is that in many (if not most) cases, it is not a solitary activity taking place in a void. Instead, it involves interactions with others and many of these interactions have a 'face-to-face' nature. *Cities, by bringing together a large number of people, may thus facilitate learning*. Put differently, the learning opportunities offered by the cities could provide a strong justification for their own existence.

Learning mechanisms have received a substantial share of attention in descriptive accounts of agglomeration in cities. Marshall (1890) already emphasised how cities favour the diffusion of innovations and ideas.[57] Following Jacobs (1969), numerous authors have stressed how the environment offered by cities improves the prospects for generating new ideas. Moreover, the advantages of cities for learning regard not only cutting-edge technologies, but also the acquisition of skills and 'everyday' incremental knowledge creation, diffusion, and accumulation (knowing how, knowing who, etc.), as suggested by Lucas (1988). There is also substantial body of empirical evidence regarding the advantages of cities for learning [see the chapters by Audretsch and Feldman (2004), by Moretti (2004), and by Rosenthal and Strange (2004), in this volume]. Despite all of this, agglomeration mechanisms directly dealing with learning have received much less attention in the theoretical literature than the sharing and matching mechanisms discussed in previous sections. Nevertheless, there have been a few key contributions. In this section, we explore some of these while taking the opportunity

[56] In this respect, the model developed by Helsley and Strange (1991) could provide a simple framework in which these issues could be embedded.

[57] As highlighted by Marshall (1890, IV.X.3): 'Good work is rightly appreciated, inventions and improvements in machinery, in process and the general organisation of the business have their merits promptly discussed: if one man starts a new idea, it is taken up by others and combined with suggestions of their own; and thus becomes the source of further new ideas'.

to highlight the need for further work in this area. For the purposes of presentation, we classify learning mechanisms into those dealing with knowledge generation, knowledge diffusion, and knowledge accumulation.

4.1. Knowledge generation

Following Jacobs (1969), a key issue regarding the generation of knowledge in cities is the role that diversified urban environments play in facilitating search and experimentation in innovation. Duranton and Puga (2001b) develop microeconomic foundations for such a role, building a model that justifies the coexistence of diversified and specialised cities and the agglomeration of firms at different stages of their life-cycle in cities of each type.[58]

The model builds on the standard input-sharing model described in Section 2.2. As in that model, the cost of using a given production process diminishes as more local firms use the same type of process because they can share intermediate suppliers. At the same time, urban crowding places a limit on city size and consequently on how many processes can be widely used in a city. We have already discussed these ingredients formally and shown that *the combination of localisation economies with congestion costs creates static advantages to urban specialisation.*

The main novelty of Duranton and Puga (2001b) is the simple model of process innovation that they build on top of the standard input-sharing model. They start from the assumption that a young firm needs a period of experimentation to realise its full potential – the entrepreneur may have a project, but may not know all the details of the product to be made, what components to use, or what kind of workers to hire. There are m possible ways to implement this project, but one is better than all others. This ideal production process, which differs across firms, is initially unknown. A firm can try to discover it by making a prototype with any one of the types of processes already used locally. If this process is not the right one, the firm can try different alternatives. Once a firm identifies its ideal process, which happens after using this process for a prototype or after exhausting all other possibilities, it can begin mass-production of its product. *The combination of this learning process that draws from local types of production processes with costly firm relocation creates dynamic advantages to urban diversity.*

As in Section 2.2, new cities can be created by competitive developers and migration makes workers in all cities equally well-off. Finally, firm turnover is introduced by having some firms randomly close down each period. Optimal investment then ensures they are replaced by new firms producing new products. Duranton and Puga (2001b) derive a set of necessary and sufficient conditions for a configuration in which diversified and specialised cities coexist to be a steady state. They then show that the same conditions guarantee that this steady state is stable and unique.

[58] As in the product-cycle literature and in armed-bandit models of learning, in Duranton and Puga (2001b) firms learn from their environment. A crucial difference, however, is that in Duranton and Puga (2001b) the environment is endogenous and itself shaped by firms' learning strategies.

When diversified and specialised cities coexist, it is because each firm finds it in its best interest to locate in a diversified city while searching for its ideal process, and later to relocate to a specialised city where all firms are using the same type of process. Location in a diversified city during a firm's learning stage can be seen as an investment. It is costly because all firms impose congestion costs on each other, but only those using the same type of process create cost-reducing static agglomeration economies. This results in comparatively higher production costs in diversified cities. However, bearing these higher costs can be worthwhile for firms in search of their ideal process because they expect to have to try a variety of processes before finding their ideal one, and a diversified city allows them to do so without costly relocation after each trial. In this sense, diversified cities act as a 'nursery' for firms. Once a firm finds its ideal production process, it no longer benefits from being in a diverse environment. At this stage, if relocation is not too costly, the firm avoids the congestion imposed by the presence of firms using different types of processes by relocating to a city where all firms share its specialisation.

4.2. *Knowledge diffusion*

4.2.1. *The transmission of skills and ideas*

In this section, we first present a model of skill transmission inspired by Jovanovic and Rob (1989), Jovanovic and Nyarko (1995), and Glaeser (1999). The basic idea is that proximity to individuals with greater skills or knowledge facilitates the acquisition of skills and the exchange and diffusion of knowledge. The rest of the literature is discussed below.

Consider overlapping generations of risk-neutral individuals who live for two periods. We refer to them as young in the first period and as old in the second period of their life. Time is discrete and the time horizon infinite. For simplicity there is no time discounting, no population growth, and no altruism between generations. Hence, each consumer's objective function is to maximise her expected lifetime consumption of the sole homogeneous good, which is used as numéraire.

Workers can be skilled or unskilled, and this affects their productivity: the output of an unskilled worker is $\underline{\beta}$ whereas that of a skilled worker is $\overline{\beta}$, where $\overline{\beta} > \underline{\beta}$. This productivity difference translates into wages because workers get paid their marginal product. Every worker is unskilled at birth, but can try to become skilled when young and, if successful, can use those skills when old.

Geography plays a crucial role in the acquisition of skills. At each period, each individual chooses whether to live in isolation in the hinterland or to live with other workers in one of many cities. As in Jovanovic and Rob (1989), let us assume that workers can only become skilled after some successful face-to-face interactions with skilled workers. Hence living in a city when young is necessary (but not sufficient) to acquire skills. Assume also that cities with a large skilled population offer better learning opportunities. Formally, the probability of becoming skilled in city i is given by the (exogenous) probability distribution function $f(N_i^S)$, where N_i^S is the number of skilled workers in the city, with $f' > 0$ and $f'' < 0$. Ignoring time indices for simplicity, denote V_i the (endogenous) value of becoming skilled in city i, which is explicitly derived below. As Jovanovic and Nyarko (1995) and Glaeser (1999), we assume that skilled workers are able to charge unskilled workers for the transmission of skills. For simplicity, assume that the surplus created when a young worker acquires skills, V_i, is split equally between the young and the old worker. Consequently, any young worker acquiring skills transfers $V_i/2$ to the old worker who taught him.

Note that cities provide no benefit other than better opportunities for learning. Young workers may be lured into cities to acquire skills, whereas old skilled workers may remain in cities because of the rents they can receive from transmitting their skills.[59] On the other hand, living in cities is more costly than living in the hinterland. The internal urban structure is as in Section 3.1 with commuting costs paid in final output. The cost of living in city i is thus τN_i where total population is the sum of its skilled and unskilled workers: $N_i = N_i^S + N_i^U$. Living in the hinterland, on the other hand, involves no commuting or housing costs. Hence *living in a city when young can be viewed as a risky investment in human capital: it always involves higher living costs but only in some cases does it improve one's skills and income when old.*

We use a pair of sub-indices to denote the locations chosen by a worker in each of the two periods of her life, with subindex H used for the hinterland and subindex i used for city i. The consumption expenditure of a worker living in the hinterland throughout her life is $c_{H,H} = 2\underline{\beta}$, since she has no chance of becoming skilled there. The consumption expenditure of this worker is higher than that of a worker living first in the hinterland and then moving to city i, since such a worker will not become skilled when young and thus will not be able to use her skills while living in a city when old: $c_{H,H} > c_{H,i} = 2\underline{\beta} - \tau N_i$. A worker who spends her youth in city i, is unsuccessful in acquiring skills, and moves to the hinterland when old, enjoys a consumption expenditure of $c_{i,H}^U = 2\underline{\beta} - \tau N_i$. If this worker instead lives in city j when old, she gets a lower consumption expenditure $c_{i,j}^U = 2\underline{\beta} - \tau N_i - \tau N_j < c_{i,H}^U$. Thus, old workers who are unskilled, either because they spent their youth in the hinterland or because they were unsuccessful in acquiring skills despite living in a city when young, are better-off in the hinterland. Consequently, in equilibrium, all unskilled workers in every city are young.

A worker who spends her youth in city i, is successful at acquiring skills, and moves to the hinterland when old, has a consumption expenditure of

$$c_{i,H}^S = \underline{\beta} - \frac{V_i}{2} - \tau N_i + \overline{\beta}. \tag{44}$$

[59] Alternatively, in the spirit of Jovanovic and Rob (1989), one could assume that meetings between skilled and unskilled workers may lead to imitation by the latter whereas meetings between skilled workers may lead to skill development (or knowledge creation) caused for instance by the re-combination of ideas. This alternative mechanism would also provide skilled workers with incentives to stay in cities, provided that the expected benefits of further skill development are not dominated by the costs of imitation.

Finally, a worker who spends her youth in city i, acquires skills, and lives in city j when old has an expected consumption expenditure equal to

$$E\left(c^{\mathrm{S}}_{i,j}\right) = \underline{\beta} - \frac{V_i}{2} - \tau N_i + \overline{\beta} + \frac{N^{\mathrm{U}}_j f(N^{\mathrm{S}}_j)}{N^{\mathrm{S}}_j}\frac{V_j}{2} - \tau N_j, \tag{45}$$

where $N^{\mathrm{U}}_j f(N^{\mathrm{S}}_j)/N^{\mathrm{S}}_j$ is the expected number of young unskilled worker that this worker expects to pass her skills to. Comparison of Equations (44) and (45) shows the trade-off for a skilled worker: by moving to the hinterland she saves in living costs but has to relinquish the rents associated with training unskilled workers.

We now derive a set of conditions for the existence and stability of a steady state in which all cities are identical in terms of their size and of their proportion of skilled workers, all young workers live in cities, all old skilled workers remain in cities, and all old unskilled workers move to the hinterland.[60] With all cities being identical, we can drop subindices for specific cities from the strictly urban variables V_i, N^{S}_i, and N^{U}_i, and use a common subindex C for all cities in the variables denoting the consumption expenditure of workers. In a steady state, the skilled population remains constant so that each skilled worker expects to teach one unskilled. This implies $N^{\mathrm{S}} = N^{\mathrm{U}} f(N^{\mathrm{S}})$. The value of being skilled, V, can then be calculated as

$$V = E\left(c^{\mathrm{S}}_{C,C}\right) - c^{\mathrm{U}}_{C,H} = \overline{\beta} - \underline{\beta} - \tau N. \tag{46}$$

In order to have a steady state as described above, young workers must prefer living in a city over living in the hinterland. This requires

$$f(N^{\mathrm{S}})E\left(c^{\mathrm{S}}_{C,C}\right) + \left[1 - f(N^{\mathrm{S}})\right]c^{\mathrm{U}}_{C,H} > c_{H,H}.$$

After replacement and simplification, this yields

$$f(N^{\mathrm{S}})\left(\overline{\beta} - \underline{\beta} - \tau N\right) \geqslant \tau N. \tag{47}$$

It must also be the case that old skilled workers prefer to remain in cities over moving to the hinterland. This requires $E(c^{\mathrm{S}}_{C,C}) \geqslant c^{\mathrm{S}}_{C,H}$. After replacement of Equations (44) and (45) this implies $V/2 \geqslant \tau N$. Replacing V from Equation (46) yields

$$\overline{\beta} - \underline{\beta} \geqslant 3\tau N. \tag{48}$$

Condition (47) implies that the probability of learning, $f(N^{\mathrm{S}})$, multiplied by the benefits from learning, $\overline{\beta} - \underline{\beta} - \tau N$, must offset the extra cost of living in cities while trying

[60] This differs significantly from Glaeser (1999), who focuses on the case of a single city with 'surplus' skilled labour. In his setting, all the benefits from learning for each generation are exhausted in urban crowding. A second difference that results from the first one is that in Glaeser (1999) the value of being skilled is exogenous, whereas here it depends on city size [see Equation (46)]. In a related paper, Peri (2002) explores learning in a two-location framework. However, his paper has a more macroeconomic focus than Glaeser's and assumes that learning is a technological externality for which he provides no micro-foundations.

to acquire skills, τN. Condition (48) stipulates that the benefits from teaching unskilled workers must be sufficiently large to compensate the higher cost of urban living for the skilled. It is easy to see that when the productivity difference between the skilled and the unskilled workers, $\overline{\beta} - \underline{\beta}$, is sufficiently large, there exists an urban population N which satisfies these two conditions.

We must also check the stability of this steady state with respect to small perturbations in the distribution of (skilled and unskilled) workers across cities. The entry of more unskilled workers in a city always reduces their expected consumption income, $\underline{\beta} - \tau N + f(N^{\mathrm{S}})V/2$. This is because further entry by unskilled workers increases the costs of urban live τN and also reduces the value of becoming skilled V. Regarding the entry of more skilled workers in a city, this reduces their expected consumption income,

$$\overline{\beta} - \tau N + \frac{N^{\mathrm{U}} f(N^{\mathrm{S}})}{N^{\mathrm{S}}} \frac{V}{2},$$

provided that the following condition is satisfied:

$$\left(\frac{f'(N^{\mathrm{S}})}{f(N^{\mathrm{S}})} - \frac{1}{N^{\mathrm{S}}}\right)\left(\overline{\beta} - \underline{\beta} - \tau N\right) - 3\tau < 0. \tag{49}$$

The first term on the left-hand side captures the effects of changes in the number of unskilled workers that each skilled worker expects to train (made up of a positive effect due to the higher proportion of successful apprentices and a negative effect due to having successful apprentices split between a larger number of skilled workers). The second term on the right-hand side is the negative effect of the higher congestion costs (including both the direct cost and the indirect cost operating through the reduction in the value of being skilled). This condition is satisfied provided that the learning function $f(.)$ is sufficiently concave, so that $f'(.)$ falls rapidly with the number of skilled workers. To ensure the stability of city sizes, we also need to check the effects of pairwise deviations in the numbers of skilled and unskilled workers. For the relevant Jacobian to be negative definite, so that the steady state is stable, we require

$$\begin{aligned} &\tau N f(N^{\mathrm{S}})\left[2 + f(N^{\mathrm{S}})\right] \\ &\quad - N^{\mathrm{S}}\left[2\left(N^{\mathrm{U}} - N^{\mathrm{S}}\right)\tau + \left(\overline{\beta} - \underline{\beta} - \tau N\right) f(N^{\mathrm{S}})\right] f'(N^{\mathrm{S}}) > 0, \end{aligned} \tag{50}$$

as well as the condition of Equation (49). Once again, these will be satisfied provided that $f(.)$ is sufficiently concave.

To summarise these conditions, provided that the productivity advantage of being skilled is sufficiently large and that the probability of learning is a sufficiently concave function of the skilled population in the city, there exists a steady state where all cities are identical in terms of their size and of their proportion of skilled workers, all young workers choose to live in cities to try to acquire skills, and all skilled workers remain in cities to transmit their skills. This result relies entirely on the assumption that one can only learn in cities and that the probability of learning is an increasing function of the number of local skilled workers ($f'(N^S) > 0$). That cities offer better learning opportunities was directly assumed rather than derived from a well-specified micro-structure. Glaeser (1999) goes a bit further by suggesting some micro-foundations inspired by Jovanovic and Rob (1989) and Jovanovic and Nyarko (1995). Since those frameworks do not exhibit any scale effect, Glaeser (1999) assumes that the number of meetings between skilled and unskilled workers every period increases with city size. As he makes clear, his objective is to explore the consequences of this assumption rather than to justify it. In practise, urban congestion may in fact reduce the number and quality of interactions. How to provide good micro-foundations for $f(N^S)$ with $f'(N^S) > 0$ remains an open question.[61]

4.2.2. *The diffusion of information*

Turning to the slightly different issue of the diffusion of information (as opposed to skills) and its relation to cities, two relevant strands of literature must be discussed.

There is a significant literature on social learning with strong micro-foundations [see Vives (1996), Bikhchandani, Hirshleifer and Welch (1998), Sobel (2000), for recent surveys]. This literature is often motivated by examples that are specifically spatial in nature, like the agglomeration of diners in certain restaurants, the propagation of rumours in cities, the adoption of fertilisers by some farmers and not others, and word-of-mouth learning in neighbourhoods. These models have two crucial properties. First, following Banerjee (1992) and Bikhchandani, Hirshleifer and Welch (1992) is the possibility of *inefficient herding*. Assume that firms need to make some investment, say in capacity. Demand is uncertain (e.g., it can be high or low) and each firm privately receives a noisy signal about this. Firms sequentially make their investment with knowledge of previous decisions. The first firm decides on the basis of its own signal only. Then, the second firm uses not only its own signal but also the information it infers from what the first firm did, etc. If the first two firms receive the wrong signal, they both make the wrong decision. Then, even if the third firm receives the good signal, it rationally chooses to discard it and makes the wrong investment. This is because this firm realises that the other two firms have received a different signal. This carries more weight than its own signal. Obviously any firm thereafter will also make the wrong decision.

The second important property of social learning models is the possibility of *strategic delays*. When making the timing of decisions endogenous, Chamley and Gale (1994) show that no-one wants to 'take the plunge' and invest first. The reason being that when firms expect the others to decide quickly, they find it profitable to wait so that they can learn from their decisions. Observable decisions lead to an informational externality, whereby waiting has a positive option value.

[61] In this respect, the meeting function in Glaeser (1999) could be given microeconomic foundations along the lines used to derive matching functions with increasing returns described in Section 3.2, possibly also incorporating the distinction between meetings and matches explored in Berliant, Reed and Wang (2000).

When the timing is exogenous, there are no scale effects. In most cases, the decision is crystallised after a few periods, regardless of the number of players. Models with endogenous timing are more promising in this respect. However, their precise implications with respect to the number of players still need to be worked out precisely.

There is also a literature modelling urban land use under spatial informational externalities. This second literature stands in sharp contrast with the social learning literature in that the spatial modelling is very detailed but the externality takes a fairly ad-hoc form. Following Fujita and Ogawa (1982) and Imai (1982), the primary purpose is to derive endogenously the existence of a Central Business District (CBD). This literature typically assumes that productivity in location s is a function of the density of economic activity at various locations weighted by a decay function. More precisely output is assumed to be the product of a standard production function multiplied by an externality term equal to the sum of output in other locations weighted by a decay function. Denote by Y_s the output of a homogeneous manufacturing good at location s. It is equal to

$$Y_s = \left[\int g(s, s')b\big[Y(s')\big]\,\mathrm{d}s'\right]\beta(l_s, r_s), \tag{51}$$

where $\beta(l_s, r_s)$ is a constant returns to scale production function with labour (l) and land (r) as inputs. $\int g(s, s')b[Y(s')]\,\mathrm{d}s'$ is the externality, where $g(s, s')$ is the spatial decay function which decreases in the distance between locations s and s' and $b[Y(s')]$ is the density of firms at s'. This function exhibits obvious increasing returns to scale at the city level. These stem from an increase in the number of firms either through a higher density or a physical expansion of the city.[62]

In Fujita and Ogawa (1982), this type of specification yields a rich set of possible outcomes. Depending on the importance of the spatial decay function $g(s, s')$ relative to commuting costs, many urban configurations are possible, from a purely monocentric city to complete dispersion. Cities experience a transition from a monocentric to a multicentric structure and then to complete dispersion as the spatial decay weakens. This type of model has been extended by Helsley (1990), Ota and Fujita (1993), Lucas (2001), Berliant, Peng and Wang (2002), and Lucas and Rossi-Hansberg (2002).

None of these papers offers much detail regarding the information externality nor the spatial decay function as modelled in Equation (51). In his discussion of the issue, Helsley (1990) argues that the knowledge produced in a location is a by-product of output as in Arrow (1962). Hence (51) can be viewed as a reduced form for a knowledge diffusion process, whereby knowledge diffuses through contacts between firms whose

[62] In Beckmann (1976) and Papageorgiou and Smith (1983), a similar spatial decay function is used to analyse the utility benefits derived from locating closer to other individuals. Such utility gains are argued to accrue from direct non-economic interactions between urban dwellers.

costs rises with distance.[63] Alternatively, Helsley (1990) suggests that knowledge could be in part location-specific.[64] However, these arguments can only be viewed as a first step towards a fully fledged micro-founded model of the diffusion of knowledge in cities with good micro-foundations for both the informational externality and its spatial decay.

Despite their lack of detailed micro-foundations, by focusing on agglomeration at the sub-city level, these models highlight a series of fundamental issues that have so far received insufficient attention. Improving our understanding of such issues will require much more than mechanically translating existing micro-foundations into a smaller spatial scale. Firstly, because one must deal with distinct questions, such as the allocation of land within a city across residential, commercial, and non-urban uses. Secondly, because the forces driving agglomeration at small spatial scales may be quite different from those driving agglomeration at the city level.

4.3. Knowledge accumulation

Like all growth models, models of knowledge accumulation build on two crucial sets of equations describing (i) the production of the different goods and (ii) the accumulation of factors. The theoretical literature on growth in cities has added specific urban features to both the production and the accumulation equations. In what follows, contributions related to each of these two modelling elements are examined in turn.

4.3.1. Dynamic effects of static externalities

Following Romer (1986) and Palivos and Wang (1996), the easiest option is to assume that final producers face individually constant returns to scale but aggregate increasing returns to scale, and that final output can be directly accumulated (when it is not consumed). More specifically assume a homogeneous final good produced using human capital and labour. Aggregate output in city i is given by

$$Y_i = \beta(K_i) K_i^{1-\gamma} L_i^{\gamma}, \tag{52}$$

where K_i is aggregate human capital in city i, L_i is net labour, and $\beta(K_i)$ is a productivity parameter subject to an externality from aggregate human capital. With commuting

[63] In this respect, Tauchen and Witte (1984) extend O'Hara's (1977) firm location model where each firm consumes one unit of space in the CBD by allowing for 'contacts' between them. Contacts between any two firms have a cost, which depends on their distance. The volume of bilateral contacts V also brings an unspecified gain $f(V)$. Firms can choose optimally their volume of contact with each of the other firms. More specifically, Kim (1988) shows that if the gains from contacts are of the form $f(V) = V - V \log V$ and transport costs are linear, the reduced form for the firm production function is equivalent to (51) with $g(s, S') = \mathrm{e}^{-|s-s'|}$.

[64] In a different vein, Combes and Duranton (2001) and Fosfuri and Rønde (2004) consider that knowledge is embedded in workers and diffuses only when workers move between firms. In this type of setting, the strong localised aspect of knowledge spill-overs is easily justified by the propensity of workers to change jobs within the same local labour market.

costs paid in units of time (as in Section 2.2), net labour as a function of city population, N_i, is equal to $L_i = N_i(1 - \tau N_i)$ where τ represents commuting costs. Since in equilibrium firms make no profit and factor owners all live in the city, aggregate output in city i can be divided directly between aggregate consumption, C_i, and savings. Savings can then be transformed into human capital at no cost so that

$$\dot{K}_i = Y_i - C_i, \tag{53}$$

where $\dot{K}_i$ denotes the variation in the stock of human capital in city i.

To get sustained growth, assume that the externality influencing the productivity parameter is such that $\beta(K_i) = K_i^{\gamma}$.[65] Hence, even though each worker faces decreasing returns to the accumulation of human capital, the city as a whole does not thanks to this externality in K_i. After replacement, aggregate output in city i is given by

$$Y_i = N_i^{1+\gamma}(1 - \tau N_i)^{\gamma} k_i, \tag{54}$$

where $k_i \equiv K_i/N_i$ is the average human capital per worker in the city. Workers save a constant fraction δ of their income at each period.[66] With all cities being symmetric in equilibrium, output and human capital per worker in the city keep growing at a constant rate equal to

$$\frac{\dot{Y}_i}{Y_i} = \frac{\dot{k}_i}{k_i} = \delta\big[N_i(1 - \tau N_i)\big]^{\gamma}. \tag{55}$$

Note that in this framework, growth is driven only by the externality in the city production function: $\beta(K_i) = K_i^{\gamma}$. *This externality plays two roles at the same time: engine of growth and agglomeration force*, which justifies the existence of cities. Note also that the accumulation side of the model, described by Equation (53), is completely passive. Hence we are in the case of a *static externality with dynamic effects*. There is no 'learning externality' in this model. Instead, there is a production externality at the city level that could receive any of the micro-foundations discussed in Sections 2 and 3.

Ioannides (1994) uses a structure similar to the one presented above but assumes that final goods are differentiated as in Dixit and Stiglitz (1977) and that each city produces a different set of goods as in Henderson and Abdel-Rahman (1991). This allows him to derive an urban version of Romer's (1987) growth model. Black and Henderson (1999) use a slightly different specification for both the urban production externality and commuting costs in an economy with a growing population. In their case, the externality is weaker than the one above so that if the population of cities remained constant it would not be possible to have sustained growth. However, commuting costs are paid in final

[65] See Jones (2001) for a thorough presentation of modern growth theory and a discussion of this assumption.

[66] In a more sophisticated model, δ is optimally chosen by workers and depends on their discount rate [see the chapter by Baldwin and Martin (2004) in this volume for further details].

goods so that they become relatively less costly as human capital accumulates and productivity increases. This leads population in each city to increase, which in turn fuels further growth.[67]

4.3.2. Dynamic externalities

Following Lucas (1988) and Eaton and Eckstein (1997), it is also possible to model urban growth using dynamic externalities. In this case, we can assume that cities offer no particular advantage with respect to the production of final goods. Each worker in city i faces constant returns and uses her human capital to produce a consumption good,

$$y_i = k_i l, \tag{56}$$

where k_i is the human capital of this worker and $l(< 1)$ is the fraction the worker's time spent producing. This worker also spends a fraction δ of her time accumulating human capital according to

$$\dot{k}_i = \delta f(K_i, k_i), \tag{57}$$

where $\dot{k}_i$ denotes the variation in the stock of human capital of this worker and $f(K_i, k_i)$, the 'learning function', is homogeneous of degree one in the workers human capital and the aggregate stock of human capital in the city. For simplicity, we can again set δ exogenously and assume that initially all workers have the same level of human capital. Further assume that commuting costs are paid in units of time as in the previous subsection, so that $l = 1 - \delta - \tau N_i$. Output per worker is then equal to $y_i = k_i(1 - \delta - \tau N_i)$. Then, by (53), the growth in the stock of human capital and output is given by

$$\frac{\dot{y}_i}{y_i} = \frac{\dot{k}_i}{k_i} = \delta f(N_i, 1). \tag{58}$$

Unlike in the previous subsection, growth is now driven by an externality in the accumulation of human capital in the city: $f(K_i, k_i)$. Here we can speak of a *dynamic externality*. Again, *this externality plays a dual role as engine of growth and agglomeration force*.[68] However, as in Section 4.2, this function is ad-hoc and proper micro-foundations are still missing.

[67] See also Bertinelli and Black (2002). They assume an externality of aggregate human capital in the production function but there is a time-lag before this externality materialises into higher productivity. In a different context, Rauch's (1993) specification is also such that output per worker in a given period is a positive function of the number of firms at the previous period. This type of specification generates interesting dynamics but strong micro-foundations are again missing.

[68] Note that in this particular model, cities are possibly too small in equilibrium because the positive human capital externality is not internalised by workers. This is by no means a general result. Models of Schumpeterian growth following Aghion and Howitt (1992) typically imply that the equilibrium growth rate may be too large.

Instead of using embodied knowledge (i.e., human capital) as accumulation factor, it is also possible to use disembodied knowledge (i.e., blueprints) following Romer (1990). In this case, providing micro-foundations seems easier because the accumulation equation becomes a production function for innovations so that the mechanisms described in Sections 2, 3, and 4.1 can be used. For instance, Helsley and Strange (2002) use a matching argument between entrepreneurs and specialised inputs to justify why cities favour innovation.

However, sustained growth also requires that new innovations are proportional to the quantity of past innovations. A simple way to do this is to argue that new innovations have a public good property and add to the existing stock of knowledge. That is, there are knowledge spill-overs. For cities to play an important role in the innovation process, these spill-overs must be local in scope.[69] Again, proper micro-foundations for local knowledge spill-overs are still missing as highlighted earlier.

5. Concluding comments

The literature on the microeconomic foundations of urban agglomeration economies has made enormous progress since the publication of the first two volumes of this *Handbook* series in 1984 and 1987. Partly, this follows progress made in related fields of research, such as industrial organisation, labour economics, or growth theory. However, one of the conclusions we can draw from this chapter is that the important insights were gained not by mechanically adapting models developed in other fields but instead by carefully combining them with ideas that already existed in urban economics.

Our knowledge of the microeconomic foundations of urban agglomeration economies is now sufficiently developed for a few general conclusions to emerge. First, different microeconomic mechanisms may be used to justify the existence of cities. These mechanisms generate final outcomes that are observationally equivalent in most (but not all) respects. This 'Marshallian' equivalence is partly good news in the sense that the concept of urban agglomeration economies is robust to many different specifications and microeconomic mechanisms. But this equivalence is also partly bad news because empirically identifying and separating these mechanisms becomes very difficult.[70] Such identification is, however, crucial from a policy perspective. As discussed throughout this chapter, the market failures associated with alternative mechanisms differ and so do the corrective policies that they call for. We hope that future theoretical work on the microeconomic foundations of urban increasing returns will pay more attention to these issues and will attempt to derive 'unique' (or at least more specific) predictions that can serve for empirical identification.

[69] See Grossman and Helpman (1995) for a thorough discussion of the effects of the scope of spill-overs on local growth in a trade context.

[70] All the more so because the benefits from agglomeration may not percolate through wages or output per worker but instead accrue directly to workers as shown in Section 3.1.

Second, heterogeneity (of workers and firms) is at the root of most if not all the mechanisms explored in this chapter. It is very difficult to conceive how interactions within an 'army of clones' could generate sufficient benefits to justify the existence of modern cities. Empirically, it is important to know at which level heterogeneity really matters. Do the gains arise from some heterogeneity between suppliers in the same narrowly defined industry or is it between firms that belong to very different sectors? This re-statement of the old 'localisation vs. urbanisation' debate will be tough to resolve empirically. Furthermore, although heterogeneity appears to play a fundamental role, its current treatment in existing models is rather thin. Firms in most models differ only in terms of the horizontal characteristics of the goods that they produce. Empirical work will face considerable difficulties to deal with this form of heterogeneity as horizontal differentiation is notoriously difficult to measure. At the same time, the coexistence of firms of very different size, levels of productivity, and dynamic evolutions is an unavoidable fact. We hope that future theoretical developments will not lag behind empirical work but instead inform it and make progress in the same direction.

Third, incomplete information also often plays a crucial role. Cities make it easier to find inputs (be it workers, intermediate goods, etc.) and customers, to experiment, and to discover new possibilities. This idea is particularly transparent in learning models, but it is also at the heart of matching models as well as of some sharing models. This suggests that the benefits from cities are likely to be more important when the economic environment is uncertain and quickly changing.

Fourth, this chapter also highlights that sharing and matching mechanisms are well developed. However, the micro-foundations of learning mechanisms, and especially of knowledge spill-overs, are far less satisfactory. Given the importance that such spill-overs appear to play in our perception not only of cities but also of growth and innovation, better and more micro-founded models of learning and spill-overs ought to be an important priority for research in this area.

Finally, we also know much more about the sources of agglomeration economies at the level of cities [or for that matter at the level of regions – see Ottaviano and Thisse (2004) in this volume] than at smaller spatial scales. Yet much of the public interest in urban issues relates to local aspects of land use that affect the immediate environment in which people live and work. Studying the micro-foundations of the micro-spatial aspects of agglomeration ought to be another research priority.

Acknowledgements

We are grateful to the editors, to Johannes Bröker, Masa Fujita, Mike Peters, Frédéric Robert-Nicoud, and to the participants at the 2002 NARSA meetings for comments and suggestions. Funding from the Social Sciences and Humanities Research Council of Canada is gratefully acknowledged by the second author.

References

Abdel-Rahman, H.M. (1988). "Product differentiation, monopolistic competition and city size". Regional Science and Urban Economics 18 (1), 69–86.

Abdel-Rahman, H.M. (1990). "Sharable inputs, product variety, and city sizes". Journal of Regional Science 30 (3), 359–374.

Abdel-Rahman, H.M. (1994). "Economies of scope in intermediate goods and a system of cities". Regional Science and Urban Economics 24 (4), 497–524.

Abdel-Rahman, H.M. (1996). "When do cities specialize in production?" Regional Science and Urban Economics 26 (1), 1–22.

Abdel-Rahman, H.M., Anas, A. (2004). "Theories of systems of cities". In: Henderson, J.V., Thisse, J.-F. (Eds.), Handbook of Regional and Urban Economics, vol. 4. Elsevier, Amsterdam, pp. 2293–2339. This volume.

Abdel-Rahman, H.M., Fujita, M. (1990). "Product variety, Marshallian externalities, and city sizes". Journal of Regional Science 30 (2), 165–183.

Abdel-Rahman, H.M., Fujita, M. (1993). "Specialization and diversification in a system of cities". Journal of Urban Economics 33 (2), 159–184.

Aghion, P., Howitt, P. (1992). "A model of growth through creative destruction". Econometrica 60 (2), 323–351.

Alonso, W. (1964). Location and Land Use; Toward a General Theory of Land Rent. Harvard Univ. Press, Cambridge, MA.

Amiti, M., Pissarides, C.A. (2002). "Trade and industrial location with heterogeneous labour". Processed. London School of Economics.

Anderson, S.P., de Palma, A., Thisse, J.-F. (1992). Discrete Choice Theory of Product Differentiation. MIT Press, Cambridge, MA.

Arnott, R.J., Stiglitz, J.E. (1979). "Aggregate land rents, expenditure on public goods, and optimal city size". Quarterly Journal of Economics 93 (4), 471–500.

Arrow, K.J. (1962). "The economic implications of learning by doing". Review of Economic Studies 29 (3), 155–173.

Audretsch, D.B., Feldman, M.P. (2004). "Knowledge spillovers and the geography of innovation". In: Henderson, J.V., Thisse, J.-F. (Eds.), Handbook of Regional and Urban Economics, vol. 4. Elsevier, Amsterdam, pp. 2713–2739. This volume.

Bairoch, P. (1988). Cities and Economic Development: From the Dawn of History to the Present. Univ. of Chicago Press, Chicago.

Baldwin, R.E., Martin, P. (2004). "Agglomeration and regional growth". In: Henderson, J.V., Thisse, J.-F. (Eds.), Handbook of Regional and Urban Economics, vol. 4. Elsevier, Amsterdam, pp. 2671–2711. This volume.

Banerjee, A.V. (1992). "A simple model of herd behavior". Quarterly Journal of Economics 107 (3), 797–817.

Baumgardner, J.R. (1988). "The division of labor, local markets, and worker organization". Journal of Political Economy 96 (3), 509–527.

Becker, G.S., Murphy, K.M. (1992). "The division of labor, coordination costs, and knowledge". Quarterly Journal of Economics 107 (4), 1137–1160.

Becker, R., Henderson, J.V. (2000). "Intra-industry specialization and urban development". In: Huriot, J.-M., Thisse, J.-F. (Eds.), Economics of Cities: Theoretical Perspectives. Cambridge Univ. Press, Cambridge, UK, pp. 138–166.

Beckmann, M.J. (1969). "Distribution of urban rent and residential density". Journal of Economic Theory 1 (1), 60–67.

Beckmann, M.J. (1976). "Spatial equilibrium in the dispersed city". In: Papageorgiou, Y.Y. (Ed.), Mathematical Land Use Theory. Lexington Books, Lexington, MA, pp. 117–125.

Berliant, M., Konishi, H. (2000). "The endogenous formation of a city: Population agglomeration and marketplaces in a location-specific production economy". Regional Science and Urban Economics 30 (3), 289–324.

Berliant, M., Wang, P. (1993). "Endogenous formation of a city without agglomerative externalities or market imperfections: Marketplaces in a regional economy". Regional Science and Urban Economics 23 (1), 121–144.

Berliant, M., Peng, S.-K., Wang, P. (2002). "Production externalities and urban configuration". Journal of Economic Theory 104 (2), 275–303.

Berliant, M., Reed III, R.R., Wang, P. (2000). "Knowledge exchange, matching, and agglomeration". Discussion Paper 135. Federal Reserve Bank of Minneapolis.

Bertinelli, L., Black, D. (2002). "Urbanization and growth". Processed. Center for Operations Research and Econometrics, Université Catholique de Louvain.

Bikhchandani, S., Hirshleifer, D., Welch, I. (1992). "A theory of fads, fashion, custom, and cultural-change as informational cascades". Journal of Political Economy 100 (5), 992–1026.

Bikhchandani, S., Hirshleifer, D., Welch, I. (1998). "Learning from the behavior of others: Conformity, fads, and informational cascades". Journal of Economic Perspectives 12 (3), 151–170.

Black, D., Henderson, J.V. (1999). "A theory of urban growth". Journal of Political Economy 107 (2), 252–284.

Borukhov, E., Hochman, O. (1977). "Optimum and market equilibrium in a model of a city without a predetermined center". Environment and Planning A 9 (8), 849–856.

Brueckner, J.K. (1987). "The structure of urban equilibria: A unified treatment of the Muth-Mills model". In: Mills, E.S. (Ed.), Handbook of Regional and Urban Economics, vol. 2. North-Holland, Amsterdam, pp. 821–845.

Brueckner, J.K. (2000). "Urban growth models with durable housing: An overview". In: Huriot, J.-M., Thisse, J.-F. (Eds.), Economics of Cities: Theoretical Perspectives. Cambridge Univ. Press, Cambridge, UK, pp. 263–289.

Brueckner, J.K., Thisse, J.-F., Zenou, Y. (1999). "Why is central Paris rich and downtown Detroit poor? An amenity-based theory". European Economic Review 43 (1), 91–107.

Brueckner, J.K., Thisse, J.-F., Zenou, Y. (2002). "Local labor markets, job matching, and urban location". International Economic Review 43 (1), 155–171.

Buchanan, J.M. (1965). "An economic theory of clubs". Economica 32 (125), 1–14.

Burchfield, M., Overman, H.G., Puga, D., Turner, M.A. (2003). "Sprawl: A portrait from space". Processed. University of Toronto.

Burdett, K., Shi, S., Wright, R. (2001). "Pricing and matching with frictions". Journal of Political Economy 109 (5), 1060–1085.

Butters, G.R. (1977). "Equilibrium distributions of sales and advertising prices". Review of Economic Studies 44 (3), 465–491.

Chamberlin, E.H. (1933). The Theory of Monopolistic Competition. Harvard Univ. Press, Cambridge, MA.

Chamley, C., Gale, D. (1994). "Information revelation and strategic delay in a model of investment". Econometrica 62 (5), 1065–1085.

Coles, M.G. (1994). "Understanding the matching function: The role of newspapers and job agencies". Discussion Paper 939. Centre for Economic Policy Research.

Coles, M.G., Eeckhout, J. (2003). "Indeterminacy and directed search". Journal of Economic Theory. In press.

Coles, M.G., Smith, E. (1998). "Marketplaces and matching". International Economic Review 39 (1), 239–255.

Combes, P.-P., Duranton, G. (2001). "Labour pooling, labour poaching, and spatial clustering". Discussion Paper 2975. Centre for Economic Policy Research.

Cronon, W. (1991). Nature's Metropolis: Chicago and the Great West. Norton, New York.

DeCoster, G.P., Strange, W.C. (1993). "Spurious agglomeration". Journal of Urban Economics 33 (3), 273–304.

Diamond, P.A. (1982). "Aggregate demand management in search equilibrium". Journal of Political Economy 90 (5), 881–894.
Dixit, A.K., Stiglitz, J.E. (1977). "Monopolistic competition and optimum product diversity". American Economic Review 67 (3), 297–308.
Duranton, G. (1998). "Labor specialization, transport costs, and city size". Journal of Regional Science 38 (4), 553–573.
Duranton, G. (2000). "Urbanization, urban structure, and growth". In: Huriot, J.-M., Thisse, J.-F. (Eds.), Economics of Cities: Theoretical Perspectives. Cambridge Univ. Press, Cambridge, UK, pp. 290–317.
Duranton, G., Puga, D. (2000). "Diversity and specialisation in cities: Why, where and when does it matter?" Urban Studies 37 (3), 533–555.
Duranton, G., Puga, D. (2001a). "From sectoral to functional urban specialisation". Discussion Paper 2971. Centre for Economic Policy Research.
Duranton, G., Puga, D. (2001b). "Nursery cities: Urban diversity, process innovation, and the life cycle of products". American Economic Review 91 (5), 1454–1477.
Eaton, J., Eckstein, Z. (1997). "Cities and growth: Theory and evidence from France and Japan". Regional Science and Urban Economics 27 (4–5), 443–474.
Economides, N. (1989). "Symmetric equilibrium existence and optimality in differentiated products markets". Journal of Economic Theory 47 (1), 178–194.
Economides, N., Siow, A. (1988). "The division of markets is limited by the extent of liquidity (spatial competition with externalities)". American Economic Review 78 (1), 108–121.
Ellison, G., Fudenberg, D. (2003). "Knife-edge or plateau: When do market models tip?" Quarterly Journal of Economics 118 (4), 1249–1278.
Ellison, G., Fudenberg, D., Mobius, M. (2004). "Competing auctions". Journal of the European Economic Association. In press.
Ethier, W.J. (1982). "National and international returns to scale in the modern theory of international trade". American Economic Review 72 (3), 389–405.
Flatters, F., Henderson, J.V., Mieszkowski, P. (1974). "Public goods, efficiency, and regional fiscal equalization". Journal of Public Economics 3 (2), 99–112.
Fosfuri, A., Rønde, T. (2004). "High-tech clusters, technological spillovers and trade secret laws". International Journal of Industrial Organization 22 (1), 45–65.
Fujita, M. (1988). "A monopolistic competition model of spatial agglomeration: A differentiated product approach". Regional Science and Urban Economics 18 (1), 87–124.
Fujita, M. (1989). Urban Economic Theory: Land Use and City Size. Cambridge Univ. Press, Cambridge, UK.
Fujita, M. (2000). "Thünen and the new economic geography". Discussion Paper 521. Kyoto Institute of Economic Research.
Fujita, M., Hamaguchi, N. (2001). "Intermediate goods and the spatial structure of an economy". Regional Science and Urban Economics 31 (1), 79–109.
Fujita, M., Krugman, P.R. (1995). "When is the economy monocentric? Von Thünen and Chamberlin unified". Regional Science and Urban Economics 25 (4), 508–528.
Fujita, M., Krugman, P.R. (2000). "A monopolistic competition model of urban systems and trade". In: Huriot, J.-M., Thisse, J.-F. (Eds.), Economics of Cities: Theoretical Perspectives. Cambridge Univ. Press, Cambridge, UK, pp. 167–216.
Fujita, M., Mori, T. (1996). "The role of ports in the making of major cities: Self-agglomeration and hub-effect". Journal of Development Economics 49 (1), 93–120.
Fujita, M., Mori, T. (1997). "Structural stability and evolution of urban systems". Regional Science and Urban Economics 27 (4–5), 399–442.
Fujita, M., Ogawa, H. (1982). "Multiple equilibria and structural transition of non-monocentric urban configurations". Regional Science and Urban Economics 12 (2), 161–196.
Fujita, M., Thisse, J.-F. (2002). Economics of Agglomeration: Cities, Industrial Location, and Regional Growth. Cambridge Univ. Press, Cambridge, UK.

Fujita, M., Krugman, P.R., Mori, T. (1999). "On the evolution of hierarchical urban systems". European Economic Review 43 (2), 209–251.

Gabszewicz, J.J., Thisse, J.-F. (1992). "Location". In: Aumann, R.J., Hart, S. (Eds.), Handbook of Game Theory with Economic Applications, vol. 1. North-Holland, Amsterdam, pp. 281–304.

Gerlach, K.A., Rønde, T., Stahl, K. (2001). "Firms come and go, labor stays: Agglomeration in high-tech industries". Processed. University of Mannheim.

Glaeser, E.L. (1999). "Learning in cities". Journal of Urban Economics 46 (2), 254–277.

Gobillon, L., Selod, H., Zenou, Y. (2003). "Spatial mismatch: From the hypothesis to the theories". Discussion Paper 3740. Centre for Economic Policy Research.

Grossman, G.M., Helpman, E. (1995). "Technology and trade". In: Grossman, G.M., Rogoff, K. (Eds.), Handbook of International Economics, vol. 3. North-Holland, Amsterdam, pp. 1279–1337.

Grossman, G.M., Helpman, E. (2002a). "Outsourcing in a global economy". Working Paper 8728. National Bureau of Economic Research.

Grossman, G.M., Helpman, E. (2002b). "Integration versus outsourcing in industry equilibrium". Quarterly Journal of Economics 117 (1), 85–120.

Hall, R.E. (1979). "Theory of the natural unemployment rate and the duration of employment". Journal of Monetary Economics 5 (2), 153–169.

Hart, O. (1995). Firms, Contracts, and Financial Structure. Oxford Univ. Press, Oxford.

Helsley, R.W. (1990). "Knowledge production in the CBD". Journal of Urban Economics 28 (3), 391–403.

Helsley, R.W., Strange, W.C. (1990). "Matching and agglomeration economies in a system of cities". Regional Science and Urban Economics 20 (2), 189–212.

Helsley, R.W., Strange, W.C. (1991). "Agglomeration economies and urban capital markets". Journal of Urban Economics 29 (1), 96–112.

Helsley, R.W., Strange, W.C. (2002). "Innovation and input sharing". Journal of Urban Economics 51 (1), 25–45.

Henderson, J.V. (1974). "The sizes and types of cities". American Economic Review 64 (4), 640–656.

Henderson, J.V. (1985). "The Tiebout model: Bring back the entrepreneurs". Journal of Political Economy 93 (2), 248–264.

Henderson, J.V., Abdel-Rahman, H.M. (1991). "Urban diversity and fiscal decentralization". Regional Science and Urban Economics 21 (3), 491–509.

Henderson, J.V., Becker, R. (2000). "Political economy of city sizes and formation". Journal of Urban Economics 48 (3), 453–484.

Holmes, T.J. (1999). "Scale of local production and city size". American Economic Review Papers and Proceedings 89 (2), 317–320.

Imai, H. (1982). "CBD hypothesis and economies of agglomeration". Journal of Economic Theory 28 (2), 275–299.

Ioannides, Y.M. (1994). "Product differentiation and economic growth in a system of cities". Regional Science and Urban Economics 24 (4), 461–484.

Jacobs, J. (1969). The Economy of Cities. Random House, New York.

Jones, C.I. (2001). Introduction to Economic Growth, second ed. Norton, New York.

Jovanovic, B. (1997). "Learning and growth". In: Keps, D.M., Wallis, K.F. (Eds.), Advances in Economics and Econometrics: Theory and applications, vol. 2. Cambridge Univ. Press, Cambridge, UK, pp. 318–339.

Jovanovic, B., Nyarko, Y. (1995). "The transfer of human capital". Journal of Economic Dynamics and Control 19 (5–7), 1033–1064.

Jovanovic, B., Rob, R. (1989). "The growth and diffusion of knowledge". Review of Economic Studies 56 (4), 569–582.

Kim, H.-S. (1988). "Optimal and equilibrium land use patterns of a city – A nonmonocentric approach". PhD thesis. Brown University.

Kim, S. (1989). "Labor specialization and the extent of the market". Journal of Political Economy 97 (3), 692–705.

Kim, S. (1990). "Labor heterogeneity, wage bargaining, and agglomeration economies". Journal of Urban Economics 28 (2), 160–177.
Kim, S. (1991). "Heterogeneity of labor markets and city size in an open spatial economy". Regional Science and Urban Economics 21 (1), 109–126.
Kim, S., Margo, R.A. (2004). "Historical perspectives on U.S. economic geography". In: Henderson, J.V., Thisse, J.-F. (Eds.), Handbook of Regional and Urban Economics, vol. 4. Elsevier, Amsterdam, pp. 2981–3019. This volume.
Klein, B., Crawford, R.G., Alchian, A.A. (1978). "Vertical integration, appropriable rents, and the competitive contracting process". Journal of Law and Economics 21 (2), 297–326.
Konishi, H. (2000). "Formation of hub cities: Transportation cost advantage and population agglomeration". Journal of Urban Economics 48 (1), 1–28.
Koopmans, T.C. (1957). Three Essays on the State of Economic Science. McGraw–Hill, New York.
Krugman, P.R. (1991a). "Increasing returns and economic geography". Journal of Political Economy 99 (3), 484–499.
Krugman, P.R. (1991b). Geography and Trade. MIT Press, Cambridge, MA.
Krugman, P.R. (1993a). "On the number and location of cities". European Economic Review 37 (2–3), 293–298.
Krugman, P.R. (1993b). "First nature, second nature, and metropolitan location". Journal of Regional Science 33 (2), 129–144.
Lagos, R. (2000). "An alternative approach to search frictions". Journal of Political Economy 108 (5), 851–873.
Lucas Jr., R.E. (1988). "On the mechanics of economic development". Journal of Monetary Economics 22 (1), 3–42.
Lucas Jr., R.E. (2001). "Externalities and cities". Review of Economic Dynamics 4 (2), 245–274.
Lucas Jr., R.E., Rossi-Hansberg, E. (2002). "On the internal structure of cities". Econometrica 70 (4), 1445–1476.
Marshall, A. (1890). Principles of Economics. Macmillan, London.
Matouschek, N., Robert-Nicoud, F. (2002). "The role of human capital investments in the location decision of firms". Processed. University of Geneva.
McLaren, J. (2000). "'Globalization' and vertical structure". American Economic Review 90 (5), 1239–1254.
Mills, E.S. (1967). "An aggregative model of resource allocation in a metropolitan area". American Economic Review Papers and Proceedings 57 (2), 197–210.
Mirrlees, J.A. (1972). "The optimum town". Swedish Journal of Economics 74 (1), 114–135.
Moretti, E. (2004). "Human capital externalities in cities". In: Henderson, J.V., Thisse, J.-F. (Eds.), Handbook of Regional and Urban Economics, vol. 4. Elsevier, Amsterdam, pp. 2243–2291. This volume.
Mortensen, D.T., Pissarides, C.A. (1999). "New developments in models of search in the labor market". In: Ashenfelter, O., Card, D. (Eds.), Handbook of Labor Economics, vol. 3. Elsevier, Amsterdam, pp. 2567–2627.
O'Hara, D.J. (1977). "Location of firms within a square central business district". Journal of Political Economy 85 (6), 1189–1207.
Oron, Y., Pines, D., Sheshinski, E. (1973). "Optimum vs. equilibrium land use pattern and congestion toll". Bell Journal of Economics and Management Science 4 (2), 619–636.
Ota, M., Fujita, M. (1993). "Communication technologies and spatial organization of multi-unit firms in metropolitan areas". Regional Science and Urban Economics 23 (6), 695–729.
Ottaviano, G.I.P., Thisse, J.-F. (2004). "Agglomeration and economic geography". In: Henderson, J.V., Thisse, J.-F. (Eds.), Handbook of Regional and Urban Economics, vol. 4. Elsevier, Amsterdam, pp. 2563–2608. This volume.
Palivos, T., Wang, P. (1996). "Spatial agglomeration and endogenous growth". Regional Science and Urban Economics 26 (6), 645–669.
Papageorgiou, Y.Y., Smith, T.R. (1983). "Agglomeration as local instability of spatially uniform steady-states". Econometrica 51 (4), 1109–1119.

Papageorgiou, Y.Y., Thisse, J.-F. (1985). "Agglomeration as spatial interdependence between firms and households". Journal of Economic Theory 37 (1), 19–31.

Peri, G. (2002). "Young workers, learning, and agglomerations". Journal of Urban Economics 52 (3), 582–607.

Peters, M. (1991). "Ex-ante price offers in matching games nonsteady states". Econometrica 59 (5), 1425–1454.

Petrongolo, B., Pissarides, C.A. (2001). "Looking into the black box: A survey of the matching function". Journal of Economic Literature 39 (2), 390–431.

Pines, D., Sadka, E. (1986). "Comparative statics analysis of a fully closed city". Journal of Urban Economics 20 (1), 1–20.

Pissarides, C.A. (1979). "Job matchings with state employment agencies and random search". Economic Journal 89 (356), 818–833.

Rauch, J.E. (1993). "Does history matter only when it matters little? The case of city-industry location". Quarterly Journal of Economics 108 (3), 843–867.

Rivera-Batiz, F. (1988). "Increasing returns, monopolistic competition, and agglomeration economies in consumption and production". Regional Science and Urban Economics 18 (1), 125–153.

Romer, P.M. (1986). "Increasing returns and long-run growth". Journal of Political Economy 94 (5), 1002–1037.

Romer, P.M. (1987). "Growth based on increasing returns due to specialization". American Economic Review Papers and Proceedings 77 (2), 52–62.

Romer, P.M. (1990). "Endogenous technological-change". Journal of Political Economy 98 (5), S71–S102.

Rosen, S. (1983). "Specialization and human-capital". Journal of Labor Economics 1 (1), 43–49.

Rosenthal, S.S., Strange, W.C. (2004). "Evidence on the nature and sources of agglomeration economies". In: Henderson, J.V., Thisse, J.-F. (Eds.), Handbook of Regional and Urban Economics, vol. 4. Elsevier, Amsterdam, pp. 2119–2171. This volume.

Rotemberg, J.J., Saloner, G. (2000). "Competition and human capital accumulation: a theory of interregional specialization and trade". Regional Science and Urban Economics 30 (4), 373–404.

Salop, S.C. (1979). "Monopolistic competition with outside goods". Bell Journal of Economics 10 (1), 141–156.

Sato, Y. (2001). "Labor heterogeneity in an urban labor market". Journal of Urban Economics 50 (2), 313–337.

Schulz, N., Stahl, K. (1996). "Do consumers search for the highest price? Oligopoly equilibrium and monopoly optimum in differentiated-products markets". RAND Journal of Economics 27 (3), 542–562.

Scotchmer, S. (2002). "Local public goods and clubs". In: Auerbach, A.J., Feldstein, M. (Eds.), Handbook of Public Economics, vol. 4. Elsevier, Amsterdam, pp. 1997–2042.

Serck-Hanssen, J. (1969). "The optimal number of factories in a spatial market". In: Bos, H.C. (Ed.), Towards Balanced International Growth. North-Holland, Amsterdam, pp. 269–282.

Small, K.A. (1992). Urban Transportation Economics. Harwood Academic, Chur.

Smith, A. (1776). An Inquiry into the Nature and Causes of the Wealth of Nations. W. Strahan & T. Cadell, London.

Sobel, J. (2000). "Economists' models of learning". Journal Economic Theory 94 (2), 241–261.

Solow, R.M. (1973). "Congestion cost and the use of land for streets". Bell Journal of Economics and Management Science 4 (2), 602–618.

Spence, M. (1973). "Job market signaling". Quarterly Journal of Economics 87 (3), 355–374.

Spence, M. (1976). "Product selection, fixed costs, and monopolistic competition". Review of Economic Studies 43 (2), 217–235.

Stahl, K. (1982a). "Differentiated products, consumer search, and locational oligopoly". Journal of Industrial Economics 31 (1/2), 97–113.

Stahl, K. (1982b). "Location and spatial pricing theory with nonconvex transportation cost schedules". Bell Journal of Economics 13 (2), 575–582.

Stahl, K., Walz, U. (2001). "Will there be a concentration of alikes? The impact of labor market structure on industry mix in the presence of product market shocks". Working Paper 140. Hamburg Institute of International Economics.
Starrett, D.A. (1974). "Principles of optimal location in a large homogeneous area". Journal of Economic Theory 9 (4), 418–448.
Starrett, D.A. (1978). "Market allocations of location choice in a model with free mobility". Journal of Economic Theory 17 (1), 21–37.
Stigler, G.J. (1951). "The division of labor is limited by the extent of the market". Journal of Political Economy 59 (3), 185–193.
Stiglitz, J.E. (1977). "The theory of local public goods". In: Feldstein, M.S., Inman, R.P. (Eds.), The Economics of Public Services. Macmillan, London, pp. 274–333.
Tauchen, H., Witte, A.D. (1984). "Socially optimal and equilibrium distributions of office activity: Models with exogenous and endogenous contacts". Journal of Urban Economics 15 (1), 66–86.
Tharakan, J., Tropeano, J.-P. (2001). "On the impact of labour market matching on regional disparities". Processed. Université Paris 1.
von Thünen, J.H. (1826). Der Isolierte Staat in Beziehung auf Landwirtschaft und Nationalökonomie. Perthes, Hamburg. English Translation: The Isolated State. Pergamon Press, Oxford, 1966.
Venables, A.J. (2002). "Labour sorting by cities: Partnerships, self-selection, and agglomeration". Processed. London School of Economics.
Vickrey, W.S. (1977). "The city as a firm". In: Feldstein, M.S., Inman, R.P. (Eds.), The Economics of Public Services. Macmillan, London, pp. 334–343.
Vives, X. (1996). "Social learning and rational expectations". European Economic Review 40 (3-5), 589–601.
Wang, P. (1990). "Competitive equilibrium formation of marketplaces with heterogeneous consumers". Regional Science and Urban Economics 20 (2), 295–304.
Wang, P. (1993). "Agglomeration in a linear city with heterogeneous households". Regional Science and Urban Economics 23 (2), 291–306.
Williamson, O.E. (1985). The Economic Institutions of Capitalism: Firms, Markets, Relational Contracting. Free Press, New York.
Wolinsky, A. (1983). "Retail trade concentration due to consumers' imperfect information". Bell Journal of Economics 14 (1), 275–282.
Zhang, Q. (2002). "Micro-foundations of local business cycles". Processed. University of Texas at Austin.

Chapter 49

EVIDENCE ON THE NATURE AND SOURCES OF AGGLOMERATION ECONOMIES

STUART S. ROSENTHAL

Department of Economics and Center for Policy Research, Syracuse University, Syracuse, NY 13244-1020, USA
e-mail: ssrosent@maxwell.syr.edu
url: http://www-cpr.maxwell.syr.edu/faculty/rosenthal/

WILLIAM C. STRANGE

Rotman School of Management, 105 St. George St., University of Toronto, Toronto, ON M5S 3E6, Canada
e-mail: wstrange@rotman.utoronto.ca
url: http://www.rotman.utoronto.ca/~wstrange/

Contents

Handbook of Regional and Urban Economics, Volume 4. Edited by J.V. Henderson and J.F. Thisse

DOI: 10.1016/S0169-7218(04)07049-2

Abstract

This paper considers the empirical literature on the nature and sources of urban increasing returns, also known as agglomeration economies. An important aspect of these externalities that has not been previously emphasized is that the effects of agglomeration extend over at least three different dimensions. These are the industrial, geographic, and temporal scope of economic agglomeration economies. In each case, the literature suggests that agglomeration economies attenuate with distance. Recently, the literature has also begun to provide evidence on the microfoundations of external economies of scale. The best known of these sources are those attributed to Marshall (1920): labor market pooling, input sharing, and knowledge spillovers. Evidence to date supports the presence of all three of these forces. In addition, there is also evidence that natural advantage, home market effects, consumption opportunities, and rent-seeking all contribute to agglomeration.

Keywords

agglomeration economies, productivity, external economies, microfoundations, urban growth

JEL classification: R0, O4, D2, C1

1. Introduction

The degree of concentration of economic activity is striking. Roughly 75% of Americans live in cities as defined by the Census Department, and yet cities occupy only 2% of the land area of the lower 48 states. A similar story could be told for any other developed county: labor and capital are both heavily concentrated in cities.

It is not just aggregate activity that is agglomerated. Individual industries are concentrated too. Figure 1, for instance, presents the density of employment in the furniture industry (SIC). Most of the country has almost no employment in the industry, as the map shows. The map also shows that the counties that do have employment are not randomly scattered across the U.S. They are disproportionately located in the western part of North Carolina and in other nearby locations. Clearly, furniture is an industry that makes use of particular raw materials, especially wood. Forestry is an important industry in North Carolina and elsewhere in the Southeast, so the location is sensible because of the access it offers to raw materials. But there are a lot of other equally sensible locations elsewhere in the county, from Maine to Oregon. Clearly, something beyond locating near raw materials sources is taking place.

The macro pattern of Figure 1 repeats itself in Figure 2, a map of the location of software producers (SIC 7371–7373 and 7375) in the vicinity of San Francisco. The map reports both the locations of existing establishments and the locations where new establishments are created (births). As can readily be seen, both are concentrated. In this case, there is no material input that is analogous to trees. Despite this, activity is highly concentrated in what is known as the Silicon Valley north of San Jose and in San Jose itself. Again, something is going on that is leading to this kind of geographic concentration.

This chapter will survey empirical work on the forces that lead to concentration, both of industries in clusters and of aggregate activity in cities. These forces are known variously as agglomeration economies or external economies of scale. In surveying the empirical work, the chapter will be concerned with two related questions: what is the nature and what are the sources of the increasing returns that produce agglomeration? In considering the nature of agglomeration economies we will be concerned with a number of smaller questions. Are they local, as seems to be the case in software, or do they operate at a regional scale, as seems to be the case for furniture? Are they restricted to individual industries like software and furniture, or are their effects comprehensive, extending across all activities? What is the dynamic nature of agglomeration economies? Are the effects of proximity felt immediately or does agglomeration have its positive effect on productivity only with a lag? Finally, are the effects dependent simply on the amount of activity that takes place somewhere, or is the nature of local interactions important to the process of agglomeration? All of these questions relate to what we will define as the scope of agglomeration economies. The empirical answers to these questions will be discussed together in Section 2.

The second broad question concerns the sources of agglomeration economies. Marshall (1920) suggests three. The first of these is the sharing of inputs whose production

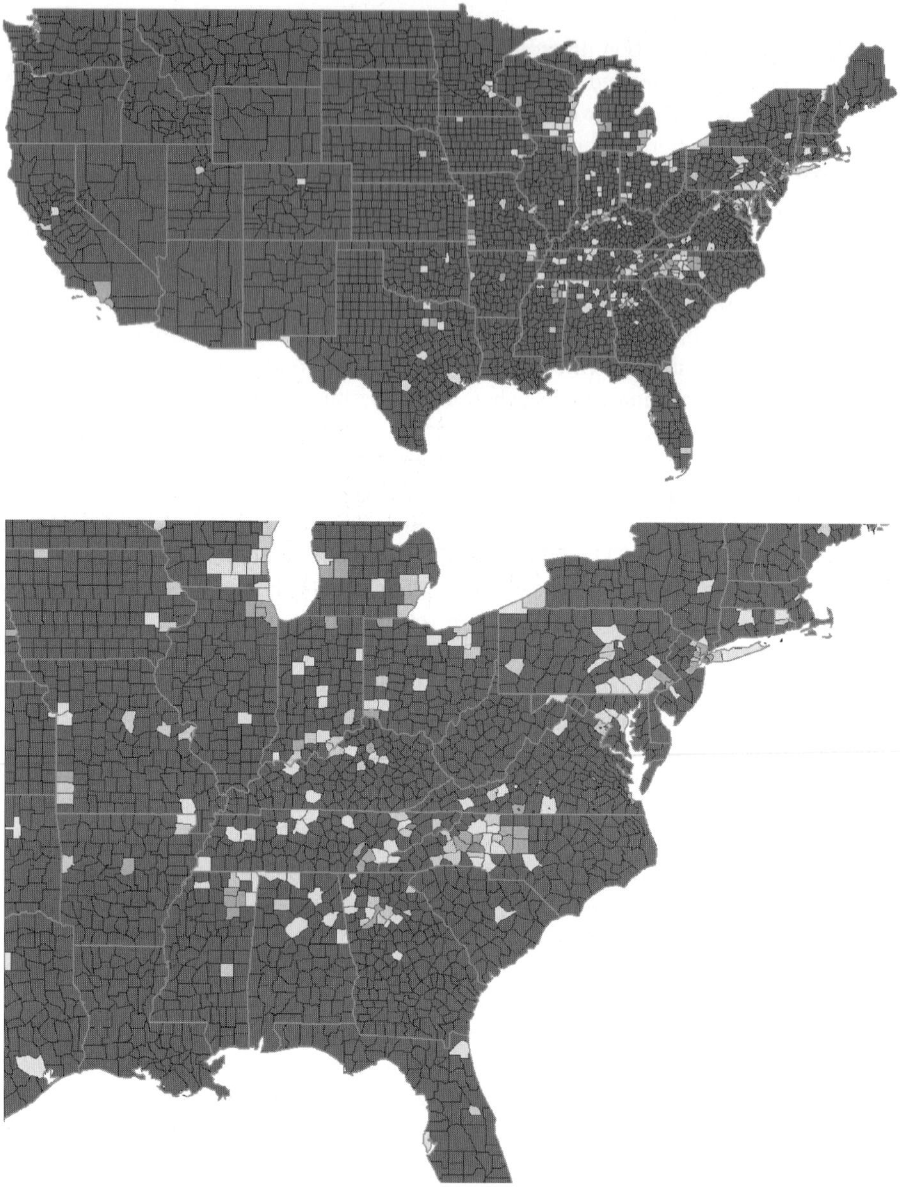

Figure 1. Furniture employment (SIC 25) per square mile. Fourth quarter 2002; source: Dun and Bradstreet. Red: greater than 10; orange: 4 to 10; dark yellow: 2 to 3; light yellow: 1 to 2; green: 0. For a colour reproduction of this figure see the colour figures section, page 3053.

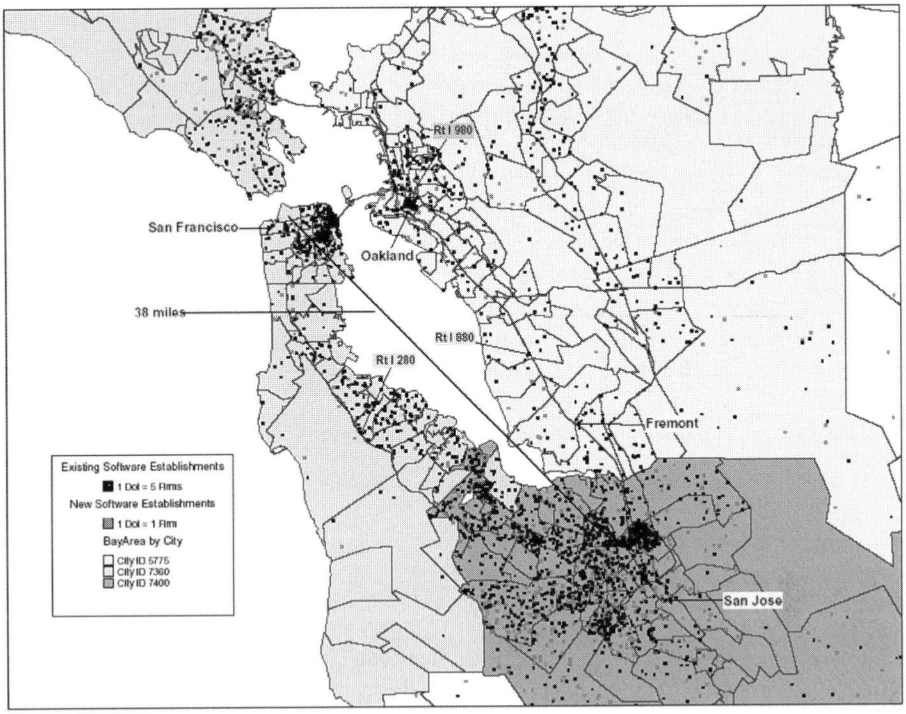

Figure 2. Existing and new software establishments in Silicon Valley. Fourth quarter 1997; source: Dun and Bradstreet. For a colour reproduction of this figure see the colour figures section, page 3054.

involves internal increasing returns to scale. The second is labor market pooling, where agglomeration allows a better match between an employer's needs and a worker's skills and reduces risk for both. The third source is spillovers in knowledge that take place when an industry is localized, allowing workers to learn from each other.[1] Other sources have been suggested more recently. These include home market effects, where the concentration of demand encourages agglomeration, and economies in consumption, where cities exist because people like the bright lights. On the negative side, it has also been suggested that agglomeration is related to rent-seeking, with inefficient mega-cities arising more frequently in undemocratic countries. This so-called urban primacy has many effects, with one being to redistribute the government's expropriated resources among the urban mob. Section 3 considers the empirical work that has addressed these issues.

Sections 2 and 3 review an econometric literature that is only about thirty years old. This literature has made substantial progress, especially in recent years as more refined

[1] In another chapter in this volume, Duranton and Puga (2004) propose a different taxonomy: matching, sharing, and learning.

data have become available. This has allowed researchers to ask questions that could not have been asked with more aggregate data. For example, evaluating the geographic extent of agglomeration economies is not possible without geographically refined data. Access to better data has also enabled researchers to answer old questions with greater precision, such as whether agglomeration economies are industry-specific or extend to the entire city. Despite the impressive record of progress of this program of formal econometric work, we believe there is much to be learned from less formal research. In Section 4, we consider some representative case studies. This is obviously a much older way to understand the facts that bear on agglomeration than through regression analysis. Even so, we believe it is an important part of the entire empirical story, both confirming and placing in context the formal empirical work and identifying important details in the big picture of agglomeration that the formal work misses.

We now turn to the scope of agglomeration economies.

2. The scope of urban increasing returns

2.1. Introduction

External economies exist when the scale of the urban environment adds to productivity. There are at least three dimensions over which these externalities may extend. We refer to the extent of the externality as its scope. The first and most familiar is the industrial scope. This is the degree to which agglomeration economies extend across industries, possibly even across all industries in a city, rather than being confined within industry boundaries. This distinction is well-known, with the economies of scale that arise from spatial concentration of activity within a given industry being known as localization economies. The externalities that arise from the concentration of all economic activity, or from city size itself, are known as urbanization economies. As will become apparent, empirical evidence in the literature suggests that as agents become closer in industrial space (i.e., their production processes become more similar), then there is greater potential for interaction.

The second kind of scope is geographic. Nearly every textbook in urban economics begins by explaining why cities exist. The answer is that proximity is advantageous. Thus, the discussion of agglomeration begins with the idea that geographic distance is crucial to understanding cites. The aspect of geographic distance that will matter most here is the attenuation of agglomeration economies with distance: if agents are physically closer, then there is more potential for interaction.

The third kind of scope is temporal. It is possible that one agent's interaction with another agent at a point in the past continues to have an effect on productivity in the present. For example, learning may take place only gradually, and awareness of a location's supply chain possibilities may take time to develop. Of course, such knowledge can decay over time. This means that in addition to the fairly well-known static agglomeration economies, there may also be dynamic agglomeration economies. That two agents who are separated temporally continue to affect each other is logically similar to the way that agents who are separated in physical or industrial space interact. The degree to which these time-separated interactions continue to be potent defines the temporal scope of agglomeration economies.

This section will examine recent empirical studies that shed light on each of these three aspects of the scope of external economies of scale. Table 1 provides a selective overview of the literature. We will begin by characterizing how one might proceed given a hypothetical "perfect" data set, free of measurement error, with no omitted variables, and including instruments that resolve all issues related to endogenous regressors. Against the backdrop of this ideal, we will discuss estimation strategies have been pursued in the presence of the imperfect data sets that actually are available. We then examine the evidence on the industrial, geographic, and temporal scope of agglomeration. Finally, we conclude the section by discussing empirical literature that sheds light on the manner in which the industrial organization and business "culture" of the local economy affects the generation and reception of external economies of scale.

Table 1
The scope of agglomeration economies

Issue	Paper	Key finding
Industrial scope	Moomaw (1981, 1983), Nakamura (1985), Calem and Carlino (1991)	Urbanization
	Nakamura (1985), Henderson (1986), Sveikauskas (1975), Henderson, Kuncoro and Turner (1995), Rosenthal and Strange (2001), Henderson (2003a)	Localization
	Glaeser et al. (1992)	Diversity
Temporal scope	Glaeser et al. (1992), Henderson, Kuncoro and Turner (1995), Henderson (1997)	Past agglomeration causes growth
	Glaeser and Maré (2001)	Lags in wage effects
Geographic scope	Rosenthal and Strange (2003), Ciccone (2002)	Attenuating effects
	Dekle and Eaton (1999)	National effects
	Ciccone and Hall (1996), Ciccone (2002)	Employment density
Organizational/ competitiveness	Glaeser et al. (1992), Henderson, Kuncoro and Turner (1995), Combes (2000b), Rosenthal and Strange (2003)	Competition
	Rosenthal and Strange (2003)	Small firms generate more
	Henderson (2003a)	Small firms receive more

A should ideally include the amount of economic activity present in a variety of different industries at different distances in industrial space from j. This would allow one to determine the industries that benefit from proximity. Including measures of physical distance would allow one to determine how close establishments need to be in order to benefit from their agglomeration. Finally, it would also be desirable to allow for dynamic externalities and consider the impacts of historic activity. Obtaining all these controls is a daunting challenge. Thus, most models of agglomeration bear on one or perhaps two of the key aspects of scope, but never all three.

2.2.3. *Estimating the production function: omitted variables and simultaneity*

The most natural way to understand agglomeration economies is to directly estimate the production function, (2.2). In carrying out this estimation, it is necessary to have measures of the various elements of x_j, including employment, land, capital, and materials. Labor inputs are perhaps the easiest to measure, since many data sets provide counts of workers, hours worked, and on occasion, proxies for skill level (e.g., education). Data on purchased materials are available in some data sets, but data on materials produced internally typically are not. See Ciccone and Hall (1996) and Henderson (2003a) for discussions of this issue. Few data sets make available measures of land use and information on the stock of capital, information essential to estimating (2.2). Thus, a fundamental challenge that must be faced in estimating a production function is in finding data on inputs.

The issue of measurement error has been central to the literature since the outset. Because this is an old issue and one that has already been surveyed with considerable care [Eberts and McMillen (1999)], our treatment will be relatively brief. First, it is clear that the absence of data on capital can affect the estimates. For instance, Sveikauskas (1975) lacks data on capital. As Moomaw (1983) points out, however, if capital is used more intensively in large cities, then the error terms will be positively correlated with the city size terms, leading to upward bias in coefficient estimates. In fact, Moomaw shows that this can inflate estimates by a factor of four.[3] Second, land is also an important input, and its contribution to production is also difficult to measure. Land will be used less intensively in large cities, so presumably this omission would lead to downward bias in the estimates.

A more recent effort to estimate (2.2) directly is Henderson (2003a). We believe that this paper is a model of a productivity-based study of agglomeration, coming closest to the ideal that we discussed at the beginning of the section. In this paper, Henderson constructs a panel of plant-level data from the Longitudinal Research Database (LRD) including measures of the capital stock, materials, and labor. Using the LRD's micro-data, Henderson controls for industrial scope in the usual way by dividing activities

[3] A related literature considers the impact of public infrastructure (i.e., roads and bridges) on productivity. See Holtz-Eakin (1994). These studies also wrestle with measuring private capital.

into those that take place within a given industry and those that do not. Henderson also draws on the panel structure of the data to address issues related to the temporal scope of agglomeration. For the most part, Henderson considers county and MSA-level indicators, rather than using variables that directly reflect proximity. An exception to this is some analysis of neighboring counties. While Henderson's work is also noteworthy for the careful treatment of the data, the strength of the empirical work rests primarily with the use of plant-level information and detail on purchased factor inputs available from the confidential LRD files. While these data appear to offer some of the best opportunities for making contributions to the understanding of agglomeration, access to them is tightly guarded. This means that many researchers choose to work with other less ideal data.[4]

Even when plant-level data are available, direct estimation of equations such as (2.2) requires that the analyst address challenging endogeneity problems. Agglomeration economies enhance plant productivity, but successful entrepreneurs also seek out productive locations. If overachieving entrepreneurs were disproportionately found in agglomerated areas, this would cause one to overestimate the relationship between agglomeration and output. Henderson initially attempts to address this problem through two-stage least squares (2SLS) using local environment measures as instruments. The instrument list includes cross-sectional MSA attributes such as the market potential of the MSA, county air quality attainment status and other variables thought to be strictly exogenous. However, Henderson notes that these regressors make weak instruments, rendering the 2SLS approach ineffective.[5]

Next, Henderson (2003a) estimates a version of (2.2) drawing on the panel structure of his data and imposing constant slope coefficients over time. Time-differencing the data, he estimates this system by generalized method of moments (GMM) using predetermined industry environment variables as instruments (e.g., lagged levels of different types of local employment). Once more, however, Henderson finds that the instruments are weak, though not as weak as the cross-sectional instruments for the 2SLS model. In addition, by using predetermined data for instruments in conjunction to differencing the data over time, he is forced to dramatically reduce the sample over which the estimation is conducted.

After experimenting with both 2SLS and GMM, Henderson concludes that controlling for endogeneity through the use of fixed effects is superior. Specifically, he estimates his productivity equation including MSA-time specific fixed effects in addition to plant fixed effects. By adding the MSA-time fixed effects the hope is that this will capture the influence of unobserved attributes that might have drawn a given entrepreneur

[4] In order to gain access to the LRD data researchers must become sworn "employees" of the U.S. Census and conduct their research in a secure room at one of the Census research stations set up for such purposes. Census research stations are currently found in Washington, DC, Boston, Pittsburgh, Chicago, and San Francisco. In addition, access to the confidential Census files is costly and requires a level of funding typically only available from a major grant.

[5] See Hanson (2001) for more on the endogeneity issue.

to the area and that might otherwise be correlated with the error term in the estimating equation. Including MSA-time specific fixed effects is appealing and may well be one of the most effective ways to address the endogenous nature of the local industrial environment. Nevertheless, even this approach may still be exposed to endogeneity problems because the presence of a plant in a given MSA and time period represents the outcome of a profit-maximizing choice.

2.2.4. *Indirect strategies for measuring the influence of agglomeration on productivity*

Estimating the production function directly is not the only way to look for evidence of agglomeration economies. Because of the challenges associated with that approach, many recent studies have begun to favor one of four indirect approaches.

The first of these is to consider growth. Glaeser et al. (1992) and Henderson, Kuncoro and Turner (1995), for example, examine the impact of MSA-level agglomeration on employment growth. In the case of Glaeser et al. (1992), growth is measured using data from the County Business Patterns while Henderson, Kuncoro and Turner (1995) rely on the Census of Manufactures. The idea here is that agglomeration economies enhance productivity and productive regions (e.g., MSAs) grow more rapidly as a result.

Studying the growth of total employment presents different challenges than estimating productivity directly. Data on total employment are often readily available and the analysis lends itself to linear regressions. However, existing employers are constrained by prior choices, most importantly the level and kind of capital previously installed. Those fixed factors affect how the employer values the marginal worker, and consequently how it changes its employment level in response to a change in its environment. In principle, this difficulty can be overcome by looking at changes in total employment over a sufficiently long time frame so that there are no fixed factors and all establishments are effectively new. Even then, one still has to address endogeneity problems: not only is the growth of total employment in a given area sensitive to the composition of employment in the area (an agglomeration effect), but growth affects the level and composition of employment. Implementing this approach, therefore, ideally requires a long panel and effective instruments to control for endogenous variables. The primary approach used to address this problem in the Glaeser et al. (1992) and Henderson, Kuncoro and Turner (1995) papers is to use deeply lagged levels of past conditions of the MSAs as regressors.[6]

A different approach to studying the scope and effect of agglomeration on productivity has been to focus on births of new establishments and their employment. This approach was taken by Carlton (1983) and by Rosenthal and Strange (2003). The idea here is that entrepreneurs seek out profit-maximizing locations and are disproportionately drawn to the most productive regions. As with the other approaches, focusing on

[6] Glaeser et al. (1992) use 1956 employment levels to help explain growth over the 1956 to 1987 period. Henderson, Kuncoro and Turner (1995) use 1970 employment levels to help explain growth over the 1970 to 1987 period.

births has both advantages and disadvantages. On the positive side, data on purchased factor inputs (e.g., capital stock, labor, materials, and land) are not required, new establishments are largely unconstrained by previous decisions, and new establishments make their location and employment decisions taking the existing economic environment as exogenously given.

Studying plant births also presents difficulties. The principal drawback is that many locations do not receive any births in a given period, which can lead to technical challenges on the econometric side. In addition, births are more likely to occur in areas where there is already an existing concentration of industrial activity as spinoffs. Rosenthal and Strange (2003) control the zeros problem by using tobit models and comparing results to those from probit models that look for positive versus zero births. In addition, Rosenthal and Strange (2003) control for "churning" effects by studying zipcode level employment data and including MSA fixed effects as control variables. Even if an entrepreneur is tied to the local MSA because of past employment and other factors, the entrepreneur will still seek out the profit maximizing location within the MSA.

The third approach used to examine the scope and influence of agglomeration is to study wages. This approach rests on the assumption that in competitive markets labor is paid the value of its marginal product. Even without perfect competition, in more productive locations, wages will therefore be higher. Recent examples of this approach include Glaeser and Maré (2001) and Wheaton and Lewis (2002). An advantage of this approach is that wage data are readily available. Moreover, by focusing on wages this makes feasible the use of a variety of widely available datasets, such as the public access version of the Census, the Consumer Population Survey (CPS), and various panel studies including the Panel Study of Income Dynamics (PSID). Here too important issues associated with omitted variables and endogenous regressors arise. Glaeser and Maré (2001) provide a particularly careful discussion of these problems, a discussion to which we will return later in this section.

The final approach is to use rents. The idea here stems from the quality-of-life literature [Rosen (1979) and Roback (1982)]. If firms are paying higher rents in a particular location all else equal, then the location must have some compensating productivity differential.[7] Dekle and Eaton (1999) use this approach to measure agglomeration economies in Japan. One difficulty with implementing this approach is finding reasonably refined data on rents. For instance, Dekle and Eaton are forced to use housing rent data as a proxy for commercial and industrial rents.

An additional and potentially tricky issue in looking at agglomeration through wages or rents is that in theory, productivity differentials should be capitalized in both wages and rents. The degree they are captured in one or the other depends on elasticities in the markets for land and labor and also on the presence of other local attributes like natural amenities. Thus, although positive evidence of wage or rent capitalization is evidence

[7] See Blomquist, Berger and Hoehn (1988), Gyourko and Tracy (1991), and Gabriel and Rosenthal (2004) for empirical work in this area.

of the existence of agglomeration economies, the absence of evidence of capitalization into one of the two is not evidence of the absence of agglomeration economies. For instance, if households prefer big cities because of amenities associated with big city life, this will work to raise rents and reduce wages in big cities. If firms find big city workers to be more productive, this works to raise wages and rents. If the household amenity effect is sufficiently large, this will lead to lower wages and higher rents in big cities despite the existence of agglomeration economies. Of course, the empirical relevance of this point depends on the degree to which amenity and firm productivity effects are correlated. If firms and households care about different things, for example, if firms care about proximity to firms in the same industry and households care about having a baseball team, then this problem would not arise.

2.3. *Industrial scope*

2.3.1. *Urbanization or localization economies*

The oldest debate in the empirical literature on agglomeration economies concerns industrial scope. Specifically, the debate concerns whether agglomeration economies are related to the concentration of an industry or to the size of a city itself, regardless of competition. In other words, the debate concerns the relative importance of localization and urbanization economies.

The earliest precise discussion of the microfoundations of agglomeration stemming from localization is in Marshall's (1920). Over a hundred years later, the analysis remains fresh:

> When an industry has thus chosen a locality for itself, it is likely to stay there long: so great are the advantages which people following the same skilled trade get from neighborhood to one another. The mysteries of the trade become no mysteries; but are as it were in the air, and children learn many of them unconsciously ... Employers are apt to resort to any place where they are likely to find a good choice of workers with the special skill which they require ... The advantages of variety of employment are combined with those of localized industries in some of our manufacturing towns, and this is a chief cause of their continued economic growth. [Marshall (1920, 271)]

Famous modern examples of highly localized industries include computers (Silicon Valley, Route 128 in Boston) and carpets (Dalton, Georgia), but also less well-known concentrations such as that of furniture manufacturing in High Point North Carolina as discussed in the Introduction.

An equally influential discussion of microfoundations related to the industrial scope of spatial concentration is found in Jacobs (1969). In contrast to Marshall's treatment of urban specialization, Jacobs stresses the importance of urban diversity. Her argument is that diversity fosters cross-fertilization of ideas. For instance, she notes that New

York's brassiere industry evolved not from the lingerie industry but from dressmakers' innovations.

This emphasis is clearly different than Marshall's, and this had led to the discussion of localization vs. urbanization being characterized as a contest between Marshall and Jacobs. This is not completely fair to Marshall, who explicitly recognized the value of urban diversity, both as a way to achieve domestic complementarity and to reduce risk:

> On the other hand a localized industry has some disadvantages as a market for labour if the work done in it is chiefly of one kind, such for instance as can be done only by strong men. In those iron districts in which there are no textile or other factories to give employment to women and children, wages are high and the cost of labour dear to the employer, while the average money earnings of each family are low. But the remedy for this evil is obvious, and is found in the growth in the same neighbourhood of industries of a supplementary character. Thus textile industries are constantly found congregated in the neighbourhood of mining and engineering industries, in some cases having been attracted by almost imperceptible steps; in others, as for instance at Barrow, having been started deliberately on a large scale in order to give variety of employment in a place where previously there had been but little demand for the work of women and children ... A district which is dependent chiefly on one industry is liable to extreme depression, in case of a falling-off in the demand for its produce, or of a failure in the supply of the raw material which it uses. This evil again is in a great measure avoided by those large towns or large industrial districts in which several distinct industries are strongly developed. If one of them fails for a time, the others are likely to support it indirectly; and they enable local shopkeepers to continue their assistance to workpeople in it. [Marshall (1920, pp. 273–274)]

Various studies have attempted to identify the impact of urbanization economies. As above, because this older work is nicely reviewed elsewhere [Eberts and McMillen (1999)], our discussion of this issue will be selective. Shefer (1973) considered a cross-section of MSAs and a group of industries, concluding that doubling city size would increase productivity by between 14 and 27%. Sveikauskas (1975) found only an increase of 6–7%, which is more in line with later work in this area. Segal (1976) improved on the capital stock measures of the earlier studies, and found that productivity was roughly 8% higher in cities with populations of two million or more. Fogarty and Garofalo (1978) find an increase in productivity of about 10% when city population is doubled. Moomaw (1981) finds the increase to be 2.7%. Tabuchi (1986) finds that doubling population gives a 4.3% increase in productivity. In sum, doubling city size seems to increase productivity by an amount that ranges from roughly 3–8%.[8]

The relative impact on productivity of localization and urbanization together are examined by Nakamura (1985) and Henderson (1986). Nakamura considers Japan, while

[8] Combes, Duranton and Gobillon (2003) find slightly smaller estimates after controlling for worker skills in a study using French wage data. Cingano and Schivardi (2003) also find a smaller estimate.

Henderson considers the U.S. and Brazil.[9] Both estimate production functions separately for two-digit manufacturing industries. Urbanization is proxied by total employment in the city. Localization is proxied by employment in the industry. While there is evidence of urbanization economies in several industries, there is evidence of localization economies in more. Some industries exhibit no evidence of external economies at all. Nakamura summarizes his work as finding that a doubling of industry scale leads to a 4.5% increase in productivity, while a doubling of city population leads to a 3.4% increase. Henderson finds almost no evidence of urbanization economies and substantial evidence of localization. Taken together, Henderson and Nakamura are more favorable to the existence of localization economies than urbanization economies. In addition, the variation across industries strongly suggests that one ought to estimate agglomeration economies separately for different industries.

Other papers have considered both localization and urbanization together. Moomaw (1983) finds evidence of both. In a births model, Rosenthal and Strange (2003) consider the impacts of own-industry and total employment in an analysis that directly considers the geographic scope of agglomeration economies. They find stronger evidence of localization. Most recently, Henderson (2003a) also finds localization effects to be strongest.

2.3.2. Specialization and diversity

There are other ways to specify industrial scope. One is to consider the degree to which a city's employment is specialized. This is typically measured as the share of a city's employment in a particular industry [i.e., Glaeser et al. (1992) and Henderson, Kuncoro and Turner (1995)]. Glaeser et al. consider growth over the period 1956–1987 of industries that were among a city's top six in 1956. All industries are grouped together in the estimation. They find that specialization does not encourage growth. Henderson et al. also consider growth, in this case from 1970–1987. They estimate separately for eight industries, three that were rapidly evolving high-technology industries during the period covered by the data and five that were mature industries with stable technologies. For the high-technology industries, they also find specialization to lack a positive effect on growth. For the mature industries, in contrast, they find a positive effect of specialization. This result is parallel to Duranton and Puga (2001a), who use French data to show that while new industries evolve in diverse cities, they move to specialized ones after reaching maturity.

Combes (2000b) argues that this specialization analysis must be viewed with some caution. The issue is in the interpretation of the specialization variable. Henderson, Kuncoro and Turner (1995) note that an increase in specialization holding sectoral employment constant leads to more growth among the mature industries. Combes notes that

[9] It is interesting to note that Henderson's (1986) use of the refined Brazilian data was made possible by a mistake where data that should have been censored were not. This suggests that obtaining data that gets close to that required for ideal estimation has at least some element of luck to it.

the only way that specialization could be greater holding sectoral employment constant would be for the entire city to become smaller. Thus, the result that specialization encourages growth could be interpreted as saying that small cities grow more quickly. Controlling for total city employment instead of sectoral employment gives an entirely different picture, one where specialization fails to encourage growth.

Another issue that complicates interpretation of specialization variables concerns absolute versus relative effects. Explicit theories of the microfoundations of agglomeration economies have nearly always been based on the idea that an increase in the absolute scale of activity has a positive effect. For instance, more workers allows better matching in Helsley and Strange (1990). This sort of model suggests that an increase in the scale of an industry increases productivity. It does not make direct predictions regarding the impact of the industry's share of employment in a particular city or regarding the city's share in the industry relative to other cites. The city share of employment variable is typically introduced as a kind of net effect. The absolute scale of own-industry activity has a positive effect if localization economies are at work, but if the city's share of employment in the industry is small, that means that there is a lot of other activity in the city. Through congestion, this could have a negative effect. Presumably, the relative share variable matters in the context of a firm selecting the location that has the greatest net effect as described above.[10]

The flip side of specialization is diversity, a different way to conceive of an urbanization economy. Considering the diversity of employment rather than simply city size is very much in the spirit of Jacobs, whose many stories capture the idea that a city's diversity of activity can breed cross-fertilization of technology and so lead to innovation and growth. The idea of diversity being important was developed prior to Jacobs by Chinitz (1961), who argues that its diversity was one reason that New York performed better than did Pittsburgh after World War II. The issue of diversity has been addressed in various ways in the literature.

As noted above, Glaeser et al. (1992) consider the determinants of the growth of the largest six industries within a given MSA. To evaluate what they call "Jacobs externalities", they control for the fraction of MSA employment in the MSA's 7th through 12th largest industries. A large MSA employment share in the 7th through 12th largest industries in the MSA is indicative of a diverse industrial base. As an alternative, Henderson, Kuncoro and Turner (1995) use a Herfindahl–Hirschman index (HHI) of employment diversity at the MSA level. As usual, HHI measures the aggregate difference between a city's sectoral employment pattern and one that would arise if employment were uniformly distributed. Rosenthal and Strange (2003) also use a Herfindahl measure calculated in the same manner, except their measure is based on zipcode level employment and they also include MSA fixed effects in their models. The MSA fixed effects capture the influence of broader MSA-wide diversity effects, while the Herfindahl controls

[10] We discuss specialization further in the context of labor market pooling in Section 3.

for within-MSA variation in employment diversity. These measures all capture the absolute level of employment diversity in a given region, regardless of whether that region is defined based on MSA boundaries, zipcodes, or other geographic dimensions.

The results of these papers are fairly consistent. Glaeser et al. (1992) find that diversity encourages growth. Rosenthal and Strange (2003) find that diversity encourages births. Henderson, Kuncoro and Turner (1995) find diversity to encourage growth among high-technology firms. Given the different specifications and the variety of industries considered, these results together strongly suggest that diversity is helpful. This is consistent with Jacobs, but it is not inconsistent with Marshall. In any case, the importance of the diversity of the rest of the city's employment does not itself rule out a parallel effect associated with the concentration of employment in a particular industry.

2.3.3. *Other work on industrial scope*

The issue of industrial scope has been considered extensively. In addition to the growth studies mentioned above, Combes (2000a) considers the effects of industrial scope on growth in France over the period 1984–1993. As he persuasively points out, it is worthwhile to consider agglomeration economies separately across countries. In France, labor mobility is lower than in the U.S., as it is in the rest of Europe. Further, European unemployment rates are higher. Either of these could impact the urban development process, and so it makes sense to analyze the process of agglomeration separately in the European environment. Combes finds that there is a substantial difference between the results for service industries and manufacturing. For manufacturing, specialization and diversity both have negative impacts on growth in all but a few sectors. For services, specialization continues to have a negative effect, but the effect of diversity becomes positive. It is worth pointing out that Combes' data includes 341 employment areas that cover the whole territory of France. This means that there is less likely to be a selection problem than in papers that have confined their analysis to urban areas only. This point is also made in Rosenthal and Strange (2003).

A different approach is taken by Wheaton and Lewis (2002). They identify an urban wage premium associated with both an increase in the concentration of own-industry employment in the city and with an increase in the specialization of the city in the industry. Agglomeration economies have been studied by looking at rents by Dekle and Eaton (1999), who look only at the effects of aggregate activity. Hence, they provide evidence of urbanization.

2.3.4. *Continuity and industrial scope*

In conclusion, it should be emphasized once more that, relative to the ideal approach outlined earlier, most papers to date have adopted restrictive treatments of industrial scope. The standard approach has been to distinguish between activity in an establishment's own industry from activity outside of the own industry. Thus, the question of the rate at which agglomeration economies attenuate as nearby activity becomes increasingly dissimilar is virtually unexplored. This is not surprising. While the concept of industrial distance has some useful parallels to geographic distance, the analogy is not exact. That is because the way to measure the geographic distance between two locations is clear. The distance between two industries is not. The closest that anyone comes to defining industries in a way that captures industrial distance is in the Cluster Mapping Project described in Section 4. That project defines 41 clusters of "related" industries based on supply relationships, the similarity of production, and so forth. However, the exact algorithm by which clusters are defined is proprietary, which is obviously a serious obstacle to economists using this sort of procedure.

The paper in the economics literature that makes the most substantial progress in characterizing industrial distance is Ellison and Glaeser (1997). They characterize the extent of co-agglomeration among two digit industries, showing that there are many instances of industries apparently affecting each other. They also consider the forces that govern co-agglomeration, showing that when there are upstream–downstream linkages, co-agglomeration is greater. In sum, Ellison and Glaeser (1997) provide strong evidence suggesting further consideration of industrial distance to be warranted.

A recent paper by Duranton and Puga (2001b) also makes some progress in this direction. They show that increasingly cities are organized not so much around traditional industrial classifications, but instead along functional lines. Specifically, they show that cities emphasize managerial and information oriented activity of the type that benefits from face-to-face contacts. Thus, the era of the one-industry town may be waning.[11]

2.4. Geographic scope

Until very recently the standard approach has been to define geography based on political boundaries such as states, MSAs, and counties. Establishment and industrial activity is then grouped within these locations treating all entities within a given location as being located at precisely the same spot. In addition, researchers have typically assumed, usually implicitly, that activity outside of a location has no effect on activity within the location. In other words, spatial lags are ignored. Studies that fit this characterization include those of Glaeser et al. (1992) and Henderson, Kuncoro and Turner (1995).

An important departure from this tradition is Ciccone and Hall (1996). In explaining state-level labor productivity, they include measures of county-level employment density. Since the theory of agglomeration is almost entirely concerned with density,

[11] It is worth pointing out that most of the papers that we have studied in this review consider the agglomeration of manufacturing industries. This is problematic given the central role of the service sector in the economies of cities today. Kolko (1999) helps to remedy this shortcoming by considering the agglomeration of service industries. He finds that the need for the sort of labor found in cities is a continuing agglomerative force, with this access continuing to be valuable even with improvements in information technology that allow communication at a distance.

this approach is welcome. They find a positive effect of density, with a doubling associated with roughly a 5% increase in productivity. Of course, states are large, and this approach implicitly supposes that an establishment in Buffalo is closer to one in New York City than would be an establishment in northern New Jersey. In a follow-up paper based on European data, Ciccone (2002) finds effects that are only slightly smaller than in the U.S. He finds that the elasticity of labor productivity with respect to employment density is 4.5% in Europe, compared to 5% in the U.S.

Dekle and Eaton (1999) use rents to consider agglomeration economies using Japanese prefecture-level data. For both finance and manufacturing, they find evidence of agglomeration economies, although the magnitude is roughly one-quarter of the Ciccone and Hall (1996) estimate. They also find evidence that an increase in activity across all of Japan increases productivity in any prefecture, which suggests a large geographic scope.

More recently still, Rosenthal and Strange (2003) provide a micro-level analysis of the geographic scope of agglomeration economies. The environment of an establishment is measured by constructing rings around the centroid of the establishment's zipcode. Rings of 1, 5, 10, and 15 miles are included. For five of the six industries studied (computer software, apparel, food processing, machinery, and fabricated metals) new arrivals are more likely to be attracted to zipcodes as employment in the own industry within one mile increases. Employment in the own industry just five miles away, however, has a much smaller effect, as does employment further out in the ten and fifteen mile rings. It is worth pointing out, however, that for some industries the effect remains significant at fifteen miles. In sharp contrast, employment outside of the own industry has an inconsistent and frequently insignificant effect.

These results are important because they provide evidence that agglomeration economies may attenuate rapidly across geographic space. Indirect evidence consistent with these results is also provided in Henderson (2003a). He finds that employment activity in a plant's own county affects plant productivity. But employment activity in neighboring counties is not found to affect the plant's productivity.

Rosenthal and Strange (2001) also provide indirect evidence that agglomeration economies attenuate across geographic space. In this paper, the level of agglomeration for individual 4-digit SIC industries is regressed on industry characteristics in an attempt to identify the micro-determinants of the sources of agglomeration economies (e.g., labor pooling, knowledge spillovers, shared inputs). The study uses the Ellison–Glaeser (1997) index of agglomeration calculated at the zipcode, county, and state levels of geography. We will discuss the paper's conclusions regarding microfoundations in Section 3. At this point, we emphasize just those results that have a geographic dimension. The first of these is that reliance on factors sensitive to shipping costs (manufactured inputs, natural resource inputs, and perishability of products) influences agglomeration at the state level. In contrast, knowledge spillovers impact highly localized agglomeration, while labor impacts agglomeration at all levels of geography. This is consistent with attenuation of agglomeration economies, with the geographic scope differing for the various agglomerative forces. It seems sensible to us that knowledge spillovers would have a different geographic scope than would, for instance, input sharing.[12]

Finally, Ellison and Glaeser (1997) present a measure of an industry's concentration, and compare this index at different levels of geography. This leads them to conclude that much of the effects are localized, but that there are also spillovers. In a follow-up paper on measuring localization, Duranton and Overman (2002) find geographic localization to take place at a relatively small scale, less than fifty kilometers.

2.5. Temporal scope

The key issue regarding the temporal scope of agglomeration economies is whether agglomeration economies are static or dynamic. This issue is touched on in the growth models of Glaeser et al. (1992) and Henderson, Kuncoro and Turner (1995). Both of these papers show that the characteristics of a city can impact its growth over a period of twenty years or more. This does not necessarily mean that the economic environment twenty years or so earlier continues to have a direct impact on growth. Instead, the effect may be indirect, an accumulation of much shorter direct effects over the period. For example, externalities arising from shared inputs make a city more attractive and draw additional industry to the local area. As this occurs, the ability to share inputs further increases, contributing to further growth of the urban area.[13] Although this is clearly a dynamic process, it is not a direct dynamic effect with a twenty-year reach. A different estimating strategy would be required to estimate that kind of effect.

The direct dynamic effect is most naturally thought of as a knowledge spillover, although it could take other forms. The idea is that if knowledge were to take time to accumulate, having a lot of activity a few years ago could directly influence today's productivity. In a sense, urban areas can be thought of as schools in which managers and workers can continually add to their skills. As the time spent in a local environment increases, knowledge of local business contacts and Marshall's "secrets of the trade" would also increase. Two otherwise identical enterprises in the same city may therefore benefit differently from the local agglomeration depending on how long each has been present. Similarly, two otherwise identical cities would offer different sorts of increasing return depending on their histories. We refer to the historical component of agglomeration economies as their temporal scope. The parallel to distance is natural. Two establishments at a physical distance have less effect on each other. The same is true for two establishments at a greater industrial distance from each other. Likewise, the effect is likely smaller for two establishments who are farther apart in time.

Henderson (1997) is the paper that most directly addresses the temporal scope of agglomeration economies. He uses lags and differencing methods to identify the impact

[12] It should also be emphasized that the geographic scope of different sources of agglomeration economies has only occasionally been considered. This issue is addressed more fully in Section 4.

[13] See Rauch (1993b) or Helsley and Strange (2001) for models of this kind of dynamic growth.

on growth of the local environment at some point in the past. As usual, he estimates separate models for different industries. Again, as usual, the estimates vary by industry, with some having externalities with a long temporal scope and others having externalities that are closer to being static. The largest effects on productivity are typically from own-industry employment at two to five years in the past. Henderson speculates that these lagged effects may arise because it takes time to learn from neighbors. If the knowledge does not lead to portable increases in productivity, which would be the case with knowledge about local networks, then mobility across locations may be reduced.

A more recent paper by Glaeser and Maré (2001) takes a different approach to the temporal scope of agglomeration economies. They employ three different major datasets, drawing on the advantages of each to offset limitations of the others.[14] The estimation involves individual wage rates being regressed on a variety of local attributes and worker characteristics. The key result is that workers earn higher wages in large cities, with the urban wage premium equaling 33%. It is possible that this result could be explained by selection instead of by agglomeration economies. This possibility is addressed by looking at the effects of urbanization on recent migrants. The key idea is that if selection is at work, then recent migrants would receive higher wages since they would be, by hypothesis, the most able. The conclusion of this analysis is that there remains a substantial urban wage premium, perhaps 20%.

The part of the analysis that bears most closely on the temporal scope of agglomeration economies comes from considering the timing of the urban wage premium. Glaeser and Maré (2001) report evidence that long-time residents in bigger cities earn a premium over workers newly arrived to the same city. In addition, they find that when long-time urban workers leave their city, their wages in their new location are higher the larger the size of the previous city of residence. These results complement those of Henderson (1997) and provide further evidence that agglomeration economies have a dynamic component. However, neither Henderson (1997) nor Glaeser and Maré (2001) address the mechanism by which the dynamic spillover occurs. Both here as in many other part of this literature, therefore, further research is warranted.

2.6. *Industrial organization, "culture", and the transmission of agglomeration economies*

Thus far, we have dealt with agglomeration economies as technological phenomena. The results that we have reported address the degree to which external economies in production exist and their industrial, geographic, and temporal scope. At this point, we will discuss a rather different approach to agglomeration economies, one that stresses incentives and organizational considerations rather than technology. As will become apparent, these considerations influence the degree to which a given pattern of agglomeration creates external economies.

[14] The datasets studied include the PSID, the National Longitudinal Survey of Youth (NLSY), and the decennial Census.

2.6.1. Competition

The key idea here is found in Porter (1990). He argues based on case evidence (to be discussed in Section 4) that local competition encourages innovation by forcing firms to innovate or fail. In this view, for any given set of industrial clusters, competitive pressure enhances productivity. Since a firm's competitors are by definition within its own industry, this is a localization-based view of agglomeration. A different possibility, one that Glaeser et al. (1992) ascribe to Marshall (1920), Arrow (1962), and Romer (1986), is that the presence of local competition will decrease productivity because of incomplete appropriation of the returns from innovation.

Glaeser et al. (1992) test these ideas in the growth models discussed earlier. They include as a regressor the ratio of establishments per employee in a city for a given industry relative to establishments per employee for the entire U.S. As this ratio decreases the local environment in the given industry is thought to become more competitive. Measuring local competition in this manner, Glaeser et al. find that an increase in competition is positively associated with growth.[15]

In related work, Henderson (2003a) considers the influence of the average size of plants in the establishment's own industry and county on individual plant productivity. He also controls for the number of own-industry plants present in the county, along with other plant-specific attributes, industry-time fixed effects, and plant-location fixed effects. Henderson finds that average employment per plant does not positively affect productivity for the high-tech and machinery industries. In contrast, the number of plants in the own industry in the plant's county does positively affect productivity among high-tech industries (the effect is insignificant for machinery). He interprets these findings as providing evidence that localization economies arise from the presence of establishments *per se*, rather than size of the establishment.

Rosenthal and Strange (2003) employ similar competition variables when studying the number of births of new establishments and their employment. The specific controls are the number of establishments per worker in the establishment's own industry and the number of establishments per worker in other industries. Both of these variables are measured at the zipcode level. For all six industries studied, results indicate that average establishment size outside of the own industry has a significant negative influence on arrivals of new establishments. But for five of the six industries average establishment size within the own industry has a significant and positive influence on arrivals, while for the sixth industry this variable is insignificant. The own-industry finding echoes results from Glaeser et al. (1992). As in that paper, one possible interpretation is that the presence of smaller establishments implies a more competitive environment and that competition is good for growth. But, as will be discussed below, an alternative

[15] Glaeser et al. (1992) also note that this result could reflect the fact that smaller establishments grow more quickly. That interpretation is consistent with empirical evidence from the industrial organization literature. See, for example, Evans (1987).

interpretation is that establishment size may be associated with a different way of doing business. In particular, smaller establishments may be more flexible and open to nearby companies, and therefore might make good neighbors.

2.6.2. *Industrial organization and business culture*

The other key idea in this section is due to Saxenian (1994). In her comparison of the differences in performance between the Silicon Valley and Boston's Route 128, she argues that local technological capabilities are not the fundamental source. The primary cause is instead the differences in local industrial organization and culture. The key difference is that the Silicon Valley is in some sense more entrepreneurial than Route 128. Saxenian's analysis is discussed further in Section 4. We will at this point instead discuss attempts to understand the nature of agglomeration by estimating the kinds of effects that Saxenian identifies.

In a model of births, Rosenthal and Strange (2003) look in two ways for evidence of an impact of firm size. First, they partition the agglomeration variables according to the size of the establishment in which a neighboring employee works. This allows the estimation of different agglomerative effects for a worker in a small firm compared to a worker in a large firm. The idea is that the small firm is likely to be more open, with a greater external effect being the predicted result. The second organizational regressor is based on whether the employee works at a subsidiary establishment or at an independent establishment. The latter is presumably more open, while the former is presumably more closed.

The results of this estimation are at least partly consistent with Saxenian. Adding an additional employee at a small firm typically has a significant and positive effect on births and new firm employment. Adding the employee at a large firm typically has an insignificant effect. To the extent that small firms are more open, this result is consistent with Saxenian. The performance of the subsidiary/nonsubsidiary variable is unexpected, with an extra worker at a subsidiary establishment having a larger effect. This is not consistent with Saxenian, suggesting as it does that corporate establishments may have larger effects on the productivity of neighbors. One possible explanation for this result may be that in some sense the quality of the interactions with nearby employees of subsidiary plants is greater than those of nearby independent plants. However, the reason for such quality differentials remains to be explored.

Henderson (2003a) also considers establishment size, but in a different way. He finds that small firms enjoy a larger increment to their productivity as own-industry employment increases in the same city. This result on how firm size can impact the reception of agglomerative spillovers complements the Rosenthal–Strange (2003) result on how firm size can impact the transmission of agglomerative spillovers. Both are consistent with Saxenian.

Florida and Gates (2001) take a very different approach to the quantification of a city's environment. They find that cities that have many "bohemians", defined as artistic occupation categories, tend to innovate more than do less creative cities. Similarly, cities with large gay populations are also more innovative. The results are interpreted as suggesting that tolerant environments are more innovative. While one would not want to read too much into these sorts of correlations, they are consistent with the idea that culture matters.

2.6.3. *The urban rat race*

Another agglomeration effect can be shown to follow from the different incentives possessed by urban residents. Specifically, cities can either inspire or require hard work of their residents, a kind of urban rat race. Rosenthal and Strange (2002) consider this issue by looking at the connection between agglomeration and work behavior. The paper begins by looking at the facts: urbanization is shown to be positively related to work hours for full-time workers in professional occupations, even after controlling for individual worker attributes and for occupational fixed effects. However, that pattern largely disappears after controlling for the localization of the worker's occupation. In addition, the pattern is never present among non-professional workers.

To investigate the source of these effects, two simple models are specified: a selection model in which hard working individuals choose to locate in an active professional environment, and an urban rat race model in which proximity to workers of a similar type causes individuals to work longer hours. If the intrinsic taste for hard work persists over time, then the selection model implies that workers of all ages should work longer hours in agglomerated environments. In contrast, the rat race model is based on the idea that competition encourages individuals to work longer hours when it is important to be noticed. This effect is likely most pronounced among young professionals who have the most to gain from reputation building.

The paper employs differencing methods to test for the presence of these effects using 1990 Census data on full-time workers. For professional workers in their 30's (defined as "young") and 40's (defined as "middle-aged"), work hours are longer in locations where the density of employment in the worker's occupation is high. No such effect is present for non-professional workers of any age. Adding controls for the proximity to rivals with whom the worker is most likely to compete – defined as individuals who earn a similar wage in the national wage distribution for the worker's occupation – does not change this result. Findings based on this specification also indicate that both young and middle-aged professional workers work longer hours in areas with a high concentration of individuals in their professions. In addition, young professionals are found to work longer hours when both rivals are present and the rewards to advancement are high. Absent such potential rewards, the presence of rivals does not differentially affect the work habits of young versus middle-aged professionals. It should also be noted that these results are robust to controls for occupation fixed effects and also the concatenation of occupation and MSA fixed effects (over 6000 fixed effects in all). On the whole, this work confirms the long held belief that cities attract industrious workers. The research also seems to identify an overlooked aspect of the urbanization–productivity relationship, that cities encourage hard work.

3. The sources of urban increasing returns

As noted earlier, there are many potential sources of agglomeration economies. A complete understanding of urban development clearly requires that these sources be understood. Some of these microfoundations were suggested by Marshall (1920), including knowledge spillovers, labor market pooling, and input sharing. There are many other causes of agglomeration that were not discussed by Marshall, including home market effects, urban consumption opportunities, and rent-seeking. The literature on the theoretical microfoundations of agglomeration economies is surveyed in another chapter [Duranton and Puga (2004)]. This section will consider econometric evidence on microfoundations. Table 2 provides an overview of some of the studies to be discussed. Three

Table 2
The Marshallian microfoundations of agglomeration economies

Microfoundation	Paper	Key results
Natural advantage	Kim (1999), Ellison and Glaeser (1999)	Factor endowments matter
Input sharing	Holmes (1999)	More purchased inputs in clusters
Labor market pooling	Diamond and Simon (1990)	Labor market risk capitalized in wages
	Kahn and Costa (2001)	High-education married locate in large cities
Knowledge spillovers	Jaffe, Trajtenberg and Henderson (1993)	More citations of a patent in the same MSA, controlling for industry effects
	Rauch (1993a), Moretti (2000)	City average education raises wage
Home market effects	Davis and Weinstein (1999)	For some industries, regional development explained by market access
Consumption	Tabuchi and Yoshida (2000)	Real wages lower in cities (reflecting consumption possibilities)
	Glaeser, Kolko and Saiz (2001)	Various measures of consumption possibilities predict growth
	Waldfogel (2003)	Agglomeration enhances consumption possibilities in radio listening
Rent seeking	Ades and Glaeser (1995)	Dictatorship predicts mega-cities
	Henderson (2003b)	Dictatorship encourages urban primacy, which discourages growth
Multiple	Rosenthal and Strange (2001)	Evidence of labor market pooling at state, county, and zipcode levels of geography; of knowledge spillover and input sharing at zipcode and state levels
	Dumais, Ellison and Glaeser (1997)	Strongest evidence for labor market pooling, some evidence for knowledge spillovers and input sharing
	Audretsch and Feldman (1996)	Evidence of input sharing and knowledge spillovers at the state level

other chapters will also consider this sort of evidence [Audretsch and Feldman (2004), Moretti (2004), and Head and Mayer (2004)], so in some places, we will refer to them.

As in Section 2, it is helpful to begin by considering how an ideal empirical analysis would proceed. Clearly, the same sort of evidence that would have been required to estimate the contributions of urbanization and localization would be required to identify the microfoundations of agglomeration economies. In fact, even more detailed data would be needed, since it would no longer be sufficient to observe the contribution of own-industry employment to productivity. Instead, it would be necessary to observe the specific channels by which own-industry activity impacts productivity. For instance, in evaluating plant level productivity, information on the local knowledge that spilled-in would be required. Regarding inputs and workers, the data would have to include information on the quality of the match between worker and input and the employing firm. It is hard to imagine the ideal data ever being available, and so some sort of econometric compromise is necessary.

3.1. Increasing returns or natural advantage?

We will begin by considering an approach that looks at microfoundations in a negative way. Estimates of the impact of agglomeration on productivity reviewed in Section 2 should be interpreted as providing an upper bound on the magnitudes of the various sorts of agglomeration economies. This is because agglomeration arises both because of the benefits of locating in areas endowed with natural advantages and also because of the influence of agglomeration economies. The estimated impact of agglomeration economies, therefore, can be refined by determining the share of productivity that can be attributed to a location's natural advantage instead of to agglomeration economies.

The potential role of natural advantage is easy to see. The steel industry in North America, for example, was initially concentrated in the Great Lakes region largely because of the presence of iron ore and coal. Similarly, it is certainly true that at least part of California's growth can be attributed to its climate, which would allow employers to pay lower wages than where the weather was less pleasant. In order to analyze the sources of agglomeration economies, it is therefore necessary to begin by looking at the degree to which natural advantage explains location.

There is a long history of empirical research on industrial location that has considered the role of natural advantage. As always, Marshall (1920, p. 269) is seminal, noting that:

> Many various causes have led to the localization of industry, but the chief causes have been physical conditions; such as the character of the climate or the soil, the existence of mines and quarries in the neighborhood, or within easy access by land or water.

Fuchs (1962) is an exhaustive North American reference, documenting the importance of access to resources for manufacturing industries.

Natural advantage has also been considered more recently. Kim (1995, 1999) and Ellison and Glaeser (1999) have argued that natural advantages are very important in determining agglomeration. This means a smaller role for increasing returns in the process of agglomeration. Looking at agglomeration between 1860–1987, Kim (1995) regresses a location quotient, measuring the concentration of industry, against measures of plant size, natural resources, and industry and time dummies. The positive coefficient on the natural resources variable is interpreted as being consistent with an important role for natural advantage in determining agglomeration.[16] Over a slightly different period, 1880–1987, Kim (1999) estimates a Rybczynski equation, regressing state employment in a given industry on factor endowments. This approach assumes that all factors of production are immobile, including labor. It is maintained that the residuals in this estimation are upper bounds on the strength of agglomeration economies. In a similar way, Ellison and Glaeser (1999) employ predicted state level employment variables to account for the importance of natural advantage in agglomeration. Both Kim and Ellison and Glaeser conclude that natural advantage is important. Specifically, Ellison and Glaeser show that the percentage of agglomeration that is predicted by the natural advantage proxies is roughly 20%. Ellison and Glaeser argue that the proxies are imperfect, and so the fraction of agglomeration that could possibly be explained is larger than 20%. Exactly how much larger is unclear, which seems to leave a lot of agglomeration unexplained by the natural advantage proxies.

A more serious issue in interpreting these results is that they assume all factors of production to be immobile, including labor. It is, of course, precisely the mobility of labor that leads to agglomeration in the presence of external increasing returns in production. Or in reverse: external increasing returns lead to the agglomeration of labor. Attributing the productivity of agglomerated labor to natural advantage seems, therefore, to be questionable, at least for more recent periods (i.e., labor probably was fairly immobile in the early periods considered by Kim (1999)).

3.2. What do the productivity studies have to say about microfoundations?

Not much. Although claims are made regarding the nature of the externalities that are measured, it can be shown that agglomeration economies whose sources are knowledge spillovers, labor market pooling, or input sharing all manifest themselves in pretty much the same way. To see this, suppose that a firm's profits equal $g(A)f(x) - c(x) + \varepsilon$, where A is an index of agglomeration economies, x is a vector of the traditional inputs of production, and ε is an independent and identically distributed error term, distributed across establishments according to the cumulative distribution function $\Phi(\varepsilon)$. The first-order conditions for optimal input demands are of the form $g(A)\partial f/\partial x_i = \partial c/\partial x_i$

[16] He argues that there is little evidence of external economies impacting regional specialization. This conclusion is based on the fact that high-technology industries are not significantly more concentrated than are other industries and on the claim that theories of agglomeration imply that high-technology industries are more sensitive to external economies. The fact is interesting, but the claim, while tempting, is not an immediate consequence of any theories of agglomeration of which we are aware. In fact, Duranton and Puga (2001a) note that specialized cities are attractive for mature industries.

where x_i is an input (i.e., labor) and $\partial c/\partial x_i$ is the marginal cost of the input (i.e., the wage). An increase in $g(A)$ from any source will lead to higher productivity, higher employment of the input and, through the usual derived demand channel, to an increase in the price of the input. Thus, high productivity, employment, wages, and rents reflect the presence of agglomeration economies. They are not, however, evidence of any particular agglomeration economy.

The same observational equivalence holds for growth. This point is made precisely in Helsley and Strange (2001). The thrust of the argument is as follows. Growth requires profitability. Profitability requires productivity, which may be enhanced in a dynamic sense by agglomeration economies. Suppose that each firm, actual or potential, requires a specific heterogeneous input, indexed by y in the characteristic space, which is taken to be the unit circle. Prior activity makes these inputs available. The greater the amount of prior activity, the thicker will be the input market. This means that agglomeration can enhance growth by allowing future activity to be carried out at lower cost, since the costs of adjusting pre-existing inputs will decrease with the amount of activity. Thus, growth fosters agglomeration by making inputs available to entrepreneurs. However, the input can be anything: a supply channel developed by existing firms, a labor market pool that prior employment has created, or an idea that flows from existing activity. As long as current activity creates something that future entrepreneurs can draw from (physical inputs, a labor pool, or local knowledge), agglomeration will enhance growth.

This observational equivalence is somewhat unfortunate, since it means that the well-developed literature on the scope of agglomeration does not directly shed a lot of light on the microfoundations of agglomeration economies. There have occasionally been instances where results on a growth–localization or growth–diversity relationship were interpreted as knowledge spillovers. While it is true that knowledge spillovers are certainly one possible channel by which growth could be influenced by localization or by diversity, it is not the only one. These claims should, therefore, be taken with some caution.

In order that the productivity studies could be interpreted as bearing on the microfoundations of agglomeration economies, it is necessary to interpret the results in a more structural way. Two approaches of this kind have been suggested. One, proposed by Glaeser and Maré (2001), is to look to the dynamic structure of agglomeration economies for evidence of microfoundations.[17] As noted in the previous section, they find the positive effect of urbanization on wages to occur with a lag. One is tempted to interpret this result as reflecting knowledge spillovers among workers, with the slow increase in wage reflecting the accumulation of knowledge. The other approach, proposed by Henderson (2003a) is to look at the effect of the number of firms, rather than their employment levels, on the productivity of neighbors. He argues that this variable is more likely to capture knowledge spillovers than other microfoundations. For this to

[17] Glaeser and Maré (2001) are explicitly aware of the observational equivalence problem, noting that an increase in wages can reflect any sort of agglomeration economy.

be true, it must be the case, however, that the amount of knowledge that can spill out from a firm does not increase with its activity level. It must also be true that the spilling out of knowledge must be independent of the number of workers with the knowledge. An equivalent interpretation of a positive sign on a numbers variable would be that each firm needs its own input, and so the market thickness effects in the input market would depend on numbers and not levels. Of course, this interpretation has the same sort of qualifications that the knowledge spillover interpretation did. It does seem clear, nonetheless, that an effect of the number of firms rather than their employment levels is not consistent with the idea of labor market pooling.

In sum, the many excellent studies of productivity have told us about the existence of agglomeration economies and also about their scope across industries, locations, and time. They have not, however, had much to say about the sources of agglomeration economies. These approaches are the subject of the rest of this section.

3.3. Individual microfoundations

One way to analyze the sources of agglomeration economies without being able to make inferences from data on productivity, growth, or wages is to look at proxies for the microfoundation. For example, although it is difficult to link Marshallian input sharing directly to productivity, it may be possible to determine when input sharing is taking place. By relating this information to location patterns, one may be able to assess the theoretical claims on input sharing and agglomeration. In principle, this method can be applied to the other Marshallian microfoundations of labor market pooling and knowledge spillovers, as well as to other potential sources such as urban consumption opportunities.

3.3.1. Input sharing

Marshall's notion of input sharing depends crucially on the existence of scale economies in input production. If there were no scale economies, then a downstream firm could procure inputs at the same low price in isolation as it could in the midst of other similar firms. In the case where there are scale economies, however, the isolated firm will be at a disadvantage. Only downstream firms located where the industry is concentrated will be able to outsource their input demands to producers who are able to achieve an efficient scale of production.

Holmes (1999) considers the connection between the characteristics of a firm's location – concentrated or not – on input sharing. His insightful treatment of employment concentration is based on U.S. Census data on manufacturing from 1987 at the establishment level. This is matched with data on purchased inputs, also from the Census, that is available for locations. The locations by which this is defined vary by industry.[18]

[18] For instance, he notes that data on purchased inputs for the creamery butter industry is partitioned into only two locations: Wisconsin and the rest of the U.S.

Dividing purchased inputs by sales gives purchased input intensity, which is his measure of vertical disintegration and therefore of input sharing. These data are used in two ways. First, the differences between purchased input intensity between the most concentrated location and the rest of the U.S. are compared. This analysis shows that the most concentrated industries exhibit a relationship that is consistent with input sharing. For instance, the pantyhose industry is concentrated in North Carolina with 62% of national employment, and purchased input intensity of 53%, compared to 40% nationally. This pattern is repeated for other concentrated industries.

The second approach uses regression analysis. The dependent variable is the difference between purchased input intensity and industry mean purchased input intensity. This is regressed on the amount of same-industry employment in the establishment's own county and in other counties whose geographic centers are within fifty miles, again differenced from an industry mean. The results are again consistent with input sharing. Averaging across industries, moving from an unconcentrated location (499 or fewer neighboring employees in the same industry) to a concentrated location (10,000–24,999 neighboring employees) results in a 3% increase in purchased input intensity. Of course, as noted in Section 2, there is nothing in the theory to suggest that the effects would be the same across industries. To deal with this, Holmes considers the ten most concentrated industries. For these, he finds an effect that is roughly twice as large. In sum, there is consistent evidence of a positive relationship between vertical disintegration and industrial concentration that is strongly suggestive of Marshallian input sharing.

If there were input sharing, one would also expect there to be a greater fraction of input suppliers carrying out specialized functions. Thus, with highly refined data it might be possible to test for the existence of input sharing by looking for the presence of specialized input suppliers at locations where an industry is concentrated. Unfortunately, the nature of industry classification, specifically the practice of putting vertically linked stages of production into the same category, makes this test difficult to carry out. Holmes notes that the textile industry is defined in a way that overcomes this difficulty. He therefore uses the industry's specialized finishing plants (SIC 226) and the entire textile industry (SIC 22) to look for a relationship between the fraction of specialized plants and his measure of industry concentration. The relationship among the median specialized input fraction and concentration is exactly consistent with the existence of input sharing.[19]

In our view, the work by Holmes (1999) offers the most direct and compelling evidence to date of the importance of input sharing as a source of agglomeration economies. Even here, however, interpretation issues arise. In particular, plants with idiosyncratically strong tendencies to rely on shared inputs will naturally seek out locations where such opportunities are present, while agglomeration itself enhances opportunities for input sharing. From an econometric perspective, this implies that plant location is endogenous causing Holmes to overestimate the causal influence of agglomeration on opportunities for input sharing. Nevertheless, the positive relationship identified

[19] In a related paper, Ono (2002) finds there to be more outsourcing in large cities.

in Holmes' work between input sharing and agglomeration can only arise if agglomeration facilitates such opportunities. In that sense, findings by Holmes (1999) unambiguously support the presence of input sharing as a source of agglomeration economies.[20]

Several other papers also provide evidence supportive of the role of input sharing. The importance of input sharing at the macro level is touched on in Bartlesman, Caballero and Lyons (1994). They present a growth model that uses panel data methods to consider the possible presence of thick market effects on productivity. While this analysis is not focused on cities, it does seem to be relevant. The key result of the "within" estimates – drawing on temporal variation to identify effects – is the finding that customer thickness has a large effect on growth, but supplier thickness does not. The "between" results – estimates that draw on cross-sectional variation to identify effects – are exactly opposite. The cross-sectional results show a strong reduced form relationship between supplier thickness and productivity. Together, Bartlesman, Caballero and Lyons (1994) reconcile these findings by observing that over the short-term customers are crucial. Over the long term, it is the suppliers who matter most.

Holmes and Stevens (2002) is also relevant to input sharing, although it does not address the issue directly. They find that establishment size is larger where an industry is concentrated. This result is identified using a "size coefficient", equal to the ratio of the mean establishment size (measured in value of output) at a location to the mean size in the sector across the U.S. This result contrasts with Vernon's (1960) analysis of firm sizes in the New York region. It does not, of course, directly address the degree of vertical integration. In sum, the papers reviewed above provide fairly strong evidence that input sharing is important, both for cities and overall.[21]

3.3.2. Knowledge spillovers

Knowledge spillovers may be the most interesting of the microfoundations, speaking as they do to so many different areas of economics, including growth theory and the economics of human capital. There is no doubt, however, that knowledge spillovers are difficult to identify empirically. Unlike input sharing, for instance, knowledge is often exchanged without being bought and sold – the word "spillover" is important [see Helsley and Strange (2002)]. Even if there is an exchange, it is more likely to be a complicated joint venture between organizations, the kind of transaction for which data are routinely collected. Thus, the econometrician faces many challenges in measuring knowledge spillovers.

One way to deal with the challenges is to look for direct evidence of knowledge spilling over. This has the obvious advantage of its directness, but it does not directly

[20] The R^2 values in the input share regression in Holmes (1999) are also quite low. Although to some extent this is to be expected given that Holmes differences away the industry means from the data, the very low R^2 values are suggestive that other unspecified factors also contribute to input sharing.

[21] There are many papers in the tradition of the New Economic Geography that also consider input sharing as a possible source of agglomeration. See the chapter by Head and Mayer (2004) for a discussion.

tie the knowledge spillover to either agglomeration or productivity. One example of this kind of research is Jaffe, Trajtenberg and Henderson (1993). They provide probably the most compelling evidence to date for the idea that knowledge spillovers are important and that such spillovers attenuate with geographic distance. They identify a "paper trail" of knowledge spillovers in the location of patent citations. The key result is that patent citations are highly spatially concentrated, with citations 5 to 10 times as likely to come from the same SMSA as control patents. Other papers looking at knowledge spillovers in this way include Jaffe (1989) and Acs, Audretsch and Feldman (1992).[22] It is important to remember that even in this kind of research, the issue of industrial scope remains.

This kind of research has proceeded in parallel with work that has attempted to study the impact of industry characteristics on innovation, presumably the most important direct outcome of knowledge spillovers. Of course, innovative activity in the broadest sense is very difficult to measure, forcing researchers to use narrower proxies. One example of this kind of research is Audretsch and Feldman (1996). In addition to looking as well at the determinants of agglomeration (see below), they consider the impact of agglomeration on innovation. Their measure of innovation is based on a count of significant product introductions by the Small Business Administration in 1982. Those data are not commonly collected and are particularly valuable. Audretsch and Feldman (1996) regress the spatial concentration of innovative activity conditional on a number of local and industry specific attributes, including university research in the field, expenditures on research and development, and the availability of skilled labor. They also control for the industry-specific spatial concentration of manufacturing activity. Results confirm that knowledge oriented industries have more spatially concentrated innovative activity, consistent with the presence of knowledge spillovers.

This strand of the literature is surveyed fully in another chapter [Audretsch and Feldman (2004)], so we will not comment on it further. Instead, we will move on to consider a related strand of the urban literature that deals with human capital externalities. Since this literature is also the subject of another chapter [Moretti (2004)], our goal will be simply to characterize how the human capital literature relates to the microfoundations of agglomeration economies. We will consider only highlights from the literature, and not even all of them.

The key idea in these papers is that workers are the primary vehicle of knowledge spillovers. This seems to be what Marshall had in mind in his discussion of Sheffield cutlery workers taking advantage of the secrets of their trade that are available as local public goods. Rauch (1993a) considers this issue by looking at the impact of the average level of education on wages and rents. Using a hedonic model in the spirit of Roback (1982), he shows that the presence of public good effects should increase wages where

[22] Almeida and Kogut (1999) employ the Jaffe, Trajtenberg and Henderson (1993) methodology to look at the characteristics of regions impact knowledge spillovers. Their key result is that regions differ in the way that knowledge spills-over, a result reminiscent of Saxenian (1994).

average education levels are high, since workers will be more productive and employers will be willing to pay high wages in competing for them. In addition, his model shows that rents will be high too, since the productivity enhanced high wages will naturally be capitalized into housing prices.

Rauch employs 1990 Census data to test these predictions. The primary conclusion is that both wages and rents rise significantly with average education. The magnitudes are nontrivial, with a one year increase in average schooling leading to an increase of 3% in wages and 13% in rents. One potential difficulty with this result is that schooling, whether at the average or individual level, is endogenous. Acemoglu and Angrist (1999) use compulsory schooling laws as an instrument for the local level of education. They then estimate the effects of local education, finding a positive effect, but one that is small and insignificantly different from zero. Following up on Rauch, Moretti (2000) considers the impact of the presence of college graduates on a city's wages. He finds a positive effect of this kind of human capital. Together with Rauch and Acemoglu–Angrist, this might suggest that the human capital externalities depend on highly educated workers.

One objection that one can make to looking at the effects of local education levels as a way to understand knowledge spillovers is that the exact channel of interaction is unspecified. Charlot and Duranton (2002) address this issue using survey data. They find reported workplace communication to be more extensive in urban areas. They then show this communication to impact wages. This impact is small, however, amounting to roughly one-tenth of the urban education premium. This may mean that the education premium depends on something other than knowledge spillovers or that the surveys do not uncover all of the knowledge spillovers that take place. The issue of human capital in cities continues to receive considerable attention. As noted above, we believe that with only a few exceptions, the literature has provided little compelling evidence on the mechanism by which knowledge spillovers are transmitted.

3.3.3. Labor market pooling

There are two related interpretations of labor market pooling. One is that workers should be better matched in large cities (an urbanization effect) or in industrial concentrations (a localization effect). It is not clear how one might assess the quality of a worker's match. One possibility would be to look at termination rates, controlling for measures of the health of the local economy and the industry. To the extent that bad matches lead to termination, this would be one way to look for direct evidence of labor market pooling. However, in the absence of a good replacement, a firm would be less likely to fire a worker of any given match quality. Thus, the viability of this approach is unclear. Another possible approach to identifying labor market pooling would be to look at turnover. The implications of the labor-market pooling hypothesis are that workers can readily change jobs and that firms can just as readily change employees. This has the same difficulty as using termination, however, since it is not clear that turnover would actually occur in a thicker labor market.[23] Another way to look at match quality is to look at specialization. In this vein, Baumgardner (1988) shows that physicians perform a narrower range of activities in large markets. This confirmation of Smith on the division of labor is also consistent with Marshallian labor market pooling in that it shows that agglomeration can foster specialization.

The other interpretation of labor market pooling is that it is fundamentally about risk. Workers and firms confront two kinds of risk in choosing to work for a particular employer in a particular city. One is worker and firm-specific: for reasons particular to the match between worker and firm, the employment relationship may be terminated. Assuming that the termination did not result from exiting the labor market completely, the worker needs another job, and the firm needs another worker. If the worker's skills and the firm's labor requirements are specific to an industry, then these needs will be easier to meet in a location where the industry is concentrated. Thus, the worker and firm-specific risk will be reduced by localization.

The second source of risk is industry-specific. Suppose that industries are subject to shocks. In this case, an industry shock could result in a worker losing a job. The worker will not find getting a job to be easy if the rest of the employers in the area are in the same negatively shocked industry. Thus, locating in a specialized city exposes a worker to greater risk. This analysis implies that industry specific shock discourages localization, while the match-specific shocks described above encourage it. It is, therefore, an empirical question of how the degree of local specialization impacts the labor market.[24]

Simon (1988) considers the relationship between the unemployment rate and a city's specialization. The latter is measured using an industry-based Herfindahl index. He shows that unemployment is greater the more specialized is a city, which is consistent with the industry-specific shocks being important. To the extent that risk is greater in a specialized city, then workers will require higher wages as compensation. Diamond and Simon (1990) address this issue, showing that workers demand higher wages in more specialized cities. This effect is tied to risk by showing that the higher wages are related to the specific measures of the cyclical variability of an industry's employment. In sum, this work is a formal treatment of Hoover's (1948) idea that one of the benefits of urbanization is the diversification it provides against sector-specific shocks to the local economy.

23 Recent evidence on turnover is provided by Fallick, Fleischman and Rebitzer (2003) and Di Addario and de Blasio (2003). Fallick et al. find that computer industry worker mobility rates are greater in the Silicon Valley than outside of California. This effect is not found for other industries. Di Addario and de Blasio also fail to find a general increase in job mobility in the Italian Industrial Districts, which are considered by many to be European cousins of the Silicon Valley.

24 A related point is made by Krugman (1991), who shows that if demand shocks are uncorrelated across individual establishments within a given industry, then firms operating in a pooled environment face an elastic labor supply function, enjoy stable wages, and are able to expand and contract during good and bad times. Krugman shows the benefits firms gain from the pooled environment during good times more than offset costs that arise from their inability to offer lower wages during bad times. On average, firms earn higher profits in the pooled environment, even when firms are risk neutral.

The notion that risk is lower and matches are better in large cities is crucial in Costa and Kahn (2001). They consider "power couples", defined as married couples where both partners have at least a bachelor's degree. They document a substantial increase in the fraction of these couples located in large cities, from 32% in 1940 to 50% in 1990. This is an increase that is substantially greater than the increase in the population of the large cities over that period. One explanation for this is that these couples met and married in large cities. Another is that large cities offer a resolution to the dual career problem by increasing the probability that both partners will be able to find jobs that are closely matched to their abilities. They test between these hypotheses by looking at the differences between power couple location patterns and the location patterns of other types of couples, singles, and "potential" couples (referred to as "incidental" couples in the paper). Using the differencing strategy, Costa and Kahn (2001) conclude that 36% of the increase in the concentration of power couples in large cities is explained by the dual career hypothesis.[25] This story is very much in the spirit of the statistical explanations of agglomeration economies that have been offered since Marshall (1920) and Hoover (1948). It has important implications for the future of cities. If the productivity of the highly educated is crucial for economic performance [as in Moretti (2000)] and if these workers continue to marry each other, then large cities will have at least one large productivity advantage relative to small cities.

3.3.4. Home market effects

Marshall is properly regarded as the first word on agglomeration economies. He is not the last. Various other explanations for agglomeration have been proposed.

One of these is the home market effect. Suppose that increasing returns lead to the concentration of employment into a large factory. This in turn, creates a large market, which, in the presence of transportation costs induces other firms to choose the same location. The idea here is that the interaction between internal scale economies in production and transport costs lead to a "magnification", where home market size expands in a self-reinforcing process of agglomeration.

One of the first formal treatments of the home market effect is Krugman (1980). Davis and Weinstein (1996) look at the relative magnitude of home market effects based on increasing returns and the more traditional Heckscher–Ohlin effects in a sample of OECD countries. They find substantially stronger evidence for Heckscher–Ohlin. A followup paper, Davis and Weinstein (1999), looks at regional agglomeration, instead of international, by considering data on Japanese prefectures. Here, in contrast, there are substantial increasing returns effects in eight out of the nineteen manufacturing industries that they study. This leads them to conclude that the home market effect may be an important determinant of regional concentration, of which the agglomeration into cities is an important instance.

[25] The use of difference-in-difference estimation methods in Costa and Kahn (2001) is highly effective. We believe that this approach could prove useful in the study of other problems in the agglomeration literature.

In a number of careful papers looking at location patterns on the U.S.–Mexico border before and after NAFTA, Hanson (1998a, 1998b) also looks at home market effects, among other things. He finds that increases in the openness of the Mexican market led to a substantial shift in the economic geography of manufacturing, with a new concentration near the border arising and the traditional concentration around Mexico City declining. This is consistent with what one would expect as trade liberalization makes the home market less important.

Taken together, these papers provide evidence of the existence of home market effects. A more complete survey of this literature is provided in another chapter [Head and Mayer (2004)].

3.3.5. Consumption

There has recently been work on agglomeration that has emphasized the consumption possibilities of large cities as sources of agglomeration. This is in clear contrast to the traditional analysis of agglomeration that has focused on the ability of cities to enhance productivity. Glaeser, Kolko and Saiz (2001) argue that there are four fundamental ways that large cities enhance consumption. First, there may be goods and services available in large cities that are not available elsewhere (i.e., opera or restaurants). Second, large cities may offer various aesthetic charms (i.e., the Los Angeles climate or Paris architecture). Third, large cities may allow the provision of public goods that would not be possible in a smaller place (i.e., specialized schools). Fourth, the relatively dense settlement of a large city allows speed of interaction that would not be possible in a smaller city (i.e., social interactions).

Glaeser, Kolko and Saiz (2001) present several different kinds of evidence to indicate the importance of consumption for cities. One is the rise of reverse commuting, which grew by 2.79% between 1980 and 1990, and at a roughly similar pace in the two previous decades. This suggests that some individuals working at suburban sites are willing to incur higher central city house prices (quality adjusted) for the opportunity to enjoy central city consumption amenities. Another kind of evidence emerges from reduced-form regressions of urban growth on various measures of a city's consumption possibilities. A temperate climate is a strong predictor of growth, as are the presence of museums and theaters. Cities with a large number of bowling alleys did not grow. Of course, there may be problems of endogeneity in that growth helps to finance cultural amenities while cultural amenities and public infrastructure can promote growth. Finally, Glaeser et al. also present evidence of an increasing concentration of wealth in central locations. On balance, the patterns noted by Glaeser et al. are consistent with the idea that consumption possibilities are a source of agglomeration economies.

Waldfogel (2003) and George and Waldfogel (2003) also deal with the implications of agglomeration for consumption. The key idea is that a larger market may allow goods to be more closely tailored to individual consumers' tastes. Waldfogel (2003) examines radio listening patterns, and finds that the average fraction of the population listening to radio increases by 2 percent with a one million person increase in a city's population.

This result is analogous to urbanization effects in manufacturing productivity. Waldfogel also finds that the number of radio stations targeting African American and Hispanic groups increases with the size of those populations apart from city size per se. This result is analogous to localization effects in manufacturing productivity. These patterns are mirrored in George and Waldfogel (2003), who analyze the newspaper purchases at the zipcode level. They find consumption externalities, with black newspaper purchases increasing with the size of the black community and decreasing with the size of the white community. White newspaper purchases, in contrast, increase with the size of the white community but are unaffected by the size of the black community. These findings suggest that local newspapers cater to the tastes of their dominant customer group, within group preference externalities are positive, and across group externalities are negative.

Tabuchi and Yoshida (2000) look at nominal and real wages to arrive at estimates of the relative strengths of the production and consumption inducements to agglomeration. They find that the elasticity of nominal wage with respect to city size is 10%. Since firms would not pay higher wages in larger cities unless there were also a corresponding increase in productivity, this nominal wage effect is interpreted as a traditional agglomeration economy in production. The elasticity of real wage with respect to city size is between −7 and −12%, depending on specification. This is interpreted as an agglomeration economy in consumption: workers acceptance of lower real wages in cities implies a corresponding consumption benefit.

The idea that workers would be willing to give up real wage to enjoy a city's consumption amenities is a central feature of a related literature on urban quality of life [e.g., Blomquist, Berger and Hoehn (1988), Gyourko and Tracy (1991)]. In that literature, the value that workers place on the opportunity to live in one city over another is measured by the difference in real wage necessary for the worker to be indifferent between the two areas. Gabriel and Rosenthal (2004) extend that idea to also measure the quality of a city's business environment – equal to the sum of land rent and wage a firm would be willing to incur for the opportunity to locate a worker in a given city. They create and analyze a panel of such measures for 37 cities over the 1977 to 1995 period. Results support the idea that cities attractive to industry grow larger, which is consistent with standard arguments in the agglomeration literature.

3.3.6. Rent-seeking

Marshall's analysis of agglomeration is that cities exist and industries concentrate because this sort of agglomeration is useful. This need not be the case. Ades and Glaeser (1995) demonstrate a relationship between rent-seeking and the formation of mega-cities, the "urban giants" that are homes to disproportionate shares of their countries' populations. Using a cross-section of 85 countries, they find that economic factors are part of the explanation of this kind of urban primacy. Specifically, tariff barriers lead to a larger degree of urban primacy, and the development of an inter-city transport network leads to less. Political factors are even more important than economic ones. Ades and Glaeser (1995) show this by constructing an index of political instability based on the numbers of coups, revolutions, and strikes. This index is shown to be associated with greater urban concentration. Centralized political systems – measured by an index of political rights such as voting procedures – have the same effect. For instance, an unstable dictatorship has 37% of its urban population in the largest city, while a stable democracy has only 23%. Of course, political stability and political rights are potentially endogenous to the level of urbanization. In order to address the issue of causality, Ades and Glaeser instrument using predetermined political characteristics, regional political characteristics, and regional infrastructure. In addition, they use the timing of urban growth to address the causality issue. The results of both procedures lead Ades and Glaeser to conclude that politics contributes to spatial concentration.

In order to be more specific about the mechanisms by which this occurs, Ades and Glaeser consider a number of case studies of urban gigantism. These cases consider classical Rome, Tudor and Stuart London, Edo during the period of the Shoguns, Buenos Aires around 1900, and Mexico City today. All of these had at least some element of the political causation of urban primacy. In Rome, for example, citizens could avail themselves of the fruits of empire by locating in the capital city and accepting imperial bread in return for not challenging the current ruler. In Mexico's centralized government, albeit nominally a federal one, it is possible to obtain valuable patronage (i.e., land), by locating in Mexico City. The implicit threat of a riot is parallel to the Roman situation. In sum, the ability to engage in rent-seeking seems to be one force that leads to the concentration of population in mega-cities.

Henderson (2003b) takes this analysis a step further. This paper also considers the determinants of urban primacy. As in Ades and Glaeser (1995), centralization, specifically a non-federal system, is shown to be positively related to urban primacy. Having a poor national road network also has a strong effect. The additional step in Henderson is the consideration of the impact of primacy on growth. As in Williamson (1965), this effect is shown to be significantly negative. For instance, for Argentina to be one standard deviation above its best level of primacy (around 0.25) would cost 1.3% growth. This is a striking result. It implies that anything that leads to excessive urban concentration – politics or roads or something else – can have substantial negative effects on economic performance.

Holmes (1998) establishes the importance of public policy in general by looking at location patterns around borders. More precisely, he uses the presence of a right-to-work law as a discrete proxy for a state's attitudes towards business. He shows that there is a discontinuous and negative change moving across a border from into a state with a right-to-work law from one without such a law. Thus, the problem of rent-seeking can be seen as part of broader pattern of public policy impacting location. [26] In contrast, Carlton (1983) finds a more moderate effect of public policy instruments in his study of firm location.

[26] Note, however, that there is nothing in the Holmes (1998) paper that suggests that a shift of manufacturing activity a short distance across state borders is inherently inefficient. This is in contrast to the Ades and Glaeser (1995) and Henderson (2003b) papers where excessive urbanization does implicitly imply a less than efficient allocation of activity across locations.

3.4. The relative importance of Marshallian microfoundations

A number of factors have been identified by theory as possibly having led to agglomeration. We have thus far looked at tests for the importance of these factors that are separate in the sense that they usually consider only one or at most two of the possible microfoundations. It would obviously be helpful if it were possible to disentangle the relative importance of these.

In the absence of data that would allow direct tests of the relative impact of, for instance, the three Marshallian microfoundations on productivity, other approaches must be employed. A natural one is to use the variation among industries to identify the impact of microfoundations. This section reviews papers that have, in different ways, followed this broad approach.

Audretsch and Feldman (1996) use a state-level spatial statistic to measure geographic concentration, both of aggregate employment and of innovation. The statistic is defined as $G = \sum_i (x_i - s_i)^2$, where x_i is location i's share of total employment and s_i is the location's share of employment in a particular industry. It takes on a value of zero when an industry is allocated across space in exactly the same way as total employment. It takes on a value close to one (depending on the size of the industry itself) when the industry is completely concentrated in one location.

Audretsch and Feldman begin by considering the determinants of the concentration of innovation. Controlling for the overall level of industrial concentration, which would lead to the concentration of innovation even in the absence of knowledge spillovers, they consider the determinants of the concentration of innovation. They show that innovation is more concentrated in an industry with a high ratio of R&D to sales, a greater reliance on skilled labor, and where more university research is devoted to research relevant to that industry.

Having looked at the concentration of industry, it is natural to look also at the concentration of production. Audretsch and Feldman (1996) show that industries are more concentrated when the share of inputs purchased from mining and agriculture is greater, confirming the previously reported results on natural advantage. An industry is also more concentrated the greater are the R&D/sales ratio and the proportion of skilled labor. Both of these are consistent with knowledge spillovers playing a role in the process of agglomeration. The latter may also be interpreted as being consistent with the labor market pooling hypothesis, since it is likely that skilled labor is more specialized than is unskilled labor. This would mean that both firms and workers would suffer more if close matches were difficult to find, which is the heart of the pooling analysis. Audretsch and Feldman also find that a greater mean shipping distance of output, which they interpret as a proxy for transport costs, increases concentration. This may be problematic, since if an industry were to concentrate for other reasons, it would find itself shipping its output a greater distance.

From an econometric perspective, the principal challenge Audretsch and Feldman (1996) face in this exercise is to control for the endogenous relationship between spatial concentration of an industry's innovative activity and the spatial concentration of the industry's production. They address this by re-estimating their model by 3SLS using natural resources and transportation costs as instruments for the innovation variable and university research as the instrument for the production variable. Results from this final exercise are quite similar to those from the ordinary least squares regressions.

Rosenthal and Strange (2001) also consider the determinants of agglomeration. This paper employs the Ellison and Glaeser (1997) index of spatial concentration instead of using the spatial G as in Audretsch and Feldman (1996). The difficulty with this statistic is that $G > 0$ does not necessarily imply that an industry is over-concentrated. If the industry was made up of a small number of large plants, and there was no agglomerative force – either an externality or a natural advantage – then G would take on a large value simply because of the industrial organization of the industry.

To address this problem, Ellison and Glaeser propose the following index of concentration: $\gamma = [G - (1 - \sum_i x_i^2)H]/[(1 - \sum_i x_i^2)(1 - H)]$. $H = \sum_j z_j^2$ is a Herfindahl index of the J plants in the industry, with z_j representing the employment share of the jth plant. For a perfectly competitive industry with a large number of small plants, H approaches zero and γ approaches $G/(1 - \sum_i x_i^2)$.[27] In this case, G measures spatial concentration without any contamination associated with industrial organization. More generally, γ takes on a value of zero when an industry is as concentrated as one would expect from a random location process, while a positive value of γ indicates excess concentration. The index is used to measure the level of spatial concentration among manufacturing industries at the zipcode, county, and state levels, in the fourth quarter of 2000.

These measures are regressed on a large number of industry characteristics, including proxies for the three Marshallian microfoundations and controls for transport costs and natural advantage. The Marshallian regressors include a measure of prior innovation in the industry and the use of both manufactured and service inputs. The model also includes variables that proxy the importance of labor market pooling by characterizing the degree of labor specialization in the industry, including labor productivity, the number of manager's per production worker, and the educational characteristics of an industry's workforce. The regressions are carried out using 4-digit manufacturing industries as observations. In addition, all of the regressions are estimated separately for concentration at the zipcode, county, and state levels, since the causes of agglomeration could well differ at different levels of geographic aggregation.

The paper's results provide evidence of the importance of all three sources of localization economies. The evidence is strongest for labor market pooling, with proxies having a positive impact on agglomeration at all levels of geography. The proxies for knowledge spillovers impact agglomeration positively only at the zipcode level. Reliance on manufactured inputs or natural resources positively affects agglomeration at the state

[27] The $(1 - \sum_i x_i^2)$ term is included in order that the index have the property that $E(\gamma) = 0$ when neither agglomerative spillovers nor natural advantage are present [see Ellison and Glaeser (1997) for details]. For the state, county, and zipcode levels that Rosenthal and Strange (2001) consider, $(1 - \sum_i x_i^2)$ is close to one, taking on values of 0.9997, 0.9954, and 0.9578, respectively.

level but has little effect on agglomeration at lower levels of geography. The same is true for the perishability of output, a proxy for transportation costs. In contrast, reliance on service inputs reduces state-level agglomeration. Taking all of these results together, an interesting pattern emerges, with industry attributes sensitive to shipping costs (reliance on manufactured inputs, reliance on natural resource inputs, marketing of perishable products) influencing agglomeration at the state level, knowledge spillovers impacting highly localized agglomeration, and labor impacting agglomeration at all levels of geography. These findings are largely robust, holding in both ordinary least squares (OLS) and 2-digit Standard Industry Classification (SIC) fixed effect specifications, with alternative MSA-based measures of geography, and when industries are aggregated from the 4-digit to the 3-digit level.

In related work, Lovely, Rosenthal and Sharma (2004) examine the spatial concentration of headquarter activity of exporters. Exporting requires specialized knowledge of foreign markets and should, therefore, contribute to spatial concentration. Lovely et al. test that idea by applying differencing methods to 4-digit industry-level data for the fourth quarter of 2000. Using data comparable to that in Rosenthal and Strange (2001), they find that when export related information is difficult to obtain, exporter headquarter activity is more highly agglomerated relative to headquarter activity in the domestic-only sector of the same industry. These findings support the idea that the need to acquire information contributes to agglomeration. However, the results do not identify the mechanism by which the need to acquire information contributes to agglomeration.

Another approach is taken by Dumais, Ellison and Glaeser (1997).[28] They look at the microfoundations of agglomeration economies by considering which industries co-agglomerate. Specifically, they consider the patterns of growth in industries, and look at the degree to which industries grow more robustly in locations where other industries use similar labor mixes, are related as suppliers of inputs or demanders of outputs, or are linked technologically. They consider several patterns of growth, including new firm births, old firm births, and closures (negative growth). They also consider a reduced form levels model, regressing the level of employment as a function of the environment created by co-agglomerated industries.

The key to this paper is its clever treatment of the relationships among industries. Input and output relatedness are defined relative to state level industrial mixes. Thus, if an industry employed a lot of fabricated metals, one would expect that if input sharing were an important agglomerative force, then the industry would be more likely to be found in states with a lot of fabricated metal production. Similarly, the fabricated metal producers would be expected to locate near their downstream consumers for the same reason. The labor mix fit is defined as the difference between an industry's employment shares by occupation and the state shares outside of the industry. This measure

[28] This is a deliberate reference to the working paper, rather than to the published paper of the same title, Dumais, Ellison and Glaeser (2002), since the latter omits the material on the sources of agglomeration economies.

is then interacted with a plant closure rate to directly address the notion that it is the risk of job loss that prompts labor market pooling. The knowledge spillover variable is calculated relative to industry mix. Two weighting schemes for intellectually related industries are employed. The first is Scherer's (1984) technology flow matrix, which was calculated from R&D and patent data. This estimates the degree to which innovative activity in one industry is likely to benefit another industry. Thus, it captures one sort of knowledge spillover: public good aspects of R&D activity. It does not really capture Marshall's "secrets of the trade". The other weighting scheme is calculated based on the co-ownership of firms in different industries. It is designed to capture scope economies, which are presumably related to the potential for intellectual spillover between industries. Again, this is a partial proxy, but as Dumais et al. note, knowledge spillovers are very difficult to capture.

These variables are used in the estimation of a number of growth models along with proxies for state level employment and standard agglomeration economies that lead firms in an industry to locate together. The model also includes state and industry fixed effects. The kinds of growth considered include new firm births, old firm births (both instances of expansion) and closure. Four sets of five year changes are used over the 1972–1992 period. The preferred specification is nonlinear (the log of 1 plus the change in employment) to deal with outliers.

While there is evidence that is consistent with all three Marshallian microfoundations, the strongest evidence by far is for the labor mix variable. The evidence on input sharing is mixed, with the presence of likely customers encouraging only new firm births, while the presence of likely input source encourages only old firm births (new plants). Neither has an impact on closures. The knowledge spillover variables have somewhat stronger effects, with the scope-economies proxy having more impact than the technology-flows proxy. One potential difficulty with this approach – recognized by Dumais et al. – is that in spatial equilibrium, the marginal impact of various sources of agglomeration economies on growth is zero, complicating efforts to uncover evidence of the sources of external economies. One way to deal with this is to regress levels of employment on the proxies. All of them are significant in this model, except for the presence of input suppliers.

Two recent papers have also addressed multiple microfoundations. Holmes (2002) considers the sources of agglomeration economies for sales offices. He employs differences between of high- and low-demand products to identify the degree to which market concentration and knowledge spillovers contribute to concentration. He finds that the former accounts for approximately half of the concentration of sales offices. Rigby and Essletzbichler (2002) consider impacts of various proxies for microfoundations on productivity using micro data from the LRD. These proxies are close to those used by Dumais, Ellison and Glaeser (1997), including measures of similarity for inputs, labor, and technology. They find evidence of all three Marshallian microfoundations. This paper's methodology clearly goes far beyond the old localization vs. urbanization question by focusing on the impacts of specific Marshallian agglomeration economies on productivity. In that sense, this paper approaches the ideal discussed at the beginning of this section.

Identifying the sources of agglomeration economies by looking across industries has the problem of constraining different industries to be affected by agglomeration in the same way. One way around this would be to focus on a particular industry. Holmes (1999) treatment of the textile industry is one example of this. A more extensive industry study is Klepper (2001), who considers the car industry. Klepper documents a number of patterns. First, the industry was dominated for the better part of a century by four highly successful companies that were founded in Detroit. Their founders had experience in related industries, including carriages and engines. Second, there were unusually many spinoffs in Detroit in the early stages of the industry (prior to 1916). Third, the spinoffs usually located near their parent firms. For instance, 50 of the 61 spinoffs of Detroit area automakers chose to locate in Detroit. Fourth, the spinoffs of successful companies themselves experienced greater success, a heritage effect. In fact, in a model of survival, although a Detroit dummy is significant in a simple model, it is not in a model that controls for corporate heritage. In addition, the spinoffs of successful companies have lower hazards even when they do not locate in Detroit.

Klepper's interpretation of these patterns is not favorable to standard theories of agglomeration. He argues that Marshallian agglomeration economies should have benefited all firms and not just the spinoffs of the early successful firms in the industry. On the other hand, the success of the early giants of the industry and the high rate of spinoffs in Detroit can be seen as being consistent with Marshallian notions of agglomeration. In any case, Klepper's work in this area is a compelling example of an agglomeration economy that operates through the specific channel of spinoffs. This would seem more consistent with a particular kind of knowledge spillovers than one that emphasizes input sharing or labor market pooling.[29]

4. Case evidence

Thus far, this chapter has considered the econometric evidence on the scope and sources of agglomeration economies. One of the chapter's themes has been the impact of increasingly refined data on the kinds of research being carried out. For instance, as noted in Section 2, the ability to geocode plant level data has made possible research that considers the geographic scope of agglomeration economies. This kind of analysis allows the study of the particulars of agglomeration economies, of which there are many.

Of course, even the most refined data set and most sophisticated econometric techniques will not be able to address all of the idiosyncratic conditions that contribute to

[29] Klepper and Simons' (2000a, 2000b) are analyses of the tire and television industries. Although agglomeration is not their central focus, like Klepper (2001), these papers make compelling cases for the use of industry studies in understanding industry location.

agglomeration. Thus, there is much to be learned about the nature of agglomeration from case studies. There is far more evidence of this kind than we can review in one brief section. We will, therefore, limit our discussion to three kinds of case studies, each shedding considerable light on the microfoundations of agglomeration economies: Hoover and Vernon (1959) and others on external economies in New York, Porter (1998) and others on clusters and competitiveness, and Saxenian (1994) on cultural and organizational differences between the Silicon Valley and Boston's Route 128.

4.1. The New York Metropolitan Region Study

The New York Metropolitan Region Study took place around 1960. It produced nine books, and a number of other reports. The motivation for the project was practical. The Regional Plan Association wanted to understand and thus forecast the growth of Greater New York City. It is not hard to see that the relevance of this project goes far beyond New York City. Two particularly notable volumes produced in this study were Hoover and Vernon (1959) and Vernon (1960), the latter being a summary.

The key idea from this project that concerns us here is external economies. These are defined as "... 'economies' which establishments obtain through sharing the services of specialists external to themselves" [Vernon (1960, p. 9)]. It is argued that these external economies have been central throughout New York's history. Early, traders benefited from scheduled sailings, wholesalers, and ship brokers not available elsewhere. Later, traders benefited from investments in the harbor, canals, and railroads. These shared inputs in trade later became foundations of shared inputs in finance, with maritime insurance underwriting forming a basis for other kinds of investment. Thus, static external economies affecting one industry became dynamic, and came to affect the city's entire economy.

The heart of urban sharing is communication. If it were possible to make use of Vernon's specialists at a distance, then incurring the costs of urbanization would be uneconomical. The reason that it is not possible to escape from the city in this way is that interactions are, in Vernon's usage, "unstable". A clothing designer does not know the button that best suits a dress until the dress is already under design. Only a particular button will do, and time is of the essence. Because of this, the designer communicates closely with supporting suppliers. It is this kind of interaction that is at the heart of external economies. Vernon reports that in a sample of "communication-oriented industries", 77.5% were located in New York City proper, a testament to the value of proximity [Vernon (1960, p. 123)]. A corollary of this is that urban concentration allows small firms to survive and even thrive. Vernon (1960, p. 110) reports that although the Core of the region contains 49.6% of manufacturing employment, but 61.2% of the region's employment at small firms (60 employees or fewer) and only 7.7% of the employment at large firms (more than 240 employees).

The analysis of external economies in the New York Metropolitan Region Study provides insights that complement the findings of the econometric work that we have reviewed in this chapter. The treatment of the central role of the transportation sector is one example. It shows how one specific industry, shipping, fostered the development of another, mercantile trade, and ultimately led to the development of yet another industry, finance. These are the kinds of specific relationships between various economic activities that can be handled nicely in a case analysis, but may get lost in formal econometrics.

The New York Metropolitan Region Study has also been valuable as a source of inspiration for econometric work. Vernon's analysis of the industrial organization of New York's textile industry has the important conclusion that small firms and large cities naturally go together. As noted above, Holmes and Stevens (2002) look at this relationship across industries and across the county. Somewhat surprisingly, they find that plants in concentrated environments are on average larger rather than smaller. Their interpretation of this result is that it is the increased productivity associated with the concentration that allows the plants to become larger. Vernon's result is shown to apply to a specific industry in a specific city, with the lesson being that as valuable as case analysis may be, it is dangerous to draw universal conclusions from a single case.

4.2. *Regional Clusters of Innovation Project*

This research has a practical motivation that parallels the New York Metropolitan Region Study, with the goal being to achieve an understanding of the forces that govern competitiveness in the hope of fostering it. The basic approach is found in Porter (1990). The heart of the approach is that a business will become more productive when factor markets are favorable, when suppliers are available, when consumers are demanding, and when competitive pressures compel sustained innovation.

The reason that this analysis is relevant here is that these conditions are more likely to be present when an industry is spatially concentrated [Porter (1998)]. The concentration is referred to as a "cluster". The Cluster Mapping Project[30] offers the following definition:

> A cluster is a geographically proximate group of interconnected companies and associated institutions in a particular field, including product producers, service providers, suppliers, universities, and trade associations. Clusters arise out of the linkages or externalities that span across industries in a particular location.

The Cluster Mapping Project identifies 41 clusters in North America, including, for example, Aerospace engines, with 18.26% of national employment in Hartford, and another 18.0% in Cincinnati and Phoenix together.

Recently, the Regional Clusters of Innovation Project has looked at the competitiveness of five specific metropolitan areas: San Diego, Wichita, North Carolina's Research Triangle, Pittsburgh, and Atlanta. As of this writing, preliminary reports are available for the first three, as is a national report.[31] These reports provide detailed portraits of

[30] http://data.isc.hbs.edu/isc/cmp_data_glossary.jsp.

[31] http://www.compete.org.

Twenty-first Century cities in much the same way that the New York Metropolitan Region Project painted a picture of post-war New York.

This analysis adds to the econometric work on agglomeration in several ways. First, by focusing on clusters, which are explicitly defined to include related industries, some of the problems associated with a narrow treatment of industry scope (see Section 2) are mitigated. Second, by focusing on policy towards agglomeration, the projects show the importance of institutions for the process of agglomeration. For instance, it is argued that all levels of government have a potential to foster productive patterns of agglomeration. Local taxes and state funding for universities are two examples. Informal organizations can have an impact too. One example of this is the alumni organization UCSD CONNECT, which helps establish and maintain links that can be valuable in rapidly changing industries such as pharmaceuticals. The bottom line of this analysis is that institutions matter for agglomeration, a point that is only tangential to most of the econometric literature.

4.3. Regional advantage

Probably the most famous instance of clustering is the Silicon Valley. That the Santa Clara Valley was not the only possible center for the computer industry is the subject of a joke among programmers, who refer to the location of their jobs relative to the Valley's fictitious silicon mines. Saxenian (1994) deals with the forces that operated on the industry in the late-20th century. She points out that in the mid-1970s, both Boston (especially around Route 128) and the San Jose to Palo Alto corridor (the so-called Silicon Valley) were essentially equal in their positions as centers of electronics and high-technology. The next decade witnessed a movement offshore of semiconductor production, which hurt the Silicon Valley, and a shift away from minicomputers, which hurt Route 128. The Silicon Valley made its well-known and successful transition to software and other computer related industries. Route 128 had more difficulties. There are two explanations for this divergence. One is that either location could have become dominant in software based on its characteristics, but that the random hand of history selected the Silicon Valley as the industry core. The other explanation is that the locations did not have identical characteristics, and that the Silicon Valley offered a more productive environment.

Both locations had many of the characteristics that could be expected to attract high-technology employment including educated workforces and proximity to research universities. Saxenian argues that the key difference between the Silicon Valley and Route 128 is in their industrial systems. In her view [Saxenian (1994, p. 7)], a local industrial system has "three dimensions: local institutions and culture, industrial structure and corporate organization". Regarding the Silicon Valley, she maintains [Saxenian (1994, p. 37)] that

> The decentralized and fluid environment accelerated the diffusion of technological capabilities and know-how within the region... When engineers moved between

> companies, they took with them the knowledge, skills, and experience acquired at their previous jobs.

In contrast, Route 128 is presented by Saxenian as being relatively rigid and hierarchical, while the Silicon Valley is presented as being flexible and entrepreneurial. This certainly seems to be the view of the industry. Saxenian quotes Jeffrey Kalb, an entrepreneurial refugee from the Digital Electronics corporation:

> There's a fundamental difference in the nature of the industry between Route 128 and [the Silicon Valley]. Route 128 is organized into large companies that do their own thing... It's very difficult for a small company to survive in that environment... The Valley is very fast-moving and start-ups have to move fast. The whole culture of the Valley is one of change. We laugh about how often people change jobs. The joke is that you can change jobs and not change parking lots. There's a culture associated with that which says that moving is okay, that rapid change is the norm, that it's not considered negative on your resume... So you have this culture of rapid decisions, rapid changes, which is exactly the environment that you find yourself in as a startup.

Thus, the key difference between the two locations is neither a natural advantage (silicon mines) nor a traditional agglomeration economy. It is instead a difference in the organization of resources that drives the difference. The difficulty of quantifying these sorts of organizational differences [Rosenthal and Strange (2003) notwithstanding] are one of the reasons that a case approach like Saxenian's is valuable.

Given his importance in the study of agglomeration, it seems appropriate to give the last word here to Marshall, who in some sense appreciated the importance of intangible aspects of the economic environment as implied at least loosely by Marshall in 1920 (1920, p. 270):

> We have seen how physical nature acts on man's energies... but we have also seen how the use he makes of these advantages depends on his ideals of life, and how inextricably therefore the religious, political and economic threads of the world's history are interwoven....

5. Conclusion

This chapter has considered the empirical literature on agglomeration economies. Some of the questions in the literature are relatively old, such as the debate over whether localization or urbanization economies are of greater importance. Other questions are relatively new, such as the consideration of the geographic, temporal, and organizational dimensions of agglomeration economies. Likewise, attempts to understand the microfoundations of agglomeration economies are also relatively recent.

Whether the questions are old or new, the answers are potentially of considerable importance for policy. For instance, the increased integration and size of the European

Union has led to interest in the degree to which a core–periphery regional development pattern is likely to emerge. Since this depends on the nature of agglomeration economies, so too should regional development policy. Similar issues confront policymakers in the rest of the world. For example, the Silicon Valley is perceived as a success that other locations would like to duplicate. Doing so obviously depends on the nature and sources of agglomeration economies.

As this review indicates, there is a lot that we do not yet know about agglomeration economies. We believe, however, that recent developments in the literature gives cause for optimism. Increasingly, researchers have made use of large micro data sets that have allowed for ever more refined studies of agglomeration. Such data sets allow for more reliable estimation, and also help resolve a variety of econometric problems. They also allow for the consideration of issues like the micro geographic scope of agglomeration that earlier data sets could not address. We are, therefore, confident that the impressive progress of recent years will continue, closing the gaps in knowledge that this review has identified.

Acknowledgements

We are grateful to Gilles Duranton, Vernon Henderson, Jacques Thisse and the participants of a presentation at the North American Regional Science Association Meetings in November, 2002. Any errors are ours alone. We are also grateful for the financial support of the National Institute of Aging, the Connaught Fund at the University of Toronto, and the Social Sciences and Humanities Research Council of Canada.

References

Acemoglu, D., Angrist, J. (1999). "How large are the social returns to education? Evidence from compulsory schooling laws". NBER Working Paper No. 7444.

Acs, Z.J., Audretsch, D.B., Feldman, M.P. (1992). "Real effects of academic research: Comment". American Economic Review 82 (1), 363–367.

Ades, A.F., Glaeser, E.L. (1995). "Trade and circuses: Explaining urban giants". Quarterly Journal of Economics 110, 195–227.

Almeida, P., Kogut, B. (1999). "Localization of knowledge and the mobility of engineers in regional networks". Management Science 45 (7), 905–917.

Arrow, K.J. (1962). "Economic welfare and the allocation of resources for invention". In: Nelson, R.R. (Ed.), The Rate and Direction of Inventive Activity. Princeton Univ. Press, Princeton, NJ, pp. 609–626.

Audretsch, D.B., Feldman, M.P. (2004). "Knowledge spillovers and the geography of innovation". In: Henderson, J.V., Thisse, J.-F. (Eds.), Handbook of Regional and Urban Economics, vol. 4. Elsevier, Amsterdam, pp. 2713–2739. This volume.

Audretsch, D.B., Feldman, M.P. (1996). "R&D spillovers and the geography of innovation and production". American Economic Review 86 (3), 630–640.

Bartlesman, E.J., Caballero, R.J., Lyons, R.K. (1994). "Customer and supplier-driven externalities". American Economic Review 84 (4), 1075–1084.

Baumgardner, J.R. (1988). "Physicians' services and the division of labor across local markets". Journal of Political Economy 96 (5), 948–982.

Blomquist, G., Berger, M., Hoehn, J. (1988). "New estimates of the quality of life in urban areas". American Economic Review 78, 89–107.

Calem, P.S., Carlino, G.A. (1991). "Urban agglomeration economies in the presence of technical change". Journal of Urban Economics 29, 82–95.

Carlton, D.W. (1983). "The location and employment choices of new firms: An econometric model with discrete and continuous endogenous variables". Review of Economics and Statistics 65, 440–449.

Charlot, S., Duranton, G. (2002). "Communication externalities in cities". London School of Economics Working Paper.

Chinitz, B.J. (1961). "Contrasts in agglomeration: New York and Pittsburgh". American Economic Review 51, 279–289.

Ciccone, A. (2002). "Agglomeration effects in Europe". European Economic Review 46, 213–227.

Ciccone, A., Hall, R.E. (1996). "Productivity and the density of economic activity". American Economic Review 86, 54–70.

Cingano F., Schivardi F. (2003). "Identifying the sources of local productivity growth". Journal of the European Economic Association. In press.

Combes, P.-P. (2000a). "Economic structure and local growth, France, 1984–1993". Journal of Urban Economics 47, 329–355.

Combes, P.-P. (2000b). "Marshall–Arrow–Romer externalities and city growth". CERAS Working Paper No. 99-06.

Combes, P.-P., Duranton, G., Gobillon, L. (2003). "Wage differences across French local labor markets: Endowments, skills, and interactions". Working Paper.

Costa, D.L., Kahn, M.E. (2001). "Power couples". Quarterly Journal of Economics 116, 1287–1315.

Davis, D.R., Weinstein, D.E. (1996). "Does economic geography matter for international specialization?" NBER Working Paper No. 5706.

Davis, D.R., Weinstein, D.E. (1999). "Economic geography and regional production structure: An empirical investigation". European Economic Review 43, 379–407.

Dekle, R., Eaton, J. (1999). "Agglomeration and land rents, evidence from the prefectures". Journal of Urban Economics 46, 200–214.

Di Addario, S., de Blasio, G. (2003). "Labor market pooling: Evidence from the Italian industrial districts". Bank of Italy Working Paper.

Diamond, C.A., Simon, C.J. (1990). "Industrial specialization and the returns to labor". Journal of Labor Economics 8 (2), 175–201.

Dumais, G., Ellison, G., Glaeser, E. (1997). "Geographic concentration as a dynamic process". NBER Working Paper No. 6270.

Dumais, G., Ellison, G., Glaeser, E. (2002). "Geographic concentration as a dynamic process". Review of Economics and Statistics 84 (2), 193–204.

Duranton, G., Overman, H.G. (2002). "Testing for localisation using micro-geographic data". London School of Economics Working Paper.

Duranton, G., Puga, D. (2001a). "Nursery cities: Urban diversity, process innovation, and the life-cycle of products". American Economic Review 91 (5), 1454–1477.

Duranton, G., Puga, D. (2001b). "From sectoral to functional urban specialisation". University of Toronto Economics Department Working Paper.

Duranton, G., Puga, D. (2004). "Micro-foundations of urban agglomeration economies". In: Henderson, J.V., Thisse, J.-F. (Eds.), Handbook of Regional and Urban Economics, vol. 4. Elsevier, Amsterdam, pp. 2063–2117. This volume.

Eberts, R.W., McMillen, D.P. (1999). "Agglomeration economies and urban public infrastructure". In: Cheshire, P., Mills, E.S. (Eds.), Handbook of Regional and Urban Economics, vol. 3. North-Holland, New York, pp. 1455–1495.

Ellison, G., Glaeser, E. (1997). "Geographic concentration in U.S. manufacturing industries: A dartboard approach". Journal of Political Economy 105, 889–927.
Ellison, G., Glaeser, E. (1999). "The geographic concentration of an industry: Does natural advantage explain agglomeration?" American Economic Association Papers and Proceedings 89, 311–316.
Evans, D.S. (1987). "Tests of alternative theories of firm growth". Journal of Political Economy 85 (4), 657–674.
Fallick, B.C., Fleischman, C., Rebitzer, J. (2003). "Job hopping in the Silicon Valley: The micro-foundations of an industry cluster". Case Western Reserve University Working Paper.
Florida, R., Gates, G. (2001). Technology and Tolerance: The Importance of Diversity to High-Tech Growth. Brookings Institution, Washington, DC.
Fogarty, M.S., Garofalo, G.A. (1978). "Urban spatial structure and productivity growth in the manufacturing sector of cities". Journal of Urban Economics 23, 60–70.
Fuchs, V. (1962). Changes in the Location of Manufacturing in the U.S. Since 1929. Yale Univ. Press, New Haven.
Gabriel, S.A., Rosenthal, S.S. (2004). "Quality of the business environment versus quality of life: Do firms and households like the same cities?" The Review of Economics and Statistics 86 (1).
George, L., Waldfogel, J. (2003). "Who benefits whom in daily newspaper markets?" Journal of Political Economy. In press.
Glaeser, E.L., Maré, D.C. (2001). "Cities and skills". Journal of Labor Economics 19 (2), 316–342.
Glaeser, E., Kolko, J., Saiz, A. (2001). "Consumer city". Journal of Economic Geography 1, 27–50.
Glaeser, E.L., Kallal, H.D., Scheinkman, J.A., Shleifer, A. (1992). "Growth in cities". Journal of Political Economy 100, 1126–1152.
Gyourko, J., Tracy, J. (1991). "The structure of local public finance and the quality of life". Journal of Political Economy 99 (4), 774–806.
Hanson, G.H. (1998a). "Regional adjustment to trade liberalization". Regional Science and Urban Economics 28 (4), 419–444.
Hanson, G.H. (1998b). "North American economic integration and industry location". Oxford Review of Economic Policy 14 (2), 30–44.
Hanson, G.H. (2001). "Scale economies and the geographic concentration of industry". Journal of Economic Geography 1, 255–276.
Head, K., Mayer, T. (2004). "The empirics of agglomeration and trade". In: Henderson, J.V., Thisse, J.-F. (Eds.), Handbook of Regional and Urban Economics, vol. 4. Elsevier, Amsterdam, pp. 2609–2669. This volume.
Helsley, R.W., Strange, W.C. (1990). "Agglomeration economies and matching in a system of cities". Regional Science and Urban Economics 20, 189–212.
Helsley, R.W., Strange, W.C. (2001). "Innovation and input sharing". Journal of Urban Economics 51 (1), 25–45.
Helsley, R.W., Strange, W.C. (2002). "Knowledge barter". University of Toronto Faculty of Management Working Paper.
Henderson, J.V. (1986). "Efficiency of resource usage and city size". Journal of Urban Economics 19, 47–70.
Henderson, J.V. (1997). "Externalities and industrial development". Journal of Urban Economics 42, 449–470.
Henderson, J.V. (2003a). "Marshall's scale economies". Journal of Urban Economics 53, 1–28.
Henderson, J.V. (2003b). "The urbanization process and economic growth: The so-what question". Journal of Economic Growth 8, 47–71.
Henderson, J.V., Kuncoro, A., Turner, M. (1995). "Industrial development in cities". Journal of Political Economy 103, 1067–1085.
Holmes, T.J. (1998). "The effects of state policies on the location of manufacturing: evidence from state borders". Journal of Political Economy 106 (4), 667–705.
Holmes, T.J. (1999). "Localization of industry and vertical disintegration". Review of Economics and Statistics 81 (2), 314–325.

Holmes, T.J. (2002). "The role of cities: evidence from the placement of sales offices". Federal Reserve Bank of Minneapolis Research Department Staff Report 298.

Holmes, T.J., Stevens, J.J. (2002). "Geographic concentration and establishment scale". Review of Economics and Statistics 84 (4), 682–691.

Holtz-Eakin, D. (1994). "Public sector capital and the productivity puzzle". Review of Economics and Statistics 76 (1), 12–21.

Hoover, E.M. (1948). The Location of Economic Activity. McGraw–Hill, New York.

Hoover, E.M., Vernon, R. (1959). Anatomy of a Metropolis. Harvard Univ. Press, Cambridge, MA.

Jacobs, J. (1969). The Economy of Cities. Vintage, New York.

Jaffe, A.B. (1989). "Real effects of academic research". American Economic Review 79 (5), 957–970.

Jaffe, A.B., Trajtenberg, M., Henderson, R. (1993). "Geographic localization of knowledge spillovers as evidenced by patent citations". Quarterly Journal of Economics 108, 577–598.

Kim, S. (1995). "Expansion of markets and the geographic distribution of economic activities: The trends in U.S. regional manufacturing structure, 1860–1987". Quarterly Journal of Economics 110 (4), 881–908.

Kim, S. (1999). "Regions, resources and economics geography: Sources of U.S. regional comparative advantage, 1880–1987". Regional Science and Urban Economics 29, 1–32.

Klepper, S., (2001). "The evolution of the U.S. automobile industry and Detroit as its capital". Carnegie Mellon Working Paper.

Klepper, S., Simons, K.L. (2000a). "Dominance by birthright: Entry of prior radio producers and competitive ramifications in the U.S. television receiver industry". Strategic Management Journal 21, 997–1016.

Klepper, S., Simons, K.L. (2000b). "The making of an oligopoly: Firm survival and technological change in the evolution of the U.S. tire industry". Journal of Political Economy 108 (4), 728–760.

Kolko, J. (1999). " Can I get some service here? Information technology, service industries, and the future of cities". Harvard University Working Paper.

Krugman, P.R. (1980). "Scale economies, product differentiation, and the pattern of trade". American Economic Review 70, 950–959.

Krugman, P.R. (1991). Geography and Trade. MIT Press, Boston.

Lovely, M., Rosenthal, S., Sharma, S. (2004). "Information, agglomeration and the headquarters of U.S. exporters". Regional Science and Urban Economics. In press.

Marshall, A. (1920). Principles of Economics. Macmillan, London.

Moomaw, R.L. (1981). "Productivity and city size: a critique of the evidence". Quarterly Journal of Economics 96, 675–688.

Moomaw, R.L. (1983). "Is population scale a worthless surrogate for business agglomeration economies?" Regional Science and Urban Economics 13, 525–545.

Moretti, E. (2000). "Estimating the social return to higher education". NBER Working Paper No. 9018.

Moretti, E. (2004). "Human capital externalities in cities". In: Henderson, J.V., Thisse, J.-F. (Eds.), Handbook of Regional and Urban Economics, vol. 4. Elsevier, Amsterdam, pp. 2243–2291. This volume.

Nakamura, R. (1985). "Agglomeration economies in urban manufacturing industries: a case of Japanese cities". Journal of Urban Economics 17, 108–124.

Ono, Y. (2002). "Outsourcing business services and the scope of local markets". Federal Reserve Bank of Chicago Working Paper.

Porter, M. (1990). The Competitive Advantage of Nations. Free Press, New York.

Porter, M. (1998). "Clusters and the new economics of competition". Harvard Business Review (November–December).

Rauch, J. (1993a). "Productivity gains from geographic concentration of human capital: Evidence from the cities". Journal of Urban Economics 34, 380–400.

Rauch, J. (1993b). "Does history matter only when it matters little?" Quarterly Journal of Economics 108, 843–867.

Rigby, D.L., Essletzbichler, J. (2002). "Agglomeration economies and productivity differences in U.S. cities". Journal of Economic Geography 2, 407–432.

Roback, J. (1982). "Wages, rents, and the quality of life". Journal of Political Economy 90, 1257–1278.

Romer, P. (1986). "Increasing returns and long run growth". Journal of Political Economy 94, 1002–1037.
Rosen, S. (1979). "Wage-based indexes of urban quality of life". In: Mieszkowski, P., Straszheim, M. (Eds.), Current Issues in Urban Economics. Johns Hopkins Univ. Press, Baltimore, pp. 391–429.
Rosenthal, S.S., Strange, W.C. (2001). "The determinants of agglomeration". Journal of Urban Economics 50, 191–229.
Rosenthal, S.S., Strange, W.C. (2002). "The urban rat race". Syracuse University Working Paper.
Rosenthal, S.S., Strange, W.C. (2003). "Geography, industrial organization, and agglomeration". Review of Economics and Statistics 85 (2), 377–393.
Saxenian, A. (1994). Regional Advantage: Culture and Competition in Silicon Valley and Route 128. Harvard University, Cambridge, MA.
Scherer, F. (1984). "Using linked patent data and R&D data to measure technology flows". In: Griliches, Z. (Ed.), R&D, Patents, and Productivity. Univ. of Chicago Press, Chicago.
Segal, D. (1976). "Are there returns to scale in city size?" Review of Economics and Statistics 58, 339–350.
Shefer, D. (1973). "Localization economies in SMSAs: A production function analysis". Journal of Regional Science 13, 55–64.
Simon, C.J. (1988). "Frictional unemployment and the role of industrial diversity". Quarterly Journal of Economics 103, 715–728.
Sveikauskas, L.A. (1975). "The productivity of cities". Quarterly Journal of Economics 89, 393–413.
Tabuchi, T. (1986). "Urban agglomeration, capital augmenting technology, and labor market equilibrium". Journal of Urban Economics 20, 211–228.
Tabuchi, T., Yoshida, A. (2000). "Separating agglomeration economies in consumption and production". Journal of Urban Economics 48, 70–84.
Vernon, R. (1960). Metropolis 1985. Harvard Univ. Press, Cambridge, MA.
Waldfogel, J. (2003). "Preference externalities: An empirical study of who benefits whom in differentiated product markets". RAND Journal of Economics. In press.
Wheaton, W.C., Lewis, M.J. (2002). "Urban wages and labor market agglomeration". Journal of Urban Economics 51, 542–562.
Williamson, J. (1965). "Regional inequality and the process of national development". Economic Development and Cultural Change 13, 3–45.

Chapter 50

NEIGHBORHOOD EFFECTS

STEVEN N. DURLAUF

Department of Economics, University of Wisconsin, 1180 Observatory Drive, Madison, WI 53706-1393, USA
e-mail: sdurlauf@ssc.wisc.edu

Contents

Handbook of Regional and Urban Economics, Volume 4. Edited by J.V. Henderson and J.F. Thisse

DOI: 10.1016/S0169-7218(04)07050-9

Abstract

This paper surveys the modern economics literature on the role of neighborhoods in influencing socioeconomic outcomes. Neighborhood effects have been analyzed in a range of theoretical and applied contexts and have proven to be of interest in understanding questions ranging from the asymptotic properties of various evolutionary games to explaining the persistence of poverty in inner cities. As such, the survey covers a range of theoretical, econometric and empirical topics. One conclusion from the survey is that there is a need to better integrate findings from theory and econometrics into empirical studies; until this is done, empirical studies of the nature and magnitude of neighborhood effects are unlikely to persuade those skeptical about their importance.

Keywords

identification, neighborhood effects, stratification, segregation, multiple equilibria, networks

JEL classification: C25, I30, R00

> "...in a neighborhood with a paucity of regularly employed families and with the overwhelming majority of families having spells of long term joblessness, people experience a social isolation that excludes them from the job network system that permeates other neighborhoods and that is so important in learning about or being recommended for jobs... And as the prospects of employment diminish, other alternatives such as welfare and the underground economy are not only increasingly relied on, they come to be seen as a way of life... Thus in such neighborhoods the chances are overwhelming that children will seldom interact on a sustained basis with people who are employed or with families that have a sustained breadwinner. The net effect is that joblessness, as a way of life, takes on a different social meaning: the relationship between schooling and post-school employment takes on a different meaning. The development of cognitive, linguistic and other education and job related skills necessary for the world of work in the mainstream economy is thereby relatively adversely affected. In such neighborhoods, therefore, teachers become frustrated and do not teach and children do not learn. A vicious cycle is perpetuated through the family, through the community and through the schools".
>
> William Julius Wilson, *The Truly Disadvantaged* (1987, p. 57)

1. Introduction

This chapter provides an overview of research on neighborhood effects in economics and other social sciences. In the last 15 years, there has been a renaissance of interest among economists in the social determinants of individual behavior and aggregate outcomes. Within the areas of urban, labor and family economics, much of this focus has centered on neighborhood effects. One reason for this is that a body of studies has argued that neighborhood influences, especially those defined by geographic residence, are important in understanding the persistence of inner city poverty; William Julius Wilson's *The Truly Disadvantaged* is probably the best known exposition of this argument. Another reason, stressed in Manski (2000), is that methodological advances in economic theory have provided ways to incorporate a range of spillover effects into rigorous microeconomic models. One source of these developments that Manski emphasizes is endogenous growth theory; many neighborhoods models incorporate spillover effects that, at least in their formal structure, are very similar to those found in growth contexts. In addition, the analysis of neighborhood effects in game theory (often called local interactions in this literature) has become an active area of research. This work does not require that neighborhoods be defined by geographic proximity; but does rely on some notion of proximity versus distance in "social space", a notion that is given content in Akerlof (1997). While the primary focus of this survey is residential neighborhood effects, a number of other forms of neighborhoods and associated effects will also be discussed.

The great bulk of the new neighborhood effects literature has focused on the consequences of neighborhood effects for individual behavior and for neighborhood composition; typically, the forms of these effects are taken as given. This is true even for the study of neighborhood effects in residential communities and schools, which constitute by far the main application of neighborhood effects to the study of substantive empirical phenomena. On the other hand, the microeconomic justifications given for residential neighborhood effects cover many of the motivations for the modern neighborhood effects literature.

What sorts of residential neighborhood effects are posited in the current literature?[1] One reason why neighborhoods affect their members, and the one whose microeconomic foundations are best justified (since they are merely a consequence of the rules for educational finance that exist in the U.S.) is the local public finance of education. Hussar and Sonnenberg (2001) and Murray, Evans and Schwab (1998) document the large differences in per pupil expenditures that persist across districts in the United States; this persistence is remarkable since state and federal programs at least implicitly designed to equalize expenditure are responsible for about 50% of public educational expenditure for kindergarten through grade 12 in the U.S.[2] To be clear, there is considerable controversy concerning the relationship between school expenditures and inequality, well summarized in the survey by Hanushek (1986) and by the papers in Burtless (1996). My own reading of this literature suggests that while a general relationship between school expenditures per capita and educational quality has proven hard to establish, schools in poor communities probably do suffer because of lack of resources. Hence very poor neighborhoods probably affect children along this dimension.

Outside of school finance, neighborhood effects have explicitly been justified along sociological and/or psychological lines. As such, they constitute forms of social interactions, which have themselves become a growing area of research; see Blume and Durlauf (2001), Brock and Durlauf (2001b) and Manski (2000) for surveys/overviews. One example of social interactions that is germane to neighborhoods is role model effects, in which the behavior of one individual in a neighborhood is influenced by the characteristics of and earlier behaviors of older members of his social group. Another form of social interactions is peer group influences; these differ from role model effects because they refer to contemporaneous behavioral influences and so may be reciprocal. Role model and peer group influences are both usually understood to produce some sort of imitative behavior, either contemporaneous or across age cohorts. This imitative behavior may be due to:

[1] Neighborhood effects have generally not included agglomeration externalities, although these presumably play a role in cases such as the provision of education. See Fujita and Thisse (2002) for an outstanding survey of agglomeration models; Duranton and Puga (2003) and Ottaviano and Thisse (2003) in this volume are also valuable reviews of the relevant issues.

[2] Murray, Evans and Schwab (1998, p. 799), find that the ratio of per pupil expenditures for the 95th percentile to the 5th percentile across U.S. schools was 2.72 in 1972, 2.22 in 1982 and 2.40 in 1992. These authors also find that court mandated reduction of educational disparities within states have been efficacious. Hussar and Sonnenberg (2001) find some overall reduction in expenditure disparities at the district level between 1980 and 1994, but caution that the decreases are not uniform across states and that large differences persist.

(1) psychological factors, an intrinsic desire to behave like certain others,
(2) interdependences in the constraints that individuals face, so that the costs of a given behavior depend on whether others do the same, or
(3) interdependences in information transmission, so that the behavior of others alters the information on the effects of such behaviors available to a given individual.[3]

Each of these types of imitative behavior implies that an individual, when assessing alternative behavioral choices, will find a given behavior relatively more desirable if others have previously behaved or are currently behaving in the same way. Hence the relative desirability of staying in school is higher when adults in a community are college graduates or when one's peers are also staying in school.

One important reason why neighborhood effects have received much recent attention is that they provide a way of understanding why poverty traps might exist. To see the logic behind this claim, suppose that educational investment decisions exhibit strong role model influences, so that the decision to attend college for each high school graduate in a community is strongly (and positively) related to the percentage of college graduates among adults in a community. Such interdependence in behaviors creates the possibility that if one has two communities, one where the adults are all college graduates, and a second where none are, that these communities will converge to different levels of college attendance in a steady state. High and low college attendance rates are each reinforced across time as high (low) attendance rates among the current pool of adults lead to high (low) attendance rates among high school graduates, who in the future will influence the high school graduates to collectively exhibit high (low) rates as well. One way to think about a poverty trap is that a community, if initially comprised of poor members, will remain poor across long time periods, even generations. Intertemporal social interactions (i.e., social interactions in which choices made at one time affect others in the future) provide precisely this sort of dependence. An important antecedent to this idea is due to Loury (1977) in his construction of a theory of persistent racial inequality; ethnicity may be regarded as a sort of neighborhood in social space.

A related notion of a poverty trap may be identified when one thinks about peer group effects. When the behavior of one member of a group is sufficiently positively dependent on the behaviors of others, this creates a degree of freedom in behavior of the group as a whole. Contemporaneous dependences in behavior mean that the members of a group will behave similarly. At the same time, these effects, when sufficiently strong, mean that the characteristics of the individuals involved will not uniquely determine what the group actually does. Dependence on history, reactions to common influences, etc. may

[3] Streufert (2000) shows how these interdependences can affect human capital formation by modeling how observations of adults in a community can affect inferences about the economic benefits to education. In his analysis, self-selection into neighborhoods means that inferences by the young about this trade off are biased. Streufert shows how under plausible assumptions, children in disadvantaged neighborhoods can be led to underestimate the returns to education, although this is not a logical implication of neighborhood self-selection. Related results are obtained by Roemer and Wets (1995).

determine which sort of average behavior actually transpires. The key idea, however, is that strong contemporaneous dependences in behavior lead to multiple possibilities for self-reinforcing behavior in groups. Within a given behavioral configuration, each individual is acting "rationally" in the usual sense. That does not mean that each self-consistent configuration is equally desirable from the perspective of the members of the group. Another definition of a poverty trap is a socially undesirable (in the sense of producing poverty across a community) collection of behaviors in which the behaviors are mutually reinforcing and so individually rational.

Neighborhood effects are also important as they may reinforce the effects of changes in private incentives. Suppose one is considering whether to provide college scholarships to randomly chosen students across a set of high schools versus concentrating the scholarships among students within a given school. If the objective of the program is to alter high school graduation rates, then the presence of social interactions can, other things equal, mean that the concentration of the scholarships will be more efficacious. Assuming the direct incentive effect of the scholarships is the same for students across schools, the advantage of concentrating the scholarships in one school is that they will induce neighborhood effects that affect all students in the school, including those who have not been offered scholarships. More generally, neighborhood effects can amplify the effects of altering private incentives; this amplification is sometimes known as a "social multiplier" following Cooper and John (1988) and Manski (1993). The presence of social multipliers has important implications for the design of policies that have yet to be explored. In addition, perspectives on inequality that are driven by the effects of neighborhoods on individuals have important implications for how one conceives of notions such as equality of opportunity, and so has direct bearing on the assessment of alternative redistributive policies, see Durlauf (1996c, 1999, 2001) for discussion.[4]

The basic structure and implications of residential neighborhoods models suggest that the notion of neighborhoods may have general application in social science contexts. In fact, there are now a number of disparate research directions each of which focuses on populations of agents who are organized into groupings in which interactions occur; at least abstractly, these different analyses employ the idea of neighborhood effects. Examples of phenomena that have been studied using such ideas include:

(1) economic growth and industrial development in which spillovers occur between technologically similar industries [Durlauf (1993)],

(2) economic development and market growth in which direct trading links between individual agents determine the extent of markets [Kelly (1997)] and

[4] In this work, I argue that neighborhood effects and related social interactions constitute a "memberships theory of inequality and poverty" in the sense that group memberships play a primary role in determining both cross-section inequality and social mobility over time. The role of groups in generating inequality is argued to matter both in assessing the ethical justifications for redistributive policies as well as having implications for the form of the policies. In the current context, neighborhood effects have obvious implications for the efficacy of government policies to redistribute neighborhood memberships as an antipoverty policy, for example.

(3) business cycles in which local demand spillovers between industries arrayed on a lattice produce persistent aggregate fluctuations [Bak et al. (1993)].

Hence, one part of this review will focus on contexts other than residence where neighborhood effects have proven to be a valuable research direction; for example, the themes considered here are likely to be relevant for a variety of urban and regional issues.

Finally, it should be noted that many of the assumptions and properties of neighborhoods effects models are similar to those found in various strands of literature, including regional and urban economics. For example, they are related to discrete choice models of location decisions of firms and workers such as Anas and Xu (1999).[5] For a second and more general example, there exist many parallels between the analysis of how neighborhood effects determine the equilibrium allocations of agents across neighborhoods and models of spatial competition, see Anderson, de Palma and Thisse (1992, Chapters 8 and 9) for a detailed description of spatial competition using logistic models that in many ways are similar to those developed for neighborhood effects by Brock and Durlauf. These similarities are exploited in Grilo, Shy and Thisse (2001) who study how the equilibrium in a spatial duopoly model is affected by the presence of conformity or vanity effects. In fact, I believe the modern neighborhood effects literature would have progressed more quickly had there been greater attention to the existing body of regional and urban economic theory.

The neighborhood effects literature is quite disparate and no survey could cover the full range of theoretical models and empirical studies contained in the existing literature. Instead, the goal of this survey is to identify some of the major research questions that unify the many analyses as well as to highlight some of the weaknesses in the literature. To do this, the survey will work sequentially from theory to econometrics to empirical work. Section 2 provides an overview of theoretical work on neighborhood effects. The discussion focuses on both the implications of neighborhood effects on aggregate behavior and on the role of these effects in determining neighborhood composition. Section 3 provides some analysis of econometric issues that arise in the study of neighborhood effects. Section 4 reviews the existing empirical literature that directly addresses neighborhood effects. Section 5 reviews a body of studies that, while not directly focusing on neighborhood effects, nevertheless speaks to the importance of such effects. Section 6 contains summary and conclusions.

2. Theory

Theoretical models incorporating neighborhood effects involve two types of basic questions. First, how do the characteristics of a neighborhood affect the decision making of

[5] Note also that the Brock and Durlauf (2001a, 2002, 2003) models of discrete choice with neighborhood effects are formally similar to the quantal games model of McKelvey and Palfrey (1995) and the approach to bounded rationality in Nash games developed by Chen, Friedman and Thisse (1997).

its members, and in the aggregate, the behaviors in the neighborhood as a whole? Second, how does the presence of neighborhood effects influence memberships in neighborhoods and in the aggregate, determine the configuration of the population across neighborhoods? While these questions of course interact throughout the theoretical literature, they are best understood as distinct.

2.1. Choice within neighborhoods

I first consider the abstract problem of how neighborhood effects influence individual choices and thereby produce interesting neighborhood behaviors in the aggregate. Consider I individuals who are members of a common neighborhood denoted as n. Each individual i, makes a choice ω_i (a choice that is taken from the elements of some set of possible behaviors Ω_i). This individual-level decision will produce a probabilistic description of the choice given certain features of the individual and his neighborhood. The goal of the analysis is to construct a probability measure $\mu(\cdot)$ for the vector of choices of all members of the group, ω, that is consistent with these individual-level probability measures and understand how neighborhood effects determine its properties. Since others influence individual agents, it is useful to define $\omega_{n,-i}$ as the vector of all choices other than that of agent i.

From the perspective of individual decision making, one may distinguish between four sorts of influences on observed behaviors. These influences have different implications for how one models the choice problem. These components are:

- X_i, a vector of deterministic (to the modeler) individual-specific characteristics associated with individual i,
- ε_i, a vector of random individual-specific characteristics associated with i,
- Y_n, a vector of predetermined neighborhood-specific characteristics, and
- $\mu_i^e(\omega_{n,-i})$, the subjective beliefs individual i possesses about behaviors of others in his neighborhood, described as a probability measure over those behaviors.

Each of these components will be treated as a distinct argument in the payoff function that determines individual choices. The terms Y_n and $\mu_i^e(\omega_{n,-i})$ constitute neighborhood effects. Following Manski (1993), who draws from the sociology literature in this regard [cf. Blalock (1984)], I will refer to Y_n as a contextual effect and $\mu_i^e(\omega_{n,-i})$ as an endogenous effect, in order to distinguish those neighborhood effects that are determined by characteristics of neighborhood members as opposed to those effects that are determined by the contemporaneous behaviors of neighborhood members. The assumption that individuals are affected by their beliefs about the behaviors of others rather than by the actual behaviors is made for analytical convenience.

Even though the neighborhood effects terms may be "nonstandard" in the context of standard decision problems, individual choices are still defined via the maximization of some individual payoff function $V(\cdot)$; given the notation we have introduced, individual choices are thus assumed to follow

$$\omega_i = \underset{\omega \in \Omega_i}{\arg\max}\, V\big(\omega_i, X_i, \varepsilon_i, Y_n, \mu_i^e(\omega_{n,-i})\big). \tag{1}$$

In order to close this model, it is necessary to describe how beliefs about the behaviors of others are determined. The benchmark assumption in this literature is that beliefs are rational in the sense that

$$\mu_i^e(\omega_{-i}) = \mu\big(\omega_{-i} \mid \varepsilon_i, Y_n, X_j, \mu_j^e(\omega_{-j})\ \forall j\big). \tag{2}$$

Notice that all uncertainty about the behaviors of others depends upon the fact that agent i cannot observe the random payoff terms ε_j for agents other than himself. The existence of an equilibrium set of behaviors within a neighborhood is thus a fixed point problem, i.e., determining what subjective conditional probabilities concerning the behavior of others correspond to the conditional probabilities produced by the model when behaviors are based on those subjective beliefs.

Equation (1) is often simplified in two ways. First, the role of endogenous neighborhood effects is reduced to the expected value of the average choice of others, $\overline{\omega}_{-i} = (I-1)^{-1}\sum_{j\neq i}\omega_j$. This assumption reduces the possible endogenous effects to a single moment of the distribution of behaviors. Second, it is often the case that ε_i is set equal to zero for all neighborhood members, eliminating uncertainty about the behavior of others. When these assumptions are made, individual decisions will solve

$$\omega_i = \operatorname*{arg\,max}_{\omega\in\Omega_i} V(\omega_i, X_i, Y_n, \overline{\omega}_{-i}). \tag{3}$$

This simplified version of the neighborhoods effects model makes clear that the interesting implications of the effects depends on the feedbacks between the choices of each individual. Neighborhoods models typically assume that these feedbacks represent a form of complementarity between choices. For the payoff function described in (3), complementarity[6] means that if $\omega^{\text{low}} < \omega^{\text{high}}$, and $\overline{\omega}_{-i}^{\text{low}} < \overline{\omega}_{-i}^{\text{high}}$, then

$$\begin{aligned} &V\big(\omega^{\text{high}}, X_i, Y_n, \overline{\omega}_{-i}^{\text{high}}\big) - V\big(\omega^{\text{low}}, X_i, Y_n, \overline{\omega}_{-i}^{\text{high}}\big) \\ &\quad > V\big(\omega^{\text{high}}, X_i, Y_n, \overline{\omega}_{-i}^{\text{low}}\big) - V\big(\omega^{\text{low}}, X_i, Y_n, \overline{\omega}_{-i}^{\text{low}}\big). \end{aligned} \tag{4}$$

(It is straightforward to modify the definition of complementarity in (4) to account for how beliefs about the average choice of others, rather than realized choices, affect individuals.) Complementarity is a fundamental property for interdependent decision making because it implies that higher choice levels of others make higher choice levels relatively more attractive, thereby creating incentives for members of a common neighborhood to behave similarly. In fact, the simplified neighborhood model (3) is an example of the class of coordination models studied in Cooper and John (1988) and generalized in Milgrom and Roberts (1990). Cooper and John establish, when Ω is an

[6] When $V(\cdot)$ is twice differentiable, then the definition I employ is equivalent to requiring positive cross-partial derivatives between ω_i and ω_{-i}. I prefer the definition of complementarity given by Equation (4) both because it is more general and because it better communicates the implications of complementarity for individual decision making. I will use the cross-partial derivative definition when discussing papers that employ it.

interval of the real line and $V(\cdot)$ is twice differentiable, that complementarity is necessary for the presence of multiple equilibria.[7] Intuitively, when complementarities are strong enough they imply that there exists a degree of freedom in the determination of individual and aggregate outcomes in the sense that complementarities dictate that individuals act similarly in equilibrium but do not specify their actual behaviors. In the neighborhoods context, this is important because multiple equilibria create the possibility that two neighborhoods with similar observables (i.e., distributions of X_i within each neighborhood n and levels of Y_n) can exhibit different aggregate behaviors.

The exact relationship between complementarities and multiple equilibria in a neighborhood will be quite complicated and will depend on the relationship between the joint distribution of the different determinants of individual choice within a neighborhood. The interplay of different choice determinants may be seen in a model due to Brock and Durlauf (2001b). In this model, members of a neighborhood make binary choices that are coded -1 and 1. Agent payoffs are

$$V_i = k\omega_i + cX_i\omega_i + dY_n\omega_i + Jm_n\omega_i + \varepsilon_i(\omega_i) \tag{5}$$

where k, c, d, and J are behavioral parameters and $m_n = I^{-1}\sum_{i=1}^{I} E(\omega_i \mid Y_n, X_j\ \forall j)$ is the (rational) expected average choice in the neighborhood; this expectation is calculated under the assumption that each agent knows the values of the contextual effects and the individual characteristics of the neighborhood members.[8] Notice that

$$\frac{\partial^2 V_i}{\partial m_n \partial \omega_i} = J,$$

hence an (expectations-based) complementarity is present and measured by this parameter. The random utility terms $\varepsilon_i(\omega_i)$ are assumed to be independent across individuals and to be negative exponentially distributed, i.e.,

$$F\big(\varepsilon_i(1) - \varepsilon_i(-1) \leqslant z\big) = \frac{1}{1+\exp(-\beta z)}.$$

Under these assumptions, it is straightforward to show that the expected average choice solves

$$m_n = \int \tanh(\beta k + \beta c X + \beta d Y_n + \beta J m_n)\,\mathrm{d}F_{X,n}. \tag{6}$$

In this expression,

$$\tanh(x) = \frac{\exp(x) - \exp(-x)}{\exp(x) + \exp(-x)}$$

[7] Cooper and John prove this under the additional condition that $X_i = X_j$, $\forall i, j$, which allows them to model all choice decisions as identical.

[8] For ease of exposition, I ignore the fact that each individual knows his own realization of $\varepsilon_i(1)$ and $\varepsilon_i(-1)$ when forming beliefs about the average choice in the neighborhood. Brock and Durlauf (2001a) explicitly develop this model when agents are affected by the average choice of others, thereby dealing with this issue.

and $F_{X,n}$ is the empirical distribution of X_i within n. Characterizing the conditions for multiple equilibria is thus quite difficult even in this simple context, once one introduces heterogeneity across agents. For the special case where $X_i = X_n$ (so that all individual heterogeneity is generated by the unobserved $\varepsilon_i(\omega_i)$) one can give a precise characterization of the number of equilibria.

PROPOSITION 1 (Number of equilibria in the Brock and Durlauf (2001a) model of binary choice with neighborhood effects). *Under the model* (5) *and* (6), *if* $X_i = X_n$, *then there exists for each value of* $k + cX_n + dY_n$ *a threshold* $H > 1$, *monotonically increasing in* $|k + cX_n + dY_n|$ *such that*

(i) *if* $\beta J < H$, *then there is a unique solution to* (6),

(ii) *if* $\beta J > H$, *there exist three solutions to* (6).

One can show that the extremal equilibria (i.e., the equilibria associated with the values of m_n that are largest and smallest in absolute value) are stable.

This proposition is useful as it illustrates how the predetermined incentives to make one choice or another, the strength of complementarity in choices, and the degree of heterogeneity across agents collectively determine the number of equilibria for a neighborhood. When predetermined incentives $(k + cX_n + dY_n)$ are sufficiently strong relative to βJ, then the equilibrium is unique. Intuitively, βJ is smaller either when complementarities are relatively weak (J is small) or unobserved heterogeneity is large (β is small). It is easy to see why weak complementarities militate against multiple equilibria. Why does β play a role? Intuitively, high degrees of heterogeneity mean (since the density of $\varepsilon_i(1) - \varepsilon_i(-1)$ is symmetric) that a large percentage of the agents in the neighborhood make choices having experienced relatively large draws of $|\varepsilon(1) - \varepsilon(-1)|$. When this is so, the percentage of agents whose decisions may be changed by the number of agents behaving similarly is relatively small, which can eliminate the possibility of multiple reinforcing configurations of behaviors.

Analogous results may be obtained when one moves to 3 or more choices [Bayer and Timmins (2002) and Brock and Durlauf (2002, 2003)]. To describe neighborhood effects in this context, it is necessary to generalize (5). When agents face L possible choices, this may be done by assuming that i's utility for choice $l \in \{0, \dots, L-1\}$ is described by

$$V_{i,l} = k_l + c_l X_i + d_l Y_n + J_l p_{i,l} + \varepsilon_{i,l} \tag{7}$$

where $p^e_{i,l}$ is the expected percentage of agents in the neighborhood making that choice when rational expectations are imposed. Relative to the binary case one important difference is that one needs to account for differential effects of individual, contextual, and endogenous effects on choice-specific payoffs; this is done by allowing the coefficients in (7) to be choice-dependent. When the random terms are double exponentially distributed, i.e., $\mu(\varepsilon_{i,l} \leqslant z) = \exp(-\exp(-\beta\varsigma + \gamma))$,[9] one has a multinomial logit model of

[9] γ is Euler's constant.

choice with neighborhood effects. Brock and Durlauf (2002, 2003) provide results on the unique versus multiplicity of equilibria for this model and show how these findings generalize to other error densities.

Once one allows for general forms of heterogeneity, for example, by allowing the individual characteristics X_i to vary across individuals, models of choice within neighborhoods rapidly become analytically intractable. This suggests that computer simulations will play an increasingly important role in studying these models, particularly as their microeconomic structures are enriched. Examples of local interactions structures that have been analyzed using a combination of analytics and computer simulations include Bell (2002) and Oomes (2003).

Complementarities within neighborhoods have implications for aggregate data beyond the possibility of multiple equilibria. This possibility was recognized in a paper by Glaeser, Sacerdote and Scheinkman (1996). The paper is also interesting as an example of a neighborhood interaction structure that is local in the sense that an individual is affected by immediate neighbors as opposed to the average behavior of the neighborhood as a whole.

In the Glaeser, Sacerdote and Scheinkman (1996) model, $2n + 1$ agents face binary choices (in their context, on whether or not to engage in criminal activity). Agents are assumed to come in three types indexed by $\{0, 1, 2\}$; $A(i)$ denotes the type of agent i. Agent heterogeneity is thus modeled via the distribution of types in a population. Mapping their model into the binary choice framework I have already described, each is associated with a payoff function

$$V_i = k_{A(i)}\omega_i + J_{A(i)}\omega_i\omega_{i-1}. \tag{8}$$

The substantive difference between this payoff function and payoffs as described by (5) are two-fold. First, there is no unobserved heterogeneity in individual payoffs due to differences in X_i or $\varepsilon_i(\omega_i)$; rather heterogeneity appears because different types are associated with different values of the parameter k in the payoff function. Second, neighborhood effects are restricted to pairs of nearest neighborhoods within a neighborhood, since the decision of each agent is assumed to only depend on one other agent. Metaphorically, agents live on a 1-dimensional block and only care about their neighbor to the left.

The recursive structure of interactions makes the analysis of individual decisions relatively easy since there are no reciprocal feedbacks between individual decisions; while the choice of $i - 1$ affects i, the choice of i does not affect $i - 1$. As a result, no issues arise of individuals making choices in order to alter the behavior of others. Nevertheless structures of this type can produce complex behaviors because the bilateral interactions across individuals indirectly connect all members of a neighborhood.

Glaeser, Sacerdote and Scheinkman close this model by specifying the three types of agents. Type 0 agents always choose $\omega_i = -1$; this may be generated by $k_0 < 0$, $J = 0$. Type 1 agents always choose $\omega_i = 1$; this behavior may be generated by $k_1 > 0$, $J = 0$. Type 2 agents always make the same choice as his neighbor, which will occur if $k_2 = 0$, $J > 0$. The distribution of agent types is assumed to be random; this randomness makes the behavior of each individual unpredictable to the modeler. These assumptions on heterogeneity may be shown to imply that there is a unique equilibrium set of choices in the neighborhood. Glaeser, Sacerdote and Scheinkman assume agent types are independent across individuals and distributed with fixed probabilities p_A.

These assumptions on heterogeneity may be shown to imply that there is a unique equilibrium set of choices in the neighborhood. This uniqueness is consistent with the goal of the analysis, which is to show how endogenous neighborhood effects influence the volatility of average crime rates across neighborhoods. Defining $p = p_1/(p_1 + p_2)$ and $\pi = p_0 + p_1$, Glaeser, Sacerdote and Scheinkeman prove that the normalized sample average $(2n + 1)^{-1/2} \sum_i \omega_i$ obeys the following central limit theorem:

PROPOSITION 2 [Limiting behavior of average choice in the Glaeser, Sacerdote and Scheinkman (1996) model].

$$(2n+1)^{-1/2} \sum_i \omega_i \Rightarrow_w N\left(0, \frac{p(1-p)(2-\pi)}{\pi}\right). \tag{9}$$

What makes this proposition important is that it provides a description of how endogenous neighborhood effects influence the dispersion of average behaviors across neighborhoods. To see this, observe that if there were no neighborhood effects, this would mean that all agents are of type 0 or 1. In this case, the variance term in the proposition would reduce to $p(1 - p)$. As the percentage of type 2 agents increases, the variance term also increases, and becomes unbounded when $\pi = 0$. This model thus illustrates that even when neighborhoods exhibit unique equilibria, neighborhood effects multiply the effects of idiosyncratic shocks and thereby increase the variance in the average behaviors that are observed.

2.1.1. The statistical mechanics of neighborhood interactions

The Brock and Durlauf (2001a) and Glaeser, Sacerdote and Scheinkman (1996) models are mathematically equivalent to models that have appeared in the statistical mechanics literature in physics and mathematics. (Models of this type are also known as interacting particle system models or random field models.) Statistical mechanics models specify a particular topology of interactions for agents within a population and explore the implications of this topology for the distributions of behaviors of the agents.[10] These interaction topologies are often local in the sense that agents are usually arrayed in some space with the strength of direct interactions determined by distance; one may think of collections of elements that directly interact as neighborhoods. Mathematical structures

[10] In physical contexts, the agents are objects such as atoms and so are not purposeful as they must be in modeling human agents; this distinction must be kept in mind when considering how to adapt statistical mechanics models to social science contexts. The failure to do so is a serious limitation of much of the recent work on economic complexity; see Durlauf (2003).

that describe populations that are comprised of neighborhoods in this sense were in fact originally developed in the context of statistical mechanics, where many fundamental phenomena such as magnetization may be described as aggregate properties of a large number of interacting elements. For the purposes of socioeconomic phenomena, statistical mechanics models allow one to analyze alternative forms of neighborhood interactions. For example, one can analyze environments where the direct payoff interdependences between members of a neighborhood are uniform as is done in Brock and Durlauf or analyze cases where direct interdependences occur between nearest neighbors as in Glaeser, Sacerdote, and Scheinkman. One of the key ideas in this literature is that overlapping neighborhoods create population-wide interdependences in behaviors, which is the basis of Proposition 2 above. Durlauf (1997), Ioannides (1997) and Kirman (1997) provide different perspectives on the use of these models in social science contexts.

Ideas from the statistical mechanics literature have begun to appear in the economics literature, as these models possess a number of interesting properties. Among these properties I would identify.

Multiple equilibria and nonergodicity. One way to understand the structure of statistical mechanics models is to think of them as probability descriptions. Following the language employed in the description of the basic model of choice with neighborhood effects, the preferences, constraints and beliefs of the agents produce a set of conditional probability measures that describe each individual's behavior given the behaviors and/or characteristics of others. An equilibrium in the model is a joint probability measure that is consistent with these conditional probability measures. When more than one such measure exists, the model exhibits multiple equilibria. The mathematical term for such multiplicity is nonergodicity.

Phase transition. A model exhibits phase transition if its properties qualitatively change for a small change in a parameter value. Phase transitions are thus a way of describing when threshold effects occur in an environment. The Brock and Durlauf model exhibits a phase transition around the threshold H; the number of equilibria in the model changes as the compound parameter βJ is moved above the threshold.

Universality. Statistical mechanics models often have aggregate properties that do not depend on the specifics of the interaction structure; so that different interaction structures will produce identical aggregate behaviors. For an example of universality, one can show that equilibrium average choice levels in the version of the Brock and Durlauf model described by Proposition 1 are unchanged if one replaces the payoff function with

$$V = k\omega_i + cX_n\omega_i + dY_n\omega_i + J\omega_i\frac{1}{2}\sum_{j\in\{i-1,i+1\}} E(\omega_j \mid X_n, Y_n) + \varepsilon_i(\omega_i). \quad (10)$$

That being said, universality is largely an unexplored property in economics contexts. From the perspectives of neighborhood effects, these models are interesting as they allow for the exploration of a range of alternative interaction structures. I regard the study of universality to be one of the most important future directions in this literature since there are generally no good empirical reasons to favor any particular neighborhood interaction structure over another.

The first example of a statistical mechanics model to appear in economics appears to be due to Föllmer (1974). Föllmer considered a population of individuals arrayed on a torus formed by the 2-dimensional integer lattice $\mathbb{Z}^2$. (To visualize this torus, think of a $K \times K$ lattice where the edges are matched up, producing a doughnut shape, to ensure each element has 4 neighbors within 1 unit distance, and let $K \Rightarrow \infty$.) In this model, each individual is associated with one of two utility functions; following the earlier discussion, the utility function associated with an agent is indexed by $\omega_i \in \{-1, 1\}$. Föllmer's objective was to determine whether, if each individual has an equal unconditional probability of being associated with either utility function, the aggregate population would converge (as population size grew) to one where half of the population is associated with each utility function. Föllmer assumed that each individual's probability of having a particular utility function was a function of his nearest neighbors, i.e.,

$$\mu(\omega_i \mid \omega_{-i}) \propto \exp\left(J\omega_i \sum_{|j-i|=1} \omega_j\right) \tag{11}$$

with $J > 0$. Föllmer (1974) shows that the average preference structure in the population, $\bar{\omega}$, obeys the following proposition.

PROPOSITION 3 [Average preferences in the Föllmer (1974) model of interdependent utility functions]. *There exists a* $\bar{J}$ *such that under the conditional probability structure* (11):

(i) *if* $J < \bar{J}$, *then* $\bar{\omega} = 0$ *for every realization of the process,*
(ii) *if* $J > \bar{J}$, *then there exist values* $m_+ > 0$ *and* $m_- < 0$, *such that* $|m_+| = |m_-|$ *and*

$$\mu(\bar{\omega} = m_+) = \mu(\bar{\omega} = m_-) = 0.5. \tag{12}$$

In the Föllmer model, J measures the strength of interdependence in preferences between nearest neighbors on the lattice; notice how the analogous parameter appears in the Brock and Durlauf (2001a) and Glaeser, Sacerdote and Scheinkman (1996) models. The theorem states that when this interdependence exceeds a certain threshold, then each sample path realization will tip toward one of the two utility functions predominating in the aggregate economy, even though there are no ex ante differences in the probabilities of either outcome. As such, the model is nonergodic.

Part of the growth of statistical mechanics models has occurred in the context of game theory; this work is an important advance over Föllmer (1974) in that this original work did not have any behavioral foundations. In a seminal paper, Blume (1993) has provided a rigorous game-theoretic formulation of lattice interaction structures of this type. This paper is also important in that it illustrates how the technical assumptions that underlie these models have substantive implications for individual behavior. One important advance Blume (1993) makes relative to Föllmer (1974) is the construction of a continuous time version of the model that allows agents to update their choices asynchronously. This allows Blume to use a Nash equilibrium concept to analyze the model. Ellison (1993) provides a related analysis of local interactions of this type, with an emphasis on the speed at which the population convergences to its limiting behavior. Ellison shows how local interactions, placed in a learning context, can slow down convergence relative to a model where agents react to all other choices, as occurs in Brock and Durlauf. Anderlini and Ianni (1996) extend work of this type to a context where individuals play a sequence of games with randomly selected neighbors, showing how the steady state behavior of such a model differs from the case where interactions are not local. Put differently, Anderlini and Ianni show that local interactions can allow a diversity of strategies to coexist in equilibrium even when all agents are playing the same (in this case, coordination) game. Recent analyses of equilibrium properties of statistical mechanics models include Blume and Durlauf (2002) and Scheinkman and Horst (2003); the former paper studies the dynamics of statistical mechanics models where interactions are common across all members whereas the latter is useful in its analysis of the relationship between the description of local neighborhoods for complementarities and the description of conditional probabilities for individual choices given the choices of others in the population.

A number of papers have employed statistical mechanics models to understand substantive phenomena. The notion of neighborhood differs across contexts; what makes the abstract notion of neighborhood useful is the implicit assumption in all of these models that agents are arrayed in some space in which distances between agents may be defined, and where these distances influence interactions. Some examples of these applications include:

Business cycles. Bak et al. (1993) develop a model of sectoral interactions based on order flows between intermediate and final good producers. When production exhibits nonconvexities, idiosyncratic producer-level shocks are able to produce aggregate business cycles. Oomes (2003) studies the role of local demand interactions in producing spatial persistence in unemployment. Interestingly, she finds that when labor may be hired in continuous quantities, the long-run distribution of unemployment is uniform across locations whereas if labor is a binary variable, spatial differences may persist indefinitely; this role for nonconvexities echoes Bak et al. Recently, Bell (2002) provides an interesting mix of local and global interactions in a model in which preferences are influenced by neighborhood effects whereas global effects are introduced via prices. Bell shows that these two effects can combine to produce rich cross-section diversity and aggregate cycles.

Economic growth. Durlauf (1993) studies a model of interacting industries in which individual industries are arrayed on a 1-dimensional lattice. Distances between industries on the lattice are interpreted as reflecting technological similarity. In the model, the choice between a high productivity (with high fixed cost) versus a low productivity technology by industry i at t depends on the technology choices of industries $i-k$ to $i+l$ at $t-1$, thereby allowing each industry to be affected by an arbitrarily large (although finite) span of neighboring industries. Durlauf (1993) shows how this model can produce development traps and explain industrial development using the idea of backwards and forwards linkages due to Albert Hirschman. Kelly (1997) develops a model of local transportation linkages and economic development that captures Adam Smith's insights on market size and specialization; this model is discussed in the context of networks and neighborhoods below.

Land use. Irwin and Bockstaed (2002) show how neighborhood interactions can affect long-term patterns of land use. In this model, the decision to develop a given parcel of land is affected by the development state of neighboring parcels. This model is shown to produce fragmented patterns of development on urban/rural fringes that are consistent with observed patterns. One interesting feature of this analysis is that it finds that the neighborhood effects for land development are negative, which may reflect congestion effects.

Technology adoption. Allen (1982) uses statistical mechanics models to analyze technology adoption when network externalities are restricted to local neighborhoods. An and Kiefer (1995) also consider the question of technological adoption and provide conditions under which more efficient technologies are adopted and when they are not.

Financial markets. Brock (1993) develops a general statistical mechanics approach to financial markets and shows how the interactions that underlie these models may be used to interpret a range of stylized facts concerning time varying volatility and market volume in financial markets. These ideas have been pursued in recent work such as Cont and Bouchard (2000) and Focardi, Cincotti and Marchesi (2002) who consider neighborhoods defined by random connections to show how stock market crashes may arise. One problem with efforts such as these (unlike Brock's work), which are part of the growing "econophysics" literature [cf. Mantegna and Stanley (1999) is a well-written introduction] is that they have weak microeconomic foundations, as discussed in Durlauf (2003).

Finally, it should be noted that within game theory there has emerged a rich literature on local interactions that does not use statistical mechanics properties explicitly, although the mathematical structures are similar. Eshel, Samuelson and Shaked (1998) explore the evolution of different behavioral types when the payoffs from different strategy choices are determined by play with neighbors and show how altruistic behavior can survive in such a context; Nowak, Bonheoffer and May (1994) and Nowak and May (1993) study similar environments. Perhaps the most general and deep treatment of local interactions models in game theory is Morris (2000) who analyzes these structures with great generality and establishes conditions under which behaviors that originate among a finite set of players can spread across a population given arbitrary local interaction structures.

2.2. Equilibrium neighborhood configurations

The presence of contextual effects Y_n and endogenous effects $\mu_i^e(\omega_{n,-i})$ in individual payoff functions implies that a complete theory of neighborhood effects must account for how neighborhoods are formed in the presence of these effects. From the perspective of an abstract choice problem, individual neighborhood choices may be thought of as

$$\max_{n \in N} V^*(x_i, Y_n, \rho_n) \tag{13}$$

where $V^*(x_i, Y_n, \rho_n)$ is the expected utility associated with neighborhood n, and ρ_n denotes any additional variables that affect this payoff; typically, this will be the rental price to residence. Notice that this payoff calculation requires that agents form beliefs about which equilibrium will emerge in a neighborhood when multiple equilibria exist. An equilibrium in an endogenous neighborhoods model is a configuration of agents across neighborhoods such that each agent solves (13) and the resulting values of Y_n are those that are generated by this configuration. Put differently, the neighborhood choices of individual agents help determine the effects in a neighborhood, so location decisions need to exhibit self-consistency.

The key theoretical feature of interest in these types of models concerns how individuals with different attributes are allocated across neighborhoods; this allocation will determine the extent to which different neighborhoods will exhibit different contextual effects; without such differences, the only way that neighborhoods may affect inequality is via multiple equilibria. The most common attribute that is studied in this literature is income, although other attributes have been considered, as is discussed below. Much of the interest in neighborhood configurations, in turn, focuses on the extent to which neighborhoods are stratified by income or other attributes. Neighborhoods are said to be stratified with respect to an attribute x_i if it is the case that the supports of the intra-neighborhood distributions of x_i do not overlap except at endpoints. Stratification by income, for example, provides a basis for understanding persistence in economic status across generations: poor families are consigned to poor neighborhoods, whose effects make it more likely their children are poor, etc.

As is well understood in the urban economics literature, modeling equilibrium allocations of individuals across neighborhoods involves a number of subtleties. In order to understand the essential features of these types of models, I describe a simple framework developed in Benabou (1996a), which is adapted to the notation I have employed and makes clear the issues that arise with respect to the question of whether equilibrium neighborhood configurations are stratified.

I work with a simplified version of the Benabou model that is modified to correspond to previous notation. The population is assumed to consist of a continuum of agents with associated measure I who may live in one of two neighborhoods, each of size $I/2$ and denoted as A and B. Residence in a neighborhood entails the payment of rents ρ_j, $j = A, B$; these rents go to an absentee landlord. There are two types of agents, denoted by whether they are associated with individual characteristics x^{high} or x^{low}; the characteristic is a scalar. Let θ denote the percentage of x^{high} agents. All contextual effects derive from the average value of x_i within the neighborhood, which is denoted as $\bar{x}_n$. The payoff to a given neighborhood can therefore be written as $V^*(x_i, \bar{x}_n, \rho_n)$.

What conditions determine whether the equilibrium allocation of families across neighborhoods is stratified by x? Benabou answers this question by considering how individual agents are willing to trade off the rental price ρ_n against the neighborhood characteristic $\bar{x}_n$. Specifically, for each individual, one may define the function $R(x_i, \bar{x}_n, \rho_n)$ which characterizes the marginal tradeoff between ρ_n and $\bar{x}_n$ that leaves utility unchanged at a given V_0. This tradeoff implicitly describes how different agents will react to changes in relative neighborhood rental prices. This function may be derived by differentiating the payoff function with respect to ρ_n and $\bar{x}_n$ when utility is held constant, i.e.,

$$V^*_{\bar{x}_n}(x_i, \bar{x}_n, \rho_n)\,\mathrm{d}\bar{x}_n + V^*_{\rho_n}(x_i, \bar{x}_n, \rho_n)\,\mathrm{d}\rho_n = 0$$

$$\Rightarrow \quad R(x_i, \bar{x}_n, \rho_n) = \frac{\mathrm{d}\rho_n}{\mathrm{d}\bar{x}_n} = -\frac{V^*_{\bar{x}_n}(x_i, \bar{x}_n, \rho_n)}{V^*_{\rho_n}(x_i, \bar{x}_n, \rho_n)}. \tag{14}$$

The properties of $R(x_i, \bar{x}_n, \rho_n)$ determine whether neighborhoods are stratified in equilibrium. The following proposition is proven in Benabou (1996a).

PROPOSITION 4 [Stratification in the Benabou (1996a) model of endogenous neighborhoods]. *If $R(x_i, \bar{x}_n, \rho_n)$ is increasing in x_i, then the only stable equilibrium configuration of families is one that is stratified.*

Benabou's result may be stated directly in terms of willingness to pay; here I follow the excellent exposition in Becker and Murphy (2000). For each agent, let $f(x_i, \bar{x}_n)$ denote the willingness to pay for neighborhood n. Without loss of generality, assume that $\theta > 1/2$. Under the assumption that this function is strictly increasing in x_i, stratification in the sense described in Proposition 4 will occur if (letting neighborhood A denote the "better neighborhood") there exists a pair of rental prices P_A and P_B such that

$$f(x^{\mathrm{high}}, x^{\mathrm{high}}) - f(x^{\mathrm{high}}, x^m) = P_A - P_B \tag{15}$$

and

$$f(x^{\mathrm{low}}, x^{\mathrm{high}}) - f(x^{\mathrm{low}}, x^m) < P_A - P_B \tag{16}$$

where x^m denotes the average x value for a neighborhood that contains $\theta I - (I/2)x^{\mathrm{high}}$ agents. These conditions are equivalent to those in the Benabou theorem, since a greater willingness to pay by affluent families is an implication of the assumption that $R(x_i, \bar{x}_n, \rho_n)$ is increasing in x_i.

Why does stratification require that the willingness to pay for a better neighborhood is increasing in the individual attribute x? As Benabou explains, when this condition holds, any deviation of neighborhood composition away from symmetry will induce x^{high} families to move to the higher $\bar{x}_n$ neighborhood. Benabou's analysis makes clear that the presence of neighborhood effects is not sufficient to produce equilibrium stratification; what is additionally required is that there is a positive correlation between the attribute and willingness to pay for the average of the attribute.

What factors contribute to the fulfillment of conditions necessary for stratification, as delineated in Proposition 4 or in (15) and (16)? Benabou (1996a) provides a typology of different factors. With respect to neighborhood effects per se, one factor that contributes to the conditions necessary for stratification to occur is associated with complementarity between individual and neighborhood attributes, i.e.,

$$\frac{\partial^2 V^*_{x_i \bar{x}_n}(x_i, \bar{x}_n, \rho_n)}{\partial x_i \partial \bar{x}_n} > 0;$$

this condition is in fact sufficient under the set of assumptions in Benabou (1996a, Proposition 2) to ensure stratification. This is unsurprising as complementarity between individual and group attributes means that the benefits to high $\bar{x}_n$ neighborhoods are greater for high x_i types. Benabou also shows that other factors can contribute to stratification even when complementarity does not hold. One reason why stratification may still occur is via financial market imperfection, e.g., the ability of x^{high} agents to borrow at lower interest rates than others. This argument is closely related to the role of capital market imperfections in perpetuating inequality originally studied by Loury (1981). In Loury's model, families are unable to borrow to educate their children because they are unable to commit their children to repay these loans; thereby producing interfamily inequality in the marginal value of educational expenditures. A related phenomenon occurs in the context of neighborhoods models in that financial market imperfections can keep poorer families from being able to enter neighborhoods even when they would benefit more from the various neighborhood effects than the current residents.

The neighborhoods literature contains a range of alternative specifications of neighborhood models; recent examples include Benabou (1993, 1996a), de Bartolome (1990), Durlauf (1996a, 1996b), Epple, Filimon and Romer (1984), Epple and Platt (1998), and Fernandez and Rogerson (1996, 1997), Hoff and Sen (2000), and Nechyba (1997). Table 1 is a summary of some of the features of these models. Earlier models that are driven by similar ideas include Miyao (1978) who did early work on the stability of community segregation, though for that model the main driving mechanism is a desire to be with others of one's type. There is still no consensus as to the most useful general framework. One reason for this is that multiple neighborhoods models, both in the specific context I address as well as the broader urban economics literature, pose a number of theoretical complications. One complication arises from the need to ensure the existence of majority voting equilibria for neighborhood tax rates.[11] More generally, the construction of a neighborhoods model in which an equilibrium exists requires a number of modeling choices, including both the details of neighborhood structure

[11] Typically, expenditures are determined by taxes (i.e., there is no interneighborhood borrowing) with an equilibrium tax rate defined as one such that no single alternative would defeat it in an election.

Table 1
Models of neighborhood formation

Model	Neighborhood structure	Sorting mechanism	Neighborhood effects	Equilibrium allocations
Benabou (1993)	2 equally sized neighborhoods for ex ante identical individuals	Rental price differences between neighborhoods	Peer effect via lower human capital investment costs when others have invested	Stable stratified equilibria exist
Benabou (1996a)	2 equally sized neighborhoods for individuals of two types for characteristic that is valued in peers	Rental price differences between neighborhoods	Mean characteristic in neighborhood is valued	Stable stratified equilibria exist and are linked to several aspects of the microstructure
de Bartolome (1990)	2 neighborhoods of fixed size	Rental prices and education/tax packages.	Ability level of peers affects value of educational expenditure	Stratified versus integrated equilibria depend on strength of peer effects; integration requires "intermediate" degree of interactions
Durlauf (1996a)	Number and size of neighborhoods are endogenous	Neighborhoods may erect income barriers	Local public finance; distribution of incomes in neighborhood also increases productivity of educational expenditure	All equilibria are stratified
Durlauf (1996b)	Number and size of neighborhoods are endogenous	Housing prices	Local public finance; distribution of incomes in neighborhood also increases productivity of educational expenditure	All equilibria are stratified
Epple and Platt (1998)	J neighborhoods of arbitrary size	Differences in property tax, lump sum subsidies	Local public finance	Partial stratification

Table 1
(*continued*)

Model	Neighborhood structure	Sorting mechanism	Neighborhood effects	Equilibrium allocations
Epple, Filimon and Romer (1984)	J neighborhoods of arbitrary size	Differences in property tax rates and public good provision	Local public finance; no spillover effects	Stable stratified equilibria exist under assumptions ensuring willingness to pay for public goods is increasing in income
Fernandez and Rogerson (1997)	2 neighborhoods	Tax and education expenditure differences; zoning is modeled as minimum housing consumption level	Local public finance; no spillover effects	All stable equilibria are stratified; zoning increases ability of richer families to isolate themselves from others
Fernandez and Rogerson (1996)	J neighborhoods for $I > J$ income classes	Differences in income taxes and public education provision	Local public finance; no spillover effects	All stable equilibria are stratified
Hoff and Sen (2000)	J neighborhoods of equal size	Differences in rental and house prices	Value of home is affected by expenditures of neighbors	Stable stratified equilibria exist
Nechyba (1997)	J neighborhoods of fixed size	Housing prices	Local public finance	Under plausible assumptions, agents stratify by preferences and income

(number, fixed or variable neighborhood size, nature of housing market) and the nature of heterogeneity across individuals.

One important set of differences in various neighborhood models concerns the specification of neighborhood structure. Model assumptions vary in terms of the number of neighborhoods, the size of neighborhoods, the degree of heterogeneity in agents, and the mechanisms that determine neighborhood membership. In Benabou (1996a) and most of the analysis in Becker and Murphy (2000), it is assumed that there are two types of agents and two equally sized communities. Associated with these two neighborhoods are rental prices; these prices determine why some families prefer to be in the lower quality neighborhood. Epple, Filimon and Romer (1984) study an environment with a fixed number of communities but with no restrictions on community size. Neighborhood entry is free; differences in neighborhood choices occur on the basis of the tax/education combinations that they offer; there are no costs to residing in a particular neighborhood. Fernandez and Rogerson (1996) analyze a similar model with J communities and I (greater than J) income types. By eliminating the housing consumption decision and placing taxes on income rather than housing consumption, as is done in Epple, Filimon and Romer (1984), they achieve some valuable simplifications that render the environment useful for policy analysis, albeit at the cost of some realism. Durlauf (1996a) allows for the number of neighborhoods and their respective sizes to be endogenous, but does this at the cost of modeling neighborhood entry as a club in which existing members may be vetoed by current members using income requirements for neighborhood membership; Durlauf (1996b) shows how to support this allocation with house prices for particular choices of preferences and the human capital production function. Hoff and Sen (2000) make the interesting extension to these types of models by enriching the housing options a neighborhood offers to allow for renters as well as homeowners. For this range of specifications, the equilibrium neighborhood allocations are, under intuitive assumptions on preferences and the various technologies that appear (e.g., production of human capital), stratified by income which is the single dimension along which families differ.

While the stability of stratified equilibria appears to be robust to a range of alternative specifications of neighborhood structure and the rules that determine neighborhood membership, it is possible to identify two ways in which this finding is sensitive to substantive microeconomic assumptions. First, it is possible that the willingness to pay differential needed for equilibrium stratification will fail to hold: de Bartolome (1990), analyzing a model in which families differ according to the ability level of their children, provides conditions under which two communities can coexist, each of which is mixed. Becker and Murphy (2000) work with a version of the two-neighborhood Benabou (1996a) model and illustrate how mixed communities can coexist; they do this by relaxing the ability to pay assumption that underlies the Proposition 4.

Perhaps more fundamental, stratification depends on the assumption that families are distinguished along a single dimension. As such, much of the richness of neighborhood decisions has been assumed away. This is understandable given the difficulties that exist in developing neighborhood models with multiple levels of heterogeneity. However, there have been important recent advances in this regard. While not focusing explicitly on neighborhoods (they study allocations across private and public schools) Epple and Romano (1998) consider a model in which families differ by both child ability and parental income. Their model produces an equilibrium in which schools are ordered according to quality but in which sorting occurs along the two dimensions of income and ability. While extrapolating their results to a neighborhood context is not straightforward (since schools are allowed to offer financial incentives to influence their composition), their findings suggest an important dimension along which current models of neighborhood formation should be generalized. In the context of neighborhood formation, Epple and Platt (1998) and Nechyba (1997) provide equilibrium models where agents differ with respect to preferences as well as income. Epple and Platt (1998) allow for costless movement across neighborhoods whereas Nechyba (1997) restricts neighborhood sizes and introduces a fixed stock of heterogeneous houses that may be traded. Two attractive features of the Epple and Platt (1998) model are: (1) voters account for the consequences for neighborhood composition when voting over tax rates, a possibility whose importance was earlier shown in Epple and Romer (1990), and (2) renters and homeowners may both be present in a neighborhood. While neither of these analyses includes spillover effects, they are, in my view, important stepping-stones for future work. Even though there exists substantial stratification of neighborhoods by income, there is also considerable overlap in the income supports of neighborhoods [see Jargowsky (1997) for a broad overview]; an empirically successful theory needs to account for this mixing. And of course, the logic of the Tiebout approach to community formation places primary weight on preferences as the source of segregation, not income per se.[12]

The vast majority of studies of neighborhood formation focus on rents or prices as the mechanism by which neighborhood memberships are restricted. As such, these models typically ignore the role of zoning restrictions in influencing neighborhood composition. Zoning, in this context, may be thought of as placing a requirement on the number of units of housing (perhaps measured in terms of quality) that a homeowner must possess in order to reside in a given neighborhood. As originally shown by Hamilton (1975), these effects can be first order. For example, Hamilton develops a model in which perfect sorting of neighborhoods by income occurs when the number of neighborhoods is variable. One exception to this lack of attention to zoning is Fernandez and Rogerson (1997), who study zoning in the context of a two-community model with local finance of education. Working with a model in which equilibrium allocations of families across neighborhoods are stratified by income, they show that the introduction of zoning (both exogenous and endogenously chosen by neighborhood members) alters the allocation of families across neighborhoods by making the high-income neighborhood more exclusive. Interestingly, zoning does not necessarily increase the disparity in per pupil educational expenditures across districts. The reason for this is that the greater exclusivity

[12] This discussion does not exhaust the reasons why neighborhoods are mixed by income. Frankel (1998) for example, shows that information imperfections can generate incentives for high-income families to live near low-income families because of the effects of low-income families on neighborhood consumption goods prices. It is not clear how important this is empirically, although the argument is quite clever.

of the richer neighborhood raises the average income of the poorer neighborhood and therefore can, in equilibrium, reduce the gap in interneighborhood expenditures. Fernandez and Rogerson (1997) do not analyze the role of zoning in models with neighborhood effects other than those induced by the public provision of education; this would be a useful extension of their work.

2.2.1. Segregation

Most of the modern neighborhood effects literature has assumed that preferences over neighborhood composition are associated with the effects of composition on "economic" outcomes such as human capital accumulation. Segregation models, in contrast, focus on how neighborhoods evolve when individuals have a preference with others of similar ethnicity; these preferences are taken as a primitive with no suggestion that ethnicity matters in any other sense.

Modern models of neighborhood effects and segregation originate in the classic work of Schelling (1969, 1971). Schelling's work was motivated by the desire to understand the phenomenon of neighborhood "tipping", which refers to the claim that the Black/White composition of neighborhoods would, when the percentage of Blacks reached around 30%, precipitously shift to a very high percentage of Blacks. Schelling's goal was to see whether this type of behavior (as well as the fact that racial segregation levels in the U.S. are very high) could be explained without recourse to the assumption that Whites preferred all White or nearly all-White neighborhoods. In contrast, Schelling considered preferences in which individuals were indifferent to the racial composition of a neighborhood until the percentage of individuals of the same type dropped below a certain threshold. Preferences of this type are "nonracist" in the sense that segregation is not strongly preferred to alternative configurations. Schelling considered a model of a population of Blacks and Whites arrayed across points in a 2-dimensional lattice. In this model, agents sequentially consider whether to move to another site on the lattice (moves are only permitted to open sites). Agents would choose to move if and only if: (1) the percentage of their nearest neighbors of different ethnicity was above a certain percentage and (2) a preferred location was open. Remarkably, Schelling found that for a range of moving thresholds, this population would essentially completely segregate itself over time.

Why does this occur? Notice that Schelling assumes that agents act myopically and sequentially. These assumptions ensure that when an agent moves, it is always towards a neighborhood with a higher percentage of his own group than the one he currently occupies. Further, notice that blocks of homogeneous agents (i.e., groups of agents such that a boundary of homogeneous agents may be defined) will always have interiors where no agents wish to move; when movements of agents extend the boundary of a block, this automatically increases the number of spaces where agents will be content to be completely segregated. Together, these features mean that individual moves in the Schelling model typically increase the level of segregation and that some increases in segregation increase the size of stable segregated groups. Together these factors lead to Schelling's finding that for "most" initial conditions, complete segregation occurs asymptotically. Schelling's findings turn out to be relatively general and have been formalized in theoretical work by Granovetter and Soong (1988) and Young (1998); the latter is noteworthy in recasting Schelling's work in the context of evolutionary game theory. In related work, Mobius (2000) shows how random fields methods may be applied to Schelling-type models in ways that allow for richer neighborhood configurations than have previously been studied; this latter work suggests methods in statistical mechanics [cf. Brock and Durlauf (2001a, 2001b) and Durlauf (1997)] may prove to be generally useful in the modeling of segregation dynamics.

Recent work has shown how the emergence of segregation occurs in the presence of alternative preferences to those studied in the original Schelling work. Panes and Vriend (2003) show how segregation emerges even when agent preferences prefer integration to all other outcomes. This work is a valuable extension to Schelling in that it both shows that even a strict preference for integration can be overcome by a dislike of being isolated. Bruch and Mare (2003) consider alternative preferences which smooth out the behavior of individuals in the sense that the decision to move from a neighborhood is no longer a zero/one function of a threshold; simulation evidence in that paper finds introducing smoothness in individual decisions strongly reduces long-run levels of segregation.

While Schelling-type models have provided fundamental insights into the emergent nature of segregation, it is important to recognize their limitations. First, I am unaware of any version of the Schelling model that introduces a well-developed housing market. [Mobius (2000) and Zhang (2003) introduce housing prices, but these prices are not generated as a consequence of market clearing; rather, they constitute an additional cost associated with neighborhood composition that is related to demand conditions.] Second, these models have yet to incorporate forward-looking behavior on the part of agents. Hence, agents make neighborhood location decisions without regard to whether these decisions will be changed in the future. As a result, these models rely on agents making residential location decisions without consideration of the future characteristics of a neighborhood. These limitations have rendered the Schelling approach somewhat hard to interpret in light of the rationality postulates of standard economic theory.

One additional concern stems from the fact that the Schelling model has not been subjected to much empirical scrutiny. For this reason, Easterly (2003) is important. Easterly argues that while approximately 10% of American urban census tracts shifted from majority White to majority Black between 1970 and 2000, there is little evidence that these changes are well explained by the initial shares of Whites in the population, as the pure Schelling model predicts. Hence, it seems important to embody microeconomic foundations into the Schelling framework in a way that can incorporate other factors that influence neighborhood choice, factors that of course are precisely what the neighborhood effects literature studies. Sethi and Somanathan (2001) is a valuable contribution in this regard as it models neighborhood choice when individuals have preferences over both the ethnicity and the income levels of neighbors. An evaluation of the empirical implications of this model would facilitate an extension of Easterly's analysis.

2.3. Neighborhoods and networks

A final area where neighborhood effects have been analyzed concerns their role in constituting social networks. To make this discussion concrete, it is useful to think about a population of agents in which some topology describes who directly communicates with whom. Information can only travel across direct communication links between individuals. One can then think about a neighborhood as a set of agents who are all capable of mutual communication via the network. Conceiving of neighborhoods in this way may be useful in understanding phenomena such as the transmission of information about job opportunities, as is discussed below. Social networks as a whole constitute a sufficiently large area to be far beyond the scope of this chapter [see Jackson (2003) for a survey of recent theoretical developments in modeling networks]. Rather, I focus on a few aspects of this literature that most closely relate to issues of how neighborhood effects produce inequality.

One of the important general questions concerning networks is what sorts of networks emerge from a given set of direct links between agents. Following work such as Kirman (1983) and Ioannides (1990) this question may be studied formally using a model in which there are I agents. Suppose each agent has a certain number of direct connections and that these connections are reciprocal, so that if i is connected to j, then j is connected to i. This environment is thus an example of a graph where the agents constitute vertices and the direct connections constitute edges. Neighborhoods are defined as groups of agents all of whom are directly or indirectly connected; i is indirectly connected to k if there is a set of agents $j_1, j_2, \ldots, j_l$ such that i is directly connected to j_0, j_0 is directly connected to j_1 and so on, with j_l directly connected to k. Different configurations of a fixed number of edges will thus induce different neighborhood structures.

From this perspective, it is clear that the structure of networks in a population will depend on both the number of direct connections between agents as well as their distribution. It is possible to form a common network for I agents from as few as $I - 1$ direct links. Similarly, since for any subset of J agents, it is possible to identify $J(J - 1)$ distinct links, it is possible for $I - 1$ links to leave most agents isolated. The natural question that arises from this structure concerns identifying which network structures are most "likely" in the space of possible configurations of direct links. This question may be answered using random graph theory, which originates in the work of Erdos and Renyi (1960). Formally, suppose that each pair i and j are directly connected with probability $p(I)$ and that direct connections are independently distributed. The dependence of the probability of a direct connection on population size is important. If the probability is not so dependent, then the number of direct connections for each agent grows linearly in population size; in contexts such as word-of-mouth communication linear growth of direct connections would be unappealing.

Under these assumptions on direct connection probabilities, the following proposition [taken from Palmer (1985, Chapter 4)] holds:

PROPOSITION 5 (Neighborhood size and direct connection probabilities).

(i) *If* $p(I) < 1/I$, *then as* I *grows, the largest neighborhood in the population will be of order* $\log I$.

(ii) *If* $p(I) = c/I$, $c > 1$, *then as* I *grows, the largest neighborhood in the population will be of order* I.

(iii) *If* $p(I) = c \log I/I$, $c > 1$, *then as* I *grows all agents will be members of a common neighborhood.*

This proposition illustrates how the distribution of neighborhoods exhibits two distinct phase transitions. First, as the probability of a direct connection moves above $1/I$, so that the expected number of connections in the aggregate population exceeds I, the size of the largest neighborhood qualitatively changes. While the population is broken up into many relatively small (when compared to the overall population size) neighborhoods, once the direct connection probability exceeds the first threshold, a large neighborhood emerges. (This is known as the giant component in the random graph literature.) One can show that the order of this neighborhood is unique. Second, as the probability moves above $c \log I/I$, multiple neighborhoods disappear as I becomes large. What sort of substantive interpretation may be given to this property? If neighborhood effects derive from the role of social networks in pooling information, as might occur in labor contexts, then the "quality" of the information available to a given individual may depend on the size of his network. One interpretation of the emergence of an underclass, consistent with Wilson (1987) and formalized in work such as Finnerman and Kelly (2003) is equivalent to the emergence of a subset of the population that is isolated from the information flows available to others.

Random graph techniques have been applied in several contexts. Kirman (1983) appears to be the first to suggest this methodology to study how local interactions lead to aggregate interactions. This analysis focuses on the question of whether local trading networks will lead to price uniformity in a population; the assumption being that arbitrage ensures prices are common across all bilateral trades in a common neighborhood. Ioannides (1990) is the first to recognize the full power of the threshold theorems in random graph theory and uses a random graph framework to study risk sharing among traders, analyzing the relationship between trading probabilities and the number of agents whose risk is pooled via within neighborhood trading. Other work has employed a random graph structure to analyze dynamic questions. For example, Kelly (1997) develops a model of specialization and economic growth in which transportation linkages between individual sites increase the extent of the market and can produce accelerated growth. His analysis exploits a theorem due to Bollabas and Thomason (1987) that shows that threshold properties such as Proposition 5 are in a certain sense generic to random graphs, a result that should prove to have wide applicability in economic contexts. Durlauf (1996d) uses random graph methods to build a model of business cycles out of neighborhood interactions; in this context neighborhoods define groups of traders who are connected directly and indirectly with larger neighborhoods producing demand externalities for individual agents. However, it seems fair to conclude that random graph methods for linking neighborhoods and aggregate outcomes have not proven to be a major tool in modeling neighborhood effects, at least yet. I believe this is for two reasons. First, random graph methods are difficult to work with and so relaxation of various assumptions that are unnatural from an economist's perspective (e.g., the independence of bilateral connection assumption or the lack of heterogeneity in bilateral connection probabilities) has yet to be achieved and is certain to be extremely difficult. Second, the random graph models that have appeared, with the exception of Kelly (1997) typically treat bilateral connections nonstrategically, whereas in many cases such as the development of communications relationships, one would expect these links to be choice variables.

Networks and neighborhoods have also been jointly studied in the context of labor markets and information transmission. From the perspective of neighborhood effects, this work is especially important as it represents the best articulated effort to develop microeconomic foundations for neighborhood effects in the sense that networks models develop neighborhood effects as a consequence of information imperfections; as I have argued above, the literature typically takes neighborhood effects as a primitive. The basic objective of the labor markets/social networks literature is to understand the role of local contacts in the transmission of information about jobs. It is generally accepted that approximately $1/2$ of all job vacancies are filled by individuals who knew someone working at the firm with the vacancy. To the extent job information is transmitted across neighbors, this creates a basis for neighborhood effects: higher employment rates in a neighborhood will imply more rapid transmission of information about job openings in a neighborhood. Montgomery (1990a) provides an early formal analysis of job acquisition and social networks. Montgomery (1990b) and Finnerman and Kelly (2003) explicitly consider the implications of differences in labor-market conditions across neighborhoods for persistent inequality. Finnerman and Kelly (2003) is noteworthy in developing a model in which the relationship between job opportunities and the density of job referrals in a neighborhood exhibits threshold behavior so that neighborhoods with referral densities below a certain level produce a pool of never employed workers with probability 1. Krauth (2003) provides a model in which neighborhoods are defined by groups of directly and indirectly connected individuals; by embedding this information structure in a Mortensen–Pissarides job matching model, Krauth (2003) shows how small changes in neighborhood composition can induce large changes in unemployment. In very recent work, Calvo-Armengol and Jackson (2003) develop a sophisticated analysis of labor-market inequality and social networks for general graph structures to describe the networks. This model provides ways of understanding wage inequality in the context of neighborhoods when understood as social networks. An interesting outstanding question is whether the findings of authors such as Calvo-Armengol and Jackson (2003) can be enriched with random graph ideas in order to produce a theory of persistent differences in networks.

2.4. Stratification and efficiency

A final area of theory concerns the efficiency of allocations of agents across neighborhoods in the presence of neighborhood effects.

One question concerns the efficiency of stratified allocations. To understand this, suppose that a planner faces the problem of allocating $L \times I$ agents in coalitions of size L. Agents are associated with exogenous characteristics x_i and each coalition has a payoff $V(x)$ where x denotes the vector of characteristics of the L coalition members. $V(x)$ is strictly increasing in x, so the individual characteristics may be thought of as measures of ability or education. Finally, assume that $V(x) = V(x')$, if x' is a permutation of the elements of x; this simply means that the order of elements in x does not matter.

As stated, the allocation problem here is essentially the marriage problem studied in Becker (1973), in which the question was what allocation of men and women into couples will produce the highest quality children. In Becker's original formulation, the efficiency of mating the highest quality male with the highest quality female, etc. depended on whether the marriage production function exhibited complementarities between the qualities of the spouses. Extending the definition described in Equation (4), complementarity in $V(x)$ means that if one fixes a subset of k elements of x at some value $\bar{z}$ and partitions $x = y, \bar{z}$, then the function $V(y \mid \bar{z})$ has the property that $V(y \mid \bar{z}) - V(y' \mid \bar{z})$ is increasing in $\bar{z}$ if $y \geqslant y'$.

Recent developments in economic theory make it simple to study this problem of efficient stratification in the presence of increased differences. Under mild technical conditions [see discussion in Milgrom and Roberts (1990) and Topkis (1998)], complementarity is equivalent (under weak technical conditions) to supermodularity of a function. Let $x \vee y$ denote a vector formed by the maximum of each of the corresponding elements of x and y and let $x \wedge y$ denote the vector formed by the minimum of each of the corresponding elements of x and y. The function $V(x)$ is supermodular if

$$V(x) + V(y) \leqslant V(x \vee y) + V(x \wedge y). \tag{17}$$

As shown in Durlauf and Seshadri (2003), this condition, when combined with the assumption that $V(x)$ is permutation invariant, immediately implies that stratification is efficient for the problem that has been described.

As argued in Durlauf and Seshadri (2003), however, the relationship between complementarity and efficiency of stratification relies on two assumptions beyond complementarity: (1) all coalitions are of equal size, and (2) coalition memberships do not alter individual behaviors. Hence, there is no presumption that stratification is efficient in more general contexts even when complementarities are present within neighborhoods.

A separate question concerns the efficiency of competitive equilibria in neighborhoods models. This question has been studied in a range of contexts, e.g., de Bartolome (1990), Becker and Murphy (2000) and Benabou (1993, 1996a). These different models produce the common result that there is no guarantee that equilibrium allocations of families across neighborhoods are efficient; further, it is possible to identify conditions under which the level of stratification is higher than is dictated by efficiency.

Benabou's (1996a) argument is very insightful and follows from an analysis of the total human capital produced by an allocation of families. For a given family, the human capital of an offspring is determined by $f(x_i, \bar{x}_n)$, where as above, $\bar{x}_n$ is the average of x in neighborhood n. Notice that $\bar{x}_n = \pi_n x^{\text{high}} + (1 - \pi_n)x^{\text{low}}$ where π_n equals the fraction of x^{high} agents in neighborhood n, Benabou contrasts the equilibrium allocation of families with the allocation that maximizes total human capital, which may be represented as

$$\begin{aligned}\max_{\pi_A, \pi_B}\ & \pi_A f\big(x^{\text{high}}, \pi_A x^{\text{high}} + (1 - \pi_A)x^{\text{low}}\big) \\ & + (1 - \pi_A) f\big(x^{\text{low}}, \pi_A x^{\text{high}} + (1 - \pi_A)x^{\text{low}}\big) \\ & + \pi_B f\big(x^{\text{high}}, \pi_B x^{\text{high}} + (1 - \pi_B)x^{\text{low}}\big) \\ & + (1 - \pi_B) f\big(x^{\text{low}}, \pi_B x^{\text{high}} + (1 - \pi_B)x^{\text{low}}\big)\end{aligned} \tag{18}$$

subject to the constraint

$$\pi_A + \pi_B = 2\theta \tag{19}$$

which simply means that all agents are allocated to one of the neighborhoods. (Recall that θ is the percentage of x^{high} agents in the population.) His analysis shows how the efficiency or inefficiency of the equilibrium level of stratification depends on the interplay of several factors. One factor that matters is the cross partial derivative $\partial^2 f(x_i, \bar{x}_n)/(\partial x_i \partial \bar{x}_n)$; when this is negative, it implies that the marginal benefit to an x^{low} family from a good neighborhood is higher than that of an x^{high} family.[13] This negative cross partial contributes to inefficiency in the equilibrium level of stratification. A second factor that Benabou identifies is $\partial^2 f(x_i, \bar{x}_n)/\partial \bar{x}_n^2$; when this second derivative is negative, the marginal value to an individual of higher average quality is decreasing in the level of the average quality, so that inefficiency in the equilibrium allocation of neighborhood memberships can occur for a broader range of (other) features of the model.

Another approach to analyzing the efficiency of equilibrium stratification is via an analysis of willingness to pay. Becker and Murphy (2000) and de Bartolome (1990) provide particularly lucid discussions in the context of a model where the equilibrium allocation of families leads to a mix of x^{high} and x^{low} families in each neighborhood. They show that the equilibrium level of stratification is inefficient if the willingness to pay function is concave in π_n. Intuitively, when this function is concave, the conditions for the competitive allocation of families imply that the transposition of an x^{low}

[13] Observe that the sign of this cross-partial derivative also matters for the equilibrium level of stratification in Proposition 4, and indicates why it is possible for stratification to be efficient. Intuitively, even though the effects of changes in neighborhood composition are not internalized, if agents with high x_i values exhibit greater willingness to pay for high x_n neighborhoods because of the production complementarity that is described, then the stratification that is induced is efficient.

family from the worse neighborhood and an x^{high} family from the better neighborhood produces a net increase in the willingness to pay when families are aggregated across neighborhoods.

The Benabou (1993, 1996a), Becker and Murphy (2000) and de Bartolome (1990) results reflect the externalities implicit in neighborhood effects. No markets exist to compensate families for the positive neighborhood effects they engender; since the effects are not internalized, there is no presumption that the equilibrium allocation of families across neighborhoods is efficient, although it may be, as discussed in footnote 8 above.

The argument as to why inefficient levels of segregation may emerge does not account for the effect of contemporaneous neighborhood allocations on future levels of individual characteristics, which is one of the reasons given by Durlauf and Seshadri (2003) that Becker's findings on the efficiency of assortative matching may break down in some cases. One clear channel where such considerations matter is human capital, which is the focus of an important analysis by Benabou (1996b). This paper studies efficiency related issues in the context of neighborhoods, human capital accumulation and growth. In Benabou's model, human capital accumulation is determined in local communities via local finance of education and possible neighborhood-specific spillover effects. From the perspective of individual families, human capital for a child is maximized as the distribution of incomes in the community is shifted to the right. At the same time, the productivity of human capital for adults is determined by the aggregate human capital among all adults in the population. The efficiency of stratification versus integration thus depends on the nature of the dynamic effects of integration versus integration on the distribution of human capital. When economy wide spillovers are strong enough, all families are better off under integration, as affluent families sacrifice some family-specific human capital formation for a better economy-wide distribution. This possibility is studied by Cooper (1998) who argues such effects can explain why affluent families are willing to redistribute tax revenues to less affluent districts, providing a positive political economy of educational subsidies.

3. Econometrics

While the theoretical literature on neighborhood effects is now quite extensively developed, far less work has been devoted to the econometric issues that arise in identifying such influences. Nevertheless, the econometrics of neighborhood effects does provide a number of important results for conducting and interpreting empirical work. In this section and in the empirical section, I will focus exclusively on the estimation of neighborhood effects. While many studies examined the cross-section and dynamic properties of neighborhood configurations, the focus of the great majority of these studies has been on developing appropriate ways to measure levels of and changes in economic stratification and racial segregation.[14] As such, the causal mechanisms have generally not been

[14] Jargowsky (1997) is an excellent overview of economic stratification of communities; Massey and Denton (1993) is the standard reference on residential racial segregation in the United States.

explicitly addressed, and so I omit a review of the methodological issues and empirical findings in that literature.[15]

3.1. Identification

The basic econometric issues that arise in the study of neighborhood effects may be understood by considering the cross-section regression

$$\omega_i = k + cX_i + dY_{n(i)} + Jm_{n(i)} + \varepsilon_i \tag{20}$$

where, following earlier notation, X_i denotes an r-length vector of observable individual characteristics, $Y_{n(i)}$ denotes an s-length vector of contextual effects and $m_{n(i)}$ denotes the expected value of ω_i for members of neighborhood $n(i)$.[16] This equation is often referred to as the linear-in-means model. An important feature of this model is the assumption that all endogenous effects work through expectations. This assumption is most appropriate when neighborhoods are relatively large, for small neighborhoods, additional complications arise because of the effect of i's behavior on others; see Kooreman and Soetevent (2002) for discussion of estimation for small groups. This model was initially studied by Manski (1993) in a foundational paper and has subsequently been analyzed by Moffitt (2001), and Brock and Durlauf (2001b, 2003). I first consider the case where $E(\varepsilon_i \mid X_i, Y_{n(i)}, i \in n(i)) = 0$ in order to focus on questions of identification that are intrinsic to neighborhood effects as opposed to identification issues that arise because of the endogeneity of neighborhoods.

To understand why identification conditions arise in this model, observe that when beliefs are rational,

$$m_{n(i)} = \frac{k + cX_{n(i)} + dY_{n(i)}}{1 - J}. \tag{21}$$

In this expression, $X_{n(i)}$ equals the average of the X_i's in neighborhood $n(i)$ and appears in the regression because this average is one of the determinants of $m_{n(i)}$. Substituting (21) into (20), the individual choices may be expressed in terms of observables via

$$\omega_i = \frac{k}{1 - J} + cX_i + \frac{J}{1 - J} cX_{n(i)} + \frac{d}{1 - J} Y_{n(i)} + \varepsilon_i. \tag{22}$$

Equation (22) summarizes the empirical implications of the linear-in-means model. The identification problem may thus be thought of as asking whether one can recover the structural parameters in (20) from the coefficients in (22).

[15] Two recent studies, Bajari and Kahn (2003) and Bayer, McMillan and Rueben (2002), employ behavioral models to study segregation patterns and constitute very promising exceptions to my general assessment of the empirical segregation literature.

[16] Relative to earlier notation, I employ the subscript $n(i)$ rather than n since observations in a cross-section will be drawn from different neighborhoods, although more than one observation may be drawn from the same neighborhood.

Since (22) contains $2r+s+1$ regressors (and associated coefficients) whereas there are only $r+s+2$ coefficients in (20), it appears that one can recover the structural parameters from a regression of ω_i onto the various regressors, in fact the parameters of (20) are overidentified. However, this conclusion fails to account for possible collinearity between the components of (22); collinearity may potentially arise because of the presence of $X_{n(i)}$ and $Y_{n(i)}$ in the equation. For example, following the case originally studied in Manski (1993), suppose that $X_{n(i)} = Y_{n(i)}$. In this case, the modeler has no basis for distinguishing between contextual and individual effects. When this condition holds, then there are only $r+s+1$ linearly independent regressors in (22), the associated coefficients for these linearly independent regressors are identified, but they cannot be uniquely mapped back into the $r+s+2$ structural coefficients in (20); identification of the structural parameters in (20) thus fails. Manski (1993) has termed this failure of identification the reflection problem, to capture the intuition that the identification problem relates to distinguishing the direct effect of $Y_{n(i)}$ on an individual versus its indirect effect as "reflected" through the endogenous effect generated by $m_{n(i)}$.

The reflection problem as originally formulated in Manski (1993) assumes that there is a one to one relationship between individual effects and contextual effects. As such, the reflection problems may be understood as describing identification limits when there is no prior information available to allow one to identify individual and contextual influences that are distinct from one another. Such information can allow for identification.[17] Brock and Durlauf (2001b) provide the necessary conditions for identification with the following theorem.

PROPOSITION 6 (Identification in linear individual-level models with neighborhood effects). *Identification of the parameters in the linear-in-means model* (20) *requires*:

(i) *The dimension of the linear space spanned by elements of* $(1, X_i, Y_{n(i)})$ *is* $r + s + 1$.

(ii) *The dimension of the linear space spanned by the elements of* $(1, X_i, Y_{n(i)}, X_{n(i)})$ *is at least* $r + s + 2$.

The identification problem as developed here is in certain respects unique to linear models. Identification breaks down when $m_{n(i)}$ is linearly dependent on the other regressors in (20); Manski's nonidentification result specifically occurs because $m_{n(i)}$ is

[17] This breakdown of identification in the absence of prior information that restrict what variables directly influence behavior is also found in the rational expectations literature where the analogous problem concerns differentiation of the effects on a given variable of expectations of future variables from the direct effects of various current and lagged variables. Wallis (1980) provides a general treatment and Sargent (1976) provides a classic example of how the lack of prior information renders very different macroeconomic theories observationally equivalent. As suggested by Binder and Pesaran (2001) and Brock and Durlauf (2001b), the timing of neighborhood effects has important implications for identification; Brock and Durlauf (2001b), for example show how identification may hold for a dynamic version of (21) if contextual effects occur with a one period lag, i.e., $\omega_{i,t}$ depends on $Y_{n(i),t-1}$ and $m_{n(i),t}$. However, this possibility has yet to be systematically explored and, of course, this timing assumption needs to be justified.

a linear combination of 1 and $Y_{n(i)}$. Linear dependence of this type will typically not arise when individual behaviors depend on other moments of the neighborhood behavior. This is most easily seen if for a nonlinear-in-means neighborhood model of the form:

$$\omega_i = k + cX_i + dY_{n(i)} + J\phi(m_{n(i)}) + \varepsilon_i \tag{23}$$

where $\phi(m_{n(i)})$ is invertible and $\mathrm{d}^2\phi(m_{n(i)})/\mathrm{d}m^2_{n(i)} \neq 0$. The self-consistent expected average choice in a neighborhood is determined by

$$m_{n(i)} = \psi^{-1}(k + cX_{n(i)} + dY_{n(i)}) \tag{24}$$

where $\psi(m_{n(i)}) = m_{n(i)} - J\phi(m_{n(i)})$. As is clear from (24), the collinearity problem that can arise in the linear in means model cannot arise here, except for hairline cases. The logic of this example is in fact quite general. Brock and Durlauf (2001a) show that in the space of twice-differentiable functions $\phi(\cdot)$, identification will fail only for a measure zero set of $\phi(\cdot)$'s. More important for empirical work, this argument also implies that identification will hold for nonlinear probability models of choices, for example binary or multinomial choice models of the type described above or duration data models with neighborhood effects. Brock and Durlauf (2001b, 2003) provide a set of results on these cases.

One additional difference between linear and nonlinear models of neighborhood effects concerns the interpretation of estimated models that ignore endogenous effects. In the case of linear models, it is possible to interpret linear models without endogenous effects as reduced forms, if $X_{n(i)} = Y_{n(i)}$. (If this is not the case, then $X_{n(i)}$ will represent a vector of omitted variables in the reduced form.) As pointed out by Manski (1993), this means that nonzero parameters associated with $Y_{n(i)}$ are necessary for these contextual effects to be present. In contrast, for nonlinear models such as the binary choice model, this will not be the case since the omission of the endogenous effect does not produce an associated reduced form.

3.2. Self-selection

The assumption that $E(\varepsilon_i \mid X_i, Y_{n(i)},\ i \in n(i)) = 0$ is unappealing. The reason for this is immediate given our earlier discussion of equilibrium neighborhood configurations: one does not think of residential neighborhoods as exogenously determined; hence, it is natural to expect that there is a relationship between neighborhood choice, i.e., $n(i)$ and unobserved heterogeneity embodied in ε_i. This is, of course, a form of self-selection bias whose presence has motivated a vast econometric literature; see Heckman (2001) and Manski (1995) for valuable overviews.

How may self-selection be addressed and how does self-selection affect identification? To answer these questions, it is useful to rewrite the behavioral equation as

$$\omega_i = k + cX_i + dY_{n(i)} + Jm_{n(i)} + E\big(\varepsilon_i \mid X_i, Y_{n(i)},\ i \in n(i)\big) + \xi_i \tag{25}$$

where $E(\xi_i \mid X_i, Y_{n(i)}, i \in n(i)) = 0$ by construction. Following the classic approach to selection developed by James Heckman [cf. Heckman (1979)], consistent estimation of (25) requires constructing a consistent estimate of $E(\varepsilon_i \mid X_i, Y_{n(i)}, i \in n(i))$ and including this estimate as an additional regressor in (25); a key insight of Heckman (1979) is that once this is done, (25) may be estimated by ordinary least squares.

To see how this may be applied to the neighborhood context, suppose that for individual i, a choice has been made across N possible neighborhoods. Neighborhood n is associated with a latent "quality" measure $Q^*_{i,n}$ that is determined by

$$Q^*_{i,n} = \gamma Z_{i,n} + \nu_{i,n} \tag{26}$$

where $Z_{i,n}$ is a vector of observable characteristics of i that influence the quality assigned to neighborhood n and $\nu_{i,n}$ denotes an unobservable individual-specific quality term. Notice that this quality measure represents an individual-specific valuation attached to each neighborhood and may be calculated on the basis of factors including the price of neighborhood membership. Individual i is assumed to choose to reside in the neighborhood with the highest $Q^*_{i,n}$. Assume that $E(\varepsilon_i \mid X_i, Y_n, Z_{i,n}) = 0$ and $E(\nu_{i,n} \mid X_i, Y_n, Z_{i,n}) = 0\ \forall i, n$. Then, for certain parametric assumptions on the densities of ε_i and $\nu_{i,n}$, there exist analytic expressions for $E(\varepsilon_i \mid X_i, Y_{n(i)}, i \in n(i))$ that may be shown to be proportional to some $\delta(\gamma Z_i)$ where the function $\delta(\cdot)$ is determined by the parametric error assumptions and the parameter vector γ is estimable from a multinomial choice model of neighborhoods; denote this factor of proportionality as κ. A behavioral equation with neighborhood effects may thus be constructed as

$$\omega_i = k + cX_i + dY_{n(i)} + Jm_{n(i)} + \kappa\delta(\gamma Z_i) + \xi_i \tag{27}$$

and so it is possible to estimate neighborhood effects in the presence of endogenous neighborhood choice. Explicit examples of this are given in Brock and Durlauf (2003) and Ioannides and Zabel (2002b); the appendix to this chapter describes the Brock–Durlauf approach in detail.

Self-selection corrections turn out to have important implications for identification. To see this, consider two cases. First, suppose that the decision to join a neighborhood only depends upon $m_{n(i)}$. In this case (27) is now a nonlinear in means model (since $\delta(\cdot)$ is almost certainly nonlinear given the fact that the neighborhood choice decision is made among a set of discrete alternatives) and is thus identified outside of pathological cases, as shown in Brock and Durlauf (2001b). Second, suppose that Z_i consists of elements of X_i and $Y_{n(i)}$. Since $\delta(\cdot)$ is nonlinear, $\delta(\gamma Z_i)$ will be linearly independent of $(1, X_i, Y_{n(i)})$ even if Z_i is linearly dependent on $(1, X_i, Y_{n(i)})$. As such $\delta(\gamma Z_i)$ is an additional individual-level regressor whose group-level analog does not appear in the behavioral equation (20). This means that by Proposition 6, identification may be achieved.

This analysis of self-selection as a road to identification for neighborhood effects suffers from its dependence on parametric assumptions concerning the distribution of errors in (20) and (26). The particular parametric assumption made here is not essential.

What appears to be more difficult is the development of a way of employing semiparametric selection corrections to facilitate identification. The analysis of identification without strong parametric assumptions is an important next step in this research. One new approach to dealing with self-selection has been proposed by Krauth (2002). In this approach, one uses information on the degree of self-selections into groups based on observables to construct bounds on the magnitude of neighborhood effects by using this information to bound the degree of self-selection on unobservables.

3.3. Unobservables and sibling data

The estimation of neighborhood effects in the presence of self-selection is an example of the more general problem of accounting for unobservable individual and neighborhood controls. Brock and Durlauf (2001b) propose using panel data methods to eliminate neighborhood-level fixed effects; identification conditions are analyzed in great generality by Graham and Hahn (2003). Bayer and Timmins (2002) propose a strategy for accounting for unobservables when more than two neighborhoods are present based on techniques for dealing with unobservable attributes in models of consumer demand which, although not yet formally incorporated into an identification analysis, appears promising.

The most active area of work that has attempted to control for unobservables has focused on the use of siblings data. Aaronson (1998) and Plotnick and Hoffman (1999) do this in a regression context. Following the discussion in Aaronson (1998), consider a pair of siblings s in a given family i. Ignoring endogenous effects, individual behavior may be described by

$$\omega_{s,i} = k + cX_{s,i} + dY_{n(i)} + \varepsilon_i + \varepsilon_{s,i}. \tag{28}$$

In this expression, ε_i denotes an unobservable family effect. Aaronson proposes eliminating this unobserved family characteristic by differencing outcomes between siblings and estimating

$$\omega_{1,i} - \omega_{2,i} = c(X_{1,i} - X_{2,i}) + d(Y_{1,n(i)} - Y_{2,n(i)}) + \varepsilon_{1,i} - \varepsilon_{2,i}. \tag{29}$$

As such, this approach exploits the standard technique in panel data studies of eliminating fixed effects through differencing. One limitation to this method is that it does not address the self-selection issue. The reason for this, following the logic associated with (26), is that the component of the regression error that is associated with self-selection can differ across siblings if the siblings are raised in the same neighborhood at different times; the information revealed by the parent's choice of neighborhood will differ according to the parent characteristics as well as the characteristics of all neighborhoods in the choice set.

A second approach to employing sibling data to uncover neighborhood effects is proposed by Solon, Page and Duncan (2000). In this approach, one compares the covariance of outcomes for siblings in the same community and a pair of unrelated individuals in the same community and uses the values to draw inferences about the role of neighborhoods versus families as determinants of individual outcomes. To compute the relationship, one may work with (28) with ε_i omitted (the correlation approach has the virtue that it does not require X_i or Y_n to be observable); I work with covariances rather than correlations for ease of exposition. Two assumptions are imposed on this model. First, members of a common family i possess identical individual effects, i.e., $X_{1,i} = X_{2,i}$. Second, no account is made of endogenous effects. Under these assumptions, the covariance of two siblings in a common neighborhood is

$$\operatorname{cov}(\omega_{1,i}, \omega_{2,i}) = \operatorname{var}(cX_i) + \operatorname{var}(dY_n) + 2\operatorname{cov}(cX_i, dY_n) \tag{30}$$

whereas the covariance of two unrelated neighbors is

$$\operatorname{cov}(\omega_{s,i}, \omega_{s,j}) = \operatorname{cov}(cX_i, cX_j) + \operatorname{var}(dY_n) + 2\operatorname{cov}(cX_i, dY_n). \tag{31}$$

These two equations provide a way of testing the null hypothesis that neighborhood effects are zero. If $d = 0$, then it must be the case that $\operatorname{cov}(\omega_{1,i}, \omega_{2,i}) > \operatorname{cov}(\omega_{s,i}, \omega_{s,j})$; this converts immediately to a correlations inequality (the analysis has presupposed that all observations have the same unconditional variance).

The correlations approach to neighborhood effects is an interesting alternative to regression approaches. However, there are two limitations to this approach. First, the comparison of correlations provides relatively little information about the nature and magnitude of neighborhood effects. While the inequality $\operatorname{cov}(\omega_{1,i}, \omega_{2,i}) > \operatorname{cov}(\omega_{s,i}, \omega_{s,j})$ is implied by the absence of neighborhood effects, it can also hold when neighborhood effects are present. Hence, comparisons of correlations provide only a weak testing framework for neighborhood effects. Further, one cannot make firm statements about the magnitude or nature of neighborhood effects and so the assessment of policies to change neighborhood composition is not possible.

A second limitation of the method is that it imposes strong assumptions on the determinants of behaviors within families. The assumption that all individual-specific characteristics are identical within a family, i.e., $X_{1,i} = X_{2,i}$, is quite strong and would appear to rule out family background variables such as income. Perhaps more important, the model assumes that differential treatment of siblings within families may be modeled by an uncorrelated and identically distributed error term. However, this assumption is problematic as it ignores such possibilities as birth order effects in childrearing, etc. Assumptions of this type have proven to be a serious problem in other contexts. For example, the use of twins data versus other siblings in heritability studies has been strongly faulted for failing to account for childrearing differences; for a discussion of this issue and many other interpretation problems with studies that are based on correlations of this type, see Goldberger and Kamin (2002). Hence, it seems important to investigate whether the error assumptions in these models are empirically appropriate.

These limitations do not mean that correlation analyses are without interest; they are clearly useful as data summaries and suggestive of the relative importance of neighborhoods in variation across individuals. At a minimum, the correlations approach is promising as a way of providing data summaries that can help guide theoretical modeling.

4. Empirical studies

4.1. Ethnography

One important source of evidence on neighborhood effects is ethnographic studies, which are an important empirical tradition in the sociology literature. This type of evidence is underutilized in economics. While such studies obviously cannot be subjected to the sorts of empirical criteria one associates with econometrically-based empirical work, such evidence is nevertheless corroborative of quantitative studies. Further, to the extent that quantitative studies require identification assumptions of the type described in Section 3, it is possible that support for such assumptions may be taken from this source.

In the 1960s, ethnographic studies produced early, albeit controversial evidence of neighborhood effects. Lewis (1966) explicitly describes how a culture of poverty existed in poor Puerto Rican communities and ascribes a number of social ills to the norms that exist in those places. Important recent ethnographic work includes Anderson (1990, 1999) who has documented how poor inner city communities have developed codes of conduct that are conducive to high levels of violence; Liebow (1967) draws related conclusions in the context of African Americans. Duneier (1992) studies the social relationships that develop at a neighborhood restaurant and illustrates the importance of social interactions even in this very particular context.

From the evidentiary standards of economics, ethnographies are generally regarded as suspect because of their particularity and because of fears that the observer's prejudices are determining the findings. While these are certainly valid concerns, they do not imply that such studies are without insight. In particular, it seems that such studies can facilitate decisions on how to define neighborhoods in more quantitative studies and may also provide some insight into the choice of control variables.

4.2. Experiments

A second source of evidence on neighborhood effects is controlled experiments. The social psychology literature is filled with studies of how groups affect individual perceptions; see Aronson (1999) for a survey. The value of this literature is reflected in a classic experiment due to Sherif et al. (1961) known as the Robbers Cave experiment. Sherif and coworkers brought a group of middle-class teenage boys to a camp at Robbers Cave Oklahoma. For the first two weeks of the camp, interactions between the boys were not guided by the experimenters. After two weeks, the boys were randomly divided into two groups, the Eagles and the Rattlers. (The one exception to randomness was that friendships observed by the experimenters were broken up.) After these groups were formed, competitive activities such as games were organized between the groups. Sherif et al. (1961) document how these groups quickly became the source of strong feelings of identity. Members of each group developed negative stereotypes about members of the other group in terms of intelligence and honesty. This experiment makes clear how neighborhoods, even under random assignment, can influence cognition and behavior towards others.

The new experimental economics has conducted many experiments that have addressed social influences on behavior, although relatively few have focused on the sorts of influences that have motivated the neighborhood effects literature. One exception is a recent study by Falk and Ichino (2003). In this experiment, individuals are organized randomly into groups of different sizes and assigned to fill envelopes, with the compensation for the activity set independent of the group's output. In some cases, individuals worked alone. In others, individuals worked side by side. For some groups, members were informed of the different productivity levels ascribed to previous groups. In others, effort was made visible, i.e., each worker could see how hard others were working. Falk and Ichino (2003) found that there was a strong correlation in effort within pairs of workers and that the effort level of groups was strongly influenced by information about the performance of others.

While it is difficult to translate these types of findings into implications for the types of neighborhood effects that are conventionally studied, experimental evidence does strongly buttress the general claim that social influences matter.

4.3. Econometric studies with observational data

Since the pioneering work of Datcher (1982) there is now a rich empirical literature designed to assess neighborhood effects. Table 2 summarizes 25 empirical studies taken from this very large literature; the selection of studies reflects an effort to explore the range of empirical analyses that have appeared as well as some bias towards more recent work.[18]

These studies cover a wide range of individual outcomes, definitions of neighborhoods and neighborhood effects, as well as a range of econometric methodologies. Nevertheless, a few general conclusions may be drawn.

First, the bulk of empirical studies of neighborhood effects find evidence of their presence. Of course, this may reflect a publication bias against negative results. However, a researcher with a strong prior that neighborhood effects are present would not have these beliefs strongly changed by the body of observational studies.

Second, the neighborhoods effects literature is highly unsystematic in its choice of neighborhood variables by which to measure effects. One finds variables such as the median income in neighborhood, the percentage of professional and managerial workers among all workers, behaviors of neighbors, etc. Further, the choice of neighborhood variables is rarely motivated by theory. [This is less true for studies that explore information transmission such as Bertrand, Luttmer and Mullainathan (2000) or Drewianka (2003) which construct neighborhood variables to reflect contact probabilities, but even

[18] Jencks and Mayer (1990) is a standard survey of earlier empirical work on neighborhood effects. See Dietz (2002) for a useful recent overview.

Table 2
Regression studies of neighborhood effects

Study	Agents	Outcomes	Neighborhood characteristics	Findings
Aaronson (1998)	Adults with siblings at least 3 years apart	High school graduation, grade completion, college attendance	High school drop out and poverty rate for neighborhood, averaged over ages 10–18; geocode or equivalent data used when available, Zip Code otherwise	Neighborhood effects are present and generally robust
Ainsworth (2002)	8th grade students	Composite math/reading test score; time spent on homework	Composite measures of proportions of high-status adults, neighborhood stability, degree of economic deprivation, and ethnic diversity at Zip Code level	Proportion of high-status adults positively influences educational outcomes
Aizer and Currie (2002)	Mothers in California with less than 4 years of college	Utilization of publicly available prenatal care	Utilization rate among other women of similar ethnicity at 5 digit Zip Code	Peer effects matter even after controlling for spatial fixed effects; however these also matter for repeat users, thus peer effect does not seem due to information transmission
Aneshensel and Sucoff (1996)	Adolescents in Los Angeles County	Measures of mental health	Socioeconomic and ethnic characteristics of neighbors that are formed by applying cluster analysis to characteristics of 49 census tracts based on 1990 data	Neighborhood characteristics are associated with perception of danger from crime, etc., which in turn are associated with depression, anxiety, etc.
Bertrand, Luttmer and Mullainathan (2000)	Adult women	Welfare use	Network measure equal to product of percentage of neighborhood members in same language group multiplied by welfare usage rate of group; data measured at Public Use Microdata Areas and Metropolitan statistical areas of PUMS	Network measure helps predict welfare use; results robust to a range of specifications

Table 2
(*continued*)

Study	Agents	Outcomes	Neighborhood characteristics	Findings
Borjas (1995)	Adults	Educational attainment, wage rates	Percentage of neighborhood that has graduated from high school, percentage that has graduated from college, labor force participation, and additional measures	Neighborhood characteristics explain some, but not all, of persistent ethnic differences in outcomes
Brewster (1994)	Adolescent women	Nonmarital sexual activity	Income, labor market, education, and racial heterogeneity measures taken at census tract level	Premarital sexual activity associated with lower median income, higher female unemployment and higher percentage of women employed full time outside the home
Brooks-Gunn et al. (1993)	Infants age 3 and adolescents age 14–19	IQ and measure of behavioral problems at 36 months; dropping out of high school and nonmarital fertility	Percentage of families in neighborhood with income below $10,000; percentage with incomes above $30,000; various additional measures	White teenagers benefit from affluent neighbors; strength of effect appears greater for more affluent families
Case and Katz (1991)	Young men in low-income Boston neighborhoods	Criminal behavior, drug and alcohol use, church attendance, labor-market activity	Mean behavior of neighbors	Peer effects are statistically significant and qualitatively large
Corcoran et al. (1992)	Males age 25–32	Hourly wages, hours of work, family income, family income relative to needs	Median family income, male unemployment rate, percentage of female-headed families, percentage of families on welfare in Zip Code for residence in 1968	Some evidence of effects related to welfare participation rate; other variables statistically insignificant
Crane (1991)	Young women age 16–19	Dropping out of high school and teenage fertility	Percentage of workers with professional or managerial job in PUMS neighborhoods (similar to census tracts)	Job composition generally predicts both outcomes; effect is (except for Hispanics), nonlinear, stronger for worst neighborhoods

Table 2
(*continued*)

Study	Agents	Outcomes	Neighborhood characteristics	Findings
Crowder and South (2003)	Teenagers	Dropping out of high school	Index of neighborhood disadvantage based on poverty and joblessness rates, occupational structure, and additional measures	Neighborhood effects present for a range of demographic groups, particularly strong for Black teenagers in single-parent households and low-income Whites
Datcher (1982)	Males 23–32	Years of schooling, hourly wages, annual earnings	Average income and racial composition of Zip Codes	Intra- and inter-racial education and wage differences associated with each measure
Drewianka (2003)	Men and women 16–44	Marriage rates	Percentage of unmarried adults in age group and various demographic characteristics of counties of residence	Larger pools of unmarried persons reduce marriage probabilities
Evans, Oates and Schwab (1992)	Teenagers	Dropping out of high school, teen fertility	Percentage of students in school attended who are classified as economically disadvantaged under Elementary and Secondary Education Act	No evidence of neighborhood effects once endogeneity of neighborhood is controlled for by instrumental variables
Foster and McLanahan (1996)	Young adults	Dropping out of high school	Drop out rate in census tract	OLS estimates find neighborhood effects; these largely disappear if neighborhood variable is instrumented with city-level socioeconomic characteristics, although test of null hypothesis of equivalence of OLS and IV estimates fails to reject
Ginther, Haveman and Wolfe (2000)	Young adults	High school graduation, years of schooling, teen nonmarital fertility	Percentage of households with low income, percentage with high incomes, percentage White, percentage of drop outs among young adults, percentage female-headed families, adult unemployment rate	Evidence of neighborhood effects is not robust to different choices of individual family background controls; richer control sets typically reduce magnitudes and statistical significance

Table 2
(*continued*)

Study	Agents	Outcomes	Neighborhood characteristics	Findings
Hogan and Kitagawa (1985)	Black female teenagers in Chicago	Nonmarital fertility	3 category ranking of neighborhood quality based on principal components analysis of a range of census tract socioeconomic characteristics	Little evidence of neighborhood effects once parenting practices are controlled for
Ioannides (2002)	Residences	Value of improvements made to home	Endogenous effects (home improvements by neighbors) and contextual effects (socioeconomic characteristics of neighbors)	Endogenous effects strongly statistically significant; contextual effects generally not statistically significant once endogenous effects are included
Ioannides and Zabel (2002a, 2002b)	Residences	Market value of a residence; interpreted as level of housing consumption of homeowner	Endogenous effects (housing consumption level of neighbors) and contextual effects (socioeconomic characteristics of neighbors)	Both endogenous and contextual effects are present, even after self-selection and neighborhood fixed effects are accounted for
Plotnick and Hoffman (1999)	Female sibling pairs (or large sibling groups if available)	Nonmarital fertility, postsecondary education, income	Percentage of families in census tract headed by females, percentage receiving public assistance, percentage with low incomes, percentage with high incomes	Little evidence of neighborhood effects once fixed family effects are allowed
Rivkin (2001)	Young female adults	Test scores in 12th grade, teen fertility, post high school education/labor force participation	Average education of schoolmates' mothers	Neighborhood effect estimates are larger when instrumental variables used to account for self-selection

Table 2
(continued)

Study	Agents	Outcomes	Neighborhood characteristics	Findings
Sirakaya (2003)	Ex-felons on probation	Recidivism for felony crimes	Recidivism rate, time to recidivism among recidivists, range of socioeconomic and demographic characteristics of legal jurisdictions (cities or counties)	Both measures of neighborhood recidivism affect individual recidivism probabilities; results are robust to controls for unobserved heterogeneity and model uncertainty
Turley (2003)	Children under age 13	Indices of educational achievement, self-esteem, and undesirable behavior	Median income of census tract or closest equivalent in PSID geocode data, measures of social connection to neighborhood (number of years child has lived in neighborhood, number of neighborhood children known by name), racial heterogeneity (measured proportion of Blacks)	Effect of median income much stronger for Whites than Blacks; effect of median income on Blacks requires certain percentage of Blacks in neighborhood; effects of median income strong only when connections to neighborhood are above certain thresholds
Weinberg, Reagan and Yankow (2002)	Adult men	Annual hours worked	Employment rate of adult men and job density in census tract and block group, 5 additional measures used to check for robustness	Neighborhood effects matter with stronger effect in worst neighborhoods

here the variables are not derived from explicit search models.] Taken together, the evidence of neighborhood effects in this literature is largely a black box, i.e., it is difficult to translate the findings of the papers into specific microeconomic mechanisms. To be clear, this probably largely reflects the failure of the theoretical neighborhoods literature to provide more guidance on the generative mechanisms that produce neighborhood effects. As discussed in Section 1, neighborhoods models typically assume certain neighborhood variables appear in the specification of preferences, technologies or beliefs and analyze the consequences.

Third, there has been relatively little systematic attention to questions of model uncertainty. While many empirical studies of neighborhood effects check for the robustness of results along a few dimensions, this has not been done systematically. One exception is Ginther, Haveman and Wolfe (2000), who explore the robustness of estimated neighborhood effects for alternative choices of individual-level controls. They find that the magnitude and statistical significance of neighborhoods effects is very sensitive to the choice of individual-level controls. One problem with this conclusion is that it does not address the question of what information is contained when one aggregates across model specifications. Put differently, one is not so much interested in the distribution of neighborhoods effects across model specifications but in estimates of neighborhood effects that do not condition on a particular model when model uncertainty is present. Brock, Durlauf and West (2003) address this general problem drawing on Draper (1995) and other recent research in statistics. Sirakaya (2003) is unique in applying model averaging ideas to the analysis of neighborhood effects. Her analysis finds strong evidence of endogenous neighborhood effects that accounts for the information contained in each of a large set of potential models of recidivism by ex-felons on probation. This work has important implications for future work on neighborhood effects.

Fourth, relatively little systematic attention has been given to the identification problems that exist between endogenous and contextual effects. This is true at two levels. First, most studies fail to address the differences between these effects and the attendant implications for the models that are estimated. Second, to the extent that both effects are included in the same model, one does not see discussion of what assumptions are being implicitly made to allow for identification. However, there are some recent exceptions to this; examples include Drewianka (2003), Ioannides and Zabel (2002a, 2002b), Minkin (2002), and Sirakaya (2003). These studies have been able to parse the two types of effects and typically find both are present.

Fifth, efforts to control for unobserved heterogeneity have had varying effects on the analysis of neighborhood effects. From the perspective of unobserved family fixed effects, findings of neighborhood effects appear to be mixed, see for example Aaronson (1998) who finds that estimates of neighborhood effects are robust to allowing for family effects in siblings data whereas Plotnick and Hoffman (1999) do not. More recently, Aizer and Currie (2002) find evidence of neighborhood effects on the utilization of publicly funded prenatal care that is robust to the incorporation of spatial fixed effects. My own reading of the literature is that this form of unobserved heterogeneity has not been shown to be of first order concern in interpreting the existing empirical studies.

Sixth, the robustness for neighborhood effects findings to controls for self-selection appears to depend on the method employed. Evans, Oates and Schwab (1992) appear to be the first to use instrumental variables to control for self-selection. This study employed a measure of the percentage of students in a school who are disadvantaged to evaluate how neighborhood effects influence high school drop out and teen fertility rates. The measure of school-level disadvantage is instrumented with metropolitan area unemployment, college completion and poverty rates and median income. Evans, Oates and Schwab (1992) find that although neighborhood effects are statistically significant when treated as exogenous, the coefficient is statistically insignificant (with a change of sign) when it is instrumented. Foster and McLanahan (1996) employ a similar instrumental variables strategy and also find that instrumental variables estimates fail to find evidence of neighborhood effects. These results contain an important cautionary message. However, it is unclear exactly how to interpret them. It is unclear that metropolitan area instruments can account for neighborhood effects that occur conditional on a metropolitan area; a point explicitly acknowledged by Evans, Oates and Schwab. For example, the effect of neighborhood characteristics on aspirations may depend on the college completion rate among adults in a neighborhood relative to the metropolitan area. There is also a question as to the validity of the instruments. It is unclear why individual behavioral decisions do not directly depend on metropolitan area characteristics and hence why they are excluded from the original behavioral equation.

It is also possible to find cases where instrumental variables estimates of neighborhood effects do not reduce estimated magnitudes. Rivkin (2001) uses similar instruments to Evans, Oates and Schwab (1992) in a study of high school-based effects and, unlike Evans, Oates and Schwab (1992) finds that coefficient estimates using instrumental variables are larger than those in a baseline model. Rivkin (2001) does not interpret this as evidence of neighborhood effects, but argues this indicates that the types of instruments employed may, if anything, exacerbate endogeneity bias. However, there is no reason why this must be so and his results are equally consistent with the interpretation that neighborhood effects matter.

In contrast, evidence of neighborhood effects is not diminished in the one study that employs an explicit self-selection correction of the type discussed in Section 3 [Ioannides and Zabel (2002b)]. This paper finds strong evidence of neighborhood effects on housing demand even after explicitly modeling the neighborhood choice decision. While this result does require parametric assumptions on various model errors, it is suggestive that if self-selection is used as a source of information, it may prove valuable. Overall, this paper may be regarded as the best example of the integration of econometric methods into empirical work that has appeared in the neighborhoods literature.

Taken as a whole, these six observations illustrate that the empirical literature based on statistical analysis of observational data provides only limited support for the importance of neighborhood effects.

4.4. Correlation studies and sibling data

Several authors have used the correlation approach described in Section 3 to uncover neighborhood effects using sibling data. These studies have generally found little evidence of neighborhood effects. Solon, Page and Duncan (2000) analyze correlations in educational attainment using geocode data in the Panel Study of Income Dynamics (PSID) and find after controlling for some basic background characteristics, the residual correlation in neighboring children's outcomes is on the order of 0.1. Page and Solon (2001) study adult incomes of females and find that the correlation between neighboring girls is only 1/3 that of sisters. They further find that much of the correlation between neighbors is driven by income differentials between urban and nonurban areas. Duncan, Boisjoly and Harris (2001) study correlations between siblings, friends, schoolmates (members of a common grade at a school), and neighbors for measures of high school achievement and delinquency. They find that sibling correlations are much higher than the others, and that friendship correlations are much larger than neighbor and schoolmate effects. While these findings suggest a larger role for family background than neighborhood characteristics as determinants of behavior, they do not directly address the economic significance of neighborhood effects nor do they provide much insight into the effects that policies that alter neighborhood membership would have, for reasons described in Section 3.

4.5. Quasi-experiments

An important alternative to the use of observational data such as the Panel Study of Income Dynamics is the use of data in which government interventions into the residential choices of individuals are used to assess the effects of neighborhoods. Such interventions are examples of what in economics are known as "quasi-experiments", the idea being that the intervention at least partially defines groups of individuals who have or have not randomly received a treatment (drawing an analogy from biostatistics), in this case, a new group membership, thereby allowing for the measurement of group effects.

One example of such an intervention is the Gautreaux program. In 1967, Dorothy Gautreaux led a group of plaintiffs to sue the Chicago Housing Authority, claiming that placement of poor families in public housing in poor neighborhoods constituted a form of discrimination. A consent decree between the plaintiffs and the CHA resolved the case and produced a housing program that in essence assigned one group of families to other parts of Chicago and another to suburban communities outside the city. Sociologist James Rosenbaum has organized and conducted interviews with families that had participated in the program in order to determine the effects of living in suburban communities on poor families. In a series of studies [cf. Rosenbaum and Popkin (1991), Rosenbaum (1995)], he showed that families living in suburbs experienced substantially better socioeconomic outcomes along a number of dimensions. As described in Rosenbaum (1995, p. 242), these differences are particularly pronounced with respect to outcomes for children. For example, the percentage of college attendees among children whose families moved to suburbs was 54% whereas the percentage for children whose moves kept them in the city of Chicago was 21%; when one considers only 4-year colleges the attendance rates are 27% versus 4%. While these data suffer from some self-selection problems that render their causal interpretation problematic (an issue well understood by Rosenbaum), they are extremely suggestive and have greatly helped to stimulate research on neighborhood effects.[19]

The Gautreaux findings are important as they represent an early effort to provide evidence of neighborhood effects based on an external intervention into neighborhood configurations. However, the various ways in which the allocation of families across new locations in Chicago versus suburbs was determined by unobserved characteristics of the families in the program, clouded any policy inferences one could draw from the program. One consequence of this is an extended effort by the Department of Housing and Urban Development to conduct an experiment in altering neighborhood memberships that is more conducive to causal inferences. This program, the Moving to Opportunity demonstration (MTO) has been underway in five cities, Baltimore, Boston, Chicago, Los Angeles and New York since 1994. The demonstration provides housing vouchers to a randomly selected group of families; within this subsidized group, families in turn were randomly allocated between unrestricted vouchers (users are known as the Section 8 group) and vouchers that could only be used in census tracts with poverty rates below 10% (whose users are the Experimental group).[20]

Recent evaluations of the effects of the vouchers include Hanratty, McLanahan and Pettit (2001), Katz, Kling and Liebman (2001), Leventhal and Brooks-Gunn (2001, 2002), Ludwig, Duncan and Hirschfield (2001) and Rosenbaum and Harris (2001). These assessments reveal a number of interesting findings. For children, there appear to have been impressive gains for both Section 8 and MTO movers along several dimensions. Katz, Kling and Liebman (2001) conclude in the case of Boston area families that children in Section 8 and Experimental groups exhibited substantial reduction in behavioral problems (the index of behavioral problems they use is about 30% lower for the two groups than those in the control group), and that Experimental group children exhibit lower incidences of asthma attacks (approximately 50% lower than either Section 8 or control children) and injuries requiring medical attention (Experimental group children exhibited injury rates that are over 50% lower than the control group and about 30% lower than the Section 8 group). Leventhal and Brooks-Gunn (2002) also find

[19] Rosenbaum's analyses compare families that were moved to alternate public housing in Chicago to families that stayed in the suburbs; those that moved and then returned to Chicago are not included. This means the sample of suburban families differs from a random selection of families in that it consists of those families who were willing to forgo the benefits of the city (proximity to family and friends, etc.). Such families might well tend to have parents who place an unusually high value on economic achievement, so the success of their offspring, for example, might be due to this latent variable and not the suburban environment per se. While the differences in outcomes may be due to neighborhood effects rather than the self-selection of more "ambitious" families into suburbs, one simply cannot determine this from the data.

[20] See Goering (1999) for a detailed description of the MTO demonstration and Goering, Feins and Richardson (2002) for an overview of MTO findings.

that behavioral problems were reduced for children in the Section 8 and control groups for New York City families; however, they failed to find evidence of improved health outcomes. Leventhal and Brooks-Gunn (2002) also found some evidence that mental health for boys was improved by moving to better neighborhoods. Ludwig, Duncan and Hirschfield (2001) find evidence using data for families in Baltimore that neighborhood moves reduce incidents of juvenile crime, finding that moves from high to low poverty neighborhoods reduce juvenile arrests for violent crimes by a factor on the order of 30 to 50%. Rosenbaum and Harris (2001) find for the Chicago demonstration economic benefits for household heads, with employment rates for Section 8 and MTO families rising from 29.3% and 24.5% to 42.9% and 46.3%, respectively.

In contrast to children's outcomes, the effects of the MTO demonstration on adults are more mixed. Hanratty, McLanahan and Pettit (2001) find evidence that hours worked among Los Angeles families rose substantially for Section 8 and Experimental families; interestingly, the increase is over 35% larger for the Section 8 families. Leventhal and Brooks-Gunn (2001) find that substantial decreases in depression (more specifically, depressive behaviors) for Experimental families versus control families; Section 8 families exhibit no improvement. In contrast, Katz, Kling and Liebman (2001) find little effect of either type of voucher on adult economic outcomes. Goering, Feins and Richardson (2002) also report evidence from a cross-site survey that finds no evidence of voucher effects on adult welfare use or labor-market activity.

As important as the MTO demonstration is, there are limitations to the information it has provided. First, the evidence thus far only describes how the vouchers have benefited those who have employed them. Relatively high percentages of eligible families have failed to use the vouchers; for the Experimental group, the percentage of eligible families using the vouchers ranges from 34 to 61% across cities [Goering, Feins and Richardson (2002)]. At best (and to be clear this is very carefully discussed by researchers involved with MTO), one cannot extrapolate the findings to the broader population of the poor. Second, one needs to recognize that much of the benefits of the programs may be attributable to the increase in income associated with voucher eligibility as opposed to the shift in neighborhoods per se. The improvements one observed between families that employed vouchers with neighborhood poverty restrictions are much less dramatic when compared with families who were given unrestricted vouchers (which is unsurprising, of course since agents with more options should over all be better off) as opposed to those who did not receive vouchers.[21] Third, it is impossible to determine what aspects of the different neighborhoods led to improved outcomes. To give one example [one that is discussed by Katz, Kling and Liebman (2001)] the reductions in asthma rates may be due to improvements in housing quality (asthma is strongly associated with rat infestations) and nothing about the neighborhood per se. The divergence in the impact of vouchers on children versus adults is further suggestive that

[21] Rosenbaum and Harris (2001, p. 336) find, for example how among MTO movers, the percentage that said the condition of their housing is good or excellent increased from 33.9 to 80.6% after moving.

one needs to be very careful in drawing causal inferences on particular neighborhood effects from the MTO studies. Finally, there is a question of generalizability. Moving large numbers of poor families to more affluent communities will induce general equilibrium effects in terms of the location decisions of other families, the ability of schools in these neighborhoods to provide needed services, etc. One can easily imagine that the commitment of affluent families to public schools would be ended by a massive influx of poor families into their communities. Hence, one cannot simply assert that the effects of this program will be replicated if it is implemented on a wide scale; a point forcefully made in Sobel (2002). For these reasons, one cannot blithely use the MTO evidence to advocate large scale housing relocation programs as an antipoverty policy, an error one finds in Fiss (2000), for example.

While the Gautreaux program and MTO demonstration directly address the sorts of neighborhood effects that have motivated the neighborhood literature, other studies of quasi-experiments have focused more on uncovering evidence of social interactions in more restricted contexts. One context is that of college roommates, where it is straightforward to identify cases of random assignment. Sacerdote (2001) examines the effects of freshmen roommate assignments and finds they have a substantial effect on academic effort. Kremer and Levy (2003) find significant peer group effects on alcohol use. These studies employ very "clean" data compared to the larger quasi-experiments; for example, there is no issue of the take up rates that appears in residential neighborhood experiments. On the other hand, there is some question as to the applicability of the findings in roommate contexts to broader neighborhood notions since rooming contexts impose especially high levels of contact. Further, roommates create "interference" in individual choices; one can easily imagine that one low effort roommate can make it harder for others to study.

4.6. Aggregate studies

A final group of studies of neighborhood effects has focused on aggregate-level data. Glaeser, Sacerdote and Scheinkman (1996) find that crime rates across cities and precincts are both far more variable than would be predicted if individual decisions were interdependent. Topa (2001) studies interactions across physically contiguous neighborhoods in Chicago. Specifically, he estimates a nonlinear regression model in which the unemployment rate in one neighborhood is allowed to depend on the unemployment rates of adjacent communities; the nonlinear relationship is structural in the sense that it is derived from a stochastic process designed to model information transmission across neighborhoods. Topa (2001) finds spatial interdependences in neighborhood-level unemployment rates are present and quantitatively important.

One problem with this approach to studying neighborhood effects is that it equates evidence of such effects with correlation in behavior across agents. In the case of Glaeser, Sacerdote and Scheinkman (1996) correlation in the unobserved components to individual behavior will increase the variance of sample means; for Topa (2001) correlated unobservables in local neighborhoods can produce correlation in the levels of unemployment. This sort of correlation does not necessarily affect the interpretation of individual-level regressions.

An intriguing recent development in using aggregate data to uncover neighborhood effects is due to Glaeser, Sacerdote and Scheinkman (2002) and exploits a social multiplier property of peer effects. A social multiplier exists in models with endogenous interactions because feedback effects between agents imply that the effect on an individual of a change in a private variable will be lower than the effect on an individual if every member of his neighborhood experiences the same change. Glaeser, Sacerdote and Scheinkman (2002) exploit this to consider how the response of an outcome variable to some control changes at different levels of aggregation; specifically, they argue that the elasticity of an individual's behavior to a change in an individual-specific control should be smaller than the elasticity of a change in the group average behavior to the average of the control. This argument is used to show the presence of social interaction effects for cases ranging from the grade point averages of Dartmouth students considered by rooming group and dormitory and crime rates at the city, state and national level. This appears to be a very promising approach.

4.7. *Identifying neighborhoods*

All of the empirical studies that I have discussed take a particular neighborhood structure as known ex ante. This common assumption is necessitated by data limitations, i.e. the definition of neighborhood is determined by the information available in the data set and not by any substantive criteria. Important data sets such as the General Social Survey (GSS) link individual data to metropolitan areas, which clearly are far broader than the notions of neighborhood suggested by theories of social interactions; even a data set such as the PSID has limitations, as one cannot identify candidates for neighborhoods smaller than census tracts. I am unaware of any systematic evaluation of the question of the appropriate units for measuring neighborhoods. Such an analysis is clearly important if one wants to engage in policy evaluation, which requires the ability to translate regression coefficients into structural parameters.

While the size of units has not been addressed, there has been some research on the appropriate social notion of a neighborhood. As Akerlof (1997) has argued, theories of social influences naturally lead one to contemplate a social space in which individuals are situated. As emphasized there and in Akerlof and Kranton (2000), the ways in which individuals are influenced by others is strongly influenced by the set of self-perceptions that constitute identity, so that two individuals in the same physical space may experience very different social interactions.

Despite the importance of the question of neighborhood definition, there has been relatively little research on this question. Aizer and Currie (2002) is an unusual exception to this in that their analysis of the role of neighborhood effects allows ethnicity and residential proximity to jointly define the relevant interaction group for individuals (in this case less educated mothers and their use of publicly funded prenatal programs). The one systematic study of the social space in which to define neighborhoods is Conley and Topa (2002).

Conley and Topa (2002) focus on correlations in unemployment across neighborhoods in Chicago. Their analysis focuses on 75 "Community Areas" in Chicago that previous researchers have constructed from the 866 Chicago census tracts with the explicit intent of identifying areas with a common sense of community, etc. Conley and Topa use unemployment data from these community areas and construct spatial correlation functions to understand how the neighborhoods covary. However, rather than simply employ Euclidean distance to construct these functions, they construct four different notions of distance between neighborhoods:

(1) physical distance, which refers to the distance between centroids of neighborhoods,
(2) travel time distance, which refers to the time necessary to travel via public transportation from the center of one neighborhood to another,
(3) racial and ethnicity distance, which is a measure of the similarity in ethnic composition between two neighborhoods based on 9 categories,
(4) occupational distance, which is a measure of occupational similarity between two neighborhoods using 13 occupational categories.

Conley and Topa find that the measure of ethnic distance seems to be the most salient dimension along which neighborhoods exhibit spatial correlation. Once one controls for racial and ethnic distance, one finds little additional spatial correlation. However, none of the metrics appear to explain much once one accounts for racial and occupational composition within a neighborhood. Hence, Conley and Topa conclude that it is likely that social interactions, if any, occur at a lower level of aggregation. While their results are not decisive, their methodology is an important advance.

5. Additional evidence on neighborhood effects

Evidence of neighborhood effects may also be found in a number of related literatures.

5.1. *Classroom effects*

A number of authors have studied the effects of classroom composition on educational outcomes. These studies are of interest both from the perspective of the "neighborhoods" defined by classrooms and because one of the reasons why the allocation of families across residential neighborhoods may matter is because of such classroom effects. An additional virtue of these studies is that in certain respects classroom composition is more amenable to quasi-experimentation, as will become apparent below.

Within the economics literature, one of the early and still most important studies is Henderson, Mieszkowski and Sauvageau (1978). This study employed an unusually detailed data set comprised of French speaking students in Montreal for whom panel data was collected to measure language and mathematics skills; the data set allowed for a range of controls for family, teacher, and schools effects. In this study, mean IQ of classmates was employed as a measure of peer group effects. Henderson, Mieszkowski and Sauvageau (1978) found that peer effects are clearly present, but that these effects are concave in the sense that the marginal effect of an increase in mean classroom IQ is decreasing in the level of the mean IQ. This result is important, as Henderson, Mieszkowski and Sauvageau (1978) argue, because it suggests that tracking classes by IQ is inefficient if the objective of the school is to maximize average educational achievement. This work also makes clear how there are distributional consequences from classroom mixing as more able students are hurt and less able students are helped.

Hanushek et al. (2001) conduct a similar analysis using data from the University of Texas Dallas Schools Project, which has compiled a complete data set of Texas students based on tracking third-grade students in 1992 for four years. Measuring peer effects by past test score performance by students in the same grade, Hanushek et al. (2001) find that mean test score performance by others in the same grade improves student performance; unlike Henderson, Mieszkowski and Sauvageau (1978), some evidence of nonlinearity appears.

Other studies have focused on the identification of peer effects through government programs that affect classroom composition. Angrist and Lang (2002) study the effects of the Metco program in Boston, a desegregation program that sends (primarily) African American students to suburban schools. Focusing on Brookline, Massachusetts, they find that there is little evidence of any adverse peer effects induced by the transfer of lower achieving inner city students into the Brookline schools. The study does not address the effects on the inner city students themselves. Boozer and Cacciola (2001) study the peer effects using data from Project Star, a state of Tennessee program that was originally designed to assess the effects of smaller class sizes on performance. Boozer and Cacciola study the effects of the percentage of students who were previously enrolled in these small classes on the performance of their classmates in subsequent years. They find these peer effects to be nontrivial and conclude that much of the net benefit of lower class sizes is due to spillover effects. Minkin (2002) reanalyzes the Project Star data under the assumption that the strength of peer influences differs between classmates who were classmates the previous year and those who were not. Interestingly, he finds much smaller peer effects for all combinations of students than do Boozer and Cacciola.

5.2. Social capital

One literature that is closely related to the study of neighborhood effects is the literature on social capital. While social capital does not possess a precise definition, the set of ideas various authors have tried to capture with the term is well summarized in Ostrom (2000, p. 176):

> "*Social capital* is the shared knowledge, understanding, norms, rules, and expectations about patterns of interactions that groups of individuals bring to a recurrent activity... When they face social dilemmas or collective-action situations... par-

ticipants must find ways of creating mutually reenforcing expectations and trust to overcome the perverse short-run temptations they face."

As this definition makes clear, there are close connections between the sorts of non-market interactions that have been discussed in the neighborhoods effects literature and those that appear in the social capital literature.

Appeals to social capital as an important determinant of individual and aggregate behavior have become very common throughout the social sciences. Much of this work is difficult to interpret due to variation in the definition of social capital across studies, a failure to explicitly deal with identification, and a tendency for these studies to conflate any empirical correlations between a group variable with an individual outcome with a causal role for social capital; critiques of the empirical literature include Durlauf (2002) and Durlauf and Fafchamps (2003). Nevertheless, a number of social capital studies do provide empirical evidence that neighborhood characteristics help predict certain individual outcomes and so are a useful empirical corroboration of findings in the empirical literature. Durlauf and Fafchamps (2003) provide a broad overview of the empirical social capital literature; the discussion here identifies a few studies that are particularly interesting from the perspective of neighborhood effects.

One theme in the empirical social capital literature concerns the effect of family moves on children's outcomes. Specifically, a standard argument in the social capital literature is that the strength of attachment to communities is a function of stability of residents; in other words, individuals who frequently move will benefit less from the social support structures provided by neighborhoods than those who are long time residents. A number of studies have found evidence that more frequent moves are associated with a number of undesirable outcomes. In a widely cited study Hagan, MacMillan and Wheaton (1996) find, using Canadian data, that adverse effects of moves on a range of educational attainment measures is mediated by parental involvement as the effects of moves are far greater when parents appear to be less engaged with offspring (as measured by perceptions of the children). Sandefur, Meier and Hernandez (1999) find that high school completion and post-secondary enrollment are both negatively associated with the number of moves an individual experiences while growing up. Two caveats should be kept in mind when assessing these studies. First, the evidence of a statistical relationship between the number of moves and various outcomes is not uniformly strong; see for example Furstenberg and Hughes (1995) who find only weak evidence of such a relationship. Second, these studies do a poor job of accounting for the endogeneity of family moves. Clearly, family moves will be correlated with unobserved family characteristics such as parental interest in offspring. Hence, for reasons parallel to the discussion of self-selection into neighborhoods, one cannot interpret these studies causally.

From the perspective of neighborhood effects, perhaps the most important work in the social capital literature revolves around efforts to identify detailed characteristics of neighborhoods and their relationship to neighborhood quality. In this context, much of the focus has been on schools as the relevant social category as opposed to residential community. Morgan and Sørensen (1999a) is a good example in this regard. This paper studies the relationship between gains in mathematics achievement between the 10th and 12th grades for students in the National Educational Longitudinal Study of 1988. Morgan and Sørensen (1999a) find that educational gains are positively associated with the density of friendship networks (measured as the percentage of five closest friends attending the same school as the individual in the study) and negatively associated with the density of parental networks (measured as knowledge by a parent of the parents of his friends). This finding has been regarded as controversial in the sociology literature [cf. comments by Carbonaro (1999) and Hallinan and Kubitschek (1999) and the rejoinder by Morgan and Sørensen (1999b)]. These controversies relate more to the interpretation of Morgan and Sorensen's findings in the context of particular social capital theories than to the findings of how different measures of social structure predict educational achievement. One important lesson from the controversy is that even very precise measures of social structure may prove difficult to map back into specific theories of neighborhood effects.

The most important work in detailing neighborhood characteristics and associated outcomes has been produced by the Project on Human Development in Chicago Neighborhoods (PHDCN). The PHDCN is an extremely detailed data collection project that covers several hundred neighborhoods in Chicago. As described in Sampson, Morenoff, and Earls (1999, p. 639), the available data include responses to questions such as "About how often do you and people in your neighborhood do favors for each other?" and the likelihood that one's neighbors would intervene if one's child were observed skipping school.

Sampson, Morenoff and Earls (1999) use the PHDCN to study a range of social aspects of neighborhoods. In particular, they distinguish the social capital of a neighborhood as "the resource potential of personal and organizational networks" (p. 635) from the collective efficacy of a neighborhood, "a task-specific construct that relates to the shared expectations and mutual engagement by adults in the active support and social control of children" (p. 635). The purpose of this distinction is to differentiate general notions of the levels of neighborhood social resources from the use of these resources. By delineating how neighborhood members help one another, for example through monitoring one another's children, Sampson, Morenoff and Earls (1999) give a rich portrait of how neighborhoods benefit their members, illustrating how help in childrearing or trust among neighbors are important mediating variables in understanding why poor neighborhoods have adverse effects on their members.

5.3. Segregation

A number of recent studies have explored the effects of segregation on individual outcomes. Cutler and Glaeser (1997) consider a set of individual outcomes such as high school graduation, college graduation, employment status, and nonmarital fertility and explore whether these outcomes are explained, for African Americans, by the levels of racial segregation in the metropolitan areas in which they live. Evidence for this is determined via the sign and statistical significance for a variable that consists of the cross product of a dummy variable for race and a measure of segregation in the metropolitan area of residence. This variable is consistently significant and implies that segregation lowers Black outcomes. The estimated magnitudes are also quite large; according to the point estimates, 2/3's of the Black/White difference in single motherhood is explained by segregation. This paper also finds that racial segregation has substantial explanatory power beyond that associated with income segregation. Mayer (2002) studies the effect of economic segregation on years of schooling. She finds that increased variance in family incomes across census tracts reduced years of schooling among children in less affluent families; within census tract variance does not appear to matter.

Other studies have found that within-neighborhood ethnic concentrations matter for understanding individual outcomes. Borjas (1995) has argued that for the United States, within-neighborhood levels of "ethnic capital", defined as average education within an ethnic group, matters for intergenerational mobility. Clark and Drinkwater (2002) find that employment outcomes are strongly related to ethnic group percentages for a range of minorities in England and Wales.

While suggestive of neighborhood effects, mapping the findings of segregation studies into evidence on neighborhood effects is complicated. For example, the Cutler and Glaeser (1997) findings on the effects of racial segregation on African Americans may reflect differences in discrimination across different metropolitan areas; similar reasoning applies to studies of the effect of ethnic concentrations on individual outcomes. This problem is not addressed by the use of instrumental variables such as number of rivers in a metropolitan area to account for the endogeneity of segregation in a metropolitan area as such instruments may proxy for regional and historical differences in the treatment of Blacks. In the case of economic segregation, interpretation difficulties arise, for example, in that it is unclear why the variance across census tracts should be informative with respect to intraneighborhood interactions.

5.4. *Social attitudes*

The importance of neighborhoods may also be seen through the analysis of attitudes. One idea that permeates the social capital literature is that the social structure of neighborhoods can affect a range of attitudes and beliefs about other individuals and groups. This idea provides a causal mechanism as to why certain behaviors may be predicted from group characteristics. For example, to the extent that certain neighborhood characteristics induce feelings of trust and reciprocity towards others, the transfer of information about job opportunities may be facilitated. A recent study by Alesina and La Ferrara (2002) evaluates this idea using data from the GSS. Individual data on various attitudes related to trust is analyzed using data on the characteristics of the metropolitan area of respondents in the survey. Alesina and La Ferrara (2002) find that levels of trust are higher among individuals who reside in metropolitan areas with higher degrees of economic inequality and racial heterogeneity. A useful advance in this type of work would be the collection of attitudinal data for smaller units than metropolitan areas, which seem too large to well approximate the relevant neighborhoods for social interactions.

One question raised by the analysis of neighborhoods and social attitudes concerns how attitudinal data of this type translate into actual behavior. At an individual level, experimental evidence in Glaeser et al. (2000) suggests that expressions of trust in answering the GSS questions are better understood as predicting trustworthy behavior by the answerer than actual feelings of trust. At an aggregate level, this question has been indirectly addressed by a recent literature that has addressed the effect of neighborhood composition on government policies. Alesina, Baqir and Easterly (1999) find that the level of racial heterogeneity in local political jurisdictions is negatively associated with the level of government services. Alesina and La Ferrara (2000) find that racial heterogeneity is associated with lower rates of participation in community social activities, an effect that is particularly pronounced among those who possess racially prejudiced views. However, while these studies are certainly consistent with evidence that neighborhood composition affects social attitudes, one can easily imagine alternative explanations for the observed behaviors. And of course, racial composition of a community is endogenous, as usual making causal claims problematic.

5.5. *Home ownership and individual behavior*

A number of authors have studied the relationship between aspects of housing and various behaviors. One argument that has been made is that home ownership is causally associated with various socially desirable behaviors. One reason for such a relationship concerns investment in public goods. DiPasquale and Glaeser (1999) argue, for example, that homeownership increases individual incentives to invest in both local amenities as well as forms of social capital, interpreted as something that increases the degree of connectedness to others. DiPasquale and Glaeser (1999) find that for the U.S., homeowners exhibit higher levels of participation in nonprofessional organizations, greater knowledge of and participation in local politics, etc. They also find similar results for Germany, although the magnitudes of the effects are substantially smaller. Green and White (1997) find that children of homeowners are less likely to drop out of high school or to experience pregnancy as teenagers. While Green and White are quite circumspect in interpreting their results, one can apply the same causal arguments as made in DiPasquale and Glaeser. Both of these studies attempt to address the endogeneity of homeownership; DiPasquale and Glaeser (1999) use the average homeownership rate of an individual's socioeconomic class whereas Green and White use a bivariate probit specification to jointly model outcomes and homeownership, both studies acknowledge that their corrections are far from ideal.

Additional evidence of the existence of neighborhood effects may be found in Glaeser and Sacerdote (1999), who study the relationship between housing structure and various measures of social interaction. They find that individuals in larger apartments appear to have stronger social connections with neighbors than do house dwellers, but that apartment dwellers are less likely to participate in local politics. This finding, combined with a finding that street crime tends to be concentrated around large apartments, leads Glaeser and Sacerdote to conclude that apartment dwellers tend to be socially isolated from the larger communities in which they live. While the causality in this analysis is unclear, the suggestion that very localized differences in housing configurations alter individual behavior is quite intriguing from the perspective of neighborhood effects.

5.6. Geography and social customs

A final source of evidence on neighborhood effects may be developed from recent studies that explore how regional variations in certain behaviors appear to be driven by social custom. This idea is of longstanding importance in areas such as sociolinguistics, where regional variations in syntax and pronunciation persist despite the influences of mass media, cf. Chambers (1995) and Labov (2001). Recent analyses have extended this idea to substantive economic behaviors. In one important study, Young and Burke (2001) study patterns in crop-sharing contracts between landowners and tenants in Illinois. They document on how crop-sharing percentages are concentrated on simple divisions (50/50, etc.) even though there is no reason, given standard theories of contracts, for this to occur. They further show that there is substantial regional variation in these simple contracts with different shares predominating in different regions. These two facts suggest an important role for local norms in determining contract terms. Young and Burke (2003) extend this work to show that these norms have significant distributional consequences. Similar findings are developed by Burke, Fournier and Prasad (2003) in the context of medical care. This paper documents strong regional differences in the use of alternative medical treatments such as choice of coronary care and shows how these may be understood as arising from local social norms. These two applications illustrate new dimensions along which to understand how neighborhood effects matter.

6. Conclusions

The new literature on neighborhood effects covers an enormous range of theoretical, econometric and empirical issues. As such, it defies easy summary. These three components of the neighborhood effects literature are in different states of development. There now exists a reasonably well-developed theoretical literature that addresses both how neighborhood effects influence aggregate behavior and how these effects influence equilibrium neighborhood formation. In contrast, the econometrics of neighborhood effects is still in a nascent stage. The literature has identified deep identification problems that exist due to Manski's (1993) reflection problem between endogenous and contextual effects. Further, the estimation problems that exist because of self-selection and other types of unobserved heterogeneity are relatively well understood. However, work is only beginning on ways to overcome these problems so that credible empirical work may proceed. Finally, there is a large empirical literature that has explored neighborhood effects over an impressive range of behaviors. Much of this work is interesting and suggestive that neighborhood effects matter. However, this work has generally not dealt with the econometric issues that arise for neighborhoods models and so cannot be regarded as meeting the evidentiary standards of the more successful literatures in economics, for example, program evaluation.

What suggestions does this assessment raise for future research? One general implication is that future empirical work should attempt to simultaneously address behaviors within neighborhoods and neighborhood configurations via structural models. Structural models will allow for a full exploration of self-selection in neighborhoods models and allow for the analysis of policy interventions in ways beyond the current literature. One example of how neighborhood choice may help elucidate the nature and magnitude of neighborhood effects is via hedonic price arguments. With the exception of Ioannides, who only addresses this indirectly, the information embedded in house prices on neighborhood effects has yet to be exploited. Work by Nesheim (2002) and Heckman, Ekelund and Nesheim (2002a, 2002b) make important advances in the use of hedonic price models to uncover factors such as neighborhood effects.

One can also identify a number of specific challenges. It seems important to develop more realistic housing market models. A generally neglected issue is that of house market dynamics; issues of capital gains and the role of future neighborhood composition have essentially been ignored in the current literature. These are extremely hard problems and compound the general difficulties that exist in urban economic theory. Recent theoretical work by Ortalo-Magne and Rady (2002a, 2002b) on housing market dynamics may prove to be important in enriching current neighborhoods models.

Finally, I believe that much more attention needs to be paid to the microeconomic foundations of neighborhood effects. One promising approach concerns the role of self-identity in behavior, which has been introduced into economics by Akerlof and Kranton (2000). This work suggests that individual preferences and beliefs are conditioned in a fundamental fashion by the type of social identity they wish to possess and to present to others. Neighborhoods are a likely source of identity. An example of how this may be important is work by Ferguson (2001) and Ogbu (2003) on African American school performance in Shaker Heights Ohio. Shaker Heights has received much attention as it is a middle-class community that appears to have been relatively welcoming to African American families and yet in which there are substantial test score gaps between racial groups. Ogbu (2003) is particularly persuasive on the role of collective identity in conditioning factors ranging from study habits to aspirations. While work on identity suggests a role for how neighborhoods directly influence their members, related work on stigma, in particular the important recent book by Loury (2002) suggests that neighborhoods also induce effects because of the way they influence how neighborhood members perceive others. Loury's view may be interpreted as saying stigma against certain groups arises because beliefs about groups are fundamentally underidentified. In other words, stereotypical thinking can persist in a society because the experiences and information available to individuals typically cannot falsify the stereotypes. The extent to which this is so very much depends on how individuals are organized in social space. In other words, stereotypes about the poor or about certain ethnic groups survive partially because the lack of interactions with these groups alters the experiences and information possessed by others. Hence, one can see a role for neighborhood configurations in underpinning Loury's arguments. These approaches to understanding why neighborhoods matter, relying as they do on particular views of human cognition, makes clear the importance of greater data collection efforts at more disaggregated levels than one typically finds in neighborhoods studies.

To be clear, given its youth, the neighborhoods effects literature has made impressive strides in expanding economists' understanding of social influences; even more progress will certainly be made over time.

Acknowledgements

The John D. and Catherine T. MacArthur Foundation, Institute for Research on Poverty, and University of Wisconsin Graduate School have provided financial support. I thank Ritesh Banerjee, Ethan Cohen-Cole, Artur Minkin, Giacomo Rondina, and Noam Yuchtman for excellent research assistance and Jacques-Francois Thisse and J. Vernon Henderson for helpful comments.

Appendix: Selection correction for neighborhood effects regressions based on the multinomial logit model

This appendix is designed to illustrate how one can employ the Heckman-type selection corrections to account for endogeneity of neighborhood choice. The analysis is taken from Brock and Durlauf (2003). Under the assumptions that

(1) $\nu_{i,n}$ is double exponentially distributed, i.e., $\mu(\upsilon_{i,l} \leqslant \varsigma) = \exp(-\exp(-\beta\varsigma + \gamma))$ (so that neighborhood choice obeys a multinomial logit model) and

(2) ε_i is normally distributed,

arguments in Lee (1983) may by used to show that

$$\omega_i = k + cX_i + dY_{n(i)} + Jm_{n(i)} - \rho\sigma_\varepsilon\varphi_{n(i)}(\gamma Z_{i,n(i)}) + \xi_{i,n(i)} \tag{A.1}$$

where

$$\varphi_{n(i)}(\upsilon) = \phi\left(\frac{\Phi^{-1}(\Lambda_{n(i)}(\upsilon))}{\Lambda_{n(i)}(\upsilon)}\right) \tag{A.2}$$

with $\phi(\cdot)$ and $\Phi(\cdot)$ denoting the density and distribution function of a normal (0, 1) random variable and

$$\Lambda_{n(i)}(\upsilon) = \frac{\exp(\upsilon)}{\exp(\upsilon) + \sum_{n \neq n(i)} \exp(\gamma Z_{i,n})}. \tag{A.3}$$

The correction described by (A.2) and (A.3) allows for consistent estimation of the behavioral parameters in (A.1). The parameters γ are estimated in a first stage multinomial logit analysis and used to form $\varphi_{n(i)}(\gamma Z_{i,n(i)})$; $\rho\sigma_\varepsilon$ is simply a regression parameter in (A.1).

References

Aaronson, D. (1998). "Using sibling data to estimate the impact of neighborhoods on children's educational outcomes". Journal of Human Resources 33 (4), 915–946.

Ainsworth, J. (2002). "Why does it take a village? The mediation of neighborhood effects on educational achievement". Social Forces 81 (1), 117–152.

Aizer, A., Currie, J. (2002). "Networks or neighborhood? Correlations in the use of publicly-funded maternity care in California". NBER Working Paper 9209.

Akerlof, G. (1997). "Social distance and economic decisions". Econometrica 65 (5), 1005–1027.

Akerlof, G., Kranton, R. (2000). "Economics and identity". Quarterly Journal of Economics 115 (3), 715–754.

Alesina, A., Baqir, R., Easterly, W. (1999). "Public goods and ethnic divisions". Quarterly Journal of Economics 114 (4), 1243–1284.

Alesina, A., La Ferrara, E. (2000). "Participation in heterogeneous communities". Quarterly Journal of Economics 115 (3), 847–904.

Alesina, A., La Ferrara, E. (2002). "Who trusts others?" Journal of Public Economics 85 (2), 207–234.

Allen, B. (1982). "Some stochastic processes exhibiting externalities among adopters". International Economic Review 23 (3), 595–608.

An, M., Kiefer, N. (1995). "Local externalities and societal adoption of technologies". Journal of Evolutionary Economics 5 (2), 103–117.

Anas, A., Xu, R. (1999). "Congestion, land use, and job dispersion: a general equilibrium analysis". Journal of Urban Economics 45, 451–473.

Anderlini, L., Ianni, A. (1996). "Path dependence and learning from neighbors". Games and Economic Behavior 13 (2), 141–177.

Anderson, E. (1990). Streetwise: Race, Class and Change in an Urban Community. University of Chicago Press, Chicago.

Anderson, E. (1999). Code of the Street: Decency, Violence, and the Moral Life of the Inner City. Norton, New York.

Anderson, S., de Palma, A., Thisse, J.-F. (1992). Discrete Choice Theory of Product Differentiation. MIT Press, Cambridge.

Aneshensel, C., Sucoff, C. (1996). "The neighborhood context of adolescent mental health". Journal of Health and Social Behavior 37, 293–310.

Angrist, J., Lang, K. (2002). "How important are classroom effects? Evidence from Boston's Metco program". National Bureau of Economic Research Working Paper 9263.

Aronson, E. (1999). The Social Animal, 8th ed.. Worth Publishers, New York.

Bajari, P., Kahn, M. (2003). "Estimating housing demand with an application to explaining racial segregation in cities". NBER Working Paper 9891.

Bak, P., Chen, K., Scheinkman, J., Woodford, M. (1993). "Aggregate fluctuations from independent sectoral shocks: self-organized criticality in a model of production and inventory dynamics". Richerche Economiche 47, 3–30.

Bayer, P., McMillan, R., Rueben, K. (2002). "An equilibrium model of sorting in an urban housing market: a study of the causes and consequences of segregation". Mimeo. Department of Economics, Yale University.

Bayer, P., Timmins, C. (2002). "Identifying social interactions in endogenous sorting models". Mimeo. Department of Economics, Yale University.

Becker, G. (1973). "A theory of marriage: part I". Journal of Political Economy 81 (4), 813–846.

Becker, G., Murphy, K. (2000). Social Economics. Harvard University Press, Cambridge.

Bell, A. (2002). "Locally interdependent preferences in a general equilibrium environment". Journal of Economic Behavior and Organization 47 (3), 309–333.

Benabou, R. (1993). "Workings of a city: location, education, and production". Quarterly Journal of Economics 108 (3), 619–652.

Benabou, R. (1996a). "Equity and efficiency in human capital investment: the local connection". Review of Economic Studies 63 (2), 237–264.

Benabou, R. (1996b). "Heterogeneity, stratification, and growth: macroeconomic implications of community structure and school finance". American Economic Review 86 (3), 584–609.

Bertrand, M., Luttmer, E., Mullainathan, S. (2000). "Network effects and welfare cultures". Quarterly Journal of Economics 115 (3), 1019–1055.

Binder, M., Pesaran, H.P. (2001). "Life cycle consumption under social interactions". Journal of Economic Dynamics and Control 25 (1–2), 35–83.

Blalock, H. (1984). "Contextual effects models: theoretical and methodological issues". Annual Review of Sociology 10, 353–372.

Blume, L. (1993). "The statistical mechanics of strategic interaction". Games and Economic Behavior 5 (3), 387–424.

Blume, L., Durlauf, S. (2001). "The interactions-based approach to socioeconomic behavior". In: Durlauf, S., Young, H.P. (Eds.), Social Dynamics. MIT Press, Cambridge.

Blume, L., Durlauf, S. (2002). "Equilibrium concepts for social interaction models". International Game Theory Review. In press.

Bollabas, B., Thomason, E. (1987). "Threshold functions". Combinatorica 7, 509–517.

Borjas, G. (1995). "Ethnicity, neighborhoods, and human capital externalities". American Economic Review 86 (3), 365–390.

Boozer, M., Cacciola, S. (2001). "Inside the black box of project star: estimation of peer effects using experimental data". Yale University Economic Growth Center Discussion Paper 832.

Brewster, K. (1994). "Race differences in sexual activity among adolescent women: the role of neighborhood characteristics". American Sociological Review 59 (3), 408–424.

Brock, W. (1993). "Pathways to randomness in the economy: emergent nonlinearity and chaos in economics and finance". Estudios Economicos 8, 3–55.

Brock, W., Durlauf, S. (2001a). "Discrete choice with social interactions". Review of Economic Studies 68 (2), 235–260.

Brock, W., Durlauf, S. (2001b). "Interactions-based models". In: Heckman, J., Leamer, E. (Eds.), Handbook of Econometrics, vol. 5. North-Holland, Amsterdam.

Brock, W., Durlauf, S. (2002). "A multinomial choice model with neighborhood effects". American Economic Review 92, 298–303.

Brock, W., Durlauf, S. (2003). "A multinomial choice model with social interactions". In: Blume, L., Durlauf, S. (Eds.), The Economy as an Evolving Complex System III. Oxford University Press. In press.

Brock, W., Durlauf, S., West, K. (2003). "Policy evaluation in uncertain economic environments". Brookings Papers on Economic Activity. In press.

Brooks-Gunn, J., Duncan, G., Klebanov, P., Sealand, N. (1993). "Do neighborhoods affect child and adolescent development?" American Journal of Sociology 99 (2), 353–395.

Bruch, E., Mare, R. (2003). "Neighborhood choice and neighborhood change". California Center for Population Research Working Paper 002-03.

Burke, M., Fournier, G., Prasad, K. (2003). "Physician social networks and geographical variation in medical care". Mimeo. Department of Economics, Florida State University.

Burtless, G. (Ed.) (1996). Does money matter? Brookings Institution Press, Washington, DC.

Calvo-Armengol, A., Jackson, M. (2003). "Networks in labor markets: wage and employment dynamics and inequality". Mimeo. California Institute of Technology.

Carbonaro, W. (1999). "Opening the debate: on closure and schooling outcomes". American Sociological Review 64 (5), 682–686.

Case, A., Katz, L. (1991). "The company you keep: the effects of family and neighborhood on disadvantaged youths". National Bureau of Economic Research Working Paper 3705.

Chambers, J. (1995). Sociolinguistic Theory. Blackwell, Oxford.

Chen, H.-C., Friedman, J., Thisse, J.-F. (1997). "Boundedly rational Nash equilibrium: a probabilistic choice approach". Games and Economic Behavior 18, 32–54.

Clark, K., Drinkwater, S. (2002). "Enclaves, neighbourhood effects, and employment outcomes: ethnic minorities in England and Wales". Journal of Population Economics 15 (1), 5–29.

Conley, T., Topa, G. (2002). "Socio-economic distance and spatial patterns in unemployment". Journal of Applied Econometrics 17 (4), 303–327.

Cont, R., Bouchard, J.-P. (2000). "Herd behavior and aggregate fluctuations in financial markets". Macroeconomic Dynamics 4 (2), 170–196.

Cooper, R., John, A. (1988). "Coordinating coordination failures in Keynesian models". Quarterly Journal of Economics 103 (3), 441–463.

Cooper, S. (1998). "A positive theory of income redistribution". Journal of Economic Growth 3 (2), 171–195.

Corcoran, M., Gordon, R., Laren, D., Solon, G. (1992). "The association between men's economic status and their family and community origins". Journal of Human Resources 27 (4), 575–601.

Crane, J. (1991). "The epidemic theory of ghettos and neighborhood effects on dropping out and teenage childbearing". American Journal of Sociology 96 (5), 1226–1259.

Crowder, K., South, S. (2003). "Neighborhood distress and school dropout: the variable significance of community context". Social Forces. In press.

Cutler, D., Glaeser, E. (1997). "Are ghettos good or bad?" Quarterly Journal of Economics 112 (3), 827–872.

Datcher, L. (1982). "Effects of community and family background on achievement". Review of Economics and Statistics 64 (1), 32–41.

de Bartolome, C. (1990). "Equilibrium and inefficiency in a community model with peer group effects". Journal of Political Economy 88 (1), 110–133.

Dietz, R. (2002). "Estimation of neighborhood effects in the social sciences: an interdisciplinary literature review". Social Science Research 31 (4), 539–575.

DiPasquale, D., Glaeser, E. (1999). "Incentives and social capital: are homeowners better citizens?" Journal of Urban Economics 45 (2), 354–384.

Draper, D. (1995). "Assessment and propagation of model uncertainty". Journal of the Royal Statistical Society, Series B 57 (1), 45–70.

Drewianka, S. (2003). "Estimating social effects in matching markets: externalities in spousal search". Review of Economics and Statistics 85 (2), 408–423.

Duncan, G., Boisjoly, J., Harris, K. (2001). "Sibling, peer, neighbor, and schoolmate correlations as indicators of the importance of context for adolescent development". Demography 38 (3), 437–447.

Duneier, M. (1992). Slim's Table: Race, Respectability, and Masculinity. University of Chicago Press, Chicago.

Duranton, G., Puga, D. (2003). "Micro-foundations of urban agglomeration economies". In: Henderson, J.V., Thisse, J.-F. (Eds.), Handbook of Regional and Urban Economics, vol. 4. Elsevier, Amsterdam, pp. 2063–2117. This volume.

Durlauf, S. (1993). "Nonergodic economic growth". Review of Economic Studies 60 (2), 349–366.

Durlauf, S. (1996a). "A theory of persistent income inequality". Journal of Economic Growth 1 (1), 75–93.

Durlauf, S. (1996b). "Neighborhood feedbacks, endogenous stratification, and income inequality". In: Barnett, W., Gandolfo, G., Hillinger, C. (Eds.), Dynamic Disequilibrium Modelling. Cambridge University Press, Cambridge.

Durlauf, S. (1996c). "Associational redistribution: a defense". Politics and Society 24 (4), 391–410.

Durlauf, S. (1996d). "An incomplete markets model of business cycles". Computational and Mathematical Organization Theory 2 (3), 191–212.

Durlauf, S. (1997). "Statistical mechanics approaches to socioeconomic behavior". In: Arthur, W.B., Durlauf, S., Lane, D. (Eds.), The Economy as an Evolving Complex System II. Addison–Wesley, Reading, MA.

Durlauf, S. (1999). "The memberships theory of inequality: ideas and implications". In: Brezis, E., Temin, P. (Eds.), Elites, Minorities, and Economic Growth. North-Holland, Amsterdam.

Durlauf, S. (2001). "The memberships theory of poverty: the role of group affiliations in determining socioeconomic outcomes". In: Danziger, S., Haveman, R. (Eds.), Understanding Poverty in America. Harvard University Press, Cambridge

Durlauf, S. (2002). "On the empirics of social capital". Economic Journal 112, 459–479.

Durlauf, S. (2003). "Complexity and empirical economics". Mimeo. Department of Economics, University of Wisconsin at Madison.

Durlauf, S., Fafchamps, M. (2003). "The empirical study of social capital: a critical survey". Mimeo. Department of Economics, University of Wisconsin.

Durlauf, S., Seshadri, A. (2003). "Is assortative matching efficient?" Economic Theory 21 (2–3), 475–493.

Easterly, W. (2003). "The racial tipping point in American neighborhoods: unstable equilibrium or urban legend". Mimeo. Department of Economics, New York University.

Ellison, G. (1993). "Learning, local interaction, and coordination". Econometrica 61 (5), 1047–1071.

Epple, D., Filimon, R., Romer, T. (1984). "Equilibrium among local jurisdictions: toward an integrated treatment of voting and residential choices". Journal of Public Economics 24 (3), 281–304.

Epple, D., Platt, G. (1998). "Equilibrium and local redistribution in an urban economy when households differ in both preferences and incomes". Journal of Urban Economics 43, 23–51.

Epple, D., Romer, T. (1990). "Mobility and redistribution". Journal of Political Economy 99 (4), 828–858.

Epple, D., Romano, R. (1998). "Competition between private and public schools, vouchers, and peer group effects". American Economic Review 88 (1), 33–62.

Erdös, P., Rényi, A. (1960). "On the evolution of random graphs". Publications of the Mathematical Institute of the Hungarian Academy of Sciences 5, 17–61.

Eshel, I., Samuelson, L., Shaked, A. (1998). "Altruists, egoists, and hooligans in a local interaction model". American Economic Review 88 (1), 157–179.

Evans, W., Oates, W., Schwab, R. (1992). "Measuring peer group effects: a study of teenage behavior". Journal of Political Economy 100 (5), 966–991.

Falk, A., Ichino, A. (2003). "Clean evidence and peer pressure". IZA Discussion Paper 732.

Ferguson, R. (2001). "A diagnostic analysis of Black–White GPA disparities in Shaker Heights, Ohio". Brookings Papers on Education Policy, 347–414.

Fernandez, R., Rogerson, R. (1996). "Income distribution, communities, and the quality of public education". Quarterly Journal of Economics 111 (1), 135–164.

Fernandez, R., Rogerson, R. (1997). "Keeping people out: income distribution, zoning, and the quality of public education". International Economic Review 38 (1), 23–42.

Finnerman, L., Kelly, M. (2003). "Social networks and inequality". Journal of Urban Economics 53 (2), 282–299.

Fiss, O. (2000). "What should be done for those who have been left behind". Boston Review 25 (3), 1–8.

Focardi, S., Cincotti, S., Marchesi, M. (2002). "Self-organization and market crashes". Journal of Economic Behavior and Organization 49, 241–267.

Föllmer, H. (1974). "Random economies with many interacting agents". Journal of Mathematical Economics 1 (1), 41–62.

Foster, E.M., McLanahan, S. (1996). "An illustration of the use of instrumental variables: do neighborhood conditions affect a young person's chance of finishing high school?" Psychological Methods 1 (3), 249–260.

Frankel, D. (1998). "A pecuniary reason for income mixing". Journal of Urban Economics 44 (1), 158–169.

Fujita, M., Thisse, J.-F. (2002). Economics of Agglomeration: Cities, Industrial Location and Regional Growth. Cambridge University Press, Cambridge.

Furstenberg, F., Hughes, M. (1995). "Social capital and successful development among at-risk youth". Journal of Marriage and the Family 57 (3), 580–592.

Ginther, D., Haveman, R., Wolfe, B. (2000). "Neighborhood attributes as determinants of children's outcomes: how robust are the relationships?" Journal of Human Resources 35 (4), 603–642.

Glaeser, E., Laibson, D., Scheinkman, J., Soutter, C. (2000). "Measuring trust". Quarterly Journal of Economics 115 (3), 811–846.

Glaeser, E., Sacerdote, B. (1999). "The social consequences of housing". Journal of Housing Economics 9 (1), 1–23.

Glaeser, E., Sacerdote, B., Scheinkman, J. (1996). "Crime and social interactions". Quarterly Journal of Economics 111 (2), 507–548.

Glaeser, E., Sacerdote, B., Scheinkman, J. (2002). "The social multiplier". National Bureau of Economic Research Working Paper 9153.

Goering, J. (1999). Moving to Opportunity for Fair Housing Demonstration: Current Status and Initial Findings. Department of Housing and Urban Development, Washington, DC.

Goering, J., Feins, J., Richardson, T. (2002). "A cross-site analysis of initial moving to opportunity demonstration results". Journal of Housing Research 13 (1), 1–30.

Goldberger, A., Kamin, L. (2002). "Twin studies in behavioral research: a skeptical view". Theoretical Population Biology 61 (1), 83–95.

Graham, B., Hahn, J. (2003). "Identification and estimation of linear-in-means models". Mimeo. Department of Economics, Harvard University.

Granovetter, M., Soong, R. (1988). "Threshold models of segregation: Chinese restaurants, residential segregation, and the spiral of silence". Sociological Methodology 18, 69–104.

Green, R., White, M. (1997). "Measuring the benefits of homeowning: effects on children". Journal of Urban Economics 41 (3), 441–461.

Grilo, I., Shy, O., Thisse, J.-F. (2001). "Price competition when consumer behavior is characterized by conformity of vanity". Journal of Public Economics 80, 385–408.

Hagan, J., MacMillan, R., Wheaton, B. (1996). "New kid in town: social capital and life course effects of migration on children". American Sociological Review 61 (3), 368–385.

Hallinan, M., Kubitschek, W. (1999). "Conceptualizing and measuring school social networks: comment on Morgan and Sorensen". American Sociological Review 64 (5), 687–693.

Hamilton, B. (1975). "Zoning and property taxation in a system of local governments". Urban Studies 12 (2), 205–211.

Hanratty, M., McLanahan, S., Pettit, B. (2001). "The impact of the Los Angeles moving to opportunity program on residential mobility, neighborhood characteristics, and early child and parental outcomes". Report. U.S. Department of Housing and Urban Development, Office of Policy Development and Research.

Hanushek, E. (1986). "The economics of schooling: production and efficiency in public schools". Journal of Economic Literature 49 (3), 1141–1177.

Hanushek, E., Kain, J., Markman, J., Rivkin, S. (2001). "Does the ability of peers affect student achievement?" Mimeo. Hoover Institution, Stanford University. Also Journal of Applied Econometrics, in press.

Heckman, J. (1979). "Sample selection bias as a specification error". Econometrica 47 (1), 153–161.

Heckman, J. (2001). "Micro data, heterogeneity, and the evaluation of public policy: Nobel lecture". Journal of Political Economy 109 (4), 673–748.

Heckman, J., Ekelund, I., Nesheim, L. (2002a). "Identifying hedonic models". American Economic Review 92 (2), 304–309.

Heckman, J., Ekelund, I., Nesheim, L. (2002b). "Identification and estimation of hedonic models". Journal of Political Economy.

Henderson, J.V., Mieszkowski, P., Sauvageau, Y. (1978). "Peer group effects and educational production functions". Journal of Public Economics 10 (1), 97–106.

Hoff, K., Sen, A. (2000). "Home-ownership, community interactions, and segregation". Mimeo. World Bank.

Hogan, D., Kitagawa, E. (1985). "The impact of social status, family structure, and neighborhood on the fertility of Black adolescents". American Journal of Sociology 90 (4), 825–855.

Hussar, W., Sonnenberg, W. (2001). "Trends in disparities in school district level expenditures per pupil". Mimeo. National Center on Education Statistics.

Ioannides, Y. (1990). "Trading uncertainty and market form". International Economic Review 31 (3), 619–638.

Ioannides, Y. (1997). "Evolution of trading structures". In: Arthur, W.B., Durlauf, S., Lane, D. (Eds.), The Economy as an Evolving Complex System II. Addison–Wesley, Reading, MA.

Ioannides, Y. (2002). "Residential neighborhood effects". Regional Science and Urban Economics 32 (2), 145–165.
Ioannides, Y., Zabel, J. (2002a). "Neighborhood effects and housing demand". Journal of Applied Econometrics. In press.
Ioannides, Y., Zabel, J. (2002b). "Interactions, neighborhood selection, and housing demand". Mimeo. Department of Economics, Tufts University.
Irwin, E., Bockstaed, N. (2002). "Interacting agents, spatial externalities, and the evolution of residential land use patterns". Journal of Economic Geography 2, 31–54.
Jackson, M. (2003). "A survey of models of network formation: stability and efficiency". Mimeo. Division of Humanities and Social Sciences, California Institute of Technology.
Jargowsky, P. (1997). Poverty and Place: Ghettos, Barrios, and the American City. Russell Sage Foundation, New York.
Jencks, C., Mayer, S. (1990). "The social consequences of growing up in a poor neighborhood". In: Lynn, L., McGreary, M. (Eds.), Inner-City Poverty in the United States. National Academy Press, Washington, DC.
Katz, L., Kling, J., Liebman, J. (2001). "Moving to opportunity in Boston: early results of a randomized mobility experiment". Quarterly Journal of Economics 116 (2), 607–654.
Kelly, M. (1997). "The dynamics of Smithian growth". Quarterly Journal of Economics 112 (3), 939–964.
Kirman, A. (1983). "Communication in markets: a suggested approach". Economic Letters 12 (2), 101–108.
Kirman, A. (1997). "The economy as an interactive system". In: Arthur, W.B., Durlauf, S., Lane, D. (Eds.), The Economy as an Evolving Complex System II. Addison–Wesley, Reading, MA.
Kooreman, P., Soetevent, A. (2002). "A discrete choice model with social interactions: an analysis of high school teen behavior". Mimeo. Department of Economics, University of Groningen.
Krauth, B. (2002). "Simulation-based estimation of peer effects". Mimeo. Department of Economics, Simon Fraser University.
Krauth, B. (2003). "A dynamic model of job networking and social influences in employment". Journal of Economic Dynamics and Control. In press.
Kremer, M., Levy, D. (2003). "Peer effects and alcohol use among college students". National Bureau of Economic Research Working Paper 9876.
Labov, W. (2001). Principles of Linguistic Change, vol. 2: Social Factors. Blackwell, Oxford.
Lee, L.-F. (1983). "Generalized econometric models with selectivity". Econometrica 51 (2), 507–512.
Leventhal, T., Brooks-Gunn, J. (2001). "Moving to opportunity: an experimental study of neighborhood effects on mental health". Mimeo. Columbia University Teachers College, Center for Children and Families.
Leventhal, T., Brooks-Gunn, J. (2002). "The early impacts of moving to opportunity on children and youth in New York city". Mimeo. Columbia University Teachers College, Center for Children and Families.
Lewis, O. (1966). La Vida: A Puerto Rican Family in the Culture of Poverty–San Juan and New York. Random House, New York.
Liebow, E. (1967). Tally's Corner: A Study of Negro Streetcorner Men. Little Brown, Boston.
Loury, G. (1977). "A dynamic theory of racial income differences". In: Wallace, P., Lamond, A. (Eds.), Women, Minorities, and Employment Discrimination. Lexington Books, Lexington, MA.
Loury, G. (1981). "Intergenerational transfers and the distribution of earnings". Econometrica 49 (4), 843–867.
Loury, G. (2002). The Anatomy of Racial Inequality. Harvard University Press, Harvard.
Ludwig, J., Duncan, G., Hirschfield, P. (2001). "Urban poverty and juvenile crime: evidence from a randomized housing-mobility experiment". Quarterly Journal of Economics 116 (2), 655–680.
Manski, C. (1993). "Identification of endogenous social effects: the reflection problem". Review of Economic Studies 60 (3), 531–542.
Manski, C. (1995). Identification Problems in the Social Sciences. Harvard University Press, Cambridge.
Manski, C. (2000). "Economic analysis of social interactions". Journal of Economic Perspectives 14 (3), 115–136.
Mantegna, R., Stanley, H.E. (1999). Introduction to Econophysics. Cambridge University Press, New York.
Massey, D., Denton, N. (1993). American Apartheid. Harvard University Press, Cambridge.

Mayer, S. (2002). "How economic segregation affects children's outcomes". Social Forces 81 (1), 153–176.
McKelvey, R., Palfrey, T. (1995). "Quantal response equilibria for normal form games". Games and Economic Behavior 10, 6–38.
Milgrom, P., Roberts, D.J. (1990). "Rationalizability, learning, and equilibrium in games with strategic complements". Econometrica 58 (6), 1255–1277.
Minkin, A. (2002). "Heterogeneous social interactions models". Mimeo. Department of Economics, University of Wisconsin.
Miyao, T. (1978). "Dynamic instability of a mixed city in the presence of neighborhood externalities". American Economic Review 68, 454–463.
Mobius, M. (2000). "The formation of ghettos as a local interaction phenomenon". Mimeo. Department of Economics, Harvard University.
Moffitt, R. (2001). "Policy interventions, low-level equilibria, and social interactions". In: Durlauf, S., Young, H.P. (Eds.), Social Dynamics. MIT Press, Cambridge.
Montgomery, J. (1990a). "Social networks and labor-market outcomes: toward an economic analysis". American Economic Review 81 (5), 1408–1418.
Montgomery, J. (1990b). "Social networks and persistent inequality in the labor market". Mimeo. Department of Economics, University of Wisconsin.
Morgan, S., Sørensen, A. (1999a). "Parental networks, social closure, and mathematics learning: a test of Coleman's social capital explanation of school effects". American Sociological Review 64, 661–681.
Morgan, S., Sørensen, A. (1999b). "Theory, measurement, and specification issues in models of network effects on learning: reply to Carbonaro and to Hallinan and Kubitschek". American Sociological Review 64, 694–700.
Morris, S. (2000). "Contagion". Review of Economic Studies 67 (1), 57–78.
Murray, S., Evans, W., Schwab, R. (1998). "Education-finance reform and the distribution of education resources". American Economic Review 88 (4), 789–812.
Nechyba, T. (1997). "Existence of equilibrium and stratification in local and hierarchical Tiebout economies with property taxes and voting". Economic Theory 10 (2), 277–304.
Nesheim, L. (2002). "Equilibrium sorting of heterogeneous consumers across locations: theory and implications". Centre for Microdata Methods and Practice Working paper CWP08/02.
Nowak, M., Bonheoffer, S., May, R. (1994). "More spatial games". International Journal of Bifurcation and Chaos 4 (1), 33–56.
Nowak, M., May, R. (1993). "The spatial dilemmas of evolution". International Journal of Bifurcation and Chaos 3 (1), 35–78.
Ogbu, J. (2003). Black Academic Achievement in an Affluent Suburb. Lawrence Erlbaum Associates, Mahwah, NJ.
Oomes, N. (2003). "Local network trades and spatially persistent unemployment". Journal of Economic Dynamics and Control 27 (11–12), 2115–2149.
Ortalo-Magne, F., Rady, S. (2002a). "Homeownership: low household mobility, volatile housing prices, and high income dispersion". Mimeo. School of Business, University of Wisconsin.
Ortalo-Magne, F., Rady, S. (2002b). "Housing market dynamics: on the contribution of income shocks and credit constraints". Mimeo. School of Business, University of Wisconsin.
Ostrom, E. (2000). "Social capital: a fad or a fundamental concept?" In: Dasgupta, P., Seragilden, I. (Eds.), Social Capital: A Multifaceted Perspective. World Bank, Washington, DC, pp. 172–214.
Ottaviano, G., Thisse, J.-F. (2003). "Agglomeration and economic geography". In: Henderson, J.V., Thisse, J.-F. (Eds.), Handbook of Regional and Urban Economics, vol. 4. Elsevier, Amsterdam, pp. 2563–2608. This volume.
Page, M., Solon, G. (2001). "Correlations between sisters and neighboring girls in their subsequent income as adults". Mimeo. Department of Economics, University of Michigan. Also Journal of Applied Econometrics, in press.
Palmer, E. (1985). Graphical Evolution: An Introduction to the Theory of Random Graphs. Wiley, New York.

Panes, R., Vriend, N. (2003). "Schelling's spatial proximity model of segregation revisited". Mimeo. Department of Economics, University of London.
Plotnick, R., Hoffman, S. (1999). "The effect of neighborhood characteristics on young adult outcomes: alternative estimates". Social Science Quarterly 80 (1), 1–18.
Rivkin, S. (2001). "Tiebout sorting, aggregation, and the estimation of peer group effects". Economics of Education Review 20, 201–209.
Roemer, J., Wets, R. (1995). "Neighborhood effects and the distribution of income". Mimeo. Department of Economics, University of California at Davis.
Rosenbaum, E., Harris, L. (2001). "Residential mobility and opportunities: early impacts of the moving to opportunity demonstration in Chicago". Housing Policy Debate 12 (2), 321–346.
Rosenbaum, J. (1995). "Changing the geography of opportunity by expanding residential choice: lessons from the Gautreaux program". Housing Policy Debate 6 (1), 231–269.
Rosenbaum, J., Popkin, S. (1991). "Employment and earnings of low-income Blacks who move to middle class suburbs". In: Jencks, C., Peterson, P. (Eds.), The Urban Underclass. Brookings Institution Press, Washington, DC.
Sacerdote, B. (2001). "Peer effects with random assignment: results for Dartmouth roommates". Quarterly Journal of Economics 116 (2), 681–704.
Sampson, R., Morenoff, J., Earls, F. (1999). "Beyond social capital: collective efficacy for children". American Sociological Review 64, 633–660.
Sandefur, G., Meier, A., Hernandez, P. (1999). "Families, social capital, and educational continuation". Mimeo. Department of Sociology, University of Wisconsin.
Sargent, T. (1976). "Observational equivalence of natural and unnatural rate theories of macroeconomics". Journal of Political Economy 84 (3), 631–640.
Scheinkman, J., Horst, U. (2003). "Equilibria in systems of social interactions". Mimeo. Department of Economics, Princeton University.
Schelling, T. (1969). "Models of segregation". American Economic Review 59 (2), 488–493.
Schelling, T. (1971). "Dynamic models of segregation". Journal of Mathematical Sociology 1 (2), 143–186.
Sethi, R., Somanathan, R. (2001). "Inequality and segregation". Mimeo. Department of Economics, Barnard College, Columbia University.
Sherif, M., Harvey, O., White, B., Hood, W., Sherif, C. (1961). Intergroup Conflict and Cooperation: The Robbers Cave Experiment. Institute of Group Relations, University of Oklahoma, Norman. Reprinted by Wesleyan University Press, 1988.
Sirakaya, S. (2003). "Recidivism and social interactions". Mimeo. Department of Economics, University of Wisconsin.
Sobel, M. (2002). "Spatial concentration and social stratification: does the clustering of disadvantage "beget" bad outcomes?" Mimeo. Department of Sociology, Columbia University.
Solon, G., Page, M., Duncan, G. (2000). "Correlations between neighboring children and in their subsequent educational attainment". Review of Economics and Statistics 82 (3), 392–393.
Streufert, P. (2000). "The effect of underclass isolation on school choice". Journal of Public Economic Theory 2 (4), 461–482.
Topa, G. (2001). "Social interactions, local spillovers, and unemployment". Review of Economic Studies 68 (2), 261–295.
Topkis, D. (1998). Supermodularity and Complementarity. Princeton University Press, Princeton.
Turley, R. (2003). "When do neighborhoods matter? The role of race and neighborhood peers". Social Science Research 32 (1), 61–79.
Wallis, K. (1980). "Econometric implications of the rational expectations hypothesis". Econometrica 48, 49–73.
Weinberg, B., Reagan, P., Yankow, J. (2002). "Do neighborhoods affect hours worked? Evidence from longitudinal data". Mimeo. Ohio State University.
Wilson, W.J. (1987). The Truly Disadvantaged. University of Chicago Press, Chicago.
Young, H.P. (1998). Individual Strategy and Social Structure. Princeton University Press, Princeton.

Young, H.P., Burke, M. (2001). "Competition and custom in economic contracts: a case study of Illinois agriculture". American Economic Review 91 (3), 559–573.
Young, H.P., Burke, M. (2003). "On the distributional effects of contractual norms: the case of cropshare contracts". Mimeo. Department of Economics, Johns Hopkins University.
Zhang, J. (2003). "A dynamic model of racial segregation". Mimeo. Public Policy Institute of California.

Chapter 51

HUMAN CAPITAL EXTERNALITIES IN CITIES

ENRICO MORETTI

Contents

Handbook of Regional and Urban Economics, Volume 4. Edited by J.V. Henderson and J.F. Thisse

DOI: 10.1016/S0169-7218(04)07051-0

Abstract

What is the effect of an increase in the overall level of human capital on the economy of a city? Although much is known about the private return to education, much less is known about the more important question of what happens to productivity, wages and land prices when the aggregate stock of human capital in a city increases. Increases in the aggregate stock of human capital can benefit society in ways that are not fully reflected in the private return of education. Human capital spillovers can in theory increase aggregate productivity over and above the direct effect of human capital on individual productivity. Furthermore, increases in education can reduce criminal participation and improve voters' political behavior. In this chapter, I review what we know about social returns to education, with a particular emphasis on those externalities that accrue to local geographic areas. The focus of the chapter is on the empirical issues that arise in identifying these externalities and on the existing empirical evidence on their magnitude.

Keywords

education, social return, spillovers, externalities, cities

JEL classification: J0, I2, H23

1. Introduction

After 40 years of research on the relationship between education and earnings, economists have a good idea of the private benefits of human capital. We know that individuals with more education earn more, and most empirical work suggests that this difference in earnings is in fact a reflection of education per se and not a result of differences in unmeasured worker characteristics.

But despite this general agreement on the private return to education, much less is known about the social return, although economists have speculated about the possibility of externalities for at least a century. In this chapter, I review what we know about the social benefits of human capital, with a particular emphasis on those benefits that accrue to local geographic areas. Although I briefly review theories of human capital externalities, the focus of this chapter is on the empirical issues that arise in estimating these externalities and on the existing empirical evidence on their magnitude.

What is the effect of an increase in the overall level of human capital on a local economy? In the presence of externalities, the effect of aggregate schooling on aggregate earnings is not necessarily the same as the effect of individual schooling on individual earnings. These earnings externalities can be either positive or negative. On one hand, a large theoretical literature in both urban economics and macroeconomics has argued that aggregate human capital has a positive effect on productivity over and above its private effect-making human capital spillovers important factors in explaining the economic growth of cities, regions, and countries.

On the other hand, it is in theory possible that education has little effect on individual productivity, but it is simply a signal of innate ability. In this case education generates negative (pecuniary) externalities, and the effect of increases in aggregate schooling on aggregate earnings is smaller than the effect of increases in individual schooling on individual earnings.

In another branch of research, economists have hypothesized that education may have other social benefits in addition to its effect on earnings. For example, education is often thought to reduce the probability that an individual will engage in activities that generate negative externalities, such as crime. Alternatively, economists from Adam Smith to Milton Friedman have argued for public subsidies to education on the grounds that a better-educated electorate makes better decisions on policy issues that affect the economy.

The possibility that the social return to human capital differs from its private return has tremendous practical importance. For example, the magnitude of the social return to education is a crucial tool for assessing the efficiency of public investment in education, since state and local governments subsidize almost all direct operating costs of primary and secondary educational institutions. In fact, much of the argument for public education comes from the recognition that education not only rewards the educated individual, but also creates a variety of benefits that are shared by society at large.

Furthermore, the magnitude of externalities from education is important for local development policies. Local governments are increasingly interested in fostering economic growth and they have a number of alternative policy options at their disposal: subsidizing new business, changing environmental or labor standards, or developing policies to attract or create an educated labor force. Local governments must strike a balance between these options, as they may involve important trade-offs. For example, lowering environmental standards may result in a reduction in the number of educated workers if demand for environmental quality increases with education. Knowing the magnitude of the social benefits of human capital is therefore a crucial consideration in the choice of an optimal development policy.

In this chapter, I present a unified equilibrium framework with productivity spillovers. The framework indicates that geographically local spillovers can be identified either directly – by comparing the productivity of firms in cities with different overall levels of human capital, holding constant firms' individual characteristics – or indirectly, using factor prices. In the indirect approach, externalities can be identified in two ways, either by comparing the wage of workers in cities with different overall levels of human capital, holding constant workers' individual characteristics; or by comparing housing prices in these cities, holding constant houses' characteristics. The framework also clarifies the precise relationship between the estimates obtained from these three empirical strategies. I use this framework to interpret existing estimates of human capital spillovers.

The issue of endogeneity of aggregate human capital is probably the most important empirical challenge facing researchers in this area. Human capital is not distributed randomly across cities; it tends to be higher in areas with high productivity and good amenities. The reason is that workers endogenously choose where to locate based on wages, cost of living and the match between their taste and city amenities. Similarly, firms also endogenously choose where to locate based on wages, cost of land and the match between their cost function and city characteristics. Empirically, we observe that cities with a well-educated labor force tend to have better amenities, better institutions, better infrastructure, a more modern industry structure, and more technologically advanced firms than cities with a less-educated labor force. In addition, workers in cities with a well-educated labor force are likely to have unobserved characteristics that make them more productive than workers with the same level of schooling in cities with a less-educated labor force.[1]

As a consequence, it is empirically difficult to disentangle the effect of higher overall levels of human capital on productivity, wages, and land prices from the effects of these unobserved characteristics of workers and cities. The framework developed here indicates that unobserved heterogeneity of firms, workers, and cities is likely to bias least squares (OLS) estimates of the externalities, but the direction of the bias is not obvious a priori. Whether the true magnitude of the spillover is larger or smaller than the OLS estimate will depend on whether the unobserved factors that affect the relative demand

[1] For example, a lawyer in New York is likely to be different from a lawyer in El Paso, TX. Similarly, a high-school graduate in a biotech firm in San Francisco is likely to be different from a high-school graduate in an apparel plant in Brownsville, TX.

of skilled labor across cities dominate the unobserved factors that affect the relative supply of skilled labor. I discuss a number of ways to address the potential endogeneity of human capital stocks.

The empirical literature on human capital externalities should arguably have two objectives. First, it should credibly assess the magnitude of spillovers. Given the significant policy implications and a large theoretical literature that assumes the existence of human capital externalities, it is an important first step to quantify the size of such externalities, if they exist at all. A second goal should be to empirically investigate the mechanisms that give rise to externalities.

After reviewing the existing evidence, I conclude that the empirical literature provides some intriguing evidence on the existence of human capital externalities, but we are still far from a consensus on the magnitude of such externalities. The empirical literature on the subject is still very young and the econometric challenges are difficult to overcome. More work is needed before we can draw convincing conclusions about the size of human capital externalities and the mechanisms that drive them.

The remainder of the chapter is organized as follows. In the next section, I describe recent trends in the geographic distribution of education across U.S. cities. In Section 3 I briefly review theories of the social return to human capital. In Section 4, I discuss the empirical challenges that arise in estimating human capital spillovers and the existing empirical evidence on the magnitude of these spillovers. In Section 5, I turn to the social benefits of education that are not reflected in increased earnings. The last section concludes.

2. Recent trends in the geographic distribution of human capital across cities

The distribution of human capital in the United States is geographically uneven. Urban areas typically tend to have a better-educated populace than rural areas. But even among urban areas, there are substantial differences in the number of skilled individuals, as well as in the changes over time in that number. For example, the fraction of college-educated individuals in cities at the top of the education distribution in 2000 (e.g., San Francisco, CA) is four times larger than the fraction of college-educated individuals in cities at the bottom of the distribution (e.g., Danville, VA). In this section, I document recent trends in the distribution of schooling across major U.S. metropolitan areas from 1980 to 2000. I also analyze which characteristics of cities in 1990 are associated with large increases in the stock of human capital between 1990 and 2000.

My findings suggest that virtually all U.S. cities experienced increases in the fraction of educated individuals in the 1990s. The increases were on average similar to those experienced during the 1980s. But the increases were by no means uniform across cities. In particular, cities that had a relatively high fraction of educated individuals in 1990 experienced *larger* increases between 1990 and 2000 than cities that had a relatively smaller fraction of educated individuals that year. As a consequence, the distribution of human capital across cities became more unequal during the 1990s. One reason for the

Table 1
Percent and dispersion of college graduates by year

	(1) Mean	(2) Variance	(3) P75–P25	(4) P10–P90
2000	0.234	0.0044	0.088	0.172
1990	0.201	0.0037	0.070	0.152
1980	0.176	0.0028	0.073	0.121

Note. Sample includes 222 metropolitan areas.

increased concentration of human capital in some cities was the high-tech boom of the 1990s, since it benefited a handful of already highly skilled cities. But this tendency of increasing inequality in the distribution of human capital across U.S. cities during the 1990s was not a new phenomenon, as it was already in place during the 1980s.

Table 1 reports summary statistics for 222 metropolitan areas that I was able to link in 1980, 1990, and 2000. The data are from the Census of Population and Housing. Throughout the paper, the unit of analysis is the metropolitan statistical area (MSA). MSAs are defined to include local economic regions with populations of at least 100,000. Most MSAs contain more than one county. The term "city" and "MSA" will be used interchangeably in this paper. A total of 320 MSAs can be identified in the 2000 Census, but only 222 can be matched consistently across censuses.[2]

Historically, the U.S. population is characterized by a long-run trend of increasing education, since the younger cohorts are better-educated than the older ones. Column 1 in Table 1 confirms that the average fraction of college graduates across 222 cities increased from 17% in 1980, to 20% in 1990 to 23% in 2000. The fact that the share of college graduates has been steadily increasing over time is well documented, and should not come as a surprise. More interesting is the fact that the dispersion of human capital across cities also appears to be increasing. I present three measures of dispersion: variance (column 2), interquartile range (column 3) and difference between 90th and the 10th percentile. The variance increased from 0.028 in 1980 to 0.037 in 1990 to 0.088 in 2000. The other two measures of dispersion are generally consistent with such increase.

These trends in the mean and dispersion of the stock of human capital across U.S. cities are depicted graphically in Figures 1 and 2. The top panel of Figure 1 plots the percent of college graduates in 1990 on the x-axis, against the percent of college graduates in 2000 on the y-axis for each city in the sample, and it superimposes the 45 degrees line. The first thing to notice in the Figure is the wide variation in the average stocks of human capital among cities. In both 1990 and in 2000, the fraction of college graduates goes from about 10% in the least-educated cities to above 40% in the

[2] Data for 1980 and 1990 are from the individual-level 5% PUMS. Because individual-level data for the 2000 Census are not yet available, I rely on aggregate statistics provided by the Census for year 2000. One limitation of the aggregate data is that the average years of schooling is not reported. Only the percent of individuals with different level of schooling achievements in each city is reported.

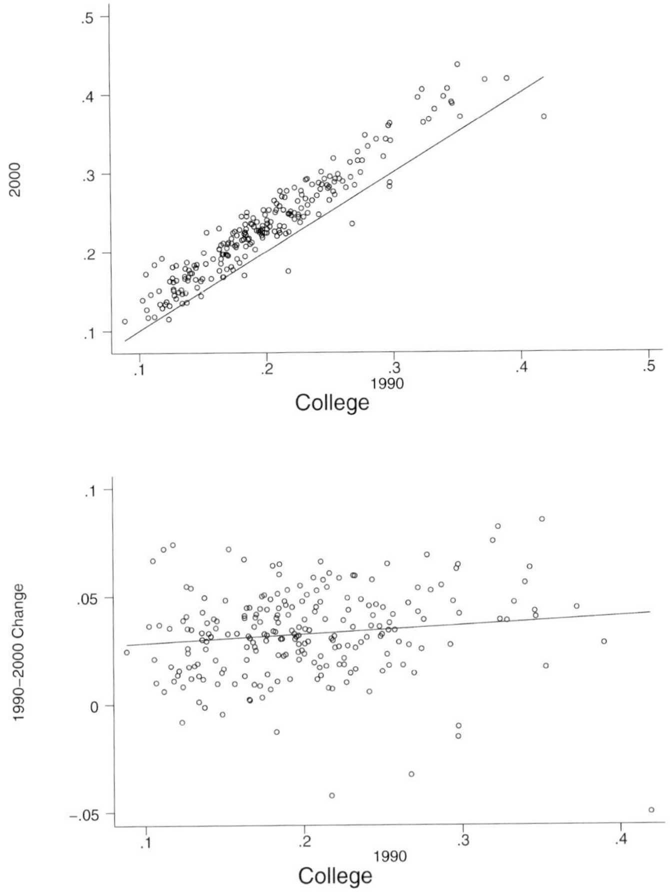

Figure 1. Changes in percent college, by city: 1990–2000.

highest-educated cities. A second feature to notice is that the stock of college graduates has increased almost everywhere. Only an handful of cities have a smaller percentage of college graduates in 2000 than in 1990. Most of the cities lie above the 45 degree line.

Third, the increase between 1990 and 2000 appears to be larger the higher the 1990 level of human capital. To see this last point clearly, the bottom panel of Figure 1 plots the percent of college graduates in 1990 on the x-axis, against the change in the percent of college graduates between 1990 and 2000 on the y-axis. Unlike the top panel, here the superimposed line is the OLS fit. The panel shows that cities that had higher levels of human capital in 1990 experienced larger increases during the 1990s. This finding is consistent with the increase in dispersion documented in Table 1. The slope (standard error) of the OLS fitted line is 0.041 (0.022).

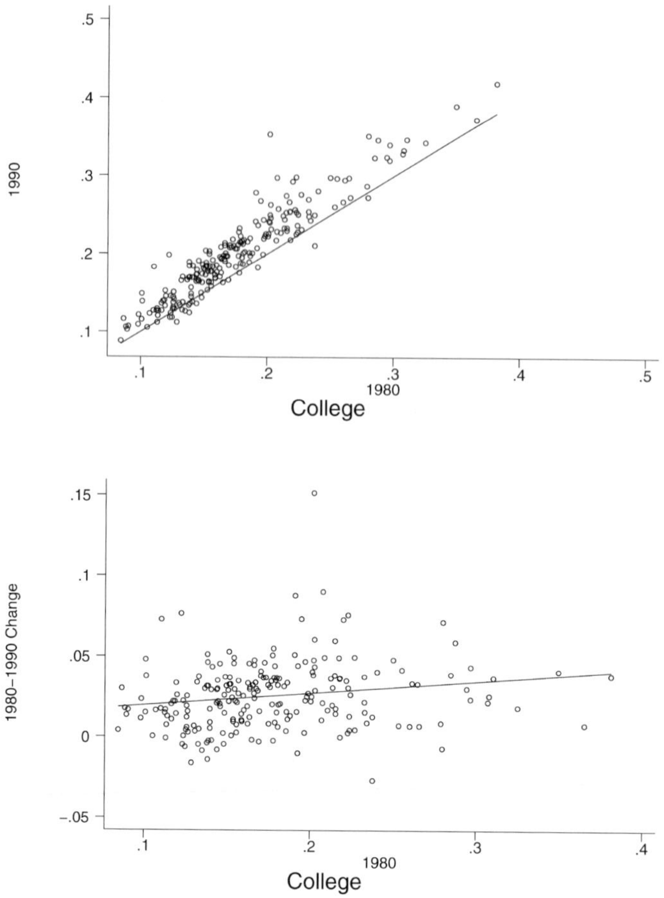

Figure 2. Changes in percent college, by city: 1980–1990.

Figure 2 shows a similar picture for the 1980s. In particular, the figure shows that the three features of the data uncovered in Table 1 are not specific to the 1990s, but have been going on much longer. The increase in dispersion is qualitatively consistent with the increase in dispersion documented in Figure 1, but the slope (standard error) of the OLS fitted line is even steeper: 0.0744 (0.0260).

To give a better sense of the distribution of human capital across cities, Table 2 lists the 15 cities with the largest and smallest per capita number of college-educated residents in 2000. San Francisco, where more than 43% of adults are college educated, appears to be the city with the largest per capita stock of human capital. Medium-sized cities that host one or more large research universities are overrepresented in the top group: examples are Madison, WI; Raleigh, NC; Gainesville, FL; Urbana-Champaign, IL; Austin, TX; College Station, TX; State College, PA; and Santa Cruz, CA. Table 3

Table 2
Cities with large and small percent of college graduates in 2000

Cities with the largest percentage	(1)	*Cities with the largest percentage*	(1)
San Francisco, CA	0.436	Jacksonville, NC	0.148
Washington, DC–MD–VA–WV	0.418	Beaumont–Port Arthur, TX	0.147
Columbia, MO	0.417	Hagerstown, MD	0.146
Madison, WI	0.406	Stockton–Lodi, CA	0.145
San Jose, CA	0.405	Huntington–Ashland, WV–KY–OH	0.144
Bloomington, IN	0.396	Modesto, CA	0.141
Fort Collins–Loveland, CO	0.395	Altoona, PA	0.139
Raleigh–Durham–Chapel Hill, NC	0.389	Ocala, FL	0.137
Gainesville, FL	0.387	Hickory–Morganton–Lenoir, NC	0.136
Champaign–Urbana, IL	0.38	Bakersfield, CA	0.135
Bryan–College Station, TX	0.37	Brownsville–Harlingen–San Benito, TX	0.134
Ann Arbor, MI	0.369	Lima, OH	0.134
Austin–San Marcos, TX	0.367	Yuba City, CA	0.132
State College, PA	0.363	McAllen–Edinburg–Mission, TX	0.129
Bloomington–Normal, IL	0.362	Johnstown, PA	0.127
Seattle–Bellevue–Everett, WA	0.359	Mansfield, OH	0.118
Rochester, MN	0.347	Vineland–Millville–Bridgeton, NJ	0.117
Santa Cruz–Watsonville, CA	0.342	Visalia–Tulare–Porterville, CA	0.115
Denver, CO	0.342	Danville, VA	0.113

Table 3
Cities with large and small changes in percent of college graduates between 1990 and 2000

Cities with the largest increases	(1)	*Cities with the largest increases*	(1)
San Francisco, CA	0.0848341	Corpus Christi, TX	0.0090711
San Jose, CA	0.0816702	Killeen–Temple, TX	0.0084904
Fort Collins–Loveland, CO	0.0750746	Yuba City, CA	0.0081555
Kenosha, WI	0.0739364	Las Cruces, NM	0.0073815
Odessa–Midland, TX	0.0718681	Salinas, CA	0.0070028
Roanoke, VA	0.0717642	Terre Haute, IN	0.0068426
Rochester, MN	0.0686671	Mansfield, OH	0.006075
Waterloo–Cedar Falls, IA	0.0670066	Montgomery, AL	0.0055255
New Bedford, MA	0.0666163	Utica–Rome, NY	0.0031253
Cedar Rapids, IA	0.0658358	Longview–Marshall, TX	0.0021987
Charleston–North Charleston, SC	0.0647602	Fresno, CA	0.001815
Colorado Springs, CO	0.0647194	Bakersfield, CA	0.0011622
Bloomington–Normal, IL	0.064214	Hickory–Morganton–Lenoir, NC	−0.001399
Asheville, NC	0.0640587	Huntington–Ashland, WV–KY–OH	−0.0046227
Madison, WI	0.0628737	Visalia–Tulare–Porterville, CA	−0.0081666
Seattle–Bellevue–Everett, WA	0.0622931	Lexington, KY	−0.0105446
West Palm Beach–Boca Raton, FL	0.0604797	Clarksville–Hopkinsville, TN–KY	−0.0128526
Fort Lauderdale, FL	0.0600323	Lafayette, IN	−0.0153243
Columbus, OH	0.0593833	Kalamazoo–Battle Creek, MI	−0.0327374
Baltimore, MD	0.0592615	Lafayette, LA	−0.0423326

lists the 15 cities with the largest and smallest changes in the per capita number of college-educated individuals between 1990 and 2000. The cities at the heart of the Silicon Valley boom experienced the largest increase. From 1990 to 2000, the share of college graduates in San Francisco and San Jose increased by 8 percentage points, almost three times the national average. The flow of young, highly-educated professionals and technicians attracted to Silicon Valley by the dot com boom in the second half of the 1990s is likely to have been a major reason for this impressive increase. As I show below, the 1990 fraction of high-tech jobs is a key predictor of the increase in the stock of human capital during the 1990s.

I now turn to a more formal analysis of the determinants of changes in the stock of human capital. Table 4 reports the coefficients from a regression of 1990–2000 changes

Table 4
Correlation between 1990 city characteristics and changes in percent of college graduates between 1990 and 2000

	(1)	(2)	(3)	(4)	(5)	(6)	(7)	(8)	(9)
College		0.066							−0.019
		(0.020)							(0.031)
Population			0.002						0.000
			(0.001)						(0.001)
Family income				0.038					0.022
				(0.008)					(0.014)
Black					−0.003				−0.027
					(0.019)				(0.020)
Hispanic					−0.030				−0.032
					(0.012)				(0.018)
Immigrants						0.0002			0.023
						(0.017)			(0.026)
Agriculture							−0.312		−0.221
							(0.066)		(0.074)
Manufacturing							0.002		−0.029
							(0.024)		(0.028)
Hi tech								0.512	0.376
								(0.131)	(0.149)
Northeast	0.037	0.024	0.007	−0.374	0.038	0.037	0.040	0.035	−0.199
	(0.003)	(0.005)	(0.015)	(0.094)	(0.003)	(0.003)	(0.003)	(0.003)	(0.144)
Midwest	0.036	0.023	0.008	−0.373	0.037	0.036	0.041	0.034	−0.197
	(0.002)	(0.004)	(0.014)	(0.095)	(0.002)	(0.002)	(0.002)	(0.002)	(0.144)
South	0.028	0.015	−0.001	−0.378	0.031	0.028	0.032	0.025	−0.201
	(0.002)	(0.004)	(0.014)	(0.093)	(0.002)	(0.002)	(0.002)	(0.002)	(0.143)
West	0.032	0.017	0.003	−0.377	0.036	0.032	0.043	0.026	−0.201
	(0.002)	(0.005)	(0.014)	(0.093)	(0.002)	(0.002)	(0.002)	(0.002)	(0.144)

Note. Standard errors in parenthesis. Entries are OLS coefficients. The dependent variable is the 1990–2000 change in percent college. Each column is a separate regression. $N = 237$.

in college share on several geographic and socio-economic indicators in 1990. I begin by analyzing whether there are differences across U.S. regions in the change in college share. Column 1 indicates that the average increase over the decade was 3.7 percentage points for Northeastern cities, a slightly smaller increase for Midwestern and Western cities, and only 2.8 percentage points for Southern cities.

In column 2, I include the percentage of college graduates in 1990. Consistent with Figure 1, I find that cities that had a large share of college graduates in 1990 further increased their share over the course of the decade. The coefficient on college share – obtained by conditioning on regional dummies – is now 0.066 larger than the unconditional coefficient reported in Figure 1.

U.S. cities differ widely in size and per capita income and it is well known that in a cross section, the share of college graduates is positively correlated with these variables. What is interesting is that the concentration of human capital in cities that are relatively larger and richer increased further during the 1990s. In particular, columns 3 and 4 indicate that the overall fraction of college graduates grew faster between 1990 and 2000 in cities that were larger and richer in 1990.

Race and ethnic background are also important predictors of cross sectional differences in human capital across cities. But as it turns out, the 1990 percentage of Blacks is not a significant predictor of changes in college share between 1990 and 2000 (column 5). On the other hand, the percentage of Hispanics is negatively correlated with changes in college share. One might expect that the fact that cities with larger Hispanic population in 1990 experienced relatively smaller increases in college share is explained by the inflow of unskilled immigrants. It is well-documented that immigrants tend to migrate to cities with high densities of immigrants. However, in column 6 I find little evidence that the 1990 fraction of immigrants is correlated with 1990–2000 changes in college share.

I now turn to the industrial structure of cities. The 1990 percentage of manufacturing jobs appears to be uncorrelated with changes in college share, while the percentage of agricultural jobs is negatively correlated with changes in college share (column 7). Perhaps the most interesting result on the correlation between industry structure and human capital is in column 8, where I focus on the relationship between the 1990 share of high-tech jobs in a city and the 1990–2000 change in college share.[3] I find that the share of high-tech jobs in a city is a strong predictor of change in college share. This is consistent with the finding in Table 2 that San Jose and San Francisco experienced the largest increase in college share over the 1990s. Finally, column 9 reports results from a specification where all the variables are included.

[3] To classify jobs as high-tech or low-tech, I use the definition of high-tech industries provided by the American Electronics Association (1997) based on 45 4-digit SIC codes. The definition is based on SIC codes, which are not exactly equivalent to the Census industry definition. In my analysis, high-tech industries include: Computers and related equipment; Scientific and controlling instruments; Guided missiles, space vehicles, and parts.

3. Theories of social returns to education

Through the chapter, I use the terms "human capital" and "education" interchangeably. The focus of this chapter is mainly empirical. Although human capital is in theory a broader concept than education, in practice most empirical studies use education to measure human capital.

After four decades of debate, there seems to be a consensus on the magnitude of the private benefits of human capital. Most empirical studies indicate that all else equal, individuals with one extra year of schooling earn about 8–12% more per year. Yet economists have speculated for at least a century that education may have additional benefits that are not reflected in the private return. If this is indeed the case, the social return to education will exceed the private return. By social return to education I mean the sum of all the benefits that accrue to society resulting from an increase in the overall level of education.

The social return to education differ from the private in the presence of externalities. I will consider three type of externalities. First, I consider what I will call productivity spillovers. Productivity spillovers arise if the presence of educated workers makes other workers more productive. In the presence of such spillovers, an increase in aggregate human capital may have an effect on aggregate productivity that is quite different from the effect of an increase in individual education on individual earnings. A large body of theoretical literature in urban and macroeconomics has argued that these types of spillovers are important determinants of economic growth.

On the other hand, it is also possible that education generates negative spillovers. For example, if education functions as a signal of productive ability, rather than enhancing productivity directly, the private return may exceed the social return.[4] In this case, increases in average schooling in a labor market may result in increases in earnings that are smaller than the private return.

Second, education may reduce the probability of engaging in activities that generate negative externalities. The most obvious example is the effect of education on criminal activities. If education reduces an individual's incentive to commit a crime, then cities with a better-educated populace will enjoy lower crime rates. Finally, economists like Adam Smith, Milton Friedman and others have argued that a better-educated electorate makes better decisions on policy issues that affect the collectivity. If this is true, cities and states with a better-educated population will elect better representatives and enact better public policies.

In the remainder of this section, I briefly review the theoretical arguments that have been proposed in support of these three sources of human capital externalities. In Sections 4 and 5 I describe the most recent empirical evidence on the magnitude of each of these externalities.

[4] This is a case where people with higher innate ability signal their higher innate productivity by enduring extra years of schooling.

For policy implications, it is important to keep in mind that not every spillover is necessarily a market failure that requires government intervention. One can think of many spillovers that are internalized. For example, an increase in the number of high skilled workers may generate positive spillovers that benefit productivity of low skill workers in the same firm. One reason for such increase in the productivity of low skilled workers is the imperfect substitution between high skill and low skill workers. Another reason is the presence of learning spillovers, if low skilled workers acquire better skills in the presence of high skilled workers. In either case, these within-firm spillovers are likely to be internalized and will be reflected in higher wages for educated workers. (I will come back to the issue of imperfect substitution in more detail in Section 4.2.1.) In this chapter, most of the analysis focuses on spillovers between firms, which are hard to internalize and therefore are market failures.

Because the geographic scope of externalities does not need to be the same for all types of externalities, the social return for a city does not need to equal the social return for a state or a country. The geographic scope of externalities is important for policy implications. For example, if spillovers have only local effects, one would argue in favor of Pigouvian subsidies to education financed at the local level, similar to those currently in place in the United States. If, however, spillovers from schooling have a broader geographical scope, so that their benefits are realized at a national level, then one would argue in favor of a federal role in public education.

From the point of view of local governments, one problem with subsidizing the production of human capital is that human capital is mobile, so that the link between production and utilization of human capital is not clear a priori. In a recent paper, Bound et al. (in press) study the relationship between production of college graduates, and their geographical distribution. Bound et al. (in press) argue that because college graduates are highly mobile, states and counties that generate large flows of new college graduates are not necessarily the ones where college graduates tend to locate.

On one hand, the production of a large number of college-educated residents in an area may lead to increases in the employment of skilled workers, if industries that are human capital intensive locate there. Examples of this phenomenon include Silicon Valley (electronics), Cambridge, MA (biotech and pharmaceutical), San Diego (medical, biotech, pharmaceutical). On the other hand, given graduates' high mobility, the link between production of college graduates and stock of college graduates may be weak. This clearly has important policy implications for states that invest heavily in public education since it is not obvious a priori what the return on such an investment is. Results in Bound et al. (in press) are not too encouraging for states like Michigan or Ohio that invest heavily in their system of public higher education. Estimates based on Census data indicate that the link between the production and use of BA degree recipients is modest. States awarding relatively large numbers of college degrees do have somewhat higher concentrations of college-educated workers, but the effect is not very large.

3.1. Productivity spillovers

The question of whether education raises a person's productivity and earnings has generated a large body of empirical literature.[5] The consensus that has emerged is that a worker's schooling does in fact raise her productivity and her earnings. For the United States in the 1990s, the private return to schooling is believed to be about 8–12%: each extra year of schooling appears to be associated with an 8–12% increase in earnings.[6]

Much less is known about the more important question of what happens to productivity and wages when the aggregate stock of educated workers increases. The fact that employers pay individual workers 8–12% more for each extra year of schooling does not necessarily imply that raising the average education in a city (or state or nation) by one year would result in a 8–12% increase in aggregate earnings. I will consider three reasons why the social return to schooling – as measured in terms of increased aggregate earnings or aggregate income – may differ from the private return that has received so much attention in the literature.

Technological externalities. While many different explanations have been proposed for positive externalities, these models can be grouped in two broad families, that I will call technological externalities and pecuniary externalities. In the first class of models, externalities are built into aggregate production functions in the form of technological increasing returns. Learning through social interaction is often cited as the mechanism through which externalities arise. Marshall (1890) is the first to argue that social interactions among workers in the same industry and location create learning opportunities that enhance productivity.

Perhaps the most influential example of the class of models where externalities are built into aggregate production functions in the form of technological increasing returns is a paper by Lucas (1988). In that paper, human capital is assumed to have two effects. First, an individual's own human capital has the standard effect of increasing her own productivity. Second, the average aggregate level of human capital contributes to the productivity of all factors of production. This second effect is an externality, because "though all benefit from it, no individual human capital accumulation decision can have an appreciable effect on average human capital, so no one will take it into account" in deciding how much to invest in human capital accumulation. In Lucas' view, human capital externalities may be large enough to explain long-run income differences between rich and poor countries.

What are the mechanisms that generate these human capital externalities? In Lucas' model the externality is simply built into the production function, but Lucas goes on

5 Although college-educated individuals clearly earn more than high-school graduates, it is possible that college graduates have higher earnings potential because of innate ability, family background, ambition and determination. If these unmeasured workers characteristics are important, college graduate would earn more than high-school graduates even in the absence of a college education.

6 See Card (1999) for a comprehensive survey of the evidence on the private return to schooling.

to argue that the sharing of knowledge and skills through formal and informal interaction is the mechanism that generates positive externalities across workers.[7] More recent models build on this idea by assuming that individuals augment their human capital through pairwise meetings with more skilled neighbors at which they exchange ideas.[8] See Duranton and Puga (2004) for a detailed survey of this class of models.

Pecuniary externalities. A second class of models explain positive human capital externalities as pecuniary externalities. Labor market pooling externalities were first proposed by Marshall (1890). One recent example is a model where job search is costly, and spillovers from education arise because of the complementarity between physical and human capital [Acemoglu (1996)]. Because of the complementarity between physical and human capital, the privately optimal amount of schooling depends on the amount of physical capital a worker expects to use. The privately optimal amount of physical capital depends on the education of the workforce. If a group of workers in a city increases its level of education, firms in that city, expecting to employ these workers, would invest more in physical capital. Since search is costly, some of the workers who have not increased their education would end up working with more physical capital and hence earn more than similar workers in other cities.

As in Lucas, the presence of skilled workers in a city generates external benefits for other workers there. Both Lucas and Acemoglu agree that the average wage of unskilled workers in a city increases with the average human capital of the labor force. But what

[7] In Lucas' words:

> We know that there are group interactions that are central to individual productivity and that involve groups larger than the immediate family and smaller than the human race as a whole. Most of what we know we learn from other people. We pay tuition to a few of these teachers, either directly or indirectly by accepting lower pay so we can hang around them, but most of it we get for free, and often in ways that are mutual – without a distinction between student and teacher. Certainly in our own profession, the benefits of colleagues from whom we hope to learn are tangible enough to lead us to spend a considerable fraction of our time fighting over who they shall be, and another fraction travelling to talk with those we wish we could have as colleagues but cannot. We know that this kind of external effect is common to all the arts and sciences – the 'creative professions'. All of intellectual history is the history of such effects.

But, Lucas argues, the external effect of human capital in not limited to academia:

> Much of economic life is creative in much the same way as is art and science. New York City's garment district, financial district, diamond district, advertising district and many more are as much intellectual centers as is Columbia or New York University.

[8] See, for example, Glaeser (1999), Peri (2002), Jovanovic and Rob (1989). Black and Henderson (1999) specifically explore human capital spillovers in urban areas. They investigate how urbanization affects the efficiency of the growth process and how growth in turn affects urbanization when human capital generates positive spillovers. Other authors focus on the importance of basic research in fostering technological innovation and productivity, the public good nature of this type of research, and the resulting positive externalities in the form of knowledge spillovers. See, for example, Arrow (1962), Griliches (1986), Jaffe, Trajtenberg and Henderson (1993), and Saxenian (1994).

distinguishes Acemoglu's story from Lucas' story is that this result does not follow from assumptions on the production function, but rather is derived from market interactions. Even though all the production functions of the economy exhibit constant returns to scale in Acemoglu, the complementarity of human capital and physical capital coupled with frictions in the job search process, generates a positive relationship between average wage and average human capital, holding constant workers' individual human capital.[9]

Although differences across cities in their *quantity* of physical capital play a central role in this model, differences in the *quality* of physical capital (technology) could arguably generate similar conclusions. Specifically, if skills and technology are complementary, it is plausible to assume that the privately optimal amount of human capital depends not only on the amount of physical capital a worker expects to use, but also on the technological level that characterizes such capital. Similarly, in models with endogenous skill-biased technical change, an increase in the supply of educated workers increases the size of the market for skill-complementary technologies and stimulates the R&D sector to spend more effort upgrading the productivity of skilled workers [Acemoglu (1998)].

Negative externalities. Another reason why the social return to schooling, as measured in terms of increased aggregate earnings, may differ from the private return is the presence of negative externalities. If education functions as a signal of productive ability, rather than enhancing productivity directly, the private return may exceed the social return. This is a case where people with higher innate ability signal their higher innate productivity by enduring extra years of schooling. If schooling is more difficult for individuals with low innate productivity than individuals with high innate productivity, then, even if schooling itself is worthless in terms of enhancing productivity, it still may be a useful screening device for employers to identify more productive job applicants. This possibility is important because it implies that one extra year in average schooling in a city (or state or nation) would result in less than an 8–12% increase in aggregate earnings.

In the most extreme version of the model, a one-year increase in average schooling in a city would have no effect on earnings. Employers would simply increase their hiring standard, and everyone would end up at the same jobs they would have had without the increase in education. In this extreme case, the private return to schooling would be 8–12%, but the social return would be 0. Although this is certainly possible in theory, this scenario is unlikely to be relevant in practice. The existing empirical evidence on private returns to schooling indicates that education has a causal effect on productivity.

[9] Empirically, manufacturing plants located in cities that have a more skilled labor force do tend to have a larger stock of human capital. This is true both in a cross section of cities and when looking at within cities changes over time. (Author's calculation using firms data from the Census of Manufacturers matched with workers data from the Census of Population.)

3.2. Crime

Besides its effects on productivity and earnings, human capital may also reduce the probability that an individual engage in socially costly activities, such as crime. Crime is a negative externality with enormous social costs. If education reduces crime, then schooling will have social benefits that are not taken into account by individuals, and most of this benefit is likely to be realized at the local level: cities with high levels of education would have lower crime rates. Given the large social costs of crime, even small reductions in crime associated with education may be economically important.

There are a number of reasons to believe that education can reduce criminal activity. First, schooling increases the returns to legitimate work, raising the opportunity costs of illegal behavior. Additionally, punishment for criminal behavior often entails incarceration. By raising wage rates, schooling makes any time spent out of the labor market more costly.

Second, schooling may directly affect the psychic rewards from crime itself. For example, Arrow (1997), discussing the social benefits of education, argues that

> Like everything else interesting about human beings, preferences are a mixture of hereditary and environment. Schools must surely have a major part, if only because they occupy a large part of a child's day. It is a traditional view that not only does education influence values but it ought to do so.

Third, schooling may alter preferences in indirect ways, which may in turn affect decisions to engage in crime. For example, education may increase one's patience (as in Becker and Mulligan (1997)) or risk aversion. A lower discount rate or higher risk aversion will reduce the probability that an individual will engage in criminal activities.

3.3. Voting

Many economists have argued that education provides social benefits through enhanced political behavior. Among many other authors, Hanushek (2002), makes this argument in his survey of public education. Interestingly, the argument that education generates externalities by improving the political behavior of voters resonates both with noted advocates of a limited role for government – such as Adam Smith and Milton Friedman – as well as with liberal proponents of a larger role of government in the economy. For example, a document by the liberal Center on National Education Policy (1996) lists several benefits of public education, including the preparation of "people to become responsible citizens". Forty years ago, Friedman (1962) made exactly the same point:[10]

[10] Even earlier, Adam Smith (1776) emphasized the benefits of increased cognitive capacity among the common people, claiming that: they are more disposed to examine, and more capable of seeing through, the interested complaints of faction and sedition, and they are, upon that account, less apt to be misled into any wanton or unnecessary opposition to the measures of government.

> A stable and democratic society is impossible without a minimum degree of literacy and knowledge on the part of most citizens and without widespread acceptance of some common set of values. Education can contribute to both. In consequence, the gain from education of a child accrues not only to the child or to his parents but also to other members of the society. The education of my child contributes to your welfare by promoting a stable and democratic society. There is therefore a significant "neighborhood effect". [...] Most of us would probably conclude that the gains are sufficiently important to justify some government subsidy.

Why might education affect political behavior? First, and most importantly, more-educated voters may have more information on candidates' and political parties' positions. The fact that better-educated citizens are likely to be more informed voters may be due to active accumulation of information during campaigns (higher newspaper readership, for example), or to a better ability to process a given amount of information (if, for example, education improves cognitive skills). According to this argument, better-educated citizens are in a position to make more informed choices at election time. By choosing better candidates, they create an externality that may benefit all citizens. A second channel through which education might affect political behavior is if education increases civic participation, for example, by raising voter turn-out rates. If increased civic participation improves social decision-making, then education may also affect the quality of political decisions.[11] If enhanced political behavior produces social benefits, then Pigouvian subsidies for education may produce more efficient education acquisition decisions. Unlike the social benefits of schooling that arise because of reductions in criminal activities, the benefits of schooling that accrue because of improved political behavior are not necessarily limited to a local area. State and national elections may benefit residents in other cities and states.

4. Estimating productivity spillovers in cities

In Section 3.1, I described alternative theoretical models based on productivity spillovers. In this section, I discuss the challenges that arise in the estimation of these spillovers, and I summarize the existing empirical evidence on their magnitude.

I begin in Section 4.1 by presenting a simple equilibrium framework that helps identify three possible strategies for estimating human capital spillovers in cities:

(1) by comparing the output (or productivity) of firms located in cities with high and low level of aggregate human capital;
(2) by comparing the wages of workers located in cities with high and low level of aggregate human capital;
(3) by comparing cost of land in cities with high and low levels of aggregate human capital.

[11] Different models have been proposed in which increased civic participation lead to better outcomes. See for example Osborne, Rosenthal and Turner (2000) and Feddersen and Pesendorfer (1996).

I then discuss possible empirical strategies for estimating spillovers using these three models. The fundamental issue in the interpretation of these three models is the presence of unobservable determinants of productivity, wages or rent that are correlated with aggregate human capital across cities. The equilibrium framework suggests that simple OLS models are likely to be biased, but the sign of the bias is not obvious a priori. I discuss alternative identifications strategies to account for unobserved heterogeneity.

A considerable portion of the discussion is devoted to empirical models based on wages (Section 4.2), since these are most prevalent in the existing literature. I discuss in detail the interpretation of wage equations in the presence of externalities, since this interpretation is complicated by the fact that increases in the stock of skilled workers in a city may affect the wage distribution even in the absence of externalities, if skilled and unskilled workers are imperfect substitutes. I review the findings of some of the existing empirical studies based on wages, productivity and land prices. Finally, in Section 4.3 I turn to models based on firm productivity. I discuss the interpretations of these models, and the existing empirical evidence.

4.1. Equilibrium with spillovers

I begin by presenting a simple general equilibrium framework of perfect competition that includes both standard demand and supply factors and spillovers from human capital. The framework identifies the effect of an increase in the relative supply of educated workers in a city on the productivity, land prices, and wages of skilled and unskilled workers. The framework, which is based on models in Roback (1982), Moretti (in press, 2002), aims to make two points. First, it indicates how human capital spillovers can be measured by relating differences across cities in firms' productivity, land prices, or wages to differences in the overall level of human capital. Second, the model identifies potential sources of unobserved heterogeneity that might bias empirical estimates of the spillover.[12]

4.1.1. Framework

The intuition is quite simple. If there are spillovers, firms and workers are more productive in cities with high overall levels of human capital. In equilibrium, firms are indifferent between cities because wages and land prices are higher in cities with high overall levels of human capital, and lower in cities with low overall levels of human capital, making unit costs similar across cities. Similarly, workers are indifferent because housing prices are higher in cities with high overall levels of human capital.

Consider two cities, A and B, and two types of labor, educated and uneducated. Workers and firms are perfectly mobile. The market structure is assumed to be perfectly competitive, so that the profits of firms are assumed to be zero. Assume that there are two

[12] See Gabriel and Rosenthal (2004) for a recent empirical application of the Roback model.

types of goods, a composite good y – nationally traded – and land h – locally traded. Each city is a competitive economy that produces y combining skilled and unskilled workers (N_1 and N_0) and capital: $y = Ag(N_0, N_1, K)$.

To introduce the possibility of human capital spillovers in the model, I allow the productivity of plants in a city to depend on the aggregate level of human capital in the city, S: $A = f(S)$. This specification is consistent with most of the explanations of spillovers suggested in the literature and described in the previous section. Note that this specification assumes that the spillover augments both capital productivity and labor productivity. Alternative assumptions are possible. For example, one could assume that human capital spillovers benefit only labor productivity, or alternatively, that they benefit only capital productivity. Empirically, it is difficult to distinguish between these alternative specifications.

Cities differ in the amenities that they offer. Workers maximize utility subject to a budget constraint by choosing quantities of the composite good and residential land, given the city amenity, v'. Because the composite good, y, is traded nationally, its price is the same everywhere and set equal to 1. Variations in the cost of living between cities depend only on variations in the price of land, p, which is assumed to be the same for all workers in the same city, irrespective of the education group. The quantity of land is fixed. Because of the perfect mobility and perfect competition assumptions, equilibrium is obtained when workers have equal utilities in all cities and firms have equal unit costs across cities.

The equilibrium for the simple case of only two cities, A and B, is described in Figure 3. The upward sloping lines in each panel represent indifference curves for the two education groups. Indirect utility of workers belonging to group j, $V_j(w_j, p, v')$, is a function of the group's nominal wage, w_j, cost of land and the amenity. The indifference curves are upward sloping because workers prefer high wages and low rent. Since workers are free to migrate, utility of workers is equalized across locations:

$$V_1(w_1, p, v') = k_1 \quad \text{and} \quad V_0(w_0, p, v') = k_0$$

for educated and uneducated workers, respectively. The downward sloping lines show combinations of wages and rents which hold constant firms' unit costs: $C_c(w_0, w_1, p) = 1$, where w_0 and w_1 are wages of uneducated and educated workers, respectively; and c indexes city. (If production functions vary across cities, for example because of spillover effects, then the unit cost functions are city-specific.) A zero-profit condition for the firms ensures that production takes place along the downward sloping curve. Thus the model has three equations (unit cost and indirect utility for each skill group) in three unknowns (w_0, w_1 and p). Point 1 in the left panel of Figure 3 represents the equilibrium combination of the educated workers' wage and the price of land in city A. Point 1 in the right panel represents the same combination for uneducated workers.

If the two cities are identical, the equilibrium in city B is the same. However, there are two ways to make the overall level of human capital higher in city B than in city A – either by increasing the relative supply of educated workers in city B, or by increasing the relative demand for educated workers in city B. I begin by considering what happens

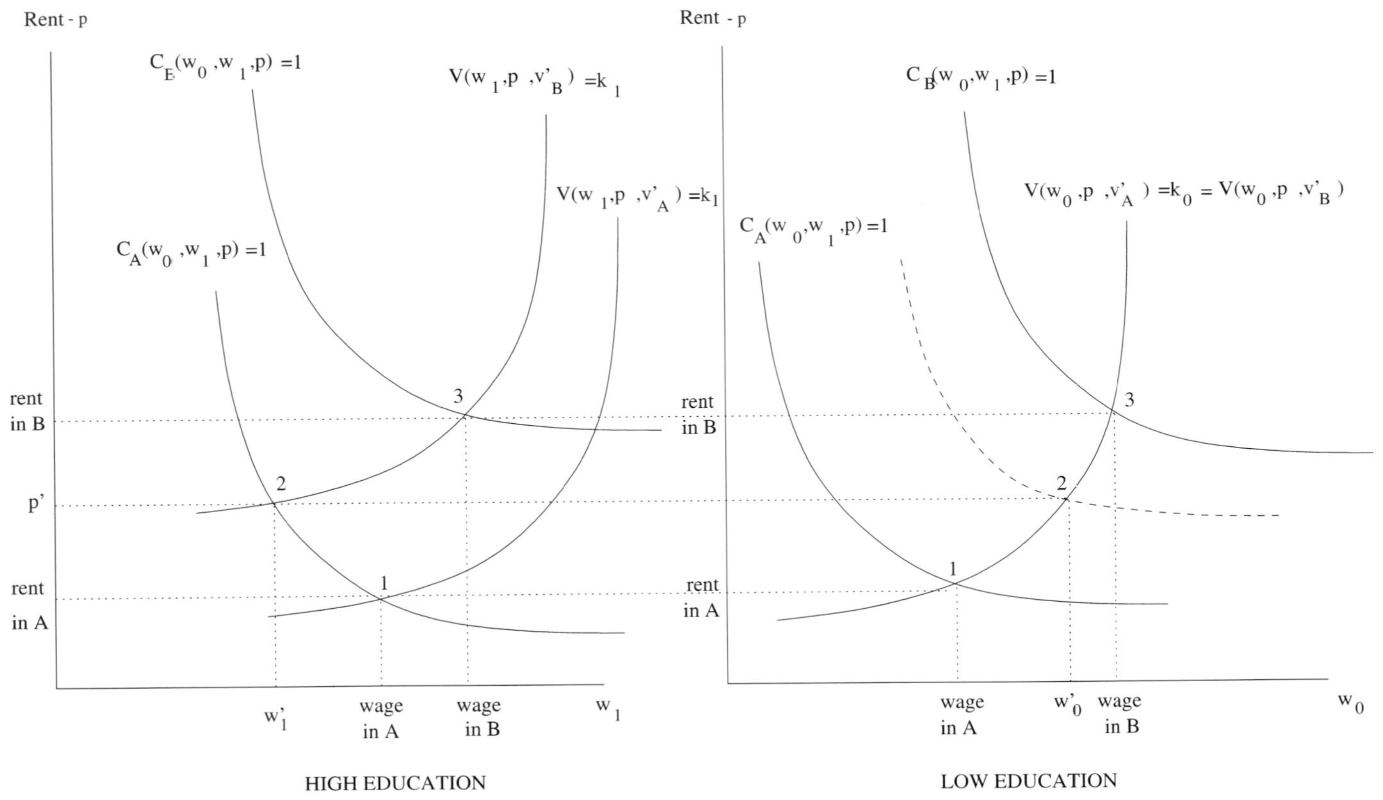

Figure 3. Equilibrium wages and rent when amenities differ across cities. Point 1 is the equilibrium in city A. Point 2 is the equilibrium in city B without spillover. Point 3 is the equilibrium in city B with spillover. The dashed lines in both panels are the isocost curves in city B without spillover. w_1 and w_0 are the nominal wage of educated and uneducated workers, respectively.

to equilibrium wages when the relative supply of educated workers is higher in B than in A.

One way of making the relative supply of educated workers higher in B than in A is to assume that city B has an higher level of the local amenity than city A ($v'_B > v'_A$) and educated workers value the amenity, while uneducated workers do not. It is important to note that, in this general framework, I interpret v' broadly, as any *exogenous* factor that increases the relative supply of educated workers.

As shown in Figure 3, the indifference curve at level k_1 of educated workers in city B is to the left of the corresponding curve in city A, while the indifference curve for uneducated workers does not change. In this context, even without externalities, the wage of the uneducated workers is higher. If there are no spillovers, the increase in the supply of educated workers in city B raises the wage of uneducated workers to w'_0 and lowers the wage of educated ones to w'_1 (point 2 in both panels of Figure 3). This is the standard result. Because of imperfect substitution, uneducated workers are now more productive in city B and because of the amenity, educated workers accept lower wages there.[13]

In the presence of spillovers, however, the combinations of wages and rents that hold firms' costs constant in city B lies to the right of the corresponding combination in city A for both groups (point 3). For educated workers, the shift of the isocost curve is caused by the spillover only; for uneducated workers the shift is caused by both complementarity (movement from 1 to 2) and the spillover (movement from 2 to 3). The distinction between complementarity and spillovers is important both for theoretical reasons as well as for policy implications. (Complementarity is clearly not a market failure). Below, I discuss how it is possible to empirically distinguish between complementarity and spillovers.

So far I have considered the case where differences in the relative number of educated workers in city A and city B are driven by differences in the relative supply. I now turn to the case where differences in the relative number of educated workers are driven by differences in the relative demand for educated workers. In Figure 4 cities are identical in term of amenities, but differ in term of technology, T. I interpret T broadly, as any *exogenous* factor that increases the relative productivity of educated workers and therefore their relative demand. To make technology differences more explicit in Figure 4, T appears in the isocost: $C(w_0, w_1, p, T)$. (Since cities are identical, the amenity is dropped from the indifference curves.) Suppose that, because of technological differences, skilled workers are particularly productive in city B and demand for them is high. Attracted by higher wages, skilled workers move to city B. In so doing, they raise average education there. Point 2 represents the equilibrium in city B if there are no spillovers. The wage of educated workers is higher because technology makes them

[13] For simplicity, we follow Roback (1982) and take the level of utility k_1 and k_0 as parameters for simplicity. Closure of the model would require that the level of utility is made endogenous. This would complicate the model, without changing its implications.

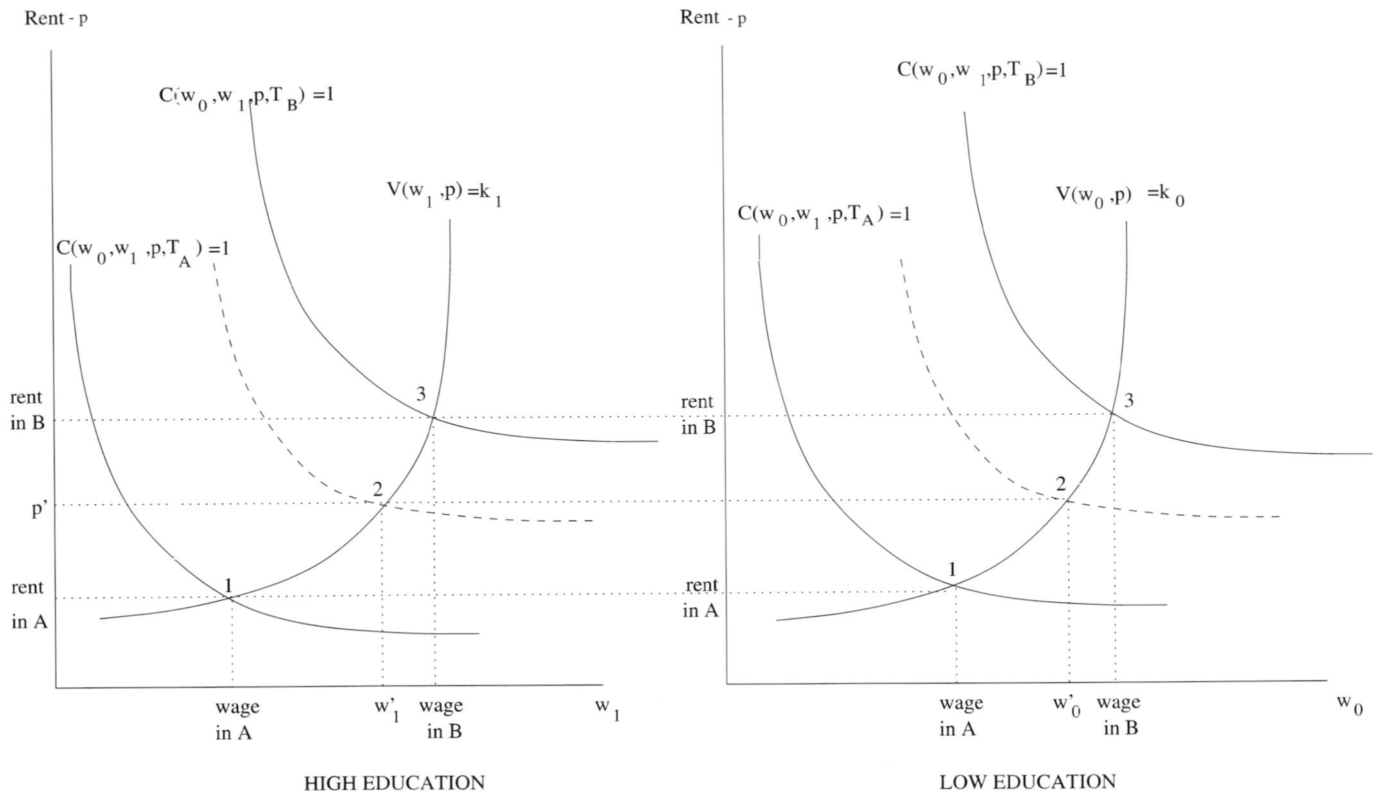

Figure 4. Equilibrium wages and rent when technology differs across cities. Point 1 is the equilibrium in city A. Point 2 is the equilibrium in city B without spillover. Point 3 is the equilibrium in city B with spillover. The dashed line in the right panel is the isocost curve in city B without spillover. w_1 and w_0 are the nominal wage of educated and uneducated workers, respectively.

more productive, while the wage of uneducated workers is higher because of complementarity. In the presence of spillovers effects, the isocost curve shifts further to the right. In this case, the true spillover effect is a shift from 2 to 3, but the observed effect is larger, from 1 to 3.

In equilibrium, both skill groups are present in both cities. Since workers are free to migrate from city A to city B, why are equilibrium wages – net of the compensating differential – not driven to equality? In this model, migration to high-wage cities leads to higher rent, making workers indifferent between cities. Although in equilibrium workers in cities with higher human capital earn higher nominal wages than workers in cities with low human capital, in real terms workers in cities with high human capital are not better off because land is more expensive.[14] A similar intuition holds for firms. Since firms are free to relocate from A to B, why is productivity not driven to equality? Wages and rent are higher in city B, making firms indifferent between cities.

Note that in this context, where cities are small open economies that face a perfectly elastic supply of labor at a fixed utility level, landowners in cities with high levels of human capital are the only real beneficiaries of the spillovers. Because land is the only immobile factor in this model, all the rent generated by the externality in terms of increased productivity is capitalized in land prices. The policy implications are not obvious. On one hand, the common U.S. system of financing public education with local property taxes seems efficient. Since landowners are the beneficiaries of the spillover, taxing land may work to internalize the externality. On the other hand, workers are mobile and heterogeneous in their tastes, and localities differ in their amenities. Under these circumstances, it is possible that municipalities that invest heavily in schooling may retain only some of the benefits. Black and Henderson (1999) present a theoretical discussion of whether local governments can successfully internalize human capital externalities.[15] And Bound et al. (in press) undertake an empirical investigation of the mobility of college graduates and its implications for local and state education policies.

It is important to realize that the model presented here assumes that cities are small relative to the whole economy, and face a perfectly elastic supply of labor at a fixed utility level, so that technology shocks do not affect the average technology for the whole economy. If the number of cities is limited and cities are large relative to the whole economy, conclusions are different, because general equilibrium effects may arise. For example, if a large city experience a large technology shock, this will result in an improvement of the average technology for the whole economy, and utility levels will in general rise.

[14] Other models achieve the same result assuming that quality of life is declining in the size of the city [Glaeser, Scheinkman and Shleifer (1995)].

[15] Black and Henderson (1999) use a dynamic framework that is more general than the one presented here, because it allows spillovers to affect economic growth.

4.1.2. Implications for empirical analysis

The model developed in the previous section predicts that the productivity of firms is higher in cities with higher overall levels of human capital. Because workers are more productive, wages are also higher in cities with higher overall levels of human capital. But for this to be an equilibrium, land prices must adjust to make workers and firms indifferent. A useful implication of this model is that there are three possible empirical strategies to identify the magnitude of human capital spillovers. We can compare productivity, wages or land prices between cities.

Using the first metric, the magnitude of the spillover can be identified by taking the difference in the unit cost functions in city A, the city with low levels of human capital, and city B, the city with high levels of human capital, holding constant the price of factors:

$$\ln c(w_{0\mathrm{A}}, w_{1\mathrm{A}}, p, S_{\mathrm{A}}) - \ln c(w_{0\mathrm{A}}, w_{1\mathrm{A}}, p, S_{\mathrm{B}}). \quad (1)$$

If there are spillovers, unit costs are lower in city B than in city A, holding constant wages and land prices.[16] Although appealing in theory, an estimation strategy based on the comparison of unit costs across cities like the one suggested by Equation (1) is hard to implement in practice because of data limitations. Large scale datasets with information on production costs for many firms in many cities are hard to obtain.

On the other hand, data on inputs and output are more readily available.[17] So, instead of identifying spillovers by comparing unit costs of otherwise identical plants located in cities with high and low levels of human capital and holding input prices fixed, one can more easily identify spillovers by comparing the output of otherwise identical plants located in cities with high and low levels of human capital, holding input quantities fixed. In the notation of the simple example in the previous section, spillovers can be measured by taking the difference in the production functions of city B and city A, holding labor and capital constant:

$$\ln\big[f(S_{\mathrm{A}})g(N_0, N_1, K)\big] - \ln\big[f(S_{\mathrm{B}})g(N_0, N_1, K)\big] = \ln f(S_{\mathrm{A}}) - \ln f(S_{\mathrm{B}}). \quad (2)$$

The second option is to measure the magnitude of the spillovers in term of land prices. The model in the previous section shows that the spillover is capitalized in land prices. If data on property values in different cities are available, estimates of the spillovers can be obtained by simply measuring differences in land prices between cities with high levels of human capital and cities with low levels of human capital. In terms of the example in the previous section, the magnitude of the spillover is simply the difference in housing

[16] Note that I now write the cost function c as a function of human capital in the city. This reduced form representation of the cost function captures the idea that in cities with higher human capital, total factor productivity is higher, so the same amount of output can be produced with less inputs.

[17] The most prominent example is the Census of Manufacturers, which provides longitudinal data on the universe of U.S. manufacturing establishments with 1 employee or more. The Census of Manufacturers has detailed information on output produces as well as capital and labor used in production.

prices between city B and city A: $(p_{\mathrm{B}} - p')$. Graphically, this is the difference in rent between point 2 and point 3 in Figure 3 or 4.

Two caveats need to be considered. First, the model assumes that land is fixed, which may not be always true. Second, there is the issue of how to empirically measure $(p_{\mathrm{B}} - p')$. Because data on land prices are difficult to obtain, researchers often rely on housing prices (adjusted for housing characteristics), which are readily available for most large cities (for example in the Census of Population and Housing). One limitation of using housing prices is that the stock of housing is not necessarily fixed.

Finally, one can use wages to measure spillovers. Most of the existing empirical studies that attempt to quantify the magnitude of human capital spillovers have focused on wages. In theory, one might think of using the difference in the wage of educated workers, $(w_{1\mathrm{B}} - w_1')$, or the difference in the wage of uneducated workers $(w_{0\mathrm{B}} - w_0')$ in the two cities, or a weighted average of the two:

$$\frac{N_1}{N_1 + N_0}(w_{1\mathrm{B}} - w_1') + \frac{N_0}{N_1 + N_0}(w_{0\mathrm{B}} - w_0').$$

Graphically, the difference in the wage of educated workers is the distance between point 2 and point 3 in the left panel of Figure 3 or 4 and the difference in the wage of uneducated workers is the distance between point 2 and point 3 in the right panel of Figure 3 or 4.

Three points are important here. First, nominal wages should be used in the empirical analysis. Wages adjusted for cost of living are not the correct dependent variable. The reason is that higher nominal wages in a city imply greater productivity. If workers were not more productive, firms producing goods that are traded nationally (such as manufacturing goods) would leave high-wage cities and relocate to low-wage cities. Some workers are employed in industries that produce output that is not traded nationally (for example, local services). But firms producing traded goods face the same price everywhere in the nation, so that, as long as there are some firms producing traded goods in every city, average productivity has to be higher in cities where nominal wages are higher [Acemoglu and Angrist (2000)].

Second, it is important to recognize that wage changes affecting workers in a city not only capture human capital spillovers, but also capture the complementarity (or imperfect substitutability) between skilled and unskilled workers. If skilled and unskilled workers are imperfect substitutes, unskilled workers benefit from an increase in the number of skilled workers even in the absence of any externality. Therefore, the average effect on wages,

$$\frac{N_1}{N_1 + N_0}(w_{1\mathrm{B}} - w_1') + \frac{N_0}{N_1 + N_0}(w_{0\mathrm{B}} - w_0')$$

reflects both the spillover effect and imperfect substitution between high- and low-education workers. The distinction is important, because, unlike human capital externalities, complementarity is not a market failure. In Section 4.2.1, I formally show the difference between complementarity and spillovers and I suggests two ways to empirically separate the two.

Finally, even controlling for the complementarity effect, the difference in wages between cities with high and low human capital is not exactly equal to the spillover, because land prices also adjust. Only in the case where no land is used in commercial production will the wage difference between cities with high and low human capital equal the spillover.

4.1.3. The consequences of unobserved heterogeneity

The discussion so far has ignored the possible presence of confounding factors that may introduce spurious correlation in the relationship between wages (or productivity or land prices) and aggregate human capital. There are many unobserved characteristics of workers and cities that affect wages and at the same time may be correlated with the overall level of human capital. A goal of the model is to identify potential sources of unobserved heterogeneity that might bias empirical estimates of the human capital spillover.

In the stylized framework developed in Section 4.1.1, unobserved heterogeneity is of two types: demand shocks that affect the relative productivity of workers with high human capital in a city; and supply shocks, that affect the relative attractiveness of a city for high human capital workers. As mentioned above, these demand and supply shocks need to be interpreted broadly, as any factor that affects the relative demand or supply of skilled workers and that is unmeasured by the econometrician.

In the presence of unobserved heterogeneity that is correlated with aggregate human capital, OLS regressions of wages on aggregate human capital can be biased upward or downward depending on the relative magnitude of unobserved demand and supply heterogeneity. To see this, consider first Figure 3, where variation in the relative number of educated workers across cities is driven by *supply* factors. To the extent that the amenity that attracts skilled workers to city B is not observed, this unobserved heterogeneity biases the OLS coefficient in a regression of wages of educated workers on share of educated workers *downward*. In Figure 3 (left panel), the true spillover is the difference between the wage at point 3 and the wage at point 2. The observed effect is instead the difference between the wage in point 3 and the wage in point 1, which is smaller than the true spillover. The intuition is straightforward. The compensating differential that skilled workers implicitly pay for the amenity is unobserved, and enters the wage of skilled workers as a negative city-specific residual. The correlation between this residual and average education is negative, as skilled workers trade some of their wage for the amenity, so that the OLS coefficient on average education is biased down.

The opposite bias arises from heterogeneity in relative labor demand. Consider Figure 4. The size of the spillover is the size of the shift from 2 to 3. But if T is unobserved, the OLS coefficient in a regression of wages of educated workers on share of educated workers assigns all of the observed correlation between wages and average education to the spillover, and yields an estimate of the spillover that is upward biased (the size of the shift from 1 to 3). Again, the intuition is clear. A positive unobserved shock to the

The wage of uneducated workers, w_0, benefits for two reasons. First, an increase in the number of educated workers raises uneducated workers' productivity because of imperfect substitution:

$$\frac{1-\alpha_0}{1-s}+\frac{\alpha_1}{s}>0.$$

Second, the spillover further raises their productivity: $(\alpha_1+\alpha_0)\gamma>0$. The impact of an increase in the supply of educated workers on their own wage, w_1, is determined by two competing forces, as I mentioned above: the first is the conventional supply effect which makes the economy move along a downward sloping demand curve:

$$\frac{\alpha_1-1}{s}-\frac{\alpha_0}{1-s}<0.$$

The second is the spillover that raises productivity.

The important feature of Equations (5) and (6) is that unskilled workers benefit from an increase in the share of educated workers in the city even in the absence of any spillovers ($\gamma=0$), but the effect on the wage of skilled workers depends on the magnitude of the spillover. If γ is large enough, the net effect for skilled workers should be positive although smaller than for unskilled workers. If $\gamma=0$, the net effect should be negative.

It is interesting to notice that an increase in the number of educated workers in a city may raise the average wage above the private return to schooling even in the absence of any spillovers ($\gamma=0$). To see this, take the derivative of average wage with respect to s minus the private return β:

$$\frac{\mathrm{d}\log(\overline{w})}{\mathrm{d}s}-\beta=s\frac{\mathrm{d}\beta}{\mathrm{d}s}+\frac{\mathrm{d}\log(w_0)}{\mathrm{d}s}+(\alpha_1+\alpha_0)\gamma, \tag{7}$$

where $\log(\overline{w})$ is the weighted average of log wages of the two groups, $\log(\overline{w})=s\log(w_1)+(1-s)\log(w_0)$; and β is the private return, defined as the difference between the wage of educated and uneducated workers $\beta=\log(w_1)-\log(w_0)$. The first component in Equation (7) is the effect of an increase of educated workers on the private return to education. This effect is negative, because as the supply of educated workers in a city increases, the private return decreases. The second effect captures the imperfect substitution between educated and uneducated workers, and is positive. The third effect reflects the spillover. In the U.S., the share of college-educated workers, s, is approximately 0.25. Therefore, the sum of the first two components,

$$s\frac{\mathrm{d}\beta}{\mathrm{d}s}+\frac{\mathrm{d}\log(w_0)}{\mathrm{d}s}=\frac{(1-s)\alpha_1-s\alpha_0}{s(1-s)}$$

is positive if the share of output that goes to college-educated workers is more than a third of the share of output that goes to less-educated workers: $\alpha_1>0.33\alpha_0$. In this case, the increase in productivity for low-education workers more than offsets the effect of the decrease in the private return to education and an increase in s raises average wages over and above the private return to schooling even in the absence of spillovers.

The distinction between imperfect substitutability and spillovers is important for the interpretation of empirical estimates. Finding that *average* wages are affected by aggregate human capital does not necessarily indicate a spillover effect: rather this finding may indicate imperfect substitution between high- and low-educated workers. This distinction is relevant not only for theoretical reasons, but also for policy reasons. The standard imperfect substitution effect is not itself a market failure. However, if human capital spillovers exist, a market failure may occur. This depends on whether the spillover takes place within or outside the firm. It is in theory possible that within-firm spillovers are reflected in the wages of educated workers, so that no market failure arises. If the spillover has effects outside the firm, however, it is likely to be a pure externality.[19]

If the spillover effect is not constant across groups (γ_j instead of γ), it is not empirically possible to separately identify externalities and imperfect substitutability. However, under the assumption that the spillover effect γ is constant across education groups, there are two ways to empirically distinguish between imperfect substitutability and externalities. First, one can estimate separate effects of changes in the fraction of highly educated workers on wages of different education groups [for example, Moretti (in press)]. By comparing the effect of an increase in the share of college graduates across education groups, it is in theory possible to shed some light on the size of the spillover. Standard demand and supply considerations suggest that the effect of an increase in college share should be positive for low-education groups and that for college graduates its sign should depend on the size of the spillover. If the spillover is strong enough, the effect for skilled workers is positive although lower than the one for unskilled workers.

Second, Ciccone and Peri (2002) propose an alternative approach – called the "constant-composition approach" – to estimate human capital externalities when highly educated workers and less-educated workers are imperfect substitutes. They propose estimating the effect of average schooling on average wages across cities, holding the relative size of each skill group constant through a re-weighting scheme. This is obtained by first estimating a city–year–education group specific conditional average wage, and then regressing these cell averages on average schooling, weighting the regression by the size of the group in a base year. The intuition is that weighting makes it possible to separate complementarity from spillovers by holding the skill distribution of the labor force in the city constant.

4.2.2. *Econometric specification*

Most of the direct evidence on the magnitude of the spillovers is based on models that regress wage on measures of the aggregate stock of human capital. The basic source

[19] One can think of the "imperfect substitutability effect" as a form of pecuniary externality. However, this type of pecuniary externality is very different from the pecuniary externalities proposed by Acemoglu that I discussed in Section 3.1.

of identification therefore consists of the comparison of wages for otherwise similar individuals who work in cities with different aggregate human capital. Typically, authors have estimated variations of the following equation

$$\log(w_{ict}) = X_{it}\beta_{ct} + \pi P_{ct} + \alpha Z_{ct} + d_c + d_t + u_{ict}, \tag{8}$$

where w_{ict} is wage of individual i living in city c in period t; X_{it} is a vector of individual characteristics, including years of schooling; P_{ct} represents a measure of aggregate human capital in city c in year t; Z_{ct} is a vector of city characteristics which may be correlated with P_{ct}; d_c represents a city fixed effect; and d_t is a year effect.

The coefficient of interest is π, which is the estimate of the effect of aggregate human capital on average wages after controlling for the private return to education. Typically, authors have measured aggregate human capital in a city, P_{ct}, using either average years of schooling or the percent of individuals with a college education. Ciccone and Peri (2002) show the conditions under which Equation (8) can be derived from the standard framework used in theoretical macro economics to model the effect of human capital on economic growth at the aggregate level [see for example, Lucas (1988) or Bils and Klenow (2000)].

A source of confusion in the existing literature has been the issue of whether nominal or real wages would be used in estimating Equation (8). From the model of Section 4.1, it should by now be clear that *nominal* wages (i.e., wages unadjusted for cost of living) are the appropriate dependent variable in Equation (8) and that no control for cost of living need to be included in Z_{ct}. In equilibrium, higher nominal wages in a city should reflect greater productivity. Although workers may be indifferent between high nominal wages and high rents on one hand, and low nominal wages and low rent on the other hand, firms still are willing to pay high nominal wages presumably only if workers are more productive.

The wage equation residual can be thought as the sum of three components:

$$u_{ict} = \mu_c\theta_i + \nu_{ct} + \varepsilon_{ict}, \tag{9}$$

where θ_i is a permanent unobservable component of individual human capital, such as ability or family background; μ_c is a factor loading which represents the return to unobserved skill in city c; ν_{ct} represents time-varying shocks to labor demand and supply in city c in period t; ε_{ict} is the transitory component of log wages which is assumed to be independently and identically distributed over individuals, cities and time.

A first source of omitted variable bias is the presence of time-varying shocks to local labor markets that are correlated with aggregate human capital. Cities differ widely in geographical location, industrial structure, technology, weather and amenities. City fixed effects sweep out the effect of *permanent* city characteristics such as the industrial structure and physical and cultural amenities that might bias a simpler cross-sectional analysis. But first-differenced models may still be biased by the presence of *time-varying* factors that are correlated with changes in human capital and wages across cities – for example, transitory productivity shocks that attract highly educated workers and raise wages: $\mathrm{cov}(\nu_{ct}, S_{ct}) \neq 0$. As argued in Section 4.1.3, the resulting OLS bias is positive (negative) if positive shocks to wages are associated with increases (decreases) in the human capital stock in a city. For example, the San Jose economy experienced an unprecedented economic expansion starting in the second half of the 1980s that was driven by the Silicon Valley computer industry boom. The same boom attracted a highly educated labor force to San Jose. On the other hand, if variation in human capital stock across cities is driven by unobserved *supply* factors, OLS is biased downward.

A second source of omitted variable bias is the presence of unobserved worker characteristics if individuals observed in cities with high human capital are better workers than individuals with the same observable characteristics who live in cities with low human capital. In terms of Equation (8), this implies that $\text{cov}(\theta_i, P_{ct}) > 0$. For example, a high-school graduate working in a biotechnology firm in San Francisco is probably different along some unobservable dimension from a high-school graduate working in a shoe factory in Miami. Similarly, a lawyer working for a Wall-Street firm in New York is likely to differ from a lawyer in El Paso, TX. This type of sorting may take place if a higher overall level of human capital in a city is associated with a higher return to unobserved ability, causing higher quality workers to move to cities with higher college share [Borjas, Bronars and Trejo (1992), Rauch (1993)]. Consider a simple Roy model where different cities reward workers' skills – both observed and unobserved – differently, and mobility decisions are based on comparative advantage. In such a model, workers are not randomly assigned to cities, but choose the city where their skills are most valued and skill–price differentials determine the skill composition of migratory flows. Cities that have an industrial structure that demands more education are also likely to offer a higher price for unobserved ability. In this case, the correlation of high P_{ct} with high wages may simply reflect higher unobserved ability of workers rather than higher productivity.

4.2.3. *Accounting for the endogeneity of human capital*

In an ideal analysis, the researcher could randomly assign different overall levels of human capital across cities and measure differences in the value of wages before sorting occurs. This experimental design would solve the econometric problems discussed in Section 4.1.3. (Note, however, that the experimental design would not solve the problem of distinguishing between complementarity and externalities discussed in Section 4.2.1). In its absence, three strategies can be used to account for endogeneity of overall levels of human capital.

First, some authors have tried accounting for time-varying shocks by controlling for observable characteristics of cities, such as racial composition or unemployment rate. It is particularly important to fully control for shocks to the relative demand for skilled labor, as they lead to overestimates of the spillover. In an effort to accomplish this goal, some researchers have used an index of demand shifts proposed by Katz and Murphy (1992). The index, a generalization of a widely used measure of between-sector demand shifts, is based on nation-wide employment growth in industries, weighted by the city-specific employment share in those industries. It captures exogenous shifts in the relative demand for different education groups that are predicted by the city industry mix.[20]

One limitation of this approach is that it is hard to argue persuasively that observables can fully account for shocks. For this reason, some studies have turned to instrumental variable techniques. This approach requires an instrument that is correlated with changes in the overall level of human capital in a city and uncorrelated with changes in unobserved factors that affect wages directly. Examples of instrumental variable used are compulsory schooling laws, child labor laws, the entry of the baby boom cohort into the labor market, and the presence of land grant colleges. The advantage of instrumental variable techniques is that a valid instrument isolates the effect of exogenous changes in human capital levels on wages. The disadvantages are that valid, exogenous instruments are rare. Furthermore, if the effect of overall human capital on wages is not homogeneous, IV estimates and OLS estimates may not be directly comparable.

As a third possible identification strategy, individual-level longitudinal data have been used. By observing the same individual over time, one can control for factors that make an individual permanently more productive. But note that if longitudinal data on multiple individuals and cities are available, individual fixed effects models are not the most general model that can be estimated. In particular, the term $\mu_c\theta_i$ in Equation (8) can be absorbed by including a set of individual $\times$ city dummies. By controlling for the individual–city match, variation that comes from movers is lost. Identification is based on stayers and comes from changes of P in a city over time. *Conditional on a city–individual match*, the longitudinal model estimates what happens to an individual's wage as aggregate human capital around her increases. The key identifying assumption is that the return to unobserved ability μ_c may vary across cities, but not over time or, if it does change over time, the change is not systematically correlated with the stock of human capital. Under this assumption, differences in the level of unobserved ability and in return to unobserved ability across cities are absorbed by individual $\times$ city fixed effects. One limitation of this longitudinal strategy is that stayers are not necessarily a random sample of the population. If stayers are different from other workers, longitudinal estimates may be biased.

[20] Different cities specialize in the production of different goods, so that industry-specific demand shocks at the national level have a differential impact on cities [Bound and Holzer (1996)]. If employment of skilled workers in a given industry increases (decreases) nationally, cities where that industry employs a significant share of the labor force will experience a positive (negative) shock to the labor demand of skilled workers. Formally, the index is

$$\text{shock}_{jc} = \sum_{s=1} \eta_{sc} \Delta E_{js}, \tag{10}$$

where s indexes two-digit industry; shock_{jc} represents the predicted employment change for workers belonging to education group j in city c; η_{sc} is the share of total hours worked in industry s in city c in 1980; ΔE_{js} is the change in the log of total hours worked in the same industry nationally between 1980 and 1990 by workers belonging to education group j. See, for example, Moretti (in press).

4.2.4. Empirical findings of wage and land price models

I now turn to a discussion of some of the empirical evidence on the magnitude of human capital externalities generated by wage models. What do we know about the magnitude of human capital spillovers? There is some indirect evidence that human capital spillover may play a role in increasing income and growth. For example, Glaeser, Scheinkman and Shleifer (1995) report that income per capita has grown faster in cities with high initial human capital in the post-war period. Findings in Glaeser and Mare (2001) arc consistent with a model where individuals acquire skills by interacting with one another, and dense urban areas increase the probability of interaction.

Yet, despite these significant policy implications, there is remarkably little systematic empirical evidence on the magnitude of human capital spillovers. Researchers have only recently begun to estimate the size of spillovers from education by comparing the wages of otherwise similar individuals in cities or states with different average levels of education. Most of these wage studies have used variants of the wage equations in Equation (8).

Rauch (1993) often cited study is the first to exploit differences in human capital across cities to identify externalities. Using the 1980 Census, he estimates a cross sectional version of Equation (8) and finds that a one year increase in average education raises wages by 3 to 5 percent in 1980. Rauch is also one of the very few researchers to examine the effect of human capital on the cost of housing. He finds that the cost of housing is higher in cities with a larger stock of human capital (holding constant housing characteristics), and concludes that spillover appear to be capitalized in land prices. A limitation of Rauch's methodology is that he does not directly account for the endogeneity of aggregate human capital. Rauch uses only one cross section and treats average schooling as historically predetermined. A second limitation is that he does not distinguish between externalities and complementarity between skilled and unskilled workers.

The correlation between wages and one measure of the overall level of human capital is shown in Figure 5, where the percentage of college graduates is plotted against the regression-adjusted average wage for 282 cities in 1990.[21] The regression-adjusted average wage is obtained by conditioning on individual education, gender, race, Hispanic origin, U.S. citizenship, and a quadratic term in potential experience. The figure shows that, *after controlling for the private return to education*, wages are higher in cities where the labor force is better educated.[22] Obviously, it is far from clear whether the association between wages and human capital uncovered in Figure 5 reflects human capital spillovers. As argued in detail in Section 4.1.3, this correlation is likely to be biased by the presence of unmeasured characteristics of workers and cities that are

[21] Calculations by the author based on the 1990 Census.

[22] Similar figures can be obtained by plotting housing cost or firms productivity against aggregate human capital.

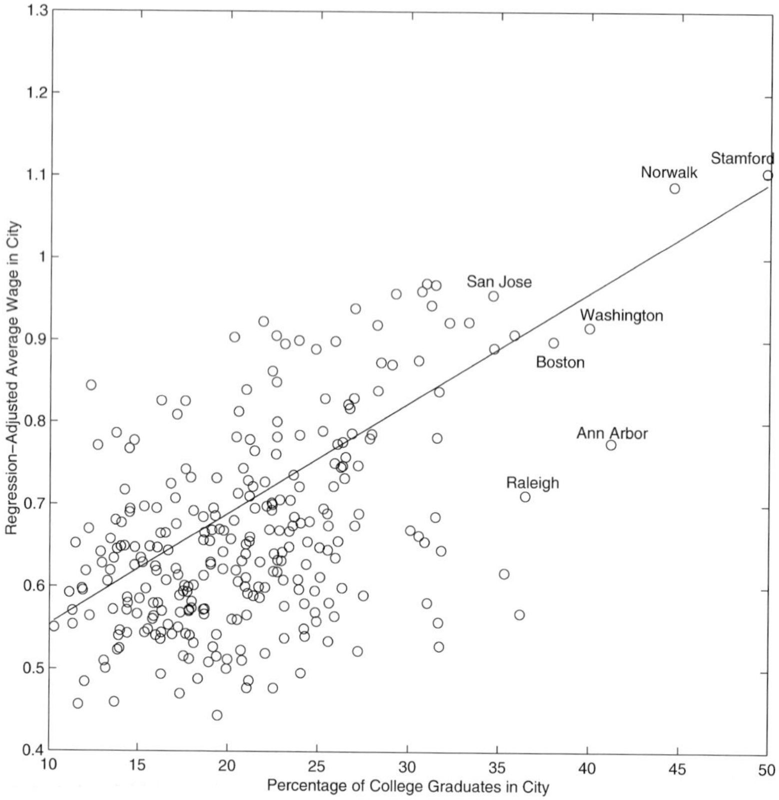

Figure 5. Correlation between regression-adjusted average wage and percentage of college graduates in 282 cities, in 1990. Regression-adjusted average wage is obtained by conditioning on individual education, gender, race, Hispanic origin, U.S. citizenship and work experience. Weighted OLS fit superimposed.

potentially correlated with the fraction of college-educated individuals across cities. Although we know that the correlation is likely to be biased, we do not know the direction of the bias. The OLS coefficient in a regression of wages on share of educated workers can be biased either downward or upward, depending on whether variation in the relative number of college-educated workers across cities is driven by unobserved *supply* factors or unobserved *demand* factors. And even if we could account for the endogeneity of college share, from the simple graph in Figure 5 we cannot distinguish between complementarities and externalities (Section 4.2.1).

Moretti (in press) attempts to address the endogeneity created by city-wide demand shocks using two instrumental variables. The first instrument is based on differences in the age structure of cities. The U.S. labor force is characterized by a long-run trend of increasing education, with younger cohorts better-educated than older ones. The second instrument used is an indicator for the presence of a land-grant college in the city.

Land-grant colleges were established by the federal Morrill Act of 1862.[23] He also tries to account for unobserved individual ability by exploiting the panel structure of the National Longitudinal Survey of Youth (NLSY) to estimate models that condition on individual × city effects.

Moretti finds that a one percentage point increase in college share in a city raises average wages by 0.6–1.2%, above and beyond the private return to education. As argued in previous sections, the finding that *average* wages are affected by the percentage of college graduates in the labor force does not necessarily indicate a spillover effect: rather this finding may indicate imperfect substitution between high- and low-education workers. For this reason, Moretti estimates the effect of changes in the fraction of highly educated workers on wages of different education groups. He finds that a one percentage point increase in the labor force share of college graduates increases the wages of high-school drop-outs and high-school graduates by 1.9 and 1.6%, respectively. It also increases wages of college graduates by 0.4%. This findings are consistent with a model that includes both conventional demand and supply factors as well as spillovers: as expected, an increase in the proportion of better-educated workers has a large positive effect on less-educated workers, and a smaller but still positive effect on the wages of the best-educated group.

Acemoglu and Angrist (2000) use state variation in child labor and compulsory school attendance laws to instrument for average schooling. They show that within state changes in these laws affect the education distribution at the "right" point, by increasing the probability of high-school graduation but not college graduation. Unlike Rauch and Moretti, Acemoglu and Angrist (2000) also address the endogeneity of individual schooling. They point out that inconsistent estimates of the private return to education will lead to inconsistent estimates of the externality, because individual and aggregate schooling are correlated.

To account for the endogeneity of individual schooling, they use quarter of birth as an instrumental variable. While their OLS estimates of the externality are qualitatively consistent with Rauch's and Moretti's OLS estimates, their IV estimates are smaller and in most cases not significantly different from zero.

The difference in findings between Acemoglu and Angrist (2000) and Moretti can be explained in part by the fact that child labor and compulsory attendance laws affect educational attainment in the lower part of the educational distribution, mostly in middle school or high school. On the contrary, Moretti identifies externalities using variation in the number of college graduates, i.e., the upper part of the distribution. It appears that a one year rise in a city's average education resulting from an increase in the number of those who finish high school has a different effect than a similar increase resulting from an increase in the number of those who go to college. A second factor that may account for the difference in estimates is the fact that Acemoglu and Angrist's analysis is at the

[23] Because the program was federal and took place more than one hundred years ago, the presence of a land-grant institution is unlikely to be correlated with local labor market conditions in the 1980s.

state level. When Moretti estimates state-level spillovers, he finds coefficients closer to those of Acemoglu and Angrist.[24]

Ciccone and Peri (2002) propose a new econometric approach – the "constant-composition approach" – to estimate human capital externalities when highly educated workers and less-educated workers are imperfect substitutes. This new approach is a generalization of the approach based on Mincer wage equations like Equation (8), and is to date the most comprehensive attempt to distinguish between complementarity and externalities. The constant-composition approach consists of estimating the effect of average schooling on average wages across cities, holding the relative size of each skill group constant with a re-weighting scheme. The weights are based on the size of each skill group in a base year.

While the re-weighting procedure accounts for the possibility of complementarity between skilled and unskilled workers, Ciccone and Peri (2002) also use a set of instrumental variables to account for the endogeneity of aggregate human capital. When they constrain highly educated workers and less-educated workers to be perfect substitutes, Ciccone and Peri (2002) find significant positive externalities, with magnitudes consistent with estimates in Rauch and Moretti. However, when they allow for imperfect substitutability, they find little evidence of positive human capital spillovers.

In a related paper, Peri (2002) models the location decisions of young and old workers as a function of human capital externalities. Using Census data, he begins by showing that the experience premium is higher in urban areas than in rural areas. For example, in 1990 a college-educated urban White male received a $2 hourly premium over the wage of a similar non-urban worker. The premium for a mature White worker was twice as large. This result indicates that young educated workers receive a lower wage premium in urban areas than their older colleagues, but in spite of this, they are overrepresented in urban areas. Why do urban areas attracts young educated workers? Peri argues that learning externalities are an important explanation. Workers learn from each other when they are young, so living in dense urban areas may raise human capital accumulation more than living in a rural area. The negative compensating differential indicates that young workers value such human capital externalities. As they grow older, the importance of knowledge spillovers diminishes, and some of them move toward non-urban areas.[25]

In most empirical applications, the geographic scope of the human capital spillover is taken as exogenous. In Conley, Flyer and Tsiang (in press), however, the scope of the spillover is allowed to vary across individuals. The stock of aggregate human capital that is relevant for an individual is defined using a measure of economic distance based on

[24] A third difference concerns the period under consideration. Most models in Acemoglu and Angrist (2000) are estimated using 1960–1980 Census data. When they add data from the 1990 Census, they find statistically significant positive estimates for the externality, when child labor laws are used as instruments. Since the private return to education increased during the 1980s, this finding may reflect a change in the social value of human capital.

[25] The evidence in Costa and Kahn (2000) offers an alternative to the learning story.

estimates of travel time between locations. They estimate the number and human capital level of potential trading partners within, say, a two hours trip for each individual. By using this economic distance metric rather than administrative geographic units like cities or provinces, they better characterize the human capital of the set of neighbors that potentially interact with each agent. Furthermore, they can identify the geographic scope of the spillover by varying the definition of the local labor market and testing how far two individuals must be for their human capital spillover to have no effect. They find significant instrumental-variable estimates of human capital externalities. They also find that externalities tend to disappear for distances further than a 90 minute trip. Conley et al. also investigate whether human capital spillovers are capitalized in land prices. They find that land prices are positively correlated with human capital stocks.

In sum, the existing *direct* empirical evidence on the magnitude of human capital spillovers is mixed. While most papers find OLS estimates that are consistent with the pattern shown in Figure 5, estimates that attempt to account for the endogeneity of aggregate human capital rarely agree. The differences across studies appear to be mostly due to differences in the particular empirical strategies adopted to account for unobserved heterogeneity. Clearly, more research is needed before we can be confident in our estimates of the magnitude of human capital spillovers.

4.3. Empirical models based on firm productivity

Having analyzed the empirical evidence based on differences in wages and land prices across cities, I now turn to evidence based on differences in productivity levels. The model in Section 4.1 indicates that if externalities exist, we should find that firms located in cities with high levels of human capital produce more output with the same inputs than otherwise similar firms located in cities with low levels of human capital. Furthermore, the model indicates that these differences between cities should coincide with observed differences in wages of workers and land prices. In equilibrium, if firms really are more productive in cities with high levels of human capital, we would expect to find that these firms incur higher labor and land costs. If this was not the case, firms (at least those producing nationally traded goods) would relocate from cities with low human capital to cities with high human capital.

4.3.1. Econometric specification

To see how spillovers can be identified by comparing the productivity of firms in cities with different level of human capital, assume that technology can be described by the following Cobb–Douglas production function:[26]

$$y_{pjct} = A_{pjct} L1_{pjct}^{\alpha_{1j}} L2_{pjct}^{\alpha_{0j}} K_{pjct}^{\beta_j}, \tag{11}$$

[26] This section is based on Moretti (2002).

where y_{pjct} is output of firm p, belonging to industry j, in city c, and year t; j indexes industry; $L1_{pjct}$ is the number of hours worked by skilled workers in the firm; $L2_{pjct}$ is the number of hours worked by unskilled workers; K_{pjct} is capital. As before, assume that A_{pjct} is a function of aggregate human capital outside the firm in the same city and unobservable productivity shocks:

$$\ln A_{pjct} = \gamma \overline{S}_{ct} + \varepsilon_{pjct}, \tag{12}$$

where $\overline{S}_{ct}$ is some measure of the overall stock of human capital among all workers in city c at time t; and ε represent unobserved heterogeneity in productivity. The coefficient of interest is γ, the external effect of education on productivity. If $\gamma = 0$, the model reduces to a standard production function without externalities.

Empirically, the production function (11) can be either estimated directly or estimated using its total factor productivity (TFP) version. The TFP version can be estimated in two steps. Under the assumption that input prices are equal to their marginal product, a plant-specific measure of TFP is easily calculated by subtracting the sum of each input cost share multiplied by the quantity of that input, from the value of the output. This estimate of TFP can then be regressed on aggregate human capital.

Like for wage models, the main concern is that there may be unobservable productivity shocks that are potentially correlated with aggregate human capital. For example, ε may reflect unmeasured firm characteristics such as the quality of machines, patents, the quality of workers and management, and the culture within the firm. Alternatively, ε may capture city characteristics that make some cities more productive than others. These may include the public infrastructure (ports, highways, or airports), weather conditions, the presence of a research universities, and efficiency of local authorities.

In general, if plants with a positive ε tend to be located in cities with a high overall level of human capital, then OLS estimates of overestimate γ.[27]

4.3.2. *Empirical findings of productivity models*

Empirical evidence suggests that knowledge spillovers may be particularly important in certain hi-tech industries. One interesting piece of evidence on knowledge externalities is a well-cited paper by Jaffe, Trajtenberg and Henderson (1993) that shows that references to existing patents that inventors include in their patent applications are likely to come from the same state or metropolitan area as the originating patent application.

[27] A similar point is made graphically in Figure 4. This is the case, for example, if unusually productive entrepreneurs are more likely to seek out productive locations; or if unusually skilled individuals are disproportionately recruited to the most productive locations. The true spillover is the difference in productivity between a plant in point 3 and a plant in point 2. But if the technology that raises productivity of educated workers in city B relative to city A is unobserved to the econometrician, a naive estimate of the spillover is the difference in productivity between a plant in point 3 and a plant in point 1, which overestimates the true spillover.

Because human capital spillovers and knowledge spillovers are invisible, most empirical studies resort to indirect evidence to test for the presence of spillovers. The studies based on wage equations described in the previous section test indirect implications of the spillover hypothesis, rather than directly measuring the spillover itself. But Jaffe, Trajtenberg and Henderson (1993) argue that patent citations offer a direct measure of spillovers, an observable paper trail in the form of citations in patents. Jaffe, Trajtenberg and Henderson (1993) use citation patterns to test the extent to which spillovers are geographically localized. Because patents are publicly available, in the absence of localized spillovers, citations would not depend on the location of the inventor.

The key empirical challenge of the paper is to distinguish between geographic patterns of patent citations caused by spillovers from patterns caused by exogenous sources of agglomeration effects. To address this issue, the authors construct "control" samples of patents that have the same temporal and technological distribution as the patent citations. To identify the presence of externalities, they compare these two patterns of geographic concentration under the assumption that the geographic correlation between the controls and originating patents is only due to exogenous agglomeration forces that are independent of spillovers. The proposed test of localization is whether the correlation is significantly greater for the cited patents than the control patents. Their findings suggest that patents citations are indeed geographically localized and that knowledge spillovers appear to be large.

Adams and Jaffe (1996) also study the composition of the knowledge transfers within and across firms. They use a TFP framework that is related to the one presented in Section 4.3.1, but instead of using the stock of human capital as their main independent variable, they focus on R&D performed in formal research labs. In particular, they postulate that a plant has an "effective stock of knowledge" that is generated in several ways: by learning-by-doing at this and other plants in the same city or industry, by informal research activities performed at the plant, by formal research of the plant's parent firm, and by formal research of other firms in the same city or industry. Empirically, they use manufacturing plant-level data to examine the productivity effects of R&D performed in a plant, outside a plant but inside the parent firm that owns the plant, and in external plants in the same geographical area or industry. They find that spillovers of R&D are important, both within and across firms – a result that is consistent with the notion that the social return to research is higher than the private return.

Interestingly, they find that the effect of parent firm R&D on plant-level productivity is diminished by both the geographical distance and the technological distance between the research lab and the plants. They interpret this finding as a reflection of the fact that communications costs rise with distance. They also provide evidence of within-industry spillover effects: R&D of other firms in the same industry does appear to affect a plant's productivity, holding industry constant. The magnitude of these spillovers is surprisingly large. The marginal product of industry R&D is approximately 40% as large as the marginal product of parent firm research.

Another piece of indirect evidence on the role of human capital spillovers on the productivity of high-tech firms is a recent paper by Zucker, Darby and Brewer (1998).

They argue that geographic differences in specialized human capital across cities is the main determinant of where and when American biotechnology industries developed. In particular, they show that the stock of human capital of outstanding scientists in certain cities – measured in terms of the number of publications reporting genetic-sequence discoveries in academic journals – plays a key role in the entry decisions of new biotech firms. This effect seems to reflect, at least in part, human capital externalities, because it is not just a reflection of the presence of universities and government research centers in areas where outstanding scientists are located.[28]

The studies described so far focus on high-tech industries. Moretti (2002) attempts to systematically assess the magnitude of human capital externalities in all industries by estimating production functions similar to those in Equation (11). Using longitudinal data, he estimates establishment-level production functions controlling for establishment-specific permanent heterogeneity, as well as time-varying industry-specific and state-specific heterogeneity. Moretti finds that productivity gains from human capital spillovers appear to be empirically relevant for manufacturing establishments in U.S. cities. However, because the stock of human capital grows slowly over time, the contribution of human capital spillovers to economic growth does not appear to be large. Estimates in the paper indicate that human capital spillovers were responsible for an average of 0.1% increase in output per year during the 1980s.[29] Most of the estimated spillover comes from high-tech plants. For non-high-tech producers, the spillover appears to be virtually zero.

Importantly, the magnitude of spillovers between plants in the same city appear to depend on their level of interaction. If input–output tables are used to measure the interaction between plants in the same city, spillovers between plants that often interact are found to be significant, while spillovers between plants that rarely interact are much smaller. This is consistent with the notion that human capital spillovers decay not only with geographic distance, but also with economic distance.

Consistent with the predictions of the theoretical model presented in Section 4.1.1, the productivity gains generated by human capital spillover appear to be offset by increased labor costs. Findings indicate that the estimated productivity differences between cities with high human capital and low human capital coincide with observed differences in wages of manufacturing workers.

4.3.3. Empirical findings of country-wide models

Although many empirical studies use cities as their unit of analysis, some studies focus on the effect of nation-wide increases in human capital on national income.[30] In gen-

[28] Audretsch and Stephan (1996) use data on IPO of biotech firms to link the location of the biotechnology firm with the location of the university-based scientists affiliated with the firm. They conclude that "while proximity matters in establishing formal ties between university-based scientists and companies, its influence is anything but overwhelming".

[29] For the average manufacturing plant in the U.S., this amounts to about $10,000 per year.

[30] See, for example, Topel (1999), Krueger and Lindahl (1998), and Bils and Klenow (2000).

eral, cities have several advantages over states, regions and countries. First, most of the geographical scope of knowledge spillover is likely to be local. Workers interact mostly at the local level. Although communications technologies like phones, e-mail and the Internet allow low-cost communication across cities, most of the interactions between individuals take place in a limited amount of space. If anything, one may argue that local spillovers are likely to arise at the neighborhood level as well as at the city level.

Second, cities are more specialized and less arbitrary economic units than countries. National boundaries that limit labor and capital mobility and national policies that encourage industrial diversification reduce the gain from factor mobility [Glaeser, Scheinkman and Shleifer (1995)].

Third, countries differ along so many variables that it is hard to interpret cross-country estimates. Legal and political institutions, cultural attitudes and social norms are important factors in determining wages and productivity of countries, and they are likely to be correlated with the aggregate level of human capital. To the extend that it is hard to convincingly control for cross countries differences in these unobservables, estimates of spillovers are hard to interpret. Looking at within countries changes over time is unlikely to solve the problem, as time-varying shocks that affect productivity and wages are likely to be highly uncorrelated with changes in human capital of the labor force. But by looking at cities within the United States, this source of unobserved heterogeneity is minimized. Although cities may have different institutions, the difference are smaller than cross-countries differences.

Finally, the lack of high quality multiple-country datasets makes cross country comparisons difficult. Available educational attainment data for many countries are noisy. Measurement error becomes an even more serious problem when looking not at cross-sectional models, but at models based on changes in education over time. For example, Krueger and Lindahl (1998) find that at least half of the variability of measured changes in schooling across countries is pure noise.[31] They re-analyze the correlation between education and growth, taking into account the measurement problems. They conclude that, on average, economic growth is positively correlated with increases in schooling, and the estimated effect is not too different from the 10 percent rate of private return to schooling. They caution, however, that cross-country evidence is relatively weak, and fraught with problems of non-comparability, measurement error, and most fundamentally, a lack of a credible "research design".

Bils and Klenow (2000) propose an overlapping generations model in which each generation learns from previous generations and human capital creates positive externality in the level of technology adoption. Although they do not estimate the model, they calibrate it using existing evidence based on Mincerian regressions of the type described in Equation (8). They conclude that schooling explains less than one-third of the empirical variation in growth rates.

[31] On the contrary, Census, CPS, and other large scale U.S. government datasets provide high quality, consistent information on schooling levels, wages and productivity for all large U.S. metropolitan areas.

(2003) find a strong effect of education on voting in the U.S. The effect appears to stem from differences in voter registration across education groups. Results from the UK, where citizens are legally responsible and actively assisted to register, show no effect of education on voting. They also find strong and persistent effects of education on civic behavior in both the U.S. and the UK. Educated adults are more likely to discuss politics with others, associate with a political group, work on community issues, and follow election campaigns in the media.

6. Conclusion

What is the effect of an increase in the aggregate level of human capital on a city economy? Although much is known about the private returns to human capital, the answer to this question is not straightforward. Increases in the skill level of a city can affect the local economy in ways that are not fully reflected in the private return of education. Human capital spillovers can in theory increase productivity over and above the direct effect of human capital on individual productivity. Furthermore, increases in education can reduce criminal participation and improve voters' political behavior.

The size of the social return to human capital has enormous policy implications. Local governments are increasingly involved in policies aimed at fostering economic growth, so a measure of the magnitude of human capital spillovers is crucial in deciding how many resources to invest in attracting skilled workers. Moreover, the magnitude of the social return to education is an important tool for assessing the efficiency of investment in public education.

Three empirical strategies are available to estimate human capital spillovers. First, human capital spillovers can be identified by comparing the productivity or the unit costs of identical plants located in cities with high and low levels of human capital. Second, spillovers can be identified by comparing land prices in cities with high and low levels of human capital; and finally spillovers can be identified by comparing wages of identical workers located in cities with high and low levels of human capital.

Despite the important policy implications and a large theoretical literature that assumes the existence of human capital externalities, the empirical literature on the magnitude of these externalities is still young. Given the limited number of empirical studies on this subject, it is still too early to draw definitive conclusions on the size of externalities. This is particularly surprising given the huge literature estimating the private return to education that has emerged in labor economics in the past four decades. Nevertheless, "economists are conspicuous by their absence" on the subject of human capital spillovers [Topel (1999)].

More research is needed to overcome the formidable identification issues that the endogeneity of human capital presents. Current research on the topic is now at a stage that is reminiscent of the literature on the private returns to education in its early stages. The empirical challenges are enormous, but the potential rewards are also large. Judging by the creativity and ingenuity that economists have shown in addressing the empirical challenges that arose in the estimation of the private return to human capital, it is not unreasonable to expect to see substantial progress on the issue of social returns in the not-too-distant future.

Acknowledgements

I thank the editors Vernon Henderson and Jacques Thisse for useful comments. I am also grateful to Luis Bertinelli, Gilles Duranton, Gerhard Glomm, Giovanni Peri, Stephanie Riegg and Stuart Rosenthal for many useful suggestions on previous versions of this chapter.

References

Acemoglu, D. (1996). "A microfundation for social increasing returns in human capital accumulation". Quarterly Journal of Economics, 779–804.
Acemoglu, D. (1998). "Why do new technologies complement skills? Directed technical change and wage inequality". Quarterly Journal of Economics 113, 1055–1090.
Acemoglu, D., Angrist, J. (2000). "How large are human capital externalities? Evidence from compulsory schooling laws". NBER Macroeconomic Annual 15.
Adams, J., Jaffe, A.B. (1996). "Bounding the effects of R&D: An investigation using matched establishment-firm data". RAND Journal of Economics 27 (4), 700–721.
American Electronics Association (1997). Area definition of the high-tech sector. Cyberstates.
Arrow, K. (1962). "Economic welfare and the allocation of resources for invention". In: Nelson, N. (Ed.), The Rate and Direction of Inventive Activity. Princeton University Press, Princeton, NJ.
Arrow, K. (1997). "The benefit of education and the formation of preferences". In: Behrman, J., Stacey, N. (Eds.), The Social Benefits of Education. University of Michigan Press.
Audretsch, D., Stephan, P. (1996). "Company–scientists location links: The case of biotechnology". American Economic Review 86 (3), 641–652.
Becker, G., Mulligan, C. (1997). "The endogenous determination of time preference". Quarterly Journal of Economics 112 (3), 729–758.
Bils, M., Klenow, P. (2000). "Does schooling cause growth?" American Economic Review 90 (5), 1160–1183.
Black, D., Henderson, J.V. (1999). "A theory of urban growth". Journal of Political Economy 107, 252–284.
Borjas, G.J., Bronars, S.G., Trejo, S.J. (1992). "Self-selection and internal migration in the United States". Journal of Urban Economics 32, 159–185.
Bound, J., Groen, J., Kezdi, G., Turner, S. (in press). "Trade in university training, cross-state variation in the production and use of college-educated labor". Journal of Econometrics.
Bound, J., Holzer, H.J. (1996). "Demand shifts, population adjustments, and labor market outcomes during the 1980s". NBER Working Paper 5685.
Brady, H.E., Verba, S. (1995). Schlozman, K.K., "Beyond SES: A resource allocation model of political participation". American Political Science Review 89 (2), 271–294.
Card, D. (1999). "Education in the labor market". In: Ashenfelter, O., Card, D. (Eds.), The Handbook of Labor Economics. North-Holland, Amsterdam.
Chiricos, T. (1987). "Rates of crime and unemployment: An analysis of aggregate research". Social Problems 34 (2), 187–211.
Ciccone A., Peri G. (2002). "Identifying human capital externalities: Theory with application to US cities". IZA Discussion Paper No. 488.

Conley, T., Flyer, F., Tsiang, G. (in press). "Local market human capital and the spatial distribution of productivity in Malaysia". Contributions to the Economics and Growth of Developing Areas.
Costa, D.L., Kahn, M.E. (2000). "Power couples: Changes in the locational choice of the college educated, 1940–1990". Quarterly Journal of Economics 115 (4), 1287–1315.
Dee, T.S. (2002). "Are there civic returns to education?" Mimeo. Swathmore College.
Duranton, G., Puga, D. (2004). "Micro-foundations of urban agglomeration economies". In: Henderson, J.V., Thisse, J.-F. (Eds.), Handbook of Regional and Urban Economics, vol. 4. Elsevier, Amsterdam, pp. 2063–2117. This volume.
Farrington, D., et al. (1986). "Unemployment, school leaving and crime". British Journal of Criminology 26, 335–356.
Feddersen, T.J., Pesendorfer, W. (1996). "The swing voter's curse". American Economic Review 86 (3), 408–424.
Freeman, R. (1983). "Crime and unemployment". Chapter 6. In: Wilson, J.Q. (Ed.), Crime and Public Policy. ICS Press, San Francisco.
Freeman, R. (1995). "The labor market". Chapter 8. In: Wilson, J.Q., Petersilia, J. (Eds.), Crime. ICS Press, San Francisco.
Freeman, R. (1996). "Why do so many young American men commit crimes and what might we do about it?" Journal of Economic Perspectives 10 (1), 25–42.
Friedman, M. (1962). Capitalism and Freedom.
Gabriel, S.A., Rosenthal, S.S. (2004). "Quality of the business environment versus quality of life: Do firms and households like the same cities?" The Review of Economics and Statistics 86 (1), 438–444.
Glaeser, E.L. (1999). "Learning in cities". Journal of Urban Economics 46 (2), 254–2334377.
Glaeser, E.L., Mare, D.C. (2001). "Cities and skills". Journal of Labor Economics 19, 316–342.
Glaeser, E.L., Scheinkman, J.A., Shleifer, A. (1995). "Economic growth in a cross-section of cities". Journal of Monetary Economics 36 (1).
Gottfredson, D. (1985). "Youth employment, crime, and schooling". Developmental Psychology 21, 419–432.
Gould, E., Mustard, D., Weinberg, B. (2000). "Crime rates and local labor market opportunities in the United States: 1979–1997". Working paper.
Griliches, Z. (1986). "Economic data issues". In: Griliches, Z., Intrilligator, M.D. (Eds.), Handbook of Econometrics. North-Holland, Amsterdam.
Grogger, J. (1998). "Market wages and youth crime". Journal of Labor Economics 16 (4), 756–791.
Hanushek, E. (2002). "Publicly provided education". In: Auerbach, A., Feldstein, M. (Eds.), The Handbook of Public Economics, vol. 3. North-Holland, Amsterdam.
Helliwell, J., Putnam, J. (1999). "Education and social capital". Working paper 9999. National Bureau of Economic Research.
Jaffe, A., Trajtenberg, M., Henderson, R. (1993). "Geographic localization of knowledge spillovers as evidenced by patent citation". Quarterly Journal of Economics 108 (3), 577–598.
Jovanovic, B., Rob, R. (1989). "The growth and diffusion of knowledge". Review of Economic Studies 56 (4), 569–582.
Katz, L.F., Murphy, K.M. (1992). "Changes in relative wages, 1963–1987: Supply and demand factors". The Quarterly Journal of Economics 107, 35–78.
Krueger, A.B., Lindahl, M. (1998). "Education for growth in Sweden and the World". Industrial Relation Section Working Paper. Princeton, NJ.
Leighley, J.E., Nagler, J. (1992). "Socioeconomic class bias in turnout, 1964–1988, The voters remain the same". American Political Science Review 86 (3), 725–736.
Lochner, L. (1999). "Education, work, and crime: Theory and evidence". Rochester Center for Economic Research Working Paper No. 465.
Lochner, L., Moretti, E. (2002). "The effect of education on crime: Evidence from prison inmates, arrests, and self-reports". American Economic Review. In press.
Lucas, R.E. (1988). "On the mechanics of economic development". Journal of Monetary Economics 22, 3–42.
Machin, S., Meghir, C. (2000). "Crime and economic incentives". Working Paper. Institute for Fiscal Studies.

Marshall, A. (1890). Principles of Economics. Macmillan, New York.

Milligan, K., Moretti, E., Oreopoulos, P. (2003). "Does education improve citizenship? Evidence from the U.S. and the UK". Journal of Public Economics. In press.

Moretti, E. (2002). "Workers' education, spillovers and productivity: Evidence from plant-level production functions". American Economics Review. In press.

Moretti, E. (in press). "Estimating the external return to higher education: Evidence from cross-sectional and longitudinal data". Journal of Econometrics.

Osborne, M.J., Rosenthal, J.S., Turner, M.A. (2000). "Meetings with costly participation". American Economic Review 90 (4), 927–943.

Peri, G. (2002). "Young workers, learning, and agglomeration". Journal of Urban Economics 52 (3), 582–607.

Powell Jr., G. (1985). "American voter turnout in comparative perspective". American Political Science Review 80 (1), 17–43.

Raphael, S., Winter-Ebmer, R. (2001). "Identifying the effect of unemployment on crime". Journal of Law and Economics 44 (1).

Rauch, J.E. (1993). "Productivity gains from geographic concentration of human capital: Evidence from the cities". Journal of Urban Economics 34, 380–400.

Roback, J. (1982). "Wages, rents and the quality of life". Journal of Political Economy 90 (6), 1257–1278.

Saxenian, A. (1994). Regional Advantage: Culture and Competition in Silicon Valley and Route 128. Harvard University Press.

Smith, A. (1776). The Wealth of Nations.

Tauchen, H., Witte, A.D., Griesinger, H. (1994). "Criminal deterrence: Revisiting the issue with a birth cohort". Review of Economics and Statistics 76 (3), 399–412.

Teixeira, R.A. (1987). Why Americans Don't Vote: Turnout Decline in the United States 1960–1984. Greenwood Press.

Topel, R. (1999). "Labor market and economic growth". In: Ashenfelter, O., Card, D. (Eds.), The Handbook of Labor Economics. North-Holland, Amsterdam.

Verba, S., Nie, N.H. (1972). Participation in America: Political Democracy and Social Equality. Harper and Row.

Viscusi, K. (1986). "Market incentives for criminal behavior". Chapter 8. In: Freeman, R., Holzer, H. (Eds.), The Black Youth Employment Crisis. University of Chicago Press, Chicago.

Weisberg, H.F., Box-Steffensmeier, J.M. (1999). Reelection 1996: How Americans Voted. Chatham House Publishers.

Witte, A.D. (1997). "Crime". Chapter 7. In: Behrman, J., Stacey, N. (Eds.), The Social Benefits of Education. University of Michigan Press, Ann Arbor, MI.

Witte, A.D., Tauchen, H. (1994). "Work and crime: An exploration using panel data". NBER Working Paper 4794.

Zucker, L.G., Darby, M.R., Brewer, M.B. (1998). "Intellectual human capital and the birth of U.S. biotechnology enterprises". American Economic Review 88 (1), 290–306.

Chapter 52

THEORIES OF SYSTEMS OF CITIES

HESHAM M. ABDEL-RAHMAN

University of New Orleans, USA
e-mail: habdelra@uno.edu

ALEX ANAS

State University of New York at Buffalo, USA
e-mail: alexanas@buffalo.edu

Contents

Handbook of Regional and Urban Economics, Volume 4. Edited by J.V. Henderson and J.F. Thisse

DOI: 10.1016/S0169-7218(04)07052-2

Abstract

Economic theories of systems of cities explain why production and consumption activities are concentrated in a number of urban areas of different sizes and industrial composition rather than uniformly distributed in space. These theories have been successively influenced by four paradigms: (i) conventional urban economics emphasizing the tension between economies due to the spatial concentration of activity and diseconomies arising from that concentration; (ii) the theory of industrial organization as it relates to inter-industry linkages and to product differentiation; (iii) the New Economic Geography which ignores land markets but emphasizes trade among cities, fixed agricultural hinterlands and the endogenous emergence of geography; (iv) the theory of endogenous economic growth. Among the issues examined are specialization versus diversification of cities in systems of cities, how city systems contribute to increasing returns in national and the global economies, the factors that determine skill distribution and income disparity between cities, the impacts of income disparity on welfare, whether population growth should cause economic activity to become more or less concentrated in urban areas, and how resources should be allocated efficiently in a system of cities. Related to the last issue, we consider models where cities are organized by local planners or developers as well as cities that self-organize by atomistic actions. A conclusion of the theoretical study of city systems is that markets fail in efficiently allocating resources across cities when certain intercity interactions are present and that a role for central planning may be necessary.

Keywords

agglomeration, cities, growth, industry structure, trade, welfare

JEL classification: H23, H41, R11, R12, R13

1. Introduction

According to a United Nations Report (1996), the World's urban population increased from 30% in 1950 to 45% in 1995 and is expected to reach 50% in 2005. In industrial countries, more people live in urban areas but the increase in urbanization has been milder, rising from 61% in 1960 to 73% in 1993. The largest cities in the world have increased from only one city with a population of over 10 million in 1950 (New York) to fifteen such cities in 1995. According to a recent *National Geographic* article, the number of such *megacities* will reach 21 in 2015 "and the number of urban areas with populations between five and ten million will shoot from 7 [in 1950] to 37. This growth will occur mainly in developing countries, those least equipped to provide transportation, housing, water, sewers. Asia and Africa, now more than two-thirds rural, will be half urban by 2025" [National Geographic (2002, p. 77), brackets ours]. While urbanists from a variety of disciplines have reacted to these rapid urbanization trends with alarm, urban economists have been patiently developing theories of city systems since the mid-1970s. These theories emphasize the benefits as well as the costs of urbanization.

Most of the non-agricultural GDP in industrialized countries is produced in urban areas and cities are where new products are developed and where virtually all of technical innovation occurs. With trade liberalization and increased globalization as exhibited by NAFTA, GATT and the ongoing expansion of the European Union, the role of national governments in international trade is becoming less important. As a result, it is increasingly convenient to view the world as a network of cities of different sizes and comparative advantages, trading with one another. Such a view of economic activity increasingly competes with traditional regional and international economics. A comprehensive theory of a system of cities is an essential component of economists' efforts to understand and model economic growth and international trade.

Modern urban economics, traced to Alonso (1964), Mills (1967) and Muth (1969) spearheaded a theory of the internal structure of a city emphasizing land markets and land use. Dixit (1973) presented perhaps the most sophisticated discussion between positive and negative scale effects of city size. The beginnings of the systems-of-cities literature within modern urban economics can be traced primarily to Henderson (1974). He synthesized this Alonso–Mills–Muth theory of a city's internal structure with the concept of Marshallian externalities [Marshall (1890)], to explain the concentration of economic activity in cities. According to Lucas (1988), cities are the engines of long-run economic growth. Such an observation is not surprising to urban economists, since under the influence of Marshall, they have long maintained that the spatial proximity of market agents in cities fosters cost savings in consumption, production, search, matching and learning, knowledge spillovers and human capital accumulation.[2] External scale economies are now crucial in the long-run endogenous growth theory [e.g.,

[2] For a review of models emphasizing the micro-foundations of spatial agglomeration and city formation using search, matching and learning see the chapter by Duranton and Puga (2004) in this volume.

Romer (1986, 1987)] and also play a key role in the theory of spatial agglomeration that is now central to all systems of cities models. Theories of city systems have been successively influenced by four paradigms:

(i) conventional urban economics emphasizing the tension between economies due to the concentration of economic activity and diseconomies arising from that spatial concentration [Mills (1967), Dixit (1973), Henderson (1974)];

(ii) the theory of industrial organization as it relates to inter-industry linkages and to product differentiation [Dixit and Stiglitz (1977), Ethier (1982)];

(iii) the theory of endogenous economic growth [Romer (1986, 1987), Lucas (1988)];

(iv) the New Economic Geography [Krugman (1991)], which ignores land markets but emphasizes trade among cities, fixed agricultural hinterlands and the endogenous emergence of geography.

An ultimate unfulfilled challenge for theories of systems of cities is to explain the number and size of cities in a national economy with given population: "*How does a specific city size distribution emerge and how does it evolve in a free market*?" and "*What is the socially optimal city size distribution and how should it evolve*?" Regularities in the size distribution of cities in both developed and developing countries have been observed. Such distributions are characterized by a hierarchical structure in which there are a relatively small number of large cities and a larger number of smaller cities, commonly described by the rank–size rule. Despite several decades of research, systems of cities theories developed to date are not rich enough to explain the empirically observed city size distributions characterized by the rank–size rule or by its variants.[3]

A second basic challenge for systems-of-cities theory is explaining the variation in industrial composition across the spectrum of city sizes and the efficiency or inefficiency of such variation. Large cities at the top of the hierarchy, like New York, London, Paris and Tokyo are characterized by a diverse industrial structure while cities all over the world tend to be more specialized, the smaller they are. Explaining this would entail theoretical models of hierarchical city size distributions with a relatively small number of large cities producing most of the goods in the economy and a larger number of smaller and more specialized cities producing only a few goods.[4] As we shall see, the existing static theory of city systems has provided a variety of insights as to why specialization versus diversification occurs. The literature has distinguished between Marshall–Arrow–Romer (MAR or localization) externalities that arise from knowledge transfers within an industry, and Jacobs (1969) (or urbanization) externalities that arise from transfers between industries. Empirical work by Glaeser et al. (1992) has claimed that cities with a diversified industrial base, hence subject to Jacobs externalities, may

[3] The rank–size rule indicates that the population of each city in a system of cities, multiplied by its population rank equals the size of the largest city. For a survey of the rank–size rule and related work, see the chapter by Gabaix and Ioannides (2004) in this volume.

[4] Lösch (1954) built descriptive models of the hierarchical distribution of economic activity over space.

grow faster than specialized cities. Henderson, Kuncoro and Turner (1995) have redressed this claim showing that MAR externalities play a bigger role in traditional industries, while Jacobs externalities are more important in modern high-technology industries. Other empirical studies suggest that labor productivity and industrial growth are positively related to the local size of the industry as well as to the industrial composition of the city in which the industry is located.[5] The theoretical literature on city systems has not yet provided an explanation as to how the rate of growth of an industry or of a city as a whole is related to city specialization or diversification.

A third challenge for theory is to explain the observed skill distribution of the labor force within and between cities in the system. In particular, large cities tend to be populated with a labor force possessing a wide variety of skills while small cities tend to be populated by a labor force with relatively specific skills. As a result observed income disparity is relatively larger in larger cities. Furthermore, this issue of income disparity within a system of cities is becoming more important to understand in an urban context given that several national studies documented that income inequality has been rising over the past two decades.[6] There has been a dramatic widening of the real gap between the wages of highly skilled and poorly skilled laborers. Thus, it is important to examine, in a theoretical framework, whether the structure of a city system and the sorting of workers among cities by skill level contributes to the observed pattern of growing wage disparities.

This chapter will survey normative as well as positive issues studied by systems of cities models. We will review the static models of city systems as well as the more recent dynamic ones. We will examine the effects of exogenous population growth as well as endogenous economic growth in a system of cities. The following are some of the questions illuminated by the literature we are surveying: What are the centripetal forces favoring concentration of economic activity in large cities versus centrifugal forces favoring dispersion of economic activity to small settlements? What determines the number and the size of cities and how does this change as population grows? What are the institutional and atomistic mechanisms by which cities are created? When do cities specialize in production and when do they diversify? When do both specialized and diversified cities coexist in a national economy? How is specialization and diversification affected by costly trade among cities? What are the factors that determine the distribution of different types of labor force in a system of cities? What are the factors that determine income disparities within an urban system and what is the impact of such income disparity on overall welfare? What are the main engines of urban growth in a system of cities? What are the sources of market failure in the allocation of resources among cities and when is central planning necessary to achieve an efficient allocation?

The organization of the chapter is as follows: Section 2 presents a simplified equilibrium model of the internal structure of a single city emphasizing the organization of

5 For survey of these empirical finding see the chapter by Rosenthal and Strange (2004) in this volume.

6 See Juhn, Murphy and Pierce (1993) for these trends in the U.S. and Machin (1996) for the UK among others.

land use around a Central Business District. This is necessary so that the reader has a clear understanding of what goes on inside each city in a system of cities and so that the link with traditional urban economics is explicit. In Section 3 our attention turns to the agglomeration economies that help form cities and to the optimal city size implied when such agglomeration economies are offset by the expansion of cities. Our exposition focuses on three commonly used models of urban agglomeration that we present in simple stylized form. These are the local public good model of public economics, the product variety model of industrial organization and the labor productivity model of Marshallian (or MAR or localization) externalities. We show that the three models are in fact perfectly equivalent and can be made to produce identical cities by the choice of a single parameter in each model. Section 4 focuses on the institutional mechanisms (developers or local governments) that can be used to form and sustain self-financing and optimally sized cities in a system of cities, provided the cities do not interact with each other. The two mechanisms are shown to be equivalent. These institutional mechanisms are contrasted with city formation under self-organization and atomistic defection. In Section 5 we provide a broad summary of historical developments in the literature on systems of cities and we identify the key issues that arise in the design of such models. The rest of the survey is devoted to examining a number of specific models from the literature, emphasizing primarily equilibrium analysis. In Section 6 we survey the basic static models of specialized and diversified city systems characterized by homogeneous labor and we investigate trade, economies of scope and increasing returns in such city systems, while in Section 7 we present static models of a city system with labor heterogeneity and income inequality. In Section 8 we provide a survey of main ideas from the literature on the efficient allocation of economic activity into a system of cities under the proper form of fiscal decentralization. The most important conclusion of this theoretical study may be that markets fail in efficiently allocating resources across cities when intercity interactions are present. Section 9 is about growth, focusing on the effects of exogenous population growth as well as endogenous economic growth. A handful of models of dynamic city systems are surveyed there. Section 10 concludes by outlining some of the challenges ahead.

2. Internal structure of cities[7]

We assume monocentric and circular cities. All production occurs at a central point (the Central Business District, or CBD).[8] We assume that producers do not use land. The only input is the labor supplied by the consumers living in the city. Each consumer

[7] Virtually all authors modeling city systems used the model presented here.

[8] This is a major drawback because as cities grow they can spawn secondary centers. Such a mechanism of subcenter formation within existing cities competes with the emergence of new cities. The literature we are surveying has not studied both processes in the same model. Some thoughts on the interaction of the two processes are presented in Section 10.

uses one unit of land for a residence (fixed lot size) and is endowed by a unit amount of time that he allocates between labor and commuting to the CBD. The time-cost of commuting a unit distance in both directions (round trip) is t, an exogenous constant. If a consumer picks his residence location to be r miles from the CBD, then his labor supply is $H(r) = 1 - tr$. We will use N to denote the number of consumer/laborers residing in the city and $\bar{r}$ to denote the radius of the city. Then, since lot sizes are uniformly equal to one, $\bar{r} = \sqrt{N/\pi}$.[9] The aggregate labor, H, supplied to the CBD is obtained by integrating over the residential area:

$$H = \int_0^{\bar{r}} 2\pi r H(r)\,\mathrm{d}r = N\bigl(1 - kN^{1/2}\bigr), \tag{1}$$

where $k \equiv 2t/(3\sqrt{\pi})$. Since k is a normalization of t, we can use either k or t to measure the unit commuting cost.

The principle that determines city structure with zero relocation costs is that identical residents achieve the same level of utility no matter where within the city they locate. Indirect utility is of the form $V(\mathbf{p}, I)$, where $\mathbf{p}$ is the market price vector of the traded goods in the economy available for the residents of the city and I is the disposable income of any resident that is available for buying those goods. Since all residents face the same $\mathbf{p}$, for the value of utility to be invariant with location within the city, the disposable income must be the same for each resident. Disposable income is defined as income less location costs (commuting costs plus the rent of the unit-sized lot).[10] Hence, for equal utility to hold, location costs must be invariant with residence location. We assume that rent at the edge of the city is zero, because there is no non-urban use for land. We assume also that each unit time spent commuting is valued at the wage rate, w. Then, commuting cost (to the CBD and back) as a function of residential distance is $C(r) = wtr$. Hence, the rent on land at radius $0 \leqslant r \leqslant \bar{r}$ is $R(r) = t(\bar{r} - r)w$. The location cost of any one resident is then $R(r) + wtr = wt\bar{r} = wtN^{1/2}/\sqrt{\pi}$, and *aggregate location cost* (*ALC*) is

$$ALC(N) = \frac{wtN^{3/2}}{\sqrt{\pi}}. \tag{2}$$

This is independent of r. We assume that a local city manager (local government or private city developer) collects all rents and redistributes the average rent to each city resident. The *aggregate land rent* thus shared (*ALR*) is:

$$ALR(N) = \int_0^{\bar{r}} 2\pi r R(r)\,\mathrm{d}r = \frac{wtN^{3/2}}{3\sqrt{\pi}}. \tag{3}$$

[9] The maximum possible radius for a city is $1/t$, since a consumer residing beyond that radius would spend all of his time commuting and would have no time to work. The maximum population that can be accommodated by such a city is therefore $N_{\max} = \pi/t^2$.

[10] Where appropriate later, we will also deduct taxes in defining disposable income.

Note that both $ALR(N)$ and $ALC(N)$ are increasing functions of the city's population, N. However, $ALC(N)$ rises three times faster than $ALR(N)$. The disposable income of any consumer can now be calculated as

$$I(N) = w + \frac{ALR(N)}{N} - \frac{ALC(N)}{N} = \left(1 - kN^{1/2}\right)w. \tag{4}$$

The consumer has this income to purchase all the goods that will be offered in the city system. Note that as N grows the disposable income falls because the marginal (and average) resident spends more time commuting in a larger city. Therefore, adding residents to the city reduces utility. Under this *centrifugal* condition, cities would not exist. To provide an economic incentive for adding residents and creating a city, we must add *centripetal* forces so that the agglomeration of people and firms generates benefits. The following section provides three stylized economies of scale models for doing this.

3. Urban agglomeration and optimal city size

The first model we present relies on a public good. This is funded collectively by the city residents and is the driver for the urban agglomeration. As more residents join the city, the average cost of the public good declines. The second model is based on consumer demand for a variety of products or producer demand for a variety of intermediate inputs. Such consumers or producers concentrate in a city in order to make a large local market that supports greater product or input variety. The third model is the case of a productivity increase from the concentration of labor in the same industry, also known in the literature as the black-box model of Marshallian externalities. One way to interpret this black-box model is that the productivity of each worker is enhanced by the innovative ideas freely contributed by the labor force working in close proximity.

In each of the models, the agglomeration results in an optimal city size: utility increases as residents are added until it peaks at some optimal city size when the centrifugal force of commuting cost and the centripetal agglomeration force are balanced at the margin. Thereafter, utility is reduced as more residents are added. We will show that the three models are equivalent in reduced form and imply the same indirect utility as a function of the city's population. More precisely, we will show that product variety in the second model is, in fact, a local public good as is also the aggregate labor supply in the third model. Each model also illustrates a different form of market failure and we discuss how it is corrected or rendered inconsequential. In Section 4, we will see how the Henry George Theorem is the appropriate mechanism for achieving the optimal city size.

In each case, we will write the indirect utility of the monocentric city of Section 2 as $V(\mathbf{p}, Q, I(N))$ where $\mathbf{p}$ is the vector of the market prices of the consumption goods, Q is the quantity of a local public good if one exists, and $I(N) = (1 - kN^{1/2})w$ is the disposable income of Section 2, with w the urban wage. To get closed-form solutions, we will specialize to the functionally separable form: $V(\mathbf{p}, Q, I(N)) = v(\mathbf{p})f(Q)I(N)$.

3.1. Local public good

A commonly cited reason for urban agglomeration is that consumers locate in close proximity in order to have access to a local public good that they finance collectively [Flatters, Henderson and Mieszkowski (1974), Stiglitz (1977), Arnott (1979), Arnott and Stiglitz (1979)]. We will assume that the city produces a private good, say good x, traded costlessly in the larger economy with price p_x and that this good is produced competitively under constant returns, with labor the only input in production. Hence, $w = p_x$. Suppose that the direct utility function is of the form $U = x^a y^\beta f(Q)$, $\alpha + \beta = 1$, where x is the quantity consumed of the locally produced good and y is the consumption of another good imported from other cities, while Q is the aggregate expenditure on the local public good. Assume that $f(Q) = Q^\mu$ where $\mu > 0$. Clearly, the source of market failure in this model is the presence of the public good. This market failure is corrected by determining Q so that consumer utility is maximized. A resident pays a lump sum tax, T, to finance the public good. Hence, $Q = TN$. Indirect utility is

$$V(\mathbf{p}, Q, I(N) - T) = \alpha^\alpha \beta^\beta p_x^{-\alpha} p_y^{-\beta}\left[w\left(1 - kN^{1/2}\right) - T\right]Q^\mu, \quad \text{where } T = \frac{Q}{N}.$$

The lump sum tax that maximizes utility, given N, is $T^* = (\mu/(1+\mu))I(N)$.[11] The after-tax utility is

$$\begin{aligned}\widetilde{V}(\mathbf{p}, N, I(N)) &\equiv V(\mathbf{p}, NT^*, I(N) - T^*) \\ &= \left(\frac{\mu}{1+\mu}\right)^\mu \left(\frac{1}{1+\mu}\right) p_x^{1+\mu-\alpha} p_y^{-\beta} N^\mu \left(1 - kN^{1/2}\right)^{\mu+1}.\end{aligned}$$

The first-best optimal city size is found by maximizing $\widetilde{V}(\mathbf{p}, N, I(N))$ with respect to N. In the functionally separable case, this optimal size is given as a fraction of the maximum possible city size, $N_{\max}$:

$$N^* = \frac{9\mu^2}{9\mu^2 + 6\mu + 1} N_{\max}. \tag{5}$$

This shows that the optimal city size increases as the unit commuting cost (k) falls (recalling from footnote 7 that $N_{\max} = 4/(9k^2)$) and increases as μ, the elasticity of utility with respect to public expenditure, increases. When $\mu = 0$, $N^* = 0$ and cities cannot exist (there is no centripetal force). And as $\mu \to \infty$, $N^* \to N_{\max}$, the centripetal force dominates causing maximally sized cities.[12]

[11] We will see in Section 4 how this optimally determined tax confiscates all of the land rent when the city population, N, is endogenous.

[12] In a variation of the public good model, Abdel-Rahman (2000) assumed that the public good is a form of infrastructure such as water, electrical or sewer system. Investment in this public good is assumed to reduce the fixed costs of setting up firms. The larger the investment in infrastructure is, the larger the number of firms that will enter the city.

3.2. Product variety and the home market effect

Agglomeration can also be caused by consumers locating in the same city to create a large home market. If the consumers value product variety, they benefit from a large home market because more unique products will emerge and be viable in a larger market. This, in turn, will drive up consumer utility providing the basis for an even larger market. Thus, suppose that each of the N consumers has a utility function that is Dixit–Stiglitz CES [Dixit and Stiglitz (1977)] given by

$$U = \left(x_0, \sum_{i=1}^{m} x_i^{\frac{\sigma-1}{\sigma}} \right)^{\frac{\sigma}{\sigma-1}}$$

where $\sigma > 1$, x_0 is a numeraire good and m is the number of varieties manufactured in the city (x_i being the consumption of the ith such variety) and assume for now that these are not traded with the other cities.[13] In Dixit–Stiglitz, part of the disposable income of the consumer is used to buy x_0. Again following Dixit and Stiglitz, we assume that each of the m products is manufactured by a different firm, and by an increasing returns technology requiring a fixed labor input, f, plus a marginal labor input, c, per unit produced. The ith firm's total cost of producing z_i units of output is then $w(f + cz_i)$. All firms pay the same wage, w, and are perfectly competitive in the labor market. In this model, the wage is taken as the numeraire price. Hence, $w = 1$. In the output market, the firms are monopolistically competitive and achieve a Chamberlin equilibrium [Chamberlin (1933)]. This imperfect competition in the output market is the basis of the market failure. Because the consumer's demands for the products are symmetrical and there is also symmetry among the many firms, the Cournot–Nash markup condition is approximately $p_i(1 - 1/\sigma) = c$, where σ is the price elasticity of the consumer's demand for each product. Hence, the equilibrium product prices are $p = (\sigma/(\sigma - 1))c$. This monopolistic markup in the differentiated goods industry is the cause of the market failure which comes about because the allocation of income between the m varieties and the numeraire good is distorted. To simplify things, we adopt a version of the Dixit–Stiglitz utility without the numeraire good. In this version, income can only be spent on the varieties and, as a result, there is no distortion and the market failure is inconsequential. The indirect utility is

$$V\big(\mathbf{p}, I(N)\big) = \left(\sum_{i=1}^{m} p_i^{1-\sigma} \right)^{1/(\sigma-1)} I(N).$$

[13] Alternatively, firms utilizing differentiated services as inputs are motivated to locate in the same city in order to create a large home market and thus increase the variety of services available to them. Krugman (1980, 1991) and Abdel-Rahman (1988) have emphasized models in which the consumer cares about consumption variety, while Abdel-Rahman and Fujita (1993) and Anas and Xiong (2003) have emphasized models in which firms producing a homogeneous product demand a variety of intermediate inputs. The former models use the Dixit and Stiglitz (1977) utility function, while the latter use the Ethier (1982) production function.

From the zero profit condition of each firm, $z = f(\sigma - 1)/c$. The aggregate labor demand is $m(f + cz) = mf\sigma$. Since the labor supply in the city is given by (1), the number of products at equilibrium is

$$m(N) = \frac{N(1 - kN^{1/2})}{f\sigma}.$$

Using this to evaluate the utility,

$$\begin{aligned} V\big(\mathbf{p}, m(N), I(N)\big) &= \big(m(N)p^{1-\sigma}\big)^{1/(\sigma-1)} I(N) = p^{-1} m(N)^{1/(\sigma-1)}\big(1 - kN^{1/2}\big) \\ &= \left(\frac{\sigma - 1}{\sigma c}\right)(f\sigma)^{1/(1-\sigma)} N^{1/(\sigma-1)}\big(1 - kN^{1/2}\big)^{\sigma/(\sigma-1)}. \end{aligned}$$

And

$$\widetilde{V}\big(\mathbf{p}, N, I(N)\big) \equiv \ln V\big(\mathbf{p}, m(N), I(N)\big) = -\ln p + \frac{1}{\sigma - 1}\ln m(N) + \ln I(N)$$

under the assumed symmetry of the varieties. This last expression, borrowed from Anas (2004) allows us to see that the consumer cares about disposable income, which decreases with city size, and the number of products that increase with city size. Only as $\sigma \to \infty$, products are viewed as perfect substitutes and variety becomes unimportant. Now define $\omega \equiv 1/(\sigma - 1)$ and note that $\omega + 1 = \sigma/(\sigma - 1)$. The optimal city size is again given by (5) where μ is now replaced by ω. As $\sigma \to \infty$ and $\omega \to 0$, all varieties are perceived as perfect substitutes. Then, N^* will be the size of a company town producing a single variety, since there is no benefit to be derived from a large home market. But as $\sigma \to 1$ and $\omega \to \infty$, $N^* \to N_{\max}$.

The consumer benefits from a larger number of goods (firms) but the fixed cost limits the number of firms at equilibrium, causing the firms to price their products above marginal cost. Hence, in Dixit and Stiglitz (1977), there is a collective incentive to tax the consumers and use the proceeds to subsidize the fixed costs of firms. This is formally equivalent to taxing consumers to pay for the public good in Section 3.1. To see this equivalence, recall that the indirect utility in the public goods model was

$$V\big(\mathbf{p}, Q, I(N) - T\big) = v(\mathbf{p})Q^{\mu}\big[\big(1 - kN^{1/2}\big) - T\big],$$

where T was the head tax so that $NT = Q$. In the current model, the number of firms (goods variety) may be viewed as a public good with after-tax utility

$$V\big(\mathbf{p}, m, I(N) - \Theta\big) = v(\mathbf{p})m^{\omega}\big[\big(1 - kN^{1/2}\big) - \Theta\big], \quad \text{where } m = N\Theta/f.$$

Maximizing this with respect to Θ, $\Theta^* = (\omega/(1 + \omega))/(1 - kN^{1/2})$, where $\omega = 1/(\sigma - 1)$. This is identical to

$$T^* = \frac{\mu}{1 + \mu}\big(1 - kN^{1/2}\big)$$

in the public good model. To complete the argument, we just need to show that the labor market clears under Θ^*. This requires

$$m = \frac{H(N)}{f\sigma} = \frac{N(1 - kN^{1/2})}{f\sigma},$$

which was shown earlier to follow from labor market clearing in the absence of any tax. That the tax is not needed to achieve the efficient allocation is a reflection of the fact that the market failure is rendered inconsequential by the absence of the numeraire good of Dixit–Stiglitz. The market allocation is efficient for a given N by laissez-faire (i.e., the efficient m is provided by the market), despite the monopolistic markup. This contrasts with the public good model of Section 3.1 where, as is well known, there is no market mechanism that can guarantee the efficient provision of the public good according to the Samuelson condition.

3.3. *Labor productivity as an external economy*

Suppose that aggregate labor, H, enters the CBD production function via two channels. First, labor is the only input purchased by each firm to produce a numeraire good under a constant-returns technology.[14] Second, it is the source of a Marshallian external effect on all firms, so that the more labor is employed in the CBD, the more productive the labor employed at each firm becomes. This is a classical Chipman (1970) type externality compatible with competitive equilibrium. The production function of firm i is $y_i = A(H)h_i$ where h_i is the labor employed by that firm, and H is the aggregate labor employed by all firms in the CBD. Because of constant returns, the aggregate CBD production function can be written as $Y = A(H)H$, where the external scale effect, $A(H)$ with $A'(H) > 0$, is the marginal and average product of labor and aggregate labor supply, $H = H(N)$, is given by (1). Let us assume that $A(H) = H^a$, $a > 0$, namely that the positive external effect increases with the total amount of labor's time devoted to work. Let us assume that the CBD labor market is competitive. Then, labor is paid its private marginal product and $w = A(H) = H^a = N^a(1 - kN^{1/2})^a$. Then, the indirect utility in the functionally separable case is

$$\widetilde{V}\big(\mathbf{p}, N, I(N)\big) \equiv V\big(\mathbf{p}, I(N)\big) = \nu(\mathbf{p})N^a\big(1 - kN^{1/2}\big)^{a+1}.$$

The city size, measured in population N at which this utility is maximized, is again given by (5) but now μ is replaced by a. When $a = 0$, there are no external returns to scale and $N^* = 0$. But as $a \to \infty$, $N^* \to N_{\max}$.

Market failure in this model arises from the fact that individual firms do not have an incentive to reward labor for the positive externality it confers on production. More precisely, the social marginal product (*SMP*) of labor is $A'(H)H + A(H) > A(H)$,

[14] In this model there is no explicit public good, so we will assume that $f(Q) = 1$ or equivalently that $V_Q = 0$.

where $A(H)$ is private marginal or average product (*PMP*). $SMP - PMP = A'(H)H$ and if producers were to cover the gap, they would incur losses. The income needed to cover the gap must be derived from another source and, as we shall see in Section 4, this source in the first-best case is the aggregate land rent. Assume for now that labor is paid its *SMP* from any source, $w = A'(H)H + A(H) = (1+a)H^a$. The functionally separable indirect utility derived above is now just multiplied by $1+a$ and, hence, the optimal city size, N^*, remains unaffected by the market failure. This model is also reduced-form-equivalent to the previous two. In this case, the city's labor force itself is equivalent to a public good. Write the after-tax indirect utility as $V = H^a(1 - kN^{1/2} - G)$ where G is the head tax and impose the constraint $GN - sH = 0$, where s is the subsidy per unit of labor. Optimizing with respect to G, given N and s, we get

$$G^* = \frac{a}{1+a}\left(1 - kN^{1/2}\right).$$

3.4. Discussion and notes on the literature

We saw that, in each of the models discussed, the reduced form indirect utility is of the form $\widetilde{V}(\mathbf{p}, N, I(N))$ with $\partial\widetilde{V}/\partial N > 0$ given $I(N)$, $\partial\widetilde{V}/\partial I(N) > 0$ and $\partial I(N)/\partial N < 0$. At the optimal size, N^*, the marginal agglomeration benefit from adding one more resident to the city just equals the marginal disutility from the increase in aggregate location cost:

$$\left.\frac{\partial\widetilde{V}(\cdot)}{\partial N}\right|_{N=N^*} = \left.\left(\frac{\partial\widetilde{V}(\cdot)}{\partial I(N)}\right)\left(-\frac{\partial I(N)}{\partial N}\right)\right|_{N=N^*}.$$

There is an important difference between the public good model of Section 3.1 on the one hand, and the product variety and labor productivity models of Sections 3.2 and 3.3, on the other. As is well known, given population N, there is no market structure that guarantees the optimal provision of the public good, Q, in Section 3.1. In Section 3.2, as we saw, laissez-faire provides the optimal diversity, m, given N, despite the markup imperfection, provided that there is no numeraire good as in Dixit and Stiglitz (1977). Likewise, in Section 3.3, the laissez-faire allocation is also efficient given N, provided that there is full employment.

The above three models of city formation have been used widely, but they are not the only ones. Helsley and Strange (1990) developed an alternative model with micro-economic underpinnings different from those discussed above. In their model, both the firms producing in the CBD as well as the workers/consumers hired by the firms are horizontally differentiated on the same unit circle. For a firm, its position on the unit circle identifies the firm's skill requirements in the labor market and for a worker, position on the unit circle identifies the skills that worker possesses. Workers are more productive when they work for firms with the skill requirements that best match theirs. Firms know only the expected skills of the workers they hire. As more firms enter the CBD, firm density on the unit circle increases, the labor market becomes thicker and workers are better matched to firms. Hence, productivity increases. Firms have fixed costs, so that each firm must command a finite range of laborer skills and the unit circle does not fill up with firms. Wages and profits are determined by a simple bargaining mechanism.

4. City formation mechanisms

Each of the models discussed in Section 3 calls for collective action to setup a city. In the first model, a tax was needed to finance the public good, while in the second (with the numeraire good present) the tax would be needed to subsidize firm entry costs in order to increase the city's product variety. In the third model, the gap between the social and private marginal products of labor would be closed by a Pigouvian subsidy to labor. In this section we will examine the relationship between the public expenditure, the tax structure and the population size at the optimum.

We will consider two planned city formation mechanisms. In the first, the city is set up and managed by a utility-maximizing local government representing the community of the city's residents. The government also decides the population of the city. In the second mechanism, there is a city developer who maximizes profit from city development, but must compete for residents in a national market. To attract residents to his city, the developer must be sure to setup and finance the city in such a way that residents moving into the city (recall that moving costs are zero) cannot do worse than achieving a reservation utility level. These two mechanisms will be shown to be equivalent under the assumption that the city-development market is contestable and that there is no limit to the number of cities.[15]

4.1. *Community planning: welfare maximization*

It is most natural to consider the problem of city formation in the context of the public good model presented in Section 3.1.[16] Suppose that a local planner or government sets a head tax, T, to be paid by each resident joining the city and uses the aggregate tax revenue to pay for the public good. Thus, $TN - Q = 0$. The government maximizes the utility of the representative city resident. The government will determine Q, N and T while land rents, $\mathbf{p}$ and w are determined by the markets. The problem of the local government is to solve:

$$\text{Maximize}_{Q,N,T} U = V\big(\mathbf{p}, Q, I(N)\big) \quad \text{subject to:}$$

$$NT - Q = 0,$$

[15] The assumption that there is no limit to the number of cities is not realistic because space on the earth or in any given national territory is limited. However, all systems-of-cities models except those in the tradition of the New Economic Geography ignore this feature.

[16] Not only is the exposition of the public good model easier, but indirectly the discussion also applies to the models of Sections 3.2 and 3.3 since we showed that the number of firms producing varieties or the labor force are implicitly public goods.

$$I(N) - w + T + \frac{ALC(N)}{N} - \frac{ALR(N)}{N} = 0.$$

We may optimize after substituting $I(N)$ into the utility and then forming the Lagrangian, $\Im$, with Lagrangian multiplier λ assigned to the tax budget constraint. The first-order conditions with respect to Q, T and N are respectively as follows:

$$\Im_Q: \quad \frac{\partial V}{\partial Q} - \lambda = 0;$$

$$\Im_T: \quad -\frac{\partial V}{\partial I} + \lambda N = 0;$$

$$\Im_N: \quad \frac{\partial V}{\partial I}\frac{\partial I}{\partial N} + \lambda T = 0.$$

Solving the first for λ and plugging that into the second, we get

$$N\frac{\partial V/\partial Q}{\partial V/\partial I} = 1. \tag{6}$$

Given N and T, this condition – known as the Samuelson condition – can be solved for the optimal level of the public expenditure, $Q^*(T, N)$. The right side is the marginal cost of the public good measured as a dollar of public expenditure, while the left side is the aggregate willingness to pay for a dollar of public expenditure, measured as the marginal rate of substitution between the public good and after-tax disposable income, summed over all the N residents. Next, we can substitute for λ and for $T = Q/N$ in the third constraint. The resulting condition is

$$Q = \left[\frac{-\partial I/\partial N}{\frac{\partial V/\partial Q}{\partial V/\partial I}}\right] N. \tag{7}$$

Given, Q and T, this equation can be solved for the optimal population $N^*(Q, T)$.

Two important facts are revealed by (7). First, note that the bracket evaluated at the optimal solution gives the optimal tax, T^*. Note that the denominator inside the bracket is the marginal rate of substitution and, from the Samuelson condition, (6), it equals $1/N$. Then the bracket can also be written as $[\cdot] = (-\partial I/\partial N)N$. The parenthesis is the marginal cost imposed on each city resident from the addition of a new resident. This marginal cost is expressed as a decrease in after-tax disposable income due to increased rent plus commuting cost net of redistributed (average) land rent. Multiplying by N gives the after-tax disposable income reduction over *all* residents caused by the addition of the marginal resident to the city. The first important fact, therefore, is that each resident is levied a Pigouvian tax equal to the social marginal cost the resident imposes on the city.

The second important fact is that the tax imposed on each resident is equal to the average land rent in the city. This can be seen directly by evaluating the derivatives and thus showing that

$$T^* = [\cdot] = \frac{ALR(N^*)}{N^*} = \frac{k}{2}(N^*)^{1/2}.$$

Hence, the optimal Pigouvian tax summed over all residents confiscates the entire land value of the city. This result, in turn, is known as the Henry George Theorem: optimizing welfare with respect to the number of residents in the city, N^*, requires levying a Pigouvian tax, T^*, on each resident the proceeds of which over all residents confiscates the city's aggregate land value, $ALR(N^*)$ – hence, causing no distortion – and using these proceeds solely to finance the optimal quantity of the public good, Q^*, implied by the Samuleson condition.

4.2. *City development*

In the foregoing, the community planner sets the population of the city without considering the alternatives which residents can obtain by going elsewhere. The planner must make sure that the maximum utility which residents can obtain by joining his city is higher than what they can get elsewhere and that there are enough potential residents available to draw from. This model obviously ignores the possibility of competition from other community planners setting up similar cities. It has been argued that with no limit on the number of cities that can emerge, competition among cities – under the assumption of costless consumer mobility among cities – would imply that the residents of all cities must be at the same utility level. Such an observation has led to a stylized model of city development in which each city is set up and managed by a profit-maximizing developer who is a utility taker. It is assumed that the developer owns all the land the city will need (having bought such a land from alternative users that do not suspect that a city will replace them) and then proceeding to sell each parcel to the highest bidder. Because this is the behavior of a perfectly price discriminating monopolist, it is immediately obvious that it is efficient and, hence, it is equivalent to assuming that the developer lets the land market for residences operate competitively. The developer pays for the public good out of the land rental proceeds. The developer chooses the level of public expenditure and the number of residents in such a way that each resident will not do worse than the national reservation utility level. If cities are set up and city developers make a profit, then new developers will enter the city-development market and will set up competing new cities. Such competition will cause all rents on land being invested in the local public good and developers making zero profits.

Suppose that $\overline{U}$ is the exogenous national reservation utility level. The developer of a representative city in the public good case must solve the following problem:

$$\text{Maximize}_{Q,T,N}\Pi = TN - Q \quad \text{subject to}$$

$$V\left(Q, w - T - \frac{ALC(N)}{N} + \frac{ALR(N)}{N}\right) - \overline{U} = 0.$$

The first-order condition with respect to Q, T and N are as follows, where μ is the Lagrangian multiplier of the utility constraint:

$$\Im_Q: \quad \frac{\partial V}{\partial Q} - \frac{1}{\mu} = 0;$$

$$\Im_T: \quad -\frac{\partial V}{\partial I} + \frac{1}{\mu} N = 0;$$

$$\Im_N: \quad \frac{\partial V}{\partial I}\frac{\partial I}{\partial N} + \frac{1}{\mu} T = 0.$$

These are identical with the corresponding first-order conditions of the community planning (Section 4.1) problem. The two problems yield an identical optimizing solution Q^*, T^*, N^* with $1/\mu^* = \lambda^*$ if $\overline{U}$ in the city-development problem equals U^* in the community welfare maximization problem.

We now turn to the labor productivity problem of Section 3.3. In this case the source of the agglomeration economy is the external returns to scale in the CBD production. A city developer solves:

$$\text{Maximize}_{N,S} \Pi = ALR(N) - SN \quad \text{subject to}$$

$$A\big(H(N)\big) + S - \frac{ALC(N)}{N} = \hat{I},$$

where $H(N)$ is the aggregate labor supply given by (1). The developer rents out all the land in the land market, organized competitively, collecting aggregate rent $ALR(N)$ and paying out a subsidy, S, to each resident. Because workers are freely mobile between cities, the developer must set the subsidy so that workers get the national disposable income, $\hat{I}$, that prevails in other cities set up by competing developers. $A(H(N))$ is the average product and the private income of the worker and $ALC(N)/N$ is the location cost of a worker in a city with N workers. Solving for S from the constraint and plugging the result into the objective and simplifying using (2) and (3), it becomes

$$\Pi = A\big(H(N)\big)N - kN^{3/2} - \hat{I}N,$$

where the second term is the aggregate commuting cost. This suggests that we can alternatively view the developer as owning all production, collecting all rents, selling the output in the national market, paying all commuting costs (the second term) and paying each worker $\hat{I}$. With many competing developers setting identical cities, the developer makes zero profit. The first-order condition together with zero profit gives

$$S^* = \frac{1}{2}kN^{*1/2} = N^* A'\big(H\big(N^*\big)\big)H'\big(N^*\big).$$

This says that the subsidy per person equals the per capita rent which, in turn, equals the difference between the social and average product of the worker. Hence, once again, the Pigouvian subsidy confiscates the total land rent, causing no distortion.

The efficiency results provided above are a direct consequence of contestability in the city formation market. Hence, the absence of large sunk costs is crucial. But if sunk costs required for city formation are large and developers are not utility takers, Helsley and Strange (1994) showed that in a game-theoretic framework with a fixed finite number of cities, the system of cities will be inefficient. This inefficiency is due to the strategic interaction between developers [Scotchmer (1986)]). In another strategic community development model, Henderson and Thisse (2001) examined the equilibrium formation of communities in which the number of communities is endogenous and the communities are differentiated by the income of their residents. Profit-maximizing developers that interact strategically choose the level of provision of a public good, an entry fee and a unit price for housing to attract households with different incomes to their community. The internal spatial structure of the communities is ignored.

4.3. *Self-organization by atomistic defection: are developers needed?*

Collective mechanisms of city formation relying on developers or local governments are not entirely realistic. An alternative view is that cities are formed, develop, evolve not by centralized action but by the atomistic decisions of consumers and firms. Under this view, consumers are assumed to be myopic and to act independently. They move to an alternative city when they can get a higher utility there. This alternative paradigm, known also as *self-organization*, is more realistic and gives rise to a variety of positive and normative questions about city formation. In the literature, Henderson has repeatedly emphasized the role of developers setting up cities, especially in the United States. On the other hand, Krugman's New Economic Geography has emphasized the formation of cities by a cumulative process caused by the defection of economic agents from other places (including from cities established earlier). The view that developers set up cities is an idealization. In the U.S. developers sometimes play an important role in setting up suburban subdivisions and in some cases whole towns or edge cities. But once these are set up, the developers sell and additional growth happens by atomistic defections. Local governments take over from initial developers but do not behave like the community welfare maximizers of Section 4.1.

It is important to identify the conditions under which developers are needed for cities to emerge, to emerge at the optimal time and to guarantee that cities have the optimal industrial composition. Autarkic optimal size is given by Equation (5) or one of its variants discussed in Section 3. Efficiency of the city system occurs when all cities are so sized. Then, shifting a resident from one city to another reduces utility in both cities. Hence, such an efficient equilibrium is also stable. There is strong agreement in the literature that this efficient and stable outcome cannot be guaranteed by atomistic defection. Henderson (1974), Anas (1992), Pines (2000) and Henderson and Becker (2000) have all presented analyses in which, under self-organization, existing cities get grossly overpopulated before new cities emerge.

To see the reason why, in the case of symmetric cities, cities emerge too late, suppose that a total population P must be divided between two city populations[17] N_1, N_2 such that $N_1 + N_2 = P$. The one-city possibilities of $N_1 = P$, $N_2 = 0$ and $N_1 = 0$, $N_2 = P$ are allowed. Assume that the two cities do not interact with each other and that each consumer is also a firm producing and consuming his own output. Cities can exist because the productivity of each consumer increases with the population of the city (the model of Section 3.3 applies). Pretend that the only action of the city government is to collect and redistribute land rent to its residents. Equilibrium requires consumers deciding in which city to locate and moving freely from the lower utility city to the higher utility one, and thus equalizing utilities. Clearly, the symmetric allocation, $N_1 = N_2 = P/2$, is always an equilibrium but it is not always stable or always optimal. The one-city allocations are also equilibria.[18] There are also asymmetric equilibria with both cities populated. Suppose that N^* is the population level where utility peaks in a city. Then there are two such asymmetric equilibria where utilities are equal: $V(N_1) = V(P - N_1)$. In one of these $N_1 < N^*$ and in the other $N_1 > N^*$. The conclusions depend strictly on the assumed shape of the locus of the asymmetric equilibria in (N_1, N_2) space. In this space, the vertical and horizontal axes correspond to the one-city equilibria and the 45 degree line corresponds to the symmetric equilibria. The slope of the asymmetric equilibria locus is negative everywhere. Anas (1992) assumes that the asymmetric locus is convex to the origin and does not cut the axes. This corresponds to the situation where agglomeration economies build up quickly with city size but decline gently once autarkically optimal city size is reached. There are two regimes separated by a bifurcation point.[19] For $P < 2N^*$, there are three equilibria. These are the two one-city equilibria that are locally stable and the symmetric equilibrium that is locally unstable. For $P > 2N^*$, there are five equilibria. These are the two one-city equilibria, the symmetric equilibrium and the two asymmetric equilibria. In this regime, the one-city equilibria continue to be locally stable, the symmetric equilibrium becomes locally stable, but the asymmetric equilibria are unstable. Now suppose that we start from a very low P, letting it grow exogenously. Since, for low P, the symmetric equilibrium is unstable, we will start with one city. At what point will a second city emerge under atomistic defection of a small population increment from the first? The answer is that in all likelihood this will never happen. For this to happen at some P, the asymmetric equilibrium locus would have to become asymptotic to the two axes. Only in that case, the migration of a single agent from the established city to the virgin site of the second city could establish a higher utility causing a catastrophic cumulative migration process to ensue, ending on a symmetric equilibrium. Otherwise, population will continue to be stuck in the first city, regardless of how overpopulated the first city becomes. Clearly, under these circumstances, atomistic migration fails and a developer or government is needed to start the

[17] This presentation borrows heavily from Anas (1992).

[18] But this requires that $U(P) > U(0)$. If not, then a one-city equilibrium is unstable even under the slightest population perturbation.

[19] The bifurcation pattern is identical to the *pitchfork bifurcation* of Krugman.

second city. That is because a developer or government can orchestrate the simultaneous migration of a critical mass of agents from the first city to establish the second.

It is also shown in Anas (1992) that the socially optimal time when the second city should be set up is t^* such that $V(P(t^*)) = V(P(t^*)/2)$. For most reasonable utility functions, this point in time is much earlier than the point in time when atomistic defection might cause the second city to self-organize. From this we can conclude that with a small number of cities the market process causes new cities to be set up too late if at all. Exceptions to the case examined by Anas do exist. Pines (2000) examined a case in which the autarkic utility curve rises to the optimal city size, N^*, thereafter falling steeply. Although it is hard to produce a realistic example of such a case, his results are interesting only because he assumed that utility falls to zero with sufficiently high population. That causes the asymmetric locus to cut both axes. In this case, atomistic defection can start a new city, but only if that atomistic defection can happen at a precise point in time. If that happens, then the cumulative process evolves smoothly with the original city declining and the new one rising in population until the symmetric equilibrium is reached. Otherwise, if that exact point in time is missed, atomistic defection would still work but only by causing a catastrophic migration process.

In all of the above-mentioned papers, the authors assumed situations in which new cities are intended to be identical to existing ones. Anas and Xiong (2004) examine a setup in which there are two industries. A homogeneous and competitive final good (manufactures) industry uses differentiated, monopolistically competitive services as intermediate inputs. If these inputs are not locally available, the final goods producers will import them from other cities. Optimal city size exists because the differentiated inputs impart an external scale economy on production (see Section 3.2). Suppose that initially there is only one city producing its own services for the use of the final good industry. It is shown that either services or manufactures can move out and set up a second smaller city at an available site by purely atomistic defection with such a new city growing smoothly from infinitesimal size.[20] This means that developers are not needed to set up the new city. They also show that the new city can emerge before the existing one is overpopulated and emerge at the optimal time.

5. Key issues and a summary of historical developments in the literature

We now wish to provide a characterization of the issues that arise in the specification of models of city systems and to follow that with a brief and broad overview of the historical developments that have occurred in the literature.

5.1. Key issues

To our knowledge, all models of systems-of-cities in existence assume that a system of cities is characterized by the costless migration of economic agents (consumers and

[20] Hadar and Pines (2003) have extended the analysis.

firms) among the cities. This assumption, though highly objectionable, forms the basis of an equilibrium principle, namely that cities are organized in such a way that, in equilibrium, agents of the same type are indifferent about the city in which they locate.[21] For example, cities with better local public goods or higher natural amenities should offer workers lower wages in the labor market and higher land rents in the land market, a form of compensating differentials. At equilibrium, these compensating differentials result in equal utility in all cities for agents of the same type.

Beyond this principle of costless migration, city-system models face a large number of basic questions that must be resolved in one way or another in specific models. Forming a clear list of such questions is essential for understanding and classifying the various contributions. Our list – which we believe is complete – consists of fourteen categories of questions.

1. *Are cities in the system identical in size and in industrial composition or are they different?* Cities may be identical in the composition of industries or they may differ. If a city contains only one industry, it is referred to as a *specialized city*. If it contains all of the modeled industries (or at least more than one) it is called a *diversified city*. All models of city systems have either specialized or diversified cities. See our discussion in Section 6.2.
2. *Is the number of commodities produced in the city system predetermined or endogenously determined?* Henderson (1974) and Wilson (1987) have emphasized alternative models with a predetermined number of commodities, whereas the New Economic Geography of Krugman (1991) emphasized models with an endogenously determined number of goods.
3. *Are city industries perfectly or imperfectly competitive or a mix of the two?* Again, Henderson (1974) and Wilson (1987) model industries as competitive, whereas Henderson and Abdel-Rahman (1991) and the New Economic Geography model them as imperfectly competitive. Abdel-Rahman (1990b, 1994) and Anas and Xiong (2003) examined models with both perfect and imperfectly competitive industries.
4. *Are cities in the system composed of homogeneous or heterogeneous worker/laborers? Is this heterogeneity exogenously imposed or endogenously determined?* Both types of models exist in the literature. See our discussion on models with labor heterogeneity in Section 7.
5. *Are cities set up by community planners (local governments) or developers, or do they become self-organized by atomistic defection of economic agents from existing cities?* Henderson and Becker (2000) presented a comparison of these city formation mechanisms. See also our discussion in Sections 4.1–4.3.
6. *How are cities linked with each other?* There is a variety of potential linkages that must be addressed. The most basic, as explained above, is costless migration

[21] There are, however, models of costly migration among countries by Hercowitz and Pines (1991) that could also be applied to intercity migration.

among cities. Are commodities produced in different cities traded among cities? Do agents located in one city own endowments (e.g., land shares) in other cities? Are public goods provided in one city excludable from residents of other cities? Namely, are they local or semi-local public goods? In city-system models with Dixit–Stiglitz varieties that are traded [e.g., Hadar and Pines (2004) or Anas and Xiong (2003, 2004)], the number of varieties produced in a city is equivalent to a semi-public good.

7. *What is the nature of transportation costs for goods traded between cities?* In the literature, the assumption of zero transport costs (in Henderson and Wilson type models) and that of positive iceberg transport costs (in Krugman type models) have played important roles.
8. *What is the nature of externalities operating within and between cities? Are these black-box technological externalities or pecuniary externalities arising from market transactions?* Our discussion in Section 3 illustrated the public good and variety models in which externalities are pecuniary and the labor productivity model in which the externality is technological.
9. *Is the number of cities in the city system predetermined and fixed or is the number and type of cities endogenously determined?* Both cases have been examined rather extensively. See, for example, Hadar and Pines (2004) or Tabuchi (1998) for the former and Henderson and Abdel-Rahman (1991), Anas (2004), Anas and Xiong (2003) for the latter.
10. *Does the city system have an explicit spatial dimension (e.g., cities located on a circle or a linear space) or is the geography abstract or highly simplified?* Treatment of cities on an explicit spatial geography has appeared only in the New Economic Geography [Krugman (1991)]. All other models of systems of cities are formulated on an abstract geography with zero transportation cost or positive transport costs but symmetrically located cities.
11. *Is the internal structure of cities (land market) treated explicitly or is it suppressed?* A simplified model of internal city structure, such as that of Section 2 is standard in the literature, except for the basic models in the New Economic Geography that ignore internal structure when dealing with city systems.
12. *Is the city system linked with a rural (non-urban) sector in the economy?* Kanemoto (1980) and Anas and Xiong (1999) present a system of cities with a rural sector and costless rural to urban migration, whereas in the standard approach of the New Economic Geography [e.g., Fujita, Krugman and Venables (1999)], rural workers are distributed over space and are treated as immobile.
13. *Does the city-system model generate unique or multiple equilibria under the same parameter values? Are there symmetric equilibria (where all cities are identical) as well as asymmetric equilibria (where cities differ in sizes or types)?* The presence of externalities in city systems has resulted in models where multiple equilibria are known to arise and are prevalent. But virtually all authors focus on the symmetric equilibria.

14. *What are the sources of market failure in the system of cities and what are the differences between market equilibrium and first-best and second-best allocations*? Our discussion of Sections 3 and 4 highlighted several types of market failure at the city level and Section 8 extends this efficiency discussion to the entire system of cities with a potentially unlimited number of sites where cities can emerge.

5.2. Historical development of the field

Historically, the development of models of systems of cities has proceeded as follows. In the earliest models by Henderson (1974), industries are perfectly competitive producing homogeneous goods and the number of such goods produced in the city system is predetermined. Increasing returns at the city level arise from Marshallian localization (industry-specific) externalities and not from pecuniary market transactions. There may be goods that are locally consumed and other goods that are traded between cities. However, trading costs are always assumed zero. Hence, as we shall see later, different traded goods are not produced in the same city because doing so would crowd the land market, raising rents and commuting costs without any offsetting benefit. The number of cities is endogenous since city developers are free to enter and form new cities according to the Henry George Theorem. Hence, city sizes are efficient. Geography is suppressed and there is no rural sector. Generally, there is a unique equilibrium (or if multiple equilibria exist, these are not specified or not examined).

A second line of modeling is based on the literature of local public goods as it applies to city formation [Stiglitz (1977)]. Wilson (1987) proposed a model in which there are two tradable private goods produced under constant returns with land and labor and without any localization economies. A third, non-traded good is a local public good. The cost of trading the two private goods among cities is again zero and again there is no rural sector. In such a model, the autarkic optimal city size is determined as an inverse U-shaped function of the city's labor force. This shape reflects the fact that the per-capita cost of the public good decreases as population is added to the city (see Section 3.1) while the marginal product and, hence, the wage received by each person also decreases. Thus, an optimal city size exists in such a model even without any commuting cost. The key question in such a model addressed by Wilson is whether the two private goods industries will locate in the same city or in separate specialized cities and how to locate them optimally. In contrast to the Henderson-type model, as we shall see, the Wilson type model has been shown to result in specialization even in the absence of land-market crowding effects (e.g., commuting costs).

In the late eighties, Hobson (1987), Abdel-Rahman (1988) and Rivera-Batiz (1988) and Abdel-Rahman and Fujita (1990) adapted the Dixit and Stiglitz (1977) model of product differentiation and monopolistic competition to an urban setting, starting models that differed considerably from those of Henderson and Wilson. In these models, firms are treated as imperfectly competitive according to Section 3.2 and subject to internal economies of scale, each firm producing a unique differentiated product. These are either final products sold to consumers [as in Dixit and Stiglitz (1977)] or intermediate products used as inputs in the production of homogeneous final products [Ethier (1982)]. By the free entry of firms, the number of goods is made endogenous and – as explained in Section 3.2 – the variety of these goods is a pecuniary external scale economy at the city level. The differentiated goods are assumed to be city-specific and are not traded between cities. As in the Henderson models, geography is again unspecified and there is no rural sector. Welfare analysis as well as market equilibrium are of interest. Because different industries can locate in the same city to share differentiated intermediate inputs, a variation of these product differentiation models have also been used by Abdel-Rahman (1990b) to explain urban diversity as we will see in more detail in Section 6.3.

In all of the above models, the system consists of specialized or diversified cities. However, in developed and developing countries specialized as well as diversified cities coexist. In an attempt to generate more realistic city system, Abdel-Rahman and Fujita (1990) and Abdel-Rahman (1996) adopted the idea of economies of scope in production to an urban setting which leads to the coexistence of specialized and diversified cities in equilibrium. But specialization versus diversification can also be explained without assuming economies of scope. In Anas (2004) and Anas and Xiong (2003), as we shall see, urban diversity versus specialization is explained as a result of the interplay of trading costs, on the one hand, and urban location costs on the other. In Duranton and Puga (2001), specialized and diversified cities coexist as a result of a dynamic model in which the city choice decisions of the firm are tied to the product cycle in a dynamic model.

Another development is based on the ideas in Krugman (1991) and is now called the New Economic Geography (NEG). In this type of model, the industry structure is again of the Dixit–Stiglitz–Ethier type. But there are several important additional features all introduced by Krugman. First, unlike in the other two model types, trading cost is positive and of the iceberg type. Second, self-organization under atomistic defection (not developers or community planners) is the city-formation mechanism. There is either a predetermined number of cities or, at least, not an unlimited number. In the basic versions of these models, cities do not have land markets and are treated as points. Multiple equilibria, not welfare analysis is the focus of the analysis. Most importantly, a rural sector with immobile farmers is usually present and plays a key role in the formation and location of cities. A specific but simple geography (e.g., line or circle) is usually treated. City systems are derived by complex simulation exercises [see Fujita and Mori (1997) and Fujita, Krugman and Mori (1999)].

Finally, most models of city systems assumed that cities are populated with identical households/workers. Helsley and Strange (1990), Kim (1991), Henderson and Becker (2000), and Abdel-Rahman and Wang (1995, 1997) introduced models with multiple but exogenously defined worker types. Abdel-Rahman (2002) developed a model in which the skill distribution of workers within the system of cities is determined endogenously through self-selection.

6. Homogeneous labor

We now turn to the most basic models of city systems under the assumption of homogeneous labor, and discuss the most important issues that have been studied using such models. These are the presence of constant returns in the extensive margin as new cities are formed when cities are not interacting, the industrial specialization versus diversification of cities, the presence of economies of scope among industries and how this affects the formation of diversified cities, the importance of trade among cities producing manufactures and/or differentiated products and how such trade causes the emergence of increasing returns with respect to the aggregate population of the city system.

6.1. *The simplest case: identical isolated cities*

The simplest city-system model consists of n identical cities that have no interaction except that the consumers are free to migrate costlessly among cities establishing an equal-utility equilibrium. Each city is set up at the autarkic efficient size of N^* consumers so that $nN^* = P$, the national or regional population. Although the number of cities must be an integer, it is commonly assumed that P is large enough relative to N^* so that n is treated as a continuous variable to give a good approximation. City economies may be according to one of the three models discussed in Section 3 and may be setup by a developer, a local government or self-organize under atomistic defection. Assuming large P, $n = P/N^*$ is a stable equilibrium since with this number of cities, consumers in each city will achieve the highest level of utility and thus atomistic defection to other cities could not result in higher utility. Similarly, if cities were set up by developers and $n > P/N^*$, each city is smaller than optimal size and city developers make losses. Some of them must exit the market, $N \to N^*$ and $n \to P/N^*$. Conversely, if $n < P/N^*$, each city is larger than optimal size and developers make positive profits. New developers should emerge with n and N tending to equilibrium again.

What are possible reasons why the cities do not have any interaction? According to the local public good model of Section 3.1, each city produces the same local public good and the same consumption good. Hence, nothing is gained by trading these goods. According to the model of Section 3.3, all cities would produce the same consumption good, again there being no reason to trade. City output would be consumed locally and any excess could be exported to the rest of the world from the CBD. In the case of the product variety model of Section 3.2, however, things are a bit different. In this case, because consumers have an extreme taste for variety (or producers an extreme bias for input variety) they would have a strong desire to not only consume their local varieties but to also import all other varieties produced in the other cities. For such cities not to trade differentiated goods, intercity trading costs have to be infinitely high, an extreme case.

The most important property of a city system with isolated non-interacting cities is a result established in the early papers of Henderson (1974), Upton (1981) and Henderson and Ioannides (1981). According to this result, even though each city is subject to internal economies of scale with respect to city population, due to centripetal forces such as those of Section 3, the city system on aggregate exhibits constant returns to scale at the extensive margin. As the aggregate population, P, grows, this constant returns is maintained by spawning new identical cities of size N^*, with all aggregates such as gross product growing at the rate of population growth. This property illustrates the importance of an economy being able to spawn new cities. When this is not possible, additional population growth must be accommodated in existing cities and these cities become larger than their autarkic optimal size and causing welfare losses.

6.2. Specialization versus diversification

A central issue is whether cities in the system will be specialized or diversified in production. Specialization occurs when production in the city consists of only one industry. Diversification is normally defined as two or more industries co-locating in the same city. The simplest way to study the problem is to assume that there are just two industries and then explore the conditions under which these two industries will locate in the same city.

6.2.1. Specialization

Suppose that the two industries have no direct connection with one another. Each produces a homogeneous good that can be traded among the consumers of the city system. Then, there are two opposing effects that must be considered. Although the literature has not been explicit about these effects, we will try to describe them carefully here.[22] The first may be called the *trading-economy effect*. This means that if each city contains both industries producing enough output to meet the local demand for both goods, then the city need not import either good. Such a diversified city saves importation cost for its residents and raises their utility. The second effect is the *crowding-out effect*. This means that if a city contains two industries it will be larger in labor force and in population. Average commuting costs will be larger in such a city lowering utility. Thus, unrelated constant returns to scale industries crowd each other out in land markets favoring the specialization of cities.

This crowding-out effect does not exist in Krugman's New Economic Geography because in those models cities are typically modeled as not having any land markets. On the other hand, in the Henderson type models with traded goods, the cost of trading goods among cities is always assumed to be zero. Hence, the trading-economy effect is non-existent. Then, the crowding-out effect remains unopposed and cities are always specialized. We can easily generalize this intuition to $k = 1, \ldots, K$ industries as long as there is no limit on the number of cities that can be formed. Suppose that all goods

[22] We follow Anas and Xiong (2003) who discuss these two effects explicitly.

can be traded within and among cities at zero cost. Then, there will be n_k specialized cities of type-k containing industry k and N_k residents. Given a total population P, $\sum_{i=1}^{K} n_k N_k = P$. Each of these cities will be set up at the efficient size implied by the economies of scale of their respective industry. If the efficient size of a city specializing in good $k+1$ is larger than the efficient size of a city specializing in good k, rents in a type-k city will be higher. To compensate, so that utility is invariant among cities, wages in the type $k+1$ city should also be higher than those in the type k. Meanwhile, the number of cities of each type will adjust so that the total quantity of each good k demanded in the city system is supplied.

The above specialization result may be contrasted with that which occurs in the model by Wilson (1987) described earlier. Recall that in that model there were homogeneous consumer-workers, two industries without localization economies, zero trading cost and a city-specific public good. It was assumed that developers set up cities. Hence, a city would be specialized if the developer found it beneficial to allow production of only one good in his city. This is an argument for specialization and trade based on the theory of clubs rather than on the theory of localization externalities. Papageorgiou and Pines (1999) provide an analysis of this model, arguing that whether cities will be specialized or diversified at the optimum of the city system depends on the asymmetry between the technologies for producing the two private goods and on the complementarities between private and public good production. Typically, in the optimum of a system of specialized cities, one will be larger than its autarkic size and the other smaller, and trade of the specialized goods will take place. At such an optimum, the city with the larger public good provision is overpopulated, pays a lower wage and has higher rents (the theory of compensating differentials) and the two types of cities differ in consumption mix as well, because the city-specific wage (determined by the city-specific marginal product of labor) means that the relative prices of the two goods are different depending on the type of city one lives in.

6.2.2. Economies of scope

One way to depart from the completely specialized city system is to assume linkages between the various industries. Perhaps the most obvious way of doing so is to assert economies of scope when the two goods are produced together in the same city. See Panzar and Willig (1981) for the non-spatial theory of economies of scope and for its relation to agglomeration economies, see Goldstein and Gronberg (1984).[23]

Abdel-Rahman (1990a) developed the first spatial model of asymmetric economies of scope. There are two homogeneous goods where the production functions are $x_1 = f(H_1, H_2)h_1$ with $f_1, f_2 > 0$ and $x_2 = g(H_2)h_2$ with $g_1 > 0$, where x_1, x_2 are

[23] See Helsley and Strange (1993) for a non-spatial micro foundation model of urban agglomeration in which matching in the used-assets capital market enhances the salvage value of the assets from failed projects. For a review of models based on search, learning and matching, see Duranton and Puga (2004) in this volume.

the outputs of firms in industry 1 and 2, respectively, h_1, h_2 are labor inputs in the firms and H_1, H_2 are aggregate labor inputs at the level of the industries. Thus, industry 1 has *urbanization economies* [Jacobs (1969)] because it reflects external economies of scale that operate across industries in the same city. Industry 2 has *localization economies* [Marshall (1890)]. The author examined a system consisting of a diversified city and a city specializing in industry 2. The main result is that the diversified city can be larger in equilibrium than the specialized city if at least one of the industries exhibits decreasing returns to scale at some point.

In Abdel-Rahman and Fujita (1993) economies of scope are modeled on the cost side. It is assumed that developers can set up cities, minimizing location plus production costs. There are again two final goods ($i = 1, 2$) with cost functions $C_i = F_i + c_i X_i$. F_i is a fixed cost that must be incurred for production to start and c_i is a constant marginal cost. X_i is industry output. Since trading costs are zero, pure specialization would occur with each city producing only one of the goods. To offset this, it is assumed that when the two goods are produced in the same city, then the fixed cost of production is $F_d < F_1 + F_2$. The cost of producing both goods in such a city is then $C_d = F_d + c_1 X_1 + c_2 X_2$. Clearly, if such fixed cost savings are not sufficiently high, cities will be specialized because the crowding-out effect is not completely offset by the cost savings of joint production. But if these savings are sufficiently high all of the cities in the system will be diversified producing both goods. There are also mixed equilibria with some cities diversified while others are specialized in one good. The mixed equilibria, in which the specialized city produces good 1, would result if $F_d > F_1$ but $F_d < F_2$. The authors showed that the diversified cities would be larger than the specialized ones.

A related paper is by Abdel-Rahman (1994). In this model there are two constant returns final goods industries producing goods traded at zero cost. Each produces using homogeneous labor plus a service specialized to that industry. Services are assumed not to be tradable among cities. The production of the two services is subject to economies of scope. In this case the saving from joint production can occur either in the fixed or the variable cost of service production. Again, when the saving from joint production of services is not high, pure specialization occurs with each city producing one final and its related intermediate good. In this case, the existence of cities is dependent on the presence of a scale economy (fixed cost) in the production of the service. Conversely, if the savings from the joint production of the two services are sufficiently high, all cities are purely diversified in equilibrium, each producing both final goods and both services. If the economy of scope lowers variable costs rather than fixed costs then a mixed equilibrium exists in which the specialized and diversified cities co-exist and, in such an equilibrium, the specialized cities can be larger than the diversified ones.

The above models treat the economy of scope as a black box because they do not show explicitly the source from which the productivity gains or the cost savings arise. A model that does so explicitly is the sharable inputs model of Abdel-Rahman (1990b). The city produces a traded good and a local public good. Both production processes are constant returns and use a homogeneous labor input plus the entire variety of differentiated, non-traded services also produced in the city. These shared services are monopolistically competitive as in Ethier (1982).

6.2.3. *Diversification without economies of scope*

While the above models achieve diversification by imposing economies of scope in the production process, it is more challenging to do this without imposing such a relationship. In fact, when economy of scope is imposed, the result of diversification in cities follows almost directly from the premise of the model. The obvious alternative is to assume that the two final goods industries are unrelated in production and that the two goods are costly to trade. If these goods are sufficiently costly to trade, then there will be a significant trading-economy effect to offset the crowding-out effect. Abdel-Rahman (1996) presents such a model. In this model, there are two final goods that can be traded among cities. One of these is traded for consumption while the other is used to produce commuting which is assumed to require monetary as opposed to time expenditure. Each manufacturing industry uses labor and differentiated services specialized to that industry. The specialized services are monopolistically competitive, as in the previous models. Because the industries do not use the same services, there are no economies of scope. Like in all Abdel-Rahman models, the services cannot be traded among cities. Two equilibria are analyzed. The first occurs when the cost of trading manufactures among cities is sufficiently low. Then all cities are specialized in one of the goods and its associated services at equilibrium. Clearly, this is because the crowding-out effect dominates the trading-economy effect. In the second type of equilibrium, all cities are identical and purely diversified. Each city produces both manufactures and the associated services for each and there is no trade. This equilibrium occurs when trading costs are so high that the trading-economy effect dominates the crowding-out effect.

6.2.4. *Intercity trade of services*

In all of the preceding models with services, the fact that these services cannot be traded provides the source of the industry-level scale economy. But is the assumption that services cannot be traded realistic? On the one hand, Abdel-Rahman and Fujita (1990) have described these producer services as "repair and maintenance services, engineering and legal support, transportation and communication services, and financial and advertising services." While some of these services are difficult to export to other cities, it is increasingly true that communication, financial (banking, insurance, investment) and advertising services are traded among cities. The recent adoption of the Internet as a communication device has increased trading of such services. Hence, the assumption that services can be traded among cities at some cost while final goods are also tradable at some other cost appears realistic. This has been examined in Anas and Xiong (2003). The setup of their model is similar to Abdel-Rahman (1996) but differs in several minor and one major respect. The minor differences are that commuting within cities costs time not money and that both final goods are consumed (rather than one being used to pay for commuting). The major difference is that both services and final goods are tradable among the cities but at different unit cost rates. The final goods (manufactures) are produced using labor and the largest possible variety of services special to that industry. Hence, each manufacturer will import all services of his industry from all other cities that produce them as well as use his locally available services. By assuming that the two industries are symmetric in technology and that the demand for their products is also symmetric, the analysis is greatly simplified. Two equilibria are analyzed using these assumptions of symmetry. In one all cities are diversified (containing both manufacturing industries and their associated services). In the other equilibrium, half of the cities are specialized in each manufacture and its associated services. The number of cities and the size of a city are the same in the two equilibria. Hence, the size of an industry located in a diversified city is half as big as it would be if the same industry were located in a specialized city. This means that a firm located in a diversified city will have exactly half the number of local services available to it than a firm located in a specialized city. This is exactly how the crowding-out effect operates in the model. On the other hand, the trading-economy effect means that there will be no trading of manufactures if all cities are diversified. It is shown that either equilibrium can yield higher utility, depending on various parameters of the model. For example, increasing the share of services in production favors specialized cities since, in such cities, more services are locally available and fewer have to be imported. For the same reason, if services are more expensive to trade, this favors specialization. Conversely, if manufactures are expensive to trade, this increases the savings from the trading-economy effect and favors the equilibrium of diversified cities. If commuting cost increases, cities become smaller and there are fewer service varieties available locally, which increases the utility of a specialized city relative to a diversified city because in the specialized city there are more service varieties locally.

6.2.5. *Product cycles*

Most recently, specialization and diversification has been analyzed in a dynamic model that resulted in system of cities in which diversified and specialized cities co-exist. Duranton and Puga (2001) developed the first model of product cycles in the systems of cities literature.[24] In this model, a metropolitan area plays the role of a nursery for new products. They employed a model of product development where firms experiment with prototypes in a diversified city until they find the ideal production process. After the firm identifies the ideal production process, it moves to a specialized city to start mass production. The main result of the paper is to identify the conditions that result in a unique steady state in which specialized and diversified cities coexist. However, the size of the diversified city is the same as that of the specialized one, which is not consistent with

[24] Henderson, Kuncoro and Turner (1995) had provided empirical support for this product cycle model in a system of cities.

empirical observation nor with other theoretical models that result in the co-existence of diversified and specialized cities.[25]

6.3. Increasing returns with traded varieties

In some of the models discussed above, the presence of costly trade among cities was the basis for the incentive to save trading costs and, hence, played a major role in whether two industries would locate in the same city or not. A second important consequence of trade among cities is the possible emergence of increasing returns in aggregate national population. Recall that in the models of city systems with isolated cities (see Section 6.1), the city system exhibited constant returns in the extensive margin as cities were created in response to population growth.

To see how trade among cities can induce increasing returns in aggregate population, we may construct a simple extension of the model of product variety that we examined in Section 3.2. In that model, we looked at only one city producing m manufactures in equilibrium, in symmetric industries. Consumers viewed these products as imperfect substitutes and had a strong enough taste for variety to want to consume all of these products at any price. What would happen if we had n such identical cities each producing m varieties of manufactures distinct from those produced in any other city? Henderson and Abdel-Rahman (1991) provided an answer, but they assume zero trading costs. Following Anas (2004), we assume an abstract geometry in which the n cities are located symmetrically with respect to one another. We assume, as he does, iceberg transport costs so that $1/\tau$ is the multiple of the demanded quantity of any manufacture that must be shipped from one city to any other. When $\tau = 1$, the cost of transportation is zero and when $\tau = 0$, the cost of transportation is infinitely high. Given that P is the national population in the entire city system and given that each city is set up at its autarkic efficient size, N, the number of symmetric cities in this economy will be $n = P/N$.

We may easily examine two aggregate quantities in this economy. One is the level of utility and the other is the *gross domestic product* (GDP) of the economy. Starting with the latter and using previously derived quantities (see Section 3.2),

$$\mathrm{GDP} = nmz = \frac{P}{N}\frac{N(1-kN^{1/2})}{f\sigma}\frac{f(\sigma-1)}{c} = \frac{\sigma-1}{\sigma c}\bigl(1-kN^{1/2}\bigr)P.$$

GDP grows linearly with national population (or per-capita GDP is constant). Hence, there are no increasing returns. This is not at all surprising since the benefits of variety occur on the demand side not on the supply side. Turning to utility, we write the direct utility first by recognizing the symmetry we have imposed. It is

$$U = \bigl[mx_i^{(\sigma-1)/\sigma} + (n-1)mx_{-i}^{(\sigma-1)/\sigma}\bigr]^{\frac{\sigma}{\sigma-1}}$$

[25] For models in which diversified and specialized cities co-exist, see Abdel-Rahman and Fujita (1990) and Abdel-Rahman (1994) discussed earlier.

where x_i is the quantity of each variety the consumer buys that is produced in his own city and x_{-i} is the quantity of each variety the consumer buys that is produced in each of the other cities. At this point, it is convenient to switch to the indirect utility which takes the form,

$$V = \left[mp^{1-\sigma} + (n-1)m\left(\frac{p}{\tau}\right)^{1-\sigma} \right]^{1/(\sigma-1)} I(N).$$

Using the previously derived quantities to make substitutions, we get

$$V = p^{-1}\left[N + (P-N)\tau^{\sigma-1}\right]^{1/(\sigma-1)}\left(1 - kN^{1/2}\right)^{\sigma/(\sigma-1)}.$$

Taking the first derivative with respect to P,

$$\frac{\partial V}{\partial P} = \frac{\tau^{\sigma-1}}{p(\sigma-1)}\left(1 - kN^{1/2}\right)^{\sigma/(\sigma-1)}\left[N + (P-N)\tau^{\sigma-1}\right]^{(2-\sigma)/(\sigma-1)}.$$

Thus we see that utility increases with aggregate population except in the case of $\tau = 0$, when cities do not trade because trading cost is prohibitively high. Furthermore, when the taste for variety is sufficiently strong ($\sigma < 2$) then utility increases with P at an increasing rate. In a system of cities model in which producers used all the input varieties while consumers purchased the homogeneous output of these producers, per capita GDP would increase with population, but utility would not.

How would increasing returns with respect to national population become exhausted? There are no models in the literature that directly analyze this issue. One obvious answer is that the land limitation of countries [present in Anas and Xiong (1999)] and the limited number of sites with certain amenities such finite seashore [present in Helpman and Pines (1980)] would at some point restrict returns from additional population growth as land on which new cities can be set up diminishes.

7. Heterogeneous labor

A common feature of all the models discussed in Section 6 is that they ignore the heterogeneity of consumers and workers. Models with such heterogeneity fall into two groups:

(1) those that exogenously introduce different types of workers, and
(2) those that generate the types of workers endogenously.

Helsley and Strange (1990) and Kim (1991), permit horizontal differentiation among workers in a model in which productivity gains are driven by better matching between workers and firms. However, in their model, all cities are identical and all workers achieve the same equilibrium expected utility. Henderson and Becker (2000), Abdel-Rahman (1998) and Abdel-Rahman and Wang (1995, 1997) have different types of exogenously specified workers achieving different utility levels in equilibrium, while Abdel-Rahman (2002) endogenously generates household types.

In Abdel-Rahman (1998), there are skilled and unskilled workers and with leisure in the utility function. Cities in this model are formed due to investment in public infrastructure. The model generates a system of two types of cities in which one type produces a food product with unskilled workers, and the other type produces a high-tech manufacturing product with the use of skilled workers. Workers sort themselves into these two types of cities. The model identifies the determinants of income inequality, which includes productivity and infrastructure effects. Then, the paper analyzes the impact of income inequality on social welfare.

In Henderson and Becker (2000), there are households who are either entrepreneurs or workers, but in this case both types locate in the same city and the model results in a system of identical cities. Cities are formed due to an externality resulting from intra-industry specialization as in Becker and Murphy (1992). The paper examines city formation by large land developers as well as self-organization and a combination of both. The main focus is efficiency of equilibrium and the requirement to achieve efficiency under different city formation mechanisms.

Abdel-Rahman and Wang (1995, 1997) examine a situation in which the national population of workers is exogenously divided into unskilled and skilled laborers. The unskilled workers are homogeneous while the skilled workers are distributed uniformly on the unit circle. The economy has two goods: food requiring unskilled labor input and a high-tech good requiring input from skilled workers. The food industry is subject to a localization economy, a decrease in the average cost of providing a form of city-specific infrastructure that facilitates food production. The two goods can be traded among the cities at zero cost. Clearly, the setup just described favors specialization since there are no direct connections between the industries. Thus, there is neither a trading-economy effect, nor economies of scope, nor input sharing to oppose the crowding-out effect that would occur if both goods were to be produced in the same city. Because of this, the equilibrium would have a core–periphery structure. There would be peripheral cities accommodating unskilled workers only, specializing in the production of food and core cities accommodating the skilled workers specializing in the production of the high-tech good.

An important question is whether at equilibrium all core cities would be identical accommodating workers of all skills or whether they would be different, accommodating workers of a subset of skill ranges. The authors assume that firms cannot setup new cities taking with them workers whose skills are best matched with the firms, i.e., coalitions of workers and firms are not allowed. This condition is insured by assuming that firms do not know a priori the skills of their workers nor workers the skill requirements of firms and that firms and workers cannot sign pre-migration contracts after matching up in one city and prior to relocating to another. Thus, a worker migrating to a new city expects to incur search costs after arriving there. Although this assumption is perhaps somewhat artificial, it ensures that high-tech cities will all be symmetric in equilibrium. As in Helsley and Strange (1990) such cities will accommodate more than one firm since the density of firms on the unit circle confers a productivity economy. The authors examine a special equilibrium outcome in which the core consists of a single large metropolis while the periphery consists of many identical and smaller cities specializing in food production and accommodating only unskilled workers. In the first paper, a symmetric Nash wage bargaining rule, as in Diamond (1982), determines a uniform wage for all skilled workers regardless of how well they are matched to their firms. However, the income of the skilled core workers is higher than that of the peripheral unskilled workers. In the second model, the Nash wage bargain is asymmetric so that firms can differentially reward workers with whom they are better matched. It is assumed that the better-matched workers have higher bargaining power and extract a higher wage. As a result, the second model produces income inequality within the core as well as between the core and the periphery. Unearned income does not play a role in the income distribution because the authors assume that all land is publicly owned and that local planners or city developers use the aggregate land rent to finance the source of the city-level scale economy. In the peripheral cities, the aggregate rents are used to pay for the local infrastructure investment, while in the core the aggregate rent is used to subsidize the fixed costs of the firms. The main claim of these two papers is that changes that improve efficiency can worsen income inequality. For example, the authors show that lower search costs and better matching in the high-tech industry cause the income distribution to become more unequal.

An extension of the above work is by Abdel-Rahman (2002). In this paper, all workers are homogeneous in skills a priori but are vertically differentiated in innate ability defined as the uniform distribution on a unit interval. However, educational investment is endogenous in the model in the sense that each worker may decide whether to acquire specialized training that causes his productivity to rise to a higher level and enables him to obtain a higher wage. If a worker decides not to acquire specialized training, he gets only a basic level of education that is provided as a public good. Only one good is produced, but there are two technologies for producing it. The good may be produced by a basic technology that utilizes workers who get only basic education or it can be produced by a specialized technology that utilizes workers who choose to acquire skills. At equilibrium, workers with higher a priori abilities can acquire skills more cheaply and all workers above a certain reservation ability level choose to acquire skills. The skills acquired are proportional to ability. Because the good is homogeneous, there is again no trading between cities and each city is self-sufficient at equilibrium. There are, however, several types of equilibria. If all workers acquire specialized training, all cities are identical high-technology cities. If no one acquires specialized training, all cities are identical low-technology cities. If, as is most realistic, if only some of the workers acquire specialized training then there are two types of specialized cities co-existing. One type is a high-technology city populated by skilled workers only and the other, a low-technology city populated by unskilled workers. Under realistic parameter values, there would be one or only a few high-technology cities and many low-technology cities. The lowest ability consumer living in a high-technology city would be indifferent between this situation and that of living in a low-technology city.

8. Efficiency and the role of central planning in city systems[26]

In Section 4 we examined optimal resource allocation within individual cities which do not interact. In Sections 6 and 7 we reviewed a variety of equilibrium models of systems of cities, making only slight reference to several issues of optimal resource allocation in such a system. We now pass to a more comprehensive treatment of issues of efficient resource allocation in a system of cities, where such cities may or may not interact with each other.

Henderson (1977), Helpman and Pines (1980) and Kanemoto (1980) were the first to pose problems of optimal resource allocation in a system of cities while some general issues have been laid out by Hochman (1981, 1997).[27] In Helpman and Pines, there is a large number of sites where cities can be set up. Each site is endowed with a different level of a natural amenity. Their model is a variant of the public goods model of Section 3.1. The quality of the public good created in a city is higher, the higher is the level of the natural amenity and the higher is the public expenditure. In addition, consumers derive utility from a composite good and from private lot size. In contrast to the model in Section 2, used in virtually all system of cities models, their lot size increases with distance from the CBD [also true in Henderson (1977) and in Kanemoto (1980)]. The main result is that it is first-best efficient to allocate more population to the sites with the highest amenity levels. However, the presence of commuting cost limits city sizes and, hence, causes sites with lower amenity levels to also be developed. If the importance of the public good in the utility function is high relative to that of residential lot size, then the optimal allocation implies large cities at high population densities that are set up at sites of high amenity. If, on the other hand, land is more important in tastes than is the public good, then there is a larger number of smaller cities with lower densities developed at the lower amenity sites. To decentralize the first-best optimum, each city can be set up by an independent developer, acting as in Section 3.1, setting up the city at its autarkic-efficient size. The developer collects the local aggregate land rent and invests it in the public good, while letting the land market allocate lot sizes. The role that falls on the central planner is to simply specify which sites should be developed.

First-best central planning can also be examined in the context of the labor productivity model of Section 3.3. Suppose that, as in, e.g., Black and Henderson (1999), there are two industries with aggregate production functions $A_i(H_i)H_i$, where $i = 1, 2$ is the

[26] We will focus on systems of cities models with the number of cities endogenous and many. Anas (1992), Tabuchi (1998), Pines (2000), Papageorgiou and Pines (1999, 2000), Hadar and Pines (2003, 2004) have addressed various issues of optimal resource allocation when there are just two cities. Henderson (1977) treated a large number of cities, but not large enough to assume away lumpiness problems. In this case, the efficient allocation of population between cities requires the equalization of the gap between social marginal product and social marginal cost, whereas an equilibrium allocation would equalize private marginal returns to labor.

[27] Kanemoto (1980) dealt with formulations corresponding to the labor productivity case as well as the public goods case.

industry, and H_i is the labor supplied to industry i. The two goods can be traded at zero cost leading to complete specialization of cities by industry. The utility function is $U = x_i^\alpha y_i^\beta$, $\alpha + \beta = 1$, where $i = 1, 2$ denotes the city type, with cities of type 1 producing good x and cities of type 2 producing good y. The central planner's first-best resource allocation problem can be stated as:

$$\mathrm{Max}_{x_1,x_2,y_1,y_2,n_1,n_2,N_1,N_2,U}\, U \quad \text{subject to:}$$

$$x_1^\alpha y_1^\beta - U = 0, \qquad x_2^\alpha y_2^\beta - U = 0,$$

$$n_1 N_1 x_1 + n_2 N_2 x_2 - n_1 A_1(H_1) H_1 = 0,$$

$$n_1 N_1 y_1 + n_2 N_2 y_2 - n_2 A_2(H_2) H_2 = 0,$$

$$n_1 N_1 + n_2 N_2 - P = 0.$$

This says that the central planner maximizes the equal utility level by deciding per capita consumptions in each city, the city sizes of each type and the number of cities of each type given aggregate population and a monocentric organization of each city as in Section 2. Hence, from Section 2, $H_i = N_i(1 - kN_i^{1/2})$ is the labor supply in a type i city. The third and fourth constraints conserve the system-wide output of each good, while the last constraint conserves population. The solution is one in which the result of Section 3.3 holds exactly: in each city, the local aggregate rents should be used to pay the subsidies that cover the gap between social marginal and average products. So, in the decentralized optimum, a different developer may set up each city, while the central planner indicates the type of each city and determines the number of each type (n_1, n_2) by issuing a license to each city developer.

In the above examples we see that the Henry George Theorem holds in the decentralized first-best optimum. The reason is that the agglomeration economy (public good in Helpman and Pines (1980) or labor productivity in the above formulation) exists only at the city level. The theorem fails to hold, when – with the number of cities endogenous – adding population to one city confers positive or negative external effects on other cities. A demonstration of this can be constructed using the model of product variety discussed in Section 3.2. Consider the extension of that model to a system of cities as formulated by Anas (2004). He assumes that all cities are symmetrically located with respect to one another and that all varieties are traded nationally with positive iceberg trading cost. In such a setting, he shows that the first-best optimal resource allocation problem of the central planner is:

$$\mathrm{Max}_{x_i,x_{-i},m,z,N}\, U(x_i, x_{-i}, m, z) = \left[m x_i^{(\sigma-1)/\sigma} + \left(\frac{P}{N} - 1\right) m x_{-i}^{(\sigma-1)/\sigma} \right]^{\sigma/(\sigma-1)}$$

given P and subject to:

$$N x_i + \left(\frac{P}{N} - 1\right) N x_{-i} \left(\frac{1}{\tau}\right) - z = 0,$$

$$m(f + cz) - N\left(1 - kN^{1/2}\right) = 0,$$

$$N_{\min} \leqslant N \leqslant N_{\max}.$$

Here, m is the number of firms (varieties) allocated to each city, N is the population allocated to each city with P/N the number of cities implied (where P is the national population), z is the output produced by each firm, x_i is the quantity consumed of each local variety, and x_{-i} the quantity consumed of each imported variety. The first constraint conserves the output of each firm, while the second conserves the allocation of labor in each city. In the third constraint, $N_{\min}$ is the population necessary to produce a single variety, indicating minimum possible city size.

Two diametrically opposed special cases of the above formulation appeared in the earlier literature. One is that of Abdel-Rahman and Fujita (1990). They implicitly assumed that the cost of trading varieties between cities is infinite ($\tau = 0$). Since, in their model, varieties cannot be traded, the economy should produce each variety in every city and there will be no externalities conferred on one city when adding population to another. In this extreme case, the Henry George rule holds again and developers acting as in Section 4.2 decentralize the first-best optimal allocation with the number of local varieties behaving like a public good and land rents subsidizing fixed costs of setting up firms. The opposite case is one where varieties can be imported from other cities at zero cost ($\tau = 1$). This was assumed in Henderson and Abdel-Rahman (1991). Under their assumption, complete specialization is optimal and each variety is produced in a separate town of minimal size.

Anas (2004) showed that this complete specialization equilibrium occurs under any positive transport cost ($0 < \tau < 1$) as long as national population, P, is fairly large. In the complete specialization equilibrium, each city produces a homogeneous composite good and a single variety that is exported to all other cities. Note that the externality is at the level of aggregate population. Adding more people to the system allows more traded varieties to be produced in new specialized cities causing welfare to increase in every city. City size is determined by the labor needed to produce a single variety plus the locally needed composite good (if one exists). It is not surprising that complete specialization should be optimal when varieties can be traded at zero cost [as Henderson and Abdel-Rahman (1991)] had assumed, because there is no trading cost to save from the two products being produced in the same city. But the result in Anas (2004) that complete specialization is optimal even with positive trading cost is surprising. This occurs because as national population increases the centrifugal forces arising from trading are strengthened.

Hochman (1997) has examined a generalization of functional forms for the complete specialization case. His key point is that each specialized town is a natural monopoly (the marginal cost curve is everywhere below the average cost curve). He notes the presence of two distortionary effects:

(1) the inefficiency of monopolistic competition causes more varieties (cities) at the optimum;

(2) each firm (city) ignores the advantages of an increase in the number of varieties and this causes fewer and larger cities at the optimum as compared to the laissez-faire equilibrium.

The optimum allocation requires marginal cost pricing. This results in optimal cities being larger and each city producing more of its variety. Because the marginal cost curve is below the average cost curve, marginal cost pricing requires a subsidy being given to the firm as in the classic problem of natural monopoly regulation. However, the Henry George rule fails since the local aggregate land rent falls short of the aggregate subsidy required and the local government has neither the means nor the incentive to pay out such a subsidy. This means that, to achieve the first-best optimum, the central planner should subsidize each variety via a head tax levied on each consumer. As shown in Hochman (1997), this subsidy can be per unit of the variety produced or, as shown by Henderson and Abdel-Rahman (1991), it can be lump sum and equal to the fixed cost of the firm. Furthermore, when each completely specialized city produces a local variety and a homogeneous good as well, as was true in the non-spatial model of Dixit and Stiglitz (1977), then Henderson and Abdel-Rahman (1991) and Hochman (1997) conclude that neither the Henry George Theorem holds, nor can the planner's first-best optimum be decentralized.

There are other contexts in which central planners are shown to be essential. Anas and Xiong (2003) present a model in which two homogeneous goods are traded at cost among cities and so are the varieties that are used as intermediate inputs in the production of these goods. Under the same parameter values (including the unit iceberg trading costs) they examine two possible equilibria. In the first type of equilibrium, each city specializes in only one homogeneous good and produces some input varieties locally. In the second type of equilibrium, each city is diversified producing both homogeneous goods and varieties. Depending on parameter values, either one of the two equilibria can yield higher utility (and be optimal). Without a central planner, such an optimum may not be achievable. A planner is needed to specify the industry mix of the cities according to the optimum allocation. Without such planning, the city system can get stuck in the inferior equilibrium.

Yet another context in which central planning is necessary to achieve the optimum is illustrated by Anas and Xiong (1999). In this model, when cities are formed, there is a benefit to the rural sector in that rural population densities decrease and agricultural productivity increases. Hence, the optimum involves a cross-subsidy from rural to urban workers.

9. Growth

One basic challenge is to explain how the city size distribution evolves over time as population grows exogenously or as endogenous economic growth occurs. A hypothesis that has found some support in the literature is the *parallel growth hypothesis*. According to this hypothesis, population growth causes cities of different sizes to grow at the same rate so that at any moment in time the relative sizes of alternative cities are unchanged. Eaton and Eckstein (1997) provide empirical support for the parallel growth hypothesis. They observed that the relative populations of the top 40 urban areas in France (1876–1990) and Japan (1925–1985) remained essentially unchanged. Black and Henderson (1999, p. 254) provided further support for this hypothesis: "Despite entry of new metropolitan areas, the relative size distribution of cities is astonishingly stable over time, exhibiting no tendency to collapse ("converge" to a common city size), spread, go bimodal, and so forth, with the actual distribution fluctuating little between decades." The parallel growth hypothesis may be questioned by observing the emergence of megacities all over the world, an observation we noted in the Introduction. If the trend were to continue, sometime in the future an increasingly large proportion of the world's population could come to reside in such megacities.

9.1. Exogenous population growth

The evolution of a city size distribution over time may be viewed as a tug-of-war between centripetal and centrifugal forces. These are not only operative at the level of an individual city, determining the size of that city as we saw in Sections 2 and 3, but they are also operative at the system of cities level. Centripetal forces favor concentration of economic activity in a small number of large cities, while centrifugal forces favor concentration of economic activity in a large number of small cities. The key question is whether population growth modifies the relative strength of these two opposing forces. If, as population grows, the centripetal forces become increasingly strong relative to the centrifugal force then the number of cities could decline with their sizes increasing. Conversely, if the centrifugal forces become increasingly strong with population growth, then the number of cities should increase with city sizes decreasing.

For a system of identically sized cities (e.g., a flat city-size distribution), this question has been posed in Anas (2004). Suppose that the exogenous system-wide population is expressed as $P(t) = n(t)N(t)$, where t is time, $n(t)$ is the number of cities as a function of time and $N(t)$ is the size of a single city. In the simplest Henderson-type setup that was examined in Section 6.1, cities are isolated (do not interact with each other); hence as population grows, city size remains unchanged while more cities are spawned. However, as we saw in Section 7, when the cities trade with each other, then the creation and size of one city confers an externality on all the others. Then, depending on the nature of trade, cities grow or shrink in size on the growth path. Anas (2004) identifies:

(a) concentration ($\dot{P}(t) > 0 \Rightarrow \dot{n}(t) < 0,\ \dot{N}(t) > 0$),
(b) balanced growth ($\dot{P}(t) > 0 \Rightarrow \dot{n}(t) \geqslant 0,\ \dot{N}(t) \geqslant 0$),
(c) de-agglomeration ($\dot{P}(t) > 0 \Rightarrow \dot{n}(t) > 0,\ \dot{N}(t) < 0$).[28]

[28] Kanemoto (1980) and Henderson and Ioannides (1981) have examined exogenous growth without trade.

Clearly, which pattern obtains will depend on how the theoretical model is specified. In Anas (2004) the model subjected to this test is that inspired by the assumptions of the New Economic Geography (NEG) adapted by him to a system-of-cities context. There is no agricultural sector as in the NEG,[29] but instead cities are organized as in Section 2 and the number of cities is endogenous. This urban economy of n cities produces m varieties and all nm varieties in the city system are consumed by each of the consumers, hence traded among the cities subject to iceberg transportation cost as in the NEG. The focus is the optimal behavior of the city system under a hypothetical central planner. Anas proves that such a city system *always* produces the third pattern of de-agglomeration in its most extreme form. As population increases exogenously, new cities are spawned on the welfare maximizing path but each city continues to get smaller and smaller until, eventually, all cities suddenly become completely specialized mini-factory towns producing a single variety that is traded to all the other cities. This result is extremely robust. Provided sufficient population growth occurs, this optimal de-agglomeration result is inevitable for all finite values of the Dixit–Stiglitz elasticity of substitution and the unit iceberg trading cost. What causes this robust de-agglomeration is the consumer's extreme taste for more varieties stemming from the Dixit–Stiglitz utility that is so central to the New Economic Geography as well as to the monopolistic-competition-based city size models of Abdel-Rahman and Fujita (1990). For a given aggregate population, more national varieties can be produced by splitting the population into small specialized towns because smaller towns require less commuting, afford more labor hours and in this way allow more varieties to be produced.

There are important implications of this result. *First*, it means that under NEG type of assumptions, observed city size distributions with cities getting larger as the world population grows cannot be efficient unless the population growth is accompanied by steep declines in the unit cost of commuting or by steep increases in the cost of trading goods and services between cities. Historically, it is true that commuting costs have fallen, but they have stabilized in recent times. But the cost of trading between cities has also fallen, not risen. This means that city-system theories that rely on Dixit–Stiglitz tastes (or on Ethier production functions) with intercity trading of differentiated goods and services may not be useful for modeling actual urbanization trends. *Second*, the de-agglomeration result suggests how better theory may be developed by modeling trade among cities in a more realistic manner.

9.2. *Endogenous economic growth*

Palivos and Wang (1996) constructed a one-sector, one factor dynamic equilibrium model of a single city in which city growth is endogenous. In this model, the engine of urban growth is the spillover of knowledge among individuals as in Romer (1986). The black-box production function of the only consumption good is $y = Ak^{\alpha}K^{1-\alpha}$

[29] For a criticism of the treatment of agriculture in the NEG, see Pines (2001).

where k and K denote per capita and aggregate human capital in the city. Thus, higher population in the city implies higher aggregate human capital stock and thus higher productivity at the individual level (due to interpersonal spillovers). As in all urban models, the growth of the city is bounded due to the rise in the average transportation cost as a result of the physical increase in the size of the city (see Section 2). It is assumed that the consumer has a constant elasticity of intertemporal substitution and a constant rate of time preference. The paper characterized the steady-state equilibrium growth path in a decentralized economy as well as the socially optimal growth path. In the decentralized economy, each agent determines the paths of consumption and investment in human capital and a developer determines the city's population. In the social optimum, the developer chooses the optimal growth path of consumption and investment as well as the population. The main result of the paper is that the optimal city size and growth rate are lager on the optimal path than on the equilibrium path, because central planning by the developer internalizes the spillover externality. The model is identical in form to the labor productivity model of city size described in Section 3.3 and, hence, the aggregate human capital level is equivalent to a public good. Unfortunately, the authors do not examine the implications of their model in a system of cities framework.

Ioannides (1994) synthesized the Dixit–Stiglitz model of product diversity and monopolistic competition (see Section 3.2) with Romer's (1987) model of increasing returns due to specialization. In this model, which employs an overlapping generations formulation, consumers invest their life savings in urban overhead capital, enabling producers to constantly create new product varieties. Because the cost of trading varieties between cities is zero, there is no home market effect and, as in Henderson and Abdel-Rahman (1991), each variety is produced in a separate and completely specialized city organized by a developer. Thus, growth in the economy is tied to the growth in the number of varieties, same thing as the growth in the number of cities. In the steady state of such a model, with all cities identical, a balanced agglomeration path is exhibited with the number of cities growing at the same rate as aggregate population and the size of each city remaining constant.

Black and Henderson (1999) developed a model of urban growth of a system of two types of cities. The economy produces an intermediate and a final good. Production of the final good requires the intermediate good as an input, but because the cost of shipping the intermediate good is assumed to be zero, locating the two goods in the same city causes only crowding effects with no offsetting benefit. Hence, at equilibrium there are two types of specialized cities, one city type producing the intermediate good while the other type specializing in the final good and importing the intermediate good. Both goods are produced using workers. Each worker is a firm. The production function of a worker uses that worker's human capital as an input, but a worker's productivity depends on two external effects as well. One of these is the total number of workers in the same city. This measures the Marshallian flow of creative ideas or information that can be obtained freely from other workers. The other external effect is the average level of human capital in the city measuring the richness of the information flowing from the labor force. This formulation is equivalent to the labor productivity model of our Section 3.3. At the level of the worker production is constant returns, but the social marginal product exceeds the private marginal product because of the external effects. Under the assumption that all workers are identical, each worker's human capital level equals the average level of human capital in the city of that worker. Each city is set up by a developer (see Section 4.2) and is self-financing under the Henry George rule. Equilibrium as well as socially optimal growth paths are analyzed.

In models with several types of cities and human capital accumulation at the level of a worker, a problem arises from the interaction of the migration decision with the human capital accumulation decision. That is because workers would choose to switch cities over their lives and they would accumulate human capital according to the sequence of city types they resided in.[30] To avoid this complexity, Black and Henderson assume that workers belong to an infinitely lived dynasty that is centrally administered. The size of the dynasty grows exogenously at a constant rate. The dynasty maximizes the lifetime discounted utility of its representative member (a worker). Each worker is allocated the same amount of consumption regardless of the city type in which that worker lives. The workers' savings (income net of commuting, rent and consumption) becomes new human capital. The dynasty allocates the human capital contributed by its workers in a city to its newborn members in that city. The dynasty also decides what fraction of its members should live in type 1 and type 2 cities. The model provides a framework for studying the effects of urbanization and city size distribution on economic growth as well as the effects of economic growth on urbanization, since the number of each type of city is endogenously determined. At steady state, the model can replicate each of the growth patterns identified above (concentration in fewer cities, balanced growth and de-agglomeration). More precisely, the number of cities increases if human capital accumulation is not strong enough. Otherwise, if human capital accumulation is strong enough, then the number of cities decreases. City sizes for each city type grow at approximately twice the rate of human capital accumulation. Thus, the model replicates the parallel growth hypothesis.[31] The social optimum involves higher consumption and human capital accumulation relative to the equilibrium since, in the equilibrium, the positive externalities from the localization of production are not internalized.

Black and Henderson mention that between 1900 and 1950, the average metropolitan population in the U.S. tripled, while the number of metro areas doubled under a national population growth rate of 1.4% per year. In the same period, the percentage

[30] Eaton and Eckstein (1997) treat migration more realistically in that individual consumers migrate from city to city over their lives but become assimilated to the average human capital level of the city in which they reside. However, in their model, the number of cities is constant and not endogenous As explained in the introduction, Black and Henderson and Eaton and Eckstein claim empirical support for the parallel growth hypothesis.

[31] The fact that all three growth patterns are possible under human capital accumulation is an important result because in models of city systems based on the New Economic Geography under costly trade between cities but no human capital, city sizes continually decrease under exogenous population growth [see Anas (2004) for the proof].

of the 17-year-old population that had completed high school rose nine-fold from 6.3 to 57.4 percent nationally (p. 254). These numbers correspond to a compound national population growth rate ($\dot{P}/P$) of 1.4% per year, a city size growth rate ($\dot{N}/N$) of 2.2% per year, a growth rate in the number of metro areas ($\dot{n}/n$) of 1.396% per year, and a human capital growth rate ($\dot{h}/h$) of 4.5% per year. From $P = Nn$, it follows that

$$\frac{\dot{n}}{n} + \frac{\dot{N}}{N} = \frac{\dot{P}}{P}.$$

In the model, city growth is proportional to human capital growth by the equation

$$\frac{\dot{N}}{N} = 2\varepsilon \frac{\dot{h}}{h}$$

where ε is the elasticity of income with respect to human capital. From the annualized growth rates given above, it is implied that $\varepsilon = 0.244$ (a 10% increase in human capital should generate only a 2.44% increase in income). Meanwhile, from

$$\frac{\dot{n}}{n} = \frac{\dot{P}}{P} - \frac{\dot{N}}{N} = 0.014 - 0.022 = -0.008,$$

implying a slight annual rate of decrease in the number of cities, not the doubling observed by Black and Henderson. The empirical part of the paper reports regressions that establish a strong association between metropolitan-area human capital levels and metropolitan populations. However, the fact that the theoretical model does not appear consistent with the data (as just explained) may be suggestive that human capital growth rates may be only part of the explanation for predicting city growth rates.

10. Challenges ahead

Systems of cities models are challenged by several empirical observations that have gained relevance and validity in recent decades. The first of these is the apparently growing trend toward larger and larger cities and the concentration of the world's population in such cities. This is sometimes referred to as the primacy phenomenon and is recognized as a persistent violation of the rank–size rule. As we saw earlier, existing models of human capital accumulation in cities do not capture this phenomenon because they have so far focused exclusively on the parallel growth hypothesis. Growth models are needed to explain how some cities grow relatively larger than others and how they become diversified as they grow. Yet, there is no dynamic model at the present time that captures the relationship between growth and diversification. The intuitive notion that diversification speeds up the growth process has found some empirical support [Glaeser et al. (1992)] but a solid theory is sorely lacking.

A second area of concern is the growth of polycentric cities all over the world. While this trend has been widely recognized [see Anas, Arnott and Small (1998)], all systems of cities models to date have relied on the monocentric model of an urban area (see

Section 2). The problem with this approach is that it suppresses an important margin across which dispersion takes place. As population grows, new cities are set up. But instead of accommodating additional population in new cities, existing cities can spawn new subcenters. Subcenter formation is a major way in which existing cities get bigger, accommodating a larger economic base. Some urban economists have developed models of subcenter formation and urban job dispersion [see Anas and Kim (1996), Anas and Xu (1999) for completely closed general equilibrium formulations based on pecuniary externalities or Lucas and Rossi-Hansberg (2002) for models based on Marshallian spillovers], but these have not been integrated into systems of cities models. These thoughts are not unrelated to those in the previous paragraph, because the ability to form subcenters encourages bigger and bigger cities and the spawning of urban subcenters in turn may be a major determinant of faster economic growth.

Finally, the idea of iceberg trading cost introduced into the New Economic Geography by Krugman (1991), hides strong dispersive tendencies. As shown in Anas (2004), cities vanish under population growth except in the case where trading costs are infinite. This suggests that the setup of the NEG can benefit greatly by a synthesis of the NEG with the models of human capital accumulation surveyed in Section 9, in order to more meaningfully explore the role of trade on city formation in a growing economy.

Acknowledgements

An earlier version of this chapter was presented at the 49th North American Meetings of Regional Science Association International, held in San Jose, Puerto Rico in November 2002. We are grateful to Robert Helsleg, our discussant, to David Pines for his careful reading of the paper and for his detailed comments and to the editors of this volume for several suggestions about the exposition.

References

Abdel-Rahman, H.M. (1988). "Product differentiation, monopolistic competition and city size". Regional Science and Urban Economics 18, 69–86.

Abdel-Rahman, H.M. (1990a). "Agglomeration economies, types, and sizes of cities". Journal of Urban Economics 27, 25–45.

Abdel-Rahman, H.M. (1990b). "Shareable inputs, product variety, and city sizes". Journal of Regional Science 30, 359–374.

Abdel-Rahman, H.M. (1994). "Economies of scope in intermediate goods and a system of cities". Regional Science and Urban Economics 24, 497–524.

Abdel-Rahman, H.M. (1996). "When do cities specialize in production?" Regional Science and Urban Economics 26, 1–22.

Abdel-Rahman, H.M. (1998). "Income disparity, time allocation and social welfare in a system of cities". Journal of Regional Science 38, 137–154.

Abdel-Rahman, H.M. (2000). "Multi-firm city versus company town: a microfoundation model of localization economy". Journal of Regional Science 40, 755–769.

Abdel-Rahman, H.M. (2002). "Does the structure of an urban system affect income disparities?" Journal of Regional Science 42, 389–410.

Abdel-Rahman, H.M., Fujita, M. (1990). "Product variety, Marshallian externalities and city sizes". Journal of Regional Science 30, 165–183.

Abdel-Rahman, H.M., Fujita, M. (1993). "Specialization and diversification in a system of cities". Journal of Urban Economics 33, 189–222.

Abdel-Rahman, H.M., Wang, P. (1995). "Toward a general-equilibrium theory of a core–periphery system of cities". Regional Science and Urban Economics 25, 529–546.

Abdel-Rahman, H.M., Wang, P. (1997). "Social welfare and income inequality in a system of cities". Journal of Urban Economics 41, 462–483.

Alonso, W. (1964). Location and Land Use. Harvard University Press, Cambridge, MA.

Anas, A. (1992). "On the birth and growth of cities: laissez-faire and planning compared". Regional Science and Urban Economics 22, 243–258.

Anas, A. (2004). "Vanishing cities: what does the New Economic Geography imply about the efficiency of urbanization?" Journal of Economic Geography, 181–199.

Anas, A., Arnott, R.J., Small, K. (1998). "Urban spatial structure". Journal of Economic Literature 36, 1426–1464.

Anas, A., Kim, I. (1996). "General equilibrium models of polycentric urban land use with endogenous congestion and job agglomeration". Journal of Urban Economics 40, 217–232.

Anas, A., Xiong, K. (1999). "Public investment in a core–periphery model". Working Paper. State University of New York at Buffalo.

Anas, A., Xiong, K. (2003). "Intercity trade and the industrial diversification of cities". Journal of Urban Economics 54, 258–276.

Anas, A., Xiong, K. (2004). "The formation and growth of specialized cities: efficiency without developers or Malthusian traps". Regional Science and Urban Economics. In press.

Anas, A., Xu, R. (1999). "Congestion, land use and job dispersion: a general equilibrium analysis". Journal of Urban Economics 45 (3), 451–473.

Arnott, R.J. (1979). "Optimal city size in a spatial economy". Journal of Urban Economics 6, 65–89.

Arnott, R.J., Stiglitz, J.E. (1979). "Aggregate land rents, expenditure on local public goods and optimal city size". Quarterly Journal of Economics 93, 471–500.

Becker, G., Murphy, K. (1992). " The division of labor, coordination costs, and knowledge". Quarterly Journal of Economics 107, 1137–1160.

Black, D., Henderson, J.V. (1999). "A theory of urban growth". Journal of Political Economy 107 (2), 252–284.

Chamberlin, E.H. (1933). The Theory of Monopolistic Competition. Harvard University Press, Cambridge.

Chipman, J.S. (1970). "External economies of scale and competitive equilibrium". Quarterly Journal of Economics 84, 347–385.

Diamond, P. (1982). "Aggregate demand management in search equilibrium". Review of Economic Studies 49, 217–227.

Dixit, A. (1973). "The optimum factory town". Bell Journal of Economics and Management Science 4, 637–654.

Dixit, A., Stiglitz, J.E. (1977). "Monopolistic competition and optimal product diversity". American Economic Review 67, 297–308.

Duranton, G., Puga, D. (2001). "Nursery cities: urban diversity, process innovation, and the life cycle of products". American Economic Review 91, 1454–1477.

Duranton, G., Puga, D. (2004). "Micro-foundations of urban agglomeration economies". In: Henderson, J.V., Thisse, J.-F. (Eds.), Handbook of Regional and Urban Economics, vol. 4. Elsevier, Amsterdam. This volume.

Eaton, J., Eckstein, Z. (1997). "Cities and growth: theory and evidence from France and Japan". Regional Science and Urban Economics 27, 443–474.

Ethier, W. (1982). "National and international returns to scale in the modern theory of international trade". American Economic Review 72, 389–405.
Flatters, F., Henderson, J.V., Mieszkowski, P. (1974). "Public goods, efficiency and regional fiscal equalization". Journal of Public Economics 3, 99–112.
Fujita, M., Krugman, P., Mori, T. (1999). "On the evolution of hierarchical urban systems". European Economic Review 43, 201–259.
Fujita, M., Krugman, P., Venables, A.J. (1999). The Spatial Economy: Cities, Regions, and International Trade. MIT Press, Massachusetts.
Fujita, M., Mori, T. (1997). "Structural stability and evolution of urban systems". Regional Science and Urban Economics 27, 399–442.
Gabaix, X., Ioannides, Y.M. (2004). "The evolution of city size distributions". "Theories of systems of cities". In: Henderson, J.V., Thisse, J.-F. (Eds.), Handbook of Regional and Urban Economics, vol. 4. Elsevier, Amsterdam. This volume.
Glaeser, E., Kallal, H.D., Scheinkman, J.A., Shleifer, A. (1992). "Growth in cities". Journal of Political Economy 100, 1126–1152.
Goldstein, G.S., Gronberg, T.J. (1984). "Economies of scope and economies of agglomeration". Journal of Urban Economics 16, 63–84.
Hadar, Y., Pines, D. (2003). "On the market failure in a Dixit–Stiglitz setup with two trading cities". Journal of Public Economic Theory 5 (4), 549–570.
Hadar, Y., Pines, D. (2004). "Population growth and its distribution between cities: positive and normative aspects". Regional Science and Urban Economics 34 (2), 125–154.
Helpman, E., Pines, D. (1980). "Optimal public investment and dispersion policy in a system of open cities". American Economic Review 70, 507–514.
Helsley, R.W., Strange, W.C. (1990). "Matching and agglomeration economies in a system of cities". Regional Science and Urban Economic 20, 189–212.
Helsley, R.W., Strange, W.C. (1993). "Agglomeration economies and urban capital markets". Journal of Urban Economics 29, 96–112.
Helsley, R.W., Strange, W.C. (1994). "City formation with commitment". Regional Science and Urban Economics 24, 373–390.
Henderson, J.V. (1974). "The sizes and types of cities". American Economic Review 64, 640–656.
Henderson, J.V. (1977). Economic Theory and the Cities. Academic Press, New York.
Henderson, J.V., Abdel-Rahman, H.M. (1991). "Urban diversity and fiscal decentralization". Regional Science and Urban Economics 21, 491–510.
Henderson, J.V., Becker, R. (2000). "Political economy of city sizes and formation". Journal of Urban Economics 48, 453–484.
Henderson, J.V., Ioannides, Y.M. (1981). "Aspects of growth in a system of cities". Journal of Urban Economics 10, 117–139.
Henderson, J.V., Kuncoro, A., Turner, M. (1995). "Industrial development in cities". Journal of Political Economy 103 (5), 1067–1090.
Henderson, J.V., Thisse, J.-F. (2001). "On strategic community development". Journal of Political Economy 109, 546–569.
Hercowitz, Z., Pines, D. (1991). "Migration with fiscal externalities". Journal of Public Economics 46 (2), 163–180.
Hobson, P. (1987). "Optimal product variety in urban areas". Journal of Urban Economics 22, 190–197.
Hochman, O. (1981). "Land rents, optimal taxation and local fiscal independence in an economy with local public goods". Journal of Public Economics 15, 290–310.
Hochman, O. (1997). "More on scale economies and cities". Regional Science and Urban Economics 27, 373–397.
Ioannides, Y. (1994). "Product differentiation and economic growth in a system of cities". Regional Science and Urban Economics 24, 461–484.
Jacobs, J. (1969). The Economy of Cities. Vintage, New York.

Juhn, C., Murphy, K., Pierce, B. (1993). "Wage inequality and rise in returns to skill". Journal of Political Economy 101, 410–442.

Kanemoto, Y. (1980). Theories of Urban Externalities. North-Holland, Amsterdam.

Kim, S. (1991). "Heterogeneity of labor markets and city size in an open spatial economy". Regional Science and Urban Economics 21, 109–126.

Krugman, P. (1980). "Scale economies, product differentiation and the pattern of trade". American Economic Review 70, 950–959.

Krugman, P. (1991). "Increasing returns and economic geography". Journal of Political Economy 99, 483–499.

Lösch, A. (1954). Die Räumliche Ordnung der Wirtschaft. Yale University Press, New Haven. Translated by Woglom, W.H. and Stopler, W.F. as *The Economics of Location*.

Lucas, R. (1988). "On the mechanics of economic development". Journal of Monetary Economics 22, 3–42.

Lucas, R., Rossi-Hansberg, E. (2002). "On the internal structure of cities". Econometrica 70 (4), 1445–1476.

Machin, S. (1996). "Wage inequality in the UK". Oxford Review of Economic Policy 12, 47–64.

Marshall, A. (1890). Principles of Economics. MacMillan, London.

Mills, E.S. (1967). "An aggregative model of resource allocation in a metropolitan area". American Economic Review 61, 197–210.

Muth, R. (1969). Cities and Housing. University of Chicago Press, Chicago, IL.

National Geographic (2002). "Megacities: the coming urban world". National Geographic (December), 70–99.

Palivos, T., Wang, P. (1996). "Spatial agglomeration and endogenous growth". Regional Science and Urban Economics 26, 645–670.

Panzar, J.C., Willig, R.D. (1981). "Economies of scope". American Economic Association Papers and Proceedings 71, 268–272.

Papageorgiou, Y., Pines, D. (1999). An Essay on Urban Economic Theory. Kluwer Academic, Boston.

Papageorgiou, Y., Pines, D. (2000). "Externalities, indivisibilities, nonreplicability and agglomeration". Journal of Urban Economics 48, 509–535.

Pines, D. (2000). "On alternative urban growth patterns". Unpublished manuscript. The Eitan Berglas School of Economics, Tel-Aviv University.

Pines, D. (2001). "New economic geography: Revolution or counter revolution?" Journal of Economic Geography 1, 139–146.

Rivera-Batiz, F.L. (1988). "Increasing returns, monopolistic competition and agglomeration economies in consumption and production". Regional Science and Urban Economics 18, 25–153.

Romer, P. (1986). "Increasing returns and long-run growth". Journal of Political Economy 94, 1002–1037.

Romer, P. (1987). "Growth based on increasing returns due to specialization". American Economic Review 77, 56–62.

Rosenthal, S.S., Strange, W.C. (2004). "Evidence on the nature and sources of agglomeration economies". In: Henderson, J.V., Thisse, J.-F. (Eds.), Handbook of Regional and Urban Economics, vol. 4. Elsevier, Amsterdam, pp. 2119–2171. This volume.

Scotchmer, S. (1986). "Local public goods in an equilibrium: how pecuniary externalities matter". Regional Science and Urban Economics 16, 463–481.

Stiglitz, J.E. (1977). "The theory of local public goods". In: Feldstein, M.S., Inman, R.P. (Eds.), The Economics of Public Services. MacMillan, London.

Tabuchi, T. (1998). "Urban agglomeration and dispersion: a synthesis of Alonso and Krugman". Journal of Urban Economics 44, 333–351.

United Nations (1996). United Nations Human Development Report. United Nations Development Program, Washington, DC.

Upton, C. (1981). "An equilibrium model of city sizes". Journal of Urban Economics 10, 15–36.

Wilson, J.D. (1987). "Trade in a Tiebont economy". American Economic Review 77, 431–441.

Chapter 53

THE EVOLUTION OF CITY SIZE DISTRIBUTIONS

XAVIER GABAIX

MIT and NBER, USA
e-mail: xgabaix@mit.edu

YANNIS M. IOANNIDES

Tufts University, USA
e-mail: yannis.ioannides@tufts.edu

Contents

Handbook of Regional and Urban Economics, Volume 4. Edited by J.V. Henderson and J.F. Thisse

DOI: 10.1016/S0169-7218(04)07053-4

Abstract

We review the accumulated knowledge on city size distributions and determinants of urban growth. This topic is of interest because of a number of key stylized facts, including notably Zipf's law for cities (which states that the number of cities of size greater than S is proportional to $1/S$) and the importance of urban primacy. We first review the empirical evidence on the upper tail of city size distribution. We offer a novel discussion of the important econometric issues in the characterization of the distribution. We then discuss the theories that have been advanced to explain the approximate constancy of the distribution across very different economic and social systems, emphasizing both barebone statistical theories and more developed economic theories. We discuss the more recent work on the determinants of urban growth and, in particular, growth regressions, economic explanations of city size distributions other than Gibrat's law, consequences of major shocks (quasi natural experiments), and the dynamics of U.S. urban evolution.

Keywords

city size distribution, Gibrat's law, Hill estimator, persistence of city size distributions, power laws, random growth, urban growth, urban hierarchy, urban primacy, Zipf regression, Zipf's law

JEL classification: C2, N9, R1

1. Introduction

The evolution of city size distributions has attracted sustained interest by researchers over a long period of time. The existence of very large cities, the very wide dispersion in city sizes, the remarkable stability of the hierarchy between cities over decades or even centuries, and the role of urbanization in economic development are all particularly interesting qualitative features of urban structure worldwide. Another surprising regularity, Zipf's law for cities [Zipf (1949)], has itself attracted considerable interest by researchers. Therefore, it is tempting to see the urban evolution of different economies through the persistence of certain patterns in city size distribution worldwide. It is of special interest for a theory to predict Zipf's law and other empirically important features.

The chapter reviews the theoretical underpinnings and accumulated knowledge on the evolution of city sizes. It puts considerable emphasis on Zipf's law for cities. After it identifies the empirical record on Zipf's law, the chapter turns next to technical issues, which are associated with the sort of econometric evidence on which empirical Zipf's law currently rests, and to more ambitious empirical investigations of Zipf's law with city data. The chapter reviews the implications for city size distributions of major analytical developments in urban economics and related areas in economics over the last forty years or so and contrasts them with the empirical literature. The chapter also examines the general empirical evidence on the evolution of city size distributions in the U.S. as well as internationally.

The predictions of economic theory may be classified as emanating from roughly two major traditions. These traditions coexist and are not construed as being mutually exclusive; they are merely meant to serve as categories for organizing the literature. One is associated with urban economics, that is, in particular, systems of cities theories. A second is associated with economic geography or analytical geography, more generally. The urban structure reflects such important economic forces as increasing returns possibly at various levels (which produce centripetal forces), congestion (which produces centrifugal forces), trade (intracity, intercity and international) and non-market interactions, all of which play important roles in both of these traditions. Both of these traditions in the literature yield predictions about size distributions that are in some sense aspatial and emphasize in varying degrees of differences across cities in terms of specialization. The chapter emphasizes theories and applications that examine the evolution of the city size distribution in a given economy as an outcome of forces that lead to appearance of new and to decline of existing cities. This is also stressed by the most recent research on urban structure, as we see in more detail further below.

2. Zipf's law for the upper tail of the city size distribution

We fix ideas and set notation by starting from the statistical regularity known as Zipf's law for cities. As early as Auerbach (1913), it was proposed that the city size distribution could be closely approximated by a power law distribution.[1]

2.1. *Zipf's law: definitions*

Let S_i denote the normalized size of city i, that is, the population of city i divided by the total urban population.[2] City sizes are said to satisfy *Zipf's law* if, for large sizes S, we have

$$P(\text{Size} > S) = \frac{a}{S^{\zeta}}, \tag{1}$$

where a is a positive constant and $\zeta = 1$. That is, the size of a city times the percentage of cities with larger size equals a constant.

An approximate way of stating Zipf's law, the so-called rank–size rule, is a deterministic rule that follows from the definition: the second largest city is half the size of the largest, the third largest city is a third of the size of the largest city, etc. That is, if we rank cities from largest (rank 1) to smallest (rank n), and denote their sizes $S_{(1)} \geqslant \cdots \geqslant S_{(n)}$, respectively, the rank i for a city of size $S_{(i)}$ is proportional to the proportion of cities greater than i. Therefore, by rewriting Equation (1) we have: $S_{(i)} \simeq k/i$ for some constant k.

It is important to bear in mind that even if Zipf's law holds perfectly, the rank–size rule would hold only approximately.[3] Still, it is very useful to visualize Zipf's law.

To do this, we take a country (for instance the United States), and order its cities by population: New York has rank 1, Los Angeles has rank 2, etc. We then draw a graph, known as Zipf's plot (see Fig. 1): on the y-axis, we place the log of the rank (New York has log rank $\ell n\, 1$, Los Angeles log rank $\ell n\, 2$); on the x-axis, the log of the population of the corresponding city (which will be called the "size" of the city). We take, like Krugman (1996a, p. 40), the 135 American metropolitan areas listed in the

[1] It is important to point out that there is no universally accepted definition of a *city* for statistical purposes. In the U.S. context, research has been conducted with both city proper data and data for metropolitan statistical areas. Differences in data availability worldwide may make international comparisons tricky. Rosen and Resnick (1980) show that the Pareto exponent of city size distributions tend to be closer to 1 when agglomerations are more carefully constructed, i.e., are closer to "true" agglomerations rather than administratively defined "cities". We return to this below.

[2] Talking about steady-state distributions requires a normalization of this type.

[3] See Gabaix (1999a, Proposition 4) for a precise statement of the rank–size rule, and the goodness of fit one can expects from it. The rank–size rule is a good approximation for cities of high rank, but not for the largest cities. For instance, the rank–size rule says that ratio of the largest city to second largest city is 2. But Zipf's law implies that this ratio is widely variable, indeed has a smallest 95% confidence interval equal to $[1, 20]$. This comes from the Rényi theorem described in Section 2.2.2, which says that $P(S_{(1)}/S_{(2)} > x) = 1/x$ for $x > 1$. So $[1, 1/.05]$ is the smallest 95% confidence interval for $S_{(1)}/S_{(2)}$.

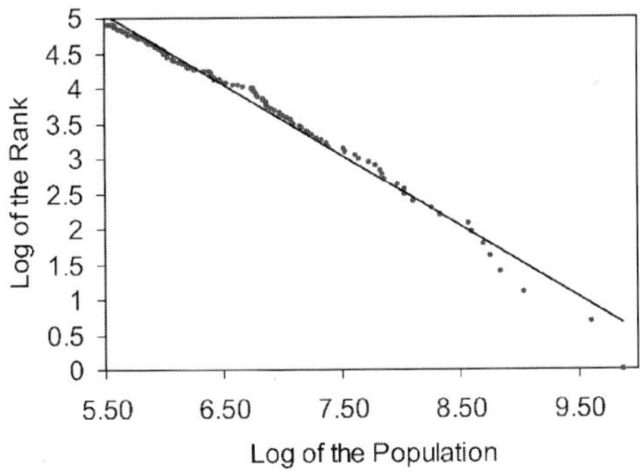

Figure 1. Log size vs log rank of the 135 U.S. metropolitan areas in 1991 listed in the Statistical Abstract of the United States (1993).

Statistical Abstract of the United States for 1991.[4] The result is something very close to a straight line. This is rather surprising, because there is no tautology causing the data to automatically generate a straight line. Furthermore, fitting a linear regression yields:

$$\ln \text{Rank} = 10.53 - \underset{(0.010)}{1.005} \ln \text{Size}, \tag{2}$$

where the standard error is in parentheses, and the R^2 is 0.986. The slope of the regression line is very close to -1, and is measured with very high precision. Returning to levels yields a very close approximation to the rank–size rule. As we argue further below, power laws like the one reported in Equation (2) fit empirical city size distributions quite well. Still, it is important to approach the issue rigorously in terms of econometric arguments.

Our approach in reviewing the literature on the evolution of city size distributions emphasizes conditions, theoretical or empirical, under which one may replicate with accuracy empirical regularities in city size distributions worldwide. We are interested in economic theories with behavioral foundations that predict such empirical regularities as Zipf's law, and others as well, but do not insist that the evidence on city size distributions be used to discriminate among those theories.

Some definitions are in order. A *power law* is a distribution function of the type $P(\text{Size} > S) \sim a/S^{\zeta}$ for large S. The positive number ζ is called the *power law exponent*. The literature sometimes uses the terms *Pareto law* (respectively *Pareto exponent*)

[4] The Statistical Abstract of the U.S. lists all the agglomerations with size above 250,000 inhabitants. The exponent ζ is sensitive to the choice of the cutoff size above which one selects the cities. For a lower cutoff, the exponent ζ is typically lower. We come back to this issue, and a possible explanation, in Section 2.4. The statistical literature [Embrechts, Kluppelberg and Mikosch (1997)] offers ways to discipline the selection of the cutoff, but those optimum cutoff techniques have not, to our knowledge, been used in the context of the city size distribution.

instead of power law (respectively power law exponent). *Zipf's law* is the statement that $\zeta = 1$.[5] *Gibrat's law* states that the growth rate of an economic entity (firm, mutual fund, city, etc.) of size S has a distribution function with mean and variance that are independent of S.[6] Those conditions will be sometimes referred to respectively as Gibrat's law for means and Gibrat's law for variances.

2.2. *Statistical methods to measure power law exponents*

We discuss next why a power law exponent ζ is notoriously difficult to estimate with city size and rank data. Embrechts, Kluppelberg and Mikosch (1997) provides a very useful review of the different methods. We will present the two most commonly used, the Zipf regression and the Hill estimator. Both present pitfalls important to bear in mind.

2.2.1. *The Zipf regression method and its pitfalls*

With n cities of ordered sizes $S_{(1)} \geqslant \cdots \geqslant S_{(n)}$, the Zipf regression fits an ordinary least squares (OLS) regression of the log rank i on the log size $S_{(i)}$ of the type (2):

$$\ell n\, i = A - \zeta_n\, \ell n\, S_{(i)}. \tag{3}$$

This procedure is the most commonly used in the empirical literature. One can show for large n, the coefficient ζ_n tends with probability 1 to the true ζ.

The advantage of this procedure is that it yields a visual goodness of fit with the power law. For large samples, such as with financial data, it is reasonably accurate. However, it has pitfalls in small samples. We provide next a Monte Carlo analysis of this phenomenon.

We fix n, the number of cities, and draw n i.i.d. city sizes S_i from an exact power law with coefficient 1.[7] So Zipf's law holds perfectly in our Monte Carlo simulations. Take for instance a sample $n = 100$. We get a mean exponent $E[\zeta_{100}] = 0.94$, so that *the OLS procedure on average underestimates the value of* ζ, here by an amount 0.06. One can interpret the origin of the bias in the following way: the expected value of the ratio between $S_{(2)}$ and $S_{(1)}$ is 0.5, but the smallest 95% confidence interval for $S_{(1)}/S_{(2)}$ is $[1, 20]$ (see Footnote 3). So typically, the value of $S_{(1)}$ will be above the value predicted

[5] This definition implies that the variance of S is infinite for $\zeta < 2$, and the mean is infinite for $\zeta < 1$. This is, strictly speaking, impossible, as the distribution of S is bounded above (by the total urban population in the case of absolute sizes, or 1 in the case of normalized sizes). So a more rigorous definition should be that the density is $p(S) = a'/S^{\zeta+1}$ for S over a range $[S_1, S_2]$ over which the power law applies, and $p(S)$ can be arbitrary elsewhere. Empirically, this range $[S_1, S_2]$ typically include the top 100 or so cities.

[6] It is sometimes used in the literature to mean that the distribution of growth rates of firms of size S is independent of S, not just the first and second moments.

[7] Concretely, we draw n i.i.d. variables u_i uniformly distributed in $[0, 1]$, and construct the sizes as $S_i = 1/u_i$ and rank them.

by the linear regression with slope -1. In other words, the size of the largest city will look "too big". The best OLS fit will correct this by making the slope less steep, so that the best fit value of ζ_n will be less than the true value of ζ.

OLS regression reports an average standard error $\sigma^{\text{nominal}}(\zeta_{100}) = 0.013$, but the true standard error is $\text{var}(\zeta_{100})^{1/2} = 0.13$. Hence a 95% confidence interval for ζ_n is [0.68, 1.20], when a naive view of OLS would one lead to expect [0.974, 1.026]. This shows that the nominal standard errors reported in the OLS regression considerably *underestimates* the true standard error on the estimated coefficient. As a result, *taking the OLS estimates of the standard errors at face value will lead one to reject Zipf's law much too often*. For references, we report the results of Monte Carlo simulations in Table 1 and the associated Zipf's law estimations for $n = 20, 50, 100, 200, 500$. The reason for those low nominal standard errors is that the ranking procedure creates positive correlations between the residuals, whereas the OLS standard error assumes that the errors are independent. So the total amount of error is understated by OLS. Actually, one can show that the true standard error is

$$\text{var}(\zeta_n)^{1/2} \sim \zeta(2/n)^{1/2} \quad \text{for large } n.\text{[8]} \tag{4}$$

In Table 2, we replicate the study with the other OLS-based approach used in the literature, that is, regressions of log size on log rank:

$$\ell n\, S_{(i)} = A' - \alpha_n\, \ell n\, i. \tag{5}$$

For very large n, under the null of a power law with exponent ζ, α_n tends to $\alpha = 1/\zeta$. The results are similar to those of Table 1. The estimate of α_n is now biased upward. The origins of the upward bias are presumably the same as those of the downward bias of ζ_n, as $\alpha = 1/\zeta$. The true standard error on α_n are slightly higher than those on ζ_n. So if one chooses an OLS procedure, regression (3) is preferable to regression (5).

We conclude by discussing a pitfall associated with an augmented Zipf regression. That is, the literature reports regressions of log rank, $\ell n\, i$, against log size, $\ell n\, S_{(i)}$, and

Table 1
Statistics on the OLS coefficient ζ_n from regression (3), assuming that Zipf's law holds perfectly ($\zeta = 1$)

Value of the number n of cities in the sample	20	50	100	200	500
Mean ζ_n	0.90	0.92	0.94	0.96	0.98
Mean nominal OLS standard error on ζ_n	0.048	0.023	0.013	0.0078	0.0037
True standard error on ζ_n	0.28	0.18	0.13	0.098	0.063
Approximate true standard error on ζ_n : $\sqrt{2/n}$	0.31	0.20	0.14	0.100	0.063
True 95% confidence interval for ζ_n	[0.37, 1.43]	[0.57, 1.27]	[0.68, 1.20]	[0.77, 1.15]	[0.85, 1.10]

The values come from 20,000 Monte Carlo simulations for each value of n. Under a general null of power law distribution with exponent ζ, the value for the statistics on ζ_n are those of the table multiplied by ζ. $\sqrt{2/n}$ is the asymptotic approximation of the true standard error on ζ_n, as discussed in the text.

[8] See Gabaix and Ioannides (2003) for the derivation.

Table 2
Statistics on the OLS coefficient α_n from regression (5), assuming that Zipf's law holds perfectly ($\alpha = 1/\zeta = 1$)

Value of the number n of cities in the sample	20	50	100	200	500
Mean α_n	1.14	1.08	1.05	1.03	1.02
Mean nominal OLS standard error on α_n	0.065	0.029	0.016	0.0086	0.0039
True standard error on α_n	0.33	0.20	0.14	0.099	0.063
Approximate true standard error on α_n : $\sqrt{2/n}$	0.31	0.20	0.14	0.100	0.063
True 95% confidence interval for α_n	[0.51, 1.76]	[0.69, 1.47]	[0.78, 1.33]	[0.84, 1.23]	[0.89, 1.14]

The values come from 20,000 Monte Carlo simulations for each value of n. Under a general null of power law distribution with exponent ζ, the value for the statistics on α_n are those of the table multiplied by $1/\zeta$. $\sqrt{2/n}$ is the asymptotic approximation of the true standard error on α_n, as discussed in the text.

its square:

$$\ell n\, i = a + b\,\ell n\, S_{(i)} + c(\ell n\, S_{(i)})^2. \tag{6}$$

A coefficient c statistically different from 0 is interpreted as a departure from Zipf's law. It may be a statistical artifact, however. To show this, we perform Monte Carlo simulations like above with n cities drawn from Zipf's law. We run (6) and count the frequency at which the t-statistic on c is greater than 1.96 in absolute value, which would naively lead one to detect a deviation from Zipf's law. For $n = 20$, 50, 100, 200 and 500, one finds a statistically significant coefficient c, respectively 65, 78, 85, 90 and 93% of the time. Hence *in the OLS regression in Equation* (6), *one will often find a statistically significant coefficient c, even if Zipf's law holds perfectly*. This fact has bearing on whether it is appropriate to reject Zipf's law on the strength of econometric evidence of a statistically significant quadratic term in OLS regressions of rank against the logarithm of size. We return to this in the discussion below of Black and Henderson (2003).

We conjecture that the reason why in regression (6) the coefficient c is typically found significant is the same as the reason why OLS has too low a nominal standard error on the ζ term in regression (3). That is, the positive correlations between residuals that are introduced by ranking cause the true amount of noise in the regression to be understated. All nominal standard errors are too low and, in particular, the coefficient c appears to be as significant from 0 too often.

To conclude, if one wants to rely on OLS to estimate ζ, the safest thing to do is to use a Monte Carlo simulation with the sample size n in order to get the expected value of the bias and the true standard error of the estimator. One can also get the value of the bias by interpolation from our Tables 1 and 2, and using Equation (4) take the value $\zeta\sqrt{2/n}$ as an estimate of the standard error.[8]

8 More tables are provided in Gabaix and Ioannides (2003).

2.2.2. *The Hill (maximum likelihood) estimator*

An alternative procedure is the Hill estimator of ζ, the Pareto exponent in Equation (1) [Hill (1975)]. Under the null of perfect power law, it is the maximum likelihood estimator. For a sample of n cities with sizes $S_{(1)} \geqslant \cdots \geqslant S_{(n)}$, this estimator is

$$\hat{\zeta} = \frac{n-1}{\sum_{i=1}^{n-1} \ell n\, S_{(i)} - \ell n\, S_{(n)}}. \tag{7}$$

It inherits the efficiency properties of a maximum likelihood estimator.[9] An estimate of the standard error of $1/\hat{\zeta}$ is constructed the following way. One calculates the "local slopes"

$$\tau_i = i(\ell n\, S_{(i)} - \ell n\, S_{(i+1)}),$$

for $i = 1, \ldots, n-1$. The Rényi representation theorem on ordered statistics [see, e.g., Reiss (1989, 36–37)] shows that the τ_i are i.i.d. exponential variables with $P(\tau_i > \tau) = e^{-\zeta\tau}$ for $\tau \geqslant 0$. $\hat{\zeta}^{-1}$ is just the empirical mean of the slopes τ_i,

$$\hat{\zeta}^{-1} = \frac{1}{n-1} \sum_{i=1}^{n-1} \tau_i .$$

A consistent standard error uses the standard deviation of the slopes:

$$\sigma_n(1/\hat{\zeta}) = \left(\frac{\sum_{i=1}^{n-1} (\tau_i - 1/\hat{\zeta})^2}{n-2} \right)^{1/2} (n-1)^{-1/2}.$$

If $1/\hat{\zeta} \gg \sigma_n(1/\hat{\zeta})$, the delta method gives the standard error on $\hat{\zeta}$:

$$\sigma_n(\hat{\zeta}) = \hat{\zeta}^2 \left(\frac{\sum_{i=1}^{n-1} (\tau_i - 1/\hat{\zeta})^2}{n-2} \right)^{1/2} (n-1)^{-1/2}. \tag{8}$$

The properties of the Hill estimator in finite samples can be very worrisome. Embrechts et al. (1997, pp. 330–345) discuss these in great detail. The core reason for the bad non-asymptotic properties of the Hill estimator is that the true distribution may have the expansion, for large S:

$$G(S) = P(\text{Size} > S) = \frac{a}{S^{\zeta}} + \frac{b}{S^{\zeta+\gamma}} + o\left(\frac{b}{S^{\zeta+\gamma}}\right), \tag{9}$$

[9] As we discuss below, Dobkins and Ioannides (2000) actually report estimates of the Zipf exponent obtained by means of this estimator.

and $\gamma > 0$. The terms $b/S^{\zeta+\gamma}$ introduces a bias that can be very high in small samples:[10]

$$E[\hat{\zeta}] = \zeta + \frac{b\gamma}{a} E[1/S_{(i)}^{\gamma}].$$

Hence the nominal standard error (8) of the Hill estimators can also considerably underestimate the true estimation error, as it overlooks the bias term.

A number of estimators have been proposed to address these issues, but many years of research have not yielded any simple, consensus solution to this problem. The state of the art may be the sophisticated non-linear procedures advocated by Beirlant et al. (1999), Embrechts, Kluppelberg and Mikosch (1997), and Feuerverger and Hall (1999). Those procedures often directly estimate the parameters ζ, b/a and γ in the expansion (9). This is still a domain of active research.

It would be interesting to have a thorough econometric study of this issue in order to assess how important the bias problem is.[11] With those caveats in mind, we propose one more methodological remark before proceeding to a review of the empirical results.

2.3. *A methodological note: "estimate, don't test"*

Before evaluating the empirical evidence, it is useful to keep in mind an injunction of Leamer and Levinsohn (1995). They argue that in the context of empirical research in international trade, too much energy is spent to see if a theory fits exactly. Rather, researchers should aim at broad, though necessarily non-absolute, regularities. In other words, "estimate, don't test". *The main question of empirical work should be how well a theory fits, rather than whether or not it fits perfectly* (i.e., within the standard errors). With an infinitely large data set, one can reject any non-tautological theory. Consistently with this suggestion, some of the debate on Zipf's law should be cast in terms of how well, or poorly, it fits, rather than whether it can be rejected or not. For example, if the empirical research establishes that the data are typically well described by a power law with exponent $\zeta \in [0.8, 1.2]$, than this is a useful result: It prompts to seek theoretical

[10] To convey the intuition for the result, we give the following heuristic derivation. Call $y_i = -\ell n\, G(S_i)$, where $G(x)$ is the true countercumulative distribution function written in (9). Then y_i is a standard exponential variable, and the Rényi theorem implies that $u_i = i(y_{(i)} - y_{(i+1)})$ are i.i.d. standard exponentials. But

$$u_i \simeq i \frac{G'(S_{(i)})}{G(S_{(i)})}(S_{(i)} - S_{(i+1)}) = \frac{S_{(i)}G'(S_{(i)})}{G(S_{(i)})} i \frac{S_{(i)} - S_{(i+1)}}{S_{(i)}} \simeq \left(\zeta + \frac{b\gamma}{aS_{(i)}^{\gamma}}\right)\tau_i$$

so that

$$\hat{\zeta} = E[\tau_i]^{-1} \simeq \zeta + \frac{b\gamma}{a} E[1/S_{(i)}^{\gamma}].$$

[11] This bias problem can be very important in financial data [Beirlant et al. (1999)], as indeed theories of the origins of power law behavior in financial data [Gabaix et al. (2003)] welcome the possibility of a bias term $b/S^{\zeta+\gamma}$.

explanations of why this should be true. Likewise, if further research establishes a degree of confidence for Gibrat's law, then theory should fit that, within the degree of confidence that the data offer.[12]

2.4. Empirical results on cities

Before we proceed with reviewing empirical results, we wish to underscore an important data issue. That is, it matters whether one deals with urban agglomerations (i.e., metropolitan areas) or with city-proper data. Conceptually, the proper entity is the urban agglomeration as an urban economy, but often international data just give the city proper data. One would expect that the exponent ζ should be larger for city proper than the urban agglomeration data, in that urban agglomerations are not bound by legal definitions of cities-proper and therefore likely to have a longer upper tail. This point was made first by Rosen and Resnick (1980) and has been revisited recently by Brakman et al. (1999), and Brakman, Garretsen and van Marrewijk (2001). The latter report comparisons, *ibid.*, pp. 206–208, 220–221, using international data.[13] With these differences notwithstanding and unless otherwise indicated, the terms urban and metropolitan are used as synonyms throughout the chapter.

Support for Zipf's law comes from numerous country studies and comparative international evidence. Rosen and Resnick (1980), Brakman, Garretsen and van Marrewijk (2001) and Soo (2003) are the most complete empirical international comparative studies. These are typically conducted along the lines of Equation (3). Rosen and Resnick examine city size distributions for 44 countries in 1970. The average Zipf's exponent is 1.13 with a standard deviation of 0.19, with almost all countries falling between 0.8 and 1.5. Brakman, Garretsen and van Marrewijk (1999, 2001, pp. 206–208, 220–221) show that city-proper data are associated with higher Zipf exponents (mean = 1.13, S.D.= 0.19, $N = 42$) than urban agglomeration data (mean = 1.05, S.D. = 0.21, $N = 22$). Soo (2003) updates these results without altering the basic findings. He finds a Zipf coefficient of 1.105, for cities, but 0.854 for urban agglomerations.[14]

The estimated dispersion in the Zipf exponent is large. Some interpret this as mixed evidence for Zipf's law. We recall, however, that Table 1 shows that large dispersion of exponents is to be expected under Zipf's law. Looking at the average of exponent estimates, however, we see that if the average value ζ is not exactly equal to 1, it is typically in the range [0.85, 1.15]. We conclude that power laws describe well the empirical regularity, with a Zipf exponent typically around 1. Furthermore, *predicting a value in a range say* [0.8, 1.2] *may be included in the list of criteria used to judge the success of urban theories.*

[12] We wish to thank Henry Overman for suggesting this discussion.

[13] The data are available at the United Nations web site http://unstats.un.org/unsd/citydata.

[14] Soo's non-parametric examination of the estimated Zipf coefficient across countries produces a distribution that is quite close to normal, with the variations being explained better by political economy variables than by economic geography variables.

Dobkins and Ioannides (2000) report OLS estimates of ζ, that are obtained along the lines of (3) with repeated cross sections of U.S. Census data for metro areas. Their estimates decline from 1.044, in 1900, to 0.949, in 1990. They also report maximum likelihood estimates for power law distributions, along the lines of (7) with the same data, which decline from 0.953, in 1900, to 0.553, in 1990. When they use the upper one-half of the sample only, a practice that conforms to some other estimations of Zipf's law [such as Fujita, Krugman and Venables (1999), Chapter 12], the estimate of ζ declines from 1.212, in 1900, with 56 metro areas in the entire sample, to 0.993, in 1990, with 167 metro areas in the sample. Gabaix (1999b) reports an estimate equal to 1.005, using the 135 largest metro areas in 1991 as reported in the *Statistical Abstract of the United States*. (See Fig. 1.)

Despite remarkable fits obtained for Zipf's law with U.S. city size data, problems remain. Nonparametric results by Dobkins and Ioannides (2000) and a finding of a significant quadratic term in a log rank regression [according to Equation (6)] reported by Black and Henderson (2003), continue to raise genuine doubts about the validity of Zipf's law as a description of the entire distribution of city size for the U.S. We return to this issue further below when we review two very relevant recent papers. One is Duranton (2002), who compares simulation results of an interesting new model that utilizes quality ladders with the empirical distributions for U.S. and for France and explains departures from Zipf's law at both ends of the distribution. Another is Rossi-Hansberg and Wright (2003), who develop a system-of-cities inspired model that implies Zipf's law in special cases and also explains departures from Zipf's law at both ends of the distribution.

Black and Henderson (2003) examine the performance of Zipf's law with the twentieth century U.S. city size distribution data. Their criticism of Zipf's law rests on a regression of the logarithm of city rank against the logarithm of size with metro area data. (Their data differ little from the Dobkins-Ioannides data.) Their results show that the Zipf coefficient declines from 0.861 in 1900 to 0.842 when all cities are used, and increases from 1.01 in 1900 to 1.18 in 1990, when only the top one-third of the size distribution is used. Their estimate of the coefficient c of the quadratic term in Equation (6) is statistically significant. It would be useful to revisit those issues with the pitfalls described in Section 2.2.1 in mind.

The approaches to estimation of Zipf's law that we discussed above are based on working with the steady-state size distribution of cities and therefore require some notion of stability of the underlying stochastic process. Difficulties with consistent definitions of cities over time, as when metropolitan area definitions in the U.S. change over time, make it hard to rely entirely on panel data. However, Black and Henderson (2003) and Dobkins and Ioannides (2000, 2001) do work with panel data. Ioannides and Overman (2003), on the other hand, constitutes the first attempt to use the Gibrat's law to test the validity of Zipf's law. We discuss their work further below.

We wish to draw the reader's attention to sources of information that have not been fully explored. Historians have produced fascinating series of urban populations that are reported in Bairoch (1988), Bairoch, Batou and Chevre (1988), Van der Woude, de

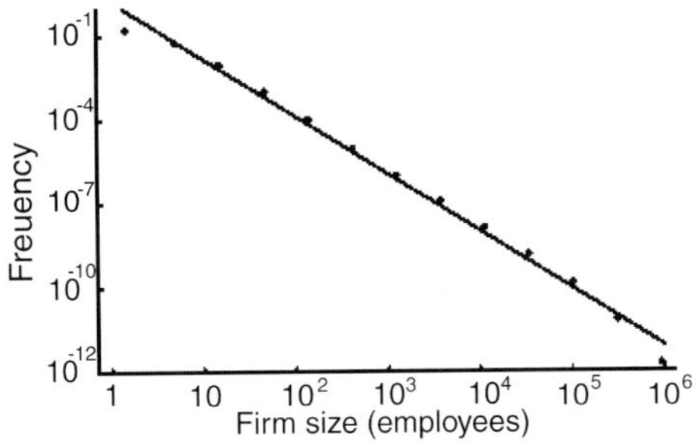

Figure 2. Log frequency $\ln g(S)$ vs log size $\ln S$ of U.S. firm sizes (by number of employees) for 1997. OLS fit gives a slope of 2.059 (s.e. $= 0.054$; $R^2 = 0.992$). This corresponds to a frequency $g(S) \sim S^{-2.059}$. *Source*: Axtell (2001).

Vries and Hayami (1990) and De Vries (1984). The casual impression of the authors is that in some decades, large cities grow faster than small cities, but in other decades, small cities grow faster. This would suggest that Gibrat's law for means holds only as a long-run average. But to our knowledge, no one has systematically used those data. They clearly deserve attention[15].

Finally, we wish to note that Zipf's law has been shown to hold for the bulk of the firm size distribution. Axtell (2001) and Okuyama, Takayasu and Takayasu (1999) present evidence for the U.S. and Japan, respectively. Our Figure 2 reproduces Axtell (2001). If the countercumulative density of the distribution is $G(x) = a/x^{\zeta}$, the density, its derivative, is $g(x) = a\zeta/x^{1+\zeta}$, so that a plot of log density vs log size will show an affine curve with slope $-(1+\zeta)$: $\ln g(x) = -(1+\zeta)\ln x + \text{constant}$. Axtell (2001) finds $\zeta = 1.059$ (S.E. 0.054) for the 5 million firms in the U.S. Census in 1997. Hence one can safely say that, except for very small and very large firms, U.S. firms follow Zipf's law. This is interesting because many of the conceptual issues that arise for cities arise also for firms. Most worked out theories of the firm would predict that many details should matter for the distribution. Fixed costs, and increasing or decreasing marginal costs, the type of competition, the cost and benefit of integration, should influence the size distribution of firms. This view of the world begs the question of why those details should have the proper values that generate Zipf's law. However, random growth models offer a simple way to understand Zipf's law. Also, though random growth seems to suggest that, in the long run, firms and cities behave like constant returns to scale economies, one does need a feature that is not constant returns to scale to generate firms and cities in the first place – for instance, a fixed cost, or an initial advantage. Perhaps this similarity of firms and

15 There is also an interesting connection between Zipf's law and Christaller's Hierarchy principle. This principle states that if an industry is present in a certain city, it tends to be present in larger cities as well. Mori, Nishikimi and Smith (2003) show that this implies a negative correlation between the average size of the cities that host an industry, and the number of those cities. They call this the Number–Average Size rule. They provide empirical evidence about this new, very interesting stylized fact.

cities will help guide some new theorizing. In any case, this strong support of Zipf's law for firms should increase one's posterior about the probability of Zipf's law for cities.

3. Random growth and Zipf's law

A first formal attempt to obtain power laws, and therefore, Zipf's law in particular, is Simon (1955). Simon assumes that urban population grows by discrete increments or "lumps". A new lump becomes a new city, with some probability; or, it goes to augment an existing city, with a probability that is proportional to the recipient city's population. Simon obtains a power law distribution as a limit of this process, but the model yields Zipf's law only as a special case. Dobkins and Ioannides (2001) confirm broad features of Simon's model, that is, that the probability of new cities appearing in the immediate vicinity of old cities and thus leading to large urban agglomerations, is increasing in the size of the existing city. Simon's model encounters some serious problems. In the limit where it can generate Zipf's law, it does not converge well, and requires that the number of cities grow indefinitely, in fact as fast as the urban population. Gabaix (1999b) and Krugman (1996b) detail these problems.

3.1. From Gibrat's law to Zipf's law

We discuss next a variant of random growth theories that builds on Gibrat (1931).[16] The conclusion is that *if different cities grow randomly with the same expected growth rate and the same variance (Gibrat's Law for means and variances of growth rate), then the limit distribution of city sizes converges to Zipf's law.* We follow here the treatment of Gabaix (1999b), who also discusses the consequences of deviation from Gibrat's law.

Specifically, the distribution of city sizes will converge to $G(S)$, given by Equation (1), if Gibrat's Law holds for city growth processes, that is, if city growth rates are identically distributed, independent of city size, and with a mean equal to the mean growth rate of the total urban population. It is straightforward to verify this claim. Let γ_t^i be the total growth of city i: $S_{t+1}^i = \gamma_{t+1}^i S_t^i$. If the growth rates γ_t^i are independently and identically distributed random variables with density function $f(\gamma)$, and given that the average normalized size[17] must stay constant and equal to 1, $\int_0^\infty \gamma f(\gamma)\,\mathrm{d}\gamma = 1$, then the equation of motion of the distribution of growth rates expressed in terms of the

[16] The first economic model with a power law may be Champernowne (1953). The classic mathematical treatment is Kesten (1973). Those random growth processes have enjoyed a renewed popularity in physics. Interesting analyses are include Levy and Solomon (1996), Marsili and Zhang (1998), Zanette and Manrubia (1997), Malcai, Biham and Solomon (1999), and Sornette (2001).

[17] One has $E[\gamma] = 1$ if all cities follow Gibrat's law. The more general condition for $E[\gamma] = 1$ is that cities in the relevant range have a growth rate that is independent of size, and that this growth rate is equal to the growth rate of the total urban population. Gabaix, Ramalho and Reuter (2004) elaborate this point in a more general context that allows birth and deaths.

countercumulative distribution function of S_t^i, $G_t(S)$, is

$$G_{t+1}(S) = \int_0^{\infty} G_t\left(\frac{S}{\gamma}\right) f(\gamma)\,\mathrm{d}\gamma.$$

Its steady-state distribution G, if it exists, satisfies

$$G(S) = \int_0^{\infty} G\left(\frac{S}{\gamma}\right) f(\gamma)\,\mathrm{d}\gamma.$$

It is straightforward to verify that $G(S) = a/S$, where a is a constant, satisfies this equation. Gabaix (1999b) examines in further detail the precise conditions that generate Zipf's law.

3.2. Deviations from Gibrat's law

3.2.1. Deviations that affect the distribution

Recognizing the possibility that Gibrat's Law might not hold exactly, Gabaix (1999b) also examines the case where cities grow randomly with expected growth rates and standard deviations that depend on their sizes. That is, the size of city i at time t varies according to:

$$\frac{\mathrm{d}S_t}{S_t} = \mu(S_t)\,\mathrm{d}t + \sigma(S_t)\,\mathrm{d}B_t, \tag{10}$$

where $\mu(S)$ and $\sigma^2(S)$ denote, respectively, the instantaneous mean and variance of the growth rate of a size S city, and B_t is a standard Brownian motion. In this case, the limit distribution of city sizes will converge to a law with a *local* Zipf exponent,

$$\zeta(S) = -\frac{S}{p(S)}\frac{\mathrm{d}p(S)}{\mathrm{d}S} - 1,$$

where $p(S)$ denotes the stationary distribution of S. Working with the forward Kolmogorov equation associated with Equation (10) yields:

$$\frac{\partial}{\partial t}p(S,t) = -\frac{\partial}{\partial S}\big(\mu(S)Sp(S,t)\big) + \frac{1}{2}\frac{\partial^2}{\partial S^2}\big(\sigma^2(S)S^2p(S,t)\big). \tag{11}$$

The local Zipf exponent that is associated with the limit distribution is given by $\frac{\partial}{\partial t}p(S,t) = 0$, can be derived and is given by:

$$\zeta(S) = 1 - 2\frac{\mu(S)}{\sigma^2(S)} + \frac{S}{\sigma^2(S)}\frac{\partial\sigma^2(S)}{\partial S}, \tag{12}$$

where $\mu(S)$ is relative to the overall mean for all city sizes.

Gabaix's theoretical contribution offers an opportunity for direct tests of the origin of Zipf's law in the form of Gibrat's Law for city growth rates. The empirical approach of Ioannides and Overman (2003) allows for a city's growth rate to depend on city size and

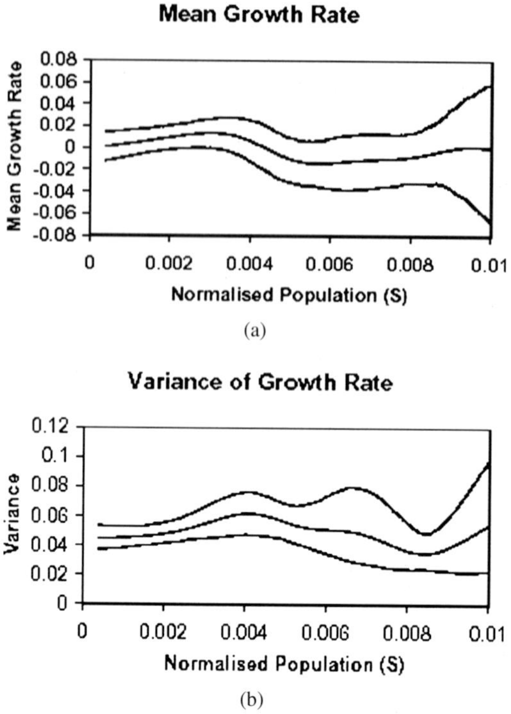

Figure 3. Non-parametric estimates of the mean and variance of the growth rate of a city of size S as a function of the size S. The figure plots the bootstrapped 95% confidence intervals. *Source*: Ioannides and Overman (2003).

to vary according to a law like Equation (10) above. To do this, they non-parametrically estimate the mean and variance of city growth rates conditional on size. This allows them to test the validity of Gibrat's Law. It appears to be confirmed. We report the graphs in Figure 3. They then use Equation (12) to directly estimate the local Zipf exponents. As we saw earlier, direct estimation of $\zeta(S)$ has turned out to be difficult to implement with standard parametric econometric procedures. However, non-parametric estimation lends itself readily to such a task. It is for this reason that Ioannides and Overman (2003) is arguably the strongest empirical confirmation to date of the validity of Zipf's law with U.S. data for metropolitan areas.

Their findings also help explain two interesting features of the size distribution of U.S. cities. First, as outlined above, estimates of the Zipf exponent for U.S. cities decline overtime. Gabaix (1999b) suggests that a possible explanation for this declining Zipf exponent is that towards the end of the period, more small cities enter, and that these small cities have a lower local Zipf exponent. The Ioannides and Overman estimations show that this suggestion is probably correct. Second, comparison of non-parametric estimates of the log rank–log size relationship to a standard parametric estimate suggests that the slope of the countercumulative function should increase absolutely and then decrease again at the upper end of the range of values, as Black and Henderson (2003) and Dobkins and Ioannides (2000) document. The Ioannides and Overman finding of a local Zipf exponent that hovers between 0.8 and 0.9 for most of the range of values of city sizes and then rises and finally falls is consistent with this pattern. *They conclude that, at least for the upper tail of the distribution, the Gibrat assumption is indeed verified.* More work is called for to look at this issue.

We can offer a simple explanation for this flattening of the Zipf curve (lower exponent ζ) for small cities, which in effect means few small cities. It is conceivable that smaller cities have a higher variance than large cities. Variance would decrease with size for small cities, and then asymptote to a "variance floor" for large cities. This could be due to the fact that large cities still have a very undiversified industry base, as the examples of New York and Los Angeles would suggest. Using Equation (12) in the baseline case where all cities have the same growth rate, which forces $\mu(S) = 0$ for the normalized sizes, gives: $\zeta(S) = 1 + \partial \ln \sigma^2(S)/\partial \ell n\, S$, with $\partial \ln \sigma^2(S)/\partial \ell n\, S < 0$ in the domain where volatility decreases with size. So potentially, this might explain why the ζ coefficient is lower for smaller sizes.

3.2.2. Deviations from Gibrat's law that do not affect the distribution

In this section we will see that the basic Gibrat process may be weakened considerably. First, the urban growth may accommodate a wide range of growth processes, as long as they contain a unit root with respect to the logarithm of city size: in particular, growth processes can have some mean-reverting component. Second, Zipf's law is compatible with the predictability present in the data (see Section 6.1) as long as the determinants themselves are not ultimately correlated with size, and mean revert at long horizons.

To examine those facts analytically, we use discrete time notation and write:

$$\ell n\, S_{it} - \ell n\, S_{i,t-1} = \mu(\chi_{it}, t) + \varepsilon_{it}, \tag{13}$$

where χ_{it} is a possibly time-varying vector of characteristics of city i; $\mu(\chi_{it}, t)$ is the expectation of city i's growth rate as a function of economic conditions at time t; and ε_{it} is white noise. In the simplest Gibrat model, ε_{it} is independently and identically distributed over time and $\mu(\chi_{it}, t)$ is constant. We examine in turn the consequence of relaxing those assumptions.

Mean reversion versus unit root in the evolution process. First, we continue to assume a constant $\mu(\chi_{is}, t) = \mu$, but we examine the consequence of relaxation of the assumption of an i.i.d. ε_{it}. We suppose a stochastic structure of the form

$$\varepsilon_{it} = b_{it} + \eta_{it} - \eta_{i,t-1},$$

where b_{it} is i.i.d., and η_{it} follows a stationary process. This gives

$$\ell n\, S_{it} - \ell n\, S_{i,0} = \mu t + \sum_{s=1}^{t} b_{is} + \eta_{it} - \eta_{i0}. \tag{14}$$

The $\sum_{s=1}^{t} b_{is}$ term in the above equation gives a unit root in the growth rate process, which is what ensures convergence to Zipf's law. The η_{it} term can have any stationarity (as long as the tails of $e^{\eta_{it}}$ are less fat than the Zipf distribution).[18] This means that, *for Zipf's law to hold, the city evolution process* (14) *can contain a mean reversion component, as long as it contains a non-zero unit root component.* Hence, in growth regressions the presence of a mean-reversion term is a priori compatible with Zipf's law – the crucial ingredient being the presence of a unit root term. Hence one can imagine that the next generation of city evolution empirics could draw from the sophisticated econometric literature on unit roots developed in the past two decades and surveyed by Stock (1994).

Economic predictability. We now examine the consequences of a non-constant $\mu(\chi_{it}, t)$ in (13). This is motivated by the empirical literature on urban growth (see Section 6.1), which obtains a predicted value for the growth rate $\mu(\chi_{it}, t)$ as a function of a vector of characteristic χ_{it} of city i. In terms of the above section, this translates into

$$\eta_{it} - \eta_{i,0} = \sum_{s=1}^{t} [\mu(\chi_{it}, t) - \bar{\mu}],$$

where $\bar{\mu}$ is the average growth rate. In view of the previous paragraph, Zipf's law requires that η_{it} be stationary. Let us unpack the economic meaning of this condition. η_{it} is stationary if:

(1.i) for a fixed χ, $\mu(\chi, t) - \bar{\mu}$ is "sufficiently" mean-reverting; or

(1.ii) for a given city i, the χ_{it}'s are "sufficiently" mean-reverting.

Case (1.i) says that the dependence on t indicates that some permanent characteristic can have impacts that are good in some time periods, bad in others. For instance the importance of temperature depends on the availability of heating systems or air conditioning. Proximity to iron ore deposits is a growth factor in some decades, and a decline factor in others. Case (1.ii) means that "good" characteristics are temporary. For instance, having better fiscal policies, or a more educated population, might be temporary, as policies and capacities change. If either (1.i) or (1.ii) hold, one sees how the growth regressions mentioned in Section 6.1 can hold. If $\sum_{s=1}^{t}[\mu(\chi_{it}, t) - \bar{\mu}]$ is not stationary, then we have case:

(2) cities with the "right" characteristics will dominate, and the city size distribution will diverge.

[18] We offer a heuristic derivation of this fact. Say that the process is $S_t = B_t H_t$, where $dB_t/B_t = b_t = \sigma\, dz_t$ is a Brownian motion with zero drift as in the simplest Gibrat process, and $H_t = e^{\eta_t}$ is an independent stationary process that follows a diffusion. S_t is reflected in the lower tail. One can write the forward Kolmogorov equation, and see that $p(B, H) = aB^{-2} f(H)$ is a solution of this equation if a is a constant and $f(H)$ is the steady-state distribution of H. It is highly plausible, though we did not attempt to prove it, that this is the unique solution for large values of B. If H has power laws less fat than 1, i.e., if $E[H] < \infty$, then $P(S > x) = aE[H]/x$ and Zipf's law holds.

This divergence could be very slow. For example, suppose that city number 50 is endowed with a permanent advantage that make it grow at a rate higher than the rest of the urban population by a rate of 1% rate per year. It will need, in order of magnitude, $T = \ln(50)/0.01 \simeq 400$ years to overtake city number 1. Hence one needs an extremely persistent advantage to ensure this divergence of the distribution. It is somewhat unlikely that such advantages can persist without decaying or being imitated, with the help of directed technological or political change. This, and the evidence on Zipf's law, suggests that (2) is not possible, and rather that we must be in cases (1.i), (1.ii), or both. It would be extremely interesting for the empirical literature on urban growth to determine this, and to examine more precisely the mechanism by which (1.i) or (1.ii) happen, as one can conjecture they do.

3.3. Economic models that deliver Gibrat's law

One could argue that a major challenge for urban theory is to deliver models that generate Gibrat's law, at least approximately. The dominant model of urban structure, that is the system of cities approach [Henderson (1974, 1988)] and the new economic geography [Fujita, Krugman and Mori (1999)] in their pure forms both fail the task of predicting a Zipf's law, and in fact not even a power law.[19]

Gabaix (1999b) offers a simple model of amenity shocks to cities, which cause intercity migration that in turn produce population shocks that are proportional to existing populations. When such amenity shocks are independent and identically distributed, the conditions of Gibrat's Law are satisfied. Gabaix (1999a) examines how extensions of such a model can be compatible with unbounded positive or negative externalities.

In a recent paper, Córdoba (2003) examines systematically the conditions for Zipf's law and concludes that "Gibrat's Law is not *an* explanation [...] but it is *the* explanation." In other words, Gibrat's law is a necessary condition for Zipf's law. In Córdoba's model at equilibrium, cities are specialized and produce one good. Cities arise because of Marshallian externalities and there are no transport costs. Córdoba shows that for Zipf's law to arise, one first needs to have a balanced growth path. Remarkably, this is possible only if:

(1) consumers have Cobb–Douglas preferences; or
(2) Marshallian external effects have equal elasticities.

If either tastes or productivity have power law distribution, one gets a power law distribution of city sizes. This power law distribution of tastes or productivity can itself come from a random growth process. The result is extended to the case of diversified cities with production of non-tradeables. One can expect that the analysis in Córdoba (2003) will motivate even more research on economic models compatible with Gibrat's law.

[19] For the latter, see several prominent reviews of Fujita, Krugman and Mori (1999), such as Anas (2001), Davis (2002), Neary (2001).

Rossi-Hansberg and Wright (2003) use ideas from the system-of-cities theory of Henderson (1974) and its urban growth application of Black and Henderson (1999) to develop a model where the urban structure eliminates local increasing returns to scale to yield constant returns to scale in the aggregate. This is accomplished by a model where local production takes place with a Cobb–Douglas production function and constant returns to scale in capital and labor services. Labor services are produced using raw labor and human capital, again with a Cobb–Douglas production function. Cities specialize completely in the production of different products. Total factor productivity affecting local production is produced in the style of endogenous growth [Lucas (1988), Romer (1990)] from total human capital and total labor in the city under Cobb–Douglas production function, is affected multiplicatively by a exogenous shock, and is external to each firm. Their specifications lead to a critical feature of the model, in that the optimal city size, that is the size that maximizes output net of commuting costs, implies that total commuting costs in each city are a constant fraction of total city output. This implies in turn that optimal city size is proportional to the square of the average product of labor. The model admits a balanced growth path along which growth is positive even if population growth is zero. Furthermore, along a balanced growth path, the growth rate of each city type may be written in terms of three components: one is proportional to the growth rate of human capital per person in each city type; a second is proportional to the rate of growth of the total factor productivity shock in the industry; and a third is proportional to the excess of the contemporaneous total factor productivity over a weighted sum of past realizations of total factor productivities. So, faster growth of human capital leads to larger cities, while faster population growth leads to smaller cities.

Proposition 4, in Rossi-Hansberg and Wright, characterizes emergence of Zipf's law in exactly two restrictive cases. One case obtains if capital is not used in production and the growth rate of the total factor productivity shock is time-independent. In this case, productivity shocks are permanent and produce permanent increases in the level of the marginal product of labor making its growth rate scale-independent. A second case obtains if industry production is according to an AK model, where there is no human capital and production is linear in physical capital, all capital depreciates after production, there is no population growth and productivity shocks are temporary. In this case, productivity shocks have a permanent effect on the marginal product of labor through the accumulation of human capital. If neither of the above conditions are satisfied, Rossi-Hansberg and Wright show that the growth rate of cities exhibits reversion to the mean and that the standard deviation of city sizes increases with the standard deviation of industry shocks. That is, if a city is large, defined as having experienced a history of productivity shocks above average, it can be expected to grow slower than average in the future, and the opposite would be true for small cities. Therefore, there would be relatively few small cities and large cities are not large enough. Consequently, the departure of the log rank–log size from the straight line associated with Zipf's Law is as found in the U.S. data. This is, of course, great progress in the long-standing effort to provide plausible microfoundations for Zipf's law for cities by delivering good news for all sides. Zipf's law can be the outcome, albeit in a special case of a very important class of models, that is, those inspired by the system-of-cities approach augmented by adopting features of the endogenous growth theory.

3.4. *Power laws at both ends of the city size distribution: random growth with exponential compounding*

Reed (2001, 2002) and Reed and Hughes (2002) advocate an interesting variant of the random growth process. This is obtained by a compounding geometric Brownian motion for city growth rates with the exponential distribution as follows. A Gibrat assumption of geometric Brownian motion but with constant instantaneous mean and variance, and given an initial state S_0, letting the process run for a fixed time T yields a size S_T that is lognormally distributed. However, if time T is exponentially distributed – for instance, if the cities "die" at a Poisson rate δ – then a power law distribution is obtained at the upper tail, which is expected, but also a power law distribution in the lower tail. Thus, the outcome is a double Pareto, with different Pareto law exponents above and below the threshold, which is given by the initial state S_0. Reed (2002) offers some evidence that this is empirically relevant, as the bottom tail of the distribution has a distribution of the type $P(S < x) \sim x^{\gamma}$ for $\gamma > 0$. The hypothesis of a non-zero death rate is likely to be indeed relevant in the lower tail of the distribution. We expect future research to be stimulated by these contributions.

4. Economic explanations for Zipf's law other than Gibrat's law

In principle, the distribution of city sizes may satisfy Zipf's law even if city growth rates do not satisfy Gibrat's Law. One such possibility, suggested by Krugman (1996b), is that the presence of Zipf's law in features of physical geography that are relevant for the properties of the urban system that adapts to them, may cause city sizes to obey it as well. Other theories may predict stable distributions for city sizes as outcomes of deterministic or random growth processes which may also satisfy Zipf's law. For example, Henderson-style systems of cities theories are not incompatible with Zipf's law for cities, in that the actual cause of Zipf's law for city sizes may be found among the underlying determinants of city sizes [Henderson (1988)].

4.1. *Zipf's law for cities coming from a power law of natural advantages*

Krugman (1996b) suggests that Zipf's law for cities might come from a Zipf's law of natural advantages. Indeed, he presents some evidence that the size of rivers follows Zipf's law. This might give rise to a power law of cities. A simple model helps thinking about those issues. Call A a index of natural advantages of a city – for instance, its proximity to the coast or the size of the river near it. Consider that the output of a city i with amenities A_i is $F(A_i, K_i, S_i)$, with F exhibiting constant returns to scale with respect to all of its arguments: K_i is the amount of capital and S_i the amount of labor in city i. Consider a model without randomness. Equalization of marginal products across cities gives $F_K(A_i, K_i, S_i) = r$ and $F_L(A_i, K_i, S_i) = w$, where r and w are the rental prices of capital and labor, respectively. The constant returns to scale assumption gives $F_K(A_i, K_i, S_i) = F_K(1, S_i/A_i, S_i/A_i)$, so that the solutions are of the type $K_i = kS_i$ and $L_i = lS_i$. The population of city i is proportional to the natural advantages of the city.

If the distribution of natural advantages across cities is power law with exponent ζ_A, (i.e., there is a b such that $P(A_i > A) = bA^{-\zeta_A}$ for A large) we get:

$$P(S_i > S) = P(A_i > S/l) = b = b(S/l)^{-\zeta_A} \sim S^{-\zeta_A},$$

so that the population distribution is power law with exponent ζ_A: $\zeta_S = \zeta_A$. Hence, if we have evidence that $\zeta_A = 1$, we would have an explanation for Zipf's law.

Obviously, more research is needed to assess this hypothesis. One of the difficulties is that the link between say the river flow f and the corresponding economic amenity A that would enter in the productivity function is not obvious. Should we have $A = f$, or $A = f^{\beta}$ for some $\beta \neq 1$? This matters, as one can show that if f is power law distribution with exponent ζ_f, relation $A = f^{\beta}$ will yield $\zeta_S = \zeta_A = \zeta_f/\beta$. Hence one has to give a reason why $\beta = 1$.

As an explanation for the persistence of city size distributions, the transmission of power laws of physical geography to city sizes needs to be refined further. For example, we know from Fujita and Mori (1997) that discontinuities in the physical landscape, such as natural ports and waterways, have important consequences for the location of cities. Still, it is clearly not the case that their actual dimensions may affect the size of cities in all instances. For example, the size of a navigable river is pertinent, but coastal location does not lend itself to such measurement. Furthermore, such theories are problematic as theories of growth when a particular physical amenity is held fixed. Clearly, this issue needs to be addressed further by the literature.

4.2. *Zipf's law for cities in models of self organization and endogenous city formation*

We review next a number of recent papers that develop models that combine several theoretical ideas. All of these papers use simulations to test their theoretical predictions.

Axtell and Florida (2001) offer a hybrid theoretical model of an urban system that predicts Zipf's law at its steady state. They attempt to "reconcile the tension between centripetal and centrifugal forces that we believe determines city sizes at the micro level, and the as-if-constant returns dynamics that seem to apply at the macro level" [*ibid.*].

Axtell and Florida propose a model of firm formation which leads to city formation by the location decisions of firms. Individual agents are myopic and interact in team production. Total team output is increasing and convex in team effort, and agents receive compensation equal to the equal shares of output. Individuals' choice of income versus leisure imply that a Nash equilibrium in effort levels exist but is Pareto-dominated by higher effort levels which are not individually rational. There exists a maximum stable size for firms beyond which groups are dynamically unstable. This implies that for firms beyond a certain size random perturbations lead to unstable adjustments. Each agent's location is originally random. Agents are allowed to move among firms or to start their own firms. When an agent starts a new firm, she selects a new location from among a finite number of locations, with a small probability, and she stays put, with a large probability. The authors claim that firms' growth rates are Laplace-distributed, their variance decreases with firm size according to a power law, wages are increasing in firm size, constant returns to scale prevail at the aggregate and city sizes obey Zipf's law.

Duranton (2002) is one of the most interesting economic models of city growth and aims at matching the observed distribution of city sizes. It actually does so very well: it offers a fairly good fit (with several free parameters), with approximate power laws for both the upper and lower tails [cf. Reed (2002)]. Several ingredients of Duranton's model are familiar to students of new economic geography. It uses the quality-ladder model of growth developed by Grossman and Helpman (1991) in an urban framework. Cities grow, or decline, as they win, or lose, industries following new innovations. So small innovation-driven technological shocks are the main engine behind the growth and decline of cities. The paper shows that observed regularities about the city size distribution are compatible with the basic building blocks of urban economics, like the existence of agglomeration economies, crowding costs, etc. In particular, these building blocks are crucial for the theory's good simulation performance.

Duranton's model has the virtue of offering a plausible explanation of the mobility of cities through the size distribution, and of generating a non-trivial such distribution from economic decisions of firms. The model does not match Gibrat's law: the mean and variance of growth rates decreases with size.[20] This is due to the fact that it does not model that larger cities do not have very diversified industrial base, which is an intuitive reason why Gibrat's law for variance may hold.

The model does match both the U.S. and French city size distributions when key parameters are calibrated based on appropriately different fundamentals.[21] Duranton's simulations show that the 10th and the 90th percentiles, that are predicted by the model, bound the U.S. distribution above the size of 220,000 inhabitants and the French distribution in its entirety. Still, in spite of his success in matching both the U.S. and French data, Duranton underscores that the real test should be whether proposed theories work well in explaining sources of urban growth and decline.

While Krugman (1996a) argues that the basic features of the urban system ought to be studied in models of self-organization, it was only until relatively recently that these newer theories were actually utilized to study empirically testable aspects of the urban system. The two most important contributions along such an approach is Brakman et al. (1999) and Brakman, Garretsen and van Marrewijk (2001). The new economic

[20] At the time of the completion of this chapter, the quantitative predictions of the model for the mean and variance of growth rates as a function of size were not made explicit, so that it was unclear how close or far they are from empirical processes.

[21] This is important because the U.S. data imply a roughly concave Zipf's curve and the French data a roughly convex one.

geography models of cities that they develop provide, in particular, for congestion costs via the specification of labor requirements for the production of the intermediate goods produced in different cities. Their simulations yield outcomes that resemble Zipf's Law. However, a Zipf coefficient near 1 is obtained only for certain parameter values which they associate with what they refer to as "industrialization", that is, large decrease in transportation costs and increasing importance of footloose industry with increasing returns to scale. Their pre- and post-industrialization scenaria are associated with Zipf coefficients exceeding 1.

5. Dynamics of the evolution of city size distributions

Eaton and Eckstein (1997) is, arguably, the most noteworthy recent study that focused on the persistence of the city size distribution and one of the most important contributions to the recent urban growth literature. The paper starts with a comparison of the dynamic evolution of the city size distribution between France and Japan. These countries have maintained national borders (that is when colonial possessions are ignored) that have remained unaltered during recent history and have urban systems with the number of cities remaining roughly constant. Eaton and Eckstein emphasize the observed persistence of the distribution over time, which they refer to as *parallel* growth of French and Japanese cities during 1876–1990 and 1925–1985, respectively. They confirm this finding by means of several alternative empirical techniques, such as Lorenz curves, Zipf regressions (logarithm of rank against logarithm of size) and non-parametric transition matrices of evolving size distributions.

They propose a theory that explains these facts and combines features of Henderson (1974) and of Lucas (1988). Their model allows for urban congestion but not intercity transportation. Persistence in the relative city size distribution is ensured by assuming that returns to learning in each city is proportional to the weighted average of human capital stocks in all cities, where the interaction coefficients are constrained to be consistent with steady-state growth. If city populations are growing at the same rate, than so are wages and consumption. Eaton and Eckstein also allow for intercity migration and examine conditions for utility costs of migration such that relative populations remove incentives for individuals to migrate. These conditions take the form of lower and upper bounds on the relative populations of two successive ranks. These bounds converge to the same quantity, if the effective rate of time discounting is equal to 0, for each city depend upon the ratio of human capitals in the respective cities and economy-wide parameters. However, while their result *does explain* the existence of *invariant* city size distributions, it does *not explain* why this distribution should obey a Zipf law, or even a power law. Nonetheless, the model is sufficiently flexible to let them set parameters that fit the data quite well. This result of parallel growth is also associated with parallel growth in total factor productivities across cities.

As the above discussion makes clear, the results of Eaton and Eckstein (1997) depend critically on conditions that bound intercity migration. Some of the earlier literature on city size distributions, such as Suarez-Villa (1988) and Tabuchi (1986), also emphasize the relationship between ad hoc laws governing intercity population flows and the stability of the city size distributions. This is, of course, not surprising. It thus appears that additional progress would be made if general models of intercity migration and trade would be built.

In the context of Eaton and Eckstein's approach, the reader naturally wonders what would happen to city size distributions in an economy marked by *expansion of its land mass and emergence of new cities.* Dobkins and Ioannides (2000) were the first to address this question recently with respect to the urban system. We next turn to questions of spatial evolution by posing them in the context of recent research on the spatial distribution of economic activity in the U.S.

5.1. Spatial concentration of economic activity in the U.S.

Before we go into details of this literature, it would be interesting to provide a broader historical perspective on the spatial concentration of economic activity in the U.S. Recent research has also examined the spatial distribution of population at different levels of aggregation. Beeson, DeJong and Troesken (1999) and Beeson and DeJong (2002) examine regional patterns of population growth at the state and county level from 1790 to 1990. They find that state-level populations show convergence while county-level populations show divergence. While initial tendencies towards convergence lasted roughly through the 1800s, in the post World War II period county-level populations have diverged. Their analysis points to the *importance of transitional dynamics* as opposed to *steady-state dynamics.* When territories opened up for settlement, growth rates were very high relative to steady states. Once such "frontier effects" have been controlled for, the tendency to divergence in the post war period is clear.

The United States transformed itself from a rural to an urban society over the last three centuries. Kim (2000) emphasizes that after a century of unremarkable growth, the 1700s, the pace of urbanization rose to historically unprecedented levels between the nineteenth and early twentieth centuries. In the twentieth century, the urban population continued to increase but in a much more dispersed manner as the suburban population increased. Throughout these developments, cities also exhibited considerable variation in their population sizes. Kim emphasizes the role of changes in regional comparative advantage and in economies of scale in transportation and local public goods for the patterns of U.S. urban development. He finds that differences in urban sizes are associated with the role of reduced market transaction costs in coordinating greater geographic division of labor. Kim (2002) looks at the dynamic evolution of urban densities. The paper documents the historical changes in population and employment densities in U.S. cities and metropolitan areas, and explores the causes of their rise and decline between the late nineteenth and the twentieth centuries.

The role of urban density has recently attracted attention in relation to the evolution of *other measures of urban size,* such as *employment.* In particular, papers by Carlino and Chatterjee (2001, 2002) point to a pronounced trend towards deconcentration of employment in the U.S. since WWII. That is, the employment share of relatively dense MSAs has declined and the share of less dense MSAs has risen. Similarly, they show that such effects also apply within MSAs. They explain these trends by means of a density-dependent congestion costs. They do not, however, estimate models for the pattern of transition. Still, these works challenge the view, based on population size studies, that the urban landscape is in some sort of steady state. Instead, they find considerable change.

5.2. *Urban evolution in the U.S.*

Dobkins and Ioannides (2000) develop a data set that tracks U.S. cities, actually metropolitan areas, from 1900 to 1990. They use contemporaneous definitions of metropolitan areas, described in detail in the Data section in *ibid.* The number of cities grows from 112 in 1900 to 334 in 1990. Many of the cities that enter the data grow from settlements physically in existence for many years, prior to the time they pass the appropriate threshold of population, that is 50,000 inhabitants. Entirely new cities also come into being, the latest one in 1944, and quickly grow large enough to be included in the data. Dobkins and Ioannides find that the U.S. urban system is characterized by *parallel growth, despite its spatial expansion.* They analyze the data in more detail, by constructing transition matrices, and track the movement of each city in the distribution relative to the others.

As noted above, Eaton and Eckstein's selection of France and Japan was motivated by their roughly stable geographical boundaries and the consistent availability of data. In contrast to such "old" countries as France and Japan, the United States has grown by continuously expanding its land mass into a well defined hinterland. New regions and cities have been brought into the U.S. urban system during the nineteenth and twentieth centuries, older regions have grown and declined, and the spatial distribution of economic activity has undergone some remarkable changes. In Europe, almost no new cities were created during the twentieth century. The U.S. urban system has developed with initial conditions quite different from those of other countries.

As Quah (1993) has forcefully argued, typical cross-section or panel data techniques do not allow inference about patterns in the intertemporal evolution of the entire cross-section distribution. They do not allow us to consider the impact over time of one part of the distribution upon another, i.e., of the development of large cities as a group upon smaller cities. Making such inferences requires one to model directly the full dynamics of the entire distribution of cities. The evolution of urbanization and suburbanization may affect individual cities so drastically as to render conventional methods of accounting for attrition totally inappropriate. As smaller urban units fuse to create larger ones, and given the small number of time series observations, non-parametric or semi-parametric distributional approaches such as the one proposed here would be the only appropriate ones. In fact, these techniques are appropriate when the sample of interest is the entire distribution, and individual observations are used to recover information about the entire distribution. The availability of data are severely restricted both in the time and the cross-section dimensions: there are only ten cross-sections, one for each of the ten census years since 1900, with 112 metropolitan areas and 334 in 1990.

The paucity of the data naturally lends itself to techniques used by Quah (1993) and Eaton and Eckstein (1997). That is, one may construct from population data a fairly low-dimensional vector indicating the frequency of cities in each of a number of suitably defined intervals (cells). Let f_t denote the frequency (density) distribution of P_{it} at time t. Eaton and Eckstein assume that f_t evolves according to a first-order autoregression (that applies to the entire distribution function (rather than scalars or vectors of numbers):

$$f_{t+1} = M \cdot f_t, \tag{15}$$

where M is a matrix of parameters. If f_t were restricted to be measures defined over a discrete set, then M in (15) is a Markov transition matrix. Absence of a random disturbance allows us to iterate (15) forward to get: $f_{t+s} = (M \cdot M \cdots M) \cdot f_t = M^s \cdot f_t$. Divergent, convergent or parallel growth may be ascertained by the properties of $f_\infty \equiv \lim_{t\to\infty} f_t$. If a limit distribution f_∞ exists, then according to the Perron–Frobenius theorem it is given by the eigenvector corresponding to the unique unitary eigenvalue of M, the non-zero solution of $[M - I]f_\infty = 0]$, where 0] denotes a column vector of zeroes. Parallel growth is understood to occur if f_∞ tends to a limit with non-zero probability over the entire support. Convergent growth would occur if f_∞ is a mass point, and divergent growth if f_∞ is a polarized or segmented distribution.

Dobkins and Ioannides (2000) and Black and Henderson (2003) adapt Equation (15) in order to allow for new cities to enter according to a frequency distribution ε_t. If the number of entrants between t and $t+1$ is I_t^n, $I_{t+1} = I_t + I_t^n$, then

$$f_{t+1} = \frac{I_t}{I_{t+1}} M_t f_t + \frac{I_t^n}{I_{t+1}} \varepsilon_t. \tag{16}$$

If M_t and $\iota_t \equiv I_t^n / I_{t+1}$ are time-invariant, then the above equation is amenable to the standard treatment. Letting M and ι be the respective time-invariant values, we may iterate Equation (16) backwards to get $f_t = (1-\iota)^t M^t f_0 + \sum_{\tau=0}^{t} [(1-\iota)M]^{t-\tau} \iota \varepsilon_\tau$, where f_0 denotes the initial distribution of city sizes.

A steady-state solution of (16) characterizes the distribution of city sizes in the long run with entry. In general, if there are few or no entrants, $\iota \approx 0$, the homogeneous solution dominates: the invariant (ergodic) distribution is a useful measure of the state of the urban system in the long run. If, on the other hand, ι is non-negligible, then the particular solution may *not* be ignored. In fact, in that case, the magnitude of the largest eigenvalue of $(1-\iota)M$ is $(1-\iota)$, and the impact of the initial conditions would be less important the higher is ι, the number of new cities that have entered over the last decade as a proportion of the new total number of cities.

In the Dobkins and Ioannides data, the values of ι_t are as follows: $\iota_{1910} = 0.194$, $\iota_{1920} = 0.067$; $\iota_{1930} = 0.051$, $\iota_{1940} = 0.019$, $\iota_{1950} = 0.012$, $\iota_{1960} = 0.229$, $\iota_{1970} = 0.136$, $\iota_{1980} = 0.245$, and $\iota_{1990} = 0.036$. These numbers suggest possibly a non-stationary series and the intertemporal variations in ι_t are interesting and worthy of special analysis.

We note that in the absence of a theory of entry of new cities, there is rather limited scope for a purely statistical analysis based on such a small number of time series observations. Entry of new cities is pursued further by Dobkins and Ioannides (2001).

The stochastic specification of Equation (16) is, in general, very complicated, especially when M_t may be time-varying. E.g., forces that cause urban growth and decline may operate quite differently at the upper level of the distribution than at the lower one, and their pattern may change over time. The distribution of new entrants has most of its mass at the lower end, which to large extent reflects the nature of our data. Even if M_t is not time-varying, it could be associated with an invariant distribution that could reflect very different properties.

By coding the position of each city relative to the others within the distribution, we are able to see whether or not specific cities move up or down in the distribution over time. Dobkins and Ioannides constructed transition matrices which are reported in *ibid.*, Appendix A.[22] The empirical transition matrices that are reported suggest that concentration at the upper end of the distribution becomes more pronounced over time: the diagonal entries are higher for higher percentiles. Another observation that follows is that most movements are to nearby cells, with very few big jumps. As one might expect in the U.S. data, there is somewhat more movement off the diagonal (compared to the French and Japanese data). Most of that movement is toward greater concentration in the time period from 1900 to 1990. However, these transition matrices have limitations. They do not pick up the full effect of "entering" cities and they do not offer us any more insight into why such changes might occur. There are undoubtedly other variables that might impact on city size distribution.

Black and Henderson (2003) confirm these results by working with a slightly different data set and a somewhat more general model. Specifically, they work with the steady-state solution of Equation (16) which does account for entry. They also interpret the increasing concentration at the upper end of the distribution as being due to scale economies and changes in technology. Since the mean city size increased four-fold and the median five-fold, medium-size cities have grown substantially. They attribute this growth less to the impact of technology through local knowledge accumulation and improved commuting and more to the effect of changes in the national demand for the output of inter-city traded services, which favors large cities. They test for the stationarity of the transition matrices, which is never close to being rejected. They also examine mobility by means of first passage times and find that upward mobility is much stronger than downward mobility. They interpret slow downward mobility as an effect of "established urban scale".

Ioannides and Overman (2004) consider, in the light of recent theoretical advances, the spatial characteristics of the U.S. urban system as it evolved over the twentieth century. These advances have highlighted the importance of spatial dimensions in understanding the evolution of urban systems: Fujita, Krugman and Venables (1999) have

[22] De Vries (1984, Chapter 7), appears to have originated the study of urbanization by means of transition matrices.

added important new spatial insights to the established literature on systems of cities [Henderson (1974, 1988)]. The system of cities approach features powerful models of intrametropolitan spatial structure, but neglected intermetropolitan spatial structure. Intermetropolitan spatial structure plays a key role in the new economic geography literature [Krugman (1991); Fujita, Krugman and Mori (1999)]. Further, as shown by Fujita and Thisse (2002), the importance of spatial dimensions is not just restricted to the new economic geography. Rather, it is a general feature of recent theoretical advances in our understanding of the economics of agglomeration.

This recent theorizing has formalized thinking about two fundamental features of any given location – the *first* and *second* "natures" – that determine the extent of development at that location. First nature features are those that are *intrinsic to the physical site itself,* independent of any development that may previously have occurred there. For example, locations on navigable rivers, with favorable climates have first nature features that might encourage development. The second nature features of a location are those that are *dependent on the spatial interactions between economic agents.*

However, these theories do not offer very precise predictions, and especially of the type that may be used to structure empirical investigations. Real life geography, the tendency for all cities to grow, the gradual convergence to some kind of equilibrium in the westward expansion of the country, the movement of population towards the Sunbelt and changes in the U.S. urban system induced by a shift over the period in industrial structure away from manufacturing and towards services are all important features in the spatial evolution of the U.S. urban system that have not yet been elaborated in the formal theory. Thus, Ioannides and Overman seek to understand first and second nature features of the U.S. urban system without restricting analysis to specific functional forms. Instead, they choose to focus predominantly on non-parametric methods proposed by Quah, *op. cit.*, that is, non-parametric estimations of stochastic kernels for the distributions of city sizes and growth rates, conditional on various measures of market potential. They show that while these relationships evolve during the twentieth century, by 1990 they stabilize so that the size distribution of cities conditional on a range of spatial variables are all roughly independent of these conditioning variables. In contrast, similar results suggest that there is a spatial element to the city wage distribution.

Their parametric estimations for growth rates against market potential, entry of neighbors, and own lagged population imply a negative effect of market potential on growth rates, unless own lagged population is also included, in which case market potential has a positive effect and own lagged population a negative one. Cities grow faster when they are small relative to their market potential.

Overman and Ioannides (2001) report non-parametrically estimated stochastic transition kernels for the evolution of the distribution of U.S. metropolitan area populations, for the period 1900 to 1990. These suggest a fair amount of uniformity in the patterns of mobility during the study period. The distribution of city sizes is predominantly characterized by persistence. Additional kernel estimates do not reveal any stark differences in intra-region mobility patterns. They characterize the nature of intra-size distribution dynamics by means of measures that do not require discretization of the city size distribution. They employ these measures to study the degree of mobility within the U.S. city size distribution and, separately, within regional and urban subsystems. They find that *different regions* show *different degrees of intra-distribution mobility. Second-tier cities show more mobility than top-tier cities.*

The results of Dobkins and Ioannides (2001) may also be considered as supportive of parallel growth. They test implications of economic geography by exploring spatial interactions among U.S. cities. They augment the data set developed in Dobkins and Ioannides (2000) by means of spatial measures including distance from the nearest larger city in a higher- tier, adjacency, and location within U.S. regions. They also date cities from their time of settlement. They find that among cities which enter the system, larger cities are more likely to locate near other cities. Moreover, older cities are more likely to have neighbors. Distance from the nearest higher-tier city is not always a significant determinant of size and growth. They find no evidence of persistent non-linear effects on urban growth of either size or distance, although distance is important for city size for some years.

6. The empirical evidence on the determinants of urban growth

6.1. *Determinants of urban growth*

Madden (1956) provides an interesting non-parametric analysis of urban growth in the United States. He emphasizes stability features in the distribution of growth rates and their evolution over time, where he notes that great dispersion coexists with considerable intertemporal variation for individual cities.

Henderson (1988), Glaeser et al. (1992) and Glaeser, Scheinkman and Shleifer (1995) examine the role of socioeconomic characteristics of city populations and of city industrial structures in economic growth. The results are detailed in this handbook by Moretti (2004).

Black and Henderson (2003) also estimate an equation for Gibrat's Law, that is for the growth rate as a function of lagged size, which yields a *statistically significant estimate for the mean reversion coefficient,* the coefficient of the logarithm of size, from -0.022 to -0.039. However, the finding of significant mean reversion may be an artifact of *measurement error.* That is, measurement error of 10% along with a standard deviation of the logarithm of size of 0.7, for the fifty largest cities, would imply an estimate coefficient of 0.02. Also, positive autocorrelation in the residual of the regression could also show up as mean reversion. In fact, the studies of Davis and Weinstein (2002) and Brakman, Garretsen and Schramm (2002), discussed below, do estimate generally positive autocorrelation for the error in such a regression.

Black and Henderson also report regressions with additional explanatory variables, that is spatially varying geographical variables like temperature, precipitation, proximity to coast (including proximity to the Great Lakes, regional dummies, and market potential variables (which are defined in an ad hoc fashion). They find that cities in warmer, drier and coastal locations do grow faster, and that regional dummies have little additional impact. Market potential has a quadratic effect on growth that diminishes as market potential rises, but it has a large effect around its mean value. Having neighbors nearby enhances growth, an effect of intercity trade. They interpret the diminution of the effect for large market potential as an outcome of *competition*. If a city is in a very high market potential area it suffers from competition: *Los Angeles benefits by being far from New York*. Still, high market potential helps large cities maintain their relative positions.

Black and Henderson are particularly careful with the estimation of the relative growth equation. Noting that the lagged city size and spatial interactions introduce endogeneity, they use lagged instruments with GMM for the unbalanced panel data for the estimation. Allowing for fixed effects and using GMM increase the absolute value of the mean reversion coefficient nearly ten-fold. This implies mean reversion that is so much stronger than is typically found in the growth literature, that it raises doubts for the reliability of these estimates. Black and Henderson also examine city sizes in relation to city types, defined in terms of industrial compositions, and find that different city types have different absolute sizes. Therefore, changes in industrial compositions change relative sizes. These results confirm important features of the system-of-cities approach.

Finally, Florida (2002) studies the impact of hard-to-measure variables such as the openness to new ideas and creativity. He uses measures and proxies, such as the fraction of the population who is foreign born or gay, a coolness and a bohemian index, all of which are not commonly used, and finds that they have a high predictive power.

We expect more studies such as those to arise, especially in non-U.S. contexts. A tighter link with the evidence on the stability of the city size distribution, such as along the lines of the distinction in Section 3.2.2, deserves serious empirical attention.

6.2. The determinants of urban primacy

Rosen and Resnick (1980) and Wheaton and Shishido (1981) show that urban concentration is negatively correlated with a country's population. Ades and Glaeser (1995) offer an empirical analysis that shows that high tariffs, high costs of internal trade and low level of international trade increase the degree of urban concentration. Interestingly, a very good predictor is a political variable: dictatorships have central cities that are, on average, 50 percent larger than their democratic counterpart. Their evidence suggests that the causation goes from political factors to urban concentration rather than the opposite.

6.3. Studies of urban growth based on quasi "natural experiments"

Davis and Weinstein (2002) and Brakman, Garretsen and Schramm (2002) offer a completely different viewpoint on the robustness of city size distributions when they are subject to unusually large aggregate shocks. These papers rely on the quasi "natural experiments" provided by the strategic bombing of, respectively, Japan and Germany, during World War II. The two studies differ, however, in their time horizons. In the former paper, the case of Japan, the time span ranges over the past 8000 years! In the latter paper, the case of Germany, it ranges from the beginning to the end of the 20th century.

These studies examine the performance of three, possibly not mutually exclusive, theories of economic geography and urban development. These are: first, *increasing returns,* defined as the combined effects on city size of knowledge spillovers, labor market pooling and costly intercity transportation either as modelled by the system of cities literature [Henderson (1974)] or by new economic geography [Krugman (1991)]; second, *random growth processes*; and third, *locational fundamentals,* by which they mean that random growth results from randomness in the physical and economic characteristics of locations themselves. Davis and Weinstein argue that these three theories, which we discuss earlier in the chapter, have very *different testable predictions* for the impact on the size distribution from a powerful but *temporary shock.*

Davis and Weinstein (2002) argue that the great deal of variation in regional densities suggests factors other than increasing returns are important in determining regional densities. The extraordinary changes in technology over the length of the study would have produced radical shifts in the urban structure over time, which are not observed. Random growth, on the other hand, is consistent with the facts, provided that the underlying stochastic process satisfies certain conditions. The locational fundamentals theory could easily explain persistence, as certain physical features of the landscape, like proximity to waterways and the ocean, have not been altered even with the intense bombing that Japan (and Germany) suffered. They interpret the great deal of persistence in population densities over time that they find as strong support of the locational fundamentals theory.

They interpret the evidence on the robustness of Japan's urban system as against the increasing returns theory and in favor of the locational fundamentals theory. They conclude that the evidence is consistent with a hybrid theory whereby locational advantages help establish basic patterns of regional densities and increasing returns, or random growth, help determine the degree of concentration. Davis and Weinstein interpret the remarkable recovery of Japan's urban system as evidence against random growth. While their results are very interesting, they need not warrant this conclusion. In the terms of Section 3.2.2 of this chapter, they show evidence for a mean-reverting component in the growth process. This is still a priori compatible with the main condition of random growth models, the presence of a unit root. They do not purport to reject the existence of such a unit root.

The same caveat applies to Brakman, Garretsen and Schramm (2002). Like Davis and Weinstein, they estimate an equation for the growth rate during $1946 + t$ and 1946, where t assumes alternative values 4, 17 and 18 in order to distinguish between short-term and long-term effects, with German city data. They separate the sample into West and East Germany, for $t = 4, 17$ and $t = 4, 18$, respectively. They conclude that when the entire of Germany and West Germany only are studied, the impact of the bombing is significant but temporary. The East German urban system, if treated separately, obeys a random walk. They attribute this difference to the different socioeconomic systems prevailing in the two parts of Germany following WW II, with East Germany having been a communist state from 1949 until its absorption into the Federal Republic of Germany in 1989. The post World War II division of Germany might have created border effects for those cities near the border. It is interesting that in spite of the prevalence of central planning in East Germany, the East German urban system might not have been altered and thus remained affected by its state at the end of WW II. In contrast, the outcome for the urban system within the free market system in West Germany was not conditioned by the bombing. They find this to be consistent with the locational fundamentals theory but not necessarily with the increasing returns theory. It is interesting that the study of the urban dynamics in Germany and Japan provides evidence for such different results. Perhaps this is due to the very different geographies of those two countries, which might have prevented the operation of market forces' altering the urban system in Japan but not in Germany.

These historical studies have clearly opened up new horizons for economic research. Still, they may be providing additional evidence on the resilience of urban systems in-the-large. For example, repeated destructions of urban settlements in Europe have always been followed by reconstruction along the earlier patterns. But it is also true, as the chapter by Hohenberg in this handbook [Hohenberg (2003)] articulates, that *persistence* of the urban structure historically must always be studied in terms of *fully dynamic models*. Such an approach finds us in full agreement.

7. Conclusion

Because Zipf's law appears to be a quite robust empirical regularity, this survey put some emphasis on it. Two related empirical regularities are Gibrat's law for means and Gibrat's law for variances. They have been less systematically studied, so more research is warranted to study their empirical validity (though initial assessments appear favorable to Gibrat's laws). These three laws offer a strong benchmark against which to measure theories of urban evolution and to organize an up to date look at the literature. The robustness of Zipf's law has also served to attract attention to the need for microfoundations.

The paper reviews a number of theories, some of them very recent, whose implications match those laws quite closely, at least approximately and within the confidence intervals in which those laws themselves hold. Most existing theories until very recently did not easily accommodate these laws. The classical urban (system of cities) theory may accommodate it as outcome of very special assumptions about preferences and technology. Some of its recent variants offer much more precise predictions and, notably, also explain departures from Zipf's law that we observe at the extremes of the city size distribution. The new economic geography literature may also accommodate it, albeit in very simple models. We do not know whether this accommodation would survive in more complex models. As the revival of interest in these topics fosters additional research with enriched theories of urban growth and development, we think that several important issues deserve attention. Notable such issues are the robustness of urban evolution, in spite of the presence of stochastic forces, and the role of economic integration and international trade.

Acknowledgements

We thank Vernon Henderson, Tom Holmes, Henry Overman (our discussant), and Jacques Thisse for very useful comments. Gabaix gratefully acknowledges the hospitality of the Russell Sage Foundation in academic year 2002–2003. Ioannides acknowledges generous support by the National Science Foundation and by the John D. and Catherine T. MacArthur, through the Research Network on Social Interactions and Economic Disparities.

Appendix: Zipf's law and urban primacy

Ordering cities by size, the k-primacy π_k is the ratio between the size of the largest city and the sum of the population of the k largest cities. Formally,

$$\pi_k = \frac{S_{(1)}}{\sum_{i=1}^{k} S_{(i)}}. \tag{A.1}$$

It lies between 0 and 1. A large π_k indicates that the largest city is quite large. In this appendix we describe the predictions of Zipf's law for this. The Rényi representation theorem cited in Section 2.2.2 gives that, for $i < j$, the difference $\ell n\ S_{(i)} - \ell n\ S_{(j)}$ can be written as

$$\ell n\ S_{(i)} - \ell n\ S_{(j)} = \sum_{h=i}^{j-1} \frac{\tau_h}{h} \tag{A.2}$$

where the τ_k are independent draws of an exponential distribution $P(\tau_k > \tau) = \mathrm{e}^{-\tau}$ for $\tau \geqslant 0$. A consequence of this is the distribution of the k first cities in a sample of n cities depends only on the ratios $(S_{(1)}/S_{(k)}, \ldots, S_{(k-1)}/S_{(k)})$ and does not depend on the specific value of n. So, to sample k-primacies (and most statistics), it is enough to draw k cities from a Zipf distribution, rather than draw n cities and take the k biggest cities. One can do that by drawing k i.i.d. random variables u_i from a uniform distribution in $[0, 1]$ and sets the sizes as $S_i = 1/u_i$. One sorts them to get the ordered sizes $S_{(i)}$. One gets the corresponding k-primacy ratio π_k. The results are reported in Table 3.

A conclusion from Table 3 is that the confidence intervals are extremely wide. This could be guessed from the result cited in Footnote 3, that under Zipf's law, the ratio of the largest city to second largest city has smallest 95% confidence interval equal to $[1, 20]$. Various authors look to explain variations in urban primacy. But Table 3 suggests that the large variations in urban primacy across countries are just what Zipf's

Table 3
Statistics on the k-primacy ratio π_k

k	2	3	5	10	50
Mean π_k	0.693	0.590	0.502	0.424	0.323
S.D. of π_k	0.140	0.172	0.193	0.205	0.208
95% C.I.	[0.506,0.975]	[0.361,0.961]	[0.251,0.944	[0.168,0.922]	[0.090,0.879]

π_k is the ratio between the size of the largest city and the sum of the population of the k largest cities. The table reports the mean of π_k, its standard deviation, and a 95% confidence interval for π_k. *Source.* Authors' calculations, based on 1 million Monte Carlo simulations for each k.

law predicts. In a sample of 44 countries, Rosen and Resnick (1980) finds a 5-primacy of 0.49 (S.D. 0.12), which is very close to the Zipf prediction, and a 50-primacy of 0.24 (S.D. 0.098). Thus Rosen and Resnick's 50-primacy number is a bit less than expected from Zipf. This maybe be due to the quality of their data. Soo (2003) finds for the 5-primacy a mean 0.50 with a standard deviation of 0.13. For the 10-primacy, he finds a mean of 0.39, with a mean of 0.13. The results are thus extremely close to the Zipf predictions.

References

Ades, A., Glaeser, E. (1995). "Trade and circuses: explaining urban giants". Quarterly Journal of Economics 110, 195–228.

Anas, A. (2001). "The spatial economy, cities, regions and international trade". Regional Science and Urban Economics 31, 601–615.

Auerbach, F. (1913). "Das Gesetz der Bevölkerungskonzentration". Petermanns Geographische Mitteilungen 59, 74–76.

Axtell, R.L. (2001). "Zipf distribution of U.S. firm sizes". Science 293, 1818–1820.

Axtell, R.L., Florida, R., (2001). "Emergent cities: A microeconomic explanation of Zipf's law". Paper presented at the Society for Computational Economics, Yale University.

Bairoch, P. (1988). Cities and Economic Development: From the Dawn of History to the Present, Christopher Braider. University of Chicago Press, Chicago.

Bairoch, P. Batou, J., Chevre, P. (1988). "The population of European cities 800–1850: Data bank and short summary of results". Centre of International Economic History Series 2. Geneva University.

Beeson, P.E., DeJong, D.N. (2002). "Divergence". Contributions to Macroeconomics 2, 1049.

Beeson, P.E., DeJong, D.N., Troesken, W. (1999). "Population growth in U.S. counties: 1840–1990". Mimeo. Department of Economics, University of Pittsburgh.

Beirlant, J., Dierckx, G., Goegebeur, Y., Matthys, G. (1999). "Tail index estimation and an exponential regression model". Extremes, 2177.

Black, D., Henderson, J.V. (1999). "A theory of urban growth". Journal of Political Economy 107, 252–284.

Black, D., Henderson, J.V. (2003). "Urban evolution in the USA". Journal of Economic Geography 3, 343–372.

Brakman, S., Garretsen, H., van Marrewijk, C. (2001). An Introduction to Geographical Economics. Cambridge University Press, Cambridge.

Brakman, S., Garretsen, H., van Marrewijk, C., van den Berg, M. (1999). "The return of Zipf: A further understanding of the rank–size distribution". Journal of Regional Science 39, 183–213.

Brakman, S., Garretsen, H., Schramm, M. (2002). "The strategic bombing of German cities during WWII and its impact on cities growth". CESifo Working Paper No. 808. CESifo, Munich.

Carlino, G., Chatterjee, S. (2001). "Aggregate metropolitan employment growth and the deconcentration of metropolitan employment". Journal of Monetary Economics 48, 549–583.

Carlino, G., Chatterjee, S. (2002). "Employment deconcentration: a new perspective on America's postwar urban evolution". Journal of Regional Science 42, 455–475.

Champernowne, D. (1953). "A model of income distribution". Economic Journal 83, 318–351.

Córdoba, J.-C. (2003). "On the distribution of city sizes". Working Paper. Rice University.

Davis, D.R. (2002). "Review of 'The Spatial Economy, Cities, Regions and International Trade', by M. Fujita, P.R. Krugman, and A.J. Venables". Journal of International Economics 57, 247–251.

Davis, D.R., Weinstein, D.E. (2002). "Bones, bombs and break points: the geography of economic activity". American Economic Review 92, 1269–1289.

De Vries, J. (1984). European Urbanization, 1500–1800. Harvard University Press, Cambridge, MA.

Dobkins, L.H., Ioannides, Y.M. (2000). "Dynamic evolution of the U.S. city size distribution". In: Huriot, J., Thisse, J. (Eds.), The Economics of Cities, Theoretical Perspectives. Cambridge University Press, Cambridge, pp. 217–260.

Dobkins, L.H., Ioannides, Y.M. (2001). "Spatial interactions among U.S. cities". Regional Science and Urban Economics 31, 701–731.

Duranton, G. (2002). "City size distribution as a consequence of the growth process". Department of Geography and Environment, London School of Economics.

Eaton, J., Eckstein, Z. (1997). "Cities and growth, theory and evidence from France and Japan". Regional Science and Urban Economics 27, 443–474.

Embrechts, P., Kluppelberg, C., Mikosch, T. (1997). Modelling Extremal Events for Insurance and Finance. Springer, New York.

Feuerverger, A., Hall, P. (1999). "Estimating a tail exponent by modelling departure from a Pareto distribution". Annals of Statistics 27, 760–781.

Florida, R. (2002). The Rise of the Creative Class: And How Its Transforming Work, Leisure Community and Everyday Life. Basic Books, New York.

Fujita, M., Mori, T. (1997). "Structural stability and evolution of urban systems". Regional Science and Urban Economics 27, 399–442.

Fujita, M., Krugman, P., Mori, T. (1999). "On the evolution of hierarchical urban systems". European Economic Review 43, 209–251.

Fujita, M., Krugman, P., Venables, A.J. (1999). The Spatial Economy. MIT Press, Cambridge, MA.

Fujita, M., Thisse, J.-F. (2002). Economics of Agglomeration. Cambridge University Press, Cambridge.

Gabaix, X. (1999a). "Zipf's Law and the growth of cities". American Economic Review, Papers and Proceedings 89, 129–132.

Gabaix, X. (1999b). "Zipf's Law for cities an explanation". Quarterly Journal of Economics 114, 739–767.

Gabaix, X., Gopikrishnan, P., Plerou, V., Stanley, H.E. (2003). "A theory of power law distributions in financial fluctuations". Nature 423, 267–270.

Gabaix, X., Ioannides, Y. (2003). "The properties of the least squares estimates of power law exponents". MIT and Tufts University.

Gabaix, X., Ramalho, R., Reuter, J. (2004). "Investor behavior and mutual fund dynamics". MIT mimeo.

Gibrat, R. (1931). Les inégalités économiques. Librairie du Recueil Sirey, Paris.

Glaeser, E., Kallal, H., Scheinkman, J., Shleifer, A. (1992). "Growth in cities". Journal of Political Economics 100, 1126–1152.

Glaeser, E.L., Scheinkman, J.A., Shleifer, A. (1995). "Economic growth in a cross-section of cities". Journal of Monetary Economics 36, 117–143.

Grossman, G.M., Helpman, E. (1991). "Quality ladders in the theory of growth". Review of Economic Studies 58, 43–61.

Henderson, J.V. (1974). "The types and size of cities". American Economic Review 64, 640–656.

Henderson, J.V. (1988). Urban Development: Theory, Fact and Illusion. Oxford University Press, Oxford.

Hill, B.M. (1975). "A simple approach to inference about the tail of a distribution". Annals of Statistics 3, 1163–1174.

Hohenberg, P.M. (2003). "The historical geography of European cities: an interpretive essay". This volume.

Ioannides, Y.M., Overman, H.G. (2003). "Zipf's Law for cities: an empirical examination". Regional Science and Urban Economics 33, 127–137.

Ioannides, Y.M., Overman, H.G. (2004). "Spatial evolution of the U.S. urban system". Journal of Economic Geography 4 (2), 1–26.

Kesten, H. (1973). "Random difference equations and renewal theory for products of random matrices". Acta Mathematica 131, 207–248.

Kim, S. (2000). "Urban development in the United States, 1690–1990". Southern Economic Journal. In press.

Kim, S. (2002). "The reconstruction of the American urban landscape in the twentieth century". Working Paper no. w8857. National Bureau Economic Research.

Krugman, P. (1991). "Increasing returns and economic geography". Journal of Political Economy 99, 483–499.

Krugman, P. (1996a). The Self-Organizing Economy. Blackwell, Oxford.

Krugman, P. (1996b). "Confronting the mystery of urban hierarchy". Journal of the Japanese and the International Economies 10, 399–418.

Leamer, E., Levinsohn, J. (1995). "International trade theory: the evidence". In: Grossman, G., Rogoff, K. (Eds.), Handbook of International Economics, vol. III. North-Holland, Amsterdam, pp. 1339–1394.

Levy, M., Solomon, S. (1996). "Dynamical explanation for the emergence of power law in a stock market model". International Journal of Modern Physics C 7, 65–72.

Lucas, R.E. Jr. (1988). "On the mechanics of economic development". Journal of Monetary Economics 22, 3–42.

Madden, C.H. (1956). "On some indications of stability in the growth of cities in the United States". Economic Development and Cultural Change 4, 236–252.

Malcai, O., Biham, O., Solomon, S. (1999). "Power-law distributions and Lévy-stable intermittent fluctuations in stochastic systems of many autocatalytic elements". Physical Review E 60, 1299.

Marsili, M., Zhang, Y.C. (1998). "Interacting individuals leading to Zipf's Law". Physical Review Letters 80, 2741–2744.

Moretti, E. (2004). "Human capital externalities and cities". In: Henderson, J., Thisse, J. (Eds.), Handbook of Regional and Urban Economics, vol. 4. Elsevier, Amsterdam, pp. 2243–2292. This volume.

Mori, T., Nishikimi, K., Smith, T. (2003). "Some empirical regularities of spatial economies: A relationship between industrial location and city size". Mimeo. Kyoto University.

Neary, P. (2001). "Of hype and hyperbolas: introducing the new economic geography". Journal of Economic Literature 39, 536–561.

Okuyama, K., Takayasu, M., Takayasu, H. (1999). "Zipf's Law in income distribution of companies". Physica A 269, 125–131.

Overman, H.G., Ioannides, Y.M. (2001). "Cross-sectional evolution of the U.S. city size distribution". Journal of Urban Economics 49, 543–566.

Quah, D. (1993). "Empirical cross-section dynamics and economic growth". European Economic Review 37, 426–434.

Reed, W. (2001). "The Pareto, Zipf and other power law". Economics Letters 74, 15–19.

Reed, W. (2002). "On the rank–size distribution for human settlements". Journal of Regional Science 41, 1–17.

Reed, W., Hughes, B. (2002). "From gene and genera to incomes and internet files: Why power laws are so common in nature". Physical Review E 66. 067103/1-4.

Reiss, R. (1989). Approximate Distributions of Order Statistics. Springer, Berlin.

Romer, P.M. (1990). "Endogenous technological change". Journal of Political Economy 98, 71–102.

Rosen, K., Resnick, M. (1980). "The size distribution of cities: an examination of the Pareto law and primacy". Journal of Urban Economics 8, 165–186.

Rossi-Hansberg, E., Wright, M.L.J. (2003). "Urban structure and growth". Working Paper. Stanford University.

Simon, H. (1955). "On a class of skew distribution functions". Biometrika 44, 425–440. Reprinted in: Models of Man: Social and Rational. Mathematical Essays on Rational Human Behavior in a Social Setting. Wiley, New York, 1957.

Soo, K.T. (2003). "Zipf's Law for cities: a cross country investigation". Working Paper. Centre for Economic Performance, London School of Economics.

Sornette, D. (2001). Critical Phenomena in Natural Sciences. Springer, Berlin.

Stock, J. (1994). "Unit roots, structural breaks, and trends". Chapter 46. In: Engle, R., McFadden, D. (Eds.), Handbook of Econometrics, vol. IV. Elsevier, Amsterdam, pp. 2740–2843.

Suarez-Villa, L. (1988). "Metropolitan evolution, sectoral economic change, and the city size distribution". Urban Studies 25, 1–20.

Tabuchi, T. (1986). "Existence and stability of city-size distribution in the gravity and logit models". Environment and Planning A 18, 1375–1389.

Van der Woude, A., de Vries, J., Hayami, A. (1990). "The hierarchies, provisioning, and demographic patterns of cities". In: Urbanization in History: A Process of Dynamic Interactions. Oxford University Press, Oxford, pp. 1–19.

Wheaton, W., Shishido, H. (1981). "Urban concentration, agglomeration economies and the level of economic development". Economic Development and Cultural Change 30, 17–30.

Zanette, D.H., Manrubia, S.C. (1997). "Role of intermittency in urban development: A model of large-scale city formation". Physical Review Letters 79, 523–526.

Zipf, G.K. (1949). Human Behavior and the Principle of Least Effort. Addison–Wesley, Cambridge, MA.

PART 2

THE DESIGN OF LOCAL GOVERNMENTS AND POLICIES

Chapter 54

URBAN POLITICAL ECONOMICS

ROBERT W. HELSLEY

University of British Columbia, Vancouver, Canada

Contents

Handbook of Regional and Urban Economics, Volume 4. Edited by J.V. Henderson and J.F. Thisse

DOI: 10.1016/S0169-7218(04)07054-6

Abstract

This chapter considers the role of economic and political institutions in the formation of local public policies. The chapter has three objectives. First, to synthesize the dominant models of local policy formation with mobile households, with particular emphasis on the objectives that are attributed to the institutions that provide collective goods. Second, to describe and model local political institutions, and consider their implications for taxes, expenditures and voting behavior. Third, to examine how institutional change, specifically the entry of new institutions in the form of private government, influences policy outcomes and the welfare of residents.

Keywords

multi-community democracy, stratification, property value maximization, developers, local political institutions, legislative decision making, the common pool problem, citizen candidates, private government, supplementary provision, supplementary regulation, potential competition, gated communities

JEL classification: D72, D78, H11, H72, H73, H77, L33, R5

1. Introduction

The "new" political economics uses the tools of modern economic analysis and game theory to study how economics and politics interact to determine public policies. In contrast to public economics, with its emphasis on the positive and normative effects of tax and spending policies, and public choice, with its emphasis on collective choice rules, political economy emphasizes the process of policy formation. Political economics is fundamentally concerned with how optimal policies are modified by political and institutional constraints. Much of modern political economics has been developed in macroeconomics, where, for example, questions about differences in public sector performance across countries are a natural concern. In this context, the political economics approach is to ask whether there are institutional differences between governments that lead to systematic variations in spending, or whether there are systematic failures in legislative decision making processes that lead to excessive levels of spending or public debt. In political economics, the emphasis is on how government policies are determined.

For better or worse, urban political economics does not exist as a well-defined field of study. This is not to say that economics and politics do not combine to determine local public policies. Surely they do. However, political economics is a very new field, and the perspectives and models of political economics have not been widely applied to urban policy issues. What follows is a selective review of a particular set of topics where local politics and urban economics intersect. Specifically, this chapter considers the role of economic and political institutions in the formation of local public policies. The chapter has three objectives. First, to synthesize the dominant models of local policy formation with mobile households, with particular emphasis on the objectives that are attributed to the institutions that provide collective goods. Second, to describe and model local political institutions, and consider their implications for taxes, expenditures and voting behavior. Third, to examine how institutional change, specifically the entry of new institutions in the form of private government, influences policy outcomes and the welfare of residents. If this chapter has a unifying theme, it is that local economic and political institutions are interesting and important.

Caplin and Nalebuff (1997) argue that institutions should be integrated more fully into economic theory. They classify economic models of institutions into three groups:

(1) models that focus on how the economic environment influences institutions,
(2) models that focus on the implications of a given institutional structure for economic outcomes, and
(3) integrated models that allow for "the influence of institutions on economic outcomes and for the influence of the environment of the institutions." (p. 307)

The models that are considered in this review fit this classification quite naturally. The models of local policy formation reviewed in Section 2 focus on how the economic environment influences the formation of communities. The models of local political institutions in Section 3 take membership as fixed, and examine the consequences of different institutions for outcomes. The models of private government in Section 4 are integrative. They consider how the institutional environment influences policy outcomes, and how the economic environment influences the formation or entry of new institutions.

2. Objectives and local policy formation

There are three basic approaches to modeling the formation of public policy at the local level. Each approach considers a system of local governments providing collective goods to mobile residents who choose between jurisdictions to maximize utility. The approaches differ fundamentally in their treatment of the problem of collective choice and in the objectives that are attributed to the institutions that provide collective goods. The first approach, pioneered by Westhoff (1977, 1979) and Rose-Ackerman (1979), assumes that community tax and spending policies are made through open agenda majority voting. The second approach, initiated by Wildasin (1979) and Brueckner (1979), supposes that local policies are chosen to maximize aggregate property values in a community. The third approach, initiated by Henderson (1974) and Stiglitz (1977), assumes that local policy is formed by profit maximizing entrepreneurial governments or developers.

2.1. *Politics*

One of the interesting consequences of the dominance of the Tiebout (1956) tradition in local public finance is that models of local government have historically paid little attention to politics or political institutions. As noted by Rose-Ackerman (1983a, 1983b) and others, Tiebout's original model can be seen as an explicit attempt to eliminate the need for politics at the local level. A metropolitan area in Tiebout's world is composed of an arbitrarily large number of competitive local governments, each offering a different bundle of taxes and public expenditures. Since each voter's ideal policy is offered by one of these local governments, an individual can always secure her most preferred policy outcome by moving. Mobility is thus a substitute for politics in the informal Tiebout tradition.

However, attempts to formalize Tiebout's insights inevitably forced authors to confront the collective choice problem, and led to the development of equilibrium models of local government in which politics play an important role. Here we briefly review the key elements of such a model, focusing on the characteristics of the political equilibrium within a community.[1]

Following Epple, Filimon and Romer (1984), consider a metropolitan area composed of a fixed number of communities with fixed geographic boundaries. Each community

[1] See Ross and Yinger (1999) for an extensive review of the literature on models of "sorting and voting", with particular emphasis on the determinants and consequences of the capitalization of fiscal variables into housing prices.

provides a congestible local public good to its residents. There are no spillovers between communities. Public good provision in each community is financed by a local tax on housing services that balances the community government's budget. The public good and tax package, or policy vector, in each community is chosen by majority rule.

Preferences are represented by the increasing and strictly quasi-concave utility function $U(g, h, x)$, where g is the level of the local public good in the consumer's community, h is housing services, and x is a composite numeraire commodity. Residents differ in income y, which is continuously distributed on a closed support.[2] Letting p^{h} represent the before-tax price of housing and t represent the local property tax rate, the budget constraint of a resident with income y is $x + ph \leqslant y$, where $p = (1+t)p^{\mathrm{h}}$ is the after-tax price. Residents are perfectly mobile, and move between communities in response to perceived differences in utility levels, which in turn reflect differences in public goods, taxes, and housing prices.

The indirect utility function of a consumer with income y is

$$V(p, y, g) \equiv \max_{h} U(g, h, y - ph) = U\big(g, h(p, y, g), y - ph(p, y, g)\big), \tag{2.1}$$

where $h(p, y, g)$ is the Marshallian demand function for housing. The assumptions made about the form of the direct utility function imply that the level sets of $V(p, y, g)$ in (g, p) space slope upward and are strictly concave. Further, the slope of such an indifference curve, $\mathrm{d}p/\mathrm{d}g = -(\partial V/\partial g)/(\partial V/\partial p)$, is assumed to be strictly increasing in income. This is an instance of the Spence–Mirrlees "single-crossing property" [Gans and Smart (1996), Edlin and Shannon (1998)]. The single-crossing property serves two important functions in this setting. First, it ensures that consumers are sorted by income in equilibrium. In particular, it ensures that each community is occupied by consumers with incomes in a connected interval, and that higher income consumers reside in communities that provide higher levels of the public good. Second, as discussed below, it ensures that there is a policy vector for each community that a majority of community residents prefers to any other.

The budget constraint of a community government is $tp^{\mathrm{h}}H - c(g, N) = 0$, where H is aggregate housing consumption in the community, N is community population, and $c(g, N)$ is the increasing and convex cost of public good provision.[3] Solving the government budget for $p = p^{\mathrm{h}} + c(g, N)/H$ (thus eliminating the tax rate), and substituting this into the indirect utility function yields a consumer's "policy preference" function

2 More recent work in this literature assumes that individuals are differentiated by income and a taste parameter. See, for example, Epple and Platt (1998), Epple and Romano (1998) and Epple, Romer and Sieg (2001).

3 If the distribution of income is $F(y)$, and this community contains all consumers with incomes in the interval $[y^-, y^+]$, then $N = F(y^+) - F(y^-)$, and, in equilibrium, housing consumption is

$$H = \int_{y^-}^{y^+} h(p, y, g)\, \mathrm{d}F(y).$$

$W(g, y) \equiv V(p^{\mathrm{h}} + c(g, N)/H, y, g)$. As noted by Persson and Tabellini (2000, p. 20), the salient assumption about individual behavior in political economics is that the consumer, as a political agent, engages in "voting, lobbying or some other form of political activity" to maximize her policy preferences. The most preferred policy or "bliss point" of a resident with income y is

$$g(y) = \arg\max_{g} W(g, y) = \arg\max_{g} V\left(p^{\mathrm{h}} + \frac{c(g, N)}{H}, y, g\right), \tag{2.2}$$

where $g'(y) > 0$ by the single-crossing condition.

The characteristics of a consumer's most preferred policy, and the political actions that follow from the pursuit of that outcome, depend in part on how the consumer expects the endogenous variables N, H and p^{h} to respond to changes in the community's tax and expenditure policy. Two different assumptions about voter expectations have been made in this literature. Prior to Epple and Romer (1991), most authors assumed voter myopia. Myopic voters treat N, H and p^{h} as fixed. In this case, the locus that describes the set of feasible (g, p) pairs from the voter's perspective (the "government services frontier", $p = p^{\mathrm{h}} + c(g, N)/H$) is increasing and convex, and the consumer's most preferred policy lies at the tangency of this locus and the highest indifference curve that the voter can reach, as shown in Figure 1. Further, the policy preferences of each consumer are "single-peaked" [Black (1948)] under these conditions: a consumer's ordering of policy alternatives is determined by their relative distances from her bliss point $g(y)$. More formally, if policy preferences are single-peaked, then for any alternative policies g'' and g', $g'' \geqslant g' \geqslant g(y)$ or $g'' \leqslant g' \leqslant g(y)$ implies $W(g'', y) \leqslant W(g', y)$.

In subsequent work, some authors have endowed voters with a limited amount of foresight regarding the impacts of policy choices on community populations and housing market outcomes. More specifically, Epple and Romer (1991) and Epple and Platt (1998) assume that voters take only the policy vectors of other communities as fixed when making political choices. This implies that each voter takes the level of utility

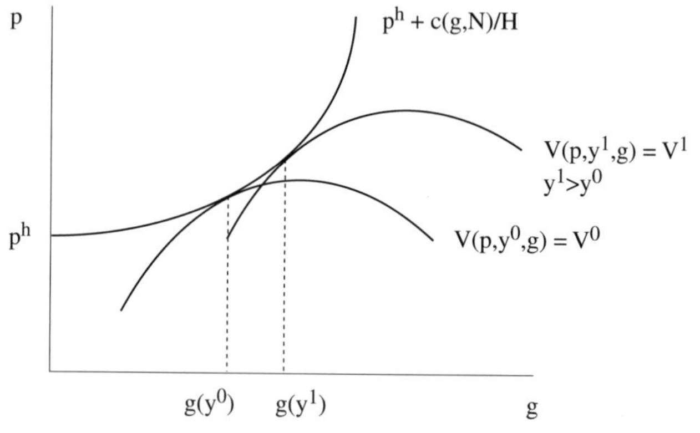

Figure 1. Preferred policies under myopia.

available in other communities as fixed, but is cognizant of how policy changes in their home community will influence population and housing market outcomes through intra-metropolitan migration. Epple, Romer and Sieg (2001) find that local policy choices in a sample of Boston communities are more consistent with this utility taking assumption than the with simpler assumption of voter myopia.

An equilibrium in this model requires that every consumer maximize utility, over goods and communities, that community budgets balance, and that community housing markets clear.[4,5] In addition, and most important for our purposes, the policy vector in each community must be a political equilibrium. In this literature, the political process is an idealized form of majority voting, sometimes called open agenda or institutionless majority rule, in which each element of the government services frontier is put against every other element in a sequence of pairwise elections until a Condorcet winner emerges. The essence of the celebrated median voter theorem [Black (1948)] is that with single-peaked policy preferences, such an equilibrium policy exists and corresponds to the median of the most preferred policies of the voters in a community.[6] Since the most preferred policy function $g(y)$ is monotonic, the median of the most preferred policies in turn corresponds to the most preferred policy of the consumer with the median income, that is, to the bliss point of the median voter.[7]

The resulting equilibrium has three properties. The first is "stratification": each community is composed of individuals with incomes in a single, connected interval.[8] The second property is "boundary indifference": the border consumer between two adjacent communities must be indifferent between them. The final property is "ascending bundles": public good levels (and housing prices) increase with the highest income in a community.

Stratification, or the sorting of consumers into imperfectly homogeneous communities, plays a role in many important policy issues. Epple and Romer (1991) show, in

4 The tradition is to close the model by assuming an exogenous housing supply function for each community. See Epple, Filimon and Romer (1984) for this convention, and Henderson (1985) for an alternative.

5 The existence of an equilibrium in the model outlined in this section has been demonstrated by Epple, Filimon and Romer (1993). However, the existence of equilibria in models of multicommunity democracy is, in general, problematic. See Caplin and Nalebuff (1997) for a general discussion. Hansen and Kessler (2001) present conditions under which an equilibrium fails to exist the original Westhoff (1977, 1979) model. The Westhoff model differs from the model described above in two ways: housing is not considered, and local public goods are financed through a proportional income tax. Nechyba (1997) provides an existence proof for a related model in which housing consumption is exogenous.

6 See Gans and Smart (1996) for a general examination of the implications of single-crossing conditions for the existence and stability of majority voting equilibria.

7 If the distribution of income is $F(y)$, and this particular community contains all consumers with incomes in the interval $[y^-, y^+]$, then the equilibrium policy of the community is $g(y^{\mathrm{M}})$, where the median income y^{M} satisfies $F(y^+) - F(y^{\mathrm{M}}) = N/2$. Median voter models of local politics have a very long history. See, for example, Bowen (1943) and Bergstrom and Goodman (1973).

8 In models with two-dimensional heterogeneity [e.g., Epple and Platt (1998)], stratification is imperfect in the sense that two residents with identical incomes (but different taste parameters) may reside in different communities in equilibrium.

contrast to the traditional view, that local redistribution may occur in equilibrium in a system of stratified communities.[9] In the case of education, stratification and local property tax finance lead to differences in educational spending and presumably outcomes across communities. Fernandez and Rogerson (1996, 1997, 1998, 1999) examine the implications of stratification for local spending on education and education finance reform, while de Bartolome (1990) considers the implications of stratification for the production of educational peer group effects. Epple and Romano (1998) use a multi-community model to study the implications of stratification for competition between public and private schools. The broader implications of stratification for knowledge spillovers, economic growth and the distribution of income are considered by Benabou (1993, 1996), Durlauf (1994, 1996a, 1996b) and Fernandez and Rogerson (2001).

There are at least three potential sources of inefficiency in this context. First, there is in general no reason to expect the preferred policy of the median voter to coincide with the policy that maximizes welfare in the community. For example, if we take utilitarianism as our normative benchmark, the optimal policy will maximize the policy preferences of the resident with the mean rather than the median income [see, for example, Persson and Tabellini (2000, Section 3.1)]. Second, the method of finance may distort consumption and production decisions. This is certainly the case with property tax finance and housing, as discussed in this context by Yinger (1982) and others. Finally, the location choices of consumers may be inefficient due to externalities associated with migration, as in de Bartolome (1990). This issue arises, in general, whenever consumers choose between a finite number of jurisdictions, and changes in the population of one community cause changes in the utility levels in others [Scotchmer (1986)].

2.2. *Property values*

Models of multicommunity democracy assume that collective choices are made through direct majority voting. Of course, there are many other political institutions that might aggregate the policy preferences of individuals in a city, including a representative institution like a city council. We will consider the role of representative local political institutions in Section 3. This subsection considers another popular, if somewhat ad hoc, rule for aggregating preferences. This is the assumption that policies are chosen to maximize property values in a community.

Following Edelson (1976), Wildasin (1979), and especially Brueckner (1979, 1982, 1983), consider a large system of small communities in which each community has an exogenous stock of houses.[10] Index the houses in a particular community by $i =$

[9] The traditional view is that local redistribution with mobile households is infeasible since generous redistributive policies will repel high-income households, and thus undermine the tax base. See Wildasin (1991) for a review of the literature on local redistribution, and an analysis of equilibrium and optimum redistribution policies in a federal system.

[10] Brueckner (1983) introduces housing production into the framework outlined here and shows that the welfare implications of property value maximization then depend on the method of finance. In particular, a head tax per house is required in order for property value maximization to lead to a first-best allocation.

$1, 2, \ldots, N$. Residents derive utility from a public good g, housing h_i and a composite numeraire commodity x according to the utility function $U(g, h_i, x)$. Public good provision is financed by a uniform tax on house value that balances the community's budget. Although residents have identical preferences, they may differ in income y. Each community is "open" in the sense that the utility level that it must offer an individual with a particular income is exogenously determined. Heuristically, this can be justified by assuming that the number of communities is arbitrarily large, and that moving between communities is costless. Denote the equilibrium utility level that a community must offer a resident with income y by $U^*(y)$.

The maximum amount that a resident with income y is willing to pay for the services offered by house i, the bid rent for house i, denoted $R_i(g, h_i, y)$, is implicitly defined by

$$U(g, h_i, y - R_i) = U^*(y). \tag{2.3}$$

Then the implicit function theorem implies

$$\frac{\partial R_i}{\partial g} = \frac{\partial U_i/\partial g}{\partial U_i/\partial x}. \tag{2.4}$$

In this open community model, the slope of the bid rent function with respect to the level of the public good is equal to the consumer's marginal rate of substitution between the public good and the numeraire. This means that the benefits of public spending are perfectly capitalized into house rents. This result plays an important role in the analysis.

The value of house i is defined as the present value of the stream of net rents that the house provides. Assuming that the house earns rent R_i in perpetuity, house value V_i is given by the asset equilibrium condition

$$V_i = \frac{1}{\theta}\big(R_i(g, h_i, y) - \tau V_i\big), \tag{2.5}$$

where τ is the property tax rate, τV_i is the property tax liability per period, and θ is the constant discount rate. Community budget balance requires $\tau \sum_i V_i = C(g, N)$, where $C(g, N)$ is the provision cost function. Then (2.5) implies that aggregate property value in the community is

$$\sum_i V_i = \frac{1}{\theta}\left(\sum_i R_i(g, h_i, y) - C(g, N)\right). \tag{2.6}$$

The critical assumption in this branch of the literature is that the community chooses the level of the public good to maximize (2.6). Of course, since resident utilities are fixed by assumption, there is nothing else to maximize in this setting. Interestingly, since all houses are owned by absentee landlords, at least in this basic version of the model, this objective implies that local policies are chosen to maximize the wealth of a group of non-residents. Using (2.4), the first-order condition for a maximum of $\sum_i V_i$

with respect to g implies

$$\sum_i \frac{\partial U_i/\partial g}{\partial U_i/\partial x} - \frac{\partial C}{\partial g} = 0. \tag{2.7}$$

Thus, the level of the public good that maximizes aggregate property value satisfies the Samuelson condition for efficient provision. In this system of open communities, aggregate property value maximization and welfare maximization are synonymous.[11] This result has been the basis of a number of tests for allocative efficiency in the local public sector.[12]

Several authors have argued that property value maximization may be the reduced form outcome of some unspecified political process. Wildasin and Wilson (1996) note that

> "in communities where significant numbers of households are owners of their own property, voting behavior may be motivated by land-value maximization considerations; to the extent that this is so, there is no real difference between a voting model and a model based on land-value maximization. Even if voters are not landowners, it is not implausible to assume that the interest of landowners is reflected in the local political process, if that process can respond to pressures brought to bear by mechanisms other than voting." (p. 179)

Many local policies seem at least consistent with the objective of property value maximization. For example, local growth controls seem to be popular with voters in part because they increase the property values of current residents.[13]

Others have tried to articulate the individual incentives and political institutions that might support property value maximization as political equilibrium, or to provide what Persson, Roland and Tabellini (1998) call "micro-political" foundations for this objective. Sonstelie and Portney (1980) argue that with perfect mobility and no limit on the number of communities, it is optimal for a resident property owner to separate consumption and investment decisions by voting for the policy vector that maximizes property value and then moving (if necessary) to the community that offers the highest level of utility.

Brueckner and Joo (1991) develop a dynamic model with imperfect mobility that examines how capitalization influences the policy preferences of current residents in a community. In particular, they show that expectations about future housing prices cause voters to consider the preferences of future residents when choosing the level of

[11] Welfare maximization can serve as an institutional objective in its own right. For example, it is reasonable to suppose that exclusive institutions like private governments [Helsley and Strange (1998)] or political parties [Caplin and Nalebuff (1997)] choose policies to maximize the welfare of their members.

[12] See Brueckner (1979, 1982) and, more recently, Deller (1990), Taylor (1995), and Hughes and Edwards (2000).

[13] See Brueckner (1995) and Helsley and Strange (1995) for complementary models of the impacts of growth controls on housing prices, and Katz and Rosen (1987) for evidence.

a durable public good. The key result is that the level of public spending that maximizes the utility of a current resident is determined by a weighted average of the net marginal benefit to the resident and the net marginal benefit to a prospective buyer of the resident's house. This implies that "the preferences of an individual who does not yet reside in the community are reflected in the voter's ideal g and thus in the choice he makes in the voting booth." (p. 457) This also implies that property value maximization only leads to the first-best outcome if the marginal valuation of the owner and the prospective buyer are equal. If current owners and future owners have difference preferences, then utility maximization and property value maximization are not equivalent. In related work, Wildasin and Wilson (1996) show that imperfect mobility can sever the tie between property value maximization and welfare maximization by giving communities an incentive to overtax less mobile workers. Sprunger and Wilson (1998) present a model with resident property owners in which imperfect mobility and uncertainty about the productivity and objectives of local governments cause the benefits of durable local public goods to be imperfectly capitalized into property values. They show that this can lead to either over- or under-provision.[14]

2.3. *Profits*

Entrepreneurial incentives play several interesting roles in the process of local policy formation. First, at a normative level, Stiglitz (1977) and Bewley (1981) argue that efficiency in a system of local governments may require the active participation of "entrepreneurial" governments or land developers. Bewley (1981) shows, through a series of examples, that mobile but myopic voters, who by assumption do not consider how their migration choices impact economic conditions elsewhere in the economy, may have no incentive to leave inefficient communities. Under these conditions, efficiency may require that governments take actions to attract or repel residents. Bewley considers several objectives that such entrepreneurial governments might pursue, including maximizing population, maximizing land values, and maximizing the government budget surplus. Following Henderson (1974), Stiglitz (1977, p. 295) notes that land developers are natural candidates to perform this active role: "The 'developer' plays a central role in this formulation [achieving efficient equilibria]. Essentially, the private developer can do anything that a centralized government can do, and, hence, if there are 'inefficiencies' he can eliminate them."

Second, at a positive level, the provision of infrastructure, public services and amenities by land or housing developers is an important part of the process of community

[14] Epple and Romer (1991) also consider the implications of capitalization for voting behavior in their model of multicommunity democracy and redistribution. In particular, they show that if non-myopic voters are homeowners rather than renters, then housing demand will depend on the possibility of capital gains associated with changes in local policy. This will change the slope of a voter's indifference curves in (g, p) space (generally causing them to become flatter), which implies that "an owner with a given endowed income will prefer a lower level of redistributive taxation than a renter with the same income." (p. 844)

formation. This is especially true in the case of so-called "private governments", as discussed in Section 4. Consequently, and following Henderson (1980), many models of community formation are based on the private provision and finance of a public good by a profit maximizing developer.[15] In these models, the policy preferences of residents are expressed through the land market, and the developer translates these expressions into a collective choice via profit maximization. As discussed below, the analysis tends to focus on how competition between developers, or more generally market structure, impacts the efficiency of the resulting equilibrium.[16] Third, and closely related, models of "profit maximizing government" [Sonstelie and Portney (1978), Epple and Zelenitz (1981)] assume that local policies are chosen by a city manager or bureaucrat to maximize the excess of tax revenue over the costs of public good provision.

To develop the basic ideas, following Helsley and Strange (1994), consider a system of monocentric community sites, where each site is owned by separate developer. The number of active developers, or the number of occupied sites, is denoted by M. For simplicity, suppose that each site is a long, narrow strip of land of width φ, and that land in each community is differentiated only by its distance from employment, concentrated at the eastern edge of the strip.[17] Assume that the opportunity cost of urban land is zero.

There are $\overline{N}$ residents in the region, and the population of a community is denoted by N. Residents are identical and perfectly mobile, and move between communities to maximize utility. There are three goods in the model: a local public good g, land consumption l, and a numeraire x. Assuming that land consumption is exogenously fixed at one unit, and that the utility function is quasi-linear, the utility of a resident may be written as $U(g) + x$, where $U(\cdot)$ is increasing and strictly concave, and land consumption has been suppressed. The budget constraint of a resident living at distance z from the employment center is $x + r(z) + tz \leqslant y$, where $r(z)$ is land rent, t is commuting cost, and y is income, which consists of exogenous labor income w and an equal share of the profits of all developers.

If U^* is the equilibrium utility level in the system, then the bid rent function for land in the community is $r(z) = y + U(g) - tz - U^*$. The market clearing condition for land implies that the boundary of a community z^* satisfies $z^* = N/\varphi$. Then the boundary

[15] There are a number of formal similarities between models of local policy formation based on profit maximization and models based on property value maximization. For example, if one interprets the absentee landowners in the basic Brueckner (1979) model of property value maximization as a single land developer, then the developer's profit is proportional to aggregate land value in (2.6).

[16] Many of the results in this literature originated in the literature on profit maximizing clubs [Scotchmer (1985a, 1985b)]. Club models typically admit more general pricing policies. For example, a club might charge both a membership fee and a per use price for the club's common facilities. Henderson and Thisse (1999, 2001), in a series of papers on the nature of small numbers competition in multi-community models, bridge the gap between developer and club models by considering optimal non-linear pricing strategies for a land developer.

[17] This specification of the geography is not essential, but does simplify the strategic interactions in the model. Somewhat surprisingly, the "shape" of a community matters in this context because it influences the curvature of a developer's best response function. See Helsley and Strange (1994) for details.

rent condition $r(z^*) = 0$ implies $r(z) = t(z^* - z) = t((N/\varphi) - z)$. Using the budget to substitute for x in the utility function and in turn substituting for $r(z)$ implies that the utility of a resident can be written as

$$V(g, N) = y + U(g) - tN/\varphi. \tag{2.8}$$

The profit of a developer equals aggregate differential land rent less the costs of public good provision,

$$\pi(g, N) = \frac{t}{2}\frac{N^2}{\varphi} - C(g), \tag{2.9}$$

where the cost function $C(g)$ is increasing and convex. Incorporating the income from land development into (2.8) yields

$$V(g, N) = w + U(g) - \frac{C(g)}{N} - \frac{tN}{2\varphi}, \tag{2.10}$$

where each resident is assumed to receive an equal share of the profits of all developers.

The efficient allocation maximizes (2.10) with respect to g and N. The first-order conditions for this problem imply $NU'(g) = C'(g)$, the Samuelson condition for efficient provision of the public good, and $\pi(g, N) = 0$. The latter condition, which implies that aggregate land rent equals the cost of public good provision, is an instance of the Henry George theorem [Stiglitz (1977), Arnott (1979)]. Whether such an efficient allocation exists depends in part on whether the aggregate population is an integer multiple of the efficient city size. If it is not, then there is a remainder of consumers who cannot be accommodated in a community of efficient size, and a first-best allocation does not exist.

The equilibrium is a Nash equilibrium in public good levels, where each developer chooses g to maximize his profit, subject to the equilibrium location decisions of residents, and taking the choices of other developers as fixed. In what follows, we focus on the symmetric equilibrium. Letting g_i represent the public good level chosen by developer i, and g_0 represent the conjectured public good level chosen by the other $(M - 1)$ developers, the migration or equal utility condition is $V(g_i, N_i) = V(g_0, (\overline{N} - N_i)/(M - 1))$. This implicitly defines the population of community i as a function of g_i and g_0:

$$N_i(g_i, g_0) = \frac{\overline{N}}{M} + \frac{\varphi}{t}\frac{M-1}{M}\big(U(g_i) - U(g_0)\big). \tag{2.11}$$

Thus, the population of community i is increasing in g_i, and decreasing in the level of the public good provided by developer i's rivals.

Developer i's problem is to choose g_i to maximize $\pi(g_i, N_i(g_i, g_0))$. The first-order condition for this problem implies

$$\frac{M-1}{M}N_i U'(g_i) - C'(g_i) = 0. \tag{2.12}$$

Thus, with a finite number of active developers, each provides too little of the local public good, relative to the first-best allocation. Underprovision arises from the strategic interactions between the communities, and in particular, from the pecuniary externality identified by Scotchmer (1985a, 1986). An increase in g_i attracts residents from other communities, causing the utility level in these other communities to rise. However, this contribution to welfare is ignored by an individual developer. The symmetric equilibrium population of each community equals $\overline{N}/M$ from (2.11).

As the population of the region and the number of active developers increases, maintaining the symmetric equilibrium size of each community at $\overline{N}/M$, (2.12) implies that the level of public good provision in each community rises. In the limit, where the population and the number of active developers are arbitrarily large, equilibrium public good provision satisfies the Samuelson rule, and is therefore efficient. Intuitively, in a very large economy, changes in the level of the public good provided by any one developer have infinitesimal impacts on utility in other communities, and the pecuniary externality disappears. This in turn implies that the population of each community approaches the first-best optimal population in the limit, and that the profit of every active developer approaches zero. Thus, under competitive conditions, the policies that arise from the actions of profit maximizing land developers are efficient.[18,19]

(2.12) and (2.11) implicitly define the reaction function of developer i, $g_i(g_0)$, where

$$\frac{\mathrm{d}g_i}{\mathrm{d}g_0} = -\frac{1}{\Delta}\frac{M-1}{M}U'(g_i)\frac{\partial N_i}{\partial g_0} < 0, \tag{2.13}$$

and $\Delta < 0$ by the second-order condition for the developer's profit maximization program. Thus, the public good levels chosen by developers are strategic substitutes. This means that if one developer chooses a higher level of the public good, it is maximizing for his rivals to choose a lower level. This implies that in a dynamic game where one developer has an opportunity to commit to a level of public good provision in advance of his rivals, the leader will choose to provide a higher level of g, and thereby capture a larger share of the regional population. Helsley and Strange (1994) show that under

[18] There are two ways to formulate the competitive hypothesis with profit maximizing developers. The first approach is utility taking, where the level of utility available in other jurisdictions is taken as fixed in the equilibrium program. In the model outlined in this subsection, developers take strategies rather than utilities as fixed. However, in the limit, that is under competitive conditions, strategy taking and utility taking are equivalent. The second approach, due to Scotchmer and Wooders (1986) and Berglas and Pines (1980) [see also Scotchmer (1994)], is price taking. In this case there is a schedule that relates the price of land (or the wage for workers) in a jurisdiction to its fiscal policies. This fixed price schedule is an analogue to a system of prices that consumers face in a competitive market for a private good. The price taking hypothesis implies that fiscal policies in one jurisdiction do not affect fiscal policies or land prices in other jurisdictions. This implies that utility in other jurisdictions is also unaffected. Thus, utility taking and price taking are equivalent in a competitive environment. Recent applications of the price taking methodology include Pines (1991) and Brueckner (2000).

[19] Scotchmer (1994) notes that developer models can fairly be criticized for being much too centralized. Helsley and Strange (1997) present a model in which there are endogenous organizational limits on the ability of developers to provide public goods.

some conditions the leader in this dynamic development game will overprovide the public good. Further, it may be in the leader's interest to choose a level of provision that deters entry by other developers, and thus prevents the formation of other communities.

The desirable welfare properties of equilibria in models with competitive land developers stand in contrast to the analysis of "profit maximizing governments" in Epple and Zelenitz (1981). Anticipating the literatures on Leviathan models of government and jurisdictional competition, they ask if competition between an arbitrarily large number of budget surplus maximizing, or rent seeking, jurisdictions can lead to an efficient allocation of resources in the local public sector.[20] In their model, each community chooses a property tax rate and a level of spending to maximize the difference between tax revenues and the costs of public goods. Residents, who consume a local public good, housing and a numeraire, are identical and perfectly mobile, but have no direct political voice in the determination of tax and spending policies.

Costless migration implies that each jurisdiction must provide the same level of utility in equilibrium. This in turn implies that housing prices must adjust to compensate for differences in tax and spending packages. For example, an increase in the tax rate in one jurisdiction causes housing prices there to fall, and causes housing prices in other jurisdictions to increase to restore equal utility. The magnitude of the changes depend on the demand and supply elasticities of housing and on the number of jurisdictions. As discussed above, as the number of jurisdictions increases, the impact of an increase in the tax rate in one jurisdiction on prices elsewhere diminishes; in the limit, as the number of jurisdictions approaches infinity, the effect is zero. This implies that, in the limit, housing prices in the home jurisdiction must change to completely offset the impact of a tax change there.

Maximizing the budget surplus subject to the housing market equilibrium discussed above, and letting the number of jurisdictions approach infinity, leads to two results. First, provision of the public good is second-best efficient (reflecting the distortionary effects of the property tax) and, second, tax revenues exceed public service costs. The latter result implies that there is a type of fiscal exploitation even when the number of jurisdictions is very large.

Henderson (1985) shows that the exploitation result does not hold if community boundaries are flexible, or more generally, if landowners and developers have an active role in the model. More specifically, he shows that with an active land market – so that the price of land is equalized across communities in equilibrium – the "bad politics" or positive profit outcome is not possible. Landowners will refuse assimilation by

[20] Brennan and Buchanan (1977, 1980) popularized the Leviathan or budget maximizing view of local government, and discussed the possibility that jurisdictional competition might have a disciplinary effect. Studies of the relationship between local decentralization and the size of government include Oates (1985), Nelson (1987), Eberts and Gronberg (1990) and Anderson and Van den Berg (1998). Most models of jurisdictional competition and rent seeking are based in the tax competition literature. See Wilson (1999) for a review, and Edwards and Keen (1996), Rauscher (1998), and Wrede (1998, 2001), Brueckner (2000) and Perroni and Scharf (2001) for recent theoretical developments.

communities that attempt to expropriate a portion of their land rents. Epple and Romer (1989) argue that as an empirical matter, the key is whether land is commonly removed from jurisdictions (through "detachments"), and they argue that it is not. They also note (as does Henderson) that with flexible boundaries we would not expect to observe capitalization of fiscal differentials within metropolitan areas.

2.4. *Complex politics*

Several authors have recently considered multi-community models with more complex specifications of the local political process. Hoyt (1999) presents a model of lobbying and public spending in a closed system of communities. The model has three components. The first is a model of the impacts of local tax and spending policies, in the spirit of Epple and Zelenitz (1981) and Henderson (1985), but with heterogeneous community sizes. Hoyt shows that the impact of a change in taxes or public spending on housing prices is smaller for a large jurisdiction.[21] The intuition is that the policies of a large jurisdiction have a discrete impact on the system-wide utility level in the metropolitan area, which weakens capitalization. So, for example, a large jurisdiction can essentially export some of a tax increase to smaller jurisdictions by reducing the system-wide utility level in the city. In contrast, for a small jurisdiction, the system-wide utility level is essentially fixed, and consequently a change in tax policy is fully capitalized into property values.

The second component is a reduced form model of political competition in which an incumbent maximizes the expected surplus from holding office, consisting of current and expected future rents. Expected future rents depend on the probability of reelection and through this on the effort (political monitoring) that voters undertake to remove the incumbent from office. The probability of remaining in office, and hence the probability of earning future rents, is assumed to be increasing in the level of the public good and decreasing in the property tax rate and monitoring effort. The third component involves residents, who are assumed to choose the level of political monitoring to maximize land value net of effort cost.

The key result is that the optimal level of political monitoring decreases with community size. Hoyt summarizes the result as follows: "In larger cities, residents have less incentive to put effort into the political process because the cost of 'bad' local politics is not as costly as it is in small cities. This is because of the incomplete capitalization of government policies into property values." (p. 167) A larger level of political monitoring in a small community will result in lower tax rates and higher public service levels. In this way, the greater incentive for monitoring in a small city improves the operation of the political system there. Of course, in the limit, if all communities become small, then the system will become open, and the differential impacts of monitoring on housing prices will disappear.

[21] Brasington (2001) provides empirical support for this result. He shows, based on a sample of housing sales in Ohio in 1991, that differences in school quality and crime rates are capitalized into housing prices, but that these effects are smaller in jurisdictions that contain a larger share of the metropolitan area population.

Caplan (2001) is also concerned with imperfect politics in a multicommunity environment. The innovation in this paper is the introduction of a model of imperfect electoral competition into a model of an urban area with many communities and a mobile population. In models of electoral competition with exogenous rents from holding office, the political equilibrium typically involves both parties adopting the preferred policy of the median voter [Downs (1957)]. However, if candidates represent different "ideologies", or have some other exogenous characteristic that is important to voters, and voters have heterogeneous ideological preferences, then the median voter may no longer be decisive. Candidates have an incentive to adopt policies that will appeal to voters with ideological preferences that more closely match their characteristics. Further, in a model in which politicians with ideologies derive utility from endogenous rents, and voters have heterogeneous ideological preferences, electoral competition may not eliminate rents in equilibrium [Persson and Tabellini (2000, Sections 3.4 and 4.3)].

Caplan considers a model with many localities, each containing two parties or candidates who care both about the level of rents they receive and about the public good level that is chosen. Parties are elected by simple majority vote. Each locality has a fixed supply of housing, and consequently capitalization is perfect. Households have heterogeneous demands for the public good and ideological preferences in the sense that their utility is higher if their preferred party is in power, ceteris paribus.

The political equilibrium features the preferred party choosing a level of rents that exactly offsets the ideological preferences of the median voter. That is, the preferred party sets the level of rents so that the median voter is just indifferent between the preferred party and the alternative. Since the consequences of imperfections in the electoral system (a positive level of rents in equilibrium) are fully capitalized into property values, it is impossible for landowners to avoid the costs of rent seeking by moving. This implies that mobility cannot discipline rent seeking in this model. Of course, Henderson's (1985) critique of fiscal exploitation in multi-community models with fixed boundaries applies here as well. This form of "bad politics" would presumably also be tempered by the actions of active landowners and developers.

3. Local political institutions

Economic models of local government generally suppress the role of political institutions. As noted in Section 2, the local political process is usually treated as an idealized form of majority rule in which residents choose policies directly through open agenda elections, and the political equilibrium within a community corresponds to the most preferred policy of the median voter. This institutionless view of local government is the basis of the large empirical literature on the demand for local public goods [Borcherding and Deacon (1972), Bergstrom and Goodman (1973), Rubinfeld (1987)], and is generally supported studies of local expenditures [Inman (1978), Turnbull and Djoundourian (1994)].

However, most local policy choices are not made directly by residents.[22,23] The vast majority of cities are governed by a local executive (a mayor or city manager) and a local legislature, the city council. This section examines how these institutions affect policy outcomes. We describe the political institutions that are most common in North American cities, examine political economy models of the operation of these and similar institutions, and review recent evidence about the importance of institutional differences and details. Since there are relatively few formal economic models of urban institutions, we will proceed in part by drawing analogies between local institutions and institutions at higher levels of government.

3.1. *The institutions and their consequences*

According to the International City/Council Management Association (ICMA), 43.7% of U.S. municipalities with populations over 2500 were governed by the combination of a mayor and a city council in 2000, while 48.3% were governed by the combination of a city council and a city manager.[24] Thus, 90% of U.S. municipalities were governed at least in part by a city council in 2000. Council members may be elected "at-large", that is, from the entire city, or by wards or districts within the city. Some cities adopt a mixed system, in which the council contains both at-large and ward representatives. Welch (1990) notes that 63% of U.S. city councils were composed of representatives elected entirely at-large in the early 1970s and that 15% of councils had both at-large and ward

[22] In the U.S., local budget referenda are probably the most important exception. However, Romer and Rosenthal (1979) show that a budget maximizing bureaucrat who has the ability to specify a "reversion" level of spending in a budget referendum, the level to which spending reverts if the proposal is defeated, will choose a reversion level that causes voters to approve spending in excess of the most preferred level of the median voter [see Rosenthal (1990) for a review]. Romer and Rosenthal (1982) find limited support for this "agenda setter" model in school district referenda in Oregon. More recently, Romer, Rosenthal and Munley (1992) find that school spending in New York State is sensitive to the requirement that all non-city school districts hold one budget referendum each year. Banks (1993) presents a signaling model in which both the preferred and revision policies are private information, and discusses earlier, related models with one-sided private information. Rothstein (1994) finds support for such a modified agenda setter model in expenditure and voting patterns in a sample of Michigan communities.

[23] Some smaller communities, primarily in New England, are governed by a particular type of direct democracy called an "open town meeting". In these communities, every eligible voter is able to "attend, speak and vote on all local municipal issues" [Fahey (1998, p. 431)]. The open town meeting form of local government presumably involves higher decision costs (including the costs of gathering information, debating issues, and voting), and lower agency and monitoring costs than representative forms [Buchanan and Tullock (1962), Sass (1991, 1992)]. In addition, open town meetings are apparently subject to relatively easy capture by local interest groups, particularly those representing public employees [Santerre (1993), Mehay and Gonzalez (1994)]. However, Deller and Chicoine (1993) present results from a property value maximization test of allocative efficiency for a sample of Maine communities, and find no evidence of differences in efficiency between direct and representative local government forms. Fahey (1998) shows, not surprisingly, that larger and more rapidly growing communities are less likely to retain the open town meeting form.

[24] Under the council–manager form, the city manager makes some high-level personnel decisions, executes contracts on behalf of the city, prepares the city budget for council approval, and enforces city laws.

representatives at that time. By 1988, the percentage of councils that relied solely on at-large elections declined to 47%, while the percentage with a mixed membership rose to 40%. According to Welch, the decline of at-large city councils was in part a response to the under-representation of minorities under this institution [see also Southwick (1997)].

The power of the executive office varies across U.S. cities. Mayors (or their offices) are traditionally classified as being either "strong" or "weak". Strong mayors have broad powers, including a veto over some city council decisions. Strong mayors also prepare the city's budget, and have hiring and firing authority over the heads of city departments. In weak mayor systems, most executive and legislative authority rests with the city council; the mayor performs largely ceremonial and organizational functions. Strong mayors are generally elected independently from members of the city council, and are more common in mayor–council systems. Baqir (2002), based on a sample of roughly 2000 U.S. municipalities in 1990, reports that 98% of mayors in mayor–council systems were independently elected, compared to 65% of mayors in council–manager systems.

Strong mayors are generally associated with fiscal discipline, and there is some support for this view in other branches in the political economics literature. For example, the literature on comparative politics suggests that presidential systems have greater accountability to voters and less collusion within and between the branches of government than parliamentary systems [Persson, Roland and Tabellini (1997, 1998, 2000)]. Persson, Roland and Tabellini (2000) show that presidential systems have lower levels of government spending as a share of national product. Inman and Fitts (1990) show that "strong" presidents (those with "independent political strength", identified from a survey of historians) were associated with lower levels of federal spending in the U.S. over the 1795–1988 period. Baqir (2002) suggests that a strong mayor may have a similar disciplinary effect on local government spending. Baqir finds support for this analogy in this study of the relationship between city council size and spending in U.S. cities. This issue is discussed in detail below.

Many studies of local political institutions in North America examine the impacts of the reform movement of the early 20th century. The reform movement brought a number of changes in local government structure that were allegedly designed to limit the exercise of private interest and patronage in city politics and promote the pursuit of public interests and professional management.[25] Some of the specific institutional changes that followed included the introduction of at-large and non-partisan elections for city council (a change that, as noted above, has since been partially reversed), the council–manager form of local government, civil service exams as a basis for appointment and promotion in the bureaucracy, and, in some areas, the replacement of the mayor–council form with a group of city "commissioners", each of whom had executive and legislative responsibility for a different city department.

[25] An alternative, and more sinister view, is that the large corporations that emerged in the Progressive Era used the reform movement as a means of directing resources toward public investments that encouraged economic growth, particularly growth in manufacturing employment. See Rauch (1995, p. 971) and the references given there.

Early studies of reform governments [e.g., Booms (1966)] expressed the hope that managerial expertise and autonomy in personnel matters could lead to lower costs for the delivery of local public services, and in particular, lower labor costs for municipal governments. However, subsequent empirical studies provide little support for this view. Morgan and Pelissero (1980) found that public expenditure levels and patterns in U.S. cities were largely unaffected by the adoption of city managers, at-large representation, and non-partisan elections. Deno and Mehay (1987) found no evidence of lower costs or wages in communities that adopted the council–manager form. Davis and Hayes (1993) found that the efficiency of police departments in Illinois was unaffected by the presence or absence of a professional city manager. Zax (1990) argued that the net effect of the movement toward at-large elections was to decrease the influence of neighborhood and partisan constituencies and increase the relative influence of municipal employees. His analysis suggests that municipal employment and compensation levels are higher in cities with non-partisan, at-large elections for city council members.

The most compelling study of the reform movement in the recent economics literature is Rauch (1995). Rauch's hypothesis is that by creating a population of career bureaucrats in city government, the reform movement put in place incentives that encouraged investment in infrastructure and other "long-gestation-period" projects. Rauch views the relationship between the city council and the bureaucracy as a principal–agent problem. Before reform, the agent, that is, the bureaucracy, is assumed to act as a political appointee who shares the council's immediate focus on retaining office. After reform, the bureaucracy is professionalized, and the agent is assumed to have some job security and therefore a longer time horizon. The agent may then use his "powers of information collection and expenditure oversight," in combination with costly or imperfect monitoring by the principal to direct resources toward longer-term projects that may further the agent's career. The implication is that this type of reform should increase the share of expenditures devoted to investment, as opposed to current public consumption. Using a panel of 144 cities over 23 years, Rauch regresses the infrastructure share of municipal expenditure on dummy variables for the use of civil service exams, the presence of a city manager, and the adoption of a commission form of local government. After accounting for the inertia generated by the durability of infrastructure investment, use of the civil service is found to have a positive impact on the share of expenditure devoted to infrastructure. Interestingly, in the cases where they are statistically significant, the presence of a city manager and the adoption of a commission form of government are both associated with lower levels of infrastructure spending.

3.2. The common pool problem in city councils

City councils are, in effect, local legislatures. One way to model the operation of a city council is by analogy with models of other legislative institutions. In that spirit, imagine a city council in which each councilor represents a well-defined local constituency. If councilors are elected by ward or district, then the constituencies will be geographic, as in most national, state and provincial legislatures. Councilors elected at-large may have non-geographic constituencies that are defined by a common ideology or policy initiative [Landbein, Crewson and Brasher (1996)]. Suppose that each councilor is motivated by holding office and that this gives her an incentive to pursue programs and policies that provide net benefits to her constituents.[26] It is generally assumed that the policies and programs that are chosen by legislatures are "distributive" in the sense that their costs are more widely distributed than their benefits [Lowi (1964), Weingast, Shepsle and Johnsen (1981)]. For example, benefits may be restricted to a particular district or group, while the supporting tax payments are made by residents of the entire city. Spending and tax choices are made by a majority vote of council members.

The literature on legislative decision making discusses a number of issues that relate to the efficiency of the policy choices that will emerge in this context. First, there is an incentive for "minimum winning coalitions" within the legislature to form for the purpose of approving distributive policies [Riker (1962)]. A minimum winning coalition is the smallest set of legislators that can guarantee passage of a proposal under majority voting. If proposals or projects have spillover costs and benefits, as distributive policies generally do, then the exclusion of the interests of delegates outside of a winning coalition will lead to inefficient choices. Second, minimum winning coalitions should be highly unstable, since excluded delegates have strong incentives to alter the coalition structure. Each member of the legislature faces some probability that he or she will be excluded from the minimum winning coalition for any particular policy proposal. Third, Weingast, Shepsle and Johnsen (1981), Shepsle and Weingast (1984), and others suggest that the resulting uncertainty helps explain the practice of "universalism", in which the size of coalitions and the set of approved projects exceed the minimum winning size. In its extreme form, universalism involves a "norm of reciprocity" in which each delegate supports the project of every other, and so a project for every delegate or constituency is approved.

More formally, following Persson and Tabellini (2000, Section 7.1), imagine that there are M seats on the city council and that the fixed population of each constituency is N. Thus, the aggregate population of the city is MN. If council members are elected by district or ward, so the constituencies are geographic, then the assumption of fixed constituencies implies that the population is immobile. Suppose that all residents are identical and, as in Section 2.3, have quasi-linear preferences of the form $U(g) + x$, where g is now per capita consumption of a publicly provided good, and x is the numeraire. All residents have the same exogenous income y. Public services are financed through lump sum taxes that balance the city's budget. Each councilor is assumed to be a perfect representative of his or her constituent group.

[26] Weingast, Shepsle and Johnsen (1981) argue that politicians have an incentive to count the resource costs of geographically earmarked programs as benefits. They refer to this as the "Robert Moses" effect: "pecuniary gains in the form of increased jobs, profits, and local tax revenues go to named individuals, firms and localities from whom the legislator may claim credit and exact tribute." (p. 648) Such "political cost-accounting" will obviously encourage individual representatives to support higher than efficient levels of public spending. For more about Robert Moses and his many effects, see Caro (1974).

Taking utilitarianism as a normative benchmark, efficient provision of public services in this symmetric setting maximizes aggregate utility $M(U(g)+x)$ subject to the resource constraint $MN(y-x-g)=0$. The first-order condition for this problem implies $U'(g)=1$: the marginal benefit of the public service should equal its marginal cost in every constituency. Represent this efficient level of provision by g^*.

In contrast, under extreme universalism, or with decentralized provision and centralized finance, each delegate chooses a level of the public service to maximize the utility of a constituent, taking the levels chosen by other delegates as fixed. Letting g^0 represent the conjectured level chosen by others, the balanced budget requirement implies that the lump sum tax τ for any group satisfies $\tau M = g + (M-1)g^0$. Thus, an individual delegate chooses g to maximize

$$y - \frac{g+(M-1)g^0}{M} + U(g). \tag{3.1}$$

The first-order condition for this problem implies $U'(g) = 1/M$. Each member of the legislature perceives that she pays only a fraction $1/M$ of the costs of the public services that she acquires for her constituents. This is known as the common pool problem. Letting g^{U} represent the level of provision under this extreme form of universalism, the concavity of $U(\cdot)$ implies $g^{\mathrm{U}} > g^*$. The common pool problem thus leads to overprovision. Persson and Tabellini (2000, p. 163) summarize the nature of the distortion as follows: "The problem here lies in the collective choice procedure, in which the tax rate is residually determined once all spending decisions have been made in a decentralized fashion. Concentration of benefits and dispersion of costs lead to excessive spending when such spending is residually financed out of a common pool of tax revenue."

The first-order condition for g^{U} implies

$$\frac{\mathrm{d}g^{\mathrm{U}}}{\mathrm{d}M} = -\frac{1}{MU''(g)} > 0 \tag{3.2}$$

by concavity. Thus, the level of overprovision increases as the constituencies become smaller, ceteris paribus. Finally, letting $G^{\mathrm{U}} = Mg^{\mathrm{U}}$ represent aggregate spending, we have

$$\frac{\mathrm{d}G^{\mathrm{U}}}{\mathrm{d}M} = g^{\mathrm{U}} + M\frac{\mathrm{d}g^{\mathrm{U}}}{\mathrm{d}M} > 0. \tag{3.3}$$

This is an instance of Weingast, Shepsle and Johnsen's (1981) "law of $1/n$": aggregate spending, and therefore the inefficiency of excessive spending, increases with the number of constituencies or the size of the legislature.

This implication of the common pool problem seems to be supported by the evidence. Landbein, Crewson and Brasher (1996), based on a sample of 192 cities in 1980, all of which have a council–manager form of government and a weak mayor, find that local government expenditure per capita is positively related to the number of elected members of the city council. Baqir (2002) finds that the size of U.S. local governments (measured by expenditures or employment per capita or expenditures as a share of total income) increases with the size of the city council. Baqir also finds that expenditures (per capita or as a share of total income) are not significantly different in councils where a majority of members are elected at-large, but that local government employment per capita is lower when at-large councilors are in the majority. However, evaluated at the sample means, employment per capita is actually higher where a majority of councilors are elected at large. This is consistent with the hypothesis that at-large councilors serve their (non-geographic) constituencies in much the same manner that ward councilors serve the interests of their wards. The positive relationship between the size of government and size of the council is unaffected by the presence of at-large elections. Baqir also examines the impact of a strong city executive, and finds that expenditures do not increase with council size when the city has a strong mayor with the power to veto city council decisions. As noted above, this is consistent with recent models and results from the literature on comparative politics.

3.3. Equilibrium models of distributive politics

The dominant approach to modeling distributive politics is contained in the literature on legislative bargaining [Baron and Ferejohn (1989), Baron (1991)]. These are game-theoretic models in which decisions are made by majority voting subject to a set of rules that govern the introduction and adjudication of proposals. For example, Lockwood (2002) focuses on how cost and benefit spillovers between constituencies determine the set of (discrete) projects that are funded under majority rule. He considers a two-stage proposal and voting game [extending Ferejohn, Fiorina and McKelvey (1987)]. In the first stage, delegates simultaneously propose sets of projects to be funded. In the second stage, delegates vote sequentially on permutations of the set of proposals where in the last round the surviving proposal is put against the status quo of no funded projects. The political equilibrium outcome consists of the set of projects that are approved in a subgame-perfect equilibrium. The key result is that, under some conditions, the set of funded projects is determined entirely by spillovers. More specifically, Lockwood presents conditions under which there is a unique political equilibrium outcome, and shows that it may take one of two forms. If all projects generate net-negative spillovers, and there are an odd number M projects in total, then the $(M+1)/2$ least harmful projects are funded. Otherwise the set of funded projects corresponds to the set of projects that generate positive net spillovers.

Besley and Coate (1999) develop a two-stage model of legislative policy choice that examines how distributive politics influences public good provision and the choice of representatives. They consider two communities with fixed populations, where residents within each community are differentiated in terms of their preference for a local public good. More specifically, the preferences of a resident of type λ in community i are given by

$$u(\lambda, x, g_i, g_{-i}) = (1-\lambda)\ln x + \lambda\big[(1-\kappa)\ln g_i + \kappa \ln g_{-i}\big], \tag{3.4}$$

where x is the numeraire, g_i is the level of the public good provided in i, g_{-i} is the level provided in the other community, and $\kappa \in [0, 1/2]$ indexes the degree of spillovers. In community i, λ_i is continuously distributed over $[0, 1]$. All residents have the same income y. The cost of one unit of either public good is $c > 0$.

To begin, consider the "decentralized" case in which local policies are chosen by a representative elected from the community [a "citizen candidate", Osborne and Slivinski (1996), Besley and Coate (1997)] by majority vote. The representative for community i chooses g_i, subject to its finance by a head tax that balances the local budget. In the second stage, the representative of community i implements the policy that maximizes her utility

$$u(\lambda_i, y - cg_i, g_i, g_{-i}) = (1 - \lambda_i)\ln y - cg_i + \lambda\big[(1 - \kappa)\ln g_i + \kappa \ln g_{-i}\big]. \tag{3.5}$$

The maximizing policy is $g_i^*(\lambda_i) = [\lambda_i(1 - \kappa)y/((1 - \lambda_i\kappa)c)]$. Composing the policy vector $(g_1^*(\lambda_1), g_2^*(\lambda_2))$ into (3.5) gives an expression for indirect utility that depends only on the types of the representatives in the two communities. These policy or candidate preference functions are single-peaked, implying that, in the first stage, each community chooses a citizen of the median type to be its representative. Thus, under decentralization, the median voter hypothesis holds.

Now suppose that each community elects a representative to the a city council, and that the council determines public good provision in both communities, subject to finance by a uniform head tax that balances the city's budget. Suppose further that power on the council is randomly allocated to one of the representatives. Let μ be the probability that the representative of community i is in power. Then, in the second stage, the representative of community i will choose the policy vector (g_i, g_{-i}) to maximize expected utility

$$\mu u\left(\lambda_i, y - \frac{c(g_i + g_{-i})}{2}, g_i, g_{-i}\right) + (1 - \mu)u\left(\lambda_{-i}, y - \frac{c(g_i + g_{-i})}{2}, g_i, g_{-i}\right). \tag{3.6}$$

Besley and Coate argue that μ parameterizes the nature of decision making within the legislature. If $\mu = 1/2$, then the policy outcome maximizes the sum of the utilities of the representatives, which corresponds loosely to the universalism norm discussed above. In contrast, if $\mu = 1$, then the policy outcome maximizes the utility of the smallest possible coalition, which consists of the representative in power.

In the second stage, voters in each community choose representatives anticipating how the outcome will influence the council's policy choice in stage one. The key result is that citizens now have an incentive to vote strategically. In particular, they must consider how their vote will influence the policies that will be chosen when their representative is not in power on the council. Besley and Coate show that the median voter in each community will now prefer that her representative have a type or preference for the public good that is higher than her own. Larger spillovers (a larger value for κ) and less legislative cooperation (a smaller μ) reduce the divergence between equilibrium type of the delegate and the type of the median voter. Thus, under centralization, the median voter hypothesis fails.

4. Private government

Private governments are voluntary, exclusive organizations that supplement services provided by the public sector. There are two broad classes of private governments. Residential private governments, sometimes called residential community associations (RCAs), common interest developments (CIDs), or homeowner associations (HOAs), exist to further the interests of residential property owners. Commercial private governments, sometimes called business improvement districts (BIDs) or business investment areas (BIAs), exist to further the interests of their member firms. Private governments are highly controversial. Garreau (1991) labels them "shadow governments", and argues that they are undemocratic, discriminatory, and operate outside of the constitutional restrictions that public governments face. This section examines the implications of private government for the provision of public services and regulation, their impact on the welfare of members and non-members, and the ability of potential competition from a private government to discipline rent seeking in the public sector.

Residential private governments are an increasingly important component of housing markets and local government systems in North America. Garreau (1991, p. 189) estimates that there may have been as many as 130,000 RCAs in the U.S. in 1988. McKenzie (1996) reports that the number of CIDs in the U.S. grew from a few hundred in 1960 to 150,000 in 1993 and that they then housed 32 million people.[27] As of 2002, the Community Associations Institute (an industry trade association) maintains that there are 231,000 RCAs in the U.S. housing 57 million Americans. The 2001 American Housing Survey from the U.S. Bureau of the Census reports that 8.9% of all households indicated that they paid community association fees in 2001. For new housing, the figure was 28%. Residential private governments provide security and sanitation services, and manage and maintain common facilities, including recreational facilities and infrastructure. They also regulate property use and individual conduct through covenants, codes and restrictions in property deeds.

There are fewer commercial private governments, but their impacts are also substantial. Pack (1992) estimates that there were 400 BIDs in the U.S. in 1992, while Mitchell's (2001) survey found 404 independently managed BIDs in the U.S. in 1999. BIDs typically provide security, marketing and sanitation services. Mitchell reports that 94% of BIDs engage in marketing, 85% provide maintenance and sanitation services,

[27] Private governments have a surprisingly long history. Reichman (1976) notes that private agreements for the use and maintenance of public facilities were used in England in 1743, and that the first private government was established in the U.S. in 1844.

and 68% provide security. Mitchell's survey also found that 88% of BIDs engaged in some form of policy advocacy, like lobbying governments on behalf of business interests. BIDs have become a key component of downtown revitalization strategies in many, if not most, major North American cities.

Private governments have five salient characteristics [Helsley and Strange (1998)].

- First, they are voluntary in the sense that they are formed by firms and households who are dissatisfied with the services provided by the public sector.
- Second, they are exclusive in the sense that they provide services only to their members.
- Third, they are part of a hierarchy of governments, and their members continue to receive and pay for services provided by the traditional public sector.
- Fourth, they are self-financing in the sense that they balance their budgets using fees and charges collected from members.
- Fifth, they are strategic: their activities interact with those of traditional governments.

There appear to be two primitive economic forces behind the growth of private government. The first is heterogeneity in demand. Restrictions on the number of communities, the difficulty of detaching land from existing communities, and the costs of moving all contribute to a community structure in which a good deal of demand heterogeneity survives the Tiebout sorting mechanism. Further, fiduciary and constitutional responsibilities often force local governments to service their entire populations with "one size fits all policies". Targeted provision of local public goods is not unheard of (local redistributive programs are certainly targeted), but it is rare. The net result is that some, perhaps most, residents find that the level of public services provided in their community does not exactly match their preferences. Private government allows high demand consumers to supplement public provision.

There also appear to be significant cost differences between public and private provision. Wolfe's (1993) meta survey of the relative costs of public and private provision for 43 services ranging from airlines to weather forecasting finds that private provision is generally less costly. Wilson (1989, p. 350) commenting on his own survey of the evidence notes that "The cost of water, street cleaning, ship maintenance, housing construction, school bus operation, and railroad track repair were all lower when done by private firms rather than government agencies." Lopez-de-Silanes, Shleifer and Vishny (1997) note that private contractors use fewer employees and pay them lower wages and benefits than government agencies do.

4.1. *Supplementary provision*

Helsley and Strange (1998) focus on the strategic interaction between a private government and the public sector. The actors in the model are a population of heterogeneous consumers, who may be firms or households, a private government, and the traditional public sector. Strategic interaction arises through a two-stage game. In stage 1, the public sector decides whether or not a private government will be allowed to form, and collects a fee from members to cover formation costs. In stage 2, the public sector and the private government choose provision levels, and consumers choose whether or not to join. The private government has narrow objectives in the sense that it is only concerned with the welfare of members. The public sector is concerned with the welfare of both members and non-members. We will consider a model of private government with a Leviathan public sector in the sequel.

The net benefit of collective good level G to a consumer of type θ is

$$\pi(G, \theta, p) = \theta f(G) - cG - p, \tag{4.1}$$

where θ indexes the value that the consumer places on G, cG is per capita cost and p is the membership price (0 for non-members). Note that provision is financed through user fees in this model, and that the per capita cost of the collective good is a constant. θ is distributed over the closed support $[\underline{\theta}, \bar{\theta}]$ according to a continuous distribution $H(\theta)$. The preferred level of spending for a type θ consumer, $G(\theta) = f'^{-1}(c/\theta)$, is increasing in θ. The level of public provision is denoted by g, and the level of private provision is denoted by γ. Helsley and Strange assume that these services are perfect substitutes: a member of the private government consumes $g + \gamma$ in total.

In the absence of a private government, the welfare maximizing choice for the public sector is $g^0 = G(E[\theta])$, where $E[\cdot]$ is the expectations operator. In this model, the public sector provides the level that is preferred by the average resident of the community. With a private government, there are three equilibrium conditions. First, consumers join the private government when it is in their interest to do so. These choices determining θ^*, the identity of the marginal member. Second, the public sector chooses g taking γ and θ^* as fixed. Third, the private government chooses γ taking g and θ^* as fixed. All these choices must be mutually consistent in equilibrium.

The resulting maximizing provision levels are $g^1 = G(E[\theta \mid \theta < \theta^*])$ for the public sector, and $\gamma^1 = G(E[\theta \mid \theta \geqslant \theta^*]) - g^1$ for the private government. Note that $g^1 + \gamma^1 = G(E[\theta \mid \theta \geqslant \theta^*])$, the level preferred by the average member. Then since $G(\theta)$ is increasing, and $E[\theta \mid \theta < \theta^*] < E[\theta] < E[\theta \mid \theta \geqslant \theta^*]$, we have $g^1 < g^0 < g^1 + \gamma^1$. The public sector responds to the existence of a private government by reducing its provision of the collective good. Thus, there is "strategic downloading" of public spending in equilibrium.[28]

The welfare effects of private government are interesting. First, the marginal member is always worse off with a private government (he faces a choice between consuming too much of the collective good and consuming too little), so the private government does not effect a Pareto improvement. Further, as in models of individual supplements to a collective good [Epple and Romano (1996), Gouveia (1997)], the equilibrium has an "ends against the middle" quality. High demanders are better off since their consumption of the collective good rises, and low demanders are better off since their consumption of the collective good falls. However, as noted above, the marginal member, and by continuity consumers near the marginal member, are worse off.

[28] Cheung (2004) finds support for this result in his study of strategic interactions between public and private government spending in California.

4.2. Supplementary regulation

Private governments engage in a variety regulatory practices. Activities that have been prohibited by the covenants, codes and restrictions that accompany membership in a CID include "flying the flag, delivering newspapers, parking pickup trucks in the driveway, kissing outside the front door, using one's own back door too much, building fences, painting the exterior certain colors, having pets, working from one's home, marrying people below a certain age, and even having children." [McKenzie (1996, p. 4)] Although these regulations seem oppressive, they have survived the test of the marketplace. CIDs appear to provide a higher level of amenities than less regulated, public developments.

Helsley and Strange (2000b) present a model of local government and social interactions that captures some of the regulatory fervor of residential private governments. The model features a population of heterogeneous agents who belong to groups, where each agent takes an action that impacts the welfare of other group members. In this model, social interactions arise from contributions to group quality, a collective good. There are two groups, an exclusive group and the remainder. The extent of secession, the size of the exclusive group, is endogenous. Group quality A_{G} is given by the average value of individual actions taken by group members.

The utility of a type θ agent is $U(\theta, a, A_{\mathrm{G}}) = y + u(\theta, a, A_{\mathrm{G}}) - ka$ where k is the cost per unit of individual action a, and θ is distributed via $H(\theta)$ on a closed support. Under these conditions, the maximizing individual action $a(\theta, A_{\mathrm{G}})$ is increasing in θ. Secession is modeled as the bifurcation of the population into two groups, where all agents above type θ^* join the private government.

The private government sets a minimum action $\underline{a}$ that is required of all members. When this minimum action is relatively large, the regulation causes some individuals to choose not to join the exclusive group. Of course there are other ways of accomplishing exclusion in such a model. If θ is observable, a manager could exclude low contributors directly. Alternatively, the group could impose a membership fee. However, regulation dominates pricing in this setting, since it both excludes low value consumers, and directly increases group quality. The quality of both groups increases in θ^*, and the quality of the exclusive group increases with the level of the minimum action $\underline{a}$.

The equilibrium is modeled as a game in which individual actions, secession and regulation occur simultaneously. There are several key results. First, all members of the low group are made worse off by secession, due to its negative impact on group quality. Thus it is not surprising that this type of secession is controversial. Second, although it is possible that some secession may be efficient, the level of secession is excessive in equilibrium. There is a migration externality associated with secession in this model [de Bartolome (1990)]: an individual who joins the exclusive group decreases the quality of both groups – she was the highest contributor in the low group and is now the lowest (perhaps regulated) contributor in the high group. Consequently equilibrium membership decisions are inefficient. Third, this implies that it would be desirable to further increase the level of regulation as a means to reduce equilibrium high group membership. This is interesting because the regulatory activities of private governments are usually met with hostility. However, this analysis shows that the many draconian regulations that these institutions impose may be useful second-best instruments.

It is also interesting to consider other objectives for the high group. Many CIDs are established by land developers who govern the organization until the community is complete and largely occupied. If the level of regulation is chosen to maximize profit, the developer will choose $\underline{a}$ to maximize the willingness to pay of the marginal member. This will lead to a lower level of regulation, ceteris paribus. However, the size of the exclusive group may be greater or smaller under profit maximization, depending on how the effects of market power compare with the migration externality discussed earlier. Of course, there is also an element of democracy to private governance in this context. Homeowner associations are typically governed by a board elected from the association's members. If there is direct voting over alternative policies, the preferences of the median member should determine policy choices. Depending on the distribution of types, there may be too much or too little regulation with democratic incentives.

4.3. Potential competition

Helsley and Strange (2000a) examine whether the threat of competition from a private government can discipline a Leviathan public sector. The paper considers four issues:

(1) how competition between a private government and the public sector influences the provision of a public service,
(2) the role of political activism in private government formation,
(3) how potential competition from a private government may contribute to public sector reform, and
(4) how the public sector responds to the threat of entry by a private government.

There are two types of consumers in the model, high and low demanders, where only high demanders join the private government. This paper, unlike those summarized above, does not consider equilibrium membership decisions. There are two institutions, the public sector and a private government, and they have different incentives and different provision costs. The private government maximizes the welfare of members. The public sector is concerned with both the welfare of the aggregate population and with the perquisites of public office, represented by the level of public provision. Thus, the public sector in this model engages in rent seeking. Each institution chooses a level of provision to maximize its objective taking the choice of the other as given. The analysis focuses on the characteristics of the resulting Nash equilibrium.

The indirect utility of a member is

$$v_{\mathrm{M}} = v(g+\gamma) - (c+r)g - c\gamma, \tag{4.2}$$

where $v(\cdot)$ is increasing and strictly concave, g is the level of public provision, γ is the level of private provision, c is private provision cost per unit and r is the public sector's cost disadvantage. The indirect utility of a non-member is

$$v_{\mathrm{N}} = \theta v(g) - (c+r)g, \tag{4.3}$$

where $0 < \theta < 1$. Nonmembers place a lower value on the public service, ceteris paribus.

The public sector's objective is to choose g to maximize

$$\Omega = \omega W + (1 - \omega)g, \tag{4.4}$$

treating γ as fixed. In (4.4), W is aggregate welfare, $W = Mv_{\mathrm{M}} + Nv_{\mathrm{N}}$, where M and N are the fixed numbers of members and non-members, respectively, and ω is the weight that is given to aggregate welfare in the public sector's objective. The first-order condition for this problem,

$$Mv'(g + \gamma) + N\theta v'(g) = (M + N)(c + r) - \frac{1 - \omega}{\omega}, \tag{4.5}$$

indicates that g is chosen so that the aggregate marginal benefit of public provision equals the aggregate marginal cost minus an adjustment that reflects bureaucratic rent seeking. Higher public sector costs (higher r) lead to a lower level of public spending, while stronger expense preferences (lower ω) lead to a higher level of public spending, other things being equal.

The private government chooses γ to maximize $W_{\mathrm{M}} = Mv_{\mathrm{M}}$ treating g as fixed. The first-order condition for this problem implies

$$v'(g + \gamma) = c. \tag{4.6}$$

(4.6) indicates that the private government chooses γ so that the marginal benefit of the public service to a member is equal to the marginal cost.

(4.5) and (4.6) implicitly define the reaction functions of the public sector $g(\gamma)$ and the private government $\gamma(g)$, respectively. The slopes of these reaction functions are

$$\frac{\mathrm{d}g}{\mathrm{d}\gamma} = -\frac{Mv''(g + \gamma)}{Mv''(g + \gamma) + N\theta v''(g)} \in (-1, 0), \tag{4.7}$$

and

$$\frac{\mathrm{d}\gamma}{\mathrm{d}g} = -1. \tag{4.8}$$

Thus, public and private provision are strategic substitutes in this model.

Let g^0 represent the level of public provision if the private government does not form, and let g^1 and γ^1 represent the equilibrium levels of public and private provision if the private government forms (see Figure 2). Assume that $g^1 > 0$: the private government never completely crowds out public spending in equilibrium. This seems realistic. Even though private provision is less costly, there may be constitutional or legislative constraints that prevent the public sector from completely withdrawing from the market. In this simple framework, it can be shown that an interior equilibrium exists provided certain boundary conditions on the reaction functions are satisfied, and that such an equilibrium features:

$$g^1 + \gamma^1 > g^0 > g^1. \tag{4.9}$$

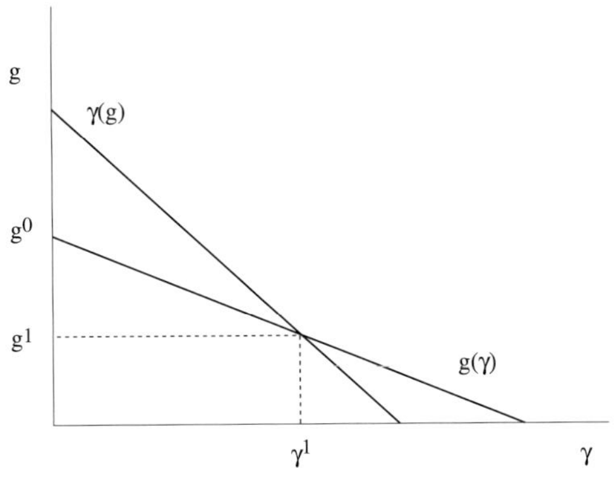

Figure 2. Equilibrium provision.

Thus, at an interior equilibrium, the private government causes a reduction in public provision. Once again, the public sector's best response to the existence of a private supplement is to effectively download some its spending. However, the private supplement more than compensates for the reduction in public spending: consumption by high-type consumers rises.

However, if $g(0) \geqslant \gamma(0)$, then there is no room in the market for a private supplement: the public sector is providing more of the public service than even the high-type consumers want. As a result, the best response of the private government is to provide $\gamma = 0$. This shows that if the bureaucrat gives little weight to the welfare of the population, so rent seeking is relatively strong, then public provision may be so large that a supplementary private government would not choose a positive provision level.

To examine private government formation, consider the following three-stage game. In stage 1, the public sector chooses g. In stage 2, members engage in political activism that may cause a private government to form. In stage 3, if the private government is active, it chooses γ. Suppose that there is a fixed cost to activism for members as a group, and that activism is undertaken provided the increase in member utility associated with the private government is larger than an individual's share of the activism cost. If the private government reduces the welfare of non-members, then activism can be inefficient in this model. In fact, if the benefits to members are large enough, a private government may form even when this reduces aggregate welfare.

In stage 1, the public sector chooses g anticipating how this will impact activism, private government formation and private provision. There are essentially two cases. First, if a private government does not form, then the public sector should choose the g that is optimal for $\gamma = 0$, namely g^0. On the other hand, if a private government forms, the public sector should choose g to maximize Ω assuming that γ follows the private government's reaction function $\gamma(g)$. In this model, the solution to this problem is γ^1, the level that was chosen in the simultaneous move provision game. This outcome (which is obviously model specific) simplifies the examination of potential competition.

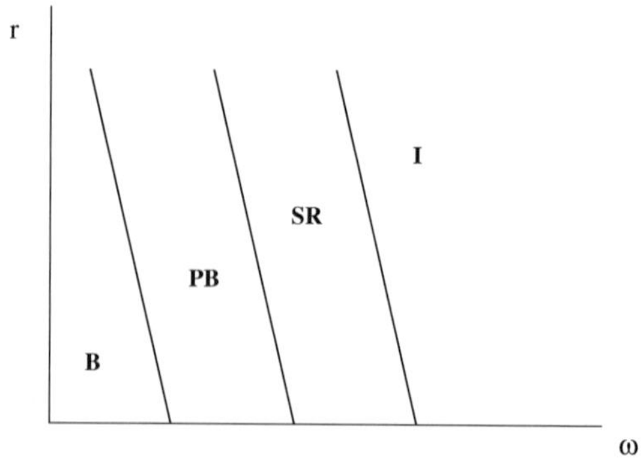

Figure 3. Entry.

Figure 3 illustrates the public sector's attitudes toward entry in this model. There are four cases or regions. For small values of ω rent seeking is so strong, and consequently public provision is so large, that there is no room for a private government. Thus, in the region labeled B, entry is blockaded. At the other extreme, for high values of ω, entry may be inevitable. This occurs if the payoff to activism is positive even when the public sector provides g^0, and is represented by the region I. Third, it is possible that the public sector leaves room for a private government to produce, but activism costs are such that the payoff to activism is negative, and so a private government does not form. We say that entry is "politically blockaded" in this case (region PB). Finally, and most interesting, if the parameters are such that entry is neither inevitable nor politically blockaded, then the public sector has a strategic choice: choose g^0 and prevent entry, or choose g^1 and accommodate it (region SR, for "strategic region").

This analysis shows that potential entry can have a very different effect on a public sector incumbent than it would have on a private firm. If there is little efficiency gain from private government, or if the public sector has strong expense preferences, it will, under some conditions, choose a high level of provision to deter entry. However, if the gain from private provision is large or if expense preferences are weak, the public sector will choose a low level of provision and welcome entry. This practice of strategic entry accommodation is entirely different than the strategic entry deterrence that is common in models with a private sector incumbent [Dixit (1980), Tirole (1988)]. There is another, more sobering, point that deserves emphasis here. Since entry is blockaded when expense preferences are high, potential competition is completely ineffective in this model in precisely the circumstances where we might think it is most important.

4.4. *Gated communities*

The most extreme form of private government is the gated community, a walled development that is designed to improve public safety by limiting public access. This type of development appears to be growing very rapidly in North America. The New

York Times has reported that 4,000,000 people lived in gated communities in the U.S. in 1995. An article in the Washington Post put the number of gated residents in California at 500,000 in 1994 [see Helsley and Strange (1999) for these and other related references]. The 2001 American Housing Survey, from the U.S. Bureau of the Census, reports that 6.6% of all households, and 14% those in new units (less than 4 years old) indicated that they live an area where "*community* access is secured with walls or fences". The percentage of houses that are gated by this definition is highest in the West (12.1%), and lowest in the Midwest (2.3%). Interestingly, within urban areas, the corresponding percentages are 8.5% for central cities, and 7.4% for suburbs.

Helsley and Strange (1999) analyze gating in a system of communities, using a model that incorporates an explicit micro-model of the market for crime. In this model, communities are controlled by developers who choose levels of gating to maximize profit, defined as revenue from land sales minus gating costs. Revenues depend on the level of crime in the community through capitalization, and the number of criminals and their target choices are endogenous. Since gating makes a community a less attractive target, it impacts the spatial distribution of crime in the urban area.

The payoff to crime in community i is

$$v_i = b(n_i) - g_i, \tag{4.10}$$

where n_i is the number of active criminals in the community, and g_i is the level of "gating", defined to include patrolling and other activities whose level can be varied. The "booty" function $b(\cdot)$ is decreasing due to congestion in criminal opportunities. The criminal labor market is closed in the sense that the payoff to criminal activity is endogenously determined by the interaction between aggregate criminal payoffs (the demand for crime) and an aggregate supply function of criminals. The supply function reflects an implicit career choice between crime and legitimate employment.

The essence of this model can be illustrated in a few simple diagrams. Figure 4 shows the equilibrium level of crime in two communities in the absence of gating. Criminal mobility equalizes v_i across the communities, and the aggregate market clearing condition determines the common equilibrium criminal payoff v^*. Figure 5 shows the impact of gating by community 1. This lowers the criminal payoff in community 1 and reduces the amount of crime there, ceteris paribus. However, this reduction in the aggregate "demand" for crime causes the equilibrium criminal payoff to fall, which leads to an increase in the level of crime in community 2 (the community can now support more criminals, since the payoff each must earn is lower), but decreases the aggregate level of crime in the metropolitan area. Thus, there is both diversion and deterrence. Gating diverts some crime to other, less protected areas, and discourages criminal activity overall by making crime less attractive relative to other "occupations".[29]

[29] LaCour-Little and Malpezzi (2001), in one of the few empirical studies of private government, found that homeowner associations, private streets and gating were associated with higher housing prices in St. Louis over the 1979–1988 period. The combination of a homeowner association and a gated street increased sales prices by roughly 26% in this sample.

examine the consequences of residential private government in a model with a housing market. Finally, there is an obvious need for empirical studies of the impacts of private government on public sector spending patterns and housing prices.

Another way for the nascent field of urban political economics to develop would be to articulate models that combine key elements from the paradigms outlined above. The obvious starting point, and one that is mentioned by Besley and Coate (1999), might be the development of a multi-community model with a representative political institution. Each community could elect a citizen candidate to the city council, which would then make policy choices. The population would presumably be mobile, and so the impacts of policies on utility would be capitalized into property values. Of course, in this setting, the common pool problem would be magnified by the relationship between the policy variables and the tax base. Under uniform property taxation, communities that are net beneficiaries of public spending will have lower liabilities due to capitalization.

Acknowledgements

I thank Richard Arnott, Keith Head, Vernon Henderson, Will Strange, Ralph Winter, and especially Jacques Thisse for helpful comments. Ron Cheung provided outstanding research assistance. The financial support of the UBC Center for Urban Economics and Real Estate is gratefully acknowledged.

References

Anderson, J.E., Van den Berg, H. (1998). "Fiscal decentralization and government size: an international test for Leviathian accounting for unmeasured economic activity". International Tax and Public Finance 5 (May), 175–190.

Arnott, R. (1979). "Optimal city size in a spatial economy". Journal of Urban Economics 6, 65–89.

Banks, J.S. (1993). "Two-sided uncertainty in the monopoly agenda setter model". Journal of Public Economics 50, 429–444.

Baqir, R. (2002). "Districting and government overspending". Journal of Political Economy 110, 1318–1354.

Baron, D.P. (1991). "Majoritarian incentives, pork barrel programs, and procedural control". American Journal of Political Science 35, 57–90.

Baron, D.P., Ferejohn, J.A. (1989). "Bargaining in legislatures". American Political Science Review 83, 1181–1206.

Benabou, R. (1993). "Workings of a city: location, education and production". Quarterly Journal of Economics 108, 619–652.

Benabou, R. (1996). "Equity and efficiency in human capital investment: the local connection". Review of Economic Studies 63, 237–264.

Berglas, E., Pines, D. (1980). "Clubs as a case of competitive industry with goods of variable quality". Economics Letters 5, 363–366.

Bergstrom, T.C., Goodman, R.P. (1973). "Private demands for public goods". American Economic Review 63, 280–296.

Besley, T., Coate, S. (1997). "An economic model of representative democracy". Quarterly Journal of Economics 112, 85–114.

Besley, T., Coate, S. (1999). "Centralized versus decentralized provision of local public goods: a political economy analysis". Working Paper 7084. National Bureau of Economic Research.
Bewley, T. (1981). "A critique of Tiebout's theory of local expenditures". Econometrica 49, 713–740.
Black, D. (1948). "On the rationale of group decision making". Journal of Political Economy 56, 23–34.
Booms, B. (1966). "City government form and public expenditures". National Tax Journal, 187–199.
Borcherding, T.E., Deacon, R.T. (1972). "The demand for services of non-federal governments". American Economic Review 62, 891–901.
Bowen, H. (1943). "The interpretation of voting in the allocation of economic resources". Quarterly Journal of Economics 58, 27–48.
Brasington, D.M. (2001). "Capitalization and community size". Journal of Urban Economics 50, 385–395.
Brennan, G., Buchanan, J.M. (1977). "Towards a tax constitution for Leviathan". Journal of Public Economics 8, 255–273.
Brennan, G., Buchanan, J.M. (1980). The Power to Tax: Analytical Foundations of a Fiscal Constitution. Cambridge University Press, New York.
Brueckner, J.K. (1979). "Property values, local public expenditure and economic efficiency". Journal of Public Economics 11, 223–245.
Brueckner, J.K. (1982). "A test for allocative efficiency in the local public sector". Journal of Public Economics 19, 311–331.
Brueckner, J.K. (1983). "Property value maximization and public sector efficiency". Journal of Urban Economics 14, 1–15.
Brueckner, J.K. (1995). "Strategic control of growth in a system of cities". Journal of Public Economics 57 (3), 393–416.
Brueckner, J.K. (2000). "A Tiebout/tax-competition model". Journal of Public Economics 77, 285–306.
Brueckner, J.K., Joo, M.-S. (1991). "Voting with capitalization". Regional Science and Urban Economics 21, 453–467.
Buchanan, J.M., Tullock, G. (1962). The Calculus of Consent. The University of Michigan Press, Ann Arbor.
Caplan, B. (2001). "Standing Tiebout on his head: tax capitalization and the monopoly power of local governments". Public Choice 108, 101–122.
Caplin, A., Nalebuff, B. (1997). "Competition among institutions". Journal of Economic Theory 72, 306–342.
Caro, R.A. (1974). The Power Broker: Robert Moses and the Fall of New York. Knopf, New York.
Cheung, R. (2004). "Strategic interactions between local governments and global governments: an empirical analysis of homeowners' associations in California". Manuscript. University of British Columbia.
Davis, M.L., Hayes, K. (1993). "The demand for good government". Review of Economics and Statistics, 148–152.
de Bartolome, C.A.M. (1990). "Equilibrium and inefficiency in a community model with peer group effects". Journal of Political Economy 98, 110–133.
Deller, S. (1990). "An application of a test for allocative efficiency in the local public sector". Regional Science and Urban Economics 20, 395–406.
Deller, S.C., Chicoine, D.L. (1993). "Representative versus direct democracy: a test of allocative efficiency in local government expenditures". Public Finance Quarterly 21, 100–114.
Deno, K.T., Mehay, S.L. (1987). "Municipal management structure and fiscal performance: do city managers make a difference?" Southern Economic Journal 53, 627–642.
Dixit, A. (1980). "The role of investment in entry deterrence". Economic Journal 90, 95–106.
Downs, A. (1957). An Economic Theory of Democracy. Harper and Row, New York.
Durlauf, S.N. (1994). "Spillovers, stratification, and inequality". European Economic Review 38, 836–845.
Durlauf, S.N. (1996a). "A theory of persistent income inequality". Journal of Economic Growth 1, 75–94.
Durlauf, S.N. (1996b). "Neighborhood feedbacks, endogenous stratification, and income inequality". In: Barnett, W.A., Gandolfo, G., Hillinger, C. (Eds.), Dynamic Disequilibrium Modeling: Theory and Applications, Proceedings of the Ninth International Symposium in Economic Theory and Econometrics. Cambridge University Press, New York, pp. 505–534.

Eberts, R.W., Gronberg, T.J. (1990). "Structure, conduct and performance in the local public sector". National Tax Journal XLIII, 165–173.

Edelson, N.M. (1976). "Voting equilibria with market based assessments". Journal of Public Economics 5, 269–284.

Edlin, A.S., Shannon, C. (1998). "Strict single crossing and the strict Spence-Mirrlees condition: a comment on monotone comparative statics". Econometrica 66 (6), 1417–1425.

Edwards, J., Keen, M. (1996). "Tax competition and Leviathan". European Economic Review 40, 113–134.

Epple, D., Filimon, R., Romer, T. (1984). "Equilibrium among local jurisdictions: toward an integrated treatment of voting and residential choice". Journal of Public Economics 24, 281–308.

Epple, D., Filimon, R., Romer, T. (1993). "Existence of voting and housing equilibrium in a system of communities with property taxes". Regional Science and Urban Economics 23 (5), 585–610.

Epple, D., Platt, G. (1998). "Equilibrium and local redistribution in an urban economy when households differ in both preferences and incomes". Journal of Urban Economics 43, 23–51.

Epple, D., Romano, R.E. (1996). "Ends against the middle: determining public service provision when there are private alternatives". Journal of Public Economics 62, 297–325.

Epple, D., Romano, R.E. (1998). "Competition between private and public schools, vouchers and peer-group effects". American Economic Review 88, 32–62.

Epple, D., Romer, T. (1989). "On the flexibility of community boundaries". Journal of Urban Economics 26, 307–319.

Epple, D., Romer, T. (1991). "Mobility and redistribution". Journal of Political Economy 99, 828–858.

Epple, D., Romer, T., Sieg, H. (2001). "Interjurisdictional sorting and majority rule: an empirical analysis". Econometrica 69 (6), 1437–1465.

Epple, D., Zelenitz, A. (1981). "The implications of competition among communities: does Tiebout need politics?" Journal of Political Economy 89, 1197–1217.

Fahey, C.A. (1998). "The choice of local government structure in Massachusetts: a historical public choice perspective". Social Science Quarterly 79, 433–444.

Ferejohn, J., Fiorina, M., McKelvey, R.D. (1987). "Sophisticated voting and agenda independence in the distributive politics setting". American Journal of Political Science 31, 169–193.

Fernandez, R., Rogerson, R. (1996). "Income distribution, communities and the quality of public education". Quarterly Journal of Economics 111, 135–164.

Fernandez, R., Rogerson, R. (1997). "Keeping people out: income distribution: zoning and the quality of public education". International Economic Review 38 (1), 23–42.

Fernandez, R., Rogerson, R. (1998). "Public education and income distribution: a dynamic quantitative evaluation of education-finance reform". American Economic Review 88 (4), 813–833.

Fernandez, R., Rogerson, R. (1999). "Education finance reform and investment in human capital: lessons from California". Journal of Public Economics 74 (3), 327–350.

Fernandez, R., Rogerson, R. (2001). "Sorting and long-run inequality". Quarterly Journal of Economics 116 (4), 1305–1341.

Gans, J.S., Smart, M. (1996). "Majority voting with single-crossing preferences". Journal of Public Economics 59, 219–237.

Garreau, J. (1991). Edge Cities: Life on the New Frontier. Doubleday, New York.

Gouveia, M. (1997). "Majority rule and the provision of a private good". Public Choice 93, 221–244.

Hansen, N.A., Kessler, A.S. (2001). "Nonexistence of equilibria in multicommunity models". Journal of Urban Economics 50 (3), 418–435.

Helsley, R.W., Strange, W.C. (1994). "City formation with commitment". Regional Science and Urban Economics 24, 373–390.

Helsley, R.W., Strange, W.C. (1995). "Strategic growth controls". Regional Science and Urban Economics 25 (4), 435–460.

Helsley, R.W., Strange, W.C. (1997). "Limited developers". Canadian Journal of Economics XXX, 329–348.

Helsley, R.W., Strange, W.C. (1998). "Private government". Journal of Public Economics 69, 281–304.

Helsley, R.W., Strange, W.C. (1999). "Gated communities and the economic geography of crime". Journal of Urban Economics 46, 80–105.
Helsley, R.W., Strange, W.C. (2000a). "Potential competition and public sector performance". Regional Science and Urban Economics 30, 405–428.
Helsley, R.W., Strange, W.C. (2000b). "Social interactions and the institutions of local government". American Economic Review 90, 1477–1490.
Henderson, J.V. (1974). "The sizes and types of cities". American Economic Review 64, 640–656.
Henderson, J.V. (1980). "Community development: the effects of growth and uncertainty". American Economic Review 70, 894–910.
Henderson, J.V. (1985). "The Tiebout model: bring back the entrepreneurs". Journal of Political Economy 93, 248–264.
Henderson, J.V., Thisse, J.-F. (1999). "On the pricing strategy of a land developer". Journal of Urban Economics 45, 1–16.
Henderson, J.V., Thisse, J.-F. (2001). "On strategic community development". Journal of Political Economy 109, 546–569.
Hoyt, W.H. (1999). "Leviathan, local government expenditures and capitalization". Regional Science and Urban Economics 29, 155–171.
Hughes, P.A.N., Edwards, M.E. (2000). "Leviathan vs. Lilliputian: a data envelopment analysis of government efficiency". Journal of Regional Science 40 (4), 649–669.
Inman, R.P. (1978). "Testing political economy's 'as if' proposition: is the median income voter really decisive". Public Choice 33, 45–65.
Inman, R.P., Fitts, M.A. (1990). "Political institutions and public policy: evidence from the U.S. historical record". Journal of Law, Economics and Organization 6, 79–132.
Katz, L., Rosen, K.T. (1987). "The interjurisdictional effects of growth controls on housing prices". Journal of Law and Economics XXX, 149–160.
LaCour-Little, M., Malpezzi, S. (2001). "Gated communities and property values". Unpublished manuscript. Washington University.
Landbein, L.I., Crewson, P., Brasher, C.N. (1996). "Rethinking ward and at-large elections in cities". Public Choice 88, 275–293.
Lockwood, B. (2002). "Distributive politics and the costs of centralization". Review of Economic Studies 69, 313–337.
Lopez-de-Silanes, F., Shleifer, A., Vishny, R. (1997). "Privatization in the United States". RAND Journal of Economics 28, 447–471.
Lowi, T. (1964). "American business and public policy: case studies and political theory". World Politics 16, 677–715.
McKenzie, E. (1996). "Homeowner association private governments in the American political system". Papers in Political Economy No. 75. University of Western Ontario.
Mehay, S.L., Gonzalez, R.A. (1994). "District elections and the power of municipal employee unions". Journal of Labor Research 15, 387–402.
Mitchell, J. (2001). "Business improvement districts and the new revitalization of downtowns". Economic Development Quarterly 15, 115–123.
Morgan, D.R., Pelissero, J.P. (1980). "Urban policy: does political structure matter?" American Political Science Review 74, 999–1006.
Nechyba, T.J. (1997). "Existence of equilibrium and stratification in local and hierarchical Tiebout economies with property taxes and voting". Economic Theory 10, 277–304.
Nelson, M.A. (1987). "Searching for Leviathan: comment and extension". American Economic Review 77, 198–204.
Oates, W.E. (1985). "Searching for Leviathan: an empirical study". American Economic Review 75, 748–757.
Osborne, M.J., Slivinski, A. (1996). "A model of political competition with citizen-candidates". The Quarterly Journal of Economics 111, 65–96.

Pack, J.R. (1992). "BIDs, DIDs, SIDs, SADs: Private government in urban America". The Brookings Review, 18–21.

Perroni, C., Scharf, K.A. (2001). "Tiebout with politics: capital tax competition and constitutional choices". Review of Economic Studies 68, 133–154.

Persson, T., Roland, G., Tabellini, G. (1997). "Separation of powers and political accountability". Quarterly Journal of Economics 112, 1163–1202.

Persson, T., Roland, G., Tabellini, G. (1998). "Towards micropolitical foundations of public finance". European Economic Review 42, 685–694.

Persson, T., Roland, G., Tabellini, G. (2000). "Comparative politics and public finance". Journal of Political Economy 108, 1121–1161.

Persson, T., Tabellini, G. (2000). Political Economics. MIT Press, Cambridge.

Pines, D. (1991). "Tiebout without politics". Regional Science and Urban Economics 21, 469–490.

Rauch, J.E. (1995). "Bureaucracy, infrastructure, and economic growth: evidence from U.S. cities during the Progressive Era". American Economic Review 85, 968–979.

Rauscher, M. (1998). "Leviathan and competition among jurisdictions: the case of benefit taxation". Journal of Urban Economics 44, 59–67.

Reichman, U. (1976). "Residential private governments: an introductory survey". University of Chicago Law Review 43, 227–306.

Riker, W.H. (1962). "The Theory of Political Coalitions". Yale University Press, New Haven.

Romer, T., Rosenthal, H. (1979). "Bureaucrats versus voters: on the political economy of resource allocation by direct democracy". Quarterly Journal of Economics 93, 563–587.

Romer, T., Rosenthal, H. (1982). "Median voters or budget maximizers: evidence from school expenditure referenda". Economic Inquiry 20, 556–578.

Romer, T., Rosenthal, H., Munley, V.G. (1992). "Economic incentives and political institutions: spending and voting in school budget referenda". Journal of Public Economics 49, 1–34.

Rose-Ackerman, S. (1979). "Market models of local government: exit, voting and the land market". Journal of Urban Economics 6, 319–337.

Rose-Ackerman, S. (1983a). "Beyond Tiebout: modeling the political economy of local government". In: Zodrow, G. (Ed.), Local Provision of Public Services: The Tiebout Model After Twenty-Five Years. Academic Press, New York, pp. 55–83.

Rose-Ackerman, S. (1983b). "Tiebout models and the competitive ideal: as essay on the political economy of local government". In: Quigley, J.M. (Ed.), Perspectives on Local Public Finance and Public Policy. JAI Press, Greenwich, pp. 23–46.

Rosenthal, H. (1990). "The setter model". In: Enelow, J., Hinich, M. (Eds.), Advances in the Spatial Theory of Voting. Cambridge University Press, Cambridge, pp. 199–234.

Ross, S., Yinger, J. (1999). "Sorting and voting: a review of the literature on urban public finance". In: Cheshire, P., Mills, E.S. (Eds.), Handbook of Regional and Urban Economics, vol. 3. North-Holland, Amsterdam.

Rothstein, P. (1994). "Learning the preferences of governments and voters from proposed spending and aggregated votes". Journal of Public Economics 54, 361–390.

Rubinfeld, D.L. (1987). "The economics of the local public sector". In: Auerbach, A.J., Feldstein, M. (Eds.), Handbook of Public Economics, vol. 2. North-Holland, Amsterdam, pp. 571–645.

Santerre, R.E. (1993). "Representative versus direct democracy: the role of public bureaucrats". Public Choice 76, 189–198.

Sass, T.R. (1991). "The choice of municipal government structure and public expenditure". Public Choice 71, 71–87.

Sass, T. (1992). "Constitutional choice in representative democracies". Public Choice 74, 405–424.

Scotchmer, S. (1985a). "Profit-maximizing clubs". Journal of Public Economics 27, 25–45.

Scotchmer, S. (1985b). "Two-tier pricing of shared facilities in a free-entry equilibrium". RAND Journal of Economics 16, 456–472.

Scotchmer, S. (1986). "Local public goods in an equilibrium: how pecuniary externalities matter". Regional Science and Urban Economics 16 (4), 463–482.
Scotchmer, S. (1994). "Public goods and the invisible hand". In: Quigley, J.M., Smolensky, E. (Eds.), Modern Public Finance. Harvard University Press, Cambridge.
Scotchmer, S., Wooders, M. (1986). "Competitive equilibrium and the core in club economies with nonanonymous crowding". Journal of Public Economics 34, 159–173.
Shepsle, K.A., Weingast, B.R. (1984). "Political solutions to market problems". American Political Science Review 78 (2), 417–434.
Sonstelie, J.C., Portney, P.R. (1978). "Profit maximizing communities and the theory of local public expenditure". Journal of Urban Economics 5, 263–277.
Sonstelie, J.C., Portney, P.R. (1980). "Take the money and run: a theory of voting in local referenda". Journal of Urban Economics 8, 187–195.
Southwick, L. (1997). "Local government spending and at-large versus district representation: Do wards result in more pork?" Economics and Politics 9, 173–203.
Sprunger, P., Wilson, J.D. (1998). "Imperfectly mobile households and durable local public goods: does the capitalization mechanism work?" Journal of Urban Economics 44, 468–492.
Stiglitz, J.E. (1977). "The theory of local public goods". In: Feldstein, M., Inman, R.P. (Eds.), The Economics of Public Services. Macmillan, London.
Taylor, L. (1995). "Allocative inefficiency of local government". Journal of Urban Economics 37, 201–211.
Tiebout, C.M. (1956). "A pure theory of local expenditures". Journal of Political Economy 64, 416–424.
Tirole, J. (1988). The Theory of Industrial Organization. MIT Press, Cambridge.
Turnbull, G.K., Djoundourian, S.S. (1994). "The median voter hypothesis: evidence from general purpose local governments". Public Choice 81, 223–240.
Weingast, B.R., Shepsle, K.A., Johnsen, C. (1981). "The political economy of benefits and costs: a neoclassical approach to distributive politics". Journal of Political Economy 89 (4), 642–664.
Welch, S. (1990). "The impact of at-large elections on the representation of Blacks and Hispanics". Journal of Politics 52, 1050–1076.
Westhoff, F. (1977). "Existence of equilibria in economies with a local public good". Journal of Economic Theory 14, 84–112.
Westhoff, F. (1979). "Policy inferences from community choice models: a caution". Journal of Urban Economics 6, 535–549.
Wildasin, D.E. (1979). "Local public goods, property values, and local public choice". Journal of Urban Economics 6, 521–534.
Wildasin, D.E. (1991). "Redistribution in a common labor market". American Economic Review 81 (4), 757–774.
Wildasin, D.E., Wilson, J.D. (1996). "Imperfect mobility and local government behavior in an overlapping generations model". Journal of Public Economics 60, 177–198.
Wilson, J. (1989). Bureaucracy. Basic Books, New York.
Wilson, J.D. (1999). "Theories of tax competition". National Tax Journal 52, 269–304.
Wolfe, C. (1993). Markets or Governments. MIT Press, Cambridge.
Wrede, M. (1998). "Household mobility and the moderate Leviathan: efficiency and decentralization". Regional Science and Urban Economics 28, 315–328.
Wrede, M. (2001). "Yardstick competition to tame the Leviathan". European Journal of Political Economy 17, 705–721.
Yinger, J. (1982). "Capitalization and the theory of local public finance". Journal of Political Economy 90, 917–943.
Zax, J.S. (1990). "Reform city councils and municipal employees". Public Choice 64, 167–177.

Chapter 55

FISCAL DECENTRALIZATION

DENNIS EPPLE[1]
Carnegie Mellon University, USA

THOMAS NECHYBA[1]
Duke University, USA

Contents

[1] Also affiliated with NBER.

Handbook of Regional and Urban Economics, Volume 4. Edited by J.V. Henderson and J.F. Thisse

DOI: 10.1016/S0169-7218(04)07055-8

Abstract

Fiscal decentralization is on the rise worldwide while barriers to factor and population mobility are declining. Greater decentralized government activity is therefore taking place in an economic environment characterized by increased competition for mobile resources, and government policy within this environment is increasingly cognizant of profound implications this combination of decentralization and mobility may have on political and economic outcomes. As these trends have become important, the academic literature across several disciplines in economics has paid increasing attention to the issues that arise from these trends. This chapter summarizes the progress that has been made in this literature – in both theoretical and empirical dimensions – while simultaneously pointing out some open questions for future research. Several important themes emerge: First, while simple versions of more general models have clarified many analytic issues, policy trade-offs are ultimately made in complicated settings rich with institutional detail. Thus, the search for a greater connection between theoretical models and data has taken on particular importance. Complex general equilibrium models of fiscal decentralization ultimately become most useful when underlying parameters within such models are determined by the data. Both calibration and structural estimation techniques are advancing this portion of the literature. Second, the last decade has seen an increasing emphasis on political forces in debates over fiscal decentralization. Not only does such decentralization carry with it potential economic benefits and costs, but political decisions are likely to be fundamentally different in a decentralized environment. Important further work on political institutions under fiscal decentralization is needed. Finally, as decentralization has been studied in multiple contexts, it has become increasingly clear that the micro-foundations of local goods and services need further theoretical and empirical investigations. Many such goods (such as crime prevention and schooling) depend on peer and neighborhood effects, and predictions can change fundamentally as such effects are introduced.

Keywords

fiscal federalism, decentralization, inter-jurisdictional competition, local governments

JEL classification: H1, H7, R1, R3, R5

1. Introduction

Both within the U.S. and in most countries around the world, fiscal decentralization seems on the rise both in the political rhetoric and in actual policy outcomes. At the same time, barriers to factor and population mobility around the world are declining. Greater decentralized government activity is therefore taking place in an economic environment characterized by increased competition for mobile resources, and government policy within this environment is increasingly cognizant of profound implications this combination of decentralization and mobility may have on political and economic outcomes. As these trends have become important over the past several decades, it is furthermore not surprising that the academic literature across several disciplines in economics has paid increasing attention to the issues that arise in this more mobile and decentralized world. This chapter attempts to summarize the progress that has been made in this literature over the past decade while simultaneously pointing out some open questions for future research.

We begin in Section 2 by providing some brief overview of stylized facts regarding fiscal decentralization around the world. Section 3 then proceeds with a discussion of the theoretical literature on fiscal decentralization and horizontal government competition.[1] The section begins with an analysis of the literature that aims to establish conditions under which Tiebout's analogy between market competition and government competition holds. The section then proceeds to a comparison of two extreme models of local government behavior – the Pigouvian welfare maximizing versus the Leviathan rent maximizing model. Neither is based on modern political economy models, but both provide insights into potential political and economic distortions that may be important under fiscal decentralization. Recent advances in the literature have, however, been focused on the more explicit modeling of political forces as well as the development of more applied and computational approaches. A discussion of these rounds out Section 3. Section 4 then considers the theoretical literature that is focused on the addition of a hierarchical dimension to decentralized government competition. Two issues are addressed: First, when considering the discrete choice of centralization versus decentralization, what are the primary forces that the recent literature has explored; and second, how do these same forces help us to evaluate the kinds and levels of hierarchical fiscal interactions. Section 5 then turns to a discussion of the empirical work on the types of theoretical issues raised in the previous two sections. This includes early work as well as innovative recent work on capitalization of fiscal variables into housing and land prices, studies of fiscal competition and efficiency, evaluations of the role of political institutions and the emergence of a promising line of empirically estimated structural models. Section 6 provides some concluding comments.

[1] By "horizontal government competition" we mean competition between governments that are not hierarchically ordered – i.e., competition between local governments or between state governments, but not competition between local and state governments. We do not use the term horizontal in the industrial organization sense of horizontally versus vertically differentiated products.

2. Increasing fiscal decentralization around the World

While fiscal and political decentralization has undoubtedly been a clear trend around the world over the past 25 years, it is not immediate how to best quantify this trend. Crude measures include official government structures (unitary versus federal) that rarely change over time and often do not give an accurate picture of actual government practices, while more continuous measures (such as the percentage of government expenditures at different government levels) may mask underlying subtleties such as the degree of control exercised by the levels of government that are officially recorded as engaging in economic activity. Nevertheless, some recent attempts to quantify worldwide trends on fiscal decentralization provide interesting insights.

Arzaghi and Henderson (2002) provide a nice synthesis of the available evidence. For a sample of 48 countries with populations in excess of 10 million in 1990, they construct a federalism index from 1960 to 1995, and they complement their analysis with a measure of the central government share in total government current consumption. Some clear trends emerge from these data. First, developed countries are generally more decentralized as measured by both the federalism index and the central government share of total government consumption. Latin American countries decentralized substantially over the period from 1980 to 1995, with the federalism index showing this block of countries as decentralized by the end of that period as the group of developed countries. Government consumption in Latin America, however, remains substantially more centralized, with developed countries spending just over 45% centrally while Latin American countries spend closer to 70% at the central level. Middle East and North African countries are by far the most centralized (with close to all government spending occurring centrally), and these countries show the least sign of decentralizing over the past several decades. All other regions exhibit substantial decreases in centralization as measured through the federalism index and at least modest decreases in centralization as measured through government spending concentration.

A more systematic analysis by Arzaghi and Henderson reveals that several economic and demographic factors seem to have large and significant impacts on the degree of centralization. In particular, per capita income, population size, and land area within a country are associated with greater decentralization, while the percent of the population that is Muslim and the degree of population centralization in the largest city in a country are associated with greater centralization. These results mirror previous cross section results by Panizza (1999) who also documents that fiscal centralization declines with greater democratization and greater ethnic fragmentation.

The general trend toward greater federalism and greater fiscal decentralization thus seems widespread and increasing. In light of this, a deeper understanding of the connection between federalism on the one hand and economic and political performance on the other is therefore in order. The remainder of this chapter attempts to provide a snap shot of where the growing academic literature on these issues stands.

3. Theoretical literature on fiscal decentralization

Much of the literature on horizontal government competition finds its origin in Tiebout's (1956) seminal article of almost five decades ago. Tiebout's provocative thesis draws an analogy between competitive markets for private goods on the one hand and competitive governments that provide mixes of local services at different tax rates on the other. Shopping plazas and malls, for instance, cater to different clienteles by providing different mixes of stores, products, restaurants, mall security, ambiance and prices, and competitive markets are largely thought to provide such services efficiently (subject to some caveats). Political jurisdictions, the Tiebout argument suggests, are similar in that they also provide different types of services (schools, police services, fire protection, street lighting, etc.), and residents gain access to these services by paying for them through taxes (and possibly through property values that may capitalize these taxes and services). Under certain loosely specified conditions, Tiebout therefore suggested that such horizontal government competition may lead to efficiency in the local public sector – with mobility of households providing the disciplining market force.

The large literature that has arisen from Tiebout's article attempts to come to terms with

(1) whether and under what precise conditions the market analogy holds, and
(2) ways of modeling in more realistic and policy relevant ways the basic Tiebout notion of household and factor mobility as an important force in local government competition.

We proceed in this section as follows: In Section 3.1, we discuss the lessons emerging from attempts to formalize Tiebout's intuition in a general equilibrium setting. Particular attention is given in this section to the success of researchers in generalizing existence and welfare theorems in relatively abstract general equilibrium models that include clubs and local jurisdictions. Sections 3.2 and 3.3 then turn to more tractable models of local government competition in which specific objective functions are assumed for local governments. In particular, Section 3.2 uses the conceptual simplification of Pigouvian local governments of homogeneous households to illustrate the kinds of externalities that may cause decentralized competition to lead to sub-optimal outcomes. Section 3.3, on the other hand, turns to the opposite extreme by assuming Leviathan local governments. Neither of these approaches comes to terms with the underlying political forces that may be relevant in an analysis of decentralized competition since both approaches exogenously specify a local objective function. Section 3.4 therefore considers recent advances in modeling politics more explicitly within a decentralized government model. Section 3.5 then considers the role of computational models that introduce greater complexities while relying on data to restrict the relevant structural parameter space.

3.1. From clubs to local public goods: *horizontal competition under local profit maximizing behavior*

General equilibrium analysis of competitive markets is built on an assumption of profit maximizing behavior by firms that are small relative to the economy and can freely enter and exit. How one can extend the assumption of profit maximization and free entry by firms to an analogous assumption on decentralized governments is not immediate. Two possible ways of modeling decentralized governments as profit maximizers with potentially free entry have emerged:

(1) Models of governments as profit maximizing clubs that provide excludable public goods or services and restrict entry through prices (and possibly through more explicit exclusionary rules).

(2) Models of governments as competing land developers that provide public goods in an attempt to maximize the value of land, or alternatively, models of governments as controlled by homeowners who seek to maximize the value of their homes.

In each of these literatures, attempts are made to answer the standard general equilibrium questions related to the existence and welfare properties of equilibria. As such, they represent the purest attempts at generalizing Tiebout's intuition by identifying conditions under which the intuition holds. No claim is made in these literatures that the models are "realistic" in the sense of being immediately applicable to applied policy analysis. Rather, the aim is to understand the potential role and the limits of horizontal government competition as a disciplining market force – much as the attempt in the Arrow–Debreu general equilibrium tradition is to arrive at an understanding of both the benefits and the limits of market competition. And, as in the Arrow–Debreu framework, the actual mechanics of the market are left relatively unspecified. However, in the case of club/developer competition, assumptions such as completeness of markets are significantly more severe than in the standard Arrow–Debreu framework – and thus leave the formalized market analogy in this section open to criticism.

3.1.1. Club competition

Among the attempts to rigorously move from a standard general equilibrium framework to one that formalizes Tiebout's intuition, *club* models come closest to models of purely private good economies and thus are the farthest removed from a model of truly competing local *jurisdictions*. They deal with neither the spatial aspects of a local economy nor the important presence of land as a crowding factor nor the political forces present within local jurisdictions. Still, club theory moves the analytical framework in the direction of incorporating commonly consumed goods within clubs, introduces notions of spillovers and crowding and specifies how markets might allocate costs of commonly consumed goods while internalizing externalities associated with club memberships – all issues relevant to horizontal government competition. The literature, which finds its origins in Buchanan's (1965) original treatment of clubs, is too large to be fully explored here, which leads us to touch only on the most recent contributions as they relate to our broader aim of discussing fiscal decentralization. A fuller treatment of clubs is provided in other handbooks [most recently by Scotchmer (2002) and Wooders (1999)].

Club goods are public goods in the sense that they can be simultaneously consumed by multiple agents, but they differ from pure public goods because of crowding in either production or consumption. Crowding in production occurs if the size or composition of the club membership affects the cost of providing the club good, while crowding in consumption arises from club size or composition entering directly into utility functions. Crowding can be *anonymous* if only the total club membership size enters the production or utility functions, or it can be *non-anonymous* if the composition of the club membership or the characteristics of club members enter independently. The good that is priced in general equilibrium club models, however, is not usually the club good itself but rather *membership* in the club.

It is in these kinds of models that Tiebout's notion has indeed survived many important tests in the sense that profit maximizing behavior by clubs leads to a first welfare theorem – equilibria, when they exist, are efficient. Existence itself, however, is not easy to establish primarily because of what has come to be known as an "integer problem": Unless the number of agents of each type is "just right" to fill up optimally sized clubs without unassigned agents being left behind, no equilibrium exists. The problem has been overcome most elegantly by Ellickson et al. (1999) who treat clubs as "small" (i.e., infinitesimal) in an economy with a continuum of agents.[2] At the same time, an important underlying assumption of this approach is that markets are "complete". While similar to assumptions required in standard Arrow–Debreu models, this assumption can seem particularly severe in the context of club models as it requires a complete set of prices for clubs of all possible populations – not just of clubs that exist in equilibrium.

Nevertheless, the model is general in the sense that agents can belong to multiple clubs, crowding can be non-anonymous, and multiple private goods are traded both within and outside of clubs. Not only is existence of an equilibrium and a first welfare theorem established, but it is further shown that the core coincides with the set of competitive equilibrium allocations.[3] The model in many ways generalizes previous results in both the club and the standard general equilibrium literatures. In a variety of other contexts, similar results on the efficiency of decentralized club economies have emerged in the past two decades. The main lesson from these models seems to be that – so long as clubs are relatively small in a competitive economy, the set of equilibria is non-empty and coincides with the core (thus also implying that all competitive equilibria are efficient).[4]

2 An alternative way of overcoming the integer problem is to define the notion of an ε-equilibrium in which there is an ε-cost to setting up new clubs. This is explored in a long literature by Myrna Wooders and John Conley [see, for example, Conley and Wooders (2001)].

3 Previous equivalence results of price taking equilibria and the core can be found in Wooders (1980) and related work.

4 Among the many applications of this intuition, one of the most relevant to policy debates has been the treatment of peer externalities in schools. Rothschild and White (1995), Epple and Romano (1998) and Caucutt (2001) demonstrate that, in line with results from the club literature, private schools can internalize these externalities through differential tuition prices. Just as in the club literature, membership in private schools is the good that is priced, and mixed private schools emerge. [Nechyba (1999), on the other hand, models privates schools as exclusionary clubs that are prohibited from differential pricing which then leads to homogenous private schools.]

Tiebout's intuition has therefore been formalized in general equilibrium models of profit maximizing *club* competition, but it is not immediately evident how much relevance these results hold for questions related to horizontal *government* competition. While crowding in production and consumption are fully introduced into club models, crowding that arises from the scarcity of land is not – and it is the link of local governments to land and housing markets that seems in many ways central to horizontal government competition. Formally, as suggested by Scotchmer (forthcoming), it is possible to interpret the Ellickson et al. (1999) club model as a local government model by interpreting one of the private goods in the model as homogeneous land. But this treats land as fully transferable between jurisdictions, implies no role for capitalization (because land, like other private goods, would command a single price regardless of where it is consumed) and loses much of what makes land unique in local public finance models. If the first step from standard general equilibrium models to Tiebout's conjecture is the introduction of clubs and club goods, the next step is then the introduction of a true model of land.

3.1.2. Introducing land, capitalization and profit maximizing land developers

Land is a peculiar type of good that is in many ways difficult to model [Berliant (1985)]. While it can be introduced in a trivial manner into club good economies (as suggested above), club models do not really become models of jurisdictions (and club goods do not really represent local public goods) unless the essential features of land are captured more fully.[5] Nevertheless, we can already see in the trivial model of land within club economies the basic reasons why a general efficiency result of the type common in club models is difficult to obtain once land is introduced. Within club models [such as that of Ellickson et al.], the efficiency result holds for trivial models of land *because land, just like bread, is transferable between clubs*. Thus, "jurisdiction boundaries" are fully endogenous and change with market conditions, and capitalization of local club goods plays no more a role in "land" markets than it does in the market for bread. This outcome of no land market capitalization turns out to be key to any full efficiency result in a local public goods economy, and any model of horizontal government competition that gives rise to equilibrium inter-jurisdictional capitalization is one in which equilibria are *not* fully efficient.

This result shows up in many different and sometimes unconnected parts of the local public finance literature. For example, in response to Oates' (1969) seminal empirical paper demonstrating large capitalization of local tax and public spending levels, Edel and Sclar (1974) pointed out that the finding of capitalization – far from being evidence of Tiebout's efficiency hypotheses, was in fact evidence against Tiebout's hypothesis. More precisely, the presence of capitalization is evidence that there is an excess demand for the type of jurisdiction in which local public choices are being capitalized, which

5 Hochman, Pines and Thisse (1995) emphasize this point in their discussion of overlapping local jurisdictions.

then implies that there is room for new jurisdictions to enter the market (thus driving down the capitalization in existing jurisdictions). In a full Tiebout equilibrium (with free entry and exit of jurisdictions), there should in fact be no capitalization of local fiscal conditions into land values (just as is the case in club models when land is introduced in a trivial way). While the presence of capitalization of local public finance variables into land values is therefore evidence in favor of Tiebout's notion of consumers "voting with their feet" by choosing jurisdictions in part based on local public finance factors, it is also evidence against Tiebout's conclusion that this consumer mobility provides a sufficiently strong disciplining force to yield a fully efficient outcome.[6]

Once clubs are tied to land (and thus become jurisdictions), the only way that the full efficiency result established in club models can then be preserved is if land is allowed to play a role similar to the role it plays when it is introduced to club models in the "trivial" manner described in the previous section. Theoretically, this can be accomplished by allowing jurisdiction boundaries to be perfectly elastic to accommodate increases or decreases in demand for a particular "jurisdiction", by permitting land within jurisdictions to be perfectly elastically supplied, or by assuming that the supply of new jurisdictions is perfectly elastic.[7] In practice, of course, none of these assumptions seem plausible in the sense of being realistic, which implies that Tiebout's full efficiency hypothesis is unlikely to hold for horizontal jurisdiction competition.

Nevertheless, the introduction of land into club models does not necessarily imply that a more constrained efficiency result cannot be obtained for models of decentralized competition among jurisdictions. One possibility that has been explored repeatedly is to model local jurisdictions as "land value maximizers" [Brueckner (1983)] for some exogenously given partition of land into competing jurisdictions. This assumption may be interpreted literally as competition among profit maximizing land developers who choose the level of local public goods knowing that such goods will in fact be capitalized into land values, or it may be interpreted more loosely as a political economy model in which homeowners cause local governments to maximize property values

6 It is important to note that "capitalization" here refers to *inter*-jurisdictional capitalization of public goods and services that are uniformly available within jurisdictions into all land values within a jurisdiction. There are at least two other types of *intra*-jurisdictional capitalization that are *not* inconsistent with Tiebout efficiency. First, to the extent that public goods or services are not uniformly accessible from all locations within a jurisdiction, capitalization within (rather than across) the jurisdiction would emerge. Examples include physically fixed public goods like parks or schools within a jurisdiction, or non-uniformity of goods such as air quality. Second, Hamilton (1976) demonstrates that financing of local public goods may be such that intra-jurisdictional capitalization emerges. For instance, if local public goods are financed through a property tax and housing quality varies within the jurisdiction, higher-quality houses are subject to negative capitalization of the expected above average property tax burden while lower-quality houses are subject to positive capitalization of the expected below average property tax burden. Hamilton demonstrates that such capitalization can be consistent with Tiebout efficiency.

7 This point is made in various ways by Epple, Zelenitz and Visscher (1978), Epple and Zelenitz (1981), Yinger (1982), Henderson (1985) and Epple and Romer (1989). The extent to which some of the assumptions – such as elastic community boundaries – are empirically realistic is debated across these papers.

(much as corporations may in fact maximize shareholder wealth [Fischel (2001)]). Unless the division of land into jurisdictions is optimal to begin with, Scotchmer (1994) then demonstrates that the competitive equilibrium under such maximizing local government behavior is *constrained* efficient (where the constraint is the way in which land is partitioned to begin with). The absence of inter-jurisdictional capitalization of local public finances into land values would be an "accident" in such a model – and would occur only if the number of jurisdictions were optimal and if jurisdiction boundaries happened to be optimally drawn given the particular primitives of the model. Any presence of inter-jurisdictional capitalization in the model would be evidence that efficiency gains could be achieved through either a redrawing of jurisdiction boundaries (i.e., a transfer of land) or an increase in the number of jurisdictions (i.e., free entry).[8] Tiebout's efficiency hypothesis – motivated by the introduction of market-like forces through consumer mobility – continues to apply when club models become models of jurisdiction competition through the introduction of land. But, the strength of the efficiency result is constrained by the process of jurisdiction formation[9] and, of course, by the degree to which competitive behavior is plausible.[10]

3.2. Government competition under local Pigouvian welfare maximization: *the role of inter-jurisdictional and intra-jurisdictional spillovers*

As we now turn away from more general attempts to formalize Tiebout's intuition and toward more specialized models, it is useful to begin with those models that abstract

[8] In addition, the integer problem dealt with in the previous section on landless clubs poses similar existence difficulties.

[9] An interesting application of the intuition emerging from these theoretical findings applies to models of local property taxation in the presence of residential zoning. Zoning can be viewed as a means of turning a property tax levied on both land and improvements of land (i.e., housing) into a tax on just land. In Hamilton (1975), jurisdictions are free to enter and exit as they provide public goods through a property tax while at the same time setting a minimum house quality level for the jurisdiction through zoning. In equilibrium, this results in house quality within jurisdictions being homogeneous which then implies that the property tax simply becomes a head tax. The tax is efficient; no capitalization emerges because of free entry of jurisdictions; and the overall outcome is efficient as households choose jurisdictions based on their willingness to pay for local public goods. In the absence of free entry of jurisdictions [Hamilton (1976)], on the other hand, and in the presence of zoning that leads to heterogenous but fixed housing quality within jurisdictions, the combination of property tax payments and capitalization within the jurisdiction leads to a similar head tax result and thus the conclusion that the property tax is once again an efficient tax. However, because of the inelasticities in land markets that arise in this alternate model, the overall equilibrium is not efficient unless the partition of houses into jurisdictions (as well as the number of jurisdictions) happens to be optimal.

[10] In the absence of competitive behavior, there is of course no particular reason to expect the efficiency result to survive. A recent literature on oligopolistic land developer models, however, provides important insights into the kinds of pricing policies that may emerge when perfect competition is relaxed. Henderson and Thisse (2001), for instance, present a model with endogenous formation of developments that provide public goods where pricing policies differ dramatically across developments. While developers of high-income areas charge higher entry fees and per unit housing prices, developers of low-income areas are predicted to subsidize housing in an attempt to keep some high-income residents. Issues that arise when community formation is analyzed in an imperfectly competitive environment fall outside the scope of our review, but readers are directed to Henderson and Thisse (2001) and references therein.

away from heterogeneity of households and from local political institutions. Since voter preferences do not conflict in this setting, a local social choice process is not faced with the task of aggregating preferences across voters and can thus simply be modeled as maximizing the utility of a representative resident. Thus, under the assumption of homogeneous households, we can assume a "Pigouvian" system of local governments – each seeking to maximize the local welfare of its population. This permits us to identify important economic forces that may arise under local government competition without being distracted by separate political considerations. These forces deal primarily with externalities of one type or another that may cause economic distortions. These distortions arise when local Pigouvian officials do not have access to a full set of policy instruments – which then leads to inter-jurisdictional spillovers, or when local expenditures inherently produce costs or benefits for other jurisdictions.[11] These cases are treated in Sections 3.2.1 and 3.2.2. At the same time, it is worth noting that much of this discussion rests on the assumption that local public goods can be modeled as an abstract g that enters utility functions identically for all residents within the jurisdiction providing g. In Section 3.23 we then turn to a brief discussion of the potential importance of considering the micro-foundations of g in particular settings. Finally, Section 3.2.4 explores inter-generational (rather than inter-jurisdictional) spillovers which have been largely ignored in much of the local public finance literature until recently.

3.2.1. Local tax spillovers

Efficiency of a local tax in models of this kind has two separate dimensions: First, in the presence of substitution effects, distortions may arise as market prices are changed through local tax policy in a manner that is standard in the public finance literature; and second, inter-jurisdictional externalities may arise as local tax policy creates spillover costs or benefits for other jurisdictions. Consider, for instance, a tax on capital. In a typical public finance framework with a closed economy, such a tax would give rise to inefficiencies by creating a wedge between the price of capital paid by firms and the price received by those who provide capital – causing various substitution behaviors within the economy. In the absence of other tax instruments, Pigouvian governments that are constrained to use capital taxes would weigh the efficiency costs of raising tax revenues against the benefits of providing public goods and services with such revenues – and would set the tax on capital such that the marginal cost from such a tax equals the marginal benefit. When capital taxes are set locally in an open economy setting, however, a second inefficiency arises despite the Pigouvian nature of the government. The

[11] Similar issues arise for regulatory rather than local fiscal policies, as, for example, in the case of growth controls [Helsley and Strange (1995), Brueckner (1990)]. In a relatively rich framework in which local Pigouvian governments provide goods, produce inputs that enhance local productivity of capital and employ environmental regulations that improve local amenities, Oates and Schwab (1988) illustrate that price taking (i.e., small) competing governments do behave efficiently in the absence of inter-jurisdictional spillovers of local regulations and expenditures. The topic is treated in a more game-theoretic context in Wildasin (1988).

welfare maximizing government would realize that capital will leave the jurisdiction as a result of an increase in the local tax on capital – and it would therefore count this as one of the costs of such a tax increase. However, if capital is not in perfectly elastic supply, capital flees to another jurisdiction, creating fiscal benefits elsewhere – resulting in a positive externality not taken into account by the local welfare maximizer. As a result, the local capital tax is underutilized.[12]

Note, however, that the latter effect does not arise if, with an increase in the tax on capital, the local government provides benefits per unit of capital equal to the increase in tax revenue per unit of local capital. For instance, a local tax on capital might be used to improve local infrastructure in such a way as to make each unit of capital within the jurisdiction more productive. Under such a scenario, the increased tax on capital would cause neither intra- nor inter-jurisdictional reallocation of capital. Thus, when benefits are directly attached to local taxes, they simply become user fees for local services. It is only when taxes on capital are used to provide services for other purposes (such as, say, public schools) that the inter-jurisdictional distortion arises – leading to underutilization of the tax. Local tax competition (resulting from local taxation of mobile factors) thus arises from inter-jurisdictional fiscal spillovers when such taxes cease to be "benefit taxes".

While, under some conditions, certain taxes like the local property tax may indeed take on the character of a benefit tax,[13] this is generally not the case. For instance, in a model of homogeneous households who each enjoy equal public goods benefits within a jurisdiction (from, say, a local school), the portion of the property tax that is levied on housing will typically generate intra- and inter-jurisdictional distortions even though the tax burden within each jurisdiction is equally disbursed.[14] While each household indeed pays taxes in proportion to the benefits they receive, marginal benefits of the local public good are not tied to marginal consumption decisions regarding housing – i.e., access to the local public school is the same regardless of how much housing a household consumes, or put still differently, marginal investments in housing capital are not made

[12] Similar issues of course arise for any tax on a base that is mobile. They also arise if the locally taxed activity is itself generating inter-jurisdictional spillovers; for instance, if a local Pigouvian government raises revenues by taxing industries that generate cross-border pollution, it will not take into account the positive inter-jurisdictional externality associated with marginal increases in local taxes.

[13] The most well-known case of this type is explored in Hamilton (1975, 1976) where local zoning combined with the property tax is shown to result in an efficient benefit tax.

[14] The portion of the property tax that falls on land rather than improvements of land (such as housing) is the traditional public finance answer for a fully efficient tax since it acts as a lump sum tax on owners of land. A well-known theorem – known as the Henry George Theorem – has developed to suggest that, in a first-best world with no distortions and with non-rival (within the jurisdiction) local public goods, 100% taxation of land rents yields the optimal level of local public goods. With rivalry, additional user fees or head taxes are required [Stiglitz (1977), Arnott (1979), Arnott and Stiglitz (1979)]. Furthermore, when multiple local public goods are provided across overlapping geographic areas, a regional government must assign property rights to particular local jurisdictions for the result to hold [Hochman, Pines and Thisse (1995)], and if non-residents own land the problem of tax exporting (mentioned in the next paragraph) may arise. For illustrative simulations regarding the potential for land taxes to raise local welfare, see Nechyba (2001).

more productive by increases in local school quality. Thus, to the extent that the property tax is a tax on (housing) capital, households will economize on capital which would then flow into other uses and other jurisdictions.[15] Both forms of inefficiency are present because the tax is not truly a "benefit tax" that acts as a user fee.[16]

While tax competition in models of competing governments with homogeneous households thus typically leads to inefficiently low taxation due to positive fiscal externalities that are not taken into account by local Pigouvian governments, there are also instances when the inter-jurisdictional fiscal externalities are negative leading to overuse of local taxes.[17] Examples include the collection of sales taxes from tourists from outside the jurisdiction,[18] or the taxation of a locally fixed industry that exports (and thus passes on a portion of its tax burden to non-residents).[19] In such cases, the local Pigouvian welfare maximizer would overutilize the particular tax to the extent to which she does not take into account the negative fiscal externality imposed on non-residents. The ability to export taxes through such methods is, however, limited by the mobility of tax bases. Excessive local sales taxes may divert consumption to other jurisdictions and locally taxed industries may move – both leading to the more traditional tax competition and thus under-utilization of the tax (as discussed above). Thus, for decentralized governments to successfully raise revenue from non-residents, they must have some form of "market power" – whether in the form of a fixed factor (that makes it difficult for an industry to move) used in the production of exported goods or in the form of locally concentrated industries with market power (e.g., Disney World in Orlando which makes possible taxation of tourists).[20]

[15] Note that this leads to a very different view of the property tax than does the model of Hamilton discussed in a previous footnote – and this difference gives rise to the well-known debate over whether the residential property tax is an efficient benefit tax or at least in part an inefficient tax on mobile capital [Mieszkowski and Zodrow (1989), Fischel (1992)]. The topic is similarly treated in Wilson (1986), Wildasin (1988, 1989).

[16] An extensive literature that focuses on the details of tax competition externalities has emerged. Mieszkowski and Zodrow (1986) focus on an analysis of the property tax as a tax on local capital in a competitive general equilibrium world, while others model tax competition in more strategic settings [Wildasin (1988, 1991), Hoyt (1991a)]. While these papers typically assume local governments face a very constrained set of tax instruments, a number of papers have also investigated the endogenous choice of local tax instruments [Bucovetsky and Wilson (1991), Hoyt (1991b), Krelove (1993), Henderson (1994, 1995), Wilson (1995, 1997), Nechyba (1997a)].

[17] In fact, Myers (1990), Krelove (1992), Wellisch (1996) investigate explicitly the potential for a decentralized solution to mobility-induced tax competition externalities through the setting of local taxes that induce tax exporting.

[18] For a recent synthesis of theoretical findings regarding commodity tax competition, see Lockwood (2001).

[19] Wellisch (2000) generalizes these into two categories: (1) source-based taxation of local rents that are partly owned by non-residents, and (2) origin-based consumption taxes that increase consumer prices paid by non-residents.

[20] Again, the inefficiency from local governments taking such "market power" into consideration when setting tax rates arises only to the extent that these taxes are not simultaneously accompanied on the margin by benefits for the taxed bases. For instance, local infrastructure investment may well benefit the owners of a fixed local resource, or taxation in the form of a sales tax of tourists in Orlando may well pay in part for public services valued by these tourists during their stay.

A final way to export local taxes involves the use of taxes that are deductible from tax obligations toward a higher level of government (such as, in the U.S., local property taxes on federal income tax forms). Such taxes are explicitly passed on in part to non-residents of the local jurisdiction which then provides direct incentives for greater local use of such tax bases by local Pigouvian welfare maximizers.

3.2.2. Local expenditure spillovers

The basic results relating to the over- or under-use of particular taxes under decentralized government competition then relate directly to whether – in a model of local welfare maximization and homogeneous households – one would expect over- or under-provision of public goods. Clearly, if a single local tax instruments on a mobile tax base is considered (and in the absence of a mechanism for this tax base to serve as a benefit tax), the fiscal externality under tax competition would lead to under-provision of local public goods [Mieszkowski and Zodrow (1986, 1989), Wilson (1986)].[21] Similarly, tax exporting – to the extent that it results in an inefficiently high use of a tax used to finance local public goods, would lead to over-provision of those goods in a local welfare maximizing framework. In addition, inter-jurisdictional spillovers of local public goods may lead to inefficiently low spending within decentralized jurisdictions for similar and well-understood reasons. If local public goods have positive spillovers (such as local road infrastructure or certain forms of environmental protection, for instance), Pigouvian local welfare maximizers will not take the benefits that are external to their jurisdiction into account when setting local public good spending levels.[22]

3.2.3. Spillovers and the micro-foundations of local public goods

While much of the literature on horizontal government competition treats local public goods as uniformly consumed by all residents of a community without the possibility of private substitutes, recent investigations of particular types of local public goods and services have begun to focus on additional spillover and externality effects that emerge when the micro-foundations of local public goods are modeled more carefully. This is likely to be a fruitful avenue for future research. Two particular strains of this emerging literature relate to the modeling of the local provision of public safety and public education. While this literature is not always framed in the Pigouvian government

[21] At the same time, it can be shown that competition among decentralized governments may also lead to greater public spending in order to attract the mobile resource if such spending raises the productivity of the mobile resource [Wilson (2000)].

[22] A related issue emerges when local governments set regulations for industries with increasing returns to scale (who may respond by "exporting" the regulatory standard to other jurisdictions) [Besharov and Zweiman (2002)].

context explored in this section, the externalities and spillovers it points to would very much be present within a Pigouvian model.

In the case of crime, for instance, Helsley and Strange (1999) explore the recent phenomenon of privately gated communities within local jurisdictions. Such communities also compete horizontally, but whether their gating expenditures are strategic complements or substitutes depends on the underlying model of crime. Furthermore, gating in one community may have externalities on others to the extent that it diverts crime to other areas.[23] Such externalities are studied in models of jurisdictional competition by Bearse (2001), Marceau (1997), and Newlon (2001). In the case of schooling, a number of micro-models [Epple and Romano (1998), Nechyba (1999), Caucutt (2001), McMillan (2001)] suggest important roles for peer effects and parental monitoring within schools. Such elements in the local public good production function can introduce important externalities within jurisdictions that are typically not modeled in the Pigouvian literature explored above.[24] In addition, private actions within the local public economy become important in these models of crime and schooling. In the case of crime, gated communities represent a kind of private government approach that either competes with or complements local public efforts to control crime. Here the nature of the private activity is again very much linked to residential location (in or outside the gated community). In the case of schooling, on the other hand, private substitutes provide a loosening of the tie between residential location and schooling. We will say more about this as it relates to schooling in the context of our discussion of applied computational models in Section 3.5. Finally, in most of our discussion of local public goods we have not considered transportation costs to places in which public goods and services can be consumed (such as public schools, parks, etc.). Examples of work that explores such issues includes Starrett (1988) and Hochman, Pines and Thisse (1995).

3.2.4. Capitalization and the internalizing spillovers across generations

Much of the literature on both the economic and political effects of decentralized government competition is focused around static models of local public goods and taxes in which local government budgets balance. Often, however, decentralized governments set policies that directly affect future generations, such as local debt policies, investments in local infrastructure or the creation of durable public amenities such as environmental quality. Some recent research has therefore focused on the question of whether horizontal government competition – through capitalization of long-run policies into land values – can effectively constrain fiscal exploitation of future generations.

The idea that local debt policies may have no impact on local wealth because of capitalization of future tax obligations into current land prices was first suggested by Oates

[23] Helsley and Strange (2000) also investigate strategic issues emerging from private governments.

[24] de Bartolome (1990) similarly stresses the role of peer externalities in local public goods economies.

(1969) and Daly (1969). Conley (2001) investigates this more formally by introducing an overlapping generations structure into a local public goods model in which current generations choose how much to invest in local durable public goods. Inter-generational spillovers are then capitalized into land values under local provision, and this induces current generations (who buy and sell land at different stages in their life cycle) to internalize such spillovers. (This is in sharp contrast to inter-jurisdictional spillovers which are not capitalized.) Conley and Rangel (2001) identify more specifically under what conditions similar internalization of inter-generational spillovers can be achieved without decentralized competition by simply tying public spending to land taxation.[25] While fiscal inter-generational spillovers (such as debt finance) could indeed be internalized simply through the use of land taxation, direct inter-generational spillovers (such as environmental degradation) require decentralized government competition in order for capitalization effects to cause current generations to internalize inter-generational externalities.[26]

3.3. Government competition under revenue maximizing governments: *local governments as Leviathan rent seekers*

While political forces have most often been incorporated into models of decentralized government competition through some form of majority rule voting (as discussed in the next section), Brennan and Buchanan (1980) suggest a very different approach to modeling such governments – an approach that is in some ways the polar opposite to the Pigouvian approach discussed in Section 3.2. In particular, Brennan and Buchanan view politicians as pure rent-seekers who provide public goods only to the extent that it enables them to gather more rents for themselves[27] – unlike citizen candidates (discussed in the next section) who care about local public goods and seek to implement their own preferences over public good and tax combinations. While tax competition as discussed for Pigouvian governments in Section 3.2 suggests local taxes will tend to be too low because of the presence of positive fiscal externalities, local taxes are predicted to be too high under Leviathan governments when local political establishments are insufficiently restrained by either political or inter-governmental competition. As a result, advocates of this "Leviathan" model of local government suggest that the more important effect of decentralized government competition is the disciplining force on local politicians that such competition introduces when tax bases are mobile, not the fiscal externalities that arise under a Pigouvian model.

[25] Earlier, Buiter (1989) and Bailey (1993) had suggested the Tiebout competition was in fact not necessary for the Oates–Daly result because of arbitrage behavior on the part of investors.

[26] Rangel (2002) focuses further on the constitutional choice of tax bases in an environment without decentralized competition – again demonstrating the importance of linking inter-generational spillovers to asset values through such instruments as land taxes. The possibility that capitalization may internalize inter-generational spillovers is independently explored in Wellisch (2000).

[27] Typically this assumption is equated to the assumption that all governments are revenue maximizers.

This intuition is treated formally by Epple and Zelenitz (1981) and links closely to the literature on club and jurisdiction competition discussed in Section 3.1. In order to focus solely on the question of whether inter-governmental competition can indeed fully restrain rent-seeking by local governments, the parsimonious model of Epple and Zelenitz assumes that all households are homogeneous and that local governments tax land/housing for the sole purpose of accruing rents. Local governments then find themselves in a game in which they set local tax rates knowing what other local governments are doing, with a symmetric equilibrium in which all tax rates are equal emerging as the outcome of the game. Even as the number of jurisdictions in the model goes to infinity (thus yielding "perfect" competition), rent-seeking politicians will levy positive tax rates so long as land/housing is not in some way perfectly elastically supplied. Rents go to zero only when the elasticity of supply of land/housing within a jurisdiction goes to infinity. Thus, the Brennan and Buchanan mechanism of restraining local government rents through decentralized competition can succeed fully only if the locally taxed good is fully mobile – either directly or through the possibility of community formation and shifting of community boundaries [Henderson (1985)].[28]

Note that neither the Pigouvian nor the Leviathan model contains any real underlying model of a local political process by which governments or government policies arise – in each case, local governments are simply in place, and a particular objective function is specified for them. Furthermore, Pigouvian and Leviathan governments represent merely extreme ends of a continuum of possible objective functions that place different weights on local social welfare and narrow government rents. This recognition has led to some recent attempts to merge the two models in order to investigate the consequences of decentralized government competition when local government institutions contain a mixture of Pigouvian and Leviathan sentiments [Rauscher (1998), Edwards and Keen (1996)]. Again, no particular political process is specified in such models, but local governments are simply assumed to exogenously care both about local social welfare and about narrow government rents. Results from such models regarding the desirability of government competition become predictably more murky, with fiscal externalities and political rent seeking pointing in opposite directions within the same model. Under certain conditions, tax competition may provide just the right amount of downward pressure on local tax rates that would otherwise be too high because of rent seeking by local governments.

A second approach to achieving a more balanced model that contains both Leviathan and Pigouvian elements is to introduce a political process under which voters provide an endogenous disciplining force on Leviathan politicians within political jurisdictions.

[28] While Epple and Zelenitz (1981) analyze the impact of changing the number of communities in their model, the model itself assumes a fixed number of communities. Henderson (1985) analyzes the same question in a framework where the number and sizes of communities are endogenous – i.e., where new communities can form and existing community boundaries can shift. These assumptions in essence bring back the perfect elasticity conditions under which inter-jurisdictional capitalization – and with it the possibility of political rents – is bid away under Tiebout competition.

This will be treated in the next section (specifically in Subsection 3.4.3) as we consider the merging of political competition ("voting with ballots") into models of decentralized government competition ("voting with feet").

3.4. Voting with feet and ballots: *adding politics to Tiebout*

In both the Pigouvian and the Leviathan model of local government, our discussion has thus far focused only on the impact of one type of competition: the horizontal competition between governments. This competitive force can give rise to fiscal externalities (Pigouvian model) or act as a disciplining force on rent seeking politicians (Leviathan model). While this is clearly the distinguishing characteristic of attempts to study decentralized rather than centralized governments, a second and potentially equally important disciplining force arises from the internal political competition that shapes local governments. We therefore turn in this section to the progress that has been made in recent years as researchers introduce politics into the competitive Tiebout framework. In most cases, this involves the introduction of some form of voting by residents within political jurisdictions. Voting can take place directly over policy alternative (Section 3.4.1) or indirectly through representatives (Section 3.4.2). While voting can serve as a disciplining force, it also has the potential to be a source of distortions. Particular issues may arise if voters have less information than politicians (Section 3.4.3), or if local political processes are influenced not merely by ballots but also by other local efforts such as lobbying (Section 3.4.4).

3.4.1. Single-dimensional policy decisions: median voter models

Perhaps the most commonly employed political model in studying local governments is the simple median voter model. Of course this model becomes meaningful only when some voter heterogeneity (and thus voter conflict) is introduced. (In the absence of such heterogeneity, voters would in fact unanimously agree to behave the same way as the local welfare maximizing government discussed in the previous section.) With voter heterogeneity, it is well known since at least Black (1948) that – when voting occurs over a single-dimensional issue space – a sufficient condition for a decisive median voter to emerge under majority rule voting is given by the assumption of single-peaked preferences. Single-peakedness thus guarantees a voting equilibrium. Equally well known are the existence problems that arise when policy spaces become multi-dimensional or when preferences over single-dimensional issue spaces are multi-peaked [Plott (1969), McKelvey (1976)]. Similarly, when private alternatives to the public good or service are available (such as, for example, private schools), voter preferences necessarily become multi-peaked [Stiglitz (1974)]. Furthermore, "partial equilibrium" single-peakedness may disappear when aggregate responses are taken into account by voters (such as when voting outcomes have implications for location choice in local public finance models).[29]

[29] Economic examples of this appear in Gans and Smart (1996).

These insights have thus placed natural limits on the extent to which median voter models can be usefully employed to study decentralized governments, but they have also resulted in important new insights on the existence of voting equilibria under more general conditions and in the development of new models that take these limitations into account.

A number of alternatives to the single-peakedness assumption have been advanced, each allowing for a wider set of circumstances under which majority rule voting results in a voting equilibrium, at least as long as the policy space remains single-dimensional. Roberts (1977) introduced a condition, termed hierarchical adherence, to study voting over income tax schedules. Drawing on Robert's result, Epple and Romer (1991) used single-crossing to characterize voting equilibrium within communities. An elegant unification is provided by Gans and Smart (1996) who define an ordinal notion of single-crossing preference profiles. With social alternatives denoted by x (ordered along a single dimension such as the unit interval), and with individuals denoted by i, the preference profile for a population satisfies single-crossing if and only if individuals can be ordered such that, for all $x < x'$, if x' is preferred by i to x, x' is also preferred to x by any $i' > i$.[30] This property can often arise quite naturally in voting models with single-dimensional issue spaces, although there exist examples in which the property cannot be invoked [Bearse, Glomm and Janeba (2001)].

A version of this condition has been used in one form or another in an important class of models that includes voters who are mobile between competing political jurisdictions. For instance, in an analysis of decentralized governments providing local redistribution, Epple and Romer (1991) analyze voter behavior in an environment where voters explicitly take into account the consequences of voting outcomes on location choices. In other models of local government competition (where voter foresight is less central to the question that is analyzed), other versions of single crossing conditions that imply greater voter myopia have also been used extensively.[31] In most of these approaches, the assumption of certain types of homogeneous preferences combined with heterogeneous income yields the natural ordering (i.e., by income) required for the preferences over the public good (or the local tax rate) to satisfy the required single crossing property.[32] A different class of multi-community models (discussed further in Section 3.4) continues to use single-peakedness rather than single crossing by assuming an even more severe form of voter myopia [Dunz (1985), Nechyba (1997b)].

[30] This single crossing condition can be defined in both weak and strong terms depending on whether the latter preference is required to be strict.

[31] Examples of such models include Westhoff (1977), Epple, Filimon and Romer (1993) and Fernandez and Rogerson (1996).

[32] However, as demonstrated in Epple, Filimon and Romer (1993), assumptions on preferences required for single crossing to hold and a multi-community equilibrium to exist can be quite severe when property taxes and housing are introduced into the model. This is discussed further below when we treat the introduction of housing into multi-community models.

Single crossing conditions have also been usefully employed to address voting equilibria in the presence of private alternatives to the local public service. Epple and Romano (1996) focus particularly on the case of education where it is natural to assume that a child is placed in either a public or a private school. Preferences over public school spending (or the tax rate funding public schools) then naturally have multiple peaks (with one peak at zero). In the context of a single community, Epple and Romano show that specialized conditions previously employed by others are in fact special cases of a broader single crossing condition, and they demonstrate the intuitive result that majority rule voting can lead to a coalition of the "ends against the middle" – with high-income private school attendees and low-income public school attendees both preferring lower taxes than middle-income public school attendees. A similar result arises in a multi-community context in Nechyba (1999) where voters are assumed to vote on public school spending conditional on their choice of where to send their child to school (thus recovering single peakedness).[33]

3.4.2. *Multi-dimensional policy decisions: structure induced equilibria and citizen candidates*

Attempts to overcome the restriction of a single dimensional issue space within a competing government setting have thus far been relatively limited. Ultimately, some additional structure needs to be imposed on the political process if voting behavior over multiple issues becomes important to the analysis. Nechyba (1997b) offers a model in which voting occurs over both local and federal levels of public good provision and uses a structure induced equilibrium concept [Shepsle (1979)]. The general approach in such structure-induced equilibria is to take multi-dimensional issue spaces and specify political structures (such as multiple levels of government or multiple single-issue committees within one government) that force voting to take place over a singe dimension at a time. A similar approach could in principle be applied to studying multiple locally provided public goods, each voted on in separate elections or referenda. This approach seems particularly applicable to situations where single-issue governments are the focus of analysis, but the imposition of the single-issue voting structure in the study of multi-dimensional decentralized political choices may be too severe in other cases. For this reason, alternatives to a median voter model are likely to play an important role in analyzing research questions that emphasize the multiple functions performed by competing decentralized governments.

One interesting structure that can be placed on majority rule voting processes focuses on voting over candidates – known as the "citizen candidates" [Osborne and Slivinski (1996), Besley and Coate (1997)] rather than direct voting over policy issues. It assumes that each citizen can choose to stand for office, and that elections occur over the set of declared candidates (whose preferences and policy making abilities may differ

[33] Hoyt and Lee (1998) use a similar assumption in a single-community model.

in a variety of ways). The winner of such elections then determines policy. Although the model is stark in assuming that a single elected representative ultimately makes all political choices, it does provide an elegant way out of the single-dimensional policy space to which median voter models are typically restricted and offers a promising tool for analyzing research questions for which a multi-dimensional issue space is critical. However, while the model has been applied to the political economy analyses of a number of topics in public economics, its application in studying competing decentralized governments remains relatively sparse.[34] This offers a potentially fruitful avenue for research.

3.4.3. *Voter information and agency problems: yardstick competition*

In all of the approaches to modeling decentralized governments discussed thus far we have implicitly assumed that voters have complete information about the political choices they face. One strand of the literature, however, has pointed out that it is likely that such information is in fact asymmetrically distributed between politicians and voters, with voters often finding it difficult to evaluate political performance. Besley and Case (1995a), using a model known as "yardstick competition" [Shleifer (1985)], have applied this intuition to the study of the behavior of competing governments. Yardstick competition models assume that, in the absence of full information, voters use outcomes in neighboring jurisdictions as information to evaluate the performance of their own local government. Just as in the case of a standard tax competition framework in which politicians take into account what happens in neighboring jurisdictions to avoid excessive outflows of local tax bases, politicians under yardstick competition also look toward their neighbors. Here, however, the concern is not over the mobility of tax bases but rather over the signal that local political choices which diverge from neighboring choices sends to voters when politicians are up for re-election. Two predictions emerge from this framework: First, if local taxes rise disproportionately (relative to neighboring districts), voters interpret this as a signal that local politicians are either ineffective or are engaged in excessive rent seeking. Second, local tax rates under yardstick competition mimic tax rates in neighboring jurisdictions.[35]

An interesting recent advance in this literature returns to the debate over the benefits of inter-governmental competition between those advocating a model of local governments as Pigouvian welfare maximizers and those that view local governments as Leviathan rent (or revenue) maximizers. Specifically, Besley and Smart (2002) consider an asymmetric information model of local politics in which voters do not know prior

[34] Besley and Coate (1999) represent one exception as they focus on issues related to fiscal federalism. Their analysis is discussed below in Section 4. Calabrese and Epple (2004) employ the citizen-candidate framework to study voting in localities over four variables: property taxes, income taxes, public good spending, and redistribution.

[35] Besley and Case (1995a) find empirical evidence for both these predictions, as do others [Revelli (2002)].

to a politician taking office whether that politician has Pigouvian or Leviathan inclinations. Rather than achieving a "mix" of Leviathan and Pigouvian models by varying the weights placed on social welfare and government rents *within an exogenous political establishment* (as in the models discussed in Section 3.3), this approach moves between the polar extremes by setting the fraction of politicians that are of one kind or another. Yardstick competition then allows voters to more easily identify local Leviathan politicians.[36]

3.4.4. *Incorporating preference intensities: lobbying through menu auctions*

When preference intensities beyond voting become of economic concern, the common-agency or "menu auction" model of Bernheim and Whinston (1986) has become "something of a workhorse model of lobbying" [Persson and Tabellini (2000)] in political economy approaches to public finance issues.[37] The model differs from traditional public finance models in that it does not assume an objective function for the government (whether Pigouvian, Leviathan or something in between), and it differs from traditional political economy models in that it specifies neither a simple voting rule on policy issues (such as the median voter rule) nor a democratic political institution (such as the citizen candidate or other structure induced political models of legislatures).[38] Rather, the model allows agents to make credible, decision-contingent promises of side payments (bribes) to a government decision maker who chooses public good and tax levels in order to maximize his own welfare. Equilibrium policy choices in an interesting subset of equilibria (those involving truth telling) are known to be efficient in this framework. Besharov (2002) introduces this framework into the local public finance literature by assuming homogenous jurisdictions with a representative government decision maker in each jurisdiction. Thus, the exogenously specified objective function of the Pigouvian or Leviathan local governments are replaced by endogenous policy choices arising from local decision makers who are influenced by side payments. The framework then permits an analysis of the role of influence costs in determining the optimal assignment of tax and spending authority to central and decentralized governments, and it permits an analysis of the desirability of constitutional constraints on central governments in the presence of influence costs.[39]

[36] However, this may cause the equilibrium to become a separating rather than a pooling equilibrium – making it less likely that Leviathan politicians mimic Pigouvian politicians when in office. In an environment where most politicians are Pigouvian, a Leviathan politician is more likely to be detected and will thus more likely choose to "get what he can" while in office. On the other hand, in an environment where most politicians are Leviathans, detection is less likely thus causing Leviathan incumbents to seek to remain in office. This leads to interesting and somewhat counterintuitive results.

[37] Grossman and Helpman (1994) first applied the model to political lobbying to study trade policy.

[38] Recent papers have, however, introduced the approach into standard political economy models; for example, Persson (1998) introduces the menu auction model into a legislative bargaining model, and Besley and Coate (2001) combine it with the citizen candidate model.

[39] Results from this analysis provide an endogenous justification for an often assumed uniformity constraint on the central government. See Section 4.1 for more details.

3.5. Toward computational models for policy analysis: *competing local governments with heterogeneous households*

A number of attempts have been made to move the theoretical literature explored thus far toward structural models that can be informed by data and used for general equilibrium policy simulations. The purpose behind these attempts has been to move the literature toward greater policy relevance by permitting more applied models that incorporate greater complexity. Given our emphasis on the importance of linking local government models to land and housing markets, we will restrict ourselves in this discussion to those computational models that explicitly include land and/or housing.[40] Sections 3.5.1 and 3.5.2 discuss two different approached to introducing housing into local public goods models and relate these to the underlying existence problems as well as the challenges of matching empirically observed house quality distributions. Sections 3.5.3 and 3.5.4 then illustrate the potential usefulness of computational models of this kind by providing a discussion of two applications of the models to policy issues (local redistribution and the decentralized provision of public schooling).

3.5.1. *Modeling land and housing*

Models that permit policy analysis through computer simulations and that explicitly introduce a housing/land market generally fall into two categories. One approach is to model housing as being supplied exogenously within each jurisdiction along an upward-sloping supply schedule, with rents typically accruing to absentee landlords and households choosing their most preferred level (given the supply schedule) at their location.[41] The second approach models housing as exogenously fixed in each jurisdiction, with each house/land combination owned by a household within the model. The nature of the housing good thus differs between these two approaches, as does the nature of ownership of houses and land.

Early attempts to include housing and land in models aimed at policy analysis were plagued by existence problems that explain why the literature developed as it has. Rose-Ackerman (1979) demonstrated that a model with a continuous housing good, local property taxation and voting generally suffers from the lack of general existence of stable equilibria. Non-convexities in budget sets arise when property taxation over a continuous housing good is used as the local policy tool under majority rule, and this technical difficulty can be overcome in one of three ways:

(i) through the use of a policy instrument other than property taxation (such as income or wealth taxation) [Konishi (1996)];

[40] As a result, we are foregoing a detailed discussion of important simulation literatures that consider government competition in the absence of land markets [as, for example, Fernandez and Rogerson (1999)].

[41] Some versions of this approach have extended the analysis to include homeowners [Epple and Romer (1991), Epple and Platt (1998)].

(ii) through the use of fairly specific functional form assumptions [Epple, Filimon and Romer (1993)];[42] or
(iii) through the introduction of discrete housing that is exogenously fixed [Dunz (1985), Nechyba (1997b)].[43]

Given the importance of property taxation in local government competition in the U.S., the assumption of income rather than property taxation may be problematic.[44] As a result, the literature has used the second and third way of resolving the existence problem depending on the types of policy questions that are analyzed.

Both approaches have advantages and disadvantages, and each leaves room for further technical advances to produce an overall more satisfying model. The first-approach models housing as a homogeneous good that can vary in quantity at each location as underlying economic conditions change. In some ways, one could argue that this incorporates a "long-run" view of housing, and models of this type can be useful in conducting policy simulations in which housing potentially increases *and decreases* at each location. At the same time, the model is somewhat artificial in a static context given that it implicitly assumes that housing at a given location can instantaneously be converted into private goods. The second approach – first introduced by Dunz (1985) and later refined by Nechyba (1997b) – on the other hand, treats housing quality at each location as exogenous and not malleable (but allows housing quality to vary across different locations within each jurisdiction). This prevents an artificial instantaneous conversion of housing to private goods but it also artificially restricts households from investing in housing at a particular location to increase size or quality. As such, it represents a more "short-run" view of housing, or alternatively a model of housing in which zoning regulations bind. Neither approach therefore accomplishes what in some sense would be ideal – a model of land and housing such that housing can be improved in the short run through investments while potentially declining in quality in the long run through depreciation (i.e., a lack of adequate investment to maintain quality). Such an approach would require a multi-period dynamic model that so far remains absent from the literature but ultimately is necessary to truly address some dynamic questions of adjustments to policy changes.

42 Epple, Filimon and Romer (1993) assume single crossing of indirect indifference curves in the house price/tax space. While examples of combinations of utility and production functions that satisfy this certainly exist and have been employed with great success in applied analysis, some common examples of functional forms do not satisfy this condition [Konishi (1996)].

43 This approach, while placing severe exogenous restrictions on housing at each location, does not require the introduction of specific functional form assumptions to achieve general existence of equilibria. Konishi (1996) and Nechyba (1997b) give a more detailed discussion of the existence problems under local property taxation.

44 While locally raised revenues in the U.S. are derived from a number of sources (with property taxes constituting approximately 35%), virtually all locally raised revenues for public schools in the U.S. come from property taxes. Since schooling is the most important locally provided service for which household mobility matters empirically, we focus on property taxation as the most relevant local tax to model in applied contexts. Local income taxes, on the other hand, are exceedingly rare.

3.5.2. *Avoiding "musical chairs" while replicating real world heterogeneity*

One of the important stylized features of housing markets in the U.S. is that, while jurisdictions can generally be ranked in terms of *average* housing quality levels, there is much overlap in the distribution of housing quality (and income) across local jurisdictions. This empirical reality is not easily replicated as an equilibrium outcome in policy models with free mobility, and this difficulty further highlights some of the existence problem inherent in multi-community models.[45] In particular, with local public goods funded through local (typically proportional) taxation, jurisdictions with high-income households face the threat of low-income households choosing to move into the jurisdiction and free riding on the contributions to the public good made by the wealthy. This can potentially lead to a non-existence result due to the "musical chairs" phenomenon of the poor "chasing" the rich who then relocate only to be chased again.[46] The solution to the existence problem lies in finding a way to allow rich districts to provide high levels of public goods without providing incentives that generate an excessive inflow of low-income free riders. Each of the two ways of modeling housing/land (discussed above in Section 3.5.1) provides a different means to overcome this existence problem while simultaneously employing data to generate the empirically observed levels of heterogeneity in housing quality and income within and across jurisdictions.

In Epple, Filimon and Romer's (1993) model of a continuous homogeneous housing good, preferences are structured in such a way as to cause the combination of housing prices and tax obligations in rich districts to be unattractive to low-income households despite the fact that rich districts provide higher levels of local public goods. If preferences are identical across households, this leads to an equilibrium in which households fully segregate based on income.[47] The "musical chairs" existence problem can thus be overcome in the continuous housing model by placing restrictions on preferences, but income heterogeneity alone does not allow the model to replicate the overlap in housing quality and income distributions across jurisdictions observed in the data. Thus, additional preference heterogeneity must be introduced such that preferences over housing varies sufficiently to produce two-dimensional stratification of household types – with some poor households who value housing relatively less being willing to consume

[45] In more abstract models, the introduction of non-anonymous crowding can generate this mixing of income types within clubs or jurisdictions and can be interpreted as a recognition of the fact that complementarities between different types may result in within-jurisdiction heterogeneity. For instance, with jurisdictions defined over large enough geographic regions, each jurisdiction is likely to require the presence of different professions (doctors, teachers, etc.).

[46] Kessler and Hansen (2001) demonstrate such a non-existence result in a model that does not have constraints imposed by a land market.

[47] Put differently, with households ordered from lowest to highest on the unit interval, jurisdictions would consist of continuous intervals of the unit interval.

a small amount of housing in rich districts in order to take advantage of the higher local public good.[48]

The Dunz/Nechyba framework of discrete and exogenously fixed housing, on the other hand, overcomes the "musical chairs" existence problem directly by fixing the housing stock in each jurisdiction and permitting capitalization to support an equilibrium. The exogenous housing stock can be interpreted as resulting from zoning or from an exogenous historical process.[49] Jurisdictions that have a relatively high housing quality will tend to produce higher levels of public goods (often with lower property tax rates), but low-income housing is exogenously limited within such jurisdictions – thus preventing an excessive inflow of low-income households seeking to free ride. No preference heterogeneity is thus required – equilibrium prices of low-quality houses in richer districts are sufficiently high relative to prices for similar houses in poorer districts to support the equilibrium presence of low-income households with identical preferences in jurisdictions that produce very different levels of public goods.[50] The process of matching the empirical distribution of house prices is also relatively straightforward and simply requires the appropriate setting of house quality distributions within each jurisdiction of the model.[51] The strong exogeneity of housing stocks also permits the introduction of various kinds of inter- and intra-jurisdictional spillovers.

3.5.3. Application 1: local redistribution

Conventional wisdom in the public finance literature has long held that redistribution is best conducted by national governments because of the constraints faced by decentralized jurisdictions subject to mobility of households. In fact, in a full Tiebout model in which jurisdictions can freely enter, local redistribution cannot emerge. However, realistic models of decentralized tax competition must incorporate the empirical reality that the number of jurisdictions is indeed limited, and this constraint makes it at least conceptually feasible that local governments could engage in limited amounts of income redistribution. It is difficult, however, to get a sense of how much such redistribution might in fact be possible when the number of local jurisdictions is limited. Epple and Romer (1991) therefore investigate this question in the context of a model with continuous housing supply with identical household preferences (but different incomes), while

48 Epple and Platt (1998) first introduce this two-dimensional stratification in a model of local income redistribution that extends Epple and Romer (1991). Later, Epple and Sieg (1999) and Epple, Romer and Sieg (2001) estimate models with two-dimensional stratification. These models are discussed in more detail in Section 6.

49 In the literature on zoning, residential exclusionary zoning has in fact been introduced as one method to stop free riders from living in communities that use proportional property taxes [Hamilton (1975)]. Fernandez and Rogerson (1997) treat zoning explicitly in a two-community model in which zoning regulations emerge endogenously.

50 If housing is relatively similar in all jurisdictions, multiple equilibria may arise in this model, but Nechyba (1997b) conjectures that this multiplicity disappears as the inter-jurisdictional variance in housing stocks increases.

51 A simple calibration method was first outlined in Nechyba (1997a) and extended in subsequent work.

Epple and Platt (1998) extend the analysis to include heterogeneous preferences (and thus incomplete stratification of income across jurisdictions). The models are calibrated to incorporate important features of U.S. data, and simulations are conducted under different assumptions of relative jurisdiction sizes and alternative assumptions regarding the fraction of homeowners as opposed to renters.

The computational method employed in these exercises then gives rise to some surprising results. First, in economies with predominantly renters, decentralized competition among local governments whose sole aim is to redistribute income under local majority rule can indeed provide substantial levels of redistribution. This feasible level of redistribution declines significantly, however, the more homeowners (as opposed to renters) participate in the political process. Homeowner preferences over levels of local redistribution differ because homeowners take into account the capital losses they will incur as local redistribution is capitalized into local house prices. While the direction of these results emerges in a purely theoretical context, the empirically relevant magnitudes emerge only under computable versions of the model as the model is matched to important features of the data. The results refine the conventional wisdom that local redistribution is severely limited: the more binding force seems to arise from internal political competition (as homeowners seek to protect their property values through local political institutions) – and not as much from economic competition between decentralized governments that bid away any residents in a race to the bottom. At the same time, important differences between models that set jurisdictions sizes differently emerge, with more local redistribution arising in larger jurisdictions.

3.5.4. *Application 2: decentralized provision of public and private schooling*

At least in the U.S., public schools are closely linked to local jurisdictions in the sense that admission to local public schools is based on the residential location of the household. Such residentially based admissions policies have long been recognized to create an important link between housing markets and the distribution of school quality across districts.[52] Housing markets in fact provide an important equilibrium force in that, when jurisdiction numbers are limited, they capitalize public school quality and local tax levels in such a way as to support an equilibrium in which large inter-jurisdictional quality differences within the public school system can be sustained as an equilibrium outcome under full mobility of households.[53] These quality differences can be the outcome of per pupil spending differences, non-pecuniary input quality differences (such as peer quality or parental involvement) or a combination of the two [Nechyba (1999)]. To the extent that this link between public schools and Tiebout forces is important, a full treatment of

[52] This link has repeatedly been demonstrated indirectly in capitalization studies from Oates (1969) through Black (1999) and in other empirical work discussed in Section 5.

[53] Such inter-jurisdictional variances in school quality can of course also emerge in models that do not include land but yield segregation of income due to restrictions on preferences [Fernandez and Rogerson (1999, 1998, 1997, 1996)].

school policy is difficult to divorce from the general equilibrium in which policies are likely to unfold.[54]

Peer effects as a component of school quality are introduced into a model of local jurisdictions by de Bartolome (1990). He studies the efficiency implications of decentralized finance in the presence of peer effects, emphasizing the trade-offs between efficiencies from varying expenditures across households and inefficiencies from stratification of peer groups. Benabou (1993, 1996) studies human capital accumulation in a general equilibrium framework in which education is locally provided and peer effects are present. Benabou demonstrates that decentralized provision of education may result in efficiency losses. This occurs if stratification of families by human capital across communities results in adverse effects on education in the low human capital community that are greater than the gains in the high human capital community. He also emphasizes that such stratification may persist despite equalization of expenditures. Durlauf (1996) studies the dynamics of income inequality when education depends on both expenditures and human capital of neighborhood residents. He establishes conditions under which stratification of families across neighborhoods can lead to persistent income inequality. In the above models, the efficiency and distributional implications of stratification depend on the way in which the benefits of peer effects vary across students with differing backgrounds. These models emphasize the importance of empirical work that might provide further evidence on the differential effects of peers on individuals.

The link between school policy, peer effects and Tiebout forces has been explored in a series of papers employing the Dunz/Nechyba model of discrete heterogeneous housing.[55] As in the case of local income redistribution (discussed in Section 3.5.3), the theoretical direction of introducing various components of the model are relatively clear, but empirically relevant magnitudes emerge only with computational analysis from calibrated (or estimated) models. In terms of insights into the nature of decentralized competition (as opposed to the introduction of multi-level government policies discussed in Section 4), the most striking result concerns the interaction of private and public schools in limiting segregation across different school districts. Versions of the model in which private school markets are not permitted result in rather extreme levels of income segregation as equilibrium housing values for the similar-quality houses are significantly higher in high-income districts. The bundling of public schools to residential locations therefore introduces a larger segregating force into the model. At the same time, when private school markets are introduced, public school quality is no longer as fully capitalized into housing prices because private schools offer alternative opportunities (divorced from residential location) to households seeking high-quality schools. Thus, private school markets introduce a desegregating force into a residentially based public school system. Most surprisingly, perhaps, income segregation is lowest when

[54] Some similar issues arise in the treatment of crime where "peer effects", spillovers and private alternatives (i.e., gated communities) are potentially important [Helsley and Strange (1999)] – as discussed in Section 3.2.3.

[55] These include Nechyba (2000, 2002, 2003a, 2003c, 2003d, in press).

public and private schools exist side-by-side. To the extent that housing remains bundled for households that choose public schools, house values continue to partially capitalize public school quality – thus providing incentives to relatively high-income households who tend to choose private schools to reside in jurisdictions with depressed housing values – i.e., poor jurisdictions with bad public schools. The capitalization of public schools into housing values – itself a segregating force – thus produces desegregation as it causes more high-income households to live in poorer districts than they would if local public choices did not distort housing prices.[56]

Epple and Romano (2003) study neighborhood schools and school choice in a model in which students differ by ability and households differ by income. Their model predicts that schools of differing quality will arise within a district (i.e., with uniform expenditure per student) that has a neighborhood school system, as well as across districts. Within districts, quality differences reflect variation in peer quality across neighborhoods and are sustained by differentials in housing prices across neighborhoods. Stratification arises due to a positive income elasticity of demand for education quality coupled with either a positive correlation of student capability and household income or with demand for educational quality rising with student capability. They also contrast outcomes in a neighborhood school system to those in a private school system with universal or flat-rate vouchers. The latter exhibits greater stratification by ability and less stratification by income than does a neighborhood public school system.[57]

4. Adding a hierarchical dimension to decentralized government competition

Many of the concerns regarding inefficient or inequitable distribution of resources that emerge from the theoretical investigation of horizontal competition motivate the interest in structuring hierarchical government interactions to improve on purely decentralized outcomes. With the theoretical literature on decentralized competition as a backdrop, we therefore now turn to the introduction of a hierarchical dimension to the models discussed thus far. Within a fuller model that includes a central government in addition to competing decentralized governments, questions regarding the appropriate level of centralization as well as the appropriate tools to be used by central governments emerge. Models that investigate such questions typically contain both centralizing and

[56] This has particular implications for the introduction of private school vouchers that unbundle the residential location and schooling choices of additional households who would otherwise choose public schools (disproportionately in better school districts) [Nechyba (1999, 2000, 2003c, 2003d), Ferreyra (2002a, 2002b)]. General equilibrium implications for central government policy toward local public schools are explored more in Section 4.

[57] Predictions of this theoretical framework are tested in Epple, Figlio and Romano (in press). Equilibrium in a system of private schools with flat-rate vouchers is studied in Epple and Romano (1998). Alternative voucher systems are analyzed in Epple and Romano (2002). And an overview of what has been and can be learned from computational approaches in education is given in Nechyba (2003b).

decentralizing forces that must be traded off against one another. In some contexts, the discrete choice between central and decentralized provision of public goods is investigated, while other models investigate the degree of optimal central government intervention into decentralized government choices. We treat the first set of questions regarding a discrete choice between centralization and decentralization in Section 4.1 and then turn to questions of fiscal interactions between central and decentralized governments in Section 4.2.

4.1. Central or local provision: *updating the "Decentralization Theorem"*

Oates (1972) framed the trade-off between centralization and decentralization as a trade-off between efficient internalization of inter-jurisdictional spillovers through centralization and efficient matching of local policies to local tastes through decentralization. Thus, fewer inter-jurisdictional spillovers[58] and greater variance in tastes should lead to greater decentralization, an insight that has come to be known as the "Decentralization Theorem" [Oates (1972)].[59] Note that this framing of the issue essentially takes a Pigouvian view of governments as maximizing welfare of its citizens, introduces Tiebout's notion of the local tailoring of public services to local tastes, and constrains the central government to providing a uniform level of public goods under centralized provision. While providing the primary starting point for analyzing federalism in economic models for several decades, the framework does not, however, incorporate the insights from much of the literature on decentralized government competition discussed thus far, and it imposes an artificial uniformity constraint on central government tax and spending policies in order to generate the trade-off that underlies the Decentralization Theorem.

The modern literature on decentralized government competition casts new light on the decentralization debate in several ways: First, the introduction of politics eliminates the need for the exogenous uniformity constraint (or alternatively provides an endogenous rationale for it) (Section 4.1.1); in fact, political forces may indeed be central to the

[58] In our discussion of Pigouvian local welfare maximizers in Section 3.2, we identified a number of such spillovers (on both the tax and spending sides) that may arise from decentralized government competition. These include the under-use of mobile tax bases under tax competition, the over-use (through tax exporting) of certain types of tax bases that involve local market power, and the under-provision of public goods with positive spillover benefits into other jurisdictions. In models with heterogeneous agents, additional mobility induced externalities may arise when local governments can "solve" local problems by providing incentives for "problem households" to move to other jurisdictions. One common example of this involves local provision of anti-poverty programs and the frequently raised fear that such programs will result in a "race to the bottom". (The subtle question for a local Pigouvian welfare maximizer in this case is to determine which population mix to consider when maximizing welfare – some initially given mix or the equilibrium mix that emerges from decentralized competition. For the case of redistribution under majority rule, our discussion in Section 3.5.2 suggests the possibility of similar under-provision of local redistribution.)

[59] Brueckner (2001) provides a recent formalization of this trade-off in terms of the issues raised in Section 3. Specifically, he models tax competition and preference heterogeneity, with the former introducing the inter-jurisdictional externality that suggests centralization may be optimal and the latter introducing the Tiebout benefit of decentralizing to permit preference sorting.

question left unaddressed by the Decentralization Theorem, although other possibilities have been informally discussed in the literature (Section 4.1.2). Second, when production functions for local public goods or services include non-pecuniary inputs that vary with local characteristics, fundamental concerns regarding "categorical equity" in the provision of certain goods [Feldstein (1975)] may be difficult to fully address through centralization (Section 4.1.3).

4.1.1. The Decentralization Theorem, politics and the "local office test"

The "Decentralization Theorem" asserts that centralization should take place only once the cost of centralization (uniformity of public goods) is outweighed by the benefits (internalization of spillovers). As suggested above, however, the theorem rests on the artificial assumption that centralized governments must tax and spend uniformly across decentralized political units. When this restriction is relaxed, it no longer becomes immediate why Pigouvian central governments could not simply set up "local offices" and mimic decentralized public goods provision to the extent that it is optimal to do so.[60] Thus, unless another opposing force is added to the Oates model, centralization is always optimal because at worst the central government can simply mimic what local governments would have done. One possible modification involves a modification of the Pigouvian nature of governments in the Oates model – either through the addition of Leviathan elements or through the explicit introduction of a political model. However, the introduction of a Leviathan element through a change in the objective function of governments away from welfare maximization and toward rent seeking (as in models discussed in Section 3.3) simply replaces one exogenously imposed decentralizing force in the Oates model with another. Instead, the most recent literature has introduced explicit political models that give rise to an endogenous decentralizing force or an endogenous reason for the existence of uniformity rules.

More precisely, Besley and Coate (1999) employ the citizen candidate framework (see Section 3.4.2) to model both local and central government provision of public goods and services without assuming constraints on the ability by central governments to vary spending across decentralized political units. They demonstrate that a trade-off between centralization and decentralization re-emerges because of the role that politics plays in the model – with decentralization emerging as optimal if spillovers are sufficiently small and centralization, despite political distortions, becoming optimal as spillovers get large. In a somewhat different context, Lockwood (2002) employs a structure induced political equilibrium model and thus also appeals to political forces as endogenously generating this type of a trade-off. Besharov (2002), on the other hand, employs a menu auction/political influence model to demonstrate that Oates' exogenous uniformity constraint on central governments might in fact have an endogenous justi-

[60] This question bears close resemblance to Coase's (1937) question regarding firms: Why can all economic activity not simply be conducted by a single firm? And it relates closely to the modern literature on the theory of the firm [Williamson (2002)].

fication after all – a justification that again arises from an underlying political story.[61] Here, centralization gives rise to greater opportunities for agents to engage in lobbying, and unless economic spillovers are sufficiently high, influence costs reduce welfare under centralization. Thus, whether politics itself generates the cost of centralization [Besley and Coate (1999), Lockwood (2002)], or whether politics gives rise to constitutionally imposed uniformity constraints [Besharov (2002)], the recent literature has focused on the introduction of political or influence models as a way of generalizing Oates' decentralization theorem when central government uniformity constraints are not exogenously imposed. In each case, decentralization becomes less attractive as inter-jurisdictional spillovers increase, and inefficiencies in political systems provide a decentralizing force.

4.1.2. Other ways to pass the "local office test"

Attempts to challenge exogenously imposed restrictions that yield the trade-offs underlying the Decentralization Theorem are relatively recent and almost solely focused on applying the political models we discussed above. More informally, however, the literature has hinted at other possible decentralizing forces that may take the place of Oates' uniformity constraint. One frequently mentioned force involves the ease with which local information can be processed by local political institutions as opposed to centralized bureaucracies [Oates (1999)]. A second involves potential gains from decentralized policy experiments in an environment characterized by uncertainty over the consequences of alternative policy proposals.[62] Neither of these has, to our knowledge, been modeled formally in a way that gives rise to endogenous advantages from decentralization. Given the similarity of the basic question to questions analyzed in the more developed modern theory of the firm [Williamson (2002)], it is likely that future research could fruitfully draw from this related literature.

4.1.3. "Categorical equity" gains and the limits of centralization

While our focus in the discussion of decentralized government competition has been primarily on efficiency considerations, a second important and policy-relevant set of considerations that naturally arise in Tiebout models with heterogeneous agents involves concerns about inter-jurisdictional equity. Even in the ideal scenario when decentralized

[61] Oates in fact seems to suggest that there are endogenous reasons for why central governments are indeed constrained (either by "typical political pressures" or "perhaps even constitutional constraints" [Oates (1999)]) to provide more uniform levels of public services at more uniform tax rates.

[62] Both of these are discussed informally in McKinnon and Nechyba (1997). Strumpf (2002) points out that it is far from obvious that policy innovation will necessarily be greater under decentralization given that an "information externality" would clearly suggest suboptimal experimentation. Neither, however, is it obvious that central governments – constrained by constitutional or political considerations, can engage in the level of optimal experimentation arising in a Pigouvian setting.

government competition leads to efficient (or constrained efficient) outcomes, the models clearly predict that outcomes in different jurisdictions will differ. This, in fact, was Tiebout's point: competition between local governments will lead to different mixes of tax and spending patterns and thus provide a menu of choices for heterogeneous households to choose among. In fact, if central government redistribution programs have generated an "equitable" distribution of household income, one might not be any more concerned about differences in local public good levels between rich and poor districts than one is concerned about the different quality of cars consumed by higher and lower-income households.

However, for certain types of local public goods and services (such as education and public safety), additional "categorical equity" concerns may arise. If this notion of equity demands equal levels of provision (or equal access to similar local public goods or services or a lack of relation between consumption levels and ability to pay),[63] the Tiebout mechanism is not particularly effective at guaranteeing such equality even if the overall income distribution is optimal in some sense. And it is on such equity grounds that central government production of some goods (or central government involvement in the production of such goods when locally produced) is frequently justified. To the extent that the production function for publicly provided goods takes only financial resources as inputs, and to the extent to which there are no alternative private markets for the provision of such goods, central government equalization of inputs can fully address such categorical equity concerns. Beyond such a simplified model of public good production, however, the general equilibrium forces that give rise to categorical inequities may continue to operate under centralization and may thus place limits on the central government's ability to fully eliminate such inequities.

This has been extensively treated in the case of public education. Ladd (1976) discusses the importance of considering both fiscal capacity (i.e., the local tax base, including industrial and commercial property) and fiscal need in determining optimal state involvement in education finance. Central government equalization of financial school inputs can indeed overcome differences in local school spending that would arise due to differences in local fiscal capacities, but fiscal needs in schools frequented by predominantly poor students is likely to be substantially higher than in schools with predominantly wealthy students because non-pecuniary inputs into school production (such as peer effects, parental involvement, teacher quality, etc.) are likely to be correlated with incomes of parents. Thus, within a model of decentralized (residentially based)

[63] The notion of categorical equity differs from typical public finance notions of equity and has a longer tradition in legal analysis. It differs from equity notions that guide our thinking about such features of economies as income distributions by placing particular emphasis on "equity" of certain types of consumption. Feldstein (1975) explains it as a principle that "singles out particular categories of services such as education and health care which are deemed to be 'fundamental interests' and asserts that individuals' consumption of these services should not be allowed to differ substantially or, alternatively, that such differences should not bear a strong relation to the individuals' ability to pay." Feldstein termed the latter version of the categorical equity notion "wealth neutrality". Arrow (1971), on the other hand, takes a utilitarian approach and arrives at conditions under which notions of categorical equity emerge as socially optimal.

school districts, inter-jurisdictional differences in school quality can emerge not only (or not even primarily) because of spending differences but rather because of accompanying differences in these non-pecuniary inputs when such inputs play an important part in the school production function. In a model of inequality in a general equilibrium model of capital accumulation with peer effects, Benabou (1996) also emphasizes that stratification may persist despite equalization of expenditures, and he demonstrates that stratification increases persistence of inequality.

Nechyba (2003a, 2002, in press) models peer influences and inputs explicitly within the Dunz/Nechyba computational model described in Section 3.5.4 and calibrates school production functions to place weights on pecuniary and non-pecuniary inputs so as to replicated private school attendance rates and public school spending levels (resulting from majority rule). Simulations comparing full centralization (and equalization) of public school spending to full decentralization by competing governments suggest that categorical inequities – while improving under centralization – continue to be substantial because of some of the very same general equilibrium forces that give rise to such inequities under decentralization.[64] Notions of categorical equity thus introduce a centralizing force, but even centralization may not be sufficiently strong to fully implement such equity notions in the presence of complexities such as non-pecuniary inputs into local public good production.[65] Epple and Romano (2003) likewise study centralization of school finance in a model in which students vary in ability and households vary in income. While centralization of school finance decreases dispersion of school qualities in their framework, stratification across schools persists due to peer effects – stratification that is little affected by the centralization of school finance.

4.2. Fiscal federalism: *hierarchical fiscal interactions between governments*

Ultimately, fiscal decentralization is rarely as extreme as suggested in Section 4.1 where the choice was treated as if full centralization and full decentralization were the only alternatives. Rather, different government services are often provided and financed through a complex set of inter-governmental fiscal institutions, including central government grants accompanied by central government constraints specifying what can and cannot be done by local governments under a given grant system. The justification for such hierarchical fiscal relationships – known as fiscal federalism – lies in attempts to combine the benefits of decentralization with the benefits of centralization. Much of the theory emanates from the literature on fiscal distortions that may arise from decentralized government competition even when local governments are Pigouvian in nature (Section 3.2) and from the desire of policymakers to achieve greater categorical equity

[64] These results are in stark contrast to the predictions from models that do not include a housing or land market and that model school production as purely a function of pecuniary inputs.

[65] Similar results of course apply to other types of publicly provided goods or services. Public safety, for instance, is clearly a function of not only pecuniary government inputs into law enforcement but also involves the characteristics of neighborhood populations – or neighborhood effects.

with respect to goods like health care, education and crime control. Oates (1972) outlined the basics of the theory by modeling local jurisdictions as single consumers that maximize utility subject to a budget constraint, and he focused on the ways in which different types of inter-governmental grants (such as matching and block grants) alter local incentives through changing local budget constraints. What type of fiscal central government intervention is optimal depends on a variety of factors including the type of problem that motivates the subsidy (Section 4.2.1), the relative levels of information available to central and local government policy makers (Section 4.2.2), the degree to which political distortions might govern hierarchical relationships (Section 4.2.3) and the extent to which local budget constraints "soften" as a result of hierarchical fiscal interactions with national governments.

4.2.1. *The theory of inter-governmental grants under Pigouvian governments with full information*

In the Oates Decentralization framework of Section 4.1, supplementing local provision of public goods with appropriately set central government matching grants causes local Pigouvian governments to internalize spillover externalities – thus maintaining the match between tastes and local public goods achieved through decentralized local policy setting while avoiding the inefficiencies from inter-jurisdictional spillovers. The central government grants can be viewed as the solution to a Prisoners' Dilemma faced by the Pigouvian local governments in the presence of inter-jurisdictional spillovers. Each would be willing to enter an agreement to take into account the benefits and costs of his own actions on other jurisdictions, but such an agreement contains all the usual incentives for each player to deviate. One way to view fiscal federalism in this context is thus to view the central government as the enforcer to the agreement – and the hierarchical fiscal institutions as the enforcement mechanism that induces each Pigouvian local government to in fact abide by the agreement to consider costs and benefits outside the local jurisdictions.[66] Central government grants can similarly be used to address categorical equity concerns across jurisdictions.

In comparing equally funded matching and block grants, the theory predicts greater local response to matching grants given the presence of substitution (price) effects in addition to income effects present in block grants. Furthermore, it predicts (under certain conditions) the same effects regardless of whether grants are given directly to local governments or indirectly to local residents through policies such as allowing local taxes to be deductible from federal tax obligations.[67] The frequent observation that the latter

[66] One portion of the literature has investigated endogenously generated transfers in decentralized systems [Myers (1990), Krelove (1992), Wellisch (1996), Silva (1997)]. Inter-regional transfers can emerge endogenously through tax exporting or through more explicit transfers to control migration. Under certain conditions, these papers demonstrate that such endogenously generated transfers are efficient.

[67] Under the current U.S. tax code, for instance, local property taxes are deductible from federal income taxes while local sales taxes are not. Of course, subsidizing local expenditures through such a mechanism does not permit for targeted subsidies to particular categories of local spending.

prediction does not seem to hold has led to a large literature (that is beyond the scope of this chapter) on what has come to be known as the "flypaper effect" – i.e., the empirical observation that where federal subsidies go (local governments versus local residents) matters to outcomes.[68] And even in the absence of inter-jurisdictional spillovers and in the presence of Pigouvian governments, central government coordination can improve on decentralized outcomes when local public goods and services (such as education, crime control, public infrastructure, etc.) are provided by *overlapping* local jurisdictions [Hochman, Pines and Thisse (1995)].

A number of different fiscal mechanisms have been proposed for the correction of different types of efficiency or equity concerns arising from decentralized provision. As suggested already, Pigouvian matching grants can control for inter-jurisdictional tax[69] and expenditure spillovers by causing local governments to fully internalize inter-jurisdictional externalities [Wellisch (2000)]. Block grants, on the other hand, may be appropriate when central governments seek to insure a minimal level of spending on particular public goods or services for categorical equity reasons [Nechyba (1996)]. In the funding of public education, the concept of wealth neutrality [Feldstein (1975)][70] provides a stronger notion of categorical equity and results in a system of jurisdiction specific matching grants. Under special circumstances, such wealth neutrality may result from a matching grant system in which central government subsidies are structured so as to insure that each locality would raise the same revenue if it set the same local tax rate, but generally such a system would result in an inverse correlation of public spending and local wealth because of strong substitutions (price) effects [Feldstein (1975), Nechyba (1996)].[71] Each of these proposals implicitly assumes that full centralization of the public service is not optimal because of the presence of at least one of the decentralizing forces discussed in Section 4.1.

4.2.2. *Information asymmetries in hierarchical fiscal relationships*

Although the assumption that local officials have more of the relevant information than central government officials (see Section 4.1.2) represents one of the arguments in favor of fiscal decentralization, this informational asymmetry is not incorporated into many

[68] Theories that have attempted to explain the flypaper effect have relied on political, institutional and behavioral explanations. A recent summary and evaluation of much of this literature is provided by Hines and Thaler (1995).

[69] Wildasin (1989) and DePater and Myers (1994) analyze this for the case of capital tax competition in different settings.

[70] Wealth neutrality arises when local expenditures on a particular public good or service are not correlated with local wealth.

[71] One concern raised in regard to matching grants based on local wealth arises from the general equilibrium prediction that such grants will lead to capitalization effects that "undo" the grants by raising property values (and thus local wealth) in poor districts and lowering values in rich districts [Inman and Rubinfeld (1979)]. In a setting in which housing quality is realistically calibrated, however, this general equilibrium effect seems to be relatively small [Nechyba (1996)].

of the treatments of hierarchical government interactions. In recent years, however, the principal–agent nature of the fiscal relationship between different levels of government has become an item of greater research interest [Wellisch (2000)], and a serious treatment of moral hazard and adverse selection issues in the area of inter-governmental grants is likely to emerge along the lines of similar treatments in industrial organization [Laffont and Tirole (1993)].

4.2.3. *Political distortions and imperfect voter information*

In Section 4.2.1, we described hierarchical fiscal interactions arising as a solution to a prisoners' dilemma faced by local jurisdictions that do not take into account the impact of their policies on other jurisdictions. In the presence of purely Pigouvian policy makers, such a solution to the prisoners' dilemma (through policies such as inter-governmental grants) can be strictly welfare enhancing. As policy makers are viewed through a more Leviathan lens, however, such coordination can become more pernicious as it could be used to protect local governments from healthy competition in much the same way as enforceable cartel agreements protect firms from such competition. Furthermore, the complexity of hierarchical fiscal relationships may obscure the connection between revenues and expenditures in the eyes of voters who may then find it more difficult to hold local governments accountable. Finally, questions have been raised as to whether it is a politically stable equilibrium to have a system in which revenues are raised at one level of government but autonomously spent at another.

In the most extreme Leviathan model, local rent-seeking politicians (in a model like Epple and Zelenitz's (1981) described in Section 3.3) would indeed find it in their interest to use central government coordination to reduce competition and thus raise political rents. But even in less extreme models, central government coordination policies may arise for reasons having little to do with welfare-enhancing policy coordination. In Nechyba (1997a), for instance, central government grants allow local residents to switch from property to income taxes even though the exclusive use of property taxes is a dominant strategy in the absence of central government coordination. If the ratio of income to property wealth is skewed to the left (with a majority of residents in each community having relatively less income than property compared to the community average), majorities would prefer such a switch in tax bases even though there is no reason to suspect an increase in general welfare from this change.[72] And, when the central government legislative process is modeled, political decisions are focused on

[72] In fact, for communities in New Jersey, the ratio of income to property wealth is skewed in exactly this way – giving rise to the prediction that voters would prefer proportional income to proportional property taxes [Nechyba (1994)]. Other explanations for the desire to limit local property taxes abound – see, for example, Vigdor (2001) and references therein, and Calabrese and Epple (2004).

funding (through grants) projects with concentrated local benefits (also termed "pork barrel projects") that may or may not be efficient.[73]

To the extent that fiscal government institutions rely on voters to hold even partially Leviathan politicians accountable, simplicity and transparency of the system is typically discussed as a virtue [Boskin (1996), Aaron and Gale (1996)]. More formally, such transparency would certainly be necessary in a yardstick competition model (see Section 3.4.3) where the activities in neighboring jurisdictions are used as a yardstick to judge the effectiveness of local politicians because voters do not have enough information to judge such effectiveness more directly. In a model that explicitly introduces lobbying and influence costs (as in Section 3.4.4), one can explicitly derive the result that politics requires constraints on hierarchical interactions – constraints that would not be optimal in a Pigouvian world [Besharov (2002)].

Finally, the literature has not yet resolved under what conditions a permanent division between provision of services (at the local level) and financing of those services (partially at the central government level) is a stable political equilibrium. McKinnon and Nechyba (1997) suggest anecdotally that, under certain assumptions, it may not be a stable equilibrium given that voters may have difficulty holding either level of government accountable, and that either central governments will impose constraints on the spending of centrally raised revenues that will in effect remove any benefits from local provision, or central governments will relinquish the funding of services over which they have little control. A formal treatment of this topic may be the subject of fruitful future research.

4.2.4. Inter-governmental grants, "soft budgets" and future generations

The danger of "soft" budget constraints in generating excessive debt under fiscal decentralization has been emphasized in the debate on the difference between competition between nation states (whose budgets are "soft" due to their ability to print currency) and sub-national governments (whose budget constraints are "hard"). This literature emphasizes the role of political constraints that credibly combine monetary centralization with fiscal decentralization to generate hard budget constraints for those political units that compete.[74] Thus, decentralized governments are forced to make economic trade-offs within their jurisdictions without being able to rely on passing costs to future

[73] Inman and Rubinfeld (1996) exposit a simple model of distributive politics of this kind. Inman (1988) argues that federal grants to U.S. states cannot be explained on either equity or efficiency grounds but can be explained as resulting from such a system of distributive politics.

[74] McKinnon (1997) and McKinnon and Nechyba (1997) provide some informal discussion of the possibility that even local budgets can become "soft" if excessively linked to central governments through inter-governmental grants. Motivated by the observation that a wave of local defaults preceded imposition of local debt limits in the U.S., Epple and Spatt (1986) develop a model in which state restrictions on local debt "harden" budget constraints by ensuring political support in state legislatures for measures that require localities to repay their debt obligations.

generations or to others taxed by the central government. Qian and Roland (1998) set up a formal framework and apply this to an analysis of economic transition in China, and Weingast (1995) argues that such considerations were important in the development of England and the U.S. in the 18th and 19th centuries.[75] A fuller and more formal treatment which identifies more precisely the conditions under which central government access to monetary policy softens local budgets and leads to exploitation of future generations remains for future research.

5. Empirical research

In this section, we discuss innovative empirical contributions within roughly the last decade. Research in the past decade has increasingly turned to empirical analysis seeking to take more explicit account of the inter-dependence among jurisdictions that arises from inter-jurisdictional mobility of households. This emphasis is reflected in work on yardstick competition, tests for fiscal inter-dependence, estimation of structural equilibrium models, and testing of effects of jurisdictional competition on public sector efficiency. A significant body of empirical research has also emerged investigating the effects of vertical inter-dependence among state and local governments as reflected, for example, in tax and expenditure limitations. Recent work has also continued an important agenda item from prior research – empirical analysis of the collective choice processes within jurisdictions. A growing body of theoretical work has focused on intra-jurisdictional choice, and empirical work has begun to follow suit. Portrayal of empirical research on the above topics is the task of this section.

5.1. Capitalization

Research on capitalization among local jurisdictions has been motivated from the outset [Oates (1969)] by an interest in testing for effects of inter-dependence among jurisdictions. In this respect, research on capitalization is an important precursor of current research on jurisdictional inter-dependence. Research on capitalization continues. Past work focused largely on testing for capitalization of fiscal differences across jurisdictions into property values. An innovative application by Black (1999) investigates capitalization within jurisdictions. In particular, she investigates the extent to which differences in school quality across neighborhood schools within a district are capitalized. A further novelty of her approach is using data for houses located near the boundaries delineating neighborhood school attendance zones. Neighborhood characteristics other than schools will tend to be similar for houses near each other across such boundaries, thus limiting the potential for confounding school differences with other neighborhood differences. There is much interest in learning whether differences

[75] For a more detailed review of this literature on "market preserving federalism", see also Oates (1999).

in public service quality are capitalized when there are neither differences in per student expenditures nor tax rates. Black finds evidence of substantial housing price variation associated with differences in measures of school quality. Her findings lend support to models discussed in Section 3.5.4 that predict that housing price differentials will support stratification across locations even when there are no differences in expenditure levels – models that also imply that expenditure equalization across communities may have little effect in reducing stratification by income and other demographic variables.

5.2. *Jurisdictional fiscal inter-dependence, competition and efficiency*

To economists, and probably to most everyone else, it is natural to think that competition among jurisdictions should stimulate providers to function more efficiently. This might occur, for example, by limiting the discretion of providers or special interests to pursue objectives that are not congruent with the interests of jurisdiction residents [Brennan and Buchanan (1980), Epple and Zelenitz (1981), Courant, Gramlich and Rubinfeld (1979)]. Tests of this hypothesis by Oates (1985) led to a substantial body of empirical research investigating whether fiscal decentralization affects public sector expenditures. Responding to research stimulated by his contribution, Oates (1989) provides an illuminating assessment of the approaches and findings from the series of papers that followed his initial contribution. His bottom line: The evidence supports the conclusion that increased competition via an increase in the number of general-purpose governments serving an area tends to restrict government spending while an increase in the number of special-district governments (e.g., water authorities) tends to increase spending, perhaps due to loss of scale economies. This conclusion highlights an issue that appears to warrant greater theoretical attention, namely research focused on better understanding the complexity of overlapping local governmental units that provide goods and services by some combination of taxation, fees, and inter-governmental revenues.

The work stimulated by Oates addresses the issue of whether spending falls with increased competition, but does not address the issue of whether resources are used more efficiently as competition increases. For many locally provided government services, measures of output are difficult to obtain. However, for education, standardized test scores and post-school earnings provide outcome measures that are comparable across school districts. Hoxby (2000a) studies the effects of school district competition on educational outcomes as well as expenditures. Since the number of school districts is potentially endogenous, Hoxby introduces the innovation by use of natural impediments to travel (e.g., rivers) as instruments for number of districts. She finds that greater competition among school districts has a significant effect both in improving educational outcomes and in reducing expenditures per student. While the both effects are of moderate size, her work suggests that decentralization not only constrains expenditures but also promote more productive use of resources.

In Section 3.4.3, we discussed research on voter information and agency problems, noting that decentralization may potentially improve governmental efficiency by providing alternatives that residents may observe in assessing how efficiently their government is functioning. In an admirable blend of theory and empirical research, Besley and Case (1995a) develop and test a model of yardstick competition. Their theoretical framework introduces imperfect information on the part of voters, presuming that incumbents know more about short-run changes in fundamentals than do voters. Electoral officials (governors) vary in competence. Voters face the task of deciding how much of a change in their state's taxes is due to a change in fundamentals and how much is due to the competence of their elected governor. Voters use outcomes in other states to obtain an assessment of the relative performance of their state government; other jurisdictions thus serving as a "yardstick". Their empirical evidence, based on jointly analyzing state taxes and gubernatorial election outcomes for U.S. states, supports the prediction that yardstick competition does indeed affect political outcomes state tax setting. This paper is one of the few to model formally the role of informational asymmetries between voters and providers and among fewer still in testing the predictions of such a model. Their paper thus serves as a yardstick for judging future contributions in this realm.

A substantial body of research has emerged, investigating inter-dependence among jurisdictions in tax and expenditure decisions. Among the first is the work of Case, Rosen and Hines (1993). They develop and test a model in which a state's expenditures may generate spillovers to neighboring states. An innovation in their approach is allowing for spatially correlated shocks as well as spillovers. Using data for a panel of states, they find evidence of strikingly large impacts; a dollar increase in spending by a state leads to an increase of seventy cents in neighboring states. Further evidence of inter-dependence of state fiscal policies is provided by Figlio, Kolpin and Reid (1999). They test for inter-dependence in setting of state welfare benefit levels. They find that states not only respond to changes in benefits by neighbors, but also that the response is asymmetric. A state tends to respond more strongly to a drop in benefits in a neighbor state than to an increase. They find, as did Case, Hines, and Rosen, that the effects arising from inter-dependence across states are large. Brueckner and Saavedra (2001) present a model to test whether there is strategic tax competition among local governments. Following the tax competition literature, their model takes populations as fixed and capital as mobile. Using data for localities in the Boston SMSA, they find that tax reaction functions slope upward, implying tax inter-dependence among local jurisdictions.

Spillovers and strategic interactions among jurisdictions will tend to lead to allocative inefficiencies. Impacts of the magnitude estimated in Case, Rosen and Hines (1993) would seem to suggest that the inefficiencies may be very large indeed. We thus need to learn more about the nature and equilibrium consequences of the inter-dependences pointed to in these empirical analyses. Does greater decentralization improve efficiency via increased competition (Hoxby) and improved voter information (Besley and Case), or are such gains offset by externalities or by inefficiencies associated with mobility of resources that localities seek to tax?

5.3. Politics, institutions and fiscal outcomes

While the evidence points to inter-dependence in fiscal policies, institutions also have been found to be important. The work of Romer and Rosenthal (1978, 1979) provides compelling evidence on this score with respect to local government referenda and agenda setting. Recent work has contributed to the agenda of studying state and local government institutions. Besley and Case (1995b) investigate whether gubernatorial term limits affect taxes and spending. As in their work on yardstick competition, competence of governors varies and must be inferred by voters from observed outcomes. In the model, performance of first-term governors affects their re-election prospects. Outcomes depend both on competence and effort, implying that, ceteris paribus, governors in their last term will perform less well than governors eligible for re-election. They find that changes in both tax and expenditure outcomes are consistent with the model's predictions.

Bohn and Inman (1995) study the effect of balanced-budget rules on state deficits using a 22-year panel for the states. They find that balanced-budget rules limiting end-of-year deficits do indeed limit deficits. Dye and McGuire (1997) find that state rules limiting local taxes retard growth in local government spending. Poterba and Rueben (1995) study the effects of local property tax limits in public employee wages, finding that more stringent property tax limits are associated with lower growth in public employee wages. Poterba (1994) studies how state institutions and politics affect state responses to the severe fiscal shocks of the late 1980s and early 1990s. He studies the effects of state constitutional restrictions on deficits and on permissible tax rates. He also investigates how adjustment to fiscal shocks is affected by party control, focusing, in particular, on whether a state has divided government and on the timing of elections. He finds that expenditure adjustments to shocks are more rapid where balanced-budget rules are stringent, and that tax increases in response to adverse shocks are smaller where tax-limitation rules are more stringent. He also finds that that single-party control increases the speed of response to fiscal shocks, and that tax increases and spending cuts are smaller in election years. The former result is consistent with findings of Alt and Lowry (1994) that states with divided government are more likely to run deficits.

As Poterba (1996) notes, the above findings with respect to budgetary institutions may be a manifestation of effects that persist even if they are not congruent with voter preferences. Alternatively, the institutions may evolve to reflect voter preferences. This is clearly a central issue in assessing the desirability of these rules and a key agenda item for future research. An important step toward addressing endogeneity of tax limitation rules is taken by Figlio (1997). He tests the effects of tax limits while allowing for potential endogeneity of the limits. He finds that correcting for potential endogeneity increases the magnitude of estimated effects of the limits. His findings are also of substantive policy interest; his results imply that tax limits are associated with higher student–teacher ratios, lower starting salaries for teachers, and lower student performance.

Adoption of limits often appears puzzling. Why would voters support restrictions at the state or national level that limit policy options available to voters at the local level?

Vigdor (2001) presents an intriguing new perspective on this question, providing a rationale for voters to support state tax limitations that affect local jurisdictions other than the one in which they reside. Why? A voter might prefer another jurisdiction more than her own if the taxes in that other jurisdiction were reduced. Voting on a referendum to support a state-imposed tax limit on local taxes provides a vehicle to act on this preference. Vigdor presents empirical evidence supporting this prediction for Proposition 2½ in Massachusetts.

The question raised by Poterba, do institutional constraints reflect voter preferences, suggests research on conditions under which policies, such as mandates by a higher to a lower-level government, will be immune to change once adopted. Calabrese (1999, 2000) provides an illuminating analysis in this respect. Prior to 1842, states determined whether their representatives to the U.S. House of Representatives were elected in single-member or multi-member districts. In 1842, the federal government adopted legislation mandating single-member districts. Why? Calabrese develops a model and empirical evidence demonstrating that the party opposite the president is advantaged by multi-member-district elections. Thus, when the same party controls the presidency and both houses, as in 1842, there is an incentive to mandate election of representatives by single-member districts. Since it is in the interest of the president to oppose a return to multi-member districts, the single-district mandate can be overridden only in the unlikely event that the party opposite the president controls two-thirds of both houses. The federal mandate adopted in 1842 endures to the present. This case illustrates that institutional change can be, essentially, irreversible. It would be of interest to investigate whether there are other institutional constraints governing state and local governments that have a similar enduring quality.

Another route by which policy is established is in the courts. For the past three decades, dating from the U.S. Supreme Court refusal to enter the fray, state courts have been the battleground for efforts to impose greater equality in education spending. Not surprisingly, there has been a great deal of variation in state court decisions. This variation provides the foundation for analyses by, Murray, Evans and Schwab (1998) testing the effects of court-mandated equalizations. They find that court mandates have, in fact, resulted in more equal spending within states. The bulk of variation in per pupil spending is now due to inter-state rather than intra-state variation.

5.4. Structural estimation of locational equilibrium models

With the exception of research on tax capitalization, most empirical work prior to the past decade took limited account of the inter-dependence among jurisdictions. Inter-jurisdictional mobility had, however, been emphasized by Goldstein and Pauly (1981) as a potential source of bias in estimating demand functions for local public goods. An innovative approach for taking account of this potential source of bias in work with micro-data was provided by Rubinfeld, Shapiro and Roberts (1987), who, in turn, build on the contribution of Bergstrom, Rubinfeld and Shapiro (1982).

As we detail in Section 3, much work has been devoted to developing theoretical models to characterize equilibrium among local jurisdictions. This work in turn has stimulated efforts to estimate "structural econometric" counterparts to these equilibrium models. Three general approaches have emerged. One is due to Epple and Sieg (1999) who estimate a model that follows on the work of Ellickson (1971), Westhoff (1977), Epple, Filimon and Romer (1984, 1993) and Epple and Platt (1998). They implement a two-stage approach, using data from the Boston SMSA. Their first stage entails choosing parameters of the model to fit the observed income distributions in each of the 92 communities in the SMSA. The second stage entails estimating the remaining parameters of the model by exploiting the necessary conditions for locational equilibrium implied by the theoretical model. A striking finding of their analysis is that a relatively parsimonious parameterization of their equilibrium model fits the 92 community income distributions in the Boston SMSA quite well. They also find that the preference parameters estimated with their approach imply the single-crossing conditions embodied in the underlying theoretical framework. Sieg et al. (2003a) extend and apply this approach to study the benefits of air pollution abatement in the Los Angeles metropolitan area. They find that the estimated benefits of pollution abatement using a framework that allows for equilibrium adjustments to air quality changes are quite different from those obtained with approaches that neglect such adjustments. A companion paper [Sieg et al. (2003b)], employs this model to investigate the distributional effects, by location and income, of air quality changes that are anticipated with implementation of air quality regulations. These authors [Sieg et al. (2002)] also generalize the model of Epple and Sieg (1999) to incorporate heterogeneous housing, and they employ this framework to define and estimate inter-jurisdictional housing price indexes.

A second approach to structural econometric modeling is developed by Bayer, McMillan and Rueben (2002). Their point of departure is the discrete-choice framework of Berry, Levinsohn and Pakes (1995), in which choice-specific unobservables are present. Their model, in the spirit of Dunz (1985) and Nechyba (1997b), takes the stock of housing in the metropolitan area as given and studies the housing choices of individuals with varying demographic characteristics. A virtue of their approach is that it is possible to allow for a relatively large set of observable characteristics of individuals. Individuals' choices of locations depend on the physical characteristics of the houses and locations as well as the demographic characteristics of the neighbors at each location. They take household employment locations as given. They estimate their model using Census micro-data for the Los Angeles metropolitan area. They can then explore via simulations how changes in the distribution of characteristics of the population would affect the equilibrium allocation of population across the set of houses in the metropolitan area. As an application of their framework, they investigate the extent to which racial segregation would change if income distributions of the different races were more to become more similar.[76] They find that this would result in increased racial segregation;

[76] The framework assumes that there are no excluded socioeconomic characteristics that are correlated with included characteristics, an assumption that is of particular importance in studying issues such as racial segregation.

members of a race could then more readily find neighborhoods with members of their own race who have similar social-economic characteristics. While they model neighborhood demographic composition as endogenous, their approach takes local government tax and expenditure policies to be exogenous. For their application to the Los Angeles basin this is a reasonable approximation given the constraints now imposed on local governments in California.

A third approach is due to Ferreyra (2002a, 2002b) who estimates an extension of the model of Nechyba (2000). Motivated by the prominent role that religious schools play in the debate on vouchers, Ferreyra introduces religious preferences into Nechyba's model. She then estimates the parameters of the model using maximum likelihood, solving for equilibrium at each evaluation of the likelihood function. Her work thus innovates both by introduction of religious preferences and by embedding the solution for equilibrium in the estimation of the parameters of the model. Her work permits policy analyses comparing equilibrium with a voucher that permits users to attend religious private schools to a voucher that can only be used at non-sectarian private schools.

Bajari and Kahn (2003) use still another approach, building on the work of Bajari and Benkard (2002). They first estimate a hedonic housing price function nonparametrically. From this, they compute taste parameters for housing and community characteristics for each household in the sample. They then study the joint distribution of these taste parameters and household demographic characteristics by regressing the former on the latter. As an application, they investigate alternative explanations of White suburbanization, concluding that suburbanization by Whites is driven by their greater demand for residence in high human capital communities and by greater demand for larger, single-family detached housing units.

5.5. *Collective choice and local fiscal institutions*

Because of their number and heterogeneity, local jurisdictions have provided a valuable base of data to test models of collective choice. At least since the work of Barr and Davis (1966), local jurisdictions have been used for such tests. New work in this domain has emerged during the last decade.

Understanding political participation has long been one of the major challenges in research on political economy. Two papers in the last decade have tested theories of participation exploiting state and local government data. Shachar and Nalebuff (1999) propose a model in which leaders influence election outcomes via the effort they exert in getting followers to vote. Thus leaders rather than individual voters make strategic decisions that influence votes, their decisions being with regard to the amount of effort to exert in a particular contest. Structural estimates of the parameters of the model are then obtained using data for U.S. presidential elections, with state party leaders modeled as choosing the effort level to exert in getting out the vote. Coate and Conlin (2001) develop still another model of turnout in which voters are members of one of two competing groups, those favoring and those opposing a referendum proposal. Their model is one in which a voter's decision about participation is based on the trade-off between the individualized cost of voting on the one hand and benefits realized from "doing one's part". They use data from Texas liquor referenda to estimate the model. The parameter estimates prove to be of reasonable magnitude, and the model outperforms two alternatives that they consider. Thus far, models of voting over local tax and expenditure decisions have typically assumed full turnout, despite the observed abysmally low turnout in many local elections. The preceding papers point to potential directions for introducing turnout in such models.

As discussed earlier in Section 4.1, a fundamental argument for decentralizing decisions to lower level governments is that such decentralization permits adoption of policies that reflect variation in preferences. Strump and Oberholzer-Gee (2002) provide a very appealing test of this premise using evidence on liquor control policies. As they note, liquor control policies provide a quite attractive case for study. There has been much variation both over time and across states in liquor control policies. The paper presents persuasive evidence that decentralization of the policy decision regarding liquor control from state to local governments is significantly greater in states where there is greater heterogeneity in preferences regarding liquor policy.

Epple, Romer and Sieg (2001) test majority rule in the context of an equilibrium model of local jurisdictions. Using data for the 92 municipalities in the Boston SMSA, they test whether public good levels are consistent with the predictions of majority rule. The results reject the myopic voting model, which has been almost universally used in modeling voting over local government tax and expenditure decisions. Their evidence suggests that more sophisticated utility-taking models may better explain the data. Given the central role that voting plays in most equilibrium models of local jurisdictions, these results point to the need for additional work in developing an empirically valid characterization of voter behavior in local elections.

5.6. *Stratification*

Stratification of population by income, race, and other characteristics within and across communities may have diverse consequences ranging from heterogeneity in preferences for local public goods, impacts on tax base, neighborhood effects, access to housing markets, and a host of other issues. In light of this, it is not surprising that the role of fiscal decentralization in influencing the extent of stratification within and across communities has been the subject of much recent research. Models that predict perfect stratification by income across communities are clearly at variance with the evidence. For example, Epple and Platt (1998) note that 19% of households in the poorest community (Chelsea) in the Boston metropolitan area in 1980 had incomes above $22,500 while 19% of households in the wealthiest community (Weston) had incomes below $22,500. Ioannides (2001) finds substantial income mixing in quite small residential neighborhoods while Ioannides and Selsen (2001) find that wealth mixing in neighborhoods is greater still.

As we have discussed previously, one potential explanation for this imperfect income sorting across communities is offered by models with heterogeneity of durable housing (e.g., Nechyba) while models with heterogeneity in preferences (e.g., Epple and Platt) provide another. Models with peer and neighborhood effects [Benabou (1993), Durlauf (1996), Epple and Romano (2003)] predict stratification within communities as well.[77] Davidoff (2003) suggests comparing the extent of stratification within communities as compared to stratification across communities as a measure of the importance of fiscal decentralization has compared to other factors affecting stratification. Using data for the Boston metropolitan area, he estimates that jurisdictions explain approximately 21% of the variation in household lifetime income. However, he argues that this overstates the extent of sorting due to fiscal decentralization. He next compares income heterogeneity across neighborhood pairs within a jurisdiction to heterogeneity in income across pairs of neighborhoods separated by a municipal boundary. Based on this analysis, he concludes that jurisdiction differences account for no more than three to four percent of income variation. Following a somewhat different tack, Daniel Aaronson (1996) investigates whether within-community income homogeneity declines after adoption of state policies that limit variation across localities in taxes and expenditures. He finds that such policies have a small but significant effect in decreasing neighborhood income homogeneity.

Rhode and Strumpf (2003) investigate how both stratification and variation in policies across jurisdictions have changed over relatively long time periods. They provide persuasive evidence that transportation costs have declined significantly over time. This, they argue, makes the kind of sorting envisioned by Tiebout less costly to achieve. They then turn to data on heterogeneity in policies across localities (e.g., municipalities and counties) and find that policies have become more homogeneous. For example, they find that the coefficient of variation of taxes per capita, measured at either the municipality or county level, was roughly half as large in 1992 as in 1890. The coefficient of variation of school spending per capita, aggregated to the county level, declined by about 25% over the same time period. They also find that differences in population characteristics (race, nativity, age) across local jurisdictions declined over this time period. They interpret these results as evidence against the Tiebout hypothesis. In doing so, they adopt a different stance than previous research regarding the predictions of the Tiebout hypothesis. Empirical analyses, beginning with the classic study by Oates (1969), have generally taken the system of municipalities in a given metropolitan area as the most natural environment for the mechanism described by Tiebout to operate. Anticipating

[77] In this chapter, we have discussed the literature on peer effects as it relates to issues associated with fiscal decentralization. Discussion of the larger literature on peer effects would take us too far afield, but research on the topic is burgeoning. Contributions include: Coleman (1996), Henderson, Mieszkowski and Sauvageau (1978), Summers and Wolfe (1977), Manski (1993), Moffitt (2001), Durlauf and Brock (2001, in press), Evans, Oates and Schwab (1992), Robertson and Symons (1996), Kremer (1997), Zimmer and Toma (1998), Hoxby (2000b), Ding and Lehrer (2001), Sacerdote (2001), Winston and Zimmerman (2003), Zimmerman (2000), Betts and Morell (1999), Arcidiacono and Nickolson (2000), Dale and Krueger (1998), Cutler and Glaeser (1997), Kremer and Levy (2003), Sacerdote (2001) and Zimmerman (1999), Betts and Morell (1999), Arcidiacono and Nickolson (2000), Epple, Newlon and Romano (2002), Hanushek et al. (2003).

this potential criticism, the authors turn to data for a single metropolitan area, where arguably the Tiebout hypothesis should have more force. In particular, they consider changes over time in the Boston SMSA. Income data permit comparisons from 1949 to 1989, and reveal little change in income heterogeneity within and between communities. Data for spending, available for a longer time interval, reveal little systematic tendency for changes in cross-community heterogeneity in spending between 1906 and 1992 for Boston municipalities. If the Boston pattern is representative of other metropolitan areas, the evidence in total suggests that the trends toward greater homogeneity observed in the national data are due to declining population heterogeneity across metropolitan areas with more modest changes in heterogeneity across communities within metropolitan areas. Whether one interprets the evidence in this paper as contacting the Tiebout hypothesis will depend, to a considerable extent, on one's view about the scope of geographic area in which the Tiebout mechanism is understood to operate.

6. Conclusions

Given the increasing trend toward fiscal decentralization and greater factor mobility, it is not surprising that substantial attention has been devoted to these topics by academic economists over the past decade. Several important themes for future research arise from our discussion in this chapter: First, while simple versions of more general models have clarified many analytic issues, policy trade-offs are ultimately made in complicated settings rich with institutional detail. As a result, while theoretical questions remain, the search for a greater connection between theoretical models and data has taken on particular importance. Complex general equilibrium models of fiscal decentralization ultimately become most useful (while retaining the rich set of trade-offs inherent in the economic environments of interest) when underlying parameters are determined by the data. Both calibration and structural estimation techniques are advancing this portion of the literature.

Second, the last decade has seen an increasing emphasis of political forces in debates over fiscal decentralization. Not only does such decentralization carry with it potential economic benefits and costs, but political decisions are likely to be fundamentally different in a decentralized environment. Important further work on political institutions under fiscal decentralization is needed and, on a more abstract level, includes a push toward a better understanding of how entire political systems compete under decentralization.[78]

Finally, as decentralization has been studied in multiple contexts, it has become increasingly clear that the micro-foundations of local goods and services need further theoretical and empirical investigations. Many such goods (such as crime prevention and schooling) depend fundamentally on peer and neighborhood effects, and predictions can

[78] This is labeled "Systems Competition" in one recent contribution to the literature [Sinn (2003)].

change fundamentally as such effects are introduced into the analysis. Similarly, locally provided goods may have private alternatives that can alter predictions when included explicitly in the analysis, and commuting costs may play important roles within urban and regional settings.

Acknowledgements

We are grateful for comments from Richard Romano, Holger Sieg, and participants at the 2002 Regional Science Association International Meetings, especially those of our discussant Will Strange and of the editors, Vernon Henderson and Jacques Thisse.

References

Aaron, H., Gale, W. (Eds.) (1996). Economic Effects of Fundamental Tax Reform. Brookings Institution, Washington, DC.

Aaronson, D. (1996). "The effect of state fiscal reform on population heterogeneity". WP-96-29. Federal Reserve Bank, Chicago.

Alt, J.E., Lowry, R.C. (1994). "Divided government and budget deficits: evidence from the states". American Political Science Review 88 (December).

Arcidiacono, P., Nickolson, S. (2000). "The mirage of peer effects: evidence from U.S. medical schools". Working paper.

Arnott, R. (1979). "Optimal city size in a spatial economy". Journal of Urban Economics 6, 65–89.

Arnott, R., Stiglitz, J. (1979). "Aggregate land rent, expenditures on public goods, and the optimal city size". Quarterly Journal of Economics 93, 471–500.

Arrow, K. (1971). "A utilitarian approach to the concept of equality in public expenditures". Quarterly Journal of Economics 85 (3), 409–415.

Arzaghi, M., Henderson, J.V. (2002). "Why countries are fiscally decentralizing". Working paper. Department of Economics, Brown University.

Bailey, M. (1993). "Note on Ricardian equivalence". Journal of Public Economics 51, 437–446.

Bajari, P., Benkard, L. (2002). Demand estimation with heterogeneous consumers and unobserved product characteristics: a hedonic approach (June).

Bajari, P., Kahn, M. (2003). Estimating housing demand with an application to explaining racial segregation in cities.

Barr, J., Davis, O. (1966). "An elementary political and economic theory of expenditures of state and local governments". Southern Economic Journal 33, 149–165.

Bayer, P., McMillan, R., Rueben, K. (2002). "An equilibrium model of sorting in an urban housing market: a study of the causes and consequences of residential segregation". Working paper.

Bearse, P. (2001). Communities, youth crime, and deterrence: a quantitative theoretic analysis.

Bearse, P., Glomm, G., Janeba, E. (2001). "Composition of government budget, non-single peakedness and majority voting". Journal of Public Economic Theory 3 (4), 471–481.

Benabou, R. (1993). "Workings of a city: location, education, and production". Quarterly Journal of Economics 108 (August), 619–652.

Benabou, R. (1996). "Equity and efficiency in human capital investment: the local connection". Review of Economic Studies 63 (2), 237–264.

Bergstrom, T., Rubinfeld, D., Shapiro, P. (1982). "Micro-based estimates of demand functions for local public goods". Econometrica 50, 1183–1205.

Berliant, M. (1985). "Equilibrium models with land: a criticism and an alternative". Regional Science and Urban Economics 15, 325–340.

Bernheim, B.D., Whinston, M. (1986). "Menu auctions, resource allocation and economic influence". The Quarterly Journal of Economics 101 (1), 1–31.

Berry, S., Levinsohn, J., Pakes, A. (1995). "Automobile prices in market equilibrium". Econometrica 63 (4), 841–890.

Besley, T., Case, A. (1995a). "Incumbent behavior: vote seeking, tax setting and yardstick competition". American Economic Review 85 (1), 25–45.

Besley, T., Case, A. (1995b). "Does electoral accountability affect policy choices? Evidence from gubernatorial term limits". Quarterly Journal of Economics 110 (3), 769–798.

Besley, T., Coate, S. (1997). "An economic model of representative democracy". Quarterly Journal of Economics 112 (1), 85–114.

Besley, T., Coate, S. (1999). "Centralized versus decentralized provision of public goods: a political economy analysis". NBER working paper 7084. Cambridge, MA.

Besley, T., Coate, S. (2001). "Lobbying and welfare in a representative democracy". Review of Economic Studies 68 (1), 67–82.

Besley, T., Smart, M. (2002). "Does tax competition raise voter welfare?" Working paper. Department of Economics, University of Toronto.

Besharov, G. (2002). "Influence costs in the provision of local public goods". Working paper. Department of Economics, Duke University.

Besharov, G., Zweiman, A. (2002). "Inefficient local regulation of local externalities". Duke University working paper.

Betts, J., Morell, D. (1999). "The determinants of undergraduate GPA: the relative importance of family background, high school resources, and peer group effects". Journal of Human Resources 107, 797–817.

Black, D. (1948). "On the rationale of group decision-making". Journal of Political Economy 56, 23–34.

Black, S. (1999). "Do better schools matter? Parental valuation of elementary education". Quarterly Journal of Economics 114 (2), 577–599.

Bohn, H., Inman, R.P. (1995). "Constitutional limits and public deficits: evidence from the states". Carnegie–Rochester Series on Public Policy (December).

Boskin, M. (Ed.) (1996). Frontiers of Tax Reform. Hoover Institution Press, Stanford.

Brueckner, J.K. (1983). "Property value maximization and public sector efficiency". Journal of Urban Economics 14 (1), 1–15.

Brueckner, J.K. (1990). "Growth controls and land values in an open city". Land Economics 66, 237–248.

Brueckner, J.K. (2001). "Fiscal decentralization with distortionary taxation: Tiebout vs. tax competition". Working paper. University of Illinois.

Brueckner, J.K., Saavedra, L.A. (2001). "Do local governments engage in strategic tax competition". National Tax Journal LIV (2), 203–229.

Brennan, G., Buchanan, J.M. (1980). The Power to Tax: Analytic Foundations of a Fiscal Constitution. Cambridge University Press, New York.

Buchanan, J.M. (1965). "An economic theory of clubs". Economica 33, 1–14.

Bucovetsky, S., Wilson, J. (1991). "Tax competition with two tax instruments". Regional Science and Urban Economics 21, 333–350.

Buiter, W. (1989). "Debt neutrality, professor Vickery and Henry George's 'single tax' ". Economics Letters 29, 43–47.

Calabrese, S. (1999). "Multimember district congressional elections". Working paper. Martin School of Public Policy, University of Kentucky.

Calabrese, S. (2000). "Multimember district congressional elections". Legislative Studies Quarterly 25 (4).

Calabrese, S., Epple, D. (2004). "On the political economy of tax limits". Working paper.

Case, A.C., Rosen, H.S., Hines jr., J.R. (1993). "Budget spillovers and fiscal policy interdependence: evidence from the states". Journal of Public Economics 52 (3), 285–307.

Caucutt, E. (2001). "Peer group effects in applied general equilibrium". Economic Theory 17, 25–51.

Coase, R. (1937). "The nature of the firm". Economica 4, 386–405.

Coate, S., Conlin, M. (2001). "Voter turnout: theory and evidence from Texas liquor referenda". Working paper (December).

Coleman, J. (Ed.) (1996). Equality of Educational Opportunity. Government Printing Office, Washington, DC.

Conley, J. (2001). "Intergenerational spillovers, decentralization and durable public goods". Working paper. Department of Economics, University of Illinois–Champaign.

Conley, J., Rangel, A. (2001). "Intergenerational fiscal constitutions: how to protect future generations using land taxes and federalism". NBER working paper 8394.

Conley, J., Wooders, M. (2001). "Tiebout economies with differential genetic types and endogenously chosen crowding characteristics". Journal of Economic Theory 98, 261–294.

Courant, P.N., Gramlich, E.M., Rubinfeld, D.L. (1979). "Public employee market power and the level of government spending". American Economic Review 69 (5), 806–817.

Cutler, D., Glaeser, E. (1997). "Are ghettos good or bad". Quarterly Journal of Economics 112 (3), 827–872.

Dale, S., Krueger. A. (1998). "Estimating the payoff to attending a more selective college: an application of selection on observables". Working paper.

Daly, G. (1969). "The burden of the debt and future generations in local finance". Southern Economic Journal 36, 44–51.

Davidoff, T. (2003). "Income sorting: measurement and decomposition". Working paper. University of California at Berkeley.

de Bartolome, C. (1990). "Equilibrium and efficiency in a community model with peer group effects". Journal of Political Economy 98 (1), 110–133.

DePater, J., Myers, G. (1994). "Strategic capital tax competition: a pecuniary externality and a corrective subsidy". Journal of Public Economics 36 (1), 66–78.

Ding, W., Lehrer, S. (2001). "Do peers affect student achievement in China's secondary schools?" Working paper.

Dunz, K. (1985). "Existence of equilibrium with local public goods and houses". SUNY-Albany Department of Economics Discussion Paper #201.

Durlauf, S.N. (1996). "A theory of persistent income inequality". Journal of Economic Growth 1 (March), 75–93.

Durlauf, S., Brock, W. (2001). "Discrete choice with social interactions". Review of Economic Studies 68 (2), 235–260.

Durlauf, S., Brock, W. (in press). "A multinomial choice model with neighborhood effects". American Economic Review.

Dye, R.F., McGuire, T.J. (1997). "The effect of property tax limitation measures on local government fiscal behavior". Journal of Public Economics 66 (3), 469–487.

Edel, M., Sclar, E. (1974). "Taxes, spending and property values: supply adjustment in a Tiebout–Oates model". Journal of Political Economy 82 (5), 941–954.

Edwards, J., Keen, M. (1996). "Tax competition and Leviathan". European Economic Review 40, 113–134.

Ellickson, B. (1971). "Jurisdictional fragmentation and residential choice". American Economic Review, Papers and Proceedings 61 (May), 334–339.

Ellickson, B., Grodal, B., Scotchmer, S., Zame, W. (1999). "Clubs and the market". Econometrica 67, 1185–1217.

Epple, D., Figlio, D., Romano, R. (in press). "Competition between private and public schools: testing stratification and pricing predictions". Journal of Public Economics.

Epple, D., Filimon, R., Romer, T. (1984). "Equilibrium among local jurisdictions: toward an integrated treatment of voting and residential choice". Journal of Public Economics 24, 281–308.

Epple, D., Filimon, R., Romer, T. (1993). "Existence of voting and housing equilibrium in a system of communities with property taxes". Regional Science and Urban Economics 23, 585–610.

Epple, D., Newlon, E., Romano, R. (2002). "Ability tracking, school competition, and the distribution of educational benefits". Journal of Public Economics 83 (1), 1–48.

Epple, D., Platt, G. (1998). "Equilibrium and local redistribution in an urban economy when households differ in both preferences and income". Journal of Urban Economics 43 (1), 23–51.
Epple, D., Romano, R. (1996). "Ends against the middle: determining public service provision when there are private alternatives". Journal of Public Economics 62, 297–325.
Epple, D., Romano, R. (1998). "Competition between public and private schools, vouchers and peer group effects". American Economic Review 88 (1), 33–62.
Epple, D., Romano, R. (2002). "Educational vouchers and cream skimming". Working paper.
Epple, D., Romano, R.E. (2003). "Neighborhood schools, choice, and the distribution of educational benefits". In: Hoxby, C.M. (Ed.), The Economics of School Choice. University of Chicago Press.
Epple, D., Romer, T. (1989). "On the flexibility of municipal boundaries". Journal of Urban Economics 26 (3), 307–319.
Epple, D., Romer, T. (1991). "Mobility and redistribution". Journal of Political Economy 99, 828–858.
Epple, D., Romer, T., Sieg, H. (2001). "Interjurisdictional sorting and majority rule: an empirical analysis". Econometrica 69 (6), 1437–1465.
Epple, D., Sieg, H. (1999). "Estimating equilibrium models of local jurisdictions". Journal of Political Economy 107 (4), 645–681.
Epple, D., Spatt, C. (1986). "State restrictions on local debt: their role in preventing default". Journal of Public Economics.
Epple, D., Zelenitz, A. (1981). "The implications of competition among jurisdictions: does Tiebout need politics?" Journal of Political Economy 89, 1197–1217.
Epple, D., Zelenitz, A., Visscher, M. (1978). "A search for testable implications of the Tiebout hypothesis". Journal of Political Economy 86, 405–425.
Evans, W., Oates, W., Schwab, R. (1992). "Measuring peer group effects: a study of teenage behavior". Journal of Political Economy 100, 966–991.
Feldstein, M. (1975). "Wealth neutrality and local choice in public education". American Economic Review 65 (1), 75–89.
Fernandez, R., Rogerson, R. (1996). "Income distribution, communities, and the quality of public education". Quarterly Journal of Economics 11 (2), 135–164.
Fernandez, R., Rogerson, R. (1997). "Keeping people out: income distribution, zoning and the quality of public education". International Economic Review 38 (1), 23–42.
Fernandez, R., Rogerson, R. (1998). "Public education and income distribution: a dynamic quantitative evaluation of education finance reform". American Economic Review 88 (4), 813–833.
Fernandez, R., Rogerson, R. (1999). "Education finance reform and investment in human capital: lessons from California". Journal of Public Economics 74 (3), 327–350.
Ferreyra, M. (2002a). "Estimating a general equilibrium model with multiple jurisdictions and private schools". Working paper. Carnegie Mellon University.
Ferreyra, M. (2002b), "Assessing voucher effects in general equilibrium". Working paper. Carnegie Mellon University.
Figlio, D. (1997). "Did the 'Tax Revolt' reduce school performance?" Journal of Public Economics 65, 245–269.
Figlio, D., Kolpin, V.W., Reid, W.E. (1999). "Do states play welfare games". Journal of Urban Economics 46 (3), 437–454.
Fischel, W.A. (2001). "Homevoters, municipal corporate governance, and the benefit view of the property tax". National Tax Journal 54 (1), 157–173.
Fischel, W.A. (1992). "Property taxation and the Tiebout model: evidence for the benefit view from zoning and voting". Journal of Economic Literature 30 (1), 171–177.
Gans, J., Smart, M. (1996). "Majority voting with single-crossing preferences". Journal of Public Economics 59 (2), 219–237.
Goldstein, G.S., Pauly, M.V. (1981). "Tiebout bias on the demand for local public goods". Journal of Public Economics 16 (2), 131–143.
Grossman, G., Helpman, E. (1994). "Protection for sale". American Economic Review 84 (2), 833–850.

Hamilton, B. (1975). "Zoning and property taxes in a system of local governments". Urban Studies 12, 205–211.
Hamilton, B. (1976). "Capitalization of interjurisdictional differences in local tax prices". American Economic Review 66, 743–753.
Hanushek, E., Kain, J., Markman, J., Rivkin, S. (2003). "Do peers affect student achievement?" Journal of Applied Economics 18.
Helsley, R., Strange, W. (1995). "Strategic growth controls". Regional Science and Urban Economics 25 (4), 435–460.
Helsley, R., Strange, W. (1999). "Gated communities and the economic geography of crime". Journal of Urban Economics 46 (1), 80–105.
Helsley, R., Strange, W. (2000). "Potential competition and public sector performance". Regional Science and Urban Economics 30 (4), 405–428.
Henderson, J.V. (1985). "The Tiebout model: bring back the entrepreneurs". Journal of Political Economy 93, 248–264.
Henderson, J.V. (1994). "Community choice of revenue instruments". Regional Science and Urban Economics 24 (2), 159–183.
Henderson, J.V. (1995). "Will homeowners impose property taxes". Regional Science and Urban Economics 24, 153–181.
Henderson, J.V., Mieszkowski, P., Sauvageau, Y. (1978). "Peer group effects and educational production functions". Journal of Public Economics 10, 97–106.
Henderson, J.V., Thisse, J.-F. (2001). "On strategic community development". Journal of Political Economy 109 (3), 546–569.
Hines, J., Thaler, R. (1995). "The flypaper effect". Journal of Economic Perspectives 9 (4), 217–226.
Hochman, O., Pines, D., Thisse, J.-F. (1995). "On the optimal structure of local government". American Economic Review 85 (5), 1224–1240.
Hoxby, C.M. (2000a). "Does competition among public schools benefit students and taxpayers?" American Economic Review 90 (5), 1209–1238.
Hoxby, C.M. (2000b). "Peer effects in the classroom: learning from gender and race variation". Working paper.
Hoyt, W. (1991a). "Property taxation, Nash equilibrium and market power". Journal of Urban Economics 34, 123–131.
Hoyt, W. (1991b). "Competitive jurisdictions, congestion and the Henry George Theorem: when should property be taxed instead of land". Regional Science and Urban Economics 21, 351–370.
Hoyt, W., Lee, K. (1998). "Education vouchers, welfare effects and voting". Journal of Public Economics 69 (2), 211–228.
Inman, R. (1988). "Federal assistance and local services in the united states: the evolution of a new federalist order". In: Rosen, H. (Ed.), Fiscal Federalism. University of Chicago Press, Chicago.
Inman, R., Rubinfeld, D. (1979). "The judicial pursuit of local fiscal equity". Harvard Law Review 92, 1662–1750.
Inman, R., Rubinfeld, D. (1996). "Designing tax policy in federalist economies: an overview". Journal of Public Economics 60, 307–334.
Ioannides, Y. (2001). "Neighborhood income distributions". Tufts University Discussion paper 2001-03.
Ioannides, Y., Selsen, T.N. (2001). "Neighborhood wealth distributions". Tufts University Discussion paper (December).
Kessler, A., Hansen, N. (2001). "(Non-) existence of equilibria in multi-community models". Journal of Urban Economics 50, 418–435.
Konishi, H. (1996). "Voting with ballots and feet: existence of equilibrium in a local public goods economy". Journal of Economic Theory 68, 480–509.
Krelove, R. (1992). "Efficient tax exporting". Canadian Journal of Economics 25 (1), 145–155.
Krelove, R. (1993). "The persistence and inefficiency of property tax finance of local public expenditures". Journal of Public Economics 51 (3), 415–435.

Kremer, M. (1997). "How much does sorting increase inequality". Quarterly Journal of Economics 112 (1), 115–139.

Kremer, M., Levy, D. (2003). "Peer effects and alcohol use among college students". NBER Working paper.

Ladd, H. (1976). "State-wide taxation of commercial and industrial property for education". National Tax Journal 29 (2), 143–153.

Laffont, J., Tirole, J. (1993). A Theory of Incentives in Procurement and Regulation. MIT Press, Cambridge, MA.

Lockwood, B. (2001). "Tax competition and tax co-ordination under destination and origin principle: a synthesis". Journal of Public Economics 81 (2), 279–319.

Lockwood, B. (2002). "Distributive politics and the cost of centralization". Review of Economic Studies 69 (2), 313–337.

Manski, C. (1993). "Identification of endogenous social effects: the reflection problem". Review of Economic Studies 60, 531–542.

Marceau, N. (1997). "Competition in crime deterrence". Canadian Journal of Economics 30 (4), 844–854.

McKelvey, R. (1976). "Intransitivities in multidimensional voting models and some implications for agenda control". Journal of Economic Theory 12, 472–482.

McKinnon, R. (1997). "Market preserving fiscal federalism in the American Monetary Union". In: Macroeconomic Dimensions of Public Finance: Essays in Honor of Vito Tanzi. Routledge, London and New York, pp. 73–93.

McKinnon, R., Nechyba, T. (1997). "Competition in federal systems: the role of political and financial constraints". In: Ferejohn, J., Weingast, B. (Eds.), The New Federalism: Can the States be Trusted? Hoover Institution Press, Stanford, CA, pp. 3–64.

McMillan, R. (2001). "Competition, parental involvement and public school performance". National Tax Journal Papers and Proceedings.

Mieszkowski, P., Zodrow, G. (1989). "Taxation and the Tiebout model: the differential effects of head taxes, taxes on land rents and property taxes". Journal of Economic Literature 27 (3), 1098–1146.

Mieszkowski, P., Zodrow, G. (1986). "Pigou, Tiebout, property taxation and the underprovision of local public goods". Journal of Urban Economics 19 (3), 356–370.

Moffitt, R. (2001). "Policy interventions, low-level equilibria, and social interactions". In: Durlauf, S., Young, P. (Eds.), Social Dynamics. MIT Press, Cambridge, MA.

Murray, S., Evans, W., Schwab, R. (1998). "Education-finance reform and the distribution of education resources". American Economic Review 88 (4), 789–812.

Myers, G. (1990). "Optimality, free mobility, and the regional authority in a federation". Journal of Public Economics 43 (1), 107–121.

Nechyba, T. (1994). "Fiscal federalism and local public finance: a general equilibrium approach with voting". PhD dissertation. University of Rochester. Unpublished.

Nechyba, T. (1996). "A computable general equilibrium model of intergovernmental aid". Journal of Public Economics 62, 363–397.

Nechyba, T. (1997a). "Local property and state income taxes: the role if interjurisdictional competition and collusion". Journal of Political Economy 105 (2), 351–384.

Nechyba, T. (1997b). "Existence of equilibrium and stratification in local and hierarchical public good economies with property taxes and voting". Economic Theory 10, 277–304.

Nechyba, T. (1999). "School finance induced migration patterns: the impact of private school vouchers". Journal of Public Economic Theory 1 (1), 5–50.

Nechyba, T. (2000). "Mobility, targeting and private school vouchers". American Economic Review 90 (1), 130–146.

Nechyba, T. (2001). "Prospects for land rent taxes in state and local tax reforms". Working paper. Lincoln Institute.

Nechyba, T. (2002). "Prospects for achieving equity or adequacy in education: the limits of state aid in general equilibrium". Working paper. Department of Economics, Duke University.

Wildasin, D. (1989). "Interjurisdictional capital mobility: fiscal externality and a corrective subsidy". Journal of Urban Economics 25, 193–212.

Wildasin, D. (1991). "Some rudimentary 'duopolity' theory". Regional Science and Urban Economics 21 (3), 393–421.

Williamson, O. (2002). "The theory of the firm as governance structure: from choice to contract". Journal of Economic Perspectives 16 (3), 171–195.

Wilson, J. (1986). "A theory of interregional tax competition". Journal of Urban Economics 19, 296–315.

Wilson, J. (1995). "Mobile labor, multiple tax instruments and tax competition". Journal of Urban Economics 38, 333–356.

Wilson, J. (1997). "Property taxation, congestion and local public goods". Journal of Public Economics 64, 207–217.

Wilson, J. (2000). "Welfare improving competition for mobile capital". Working paper. Department of Economics, Michigan State University.

Winston, G., Zimmerman, D. (2003). "Peer effects in higher education". In: Hoxby, C.M. (Ed.), College Decisions: How Students Actually Make Them and How They Could. University of Chicago Press.

Wooders, M. (1980). "The Tiebout hypothesis: near optimality in local public good economies". Econometrica 48, 1467–1485.

Wooders, M. (1999). "Multijurisdiction economies, the Tiebout hypothesis and sorting". Proceedings of the National Academy of Sciences 96 (19), 10585–10587.

Yinger, J. (1982). "Capitalization and the theory of local public finance". Journal of Political Economy 90, 917–943.

Zimmerman, D. (1999). "Peer effects in academic outcomes: evidence from a natural experiment". Discussion paper No. 52. Williams Project on the Economics of Higher Education, Williams College.

Zimmerman, D. (2000). "Peer effects in private and public schools: a cross country empirical analysis". Working paper.

Zimmer, R., Toma, E. (1998). "Peer effects in private and public schools across countries". Working paper.

Chapter 56

SPRAWL AND URBAN GROWTH

EDWARD L. GLAESER[1]

Harvard University, Cambridge, MA 02138, USA
e-mail: eglaeser@kuznets.fas.harvard.edu

MATTHEW E. KAHN

Tufts University, Medford, MA 02155, USA

Contents

[1] Also affiliated with NBER.

Handbook of Regional and Urban Economics, Volume 4. Edited by J.V. Henderson and J.F. Thisse

DOI: 10.1016/S0169-7218(04)07056-X

Abstract

Cities can be thought of as the absence of physical space between people and firms. As such, they exist to eliminate transportation costs for goods, people and ideas and transportation technologies dictate urban form. In the 21st century, the dominant form of city living is based on the automobile and this form is sometimes called sprawl. In this essay, we document that sprawl is ubiquitous and that it is continuing to expand. Using a variety of evidence, we argue that sprawl is not the result of explicit government policies or bad urban planning, but rather the inexorable product of car-based living. Sprawl has been associated with significant improvements in quality of living, and the environmental impacts of sprawl have been offset by technological change. Finally, we suggest that the primary social problem associated with sprawl is the fact that some people are left behind because they do not earn enough to afford the cars that this form of living requires.

Keywords

cars, suburbanization, sprawl, pollution

JEL classification: R14, R41

1. Introduction

In the early part of the 20th century, cities grew upward. Tenements and luxury apartment buildings replaced brownstones. Skyscrapers came to adorn urban landscapes. But at the end of the 20th century, urban growth has pushed cities further and further out. The compact urban areas of 1900 have increasingly been replaced by unending miles of malls, office parks and houses on larger and larger lots. At first, people continued to work in cities but lived in sprawling suburbs. But the jobs followed the people and now metropolitan areas are characterized by decentralized homes and decentralized jobs. In 2003 America, urban growth and sprawl are almost synonymous and edge cities have become the dominant urban form.

In this essay, we review the economic literature on sprawl and urban growth, and make four points.

- First, despite the pronouncements of academic theorists, dense living is not on the rebound. Sprawl is ubiquitous and expanding.
- Second, while many factors may have helped the growth of sprawl, it ultimately has only one root cause: the automobile. Suburbia, edge cities and sprawl are all the natural, inexorable, result of the technological dominance of the automobile.
- Third, sprawl's negative quality of life impacts have been overstated. Effective vehicle pollution regulation has curbed emissions increases associated with increased driving. The growth of edge cities is associated with increases in most measures of quality of life.
- Fourth, the problem of sprawl lies not in the people who have moved to the suburbs but rather the people who have been left behind. The exodus of jobs and people from the inner cities have created an abandoned underclass whose earnings cannot support a multi-car-based lifestyle.

1.1. *Plan of the paper*

In Section 2, we begin with a characterization of sprawl in the United States. To us, the most striking fact about sprawl in the U.S. is its omnipresence. Employment is decentralized almost everywhere and traditional downtowns now contain only a tiny sliver of overall metropolitan employment. The overwhelming majority of Americans live in medium-density census tracts miles from the city center.

After first describing the level of sprawl, in Section 3, we turn to its roots. Many authors have argued that sprawl is caused by government policies such as highway subsidies, the home mortgage interest deduction, and insufficient funding of urban public services (such as subways). Others have claimed that sprawl comes from a desire to avoid Blacks or the poor. While some of these forces abetted the rise of sprawl, the root cause of U.S. sprawl is far more prosaic – the technological superiority of the automobile. Automobiles are so much faster than previous means of transportation that in most of America they have become really the only travel mode.

Cities have always been shaped by transportation technologies. The dense walking cities of 18th century Boston and New York crowded up against their wharves. The merchants, who traveled by foot, needed to be close to their much swifter goods, which traveled by boat. In the 19th century, the omnibus and later the streetcar opened cities up. Long, parallel streets replaced winding cow paths as people, particularly the wealthy, moved to newer, less dense neighborhoods. The subway and commuter rail moved people still further away from the downtown.

As important as prior transportation innovations have been, the car has had a more dramatic effect on the city than anything before it. Unlike the earlier transportation innovations, the car has radically reshaped cities because it eliminates walking almost entirely. People who took streetcars in 1900 still had to walk from the streetcar stop to their homes or their jobs. As such, businesses and homes needed to crowd against public transportation stations. Routine shopping and many other non-work related activities were generally done on foot before the automobile. As such stores, schools and restaurants needed to be within ready walking distance of consumers. Public transportation made it possible for consumers to live far from their work, but they still needed to live at high densities. Cars have changed that and as a result, inalterably changed city living forever.

The car should be understood as having two distinct effects on population decentralization. First, as almost all analysts of sprawl recognize [e.g., Alonso (1964), Jackson (1985), Brueckner (2000)] – cars reduce transport costs, thus increasing the possible distance between residences and jobs. But cars and trucks have one other equally important effect: they eliminate the scale economies involved in older transportation technologies. Ports and railway stations were massive pieces of infrastructure, and they could not be reproduced willy–nilly throughout metropolitan areas. As a result, traditional cities clustered around the port and the railroad hub. One may think that Wall Street developed because of agglomeration economies, but the history of the downtown suggests that the fixed costs of transportation were at least as important. As trucks and cars have replaced boats and trains, these scale economies have vanished and it has become possible for employment to decentralize throughout metropolitan areas and throughout the country.

But has the move to sprawl been socially beneficial? In Section 4, we consider the welfare consequences of sprawl. While many non-economists seem to think that sprawl is an unequivocal evil, we think that generally sprawl has yielded social benefits. Sprawl has been associated with large houses and short travel times. The median housing unit in Manhattan has 820 square feet. In the suburbs of Washington, DC, the median housing unit has 1950 square feet. Across the United States, the median household lives in a housing unit with 1395 square feet (data source 1999 American Housing Survey).

The commute time differences are also dramatic. While congestion may be slowing commutes in some edge cities, in most cases, the car-based urban frontier has far shorter commutes than the old public transportation cities [Gordon, Kumar and Richardson (1991)]. Cars are just so much faster than public transportation that commutes in the old dense cities are almost always much longer than in their newer, sprawling competitors.

Thus, the average commute in New York City is the longest of any large city – 39 minutes. In the edge cities, the average commute is 21 minutes about one-half of this amount. The savings of more than 30 minutes per day in travel time represents one of the biggest welfare effects of sprawling cities. While it may be optimal to introduce policies which would force people to internalize the congestion externalities from their driving, even without those policies, commute times have plummeted in edge cities.

We then turn to the other potential costs of sprawl – social segregation and environmental damage. There is a strong logic which argues that automobiles have facilitated segregation. Cars are expensive and the new car-based cities have been much more accessible to the wealthy. Conversely, the poor have tended to circle around public transportation [Glaeser, Kahn and Rappaport (2000)].

However, across metropolitan areas, cities with more sprawl are actually less segregated, both on the basis of income and on the basis of race. In general, the car-based edge cities have much more racial integration than the older public transportation cities than they replaced. Changes in income-based segregation are harder to assess, but across cities, the presence of public transportation tends to increase the level of income-based segregation [Glaeser, Kahn and Rappaport (2000)]. Multiple transport modes provide a natural explanation for this segregation phenomenon. When there are multiple modes, the rich will live in the car zones and use the more expensive, faster mode and the poor will live in areas with greater access to the cheaper, slower mode. Car-based edge cities feature only one mode and hence have less segregation. As a result, there is more segregation in the multiple mode traditional cities.

This implies that sprawl cities may actually both reduce segregation and hurt the well being of the poor. In sprawl cities, the poor are forced to spend more on transportation services. They are less segregated but they also have less cash. Consumer expenditure surveys make it clear that the poor in sprawl cities spend less on non-car expenditures. They may indeed be the losers from sprawl.

Finally, there is the question of the environmental consequences of sprawl and car reliance. These include local air pollution, Global Warming impacts, and lost farmland.

Car cities such as Houston and Los Angeles have had high smog levels. Suburban vehicle-dependent growth leads to increased aggregate gasoline consumption. This raises the stock of greenhouse gases. Suburban growth also displaces farmland. Road construction and large suburban lots contribute to paving over farmland. Such open space offers aesthetic benefits and hard to measure "existence value" benefits.

Vehicle regulation has significantly reduced emissions per-mile over the last 30 years. As we document below, urban air quality has sharply improved in growing areas. We recognize that sprawl, through increasing driving during an era when little improvements in fleet fuel economy have been achieved, has increased greenhouse gas production. Some pollution-based taxation may increase social welfare, but current gas taxes already appear to cover most estimates of environmental damage.[1]

[1] Parry and Small (2002) argue that the United States' gasoline tax is too low while England's is too high.

Some environmental advocates have argued that sprawl destroys forest, but over the past 20 years the amount of forest cover in the U.S. has increased, not decreased. Overall, residential real estate still covers a very small amount of the country and the increases in urban land area have been irrelevant to the overall amount of forest cover [Fischel (1987)]. Forests have by and large increased because low return agricultural activities have been discontinued and replaced by forests. Indeed, there is one argument that increases in housing construction actually increase the demand for wood and therefore lead to an increase in the amount of forest cover.

While our depiction of sprawl is generally positive, we do think that the rise in car-based cities raises several important policy concerns. The first is that increasing reliance on the automobile increases the costs of failing to properly address congestion externalities. Without a more sensible approach to taxing drivers for using roads during peak travel times, it is likely that the welfare costs of traffic delays will continue to spiral [see Small and Gomez-Ibáñez (1998)]. There is a growing optimism that London's recent road pricing scheme is achieving its goals with little political backlash.

The second important policy concern is that small jurisdictions which were reasonable political units in an era of high transport costs may no longer be appropriate as the costs of movement have fallen. They make decisions which often impose externalities on neighboring jurisdictions which may well be quite costly. The most obvious example of this failure lies in the area of land use controls. Homeowners impose growth controls supposedly in an attempt to deter sprawl [Katz and Rosen (1987), Rosen and Katz (1981)]. However, these controls often simply push developers to the next town out and sprawl may indeed increase as a result of these policies. Some sprawling metropolitan areas, such as Atlanta with its Atlanta Regional Commission, have attempted to co-ordinate jurisdictional policy.

Our final policy concern relates to sprawl and the poorest Americans. As there are a large number of Americans who cannot afford automobiles, the flight to edge cities has indeed left them behind. If we accept that America will be primarily a car-based nation, then it makes sense to ask whether car-based subsidies for the poor make sense. We summarize the work of Raphael and Stoll (2001).

2. The extent of sprawl

In this section, we review key facts about the growing edge cities in the United States. Our goal is to discuss the measurement of sprawl and apply those measures to American urban data. In general, there are two concepts which come together in the popular conception of sprawl: decentralization and density. Decentralization refers to the spreading of employment and population throughout the metropolitan area. Density refers to the degree to which employment and population are centered in high-density living and working areas.

In principle, there could be decentralized, dense urban areas. These areas would be characterized by a large number of employment subcenters, where each subcenter is itself quite dense. This vision of urban sprawl is described in the work of Anas, Arnott and Small (1998), Brueckner (1979), Giuliano and Small (1991), McDonald and McMillen (2000) and McMillen and McDonald (1998), and by the edge city model of Henderson and Mitra (1996). But most popular views of sprawl seem to believe that decentralization and lower densities tend to go together. As such, when edge cities formed, they did not replace traditional dense downtowns with new dense job centers, but rather with low-density employment areas.

We will use a number of measures to capture both decentralization and density [for an extensive review of different measures see Galster et al. (2001)]. Several intuitive measures of decentralization present themselves. Of course, for any measure of decentralization, we need some idea of where the metropolitan areas center actually is located. For this, we use the 1982 Special Census Survey which asked local leaders for the exact spot which is the geographical center of their city. These surveys are surely imperfect, but in general the survey tends to pick the spot that seems to be the natural center. For example, in New York, Wall Street was picked as the city's geographical center. In metropolitan areas with multiple cities, we chose the city with the largest population and used the city center of that city.

One natural test of the validity of these estimates is to ask whether these centers do appear to be focal points for employment, or put another way, is there an unusually high concentration of employment in and around those centers. To check this, we calculated the employment density (measured as employees per mile) in the zip code that contained each city center. The data source is the Department of Commerce's Zip Code Business Patterns 1996 data [Glaeser and Kahn (2001)]. We then compare this employment density with the employment density of other zip codes in the metropolitan area. Out of 301 metropolitan areas, we found that in 180 of them, the city center zip code had the absolute highest employment density in the metropolitan area. In 270 of the MSAs, the city center zip code was among the four most dense zip codes. These city centers are not mere arbitrary definitions. They almost always measure one of the densest employment spots in the city.

Using these city centers, we calculate a number of different measures of employment and population decentralization. The first and easiest measure is the share of employment within a five-mile radius of the city center. These measures have the virtue of capturing the extent to which the population or employment is really physically close to the center of the city. Table 1 provides some basic summary statistics. Across 150 major metropolitan areas, the average city has 42.6 percent of its total employment within a 5 mile radius around its CBD. This average masks wide variation. Ten percent of cities have more than 80 percent of their employment outside of the five-mile inner ring.

The level of decentralization is striking. Figure 1 shows the cumulative distribution of jobs and people for U.S. metropolitan areas as a whole, asking what share lies within different boundaries. Across all of the different metropolitan areas, we find that only 45 percent of employment and 38 percent of population lies with 5 miles of the city center.[2]

[2] The data source for population is the 1990 Census of Population and Housing.

Table 1
Summary statistics for MSA level sprawl indicators

MSA measure for 150 major MSAs	Mean	st.dev.	10th percentile	90th percentile
Percentage of population: within inner 3 mile ring	18.26	10.82	5.78	32.9
within inner 5 mile ring	34.72	15.71	17.54	55.94
within inner 10 mile ring	63.95	16.51	40.17	86.13
Percentage of employment: within inner 3 mile ring	25.71	12.33	10.94	43.76
within inner 5 mile ring	42.59	18.09	19.29	66.67
within inner 10 mile ring	70.18	18.53	43.1	91.5
MSA average population density	2952	3969	917	4971
MSA average employment density	3900	9867	624	6519
Overall MSA population density	1008	1782	230	2031
Median person's distance in miles from CBD	7.88	2.97	4.55	11.72
Median worker's distance in miles from CBD	6.93	3.27	3.54	12.05

Average population density and average employment density are defined as the weighted average of zip code density where the weight is the zip code's share of total MSA activity. Inner rings refer to distance from the Central Business District. Median distance is the location such that 50 percentage of economic activity in the MSA is beyond that distance.

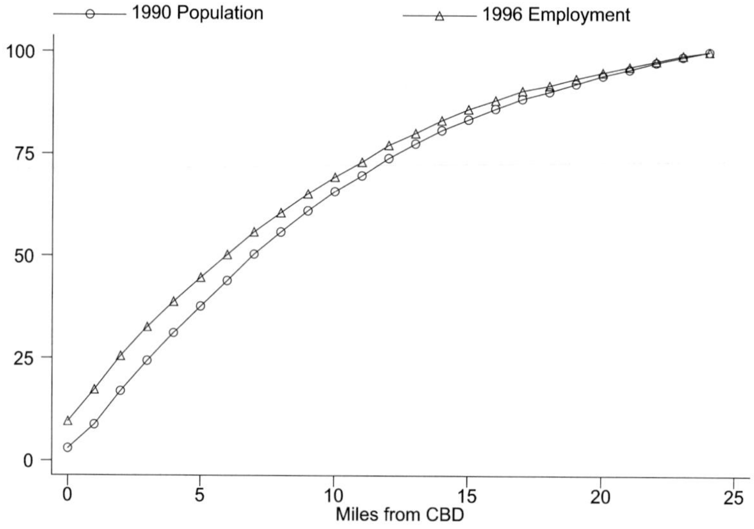

Figure 1. The spatial distribution of people and jobs within MSAs.

Population decentralization and employment decentralization go hand in hand. While, in general, jobs are more centralized than people, the cities that are centralized along one dimension are centralized along both. To show this, we estimate regression (1) separately by MSA using both employment density and population density as the dependent variables:

$$\log(\text{Density}) = a + b * \text{Distance from CBD} + e. \tag{1}$$

In this regression, the coefficient b captures the extent to which density falls with distance from the CBD.[3] This functional form can be justified using a version of the Alonso–Muth–Mills model. After estimating Equation (1) for 131 major MSAs, we took the population and employment gradient estimates of b and ran a second stage regression of the form: $b = c + g * \log(\text{population}) + \text{Region} + U$. Controlling for a MSA's region and its population, we recover a residual for each MSA for its employment and population gradient. Figure 2 shows the correlation across metropolitan areas of the employment density–distance gradient residual and the residential density–distance gradient residual. There are very few cities which have centralized employment and decentralized residences (or vice versa).

As we turn to measuring density, there are a few possible alternatives. Most obviously, one can use jobs or residents per mile in the city as a whole. This certainly fits the popular conception of density, but does little to differentiate cities where the bulk of people live in skyscrapers that are surrounded by vacant land with cities where the bulk of people live in single-family dwellings at low densities.

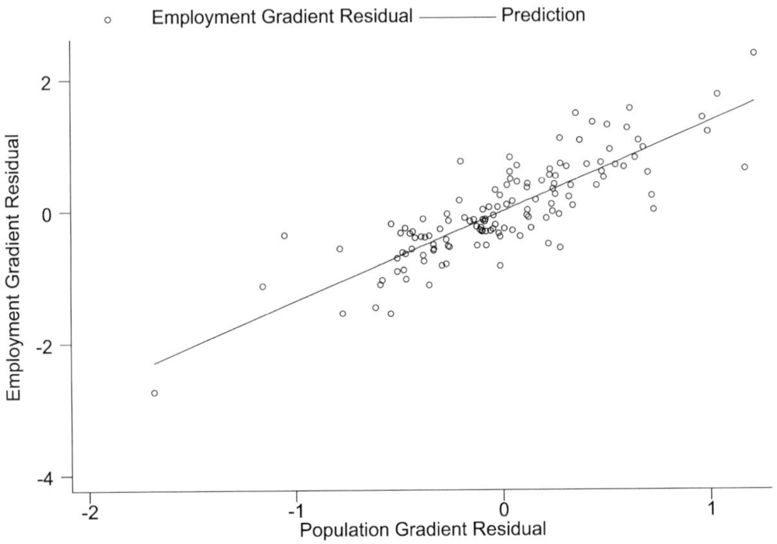

Figure 2. Cross-MSA employment and population gradients.

[3] It should be noted that when we calculate population density using the square mileage of the zip code. We are unable to incorporate the fact that there are vacant lots within zip codes. Mieszkowski and Smith (1991) are able to calculate density gradients for Houston while accounting for the presence of vacant lots.

One natural improvement is to look at density at the zip code level and to ask at what density does the average member of this city live or work, or more precisely:

$$\sum_{i=1}^{I} \frac{N_i}{N_{\text{Total}}} \frac{N_i}{A_i},$$

where A_i refers to the square mileage of the geographic subunit. The geographical unit for our employment and population data is the zip code.

The bottom of Table 1 shows that across 150 major MSAs, the average person lives in a community of density 2952 people per square mile and works in an area featuring 3900 employees per square mile. Table 2 shows that major cities differ greatly with respect to their employment densities. The average worker in New York City works at a job density five times higher than the fourth most dense city (Boston). While New York City has the highest job density index, it does not have the highest share of all metro jobs within a three-mile ring around its CBD. The left column of Table 2 shows that San Francisco is the least sprawled metro area based on this criterion.

Given that different sprawl indicators yield different rankings of major cities, in Table 3 we present a correlation matrix of seven of our indicators for 150 major metro areas. While some correlations are quite high, such as the negative correlation of −0.57 between "percent of employment within inner 3 mile ring around the CBD" and "median worker's distance in miles from the CBD", other

Table 2
High and low sprawl for 50 major metro areas

	Percentage of employment within 3 mile ring around CBD		Employment weighted MSA job density
Least sprawled			
San Francisco	48.3	New York City	108,177
Providence	46.76	Chicago	40,682
New York City	46.58	San Francisco	34,620
Springfield	41.99	Boston	20,050
Jersey City	41.76	Washington, DC	15,263
Most sprawled			
Los Angeles	7.3	Fresno	1386
New Haven	10.47	Tucson	1542
San Jose	11.41	Grand Rapids	1574
Anaheim	13.84	Saint Cloud	1654
Fort Lauderdale	14.86	Springfield	1987

Employment weighted MSA job density is constructed by taking the employment density by zip code as defined as employment per square mile and then calculating a MSA weighted average where the weight is a zip code's share of all jobs in the MSA.

Table 3
Correlation matrix for various MSA sprawl indicators

$N = 150$	Indicator	1	2	3	4	5	6
Percentage of population within inner 3 mile ring	1	1					
Percentage of employment within inner 3 mile ring	2	0.77	1				
MSA average population density	3	−0.06	0.07	1			
MSA average employment density	4	−0.13	0.13	0.9	1		
Overall MSA population density	5	−0.07	0.01	0.95	0.8	1	
Median person's distance in miles from CBD	6	−0.48	−0.49	−0.02	0.04	0.04	1
Median worker's distance in miles from CBD	7	−0.41	−0.57	−0.02	−0.02	0.06	0.89

Table 4
Work and residential densities by distance from the CBD

Distance from CBD	Population density			Job density		
in miles	Mean	st.dev.	95th percentile	Mean	st.dev.	95th percentile
0 to 5	7647	15,745	26,027	23,497	67,497	160,821
5 to 10	7433	13,509	35,385	2541	3710	8035
10 to 15	3555	4876	11,422	1926	2319	5482
15 to 20	2132	2610	7124	1508	2108	5072
20 to 25	1381	1718	4812	1216	3374	3708

We partition all zip codes by their distance from the Central Business District. Within each five mile ring, we calculate weighted population and employment density and the 95th percentile of these distributions.

correlations are quite low.[4] One interesting zero correlation is between "MSA average population density" and the "Median person's distance in miles from the CBD".

The population and job density measures provide a metric for investigating whether there are meaningful employment centers outside of core employment centers. To address this, we look at the distribution of employment densities close to the city center and away from the city center. We assign each zip code to one of five mutually exclusive and exhaustive categories based on five-mile rings around the CBD. For each of these five-mile rings, we calculate the weighted average of job and population density. Table 4 shows the distribution of these densities. Across the metropolitan U.S. as a whole, the average person works in a zip code with 10,371 workers per square mile and lives in a zip code with 5651 people per square mile. The average worker, who works in the 5 to

4 We calculate for each metro area, the distance from the CBD such that 50% of workers work further from the CBD than that point. The bottom of Table 1 shows that the median worker works at 6.9 miles from the CBD but in 10% of cities, the median worker is located more than 12 miles from the CBD.

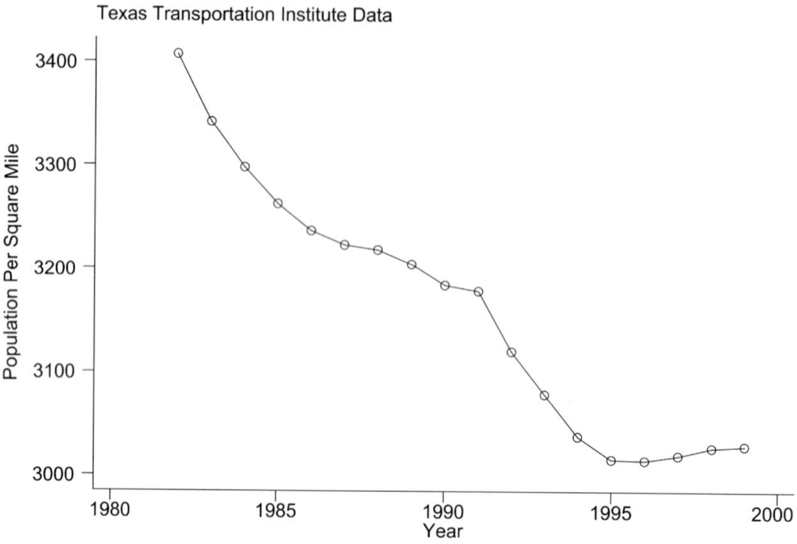

Figure 3. Population density time trend for 68 major MSAs.

10 mile ring around the CBD, works in an environment where there are 2541 workers per square mile while the average resident who lives in the five to ten mile ring around the CBD lives in a community where there are 7433 people per square mile. Outside of the inner ring, average population densities are higher than average employment densities. Employment outside of urban centers is not characterized by competing centers, but rather by dispersed employment.

Ideally, we would like to construct our sprawl measures at several points in time. Unfortunately, we can only access nationally representative employment distributions starting in the 1990s. To provide some facts about trends in density, we use population density data from the Texas Transportation Institute database. Using data from 1982 to 1999 for 68 major metropolitan areas, we graph population weighted population density over time. Figure 3 shows that population density has fallen over 10% during this period. Interestingly, the data suggest that over the last five years population density has slightly increased.

3. The causes of sprawl

The simplest framework for understanding sprawl is the Alonso–Muth–Mills monocentric model. In its pure form, this model cannot address employment decentralization, but certainly helps us to understand the basic determinants of decentralization. Consider an open city with exogenously given wage w and commuting costs of t per unit distance (all quantities are in flows per time period), where distance to the city center is denoted d.

We assume that individuals maximize a utility function defined over land area (denoted A) and a composite commodity (denoted C) or $C + \alpha \log(A)$. Commuting cost equals t times total distance spent commuting. Thus, if an individual lives d units away from the city center, the commuting time equals td and total earnings to be spent on land and the composite commodity equals $w - td$. We also allow the possibility of a government subsidy of land consumption equal to x times overall expenditure on land. This subsidy attempts to capture the potential effects of policies ranging from the home mortgage interest deduction to zoning which might increase the appeal of buying bigger or more expensive land.

The rental price per unit of land (or rent gradient) is denoted $P(d)$. Indifference among locations implies that $-P'(d)A(1-x) = t$. The first-order condition for optimal land consumption implies that $P(d)A(1-x) = \alpha$. Together, these imply that $P(d) = P_0 e^{-(td)/\alpha}$, where P_0 is the price of land at the city center. We close the model by assuming that there is a reservation location with (i) wages net of transportation costs equal to $(1-\theta_1)w - \theta_2 t$ and (ii) land costs of $\widehat{P}$.[5] Together, these assumptions imply a reservation utility of $(1-\theta_1)w - \theta_2 t - \alpha + \alpha \ln(\alpha/(1-x)\widehat{P})$. Land on the edge of the city has value of $\underline{P}$ if used for non-residential purposes. The reservation utility level implies that

$$P_0 = \widehat{P} e^{(w\theta_1 + \theta_2 t)/\alpha} \quad \text{and therefore} \quad P(d) = \widehat{P} e^{(w\theta_1 + t(\theta_2 - d))/\alpha}.$$

The outer edge of the city occurs when

$$P(d) = \underline{P} \quad \text{or} \quad \bar{d} = \theta_2 + \frac{w\theta_1 + \alpha \log(\widehat{P}/\underline{P})}{t}.$$

Two natural measures of sprawl exist in this model. The first measure is the furthest limit of the city's population. This will be the extent of the city or $\bar{d}$. The total population of the city is

$$\int_{d=0}^{\theta_2 + (w\theta_1 + \alpha \log(\widehat{P}/\underline{P}))/t} \frac{1-x}{\alpha} \widehat{P} e^{(w\theta_1 + \theta_2 t - td)/\alpha} \, \mathrm{d}d$$

or

$$\frac{(1-x)}{t} \left(\widehat{P} e^{(w\theta_1 + \theta_2 t)/\alpha} - \underline{P} \right),$$

so the average density equals

$$(1-x) \frac{\widehat{P} e^{(w\theta_1 + \theta_2 t)/\alpha} - \underline{P}}{w\theta_1 + \theta_2 t + \alpha \log(\widehat{P}/\underline{P})}.$$

[5] The parameters θ_1 and θ_2 capture the extent that changes in w and t influence the reservation utility. They measure the extent to which w and t are local parameters, or parameters that influence utility everywhere.

What variables will impact sprawl? Most obviously, things that will increase the city will tend to make it bigger and more dense. Thus, the value of $\bar{d}$ is increasing with w, θ_1, θ_2 and $\widehat{P}$ and falling with $\underline{P}$. The average density level is rising with w, θ_1, θ_2 and $\widehat{P}$, if $1 > \alpha$ (which we assume).

These comparative statics represent the pseudo-sprawl that is perceived with the growth of any city. As cities become more attractive, they grow up and out. Thus, as New York grew throughout its 400 year history, wheat fields have gotten covered and skyscrapers have gotten built. Increases in x – the subsidy to land consumption – causes density to fall, but do not impact the overall spread of the city. As long as $\widehat{P}$ is greater than $\underline{P}$, increases in α cause the density level of the city to fall and cause the overall spread of the city to rise. Thus, factors that would increase the demand for land cause the city to sprawl, using either measure.

Finally, if $1 > \alpha$ then increases in the value of t cause the city to contract and become more dense. This represents a primary comparative static of the model and the key to understanding most of the thinking about the link between transportation costs and urban sprawl. As transportation costs fall, it naturally becomes more attractive to live at further distances and commute further.[6]

Now, we follow Henderson and Mitra (1996) and others, and allow for multiple employment centers. We retain our assumptions about the utility function and transport costs, but now assume that $x = 0$. In a spatial equilibrium, all individuals must be optimizing their consumption and be indifferent across locations. Furthermore, developers must be unable to earn positive profits by creating new employment subcenters.

We will refer to the original downtown as employment subcenter zero with wage w_0 and location $d_0 = 0$. Any additional employment subcenters are denoted with subscript s are characterized by a wage, distance pair (w_s, d_s), for $s = \{1, 2, \ldots, S\}$, where $d_{s+1} > d_s$ for all s. We assume that wages in each subcenter are determined by the distance between the city center and the new subcenter. Agglomeration economies mean that proximity between the new center, and the old core are desirable and we assume that $w(d)$ in each new subcenter equals $w - zd$, where $z < t$.

The implication of $z < t$ is that we can define a vector of locations denoted $\hat{d}_s$ where individuals are indifferent between subcenter s and subcenter $s + 1$. We know that $d_s < \hat{d}_s < d_{s+1}$, because individuals who live close to a subcenter will always prefer working there to commuting elsewhere (because $z < t$). We let $\hat{d}_s$ denote the point in the interval (d_s, d_{s+1}) where for all d greater than $\hat{d}_s$, subcenter $s + 1$ is strictly preferred to subcenter s and for all d less than $\hat{d}_s$, subcenter s is strictly preferred to subcenter $s + 1$. At $\hat{d}_s$, residents are indifferent between working at the two locations, which implies that

$$\hat{d}_s = \frac{d_s + d_{s+1}}{2} + \frac{z(d_{s+1} - d_s)}{2t}.$$

[6] The overall impact on density depends critically on $\theta_2 > 0$. If $\theta_2 = 0$, then increases in transportation costs only impact the city and not the reservation locale, and increases in t cause population to fall by proportionately as much as the area of the city and there is no link between t and average density.

All residents in the interval $(\hat{d}_{s-1}, \hat{d}_s)$ commute to subcenter s. In this interval, the price gradient will equilibrate utility levels for all commuters. Thus if we let P_0^s denote the price of land at subcenter s, it must be true on the interval $(\hat{d}_{s-1}, \hat{d}_s)$, that the price vector is, $P(d) = P_0^s \mathrm{e}^{-(t|d-d_s|)/\alpha}$, and the reservation utility formula tells us that

$$P_0^s = \widehat{P}\mathrm{e}^{(w-zd_S-w(1-\theta_1)+\theta_2 t)/\alpha} = \Psi \mathrm{e}^{-zd_s/\alpha},$$

where Ψ denotes $\widehat{P}\mathrm{e}^{(w\theta_1+\theta_2 t)/\alpha}$. The density levels around each subcenter will equal $1/\alpha$ times the price.

We assume that developers can open new employment centers for a fixed cost K which is independent of the distance from the old downtown. They will continue to open these centers as long as there are profits to be made from new subcenters. In particular, we define a development equilibrium as one in which the costs of developing any new subcenter must be greater than the increase in land values that would be created by this new development. In this definition, we follow Henderson and Mitra (1996) and assume that developers are able to reap the full benefits that their construction has on property values. The logic that lies behind this condition is that presumably developers can buy up land at current prices, then develop and then resell the land at the new equilibrium prices.

There are two equilibrium conditions that are helpful for understanding the implications of this model for sprawl. First, we will develop conditions on the maximum distance between employment subcenters. This helps us to understand the degree to which employment centers will be spread throughout the metropolitan area. Second, we will provide comparative statics on the total extent of development within the area. If there are two existing subcenters, denoted $s-1$ and $s+1$, then the extra land value created by building a new subcenter (denoted s) will equal:

$$\frac{2\Psi\alpha \mathrm{e}^{-zd_{s-1}/\alpha}}{t}\Big(\mathrm{e}^{-z\phi\Delta/\alpha} + \mathrm{e}^{-(t+z)\Delta/(2\alpha)} - \mathrm{e}^{-(t+z)\phi\Delta/(2\alpha)} - \mathrm{e}^{(-(1-\phi)t\Delta-(1+\phi)z\Delta)/(2\alpha)}\Big), \tag{1}$$

where Δ denotes $d_{s+1} - d_{s-1}$ and $\phi\Delta$ denotes $d_s - d_{s-1}$. If the developer enters, he will choose d_s (or equivalently ϕ) to maximize this amount, and he will only enter if this amount (given optimal selection of ϕ) is greater than K, the costs of building a new subcenter. This leads us to our first proposition.

PROPOSITION 1. *As long as*

$$2\Psi\alpha \mathrm{c}^{-zd_{s-1}/\alpha}\left(\left(\frac{2z}{t+z}\right)^{2z/(t-z)} - \left(\frac{2z}{t+z}\right)^{(t+z)/(t-z)}\right) > tK,$$

then there exists a unique value of Δ, denoted $\widetilde{\Delta}$ at which developers earn exactly zero by building a new subcenter and locating it optimally. For values of Δ above $\widetilde{\Delta}$, developers earn positive profits by building a new subcenter and for values of Δ below $\widetilde{\Delta}$, developers lose money with new construction.

The value of $\widetilde{\Delta}$, which can be interpreted as the maximum distance between two subcenters, rises with K, and d_{s-1}, and falls with w, $\widehat{P}$, θ_1 and θ_2. The value of $\widetilde{\Delta}$ rises with z when z is small.

The impact of t on $\widetilde{\Delta}$ is ambiguous. For example, when $\theta_2 = 0$ and $z = 0$, then $\widetilde{\Delta}$ falls with t if and only if the cheapest lot in between the two centers costs more than 8.2 percent of the most expensive lost between the two centers.

The inequality

$$2\Psi\alpha \mathrm{e}^{-zd_{s-1}/\alpha}\left(\left(\frac{2z}{t+z}\right)^{2z/(t-z)} - \left(\frac{2z}{t+z}\right)^{(t+z)/(t-z)}\right) > tK$$

is needed to ensure that there exists some value of Δ at which profitable development can occur. The term $\widetilde{\Delta}$ can be thought of as the maximum distance between any two subcenters in equilibrium. Any distance that is greater than this amount implies that there are profits from new entry. As such, the value of $\widetilde{\Delta}$ gives us a measure of the degree to which employment subcenters will be spread throughout the metropolis.

When the value of K falls, we expect to see more employment subcenters. To us, this captures the role that the decline in big transportation infrastructure (rail stops, ports) and its connection to the rise of edge cities. As d_{s-1} rises, there will be fewer employment centers. This is a natural outcome of the assumption that productivity declines with distance from the center. The parameters w, $\widehat{P}$, θ_1 and θ_2, all reflect general demand for the metropolitan area. As these rise, the demand for the metropolitan area rises and the maximum density between any two employment centers declines. Declining values of z, the extent to which productivity falls with distance from the urban center, also increases the attractiveness of subcenters.

The impact of changing transport costs is ambiguous. This occurs because transport costs have a number of different effects. First, rising transport costs make long commutes less attractive and therefore increase the demand for new employment subcenters. Second, rising transport costs limits the general returns to construction, because few people can use the new subcenter.

We now turn to the determinants of the location of the employment center that is furthest from the city. We examine this edge by assuming the existence of a subcenter S, and asking whether a new developer will want to open a subcenter beyond this point. The net surplus from this development again equal the change in land values minus the cost of development. Assuming that the new center is built in an area that had been urbanized, the total increase in land value created by the new employment center equals:

$$\frac{2\alpha\Psi \mathrm{e}^{-zd_{S+1}/\alpha}}{t}\left(1 - \mathrm{e}^{-(t-z)(d_{S+1}-d_S)/(2\alpha)}\right) - \frac{t-z}{t}\underline{P}(d_{S+1} - d_S). \tag{2}$$

The value of d_{S+1} is chosen to maximize this quantity. This implies the following proposition.

PROPOSITION 2. *As long as*

$$\frac{2\alpha\Psi}{t}\left(\mathrm{e}^{-zx/\alpha} - \mathrm{e}^{-(t+z)x/(2\alpha)}\right) - \frac{t-z}{t}\underline{P}x - K$$

is positive for some positive value of x, *then there exists a value of* d_S, *denoted* $\tilde{d}_S$ *at which the returns from developing a new center further from the urban core, are equal to zero. At values of* d_S *beyond that point, development yields losses and at values of* d_S *below that point development can yield positive profits.*

The value of $\tilde{d}_S$ *is declining with* K, $\underline{P}$, *and* z *and rising with* w, θ_1, θ_2, *and* $\widehat{P}$.

These comparative statics are also straightforward. The fixed infrastructure costs are certainly crucial. When these are high, there will not be sprawl. High values of land for non-urban purposes will also deter sprawl. It is also true that as the agglomeration parameter, z, rises sprawl will decline. If z were to fall, which might come about because of improvements in information technology which facilitated the connection between edge centers and the core, this would cause sprawl to rise. Finally, just as before, an increase in variables such as w, θ_1, θ_2, and $\widehat{P}$, which make the urban area generally more attractive will increase the amount of sprawl.

These exercises have given us some sense of the likely determinants of sprawl. The basic monocentric model emphasized the importance of commuting technology, government subsidies, demand for land and basic demand for the urban area. The extended polycentric model further brought in the fixed infrastructure costs inherent in building a new subcenter, and the deterioration of productivity with distance from the core (i.e., the importance of agglomeration). We now turn to the empirical evidence on the importance of these forces.

4. Evaluating the transportation cost hypothesis

The model argues that transportation costs influence the degree of sprawl in two very different fashions. First, in the classic monocentric model, lower costs mean that the edge of the city expands and density decreases. As commuting costs fall, the amount of land area consumed increases and the edge of the city expands. Second, in the polycentric model, the switch from public transportation to cars severely reduces the fixed costs of opening new employment centers. Public transportation, even buses, requires a great deal of fixed cost infrastructure which makes large numbers of employment subcenters difficult. At the production level, the rise of the truck has made the large infrastructure inherent in rail depots unnecessary and has freed firms from the old centers. The switch from manufacturing to services also had the effect of reducing the fixed costs involved in opening new centers and increasing the advantages of locating near where people lived.

The overwhelming importance of transportation costs in these models pushes us towards the hypothesis that the ultimate driver of decentralization is the private automobile and its commercial equivalents, including the truck. In this section, we evaluate the empirical connection between sprawl and transport costs. We will do three things. First, we will begin by highlighting the remarkable fall in transportation costs over the 20th century. Second, we will show the cross-sectional relationship between the sprawl and automobile usage. Third, we will look at international evidence and show that plausibly exogenous factors that deter automobile development have led to decreases in the level of sprawl.

4.1. Transport costs over time

In the early part of the century, the Europeans had the lead in car ownership. After all, the big early innovations in the automobile occurred in Germany (with Karl Daimler's invention of the internal combustion engine) and France (where the marketing of the automobile really began). But by 1920, the Americans had leapt ahead of the Europeans as Henry Ford's mass production pushed prices down and low American densities created a strong demand. By 1950, the number of households per car reached five in America. In the European countries, this threshold would not be reached until much later. For example, despite being the home of Karl Daimler, it would take the Germans until 1970 to reach the same car ownership levels that America had reached by 1920.

Since 1950, car ownership has continued to expand. In 1950, the majority of households owned one automobile (52 percent), but only 7 percent owned two cars or more. By 1990, multi-car households were the norm. In that year, the U.S. Census reports that 11 percent of households had no car and 33.4 percent had only one car. The rest had two or more automobiles. The last Census reported that among households with two or more members, less than one-third of households had less than two cars. This should not surprise us – America's sprawl cities require a car for each adult.

In the United States, the reliance on the automobile as a means of commuting is also pretty complete. As late as 1960, 22 percent of workers took public transportation or walked and 64 percent drove (either alone or in carpool).[7] The 1960s saw the continuing decline of non-car transportation and by 1970, 78 percent drove and 16.3 percent took public transportation or walked. In 1980, 84 percent of workers drove and 6.4 percent took public transportation and 5.6 percent walked. By and large, transportation patterns have been relatively static since 1980. The share taking public transportation has continued to decline to 5.3 percent in 1990 and 4.7 percent in 2000. Carpooling has somewhat declined (presumably as incomes have increased), but the share of people commuting by car rose to 86.6 percent in 1990 and 87.9 percent in 2000. Public transit improvements to rail systems in cities such as Atlanta, Boston, Chicago, Portland and Washington, DC, have only slightly increased public transit use [Baum-Snow and Kahn (2000)]. Billions of dollars of public transit subsidies have failed to significantly increase usage despite consistently rosy ex-ante forecasts of higher ridership [Kain (1991, 1997)].

Why did the car triumph? While government policies may have subsidized this transport mode, at this point we focus on why individuals, when multiple modes are available, appear to prefer driving to taking public transportation. Cars are almost uniformly more expensive in terms of cash, both in terms of initial investment and in terms of operating costs. Public transportation twice per day rarely costs more than $2.50 (except

[7] The primary residual category is working at home which represented 7.2 percent of the population in 1960.

for taxis). While it may be possible to operate an automobile for less than $912.50 per year, in many places insurance costs alone exceed that amount. Maintenance can easily be several hundred dollars per year and parking can also be quite expensive. The car certainly did not become ubiquitous because it is cheap.

Consumer expenditure survey data bears out this claim. The average consumer unit (essentially a household) spends $6963 per year or 18.3 of their total household expenditures on initial vehicle purchase, gasoline and other vehicle expenditures (including insurance). It is the largest category of expenditure other than housing, and it dwarfs private spending on health care or apparel or entertainment for most people.[8]

Cars offer tremendous time saving advantages. While those who have spent hours stuck in traffic may have trouble believing it, the average car trip is actually much shorter than the average trip made using public transportation. The median commute time in the year 2000 for those people who drove alone to work was 24.1 minutes. The median commute time for those people who took public transportation was 47.7 minutes. The average public transportation trip takes is almost twice as long as the average trip made using the automobile. Figure 4 uses 1990 cross-city data to document the clear relationship that people who live in public transit cities have longer commutes.

Glaeser, Kahn and Rappaport (2000) investigate these time differences by mode using the 1995 National Personal Transportation Survey. We found that public transportation appears to involve a fixed time cost of approximately 16–20 minutes, regardless of length. After this fixed time costs, cars appear to be about 50 percent faster than buses

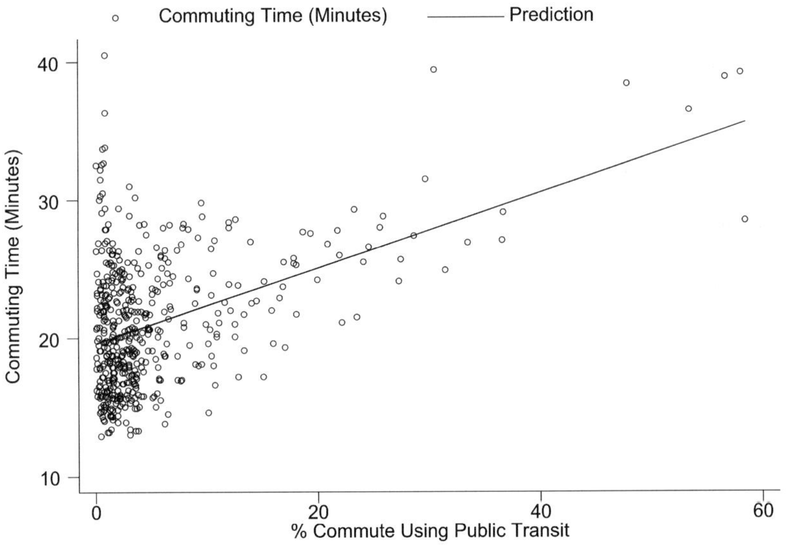

Figure 4. 1990 Cross-city variation in commute times.

[8] As urban economics tends to focus on the interaction between transportation and housing, it is worthwhile noting that approximately one-half of families' expenditures go on those two categories.

and roughly as fast as trains. It is this fixed time cost that makes public transportation so costly. The time spent walking (or driving) to the station or bus stop plus the time spent waiting for the bus or train plus the time spent walking or driving to the final destination appears to take up as much time as driving ten miles. As time has gotten more valuable, the time costs of public transportation have become more severe and the population has continued to move entirely towards the automobile.[9]

The car is certainly the most important transportation technology to impact the city over the last two centuries, but it is far from being the only one. In general, transport costs have declined and this has enabled urban growth in places which are far from raw materials and far from waterways. Moreover, technological innovations have enabled trucks to replace boats and trains. In 1947, there were three times as many employees in rail as in trucking and warehousing. By 1961, trucking employment passed rail and now it is a far bigger industry. According to the most recent U.S. Statistical Abstract, by value, trucks carry 86 percent of total commodity shipments within the U.S.

This is particularly important because trucks require much less fixed infrastructure than trains and boats. Large fixed infrastructure appears to be a large element driving the monocentric city of the past. The 19th century urban booster's fondest wish was a railroad stop in their town. The decline in the need for proximity to the port or rail depot has made the decentralization of manufacturing, and employment more generally, feasible.

4.2. *The empirical connection between cars and sprawl*

The best evidence on the claim that cars made sprawl possible is the high correlation between using automobiles and living in low-density edge cities. This type of correlation certainly does not prove that cars caused sprawl, but it is strong evidence suggesting at least cars and low-density living are very strong complements. One of the easiest ways to see this connection is to look at the correlation between urban density and driving to work across U.S. cities. In this regression, we include all U.S. cities with population levels above 25,000 and density levels that are greater than one person per every four acres.[10]

Within this sample, the overall relationship between driving to work (as a percentage of all commutes) and the logarithm of people per acre is

$$\text{(10) percent driving} = \underset{(0.027)}{1.27} - \underset{(0.003)}{0.066} * \log(\text{people/square mile}),$$

$$N = 1071, \qquad R^2 = 0.255.$$

[9] Whether the income elasticity of commuting costs equals one or not remains an open question. Calfee and Winston's (1998) contingent valuation study of household commuting costs suggests that the income elasticity of community is much less than one. One possible explanation for their finding is that richer commuters drive "more fun", higher performance vehicles.

[10] There are actually four cities in the 1990 Census that fall below this cutoff: Anchorage (AK), Juneau (AK), Butte-Silverbow (MT) and Suffolk City (VA).

Table 5
Transportation modes and times in low sprawl and high sprawl MSAs

	Whole sample	Sprawled MSAs	Centralized MSAs	Centralized MSA in Northeast
Variable				
Percentage of trips by private vehicle	86.34	91.55	81.82	72.54
Percentage of trips walked	7.39	4.65	10.19	17.53
Percentage of 1 mile or shorter trips by private vehicle	68.47	77.6	62.27	51.07
Percentage of shopping trips by private vehicle	87.06	92.93	81.8	72.25
Percentage went out to eat by private vehicle	84	90.36	77.95	69.16
Average trip time in minutes				
All trips	16.76	16.48	17	17.72
1 mile or shorter trips by private vehicle	4.7	4.52	4.85	4.86
Shopping trips	12.07	12.29	11.87	11.75
Eating trips	13.25	13.5	13.02	13.18
Non-car trips	19	17.2	19.93	21.15
Walking trips	10.59	9.68	11.01	10.67
Bus trips				35.57
Subway trips				39.04

The data source is the 1995 National Personal Transportation Survey Day Trip File. The unit of analysis is a trip. The NPTS sample covers 46 MSAs. Centralized MSAs are those above the median of the Smart Growth Index of Ewing, Pendall and Chen (2002). Sprawled MSAs have an index score below this median.

Standard errors are in parentheses. The raw correlation between these variables is more than 50 percent. The t-statistic is 19 and the coefficient has a sensible economic magnitude. As the density roughly doubles, the share that drives drops by roughly 6.6 percent.

Another way of thinking about this is in the 56 cities with density levels above 10,000 people per square mile, 38 percent of workers commute by private car and 37 percent commute using public transportation. Out of the 232 cities in the U.S. in 1990 with more than 50,000 inhabitants and density levels less than 2500 people, exactly none of them had less than 59 percent of workers commute by private car and in none of those cities did public transportation usage exceed 6.3 percent. Of the 372 cities with more than 50,000 inhabitants and density levels below 5000 people per square mile, two cities less than 55 percent of workers driving alone and three cities had public transportation usage above 13.5 percent.

In sprawled metropolitan areas, people use their cars to do everything. To document this, in Table 5, we use the 1995 National Personal Transportation Survey's Daytrip file. In this data set, the unit of analysis is a trip. Each survey participant recorded all of his trips that day. In Table 5, we report what share of these trips were taken by private vehicle for the whole sample, and then broken out by above median sprawl and below median sprawl MSAs.[11]The first row of the table shows that in MSAs which have a

[11] We partition cities based on the sprawl index presented in Ewing, Pendall and Chen (2002).

sprawl index above the median, 92% of trips are taken by car while 81% of trips are taken by car in below median sprawl cities. Even for trips less than one mile, there is large difference in car use. In sprawl areas, 78% of 1 mile or shorter trips are done by car while 62% of such trips are taken by car in low sprawl cities. While 7% of all trips are walked, in northeastern cities whose sprawl index is below the median, 18% of trips are by foot.

Because cars are such a ubiquitous feature of American life, it is hard to empirically test what happens when cars are not available. In the year 2000, in 49 out of the fifty states more than 85 percent of households own a car. Only in New York City do almost 30 percent of households not own an automobile. It is true that car ownership correlates with density across states – only 4.5 percent of the households in Wyoming and Idaho are without cars – but there is no way of making an inference about the impact of cars on sprawl using state-level variation. The range of car ownership is too narrow and the degree of car ownership is too endogenous.

To try and shed some light on this topic, we look at international evidence. In particular, we follow Ingram and Liu (1999) and Glaeser, Kolko and Saiz (2001) who look at the relationship between urban density, car ownership and gas taxes across countries. Gas taxes vary widely from country to country and places with higher gas taxes have many fewer cars per capita. Moreover, gas taxes are in part a result of the general regulatory regime and in principle instruments that impact the degree of regulation generally may be valid instruments for the level of gas taxes.

We start by showing the general connection between the degree of car ownership and the level of urban density. We use data from Ingram and Liu (1999) to look at connections between cars and urban density. In Table 6, we show these relationships. In regression (1), we regress the log of urban density (defined as people per square mile) on vehicles per-capita across a sample of 70 international cities. Controlling for real GDP per-capita and a time trend (to control for the fact that some of our observations come from different years), we find a positive correlation between low-density cities (what we call sprawl) and car ownership.

In the next regression, we replace our measure of car ownership with a measure of gas taxes provided in the Ingram and Liu (1999) data. A large amount of the international variation in the cost of operating an automobile is the result of different taxation of gasoline in different countries. For example, the price of gas per gallon is often two or three times higher in Europe than in the U.S. primarily because of government taxation of gasoline. Regressions (5) and (6) look at the connection between gas taxes and vehicle ownership. Regression (5) documents that places with higher gas taxes have lower levels of vehicle ownership.

While the fact that gas taxes are negatively associated with vehicle ownership across countries can be interpreted as a classic price effect, there is another interpretation. It is possible that vehicle ownership actually drives gas taxes and not the reverse. In countries, where a large share of people commute by car, the median voter is likely to be generally hostile to gas taxes. In countries where cars are luxury goods, gas taxes may be considerably more popular.

Table 6
International evidence on transportation and density

	log of urban density			Vehicles per-capita			log of gasoline price regime
Regression	(1)	(2)	(3)	(4)	(5)	(6)	(7)
Vehicles per-capita	−0.0047 (0.0006)		−0.0075 (0.0010)	−0.0052 (0.0013)			
Gasoline price regime		0.0134 (0.0016)			−1.7861 (0.2547)	−2.1069 (0.4545)	
Real GDP per-capita	0.0001 (0.0006)	−0.0002 (0.0000)	0.0002 (0.0000)	0.0001 (0.0001)	0.0445 (0.0019)	0.0436 (0.0025)	0.0000 (0.0000)
French legal origin dummy							0.5592 (0.1772)
Constant	9.1510 (0.1358)	8.4910 (0.1709)	8.9717 (0.1642)	9.0864 (0.1775)	64.2527 (27.2768)	95.7327 (44.3699)	4.2110 (0.1536)
Observations	70	70	70	62	70	62	62
R^2	0.776	0.7902			0.8907		0.1632
Estimation	OLS	OLS	IV	IV	OLS	IV	OLS

The data source is the Ingram and Liu (1999) International Data set. The time trend is suppressed. In regression (3), the gasoline price regime is used as an instrument for vehicles per-capita. In regression (4), legal origin dummies are used as an instrument for vehicles per-capita. In regression (6), legal origin dummies are used as an instrument for gas price regime. Vehicles per 1000 has a mean of 294 and a standard deviation of 207.4. Gasoline price regime has a mean of 70.2 and a standard deviation of 33.14. Real GDP per-capita has a mean of 8297 and a standard deviation of 4331. The cities in the sample include: Adelaide, Amsterdam, Bandung, Bangkok, Brisbane, Brussels, Chicago, Copenhagen, Denver, Detroit, Frankfurt, Guangzhou, Hamburg, Hong Kong, Jakata, Los Angeles, London, Manila, Melbourne, Munich, New York City, Osaka, Paris, Perth, Phoenix, San Francisco, Seoul, Singapore, Stockholm, Surabaya, Sydney, Tokyo, Toronto, Vienna, and West Berlin.

To address this endogeneity problem, we use country's legal origin as an instrument for the level of gas taxes. In a rich literature on the impact of legal origin, La Porta et al. (1997, 1999) have shown that most of the countries in the world have legal origins that ultimately stem from one of a small number of basic legal systems (i.e., French, British, German or Socialist). The legal origin of the country tends to be strongly correlated with a rich number of features of the government and the economy and in particular, civil law (i.e., French legal origin) countries tend to be more regulated than common law (i.e., English legal origin) countries. In regression (7), we show that gas taxes are higher (controlling for GDP per capita and the time trend) in civil law countries than in common law countries. As legal origin significantly predates the invention of the automobile, we will use this as an instrument for the level of gas taxes. In regression (6), we show that there is still a sharp relationship between gas taxes and the level of vehicle ownership when we instrument for gas taxes using legal origin.

In regressions (3) and (4), we use first gas taxes and then legal origin as instruments for the level of vehicle ownership in explaining urban population density. In regression (3), we use gas taxes as an instrument for vehicle ownership and the coefficient changes little. In regression (4), we use legal origin as an instrument for vehicle ownership (legal origins' impact of vehicle ownership runs through increased gas taxes) and we find that the results look quite similar. We conclude that across countries at least, places that make it difficult to own cars have much less sprawl. To us, this serves as at least some evidence showing the extent that sprawl is dependent on the automobile.

5. Evaluating other causes of sprawl: the demand for land and flight from blight

The rise of the automobile is certainly not the only factor driving the decentralization of population and employment. One factor that has surely played some role in explaining the increasing suburbanization of population is the demand for larger suburban lots. People who move into the suburbs are motivated to a significant degree by the desire for more living space. However, for a land-oriented view to explain the rise in suburbanization, it needs to explain why the demand for land should have risen so much over the twentieth century.

In fact, Margo (1992) proposes just such a theory. He argues that rising incomes over the past 50 years have increased the demand for land and that one-half of the increased suburbanization between 1950 and 1980 can be explained by people getting richer. His methodology is to look at the relationship between income and suburban living in 1950 and show that if that relationship stayed constant, rising incomes would have propelled a large number of people into suburban areas.

We certainly agree that rising incomes were an important factor in driving the suburbanization of population. Indeed, in our cross-national evidence above, we also found that richer countries had less dense cities, and that the coefficient on income is at least as important as the coefficient on vehicle ownership. Our view is that both the rising incomes and automobile ownership were necessary. After all, without rising incomes, Americans would not have had the money to pay for all those automobiles. However, without the automobile the car-based edge cities would really be impossible. If Margo had been able to look at the relationship between income and suburbanization in 1900, before the advent of the automobile, we suspect that this relationship would have been much weaker.

To address this theory, we look at the degree of metropolitan decentralization by city per-capita income. For each metropolitan area, we assign it to one of four mutually exclusive and exhaustive categories based on per-capita income data from the Regional Economic Information System. In Table 7, we display a number of our decentralization measures for these different quintiles. Based on MSA Average Population Density, richer MSAs feature higher population density. Across the three sprawl indicators, there is no evidence that richer MSAs are significantly more decentralized.[12] While it

[12] We recognize that a problem with comparing per-capita income across metropolitan areas is that the cost of living varies across cities.

Table 7
Sprawl as a function of MSA attributes

Each cell reports a sample average	MSA average population density	Median resident's distance to CBD in miles	Median worker's distance to CBD in miles
All	2952.00	7.88	6.93
Panel A			
MSAs in lowest 25% of per-capita income pdf	1614.00	7.62	6.26
MSAs in 25th–50th% of per-capita income pdf	2457.00	6.74	6.01
MSAs in 50th to 75th% of per capita income pdf	2661.00	8.93	7.71
MSAs in highest 25% of per-capita income pdf	5127.00	8.5	7.76
Panel B			
MSAs in lowest 25% of poverty pdf	2027.00	7.56	6.46
MSAs in 25th–50th% of poverty pdf	2924.00	7.97	6.61
MSAs in 50th to 75th% of poverty pdf	2527.00	7.19	6.23
MSAs in highest 25% of poverty pdf	3695.00	8.51	7.63
Panel C			
MSAs in lowest 25% of Black pdf	1892.00	7.14	5.89
MSAs in 25th–50th% of Black pdf	2207.00	7.3	6.14
MSAs in 50th to 75th% of Black pdf	3095.00	8.14	7.26
MSAs in highest 25% of Black pdf	3834.00	8.45	7.73
Panel D			
MSAs in lowest 25% of fragmentation pdf	2836.00	6.85	5.81
MSAs in 25th–50th% of fragmentation pdf	2872.00	8.8	7.62
MSAs in 50th to 75th% of fragmentation pdf	3641.00	7.68	6.73
MSAs in highest 25% of fragmentation pdf	3425.00	8.29	7.74

MSA per-capita income data is from the year 2000. The data source is the Regional Economic Information System. Employment data is from 1996. Demographic data on poverty and % Black is from the 1990 County Fact Book. A MSA's poverty rate and % Black is determined by its county that has the highest rate for these variables. Fragmentation represents the number of city governments within the MSA in 1962. There are 150 total MSAs.

is certainly true that richer people are more likely to own more land, the level of decentralization is so common, even in the poorest metropolitan areas, we have trouble believing that rising incomes (without the technological innovation of the automobile) would have changed the spatial structure of the country so drastically.

A second major alternative hypothesis is that the growth of the suburbs has come about because people have fled the social problems of the inner city. As forcefully argued by Mills and Lubuele (1997) and Jackson (1985), central city problems may have led people to leave and seek solace in bucolic, socially controlled suburbs. At the individual level, this theory is irrefutable. Millions of Americans have surely been directly motivated in their move to the suburbs by the desire for a more attractive social milieu. Moreover, in the case of individual cities, such as Detroit, lack of downtown amenities has surely spurred suburbanization [as in Brueckner, Thisse and Zenou (1999)].

However, the problem with this theory is that while increases in crime may spur suburbanization [see Cullen and Levitt (1999)], the trend towards suburbanization is ubiquitous. Table's 7 Panel B shows the degree of decentralizations across MSAs again dividing the metropolitan areas into quintiles. In this case, we split the metropolitan areas by the degree of central city poverty. Indeed, there is somewhat more decentralization in the metropolitan areas with more poverty. The results support the hypothesis that there has been more sprawl in more troubled cities; comparisons across groups seem to lend some credence to the Mills and Lubuele emphasis on flight from blight.[13]

However, to us the most striking thing about the table is not the small connection between inner city poverty and the degree of sprawl, but rather the fact that sprawl is so high in all five other groups. Even in the group of metropolitan areas that have the least central city poverty, the median worker works 6.5 miles away from the central business district. We conclude from this that inner city problems certainly encourage suburbanization, but that suburbanization is far too ubiquitous to be primarily the result of poor central cities.

6. Evaluating other causes of sprawl: the political roots of sprawl

A final set of theories concerning the flight to the suburbs emphasizes the role of politics. There are two variants of this hypothesis. The first variant is that federal and state governments through their favoritism of the automobile and through other anti-urban policies pushed people out of the central cities into the suburbs. This story is not particularly popular among economists, but urbanists in other disciplines are quite fond of the view that massive government spending on roads and highways, coupled with relatively low gas taxes and little subsidization of public transportation, made America's automobile culture inevitable [see e.g., Hart and Spivak (1993)].

There is certainly some truth to this view. Other governments have spent much less on roads and taxed gasoline much more severely. As we documented above, we believe strongly the high European gas taxes deter private automobile use. Indeed, total government spending on highways is somewhat awe-inspiring. According to the U.S. Department of Transportation, total highway expenditures by all levels of government reached $128.5 billion in 2000. Of that sum, $31 billion represents administration, bond interest and highway patrols. Another $31 billion represents maintenance on existence infrastructure. The remainder is new construction.

How is this vast expenditure financed? Is this actually a huge boondoggle, where motorists are subsidized by non-drivers? In fact, $81 billion is financed by user fees. A small fraction of that ($5 billion) represents tolls. The remainder comes primarily from gas taxes. Another $11 billion is paid for out of bonds which are at least supposed

[13] Of course, establishing causality is hard, as Meyer, Kain and Wohl (1965) and many others have argued, the suburbanization of population may hurt central city residents.

to be retired using future user fees. The remainder, almost $40 billion does seem to represent government subsidy. This is certainly a non-trivial subsidy and the subsidy's share of total expenditures appears to have been higher during the early era of highway construction.

However, this quantity needs to be put in the context of total automobile expenditures. If $40 billion represents $300 per household, this is tiny relative to other car related spending. The subsidy is no more than 5 percent of total per capita spending on automobile travel. By this, we do not mean to claim that subsidizing highways makes sense. However, it seems unlikely that reducing the price of automobile travel by two or three percent is likely to have made a huge difference in the transition to car-based living.

Moreover, public transportation is also subsidized. The dollar amount is not as large as the subsidy towards highways, but total government expenditure on public transportation is more than $25 billion, and only a fraction of that is returned in government revenues. There is a subsidy of highways, but it seems impossible to believe that this subsidy was the crucial determinant of the growth of America's car-based sprawl culture.

The second variant of the government caused sprawl view is that local governments are responsible for suburbanization. The most classic story is that suburbanization is a form of Tiebout sorting where people move to the suburbs to get the bundle of public goods and services that they want. There is certainly truth to this view. Suburbanites value living in their own jurisdictions and that is one thing that makes suburbs attractive. This effect is exacerbated if central cities redistribute from rich to poor [as in Brueckner (1983)]. No one can look at the development of the suburbs around Detroit and not think that the administration of Coleman Young encouraged some of the Whites to leave.

The problem with this view is that again suburbanization is only weakly correlated with the number of jurisdictions. The degree of suburbanization in Philadelphia, the most fragmented metropolitan area in the country is not higher than the degree of suburbanization in Anchorage, the least fragmented area. To study this, in Panel D of Table 7, we split metropolitan areas by their degree of political fragmentation based on data from 1962. Here we see little excess suburbanization in more fragmented communities. Suburbanization is ubiquitous, even if the non-fragmented metropolitan areas. Our point is not that Tiebout sorting does not occur. Rather, our point is that the driving force behind sprawl is not jurisdictional sorting.

A second theory about how local governments create sprawl works through the zoning process. If districts that are closer to the city center, zone and make high-density construction impossible, then this will surely increase the development of sprawl on the edge of the city. Districts on the edge, which contain primarily farmland, have no incentive to block new construction and rarely do so. In this way, the so-called Smart Growth movement may have unwittingly supported sprawl because it gave intellectual legitimacy to the idea that areas close to the city center should restrict new construction. Unless the district can actually prevent construction on the edge of the city, this type of policy will increase sprawl.

How important have land use controls actually been in creating sprawl? In particular, metropolitan areas in California, this is surely a relevant factor. However, in most of the middle of the country zoning tends to be pretty weak. Still, sprawl is particularly ubiquitous in the South and Midwest. Houston, a city with no zoning, sprawls. Again, this force may have contributed to the suburbanization of jobs and people, but it cannot have been the driving force.

A final idea about how the government may have fomented sprawl is put forward by Voith (1999). Voith argues that through the home mortgage interest deduction, the government has subsidized housing consumption and that this has induced people to consume more housing and as a result live outside of urban areas. We are skeptical about the importance of this force [see Glaeser and Shapiro (2002)], but we agree that subsidizing homeownership will also support the move to sprawl.

7. Is sprawl bad?

Finally, we turn to the fundamental question of whether sprawl deserves some major policy response. We have mentioned the primary benefits of sprawl already: a car culture that generally allows short commutes and large homes. However, these benefits may be offset by other social costs. Brueckner (2000) highlights three major areas where developers who build on the edges of cities may not be internalizing the full costs of their actions. First, these developments may increase traffic congestion. This is certainly the most obvious market failure in edge cities and we turn to the issue of congestion first.

Second, these developments may have environmental consequences. Brueckner focuses on the elimination of empty space at the edge of the city. We discuss that briefly, but rather focus on the environmental consequences of having so many drivers.

Third, developers may not pay for the full costs of the infrastructure that they use. We will not discuss this third possibility. In many cases this appears to be true, although in other cases the combination of taxes and impact fees probably pay for the costs of sprawl. We will not focus on this issue as the appropriate policy response seems obvious. If suburbanites are not paying for the costs of their infrastructure, then they should be made to do so. We suspect that in many cases, property taxes do cover the new infrastructure costs, but since there is likely to be a large amount of heterogeneity across the U.S., we will simply agree that impact fees are appropriate if developers are underpaying, and we will not discuss this topic further.

We also add two additional areas where policy concern might be merited. First, we discuss the productivity consequences of sprawl. In principle, when jobs move to the suburbs, this may reduce productivity in the city and this could yield social losses. Second, we consider the social consequences of suburbanization and ask whether there are externalities in that area that are worth addressing.

A final area that looms large as one of the major policy failures in the suburbanization context is the use of zoning laws. In theory, zoning laws provide localities with a means to induce developers to internalize externalities. However, there are two problems with zoning. First, if zoning pushes development off to the fringe of the city and this form of development has externalities, then zoning will be inefficient. Second, and we suspect more importantly, localities are incentivized to use zoning not only to internalize externalities but also to restrict supply to raise property values. This incentive means that localities will act like local monopolists and underprovide new construction. This appears to have had remarkable effects pushing real estate prices up in the 1990s and this is also a major topic for policy action.

7.1. Housing prices and quantities

Of course, the main benefit of sprawl for most consumers is cheaper, larger homes. Figure 5 reports median square footage of floor area in new one-family houses from 1973 until 2001. Over the last 20 years, news homes have grown by roughly 20%. Using the 1999 micro data from the American Housing Survey, in Table 8 we present average housing consumption for households with at least three people for people and whose income is greater than $10,000. We present separate means for center city and suburban residents and present these results for a subset of 11 major MSAs and for the whole sample. The second row shows the amount of square feet per person. In the major cities, the average central city resident has 496 square feet per person. The average suburban resident has 570 square feet per person. This difference is large. In the next rows, we show that on average suburbanites have more bedrooms and bathrooms as well.[14]

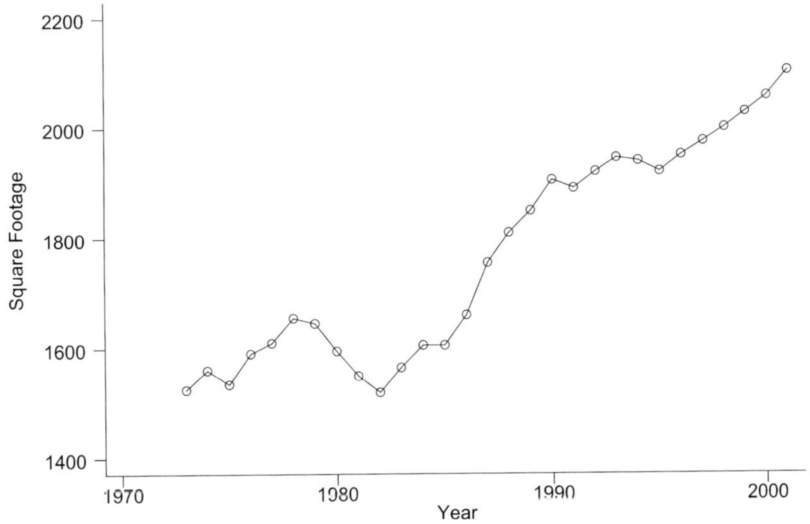

Figure 5. Median square footage of floor area in new one-family houses.

[14] Kahn (2001) uses 1997 American Housing Survey and documents that both Blacks and Whites live in larger housing units when they live in more sprawled MSAs. He uses the share of MSA jobs more than 10

Table 9
Commuting times and speeds in low and high sprawl areas

	All commuters			Auto commuters		
Miles to work	1.4110	1.3438	1.3770	1.3793	1.5775	1.8013
	(0.0151)	(0.0216)	(0.0211)	(0.0195)	(0.0378)	(0.0867)
Miles to work∗low sprawl dummy		0.1310	0.1412	0.1282	0.1770	0.2986
		(0.0301)	(0.0296)	(0.0279)	(0.0531)	(0.1187)
Residential block population density			0.0003	0.0002	0.0002	0.0002
			(0.0001)	(0.0001)	(0.0001)	(0.0001)
Constant	8.0990	8.1237	5.3122	5.2077	3.9774	3.1434
	(0.1496)	(0.1496)	(0.1860)	(0.1708)	(0.1845)	(0.2252)
MSA fixed effects	Yes	Yes	Yes	Yes	Yes	Yes
Commute distance in miles	20 or less	20 or less	20 or less	20 or less	10 or less	5 or less
Observations	13571	13571	13508	10223	7042	4076
Adjusted R^2	0.4341	0.4348	0.4589	0.5315	0.3921	0.2667

The dependent variable is the time to work in minutes. Each column reports a separate OLS regression. The data source is the 1995 National Personal Transportation Survey. The "low sprawl dummy" equals one if a MSA is above the median of the Smart Growth Index of Ewing, Pendall and Chen (2002). Standard errors are presented in parentheses. Residential block population density has a mean of 7779 and a standard deviation of 8662.

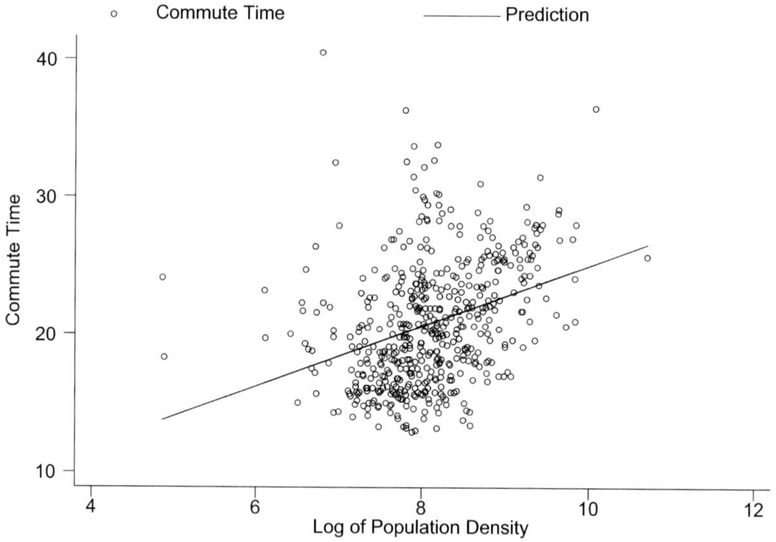

Figure 6. 1990 Cross-city relationship between commuting time and density.

7.3. Sprawl and the environment

Many of the harshest critics of suburbanization have been environmentalists. The move to edge cities has three major impacts on the environment. First, it uses up land that once used to be farmland or forest. Second, because sprawl is so car intensive, the move to sprawl may have increased car-related air pollution and increase the supply of greenhouse gas production. We consider all of these possibilities at this point.

While it is true that sprawl, by definition, increased the amount of developed land, it is worthwhile emphasizing that America is only slightly developed. Ninety-five percent of the land in this country remains undeveloped. Only 6.6 percent on non-federal land has been developed. Moreover, people start living on truly massive estates, residential development is unlikely to cover a large area of the country. For example, if every American lived on 1/4 of an acre of land, so each family of four had an acre, this would not fill up one half of the state of Texas. Thus, there is more than enough land to accommodate any reasonable level of development.

Moreover, forest cover in the U.S. is increasing, not declining. The big changes in land use in this country are the reduction of pasture and range land, not the increase in developed land. If there are environmental consequences from different forms of land use, then surely focusing on the conversion for pastures to forests is more important than anything concerning the small amount of total land that is developed. As an aside, given that sprawl needs housing and housing requires wood and wood needs forest, it may well be that the increase in sprawl has actually increased forest cover in the U.S. by increasing the demand for forest products.

Of course, the fact that the overall level of forest cover in the U.S. is rising does not mean that people have forests where they want them. There are a number of recreational, not environmental, reasons why people may want to have forests close to cities. This presumably calls for some targeted park development, not for limits on sprawl. The growth of land trusts such as the Nature Conservancy provides a free market solution for providing this local club good.[17]

Two major environmental externalities associated with driving are greenhouse gas production and local smog. Driving is a major contributor to U.S. greenhouse gas production. Between 1990 and 2000, CO_2 emissions per-capita have grown roughly 5% even though CO_2 emissions per unit of GDP have fallen over 15%. Increased driving has played a role in this increase. Both international cross-city evidence and domestic evidence shows that people drive more in more sprawled cities [Newman and Kensworthy (1998) and Kahn (2000)].

Given that there has been little change over the last 20 years in average fleet fuel economy, increased mileage translates into more fuel consumption and subsequent increases in greenhouse gas production. The recent Kyoto Protocol treaty would have required

[17] Even in Japan, the island of Honshu has approximately 56 million acres (excluding all other Japanese islands) – this is enough for all 47 million Japanese households to live in 3000 square foot homes on quarter acres, and leave 75 percent of the land area (and all other Japanese islands) unoccupied. Currently, 50 percent of Japanese households together sit on less than two percent of the available land area in the Archipelago. High Japanese densities are not the result of lack of land, but of government policies that often reflect the goals of other lobbies. Currently, only 4.7% of Japanese land is used for building.

the U.S. to reduce its greenhouse gas production by roughly 10%. Interestingly, suburbanization has increased the average driver's greenhouse gas emissions by around 10%. Annual U.S. carbon dioxide emissions per-capita equals 40,000 pounds. Every gallon of gasoline consumed creates 20 pounds of emissions. Thus, if a household, whose vehicle achieves 25 miles per gallon, reduced its driving from 22,620 to 16,950 miles a year this would reduce household emissions by over 4000 pounds [Kahn (2000)]. These mileage figures represent the sample means for suburban and city household drivers as reported in the 1995 NPTS data. The growing popularity of large fuel inefficient vehicles, such as SUVs, increases the climate change impact of suburban driving. It is possible that technological advances such as the development of a fuel efficient hydrogen car will help to offset the extra driving brought about by ongoing suburbanization [Hawken, A. Lovins and L.H. Lovins (1999)]. But, even optimists believe this will not take place for another 20 years.

Despite increased vehicle use over the last thirty years, the most polluted parts of the United States have experienced a dramatic drop in their smog levels. California has experienced sharp population growth, on going suburbanization, and due to its geography and concentration of economic activity it features the worst ozone smog problems in the nation. To document air pollution trends, we use the California Ambient Air Quality Data 1980–1999 (California EPA Air Resources Board). This CD-ROM provides all air quality readings taken in the state during this time period. In this data, the unit of analysis is a monitoring station. We partition California into two areas, the Los Angeles Basin and everywhere else in the state. The Los Angeles basin has suffered from the worst smog in the nation.

In Table 10, we break out the pollution data into two decades, the 1980s and the 1990s, and we explore pollution trends in the Los Angeles area and in the rest of the state. During both decades, total population grew by more in the Los Angeles area than in the rest of the state and vehicles per-capita continued to grow. This should have led to more smog and nitrogen dioxide pollution as car activity increases. Yet, the table highlights the sharp pollution progress in the Los Angeles basin relative to the rest of the state. In the Los Angeles basin, people living near the median monitoring station in the 1980s were exposed to 33 polluted days per year while in the 1990s their exposure fell down to 5 days a year. This extra month of clean air is striking given that the median person in the rest of the state did not gain. The bottom two rows of the table document the Los Angeles basin's progress based on two other ambient pollution criteria. Despite the growth in this region, the Los Angeles region is converging to the rest of the state's low pollution levels.

This environmental gain was achieved due to the greening of the automobile. New vintages emit much less emissions than pre-1975 makes [Kahn (2000)]. Table 11 reports California vehicle median hydrocarbon emissions by model year and calendar year. The California Air Resources Board has pulled different vehicles off of the road in different calendar years and conducted a "random roadside test". Pooling these repeated cross-sections provides evidence on the extent of the greening of fleet emissions. Each column of Table 11 reports cross-sectional facts about how vehicle emissions variation across

Table 10
Smog progress in California from 1980 to 1999

	Los Angeles basin		California outside of the Los Angeles basin	
	1980–1989	1990–1999	1980–1989	1990–1999
Percent change in population	26.5	11.9	25.4	11.4
Annual count of days when ambient ozone exceeded the national 1 hour standard	33	5	0	0
Mean of 30 highest annual 1 hour readings of ozone (parts per million)	0.149	0.112	0.086	0.083
Annual mean for nitrogen dioxide (parts per million)	0.034	0.024	0.019	0.015
Annual mean for sulfur dioxide (parts per million)	0.0034	0.0018	0.0009	0.0013

Note: The unit of analysis is an ambient monitoring station. This table's pollution entries are cell medians. The data source is the California EPA's Air Resources Board's California Ambient Air Quality Data 1980–1999. The Greater Los Angeles Area is defined as the following counties: Orange, Los Angeles, San Bernardino, Riverside, San Diego, Kern and Ventura. In each cell, there are at least 303 monitoring stations.

Table 11
California vehicle hydrocarbon emissions

	Calendar year		
Median emissions by cell	1992	1993	1996
Model year			
1965–1969	114	72	119.5
1970–1974	87	70	91
1975–1979	27	24.5	27
1980–1984	28	4	31
1985–1989	8	6.5	12
1990–1996			4

The data source is the California Random Roadside Emissions Test. This table reports sample medians for three separate cross-sectional data sets collected in 1992, 1993 and 1996. Each entry of the table reports emissions (measured in parts per million) by model year and calendar year. In calendar years 1992 and 1993, cars built after 1990 are included in the model year 1985–1989 category.

vehicle vintage types. Reading across a row of Table 11 indicates how for a given model year, a vehicle's emissions changes as it ages. Two key facts emerge from Table 11. Vehicles built after 1975 have much lower emissions than pre-1975 vehicles [Kahn (1996)]. Second, post 1975 makes continue to have lower emissions relative to pre-1975 makes even as they age. For example, the median vehicle built between 1975 and 1979 has relatively low emissions in calendar year 1992 and in 1996. This table indicates that the average air pollution externality per mile of driving is falling over time.

Indeed, throughout the U.S. most major forms of pollution are actually declining. Carbon monoxide, particulates, ozone, sulfur dioxide, and lead have all decreased significantly. Sprawl may be increasing the scale of driving, but improvements in technology are more than compensating for this increase.

This is not to say that cars should not be taxed so that they internalize the environmental consequences of driving. Older cars that produce so much of the car fleet's pollution output are natural candidates for environmental taxes. Equity considerations, poor people own older vehicles than richer people, tend to discourage such differentiated taxes.

There are negative environmental externalities due to sprawl, but they do not seem overwhelming. Forest cover in the U.S. is rising, not falling. Automobile pollution is becoming a less serious problem. Certainly, targeted responses are appropriate. Setting aside land if there is demand for empty land seems like a sensible response to overdevelopment and gas taxes seem like the right response to car pollution [see Parry and Small (2002)]. Neither calls for a wholesale end to sprawl.

7.4. Agglomeration and productivity consequences of sprawl

Another possible negative consequence of sprawl is that urban agglomeration economies may be reduced. There is a rich and impressive literature documenting the importance of agglomeration effects. This literature has shown the connection between density at the county level and agglomeration [Ciccone and Hall (1996)] and has documented that higher urban wages are not merely the result of more able workers moving to cities [Glaeser and Maré (2001)]. Rauch (1993) shows that wages are higher in cities with higher human capital workers. Jaffe, Trajtenberg and Henderson (1993) provide the best evidence that ideas do move more quickly when people are in close proximity. Lucas Jr. and Rossi-Hansberg (2002) also argue for the importance of density in speeding productivity. These papers all suggest that sprawl might indeed reduce agglomeration economies and deter overall productivity.

There is however some doubt about the level of agglomeration needed for spillovers to operate. While no one doubts that dense areas are more productive than the wilds of Sasketchewan, it is less obvious that downtown Detroit is more productive than Silicon Valley (a textbook example of sprawl). It is possible that some forms of agglomeration actually require working in a walking city. After all, the shear rush of new ideas associated with moving around Tokyo or New York is staggering. But we suspect that most agglomeration effects are based on ready access to other human being. After all, Lucas Jr. (1988) himself wrote "What can people be paying Manhattan or downtown Chicago rents for, if not for being near other people?"

It is exactly this type of reasoning that makes us suspect that sprawl is not so bad for productivity. After all, well functioning sprawl is full of people. The only difference between sprawl and conventional downtowns is that sprawl is built around the automobile, not around walking and public transportation. As such, we suspect that some sprawling car cities are more productive, and others are less so, just as some traditional cities are more productive and others not. Sprawl cities with higher levels of density and better transportation infrastructure appear (as in the case of Silicon Valley and Route 128) to be able to deliver very high levels of connection indeed.

As such, we think that some empirical evidence is appropriate to look at this issue. Again, we see this evidence as not disputing the general importance of agglomeration effects, but rather as informing the question as to whether these agglomeration effects can still work when people drive, rather than walk or take public transportation.

There are two pieces of evidence that bear on this issue. First, there is the question of whether output is less in lower-density areas. Here there is no question. Per capita incomes are higher in MSAs with higher levels of density. Across major MSAs, the overall relationship in the year 2000 was:

$$\log(\text{per capita income}) = \underset{(0.08)}{9.55} + \underset{(0.01)}{0.13} * \log(\text{job density}),$$

$$N = 139, \qquad R^2 = 0.40.$$

Standard errors are in parentheses. This relationship is quite strong and mimics at the MSA level what Ciccone and Hall (1996) found using state-level information on productivity.

However, when we repeat this regression using the share of jobs more than three miles from the city center as our measure of job decentralization, we find

$$\log(\text{per capita income}) = \underset{(0.10)}{10.05} + \underset{(0.13)}{0.27} * \text{Job sprawl},$$

$$N = 139, \qquad R^2 = 0.03.$$

In this case, a 10-percentage point increase in job sprawl increases MSA per-capita income by 2.7%. Thus, aggregate density at the MSA level matters, but the degree to which those jobs are centralized in the central city appears to be irrelevant.

A second form of evidence is to actually calculate the job density within 30 minutes drive of a central location in the new edge cities and to compare this with the job density within the traditional CBD. By our calculations, it would take 25 minutes to go about three miles using public transportation. There are 81,000 jobs within a three-mile radius of the center of downtown St. Louis. In a car, even in moderate traffic, someone should be able to travel 12.5 miles in a modern edge city. The number of jobs within three miles of downtown Palo Alto or Tyson's Corner dwarfs the number of jobs in the traditional downtowns of most older cities. As such, the edge cities are true agglomerations, they just involve using automobiles.

7.5. Social consequences of sprawl

One particularly important question about sprawl is whether it creates segregation of rich and poor or racial segregation or social isolation more generally. First, it seems quite clear that the wealthy have found it easier to take advantage of the new edge cities than the poor. As Glaeser, Kahn and Rappaport (2000) document, the poor live downtown and the rich live in suburbs. We follow Gin and Sonstelie (1992) and argue that transportation technologies play a crucial role in explaining this segregation. Because cars a re so expensive, the poor live in cities so that they can use public transportation. Glaeser, Kahn and Rappaport (2000) show that poverty rates are much higher closer to public transit stops and when areas increased access to public transportation their poverty rates increased.

While it is true that the automobile has led to the suburbanization of the wealthy, it is not clear what the solution to this problem should be. One approach might be to tax the car and push the rich back into cities. Alternatively, one might think that the right approach is to subsidize car ownership for the poor as advocated by Raphael and Stoll (2001).

One piece of information which is important in determining whether car cities should be taxed or public transportation cities should be subsidized is to ask which urban form is fundamentally more integrated. Cutler, Glaeser and Vigdor (1999) find that racial segregation is much lower in suburban census tracts than in urban census tracts. Moreover, the level of segregation has been lower in the newer, car-based cities of the west and the south than in the older, public transportation based cities of the northeast. Suburbs certainly do not seem like models of integration, but then older cities were pretty segregated as well. We take the Cutler, Glaeser and Vigdor (1999) 1970 and 1990 dissimilarity index and calculate the change in segregation over this 20 year period. In Figure 7, we graph the change in segregation with respect to the percent change in MSA population

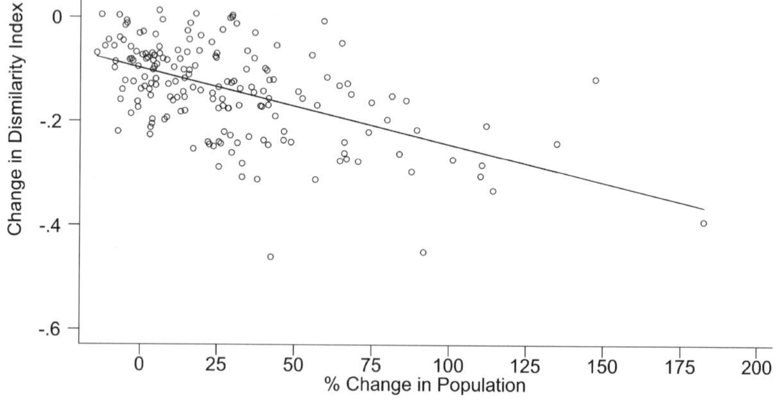

Figure 7. Racial segregation trends across MSAs from 1970 to 1990.

growth over that time period. A clear negative correlation is seen. Fast growing metro areas such as Orlando, Las Vegas, and Phoenix have experienced a sharper decline in segregation relative to slow growth areas.

The evidence on social isolation in the suburbs is quite mixed. As Putnam (1999) reports, people in suburbs are less likely to join formal social organization. Glaeser and Sacerdote (1999) show that people who live in single family detached houses are also less likely to interact with their neighbors than people who rent. The proximity involved in urban density and multi-unit buildings appears to abet connection. Presumably these facts help us to understand why some critics of suburban living argue that it is socially isolated.

However, many of these relationships are quite weak and other forms of social connection rise in the suburbs. For example, church attendance is higher in suburban areas. Time study diaries show almost no difference in the time per week spent in social activities between city-dwellers and suburbanites. As a result, we think that this is a provocative area for new research, but hardly a compelling basis for government action.

7.6. Zoning

The past ten years has seen a startling increase in housing prices in many east and west coast metropolitan areas. These increases have been highly localized. In most of the United States, housing prices are generally determined by the physical cost of construction [see Glaeser and Gyourko (2001)]. Still, in some areas and in particular in the suburbs of wealthy cities, housing prices have reached astonishingly high levels.

In principle, this increase could just be the result of rising demand for land. After all, the urban model discussed above predicts that as a city growth, the value of land that is proximity to work areas should become quite high. However, the urban model does not really explain the experience of American housing prices very well. The urban model predicts that land should be equally valued on the intensive and extensive margins. In other words, the gap in price between a house on a quarter acre lot and a house on a half acre lot should be the same as the difference between the price of the house on a quarter acre lot and the construction cost of the house. If this was not true, then the owner of the house on the half-acre lot would subdivide and build a new house on one-half of his parcel.

Glaeser and Gyourko (2001) show that these two values diverge wildly in expensive areas. In some expensive areas, the price per acre as calculated by subtracting construction cost from housing value and dividing by land area is as much as ten times as much as the price per acre found comparing equivalent houses on different size lots. This can only occur if zoning, or other development controls have stopped new construction. In deed, examination of new construction statistics in the 1990s show that expensive areas have indeed stopped allowing new construction, presumably through various forms of regulation.

This may in fact be efficient. Zoning may be internalizing externalities exactly as it is meant to. However, it seems just as likely that current homeowners are using zoning to restrict supply are thereby push up the price of their house. In this way, zoning enables homeowners to act like local monopolists and its effects may be quite costly socially. As we move forward, this area deserves more research and policy attention.

8. Conclusion

Over the past century, urban growth has taken the form of sprawl. First people and then jobs left the high density, walking and public transport cities of the 19th century. They moved into the lower density, car cities of the next century. The move to cars and trucks was important not only because it reduced transport costs, but also because it eliminate the fixed costs of rail depots and ports. These fixed costs had been a major force driving agglomeration and their disappearance has enabled employment to decentralize. Edge cities were made possible by the automobile and as long as the car remains the dominant transport mode, sprawl is likely to remain the dominant urban form.

The economic and social consequences of sprawl do not appear to be dire. Suburbanization is not linked to rapid decreases in intellectual creativity or to massive social unrest. New ideas seem to be created in Silicon Valley just as easily as they were in Detroit. After all, most theories about urban agglomeration leading to innovation stress connection, not transport mode. Since people who live in the new car cities are still quite close to their neighbors, when proximity is measured by travel time, we should not have really expected a decline in the degree of intellectual progress.

Suburbanites are less connected than city-dwellers, but the difference seems slight. Suburbs are actually more racially integrated than central cities. There is a transitional problem as the poor can not pay for cars and remain stuck in central cities and this surely deserves policy attention. But it makes more sense to give the poor car vouchers [as advocated by Raphael and Stoll (2001)] rather than to stop suburbanization.

There are some market failures associated with sprawl. Highways have a common pool problem that is not shared by rail. Either we need to be accustomed to traffic jams, as Tony Downs (1992) eloquently argued in Stuck in Traffic, or we need to figure out how to be smarter about using electronic tolls to limit congestion. Pollution is an issue, but the phase-in of vehicle emissions control technology has reduced emissions per mile faster than vehicle mileage has increased. Finally, there is the issue of zoning. Local political units work well for many things, but they appear to be restricting housing supply to raise prices and we should probably rethink our current zoning laws.

Acknowledgements

Edward L. Glaeser thanks the NSF for financial support. Jan Brueckner, Vernon Henderson, Andrei Goureev and Jacques Thisse provided extremely helpful comments.

Appendix: Proofs of propositions

PROOF OF PROPOSITION 1. The social surplus (or profits) generated by a new subcenter equals

$$\pi(\phi, \Delta, X) = \frac{2\widehat{P}e^{(w\theta_1+\theta_2 t - zd_{s-1})/\alpha}\alpha}{t}\big(e^{-z\phi\Delta/\alpha} + e^{-(t+z)\Delta/(2\alpha)} - e^{-(t+z)\phi\Delta/(2\alpha)} - e^{(-(1-\phi)t\Delta-(1+\phi)z\Delta)/(2\alpha)}\big) - K. \tag{A.1}$$

Differentiation then gives us

$$\frac{d\pi}{d\phi} = \frac{2\Psi\alpha e^{-zd_{s-1}/\alpha}}{t}\left(\frac{-z\Delta}{\alpha}e^{-z\phi\Delta/\alpha} + \frac{(t+z)\Delta}{2\alpha}e^{-(t+z)\phi\Delta/(2\alpha)} - \frac{(t-z)\Delta}{2\alpha}e^{(-(1-\phi)t\Delta-(1+\phi)z\Delta)/(2\alpha)}\right), \tag{A.2}$$

which in turn implies

$$\frac{(t-z)\phi}{2\alpha}e^{(-(1-\phi)t\Delta-(1+\phi)z\Delta)/(2\alpha)} = \frac{-z\phi}{\alpha}e^{-z\phi\Delta/\alpha} + \frac{(t+z)\phi}{2\alpha}e^{-(t+z)\phi\Delta/(2\alpha)}$$

or

$$2z + (t-z)e^{-(1-\phi)(t+z)\Delta/(2\alpha)} = (t+z)e^{-(t-z)\phi\Delta/(2\alpha)}.$$

Differentiation also gives us that

$$\frac{d\pi}{d\Delta} = \frac{\partial\pi}{\partial\phi^*}\frac{\partial\phi^*}{\partial\Delta} + \frac{\partial\pi}{\partial\Delta}$$
$$= \frac{2\Psi\alpha e^{-zd_{s-1}/\alpha}}{t}\left(\frac{-z\phi}{\alpha}e^{-z\phi\Delta/\alpha} - \frac{t+z}{2\alpha}e^{-(t+z)\Delta/(2\alpha)} + \frac{(t+z)\phi}{2\alpha}e^{-(t+z)\phi\Delta/(2\alpha)} + \frac{t(1-\phi)+z(1+\phi)}{2\alpha}e^{(-(1-\phi)t\Delta-(1+\phi)z\Delta)/(2\alpha)}\right). \tag{A.3}$$

Using the fact that

$$\frac{(t-z)\phi}{2\alpha}e^{(-(1-\phi)t\Delta-(1+\phi)z\Delta)/(2\alpha)} = \frac{-z\phi}{\alpha}e^{-z\phi\Delta/\alpha} + \frac{(t+z)\phi}{2\alpha}e^{-(t+z)\phi\Delta/(2\alpha)},$$

we can simplify this expression to

$$\frac{d\pi}{d\Delta} = \frac{2\Psi(t+z)e^{-zd_{s-1}/\alpha}e^{-(t+z)\Delta/(2\alpha)}}{2t}\big(e^{(t-z)\phi\Delta/(2\alpha)} - 1\big) > 0.$$

It is obviously true that profits are negative when Δ is sufficiently small. Now change notation and let

$$\phi\Delta = -\frac{2\alpha}{t-z}\log\left(\frac{2z}{t+z}\right),$$

then as Δ becomes sufficiently large, profits converge to

$$\frac{2\Psi\alpha e^{-zd_{s-1}/\alpha}\left(\left(\frac{2z}{t+z}\right)^{2z/(t-z)}-\left(\frac{2z}{t+z}\right)^{(t+z)/(t-z)}\right)}{t}-K,$$

which is positive when

$$2\Psi\alpha e^{-zd_{s-1}/\alpha}\left(\left(\frac{2z}{t+z}\right)^{2z/(t-z)}-\left(\frac{2z}{t+z}\right)^{(t+z)/(t-z)}\right)>tK.$$

Then continuity ensures the existence of a value of Δ, which satisfies $\pi(\phi^*(\widetilde{\Delta}(X),X),\widetilde{\Delta}(X),X)=0$.

The equality $\pi(\phi^*(\widetilde{\Delta}(X),X),\widetilde{\Delta}(X),X)=0$, which implies that

$$\frac{\partial\widetilde{\Delta}}{\partial X}=-\frac{\partial\pi}{\partial X}\bigg/\frac{\partial\pi}{\partial\Delta},$$

so that the sign of the effect of any variable X on $\widetilde{\Delta}$ is the opposite of the sign of the effect of any variable X on π. Differentiation then gives us that

$$\frac{\partial\pi}{\partial K}<0,\qquad\frac{\partial\pi}{\partial\widehat{P}}>0,\qquad\frac{\partial\pi}{\partial w}>0,$$

$$\frac{\partial\pi}{\partial\theta_1}>0,\qquad\frac{\partial\pi}{\partial\theta_2}>0\quad\text{and}\quad\frac{\partial\pi}{\partial d_{s-1}}<0.$$

When $\theta_2=0$,

$$\begin{aligned}\frac{\partial\pi}{\partial t}&=\frac{2\Psi e^{(-z(d_{s-1}+\phi\Delta))/\alpha}\alpha}{t^2}\\&\quad\times\Bigg(-(1+e^{(-t\Delta-(1-2\phi)z\Delta)/(2\alpha)}-e^{-(t-z)\phi\Delta/(2\alpha)}-e^{-(1-\phi)(t+z)\Delta/(2\alpha)})\\&\quad-\frac{\Delta t}{2\alpha}(e^{(-t\Delta-(1-2\phi)z\Delta)/(2\alpha)}-\phi e^{-(t-z)\phi\Delta/(2\alpha)}-(1-\phi)e^{-(1-\phi)(t+z)\Delta/(2\alpha)})\Bigg)\\&\quad\times\frac{1}{t}(1+e^{-t\Delta/(2\alpha)}-2e^{-t\Delta/(4\alpha)}).\end{aligned}\tag{A.4}$$

If z is small so $\phi\approx0.5$, and using the notation $x=\Delta t/(2\alpha)$ the expression in brackets can be approximated by $(2+x)e^{-0.5x}-(1+x)e^{-x}-1$. This expression equals zero (to two decimal places) when $x=2.5$ and is positive for all values below that amount and negative for all values above that amount. When $2.5=\Delta t/(2\alpha)$, then the land in between the two old subcenters traded at 8.2 percent of the value of land at the old subcenters, and is more than that amount when $2.5>\Delta t/(2\alpha)$. As such, when $z=0$, the maximum spread between two subcenters falls with t when land in between the two old subcenters costs more than 8.2 percent of land at the subcenters and rises otherwise.

$$\frac{\partial\pi}{\partial z}=\frac{-2\widehat{P}\mathrm{e}^{(w\theta_1+\theta_2 t-zd_{s-1})/\alpha}}{t}\Bigg((d_{s-1}+\phi\Delta)$$
$$\times\left(\mathrm{e}^{-z\phi\Delta/\alpha}+\mathrm{e}^{-(t+z)\Delta/(2\alpha)}-\mathrm{e}^{-(t+z)\phi\Delta/(2\alpha)}-\mathrm{e}^{(-(1-\phi)t\Delta-(1+\phi)z\Delta)/(2\alpha)}\right)$$
$$+\frac{\Delta}{2}\Big((1-2\phi)\mathrm{e}^{-(t+z)\Delta/(2\alpha)}+\phi\mathrm{e}^{-(t+z)\phi\Delta/(2\alpha)}$$
$$-(1-\phi)\mathrm{e}^{(-(1-\phi)t\Delta-(1+\phi)z\Delta)/(2\alpha)}\Big)\Bigg). \tag{A.5}$$

If $z=0$, so $\phi\approx 0.5$, this terms in brackets become

$$-(d_{s-1}+0.5\Delta)\left(1+\mathrm{e}^{-t\Delta/(2\alpha)}-2\mathrm{e}^{-t\Delta/(4\alpha)}\right),$$

which is always strictly negative. The problem is continuous, so that for low values of z, the expression will remain negative. □

PROOF OF PROPOSITION 2. Define $\pi(d_{s+1},d_s,X)$ as the net profits yielded from a new subcenter, where X refers to any other exogenous characteristic. This function equals

$$\frac{2\alpha\Psi\mathrm{e}^{-zd_{S+1}/\alpha}}{t}\left(1-\mathrm{e}^{(-(t-z)(d_{S+1}-d_S))/(2\alpha)}\right)-\frac{t-z}{t}\underline{P}(d_{S+1}-d_S)-K. \tag{A.6}$$

Also define $d^*_{S+1}(d_S,X)$ as the optimal value of d_{S+1} contingent upon the other characteristics. This is determined by the first-order condition

$$\frac{\Psi}{t}\left(-2z\mathrm{e}^{-zd_{S+1}/\alpha}+(t+z)\mathrm{e}^{(-(t+z)(d_{S+1}+(t-z)d_S))/(2\alpha)}\right)-\frac{t-z}{t}\underline{P}=0,\quad\text{or}$$

$$(t+z)P(\hat{d}_S)=2zP(d_{S+1})+(t-z)\underline{P}.$$

At the optimal level of d_{S+1},

$$\frac{\mathrm{d}\pi}{\mathrm{d}d_S}=\frac{\partial\pi}{\partial d_{S+1}}\frac{\partial d^*_{S+1}}{\partial d_S}+\frac{\partial\pi}{\partial d_S}\quad\text{or}\quad-\frac{(t-z)}{t}\left(\Psi\mathrm{e}^{((t-z)d_S-(t+z)d_{S+1})/(2\alpha)}-\underline{P}\right),$$

which is negative because $P(\hat{d}_S)>\underline{P}$. It is obvious that for a sufficiently large value of d_S, profits from a new subcenter become negative. As long as

$$\frac{2\alpha\Psi}{t}\left(\mathrm{e}^{-zd_{S+1}/\alpha}-\mathrm{e}^{-(t+z)d_{S+1}/(2\alpha)}\right)-\frac{t-z}{t}\underline{P}d_{S+1}-K$$

is positive for some value of d_{S+1}, then it is profitable to build a new subcenter when $d_S=0$. Then by continuity there must exist a value of d_S, where profits from building a new subcenter equal exactly zero.

Define $\tilde{d}_S$ as the value of d_S at which development yields exactly zero profits. From $\mathrm{d}\pi/\mathrm{d}d_S<0$, it follows that for all distances beyond that point, development yields negative profits and for all distances nearer than that point development yields positive profits.

Totally differentiating the equality $\pi(d^*_{S+1}(\tilde{d}_S(X), X), \tilde{d}_S(X), X) = 0$ yields

$$\frac{\partial \tilde{d}_S}{\partial X} = -\frac{\partial \pi}{\partial X} \Big/ \frac{\partial \pi}{\partial d_S}.$$

This tells us that the sign of $\partial \tilde{d}_S/\partial X$ is the same as the sign of $\partial \pi/\partial X$. Differentiation then tells us that

$$\frac{\partial \pi}{\partial K} < 0, \qquad \frac{\partial \pi}{\partial \widehat{P}} > 0, \qquad \frac{\partial \pi}{\partial w} > 0,$$

$$\frac{\partial \pi}{\partial \theta_1} > 0, \qquad \frac{\partial \pi}{\partial \theta_2} > 0 \quad \text{and} \quad \frac{\partial \pi}{\partial \underline{P}} < 0.$$

To see the comparative static on z, it is helpful to rewrite the basic land value change equation:

$$\begin{aligned}
&\int_{\hat{d}_S}^{d_{S+1}} \Psi\left(\mathrm{e}^{(-zd_{S+1}-t(d_{S+1}-d))/\alpha} - \mathrm{e}^{(-zd_S-t(d-d_S))/\alpha}\right) \mathrm{d}d \\
&\quad + \int_{d_{S+1}}^{\underline{d}_{\text{old}}} \Psi\left(\mathrm{e}^{(-zd_{S+1}-t(d-d_{S+1}))/\alpha} - \mathrm{e}^{(-zd_S-t(d-d_S))/\alpha}\right) \mathrm{d}d \\
&\quad + \int_{\underline{d}_{\text{old}}}^{\underline{d}_{\text{new}}} \left(\Psi \mathrm{e}^{(-zd_{S+1}-t(d-d_{S+1}))/\alpha} - \underline{P}\right) \mathrm{d}d.
\end{aligned} \tag{A.7}$$

The derivative of this with respect to z equals

$$\begin{aligned}
&\int_{\hat{d}_S}^{d_{S+1}} \Psi\left(\frac{-d_{S+1}}{\alpha}\mathrm{e}^{(-zd_{S+1}-t(d_{S+1}-d))/\alpha} + \frac{d_S}{\alpha}\mathrm{e}^{(-zd_S-t(d-d_S))/\alpha}\right) \mathrm{d}d \\
&\quad + \int_{d_{S+1}}^{\underline{d}_{\text{old}}} \Psi\left(\frac{-d_{S+1}}{\alpha}\mathrm{e}^{(-zd_{S+1}-t(d-d_{S+1}))/\alpha} + \frac{d_S}{\alpha}\mathrm{e}^{(-zd_S-t(d-d_S))/\alpha}\right) \mathrm{d}d \\
&\quad + \int_{\underline{d}_{\text{old}}}^{\underline{d}_{\text{new}}} \left(\frac{-d_{S+1}}{\alpha}\Psi \mathrm{e}^{(-zd_{S+1}-t(d-d_{S+1}))/\alpha}\right) \mathrm{d}d.
\end{aligned} \tag{A.8}$$

Since for all d within the integrals

$$\frac{d_{S+1}}{\alpha}\mathrm{e}^{(-zd_{S+1}-t(d_{S+1}-d))/\alpha} > \frac{d_S}{\alpha}\mathrm{e}^{(-zd_S-t(d-d_S))/\alpha},$$

it follows that the returns from building a new subcenter are falling with z. □

References

Alonso, W. (1964). Location and Land Use. Harvard Univ. Press, Cambridge, MA.

Anas, A., Arnott, R., Small, K.A. (1998). "Urban spatial structure". Journal of Economic Literature 36 (3), 1426–1464.

Baum-Snow, N., Kahn, M.E. (2000). "The effects of new public projects to expand urban rail transit". Journal of Public Economics 77 (2), 241–263.

Brueckner, J.K. (1979). "A model of non-central production in a monocentric city". Journal of Urban Economics 6 (4), 444–463.

Brueckner, J.K. (1983). "Central-city income redistribution and the flight to the suburbs: A stylized model". Regional Science and Urban Economics 13 (2), 177–193.

Brueckner, J.K. (2000). "Urban sprawl: Diagnosis and remedies". International Regional Science Review 23 (2), 160–171.

Brueckner, J.K., Thisse, J.-F., Zenou, Y. (1999). "Why is central Paris rich and Downtown Detroit poor? An amenity-based theory". European Economic Review 43 (1), 91–107.

Calfee, J., Winston, C. (1998). "The value of automobile travel time: Implications for congestion policy". Journal of Public Economics 69 (1), 83–102.

Ciccone, A., Hall, R.E. (1996). "Productivity and the density of economic activity". American Economic Review 86 (1), 54–70.

Cullen, J.-B., Levitt, S. (1999). "Crime, urban flight, and the consequences for cities". Review of Economics and Statistics 81 (2), 159–169.

Cutler, D.M., Glaeser, E.L., Vigdor, J.L. (1999). "The rise and decline of the American ghetto". Journal of Political Economy 107 (3), 455–506.

Downs, A. (1992). Stuck in Traffic. Brookings Institution Press, Washington, DC.

Ewing, R., Pendall, R., Chen, D. (2002). "Measuring sprawl and its impact". http://www.smartgrowthamerica.com/sprawlindex/sprawlindex.html.

Fischel, W. (1987). The Economics of Zoning Laws. Johns Hopkins Press, Baltimore.

Galster, G., Hanson, R., Ratcliffe, M.R., Wolman, H., Coleman, S., Freihage, J. (2001). "Wrestling sprawl to the ground: Defining and measuring an elusive concept". Housing Policy Debate 12 (4), 681–717.

Gin, A., Sonstelie, J. (1992). "The streetcar and residential location in nineteenth century Philadelphia". Journal of Urban Economics 32, 92–107.

Giuliano, G., Small, K.A. (1991). "Subcenters in the Los Angeles Region". Regional Science and Urban Economics 21 (2), 163–182.

Glaeser, E.L., Gyourko, J. (2001). "Urban decline and durable housing". NBER Working Paper No. 8598.

Glaeser, E.L., Kahn, M.E. (2001). "Decentralized employment and the transformation of the American city". Brookings–Wharton Papers on Urban Affairs, 1–47.

Glaeser, E.L., Maré, D.C. (2001). "Cities and skills". Journal of Labor Economics 19 (2), 316–342.

Glaeser, E.L., Sacerdote, B. (1999). "Why is there more crime in cities?" Journal of Political Economy 107 (6), S225–258.

Glaeser, E.L., Shapiro, J.M. (2002). "The benefits of the home mortgage interest deduction". NBER Working Paper No. 9284.

Glaeser, E.L., Kahn, M.E., Rappaport, J. (2000). "Why do the poor live in cities?" NBER Working Paper No. 7636.

Glaeser, E.L., Kolko, J., Saiz, A. (2001). "Consumer city". Journal of Economic Geography 1 (1), 27–50.

Gordon, P., Kumar, A., Richardson, H. (1991). "The influence of metropolitan spatial structure on commuting time". Journal of Urban Economics 26 (2), 138–151.

Hart, S.I., Spivak, A.L. (1993). Elephant in the Bedroom: Automobile Dependence and Denial Impacts on the Economy and Environment. Hope Publishing House.

Hawken, P., Lovins, A., Lovins, L.H. (1999). Natural Capitalism: Creating the Next Industrial Revolution. Little Brown, New York.

Henderson, J.V., Mitra, A. (1996). "The new urban landscape developers and edge cities". Regional Science and Urban Economics 26, 613–643.

Ingram, G., Liu, Z. (1999). "Motorization and road provision in countries and cities". World Bank Working Paper 1842.

Jackson, K. (1985). Crabgrass Frontier. The Suburbanization of the United States. Oxford University Press, London.

Jaffe, A.B., Trajtenberg, M., Henderson, R. (1993). "Geographic localization of knowledge spillovers as evidenced by patent citations". Quarterly Journal of Economics 108 (3), 577–598.

Kahn, M.E. (1996). "New evidence on trends in vehicle emissions". RAND Journal of Economics 27 (1), 183–196.

Kahn, M.E. (2000). "The environmental impact of suburbanization". Journal of Policy Analysis and Management 19 (4), 569–586.

Kahn, M.E. (2001). "Does sprawl reduce the Black/White housing consumption gap?" Housing Policy Debate 12 (1), 77–86.

Kain, J.F. (1991). "Deception in Dallas: Strategic misrepresentation in rail transit promotion and evaluation". Journal of the American Planning Association 56, 184–196.

Kain, J.F. (1997). "Cost-effective alternatives to Atlanta's rail rapid transit system". Journal of Transport Economics and Policy, 25–49.

Katz, L.F., Rosen, K. (1987). "The interjurisdictional effects of growth controls on housing prices". Journal of Law and Economics 30 (1), 149–160.

La Porta, R., Shleifer, A., Lopez-de-Silanes, F., Vishny, R. (1997). "Legal determinants of external finance". Journal of Finance 52 (3), 1131–1150.

La Porta, R., Shleifer, A., Lopez-de-Silanes, F., Vishny, R. (1999). "The quality of government". Journal of Law, Economics and Organization 15 (1), 222–279.

Lucas Jr., R.E. (1988). "On the mechanics of economic development". Journal of Monetary Economics 22 (1), 3–42.

Lucas Jr., R.E., Rossi-Hansberg, E. (2002). "On the internal structure of cities". Econometrica 70 (4), 1445–1476.

Margo, R. (1992). "Explaining the postwar suburbanization of the population in the United States; the role of income". Journal of Urban Economics 31, 301–310.

McDonald, J.F., McMillen, D.P. (2000). "Employment subcenters and subsequent real estate development in suburban Chicago". Journal of Urban Economics 48 (1), 135–157.

McMillen, D.P., McDonald, J.F. (1998). "Suburban subcenters and employment density in metropolitan Chicago". Journal of Urban Economics 43 (2), 157–180.

Meyer, J., Kain, J., Wohl, M. (1965). The Urban Transportation Problem. Harvard Univ. Press, Cambridge, MA.

Mieszkowski, P., Smith, B. (1991). "Analyzing urban decentralization: The case of Houston". Regional Science and Urban Economics 21 (2), 183–199.

Mills, E.S., Lubuele, L.S. (1997). "Inner cities". Journal of Economic Literature 35 (2), 727–756.

Newman, P., Kensworthy, J. (1998). Sustainability and Cities: Overcoming Automobile Dependence. Island Press Books.

Parry, I.W.H., Small, K.A. (2002). "Does Britain or the United States have the right gasoline tax?" March 2002 |02–12| Resources for the Future Working Paper, http://www.rff.org.

Putnam, R. (1999). Bowling Alone: The Collapse and Revival of American Community. Simon & Schuster, New York.

Raphael, S., Stoll, M. (2001). "Can boosting minority car-ownership rates narrow inter-racial employment gaps?" The Brookings–Wharton Papers on Urban Economic Affairs, 99–145.

Rauch, J.E. (1993). "Productivity gains from geographic concentration of human capital: Evidence from the cities". Journal of Urban Economics 34 (3), 380–400.

Rosen, K., Katz, L.F. (1981). "Growth management and land use controls: the San Francisco bay area experience". American Real Estate and Urban Economics Association Journal 9 (4), 321–344.

Small, A.K., Gomez-Ibáñez, J. (1998). "Road pricing for congestion management: The transition from theory to policy". In: Button, K., Verhoefs, E. (Eds.), Road Pricing, Traffic Congestion and the Environment: Issues of Efficiency and Social Feasibility. Elgar Press, Northampton, MA.

Voith, R. (1999). "Does the federal tax treatment of housing affect the pattern of metropolitan development?" Federal Reserve Bank of Philadelphia Business Review, 3–16.

Chapter 57

FACTOR MOBILITY AND REDISTRIBUTION

HELMUTH CREMER[1]

University of Toulouse, Toulouse, France
e-mail: helmut@cict.fr

PIERRE PESTIEAU[2]

CREPP, University of Liège, Liège, Belgium
e-mail: p.pestieau@ulg.ac.be

Contents

[1] Also affiliated at GREMAQ and IDEI.
[2] Also affiliated at CORE, CEPR and Delta.

Handbook of Regional and Urban Economics, Volume 4. Edited by J.V. Henderson and J.F. Thisse

DOI: 10.1016/S0169-7218(04)07057-1

Abstract

This chapter reviews recent theoretical work on the effect of factor mobility and the ensuing tax competition on the capacity of governments to raise revenue and redistribute income. It focuses on three issues: the relevance and limitations of the "race to the bottom" result, the benefits and pitfalls of partial coordination and the incidence of factors mobility on social security systems.

Keywords

factor mobility, redistribution, tax competition, tax cooperation, tax harmonization

JEL classification: H21, H23, H71, H77, R13, R51

1. Introduction

One of the main alleged pitfalls of European construction is that it would impede redistributive policies at the national level and threaten the future of the "welfare state". This allegation is widespread in political circles and in the media and the recently decided addition of ten new member states is likely to foster its intensity. A major theme in that debate is the potential loss in tax revenues as a result of tax competition. Accordingly, the integration process would exert a negative influence on the ability of member states to generate an "adequate" level of tax revenues. Over the last two decades, this debate has spawned a significant amount of academic research and the literature continues to grow at an impressive speed. While the underlying problem involves a number of different ramifications, it seems that the literature has exploded in even more directions. The purpose of this chapter is to provide a selective survey of this literature and to focus on some issues that we consider as crucial for the future of redistributive policies and social protection.[1]

Economic integration can affect redistribution in a variety of ways. In this paper we focus on one of the implications of economic integration, namely the increase in mobility of factors of production, capital and labor. The basic idea is that mobile factors can adjust their location to any interregional differentials in taxation or in benefits. National governments cannot abstract from such potential reaction when designing redistributive policies. By focusing on factor mobility, we deliberately abstract from other implications of economic integration, such as increased mobility of goods, that can also affect redistribution.[2]

The literature on factor mobility and redistribution covers two aspects of reality. Earlier work was based on the fiscal federalism literature and was exclusively devoted to the setting of a federal state. More recently, an increasing number of studies have been concerned with economic unions, also called confederations. The main difference between the two settings is that there is a central authority in a federation while such a central government typically does not exist in confederations.[3] Consequently, the two settings have different implications for the modeling of the relationship between redistribution and mobility. Our main concern being the redistributive capacities of European Union national governments, we shall concentrate on the case where no strong central government exists. However, our results also apply to a federation with a high degree of decentralization. Furthermore, we shall also discuss some transversal issues like the appropriateness of centralization or cooperation and, in particular the potential benefits of competition between national (or regional) governments.

[1] There exists several surveys which focus on other aspects of that impressive literature [see Wilson (1999), Haufler (2001), Wellisch (2000), Wildasin (1994a), Cremer et al. (1996)].

[2] Wilson and Wildasin (2003) show that the possibility of trade (in goods) may have a significant impact on the results. In particular, it may lead to an increases in taxes.

[3] Or, at least, has more limited prerogatives.

It is important at the outset to make clear that we adopt the viewpoint of the public finance literature as opposed to that of economic geography and trade theory. This implies a number of assumptions that are standard in the public finance treatment of tax competition: perfect competition, constant returns to scale technology, mobility of some factors (capital, skilled or unskilled labor) and immobility of other factors (skilled or unskilled labor, land, natural resources). These assumptions are inspired by the considered context and the desired applications; they are not always consistent. In particular, the distinction between those resources that are perfectly mobile and those that are immobile often differs significantly from one paper to the other.[4] In economic geography the standard assumption concerning labor mobility is that skilled labor is mobile whereas unskilled labor does not move. The objective pursued in that literature is to explain the dynamics of agglomerations catering to all skilled workers. In the public finance tradition, on the other hand, one of the concerns is to explain the risk for too generous region to attract low income families. To address this question it is convenient to assume that unskilled workers are the only ones to move.[5]

We will first present our benchmark model of tax competition and its implications as to reductions of tax rates and redistributive efforts; see Section 2. We show that the "race to the bottom" result arises in a most dramatic way in a small open economy setting. In such a framework, mobility and redistribution appear to be essentially incompatible. Mobility has a less extreme impact in a strategic Nash equilibrium setting with a "limited" number of countries: redistribution is adversely affected, but does not disappear altogether. In Section 3 we then review the most evident qualifications which pertain to assumptions made in the benchmark model. They concern for instance the assumptions of symmetry, constant returns to scale technology, full employment and benevolent governments. We depart from this latter assumption by discussing a political economy approach instead of a normative one. Next, in Section 4, we deal with the issue of tax cooperation and show its pitfalls. In particular, we study the issue of partial cooperation policies, i.e., cooperation agreements which are limited to a subset of the available tax instrument. A prominent example of such a reform is currently under debate and consists in imposing a minimum tax on capital incomes. Finally, we consider the incidence of labor mobility on social security schemes. This issue is likely to be of considerable importance during the next decades. It goes beyond the scope of traditional tax competition model in particular because it involves inter-generational (and thus dynamic) issues. It has only recently started to receive some attention in the literature.

[4] Wildasin (2003b) presents an attempt to overcome this difficulty. He considers a setting in which the degree of mobility of different resources is determined endogenously. For further discussion of the relevance and justification of the underlying assumptions, see also Wildasin (2003a).

[5] In many tax competition models some results (like the "the race to the bottom" property) obtain with either mobility assumption (skilled or unskilled workers).

2. The benchmark model and the "race to the bottom" result

2.1. *Setting and closed economy solution*

Consider a confederation of J identical countries, indexed $j = 1, \ldots, J$. For the sake of simplicity, we shall often concentrate on the case where J is large, so that each individual country becomes (roughly speaking) a small open economy. However, in some instances we allow for any level of $J \geqslant 2$. Within each country, competitive firms produce a single output using three factors of production: capital, K, and two types of labor, e.g., skilled, M, and unskilled L. Each country has a capital endowment of $\overline{K}$ and the number of native skilled and unskilled workers is given by $\overline{M}$ and $\overline{L}$, respectively; each worker supplies one unit of his type of labor. For the time being, we assume that both capital and skilled labor are immobile while unskilled labor is mobile. Consequently, we have $K = \overline{K}$ and $M = \overline{M}$, but L can differ from $\overline{L}$. We thus distinguish the number of natives $\overline{L}$ from the number of residents L. In other words, $\overline{L} - L$ is the net emigration if any. Once production takes place, the output is sold to residents as a final consumption. The consumption of each type of worker is equal to his net of tax income and is denoted by c^{s} and c^{u} for the skilled and unskilled, respectively. Both types of workers have the same utility function with consumption as the only argument. Skilled workers own the stock of capital; their income consists of earnings and capital income. The objective of each national government is utilitarist over the population of *natives*. National welfare it then given by

$$W = \overline{M}u(c^{\mathrm{s}}) + \overline{L}u(c^{\mathrm{u}}). \tag{1}$$

Finally, we have a constant returns to scale (CRS) production function

$$Y = F(\overline{M}, \overline{K}, L). \tag{2}$$

Using Euler's law, we can write

$$Y = w^{\mathrm{s}}\overline{M} + w^{\mathrm{u}}L + r\overline{K}, \tag{3}$$

where r is the marginal productivity of capital and w^{s} and w^{u} denote the marginal productivities of skilled and unskilled workers, respectively. We assume that $w^{\mathrm{s}} > w^{\mathrm{u}}$ is satisfied at the market equilibrium.

Tax instruments consist of (positive or negative) per unit taxes on skilled workers, τ^{M}, on unskilled workers τ^{L} and on capital τ^{K}. Assuming purely redistributive taxation (with no revenue requirement), the budget constraint of the government is given by

$$\tau^{\mathrm{M}}\overline{M} + \tau^{\mathrm{L}}L + \tau^{\mathrm{K}}\overline{K} = 0. \tag{4}$$

With perfectly competitive markets, the gross return of each factor equals its marginal product. Recalling that capital is owned by the skilled workers, the net income and consumption levels of the two types of workers are then given by

$$c^{\mathrm{s}} = w^{\mathrm{s}} - \tau^{\mathrm{M}} + (r - \tau^{\mathrm{K}})\overline{K}/\overline{M}, \tag{5}$$

$$c^{\mathrm{u}} = w^{\mathrm{u}} - \tau^{\mathrm{L}}. \tag{6}$$

Let us first of all consider the closed economy solution which is a useful benchmark. To obtain this case, we impose $L = \overline{L}$ as additional constraint. Using (1), (4)–(6), we can then write the government's problem as follows:

$$\max_{\tau^{\mathrm{K}},\tau^{\mathrm{M}},\tau^{\mathrm{L}}} \quad \overline{M}u\big(w^{\mathrm{s}} - \tau^{\mathrm{M}} + (r - \tau^{\mathrm{K}})\overline{K}/\overline{M}\big) + \overline{L}u(w^{\mathrm{u}} - \tau^{\mathrm{u}})$$
$$+ \mu\big[\tau^{\mathrm{M}}\overline{M} + \tau^{\mathrm{L}}\overline{L} + \tau^{\mathrm{K}}\overline{K}\big].$$

The first-order conditions yield $u'(c^{\mathrm{s}}) = u'(c^{\mathrm{u}})$, which implies $c^{\mathrm{s}} = c^{\mathrm{u}}$. A utilitarist national government would use the taxes to equate disposable income or consumption. This extreme solution arises because all factors are supplied inelastically and, for the time being, immobile. Consequently, all tax instruments are effectively lump-sum. Note that we just need two instruments. As long as τ^{M} is unrestricted, we can set the tax on immobile capital at any arbitrary level, including $\tau^{\mathrm{K}} = r$.[6] In any case we will have $\tau^{\mathrm{L}} < 0$, while the sign of τ^{M} is ambiguous. However, we know that the total tax paid by skilled workers (including the capital tax) is positive.

2.2. Small open economy

Let us now open the economy and allow unskilled workers to move. Assuming perfect mobility at no cost, their utility is then equated across countries. Here equality of utility is equivalent to equality of disposable income. We have thus:

$$c_j^{\mathrm{u}} = \omega \quad \forall j.$$

In the small economy case ($J \to \infty$) any individual country considers ω as given and the problem for the government can thus be written as

$$\max_{\tau^{\mathrm{L}}} \quad \overline{M}u\left(\frac{F(\overline{M}, \overline{K}, L) - \omega L}{\overline{M}}\right) + \overline{L}u(\omega), \tag{7}$$

where $L = L(\omega + \tau^{\mathrm{L}})$ is the labor demand function.[7] The specification of this welfare function reflects the assumption that the social planner takes into account the welfare of its citizens before migration (the natives) and not that of the final residents. We come back to this assumption in the next section. It is not crucial but makes the exposition simpler. With this specification, maximizing social welfare amounts to just maximizing

[6] The results in this section would not change if K were dropped altogether. We have nevertheless included it to make the model consistent with the specification used in Section 4.

[7] Which are derived in the usual way from profit maximization so that L solves $F_L(\overline{K}, \overline{M}, L) = \omega + \tau^{\mathrm{L}}$.

$\overline{M}c^{\mathrm{s}} = F(\overline{M}, \overline{K}, L) - \omega L$. One easily checks the first-order condition

$$\overline{M}\frac{\partial c^{\mathrm{s}}}{\partial \tau^{\mathrm{L}}} = (F_L - \omega)\frac{\partial L}{\partial w^{\mathrm{u}}} = \tau^{\mathrm{L}}\frac{\partial L}{\partial w^{\mathrm{u}}},$$

which implies $\tau^{\mathrm{L}} = 0$.

In the small economy setting, mobility thus has a dramatic impact on redistribution: we move from perfect income equalization achieved in the closed economy to a no redistribution equilibrium when the economy is open. This extreme conclusion is of course due to the specific assumptions we have made. In particular, the idea that the national government takes the mobile factor's income as given is rather extreme and should be qualified.

2.3. Strategic interaction: Nash equilibrium

To do so we shall now move away from the small open economy case and consider a setting of strategic interaction with a "small" number of countries ($J < \infty$). More precisely, we consider a (non-cooperative) game where the players are the J countries and where the strategic variables are tax rates, τ_j^{L}. A country's payoff is welfare given by (1), where consumption levels are evaluated at the migration equilibrium induced by the profile of tax rates. We study the Nash equilibrium of this game.

For any given profile of tax rates, mobility (and perfect competition in the labor market) imply that the allocation of low skilled workers amongst countries must satisfy

$$\sum_{j=1}^{J} L(\omega + \tau_j^{\mathrm{L}}) = J\overline{L}, \tag{8}$$

where τ_j^{L} are given and ω, the net of tax wage level, is endogenously determined. Each individual worker treats ω as given, but the countries now realize that a change in taxes will affect ω. Solving (8) yields ω as a function of the profile of tax rates: $\omega = \omega(\tau_1^{\mathrm{L}}, \dots, \tau_J^{\mathrm{L}})$. Differentiating (8) yields

$$\frac{\partial \omega}{\partial \tau_j^{\mathrm{L}}} = -\frac{\mathrm{d}L(\omega + \tau_j^{\mathrm{L}})/\mathrm{d}w^{\mathrm{u}}}{\sum_k \mathrm{d}L(\omega + \tau_k^{\mathrm{L}})/\mathrm{d}w^{\mathrm{u}}}. \tag{9}$$

In a symmetric setting wherein $\tau_j^{\mathrm{L}} = \tau^{\mathrm{L}}$ for all j, this reduces to

$$\frac{\partial \omega(\tau^{\mathrm{L}}, \dots, \tau^{\mathrm{L}})}{\partial \tau_j^{\mathrm{L}}} = -\frac{1}{J}, \tag{10}$$

and one has $\partial \omega / \partial \tau_j^{\mathrm{L}} = 0$ (i.e., the small economy assumption) only for J tending to infinity.

The payoff function of national government j is now obtained by substituting $\omega = \omega(\tau_1^{\mathrm{L}}, \ldots, \tau_J^{\mathrm{L}})$ into the objective function considered in expression (7), yielding

$$\overline{M}u\left(\frac{F(\overline{M}, \overline{K}, L_j) - \omega(\tau_1^{\mathrm{L}}, \ldots, \tau_J^{\mathrm{L}})L_j}{\overline{M}}\right) + \overline{L}u\left(\omega\left(\tau_1^{\mathrm{L}}, \ldots, \tau_J^{\mathrm{L}}\right)\right), \tag{11}$$

where $L_j = L[\omega(\tau_1^{\mathrm{L}}, \ldots, \tau_J^{\mathrm{L}}) + \tau_j^{\mathrm{L}}]$. To determine country j's best reply, we maximize (11) with respect to τ_j^{L}. The first-order condition is given by

$$u'(c^{\mathrm{s}})\tau_j^{\mathrm{L}} \frac{\mathrm{d}L_j}{\mathrm{d}w^{\mathrm{u}}}\left(\frac{\partial \omega}{\partial \tau_j^{\mathrm{L}}} + 1\right) + \left[\overline{L}u'(c^{\mathrm{u}}) - L_j u'(c^{\mathrm{s}})\right]\frac{\partial \omega}{\partial \tau_j^{\mathrm{L}}} = 0, \tag{12}$$

and the Nash equilibrium is defined by the system of J identical equations specified by (12), $j = 1, \ldots, J$. Assuming a symmetric equilibrium with $\tau_j^{\mathrm{L}} = \tau^{\mathrm{L}}$ (and thus $L_j = \overline{L}$) for all j, making use of (10) and rearranging yields the following characterization of the solution:[8]

$$\frac{\tau^{\mathrm{L}}}{\overline{L}} \frac{\mathrm{d}L}{\mathrm{d}w^{\mathrm{u}}}\left(\frac{J-1}{J}\right) - \frac{1}{J}\left[\frac{u'(c^{\mathrm{u}}) - u'(c^{\mathrm{s}})}{u'(c^{\mathrm{s}})}\right] = 0. \tag{13}$$

The first implication of (13) is that complete ($c^{\mathrm{u}} = c^{\mathrm{s}}$) or "excessive" redistribution ($c^{\mathrm{u}} > c^{\mathrm{s}}$) cannot occur at a symmetric equilibrium. To see this, observe that with $c^{\mathrm{u}} \geqslant c^{\mathrm{s}}$, the term in brackets is negative so that with $\mathrm{d}L/\mathrm{d}w^{\mathrm{u}} < 0$ we must have $\tau^{\mathrm{L}} > 0$, which in turn contradicts $c^{\mathrm{u}} \geqslant c^{\mathrm{s}}$.[9] Consequently, the term in brackets is positive as $c^{\mathrm{u}} < c^{\mathrm{s}}$ and (with finite J) we obtain $\tau^{\mathrm{L}} < 0$ so that there is some redistribution. Regarding the other two tax instruments, τ^{M} and τ^{K}, we have again one degree of freedom exactly like in the closed economy case. With $\tau^{\mathrm{L}} < 0$ we know from the budget constraint that the skilled have to pay a positive total tax. However, to levy this total amount we need just one instrument and the other tax can be set at any arbitrary level. When J tends to infinity, τ^{L} tends to 0 and we obtain the small open economy as a limit case of this Nash equilibrium setting. Similarly, when J "tends to 1", we obtain the closed economy solution with $u'(c^{\mathrm{u}}) = u'(c^{\mathrm{s}})$ as a limit case.[10] Under some additional assumptions, one can also show that $|\tau^{\mathrm{L}}|$ increases as J decreases. Put differently, the equilibrium transfer to the unskilled decreases as the number of countries increases. Observe also that the elasticity $(\partial L/\partial w^{\mathrm{u}})(w^{\mathrm{u}}/\overline{L})$ plays a Ramsey-type role: the higher it is (in absolute value), the lower will be the transfer.

To sum up, we have seen that *in the case of a small economy (or at a Nash equilibrium when J tends to infinity) there is a race to the bottom and the bottom implies no tax and*

[8] Existence of equilibria has been studied by Laussel and Le Breton (1998) and Bayindir-Upman and Ziad (2002).

[9] Recall that $w^{\mathrm{u}} < w^{\mathrm{s}}$ and that capital is owned by the skilled.

[10] This statement has of course to be qualified because J is a discrete variable in our setting. The property we announce is based on taking the limit of the equilibrium condition (13) while taking J as a continuous variable.

thus no redistribution at all. The race is not that radical when the number of countries is reduced and there is strategic interaction among countries. Nevertheless, the basic conjecture that mobility puts downward pressure on redistribution goes through. We have obtained this result in a setting where the unskilled and thus the beneficiaries of redistribution are mobile. Similar conclusions would however hold if instead the skilled (net tax payers) or capital were mobile.[11]

We shall now review a number of qualifications which have to be made to assess the practical relevance of this result. Before proceeding, however, it is important to stress that the downward pressure on redistribution does not arise because of mobility per se. It arises first and foremost because of the non-cooperative behavior of the countries. Like most of the tax competition literature, we have considered a Nash equilibrium and it is well known that Nash equilibria are typically not optimal. This problem can be overcome, at least in principle, through cooperation. In Section 4 we come back to this issue and show how to reach an optimal solution in an open economy through cooperation. There we will also introduce two mobile factors (L and K), thereby allowing for the possibility of "partial cooperation".

3. Qualifications

Our benchmark model is highly stylized. It is solely meant to be illustrative and to bring across the main points in the simplest possible way. To assess its relevance and its policy implications a certain number of qualifications pertaining to some of the basic assumptions are in order. We start with the assumption of symmetry: symmetry in the initial conditions and symmetry in the solutions.

3.1. National asymmetries

In the benchmark model we have adopted an assumption of identical countries. It is clear that if we relax this assumption, the solution is likely to be asymmetrical as well and this brings in the added complication that productive efficiency can be violated (marginal products of mobile factors may differ between countries). Furthermore, and most significantly from our perspective, *under asymmetry it is no longer necessarily true that mobility leads to less redistribution, at least not in all countries.* To see this, consider a two-country setting and assume that country 1 does not care about income inequality and thus maximizes total (or equivalently *per capita*) income of its natives. Country 2, on the other hand, is averse to inequality [it has an objective function similar to (1)]. Except for this difference in preferences, countries are identical. Both are concerned by

[11] Among the often cited papers that have discussed the race to bottom as resulting from factor mobility: Bucovetsky (2003), Christiansen, Hagen and Sandmo (1994), Gordon (1983), Oates and Schwab (1988), Lopez, Marchand and Pestieau (1998), Schjelderup (1997), Sinn (1990), Wildasin (1992, 1997), Wilson (1980, 1982).

the welfare of their native citizens whether or not they move away. Further, we assume here that the skilled workers are mobile whereas the unskilled are not. In this case, it is clear that upon integration, country 2 will find it very difficult to redistribute income and in any case, it will end up with less skilled workers than it started with. In other words, for this country redistribution decreases as a result of mobility. However, country 1 may very well end up with more redistribution that it would do in autarky. To see this note that country 1 simply sets a zero tax under autarky. Under mobility, it will then tend to "import" skilled workers. Consequently, it may find it interesting to impose a positive tax on the skilled albeit for strategic reasons rather than for redistributive ones. This is because part of the taxed skilled are immigrants who do not count in the welfare functions. Put differently, part of the tax is exported and total revenue of the natives is maximized if the skilled are taxed while proceeds are redistributed to the unskilled.

This type of "peculiar" outcome has been obtained by a number of authors in different settings. Leite Monteiro (1997), Wildasin (1994a, 1994b) and Epple and Romer (1991) all provide examples of cases where mobility can induce one of the two regions to effect more redistribution that in autarky.

Asymmetry in objective functions is not the only one. There can also be asymmetry in population size and also in capital endowment. Contributions on that question are generally cast in a model of capital mobility. Bucovetsky (1991) and Wilson (1991) both consider the case of countries that have the same capital labor ratio but differ in population size. They show that the less populated country enjoys a higher level of welfare following capital integration. This is known as the *small region advantage*. Peralta and van Ypersele (2002) obtain the same result in a setting when both population size and capital labor ratio are different at the start. They also show that when the population is the same, a country with a smaller capital labor ratio tends to loose from tax competition.

3.2. *Objective function with varying population*

When labor is mobile, one faces the problem of varying population size. With endogenous population, measuring social welfare has always been a controversial issue. Population economists are very familiar with the debate between Mills and Bentham or, more specifically, between aiming at maximum total utility or at maximum *per capita* utility. With the former, there is a bias towards favoring a population as large as possible; on the contrary, with the latter there is a Malthusian bias. To circumvent this difficulty several approaches have been used in the literature.

First of all, there is the approach used in the Tiebout tradition, wherein the regional government – in fact a municipality – maximizes land value. Alternatively, a number of authors have adopted a public choice view (in particular, the median voter approach). Residents vote for the regional tax spending package. Assuming that most people do not move, the majority is hardly concerned with the welfare of the migrants – in or out – and if they are, this will be out of altruism. Brown and Oates (1987) and Wildasin (1991) have adopted this view.

Another way to circumvent the difficulty raised by an endogenous population is to assume a mobility-free criterion such as citizenship. In our benchmark model, we have assumed that national governments are exclusively concerned by the welfare of the "native citizens" whether or not they stay in their region of origin. Similarly, Leite Monteiro (1997) uses an utilitarian social welfare function involving only the natives regardless of location.

If we take $u(\cdot)$ as the utility function of either types of worker in country j, one can have two types of utilitarian social objectives:

$$W = \overline{M}u(c^{\mathrm{s}}) + \overline{L}u(c^{\mathrm{u}}), \tag{B}$$

like in our benchmark model, or alternatively

$$W = \overline{M}u(c^{\mathrm{s}}) + Lu(c^{\mathrm{u}}), \tag{M}$$

where the government cares about residents irrespective of their origin. Recall that $\overline{L}$ is the number of unskilled citizens (natives or initial residents) and L that of unskilled workers (residents after mobility takes places). One can easily show that those two objectives yield different solutions. When the weight is endogenous as in (M) and migration is costless, the initial distribution of the population across countries (i.e., the value of $\overline{L}$) is irrelevant and the solution tends to be closer to aggregate efficiency.

One clearly faces a rather difficult problem with objective (B). What makes a nation is a dynamic and complex process. It takes years for new immigrants to receive the same weight as long term residents in the political process of a region. In that respect, Michel, Pestieau and Vidal (1998) consider an important feature of countries with immigration, that is the progressive process of adjustment and assimilation. In the beginning, newcomers have little, if any, weight in the social welfare function. After some time (a decade or a generation), they become full fledged citizens; they can vote and have the same weight as any other national. This specification offers the advantage of being quite realistic and makes redistribution evolve over time, which is consistent with what can be observed. In autarky one can have a lot of redistribution. If the country opens to immigration of unskilled workers, the new migrants have no weight at the beginning and this implies less redistribution. After a while, when they become full fledged citizens, redistribution develops anew.

The possibility of differential tax treatment of immigrants makes a big difference. This is essential to preserve the efficacy of redistributive policies that involve only nationals. In Western European countries, there is a significant immigration from outside of the economic union. Some of it is illegal and of course there is considerable potential for much more. Those immigrants do receive unequal treatment compared with those from the European Union area, and this is specially true for illegal ones. Indeed, the denial of fiscal and social benefits to illegal migrants seems to be part of a deliberate employment policy.

This is not an abstract issue. The Scientific Council of the German Ministry of Finance has recently proposed to replace the traditional employment principle with a "delayed" integration principle in the assignment of individuals to jurisdictions in terms of taxation, social insurance and social assistance in Europe.[12]

Moving from the employment principle to the origin principle implies that individuals are taxed and received benefits in their home country. It has obvious efficiency advantages and safeguards the welfare state. It has also serious disadvantages; in particular, it is much harder to enforce and it raises ethical problems.

3.3. *Benevolent governments*

The tax competition literature generally assume national governments that are benevolent maximizers of social welfare. At times it assumes decision making based on majority voting in which case the median voter essentially "becomes" the social planner.[13] In either case, what matters are the preferences of citizen or residents and national authorities always choose a Pareto-efficient outcome (from their perspective and conditional on the behavior of other countries). In such a world, tax competition tends of course to be a bad thing for it imposes additional constraints on otherwise welfare maximizing authorities. Mobility in itself may of course be efficiency enhancing, but the lack of cooperation between national tax policies unavoidably tends to lower welfare.

The public choice literature, in contrast, has a radically different perception of how the policy making process works. In particular, Brennan and Buchanan (1980) suggest that governments generally lack accountability, especially higher levels of government. Therefore, there is room for policy makers to pursue their own personal goals, rather than serving the interest of the public. The personal interest of policy makers will typically result in too high levels of public expenditures. To account for the possibility of non-benevolent behavior on behalf of public authorities, public choice economists often assume a Leviathan-type government that is an untrustworthy revenue maximizer. Accordingly, governments have the tendency to set tax rates that are too high from a social point of view. In that case, tax competition will serve the valuable task of taming the Leviathan. In particular, it forces governments to reduce taxes, which improves the conditions for an efficient mix of taxes and public expenditures [McLure (1986)].

Edwards and Keen (1996) try to reconcile the two opposing views on governments. They develop a model of tax competition where the government is characterized by properties of both the benevolent maximizer of social welfare and the Leviathan revenue maximizer. Consequently, the cost of tax competition related to fiscal externalities should be weighed in the Edwards–Keen model against the gains of tax competition associated with the disciplining impact on the Leviathan. Within their setting, Edwards and Keen derive an explicit condition regarding government behavior under which tax competition harms social welfare. In particular, welfare increases only if the fraction

[12] See Richter (2001) and Sinn (1994).

[13] The classical paper on this is Epple and Romer (1991). More recently, Hindriks (2001) analyzes also a model with imperfect mobility of the poor and the rich and with redistribution chosen by majority. He shows that greater mobility of the poor can increase the extent of redistribution.

of government spending that represents "pure waste" exceeds the responsiveness of the mobile factor (capital in their case) to taxes. Hence, if capital is very elastic, tax competition is unlikely to be beneficial for this would require a very high fraction of the Leviathan-component of public spending.[14]

3.4. Constant returns to scale

The tax competition literature usually starts from the assumption that technology has constant returns to scale and that there is at least one immobile factor. As a consequence, one ends up with interior solutions and avoids the unpleasant outcome of empty communities or depopulated countries. One cannot have all mobile factors flowing into a single country: their marginal productivity would vanish relative to what it is in the other countries. Another standard assumption is that of perfect competition.

There is however an increasing awareness that in both national and supranational area there are such things as core regions, heavily populated and technically very modern, and peripheral regions, retaining only traditional and local activities and being progressively depopulated. The question is then raised of whether such an outcome is socially desirable and if not, how to correct it.

To account for interregional disparities, economist geographers depart from the neoclassical world of constant returns to scale and perfect competition in which economic integration does neither amplify nor dampen geographical discrepancies. With increasing returns to scale and imperfect competition, labor mobility generates the emergence of modern and traditional sectors. Unskilled workers are assumed to be much less mobile than skilled workers. The latter will move to the modern sector where they produce a differentiated good that is monopolistically competitive and costly traded.

In these models mobility and transport costs are introduced and play an important role. For example, Ottaviano and Thisse (2002) have a model in which the market outcome is socially desirable when transport costs are either high or low. In the first case, activities are dispersed and this is efficient. In the second case, they are agglomerated and again this is efficient. In contrast, with intermediary transport costs, the market leads to a polarization between modern and traditional sectors whereas optimality recommends a balanced allocation of activities.

3.5. Full employment

In tax competition literature, full employment is generally assumed and redistribution is typically epitomized by income tax-transfer schemes and, more rarely, by social insurance schemes. This is somewhat surprising as there is a huge debate in political circles

[14] In the same line, see Keen and Kotsogiannis (2002, 2003) and Kelders and Kölhenbürger (2003), who argue that tax competition does not necessarily imply undertaxation in federal systems with tax incentives arrangements. See also Wilson and Wildasin (2003).

on the issue of attracting foreign investment to boost domestic employment and on the robustness of social insurance schemes to tax competition. More specifically, the belief is widespread that fostering employment through wage subsidies and providing unemployed with generous compensations are conflicting objectives in a setting of factor mobility and tax competition.

There exists some papers trying to integrate unemployment in tax competition models. They typically focus on capital mobility. Lejour and Verbon (1994, 1996), for instance, develop a two-country model where wages are determined through a union-firm bargaining process, and where capital is imperfectly mobile across countries. A payroll tax is levied to finance an unemployment benefit. The government chooses the payroll tax which in turn determines the unemployment benefits, so as to maximize a weighted sum of the utilities of workers and capital owners. Their setting relies on a number of specific assumption. In particular, it assumes, that the wage elasticity of labor demand is larger than one. Lejour and Verbon show that opening borders to capital reduces the payroll tax and that, with mobile capital, a coordinated rise in the countries' payroll tax would increase the countries' weighted sum of individual utilities.

In a more recent paper, Fuest and Huber (1999b) also assume that wages are subject to union-firm bargaining. However, contrary to Lejour and Verbon (1996) individuals' labor supply is elastic. Accordingly the wage bargaining process results in all individuals being employed but rationed in their labor supply (underemployment). In each country a wage tax and a source-based capital tax are used along with a 100% profit tax to finance the provision of a public good rather that an unemployment benefit. Taking into account the mobility of capital across countries, each country's government chooses its fiscal instruments so as to maximize the utility of its representative citizen. Huber and Fuest show that if governments do not account for the effects of their policy on the wage bargaining process, a coordinated increase in either the wage tax or the capital tax (the other tax being kept constant) results in a reduction of welfare. However, if they account for the effect of their policy, the result is shown to depend upon the wage elasticity of labor demand; the cooperation measures considered above lead to a fall in welfare if this elasticity is smaller than one and to a rise in welfare otherwise.

Lozachmeur (2003) develops a model in the vein of Harris and Todaro in which there is unemployment and potential migrants equate their expected utility across countries. Mobility and fiscal competition lead to underprovision of unemployment benefits. Using a common framework of analysis, Richter and Schneider (2001) and Koskela and Schöb (2002) show that the optimal tax on mobile capital need not be zero if there are distortions in the labor market. This conclusion holds under both unemployment and underemployment. In particular, they show that, if wages are the result of bargaining between unions and firms, the tax on capital depends not only on the properties of the production function but also on the restrictions on other fiscal instruments, such as profit and wage taxes.

The issue of fiscal competition with distorted labor markets has also been investigated by Gabszewicz and van Ypersele (1996). They develop a political economics model where some minimal wage is chosen by majority voting and results in unemployment.

They show that opening borders to capital flows has a depressing effect on the minimal wage.

Finally, Leite Monteiro, Marchand and Pestieau (2003) analyze how capital income taxation can be used to fight structural unemployment. In a model that generalizes Lejour and Verbon (1996) they consider a setting of wage bargaining, where each country has to decide on employment-enhancing policies and on redistributive policies aimed at the unemployed. Contrary to the case where wages are exogenously given, the chosen level of employment subsidy may be lower with capital mobility. This result, which seems counter-intuitive, is explained by the fact that unions do not fully account for all the effects of their wage choice on the expected utility of their members. In particular, the change in the interest rate induced by the choice of the union's wage affects the elasticity of labor demand. The choice of the country's employment subsidy in a closed economy setting will then account for this myopic behavior of unions. Opening the borders to capital flows may then lower the employment subsidy. To sum up, introducing unemployment in the analysis does not modify the standard conclusion as long as unemployment is based on a simple story such as fixed wage. With flexible labor supply and wage bargaining, on the other hand, factor mobility does not necessarily result in lower taxes.

4. Tax competition and tax cooperation

We have seen that under mobility, net factor returns are linked so that the redistribution of income becomes a public good the benefits of which extend to the enlarged factor market itself. From there, a number of authors starting with Stigler (1957), view redistribution as a responsibility of the central (federal) government. Accordingly, grants from the central government to lower-level governments, or preferably direct taxation of households by the central government, can be used to internalize the fiscal externalities associated with income redistribution and, hence, to achieve a more satisfactory outcome.

In terms of our benchmark model, full redistribution can be achieved by entrusting the central government with the appropriate tax instruments. The proposition that central governments should take primacy in equity aspects of tax polity, and be assigned the tax bases that are mobile at lower levels, is directly inspired by the theory of fiscal federalism. It clearly calls for several qualifications particularly when applied to an economic union without powerful central authority rather than to a standard federal state.

As a matter of fact, the centralization of the redistributive functions has been questioned even in the fiscal federalism setting where a central government does exist, in particular on informational grounds. It raises further objections in a confederate setting without any central authority. The relevant issue then become one of cooperation to overcome the inefficiencies created by non-cooperative behavior.

We have already mentioned in Section 2 that a globally first-best optimal outcome can be reestablished through "full cooperation" on all relevant policy instruments. This is of course a somewhat naive view for it neglects the problem of enforceability of co-operation agreements as well as possible informational problems.[15] Another limitation of this results is that in reality an across the board cooperation on *all* relevant tax instruments may be quite difficult to achieve. *A piece-meal approach involving only partial cooperation (or harmonization) appears to be more reasonable to expect.* But then the welfare impact of the cooperation policy is less straightforward to assess. For instance if the EU countries were to agree on minimum tax rates on capital incomes, this might lead to fiercer tax competition for the setting of other tax instruments.

The potential pitfalls of partial cooperation were first discussed by Cremer and Gahvari (2000) in a setting with a single tax but with the possibility of tax evasion. These authors have shown that the harmonization of statutory tax rates, may induce countries to cut down on enforcement policies, thereby reintroducing tax competition through the back-door. More recently, the same authors have a setting of tax competition with two instruments in the context of environmental taxation; see Cremer and Gahvari (2002a, 2002b). They show that when countries agree on minimum taxes on polluting (final) goods, tax competition may be shifted to emission taxes (collected at the production level).

To address the issue of tax cooperation in particular that of partial cooperation, we will now slightly complicate our canonical model. This brings us close to the specification recently used by Marchand, Pestieau and Sato (2003) by which our analysis in this section is inspired. To make room for tax competition on more than one instrument, we now consider two mobile factors, capital and unskilled labor, and an immobile factor, skilled labor. We show that tax competition along with the small open economy assumption leads to a zero tax on *both* mobile factors. With tax cooperation this can be avoided. *Then we show that partial cooperation can be harmful.*[16] Finally, we discuss some other issue of tax cooperation.

4.1. Tax competition and tax cooperation with two mobile factors

We consider the benchmark model with a *large* number of identical countries $j = 1, \ldots, J$. To reflect the assumption that capital K is now mobile, along with unskilled labor, L, the CRS production function (2) is rewritten as

$$Y_j = F\left(\overline{M}_j, K_j, L_j\right).$$

The country index j which so far was dropped for simplicity will be systematically used in this section to avoid confusions. Since $\overline{M}$ is immobile and identical across countries, one can normalize it to 1 and write

$$Y_j = F(1, K_j, L_j), \tag{14}$$

[15] An alternative suggested by Cardarelli, Taugourdeau and Vidal (2002) is to adopt a repeated game setting. They show that under some assumptions full efficiency can be achieved.

[16] See also Fuest (1995) and Fuest and Huber (1999a).

where the earnings of skilled labor is

$$F_M^j = Y_j - K_j F_K^j - L_j F_L^j. \tag{15}$$

The (initial) capital stock $\overline{K}$ continues to be held by the skilled; it is identical in all countries. Similarly, the number of native unskilled is $\overline{L}$ in all countries. As seen in Section 2, without mobility we have full redistribution with $c^{\mathrm{s}} = c^{\mathrm{u}}$.

Perfect mobility of factors L and K implies that their net returns are equated across countries. Namely,

$$F_K^j - \tau_j^{\mathrm{K}} = \varrho, \quad j = 1, \ldots, J, \tag{16}$$

and

$$F_L^j - \tau_j^{\mathrm{L}} = \omega, \quad j = 1, \ldots, J, \tag{17}$$

where ϱ and ω denote the net interest rate and net wage, respectively, in the world markets. This implies the following factor demands:

$$K_j = K_j\left(\varrho + \tau_j^{\mathrm{K}}, \omega + \tau_j^{\mathrm{L}}\right) \tag{18}$$

and

$$L_j = L_j\left(\varrho + \tau_j^{\mathrm{K}}, \omega + \tau_j^{\mathrm{L}}\right). \tag{19}$$

We distinguish in each country the initial endowments of factors, denoted by $\overline{K}$ and $\overline{L}$, that are the same across countries and the actual levels of factors used, denoted by K_j and L_j. At the equilibrium of the world factor markets, we must have the following equalities:

$$\sum_j K_j\left(\varrho + \tau_j^{\mathrm{K}}, \omega + \tau_j^{\mathrm{L}}\right) = J\overline{K} \tag{20}$$

and

$$\sum_j L_j\left(\varrho + \tau_j^{\mathrm{K}}, \omega + \tau_j^{\mathrm{L}}\right) = J\overline{L}. \tag{21}$$

Since countries are identical, the following properties hold at the symmetric equilibrium:[17]

$$\frac{\partial \omega}{\partial \tau_j^{\mathrm{L}}} = -\frac{1}{J}, \qquad \frac{\partial \varrho}{\partial \tau_j^{\mathrm{K}}} = -\frac{1}{J},$$

[17] To show this, let us first totally differentiate the optimality conditions (16) and (17). This yields: $K_r^j \equiv \partial K_j / \partial r_j = S_j^{-1} F_{LL}^j(1, K_j; L_j)$, $L_w^j = S_j^{-1} F_{KK}^j(\cdot)$ and $K_w^j = L_r^j = -S_j^{-1} F_{KL}^j(\cdot)$, where $S_j = F_{KK}^j(\cdot) F_{LL}^j(\cdot) - (F_{KL}^j(\cdot))^2 > 0$. In order to determine $\mathrm{d}\varrho/\mathrm{d}\tau_j^{\mathrm{K}}$ and $\mathrm{d}\omega/\mathrm{d}\iota_j^{\mathrm{K}}$, we then differentiate (20) and (21) with respect to ϱ, ω and τ_j^{K}, which gives $\sum_i K_r^i \,\mathrm{d}\varrho + \sum_i K_w^i \,\mathrm{d}\omega = -K_r^j \,\mathrm{d}\tau_j^{\mathrm{K}}$ and $\sum_i L_r^i \,\mathrm{d}\varrho + \sum_i L_w^i \,\mathrm{d}\omega = -L_r^j \,\mathrm{d}\tau_j^{\mathrm{K}}$. Solving this system of two equations yields $\mathrm{d}\varrho/\mathrm{d}\tau_j^{\mathrm{K}} = -1/J$ and $\mathrm{d}\omega/\mathrm{d}\tau_j^{\mathrm{K}} = 0$ at the symmetric equilibrium where $K_j = \overline{K}$ and $L_j = \overline{L}$, $j = 1, \ldots, J$. The other derivatives, $\partial\varrho/\partial\tau_j^{\mathrm{L}} = 0$ and $\partial\omega/\partial\tau_j^{\mathrm{L}} = -1/J$, are obtained in the same way.

which generalizes (10). When J tends to infinity,

$$\frac{\partial\omega}{\partial\tau_j^{\mathrm{K}}} = \frac{\partial\varrho}{\partial\tau_j^{\mathrm{L}}} = 0$$

so that ω and ϱ are taken as given by each country. This is once again the small economy case on which we concentrate for the rest of this section.

We now turn to the implication of factor mobility on the redistributive tax policy. Each national government maximizes

$$W_j = u\left(c_j^{\mathrm{s}}\right) + \overline{L}u(\omega).$$

From each country's perspective maximizing W_j amounts to maximizing c_j^{s}:

$$c_j^{\mathrm{s}} = F_j - \varrho K_j - \omega L_j + \varrho\overline{K}. \tag{22}$$

This yields the following first-order conditions:

$$\frac{\partial c_j^{\mathrm{s}}}{\partial\tau_j^{\mathrm{K}}} = \tau_j^{\mathrm{K}}\frac{\partial K_j}{\partial\tau_j^{\mathrm{K}}} + \tau_j^{\mathrm{L}}\frac{\partial L_j}{\partial\tau_j^{\mathrm{K}}} = 0, \tag{23a}$$

$$\frac{\partial c_j^{\mathrm{s}}}{\partial\tau_j^{\mathrm{L}}} = \tau_j^{\mathrm{K}}\frac{\partial K_j}{\partial\tau_j^{\mathrm{L}}} + \tau_j^{\mathrm{L}}\frac{\partial L_j}{\partial\tau_j^{\mathrm{L}}} = 0. \tag{23b}$$

Since ϱ and ω are taken as given, the effect of a change in τ_j^{K} on either K_j or L_j is the same as the effect of a change in $r_j \equiv \varrho + \tau_j^{\mathrm{K}}$ and the same holds for τ_j^{L} with $w_j \equiv \omega + \tau_j^{\mathrm{L}}$. We can thus rewrite:

$$\frac{\partial c_j^{\mathrm{s}}}{\partial\tau_j^{\mathrm{K}}} = \tau_j^{\mathrm{K}}K_r^j + \tau_j^{\mathrm{L}}L_r^j = 0, \tag{24a}$$

$$\frac{\partial c_j^{\mathrm{s}}}{\partial\tau_j^{\mathrm{L}}} = \tau_j^{\mathrm{K}}K_w^j + \tau_j^{\mathrm{L}}L_w^j = 0, \tag{24b}$$

where the partial derivatives K_r^j, L_r^j, K_w^j, L_w^j are derived in footnote 17 and are given by

$$K_r^j \equiv \frac{\partial K_j}{\partial r_j} = \frac{F_{LL}(1,\overline{K},\overline{L})}{\overline{S}}; \qquad L_w^j \equiv \frac{\partial L_j}{\partial w_j} = \frac{F_{KK}(1,\overline{K},\overline{L})}{\overline{S}}, \tag{25}$$

$$K_w^j = \frac{\partial K_j}{\partial w_j} \equiv L_r^j = \frac{\partial L_j}{\partial r_j} = \frac{-F_{KL}(1,\overline{K},\overline{L})}{\overline{S}}, \tag{26}$$

with

$$\overline{S} = F_{KK}(\overline{1},\overline{K},\overline{L})F_{LL}(1,\overline{K},\overline{L}) - F_{KL}^2(1,\overline{K},\overline{L}) > 0.$$

Note for future reference that at the symmetric equilibrium the derivatives of the demand functions for K_j and L_j in (23a) and (23b) are identical across countries and only depend upon $\overline{K}$ and $\overline{L}$.

With $\overline{S} > 0$, the solution to (24a)–(24b) is given by $\tau_j^{\mathrm{K}} = \tau_j^{\mathrm{L}} = 0$. In the small open economy setting adopted here where the world prices of mobile factors are taken as given by each country, redistributive taxes and subsidies are equal to zero.

This solution is to be contrasted with that obtained in autarky. It is also to be compared with that obtained in a cooperative framework in which national governments agree on (and commit to) a policy which maximizes the utility of a representative country. In our setting of identical countries, this cooperative solution would be the same as the autarchic one, that is, it would imply equal disposable income for the two types of individuals within and across countries; see Section 2. Observe that to achieve this solution, the agreement must concern all tax instruments, or, to be more precise as many tax instruments as there are degrees of freedom. This would require for instance a uniform subsidy ($-\tau^{\mathrm{L}}$) on earnings and a tax on capital income (τ^{K}) that would be set so as to equate disposable incomes.[18]

For a number of reasons pertaining mainly to political economy, it is often difficult to find an agreement on all tax instruments. At best, one can expect that there will be an agreement around what is the most shocking consequence of tax competition, the fact that some "symbolic" sources of income, typically capital, fully escape taxation.[19] To account for this difficulty, we shall now study partial cooperation measure. In particular, we shall study the implications of agreement on a certain level (strictly positive) of taxation of capital, while the other tax instruments continue to be set non-cooperatively. In our symmetrical setting this minimum rate is binding in all countries.[20]

4.2. *Partial tax cooperation*

Starting from the *laissez-faire* situation, we thus now turn to the case where only some partial cooperation is possible. We consider the implications of a coordinated increase in τ_j^{K} to a "minimum rate", denoted $\hat{\tau}^{\mathrm{K}} > 0$, while the other tax τ_j^{L} is free to vary the way the countries decide. Let be this minimum rate that all countries are forced to apply. This means that condition (24b) remains relevant and determines each country's choice of τ_j^{L}:

$$\hat{\tau}^{\mathrm{K}} K_w^j + \tau_j^{\mathrm{L}} L_w^j = 0, \tag{27}$$

[18] Recall that there is a third instrument, namely τ^{M} which is determined as residual to achieve budget balance. While this third instrument does not explicitly appear in our analysis, its availability is accounted for in the expressions. In particular it ensure that there are effectively two degrees of freedom so that the study of partial coordination is meaningful in the first place.

[19] See on this Huizinga (1995).

[20] This would not necessarily be the case under asymmetry.

while Equation (24a) relative to the choice of τ_j^{K} does not hold anymore. Consequently, the equilibrium level of τ_j^{L} is now conditional on $\hat{\tau}^{\mathrm{K}}$, the tax rate on capital. Under symmetry this level is obtained from a single equation, namely (27). Furthermore, in this equation K_w^j and L_w^j are effectively constants; see Equations (25) and (26). This is because as long as the equilibrium remains symmetric, each country uses $\overline{K}$ units of capital and $\overline{L}$ unskilled workers.[21] This simplifies the analysis considerably.

To determine the effect of a small coordinated increase in $\hat{\tau}^{\mathrm{K}}$ on τ_j^{L}, we totally differentiate (27) with respect to the tax rates:

$$K_w^j \, \mathrm{d}\hat{\tau}^{\mathrm{K}} + L_w^j \, \mathrm{d}\tau_j^{\mathrm{L}} = 0,$$

which yields

$$\frac{\mathrm{d}\tau_j^{\mathrm{L}}}{\mathrm{d}\hat{\tau}^{\mathrm{K}}} = -\frac{K_w^j}{L_w^j} = \frac{F_{KL}(1, \overline{K}, \overline{L})}{F_{KK}(1, \overline{K}, \overline{L})}. \tag{28}$$

Consequently, and with $F_{KK} < 0$, $\mathrm{d}\tau_j^{\mathrm{L}}/\mathrm{d}\hat{\tau}^{\mathrm{K}}$ has the *opposite* sign of $F_{KL}(1, \overline{K}, \overline{L})$. Also recall that in the small open economy case we start from $\tau_j^{\mathrm{L}} = 0$. Consequently, when capital and low skilled labor are complements ($F_{KL}(1, \overline{K}, \overline{L}) > 0$) imposing a positive tax on capital will result in a negative tax (a subsidy) on the low skilled. This appears to be a move in the right direction for it brings us closer to the optimum. On the other hand, when the two factors are substitutes ($F_{KL}(1, \overline{K}, \overline{L}) < 0$), we will have $\tau_j^{\mathrm{L}} > 0$ so that the low skilled now pay taxes which will benefit the high skilled. In other words, we have a case of reverse redistribution. *This suggests that the cooperation on the capital tax can be expected to have a positive impact on welfare only in the case where lower skilled labor and capital are complements. When they are substitutes, the cooperation appears to have perverse effects on redistribution.*

To confirm this, let us study the impact on consumption levels and on welfare. Recall that the consumption of unskilled workers is $c_j^{\mathrm{u}} = \omega$ so that the consumption of the skilled workers (and capital owners) is given by $c_j^{\mathrm{s}} = F(1, \overline{K}, \overline{L}) - \overline{L}\omega$. Using (17) along with the property that F_L^j does not change, we obtain

$$\frac{\mathrm{d}c_j^{\mathrm{u}}}{\mathrm{d}\hat{\tau}^{\mathrm{K}}} = -\frac{\mathrm{d}\tau_j^{\mathrm{L}}}{\mathrm{d}\hat{\tau}^{\mathrm{K}}} = -\frac{F_{KL}(1, \overline{K}, \overline{L})}{F_{KK}(1, \overline{K}, \overline{L})} \tag{29}$$

and

$$\frac{\mathrm{d}c_j^{\mathrm{s}}}{\mathrm{d}\hat{\tau}^{\mathrm{K}}} = \overline{L}\frac{\mathrm{d}\tau_j^{\mathrm{L}}}{\mathrm{d}\hat{\tau}^{\mathrm{K}}} = \overline{L}\frac{F_{KL}(1, \overline{K}, \overline{L})}{F_{KK}(1, \overline{K}, \overline{L})}. \tag{30}$$

[21] Put differently, while the possibility of factor mobility has a dramatic impact on tax rates, there will be no effective mobility *at the symmetric equilibrium*.

To understand these expressions it is important to realize that while each country considers ω as constant (and independent of the policy decisions of a single country), the net wage ω does change following the increase in capital taxation (which applies to all countries). This is brought out clearly by expression (17).

Turning to social welfare, we then obtain

$$\frac{\mathrm{d}W_j}{\mathrm{d}\hat{\tau}^{\mathrm{K}}} = \overline{L}u'\big(c_j^{\mathrm{u}}\big)\frac{\mathrm{d}c_j^{\mathrm{u}}}{\mathrm{d}\hat{\tau}^{\mathrm{K}}} + u'\big(c_j^{\mathrm{s}}\big)\frac{\mathrm{d}c_j^{\mathrm{s}}}{\mathrm{d}\hat{\tau}^{\mathrm{K}}} = \overline{L}\big[u'\big(c_j^{\mathrm{s}}\big) - u'\big(c_j^{\mathrm{u}}\big)\big]\frac{F_{KL}(1,\overline{K},\overline{L})}{F_{KK}(1,\overline{K},\overline{L})}.$$

By assumption we have in the *laissez-faire* with no tax $c_j^{\mathrm{s}} > c_j^{\mathrm{u}}$ and thus $u'(c_j^{\mathrm{s}}) < u'(c_j^{\mathrm{u}})$. When moving away from that situation by increasing marginally τ^{K} in a coordinated way ($\mathrm{d}\hat{\tau}^{\mathrm{K}} > 0$), we conclude that

$$\mathrm{d}W_j \lesseqgtr 0, \qquad \mathrm{d}c_j^{\mathrm{u}} \lesseqgtr 0 \quad \text{and} \quad \mathrm{d}c_j^{\mathrm{s}} \gtreqless 0 \quad \text{if} \quad F_{KL}(1,\overline{K},\overline{L}) \lesseqgtr 0.$$

This confirms our conjecture made above. In particular, when $F_{KL}(1,\overline{K},\overline{L}) < 0$, namely when the two mobile factors are substitutes, a minimum tax on capital income proves to be welfare decreasing. With complements, on the other hand, welfare increases.

To understand the intuition behind these results we have to return to the impact of capital tax harmonization on τ_j^{L} as shown by (28). The bottom line is than when the two mobile factors are complements, reducing tax competition on one of the taxes creates a spillover for the other tax as it also relaxes tax competition there. To be more precise, when $\hat{\tau}^{\mathrm{K}}$ is increased (above the Nash equilibrium level) each country would like to unilaterally decrease the tax on capital and thus to increase the net return of this factor. This can be achieved indirectly by subsidizing the complementary factor namely unskilled labor. *With substitutes, on the other hand, we get the opposite effect*: *the cooperation juts shifts the tax competition from one instrument to the other.* Each individual country will now be tempted to indirectly increase the return on capital by *increasing* the tax on the substitute (unskilled labor). Consequently countries compete in another tax instrument instead and the overall outcome is worse than the *laissez-faire*.[22]

4.3. Centralization and/or coordination: further discussion

We have pointed out in Section 3.3 that tax competition may be welfare improving when governments are not benevolent. When this is the case, coordination will of course not have a positive impact on welfare. To conclude our review of the issue of coordination, we shall now sketch a few additional potential pitfalls to coordination and/or centralization. The issues we review arise because of informational problems. First, we shall

[22] The interpretation is complicated by the fact that one factor (capital) should be taxed, while the other one (unskilled labor) should be subsidized. Reinforced tax competition then translates into a *higher* tax (lower subsidy) on unskilled labor (which each country would like to "repel").

contrast the tax competition literature with the Tiebout hypothesis under which mobility (and competition between local governments) plays an important role for preference revelation. Second, we shall discuss Pauly's application of the Tiebout model to the context of redistribution. In these two settings the underlying information failure is that individual preferences (willingness to pay) for public goods (or redistribution) are not observable. Our third and last point is based on a different type of information asymmetry, namely that between central and local authorities. Consequently, redistribution between regions or countries by a central (supra-national) authority may be problematic, even when policy makers are benevolent.

4.3.1. Fiscal federalism versus Tiebout hypothesis

By assuming at the outset that regions consist of heterogenous individuals, the theory of fiscal federalism brings a bias towards the centralization of the redistributive functions. One could assume instead that people freely move across regions looking for the pattern of taxes and services fitting their tastes and their income. Such a process by which mobility alone would be enough to secure efficiency in patterns of local public expenditure and taxation is known as the Tiebout hypothesis. Under some assumptions, it does not only imply efficiency but also homogeneity of communities.[23]

If the Tiebout hypothesis were verified, it would mean that the main question of this paper, that is of the efficacy of redistributive policies within regions being challenged by fiscal competition would appear groundless. There would be no need for redistribution at the regional level if before tax income were equalized by mobility. Yet, there is another issue which is that of redistribution across regions. Such redistribution calls for a central authority. Coming back to Tiebout's hypothesis and without engaging a long and intricate debate, it suffices to note that it makes sense in the context of mobility within and to a lesser extent between municipalities but not between regions or nations. Further, even within that particular setting, it relies on quite unrealistic assumptions that have not been empirically validated. This does not mean that people do not express their discontent with the pattern of regional fiscal policy by moving to regions they find more congenial. It implies that this process does not in general yield an efficient outcome.

4.3.2. Redistribution as a local public good

The traditional fiscal federalism setting implies heterogeneity within regions and the conventional wisdom is that redistribution should be centralized. Two main questions can be raised. First, does there exist a central government capable of such redistribution? If not, what are the alternative policies? Second, are there not any arguments in favor of decentralizing redistribution? We first answer this latter question.

The arguments in favor of giving the central government exclusive responsibility for redistribution are indeed not clear-cut. Pauly (1973) makes a case for entrusting regional

[23] The original paper is Tiebout (1956); see also the survey by Schotchmer (2002).

governments with some redistributive functions. He assumes a particular type of utility interdependencies. The utility of the rich is an increasing function of the poor's income. Further, higher weight is given to the poor belonging to the region than to those living elsewhere. In other words, income redistribution is of the nature of a local public good. Differences in tastes and incomes may dictate a different amount of redistribution over regions. In this case, as in the case of any other local public good, decentralization might be desirable. Pauly considers various levels of mobility. The case for decentralizing redistribution is stronger the less mobile are individuals, the more dissimilar are tastes for redistribution over regions, and the more redistribution is implied by Pareto-efficiency. In other words, his model seems to fit the European Union more than federal countries such as the United States.

To sum up, both Tiebout and Pauly provide arguments for letting regional governments achieve their own redistribution, but neither one addresses the other important issue of redistribution across regions which clearly calls for some centralization. For Tiebout, equality of income results from mobility; for Pauly, mobility is limited and redistribution is a local public good better supplied at the regional level. In a sense, both of these arguments provide additional support for the idea that competition between local authorities may have positive effects. In Section 3.3 we have reviewed the arguments that plead in this direction on the basis of rent seeking behavior on behalf of governments. The arguments presented here are different for they continue to apply when governments are benevolent. Instead they point to the idea that competition may be an effective way for preference revelation in a context of asymmetric information.

4.3.3. *Centralization versus cooperation*

We now come to the question of whether a central government is capable of redistribution. In that regard, it is again important to underline the differences between a federal setting, such as that of the United States, and a confederal one, such as the European Union. In a confederation the costs of mobility (particularly labor mobility) are higher that in a federation. More importantly, in the European Union case, there is no real central government. In other words, one cannot discuss the issue of centralization versus decentralization in the same way as in a federal state. Reforms towards efficiency or equity have to be approached from the viewpoint of negotiation, cooperation and above all Pareto-improving moves. Welfare improvements are not sufficient, as the prevailing decision rule is most often unanimity. Thus the usual debate over centralization versus decentralization is changed into a debate over Pareto-improvement with and without compensations.

In the perfectly symmetric case, the first-best allocation can easily be achieved by cooperative agreement. Alternatively, if the central government imposes some minimum standards of taxation that yield the optimal solution, these ought to be unanimously agreed upon. Most often, however, there is no perfect symmetry. Then, it is likely that moving towards the first-best optimal solution involves different gains across countries or even losses in some. In this case, compensatory schemes or logrolling procedures have to be considered. Note however that even in asymmetric cases, some minimum standards can be Pareto-improving.

Wildasin (1991) examines an economic union within what he calls a common labor market such as assumed here. He allows for corrective subsidies by a central government and reaches the striking result that with optimal subsidies the tax rates on mobile taxpayers should be equalized across regions. This implies that regions with weaker preferences for redistribution should receive larger subsidies. There is however a problem with Wildasin's argument. Even if one restricts the corrections of Nash equilibria to Pareto corrections, they imply side payments. In other words, the optimal scheme is such that in a two region setting the less redistributive one is compensated so as to allow for productive efficiency and impose the same tax as the more redistributive region. Even though such a scheme ought to be unanimously supported, its actual implementation might be difficult. In a subsequent paper, Wildasin (1994a) considers a setting with mobile recipients of income transfers and shows that a region subject to labor immigration may gain by paying some transfers to workers in the source region so as to reduce the level of immigration.

Also related to the debate of centralization versus cooperation is the availability of information for different levels of governments. It is argued that lower levels authorities (being "closer" to these tax base) have better information to implement the tax system, and this is a point in favor of decentralization. But once again this advantage seems to be different in federal and confederal systems.[24]

5. Intergenerational redistribution and tax competition

Tax competition such as usually approached (and reviewed in the previous sections) suggests that countries underprovide public goods and reduce redistributive policies. This is because the threat of capital flight and of loss of skilled labor along with the risk of unskilled labor inflow would prompt individual countries to set tax rates that are too low from a supranational welfare perspectives. More recently economists have started investigating the *open economy aspects of intergenerational redistribution and particularly those of pension schemes.* This raises interesting questions which go beyond the scope of the traditional tax competition literature. For example, there is issue of the co-existence of pay-as-you-go (PAYG) and of fully funded (FF) pension systems within an economic union. For our purpose, the main difference between the two systems is that PAYG generates an intergenerational transfer at the expense of future generations, while a FF system does not imply such a transfer. Can the two systems co-exist in the long run and, if so, what type of adjustments will be induced by economic integration?

[24] The role of asymmetric information between central and local governments has been discussed over the last decades. The idea that local governments have better knowledge of needs, preference or resources of individuals that the central government is often advanced in favor of some decentralization. See on this Bucovetsky, Marchand and Pestieau (1998), Cremer and Pestieau (1996a, 1996b), Cremer, Marchand and Pestieau (1996).

These question arises for two reasons. First, the two systems have different implications in terms of capital accumulation and in autarky the rate of return on capital will thus tend to differ between countries. Under mobility this will give rise to capital movements which will may have a significant impact on the individual countries. Second, under a PAYG system, individuals are effectively born with a debt towards the previous generation(s). Their contributions will have to pay for the retirement benefits of their (grand) parents. When they are mobile, young workers can, however, escape from this liability by moving to a country with a FF system.

We shall now briefly discuss some of these problems. There are two main streams of literature which differ mainly by the underlying source of mobility: capital only or capital and labor. We start with a setting where capital is the only mobile factor.

5.1. Capital mobility

To illustrate the issue that arise, consider a two-country, two overlapping-generation model.[25] In country $j = A, B$ at time t identical consumers maximize

$$u\left(c_t^j, d_{t+1}^j\right)$$

subject to the budget constraints

$$c_t^j = w_t^j - \tau_t - s_t^j \quad \text{and} \quad d_{t+1}^j = s_t^j\left(1 + r_{t+1}^j\right) + p_{t+1}^j,$$

where τ is the payroll tax; p, the pension benefit; c and d, first- and second-period consumption; s, savings; and w and r, wage and interest rate. Initially both countries are identical but for one aspect, namely the type of pension system. Country A has a "pay-as-you-go" (PAYG) pension system. Consequently, it offers an implicit rate of return which equals the rate of population growth n. The relationship between contributions and benefits is then given by

$$(1 + n)\tau_t = p_t^A.$$

Country B has a "fully-funded" system so that pension benefits are determined according to

$$\left(1 + r_{t+1}^B\right)\tau_t = p_{t+1}^B.$$

For the sake of simplicity we use a log linear utility function which has the nice property that consumers spend a fixed proportion, $(1 - \sigma)$, of lifetime income on first-period consumption and a proportion σ on second-period consumption. Consequently, savings in country A are given by

$$s_t^A = \sigma\left[w_t^A - \tau\frac{r_{t+1}^A - n}{1 + r_{t+1}^A}\frac{1 - \sigma}{\sigma}\right].$$

[25] We closely follow Casarico (2000).

In country B, on the other hand, saving is simply

$$s_t^B = \sigma w_t^B .$$

Production is represented by a CRS production function. In *per capita* terms, we have

$$y^j = f(k^j),$$

with y^j is output per worker and k^j, capital per worker. Assuming perfect competition, equilibrium factor prices are:

$$r_t^j = f'(k_t^j) \quad \text{and} \quad w_t = \omega(k_t^j) = f(k_t^j) - f'(k_t^j)k_t^j . \tag{31}$$

Finally, in a closed economy we have the equality between saving and capital accumulation:

$$(1+n)k_{t+1}^j = s_t^j .$$

In the steady state we have

$$(1+n)k^j = \sigma\left[\omega(k^j) - \tau^j x^j \frac{f'(k)-n}{1+f'(k)} \frac{1-\sigma}{\sigma}\right],$$

where $x^A = 1$ and $x^B = 0$.

Assuming dynamic efficiency, namely $r^j > n$, one obtains

$$k^A < k^B, \qquad r^A > r^B \quad \text{and} \quad w^A < w^B, \tag{32}$$

as well as $u^A < u^B$. In words, capital stock, wage rate and utility will be smaller, while the interest rate will be larger in the country with the PAYG system. These are standard properties which are mainly due to the fact that with $r > n$, PAYG offers a lower return than FF.

Let us now introduce perfect capital mobility with the consequence that both rates of interest must be equal. This quite clearly requires capital flows from B to A. In the new steady state, we have $k^A = k^B = k^w$ and thus equality between interest rates and wages. We use the superscript w for the perfect capital mobility steady-state solutions. We thus have

$$k^A < k^w < k^B; \qquad r^B < r^w < r^A; \qquad w^A < w^w < w^B .$$

In terms of welfare, outcomes vary between countries and generations. In country A, future generations are positively affected by capital mobility; in country B, the effect is ambiguous.

This analysis is of limited scope: it simply shows the incidence of economic integration on two countries with different pension system. In terms of output countries with PAYG seem to gain relative to countries with FF. In that reasoning we take the basic parameter τ, the payroll tax as given. Pemberton (1999, 2000) goes one step further. He assumes that a PAYG system is redistributive and thus generates welfare gains up to a certain limit for a given capital stock. He then distinguishes two settings. In the first one, countries are isolated or equivalently, they are integrated but play cooperatively. In this setting the optimal choice of τ is made considering its direct impact on social welfare (redistribution) and its indirect impact through capital decrease (production). If we write social welfare in the steady state as a function of τ and k, the social planner's problem is

$$\max_{\tau} \quad V\big(\tau, k(\tau)\big),$$

which yields

$$V_\tau + V_k \frac{\partial k}{\partial \tau} = 0,$$

with V_τ and V_k positive and $\partial k/\partial \tau < 0$.

Let us come to the second setting, that of a small open economy with given rate of interest and thus, from (31) also given (steady-state per-capita) capital stock. Put differently, k is no longer a function of τ. The planner's problem then becomes

$$\max_{\tau} \quad V(\tau, k)$$

and the optimal level of taxation is given by $V_\tau = 0$. Consequently, we obtain a value of τ which is higher than in autarky or in a cooperative solution. Pemberton (1999) compares the effect of a go-it-alone shift to FF in a single country with a world-wide shift. He shows that an isolation paradox may arise: each country may not switch to a FF system because some of its residents may loose. Yet the switch would be Pareto improving if all the countries simultaneously switched. The isolation paradox can be interpreted, once again, as a coordination failure.

5.2. Mobility of labor and capital

We now add the mobility of labor and assume that young workers (and payroll taxpayers) can choose their country of residence. Mobility of labor and capital with pensions systems is particularly interesting because it implies two equilibrium conditions that are likely to be incompatible. The first one is the consequence of capital mobility. Assuming a CRS technology, the equality of rate of return on capital leads to the equality of wage across regions. Using the above notation, one has $r^A = r^B = r$ and thus

$$w^A = w^B = w.$$

Then, we also have the labor mobility equilibrium which satisfies:

$$\begin{cases} 0 < L^A, L^B < N^A + N^B & \text{for } w^A - \tau^A \dfrac{r-n}{1+r} = w^B, \\ L^A = 0, & \qquad\qquad\qquad\qquad < , \\ L^A = N^A + N^B, & \qquad\qquad\qquad\qquad >, \end{cases} \tag{33}$$

where N^j is the population of workers in region j before migration and L^j is the population of workers after migration. Recall that country A has a PAYG system while pensions are FF in country B.

It is clear from these conditions that to obtain an interior solution we need $\tau^A = 0$, so that *the PAYG system will have to disappear: taxes are zero or they are positive and all potential payroll taxpayers leave the country. Either way, no revenue can be raised to finance the PAYG pensions.* For the young generation this effectively implies a switch to a FF system. Older individuals, however, and especially those who are already retired when integration occurs are bound to loose in the process as the financing of their retirement benefits is jeopardized.

We can easily extend our analysis to the case of two PAYG systems of possibly different size. When A and B both have PAYG systems the condition for an interior migration equilibrium is given by

$$w^A - \tau^A \frac{r-n}{1+r} = w^B - \tau^B \frac{r-n}{1+r},$$

which in turn requires $\tau^A = \tau^B$ so that contribution rates (and thus benefits) must be equalized. Otherwise, one of the two countries, that with the higher τ^j will be emptied of its young workers, the old retirees being left behind without pension benefits. Consequently, we have the result by Homburg and Richter (1993) [see also Breyer and Kolmar (2002)] that *harmonization is necessary on efficiency grounds when households can freely migrate between regions.* To avoid such extreme solutions, a number of authors have introduce additional features: differential fertility rates, decreasing returns to scale, mobility costs, public goods.[26]

With labor mobility, differentials in the net benefits that individuals can expect from public pensions [in the above example $-\tau^j(r-n)/(1+r)$] alter the payoff to migration and can influence the international allocation of labor. Wildasin (1999) estimates the change in the present value of lifetime wealth for representative workers in 7 European Union countries that results from switching from one public pension program to another. He shows that moving between certain countries can result in an increase of 15% or even more in lifetime wealth. As he points out, differentials in net benefits create fiscal incentives for inefficient labor allocation. We expect increased mobility to lead to a reduction in differences in intergenerational redistribution over time.

6. Conclusion

In this survey, we have focused on the effect of factor mobility on the capacity of national governments to redistribute income. As emphasized in most studies surveyed, mobility makes it difficult to efficiently tax or subsidize mobile factors, whatever they

[26] See also Jousten and Pestieau (2002).

are, capital or labor. To a certain extent, the effects of labor and capital mobility are alike, which is a bit surprising. There are however some differences. First, labor income tax base tends to be empirically much broader than that of capital income. Second, and more importantly, the similarity hinges upon the assumption that the national governments are concerned by the welfare of all mobile nationals regardless of their location.

Another distinction concerns the possibility of formal or informal discrimination between an incoming factor of production and a long time established one. In the case of capital mobility and given the source based principle, it often happens that foreign capital income is subject to a lower tax, if any, than domestic capital income. In the case of labor mobility, and specifically of low skill labor, the residence based principle applies and differential tax treatment is hardly conceivable except in the treatment of illegal migration.

Regardless of these differences, we have seen that in general, factor mobility makes it difficult to conduct the same redistribution policies as would be conducted in autarky. This is where one thinks of centralization or cooperation. We have seen that in a number of cases the type of equilibrium with lower redistribution was of the Pareto-inferior type. In other words, cooperation is feasible. However, in many real-life asymmetrical situations, the non-cooperative solution is not of that type. Further, besides regional income redistribution, there is another issue, namely that of redistribution across regions for which a certain centralized compelling authority is unavoidable.

We have also pointed out another possible pitfall of cooperation which arises because a coordinated setting of *all* relevant tax instruments may not be a realistic perspective. A piece-meal approach involving only partial cooperation (or harmonization) appears to be more reasonable to expect. But then the welfare impact of the cooperation policy is less straightforward to assess. For instance, if the EU countries were to agree on minimum tax rates on capital incomes, this might lead to fiercer tax competition for the setting of other tax instruments.

Finally, we have briefly reviewed some recent contributions which go beyond the scope of the traditional tax competition literature. They study open economy aspects of intergenerational redistribution and particularly those of pension schemes. In particular, there is the issue of the co-existence of pay-as-you-go and of fully funded pension systems within an economic union. The question is whether such a co-existence can be sustained and if yes, what type of adjustments will be induced by economic integration.

Acknowledgements

We thank the editors, Vernon Henderson and Jacques Thisse for their helpful comments and suggestions.

References

Bayindir-Upman, T., Ziad, A. (2002). "Existence of equilibria in a basic tax competition model". Mimeo.

Brennan, G., Buchanan, J.M. (1980). The Power to Tax: Analytical Foundations of a Fiscal Constitution. Cambridge Univ. Press, Cambridge, UK.

Breyer, E., Kolmar, M. (2002). "Are national pension systems efficient if labor is (im)perfectly mobile?" Journal of Public Economics 83, 347–374.

Brown, C.C., Oates, W.E. (1987). "Assistance to the poor in a federal system". Journal of Public Economics 32, 307–330.

Bucovetsky, S. (1991). "Asymmetric tax competition". Journal of Urban Economics 30, 167–181.

Bucovetsky, S. (2003). "Efficient migrations and income tax competition". Journal of Public Economic Theory 5, 249–278.

Bucovetsky, S., Marchand, M., Pestieau, P. (1998). "Tax competition and revelation of preferences for public expenditure". Journal of Urban Economics 44, 367–390.

Cardarelli, R., Taugourdeau, E., Vidal, J.-P. (2002). "A repeated interactions model of tax competition". Journal of Public Economic Theory 4, 19–38.

Casarico, A. (2000). "Pension systems in integrated capital markers". Topics in Economic Analysis and Policy 1, 1–17.

Christiansen, V., Hagen, K.P., Sandmo, A. (1994). "The scope for taxation and public expenditure in an open economy". Scandinavian Journal of Economics 96, 289–309.

Cremer, H., Gahvari, F. (2000). "Tax evasion, fiscal competition and economic integration". European Economic Review 44, 1633–1657.

Cremer, H., Gahvari, F. (2002a). "Environmental taxation, tax competition and harmonization". Mimeo. University of Toulouse.

Cremer, H., Gahvari, F. (2002b). "Environmental taxation and partial harmonization in open economies". Mimeo. University of Toulouse.

Cremer, H., Pestieau, P. (1996a). "Distributive implications of European integration". European Economic Review 40, 747–758.

Cremer, H., Pestieau, P. (1996b). "Income redistribution in an economic union: the trade-off between inter- and intra-national redistribution". International Taxation and Public Finance 4, 325–336. Also in: The Economics of Globalization: Policy Perspectives from Public Economics. Cambridge Univ. Press, Cambridge, UK, 1999, pp. 143–155.

Cremer, H., Marchand, M., Pestieau, P. (1996). "Interregional redistribution through tax surcharge". In: International Taxation and Public Finance, vol. 3, pp. 157–174. Also in: Wildasin, D. (Ed.), Fiscal Aspects of Evolving Federations. Cambridge Univ. Press, New York, 1997, pp. 63–81.

Cremer, H., Fourgeaud, V., Leite Monteiro, M., Marchand, M., Pestieau, P. (1996). "Mobility and redistribution. A survey of the literature". Public Finance 51, 325–352.

Edwards, J., Keen, M. (1996). "Tax competition and Leviathan". European Economic Review 40, 113–134.

Epple, D., Romer, T. (1991). "Mobility and redistribution". Journal of Political Economy 99, 828–858.

Fuest, C. (1995). "Interjurisdictional competition and public expenditure: is tax coordination counterproductive?" Finanzarchiv 52, 478–496.

Fuest, C., Huber, B. (1999a). "Can tax coordination work?" Finanzarchiv 56, 443–459.

Fuest, C., Huber, B. (1999b). "Tax coordination and unemployment". International Tax and Public Finance 6, 7–26.

Gabszewicz, J.J., van Ypersele, T. (1996). "Social protection and political competition". Journal of Public Economics 61, 193–208.

Gordon, R.H. (1983). "An optimal taxation approach to fiscal federalism". Quarterly Journal of Economics 98, 567–586.

Haufler, A. (2001). Taxation in a Global Economy. Cambridge Univ. Press, Cambridge, UK.

Hindriks, J. (2001). "Mobility and redistribution politics". Journal of Public Economic Theory 3, 96–120.

Homburg, S., Richter, W. (1993). "Harmonizing public debt and public pension schemes in the European Community". Journal of Economics Supplement 7, 51–64.

Huizinga, H. (1995). "International interest withholding taxation: prospects for a common European policy". International Tax and Public Finance 1, 277–291.

Jousten, A., Pestieau, P. (2002). "Labor mobility, redistribution and pension reform in the European Union". In: Feldstein, M., Siebert, H. (Eds.), Pensions Reforms. Where does Europe stands? Univ. of Chicago Press for NBER, Chicago.

Keen, M., Kotsogiannis, C. (2002). "Does federation lead to excessive high taxes". American Economic Review 92, 363–370.

Keen, M., Kotsogiannis, C. (2003). "Leviathan and capital tax competition in federations". Journal of Public Economic Theory 5, 177–200.

Kelders, Ch., Kölhenbürger, M. (2003). "Tax incentives in fiscal federalism: an integrated perspective". Unpublished. CESifo, Munich.

Koskela, E., Schöb, R. (2002). "Optimal factor income taxation in the presence of unemployment". Journal of Public Economic Theory 4, 387–404.

Laussel, D., Le Breton, M. (1998). "Existence of Nash equilibria in models of fiscal competition". Regional Science and Urban Economics 28, 283–296.

Leite Monteiro, M. (1997). "Redistributive policy with labor mobility across countries". Journal of Public Economics 65, 229–244.

Leite Monteiro, M., Marchand, M., Pestieau, P. (2003). "Redistribution with capital mobility and union's wage setting". Journal of Public Economic Theory 59, 212–226.

Lejour, A.M., Verbon, H.A. (1994). "Labour mobility and decision making on social insurance in an integrated market". Public Choice 79, 161–185.

Lejour, A.M., Verbon, H.A. (1996). "Capital mobility, wage bargaining and social insurance policies in an economic union". International Tax and Public Finance 3, 495–514.

Lopez, S., Marchand, M., Pestieau, P. (1998). "A simple two-country model of redistributive capital income taxation". Finanzarchiv 55, 445–460.

Lozachmeur, J.-M. (2003). "Fiscal competition, labor mobility and unemployment". Finanzarchiv 59, 212–226.

Marchand, , M., Pestieau, , P., Sato, , M. (2003). "Can piecewise fiscal coordination be welfare improving? A model of income redistribution". Journal of Urban Economics 54, 451–458.

McLure, C. (1986). "Tax competition: Is what's good for the private goose also good for the public gander?" National Tax Journal 39, 341–348.

Michel, Ph., Pestieau, P., Vidal, J.-P. (1998). "Labor mobility and redistribution with evolving altruism: the case of a small economy". Regional Science and Urban Economics 28, 363–377.

Oates, W.E., Schwab, R.M. (1988). "The allocative and distributive implications of local fiscal competition". Working Paper 88-38. Department of Economics, University of Maryland.

Ottaviano, G.I.P., Thisse, J.-F. (2002). "Integration, agglomeration and the political economics of factor mobility". Journal of Public Economics 83, 429–456.

Pauly, M.V. (1973). "Income redistribution as a local public good". Journal of Public Economics 2, 35–58.

Pemberton, J. (1999). "Social security: national policies with international implications". Economic Journal 109, 492–598.

Pemberton, J. (2000). "National and international privatisation of pensions". European Economic Review 44, 1873–1896.

Peralta, S., van Ypersele, T. (2002). "Capital tax competition among an arbitrary number of asymmetric countries". CORE DP 2002/31.

Richter, W. (2001). "Delayed integration of mobile labor: a principle for coordinating taxation, social security and social assistance". Unpublished.

Richter, W., Schneider, K. (2001). "Taxing mobile capital with labour market imperfections". International Tax and Public Finance 8, 245–262.

Schjelderup, G. (1997). "Optimal income taxation and international labour mobility". Bulletin of Economic Research 49, 327–349.

Schotchmer, S. (2002). "Local public goods and clubs". In: Auerbach, A., Feldstein, M. (Eds.), Handbook of Public Economics, vol. 4. North-Holland, Amsterdam, pp. 1999–2041.

Sinn, H.-W. (1990). "Tax harmonization and tax competition in Europe". European Economic Review 34, 489–504.

Sinn, H.-W. (1994). "How much Europe? Subsidiarity, centralization and fiscal competition". Scottish Journal of Political Economy 41, 85–107.

Stigler, G.J. (1957). "The tenable range of functions of local governments". In: Federal Expenditure Policy for Economic Growth and Stability. Reprinted in: Phelps, E.S. (Ed.), Private Wants and Public Needs, revised ed. Norton, New York, 1965.

Tiebout, C.M. (1956). "A pure theory of local expenditures". Journal of Political Economy 64, 416–424.

Wellisch, D. (2000). The Theory of Public Finance in a Federal State. Cambridge Univ. Press, New York.

Wildasin, D.E. (1991). "Income redistribution in a common labor market". American Economic Review 81, 757–774.

Wildasin, D.E. (1992). "Relaxation of barriers to factor mobility and income redistribution". In: Pestieau, P. (Ed.), Public Finance in a World of Transition. Proceedings of the 47th Congress of the International Institute of Public Finance. Public Finance/Finances Publiques 47 (supplement), 216–230.

Wildasin, D.E. (1994a). "Income redistribution and migration". Canadian Journal of Economics 27, 637–656.

Wildasin, D.E. (1994b). "Public pensions in the EU: migration incentives and impacts". In: Panagariya, A., Portney, P.R., Schwab, R.M. (Eds.), Environmental Economics and Public Policy: Essays in Honor of Wallace E. Oates. Edward Edgar.

Wildasin, D.E. (1997). "Income distribution and redistribution within federations". Annales d'Economie et de Statistique 45, 291–313.

Wildasin, D.E. (2003a). "Fiscal competition: an introduction". Journal of Public Economic Theory 5, 169–177.

Wildasin, D.E. (2003b). "Fiscal competition in space and time". Journal of Public Economics. In press.

Wilson, J.D. (1980). "The effect of potential emigration on the optimal linear income tax". Journal of Public Economics 14, 339–353.

Wilson, J.D. (1982). "Optimal linear income taxation in the presence of emigration". Journal of Public Economics 18, 363–379.

Wilson, J.D. (1999). "Theories of tax competition". National Tax Journal 52, 269–304.

Wilson, J.D., Wildasin, D.E. (2003). "Tax competitions: bone or boon". Journal of Public Economics. In press.

PART 3

ECONOMIC GEOGRAPHY AND THE GEOGRAPHY OF MODERN ECONOMIES

Chapter 58

AGGLOMERATION AND ECONOMIC GEOGRAPHY

GIANMARCO OTTAVIANO[1]

Università di Bologna, Italy
e-mail: ottavian@economia.unibo.it

JACQUES-FRANÇOIS THISSE[2]

CORE, Université catholique de Louvain, Belgium

CERAS, École nationale des ponts et chaussées, France
e-mail: thisse@core.ucl.ac.be

Contents

[1] Also affiliated with FEEM and CEPR.
[2] Also affiliated with INRA-CESAER and CEPR.

Handbook of Regional and Urban Economics, Volume 4. Edited by J.V. Henderson and J.F. Thisse

DOI: 10.1016/S0169-7218(04)07058-3

Abstract

Peaks and troughs in the spatial distributions of population, employment and wealth are a universal phenomenon in search of a general theory. Such spatial imbalances have two possible explanations. In the first one, uneven economic development can be seen as the result of the uneven distribution of natural resources. This is sometimes called 'first nature' and refers to exogenously given characteristics of different sites. However, it falls short of providing a reasonable explanation of many other clusters of activities, which are much less dependent on natural advantage. The aim of geographical economics is precisely to understand what are the economic forces that, after controlling for first nature, account for 'second nature', which emerges as the outcome of human beings' actions to improve upon the first one. Specifically, geographical economics asks what are the economic forces that can sustain a large permanent imbalance in the distribution of economic activities. In this paper, we focus on the so-called 'new economic geography' approach. After having described some of the main results developed in standard location theory, we use a unified framework to survey the home market effect as well as core–periphery models. These models have been criticized by geographers because they account for some spatial costs while putting others aside without saying why. Furthermore, core–periphery models also exhibit some extreme features that are reflected in their bang–bang outcomes. We thus move on by investigating what the outcomes of core–periphery models become when we account for a more complete and richer description of the spatial aspects that these models aim at describing. We conclude by suggesting new lines of research.

Keywords

agglomeration, economic geography, monopolistic competition, increasing returns, transport costs

JEL classification: F12, F16, R12

1. Introduction

Peaks and troughs in the spatial distributions of population, employment and wealth are a universal phenomenon in search of a general theory. At a high level of abstraction spatial imbalances have two possible explanations.[3] First of all, uneven economic development can be seen as the result of the uneven distribution of natural resources. This is sometimes called 'first nature' and refers to exogenously given characteristics of different sites, such as the type of climate, the presence of raw materials, the proximity to natural ways of communication, etc. First nature is clearly important to explain the location of heavy industries during the Industrial Revolution, because the proximity of raw materials was a critical factor, or why Florida keeps attracting so many (retired) people. However it falls short of providing a reasonable explanation of many other clusters of activities, which are much less dependent on natural advantage (think of the metropolitan area of Tokyo or the Silicon Valley).[4]

The aim of geographical economics is precisely to understand what are the economic forces that, after controlling for first nature, account for 'second nature', which emerges as the outcome of human beings' actions to improve upon the first one. From a methodological point of view, geographical economics starts with considering an initial situation in which space is homogeneous and production activities are equally present at all sites. Then, it asks what are the forces that can allow a *small* (possibly temporary) asymmetric shock across sites to generate a *large* permanent imbalance in the distributions of economic activities. Among the various classes of models that have been put forth to address this question, we focus on the so-called *new economic geography* (in short NEG).

NEG has been initiated by three authors, namely Fujita (1988), Krugman (1991) and Venables (1996) who all use general equilibrium models with monopolistic competition. Most models in NEG assume the existence of two sectors, the 'modern' and the 'traditional' sectors. At the time of the Industrial Revolution, the modern sector was *manufacturing*. The geographical concentration of industry generated an additional demand for manufactured goods, as shown by the history of the Manufacturing Belt in the United States or the development of the Ruhr in Germany. Today, the modern sector is the *service industry* in which firms do not only supply consumers and manufacturing firms, but also serve each other. The tendency toward agglomeration is thus strengthened by the fact that business services tend to work more and more for headquarters and research labs of manufacturing firms, which remain mostly located in large urban

[3] Unevenness arises across countries in the world, across regions and cities within a country, and across neighbors within a city. In this chapter, we focus mainly on explanations dealing with the first two levels of analysis – countries and regions.

[4] Strong regional imbalances arose during the Industrial Revolution. According to Pollard (1981) who paid due attention to the regional aspects of the industrialization of Europe, "industrialization remained a local phenomenon" (p. 32), and hence "it is perhaps unnecessarily inexact to talk of England and the Continent rather than, say, of Lancashire and the Valley of the Sambre-Meuse" (p. 41).

agglomerations. Thus, our point is that 'what the two sectors are' changes with the stage of development of the economy as well as with the epoch under consideration.

The main results obtained by NEG after one decade of research have been synthesized in a book written by the same authors [Fujita, Krugman and Venables (1999)]. During this period, there have been endless debates involving economists, geographers and regional scientists about what was really 'new' in the NEG [see, e.g., Isserman (1996) and Martin (1999)]. By now, it is widely recognized that many ideas had been around for a long time in the works of economic geographers and location theorists.[5] We survey these ideas in Section 2 and conclude that, despite several early and outstanding contributions, it is fair to say that economic geography and location theory lay for long in the periphery of mainstream economic theory. The reason for such a peripherality is likely to be found in the difficulty for the competitive paradigm, which has dominated so much economic research, to explain the formation of economic agglomerations. Indeed, as shown by Starrett (1978), cities, regional specialization and trade *cannot* arise at the competitive equilibrium of an economy with a homogeneous space. The reason for this somehow amazing and seldom mentioned result is the presence of space-specific nonconvexities that prevent the existence of a nontrivial competitive equilibrium.

NEG may be viewed as an attempt to overcome this theoretical deadlock. It does so by connecting trade and location theories, a research target put forward several years ago by Ohlin, Hesselborn and Wijkman (1977).[6] In this perspective, modern theories of agglomeration are very much dominated by a simple principle: *a market place is the core of the economy because this place is its main market*. We illustrate this point in Section 3 by means of what is called the 'home market effect' (henceforth, HME). According to Helpman and Krugman (1985, p. 197), once transport costs are explicitly accounted for, this effect arises when imperfectly competitive industries tend to concentrate their production in their larger markets and to export to smaller ones.[7] Stated differently, the HME has the features of a 'gravitational force' that attracts imperfectly competitive sectors towards larger markets. Accordingly, it allows small permanent shocks to market size to generate large permanent disparities in the location of firms. For this reason, the HME is the basic ingredient that lies at the heart of most models of agglomeration. Its historical relevance in the industrialization of Europe is emphasized by Pollard (1981) for whom, even though there are examples of export-led developments,

[5] See Fujita and Thisse (2002) for an integrated overview of new economic geography and standard location theory.

[6] Note that agglomeration may arise even when transport costs are sufficiently high for trade not to occur. In the framework described in Section 4.1, the spatial equilibrium pattern is then determined by the ratio of the mobile to the immobile factor: the larger this ratio, the larger the agglomeration [Behrens (2004)]. Hence, contrary to general beliefs, agglomeration is not a 'by-product' of trade; it may also emerge in an autarkic world.

[7] In this chapter, transport costs are broadly defined to include all impediments caused by distance, such as shipping costs per se, tariff and non-tariff barriers to trade, different product standards, difficulty of communication, and cultural differences.

"it is obviously harder to build up an industrial complex without the solid foundation of a home market" (p. 249). We discuss the reasons that may explain why such an effect exists and uncover its relationships with standard location theory. In particular, we argue that the market equilibrium is the outcome of the interplay between two opposing forces, a market-crowding force and a market-access force, very much as in spatial competition à la Hotelling. Using two different models of monopolistic competition, we show that, in the case of two regions, *a more than proportionate fraction of the modern sector is established within the larger region*. Very much as in standard location theory, physical capital is a disembodied factor, which can be used in either region and moves from one region to the other seeking the highest *nominal* rate of return.

The main limit of the HME is that, on its own, it is not able to explain why even small *temporary* shocks can have large permanent effects on the economic landscape. This is achieved by the models discussed in Section 4. They may be subdivided into two categories according to whether or not labor is mobile. The first category assumes that part of the labor force is mobile (Section 4.1). Unlike the models of Section 3 in which the capital-owners repatriate all their earnings where they live, the core–periphery (in short CP) model assumes that mobile workers spend their income in the region in which they are active. In other words, the production factor is now embodied in workers and this difference suffices to give rise to circular causation in locational decisions. When transport costs are sufficiently low, such an ex-post immobility of income exacerbates the transient HME caused by a temporary shock to market size. The result is that *all firms belonging to the modern sector end up with locating within a single region* (the 'core'), the other region being specialized in the traditional sector (the 'periphery'). In other words, workers' mobility strengthens much more than proportionally the initial advantage given by a larger initial market size, thus leading to the 'amplification' of the HME. By contrast, when transport costs are sufficiently high, the HME vanishes in that each region ends up with the same size. Under these circumstances, each factor gets the same earning regardless of its location, very much as in the neoclassical Heckscher–Ohlin setting. Although the idea is not new, the CP model is the first general equilibrium model that produces an uneven economic space from an otherwise even physical space as a consequence of low transport costs and mobile production factors. Compared to the HME models, one distinguishing feature of CP models is that human capital moves seeking the highest *real* rate of return.

Armchair evidence shows, however, that agglomeration arises even in the absence of labor mobility. This leads us to investigate the second category of models in which 'vertical linkages' of the type stressed by Venables (1996) is the main reason for the existence of agglomeration (Section 4.2). Even though all workers stay put, the size of a regional market remains variable because of input–output linkages. The reason is that, whenever a firm sets up in a particular region, the local size of its upstream and downstream markets expand.

Models in NEG have been criticized by geographers and location theorists because they account for 'some' spatial costs while putting 'others' aside without saying why.

Table 1

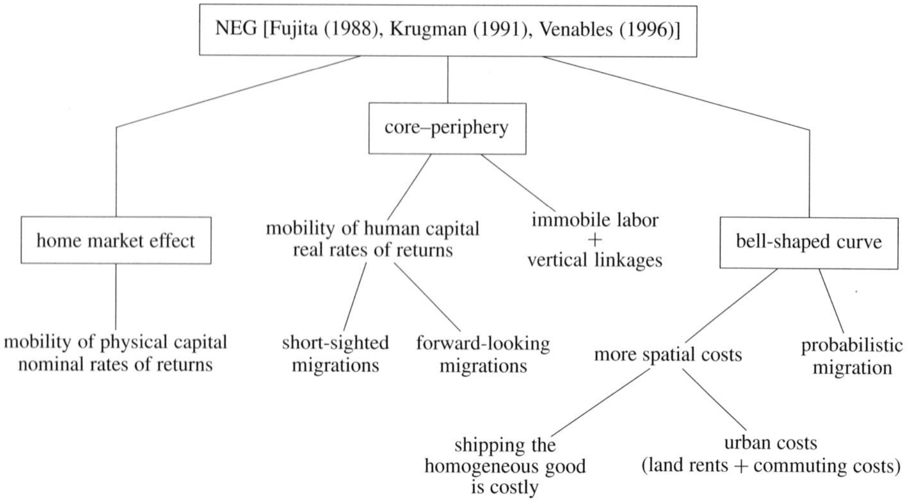

First, transport costs of the output of the traditional sector are not zero in the real world. Second, the agglomeration of the modern sector within a region gives rise to urban costs that typically increase with the size of the corresponding population. To be sure, all these costs have declined since the beginning of the Industrial Revolution but they did not do so at the same speed. Thus, what matters for the space-economy is their relative variation over time. Furthermore, CP models share with Bertrand's setting some unpleasant and extreme features that are reflected in their 'bang–bang' outcomes: only full agglomeration and full dispersion may occur, whereas changes in the spatial pattern are always catastrophic. This does not strike us as being plausible. As argued by Hotelling (1929) long ago, such results arise because the modeling strategy is often too simple: more meaningful models should account explicitly for some heterogeneity across agents. The purpose of Section 5 is to investigate what the CP model becomes when we account for a more complete and richer description of the spatial aspects that this model aims at describing.

In Section 6, we suggest new lines of research. Before proceeding, a last comment is in order. The contributions in NEG have flourished during the last decade. Instead of providing a superficial overview of the field, we have chosen to concentrate on the main ideas and results within a unified framework that slightly departs from the most standard models. This framework is summarized in Table 1, whereas extensions are mentioned in footnotes where the reader may find additional references for future reading.[8]

[8] In the chapter by Richard Baldwin and Philippe Martin (2004), the reader will find a discussion of agglomeration forces that are growth-specific.

2. The legacy of location theory

The objective of location theory is to answer the question: why some particular production activities (such as plants, offices, public facilities, etc.) choose to establish themselves in some particular places of a given space? This question can be broken in two sub-questions as to the location of a firm and the location of an industry. As to the former, one may ask: why does an isolated firm faces a location problem and how does it solve it? As to the latter, one may ask: how are firms' locational decisions intertwined? The purpose of this section is to show that earlier contributions in location theory have uncovered several of the main ideas used in NEG to answer the above questions. We do not intend to provide here an exhaustive survey of what had been accomplished by economists in pre-Krugman times but, more modestly, to show that the main ingredients had already been there, sometimes for a long period. This will allow us to assess why there is an 'N' in NEG.

2.1. The location of a firm

The location problem of a firm arises because some of its activities are indivisible. In Koopmans's (1957, p. 154) words:

> "without recognizing indivisibilities – in human person, in residences, plants, equipment, and in transportation – urban location problems, down to those of the smallest village, cannot be understood."

More precisely, for the location problem of a firm to be not trivial, there must be some sort of increasing returns at the plant level as well as transport costs: increasing returns lead the firm to concentrate its production in a few plants, whereas transport costs raise the issue of where to locate these plants.

2.1.1. Increasing returns vs. transport costs

The fundamental trade-off of economic geography between increasing returns and mobility costs has been recognized by various scholars interested in the formation of human settlements. This should not come as a surprise because increasing returns and mobility costs may take quite different forms, thus making them applicable to a wide range of situations. One example is provided by the following statement made by W.M. Flinders Petrie in his *Social Life in Ancient Egypt* published in 1923:

> "It has been noticed before how remarkably similar the distances are between the early Nome capitals of the Delta (twenty-one miles on an average) and the early cities of Mesopotamia (averaging twenty miles apart). Some physical cause seems to limit the primitive rule in this way. Is it not the limit of central storage of grain, which is the essential form of early capital? Supplies could be centralised up to ten miles away; beyond that the cost of transport made it better worthwhile to have a nearer centre."

This echoes Lösch (1940) who writes about two decades later:

> "We shall consider market areas that are not the result of any kind of natural or political inequalities but arise through the interplay of purely economic forces, some working toward concentration, and other toward dispersion. In the first group are the advantages of specialization and of large-scale production; in the second, those of shipping costs and of diversified production." (p. 105 of the English translation)

Observe that the same trade-off has been modeled by Kuehn and Hambuger (1963) in a planning context: given a spatial distribution of requirements for a particular commodity, fixed costs must be incurred for locating the facilities that produce this commodity and transport costs must be borne to ship it from the facilities to the consumers. The aim of the model is then to determine the number and locations of facilities so as to minimize the sum of production and transport costs.[9]

2.1.2. Weber and the location of the firm

The oldest formal analysis of the location of a firm is the minisum location problem, which consists in locating a plant in the plane. The aim is to minimize the weighted sum of Euclidean distances from that plant to a finite number of sites corresponding to the markets where the plant purchases its inputs and sells its outputs; the weights represent the quantities of inputs and outputs bought and sold by the plant, multiplied by the appropriate freight rates [Weber (1909)]. When the sites are not collinear, the minisum problem has no analytical solution and one must pertain to an algorithm to solve it. However, it is possible to derive special, but meaningful, results. A site is said to be a *dominant place* if its weight is greater than or equal to the sum of the weights of all the other sites. In this case, the dominant place is the optimal solution to the minisum problem [Witzgall (1964)]. Such a simple result may explain the locational decision made by seemingly different firms to set up in a large metropolitan area as well as it allows one to understand the location of steel mills next to the iron mines in the 19th century and later next to their main markets.

Since the 1960s, the focus in firm location theory has moved from the least transport cost approach to the more standard microeconomic approach of profit maximization. The corresponding integration of additional variables within the Weberian framework has permitted a better understanding of the influence of several economic and geographic factors in electing a location. This is exemplified by the work of Sakashita (1967) who demonstrates that, in the case of a segment connecting the market and the input source, the firm always chooses to set up at one of the two endpoints and never at an intermediate point. For that, freight rates have to be constant or to taper off as the distance covered increases, a condition that characterizes all modern transport technologies. Thus, models in firm location theory tell us something fundamental for the space-economy: *new firms have a high propensity to settle at places where economic activities are already established.*

[9] See, e.g., Hansen et al. (1987) for an economic-oriented survey of this model and of related ones.

2.2. The location of an industry

In location theory, the passage from a firm to an industry is not smooth because the locational decisions of several firms can hardly be studied within a perfectly competitive framework.

2.2.1. Starrett and the breakdown of the competitive price mechanism

The most elegant and general model of a competitive economy is the Arrow–Debreu model. The economy is formed by agents (firms and consumers) and by commodities (goods and services). A firm is characterized by a set of production plans, each production plan describing a possible input–output relation. A consumer is identified by a relation of preference, by a bundle of initial resources and by shares in the firms' profits. Roughly speaking, when firms' technologies exhibit nonincreasing returns to scale, there exist market prices (one per commodity), a production technology for each firm and a consumption bundle for each consumer that satisfy the following conditions: at the prevailing prices

(i) supply equals demand for each commodity;

(ii) each firm maximizes its profit subject to its possible production technologies; and

(iii) each consumer maximizes her utility under her budget constraint defined by the value of her initial endowment and her shares in firms' profits.

In a world à la Arrow–Debreu, a commodity is defined not only by its physical characteristics, but also by the place where it is available, even though the same good does change nature when shipped. The same good traded at different places is treated, therefore, as different commodities. Within this framework, choosing a location is part of choosing commodities. Hence, the Arrow–Debreu model aims at integrating spatial interdependence of markets into general equilibrium in the same way as other forms of interdependence. Unfortunately, the spatial impossibility theorem by Starrett (1978) shows that things are not that simple.

To illustrate the nature of the problem, consider the extreme case of a *homogeneous* space with a finite number of locations. By a homogeneous space, we mean the following two conditions:

(i) the production set of a firm is the same in all locations and

(ii) consumers' preferences are the same at all locations.

Such an assumption is made in order to control for the impact that first nature may have on the distribution of economic activity. This is because we are interested in finding economic mechanisms that explain agglomeration without appealing to physical attributes of locations or technological externalities (second nature). For the rest, the economy follows the lines of the competitive framework as described in the foregoing. Then, we have:

THEOREM 1 (The spatial impossibility theorem). *Consider an economy with a finite number of locations and a finite number of consumers and firms. If space is homogeneous, transport is costly and preferences are locally nonsatiated, then there is no competitive equilibrium involving transportation.*

What does it mean? If economic activities are perfectly divisible, a competitive equilibrium exists and is such that each location operates as an autarchy. For example, if consumers have the same preferences and identical initial endowments, regions have the same relative prices and the same production structure (backyard capitalism). This is hardly a surprising outcome since, by assumption, there is no reason for the economic agents to distinguish among locations and since each activity can operate at an arbitrarily small level. It is worth stressing, however, that the autarchic equilibrium does not necessarily involve a uniform distribution of activities.

Once economic activities are *not* perfectly divisible, they have an *address* in space. Then, as observed by Starrett, the transport of some goods between some places becomes unavoidable:

> "as long as there are some indivisibilities in the system (so that individual operations must take up space) then a sufficiently complicated set of interrelated activities will generate transport costs" [Starrett (1978), p. 27]

In this case, the spatial impossibility theorem tells us that no competitive equilibrium with trade across locations exists. Since activities are not perfectly divisible (thus implying the presence of nonconvexities in the economy), firms and consumers may want to be separate because each must choose to use a positive amount of land that cannot be made arbitrarily small, even though the individual land consumption is endogenous. Physical separation and the homogeneity of space then place firms and consumers in a relation of symmetry such as the only spatial factor that matters to them is their position relative to the agents with whom they trade. In this context, *the fact that shipping goods is costly and that agents have an address generates nonconvexities in production or consumption sets that prevent the competitive setting from handling such a system of exchanges*. It is in that sense that the Arrow–Debreu framework fails to handle the spatial question: competitive equilibria, when they exist, involve no trade across locations.[10]

If we want to understand something about the spatial distribution of economic activities, especially the formation of major economic agglomerations, it follows from the spatial impossibility theorem that we must assume either that *space is heterogeneous* (as in the neoclassical theory of international trade or in land use models à la von Thünen), or that *externalities* exist and are many (as in modern urban economics), or that *markets are imperfect* (as in spatial competition theory or in economic geography). Although it is obvious that space is heterogenous, diversity of resources seems weak as a sole

[10] For a more detailed discussion, see Fujita and Thisse (2002, Chapter 2).

explanation for the existence of large metropolises as well as for the persistence of substantial regional income inequalities. For this reason, in what follows, we consider the other two explanations.

2.2.2. Cities and product variety

Whereas Marshallian externalities have a long standing tradition in modeling the supply side of a spatial economy,[11] it is less known that they also operate on the demand side. In a very insightful – but not much quoted – paper, Haig (1926) argues that cities offer a great number of people a large assortment of consumption goods and services. He views the advantages associated with variety (*varietas delectat*) as being so large that the question is changed from "Why live in the city?" to "Why not live in the city?" In other words, migration to a large city may be explained purely by a consumption motive:

> "in a large city an individual may derive a higher utility from spending a given amount of income than in a small town ... even if the prices for commodities obtainable at both locations are higher in the former than in the latter." [Stahl (1983), p. 318]

a result which follows directly from the convexity of preferences. What will then influence the development of an urban center is the cost of delivering such assortments in the countryside. We thus have the main ingredients that govern the agglomeration and dispersion forces at work in NEG models. In addition, Haig observes that

> "The great bulk of population ... must work and must consume most of what they earn where they earn it. With them consumption and production is practically a simultaneous process and must be carried on for the most part in the same place. To them location is of interest both in its effects upon production and in its effects upon consumption." (pp. 185–186)

This drives the formation of an agglomeration in the CP model: when workers move, they do so with their expenditures as well as with their labor.

Along the same lines, Lampard (1955) makes it clear that a variety-like argument similarly applies to intermediate goods used by firms because "the principal function of the city today in terms of employment it creates is the provision of services rather than manufactures."

2.2.3. Hotelling and spatial competition

Ever since the pioneering work of Hotelling (1929), it is generally accepted that competition for market areas is an agglomeration force that would lead sellers to congregate,

[11] See the chapter by Gilles Duranton and Diego Puga (2004) in this volume for a survey of the microeconomic underpinnings of such externalities.

a result known as the principle of minimum differentiation. The two ice-cream men problem provides a neat illustration of this principle. Two merchants selling the same ice-cream at the same fixed price compete in location for consumers who are uniformly distributed along a beach of length L; each consumer purchases one cone of ice-cream from the nearer firm. Since Lerner and Singer (1937), it is well known that the unique Nash equilibrium of this game is given by the location pair $s_1^* = s_2^* = L/2$. In words, the two ice-cream sellers choose to locate back to back at the market center. This is due to the so-called 'market area effect': each seller's profit is an increasing function of the fraction of the beach to which she has privileged access.

However, things become more complex when (mill) prices are brought into the picture. Hotelling considers a two-stage game where the firms first simultaneously choose their locations and afterwards their prices. The market equilibrium may then be viewed as the interplay between a dispersion force and an agglomeration force. To illustrate how this trade-off works, let $\pi_1^* = \pi_1(p_1^*, p_2^*, s_1, s_2)$ be firm 1's profit evaluated at the equilibrium prices $p_i^*(s_1, s_2)$ corresponding to the location pair $s_1 < s_2$. Then, since $\partial\pi_1^*/\partial p_1^* = 0$, we have:

$$\frac{d\pi_1^*}{ds_1} = \frac{\partial\pi_1}{\partial p_2}\frac{\partial p_2^*}{\partial s_1} + \frac{\partial\pi_1^*}{\partial s_1}.$$

In general, the terms in the right-hand side of this expression can be signed as follows. The first one corresponds to the *price effect* (the desire to relax price competition) and is expressed by the impact that a change in firm 1's location has on price competition. Since goods are spatially differentiated, they are substitutes so that $\partial\pi_1/\partial p_2$ is positive; because goods become closer substitutes when s_1 increases, $\partial p_2^*/\partial s_1$ is negative. Hence the first term is negative: this is the dispersion force. The second term, which corresponds to the *market area effect*, is positive: this is the agglomeration force. Consequently, the impact of reducing the inter-firm distance upon firms' profits is a priori undetermined. Nevertheless, as established by d'Aspremont, Gabszewicz and Thisse (1979), if transport costs are quadratic, a unique price equilibrium exists for any location pair and the two firms wish to set up at the endpoints of the market. In other words, *price competition is a strong dispersion force* .

This dispersion of firms turns out to be very sensitive to a particular assumption of the model, namely firms sell a homogeneous good. Following Haig and NEG, we find it more realistic to assume that they sell differentiated products whereas consumers like product variety. Consequently, even if prices and locations do not vary, they do not always purchase from the same vendor. The idea that consumers distribute their purchases between several sellers is not new in economic geography and goes back at least to Reilly (1931) who formulated the so-called *gravity law of retailing*. Such a behavior is naturally modeled by discrete choice theory. In the special case of the logit [McFadden (1974)], a consumer at x buys from firm i with a frequency given by

$$\mathbf{P}_i(x) \equiv \frac{\exp[-(p_i + t|x - s_i|)/\upsilon]}{\sum_{j=1}^{M}\exp[-(p_j + t|x - s_j|)/\upsilon]} \tag{1}$$

where t is the transport rate (transport costs are linear in distance) and υ the degree of product differentiation.[12] Let c be the common marginal production cost. Then, we have [de Palma et al. (1985)]:

PROPOSITION 2 (The principle of minimum differentiation). *Assume that firms choose simultaneously their prices and locations. If consumers' purchasing behavior is described by* (1) *and if* $\upsilon/tL \geqslant 1/2$ *holds, then* $p_i^* = c + \upsilon n/(n-1)$ *and* $s_i^* = L/2$, $i = 1, \ldots, n$, *is a Nash equilibrium.*

Therefore, firms choose to agglomerate at the market center when their products are differentiated enough, when transport costs are low enough, or both.

Considering a more general setting in which the optimal behavior of a firm depends on what households and other firms do, while the optimal behavior of a household depends on what firms and other households do, Papageorgiou and Thisse (1985) describe the process of interaction between the two classes of agents as follows:

> "Households are attracted by places where the density of firms is high because opportunities there are more numerous, and they are repulsed by places where the density of households is high because they dislike congestion. Firms are attracted to places where the density of consumers is high because there the expected volume of business is large, and they are repulsed by places where the density of sellers is high because of the stronger competition prevailing there." (p. 20)

Those authors then show that, when varieties are sufficiently differentiated and/or transport costs are low enough, the interaction among firms and households leads to a spatial equilibrium in which both sellers and customers distribute themselves according to two bell-shaped curves that sustain each other. This confirms, within a broader framework, Hotelling's principle of minimum differentiation.[13]

2.3. Where did we stand in 1990?

Putting all those things together, it follows that the legacy of location theory can be summarized in five points:

[12] It is worth noting here that the logit and the CES, which is extensively used in NEG, are closely related in that both models can be derived from the same distribution of consumer tastes; the only difference is that consumers buy one unit of the product in the former and a number of units inversely related to its price in the latter [Anderson, de Palma and Thisse (1992, Chapters 3–4)]. In addition, this revised version of the standard model of spatial competition is such that each firm competes with every other firm, regardless of their location, as in monopolistic competition models used in subsequent sections. See Anderson and de Palma (2000), for a synthesis of localized and nonlocalized competition models.

[13] Using random preferences, Anas and Xu (1999) have cast trip dispersion within a general equilibrium framework and show how agglomeration of firms and consumers may arise in an otherwise competitive model. This does not contradict the spatial impossibility theorem because preferences are now defined conditionally on the distribution of firms.

(I) the economic space is the outcome of a trade-off between various forms of increasing returns and different types of mobility costs;
(II) price competition, high transport costs and land use foster the dispersion of production and consumption; therefore
(III) firms are likely to cluster within large metropolitan areas when they sell differentiated products and transport costs are low;
(IV) cities provide a wide array of final goods and specialized labor markets that make them attractive to consumers/workers; and
(V) agglomerations are the outcome of cumulative processes involving both the supply and demand sides.[14]

Consequently, *the space-economy has to be understood as the outcome of the interplay between agglomeration and dispersion forces*, an idea put forward by geographers and regional scientists long ago, *within a general equilibrium framework accounting explicitly for market failures*.

Those five points capture also the main ingredients of NEG with a focus on pecuniary rather than technological externalities. Thus, there is little new about them. Nevertheless, before NEG they were not knitted together and were often available only in specialized studies. In addition, they were (at best) developed within partial equilibrium models. Therefore, *what was missing was a general equilibrium framework with imperfect competition connecting these various insights and allowing for a detailed study of their interactions*. Here lies the main contribution of NEG: "to combine old ingredients through a new recipe," even though Paul Krugman failed to acknowledge (and probably was not aware of) most of them when he published his *Journal of Political Economy* paper.

3. Where do firms locate: the home market effect

The first step to understand how NEG models work is to consider the home market effect (HME). In the case of a two-region economy, the HME implies that the location with larger local demand succeeds in attracting a more than proportionate share of firms in imperfectly competitive industries. This pattern of demand-driven specialization maps into trade flows and generates the theoretical prediction that large regions should be net exporters of goods produced under increasing returns and imperfect competition. The HME deals with the location of an industry when the spatial distribution of consumers is fixed, a topic investigated by Lösch (1940, Chapter II) and extensively studied in location theory since then. There are differences, however. In standard location theory, space is represented by a one- or two-dimensional space [Eaton and Lipsey (1977), Beckmann and Thisse (1986)]; space is here described by two regions, as in

[14] The connections with early regional development theories, such as Myrdal (1957), have been made clear by Krugman himself from the very beginning of his work. This is why they have not been discussed here.

trade theory. Even though poorer from a spatial point of view, the HME is nevertheless much richer in terms of microeconomic content. Having said that, the intuition behind the HME lies in standard location theory. Since a profit-maximizing firm also minimizes the transport costs it incurs when delivering its output, everything else equal it will locate in the larger market, which corresponds to a dominant place in the sense of Weber (see Section 2.1.2). Nevertheless, not all firms will locate in the bigger market because positive transport costs allow firms to relax price competition by locating far from their competitors (see Section 2.2.3). Hence some firms may want to set up in the smaller market.

The HME has been generally discussed under monopolistic competition. On such a market structure are also generally based all existing models in NEG. For this reason, we choose to focus all that follows on monopolistic competition. However, we want to stress that, despite major differences in market structure, the HME bears some strong resemblance with the principle of minimum differentiation discussed in Section 2.2.3. In both cases, consumers are dispersed and firms lure to the location with the highest potential for demand: the larger market in trade theory and the market center in spatial competition.

3.1. *The market structure problem*

In his review of Chamberlin's (1933) book, Kaldor (1935) claims that a firm affects the sales of its neighboring firms, but not distant ones. The impact of its price reduction is, therefore, not symmetric across all locations. In other words, there are good reasons to believe that competition across locations is inherently oligopolistic [Eaton and Lipsey (1977), Gabszewicz and Thisse (1986)]. Unfortunately, models of spatial competition are plagued by the frequent nonexistence of an equilibrium in pure strategies [Gabszewicz and Thisse (1992)]. Thus, research has faced a modeling trade-off: to appeal to mixed strategies, or to use monopolistic competition in which interactions between firms are weak. For the sake of simplicity, Krugman and most of the economics profession have retained the second option, which is not unreasonable once we address spatial issues at a macro-level. In addition, models of monopolistic competition have shown a rare ability to deal with a large variety of issues related to economic geography, which are otherwise unsatisfactorily treated by the competitive paradigm [Matsuyama (1995)]. However, it should be kept in mind that spatial competition should not be missed at the micro-level.

In the Dixit and Stiglitz (1977) setting, *monopolistic competition* emerges as a market structure determined by consumers' heterogeneous tastes and firms' fixed requirements for limited productive resources. On the demand side, the set of consumers with different tastes are aggregated into a representative consumer whose preferences exhibit *love for variety*: her utility is an increasing function not only of the amount of each variety of a horizontally differentiated good, but also of the total number of varieties available.[15] On the supply side, production exhibits economies of scale within varieties but no economies of scope across varieties, thus implying a one-to-one relationship between firms and varieties. Consequently, each firm supplies one and only one variety (monopolistic). However, there are no entry or exit barriers so that prices are just enough to cover average cost (competition). Finally, firms are so many that they do not interact directly but only indirectly through aggregate demand effects. Formally, we assume that there is a *continuum of firms*.

The continuum approach does not imply the absence of interactions among firms. Indeed, each firm must figure out what will be the total output (or, alternatively, the average price index) in equilibrium when choosing its own quantity or price, or when deciding whether to enter the market. This is not what we encounter in a differentiated oligopolistic market when individual decisions made by competitors are needed by each firm. Here, we have a setting in which each firm must know only a global statistics about the market but not its details. We believe that using a statistics of the market is a particularly appealing way to capture the idea of monopolistic competition because it saves the essence of competition by forcing each firm to account for the aggregate behavior of its competitors.

Furthermore, the continuum assumption is probably the most natural way to capture Chamberlin's intuition regarding the working of a 'large group' industry, while allowing us to get rid of the 'integer problem' which often leads to inelegant results and cumbersome developments. Note also that, unlike oligopoly theory, which is plagued by the differences between the Bertrand and Cournot settings, the distinction between price competition and quantity competition becomes immaterial in monopolistic competition. Indeed, being negligible to the market, each firm behaves as a monopolist on the residual demand, which makes it indifferent between using price or quantity as a strategy. Last, this modeling strategy allows one to respect the indivisibility of an agent's location (her 'address') while avoiding to appeal to the existence of strong nonconvexities associated with large agents. At the same time, it leads to a description of the regional shares of economic and demographic magnitudes by means of continuous variables.

Although we consider only specific models of monopolistic competition such as the CES and the linear models, we expect the results obtained in these two different settings to be representative of general tendencies.

3.2. The framework and two models

We consider a $2 \times 2 \times 2$ setting. The economic space is made of two regions (A and B). The economy has two sectors, the 'modern' sector X and the 'traditional' sector Z. There are two production factors, capital (H) and labor (L).

[15] The CES utility used by Dixit and Stiglitz is indeed an aggregate for a particular population of heterogeneous consumers [Anderson, de Palma and Thisse (1992, Chapters 3–4)]. Even though their intellectual origins differ, preference for variety is formally similar to the gravity law of retailing mentioned in Section 2.2.3.

For the HME to arise, the two regions must differ in their expenditures. This could happen for various reasons and we find it convenient to consider a simple setting. The economy is endowed with H capitalists and L workers each supplying one unit of their corresponding factor inelastically. Capital services, but not capital-owners who stay put, are perfectly mobile between regions whereas labor is immobile. Specifically, workers are distributed so that a fraction $\theta \in (0, 1)$ resides in region A: $L_A = \theta L$. Without loss of generality, that region is assumed to host a larger number of workers ($\theta > 1/2$). To rule out comparative advantage à la Heckscher–Ohlin, capitalists are distributed according to the same fraction θ in region A: $H_A = \theta H$. Relative factor endowments are then the same across regions.

The Z-sector produces a homogeneous good under constant returns to scale and perfect competition. In particular, one unit of output requires one unit of L. Profits maximization then yields $p_i^Z = w_i$ where w_i is the wage. This good is costlessly traded between regions so that its price is the same everywhere: $p_A^Z = p_B^Z$. It is convenient to choose the homogeneous good as the numéraire, implying $p_A^Z = p_B^Z = 1$ and $w_A = w_B = 1$.

The X-sector produces a continuum of horizontally differentiated varieties under increasing returns. Each variety is supplied according to the same increasing-return technology: the production of $x(s)$ units of variety s requires a fixed amount f of capital and a variable amount $mx(s)$ of labor so that the total cost of the firm producing variety s is given by

$$TC_i(s) = r_i f + w_i m x_i(s) \tag{2}$$

where r_i is the rental rate of capital in region i. Because there are increasing returns to scale but no scope economies, each variety is produced by a single firm. Indeed, since consumers have a preference for variety, any firm obtains a higher share of the market by producing a differentiated variety than by replicating an existing one. Furthermore, shipping a variety across regions is costly but intraregional transport costs are zero.[16] We assume that regional markets are *segmented*: each firm sets a delivered price specific to the market in which its variety is sold.[17] In the first model discussed below (Section 3.2.1), demands have the same elasticity across locations so that both mill and discriminatory pricing policies yield the same equilibrium prices and outputs. This equivalence no longer holds in the second model (Section 3.2.2).

The market equilibrium is the outcome of the interplay between a dispersion force and an agglomeration force, very much as the spatial competition model à la Hotelling. The

16 This shows once more the trade-theory origin of most NEG models. Intraregional transport costs should also be positive but different from the interregional transport costs. By changing the value of these costs, one may study the impact of the quality of transport infrastructures on the distribution of activities. See Martin and Rogers (1995) for a first attempt along these lines.

17 There are many good reasons to believe that firms want to use spatial separation to segment their market [Thisse and Vives (1988)], whereas empirical work confirms the assumption that international, or even interregional, markets are still very segmented [Greenhut (1981), Head and Mayer (2000)].

agglomeration force lies in *market access*: the transport cost saving provided by locating in the larger region, the counterpart of the market area effect in spatial competition. The dispersion force lies in *market crowding*: the fiercer competition that arises when firms locate back to back, which corresponds to the price effect in spatial competition. Hence, the forces are the same, even though we consider two locations here, whereas there is a continuum of locations in spatial competition. The main difference is that we use here a general equilibrium framework instead of a partial equilibrium model.

Let $\lambda \in [0, 1]$ be the fraction of capital employed in region A so that $(\theta - \lambda)H < 0$ (respectively > 0) measures the extent of capital flows into (respectively out of) A. Denote by $r_i(\lambda)$ the rental rate of capital in region $i = A, B$ when its spatial distribution is $(\lambda, 1 - \lambda)$. A *spatial equilibrium* arises at $\lambda \in (0, 1)$ when

$$\Delta r(\lambda) \equiv r_A(\lambda) - r_B(\lambda) = 0$$

or at $\lambda = 0$ when $\Delta r(0) \leqslant 0$, or at $\lambda = 1$ when $\Delta r(1) \geqslant 0$. Such an equilibrium always exists when $r_i(\lambda)$ is a continuous function of λ [Ginsburgh, Papageorgiou and Thisse (1985)].

In the absence of a general model of monopolistic competition, we add one more 2 to the $2 \times 2 \times 2$ setting by discussing the two specific models that have been used so far in NEG.[18]

3.2.1. A nonlinear model with fixed mark-ups: CES utility and iceberg transport costs

The preference ordering of a consumer living in region i is captured by the utility function:

$$U_i = Q_i^{\mu} Z_i^{1-\mu} \tag{3}$$

where

$$Q_i = \left(\int_0^N q_i(s)^{\frac{\sigma-1}{\sigma}} \, \mathrm{d}s \right)^{\frac{\sigma}{\sigma-1}} \tag{4}$$

is the consumption of good X, Z_i the consumption of the numéraire, $q_i(s)$ the consumption of variety s of good X, and N the total number (mass) of varieties. Because each variety is negligible, $\sigma > 1$ is both the elasticity of demand of any variety and the elasticity of substitution between any two varieties.

Standard utility maximization of (3) yields CES demand by residents in region i for a variety produced in location j:

$$q_{ji}(s) = \frac{p_{ji}(s)^{-\sigma}}{P_i^{1-\sigma}} \mu Y_i \tag{5}$$

[18] In the HME context, they have been developed respectively by Martin and Rogers (1995) and Ottaviano (2001a).

where p_{ji} is the consumer price of a variety produced in j and sold in i, P_i is the local CES price index associated with (4):

$$P_i = \left[\int_{s \in n_i} p_{ii}(s)^{1-\sigma}\, ds + \int_{s \in n_j} p_{ji}(s)^{1-\sigma}\, ds \right]^{\frac{1}{1-\sigma}} \tag{6}$$

where n_i is both the set and the number of varieties produced in region i so that $n_A + n_B = N$. The regional income Y_i consists of capital rental rates (R_i) and wages $(w_i L_i)$:

$$Y_i = R_i + w_i L_i. \tag{7}$$

Thus, the representative consumer in region i maximizes utility (3) subject to the following budget constraint:

$$\int_{s \in n_i} p_{ii}(s) q_{ii}(s)\, ds + \int_{s \in n_j} p_{ji}(s) q_{ji}(s)\, ds + p_i^Z Z_i = Y_i. \tag{8}$$

Moreover, as already discussed, costlessly trade and perfect competition in sector Z together with the choice of numéraire imply $p_i^Z = w_i = 1$.[19] Trade in X, on the contrary, is inhibited by frictional trade barriers, which are modeled as iceberg costs à la Samuelson: for one unit of the differentiated good to reach the other region, $\tau \in (1, \infty)$ units must be shipped.

Due to the fixed input requirement f, capital market clearing implies that, in equilibrium, the number of firms is determined by $N = H/f$ with

$$n_A = \frac{\lambda H}{f}, \qquad n_B = \frac{(1-\lambda)H}{f} \tag{9}$$

so that *the number of active firms in a region is proportional to the amount of capital that is employed locally.*

Using (2), a typical firm located in region i maximizes profit:

$$\Pi_i(s) = p_{ii}(s) q_{ii}(s) + p_{ij}(s) q_{ij}(s) - m\big[q_{ii}(s) + \tau q_{ij}(s)\big] - r_i f$$

where, due to the choice of numéraire, the wage w_i is set equal to 1, while $\tau q_{ij}(s)$ represents total supply to the distant location j inclusive of the fraction of variety i that melts on the way. The first-order condition for profit maximization gives:

$$p_{ii}^*(s) = m\sigma/(\sigma - 1) \quad \text{and} \quad p_{ij}^*(s) = \tau m\sigma/(\sigma - 1) \tag{10}$$

for every i and j.[20] Using (10), the CES price index (6) simplifies to

$$P_i = \frac{m\sigma}{\sigma - 1}(n_i + \phi n_j)^{\frac{1}{1-\sigma}} \tag{11}$$

[19] Wage equalization holds as long as the homogeneous good is produced in both regions. That is the case when a single region alone cannot supply the economy-wide demand, i.e. when good Z has a large weight in utility (μ small) and product variety is highly valued by consumers (σ small). The exact condition is $\mu < (1-\theta)/(1-\theta/\sigma)$, which is assumed to hold from now on.

[20] Note the difference with Krugman: equilibrium prices depend on the cost of the mobile factor. Here, they are constant because the cost of the immobile factor is given.

where $\phi \equiv \tau^{1-\sigma} \in (0, 1)$ is a measure of the *freeness of trade*, which increases as τ falls and is equal to one when trade is costless ($\tau = 1$). Since the total number of X-firms is given by $N = H/f$, the price index (11) decreases (increases) with the number of local (distant) firms.

Due to free entry and exit, there are no profits in equilibrium. This implies that a firm's scale of production is such that operating profits exactly match the fixed cost paid in terms of capital. In other words, the equilibrium rental rate corresponding to (9) is determined by a bidding process for capital, which ends when no firm can earn a strictly positive profit at the equilibrium market prices. That is, a firm's operating profits are entirely absorbed by the cost of capital

$$r_i f = p_{ii}^*(s)q_{ii}(s) + p_{ij}^*(s)q_{ij}(s) - m\big[q_{ii}(s) + \tau q_{ij}(s)\big]$$

which, given (5), (10) and (11), yields

$$r_i = \frac{m x_i}{f(\sigma - 1)} \tag{12}$$

where $x_i = q_{ii}(s) + \tau q_{ij}(s)$ is the total production by a typical firm in location i.

Market clearing for a typical variety produced in region i implies

$$x_i^* = \frac{\sigma - 1}{m\sigma}\left(\frac{\mu Y_i}{n_i + \phi n_j} + \frac{\phi\mu Y_j}{\phi n_i + n_j}\right). \tag{13}$$

Using (9) and (13), we may rewrite the rental rate in region A as follows:

$$r_A(\lambda) = \frac{\mu}{\sigma H}\left[\frac{Y_A}{\lambda + \phi(1 - \lambda)} + \frac{\phi Y_B}{\phi\lambda + (1 - \lambda)}\right] \tag{14}$$

with a symmetric expression holding for region B.

For $\lambda \in (0, 1)$ the equilibrium distribution of firms solves $r_A(\lambda) = r_B(\lambda) = r$, which implies:

$$Y_A = \theta(rH + L), \qquad Y_B = (1 - \theta)(rH + L). \tag{15}$$

Plugging (15) into (14) and solving the two resulting equations for λ and r gives the (interior) equilibrium distribution of firms:

$$\lambda^* = \frac{1}{2} + \frac{1 + \phi}{1 - \phi}\left(\theta - \frac{1}{2}\right) > \theta > \frac{1}{2}. \tag{16}$$

This expression reveals the presence of the HME: *the larger region hosts a more than proportionate share of firms.*[21] In addition, λ^* rises continuously with ϕ so that the agglomeration process is smooth with respect to falling transport costs.

[21] Formally, this is equivalent to saying that the coefficient of θ in (16) is greater than 1, which is the condition used to test the presence of HME in empirical models [see the chapter by Keith Head and Thierry Mayer (2004) in this volume].

For ease of interpretation, (16) may be rewritten as follows:

$$(1+\phi)(\theta - 1/2) - (1-\phi)(\lambda^* - 1/2) = 0. \tag{17}$$

From left to right, the first term depends on the spatial distribution of consumers θ. Since the coefficient of $(\theta - 1/2)$ is positive, this term measures the market access advantage of the larger region in the presence of trade barriers. The second term in (17) depends on the international distribution of firms λ. Since the coefficient of $(\lambda^* - 1/2)$ is negative, that term measures the market crowding disadvantage of the region that hosts the larger number of firms. Lower trade barriers (τ) and a smaller elasticity of substitution (σ) make ϕ larger, thus strengthening the access advantage while weakening the crowding disadvantage. In particular, we have $\mathrm{d}^2\lambda^*/\mathrm{d}\theta\,\mathrm{d}\phi > 0$, which reveals the magnification of the HME by freer trade.

While enlightening, the CES set-up with iceberg costs faces some shortcomings. In particular, it yields a demand system in which the own-price elasticities of demands are constant, identical to the elasticities of substitutions and equal to each other across all varieties. This entails that the equilibrium mark-up is independent of the spatial distribution of firms and consumers. Though convenient from the analytical point of view, such a result conflicts with research in spatial price theory where it is shown that demand elasticity varies with distance while profits change with the level of demand and the intensity of competition [Greenhut, Norman and Hung (1987)]. Moreover, the iceberg assumption also implies that any increase in the price of the shipped good is accompanied by a proportional increase in its transport cost, which is unrealistic. All this entangles the economic meanings of the various parameters, thus leading to unclear comparative static results.

3.2.2. *A linear model with variable mark-ups: quadratic utility and linear transport costs*

To avoid some of the pitfalls of the CES and iceberg, we now consider a model that differs in the specification of preferences and transport costs. Preferences are described by the following quasi-linear quadratic utility:

$$U_i = \alpha \int_0^N q_i(s)\,\mathrm{d}s - \frac{\beta-\gamma}{2} \int_0^N [q_i(s)]^2\,\mathrm{d}s - \frac{\gamma}{2}\left[\int_0^N q_i(s)\,\mathrm{d}s\right]^2 + Z_i. \tag{18}$$

The parameters in (18) are such that $\alpha > 0$ and $\beta > \gamma > 0$. In this expression, α expresses the intensity of preferences for the differentiated product, whereas $\beta > \gamma$ means that consumers are biased toward a dispersed consumption of varieties. In particular, the quadratic utility function exhibits love for variety as long as $\beta > \gamma$. Finally, for a given value of β, the parameter γ expresses the substitutability between varieties: the higher γ, the closer substitutes the varieties. In the limit, when $\beta = \gamma$, (18) degenerates into a standard quadratic utility defined over a homogeneous product.

Standard utility maximization under (8) yields linear demands by residents in region i for a variety produced in location j:

$$q_{ji}(s) = [a - (b + cN)p_{ji}(s) + cP_i]^+ \tag{19}$$

where $[g]^+$ denotes the positive part of g, p_{ji} the consumer price of a variety produced in j and sold in i,

$$P_i \equiv n_i p_{ii} + n_j p_{ji}$$

and

$$a \equiv \frac{\alpha}{\beta + (N-1)\gamma}, \qquad b \equiv \frac{1}{\beta + (N-1)\gamma}, \qquad c \equiv \frac{\delta}{(\beta - \gamma)[\beta + (N-1)\gamma]}.$$

Clearly, P_i/N can be interpreted as the price index prevailing in region i. Thus, (19) encapsulates the idea that the demand of a certain variety falls when its own price rises not only in absolute terms (*own price effect*) but also relatively to the average price (*differential price effect*), which seems to be the essence of monopolistic competition.

On the supply side, the only difference with respect to the foregoing is that transport costs are not of the iceberg type. Specifically, the varieties of the modern sector are traded at a cost of $t > 0$ units of the numéraire per unit shipped between the two regions. Accordingly, a representative firm in i maximizes its profits, which, after using (19), are defined by

$$\Pi_i(s) = [p_{ii}(s) - m][a - (b + cN)p_{ii}(s) + cP_i]M_i$$
$$+ [p_{ij}(s) - m - t][a - (b + cN)p_{ij}(s) + cP_j]M_j - r_i f \tag{20}$$

where

$$M_A = \theta(L + H), \qquad M_B = (1 - \theta)(L + H)$$

are the numbers of consumers in regions A and B, respectively.

Market prices are obtained by maximizing profits while the rental rates of capital are determined as described above by equating the resulting profits to zero. Since we have a continuum of firms, each one is negligible in the sense that its action has no impact on the market. Hence, when choosing its prices, a firm in A accurately neglects the impact of its decision over the two price indices P_A and P_B. In addition, because firms sell differentiated varieties, each one has some monopoly power in that it faces a demand function with finite and variable elasticity. On the other hand, since the price index enters the demand function (see (19)), a firm must account for the distribution of the firms' prices through some aggregate statistics, given here by the average market price, in order to find its equilibrium price. As a consequence, the market solution is given by a Nash equilibrium in which each firm neglects its impact on the market but is aware that the market as a whole has a nonnegligible impact on its behavior.

Solving the first-order conditions for profit maximization yields the equilibrium prices:

$$p_{ii}^* = \frac{1}{2}\frac{2[a + (b + cN)m] + n_j ct}{2b + cN} = \frac{P_i}{N} - \frac{t}{2}\frac{n_j}{N} \tag{21}$$

$$p_{ij}^* = p_{jj}^* + \frac{t}{2} = \frac{P_j}{N} + \frac{t}{2}\frac{n_i}{N} \tag{22}$$

which depend on the total number of active firms as well as on their distribution between the two regions. Due to trade barriers, in both regions domestic firms price below the average prices, P_A/N and P_B/N, the more so the larger the relative number of foreign competitors; foreign firms price above average prices, the more so the larger the number of domestic competitors.

Substracting m and t from (22), we see that firms' prices net of transport costs are positive regardless of their spatial distribution if and only if

$$t < t_{\text{trade}} \equiv \frac{2(a - bm)}{2b + cN}. \tag{23}$$

The same condition must hold for consumers in B (A) to buy from firms in A (B), i.e. for the demand (19) evaluated at the equilibrium prices (21) and (22) to be positive for all λ. From now on, condition (23) is assumed to hold.

Using (23), we observe that more firms in the economy lead to lower market prices for the same spatial distribution $(\lambda, 1 - \lambda)$ because there is more competition in each local market. Similarly, both the prices charged by local and foreign firms fall when the mass of local firms increases because competition is fiercer. Equilibrium prices also rise when the degree of product differentiation, inversely measured by c, increases provided that (23) holds.

The rental rate of capital prevailing in region A can be obtained by evaluating (20) at equilibrium prices, which yields the following quadratic expression in λ:

$$r_A(\lambda) = \frac{b + cN}{f}\big[(p_{AA}^* - m)^2\theta + (p_{AB}^* - m - t)^2(1 - \theta)\big](L + H) \tag{24}$$

with a symmetric expression holding in region B.

Again, for $\lambda \in (0, 1)$ the equilibrium distribution of firms solves $r_A(\lambda) = r_B(\lambda)$ so that, by (21), (22), and (24), it equals

$$\lambda^* = \frac{1}{2} + \frac{2f(2a - 2bm - bt)}{ctH}\left(\theta - \frac{1}{2}\right) > \theta > \frac{1}{2} \tag{25}$$

when (23) is satisfied, thus revealing the presence of the HME.[22] To gain insight about this result, we rewrite (25) as follows:

$$2(2a - 2bm - bt)(\theta - 1/2) - ctN(\lambda^* - 1/2) = 0$$

[22] Note that the coefficient of θ in (25) is also larger than 1.

which shows that in equilibrium the distribution of firms is again determined by the interaction of two terms. As before, since the coefficient of $(\theta - 1/2)$ is positive in so far as (23) holds, the first term measures the market access advantage of the larger region, whereas the second term measures the market crowding disadvantage of the region that hosts a larger number of firms.

The quasi-linear quadratic set-up allows for clearer comparative statics results showing that the importance of the access advantage with respect to the crowding disadvantage grows as the own (b) and differential (c) price effects fall. In addition, more product differentiation (a smaller c) decreases the weight of market crowding. In the limit case of monopoly ($c = 0$), only market access considerations matter since a firm's operating profits are independent from other firms' locations [as in the single firm case considered by Sakashita (1967)]. The relevance of market crowding also falls as the level of fixed costs grows, that is, as the number of competing firms N decreases. Finally, transport costs t affect both market access and crowding. In particular, lower t strengthens the former and weakens the latter. The reason why is that, with lower transport costs, a larger fraction of a firm's operating profits is independent of the location of competitors. In particular, we have $\mathrm{d}^2\lambda^*/\mathrm{d}\theta\,\mathrm{d}t < 0$, which again shows the magnification of the HME by freer trade.

The results of Section 3.2 may be summarized as follows.

PROPOSITION 3 (The home market effect). *Consider an economy with two regions and two sectors. If the two regions differ only in terms of their expenditures on the modern good, then the market equilibrium involves a more than proportionate share of the modern sector in the region with larger expenditures.*

Accordingly, small permanent shocks to relative demands give rise to large permanent differences in regional sectoral specialization. This property cannot be readily extended to multi-regional set-ups. The three-region model in Krugman (1993) can be used to argue that the HME has no straightforward definition because there is no obvious benchmark against which to measure the 'more than proportionate' presence of imperfectly competitive firms. However, because the HME extends the idea of a dominant place in the Weber problem, existing results in location theory [Beckmann and Thisse (1986)] and 'classical' economic geography [Thomas (2002)] suggest, in the multiregional case, the existence of a hierarchy of regional markets, which depends on both the *size* of these markets but also their *relative position* within the space-economy.[23] Extensions along these lines would be a worthy contribution to the state of the art.

[23] When intraregional costs are taken into account, it is reasonable to assume that the larger (and richer) region has better infrastructures than the other. This amplifies the HME because higher intraregional costs amount to reducing the size of the local market [Martin and Rogers (1995)].

4. The core–periphery structure

The models discussed in the foregoing section reveal that imperfect competition and increasing returns can exacerbate exogenous differences in market size. More precisely, we have shown that small permanent shocks can give rise to large permanent differences between regions. In the present section, we discuss a framework, namely the core–periphery (CP) model originally due to Krugman (1991), which allows even small temporary shocks to cause large permanent differences between regions. The key-difference with the models of Section 3 is that now the mobile factor – skilled labor – spends its income where it is used, whereas profits were repatriated in the foregoing section.

Because changes in the spatial patterns happen when trade barriers are low, the proposed framework sheds light on the spatial aspects of the industrialization process, which may be collapsed in the following two steps described by Pollard (1981).[24] First, the symmetric pattern provides a fairly good approximation of the early configurations prevailing in Europe before the Industrial Revolution:

> "Before the industrial revolution, the gaps between different parts of Europe were much smaller than were to become later and some industrial activity not unlike that in Inner Europe was to be found almost everywhere." (p. 201)

Second, the formation of a core–periphery pattern seems to be a fair description of the way industrialization developed across regions:

> "the industrial regions took from them [their agricultural neighbors] some of their most active and adaptable labor and they encouraged them to specialize in the supply of agricultural produce, sometimes at the expense of some pre-existing industry running the risk thereby that this specialization would permanently divert the colonized areas from becoming industrial themselves." (p. 11)

4.1. The labor mobility framework

The setting departs from the one of the previous section under one major respect: H is not physical capital anymore but rather human capital that is embodied in workers. The crucial implication is that, differently from the foregoing, *a capital-owner can now offer her services only in the region where she resides*. Accordingly, H and L represent two types of workers that we call skilled and unskilled (*labor dualism*). The two types of workers differ in terms of their geographical mobility: the skilled workers are mobile between regions, whereas the unskilled workers are immobile.[25] Moreover, the unskilled workers are equally distributed between the two regions because we want regions to be a priori symmetric.

[24] The work of Tirado, Paluzie and Pons (2002) about the impact on industrial location of economic integration in 19th century Spain also seems to provide a good illustration of the previsions made by CP models.

[25] This extreme assumption is justified because the skilled are more mobile than the unskilled over long distances [SOPEMI (1998)].

The market equilibrium is again the outcome of the interplay between a market crowding effect and a market access effect. However, differently from the HME setup, the mobility of workers affects both the supply and demand sides of the region of destination (and not just the supply side), thus making the size of the local market endogenous. The reason is that firms' relocation has to be matched by skilled migration so that the two may reinforce each other. This in turn induces some skilled living in the other region to move toward the region with more firms in which they may enjoy a higher standard of living. The resulting increase in the numbers of consumers creates a larger demand for the differentiated good which, therefore, leads additional firms to locate in this region. This implies the availability of more varieties in the region in question but less in the other because of scale economies at the firm's level. Consequently, as noticed by Krugman (1991, p. 486), there is *cumulative causation* à la Myrdal because these two effects reinforce each other: "manufactures production will tend to concentrate where there is a large market, but the market will be large where manufactures production is concentrated".[26]

Formally, (9) implies that λ now measures both the fraction of firms and the fraction of skilled workers in region A. Then, denoting by $v_i(\lambda)$ the indirect utility a skilled worker enjoys in region i, a *spatial equilibrium* arises at $\lambda \in (0, 1)$ when

$$\Delta v(\lambda) \equiv v_A(\lambda) - v_B(\lambda) = 0$$

or at $\lambda = 0$ when $\Delta v(0) \leqslant 0$, or at $\lambda = 1$ when $\Delta v(1) \geqslant 0$. Such an equilibrium always exists when $v_r(\lambda)$ is a continuous function of λ [Ginsburgh, Papageorgiou and Thisse (1985)]. However, this equilibrium is not necessarily unique.

Stability is then used as a refinement to eliminate some of the equilibria. To this end, scholars have followed a well-established tradition in migration modeling by assuming that workers are attracted (respectively repelled) by regions having a utility higher (respectively lower) than the average utility. In so doing, they have also assumed that the power of attraction of a region increases with its size because larger size makes a region more "visible" to migrants. Formally, this has led to the adoption of the following *replicator*:

$$\frac{\mathrm{d}\lambda}{\mathrm{d}t} = \lambda[V_H - \lambda V_H - (1 - \lambda)V_F] = \lambda \Delta v(\lambda)(1 - \lambda). \tag{26}$$

A spatial equilibrium is (locally) *stable* if, for any marginal deviation of the population distribution from the equilibrium, the equation of motion above brings the distribution of skilled workers back to the original one. When some skilled workers move from one region to the other, we assume that local labor markets adjust instantaneously. More precisely, the number of firms in each region must be such that the labor market clearing conditions (9) remain valid for the new distribution of workers. Wages are then adjusted for each firm to earn zero profits.

[26] Observe that similar processes have been studied in spatial competition theory [Stahl (1987), Fujita and Thisse (2002, Chapter 7)].

4.1.1. CES utility and iceberg transport costs

In Krugman (1991), utility is given by (3). The corresponding indirect utility differential is

$$\Delta v(\lambda,\phi) \equiv \mu^{\mu}(1-\mu)^{1-\mu}\left\{\frac{w_A(\lambda,\phi)}{[P_A(\lambda,\phi)]^{\mu}} - \frac{w_B(\lambda,\phi)}{[P_B(\lambda,\phi)]^{\mu}}\right\} \tag{27}$$

where $w_i(\lambda,\phi)$ is the wage prevailing in region $i = A, B$.[27] Substituting (9) into (11), the price index in region A is as follows:

$$P_A(\lambda,\phi) = \frac{m\sigma}{\sigma-1}[\lambda+\phi(1-\lambda)]^{\frac{1}{1-\sigma}}\left(\frac{H}{f}\right)^{\frac{1}{1-\sigma}} \tag{28}$$

with a symmetric expression holding for P_B. The presence of P_A and P_B in (27) adds a *new* item to the list of location effects. In particular, (28) shows that, for a given wage, the region with more skilled workers, and thus more manufacturing firms, grants higher purchasing power, that is, higher consumer surplus. The reason is its lower price index as the larger number of domestic firms implies that fewer manufacturing varieties are imported and burdened by transport costs (*cost-of-living effect*). Therefore, *this additional effect teams up with the market size effect to support the agglomeration of manufactures against the market crowding effect.*

For the determination of skilled wages w_A and w_B, notice that the definition of incomes has changed to:

$$Y_A(\lambda,\phi) = \frac{L}{2} + w_A(\lambda,\phi)\lambda H, \qquad Y_B(\lambda,\phi) = \frac{L}{2} + w_B(\lambda,\phi)(1-\lambda)H. \tag{29}$$

Plugging (29) into (14) and (15) and solving the two resulting equations together for w_A and w_B gives the equilibrium skilled wages:

$$w_i^* = \frac{\mu/\sigma}{1-\mu/\sigma}\frac{L}{2}\frac{2\phi n_i + [1-\mu/\sigma+(1+\mu/\sigma)\phi^2]n_j}{\phi(n_i^2+n_j^2)+[1-\mu/\sigma+(1+\mu/\sigma)\phi^2]n_i n_j} \tag{30}$$

[27] In Krugman (1991) skilled labor is used for both the fixed and variable costs of good X. For expositional purposes, we present here the analytically solvable version of his model put forth by Forslid and Ottaviano (2003), where only the fixed cost is incurred in terms of skilled labor whereas the variable cost is paid in terms of unskilled labor. Although the modified version and the original model exhibit the same qualitative behavior, there are some quantitative differences. The break and sustain points are larger while the no-black-hole condition is less stringent in the former than in the latter. In particular, to pass from the modified version to the original model, one has to multiply μ by σ wherever it appears [see Fujita, Krugman and Venables (1999)]. All together these properties imply that agglomeration forces are weaker in the modified version. The reason is weaker demand linkages: in Krugman (1991), the expenditures of a skilled worker are equal to the total revenues of the corresponding firm, in Forslid and Ottaviano (2003) they are equal to its operating profits only, which are indeed a fraction $1/\sigma$ of firm revenues.

$$\Delta v_{\lambda\lambda}(1/2, \phi_b) = 0, \qquad \Delta v_{\lambda\lambda\lambda}(1/2, \phi_b) > 0. \tag{36}$$

Because $\lambda = 1/2$ is always an equilibrium, $\Delta V(\lambda, \phi)$ rotates around $(\lambda, \Delta V) = (1/2, 0)$ as ϕ changes. Hence, (35) says that the steady state $\lambda = 1/2$ turns from stable to unstable as soon as ϕ grows above ϕ_b. Likewise, (36) says that, when the equilibrium $\lambda = 1/2$ changes stability, two additional equilibria emerge. Due to the symmetry of the model these equilibria are symmetric. All these properties together say that the differential equation (26) undergoes a (local) pitchfork bifurcation at $\phi = \phi_b$. Moreover, the global extension of $\Delta v_{\lambda\lambda\lambda}(1/2, \phi_b) > 0$ implies that $\phi_b > \phi_s$.

The fact that transport costs at the break point are lower than at the sustain point implies that the model displays 'hysteresis' in location: once the CP equilibrium is reached, transport costs may rise above the break point before agglomeration ceases to be an equilibrium.

4.1.2. *Quadratic utility and linear transport costs*

The fact that (33) involves noninteger power variables makes the CP model not amenable to an analytical solution.[30] By contrast, Ottaviano, Tabuchi and Thisse (2002), who use the quasi-linear quadratic form (18) together with linear transport costs, have been able to obtain such a solution.[31] The indirect utility of a skilled worker is now given by

$$v_i = S_i + w_i + Z_i, \quad i = A, B$$

where

$$S_i = \frac{a^2 N}{2b} - a\int_0^N p_i(s)\,\mathrm{d}s + \frac{b + cN}{2}\int_0^N [p_i(s)]^2\,\mathrm{d}s - \frac{c}{2}\left[\int_0^N p_i(s)\,\mathrm{d}s\right]^2$$

is the consumer surplus and w_i the skilled wage.

The skilled wage prevailing in region A can be obtained by evaluating (20) at equilibrium prices, while taking into account that the numbers of consumers in the two regions are as follows:

$$M_A = \frac{L}{2} + \lambda H, \qquad M_B = \frac{L}{2} + (1 - \lambda)H$$

which yields the following expression:

$$w_A^*(\lambda, t) = \frac{b + cN}{f}\left[(p_{AA} - m)^2\left(\frac{L}{2} + \lambda H\right) + (p_{AB} - m - t)^2\left(\frac{L}{2} + (1 - \lambda)H\right)\right] \tag{37}$$

[30] Pflüger (2004) shows that using a quasi-linear, instead of a Cobb–Douglas, upper-tier utility allows for an analytical solution of the CP model described in the foregoing section. In addition, he proves that the nature of the bifurcation changes: the agglomeration process is gradual as trade costs fall.

[31] See Ludema and Wooton (2000) for a model of economic geography with $\beta = \gamma$ and quantity-setting firms.

with a symmetric expression holding in region B.

Using the equilibrium prices (21)–(22) as well as (37), the indirect utility differential is then

$$\Delta v(\lambda, t) \equiv S_A(\lambda, t) - S_B(\lambda, t) + w_A(\lambda, t) - w_B(\lambda, t)$$
$$= Dt(t^* - t) \cdot (\lambda - 1/2) \tag{38}$$

where $D > 0$ is a bundle of parameters independent of t and

$$t^* = \frac{4f(a - bm)(3bf + 2cH)}{2bf(3bf + 3cH + cL) + c^2H(H + L)} > 0.$$

It follows immediately from (38) that $\lambda = 1/2$ is always an equilibrium. Since $D > 0$, for $\lambda \neq 1/2$ the indirect utility differential has always the same sign as $\lambda - 1/2$ if and only if $t < t^*$; otherwise it has the opposite sign. When $t < t^*$, the symmetric equilibrium is unstable and workers agglomerate in region A (B) provided that the initial fraction of workers residing in this region exceeds $1/2$. In other words, agglomeration arises when transport costs are low enough, as in the foregoing and for similar reasons. In contrast, for large transport costs, that is, when $t > t^*$, it is straightforward to see that the symmetric configuration is the only stable equilibrium. Hence, the threshold t^* corresponds to both the critical value of t at which symmetry ceases to be stable (break point) and the value below which agglomeration is stable (sustain point); this follows from the fact that (38) is linear in λ.

When increasing returns are stronger, as expressed by higher values of f, t^* rises since $\mathrm{d}t^*/\mathrm{d}f > 0$. This means that *the agglomeration of the manufacturing sector is more likely, the stronger are the increasing returns at the firm's level.* In addition, t^* increases with product differentiation since $\mathrm{d}t^*/\mathrm{d}\gamma < 0$. In words, *more product differentiation fosters agglomeration.*

It is readily verified that t^* is lower than t_{trade} when the population of unskilled is large relative to the population of skilled. Although the size of the industrial sector is captured here through the relative population size of L/H and not through its share in consumption, the intuition is similar: the ratio L/H must be sufficiently large for the economy to display different types of equilibria according to the value of t, otherwise the coefficient of $(\lambda - 1/2)$ in (38) is always positive and agglomeration always prevails. Our condition does not depend on the expenditure share on the manufacturing sector because of the absence of general equilibrium income effects: small or large sectors in terms of expenditure share may either be agglomerated when t is small enough.

The quadratic set-up allows us to derive analytically the results obtained by Krugman (1991). Nonetheless it should not be viewed as substitute but rather as complement to the CES set-up. While both models are not general, each has its own comparative advantage and should be used accordingly.

The results of Section 4.1 may be summarized as follows.

PROPOSITION 4 (Core–periphery with labor migration). *Consider an economy with two regions and two sectors. The traditional sector employs only geographically immo-*

bile unskilled workers who are evenly distributed between regions. The modern sector employs also mobile skilled workers. Then, for low enough transport costs, the only stable equilibrium has the whole modern sector agglomerated within the same region.

In other words, for sufficiently low transport costs, even a small transitory shock to initially symmetric regions can give rise to large permanent regional imbalances. The different result with respect to Proposition 3 is due to the fact that some workers are now allowed to move whereas they all stay put in the setting considered in Section 3. Individuals' mobility makes market sizes endogenous, thus allowing for the emergence of cumulative causationl. When transport costs are low, the attraction of mobile consumers towards the larger market makes it even larger: as consumers relocate, its market access advantage grows whereas its market crowding disadvantage falls. Eventually, this leads to the agglomeration of all firms in one region. By contrast, when transport costs are high, the opposite holds in that market crowding now dominates market access, thus fostering the dispersion of firms.

Such result concurs with Proposition 2 in which either sufficiently low transport costs, or a sufficiently high degree of product differentiation, or both are needed for a cluster of firms to arise in an oligopoly involving dispersed consumers. The fact that agglomeration arises when transport costs are low also confirms what has been shown in spatial oligopoly theory. Therefore, it is tempting to answer Neary (2001, p. 551) that models of monopolistic competition seem to provide a reasonable approximation of what could be obtained in the (still missing) general equilibrium model with strategic interactions.[32]

4.2. *The vertical linkage framework*

In the foregoing, agglomeration arose because of the endogeneity of local market sizes due to mobile consumers. When labor is immobile across regions but perfectly mobile between sectors, the cumulative causation falls short and the symmetric equilibrium is the only stable outcome [Puga (1999)]. Another reason for the market size to be endogenous is *the presence of input–output linkages between firms*: what is output for a firm is input for another and vice versa (the 'ancillarity' industries). In this case, the entry of a new firm in a region not only increases the intensity of competition between similar firms (market crowding effect); it also increases the size of the market

[32] Throughout this section, workers care only about their current utility level when choosing a location. This is a very restrictive assumption because migration decisions are typically made on the grounds of current *and* future utility flows as well as of various costs due to search, mismatch and homesickness. It is, therefore, important to figure out how the interplay between history and expectations shapes the space-economy when workers maximize the intertemporal value of their utility flows. Somewhat different approaches have been proposed to tackle this problem, but they yield similar conclusions [Ottaviano (1999, 2001b), Baldwin (2001), Ottaviano, Tabuchi and Thisse (2002)]: when the initial distribution of economic activities is not too skewed and when transport costs take intermediate values, the common belief that the skilled will eventually agglomerate in the smaller region can reverse the historically inherited advantage of the larger region. Hence, psychological forces may overcome the historical advantage of a region.

of upstream firms-suppliers (market size effect) and decreases the costs of downstream firms-customers (*cost effect*).

The easiest way to introduce the above considerations is to model input–output linkages within the same industry.[33] Specifically, consider the model of Section 4.1.1, but with two fundamental modifications.[34] First, there is only one factor of production, labor say, which is constant and in equal supply in the two regions:

$$L_i^Z + L_i^X = L/2$$

where L_i^Z and L_i^X are region i employments in sectors Z and X, respectively. Labor can freely relocate between sectors within the same region but it is spatially immobile. As in the foregoing, this factor is used in both sectors to fulfill the variable input requirement. Again, when trade in the homogeneous good is costless, we have $w_i = p_i^Z = 1$ as long as each region is not specialized in sector X, a condition that we assume to hold throughout this section. Second, *the fixed cost of manufacturing are incurred in a composite input consisting of labor and the differentiated varieties of good X*. For simplicity, as in Krugman and Venables (1995), the composite input is assumed to be Cobb–Douglas in L_i^X and Q_i with shares $1-\mu$ and μ, respectively.[35] Accordingly, the total cost function for a typical manufacturing firm is now given by – contrast with (2):

$$TC_i(s) = P_i^{\mu} w_i^{1-\mu} f + w_i m x_i(s)$$

where P_i is given by (11).

A typical firm located in region i maximizes profit:

$$\Pi_i(s) = p_{ii}(s)q_{ii}(s) + p_{ij}(s)q_{ij}(s) - m[q_{ii}(s) + tq_{ij}(s)] - P_i^{\mu} f \tag{39}$$

where we have again set $w_i = 1$. As a result, optimal pricing is still given by (10), which allows us to rewrite (39) as

$$\Pi_i = \frac{m}{\sigma - 1} x_i - P_i^{\mu} f. \tag{40}$$

Intermediate demand implies that expenditures on manufactures now stem not only from consumers but also from firms:

$$\mu E_i = \mu Y_i + \mu n_i P_i^{\mu} f \tag{41}$$

where Y_i is consumers' income inclusive of firms' profits Π_i:

$$Y_i = \frac{L}{2} + n_i \Pi_i = \frac{L}{2} + n_i \left(\frac{m}{\sigma - 1} x_i - P_i^{\mu} f \right) \tag{42}$$

[33] In the original version of this model, Venables (1996) has an upstream and a downstream sectors. For simplicity, Krugman and Venables (1995) choose to collapse the two sectors into a single one. Here we present an analytically solvable version of Krugman and Venables (1995) due to Ottaviano (2002).

[34] See Ottaviano and Thisse (2001) for a treatment of the linear model with vertical linkages.

[35] This means that each firm consumes each and every variety as an input. Such an extreme assumption may be qualified when the CES is reinterpreted as a two-stage discrete choice model in which a single variety is chosen in the first stage and its quantity in the second [see Anderson, de Palma and Thisse (1992, Chapter 3)].

where the second equality is granted by (40). Then

$$\mu E_i = \mu\left(\frac{L}{2} + \frac{m}{\sigma - 1} n_i x_i\right).$$

Recalling (13), the X-sector market clearing condition becomes

$$x_i = \frac{\sigma - 1}{m\sigma}\left(\frac{\mu E_i}{n_i + \phi n_j} + \frac{\phi \mu E_j}{\phi n_i + n_j}\right) \tag{43}$$

which, by (41) and (42), can be rewritten as follows:

$$x_i = \frac{\sigma - 1}{m\sigma}\left\{\frac{\mu[L/2 + n_i x_i m/(\sigma - 1)]}{n_i + \phi n_j} + \frac{\phi\mu[L/2 + n_j x_j m/(\sigma - 1)]}{\phi n_i + n_j}\right\}. \tag{44}$$

For $i = A, B$, (44) generates a system of linear equations that can be solved to obtain x_A and x_B as explicit functions of the numbers of active firms n_A and n_B. Standard derivations yield

$$x_i = \frac{\sigma - 1}{m}\frac{\mu}{\sigma - \mu}\frac{L}{2}\frac{2\phi n_i + [1 - \mu/\sigma + (1 + \mu/\sigma)\phi^2]n_j}{\phi(n_i^2 + n_j^2) + [1 - \mu/\sigma + (1 + \mu/\sigma)\phi^2]n_i n_j} \tag{45}$$

which is the same as in 3.2.1

We are now ready to analyze the entry decision of firms in the two regions. As before, we assume that agents are short sighted: firms enter when current profits are positive and exit when they are negative. Specifically, their flow is regulated by the following simple adjustment:

$$\frac{\mathrm{d}n_i}{\mathrm{d}t} = \begin{cases} \Pi_i(n_i, n_j, \phi) & \text{if } n_i > 0 \\ \max\{0, \Pi_i(n_i, n_j, \phi)\} & \text{if } n_i = 0 \end{cases} \tag{46}$$

where, by (40) and (45),

$$\Pi_i(n_i, n_j, \phi) = \frac{\mu/\sigma}{1 - \mu/\sigma}\frac{L}{2}\frac{2\phi n_i + [1 - \mu/\sigma + (1 + \mu/\sigma)\phi^2]n_j}{\phi(n_i^2 + n_j^2) + [1 - \mu/\sigma + (1 + \mu/\sigma)\phi^2]n_i n_j} - \left(\frac{m\sigma}{\sigma - 1}\right)^{\mu}(n_i + \phi n_j)^{\frac{\mu}{1-\sigma}} f.$$

Unlike the CP model, *the vertical linkage model cannot be reduced to a unique differential equation* because the total number of firms is variable.

Given (46), a spatial equilibrium arises at (n_A^*, n_B^*), with both $n_A^*, n_B^* > 0$, when $\Pi_i(n_i^*, n_j^*, \phi) = 0$ for $i = A, B$. It may also arise at $(n_A^*, n_B^*) = (n_A^0, 0)$, with $n_A^0 > 0$, when $\Pi_A(n_A^0, 0, \phi) = 0$ and $\Pi_B(n_A^0, 0, \phi) < 0$; similar conditions define agglomeration in B. As in the CP model, equilibria may be multiple and stability is used to dismiss some of them.

Consider first an agglomerated configuration with all active firms in, say, region A: $n_A = n_A^0$ and $n_B = 0$. This is a stable equilibrium for (46) if and only if

$$\Pi_A\left(n_A^0, 0, \phi\right) = 0 \tag{47}$$

so that no firm in A is willing to enter or exit, and

$$\Pi_B\left(n_A^0, 0, \phi\right) < 0 \tag{48}$$

so that no firm is willing to start production in B. It is readily verified that (47) is satisfied if and only if n_A^0 is such that

$$n_A^0 = \left[\frac{\mu/\sigma}{1-\mu/\sigma}\frac{L}{f}\left(\frac{\sigma-1}{m\sigma}\right)^{\mu}\right]^{\frac{1}{1+\frac{\mu}{1-\sigma}}}. \tag{49}$$

Moreover, (48) is met if and only if

$$\frac{[1-\mu/\sigma + (1+\mu/\sigma)\phi^2]}{2\phi^{1+\frac{\mu}{1-\sigma}}} - 1 < 0$$

which implies that the condition for agglomeration to be a stable equilibrium in the present model is the same as in the CP model: ϕ must be larger than the sustain point ϕ_s as defined by (34).

Turning to interior equilibria, standard but tedious analysis reveals that the loci $\Pi_A(n_A, n_B, \phi) = 0$ and $\Pi_B(n_A, n_B, \phi) = 0$ always cross at least once and no more than thrice. In particular, they always cross at the symmetric outcome in which n_A and n_B are both equal to

$$n^* = 2^{-\frac{1-\sigma}{1-\sigma+\mu}}(1+\phi)^{-\frac{\mu}{1-\sigma+\mu}} n_A^0 \tag{50}$$

where n_A^0 is given by (49) and independent of ϕ. As a result, while the number of active firms with agglomeration is invariant to trade barriers, the number of those active in the symmetric equilibrium is not.

The symmetric equilibrium is stable as long as the two eigenvalues of the Jacobian of (46) are negative at $n_A = n_B = n^*$. Taking into account the fact that the total output $n_A x_A + n_B x_B = [(\sigma-1)\mu L]/[(\sigma-\mu)m]$ is independent of the numbers of firms n_i gives a first eigenvalue $\partial\Pi_A/\partial n_A + \partial\Pi_B/\partial n_A$, which is always negative. As to the second eigenvalue $\partial\Pi_A/\partial n_A - \partial\Pi_B/\partial n_A$, its sign is negative (respectively positive) whenever $\phi <$ (respectively $>$) ϕ_b. Thus, in the vertical-linkage model we have not only the same sustain point (ϕ_s) and the same break point (ϕ_b) but also the same no-black-hole condition ($\mu < \sigma - 1$) as in the CP model.

Finally, under the no-black-hole condition, (50) reveals that n^* is an increasing function of ϕ. The freer trade is, the larger the number of active firms: trade integration fragments the market. Moreover, under symmetry the number of active firms in each region is larger than the total number of firms under agglomeration ($n^* > n_A^0$). Therefore, differently from the CP framework, in the vertical-linkage model, *agglomeration defragments the market and reduces product variety*.

To sum up, also with vertical linkages, small transitory shocks can have large permanent effects:

PROPOSITION 5 (Core–periphery with vertical linkages). *Consider an economy with two regions and two sectors. The traditional sector employs only geographically immobile workers who are evenly distributed between regions. The modern sector employs also intermediate inputs supplied by the industrial firms. Then, for low enough transport costs the only stable equilibrium has the whole modern sector agglomerated within the same region.*

This result differs from Krugman and Venables (1995) who obtain the following pattern as transport costs fall: dispersion–agglomeration–redispersion. This difference is due to the fact that we assume here that regions never fully specialize in the production of the differentiated good. This is not an innocuous assumption because it insures that the agglomeration of firms within a region does not trigger wage divergence between regions. *When wages increase with the number of firms setting in the core, beyond some threshold freer trade may lead to the redispersion of the modern sector because local wages are too high.* Giving a full analytical treatment of this model is a task beyond our reach and we refer the reader to Puga (1999) for what is probably the best analysis of this model and of several other generalizations, the most important of which is covered in the subsequent section.

5. The bell-shaped curve of spatial development

The NEG models surveyed in Sections 3 and 4 provide possible explanations for a certain number of stylized facts summarized in the introduction. Yet, they rest on a set of very peculiar assumptions. Moreover, the explanation of other stylized facts remains beyond their reach. In this section we consider the most important of the unexplained facts to show that NEG models can be made both less theoretically restrictive and more empirically appealing by removing some of their most peculiar assumptions.

In terms of stylized facts, there exists a strand of literature that connects the evolution of the spatial distribution of population and industry to the various stages of economic development [Williamson (1965)]. These authors argue that a high degree of urban concentration together with a widening urban–rural wage differential is expected to arise during the early phases of economic growth. As development proceeds, spatial deconcentration and a narrowing wage differential should occur. Hence, *the emergence of a core–periphery structure would be followed by a phase involving interregional convergence.*

Such a bell-shaped relation between the degree of spatial concentration of economic activities and the degree of goods and factors mobility (the so-called 'bell-shaped curve of spatial development') does not arise in either the HME nor the CP models presented so far. Here we survey some recent contributions that overcome that limitation. For ease of exposition, we name the traditional (respectively modern) sector 'agriculture' (respectively 'industry') as in Krugman (1991).

5.1. More on spatial costs

A first somewhat awkward assumption of the models of Sections 3 and 4 is that the transport cost of one good is taken into account whereas the transport cost of the other is neglected. There is no evidence that shipping a differentiated good costs much more than shipping a homogeneous good [Rauch (1999)]. The role of the traditional sector is very modest in the HME and CP models: it permits trade imbalances in the industrial good. A second unsatisfactory assumption is that the agglomeration of workers into a single region does not involve any agglomeration costs. Yet, it is reasonable to believe that a growing settlement in a given region will often take the form of an urban area, typically a city in which land becomes a critical commodity. In what follows we remove these assumptions and show that a bell-shaped curve of spatial development may indeed emerge. Interestingly, what is crucial for the spatial organization of the economy is *the value of the transport cost relative to the additional spatial cost taken into consideration*. Specifically, agglomeration forces are strongest when the cost of shipping the industrial good takes intermediate values.

Surprisingly enough, dealing with transport costs in the case of two sectors does not appear to be a simple task. In the model proposed by Krugman (1980), which is very similar to the one considered in Section 3.2.1, Davis (1998) shows that *the HME vanishes when both the industrial and the agricultural goods are shipped at the same cost*. The intuition is fairly straightforward. Suppose that both regions produce their own requirements of the agricultural good, so that industry is distributed according to region size. If some firms are relocated into the large region, then trade in the industrial good falls whereas trade in the agricultural good rises. Transport costs being the same for the two goods, one expects total transport costs in the economy to rise, thus implying that the shifted firms find the move unprofitable.

The issue is more involved in CP models. To our knowledge, the first analytical solution has been provided by Picard and Zeng (2003) who use the linear model of Section 4.1.2. They assume that the agricultural good is differentiated and that region $i = A, B$ is specialized in the production of variety i.[36] Preferences are quadratic and given by

$$U_i^a = U_i + \alpha_a\left(q_A^a + q_B^a\right) - \frac{\beta_a - \gamma_a}{2}\left[\left(q_A^a\right)^2 + \left(q_B^a\right)^2\right] - \frac{\gamma_a}{2}\left(q_A^a + q_B^a\right)^2$$

where U_i is given by (18) and q_i^a the quantity of variety i of the agricultural good. As usual, the first-order conditions yields the demands for this good in region A as follows:

$$q_{ji}^a = a_a - (b_a + 2c_a)p_{ji}^a + c_a\left(p_{ii}^a + p_{ji}^a\right)$$

[36] When the agricultural good is homogenous, dispersion always prevails as soon as τ_a is positive [Picard and Zeng (2003)]. See also Fujita, Krugman and Venables (1999, Chapter 7).

where

$$a_a \equiv \frac{\alpha_a}{\beta_a + \gamma_a}, \qquad b_a \equiv \frac{1}{\beta_a + \gamma_a}, \qquad c_a \equiv \frac{\rho_a}{(\beta_a - \gamma_a)(\beta_a + \gamma_a)}.$$

Shipping one unit of each variety of the agricultural good requires $t_a > 0$ units of the numéraire. Picard and Zeng (2003) then show that the utility differential (38) becomes

$$\Delta v(\lambda, t, t_a) = U_A^a - U_B^a = \left[Dt(t^* - t) + Gt_a^2\right] \cdot (\lambda - 1/2)$$

where $G > 0$ is a bundle of parameters independent of t and t_a. For any given t_a, the expression $Dt(t^* - t) + Gt_a^2$ may have one, two or no zeros. Clearly, there exists a value of t_a for which it has a single zero, which is denoted $\bar{t}_a$. When $t_a < \bar{t}_a$, the equation $Dt(t^* - t) + Gt_a^2 = 0$ has two real and distinct roots $\bar{t}_1$ and $\bar{t}_2$. Hence, it is immediate to show the following result:

PROPOSITION 6 (Shipping the agricultural good is costly). *Consider the CP model with labor migration of Section* 4.1. *If agricultural shipping costs are low, then the market equilibrium has all industrial firms located in the same region whenever their own transport costs take intermediate values; otherwise, the symmetric configuration is the only stable spatial equilibrium. By contrast, if agricultural shipping costs are large enough, dispersion always prevails.*

In the present context, economic integration has two dimensions described by the parameters t and t_a. When shipping the agricultural good is sufficiently cheap, the spatial distribution of industry is bell-shaped with respect to its own transport cost but changes in regimes remain catastrophic. It is interesting to point out that while dispersion arises for both high and low transport costs, this happens for very different reasons. In the former case, firms are dispersed due to the crowding effect on the industrial good market; in the latter, the working force is the price differential of the agricultural good. A new result also emerges: when shipping the agricultural good is expensive, industry is always dispersed. All of these agree with the simulations reported on by Fujita, Krugman and Venables (1999, Chapter 7) for a similar extension of Krugman's (1991) model and show that *the level of the agricultural good's transport costs matters for the location of industrial firms.*[37]

[37] Tabuchi (1998) and Ottaviano, Tabuchi and Thisse (2002) assume that the (main) dispersion force rests on land consumption, which rises with the size of the population established within the same region whereas firms set up in a regional employment center. Using the two models of Section 4.1, these authors show that the existence of commuting costs within each regional cluster is sufficient to yield dispersion when the transport costs are sufficiently low. Hence, as transport costs fall, the economy involves dispersion, agglomeration, and redispersion. In other words, sufficiently high commuting costs always yield dispersion. This is strikingly similar to Proposition 6, but redispersion is now triggered by the crowding of the land market. In the present context, we may assume that there is no farmers without annihilating the dispersion force. If $L = 0$, it is readily verified that the economy moves from agglomeration to dispersion when transport costs fall, thus confirming the numerical results obtained by Helpman (1998). Note also that a bell-shaped curve arises in the vertical linkage model of Krugman and Venables (1995) when unskilled labor is replaced by land.

5.2. Heterogenous workers

Another unappealing assumption of the NEG models considered in Sections 3 and 4 is that individuals have the same preferences. Although this assumption is not uncommon in economic modeling, it seems highly implausible that all potentially mobile individuals will react in the same way to a given real wage gap between regions. Some people show a high degree of attachment to the region where they were born; they will stay put even though they may guarantee to themselves higher real wage in other places. In the same spirit, life-time considerations such as marriage, divorce and the like play an important role in the decision to migrate. Finally, regions are not identical and exhibit different natural and cultural features. Typically, individuals differ in their reactions to these various factors. Although individual motivations are difficult to model, Tabuchi (1986) has argued that it is possible to identify their aggregate impact on the spatial distribution of economic activities by using discrete choice theory. Stated differently, a discrete choice model can be used to capture the matching between individuals and regions. Tabuchi and Thisse (2002) have then combined the CP model of Section 4.2 with the logit in order to asses the impact of heterogeneity in migration behavior.[38]

Let $\upsilon_r(\lambda)$ be the indirect utility obtained from consuming the industrial and agricultural goods in region r. Then, the probability that a worker will choose to reside in region r is given by the logit formula:

$$\mathbf{P}_r(\lambda) = \frac{\exp[\upsilon_r(\lambda)/\upsilon]}{\exp[\upsilon_r(\lambda)/\upsilon] + \exp[\upsilon_s(\lambda)/\upsilon]}. \tag{51}$$

In (51), υ expresses the dispersion of individual tastes: the larger υ, the more heterogenous the workers' tastes about their living place. When $\upsilon = 0$, workers are homogeneous and behave as in Section 4.1. In the present setting, it should be clear that the population of skilled workers changes according to the following equation of motion:

$$\frac{\mathrm{d}\lambda}{\mathrm{d}t} = (1-\lambda)\mathbf{P}_A(\lambda) - \lambda\mathbf{P}_B(\lambda) \tag{52}$$

where the first term in the RHS of (52) stands for the fraction of people migrating into region A, while the second term represents those leaving this region for region B. A spatial equilibrium λ^* arises when $\mathrm{d}\lambda/\mathrm{d}t = 0$. Tabuchi and Thisse (2002) show that the sign of $\partial\lambda^*/\partial t$ is identical to the sign of $Dt(t^* - t) - 4\upsilon$. It is then readily verified that $\upsilon = \upsilon^* \equiv D(t^*)^2/16$ is a zero of the discriminant of this expression. Accordingly, when $\upsilon < \upsilon^*$, the equation $Dt(t^* - t) - 4\upsilon = 0$ has two real and distinct real roots t_1^* and t_2^*. The following result then holds.

38 This assumption turns out to be empirically relevant in migration modeling [Anderson and Papageorgiou (1994)], while it is analytically convenient without affecting the qualitative nature of the main results. See also Section 2.2.3.

PROPOSITION 7 (Probabilistic migration behavior). *Consider the CP model with labor migration of Section* 4.1. *Assume that workers differ in terms of attachment to the two regions. If workers' heterogeneity is small, the market equilibrium involves full dispersion for high transport costs; when transport costs take intermediate values, the industry is partially agglomerated, with the gap between regions being a bell-shaped function of transport costs; finally, the industry is again fully dispersed once transport costs are sufficiently low. If workers' heterogeneity is large, complete dispersion always prevails.*

In other words, when $t < t_1^*$ workers are dispersed as long as $\upsilon > 0$; whereas they would be agglomerated in the standard case because $t_1^* = 0$ and $t_2^* = t^*$ for $\upsilon = 0$. When heterogeneity is positive but weak, industry displays a *smooth bell-shaped* pattern. Furthermore, full agglomeration never arises and the economy moves away from dispersion in a noncatastrophic manner. By contrast, when υ is large enough, there is always dispersion. Hence, we may then conclude that taste heterogeneity is a strong dispersion force that deeply affects the formation of the space-economy.[39] Thus, workers' heterogeneity has the same type of impact on the space-economy as positive commuting costs within each region and positive transport costs for the agricultural good. The main difference lies in the smoothness of the process. Finally, note that redispersion as motivated here may be viewed as a return to some form of "first nature" because, eventually, workers choose to reside in the region that give them the best match according to some noneconomic attributes.

6. Where do we go from here

In a world of globalization, it is tempting to foresee the 'death of distance' and, once the impediments to mobility have declined sufficiently, to wait for the predictions of the neoclassical theory of factor mobility to materialize. According to this theory, production factors respond to market disequilibrium by moving from regions in which they are abundant toward regions in which they are scarce. In the simplest model with capital and labor as the only inputs, in equilibrium the capital–labor ratio is equal across regions, thus implying that each factor receives the same return in both regions. As a consequence, there would be no reasons anymore to worry about where economic activities do take place.

Yet, such a result clashes with most regional policy debates in industrialized countries, which implicitly assume that there is 'too much' spatial concentration in economic activity. Regional planners and analysts point to the inability of the market to organize the space-economy in an efficient way and forcefully argue that public intervention is needed. At the same time, they fail to explain the nature of the market failure. This is what the spatial impossibility theorem accomplishes: once space is explicitly introduced in the neoclassical model, nontrivial market outcomes are inefficient.

[39] Similar conclusions are obtained by Murata (2003) for the Dixit–Stiglitz iceberg model.

NEG models investigate the nature of the interplay between imperfect competition, plant-level returns to scale and the associated pecuniary externalities. They show that even small transitory shocks can have large permanent effects on the economic landscape. This is consistent with the emergence of a *putty-clay economic geography* that seems to be one of the main features of modern economies: the steady fall in transport costs seems to allow for a great deal of flexibility on where particular activities can locate, but once spatial differences develop, locations tend to become quite rigid.[40] Hence *regions that were once similar may end up having very different production structures.* Nonetheless, we have also seen that such an extreme agglomeration may give rise to various forms of price differentials that can trigger a process of redispersion, or that more sophisticated migration behavior may prevent the emergence of a single core. Thus, it is fair to say that no definitive conclusion emerges, even though the case for agglomeration seems to be strong.

Several issues remain untouched or are, at the very least, poorly understood. First, someway paradoxically, NEG models have fallen short of full-fledged welfare analysis.[41] One exception can be found in Ottaviano and Thisse (2002), who provide a new welfare analysis of agglomeration. They argue that, while natural due to the many market imperfections that are present in new economic geography models, such an analysis has been seldom touched due to the limits of the standard CES approach. What they show is that the market yields agglomeration for values of the transport costs for which it is socially desirable to keep activities dispersed. In particular, while they coincide for high and low values of the transport costs, *the equilibrium and the optimum differ for a domain of intermediate values.* This opens the door to regional policy interventions grounded on both efficiency and equity considerations. More work is called for here to confirm this preliminary result.[42]

Another drawback of the NEG models is the assumption of a two-region setting borrowed from trade theory. By their very nature, such models are unable to, explain the rich and complex hierarchy that characterizes the space-economy. In addition, if they allow one to better understand *why* agglomeration occurs, those models have little to say about *where* it arises. Therefore, one major step on the research agenda is the study of a multiregional system whose aim is to understand why some regions are more successful than others. To accomplish this task, we need to account for the actual geography of these regions, something that trade theorists have put aside. Moving into this direction also requires the study of the role of nonmarket institutions, such as organized interests and the polity, in the process of spatial development. This is a hard but exciting task.[43]

[40] In this respect, the chapter by Paul Hohenberg (2004) devoted to the historical urban geography of Europe is striking.

[41] See, however, Krugman and Venables (1995) and Helpman (1998) for some numerical developments about the welfare implications of agglomeration in related models.

[42] Other recent contributions to the welfare analysis of agglomeration can be found in Baldwin et al. (2003) and Charlot et al. (2003).

[43] A first attempt in this direction is Robert-Nicoud and Sbergami (2004) who show how a political process may weaken, or even reverse, the home market effect studied in Section 3.

Another fundamental question is related to the fact that local labor markets are modeled in a very simple way in NEG: operating profits are used to pay the skilled workers.[44] In particular, these models do not help understand why unemployment persists in areas included in or adjacent to prosperous regions. Given the social importance of the issue at stake, one should investigate the possible reasons for the existence of a geography of employment that shows strong regional disparities. In addition, it is worth stressing that labor markets are probably the most regulated ones in Europe, with national institutions varying sometimes substantially across countries. Here too, we ignore what the impacts of such institutions are on the spatial organization of economic activities. Last, labor mobility between sectors should be studied in relation to the way regional prospects interfere with the training level of local workers. Clearly, more work is called for in these various directions for the NEG models to permit the design of what could be more effective regional development policies.[45]

Finally, NEG has very much relied on the development of new, but specific, models of monopolistic competition. Future progress in the field (and in others) will largely depend on the economists' ability to tame increasing returns and imperfect competition within more general models than those used so far. Building such models is a 'must' that will require much more imagination.

Acknowledgements

We thank A. Anas, K. Behrens, S. Brakman, H. Garretsen, J. Hamilton, K. Head, V. Henderson, T. Mayer, Y. Murata, M. Pflüger, E. Paluzie, P. Picard, D. Puga, F. Robert-Nicoud, T. Tabuchi, and C. Terra for helpful comments and discussions. This research was supported by the Ministère de l'éducation, de la recherche et de la formation (Communauté française de Belgique), Convention 00/05-262. Both authors are also grateful to the RTN Program of the European Commission for financial support.

References

Anas, A., Xu, R. (1999). "Congestion, land use, and job dispersion: a general equilibrium model". Journal of Urban Economics 45, 451–473.

Anderson, S.P., de Palma, A. (2000). "From local to global competition". European Economic Review 44, 423–448.

[44] Picard and Toulemonde (2004) offer an alternative, promising way to deal with some aspects of the labor market.

[45] Baldwin et al. (2003) provide a detailed survey of the various policy implications of NEG models grounded on welfare analysis. In particular, they show that many standard regional policies, which often use *ceteris paribus* arguments, may well deliver outcomes that vastly differ from those expected. By taking into account several general equilibrium effects usually neglected, these models provide a new framework to think about the design of regional policies.

Anderson, S.P., de Palma, A., Thisse, J.-F. (1992). Discrete Choice Theory of Product Differentiation. MIT Press, Cambridge, MA.

Anderson, W.P., Papageorgiou, Y.Y. (1994). "An analysis of migration streams for the Canadian regional system, 1952–1983. 1. Migration probabilities". Geographical Analysis 26, 15–36.

Baldwin, R.E. (2001). "Core–periphery model with forward-looking expectations". Regional Science and Urban Economics 31, 21–49.

Baldwin, R.E., Forslid, R., Martin, Ph., Ottaviano, G.I.P., Robert-Nicoud, F. (2003). Economic Geography and Public Policy. Princeton University Press, Princeton.

Baldwin, R.E., Martin, P. (2004). "Agglomeration and regional growth". In: Henderson, J.V., Thisse, J.-F. (Eds.), Handbook of Regional and Urban Economics, vol. 4. Elsevier, Amsterdam, pp. 2671–2712. This volume.

Beckmann, M.J., Thisse, J.-F. (1986). "The location of production activities". In: Nijkamp, P. (Ed.), Handbook of Regional and Urban Economics, vol. 1. North-Holland, Amsterdam, pp. 21–95.

Behrens, K. (2004). "Agglomeration without trade: how non-traded goods shape the space-economy". Journal of Urban Economics 55, 68–92.

Chamberlin, E.H. (1933). The Theory of Monopolistic Competition. Harvard University Press, Cambridge, MA.

Charlot S. Gaigné C. Robert-Nicoud F. Thisse J.-F. (2003). "Agglomeration and welfare: the core–periphery model in the light of Bentham, Kaldor, and Rawls". CORE Discussion Paper N° 2003/39.

d'Aspremont, C., Gabszewicz, J.J., Thisse, J.-F. (1979). "On Hotelling's "stability in competition" ". Econometrica 47, 1045–1050.

Davis, D.R. (1998). "The home market effect, trade, and industrial structure". American Economic Review 88, 1264–1276.

de Palma, A., Ginsburgh, V., Papageorgiou, Y.Y., Thisse, J.-F. (1985). "The principle of minimum differentiation holds under sufficient heterogeneity". Econometrica 53, 767–781.

Dixit, A.K., Stiglitz, J.E. (1977). "Monopolistic competition and optimum product diversity". American Economic Review 67, 297–308.

Duranton, G., Puga, D. (2004). "Micro-foundations of urban agglomeration economies". In: Henderson, J.V., Thisse, J.-F. (Eds.), Handbook of Regional and Urban Economics, vol. 4. Elsevier, Amsterdam, pp. 2063–2117. This volume.

Eaton, B.C., Lipsey, R.G. (1977). "The introduction of space into the neoclassical model of value theory". In: Artis, M., Nobay, A. (Eds.), Studies in Modern Economics. Blackwell, Oxford, pp. 59–96.

Faini, R. (1999). "Trade unions and regional development". European Economic Review 43, 457–474.

Forslid, R., Ottaviano, G.I.P. (2003). "An analytically solvable core–periphery model". Journal of Economic Geography 3, 229–240.

Fujita, M. (1988). "A monopolistic competition model of spatial agglomeration: A differentiated product approach". Regional Science and Urban Economics 18, 87–124.

Fujita, M., Krugman, P., Venables, A.J. (1999). The Spatial Economy. Cities, Regions and International Trade. MIT Press, Cambridge, MA.

Fujita, M., Thisse, J.-F. (2002). Economics of Agglomeration. Cities, Industrial Location, and Regional Growth. Cambridge University Press, Cambridge.

Gabszewicz, J.J., Thisse, J.-F. (1986). "Spatial competition and the location of firms". In: Gabszewicz, J.J., Thisse, J.-F., Fujita, M., Schweizer, U. (Eds.), Location Theory. Harwood Academic, Chur, pp. 1–71.

Gabszewicz, J.J., Thisse, J.-F. (1992). "Location". In: Aumann, R.E., Hart, S. (Eds.), Handbook of Game Theory with Economic Applications, vol. 1. North-Holland, Amsterdam, pp. 281–304.

Ginsburgh, V., Papageorgiou, Y.Y., Thisse, J.-F. (1985). "On existence and stability of spatial equilibria and steady-states". Regional Science and Urban Economics 15, 149–158.

Greenhut, M.L. (1981). "Spatial pricing in the United States, West Germany and Japan". Economica 48, 79–86.

Greenhut, M.L., Norman, G., Hung, C.-S. (1987). The Economics of Imperfect Competition. A Spatial Approach. Cambridge University Press, Cambridge.

Haig, R.M. (1926). "Toward an understanding of the metropolis. I. Some speculations regarding the economic basis of urban concentration". Quarterly Journal of Economics 40, 179–208.
Hansen, P., Labbé, M., Peeters, D., Thisse, J.-F. (1987). "Facility location analysis". In: Hansen, P., Labbé, M., Peeters, D., Thisse, J.F., Henderson, J.V. (Eds.), Systems of Cities and Facility Location. Harwood Academic, Chur, pp. 1–70.
Head, K., Mayer, T. (2000). "Non-Europe. The magnitude and causes of market fragmentation in the EU". Weltwirtschaftliches Archiv 136, 284–314.
Head, K., Mayer, T. (2004). "The empirics of agglomeration and trade". In: Henderson, J.V., Thisse, J.-F. (Eds.), Handbook of Regional and Urban Economics, vol. 4. Elsevier, Amsterdam, pp. 2609–3670. This volume.
Helpman, E. (1998). "The size of regions". In: Pines, D., Sadka, E., Zilcha, I. (Eds.), Topics in Public Economics. Theoretical and Applied Analysis. Cambridge University Press, Cambridge, pp. 33–54.
Helpman, E., Krugman, P.R. (1985). Market Structure and Foreign Trade. MIT Press, Cambridge, MA.
Hohenberg, P.M. (2004). "The historical geography of European cities: an interpretive essay". In: Henderson, J.V., Thisse, J.-F. (Eds.), Handbook of Regional and Urban Economics, vol. 4. Elsevier, Amsterdam, pp. 3021–3052. This volume.
Hotelling, H. (1929). "Stability in competition". Economic Journal 39, 41–57.
Isserman, A.M. (1996). "It's obvious, it's wrong, and anyway they said it years ago? Paul Krugman and large cities". International Regional Science Review 19, 37–48.
Kaldor, N. (1935). "Market imperfection and excess capacity". Economica 2, 35–50.
Koopmans, T.C. (1957). Three Essays on the State of Economic Science. McGraw–Hill, New York.
Krugman, P.R. (1980). "Scale economies, product differentiation, and the pattern of trade". American Economic Review 70, 950–959.
Krugman, P.R. (1991). "Increasing returns and economic geography". Journal of Political Economy 99, 483–499.
Krugman, P.R. (1993). "The hub effect: or, threeness in international trade". In: Ethier, W.J., Helpman, E., Neary, J.P. (Eds.), Theory, Policy and Dynamics in International Trade. Cambridge University Press, Cambridge.
Krugman, P.R., Venables, A.J. (1995). "Globalization and the inequality of nations". Quarterly Journal of Economics 60, 857–880.
Kuehn, A.A., Hambuger, M.J. (1963). "A heuristic program for locating warehouses". Management Science 9, 643–666.
Lampard, E.E. (1955). "The history of cities in the economically advanced areas". Economic Development and Cultural Change 3, 321–342.
Lerner, A., Singer, H.W. (1937). "Some notes on duopoly and spatial competition". Journal of Political Economy 45, 145–186.
Lösch, A. (1940). Die Räumliche Ordnung der Wirtschaft. Gustav Fischer, Jena. English translation: The Economics of Location. Yale University Press, New Haven, CN, 1954.
Ludema, R.D., Wooton, I. (2000). "Economic geography and the fiscal effects of regional integration". Journal of International Economics 52, 331–352.
Martin, R. (1999). "The new 'geographical turn' in economics: some critical reflections". Cambridge Journal of Economics 23, 65–91.
Martin, Ph., Rogers, C.A. (1995). "Industrial location and public infrastructure". Journal of International Economics 39, 335–351.
Matsuyama, K. (1995). "Complementarities and cumulative process in models of monopolistic competition". Journal of Economic Literature 33, 701–729.
McFadden, D. (1974). "Conditional logit analysis of qualitative choice behavior". In: Zarembka, P. (Ed.), Frontiers in Econometrics. Academic Press, New York, pp. 105–142.
Murata, Y. (2003). "Product diversity, taste heterogeneity, and geographic distribution of economic activities: Market vs. non-market interactions". Journal of Urban Economics 53, 126–144.
Myrdal, G. (1957). Economic Theory and Underdeveloped Regions. Duckworth, London.

Neary, J.P. (2001). "Of hype and hyperbolas: introducing the new economic geography". Journal of Economic Literature 39, 536–561.
Ohlin, B., Hesselborn, P.O., Wijkman, P.M. (Eds.) (1977). The International Allocation of Economic Activity. Macmillan, London.
Ottaviano, G.I.P. (1999). "Integration, geography, and the burden of history". Regional Science and Urban Economics 29, 245–256.
Ottaviano G.I.P. (2001a). "Home market effects and the (in)efficiency of international specialization". Mimeo. GIIS.
Ottaviano, G.I.P. (2001b). "Monopolistic competition, trade, and endogenous spatial fluctuations". Regional Science and Urban Economics 31, 51–77.
Ottaviano G.I.P. (2002). "Models of 'new economic geography': factor mobility vs. vertical linkages". Mimeo. GIIS.
Ottaviano, G.I.P., Tabuchi, T., Thisse, J.-F. (2002). "Agglomeration and trade revisited". International Economic Review 43, 409–436.
Ottaviano, G.I.P., Thisse, J.-F. (2001). "On economic geography in economic theory: increasing returns and pecuniary externalities". Journal of Economic Geography 1, 153–179.
Ottaviano, G., Thisse, J.-F. (2002). "Integration, agglomeration and the political economics of factor mobility". Journal of Public Economics 83, 429–456.
Papageorgiou, Y.Y., Thisse, J.-F. (1985). "Agglomeration as spatial interdependence between firms and households". Journal of Economic Theory 37, 19–31.
Pflüger, M. (2004). "A simple, analytically solvable, Chamberlinian agglomeration model". Regional Science and Urban Economics. In press.
Picard, P., Toulemonde, E. (2003). "Regional asymmetries: economies of agglomeration versus unionized labor markets". Regional Science and Urban Economics 33, 223–249.
Picard, P., Toulemonde, E. (2004). "Endogenous qualifications and firms' agglomeration". Journal of Urban Economics 55 (3), 458–477.
Picard, P., Zeng, D.-Z. (2003). "Agricultural sector and industrial agglomeration". CORE Discussion Paper N°2003/22.
Pollard, S. (1981). Peaceful Conquest. The Industrialization of Europe 1760–1970. Oxford University Press, Oxford.
Puga, D. (1999). "The rise and fall of regional inequalities". European Economic Review 43, 303–334.
Rauch, J.E. (1999). "Network versus markets in international trade". Journal of International Economics 48, 7–35.
Reilly, W.J. (1931). The Law of Retail Gravitation. Pilsbury, New York.
Robert-Nicoud, F., Sbergami, F. (2004). "Home-market vs. vote-market effect: location equilibrium in a probabilistic voting model". European Economic Review 48, 155–179.
Sakashita, N. (1967). "Production function, demand function and location theory of the firm". Papers and Proceedings of the Regional Science Association 20, 109–129.
SOPEMI (1998). Trends in International Migration. OECD, Paris.
Starrett, D. (1978). "Market allocations of location choice in a model with free mobility". Journal of Economic Theory 17, 21–37.
Stahl, K. (1983). "A note on the microeconomics of migration". Journal of Urban Economics 14, 318–326.
Stahl, K. (1987). "Theories of urban business location". In: Mills, E.S. (Ed.), Handbook of Regional and Urban Economics, vol. 2. North-Holland, Amsterdam, pp. 759–820.
Tabuchi, T. (1986). "Existence and stability of city-size distribution in the gravity and logit models". Environment and Planning A 18, 1375–1389.
Tabuchi, T. (1998). "Agglomeration and dispersion: a synthesis of Alonso and Krugman". Journal of Urban Economics 44, 333–351.
Tabuchi, T., Thisse, J.-F. (2002). "Taste heterogeneity, labor mobility and economic geography". Journal of Development Economics 69, 155–177.

Thisse, J.-F., Vives, X. (1988). "On the strategic choice of a spatial price policy". American Economic Review 78, 122–137.

Thomas, I. (2002). Transportation Networks and the Optimal Location of Human Activities. A Numerical Geography Approach. Edward Elgar, Cheltenham, UK.

Tirado, D.A., Paluzie, E., Pons, J. (2002). "Economic integration and industrial location: the case of Spain before World War I". Journal of Economic Geography 2, 343–363.

Venables, A.J. (1996). "Equilibrium locations of vertically linked industries". International Economic Review 37, 341–359.

Weber, A. (1909). Über den Standort der Industrien. J.C.B. Mohr, Tübingen. English translation: The Theory of the Location of Industries. Chicago University Press, Chicago, 1929.

Williamson, J. (1965). "Regional inequality and the process of national development". Economic Development and Cultural Change 14, 3–45.

Witzgall, C. (1964). "Optimal location of a central facility: mathematical models and concepts". National Bureau of Standard Report 8388, Washington, DC.

Chapter 59

THE EMPIRICS OF AGGLOMERATION AND TRADE

KEITH HEAD

Faculty of Commerce, University of British Columbia, 2053 Main Mall, Vancouver, BC, Canada V6T1Z2
e-mail: keith.head@ubc.ca

THIERRY MAYER[1]

Université de Paris I Panthéon Sorbonne (TEAM), Paris, France
e-mail: tmayer@univ-paris1.fr

Contents

[1]Also affiliated with CEPII, CERAS and CEPR.

Handbook of Regional and Urban Economics, Volume 4. Edited by J.V. Henderson and J.F. Thisse

DOI: 10.1016/S0169-7218(04)07059-5

Abstract

This chapter examines empirical strategies that have been or could be used to evaluate the importance of agglomeration and trade models. This theoretical approach, widely known as "New Economic Geography" (NEG), emphasizes the interaction between transport costs and firm-level scale economies as a source of agglomeration. NEG focuses on forward and backward trade linkages as causes of observed spatial concentration of economic activity. We survey the existing literature, organizing the papers we discuss under the rubric of five interesting and testable hypotheses that emerge from NEG theory. We conclude the chapter with an overall assessment of the empirical support for NEG and suggest some directions for future research.

Keywords

new economic geography, home market effects, spatial concentration, trade barriers

JEL classification: F12, R12

1. Introduction

In the 1990s, theorists developed a new approach to understanding why some regions seem to attract a disproportionate share of economic activity. Widely known as "New Economic Geography" (NEG), this approach emphasizes the interaction between trade costs and firm-level scale economies as a source of agglomeration. The dictionary provides two senses for the word agglomeration. The first is that of a process by which things come together. The second is the description of a pattern, namely one in which economic activity is spatially concentrated. NEG starts with the observed pattern of agglomeration and postulates a process through which it might have emerged: Producers and consumers co-locating to exploit plant-level scale economies while minimizing trade costs. NEG therefore specifically focuses on trade linkages as causes of observed spatial concentration of economic activity.

"New economic geography has come of age" as Neary (2001) recently wrote in a mildly skeptical review for the *Journal of Economic Literature*.[2] While this statement seems deserved for theory, the empirical literature treating the same questions remains unsettled in both methodology and results. There is no agreed upon regression to estimate, nor even a consensus dependent variable to explain. As a result, empirical papers addressing various aspects of agglomeration and trade are difficult to compare. The Fujita, Krugman and Venables (1999) and Baldwin et al. (2003) books devote a few paragraphs each to empirical work and emphasize that the time has now come to devote greater research efforts to the empirical validation or falsification of the framework. Overman, Redding and Venables (2001) and Hanson (2001) are early surveys of empirical work on NEG. Brakman, Garretsen and van Marrewijk (2001) provide the first textbook where many empirical aspects of NEG are covered in detail. Since those surveys were written, the literature has continued to grow in many directions. Here we attempt to weave together the disparate strands of the empirics of agglomeration and trade and outline the important and challenging questions for future research.

The chapter starts with the definition and delimitation of the field in Section 2, where we organize the paper around five empirical propositions that we believe capture the essential insights offered by the theory. Section 3 emphasizes the central role of market potential in determining location patterns in those models and provides a method of measurement directly derived from theory. Then, each of the remaining sections covers one of the five empirical propositions identified in Section 2. The empirical work on the impact of market potential on factor prices and factor movements is covered in Sections 4 and 5, respectively. The benefits that regions can enjoy from a large domestic demand ("home market effects") have been subjected to important empirical tests

[2] There are now at least three monographs – Fujita, Krugman and Venables (1999), Fujita and Thisse (2002), and Baldwin et al. (2003) – authored by combinations of leading theorists in the field that provide thorough analyses of the theoretical aspects of the literature.

that we survey in Section 6. The impact of trade integration on the level of agglomeration is one of the most sensitive questions of this field. We describe existing results and consider new ways to test this proposition in Section 7. The last proposition that has perhaps been most emblematic of NEG models because of its spectacular nature is the possibility of disproportionately strong effects of small, temporary shocks. "Spatial catastrophes", where short-lived shocks can have permanent impacts on location patterns, have been very recently subject to empirical testing, which we cover in our Section 8. We conclude the chapter with an overall assessment of the empirical support for NEG and suggest some directions for future research.

2. Defining, delimiting, and testing the NEG

The label "new economic geography" is unfortunate in a number of respects. First, it raises hackles by claiming as novel that which some already considered to be well-known, but under-appreciated work. More importantly, the label gives no clear indication of the contents. This means that the same label might be used to describe quite different areas of inquiry. Finally, it is not clear what one should call later work that might supersede the current approach. However, in linguistic choice as with location choice, there is often a gain from following the decisions of predecessors. We therefore adhere to common usage in taking "new economic geography" (or NEG) to refer to theories that follow the approach put forward in Krugman's (1991b) book and, particularly his *Journal of Political Economy* article [Krugman (1991a)]. While we do not wish to denigrate the contributions preceding and following these two pieces, their huge influence is an empirical fact. A *Web of Science* search shows that these two works received a combined total of over 1000 journal citations since they were written.

Ottaviano and Thisse (2004) point out in their chapter of this Handbook that many of the ingredients of new economic geography were developed many decades before Krugman's (1991a) paper. Indeed they suggest that the main contribution of NEG was to "combine old ingredients through a new recipe". Krugman and many of the other 1990s contributors to NEG gave little acknowledgement to its antecedents in regional science and location theory. Rather, they approached economic geography with perspectives developed from "new trade" theory. Indeed, the concluding section of Krugman (1979) anticipates many of the model elements and results that would appear over a decade later:

> "... suppose that there are two regions of the kind we have been discussing and that they have the same tastes and technologies. There is room for mutual gains from trade, because the combined market would allow for both greater variety of goods and a greater scale of production. The same gains could be obtained without trade however, if the population of one region were to migrate to the other. In this model, trade and growth in the labor force are essentially equivalent. If there are impediments to trade, there will be an incentive for workers to move to the region

which already has the larger labor force. This is clearest if we consider the extreme case where no trade in goods is possible but labor is perfectly mobile. Then the more populous region will offer both a greater real wage and a greater variety of goods, inducing immigration. In equilibrium, all workers will have concentrated in one region or the other. Which region ends up with the population depends on initial conditions; in the presence of increasing returns history matters." [Krugman (1979, p. 478)]

This quote shows that the main elements of the stories formalized in the 1990s economic geography literature had already been anticipated by Krugman in the late 1970s. Krugman certainly did not originate all the ideas currently associated with NEG. However, the approach he popularized drew heavily on his own earlier work on trade patterns.

2.1. Essential ingredients for NEG

Five essential ingredients distinguish NEG models from other approaches to understanding the geography of economic activity. We do not wish to imply that they were novel contributions of NEG or new trade but rather that they are useful indicators for categorization.

(1) *Increasing returns to scale (IRS) that are internal to the firm.* NEG models assume a fixed, indivisible amount of overhead required for each plant. NEG models *do not* assume any pure technological externalities that would lead directly to external scale economies.

(2) *Imperfect competition.* With internal increasing returns, marginal costs are lower than average costs. Hence, one cannot assume perfect competition because firms would be unable to cover their costs. The vast majority of the literature goes on to assume a particular market structure and accompanying functional forms for demand: Dixit and Stiglitz' (1977) model of monopolistic competition.[3]

(3) *Trade costs.* The outputs and inputs used by firms are tradeable over distances but only by incurring costs. These costs are often assumed to be proportional to the value of the goods traded.

(4) *Endogenous firm locations.* Firms enter and exit in response to profitability at each possible location. The assumption of increasing returns implies that firms have an incentive to select a single production site and serve most consumers at a distance. If plant-level fixed costs were negligible, the firm would replicate itself everywhere (a la McDonalds).

[3] Recent work by Ottaviano, Tabuchi and Thisse (2002) shows that a linear model of monopolistic competition retains most of the key predictions obtained from the Dixit–Stiglitz structure. Results by Combes (1997), Head, Mayer and Ries (2002), and Feenstra, Markusen and Rose (2001) suggest that NEG models could also rely on Cournot competition with free entry.

(5) *Endogenous location of demand.* Expenditure in each region depends upon the location of firms. Two mechanisms for the mobility of demand have been proposed:
   (a) Mobile workers who consume where they work [Krugman (1991a)].
   (b) Firms that require the outputs of their sector as intermediate inputs [Krugman and Venables (1995)].

Ingredients (1)–(4) all appeared in the new trade literature, and in particular gave rise to the *home market effects* identified in Krugman (1980). With these assumptions, agglomeration can arise but only through the magnification of initial region size asymmetries. The key innovation of NEG relative to new trade is assumption (5). Without (5), symmetric initial conditions can be expected to lead to symmetric outcomes. With all five assumptions, initial symmetry can be broken and agglomerations can form through a process of circular causation. This is perhaps the basis for the Davis blurb on the back of Fujita, Krugman and Venables (1999) that "the work is an even more radical departure from orthodoxy than the new trade theory of the 1980s".

2.2. *Alternative explanations of agglomeration*

If NEG comprises models with these five ingredients, what are the competing explanations of economic geography? Empirical work testing NEG-based hypotheses benefits from the consideration of a set of *plausible alternatives*. Prominent alternatives to NEG include

- *Natural advantages* [see Ellison and Glaeser (1997, 1999)] – also known as "First Nature" [Krugman (1993)] and "locational fundamentals" [Davis and Weinstein (2002)] – and the closely related "factor proportions theory" take the geographic distribution of productive resources as exogenous and use it to explain the geographic distribution of production.
- *Human capital externalities* models link the return to skill in a location to the number of skilled workers there. High skill areas tend to attract larger numbers of employers of skilled workers. Marshall (1920) describes this mechanism for agglomeration. Formal models were developed by Krugman (1991b) and Helsley and Strange (1990). Human capital externalities are central in Lucas' (1988) theory of economic development. Empirical applications are covered in the Moretti (2004) chapter of this volume.
- *Technological externalities/Knowledge spillovers.* Producers benefit from spatial proximity of their counterparts in the same industry via flows of productive knowledge.

The Rosenthal and Strange (2004) chapter of this volume considers the empirical evidence in favour of each of these microfoundations for agglomeration. Our chapter, in contrast, focuses its attention on work that has a direct bearing on the validity of the NEG approach.

In any type of empirical testing of NEG predictions, we think an important issue is that the researcher should keep in mind the presence of the alternative explanations outlined above. Ideally, the empirical procedures employed should incorporate one or more *discriminating hypotheses* that can help differentiate NEG-type mechanisms from natural advantages or "pure externalities" explanations for the level of agglomeration observed in the data. Davis and Weinstein (1996), which we cover in detail, proposed a first empirical test along this route, trying to discriminate between NEG and the explanatory framework of traditional trade theory. While discrimination often proves difficult in this type of modelling, we believe the literature would progress in an important way by following this path, through the application of discriminating tests to a broader set of issues.

2.3. Testing NEG propositions

For guidance, we think it useful to refer to Leamer and Levinsohn's (1995) influential chapter on the empirical evidence on international trade theory. This chapter is known by many empirical trade economists for its puzzling injunction to "estimate, don't test". Its more useful contribution is the process of laying out clear and compelling propositions derived from theory that can be subjected to empirical scrutiny (i.e., tested).

Leamer and Levinsohn (1995) council empiricists to steer a middle road between "taking theory too seriously" and "treating theory too casually". A related way to state the problem is in terms of the classical statistical problems of Types I and II error. In doing empirical work on NEG, we want to avoid interpreting results as rejecting NEG when it actually offers valuable insights. This might occur if our tests hinge on some highly fragile aspect of the theory rather than its core empirical content. Conversely, we do not want to confirm the validity of NEG based on results that are consistent with NEG but would also be equally consistent with alternative theories.

Two examples illustrate these problems. In terms of "false confirmations", consider the following quote from Baldwin et al. (2003): "Exhibit A is the concentration of economic activity in the face of congestion costs. Two bedroom houses in Palo Alto, California routinely change hands for hundreds of thousands of dollars while houses in northern Wisconsin can be had for a song. Despite the high cost of living and office space, Silicon Valley remains attractive to both firms and workers while economic activity in northern Wisconsin languishes." While high housing prices within agglomerations are consistent with NEG, they are also consistent with the three alternative theories of spatial variation in economic activity. Indeed, the natural advantages theory seems consistent with the facts above. In particular, the superior climate in the San Francisco Bay Area (temperatures averaging 49 °F (9.5 °C) degrees in January versus 14 °F (−10 °C) in Green Bay in Northern Wisconsin) could push up housing prices and raise economic activity there.

False rejections can arise from the failure of the actual data to exhibit certain features that models exhibit only as a consequence of simplifying assumptions rather than as a result of the fundamental mechanism the model proposes. For example, Krugman (1991a) predicts that the distribution of manufacturing activity across regions will be either perfect symmetry or complete concentration in one region. Actual data for Europe or North America show that all major regions contain some manufacturing workers but they are far from evenly distributed. Before we reject NEG based on this data, we should recognize that models including all 5 of the identifying features of NEG are consistent with these facts [Tabuchi and Thisse (2002)].

Our review of the empirics of agglomeration and trade is organized around 5 propositions that emerge from the most well-known NEG models. In some cases we include alternative or subsidiary formulations of a given proposition.

(1) *Market potential raise local factor prices.* A location whose access to major markets and suppliers is not impeded by large trade costs will tend to reward its factors with higher wages and land rentals.

(2) *Market potential induces factor inflows.* Capital will be drawn to areas with good access to major markets for final goods and major suppliers of intermediate inputs (backward linkages). Workers favour locations with good access to suppliers of final goods (forward linkages).

(3) *Home market/magnification effect* (HME). Regions with large demand for increasing returns industries account for an even larger share of their production. Put another way, the larger of two regions will be a net exporter to the smaller region in industries characterized by plant-level increasing returns.

(4) *Trade induces agglomeration* (TIA). In an industry featuring increasing returns and partially mobile demand, a reduction in trade costs facilitates spatial concentration of producers and consumers.

(5) *Shock sensitivity.* A temporary shock to economic activity in a location can permanently alter the pattern of agglomeration.

3. Preliminaries: defining and measuring market potential

The primary mechanisms at work in NEG are the market size effects first identified in Krugman (1980). Krugman (1980) developed the basic model combining monopolistic competition and trade costs. He then explored two implications, which we will refer to as the "price" and "quantity" aspects of the market size effect.

The price effect emerges in a one sector model. If the resources employed in each country in each sector are fixed by full-employment and trade balance considerations, then the zero profit condition implies that the smaller country must pay lower wages. Otherwise, firms would prefer to locate in the large country and serve the small one through exporting.

Krugman (1980) illustrates the quantity effect in a very stylized setting involving equal-sized countries, two industries, and "mirror-image" preferences. Helpman and Krugman (1985) later provided a more satisfactory development of the quantity market size effect. As with the price version, the country with the larger market is appealing because it allows the producer to economize on trade costs. If wages do not rise to eliminate this advantage, then a disproportionate share of the producers will locate in the large market. This result is usually referred to as the "home market effect" or the "magnification effect".

The rest of this section will proceed as follows. First we will show how trade costs influence trade flows and introduce the critical parameter, ϕ_{ij}, measuring accessability of a given market i to imports from source j. Then we derive what might be thought of as the fundamental equation of NEG: the relationship between the prospective profitability of a location and its "real market potential". Then we consider the effect of market potential on factor prices and location decisions in subsequent sections.

3.1. Measuring access to markets

We employ the Dixit–Stiglitz–Krugman model of monopolistic competition and trade in a multi-region setting. Let $\mu_i Y_i$ denote expenditures by region i on the representative industry. In theoretical models it is standard to make industry-level expenditure be exogenous by assuming an upper-level utility function that is Cobb–Douglas with expenditure parameter μ_i, thus giving rise to fixed expenditure shares out of income, Y_i. The sub-utility is a constant elasticity of substitution (CES) aggregate of differentiated varieties produced in the considered industry, with σ representing an inverse index of product differentiation.[4] In this model, σ plays several "roles", being in particular an inverse measure of the markup and available economies of scale. This parsimony is useful in theory but dangerous in applications.

The amount spent by consumers from region i for a representative variety produced in region j is given by

$$p_{ij}q_{ij} = \frac{p_{ij}^{1-\sigma}}{\sum_k n_k p_{ik}^{1-\sigma}} \mu_i Y_i, \tag{1}$$

where p_{ij} is the delivered price faced by consumers in i for products from j. It is the product of the mill price p_j and the *ad valorem* trade cost, τ_{ij}, paid by consumers. Trade costs include all transaction costs associated with moving goods across space and national borders. We can see from (1) that trade costs influence demand more when there is a high elasticity of substitution, σ. Indeed many results in Dixit–Stiglitz-based models depend on the term $\phi_{ij} \equiv \tau_{ij}^{1-\sigma}$, that Baldwin et al. (2003) punningly refers to as the "phi-ness" of trade.

The total value of imports (including trade costs) from all n_j firms based in region j will be denoted m_{ij}:

$$m_{ij} = n_j p_{ij} q_{ij} = n_j p_j^{1-\sigma} \phi_{ij} \mu_i Y_i P_i^{\sigma-1}, \tag{2}$$

[4] The *taste for variety* of each consumer represented by the CES functional form is not essential to the model, as the same aggregate demand structure can be obtained with a model of *variety of tastes* when the variance of consumer preferences is described by a logistic distribution [Anderson, de Palma and Thisse (1992)].

where $P_i = (\sum_k n_k p_k^{1-\sigma} \phi_{ik})^{1/(1-\sigma)}$. Fujita, Krugman and Venables (1999) refer to P_i as the "price index" in each location. It is a generalized mean of the delivered costs of all the suppliers to location i that assigns increasing weight to sources that have a large number of suppliers, n_k, or good access to market i, measured by a high ϕ_{ik}. Thus a location that is served by a large number of nearby and low-price sources will have a low P_i and will therefore be a market where it is difficult to obtain a high market share.

Equation (2) can be manipulated to obtain an estimate of ϕ_{ij}. First, divide m_{ij} by m_{ii}, the region i's imports from itself. The $\mu_i Y_i P_i^{\sigma-1}$ cancel since they apply to i's imports from all sources. The remaining expressions involve relative numbers of firms and relative costs in i and j. These ratios can be eliminated by multiplying by the corresponding ratio for region j: m_{ji}/m_{jj}. The result is

$$\frac{m_{ij}m_{ji}}{m_{ii}m_{jj}} = \frac{\phi_{ij}\phi_{ji}}{\phi_{ii}\phi_{jj}}. \tag{3}$$

The standard practice in NEG models is to assume free trade within regions, i.e., $\phi_{ii} = \phi_{jj} = 1$ and symmetric bilateral barriers $\phi_{ji} = \phi_{ij}$. These assumptions lead to a very simple estimator for ϕ_{ij}:

$$\hat{\phi}_{ij} = \sqrt{\frac{m_{ij}m_{ji}}{m_{ii}m_{jj}}}. \tag{4}$$

The numerator requires only trade flow data expressed according to industry classifications. The denominator factors are each region's "imports from self" (or, equivalently, "exports to self"). They are calculated as the value of all shipments of the industry minus the sum of shipments to all other regions (exports).

It therefore is fairly easy to give a feeling of the extent of current trade freeness among the biggest industrialized countries for which bilateral trade flows and production figures are readily available. We use here the database recently made available by the World Bank[5] combined with the OECD STAN database (the Appendix gives details about this data) in order to calculate values of trade flows and $\hat{\phi}_{ij}$ for distinctive pairs of countries in 1999. We opt for the United States–Canada and France–Germany as our pairs of countries.

Recalling that $0 < \hat{\phi}_{ij} < 1$ with 0 denoting prohibitive trade costs, the overall level of trade costs in Table 1 seems to be very high. We can obtain from $\hat{\phi}$ an estimate of the ad valorem equivalent of all impediments to trade between the United States and Canada. The calculation requires an estimate of the price elasticity σ. Using the lowest Head and Ries (2001) estimate of σ for U.S.–Canada trade in manufactured goods (8), trade costs have an ad valorem equivalent ranging from $\tau - 1 = 0.717^{-1/7} - 1 = 4.9\%$ for Canada–U.S. auto trade to just over 36% for Canada–U.S. trade in clothing and Germany–France trade in autos. With the exception of North American auto trade, the

[5] http://www1.worldbank.org/wbiep/trade/data/TradeandProduction.html.

Table 1
The ϕ-ness of trade in 1999 for North America and Europe, selected industries, import values in millions of US$

Country	Foreign source (m_{ij})	Domestic source (m_{ii})	Odds (m_{ij}/m_{ii})	$\hat{\phi}$
		Textiles, apparel and leather		
Canada	3232.48	6275.55	0.515	0.111
U.S.	3437.03	144731.00	0.024	
Germany	1955.14	9742.13	0.201	0.130
France	1604.72	19095.45	0.084	
		Motor vehicles and parts		
Canada	41069.02	13257.20	3.098	0.717
U.S.	58776.02	354653.00	0.166	
Germany	7468.84	101719.28	0.073	0.114
France	9842.01	55179.41	0.178	

level of trade freeness appears to be quite low, even though we have chosen pairs of countries known for their high levels of formal trade integration.

The starkest predictions of NEG models deal with the possibly dramatic consequences of trade liberalization on agglomeration. It is often assumed that we live in an era of trade integration and that would here translate into a trend of rising $\hat{\phi}$ over time. Do we actually observe this trend in the $\hat{\phi}$ data?

We consider, in Figure 1, the evolution of trade freeness for three distinctive country pairs. We can indeed see that international trade is getting easier over the recent period. The rate of progress is not the same for all country pairs, with North America being

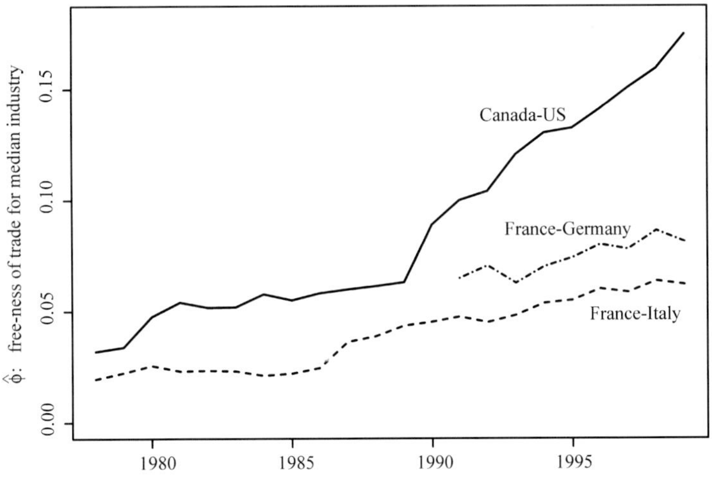

Figure 1. Evolution of median-industry ϕ-ness of trade.

the fastest integrating region since the end of the eighties. The pace of trade integration also seems to be more important since the late eighties in the European Union, as can be seen from the France–Italy combination for which a longer time period is available.[6] It is noteworthy that the change in the pace of integration for the median industry seems to correspond in both regions to the starting date of implementation of a major trade liberalization agreement (the U.S.–Canada Free Trade Agreement in January 1989 and the Single European Act in January 1987). This observed rise in $\hat{\phi}$ is a sort of pre-requisite for any test of the main predictions of NEG models: although remaining at surprisingly low levels, the integration of the world economy is rising, which corresponds to the typical thought experiment of NEG theoretical predictions.

3.2. *Profits as a function of market potential*

Returning to the firm's location decision, total production cost in each region is assumed to take the form $c_j q_j + F_j$. Increasing returns come from a plant-specific fixed costs F_j, q_j is the total output of the representative firm in j and c_j is the constant marginal cost of production. Each firm maximizes the following gross profit function for each market: $\pi_{ij} = (p_j - c_j)\tau_{ij} q_{ij}$. The resulting mill prices are simple mark-ups over marginal costs:

$$p_j = \frac{c_j \sigma}{\sigma - 1}.$$

The gross profit earned in each market i for a variety produced in region j is given by $\pi_{ij} = (p_{ij} q_{ij})/\sigma$. Substituting in Equation (2) and then summing the profits earned in each market and subtracting the plant-specific fixed cost, F_j, we obtain the net profit to be earned in each potential location j:

$$\Pi_j = \frac{1}{\sigma} c_j^{1-\sigma} \mathrm{RMP}_j - F_j, \tag{5}$$

where $\mathrm{RMP}_j = \sum_i \phi_{ij} \mu_i Y_i P_i^{\sigma-1}$. RMP is an abbreviation of Real Market Potential. Redding and Venables (2004) derive the same term (except they do not use ϕ_{ij} notation) and call it market access. To maintain continuity with prior work [from Harris (1954) to Fujita, Krugman and Venables (1999)], we instead employ the term *market potential*. The "real" is added in order to contrast it with an alternative formulation that we refer to as Nominal Market Potential or $\mathrm{NMP}_j = \sum_i \phi_{ij} \mu_i Y_i$. The "nominal" refers to the absence of an adjustment for variation in the price index term P_i.

Davis and Weinstein (2003a) use a variant of NMP in which they set $\phi_{ij} = d_{ij}^{\delta}$ where d_{ij} is the distance between locations i and j and δ is the coefficient on $\ln d_{ij}$ in a gravity

6 Note that the fact that trade is consistently freer in the Franco-German than in the Franco-Italian combination is consistent with the smaller bilateral distance in the former as compared to the latter [411 against 550 miles in Head and Mayer (2000)].

equation estimation using industry-level bilateral trade. Since usual estimates of δ do not differ greatly from minus one,[7] $1/d_{ij}$ is a reasonable approximation for ϕ_{ij}. Further assuming the share of income devoted to each industry does not vary across countries, one obtains $\text{NMP}_j \propto \sum_i Y_i/d_{ij}$, where Y_i is an aggregate measure of demand such as GDP or retail sales. Thus, NMP is proportional to the original formulation of market potential used by Harris (1954) and in subsequent work of geographers.

Nominal Market Potential is intuitively appealing and not very difficult to implement empirically. However, the omission of the price index adjustment $P_i^{1-\sigma}$ effectively severs the link with the underlying profit maximization problem. The reason is simple. Large demand translates into large profits if profit margins and market shares are high. The more competitors there are in a given location, and the more competitors that have low-cost access to that location, and the lower the marginal costs of those local and nearby competitors – that is to say, the lower is P_i, the lower will be any particular firm's share of market i. In other words, a large market that is extremely well-served by existing firms might offer considerably less potential for profits than a smaller market with fewer competitors in the vicinity. NMP might still be useful for some purposes. For instance, since it does not depend on locations of firms or on industry-level costs, both of which are endogenous in economic geography models, NMP might be a good instrument for RMP. However, a regression that includes just NMP is, at best, a reduced form whose coefficients must be interpreted with great caution.

4. Market potential raises factor prices

The impact of market potential on factor prices can be seen by solving for the variable costs in region j that would set the profit equation, (5), equal to zero.

$$c_j = \left(\frac{\text{RMP}_j}{\sigma F_j}\right)^{1/(\sigma-1)}.$$

Suppose, following Redding and Venables (2004), that c_j is function of wages (w), prices of other primary factors (v), and intermediate input prices. If all firms use the same basket of intermediates, then P_j is also the appropriate intermediate price index. Assuming a Cobb–Douglas form, we obtain $c_j = P_j^{\alpha} w_j^{\beta} v_j^{\gamma}$. Suppose further that fixed costs are proportional to variable costs, i.e., $F_j = f c_j = f P_j^{\alpha} w_j^{\beta} v_j^{\gamma}$ where f is a constant determining the strength of increasing returns. After making substitutions and rearranging, we have

$$\beta \ln w_j + \gamma \ln v_j = -\frac{1}{\sigma}\ln(\sigma f) + \frac{1}{\sigma}\ln \text{RMP}_j - \alpha \ln P_j. \tag{6}$$

[7] Disdier and Head (2003) find a mean of −0.87 in meta-analysis of 896 coefficients supplied by 55 different papers.

Redding and Venables (2004) and Hanson (1998) proceed to the empirical implementation of various versions of this equation linking factor prices to market potential.[8] There are three terms to be estimated in the complete version of this equation. The two most important concern the real market potential on one hand and the price index on the other hand. Note that (6) is closely linked to (5): high RMP for a region predicts a relatively high profit for firms located there. In the long run, when free entry drives profits everywhere towards zero, the input prices have to rise to absorb those extra profits in high RMP regions.

Note also that the price index, P_j, appears twice in the factor price equation. It first appears in the RMP term where it acts as a weight on NMP, accounting for the number of potential suppliers to each market, discounted if they have poor access or charge high prices. The price index also enters as the aggregate prices of intermediate inputs. Based on the assumption that firms consume all varieties of competitors as inputs, costs are lower when those input–output linkages are relatively free from trade costs, i.e., when the price index is low, signifying that (input-supplying) competitors are relatively close from your place of production.

Equation (6) bears a close resemblance to the equation estimated by Dekle and Eaton (1999). They relate a share-weighted index of wages and land rents in Japanese prefectures to a term that sums across incomes discounted by distance. There are important differences in theoretical motivation that also result in subtle, but important, differences in specification. Dekle and Eaton (1999) assume agglomeration economies taking a technological form in which the production function has a neutral shift term that depends on nearby economic activity. Their term is a variant of NMP that assumes an exponential distance decay function. Thus, it differs from RMP because of the absence of the price index term. In principle, this distinction might be used to break the observational equivalence between NEG approaches to factor price determination and approaches that invoke spatial technological externalities.

4.1. Market potential and international income inequality

The left-hand side of (6) is a cost-share weighted sum of logged primary factor prices. A natural proxy for this is the log of GDP per capita or ln GDPC. Adding an error term, we have

$$\ln \mathrm{GDPC} = \zeta + \frac{1}{\sigma} \ln \widehat{\mathrm{RMP}}_j + \frac{\alpha}{\sigma - 1} \ln \widehat{\mathrm{SP}}_j + \varepsilon_j, \tag{7}$$

where $\mathrm{SP}_j \equiv P_j^{1-\sigma}$ stands for supply potential [referred to as "supplier access" by Redding and Venables (2004)]. This is the key equation estimated in Redding and Venables (2004). The authors obtain the RMP and SP terms needed for this regression using

[8] The first published derivation of the wage-potential equation seems to be the 1991 working paper version of Krugman (1993).

estimates from the bilateral trade equation of the model.[9] Indeed, using the fact that bilateral trade volumes $m_{ij} = n_j p_{ij} q_{ij}$, where m_{ij} is given by (2), we obtain

$$\ln m_{ij} = \text{FX}_j + \ln \phi_{ij} + \text{FM}_i, \tag{8}$$

where the variables FX_j and FM_i are exporter and importer fixed effects, respectively, with theoretical correspondence

$$\text{FX}_j = \ln\left(n_j P_j^{1-\sigma}\right) \quad \text{and} \quad \text{FM}_i = \ln\left(P_i^{\sigma-1} \mu_i Y_i\right).$$

Therefore, a bilateral trade flow regression in a first step provides estimates of ϕ_{ij} and fixed effects that can be used to construct

$$\widehat{\text{SP}}_j = \sum_i \exp(\text{FX}_i)\phi_{ij} \quad \text{and} \quad \widehat{\text{RMP}}_j = \sum_i \exp(\text{FM}_i)\phi_{ij}.$$

Equation (8) is fitted by Redding and Venables (2004) on a sample of 101 countries for the year 1994 with bilateral distance and contiguity being used to estimate ϕ_{ij} in this gravity-like regression. The two variables of interest SP_j and RMP_j are then constructed for the same set of countries in 1996 with a distinction between the *domestic and foreign components* of those potential variables. Three different sets of variables are constructed which use different proxies for ϕ_{ii}, the internal trade costs, supposed to be linked in alternative ways to the internal distance of a country approximated by $d_{ii} = (2/3)\sqrt{\text{area}/\pi}$.[10] Supplier and market potential are regressed separately because of strong correlation in the series, most of the analysis uses RMP regressions. Note that the method of calculating ϕ_{ii} relative to ϕ_{ij} has important implications for the results. It can be seen from the definition of RMP that any overestimate of freeness of internal trade relative to international trade will give higher relative weight to local GDP in the RMP calculation. In the limit, if ϕ_{ii} approaches 1 and ϕ_{ij} approaches 0 for all international trade flows, only local GDP will be considered in market potential and the estimation will be dangerously approaching a regression of GDP per capita against GDP. This issue is extremely clear when comparing results from the two last RMP specifications in their Figures 3 and 4 graphing the log of GDP per capita against the log of RMP(2) and RMP(3), respectively. The definitions of those variables are such that RMP(3) divides the coefficient applied to internal distance in ϕ_{ii} calculation by two compared to RMP(2). This systematically increases the weight of local GDP in market potential calculation and not surprisingly increases the fit of the regression as remote but high-income countries like Australia see their remoteness reduced through the larger weight put on local GDP.

[9] This two-step procedure where the first step makes use of the gravity-like prediction of bilateral trade patterns in empirical implementations of the NEG model originates in the 1998 NBER working paper version of Davis and Weinstein (2003a) and is also adopted by Head and Mayer (2002).

[10] This measure makes the assumption that each country is a disk where all producers are located in the center and consumers are located uniformly over the area.

A natural way to correct for this problem is to run regressions with only the foreign component of market potential. The authors show that this component alone can explain an impressive 35% of GDP per capita variation across the sample. The full specification with RMP(3) makes the figure rise to near 75%. Robustness checks are conducted with first inclusion of recently successful variables of the cross-country growth literature (endowments in natural resources, physical geography, quality of institutions). The NEG variables measuring access retain their influence. The problem with focusing on the foreign component is that the theory clearly calls for local wages to be increasing in the size of the local market. *Based on foreign market potential only, one would expect Canada to pay substantially higher wages than the United States.*

The ideal solution would be to construct RMP using domestic *and* foreign market potential, but to instrument for it in the regression analysis to solve the endogeneity problem (income enters on both sides of the equation). Redding and Venables (2004) take this approach, using distance to New York City, Brussels, and Tokyo as the instruments. This approach removes contemporaneous shocks to local income per capita. Since the location of these centers of high income are not themselves exogenous in the long run (i.e., why not Rio de Janeiro, Lagos, and Delhi?), we see much scope for future development of the instrumental variable approach.

4.2. *Market potential and interregional wage differences*

In a seminal paper on estimation of wage equations, Hanson (1998) adopts a similar model structure for his study of market potential inside the United States.[11] One difference is that he omits intermediate inputs and primary factors other than labor from the production function. Imposing $\alpha = \gamma = 0$ and $\beta = 1$ in (6), the iso-profit condition reduces to

$$\ln w_j = -\frac{1}{\sigma}\ln(\sigma f) + \frac{1}{\sigma}\ln \mathrm{RMP}_j = -\frac{1}{\sigma}\ln(\sigma f) + \frac{1}{\sigma}\ln\left(\sum_i \mu_i Y_i \phi_{ij} P_i^{\sigma-1}\right). \quad (9)$$

Hanson (1998) then imposes two additional equilibrium conditions. First, he assumes that free migration equalizes real wages across locations. The model follows Helpman (1998) in replacing the agricultural good in the upper-level utility function of individuals with housing. Denoting H_i as the housing stock in i and P_i^H the price of housing, real wage equalization implies $w_i P_i^{-\mu_i} (P_i^H)^{-(1-\mu_i)} = C$, $\forall i$, where C is a constant.[12]

[11] We refer here to the 2001 revised version of a paper first issued as a 1998 NBER working paper.

[12] This assumption, present in Helpman (1998), is somewhat restrictive. Indeed, imposing equality in real wages in the original Krugman (1991a) framework forces the model to be at the symmetric equilibrium, for if the equilibrium was agglomerated, it would yield a core–periphery outcome and the region hosting the manufacturing industry would pay a higher real wage as in Figure 5.2 in Fujita, Krugman and Venables (1999). However, due to the presence of the housing sector, the Helpman (1998) model can exhibit interior agglomerated equilibria that satisfy the real wage equalization assumption. This assumption, while not innocuous, seems defensible as long as the sample under consideration does not exhibit a core–periphery outcome (which is obviously very rare).

The second equilibrium condition is that housing payments equal housing expenditure: $P_i^H H_i = (1-\mu_i)Y_i$. It is then possible to replace the two price terms in (9) and obtain:[13]

$$\ln w_j = B + \frac{1}{\sigma}\ln\left[\sum_i Y_i^{\frac{\sigma(\mu-1)+1}{\mu}} w_i^{\frac{\sigma-1}{\mu}} H_i^{\frac{(\sigma-1)(1-\mu)}{\mu}} \phi_{ij}\right], \tag{10}$$

with B a function of C, μ, σ and f, constant over all locations i. The first difference of this last equation as well as a simplified version omitting the price index in the market potential (and therefore closer to nominal market potential) are estimated using a non-linear least squares estimation procedure. Concentrating on the specification most linked to theory, the principal result is that the estimated coefficients imply parameters consistent with the underlying theoretical framework, with a reasonably good overall fit (0.347 for the 1980–1990 period). The analysis produced for all 3075 U.S. counties shows that the higher are personal incomes, wages and housing stocks in proximate locations, the greater will be the local wage. An appealing feature of the approach is that the estimation of the wage equation provides estimates of key parameters of the model. This is useful *per se* but also can be used as a device to check the consistency of the results with the underlying theoretical framework. The estimate of σ ranges between 4.9 and 7.6, which corresponds to recent estimates in the literature by Head and Ries (2001) or Lai and Trefler (2002) for instance. Those values of σ are interesting first because they confirm recent results through a very different estimation strategy, but also because those estimates are consistent with reasonable values for other equilibrium relationships in the model: With those high σ, the equilibrium markup of prices over marginal costs in the model, $\sigma/(\sigma - 1)$, is between 1.15 and 1.25. The expenditure share of the IRS traded good, μ is estimated to be between 0.91 and 0.97, which lies within the 0–1 range but is much higher than the actual share of expenditures on manufactured goods.[14] Another interpretation on parameters values is that, in the Helpman (1998) model, the equivalent of the "no black hole condition" of Fujita, Krugman and Venables (1999) is that $\sigma(1 - \mu) < 1$. If this condition is not satisfied, the equilibrium is always dispersed [remember that the prediction of the model, in terms of relationship between agglomeration and trade costs, in Helpman (1998) is the reverse of Krugman's (1991a) one], independently of trade costs. All specifications yield values of parameters satisfying this condition. The econometric analysis therefore reveal that the wage equation seems to fit well the spatial variation of wages within the United States. It is noteworthy that the full implementation of the theory-based wage equation obtains a better fit than the simpler wage equation based on Harris (1954) market potential.

To give a clearer view of the extent to which geography matters in the determination of wages in the United States, Hanson (1998) then proceeds to simulations of the model

[13] Note that Hanson (1998) makes the additional assumption that $\mu_i = \mu$, $\forall i$. Also the ln function is missing for the market potential term in this version.

[14] The set of unreported robustness checks include a specification replacing the housing sector by a Krugman (1991a) freely traded agricultural product. Estimates of σ and τ are similar but μ is estimated to be between 1.5 and 2.

with the parameters estimated. The exercise simulates a negative 10% shock on the income in Illinois. The impact of this shock on wages drops very rapidly with distance: 74 kilometers away from the initial shock, wages fall by only 0.43%, in St Louis (345 kilometers away), the fall is down to 0.32%, and wages are unchanged at a distance of 885 kilometers. This extremely strong impact of distance on wage response to localized shocks is the translation of the trade cost parameter estimated which implies that travelling 2 kilometers multiplies the price of a good by $\exp(2 \times 1.97) = 51.4$ [using Hanson (1998), specification of trade costs and his estimate for the 1970–1980 regression]. This disturbingly large estimate may be a consequence of the function form of the distance decay function. Hanson (1998) assumes $\tau_{ij} = \exp(td_{ij})$, the formulation used by Krugman (1993) in his original theoretical derivation of the wage equation and by Dekle and Eaton (1999) in their empirical work. The vast empirical literature estimating gravity equations suggests that τ_{ij} should be a *power* function of distance of the form $\tau_{ij} = d_{ij}^{\delta}$, as the log of trade flows is unanimously found to decrease linearly with the log of distance (usually with slope near -1).

The above analysis by Gordon Hanson is a structural estimation of the wage equation linking positively nominal wage to market access within the United States. The chapter by Combes and Overman (2004) discusses some recent work that applies the Hanson (1998) methodology to wages in European countries. While the Hanson (1998) and Redding and Venables (2004) papers both draw on the iso-profit equation's implications for spatial wage variation, they make different assumptions about worker mobility and use very different econometric strategies. Future work should evaluate these differences and their implications.

Non-structural methods can also be useful for assessing the relationship between access and factor prices. With an important external trade liberalization, the internal geography of production is likely to change rapidly as foreign markets rise in importance to domestic producers. The quality of access to foreign consumers may gain weight in the location decision relative to former domestic centers of consumption.

Hanson (1997) takes the example of trade liberalization in Mexico which provides a natural experiment of this process, as the country experienced a 40-year period of protectionism ending abruptly in 1985, when the country liberalized foreign trade dramatically. The fact that centrally-located Mexico City concentrated such a large proportion of industrial activity before liberalization combined with the proximity, location and size of the U.S. economy, makes the evolution of wage gradients inside the Mexican economy the basis of a reduced form estimation of market access forces at work.

Hanson (1997) uses as a dependent variable the wage in each Mexican region relative to Mexico City wage in the same industry. The explanatory variables are distances to the capital and to the nearest major United States border crossing, together with the same variable interacted with a post-1985 dummy variable. Industry and year fixed effects are included. The results show indeed that distance to industry centers has a negative influence on relative wages. A 10% increase in distance to Mexico City reduces wages by 1.92% whereas the same increase in distance to the U.S. border reduces wages by 1.28%. Access to markets indeed matters for local wages. The other main prediction however receives less support. The change in trade policy occurred in 1985, but there seems to be no robust evidence of a strong change in wage gradients (diminished impact of distance to Mexico City and increased impact of distance to U.S.) after this date.[15] There is some evidence of wage compression over time from 1965 to 1988 in the country, but this movement is not much more pronounced in the end of the sample and was in fact quite stable over the period. The interpretation Hanson (1997) favors is that the older maquiladora programme (launched in 1965 and providing massive liberalization on input imports for exporting plants) had already contributed to the theoretically expected wage compression.

Even if all methodological issues have not yet been resolved, the results surveyed in this section point to an apparent empirical success of the wage equation (and more generally of the price aspect of market size effects), which constitutes an important mechanism of NEG models.

5. Market potential attracts factor inflows

With micro data one may explore how firms' and workers' location decisions depend on market and supply potential. Two types of location choices can be studied, location choice of production units by firms and location choice of individuals through migrations. Such analysis can be interpreted as empirical test of the existence of:

(1) *Backward linkages* (are firms attracted to locations with large demand for their products?).
(2) *Forward linkages* (are consumer-workers attracted to locations with high industrial production?).

5.1. Firm locations and downstream demand

Consider first the location decisions of firms. Firms wish to choose the location that leads to highest expected profits. Thus a firm will choose location j if it expects Π_j to exceed Π_k for all $k \neq j$. Firms that appear identical to the econometrician (same investment timing and industry, etc.) often choose different locations. As a result, it is conventional to assume that there are unobserved components to the profit function. When those unobserved components have a distribution given by a multivariate extreme value, parameters of the profit equation yielding location choices can be estimated by the conditional logit model initiated by Daniel McFadden. Carlton (1983) was the first to apply this model to choice of production sites by firms. Most recent work following this methodology studies the determinants of foreign affiliates' location choices (foreign

[15] The evidence of a diminishing importance of distance to Mexico City is slightly stronger in Hanson (1996). This paper (the first of this stream of work on changes in regional manufacturing activity in Mexico) focuses on regional wages in the apparel industry, for which the strength of linkages with upstream U.S. firms might be sufficiently high to yield rapid and measurable changes in location patterns.

Table 2
Downstream demand variables used in location choice studies

Reference	Origin of investors	Location choices	Demand measurement
Coughlin, Terza and Arromdee (1991)	All foreign investors	American States	State per capita income
Devereux and Griffith (1998)	United States	UK, France, Germany	Share of total apparent consumption in the industry
Friedman, Gerlowski and Silberman (1992)	All foreign investors	American States	Gravity measure of states' per capita income
Head, Ries and Swenson (1999)	Japan	American States	State personal income + sum of the contiguous states' personal income
Henderson and Kuncoro (1996)	Indonesia	Indonesian districts	District population + distance to the nearest large town

direct investment samples have the advantage of presenting relatively footloose location choices that are often concentrated over a relatively short period of time) and incorporate a variable or a set of variables accounting for the "quality" of access of each alternative location to downstream demand. Table 2 gives some examples of such work.

In general, this kind of literature only considers rather simple demand specifications that either consists solely of local income or of *ad hoc* constructions that try to incorporate both local size of demand and more distant sources of consumption. The precise construction used varies from adding the income from contiguous locations [Head, Ries and Swenson (1999)] to using a gravity-type measure of incomes bearing some resemblance with NMP [Friedman, Gerlowski and Silberman (1992)]. The vast majority of the results yield positive coefficients, confirming the intuition that firms value proximity to consumers. The structural interpretation of those coefficients is however problematic as even NMP is only a rough approximation of what a fully specified market potential variable (RMP) should be.

For many suppliers of intermediate inputs, the relevant "consumers" are downstream firms. Smith and Florida (1994) examine the location decisions of about 200 Japan-based auto parts suppliers that established factories in the United States during the 1980s. They found a strong attractive influence of the location of Japan-owned auto assembly factories. Head, Ries and Swenson (1995) exploit the Japanese institution of vertical *keiretsu* to examine the co-location of vertically related factories of 751 Japanese plants established in the U.S. between 1980 and 1990. They found that members of the same *keiretsu* tended to choose the same states. This tendency was large and statistically significant even after controlling for agglomeration effects at the industry level. Moreover, states that were adjacent to locations that had attracted *keiretsu* investment were more likely to be chosen than states with no nearby *keiretsu* investment. This suggests that a spatial nature to the linkage rather than mere emulation of location choices.

Head and Mayer (2002) explore the firms' side of location decisions based on a structural model of the market access motive. This paper studies a sample of 452 affiliates that Japanese firms established in 57 regions belonging to 9 European countries (Belgium, France, Germany, Ireland, Italy, the Netherlands, Spain, Portugal and the United Kingdom) during the period 1984–1995. When an affiliate chooses its location, the only relevant information is the ordering of profits over alternative locations. Monotonic transformations can therefore be made to the profit function (5) in order to obtain an additive expression for the profitability of each location. Specifically, we add F_j, multiply by σ, and take logs, yielding

$$V_j \equiv \ln\big[\sigma(\Pi_j + F_j)\big] = -(\sigma - 1)\ln c_j + \ln \mathrm{RMP}_j. \tag{11}$$

As in Hanson (1998) and Redding and Venables (2004), the central issue is the construction of the RMP_j variable. Head and Mayer (2002) make use of the trade equation of this model seen in Section 3.1. The methodology is, in this respect, close to Redding and Venables (2004). Estimation of a transformed version of the bilateral trade equation m_{ij} enables to obtain the parameters needed for the calculation [whereas Redding and Venables (2004) can be interpreted as a direct estimation of the entire RMP_j term].

Using $v_j = n_j p_j q^*$ as a notation for the value of production in the considered industry in region j (q^* standing for the individual output of firms, constant in this model if firms share the same technology), CL_{ij} as a dummy variable set to one for countries sharing a common language, and the assumption that trade costs are positively influenced by distance (with elasticity δ) and negatively related to common language (with elasticity λ), the estimated trade equation derived from (1) is

$$\ln\left(\frac{m_{ij}}{m_{ii}}\right) - \ln\left(\frac{v_j}{v_i}\right) = -b - (\sigma - 1)\ln\left(\frac{p_j}{p_i}\right) - \delta \ln\left(\frac{d_{ij}}{d_{ii}}\right) + \lambda \mathrm{CL}_{ij} + \varepsilon_{ij}, \tag{12}$$

where $\exp(-b)$ gives, everything else equal, the ratio of intra-national to international trade [the, large, negative impact of the political borders on trade flows first uncovered by McCallum (1995)]. The estimated parameters $(\hat{\sigma}, \hat{b}, \hat{\delta}, \hat{\lambda})$ are then used (together with industry-level apparent consumption, wages and number of competitors for each region j needed in RMP_j) to construct the market potential variable included in the location choice analysis of Japanese firms in Europe. The formulas used for the construction of trade costs are

$$\phi_{ij} = \tau_{ij}^{1-\sigma} = \mathrm{e}^{-\hat{b}+\hat{\lambda}\mathrm{CL}_{ij}} d_{ij}^{-\hat{\delta}} \quad \text{for } i \neq j \quad \text{and} \quad \phi_{ii} = \tau_{ii}^{1-\sigma} = d_{ii}^{-\hat{\delta}}.$$

The c_j variable can be given several specifications in empirical work. In their most complete setting, Head and Mayer (2002) consider typical labour market and fiscal determinants of production costs (wages, unemployment rate, social charges, corporate tax rate and regional subsidy eligibility). The paper also incorporates two proxies for other intra-industry externalities into the cost function intended to capture the possibility that clustering leads to direct economic benefits such as access to workers with specialized skills or knowledge sharing between competitors.

There are three main specifications of the market potential estimated, the first one corresponds to the theoretical equation (11), the second reduces market potential to the Harris (1954) formula which simplifies the assumed trade costs and neglects the impact of competitors on the location choice. The third specification follows Redding and Venables (2004) and separates RMP_j into local and non-local components. In nested logit estimates (a discrete choice model that allows for the correlation of error terms among location alternatives inside a same country) Head and Mayer (2002) obtain a point estimate of 1.26 on the RMP_j term. This implies that a 10% rise in the market potential of a European region yields to a 10.5% increase in the probability of this region being chosen by a Japanese investor. The near unitary effect of market potential corresponds to the theoretical prediction and the goodness of fit of the different regressions as well as the coefficients suggest a small preference for the RMP_j specification of market potential over the Harris (1954) version. However, the specification yielding the highest fit is the one separating local and non-local components of the market potential term. The striking result of this specification is that the local component of demand has a clearly dominant influence on location choices.

A last result is that the variables embodying other intra-industry externalities retain a strong positive effect on location choices regardless of the estimation technique and market potential formulation. The previous findings of agglomeration effects using the same type of variables are very common in the literature [Head, Ries and Swenson (1995), Devereux and Griffith (1998), Guimarães, Figueiredo and Woodward (2000), Crozet, Mayer and Mucchielli (2004), for instance]. Those previous results could have been caused by a mis-specification of the demand term, described as (various forms of) local income of the locations, and therefore be proven invalid when considering market potential properly. Head and Mayer (2002) show evidence of the contrary: even when final demand linkages are appropriately controlled for through the market potential term, direct agglomeration effects appear to retain a powerful role in location choices. This suggests that the *backward linkage* NEG mechanism might not be the only or even the main driver of clustering behavior by firms (at least by foreign investors).

5.2. *Worker locations and forward linkages*

What about the empirical validity of the *forward linkage*? Workers choose locations to maximize expected real wages after taking into account mobility costs. Let us denote real wages in i with ω_i, given by nominal wages divided by the aggregate price index. The latter depends on the modern sector's price index, P_i, with expenditure share μ and the traditional (often considered to be agriculture) sector price p_i^Z with share $1-\mu$. Under standard assumptions p_i^Z is normalized to one. Hence the log real wage is given by

$$\ln \omega_j = \ln w_j - \mu \ln P_j. \tag{13}$$

In the Krugman (1991a) version, worker movement is governed by a very simple equation: $\dot{\lambda}_i = \kappa(\omega_i - \bar{\omega})\lambda_i$. This formulation does not consider mobility costs and the high likelihood of heterogeneity in the cost of re-locating. Discrete choice models offer a much more realistic treatment of mobility without sacrificing tractability.[16] Suppose that utility in region j is given by $\ln \omega_j + \varepsilon_j$, where ε_j describes heterogeneous non-pecuniary benefits living in region j. The probability of moving from i to j is given by the probability that $(\ln w_j - \ln w_i) + \mu(\ln P_i - \ln P_j) - \rho + \varepsilon_j - \varepsilon_i > 0$, where ρ represents the mean relocation costs. Making distributional assumptions for $\varepsilon_i - \varepsilon_j$, we can estimate the responsiveness of location choice to proximity to producers. Although an estimation of this sort lies at the core of the propositions of NEG, we are not aware of any papers to have done so with micro data. Crozet (2000) has estimated a similar proposition with *aggregate* flow data in a structural estimation of a NEG model.

His framework incorporates a third industry, a non-traded service sector, which [as in Hanson (1998)] enables the predictions of the theoretical model to be less dramatic, the periphery always maintaining some production in the manufacturing industry. The real wage equation is then transformed to be $\ln \omega_j = \ln w_j - \mu \ln P_j^X - \psi \ln P_j^Y$, X and Y being the manufacturing and service industries, respectively. Crozet (2000) envisions a mobility cost specification similar to the one in discrete choice models with a deterministic and a random component. Keeping the same notation as above, the number of migrants from j to i is shown to be equal to

$$\mathrm{mig}_{ji} = \frac{\omega_i}{\omega_j} \frac{\varepsilon_i}{\rho_{ji}},$$

where ε_i is the probability of finding a job in location i (assumed proportional to the employment rate in i) and $\rho_{ji} \equiv (d_{ij} + cB_{ij})^{\nu}$, the bilateral mobility cost, assumed positively related to bilateral distance and non-contiguity (B_{ij} is a dummy variable set to one for contiguous regions). The central equation of the paper is obtained by using mig_{ji} together with traditional pricing rules, the proportional relationship between the number of varieties and the labour force of this model, and the definition of price indexes:

$$\mathrm{mig}_{ji} = \left(\frac{w_i}{w_j}\right)^{1-\psi} \left(\frac{L_i^Y}{L_j^Y}\right)^{\frac{\psi}{\sigma^Y - 1}} \left(\frac{\sum_k L_k^X \phi_{ki} w_k^{1-\sigma^X}}{\sum_k L_k^X \phi_{kj} w_k^{1-\sigma^X}}\right)^{\frac{\mu}{\sigma^X - 1}} \frac{\varepsilon_i}{\rho_{ji}}. \tag{14}$$

Several things can be learned from this equation. First, leaving aside relative nominal wage, this expression has some resemblance with the gravity equation. Bilateral flows of workers are positively related to the relative size of the hosting region (because a large host region produces a large share of available varieties and has therefore a low overall price index). The distance term is here related to the mobility costs. Second, the large central term in (14) is related to the nominal market potential (NMP) defined above. It indeed consists of trade cost-weighted sums of market sizes (number of workers here instead of incomes in NMP). Access [which Crozet (2000) refers to as "centrality"] is an attractive characteristic for regions here, like in the location choice of firms. However,

[16] Tabuchi and Thisse (2002) show that allowing for probabilistic migration due to taste heterogeneity has important effects in the NEG model they consider. Murata (2003) confirms this finding in a Dixit–Stiglitz–Krugman framework.

it should be noted that the reason is intrinsically different: Good access is attractive *for firms and for workers* because of their high market potential, which translates either in high expected profits [Equation (11)] or higher nominal wages [Equation (7)]. This dimension appears in the first nominal wage term of (14), but there is an additional aspect that makes access attractive for workers yielded by the large availability of nearby producers and corresponding low price index. Note that the corresponding effect for firms is yielded by low price of inputs in central places, which is given by the supply potential term ($\mathrm{SP}_j \equiv P_j^{1-\sigma}$) in Equation (7).

Crozet (2000) proceeds to a transformation of (14), yielding a structurally estimable [through non-linear least squares, very much in the spirit of Hanson (1998) and Lai and Trefler (2002)] specification. The sample consists of internal bilateral migration flows between regions of Germany (period 1983–1992), Spain (period 1983–1993), Italy (period 1983–1993), The Netherlands (period 1988–1994), and the United Kingdom (period 1980–1985).

The main results of interest here are the impact of market access on migration inflows. The estimated parameters correspond to signs and magnitudes predicted by the theoretical framework, with a good overall predictive power of the regressions. The most interesting parameters are σ and δ, the CES and the elasticity of trade costs to distance, respectively. All estimates of σ lie significantly above 1, ranging from 1.3 for the United Kingdom to 4.3 for the Netherlands. Estimates of δ are also systematically significantly positive across countries, with a very high average value of 1.8 but considerable variation across countries (over 3 in Germany to 0.5 in Spain).

Like Hanson's (1998) simulations of the geographical dissipation factor of a negative shock to Illinois income, Crozet (2000) proceeds to use parameter estimates to evaluate theoretical predictions numerically. The prediction he examines is the break point of trade costs below which the symmetrical equilibrium of his model is not stable anymore and the country should exhibit an increasing core–periphery structure. This is done for each country in terms of relative distance below which the core–periphery should be the only equilibrium. The idea can be summarized as a calculation, for each major region in the country, of a radius defining a surrounding area where the activity would tend to be "attracted" to the central region. It appears that those relative distances are very small, which means that significant core–periphery patterns can only happen on very small distances. An example from the paper is that the German region of Bayern with an internal distance of about 100 kilometers is predicted to attract all IRS activities located within a radius of 120 kilometers from its center. It does not seem to threaten any other important region. This calculation does not incorporate migration costs, and a last exercise conducted by Crozet (2000) uses all estimated parameters to calculate the equilibrium predicted number of migrants for equalized nominal wages arising from (14). The number of predicted migrants (actually roughly consistent with real ones) is strikingly low, even for very large differences in size and very small relative distances. Put together, *these results point to the empirical relevance of agglomeration forces operating through forward linkages, but those forces are likely to stay very localized, unable to generate core–periphery patterns in Europe at a large geographical level*, at least as long as labour remains so sensitive to migration costs.

6. Home market/magnification effects

There are three closely related predictions regarding the effects of market size asymmetries on the geographic distribution of industry activity that have come to be known as "home market effects". Krugman (1980) initiates the literature by demonstrating that the country with the larger number of consumers of an industry's goods will run a trade surplus in that industry. Further development of the model in Helpman and Krugman (1985) shows that the larger country's share of firms in the increasing returns industry exceeds its share of consumers. They also show that increases in a country demand lead to more than one-for-one increases in production.

6.1. *The magnification of production*

The Krugman (1980) formulation relates ratios of numbers of firms to ratios of numbers of consumers. In particular, Krugman imagines two equal size countries with different preferences. The relative size of country i's home market in terms of our notation would be μ_i/μ_j. Its relative number of firms (and relative production) would be n_i/n_j. Expressed in our notation, Equation (25) of Krugman (1980) shows that

$$\frac{n_i}{n_j} = \frac{\mu_i/\mu_j - \phi}{1 - \phi\mu_i/\mu_j}.$$

Davis and Weinstein (1996, 1999, 2003a) use the derivative to motivate their estimation:

$$\frac{d(n_i/n_j)}{d(\mu_i/\mu_j)} = \frac{1-\phi^2}{(1-\phi[\mu_i/\mu_j])^2} > 1.$$

They term this result the "magnification effect". Note that starting from a point of symmetric preferences, that is where $\mu_i = \mu_j$,

$$\frac{d(n_i/n_j)}{d(\mu_i/\mu_j)} = \frac{1+\phi}{1-\phi}.$$

Inspection of this expression reveals that increasing "free-ness" of trade leads to a magnification of the magnification effect.

Empirical work based on Krugman (1980) must confront three important issues related to the difference between model and data dimensionality. The model (as most of the subsequent theoretical work on the topic) assumes 1 factor, 2 industries, and 2 countries. These assumptions raise the following questions for empirical analysis.

(1) How can one allow for factor proportions to influence the trade pattern as in the traditional model of trade? Tests of new trade need to be compared with an alternative of H–O trade.

(2) How do we model the relationships between multiple industries? Krugman (1980) considered one industry models where balanced trade required higher wages in the large country. He also considered a two-industry model where balanced trade was achieved by making one country having "mirror image" differences in preferences. This allowed for idiosyncratic demand to determine the location of production at the industry level while retaining equal wages in equilibrium. Helpman and Krugman (1985) gives a role for absolute differences in country size by assuming that there is a zero trade-cost constant returns sector that equates wages and absorbs any trade imbalances caused by home market effects operating on the IRS industry. In actual data, the mirror image assumption certainly fails and the CRS sector probably does not have zero trade costs or the ability to absorb all trade imbalances.

(3) How do we construct demand measures in the presence of more than two countries? Indeed, how does one even formulate the home market effect hypothesis? The ratios and shares of the theoretical formulations neglect third-country effects.

In addition to these three conceptual problems, there is also a practical problem. What data should be used to measure demand differences? The obvious approach is to use something called "apparent consumption" or "domestic absorption". This starts with domestic production adds imports and subtracts exports. While the measure is sensible, it requires trade data measured in a way so as to make them comparable with production data. The underlying data are collected by different agencies (survey and census for production, customs offices for trade) using different classification systems. To make trade and production data comparable across multiple countries is even more difficult.[17]

Given these four challenges, one can understand why the first empirical tests of home market effects did not appear until 16 years after the publication of the Krugman (1980) paper that coined the term.[18] The pioneering paper, Davis and Weinstein's (1996) NBER working paper "Does economic geography matter for international specialization", was never published. Nevertheless, its methodology and discussions of its chief results appear in Davis and Weinstein (1999, 2003a). Prior to considering the results of these

[17] There are several data sets that attempt to provide compatible trade and production data for a broad set of countries, industries and years. The World Bank provides a recently assembled data set, with wide overall coverage (referenced above). The database covers the 1976–1999 period with compatible bilateral trade and production data at the ISIC 3-digit level (28 industries) for 67 countries and ISIC 4-digit level (81 industries) for 24 countries.

[18] Justman (1994) is an early empirical contribution emphasizing the importance of local demand in the production hosted by a particular location. His analysis is primarily centered on correlation coefficients between industry-level output and local demand for the good considered among 318 U.S. MSAs. Results point to some explanatory power of local demand for the good in industry supply location pattern but the link to theory is rather thin and no reference is actually made to HME or NEG theories. In fact, as emphasized by Davis and Weinstein (1999), simple correlations are not the appropriate device for hypothesis testing of agglomeration theories. All sensible theories yield a *positive relationship* between the location of supply and the location of demand, thus implying positive correlation coefficients. But correlation coefficients cannot distinguish between more than proportional from less than proportional relationships between supply and demand. A very high correlation can be associated with either a steep or a flat slope of the link between output and demand.

three papers, we shall discuss the common method and how it confronted each of the three "dimensionality" issues posed above.

Davis and Weinstein (1996, 1999, 2003a) estimate equations that they describe as being "inspired" by Krugman (1980) but adapted to allow for an important role for factor endowments. Their specification is estimated in levels, rather than the ratios analyzed by Krugman (1980). In particular, they propose that production of "goods" (the most disaggregated classification of industries available) is linearly related to variables called SHARE and IDIODEM:

$$X_{gr} = \beta_1 \mathrm{SHARE}_{gr} + \beta_2 \mathrm{IDIODEM}_{gr} + \varepsilon_{gr}. \tag{15}$$

SHARE_{gr} is not actually a share. Rather it gives a prediction for region r's production of a good if its output at the more aggregated level (X_r) were allocated across goods in the same proportion as the rest of the "world". Thus suppose we denote X_{gr} as the value of r's production of good g. Then production of the aggregate sums the goods for a given region: $X_r = \sum_g X_{gr}$. Production of rest of world for the good and the aggregate are given by $X_{gR} = \sum_{s \neq r} X_{gs}$ and $X_R = \sum_g X_{gR}$. Expressed in our notation (which suppresses the n subscript they use for industry aggregates), we have

$$\mathrm{SHARE}_{gr} = \frac{X_{gR}}{X_R} X_r.$$

The key variable in the analysis is IDIODEM. It is defined as a deviation from rest-of-world demand patterns. Recall that we defined $E_r = \mu_r Y_r$ where μ_r is an expenditure share parameter and Y_r is total income. Applying the same notation as with X, we have

$$\mathrm{IDIODEM}_{gr} = \left(\frac{E_{gr}}{E_r} - \frac{E_{gR}}{E_R} \right) X_r.$$

The term in parentheses measures demand differences. Note that it does not depend on absolute differences in country size (Y_r and Y_R cancel out in the E ratios). In the absence of idiosyncratic demand differences, that is, for $\mathrm{IDIODEM}_{gr} = 0$, Davis and Weinstein (1996, 1999, 2003a) expect $X_{gr} = \mathrm{SHARE}_{gr}$ and therefore expect β_1 to be approximately one.

The specification is augmented by a vector of endowments of land, capital, and labor by education category called Factors:

$$X_{gr} = \beta_1 \mathrm{SHARE}_{gr} + \beta_2 \mathrm{IDIODEM}_{gr} + \Omega_g \mathrm{Factors} + \varepsilon_{gr}. \tag{16}$$

They consider this specification to nest comparative advantage (via Factors) and increasing returns (via IDIODEM) in the same specification. Note that the maintained assumption throughout these studies is that Factors determine production at the level of the industry aggregates X_r.

The estimate of β_2 is the focus of the analysis. A coefficient on IDIODEM above one provides evidence of home market effects. The Davis and Weinstein (1996, 1999, 2003a) specification might be thought of as a kind of linear approximation of the true model. Around the point of symmetry then, it may be the case that β_2 provides a rough

Table 3
Davis and Weinstein's "pooled" HME estimates

	OECD, DW (1996)		Japan, DW (1999)		OECD, DW (2003a)	
SHARE (β_1)	1.103	0.259	1.033	−1.744	0.96	–
	(0.002)	(0.198)	(0.007)	(0.211)	(0.01)	
IDIODEM (β_2)	1.229	0.712	1.416	0.888	1.67	1.57
	(0.005)	(0.033)	(0.025)	(0.070)	(0.05)	(0.10)
Factors	No	Yes	No	Yes	No	Yes

estimate of what Helpman and Krugman (1985) show to be the (magnified) response of the share of production in r with respect to an increase of the share of demand located in r: $\mathcal{M} = (1+\phi)/(1-\phi)$. Davis and Weinstein (1996, 1999, 2003a) argue that a coefficient between zero and one implies a comparative advantage world with trade costs. Subsequent theoretical results by Feenstra, Markusen and Rose (2001), Trionfetti (2001), and Head, Mayer and Ries (2002) all cast doubt on this implication. With a fixed number of firms, asymmetric home bias in preferences, or national product differentiation, it is possible to observe production respond less than one-for-one to demand even in models of imperfect competition without comparative advantage. The implication *does* seem to run strongly in the opposite direction. Models of comparative advantage with constant returns are inconsistent with the magnifying effect of market size, i.e., $\hat{\beta}_2 > 1$ supports increasing returns models.

Coefficients of 0 and 1 on IDIODEM correspond, respectively, to a frictionless and autarkic CRS world. Davis and Weinstein (1996, 1999, 2003a) do not discuss the interpretation of negative coefficients. We are not aware of any model that generates a negative relationship between demand and the location of production. Consequently, a finding of $\hat{\beta}_2 < 0$ suggests either sampling error or mis-specification.

The Davis and Weinstein (1999, 2003a) results are considered by many to provide strong support for home market effects and NEG more generally. In an endnote, Fujita, Krugman and Venables (1999) write of the paper on Japanese regions published in 1999 that Davis and Weinstein "measure the importance of the home market effect and find surprisingly strong impacts". In their review of empirical evidence Baldwin et al. (2003) state that these papers find "econometric evidence that one agglomeration force – the so-called home market effect – is in operation."

Table 3 presents the pooled results from the three Davis and Weinstein (1996, 1999, 2003a) papers on home market effects (with standard errors in parentheses). The result from the 1996 and 1999 studies both indicate that controlling for factors drives the coefficient on IDIODEM below one. Thus, if one accepts the nested specification proposed by Davis and Weinstein, the pooled estimates do not support home market effects. The 2003 paper retains $\hat{\beta}_2 > 1$ after controlling for Factors but it should be noted that this specification omits SHARE. The problem with the pooled results, as noted by the authors, is that it gives a single answer as to the presence or absence of home market effects. Since industries differ, it would seem more attractive to let the data indicate

Table 4
Summary statistics on Davis and Weinstein's disaggregated IDIODEM estimates

Paper/table	Mean $\hat{\beta}_2$	Median $\hat{\beta}_2$	N	% > 1	% sig > 1	% < 0	% sig < 0
DW (1999), Japan							
Table 6	1.63	0.45	20	45%	40%	40%	5%
DW (2003a), OECD							
Table 2 (4-digit runs)	1.47	0.95	50	50%	22%	38%	4%
Table 3 (4-digit pooled)	1.20	1.02	13	54%	31%	0	0
Table 4 (3-digit runs)	4.23	0.71	24	37.5%	8.3%	37.5%	12.5%

which industries have home market effects and which ones have production patterns determined mainly by factors.

Table 4 presents some summary statistics on the disaggregated results. The average values of $\hat{\beta}_2$, the coefficient on IDIODEM, are greater than one in all four sets of results, suggesting that manufacturing industries on average have home market effects. Means can be strongly influenced by outliers. The median coefficients on IDIODEM are less than one in three sets of regressions and marginally over one in just Table 3 of the OECD study. In summary, more than half of the industry-level coefficients are less than one and a disturbingly large share are negative. One interpretation of the results is that a sizeable number of industries (11 out of 50) appear to exhibit home market effects. Another take is that the industry-level estimates are just too noisy to provide solid support for the HME.

Head and Ries (2001) consider home market effects in the context of trade liberalization between Canada and the United States, phased in over ten years starting in 1989. They base their specification on Helpman and Krugman's (1985) share equation. Helpman and Krugman (1985) developed a piece-wise linear formulation in terms of shares of consumers and producers. We reproduce here the formulation expressed in the terms of our modeling from Section 3.1 in a two region (noted i and j) framework. Let λ denote the share of producers in country i and θ to denote its share of demand. Thus, we would have $\lambda = n_i/N$ and $\theta = (\mu_i Y_i)/E$, where $E = \sum_k \mu_k Y_k$ and $N = \sum_k n_k$. For interior solutions, i.e., where n_i and n_j are both positive, the *spatial equilibrium* arises at $\lambda^* \in (0, 1)$ such that $\Pi_i(\lambda^*) - \Pi_j(\lambda^*) = 0$. Using (5), the difference in profits function writes:

$$\Pi_i(\lambda^*) - \Pi_j(\lambda^*) = \frac{1}{\sigma}\left(c_i^{1-\sigma}\mathrm{RMP}_i - c_j^{1-\sigma}\mathrm{RMP}_j\right) - (F_i - F_j).$$

To solve for the spatial equilibrium, the literature typically relies upon a particular specification of the *other* sector, referred to as agriculture or "traditional". The other sector has constant returns to scale, perfect competition, zero transport costs and a unitary labor requirement technology. It is also assumed to account for a large share of total consumer expenditures. All these conditions are used to ensure that, with this sector staying active in both economies, the price of this good is equalized, therefore equal wages prevail in both economies for the manufacturing sector as well. With identical

shows that, in the increasing returns, monopolistic competition framework, for a given share of demand from all sources (θ), a country with a higher share of customers that "buy domestic" will tend to have a higher share of the firms in the industry. Trionfetti's (2001) specification can be expressed (in terms of the notation we have already been using) as

$$\lambda_i^* = \beta_1 + \beta_2\theta_i + \beta_3\text{HB}_i + \varepsilon_i.$$

The new variable HB_i measures the share of the "home-biased" demand in industry i residing in the home-country. The coefficient on HB_i should be positive if and only if the increasing returns monopolistic competition model applies. The magnification effect, β_2, from prior specifications need not be greater than one in the presence of increasing returns *and* home bias. The key issue is not the mere existence of home-biased demand. Any symmetric avoidance of foreign varieties is observationally equivalent to a common non-tariff barrier. In the Helpman and Krugman (1985) model such symmetric home bias lowers ϕ and therefore $\mathcal{M}$ as well. The Trionfetti (2001) specification relies upon one country having more home biased customers than the other. If that is the case, firms would not simply follow demand to be close to the larger market. This might put them into a position of having to reach home-biased customers by exporting to them which is not profitable. Rather, firms will care about locating near customers in general but particularly near those who refuse to buy non-local goods. Asymmetric home bias is like an asymmetric tariff. The larger is the tariff on imports holding the tariff on exports constant, the more the incentive to locate in the protected market. Thus, Trionfetti (2001) is relying on the "import protection as export promotion" feature of increasing returns models.

Like Davis and Weinstein (2003a), Trionfetti (2001) estimates using cross-country variation in demand and production to identify coefficients at the industry level. His sample comprises eight European countries and he identifies home biased demand using input–output tables for those countries isolating for each industry the sources of demand for which the import share is below average or twice below average. Trionfetti's (2001) results offer mixed support for the home market effect. The magnification effect, β_2, is never significantly greater than one and often significantly less than one. The home-bias effect β_3 is positive and significant for 7 out of 18 industries.

Brülhart and Trionfetti (2002) propose a similar test based on a different estimate of home biased demand. They proceed in two steps, first estimating a gravity trade equation where, in the spirit of Wei (1996), flows internal to countries are added and identified by a dummy. The exponential of the coefficient on this dummy gives the extent to which countries trade "excessively with themselves", which is identified with the home bias. With such an estimate for each industry of each importing country, they can construct an IDIOBIAS variable on the same model as the IDIODEM variable (capturing deviations from the median home bias in the sample) from Davis and Weinstein (1999, 2003a) papers and run the same type of regressions as Davis and Weinstein with this new variable added.[21] The hypothesis tested is very similar to the above: Models of trade characterized by increasing returns and home bias should exhibit a positive coefficient on the IDIOBIAS variable as opposed to models of comparative advantages. Their sample comes from the OECD COMTAP database and the HME regressions concerns 6 countries (Belgium, France, Germany, Italy, Netherlands, UK), 18 manufacturing industries and 4 years (1970, 1975, 1980 and 1985). Five out of the 18 industries exhibit a response to home biased demand and therefore validate the discriminating test in favor of increasing returns. Those industries (Office machinery, Motor vehicles, Meat products, Dairy products, Paper and Printing) taken together represent around a quarter of manufacturing output of the zone.

6.3. The magnification of exports

As stated in the very beginning of this section, the original formulation of the home market effect by Krugman (1980) focused on the impact of market size on net exports of a country in IRS industries. In a two region framework, this "trade version" of the home market effect states that the region with a share of demand for the IRS good superior to one half will be a net exporter of this good. This prediction, as with the one on production shares seen in the above subsections, extends to other (though not all) popular imperfect competition models with trade costs [Head, Mayer and Ries (2002)]. Lundbäck and Torstensson (1998) implement this prediction empirically for 17 OECD countries over 49 industries (using the STAN database). Their version of the theoretical setup includes possibly different home biased preferences across countries and, as in Trionfetti (2001), this yields an additional HME prediction. In this setup, a country will produce disproportionately and be a net exporter of the goods for which the home bias of its customers is most pronounced compared to its trade partners. The empirical specification links the net trade in industry/country combinations to a measure of "demand bias" (intended to capture how demand in a country deviates from the sample's average demand for the considered industry), and a measure of home bias. This last variable is given by the residuals from a first stage regression of domestic producers market share of domestic demand on their market share of world demand for each industry. The regressions also include three more variables, two for factor endowments and one for scale economies. Results are again mixed for the HME: the demand bias variable is positive and significant in 6 out of 17 countries, significantly negative in 3 countries, and insignificant for the 8 remaining countries. The variable intended as a proxy for home bias asymmetries in preferences offers much greater support, being very significantly positive in all countries.

Three recent papers – Feenstra, Markusen and Rose (2001), Weder (2003), and Hanson and Xiang (2002) – propose tests for the HME using *bilateral* export patterns. Feenstra, Markusen and Rose (2001) estimate gravity equations and interpret a larger coefficient on exporter GNP than importer GNP as evidence of the home market effect.

[21] Note that the 2001 paper by Trionfetti follows a share regression specification which has a closer link to theory than the Davis and Weinstein (1999, 2003a) type of regression adopted in the later paper.

They find this coefficient pattern in differentiated products but not for homogeneous products. Weder (2003) finds that the ratio of UK to U.S. exports to third markets are increasing in the relative size of the UK market. It is not clear, however, whether this result violates a model of national product differentiation and constant returns if the latter allows larger countries to produce (and export) a larger number of varieties. Hanson and Xiang (2002) adopt a different definition of home market effects from what has been standard in the theory and empirical literature. This makes their results difficult to compare with those of prior studies. One important finding of this paper is that demand measures based only on national demand give quite different results from summations of proximate demand subject to a distance discount. The latter approach corresponds to the concept of nominal market potential defined earlier in this chapter and also utilized in Davis and Weinstein (2003a).

6.4. *The robustness of the relationship*

We have summarized the methods and results of ten papers that test for the home market effects (HMEs) implied by increasing returns models using the relationship between production, exports, and home demand. *The evidence on HMEs accumulated by these papers is highly mixed.* One can see some support for HMEs in some industries in some specifications. However reverse HMEs (coefficients on demand of less than one or on home biased demand of less than zero) are more frequent. These overall unsupportive results should be contrasted with the more robust results arising from wage equations seen in Section 4. The empirical success of wage equations and the less successful attempts to validate home market effects in production regressions are entirely consistent with each other. They can be interpreted in a positive way as a sign that market access mechanisms of NEG are empirically important, but generally take the form of higher factor incomes in large demand areas rather than magnified production shares of IRS industries.

Despite its robustness to alternate market structures and demand formulations, the home market effect turns out to be quite fragile in one key respect. The theoretical literature following Helpman and Krugman (1985) makes assumptions that lead to a perfectly elastic supply of labor to the increasing returns sector. This is necessary to obtain the linear share equation. In contrast, the literature on income-access effects may be seen as holding quantity constant and letting wages adjust. The more general case where market access influences the number of firms in a location, and thereby net exports, as well as the prevailing wage is much more difficult to carry out. However, Fujita, Krugman and Venables (1999) provide an illuminating investigation, that when pushed a little bit further, yields a result that can help to make sense of the results of the two empirical literatures.

Start from a symmetric equilibrium. Then totally differentiate, linearize and make substitutions. The result, as shown in Fujita, Krugman and Venables (1999), is

$$\left[\sigma\frac{1+\phi}{1-\phi}+(1-\sigma)\frac{1-\phi}{1+\phi}\right]\frac{\mathrm{d}w}{w}+\left[\frac{1+\phi}{1-\phi}\right]\frac{\mathrm{d}L}{L}=\frac{\mathrm{d}Y}{Y}. \tag{19}$$

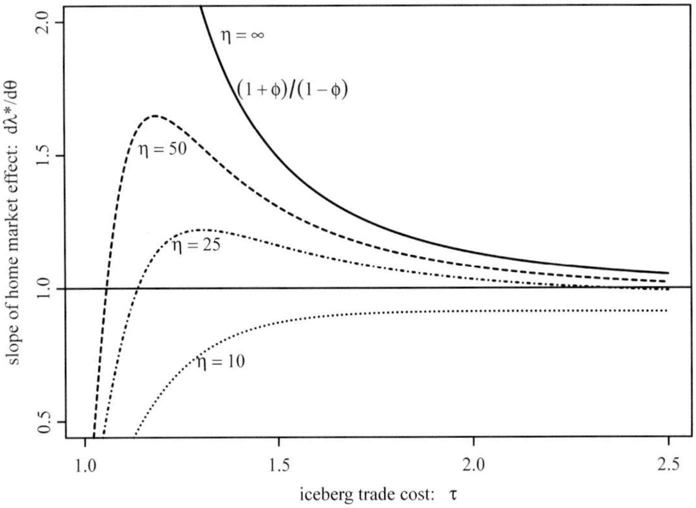

Figure 2. Home market effects with imperfectly elastic labor supply.

The supply of labour to the modern sector, L, has a wage elasticity of

$$\eta \equiv \frac{\mathrm{d}L/L}{\mathrm{d}w/w}.$$

Since, around the symmetry point, firms have all the same employment, we can write $\mathrm{d}n/n = \mathrm{d}L/L$. Finally around the point of symmetry, $\mathrm{d}\lambda^*/\mathrm{d}\theta = (\mathrm{d}n/n)/(\mathrm{d}Y/Y)$. Thus we can combine all these substitutions and re-express Equation (19) as

$$\mathrm{d}\lambda^*/\mathrm{d}\theta = \mathcal{M}/\big(1 + \big(1 + \big(\mathcal{M}^2 - 1\big)\sigma\big)/\eta\big). \tag{20}$$

As $\eta \to \infty$ we obtain $\mathrm{d}\lambda^*/\mathrm{d}\theta = \mathcal{M} = (1 + \phi)/(1 - \phi) > 1$. However, smaller elasticities of labour supply lead to bigger wages in the large market and this dampens or even destroys the home market effect. This can be seen by letting the trade costs get very large. When $\phi \to 0$, we obtain $\mathrm{d}\lambda^*/\mathrm{d}\theta = 1/(1 + 1/\eta) < 1$; as long as η is of finite (positive) value, there always exists a level of trade costs above which we obtain reverse HMEs. We illustrate in Figure 2, where $\mathrm{d}\lambda^*/\mathrm{d}\theta$ is graphed against τ for different values of the labour supply elasticity. It can be seen in this figure that large trade impediments associated with low labour supply elasticities will yield reverse home market effects (slopes inferior to one). Furthermore the monotonically decreasing relationship between the HME and trade barriers (that we refer to as "secondary magnification") is only valid in the limit when $\eta \to \infty$.

We conclude that market access is an important determinant of both the locations of producers and their factor returns. However, the prediction of a more than one-for-one response of production to demand only arises under extreme versions of more general models. Since less than unitary responses are consistent with constant returns models, the HME test is not ideal for discriminating between increasing returns and traditional models. While consistently larger than one estimates of the HME would have militated in favor of an increasing returns model, the highly mixed pattern of estimated coefficients neither supports nor falsifies the new trade foundations of NEG.

7. Trade-induced agglomeration

The work reviewed in Sections 4–6 all consider the impact of the geographic distribution of demand as an *explanatory* variable. While this empirical approach is useful and justifiable in certain contexts, it is also problematic. The key idea of NEG is that *the location of demand is jointly determined with the location of production.* In particular, the opportunity to export at low cost to immobile sources of demand allows all the mobile consumers and producers to congregate in the so-called manufacturing core. The predicted relationship between the free-ness of trade and agglomeration motivated the title of this chapter. Indeed, a large part of European academic interest in agglomeration stems from the question of whether a more united European market will lead to more spatially concentrated industry.

We begin this section with a review of work that has examined the relationship between agglomeration and trade costs, as well as the related issues of plant-level increasing returns and demand mobility. Existing work of this type is loosely related to the underlying theory. Later in this section, we consider steps that might be taken to treat the theory more seriously and review two papers that move in this direction.

7.1. Concentration regressions

The papers we present in this section may be thought of as reduced-form approaches to the hypotheses expressed verbally above. They construct concentration indexes to measure the strength of agglomeration forces over different industries and time periods, and then check whether those patterns are broadly consistent with predictions of NEG models or with other plausible stories. All papers reviewed here can be grouped as doing the following type of regression:

$$\mathrm{CONC}_s = a + b\mathrm{TRCOSTS}_s + c\mathrm{IRS}_s + d\mathrm{LINKAGES}_s + \cdots + e_s.$$

The dependent variable, CONC_s is the particular geographic concentration index of industry s. $\mathrm{TRCOSTS}_s$ and IRS_s are proxies for trade costs (τ in the model) and the degree of increasing returns ($1/\sigma$ in the model), respectively. $\mathrm{LINKAGES}_s$ measures the industry's reliance on intermediate inputs sometimes distinguishing between those that are mobile versus those that are tied to immobile natural resources. A variety of other variables (represented above as $\cdots$) can be added to this type of regressions, some intended alternative explanations for agglomeration such as endowments or technological spillovers.

7.1.1. *Concentration indexes of agglomeration*

Measuring spatial concentration of activity is a far less trivial exercise that might seem at first sight. Duranton and Overman (2002) list five properties we would expect from a meaningful concentration index. Combes and Overman (2004) add four additional *desiderata* in their chapter in this volume. Most indexes are constructed by dividing up geographic space into regions and comparing the share of activity (measured by number of firms, production, or employment) in each region with a benchmark. Two problems deserve special attention. The first is that an industry with a small number of establishments may appear to be concentrated purely by chance. This so-called lumpiness problem makes it problematic to compare industries with commonly used measures such as the locational Gini index. Ellison and Glaeser's (1997) solution to the lumpiness problem has led to wide adoption of their index, hereafter referred to as the EG index.

A second important issue that still awaits a satisfactory solution is the dependence of concentration indexes on the level and method of geographical disaggregation. When geographic units lack economic relevance, actual clusters of industries that take place across borders of those units are artificially separated. Furthermore, standard concentration indexes fail to account for the spatial proximity of those units. A concrete example illustrates these problems. In 1995, 76 establishments produced watches in France, employing 5406 people. The first départment for this industry hosted 45 of those firms, accounting for 64% of national employment of the industry (against approximately 1% of France's GDP and area). This extreme concentration pattern would be partly captured by Gini or EG indexes, and it is indeed, as this industry appears to have among the highest EG index in Table 1 of Maurel and Sédillot (1999), who use very comparable data. One thing those indexes miss is that the considered départment is Doubs, which is contiguous to Switzerland. It is therefore quite likely that the real agglomeration in the watch industry spills over the political border, a feature this type of index cannot account for. In addition, the two following départements in terms of the number of firms for the watch industry are Haute-Savoie and Jura (7.1% and 3.3% of industry's employment, respectively), which are also contiguous to Switzerland and very close to Doubs. The EG index cannot control for this additional dimension of agglomeration, as its computation would be exactly the same if Haute-Savoie and Jura were located hundreds of kilometers apart and away from Doubs.

Duranton and Overman (2002) construct a "continuous-space concentration index" that alleviates the problems associated with standard indexes. Their index uses the actual location of firms at the most detailed level available and compares bilateral distances between all pairs of firms to a counterfactual distribution emerging from a random re-location of all firms. There are two practical problems that will limit adoption of this method. First, only a few data sets provide the precise address of each producing establishment. Second, the use of simulations to construct the benchmark raises issues of replicability.

Is the picture of relative spatial agglomeration of industries actually different when using different indexes? Duranton and Overman (2002) calculate (in addition to their own index) EG indexes using 120 postcodes in the UK as geographical units. The most interesting result of the comparison for our purpose is that the two measures of agglomeration are almost uncorrelated when considering rankings of industries. The correlation between the two rankings improves significantly when only large plants are considered, but still the Spearman rank correlation between the two indexes is only equal to 0.4. This means that the results given by a discrete space index and a continuous space index might be very different. This should draw our attention to the fact that the spatial scale is very important in results using the EG index. In particular, taking a level of location units that is "too fine" can lead to an underestimation of agglomeration levels because it artificially separates clusters that sprawl over the border between units. Even worse, the ranking of industries can be radically changed by the choice of units, which endangers any attempt to *explain different concentration levels across industries*. This important problem is also apparent in Rosenthal and Strange (2001) who calculate EG indexes at the state, county and zip code level for 4-digit industries in the United States. The mean EG index goes from 0.0485 at the state level to 0.0101 at the zip code level. The correlation between the two being only 0.58.[22] Rosenthal and Strange (2001) interpret this as a possible change in determinants across geographical levels, but the inadequacy of the EG index to deal properly with spatial aggregation problems is another plausible explanation.

7.1.2. Results of concentration regressions

All users of concentration indexes acknowledge that multiple phenomena (endowments, spillovers, and NEG-type linkages for instance) – usually considered separately in theory – probably act simultaneously in a great number of industries. High values of indexes *per se* are therefore not very informative on the prevalence of NEG mechanisms in the economy. What needs to be done is to disentangle the share of each possible explanation in the observed concentration index. We now consider papers that have related concentration indexes to proxies of trade costs, increasing returns, and vertical linkages while controlling for other possible sources of agglomeration.

Since trade costs have tended to decline over time due to improvements in transport technology, and – since the end of WWII – due to reductions in trade barriers, a crude strategy is to measure how spatial concentration has changed over time. Kim (1995) examines the period from 1860 to 1987. Concentration, measured by a locational Gini index, falls until 1900, then rises to a peak around 1927 and then declines steadily until 1987, reaching a level approximately a third lower than in 1860. This non-monotonic

[22] Maurel and Sédillot (1999) also found that the average EG index rises with the level of spatial aggregation (from 0.06 for the 95 French départements to 0.09 for the 22 French régions. Ellison and Glaeser (1997) found their index to have a median value of 0.005 at the U.S. county level and 0.023 at the state level.

evolution of concentration presents a puzzle for the basic Krugman (1991a) model. Examining European data from 1972 to 1996, Brülhart (2001) finds that the average employment Gini index grows by about 18%. Interestingly, there is no evidence that the growth rate accelerates in the sub-period following the signing the Single Market Programme. In fact, contrary to the fears of increased agglomeration with trade liberalization, the average growth rate is about one third *lower* after 1986. These results are interesting but their interpretation as evidence for or against NEG relies upon the untenable assumption that trade costs are the only variable changing over time.

A more direct approach is to relate industry-level spatial concentration to industry-level proxies for trade costs. Brülhart (2001) relates variation in the Gini indexes across industries and over time to the Buigues, Ilkovitz and Lebrun (1990) classification of industries as characterized by high, medium or low NTBs. Seemingly contradictory with the basic predictions of NEG models, concentration is positively related to NTB level. Haaland, Kind and Midelfart-Knarvik (1999) find no effect for the same NTB measure. Given the crude nature (one year, low informativeness about the level of protection) of the Buigues, Ilkovitz and Lebrun (1990) measure, we should not infer much from these inconsistent results.

Ades and Glaeser (1995) provide more persuasive results using a substantially different methodology. Their data comprises a cross-section of 85 countries. Instead of concentration indexes, their dependent variable is the log of the size of the country's largest city. As they control for the population of the rest of the country, this is like measuring the share of the population in the main city. Three variables capture transport costs within each country. The first is area. Holding population constant, larger areas amount to greater average distances between buyers and sellers, and therefore larger transport costs (lower ϕ). The second and third variables measure transportation infrastructure, using, respectively expenditures on transport and communication and road density. All three variables point to a *positive* relation between trade costs and agglomeration (in the main city). This contradicts the prediction of Krugman (1991a) but is consistent with the Helpman (1998) model that reverses the relationship between agglomeration and trade costs.

Kim (1995) is one of the first papers to investigate empirically the relative explanatory power of alternative theoretical frameworks in a panel data setting. Kim (1995) regresses Gini indexes calculated in 1880, 1914, 1947, 1967, and 1987 for twenty 2-digit industries on a proxy for internal scale economies (production workers per plant), a resource intensity variable (cost of raw materials divided by value added), and two sets of industry and year fixed effects. The significant positive influence of scale economies offers some support for NEG.

Using national data from Europe, several papers have attempted to corroborate Kim's (1995) finding of a positive relationship between spatial concentration and measures of scale economies. Amiti (1999) follows Kim (1995) in using firm size as the proxy for increasing returns and in controlling for industry fixed effects. Her work suggests that European industries also exhibit a positive correlation between changes in increasing returns and changes in spatial concentration. Brülhart and Torstensson (1996) find a

0.69 rank correlation between locational Gini indexes and returns to scale estimates of Pratten (1988) in a cross-section of 18 industries. They also find a 0.63 correlation between the degree of increasing returns and a "centre–periphery bias" variable that the authors constructed by relating each industry's geographic distribution of employment to the corresponding distribution of market potential. Thus it appears that increasing returns industries are both spatially concentrated and centrally located. Moving beyond simple correlations and adding a 25 year temporal dimension to the concentration data, Brülhart (2001) finds however no significant effect for the Pratten measure of increasing returns. Haaland, Kind and Midelfart-Knarvik (1999) find that their scale economies proxy has a consistently negative impact on concentration.

Trade costs and increasing returns are the two key parameters determining agglomeration in the Krugman (1991a) version of NEG. The Venables (1996) version focuses on input–output linkages between industries. In the Puga (1999) model, this corresponds to a parameter we call α in Equation (21). Ellison and Glaeser (1997) establish a relationship between a variant of their index capturing co-agglomeration and the input–output linkages between the considered industry pairs. They construct two lists of 100 industries pairs, one consisting of the 100 downstream industries that receive the largest value of inputs per dollar value of output from a single upstream industry. The second list consists of the 100 upstream industries selling the largest portion of their output to a single industry. Out of the first (downstream) list of industry pairs, 77 industry pairs show a tendency to co-agglomerate, whereas the figure is 68 for the second list. Rosenthal and Strange (2001) use manufactured inputs per dollar of shipments as a proxy for the strength of input–output linkages in the industry (what they call "input sharing"). They find weak empirical evidence of such linkages, with statistical significance only at the state level (the significance is slightly improved when considering "young firms" that have less than 5 years of existence). Using a similar measure, Amiti (1999) finds significant positive effects of linkages on spatial concentration in Europe. In Haaland, Kind and Midelfart-Knarvik (1999) paper, input–output linkages always have a small and barely significant coefficient.

What is the take-away from the concentration regressions relating spatial concentration to proxies for the key NEG parameters? First, there is little persuasive evidence that the degree of increasing returns raises spatial concentration. Whether the absence of a statistical relationship reflects poor proxies for increasing returns or inadequate concentration indexes or the absence of an economic relationship is uncertain. Second, vertical linkages do seem to have a fairly robust relationship with concentration. We would hope that future work would follow the approach of Ellison and Glaeser (1997) in exploiting the precise nature of input–output linkages, rather than just summing over all intermediate input purchases. Last, trade costs have a highly mixed impact on geographic concentration. As will be discussed in the following section, this is not inconsistent with some versions of NEG theory. Greater concern over functional form is warranted here, as well as better measures of trade costs. Somewhat surprisingly to us, the most convincing evidence – provided by Ades and Glaeser (1995) – militates in favor of the Helpman (1998) model.

7.2. Taking NEG theory seriously

The models described in the previous subsection do not take NEG theory "too seriously". Brülhart (2001), for example, explains his goal is to "... look for stylized facts that might or might not be consistent with theoretical predictions rather than for rigorous tests of competing models." We think this approach is quite understandable for first-generation empirical assessments of NEG theories. Nevertheless, it seems worthwhile to take a closer look at the predictions of NEG.

7.2.1. Concentration predictions of NEG models

Consider first the simplest NEG model, namely the Krugman (1991a) model and its conditional concentration prediction often illustrated with the "tomahawk" subcritical bifurcation diagram. We present an example of this diagram in panel (a) of Figure 3 which replicates the version presented as Figure 5.4 in Fujita, Krugman and Venables (1999) (drawn for $\mu = 0.4$ and $\sigma = 5$). Three equilibrium configurations for the share of firms λ are associated with a gradual fall in trade costs from an initially high level: Stable dispersion only, followed by a multiple equilibria range where both dispersion and agglomeration are possible outcomes, and last stable agglomeration only, for high levels of trade integration. Location adjustment dynamics towards stable equilibria are indicated by the arrows.

Inspection of this diagram reveals that there are indeed predictions on concentration variation, but those are at the same time too simple to be verified and not simple enough to be easily implemented empirically. The basic prediction is that for levels of trade costs above the sustain point (τ_S), only dispersion can be an equilibrium, while under the break point (τ_B), only full agglomeration can be sustained as a stable equilibrium. While this simplest prediction of an abrupt and immediate change from complete symmetry to extreme agglomeration is clearly too stark to be verified, the pattern suggests a positive relationship between trade integration and concentration, which is the rationale behind much of the empirical work reviewed in Section 7.1.2. Note that this prediction can in principle be subjected to empirical test using time series (focused on the evolution of concentration indexes within each industry) or cross section data (focused on assessing which industries are correctly predicted to be dispersed of agglomerated).

There are however important issues in the implementation of such tests. Indeed, a key concern is that this model predicts *nothing like* a simple linear relationship between concentration and trade integration. In fact, it is immediately apparent from the diagram that for the vast majority of admissible parameter values, "nothing will happen" in terms of concentration after a small fall in trade costs τ. It is only somewhere between τ_S and τ_B that a considered industry will discontinuously jump from the symmetric to the agglomerated equilibrium. This prediction, sometimes referred to as catastrophic agglomeration, is summarized in the following quote:

> Catastrophe is the most celebrated hallmark of the CP model – probably because it is so unexpected. Specifically, starting from a symmetric outcome and very high

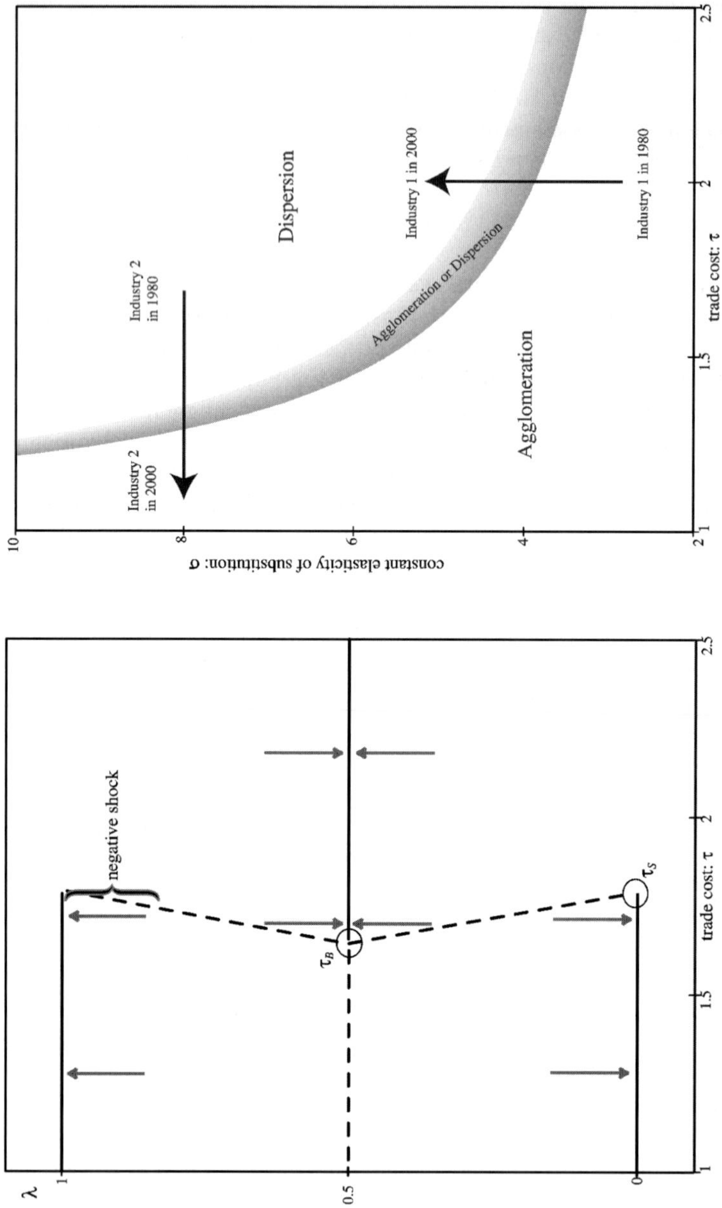

(a) Bifurcation for $\mu = 0.4$ and $\sigma = 5$

(b) Bifurcation for $\mu = 0.4$ and varying σ

Figure 3. Equilibrium configurations in the Krugman (1991a) model.

> trade costs, marginal increases in the level of trade free-ness ϕ has no impact on the location of industry until a critical level of ϕ is reached. Even a tiny increase in ϕ beyond this point causes a catastrophic agglomeration of industry in the sense that the only stable outcome is that of full agglomeration. [Baldwin et al. (2003)]

A linear regression is therefore severely *mis-specified* as even if there existed an industry where the simplest NEG model applied perfectly, the linear estimation would presumably yield a coefficient not statistically different from zero, which would likely be misinterpreted as a rejection of NEG. The expectations that should be derived from this theory are truly more complicated than a simple linear relationship and heavily dependent on the values of the parameters. The vast empirical literature (covered above and in much more depth in Combes and Overman (2004) chapter of this Handbook) trying to find evidence of NEG through linear relationships with concentration indexes as the dependent variable is therefore weakly grounded in theory (while being often both insightful and instructive). Our belief is that time has come for this type of research to now re-consider their methodological strategy and in particular think about ways to improve the specifications with a closer concern about what the models actually predict.

There are however several possible empirical implementations of the simple NEG model more consistent with theory. The bifurcation diagram can again be used here, in a version accounting for the likely variance across industries in *both* τ and σ dimensions. Panel (b) of Figure 3 uses the same sustain and break point equations to divide the σ–τ parameter space into ranges where

(i) full *agglomeration* in one location or the other are the only stable equilibria,
(ii) symmetric *dispersion* is the only stable equilibrium, and
(iii) the shaded area in which agglomerated *and* dispersed equilibria are stable.

This representation can be seen as a graphical version of Table 5.1 in Fujita, Krugman and Venables (1999).

Several empirical implementations seem possible when considering the panel (b) of Figure 3. Industry-level estimates of τ and σ can be used to give coordinates for each industry to be placed in the figure for a given set of trade partners. Measuring these parameters is not a trivial task, of course. Ideally, τ should capture a variety of sources of trade costs including transport costs, tariffs, non-tariff barriers, communication costs. Those costs are bilateral in nature (depending for instance on bilateral distance between the trading partners) and industry-specific (transport costs of concrete and semiconductor chips differ drastically).[23]

Measuring σ raises difficult issues because this parameter fulfills multiple roles in the Dixit–Stiglitz model. It is not only a differentiation parameter, but also the price elasticity of demand, an inverse index of scale economies, and an inverse measure of equilibrium markups. Using a gravity equation, coefficients on the origin country

[23] Hummels (1999) and Limao and Venables (2001) are two papers that grapple with the issue of measuring international transport costs correctly.

price term or on bilateral tariffs or freight can then be used to infer σ.[24] Alternatively, one can exploit the fact that the Lerner index in the Dixit–Stiglitz model is given by $(p-c)/p = 1/\sigma$, with p denoting price and c marginal cost. Consequently, multiplying by the output of symmetric firms in the industry, one can calculate σ at the industry level as shipments/(shipments-variable costs).[25]

With estimates of τ and σ in hand, the next step is to assess whether a cross section of industry-level concentration indexes match the predictions of the model (for instance, that industry 1 was more agglomerated than industry 2 in 1980 as predicted by the model illustrated in Figure 3). One may also look *within* industries to verify whether changes in parameters over time delivered the predicted change in agglomeration patterns. In the examples considered in Figure 3, concentration indexes can be used to assess whether industry 1 became more dispersed over the period and industry 2 more agglomerated.

7.2.2. *The diagonal Puga model*

The Krugman (1991a) model is however probably too restrictive to be used directly in empirical work following the lines just mentioned. Indeed, a particularly important feature of this model is that it predicts that high trade costs will generate dispersion and low trade costs agglomeration. The problem with this is that the Krugman (1991a) model continues to predict full agglomeration even as transport costs become tiny. This is because the dispersive forces decline with trade costs at an even more rapid rate than the agglomerative forces. With *any other congestion force unrelated to trade costs*, the equilibrium pattern of location will return to dispersion for some (low) trade costs threshold where all trade-related forces become so weak that they must be dominated by the congestion force.[26] These additional congestion forces cause *dispersion* to have a U-shaped relationship with trade costs. Reciprocally, spatial *concentration* has what Ottaviano and Thisse (2004) in this volume describe as a *bell-shaped* relationship with trade costs.[27]

Linear regressions of concentration indexes on trade costs remain inappropriate in the Puga (1999) model. The good point of the bell shape prediction in terms of empirical testing and specification is that there is at least a continuous relationship between

[24] For details on several variants of this method, see Hummels (1999), Head and Mayer (2000), Head and Ries (2001), Lai and Trefler (2002), and Erkel-Rousse and Mirza (2002).

[25] In other market structures, such as Ottaviano, Tabuchi and Thisse (2002), this simple relationship between markups and the substitution parameter does not exist.

[26] Examples of congestion forces giving rise to the bell shape include Helpman (1998), where the housing sector makes agglomeration unsustainable for very low trade costs, or comparative advantage as in Forslid and Wooton (2003). The Ottaviano and Thisse (2004) chapter also analyzes mechanisms yielding the bell. The bell-shaped prediction can be obtained through the inclusion in the NEG model of different realistic features such as impediments in inter-regional workers' mobility [Krugman and Venables (1995), enriched considerably in Puga (1999)] or heterogeneity in the tastes of workers which translates into their migration patterns [Tabuchi and Thisse (2002)].

[27] Describing the bell as an "inverted U" is both awkward and potentially confusing and should therefore be avoided.

trade costs and concentration over some range of the parameters. Unfortunately, this relationship is *not linear and worse, not monotonic*.

The Puga (1999) version of the NEG model removes the exotic dynamics of the Krugman (1991a) model while remaining analytically tractable. It is sufficiently detailed and complete to nest the Krugman (1991a) and Krugman and Venables (1995) approaches. To extend the Puga (1999) model to accommodate multiple increasing returns industries, we do have to impose a strong assumption about the input–output structure: Firms in an industry source all their intermediate inputs from their own industry. This implies a diagonal input–output (I–O) structure. We also must assume that industry expenditure shares are fixed by preferences (i.e., the upper-level utility is Cobb–Douglas). Those assumptions are restrictive, being more acceptable as approximations only for highly aggregated industries. This suggests the need for more detailed modelling of actual input–output linkages and demand substitution patterns between industries (as detailed below, this is an important contribution of Forslid, Haaland and Midelfart-Knarvik (2002) to provide predictions of a "full" model with I–O linkages between 14 industries calibrated on real data).

The parameters of interest include τ (trade costs), σ (the elasticity of substitution between varieties), μ (the share of consumer expenditure on manufactured goods), α [the share of costs constituted by purchases of intermediate goods from one's own industry, which is zero in the Krugman (1991a) model], and η [the elasticity of a region's labor supply to the manufacturing sector with respect to local agricultural wages, which Krugman (1991a) and Krugman and Venables (1995) assume to be infinite].

We therefore implement the analysis presented in Puga (1999), where he identifies the threshold transaction costs between which dispersion is unstable and we should therefore expect to observe agglomeration. This analysis is intended to illustrate what this unexplored path of empirical implementation of NEG theory could be. Let us follow his notation and define $\underline{\phi}_s$ and $\overline{\phi}_s$ as the lower and upper break points for sector s. Puga (1999) shows that these break points are solutions to the following quadratic equation in ϕ:

$$\begin{aligned}&\big[\sigma(1+\alpha)-1\big]\big[(1+\alpha)(1+\eta)+(1-\alpha)\mu\big)\big]\phi^2\\&\quad-2\big\{\big[\sigma\big(1+\alpha^2\big)-1\big](1+\eta)-\sigma(1-\alpha)\big[2(\sigma-1)-\mu\alpha\big]\big\}\phi\\&\quad+(1-\alpha)\big[\sigma(1-\alpha)-1\big](\eta+1-\mu)=0.\end{aligned}\tag{21}$$

The roots of this equation give the degrees of trade freeness $\underline{\phi}_s$ above which complete symmetry is unstable and activity starts to agglomerate, and $\overline{\phi}_s$ for which trade is so easy that the process of re-dispersion is completed and the equilibrium reverts to perfect symmetry. Although the analytical expressions of solutions to Equation (21) are not easy to manipulate, they can be calculated very easily for each sector s when one plugs in values of parameters of main interest, σ_s, μ_s and α_s. This gives for each industry the range defined by $[\underline{\phi}_s, \overline{\phi}_s]$ over which agglomeration is expected and that we can compare with $\hat{\phi}_s$ calculated from observed trade flows of country pairs representative

that agglomeration could arise endogenously, starting from a situation of perfectly symmetric countries or regions. This mirrored the effort of new trade theories a decade before to design models able to generate (intra-industry) trade in a world of seemingly identical countries in terms of endowments and technology. In empirical work, natural advantages have to be brought back in the analysis, because in the real world countries differ in their initial conditions in ways that can be expected to alter the final outcome.

A quite important point is that traditional comparative advantage constant returns with perfect competition models also give rise to predictions of increasing agglomeration accompanying trade liberalization. The increased specialization of countries in the production of the goods for which they have a comparative advantage will indeed translate into increased agglomeration of industries across space. However this relationship is predicted to be monotonic as opposed to the NEG models of the increasing returns with imperfect competition type outlined above, where the bell shape emerges. Forslid, Haaland and Midelfart-Knarvik (2002) provide a framework encompassing both input–output linkages in a Venables (1996) type model and comparative advantage patterns in order to assess which industries are predicted to exhibit the bell shape and which industries are predicted to agglomerate monotonically with trade integration. There are 14 industries linked with region-specific input–output tables (the regions are groupings of 17 West European countries into 4 European regions called Central, North, South and West). Of those 14 industries, ten are assumed to have the Dixit–Stiglitz–Krugman usual market structure, two are traded perfectly competitive sectors without trade costs and with decreasing returns to scale, and two are non-tradeable monopolistic competition services sectors. Capital, unskilled labour and skilled labour – the three primary factors of production – are assumed to be internationally immobile. Data for calculating parameters mostly comes from Eurostat, GTAP and NBER world trade flows databases. The parameters of primary interest, trade costs and elasticities of substitution, respectively come from GTAP and from scale elasticities calculation based on Pratten (1988).

The main result of interest for our purpose lies in Forslid, Haaland and Midelfart-Knarvik's (2002, Figure 3) which depicts the path of the agglomeration of each industry (as measured by the standard deviation of the distribution of the share of production of the industry in each region) with respect to trade costs. Metals, chemicals, transport equipment and machinery all exhibit a distinct bell shape in the agglomeration index with decreasing trade costs, while the other increasing returns industries in their model (and specially so textile, leather, and food products) show a monotonic increase in agglomeration. The bell-shaped industries show, as expected, the highest degree of increasing returns to scale and relatively high share of own output in their intermediate goods consumption. We can also note from this paper that those industries are predicted to be at the start of the agglomeration process; that is, in the beginning of the range of trade costs for which agglomeration increases with trade liberalization. Note however that *the amount of predicted changes in the concentration patterns is much lower in the bell-shaped industries than in the others that seem to follow more closely the predictions from comparative advantage theories*. Thus, while the theoretical interest is primarily focused on those industries, it might be that the major part of the action concerning spatial distribution of activities in Europe will take place in more traditional industries exhibiting considerably larger concentration trends. This pattern is also observed in some of the papers investigating concentration patterns in a more descriptive way (like the ones covered in Section 7.1.2).

Combes and Lafourcade (2001) also propose simulations based on a model featuring input–output linkages between imperfectly competitive industries operating in a multiple location space. Their modeling strategy however differs notably from the usual approach as they use a Cournot, segmented markets, homogenous goods model as their theoretical framework. The paper proceeds in two steps: A structural estimation of the model is followed by a simulation of transport costs reduction effects. The estimated equation relates employment per firm in each of the 341 French regions considered to two terms capturing final demand and input–output linkages. The econometric analysis involves estimation for each industry of the sole unobserved element in the model: Industry-specific transport costs (a parameter for each industry multiplying an observed average transport costs). If this parameter is insignificant, the industry is estimated to be unaffected by transport costs and the linkages at the heart of agglomeration in this model are irrelevant. Significant and positive parameters are interpreted as empirical validation of the model. The results exhibit 47 significantly positive coefficients out of 64 industries in the full version of the model.

The second step uses the transport-cost sensitivity estimates to simulate the effects of a uniform transport-cost decrease in France (up to 30%). For computational reasons, simulations have to be run for the short-run version of the model (keeping the number of plants in each location-industry at its actual level in 1993). The change in production patterns and extent of agglomeration therefore entirely arises from changes in prices and individual production by firms (both of which would be unchanged in a Dixit–Stiglitz–Krugman framework).

The simulation results show a fall in production concentration for all industries. However, spatial scale matters. At the national level, the authors offer the stark prediction of a gradual switch from a monocentric structure to a duocentric one, the area around Lyon emerging as a second important center more comparable to the area around Paris. Meanwhile, at a finer geographic scale, increased polarization of activity around the main cities of France arises from the simulations. The overall picture is therefore one of an increased number of large centers of more even size, with surrounding areas loosing their industrial base to the benefit of the local center.

Those last papers seem to correspond to the kind of "computable spatial equilibrium" work that Fujita, Krugman and Venables (1999) called for in the conclusion of their book. They use ambitious NEG theoretical modelling, extended to account for important characteristics such as precise input–output linkages between a great number of industries, in order to give insights of what those models predict when a particular experiment, such as a drop in trade costs, occurs. In that sense they bear a large inheritance from modern computable general equilibrium modelling of trade liberalization accounting for market structure imperfections. This kind of work can be viewed, as Forslid, Haaland and Midelfart-Knarvik (2002) nicely put it, as "theory with numbers, rather than empirical results". These papers show how to generate empirical predictions that are tightly linked to rich versions of underlying theory. The next step would be to find cases where reality has conducted the same type of experiment as the simulation. Then one can confront predictions from calibrated models with actual data on concentration indexes to assess the empirical validity of predictions that are tightly linked to theory.

8. Instability, persistence, and agglomeration

The existence of multiple equilibria, only some of which are stable, is a very general feature of the NEG framework. Evidence of multiple equilibria in economic geography would not directly support the NEG approach since human capital and technological externalities also generate the self-reinforcing processes that create multiple equilibria. However, evidence refuting multiple equilibria would support the "natural advantages" approach in which agglomerations occur where they do because of exogenous and unchanging features of the natural setting.

Davis and Weinstein (2002) recently examined Japanese history and devised several tests designed to detect multiple equilibria. Their results, summarized in the quote below, clearly indicates that the authors do not find a lot of support for the existence of multiple equilibria.

> "An important practical question, then, is whether such spatial catastrophes are theoretical curiosa or a central tendency in the data. Our results provide an unambiguous answer: Even nuclear bombs have little effect on relative city sizes over the course of a couple of decades. The theoretical possibility of spatial catastrophes due to temporary shocks is *not* a central tendency borne out in the data." [Davis and Weinstein (2002, p. 1284) emphasis is in the original]

The basic question is whether the geographic pattern of agglomeration is stable over time periods featuring large shocks. Natural advantages models should exhibit such stability since there is a single equilibrium, which is globally stable and should change slowly given that nature changes slowly. In contrast, NEG models – and others of similar ilk – *might* exhibit instability. Referring back to the panel (a) of Figure 3, suppose the economy has parameter values that situate it in the region of three stable equilibria. Then a moderate negative shock to an agglomeration (that is a decline in λ from a starting point of $\lambda = 1$, as illustrated with a "}") could move the economy past the dashed line to a region of the parameter space where the dynamics (shown by the arrows) now push towards the symmetric dispersed equilibrium. Thus, while a small shock would rapidly be reversed (agglomeration is locally stable), a moderate shock could cause the agglomeration to unravel. An extremely large shock could even reposition the agglomeration from one location to another.

There are two related statistical methods for examining the issues of persistence and responsiveness to shocks. First, one can simply look at the correlations between the size of current agglomerations and their size in the past. Second we can estimate the extent to which locations recover from measured shocks.

8.1. Stability of historical location rankings

The long-run correlation method calculates the raw or rank correlation between city i's current share of the relevant population, λ_{it}, and its share b years before, $\lambda_{i,t-b}$. While a high correlation is expected for small b, it seems likely that over a longer period, featuring general population increase, important economic transitions and shocks, the correlation would decline dramatically. In calculating λ_{it} one may use cities as the geographic unit as long as they are consistently defined over time. Lacking such data, Davis and Weinstein (2002) use 39 regions for which they divide regional population by regional area and obtain population density as the agglomeration measure. The most striking result from the intertemporal correlations is that 1998 population density has a 0.76 raw correlation with population density in 1600 (i.e., $b = 398$); at 0.83, the rank correlation is even higher. Thus, over a four century period in which the total population of Japan increased tenfold, the economy shifted from agriculture to manufacturing and services, the ranking of regions remained remarkably stable.

Brakman, Garretsen and Schramm (2002) investigate stability of city sizes in Germany. Unlike Japan, where mountainous terrain substantially constrains where its 126 million residents might live, Germany's physical geography exerts a less dominant influence. For 60 cities, the authors find a 0.841 rank correlation between their 1939 and 1999 populations. Since Davis and Weinstein (2002) find 0.93 rank correlation between 1920 and 1998, this suggests that Germany's agglomeration pattern is somewhat less persistent than Japan's.

One of the main messages of Davis and Weinstein (2002) is that physical geography matters a great deal for economic geography. They quote from recent theoretical monographs to establish that NEG theorists have given inadequate attention to the importance of physical geography in explaining agglomeration. Another set of researchers, most notably Jeffrey Sachs (2001) and Jared Diamond (1997), have been pushing a "geography as destiny" viewpoint. Acemoglu, Johnson and Robinson (2002) illustrate one case where early geographic advantages translated into subsequent *disadvantages*. Their experiment is the European colonization of much of the Americas, Africa, and Oceania following 1500. One might expect, under some models of NEG, that Europeans would colonize areas that already provided good markets and supplies of inputs. In that case, we might expect colonizers to choose areas that already had relatively dense and urbanized populations. In a natural advantages setting, one would expect Europeans to choose the areas with strong fundamentals, which again would probably be the areas of relatively dense inhabitation.

Acemoglu, Johnson and Robinson (2002) also argue that the urbanized areas were very likely to be the more prosperous areas based on both theory and current cross-sectional correlations between urbanization and income per capita. They raise the question of whether prosperity in 1500 would be a good forecaster of prosperity in 1995.

The answer they find is a resounding no. Incomes in 1995 are negatively related to both urbanization and population density in 1500. The currently prosperous countries tend to be ones that attracted European colonists who brought with them European institutions. The Europeans tended to treat existing population centers as locations to extract resources from and this resulted, according to Acemoglu, Johnson and Robinson (2002) in investment-depressing institutions. While this study has only a tangential connection to NEG empirics, we think it worth mentioning to elaborate on the type of historically focussed empirical work that might help to disentangle the different roles of natural advantages, self-reinforcing processes, and shocks in determining the pattern of agglomeration.

Dumais, Ellison and Glaeser (2002), following up on Ellison and Glaeser (1997), study the evolution of the EG concentration index over the period 1972–1992. One of the objectives of Dumais, Ellison and Glaeser (2002) is to investigate the pattern of industry mobility to assess "how important historical accidents are in practice and whether Krugman's charming examples are representative". An important preliminary finding is that the measured level of agglomeration of industries is very stable over time: They find a correlation coefficient of 0.92 between 1972 and 1992 EG indexes across industries [Kim (1995) finds a corresponding striking correlation of 0.64 with a different localisation index between 1860 and 1987 values].

As emphasized by the authors, this dynamic stability is compatible with different, and informative, patterns of underlying "firms demographics". One possible pattern is that, in each industry, new firms replace old or dead ones in the same locations. Another possibility is that the underlying economic forces in each industry persist over time and therefore yield this great stability in the *levels* of agglomeration, despite important changes in the precise *location* of the industry. NEG models are often characterized by historical accidents, in which a region taking an accidental lead in the production share of the IRS industry might end up attracting all firms of this industry. The linkages creating the agglomeration forces thereafter make it very difficult to "break the core" into a more dispersed pattern or relocate this core in another region. Concentrated industries because of NEG linkages should therefore be expected to be very immobile over time.

Contrary to those NEG-type expectations, Dumais, Ellison and Glaeser (2002) find that the most geographically concentrated industries do *not* exhibit any less mobility than a typical un-concentrated industry. This result therefore sheds some doubt on the hypothesis that spatial concentration would be mainly explained by mechanisms locking-in industries in the locations historically chosen by pioneering firms.

8.2. The long-term impact of temporary shocks

The long-run correlations are interesting especially when we have strong reason to believe that there were important city-specific shocks that might have impacted agglomeration patterns. It is more compelling to examine these city-specific shocks directly using the shock persistence regressions. Assuming multiplicative shocks, taking natural logs, and calculating before and after differences, one obtains

$$(\ln \lambda_{i,t+a} - \ln \lambda_{it}) = \alpha + \beta(\ln \lambda_{it} - \ln \lambda_{i,t-b}) + e_{it}, \tag{22}$$

where a is the time elapsed *after* the split point (t) and b is the time elapsed *before* the split. Thus, b is the duration of the period in which the shock occurs. The estimated value of β tells us about the dynamics. An estimate of $\hat{\beta} \approx 0$ suggests a random walk in city sizes. That is all shocks have permanent effects. On the other hand, $\hat{\beta} \approx -1$ suggests shocks undo themselves over the time frame of a years.

For Davis and Weinstein (2002), the shock period is 1940 to 1947 (i.e., $b = 7$) when Japan experienced intense bombing from Allied forces that devastated many cities. The shock recovery period is 1947 to 1960 (i.e., $a = 13$). While their motivating algebra is in terms of the log shares, they replace the difference in log shares with the growth rates in their regressions. While these will be approximately the same for small changes, we think it advisable to retain the difference-in-logs specification for contexts such as their study where there were large changes.

Note that it can be shown that if the three values of $\ln \lambda_i$ ($t + a$, t, and $t - b$) were completely independent of each other (say just random noise) then the expected coefficient on β would be -0.5. This is because λ_{it} enters negatively in the dependent variable and positively in the explanatory variable. To deal with simultaneity, Davis and Weinstein (2002) instrument for $\lambda_{it} - \lambda_{i,t-b}$ using city-specific death and destruction measures.

Davis and Weinstein (2002) estimates $\hat{\beta} \approx -1$. Thus, cities experiencing the largest population declines due to bombing tend to have the fastest postwar growth rates. By 1960, on average the population shocks have been fully reversed. Even Nagasaki and Hiroshima, victims of atomic bombs that reduced populations by 8.5% and 20%, respectively, saw their populations come back in line with their 1925–1940 growth trends as early as 1960 for Nagasaki and 1975 for Hiroshima.

Those fascinating, albeit macabre, results exhibit no evidence for the catastrophe phenomena that are possible in NEG models. However, the distance from theory of this work commands some caution in interpretation: How large should the shock be for the model to predict a change in equilibrium? One should probably employ a simulated version of the model to examine this question. An additional difficulty is that the size of the shock needed depends on the level of integration of the zone. As shown in Figure 3(a), the region of high sensitivity to shocks is only for a narrow range of τ ($1.627 < \tau < 1.807$ for the case considered in Figure 3). Outside that range, two situations are possible: When τ is very high, symmetry cannot be broken, *whatever the size of the shock*. When the actual τ is lower than the bottom of the range, much larger shocks would be required to reverse the pattern of agglomeration. Indeed, the Davis and Weinstein (2002) paper is unclear as to whether they assume Japan in that period to be in the zone where both symmetric and agglomerated equilibria coexist or in the zone where there is no stable dispersed equilibrium. The two cases have different implications: In the former, the equilibrium can jump from agglomerated to dispersed (or the reverse) with a relatively small shock compared with the shock needed in the latter situation to make the equilibrium switch from agglomeration in one region to agglomeration in another. Therefore, it is at least possible that Japan was at the time in a parameters zone where only a *reversal* of agglomerated equilibrium was possible, a switch that could only result from shocks even larger than nuclear bombing. Further empirical investigation of NEG-type persistence of temporary shocks needs to take into account that the predictions of those models are conditional on values of the parameters. This recommendation parallels the one made above about concentration index regressions.

Another caveat regarding inferences to be drawn from Davis and Weinstein's (2002) study is that this is a case where physical geography matters an exceptional amount. Japan's mountainous topography, with a small share of overall land actually suitable for large scale city locations, makes it possible that activity reverts to its original location because there is no other suitable location left to occupy. While this point might certainly have some validity for activity and population growth as a whole, it should have less importance at the industry level. This is investigated in a follow-up paper by Davis and Weinstein (2003b). In the aftermath of allied bombing on Japanese cities, they show a tendency for *specific industries* to locate back where they initially were (despite massive destruction that drastically changed the distribution of industries across cities). This finding further undermines the case for multiple equilibria in location patterns.

Brakman, Garretsen and Schramm (2002) study the impact of wartime bombing in Germany. With respect to the persistence of related shocks, they find an estimate of β equal to -0.42 for West German cities when they assume $a = 4$. This goes to -0.52 when the authors broaden the "after" window to 17 years. They use house destruction as their instrumental variable for the population shock. Oddly, in East Germany, there was no tendency towards shock reversal and urban populations appear to follow random walks. We see a value to more studies of shock persistence. From these two studies, it is tempting to conclude that the greater the constraint imposed by physical geography, the greater will be the tendency for shocks to undo themselves over time.

Combining the key results of this section, it seems that this set of recent papers shows no evidence of either catastrophes (city sizes persist despite large shocks) or historical accidents (same level of mobility between concentrated and dispersed industries). It suggests that those two celebrated characteristics of NEG models should perhaps be considered more as fascinating theoretical "exotica" rather than as robust elements of economic geography.

9. Conclusion

Theoretical work on economic geography has a long and productive history. The last decade has seen a torrent of new papers, many of which expand upon the framework developed by Krugman (1991a). This literature, often referred to by the not very descriptive title of "new economic geography", is exciting because it generates results that contrast markedly with the traditional analyses involving exogenous factor supplies and constant returns to scale. NEG theories are characterized by magnification, bifurcation, multiple equilibria, and the possibility of catastrophe.

At its conclusion, the authors of *The Spatial Economy* argued that a vital part of "the way forward" from their work would involve empirical examination of the "intriguing possibilities" raised by the new theory. They did not specify the form these examinations should take, nor has any consensus emerged on the empirical methods to be applied to NEG.

Although the theory is still being digested, a large new serving of empirical work has arrived over the last five years. This survey has attempted to organize the new empirics of agglomeration and trade into categories and then assess the collective support it provides for NEG. The diversity in approaches that characterizes this literature probably stems in large part from the difficulties inherent in testing theories involving circular causation. In terms of the results, our sense is that the dust has not settled yet. One can see a number of supportive findings but there are just as many findings that appear to undermine the new theory. The positive relation between wages and market potential looks like a sturdy result but the response of production to demand, while certainly positive, is not consistently greater than one for one. Economic activity concentrates spatially but this agglomeration cannot yet be seen as confirmation of the theories that were constructed to explain the phenomenon. There are a number of other explanations that are consistent with the data and not much yet that strongly points to the explanation offered by NEG.

The lesson to be learned from past work [and from Leamer and Levinsohn (1995)] is that methods need to be designed to connect closely to the theory but should not be reliant upon features of models that were included for tractability or clarity of exposition instead of realism. Rather we need to focus on testing the essential distinguishing features of the models that allow one to falsify them or their alternatives.

What elements of the existing empirical literature will and should continue to figure prominently in future empirics? First, trade costs are a critical parameter and further work will continue to try to estimate how they vary across industries and over time. In models based on CES demand, it is critical to identify the free-ness of trade which is a compound parameter, $\tau^{1-\sigma}$, depending on trade costs as moderated by the elasticity of substitution between varieties. Second, the concept of real market potential (demands that are summed up while discounting for distance, borders, and supply alternatives) should continue to figure in studies of the location decisions of firms and workers, as well as the determination of factor prices. More work will be required to decide how to estimate each location's real market potential. In addition we need tests to discriminate between market potential as a motive for agglomeration in contrast to other mechanisms that might generate similar empirical relationships. Indeed, while structural estimation of NEG models is a valuable approach, we believe the biggest advances will come from approaches like Davids and Weinstein's (1996, 2003a) where estimates of a single parameter can allow us to choose between plausible alternative mechanisms of economic geography.

Acknowledgements

A first version of this chapter was presented at the CEPR "Cities and Geography" conference on December 12, 2002 in Paris. We appreciate the helpful suggestions we received during this event and later from the editors, Jacques Thisse and Vernon Henderson. Pierre-Philippe Combes, Gordon Hanson, Pamina Koenig-Soubeyran, Françoise Maurel, Henry Overman, Stephen Redding, and Federico Trionfetti also provided detailed and useful comments. This paper is produced as part of a CEPR Research Network on "The Economic Geography of Europe: Measurement, Testing and Policy Simulations", funded by the European Commission under the Research Training Network Programme (Contract No: HPRN-CT-2000-00069).

Appendix: Data appendix of Figure 4

Figure 4 uses several data sets that make feasible an industry-level collection of parameters values combined with trade freeness calculation. The main issue is to find a sufficiently flexible industry classification that allows both for a reasonable level of detail in the study and good data availability. The classification used by the OECD for its

Table 5
Values of parameters used in Figure 4

IO code	Description	μ	α	σ	$\phi_{\text{fr-de}}$	$\phi_{\text{us-ca}}$
3	foodbevtob	6.78%	18.52%	4.53	0.033	0.034
4	cloth	2.34%	34.66%	6.62	0.088	0.055
5	wood	0.36%	20.38%	3.64	0.019	0.130
6	paper	0.53%	36.61%	4.34	0.035	0.112
7	chemical	0.49%	42.93%	3.89	0.138	0.202
8	drugs	0.43%	7.56%	9.53	0.051	0.044
9	petro	0.72%	6.77%	5.01	0.019	0.055
10	plastics	0.26%	22.55%	5.36	0.070	0.135
11	minerals	0.10%	15.10%	2.65	0.032	0.087
12	ferrous	0.00%	58.59%	2.32	0.098	0.095
13	non-ferrous	0.04%	49.19%	6.66	0.150	0.343
14	fabmetal	0.49%	7.49%	4.85	0.024	0.061
15	machinery	3.83%	22.61%	7.87	0.106	0.494
16	computers	1.50%	19.38%	11.02	0.543	0.807
17	electrical	1.71%	19.30%	5.88	0.078	0.262
18	radiotvcom	1.89%	32.94%	9.44	0.212	0.210
19	ships	0.16%	0.12%	7.40	0.012	0.107
20	railroad	0.31%	21.01%	7.40	0.052	0.185
21	vehicles	2.67%	49.08%	7.11	0.130	0.594
22	aircraft	0.22%	39.63%	7.40	0.812	0.207
23	instruments	0.59%	17.80%	7.43	0.100	.

IO tables is quite attractive in those respects as it has a very easy correspondence with UN industry classifications ISIC rev2 and rev3, which are widely used and are quite easy to match with trade data.

The parameters needed are μ (the share of the industry's good in overall consumption), α (the share of own industry inputs expenditures in overall costs) and σ (which has the many interpretations emphasized above). For this graph, we use the OECD IO table for Japan in 1990 which is the latest table available. μ_s is calculated as the share of domestic demand for industry s goods in total domestic demand (domestic demand being defined as private final consumption + government purchases plus purchases for investment of goods from industry s). α_s represents the share of inputs purchased from own industry in overall costs (proxied by total purchases on intermediates plus compensation of employees). σ_s is taken from Table 4 of Hummels (1999) which gives estimates for 2 digit SITC rev3 industries in 1992, easy to match with the IO classification (the average of σ values are taken when multiple SITC goods categories map into a single IO industry). The last parameter needed to compute the range defined by $[\underline{\phi}_s, \overline{\phi}_s]$ is η, fixed to 200. More work is needed on getting estimates of η from the literature and ensuring that real roots exist for lower, more realistic, values.

The calculation of $\hat{\phi}_s$ involves comparable bilateral trade and production data in a common classification for our country pairs. The trade data from the World Bank trade and production database and production figures extracted from STAN OECD database both map into IO industries and give data for a quite long time period. For Figure 4, we use 1995 data to evaluate freeness of trade (except for aircraft, for which we use 1996 for the France–Germany ϕ), a recent year that is not too remote from the years for which parameters μ, α and σ are available (see Table 5).

References

Acemoglu, D., Johnson, S., Robinson, J. (2002). "Reversal of fortune: geography and institutions in the making of the modern world income distribution". Quarterly Journal of Economics 117 (4), 1231–1294.

Ades, A., Glaeser, E. (1995). "Trade and circuses: explaining urban giants". Quarterly Journal of Economics 110 (1), 195–227.

Amiti, M. (1999). "Specialisation patterns in Europe". Weltwirschaftliches Archiv 134 (4), 573–593.

Anderson, S.P., de Palma, A., Thisse, J.-F. (1992). Discrete Choice Theory of Product Differentiation. MIT Press, Cambridge.

Baldwin, R., Forslid, R., Martin, P., Ottaviano, G., Robert-Nicoud, F. (2003). "The core–periphery model: key features and effects". In: Public Policies and Economic Geography. Princeton University Press, Princeton. Chapter 1.

Brakman, S., Garretsen, H., van Marrewijk, C. (2001). An Introduction to Geographical Economics. Cambridge University Press, Cambridge.

Brakman, S., Garretsen, H., Schramm, M. (2002). "The strategic bombing of German cities during WWII and its impact on city growth". Mimeo, http://www.few.eur.nl/few/people/vanmarrewijk/geography/further%20reading/bombingsept2002def.pdf.

Brander, J. (1981). "Intra-industry trade in identical commodities". Journal of International Economics 11 (1), 1–14.

Brülhart, M., Torstensson, J. (1996), "Regional integration, scale economies and industrial economies". Center for Economic Policy Research Discussion Paper # n1435.

Brülhart, M. (2001). "Evolving geographical specialisation of European manufacturing industries". Weltwirschaftliches Archiv 137 (2), 215–243.

Brülhart, M., Trionfetti, F., (2002). "A test of trade theories when expenditure is home biased". Mimeo. University of Lausanne.

Buigues, P., Ilkovitz, F., Lebrun, J.-F. (1990). "The impact of the internal market by industrial sector: the challenge for member states". European Economy, Social Europe (Special issue).

Carlton, D. (1983). "The location and employment choices of new firms: an econometric model with discrete and continuous endogenous variables". Review of Economics and Statistics 65 (3), 440–449.

Combes, P.-P. (1997). "Industrial agglomeration under Cournot competition". Annales d'Economie et de Statistique 45, 161–182.

Combes, P.-P., Lafourcade, M. (2001). "Transport cost decline and regional inequalities: evidence from France". Center for Economic Policy Research Discussion Paper # 2894. Revised version: http://www.enpc.fr/ceras/combes/pdf/artinf.pdf.

Combes, P.-P., Overman, H.G. (2004). "The spatial distribution of economic activities in the European Union". In: Henderson, J.V., Thisse, J.-F. (Eds.), Handbook of Regional and Urban Economics, vol. 4. Elsevier, Amsterdam. This volume.

Coughlin, C.C., Terza, J.V., Arromdee, V. (1991). "State characteristics and the location of foreign direct investment in the United States". Review of Economics and Statistics 73 (4), 675–683.

Crozet, M. (2000). "Do migrants believe in market potential?" Cahier de la MSE–Série Blanche # 2000-30. Revised version: http://team.univ-paris1.fr/teamperso/crozet/Do_migrants.pdf. Journal of Economic Geography. In press.

Crozet, M., Mayer, T., Mucchielli, J.L. (2004). "How do firms agglomerate? A study of FDI in France". Regional Science and Urban Economics 34 (1), 27–54.

Davis, D., Weinstein, D. (1996). "Does economic geography matter for international specialization?" National Bureau of Economic Research Working Paper #5706.

Davis, D., Weinstein, D. (1999). "Economic geography and regional production structure: an empirical investigation". European Economic Review 43 (2), 379–407.

Davis, D., Weinstein, D. (2002). "Bones, bombs, and break points: the geography of economic activity". American Economic Review 92 (5), 1269–1289.

Davis, D., Weinstein, D. (2003a). "Market access, economic geography and comparative advantage: an empirical assessment". Journal of International Economics 59 (1), 1–23.

Davis, D., Weinstein, D. (2003b). "A search for multiple equilibria in urban industrial structure". Mimeo presented at the CEPR workshop 'The Economic Geography of Europe: Measurement, Testing and Policy Simulations' held in Villars, 17/18 January 2003.

Dekle, R., Eaton, J. (1999). "Agglomeration and land rents: evidence from the prefectures". Journal of Urban Economics 46 (2), 200–214.

Devereux, M., Griffith, R. (1998). "Taxes and the location of production: evidence from a panel of US multinationals". Journal of Public Economics 68 (3), 335–367.

Diamond, J. (1997). Guns, Germs and Steel: The Fate of Human Societies. Norton, New York.

Disdier, A.C., Head, K. (2003). "Exaggerated reports on the death of distance: lessons from a meta-analysis". University of British Columbia mimeo.

Dixit, A., Stiglitz, J. (1977). "Monopolistic competition and optimum product diversity". American Economic Review 67 (3), 297–308.

Dumais, G., Ellison, G., Glaeser, E. (2002). "Geographic concentration as a dynamic process". Review of Economics and Statistics 84 (2), 193–204.

Duranton, G., Overman, H. (2002). "Testing for localization using micro-geographic data". Center for Economic Policy Research Discussion Paper #3379.

Ellison, G., Glaeser, E. (1997). "Geographic concentration in U.S. manufacturing industries: a dartboard approach". Journal of Political Economy 105 (5), 889–927.

Ellison, G., Glaeser, E. (1999). "The geographic concentration of industry: does natural advantage explain agglomeration?". American Economic Review Papers and Proceedings 89 (2), 311–316.
Erkel-Rousse, H., Mirza, D. (2002). "Import price-elasticities: reconsidering the evidence". Canadian Journal of Economics 35 (2), 282–306.
Feenstra, R., Markusen, J., Rose, A. (2001). "Using the gravity equation to differentiate among alternative theories of trade". Canadian Journal of Economics 34 (2), 430–447.
Forslid, R., Haaland, J.I., Midelfart-Knarvik, K.H. (2002). "A U-shaped Europe? A simulation study of industrial location". Journal of International Economics 57 (2), 273–297.
Forslid, R., Wooton, I. (2003). "Comparative advantage and the location of production". Review of International Economics 11 (4), 588–603.
Friedman, J., Gerlowski, D., Silberman, J. (1992). "What attracts foreign multinational corporations". Journal of Regional Science 32 (4), 403–418.
Fujita, M., Krugman, P., Venables, A. (1999). The Spatial Economy: Cities, Regions, and International Trade. MIT Press, Cambridge.
Fujita, M., Thisse, J.-F. (2002). Economics of Agglomeration: Cities, Industrial Location and Regional Growth. Cambridge University Press, Cambridge.
Guimarães, P., Figueiredo, O., Woodward, D. (2000). "Agglomeration and the location of foreign direct investment in Portugal". Journal of Urban Economics 47 (1), 115–135.
Haaland, J.I., Kind, H.J., Midelfart-Knarvik, K.H. (1999). "What determines the economic geography of Europe?" Center for Economic Policy Research Discussion Paper # 207.2.
Hanson, G.H. (1996). "Localization economies, vertical organization, and trade". American Economic Review 86 (5), 1266–1278.
Hanson, G.H. (1997). "Increasing returns, trade and the regional structure of wages". Economic Journal 107 (440), 113–133.
Hanson, G.H. (1998). "Market potential, increasing returns, and geographic concentration". National Bureau of Economic Research Working Paper # 6429. Revised December 2001 version: http://www-irps.ucsd.edu/faculty/gohanson/Uscnty.pdf.
Hanson, G.H. (2001). "Scale economies and the geographic concentration of industry". Journal of Economic Geography 1 (3), 255–276.
Hanson, G.H., Xiang, C. (2002). "The home market effect and bilateral trade patterns". NBER Working Paper # 9076.
Harris, C. (1954). "The market as a factor in the localization of industry in the United States". Annals of the Association of American Geographers 64, 315–348.
Head, K., Mayer, T. (2000). "Non-Europe: the magnitude and causes of market fragmentation in Europe". Weltwirschaftliches Archiv 136 (2), 285–314.
Head, K., Mayer, T. (2002). "Market potential and the location of Japanese investment in the European Union". Center for Economic Policy Research Discussion Paper # 3455. Revised version in press in Review of Economics and Statistics.
Head, K., Mayer, T., Ries, J. (2002). "On the pervasiveness of home market effects". Economica 69 (275), 371–390.
Head, K., Ries, J. (2001). "Increasing returns versus national product differentiation as an explanation for the pattern of U.S.–Canada trade". American Economic Review 91 (4), 858–876.
Head, K., Ries, J., Swenson, D. (1995). "Agglomeration benefits and location choice: evidence from Japanese manufacturing investment in the United States". Journal of International Economics 38 (3–4), 223–247.
Head, K., Ries, J., Swenson, D. (1999). "Attracting foreign manufacturing: investment promotion and agglomeration". Regional Science and Urban Economics 29 (2), 197–218.
Helpman, E. (1998). "The size of regions". In: Pines, D., Sadka, E., Zilcha, Y. (Eds.), Topics in Public Economics, Theoretical and Applied Analysis. Cambridge University Press, Cambridge, pp. 33–54.
Helpman, E., Krugman, P. (1985). Market Structure and Foreign Trade. MIT Press, Cambridge.
Helsley, R., Strange, W. (1990). "Matching and agglomeration economies in a system of cities". Regional Science and Urban Economics 20 (2), 189–212.

Henderson, J.V., Kuncoro, A. (1996). "Industrial centralisation in Indonesia". World Bank Economic Review 10 (3), 513–540.
Hummels, D. (1999). "Toward a geography of trade costs". Mimeo. University of Chicago.
Justman, M. (1994). "The effect of local demand on industry location". Review of Economics and Statistics 76 (4), 742–753.
Kim, S. (1995). "Expansion of markets and the geographic distribution of economic activities: the tends in U.S. regional manufacturing structure, 1860–1987". Quarterly Journal of Economics 110 (4), 881–908.
Krugman, P. (1979). "Increasing returns, monopolistic competition, and international trade". Journal of International Economics 9 (4), 469–479.
Krugman, P. (1980). "Scale economies, product differentiation, and the pattern of trade". American Economic Review 70, 950–959.
Krugman, P. (1991a). "Increasing returns and economic geography". Journal of Political Economy 99, 483–499.
Krugman, P. (1991b). Geography and Trade. MIT Press, Cambridge.
Krugman, P. (1993). "First nature, second nature, and metropolitan location". Journal of Regional Science 33 (2), 129–144.
Krugman, P., Venables, A. (1995). "Globalization and the inequality of nations". Quarterly Journal of Economics 110 (4), 857–880.
Lai, N., Trefler, D. (2002). "The gains from trade with monopolistic competition: specification, estimation, and mis-specification". NBER Working Paper # 9169.
Leamer, E., Levinsohn, J. (1995). "International trade theory: the evidence". In: Grossman, G., Rogoff, K. (Eds.), Handbook of International Economics, vol. 3. North-Holland, Amsterdam, pp. 1339–1394.
Limao, N., Venables, A. (2001). "Infrastructure, geographical disadvantage, transport costs, and trade". World Bank Economic Review 15 (3), 451–479.
Lucas, R. (1988). "On the mechanics of economic development". Journal of Monetary Economics 22, 3–42.
Lundbäck, E., Torstensson, J. (1998). "Demand, comparative advantage and economic geography in international trade: evidence from the OECD". Weltwirtschaftliches Archiv 134 (2), 230–249.
Marshall, A. (1920). Principles of Economics. Macmillan, London.
Maurel, F., Sédillot, B. (1999). "A measure of the geographic concentration in French manufacturing industries". Regional Science and Urban Economics 29 (5), 575–604.
McCallum, J. (1995). "National borders matter: Canada–US regional trade patterns". American Economic Review 85 (3), 615–623.
Moretti, E. (2004). "Human capital externalities in cities". In: Henderson, J.V., Thisse, J.-F. (Eds.), Handbook of Regional and Urban Economics, vol. 4. Elsevier, Amsterdam, pp. 2243–2292. This volume.
Murata, Y. (2003). "Product diversity, taste heterogeneity, and geographic distribution of economic activities: market vs. non-market interactions". Journal of Urban Economics 53 (1), 126–144.
Neary, J.P. (2001). "Of hype and hyperbolas: introducing the new economic geography". Journal of Economic Literature 39 (2), 536–561.
Ottaviano, G., Tabuchi, T., Thisse, J.-F. (2002). "Agglomeration and trade revisited". International Economic Review 43 (2), 409–436.
Ottaviano, G., Thisse, J.-F. (2004). "Agglomeration and economic geography". In: Henderson, J.V., Thisse, J.-F. (Eds.), Handbook of Regional and Urban Economics, vol. 4. Elsevier, Amsterdam, pp. 2563–2608. This volume.
Overman, H., Redding, S., Venables, A. (2001). "The economic geography of trade, production and income: a survey of empirics". Center for Economic Policy Research Discussion Paper # 2978. In: Harrigan, J., Choi, K. (Eds.), Handbook of International Trade. Blackwell, London. In press.
Pratten, C. (1988). "A survey of the economies of scale". In: Research on the "Costs of Non-Europe". Vol. 2: Studies on the Economics of Integration. Commission of the European Communities, Luxembourg.
Puga, D. (1999). "The rise and fall of regional inequalities". European Economic Review 43 (2), 303–334.
Redding, S., Venables, A. (2004). "Economic geography and international inequality". Journal of International Economics 62 (1), 53–82.

Rosenthal, S., Strange, W. (2001). "The determinants of agglomeration". Journal of Urban Economics 50, 191–229.

Rosenthal, S.S., Strange, W. (2004). "Evidence on the nature and sources of agglomeration economies". In: Henderson, J.V., Thisse, J.-F. (Eds.), Handbook of Regional and Urban Economics, vol. 4. Elsevier, Amsterdam, pp. 2119–2171. This volume.

Sachs, J. (2001). "Tropical underdevelopment". National Bureau of Economic Research Working Paper # 8119.

Smith, D., Florida, R. (1994). "Agglomeration and industry location: an econometric analysis of Japanese-affiliated manufacturing establishments in automotive-related industries". Journal of Urban Economics 36 (1), 23–41.

Tabuchi, T., Thisse, J.-F. (2002). "Taste heterogeneity, labour mobility and economic geography". Journal of Development Economics 69 (1), 155–177.

Trionfetti, F. (2001). "Using home-biased demand to test trade theories". Weltwirtschaftliches Archiv 137 (3), 404–426.

Venables, A. (1996). "Equilibrium locations of vertically linked industries". International Economic Review 37 (2), 341–359.

Weder, R. (2003). "Comparative home-market advantage: an empirical analysis of British and American exports". Weltwirtschaftliches Archiv 139 (2), 220–247.

Wei, S.-J. (1996). "Intra-national versus international trade: how stubborn are nations in global integration?" National Bureau of Economic Research Working Paper # 5531.

Chapter 60

AGGLOMERATION AND REGIONAL GROWTH

RICHARD E. BALDWIN[1]

Graduate Institute of International Studies, Geneva, Switzerland
e-mail: baldwin@hei.unige.ch

PHILIPPE MARTIN[2]

University of Paris1 Panthéon-Sorbonne, Paris, France
e-mail: martin-p@mail.enpc.fr

Contents

[1] Also affiliated with CEPR.
[2] Also affiliated with CERAS-ENPC and CEPR.

Handbook of Regional and Urban Economics, Volume 4. Edited by J.V. Henderson and J.F. Thisse

DOI: 10.1016/S0169-7218(04)07060-1

Abstract

We review the theoretical links between growth and agglomeration. Growth, in the form of innovation, can be at the origin of catastrophic spatial agglomeration in a cumulative process à la Myrdal. One of the surprising features of the Krugman [Journal of Political Economy 99 (1991) 483–499] model, was that the introduction of partial labor mobility in a standard "new trade model" with trade costs could lead to catastrophic agglomeration. The growth analog to this result is that the introduction of endogenous growth in the same type of "new trade model" can lead to the same result. A difference with the labour mobility version is that the results are easier to derive from the analytical point of view in the endogenous growth version. We show that the relation between growth and agglomeration depends crucially on capital (human or physical) mobility between regions. The absence of capital mobility is at the heart of the possibility of spatial agglomeration with catastrophe. In addition, growth alters the process of location even without catastrophe. In particular, and contrary to the fundamentally static models of the New Economic Geography, spatial concentration of economic activities may be consistent with a process of delocation of firms towards poor regions. Finally, the presence of localized technology spillovers implies that spatial agglomeration is conducive to growth.

Keywords

growth, capital mobility, agglomeration, endogenous growth, technology spillovers

JEL classification: O40, R11, R12

1. Introduction

Spatial agglomeration of economic activities on the one hand and economic growth on the other hand are processes difficult to separate. Indeed, the emergence and dominance of spatial concentration of economic activities is one of the facts that Kuznets associated with modern economic growth. This strong positive correlation between growth and geographic agglomeration of economic activities has been documented by economic historians [Hohenberg and Lees (1985) for example], in particular, in relation to the industrial revolution in Europe during the nineteenth century. In this case, as the growth rate in Europe as a whole sharply increased, agglomeration materialized itself in an increase of the urbanization rate but also in the formation of industrial clusters in the core of Europe that have been by and large sustained until now. The role of cities in economic growth and technological progress has been emphasized by urban economists [Henderson (1988), Fujita and Thisse (2002)], development economists [Williamson (1988)] as well as by economists of growth [Lucas (1988)]. At the other hand of the spectrum, as emphasized by Baldwin, Martin and Ottaviano (2001), the growth take-off of Europe took place around the same time (end of eighteenth century) as the sharp divergence between what is now called the North and the South: growth sharply accelerated (for the first time in human economic history) at the same time as a dramatic and sudden process of agglomeration took place at the world level. Hence, as put by Fujita and Thisse (2002), "agglomeration can be thought as the territorial counterpart of economic growth".

Less dramatically and closer to us, Quah's (1996) results suggest also a positive relation between growth and agglomeration. He finds that among the Cohesion group of countries (Greece, Spain, Portugal and Ireland, though there are no Irish regional data), the two countries that have achieved a high rate of growth and converged in per capita income terms towards the rest of Europe (Spain and Portugal) have also experienced the most marked regional divergence. This is consistent with the results of De la Fuente and Vives (1995), for instance, building on the work of Esteban (1994) who suggest that countries have converged in Europe but that this process of convergence between countries took place at the same time as regions inside countries either failed to converge or even diverged. There are however few direct empirical tests of the relation between agglomeration and growth. Ciccone (2002) analyses the effects of employment density on average labor productivity for 5 European countries at the Nuts 3 regional level. He finds that an increase in agglomeration has a positive effect on the growth of regions. An indirect test of the relationship is performed in the literature on localized technology spillovers. The presence of localized spillovers has been well documented in the empirical literature. Studies by Jacobs (1969) and more recently by Jaffe, Trajtenberg and Henderson (1993), Coe and Helpman (1995), Coe, Helpman and Hoffmaister (1997), Ciccone and Hall (1996) provide strong evidence that technology spillovers are neither global nor entirely localized. The diffusion of knowledge across regions and countries does exist but diminishes strongly with physical distance which confirms the role that social interactions between individuals, dependent on spatial proximity, have in such diffusion. A recent study by Keller (2002) shows that even though technology spillovers have become more global with time, "technology is to a substantial degree local, not global, as the benefits from spillovers are declining with distance." The fact that technology spillovers are localized should in theory lead to a positive link between growth and spatial agglomeration of economic activities as being "close" to innovation clusters has a positive effect on productivity. Hence, these empirical results point to the interest of studying growth and the spatial distribution of economic activities in an integrated framework. From a theoretical point of view, the interest should also be clear. There is a strong similarity between models of endogenous growth and models of the "new economic geography" (NEG). They ask questions that are related: one of the objectives of the first field is to analyze how new economic activities emerge through technological innovation; the second field analyzes how these economic activities choose to locate and why they are so spatially concentrated. Hence, the process of creation of new firms/economic activities and the process of location should be thought as joint processes. From a methodological point of view, the two fields are quite close as they both assume (in some versions) similar industrial structures namely, models of monopolistic competition which reflects the role of economies of scale in both fields.

In this chapter, we will attempt to clarify some of the theoretical links between growth and agglomeration. Growth, in the form of innovation, can be at the origin of catastrophic spatial agglomeration in a cumulative process à la Myrdal. One of the surprising features of the Krugman (1991) model, was that the introduction of partial labor mobility in a standard "new trade model" with trade costs could lead to catastrophic agglomeration. The growth analog to this result is that the introduction of endogenous growth in the same type of "new trade model" can lead to the same result. A difference with the labour mobility version is that the results are easier to derive from the analytical point of view in the endogenous growth version. In addition, growth alters the process of location even without catastrophe. In particular, and contrary to the fundamentally static models of the NEG, spatial concentration of economic activities may be consistent with a process of delocation of firms towards poor regions. In common with the static models [see the chapter by Ottaviano and Thisse (2004) in this volume], the home market effect plays here a crucial role to explain agglomeration.

The relation between growth and agglomeration depends crucially on capital mobility. Without capital mobility between regions, the incentive for capital accumulation and therefore growth itself is at the heart of the possibility of spatial agglomeration with catastrophe. In the absence of capital mobility, some results are in fact familiar to the NEG [Fujita, Krugman and Venables (1999)]: a gradual lowering of trade costs between two identical regions first has no effect on economic geography but at some critical level induce catastrophic agglomeration. In the model presented in this chapter, *in the absence of migration, "catastrophic" agglomeration means that agents in the South have no more private incentive to accumulate capital and innovate.* The circular causality which gives rise to the possibility of a core–periphery structure is depicted in Figure 1 and as usual in economic geography models is characterized by both production and demand shifting which reinforce each other. The production shifting takes the

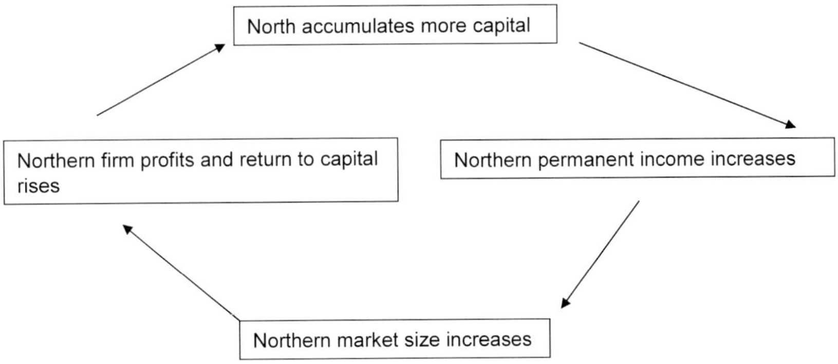

Figure 1. Demand-linked circular causality.

form of capital accumulation in one region (and de-accumulation in the other) and the demand shifting takes the form of increased permanent income due to investment in one region (and a decrease in permanent income in the other region).

Capital mobility eliminates the possibility of catastrophic agglomeration because in this case production shifting does not induce demand shifting as profits are repatriated. It is therefore stabilizing in this sense. This is in sharp contrast with labor mobility which we know to be destabilizing. However, capital mobility also makes the initial distribution of capital between the two regions a permanent phenomenon so that both the symmetric and the core–periphery equilibria are always stable.

In a second section of this chapter, we will concentrate on the opposite causality running from spatial concentration to growth. For this, we will introduce localized technology spillovers which will imply that the spatial distribution of firms will have an impact on the cost of innovation and therefore the growth rate.

This chapter uses modified versions of Baldwin (1999), Baldwin, Martin and Ottaviano (2001) and Martin and Ottaviano (1999). The first two papers analyze models of growth and agglomeration without capital mobility. In contrast to the first paper which uses an exogenous growth model, this chapter analyses endogenous growth. In contrast to the second paper, we restrict our attention to the case of global technology spillovers. The last paper presents a model of growth and agglomeration with perfect capital mobility. Baldwin et al. (2003) also treat some common themes in their Chapters 6 and 7.

2. The basic framework of growth and agglomeration

Many of the most popular economic geography models focus on labor, examples being Krugman (1991), Krugman and Venables (1995), Ottaviano, Tabuchi and Thisse (2002) and Puga (1999). These are unsuited to the study of growth. The key to all sustained growth is the accumulation of human capital, physical capital and/or knowledge capital – with the accumulation of knowledge capital, i.e., technological progress having a privileged position. We thus need a model in which capital exists and its stock is endogenous.

To present the basic elements of this literature, we organize the discussion with the help of a workhorse model. As Baldwin et al. (2003) show, introducing capital into a geography model is relatively simple. The simplest way is accomplished by the 'footloose capital' model (FC model) due to Martin and Rogers (1995). The FC model, however, takes the capital stock as given. Getting to a growth model requires us to add in a capital-producing sector.

Specifically we denote capital by K and labor by L. The capital-producing sector is referred to as the sector I (for innovation and investment, see below) and this comes on top of the two usual sectors, manufactures M and traditional-goods T. The regions (two of them) are symmetric in terms of preferences, technology and trade costs. The usual Dixit–Stiglitz M-sector (manufactures) consists of differentiated goods. Another difference is that the fixed cost is in terms of K. Each variety requires one unit of capital which can be interpreted as an idea, a new technology, a patent, machinery, etc. Production also entails a variable cost (a_M units of labor per unit of output). Its cost function, therefore, is $\pi + wa_M x_i$, where π is K's rental rate, w is the wage rate, and x_i is total output of a typical firm. Traditional goods, which are assumed to be homogenous, are produced by the T-sector under conditions of perfect competition and constant returns. By choice of units, one unit of T is made with one unit of L. The structure of the basic growth and agglomeration model is in Figure 2.

Regional labor stocks are fixed and immobile, so that we eliminate one possible source of agglomeration. Each region's K is produced by its I-sector. I is a mnemonic for innovation when interpreting K as knowledge capital, for instruction when inter-

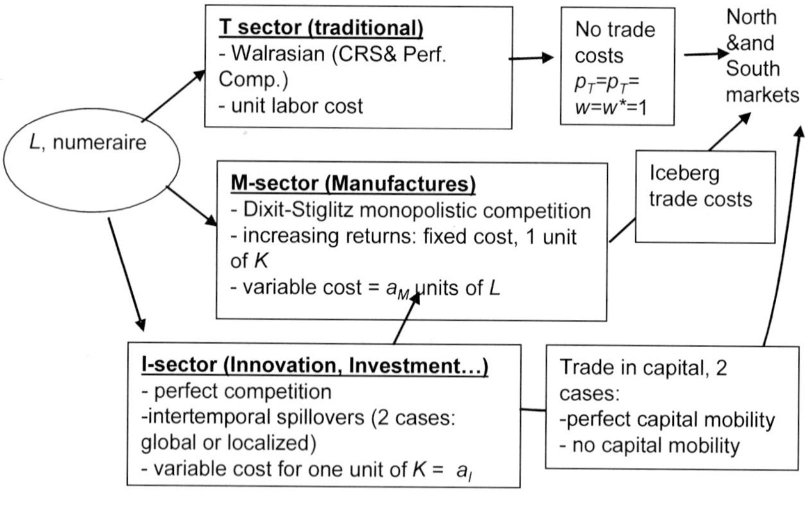

Figure 2. The basic structure of the growth and agglomeration model.

preting K as human capital, and for investment-goods when interpreting K as physical capital. One possible interpretation of the difference between the situation of capital mobility and one of capital immobility is that in the first case K is physical capital (mobility then means the delocation of plants) or as knowledge capital that is marketable and tradable through patents. The second case, capital immobility, would be more consistent with the interpretation of human capital. In this case, labor immobility implies capital immobility. The I-sector produces one unit of K with a_I units of L, so that the marginal cost of the I sector, F, is wa_I. Note that this unit of capital in equilibrium is also the fixed cost F of the manufacturing sector. As one unit of capital is required to start a new variety, the number of varieties and of firms at the world level is simply the capital stock at the world level: $K^W = K + K^*$. We note n and n^* the number of firms located in North and South, respectively. As one unit of capital is required per firm we also know that: $K^W = n + n^*$. However, depending on the assumption we make on capital mobility, the stock of capital produced and owned by one region may or may not be equal to the number of firms producing in that region. In the case of capital mobility, the capital may be produced in one region but the firm that uses this capital unit may be operating in another region. Hence, the number of firms located in one region is, in the case of capital mobility, different from the stock of capital owned by this region.

To individual I-firms, the innovation cost a_I is a parameter. However, following Romer (1990) and Grossman and Helpman (1991), a sector-wide learning curve is assumed. That is, the marginal cost of producing new capital declines (i.e., a_I falls) as the sector's cumulative output rises. Many justifications of this intertemporal externality, classic in the endogenous growth literature, are possible. Romer (1990), for instance, rationalizes it by referring to the non-rival nature of knowledge. We can summarize these standard assumptions of this literature by the following:

$$\dot{K} = \frac{L_I}{a_I}; \qquad F = wa_I; \qquad a_I = 1/K^W; \qquad K^W = K + K^* \tag{1}$$

where K and K^* are the Northern and Southern cumulative I-sector production levels. Note that spillovers are global: the North learns as much from an innovation made in the South than in the North. Below, we introduce localized technological spillovers. Following Romer (1990) and Grossman and Helpman (1991), depreciation of knowledge capital is ignored.[3] Finally, the regional Ks represent both region-specific capital stocks and region-specific cumulative I-sector production. Because the number of firms, varieties and capital units is equal, the growth rate of the number of varieties, on which we will focus, is therefore: $\dot{K}^W/K^W = g$.

We assume an infinitely-lived representative consumer (in each country) with preferences:

$$U = \int_{t=0}^{\infty} \mathrm{e}^{-\rho t} \ln Q \, \mathrm{d}t;$$

[3] See Baldwin et al. (2003) for a similar analysis with depreciation.

$$Q = C_T^{1-\alpha} C_M^{\alpha}; \qquad C_{\mathrm{M}} = \left(\int_{i=0}^{K+K^*} c_i^{1-1/\sigma} \, \mathrm{d}i \right)^{\frac{1}{1-1/\sigma}} \tag{2}$$

where ρ is the rate of time preference, σ is the constant elasticity of substitution among varieties, and the other parameters have the usual meaning. Utility optimization implies that a constant fraction α of total Northern consumption expenditure E falls on M-varieties with the rest spent on T. Optimization by agents in the North also yields unitary elastic demand for T and the CES demand functions for M varieties. The optimal Northern consumption path also satisfies the standard Euler equation with log utility which requires[4] $\dot{E}/E = r - \rho$ (r is the North's rate of return on investment) and a transversality condition. Southern optimization conditions are isomorphic.

On the supply side, free trade in T equalizes nominal wage rates as long as both regions produce some T (i.e., if α is not too large). Taking Northern labor as numeraire then $w = w^* = 1$. As for the M-sector, units are chosen such that $a_M = 1 - 1/\sigma$ so that producer prices of varieties are also normalized to 1. With monopolistic competition, equilibrium operating profit is the value of sales divided by σ. Using the goods market equilibrium and the optimal pricing rules, the operating profits are given by:

$$\pi = bB\frac{E^w}{K^w}; \qquad B \equiv \frac{s_E}{s_n + \phi(1-s_n)} + \frac{\phi(1-s_E)}{\phi s_n + 1 - s_n};$$

$$b \equiv \frac{\alpha}{\sigma}, \qquad \phi \equiv \tau^{1-\sigma},$$

$$\pi^* = bB^*\frac{E^w}{K^w}; \qquad B^* \equiv \frac{\phi s_E}{s_n + \phi(1-s_n)} + \frac{1-s_E}{\phi s_n + 1 - s_n} \tag{3}$$

where $s_E \equiv E/E^w$ is North's share of world expenditure E^w; $s_n = n/(n+n^*)$ is the share of firms which are located in the North, and $0 \leqslant \phi \leqslant 1$ is the usual transformation of trade costs such that ϕ measures the "free-ness" (phi-ness of trade), with $\phi = 0$ implying zero free-ness and $\phi = 1$ implying perfect free-ness (zero trade costs). When capital is immobile, this share is the share of capital owned by the Northern region s_K. Also, B is a mnemonic for the 'bias' in Northern M-sector sales since B measures the extent to which the value of sales of a Northern variety exceeds average operating profit per variety worldwide (namely, bE^w/K^w).

[4] See Barro and Sala-i-Martin (1995) for a derivation using the Hamiltonian approach. Intuitively, the marginal cost of postponing consumption is ρ plus the rate of decline of marginal utility which, given the log preferences is just, $\dot{E}/E$. The marginal benefit is r, the rate of return on investment. The optimal consumption path must be such that the two are equalized so that agents are indifferent to a small intertemporal reallocation of consumption.

3. The case without localized spillovers: growth matters for geography

We start with the simple extreme case considered by Grossman and Helpman (1991) where spillovers are perfectly global. This assumption is already embedded in Equation (1).

3.1. The growth equilibrium

Since the location of innovation and production are irrelevant to the innovation process (knowledge spillovers are global and depend only on past I-sector production), the worldwide equilibrium growth rate can be determined without pinning down the spatial distribution of industry (the location equilibrium). The easiest and most intuitive way of solving for growth equilibria is to use Tobin's q [Baldwin and Forslid (1997, 2000)]. The essence of Tobin's approach is to assert that the equilibrium level of investment is characterized by the equality of the stock market value of a unit of capital – which we denote with the symbol v – and the replacement cost of capital, F. Tobin takes the ratio of these, so what micro economists would naturally call the M-sector free-entry condition (namely $v = F$) becomes Tobin's famous condition $q = v/F = 1$.

Calculating the numerator of Tobin's q (the present value of introducing a new variety) requires a discount rate. In steady state, $\dot{E}/E = 0$ in both regions,[5] so the Euler equations imply that $r = r^* = \rho$. Moreover, the present value of a new variety also depends upon the rate at which new varieties are created. In steady state, the growth rate of the capital stock (or of the number of varieties) will be constant and will either be common ($g = g^*$ in the interior case) or North's g (in the core–periphery case). In either case, the steady-state values of investing in new units of K are:

$$v = \frac{\pi}{\rho + g}; \qquad v^* = \frac{\pi^*}{\rho + g}. \tag{4}$$

It can be checked that the equality, $v = F$, is equivalent to the arbitrage condition present in endogenous growth models such as Grossman and Helpman (1991). The free entry condition in the innovation sector ensures that the growth rate of the value v of capital is equal to growth rate of the marginal cost of an innovation, F, which due to intertemporal spillovers is $-g$. With $r = \rho$, and using the definition of F we get the regional qs:

$$q = \frac{\pi K^w}{\rho + g}; \qquad q^* = \frac{\pi^* K^w}{\rho + g}. \tag{5}$$

In the case of global spillovers, the common growth rate is easy to find because it does not depend on geography. The reason is simply that the cost of innovation and the

[5] To see this, use the world labour market equilibrium: $2L = \alpha E^w(1 - 1/\sigma) + (1 - \alpha)E^w + g$ which says that world labour supply can be used either in the manufacturing sector, the traditional sector or the innovation sector. It implies that a steady state with constant growth only exists if E^w itself is constant.

total size of the market do not depend on the location of firms. Hence, we can just use the special case of the symmetric equilibrium where $s_E = s_n = 1/2$ to find the growth rate.

3.1.1. Endogenous growth and the optimal savings/investment relation

Using Equation (3) in that case and imposing that Tobin's q is 1 in Equation (5), we get the following relation between growth and world expenditure $E^w : bE^w = g + \rho$ where $b \equiv \alpha/\sigma$ as is standard in the growth literature. It just says that higher expenditure by increasing profits induces more entry in the manufacturing sector, which implies a higher growth rate. The other equilibrium relation between growth and world expenditure is given by the world labor market equilibrium: $2L = \alpha E^w(1 - 1/\sigma) + (1 - \alpha)E^w + g$, which states that labor can be used either in the manufacturing sector (recall the unit labor requirement in this sector is normalized to $1 - 1/\sigma$), in the traditional sector or in the innovation sector ($\dot{K}^w$ is the production of the sector per unit of time and $F = 1/K^w$ is the labor requirement in the innovation sector). Here the relation is negative as higher expenditure implies that labor resources are diverted from the innovation sector to the manufacturing and traditional sector.

Combining the two, we find that the world level of expenditure is simply given by $E^w = 2L + \rho$. Using these equations, the growth rate of the number of varieties and of the world capital stock is given by

$$g = 2Lb - (1 - b)\rho; \quad b \equiv \frac{\alpha}{\sigma}, \tag{6}$$

g depends positively on the size of the world economy (as measured by the endowment of the primary factor) and negatively on the discount rate as in any endogenous growth model. Importantly, *when knowledge spillovers are global in scope, the equilibrium growth rate g does not depend on geography.*

Finally, a simple equilibrium relation exists between s_E and s_K, the Northern share of expenditures and the Northern share of capital ownership. It can be shown that optimizing consumers set expenditure at the permanent income hypothesis level in steady state. That is, they consume labor income plus ρ times their steady-state wealth, $FK = s_K$, and, $FK^* = (1 - s_K)$ in the North and in the South, respectively. Hence, $E = L + \rho s_K$, and $E^* = L + \rho(1 - s_K)$. Note that this is another way to check the level of world expenditure as: $E + E^* = E^w = 2L + \rho$. Thus, we get:

$$s_E \equiv \frac{E}{E^w} = \frac{L + \rho s_K}{2L + \rho} = \frac{1}{2} + \frac{\rho}{2L + \rho}\left(s_K - \frac{1}{2}\right). \tag{7}$$

This relation between s_E and s_K, can be thought as the optimal savings/expenditure function since it is derived from intertemporal utility maximization. The intuition is simply that an increase in the Northern share of capital increases the permanent income in the North and leads therefore to an increase in the Northern share of expenditures.

3.1.2. The role of capital mobility

Having worked out the equilibrium growth rate and thus implicitly defined the amount of resources devoted to consumption, we can turn to working out the spatial division of industry, i.e., the location equilibrium. From now on two roads are open:

(1) We can let capital owners decide where to locate production. Capital is mobile even though capital owners are not, so that profits are repatriated in the region where capital is owned. In this case, s_n, the share of firms located in the North and s_K, the share of capital owned by the North, may be different. s_n is then endogenous and determined by an arbitrage condition that says that location of firms is in equilibrium when profits are equalized in the two regions. Because of capital mobility, the decision to accumulate capital will be identical in both regions so that the initial share of capital owned by the North, s_K, is permanent and entirely determined the initial distribution of capital ownership between the two regions.

(2) A second solution is to assume that capital is immobile. Presumably, this would be the case if we focus on the interpretation of capital being human (coupled with immobile agents). In this case, the location of production, s_n, is pinned down by capital ownership: $s_n = s_K$.

As we shall see in detail below, the capital mobility assumption is pivotal. Why is this? In standard terminology, allowing capital mobility eliminates demand-linked circular causality (backward linkages); capital moves without its owners, a shift in production leads to no expenditure shifting because profits are repatriated. When capital is immobile, any shock which favours production in one region is satisfied by the creation of new capital in that region. Since the income of the new capital is spent locally, the 'production shifting' leads to 'expenditure shifting'. Of course, expenditure shifting fosters further production shifting (via the famous home market effect), so without capital mobility, the model features demand-linked circular causality. As is well known, this form of linkage is de-stabilizing, so – as we shall see in detail below – capital mobility in a growth model is a stabilizing force.

Because the case of capital mobility is simpler, we start with it.

3.2. Perfect capital mobility: the location equilibrium

With capital mobility, an obvious question arises: where does capital locate? Capital owned in one region can be located elsewhere. Again, the arbitrage condition, which implies that profits across regions need to be equal for firms to be indifferent between the two locations, pins down the equilibrium location of firms. Using Equation (3), and imposing the equality of profits, we get that there is no more incentive for relocation when the following relation between s_n and s_E is satisfied:

$$s_n = \frac{1}{2} + \frac{1+\phi}{1-\phi}\left(s_E - \frac{1}{2}\right), \quad 0 \leqslant s_n \leqslant 1, \tag{8}$$

where the equilibrium s_n equals unity or zero when the s_n implied by (8) is outside the zero-unity range. This is an example of the "home market" effect. Since $(1+\phi)/(1-\phi)$ is greater than one, this relationship tells us that a change in market size leads to a more than proportional change in the spatial allocation of industry.

Combining Equations (7) and (8), we get the equilibrium relation between the share of firms located in the North, s_n, and the share of capital owned by the North, s_K:

$$s_n = \frac{1}{2} + \frac{\rho}{2L+\rho}\frac{1+\phi}{1-\phi}\left(s_K - \frac{1}{2}\right), \quad 0 \leqslant s_n \leqslant 1. \tag{9}$$

Note also that if the initial distribution of capital in the North is such that $s_K > 1/2$, then more firms will be located in the North than in the South: $s_n > 1/2$. An increase in the share of capital in the North, s_K, induces relocation to the North as it increases expenditure and market size there. Note also that lower trade costs (higher ϕ) will reinforce the home market effect, implying that an unequal distribution of capital ownership will translate in an even more unequal distribution of firms.

3.2.1. *Stability of the location equilibrium*

It is easy to see that the division of industry described above will not change over time. With perfect capital mobility, operating profits have to be the same in both regions which also implies that the value of capital has to be the same in both regions. Hence, $\pi = \pi^*$ and $q = q^* = 1$. This, together with the assumption of constant returns to scale, and the assumption of global spillovers (implying that the cost of innovation is the same in both regions) means that the two regions will accumulate capital at the same constant rate so that any initial distribution of capital is stable. Moreover, since neither backward nor forward linkages operating in this model with capital mobility, no "catastrophic" agglomeration scenario can unfold [see Martin and Ottaviano (1999)]. Hence, the equilibrium described by (9) is always stable. In particular, the symmetric equilibrium where $s_n = s_K = 1/2$, is always stable for any level of trade costs.

To see this point in more detail, one can analyze the effect of a small increase in s_n and check the impact of this perturbation on the ratio of profits in the North to profits in the South. That is, we ask the question whether an increase in geographic concentration in the North decreases or increases the incentive to relocate in the North. The symmetric equilibrium is stable if and only if $\partial(\pi/\pi^*)/\partial s_n$ is negative. Indeed, this is the case for all positive levels of trade costs since, evaluated at the equilibrium geography:

$$\frac{\partial(\pi/\pi^*)}{\partial s_n} = -\frac{(1-\phi)^2}{(1+\phi)^2}\frac{1}{s_E(1-s_E)} < 0.$$

Evaluated at the equilibrium given by (9), an exogenous increase in the share of firms located in the North always decreases relative profits there, so that it leads firms to go back to the South. The location equilibrium determined in (9) is always stable. The reason is that when more firms locate in the North, this increases competition there (and decreases it in the South).

3.2.2. Does capital flow from rich to poor?

An interesting question that can be analyzed in this framework is: "Do firms relocate towards the North or towards the South?" In economic geography models without growth, industrial concentration implies that firms are destroyed in the South and built in the North. Here, the relocation story is richer because of the constant creation of new firms. To see what is the direction of relocation we need to look at the difference between the share of capital owned by the North and the share of firms located in North. The expression is easier taking ratios, so:

$$s_K - s_n = 2\frac{L(1-\phi) - \rho\phi}{(1-\phi)(2L+\rho)}\left(s_K - \frac{1}{2}\right). \tag{10}$$

In the symmetric equilibrium, where both regions are endowed originally with the same amount of capital there is no relocation of course. If the initial distribution of capital is such that $s_K > 1/2$, so that the North is richer than the South, then the direction of the capital flows is ambiguous; it depends on the sign of $L(1-\phi) - \rho\phi$. If this expression is positive, then $s_K > s_n$ so that some of the capital owned by the North relocates to the South.

The ambiguity of the direction of capital flows stems from the fact that it is governed by two opposite effects, namely the market crowding effect (which is a dispersion force that makes the poor capital region attractive because firms installed there face less competition), and the market access effect (which is an agglomeration force that makes the rich region attractive because of its high level of income and expenditure). The first effect dominates when trade is quite closed (ϕ is low). Note that when the rate of time preference is high or more generally when the return to capital is high, the capital rich region becomes more attractive because the market access effect is reinforced. There is a threshold level of trade costs that determines the direction of capital flows. It is given by

$$\phi^{\mathrm{CP}} = \frac{L}{L+\rho}. \tag{11}$$

When trade costs are below this level, relocation takes place towards the South and vice-versa. The reason why we attach CP (for core–periphery) to this threshold will become clear later when we analyze the case of capital immobility, as we will see that this threshold value is the one for which the symmetric equilibrium becomes unstable.

An interesting feature here is that concentration of wealth and of economic activities in the North (s_K and $s_n > 1/2$), is compatible with relocation of firms from North to South ($s_K < s_n$) when $\phi < \phi^{\mathrm{CP}}$. This comes from the introduction of growth and the fact that a larger number of newly created firms are created and owned by the North than by the South.

3.3. No capital mobility: "new growth" and "new geography"

The previous section described a growth and geography equilibrium where agglomeration forces were present,[6] but where no "catastrophe" could take place since all circular causality had been ruled out. As discussed above, eliminating capital mobility in a growth model is actually de-stabilizing since anything that changes the spatial allocation of industry and thus capital will simultaneously change that spatial allocation of expenditure. And, as is well known, the home market effect means that any change in expenditure's spatial allocation induces a knock-on change in the location of industry.

More formally, restricting capital mobility (together with the assumptions of labor immobility) has two implications. First, the number of firms and the number of units of capital owned in a region are identical: $s_n = s_K$. Second, because the arbitrage condition of the previous section does not hold, profits may be different in the two regions. This in turn implies that, contrary to the previous section, the two regions may not have the same incentive to accumulate capital so that the initial ownership of capital does not need to be permanent. This means that the analysis will be quite different from the previous section. We will ask the following questions which are the usual ones in the NEG models. Starting from an equal distribution of capital, the symmetric equilibrium, we will determine under which circumstances it remains a stable equilibrium. Then we will look at the core–periphery equilibrium and again ask when this equilibrium is stable.

3.3.1. Stability of the symmetric equilibrium

We first consider interior steady states where both regions are investing, so $q = 1$ and $q^* = 1$. Using (3) and (5) in (6), $q = q^* = 1$ and imposing $s_n = s_K$, we get:

$$s_K = \frac{1}{2} + \frac{1+\phi}{1-\phi}\left(s_E - \frac{1}{2}\right) \tag{12}$$

which of course is just (8) with s_n replaced by s_K. In other words, it now determines the location of capital ownership as well as the location of production. Together with Equation (7) which implied that production shifting led to expenditure shifting, this defines a second positive relation between s_E and s_K, i.e., expenditure shifting leads to production shifting.

The intuition is that a relative increase in Northern demand increases profits in the North and therefore the marginal value of an extra unit of capital. In other words, the

[6] We define agglomeration as the phenomenon where the concentration of economic activity creates forces that foster the concentration of economic activity. The home market effect, which did operate in the previous section, shows agglomeration forces are present since a division where $s_L = s_K > 1/2$ would not be an equilibrium. Due to the home market effect, such a division would encourage further concentration of economic activity in the North.

numerator of Tobin's q increases in the North. Hence, this raises the incentive to innovate there and the North indeed increases its share of capital s_K. The intuition is therefore very close to the "home market effect" except that it influences here the location of capital accumulation. Together with the optimal saving relation of (7), it is easy to check that the symmetric solution $s_E = s_K = 1/2$ is always an equilibrium, in particular it is an equilibrium for all levels of trade costs. The symmetric equilibrium is the unique equilibrium for which both regions accumulate capital ($q = q^* = 1$). However, the fact that there are two positive equilibrium relations between s_E and s_K, the share of expenditures and the share of capital in the North, should warn us that the symmetric equilibrium may not be stable. Indeed, in this model a 'circular causality' specific to the presence of growth and capital immobility tends to de-stabilize the symmetric equilibrium because of the demand-linked cycle in which production shifting leads to expenditure shifting and *vice versa*. The particular variant present here is based on the mechanism first introduced by Baldwin (1999) in a neo-classical growth model.

There are several ways to study the symmetric equilibrium's stability. We can first graph the two equilibrium relations between s_E and s_K, the "Permanent Income" relation (call it PI) given by Equation (7) and the "Optimal Investment" relation (call it OI) given by Equation (12). In the case where the slope of the PI relation is less than the OI relation we get the left panel of Figure 3. At the right of the permanent income relation, s_E, the share of expenditures in the North, is too low given the high share of capital owned by the North (agents do not consume enough). The opposite is true at the left of the PI relation. At the right of the optimal investment relation, s_K, the share of capital in the North, is too high given the low level of s_E, the share of expenditures in the North (agents invest too much). The opposite is true is at the left of the OI relation. This graphical analysis suggests that in this case the symmetric equilibrium is stable.

In the case where the slope of the PI relation is steeper than the OI then the same reasoning leads to the right panel of the diagram. This suggests that in this case, the symmetric equilibrium is unstable. According to this graphical analysis, the trade cost

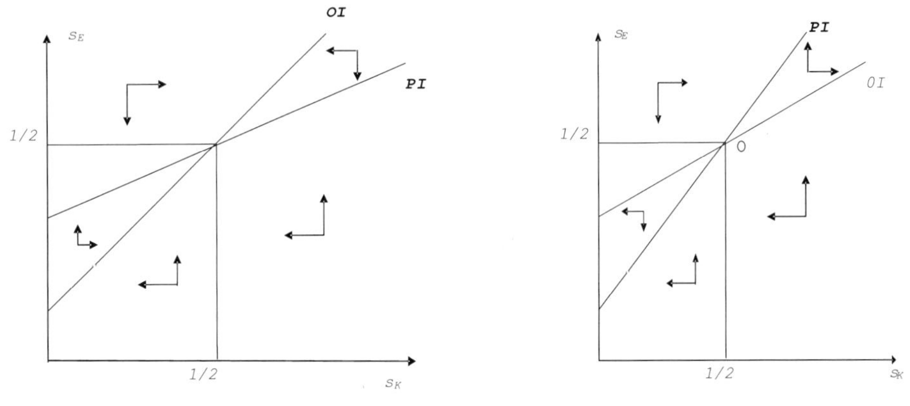

Figure 3. The Northern shares of expenditure and capital, stable and unstable cases.

below which the symmetric equilibrium becomes unstable is exactly the one for which the slope of the PI curve equals the slope of OI curve. The slope of the PI curve is $\rho/(2L+\rho)$ which is the share of capital income in total income. The slope of the OI curve is $(1-\phi)/(1+\phi)$. The two slopes are equal for a level of trade costs which we saw above: it turns out to be the threshold level, which we define as ϕ^{CP}, given by Equation (11), namely $\phi^{\mathrm{CP}} = L/(L+\rho)$. When the "free-ness" of trade is higher than this level, our graphical analysis suggests that the stable equilibrium is not stable.

To gain more intuition on this result, we can also study the symmetric equilibrium's stability in a different and more rigorous way. We can analyze the effect of an exogenous increase s_K, by a small amount and check the impact of this perturbation on Tobin's q, allowing expenditure shares to adjust according to (7). The symmetric equilibrium is stable if and only if $\partial q/\partial s_K$ is negative: in this case, an increase in the share of Northern capital lowers Tobin's q in the North (and therefore the incentive to innovate) and raises it in the South (by symmetry $\partial q/\partial s_K$ and $\partial q^*/\partial s_K$ have opposite signs). Thus when $\partial q/\partial s_K < 0$, the perturbation generates self-correcting forces in the sense that the incentive to accumulate more capital in the North falls and increases in the South. If the derivative is positive, the increase in the share of capital in the North reinforces the incentive to accumulate more capital in the North: the symmetric equilibrium is unstable in this case. Differentiating q with respect to s_K, we have:

$$\left(\frac{\partial q/q}{\partial s_K}\right)\bigg|_{s_K=1/2} = 2\left(\frac{1-\phi}{1+\phi}\right)\left(\frac{\partial s_E}{\partial s_K}\right)\bigg|_{s_K=1/2} - 2\left(\frac{1-\phi}{1+\phi}\right)^2. \tag{13}$$

This expression illustrates the two forces affecting stability. The first term is positive, so it represents the destabilizing force, namely the *demand-linked effect*. This effect was absent of the stability analysis in the case of capital mobility because an increase in profits in one region led to delocation of capital but not to more local capital accumulation. *In the case of capital immobility, the only adjustment mechanism when profits increase in one region is that agents in that region accumulate more capital up to point where the profits of accumulating capital are driven to zero.* This "local" accumulation process generates a higher permanent income and a higher level of expenditure in one region only which is the reason for the circular causality.

The negative second term reflects the stabilizing *market crowding effect*, which was the only one present in the capital mobility case. Clearly, reducing trade costs (an increase in ϕ) erodes the stabilizing force more quickly than it erodes the destabilizing demand-linkage.

Using (7) to find $\partial s_E/\partial s_K = \rho/(2L+\rho)$, the critical level of ϕ at which the symmetric equilibrium becomes unstable is defined by the point where (13) switches sign. It is easy to check that again this critical level is given by ϕ^{CP} of Equation (11).

When trade costs are high the symmetric equilibrium is stable and gradually reducing trade costs produces standard, static effects – more trade, lower prices for imported goods, and higher welfare. There is, however, no impact on industrial location, so during an initial phase, the global distribution of industry appears unaffected. As trade freeness moves beyond ϕ^{CP}, however, the equilibrium enters a qualitatively distinct phase.

The symmetric distribution of industry becomes unstable, and Northern and Southern industrial structures begin to diverge; to be concrete, assume industry agglomerates in the North. Since s_K cannot jump, crossing ϕ^{CP} triggers transitional dynamics in which Northern industrial output and investment rise and Southern industrial output and investment fall. Moreover, in a very well-defined sense, the South would appear to be in the midst of a 'vicious' cycle. *The demand linkages would have Southern firms lowering employment and abstaining from investment, because Southern wealth is falling, and Southern wealth is falling since Southern firms are failing to invest.* By the same logic, the North would appear to be in the midst of a 'virtuous' cycle.

3.3.2. The core–periphery equilibrium

In addition to the symmetric equilibrium, a core–periphery outcome ($s_K = 0$ or 1, but we will focus only on the second one where the North gets the core) can also exist. For $s_K = 1$ to be an equilibrium, it must be that $q = v/F = 1$ and $q^* = v^*/F^* < 1$ for this distribution of capital ownership: continuous accumulation is profitable in the North since $v = F$, but $v^* < F^*$ so no Southern agent would choose to setup a new firm. Defining the core–periphery equilibrium this way, it implies that it is stable whenever it exists. Using (3), (5) and (6), (7), q^* with $s_K = 1$ simplifies to

$$q^* = \frac{(1+\phi^2)L + \phi^2\rho}{(2L+\rho)\phi}. \tag{14}$$

If q^* is less than 1 when $s_K = 1$, then the core–periphery equilibrium exists and is stable as there is no incentive for the South to innovate in this case. The threshold ϕ that solves $q^* = 1$ defines the starting point of the core–periphery set. Again, this threshold is ϕ^{CP} of Equation (11). This implies that at the level of the trade costs for which the symmetric equilibrium becomes unstable, the core–periphery becomes a stable equilibrium.

When trade costs are high enough, the core–periphery equilibrium is not a stable equilibrium: in this case the South would have an incentive to innovate because the profits in the South are high enough. This is because even though the Southern market is small in this case (it has no capital income in the core–periphery equilibrium), it is protected from Northern competition thanks to high trade costs. When trade costs are low enough, this protection diminishes and the fact that the market in the South is small becomes more important: in this case, above the threshold ϕ^{CP}, it becomes non profitable to operate a firm in the South.

Using $s_K = 1$, the remaining aspects of the core–periphery steady state are simple to calculate. In particular, since $s_K = 1$, $q = 1$, and $q^* < 1$, we have that no labor is used in the innovation or manufacturing sectors in the South and all innovation is made in the North.

Note that the core–periphery outcome ($s_K = 1$) is reached only asymptotically. This is because we present a simpler version of the model where the stock of capital in the South does not depreciate and once the level of ϕ^{CP} is crossed, stays constant, whereas

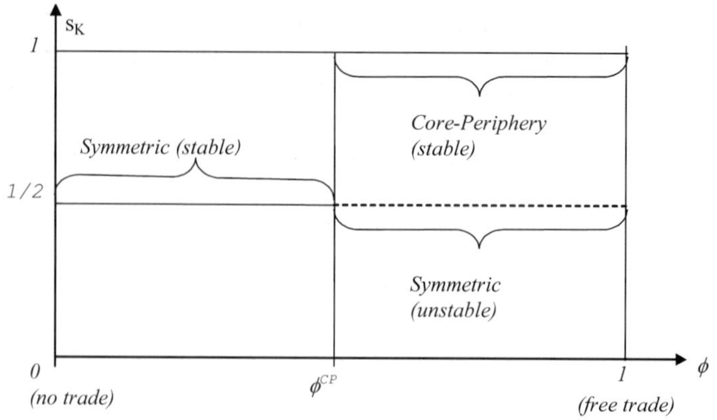

Figure 4. Stability properties of the core–periphery equilibrium.

the stock of capital in the North keeps growing at rate g. Figure 4 summarizes the model's stability properties in a diagram with ϕ and s_K on the axes.

Following the tradition of the NEG we have analyzed here the existence and stability conditions of the symmetric and core–periphery equilibria. In this simple model we can go further and analyze what would happen if we started from a situation in which the North had more capital than the South ($1/2 < s_K < 1$). It can be checked, using Equations (3), (5) and (6) that in this case $q < 1$ (and $q^* > 1$) if

$$(1 - s_K)\left(s_K - \frac{1}{2}\right)(1 - \phi)\left[\rho\phi - L(1 - \phi)\right] < 0,$$

that is, if $\phi < \phi^{\mathrm{CP}}$. Hence, in this case, the North would not innovate (the large stock of capital implies a high degree of market crowding) and the South would innovate. Hence, if we start from such an interior asymmetric equilibrium then one would converge back to the symmetric equilibrium as long as trade costs are high enough. If $\phi > \phi^{\mathrm{CP}}$, then the economy converges to the core–periphery equilibrium.

3.4. Concluding remarks

Comparing perfect capital mobility to no capital mobility, we conclude that:

- When trade costs are high, the absence of capital mobility leads to convergence between the two regions: if one region starts with more capital than the other then, the two regions converge to the symmetric equilibrium. On the contrary, with capital mobility, any initial distribution of capital ownership becomes permanent. However, some of the firms owned by the North will relocate and produce in the South. This will produce some sort of convergence in terms of GDP but not in terms of GNP.
- When trade costs are low, the absence of capital mobility leads to divergence between the two regions asymptotically, whatever the initial distribution of capital,

all the capital is accumulated and owned by one region.[7] With capital mobility, as long as all the capital is not entirely owned by the North, some firms will still produce in the South. However, some of the Southern capital will delocate to the North.

Hence, in the case of mobile capital (physical or tradable innovations such as patents), the key parameter for regional income distribution is the initial distribution of capital. In the case of immobile (human) capital, the key parameter is the level of trade costs. The regional distribution of capital affects the long term regional income distribution "only" to the extent that it determines which region becomes the core, through a small initial advantage in capital endowments for example. To simplify matters we have used a model where only one type of capital exists. To make it more realistic, in particular for the European case, it would be interesting to extend it and take into account the different natures of capital so that part of the capital is mobile and part is not.

Can we derive some policy implications from this analysis? One striking result is that when regions are not well integrated (high transport/trade costs), capital immobility is conducive to regional convergence.[8] However, when regions are well integrated, the opposite result is true. To the extent that public policies can alter capital mobility, the policy implication is clear: capital mobility, both physical and human, should be facilitated between countries which are well integrated on the trade side. In the European context, this suggests that the "single market" was right to foster free movement of goods and capital at the same time.

4. The case with localized spillovers: geography matters for growth (and vice versa)

In the previous section, we showed that growth could dramatically alter economic geography in the sense that the process of accumulation of capital teamed with capital immobility could lead to catastrophic agglomeration. However, geography had no impact on growth. This was due to the fact that we assumed global spillovers: the learning curve, which as in any endogenous growth model, was at the origin of sustained growth, was global in the sense that the North and the South would learn equally from an innovation made in any region. In this section, we analyze how localized spillovers give a role in growth to the geography of production and innovation activities.[9]

7 This result however is not general. Urban (2002) integrates a neo-classical growth model into a static geography model without physical capital mobility. Contrary to the models presented here, he shows that lower trade costs lead to convergence between the poor and the rich country. The reason is that the classic local decreasing returns effect implies that there is more incentive to accumulate capital in the poor country and in his model this effect does not depend on trade costs. On the contrary, the home market effect, the divergence force, decreases as trade costs diminish.

8 Basevi and Ottaviano (2002) modify this type of model to investigate the intermediate situation in which capital mobility is neither absent nor perfectly free.

9 Localized spillovers are not the only way that geography can affect growth. Martin and Ottaviano (2001) generate a feedback between growth and agglomeration by assuming vertical linkages rather than local

4.1. Necessary extensions of the basic model

Introducing localized technological spillovers requires a minor modification to one of the assumptions made in the previous section.[10] Equation (1) that described the innovation sector assumed global spillovers in the sense that the marginal cost of an innovation, identical in both regions, was: $F = wa_I = 1/K^W$, so that it was decreasing in the total stock of existing capital; in the Grossman and Helpman (1991), spillovers were global. Grossman and Helpman (1991) also consider the other polar of extreme where knowledge spillovers are purely local. Since the "geography of knowledge" is an important topic for policy makers and a subject that has attracted a great deal of empirical work [see the chapter of Audretsch and Feldman (2004) in this volume], it is more convenient to allow non-polar assumptions concerning knowledge spillovers as introduced by Baldwin and Forslid (2000). Specifically, suppose that these spillovers are localized in the sense that the cost of R&D in one region also depends on the location of firms (stock of knowledge capital). Hence, the Northern cost of innovation depends more on the number of firms located in the North than in the South so that Equation (1) becomes (taking into account that the wage rate is equal to 1):

$$F = a_I; \qquad a_I \equiv \frac{1}{K^W A}; \qquad A \equiv s_n + \lambda(1 - s_n), \quad 0 \leqslant \lambda \leqslant 1, \tag{15}$$

where λ (a mnemonic for learning spillovers) measures the degree of to which learning from knowledge creation in one region facilitates knowledge creation in the other region. The fully global spillovers case is where $\lambda = 1$; the fully local case is $\lambda = 0$. To put it differently, the higher the trade costs on the mobility of ideas, technologies, and innovations. The cost function of the innovation sector in the South is isomorphic.

Again the case of perfect capital mobility is easier than the case without capital mobility. Hence, we will start with the former following some of the analysis of Martin and Ottaviano (1999) and then describe the model without capital mobility following Baldwin, Martin and Ottaviano (2001).[11]

spillovers in innovation. Because the innovation sector uses manufacturing goods as an input, the location of manufacturing affects the cost of innovation through trade costs. Yamamoto (2003) presents a similar model with circular causation between growth and agglomeration coming from the vertical linkages between the intermediate goods sector and the innovation sector. A different type of geography and growth model where trade is absent is proposed by Quah (2002). The knowledge spillovers are imperfect both across space and time so that quite intuitively spatial clusters can appear. The reasoning is not very different from Grossman and Helpman (1991) who show that when knowledge spillovers are localized the increasing returns activity concentrates in one location.

[10] Here, localized technology spillovers are assumed. Duranton and Puga (2001) provide micro-foundations for the link between local diversity and innovation. Firms that innovate locate in diversified cities and then relocate in specialized cities to commence mass production.

[11] The set of basic results is enriched by other contributions. Ottaviano (1996), as well as Manzocchi and Ottaviano (2001) extend the model of Martin and Ottaviano (1999) to a three-region economy.

4.2. The case of perfect knowledge capital mobility

There are three endogenous variables that we are interested in: the growth rate g which is common to both regions in steady state; s_n, the share of firms that are producing in the North; and s_E, the share of expenditure in the North which also can be thought as a measure of income inequality between North and South. Remember that with perfect capital mobility, s_K the share of capital in the North is given by the initial distribution of capital as the stocks of capital in both regions grow at the same rate. We want to find the different equilibrium relations between these three endogenous variables.

Due to localized spillovers, it is less costly to innovate in the region with the highest number of firms (which represent also capital or innovations). This implies that, because of perfect capital mobility, all the innovation will take place in the region with a higher number of firms. Remember that due to perfect competition the value of an innovation is equal to its marginal cost. The shares of firms are perfectly tradable across regions (perfect capital mobility) so the value of capital (or firms) cannot differ from one region to another and no innovation will take place in the South. But the South will be able to simply buy (without trade costs) innovations or capital produced in the North. Hence, in the case when $s_K > 1/2$, that is when the initial stock of capital is higher in the North than in the South, we know from the previous section that this will imply that more firms will be located in the North ($s_n > 1/2$) so that all innovation will take place in the North. In this case the world labor market equilibrium will be given by:

$$2L = \frac{g}{s_n + \lambda(1 - s_n)} + \alpha\frac{\sigma - 1}{\sigma}E^W + (1 - \alpha)E^W. \tag{16}$$

Remember also that world expenditure is given by $E^W = 2L + \rho F K^W$. The value and marginal cost of capital is given by F in (15). Using this and Equation (16), we get the growth rate of capital g as a function of s_n, our first equilibrium relation:

$$g = 2bL\left[s_n + \lambda(1 - s_n)\right] - \rho(1 - b), \quad 1/2 < s_n \leqslant 1. \tag{17}$$

Compared to the growth rate derived in the previous section, this one differs because of the presence of localized spillovers: spatial concentration of firms (a higher s_n) implies a lower cost of innovation and therefore a higher growth rate. Note also that for a given geography of production (a given s_n), less localized spillovers (a higher λ) also implies a lower cost of innovation in the North (as the innovation sector in the North benefits more from spillovers of firms producing in the South) and a higher growth rate.

The arbitrage condition consistent with the assumption of perfect capital mobility requires profits to be equalized in the two locations so that $\pi = \pi^* = bE^W/K^W$. This gives the same equilibrium relation between s_n and s_E as in the previous section (Equation (8)).

To find the third equilibrium relation, one between s_E and g, remember that due to intertemporal optimization, $E = L + \rho v K$ where v is the value of capital which itself is equal to the discounted value of future profits. Using these relations, it is easy to get the last equilibrium relation:

$$s_E = \frac{1}{2} + b\frac{\rho}{g+\rho}\left(s_K - \frac{1}{2}\right). \tag{18}$$

Note that income inequality between the two regions is decreasing in the growth rate as long as the North is initially richer than in the South in capital stocks ($s_K > 1/2$). This is because the value of capital decreases with growth due to faster entry of new firms.

The equilibrium characterized by these three relations is stable for the same reasons as in the case of perfect capital mobility of the previous section. Capital mobility allows Southerners to save and invest buying capital accumulated in the North (in the form of patents or shares). Hence, *the lack of an innovation sector does not prevent the South from accumulating capital*: the initial inequality in wealth does not lead to self-sustaining divergence. No "circular causality" mechanism which would lead to a core–periphery pattern, as in the NEG models of the type of Krugman (1991), will occur.

Using Equations (8), (17) and (18), the equilibrium is the solution to a quadratic equation. One can find the trade cost such that relocation goes from North to South in the case where $s_K > 1/2$ (which implies also that $s_n > 1/2$). $s_K > s_n$ if

$$\phi < \frac{\lambda L(1-s_K) + Ls_K}{\lambda L(1-s_K) + Ls_K + \rho}.$$

Note that when all the capital is owned by the North ($s_K = 1$), then the threshold level of trade cost is again ϕ^{CP} given in the previous section. Note also that in the less extreme case where $s_K < 1$, *less localized spillovers imply, everything else constant, that relocation will take place towards the South*. The reason is that less localized spillovers imply a lower cost of innovation in the North, and therefore a lower value of capital of which the North is better endowed with. Hence, less localized spillovers generate, for a given distribution of capital, a more equal distribution of incomes and expenditures and therefore attract firms in the South.

One could analyze the properties of this equilibrium by analyzing the equilibrium location s_n. However, it is more revealing to use a graphical analysis.

Equation (8) provides a positive relation between s_n and s_E, the well-known "demand-linked" effect. In Figure 5, this relation is given by the curve $s_n(s_E)$ in the NE quadrant. Equation (17) provides a positive relation between g and s_n. This is the localized spillovers effect: when industrial agglomeration increases in the region where the innovation sector is located, the cost of innovation decreases and the growth rate increases. This relation is given by the line $g(s_n)$ in the NW quadrant. Finally, Equation (19) provides a negative relation between s_E and g. This is a "competition" effect: the monopoly profits of existing firms decrease as more firms are created; as the North is more dependent on this capital income, the Northern share of income and expenditures decreases. This relation is described by the curve $s_E(g)$ in the SE quadrant.

This graph can be used to analyze the relation between the geography of income, the geography of production and growth.

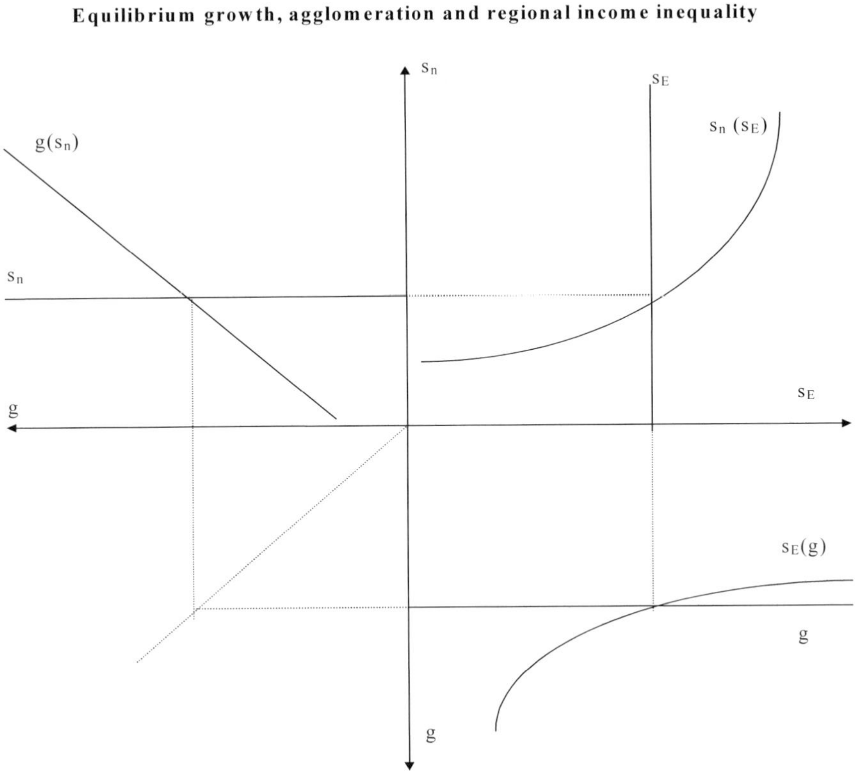

Figure 5. Spatial equity and efficiency.

4.2.1. Spatial equity and efficiency

An increase in regional inequality in capital endowments s_K shifts to the right the $s_E(g)$ in the SE quadrant. The impact is therefore an increase in income inequality and an increase in spatial inequality in the sense that s_n increases. However, because the economic geography becomes less dispersed and therefore more efficient from the point of view of localized technology spillovers, the growth rate g is higher. Hence the introduction of growth and localized spillovers in a geography model is at the origin of a trade-off between spatial equity and efficiency [see Martin (1999) for an analysis along these lines] which may have important implications for public policies.

It is also easy to analyze the impact of lower trade costs on goods (higher ϕ). For a given income disparity, it increases spatial inequality so that the schedule $s_n(s_E)$ shifts up in the NE quadrant. This in turn increases the growth rate which leads to lower income inequality, an effect that mitigates the initial impact on spatial inequality. Overall even though spatial inequality has increased, the growth rate has increased and nominal income disparities have decreased.[12,13] It is also interesting to analyze the effects of an increase in λ that is less localized technology spillovers. This can be interpreted as lowering trade costs between regions on ideas and information. Public policies that improve infrastructure on telecommunication, the Internet or education may be interpreted as affecting λ. This shifts the $g(s_n)$ to the left in the NW quadrant so that growth increases for a given geography of production. This lowers income disparities between the two regions as monopolistic profits are eroded by the entry of new firms. This in turn brings a decrease in spatial inequality on the geography of production as s_n decreases. More generally, an exogenous increase in growth will lead to less spatial agglomeration and less regional income inequality. This is important because it implies that, even in the presence of localized technology spillovers, the sign of the correlation between growth and agglomeration depends on the nature of the forces at work.

4.2.2. Welfare implications

The structure of the model is simple enough so that it is fairly easy, at least compared to the other models, to present some welfare implications. One question we can ask is whether the concentration of economic activities, generated by market forces, is too small or too important from a welfare point of view [see Baldwin et al. (2003, Chapters 10 and 11) for a more detailed analysis]. Two distortions, which are directly linked to economic geography, exist here. First, when investors choose their location they do not take into account the impact of their decision on the cost of innovation in the North where the innovation sector is located. Localized positive spillovers are not internalized in the location decision and from that point of view the "market" economic geography will display too little spatial concentration. Second, the location decision also has an impact on the welfare of immobile consumers which is not internalized by investors. This happens for two reasons. On the one hand, an increase in spatial concentration affects negatively the cost and therefore the value of existing capital so that the wealth of capital owners in both regions decreases. This affects more the North than the South. On the other hand, when spatial concentration in the North increases, consumers in the North gain because of the lower transport costs they incur. Symmetrically, consumers in the South loose. V and V^*, the indirect individual utilities of North and South, respectively, as a function of the spatial concentration s_n and of the growth rate g are given by

$$V = C + \frac{1}{\rho}\ln\left(1 + \frac{\rho s_K}{L s_n}\right) + \frac{\alpha}{\sigma(\sigma-1)}\ln\left[s_n + \phi(1-s_n)\right] + \frac{\alpha g}{\rho^2(\sigma-1)},$$

[12] Martin (1999) also shows that lowering transport costs inside the poor region will have exactly the opposite effect as it leads firms to relocate into that region.

[13] These results of course depend on the assumption that agglomeration of economic activities decreases the cost of innovation. If congestion costs exist when the agglomeration becomes too large, lowering trade costs between regions may have very different effects. Baldwin et al. (2003) show in this case that lower trade costs may lead to an equilibrium with high spatial inequality, high income inequality and low growth.

$$V^* = C + \frac{1}{\rho}\ln\left[1 + \frac{\rho(1-s_K)}{Ls_n}\right] + \frac{\alpha}{\rho(\sigma-1)}\ln[1 - s_n + \phi s_n] + \frac{\alpha g}{\rho^2(\sigma-1)} \quad (19)$$

where C is a constant. We can analyze how a change in the spatial concentration s_n affects welfare in both regions:

$$\frac{\partial V}{\partial s_n} = \frac{2L\alpha^2(1-\lambda)}{\rho^2\sigma(\sigma-1)} - \frac{s_K}{Ls_n^2 + \rho s_K s_n} + \frac{\alpha}{\rho(\sigma-1)}\frac{1-\phi}{s_n + \phi(1-s_n)},$$

$$\frac{\partial V^*}{\partial s_n} = \frac{2L\alpha^2(1-\lambda)}{\rho^2\sigma(\sigma-1)} - \frac{1-s_K}{Ls_n^2 + \rho(1-s_K)s_n} - \frac{\alpha}{\rho(\sigma-1)}\frac{1-\phi}{1-s_n+\phi s_n}. \quad (20)$$

There are three welfare effects of a change in spatial concentration. The first term is identically positive in both regions: an increase in spatial concentration increases growth because, through localized spillovers, it decreases the cost of innovation. The second term is negative in both regions: the decrease in the cost of innovation also diminishes the value of existing firms and therefore diminishes the wealth of capital owners. Because the North owns more capital than the South, this negative effect is larger in the North than in the South. Finally, the last term represents the welfare impact of higher concentration on trade costs. This welfare effect is positive in the North and negative in the South.

To analyze whether the market geography displays too much or too little concentration in the North implies to evaluate these two equations at the market equilibrium. It can be checked that as long as λ is sufficiently small (technological spillovers are sufficiently localized), the effect of an increase in spatial concentration is always positive on the North. It is interesting that the North will gain less by an increase in geographical concentration if it owns a larger share of the capital. Another way to say this is that capital owners may loose from geographical concentration in the North. *Geographical concentration in the North may improve welfare in the South.* This is in stark contrast with static economic geography models where the Southerners always loose following an increase in concentration in the North. Here the positive effect on growth may more than compensate the negative impact of concentration on trade costs and on wealth. This will be so if λ is sufficiently small (technological spillovers are sufficiently localized), and if trade costs are low enough.

4.3. *The case without capital mobility: the possibility of a growth take-off and agglomeration*

As in the case of globalized spillovers, allowing perfect capital mobility stabilizes the localized spillovers model by eliminating demand-linked circular causality. We turn now to the opposite assumption – capital immobility. As we shall see, this opens the door to some spectacular interactions between growth and geography.

Here we follow the analysis of Baldwin, Martin and Ottaviano (2001). The model is identical to the one described in the previous section except for the introduction of localized spillovers as described in Section 4.2. This has several consequences: the geography of production has now an impact on the cost of innovation so that as in Section 4.2 the global growth rate is affected by geography. The value of capital, which can differ in the two regions as capital mobility is absent, is itself affected by geography because the innovation sector is perfectly competitive. Hence, the marginal cost of capital and innovation is equal to its value. In turn, this affects wealth and expenditures in the two regions so that profits will depend on geography in this way too. This implies that the two relations between the share of capital in the North (s_K) and the share of expenditures in the North (s_E) are going to be much more complex than in the case without localized spillovers.

4.3.1. The long-run equilibria and their stability

The optimal savings/expenditure function derived from intertemporal utility maximization, which we interpreted as a permanent income relation in the previous section (Equation (8) becomes:

$$s_E = 1/2 + \frac{\rho\lambda(2s_K - 1)}{2\{2LAA^* + \rho[A(1-s_K) + A^* s_K]\}} \tag{21}$$

where A is given in (15) and A^* is the symmetric. The permanent income relation is such that s_E is always increasing in s_K: an increase in the Northern share of capital increases the Northern share of expenditures. When we consider interior steady states where both regions are investing (innovating), so that $q = 1$ and $q^* = 1$, the second relation between s_E and s_K, which we called the optimal investment one, becomes, in the presence of localized spillovers:

$$s_E = 1/2 + \frac{(2s_K - 1)(\lambda + \lambda\phi^2 - 2\phi)}{2(1-\phi^2)[A(1-s_K) + A^* s_K]}. \tag{22}$$

Note of course that $s_E = s_K = 1/2$, the symmetric equilibrium is a solution to the two equilibrium relations (23) and (24). Two other solutions to this system may exist which are given by:

$$s_K = 1/2 \pm \frac{1}{2}\sqrt{\left(\frac{1+\lambda}{1-\lambda}\right)\left(\frac{1+\lambda\Lambda}{1-\lambda\Lambda}\right)}; \qquad \Lambda \equiv \left[1 - \frac{2\rho\phi(1-\lambda\phi)}{L(\lambda + \lambda\phi^2 - 2\phi)}\right]^{-1}. \tag{23}$$

Both s_E and s_K converge to $1/2$ either as λ approaches 1 or as ϕ approaches the value

$$\phi^{\text{cat}} = \frac{L(1+\lambda) + \rho - \sqrt{(1-\lambda^2)[L(1+\lambda)+\rho]^2 + \lambda^2\rho^2}}{\lambda[L(1+\lambda) + 2\rho]} \tag{24}$$

from above. For levels of ϕ below ϕ^{cat}, these two solutions are imaginary. In addition, for levels of ϕ above another critical value,

$$\phi^{\text{CP}'} = \frac{2L + \rho - \sqrt{(2L+\rho)^2 - 4\lambda^2 L(L+\rho)}}{2\lambda(L+\rho)}, \tag{25}$$

one of the solutions is negative and the other one is above unity. Since both violate boundary conditions for s_K, the corresponding steady-state outcomes are the corner solutions $s_K = 0$ and $s_K = 1$. Note that for $\lambda = 1$, $\phi^{\text{cat}} = \phi^{\text{CP}'} = \phi^{\text{CP}}$, as defined in the previous section.

As in the case without localized spillovers, we can study the stability of the core–periphery equilibrium by analyzing the value of q^* at $s_K = 1$:

$$q^*|_{s_K=1} = \frac{\lambda[L(1+\phi^2)+\rho\phi^2]}{\phi(2L+\rho)}. \tag{26}$$

When $q^* < 1$, we then know that the core–periphery equilibrium is stable as the South has no incentive to innovate any more. It is easy to check that $q^* < 1$, when $\phi > \phi^{\text{CP}'}$.

The stability of the symmetric equilibrium can be studied following the same method as in the case without localized spillovers. We turn to signing $\partial q/\partial s_K$ evaluated at the symmetric equilibrium. Differentiating q with respect to s_K, we have:

$$\begin{aligned}\left(\frac{\partial \bar{q}/\bar{q}}{\partial s_K}\right)\bigg|_{\bar{s}_K=1/2} &= 2\left(\frac{1-\phi}{1+\phi}\right)\left(\frac{ds_E}{ds_K}\right)\bigg|_{\bar{s}_K=1/2} \\ &\quad + \frac{4}{1+\lambda}\frac{1+\phi^2}{(1+\phi)^2}\left[1-\lambda-\frac{(1-\phi)^2}{1+\phi^2}\right].\end{aligned} \tag{27}$$

Using (21) to find $\partial s_E/\partial s_K = 2\lambda\rho/[(1+\lambda)(L(1+\lambda)+\rho)]$, when evaluated at $s_K = 1/2$, we see that the system is unstable (the expression in (27) is positive) for sufficiently low trade costs (i.e., $\phi \approx 1$). The two effects discussed in the previous section in the case without localized spillovers are still present. The first positive term is the *demand-linked effect*: an increase in s_K increases North's capital income, expenditure share and local profits so that the value of an innovation (the numerator of Tobin's q) increases. The last negative term is the stabilizing *market crowding effect*. The second (positive) term is new and can be thought of as the *localized spillovers effect*: an increase in s_K implies a lower cost of innovation in the North (the denominator of Tobin's q) and therefore increase the incentive to innovate in the North.

4.3.2. *Possibility of catastrophic agglomeration*

It is possible to show that $\phi^{\text{cat}} < \phi^{\text{CP}'} < \phi^{\text{CP}}$. Hence, localized spillovers make the *catastrophic* agglomeration possible for higher trade costs. The critical level at which the expression in (27) becomes positive is ϕ^{cat}. Standard stability tests involving eigenvalues can be used to derive the same result. Figure 6 summarizes the model's stability properties in a diagram with ϕ and s_K on the axes. It shows that up to ϕ^{cat}, only the symmetric equilibrium exists and is stable. Between ϕ^{cat} and $\phi^{\text{CP}'}$, the symmetric steady-state looses its stability to the two neighboring interior steady states, which are thus saddle points by continuity. After ϕ^{CP}, only the core–periphery equilibria are stable. Note that these can be attained only asymptotically because, due to the absence of capital depreciation, the South share of capital never goes to zero even after it stops investing (i.e., after ϕ^{CP}).

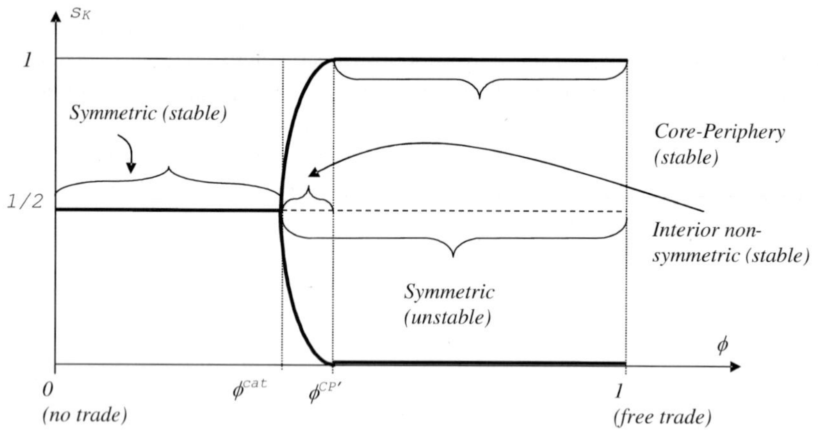

Figure 6. Stability properties of equilibria in the presence of localized spillovers.

4.3.3. *Geography affects growth*

Introducing localized technology spillovers implies that economic geography affects the global growth rate and the model generates endogenous stages of growth. In the version with capital mobility, the result that geography affects growth was already present. However, because of the absence of possible catastrophe, the relation between geography and growth was linear. This is not the case here. There are different stages of growth in the sense that if we think that trade costs are lowered with time, then as economic geography is altered in a non linear way, the growth rate itself changes in a non linear manner. When trade costs are high so that $\phi < \phi^{\text{cat}}$, the equilibrium economic geography is such that industry is dispersed between the two regions. This implies that spillovers are minimized and the cost of innovation is maximum. Using the optimal investment condition $q = q^* = 1$, and the fact that $s_K = 1/2$, it is easy to find the growth rate (see also Equation (18) using $s_K = s_n = 1/2$) in that first stage:

$$g = bL(1+\lambda) - \rho(1-b). \tag{28}$$

The growth rate of course increases with λ. Asymptotically, when $s_K = 1$, spillovers are maximized so that the cost of innovation is minimized. Again using Equation (18) with $s_K = s_n = 1$, the growth rate is in that stage:

$$g = 2bL - \rho(1-b), \tag{29}$$

which is, of course, identical to the solution when spillovers are global since in the core–periphery outcome, all innovators are located in the same region so that learning is not affected by the degree of localization λ.

The growth rate in that final stage is higher than the growth rate in the first stage when trade costs are high. In the former stage, innovation has stopped in the South which then is entirely specialized in the traditional good. In the intermediate stage, which we call the take-off stage, i.e., when trade costs are such that $\phi^{\text{cat}} < \phi < \phi^{\text{CP}'}$, the growth rate cannot be analytically found. However, it can be characterized as a take-off stage as the bifurcation of the system entails that the economy leaves a neighborhood of the symmetric steady state to reach a neighborhood of the asymmetric steady state in finite time.

To sum up, we have seen that a gradual lowering of trade costs on goods (an increase in ϕ) leads, once the trade cost passes a certain threshold, to a catastrophic agglomeration characterized by a sudden acceleration of innovation in one region (take-off) mirrored by the sudden halt of innovation in the other region. The North (the take-off region) enters a virtuous circle in which the increase in its share of capital expands its relative market size and reduces its relative cost of innovation which in turn induces further innovation and investment. In contrast, the South enters a vicious circle in which lower wealth leads to lower market size and lower profits for local firms. It also leads to an increase in the cost of innovation so that the incentive to innovate diminishes. Hence, *growth affects geography which itself affects growth and agglomeration is driven by the appearance of growth poles and sinks.*

4.3.4. *Can the periphery gain from agglomeration?*

In most geography models, agglomeration is a win–lose bargain. Residents of the region that gains the industry typically enjoys an increase in welfare while those left in the periphery see their real incomes fall. Allowing for endogenous growth opens the door to an important caveat to this pessimistic scenario.

The continual lowering of trade costs produces uneven spatial development – real per-capita income rises in the core region (since it saves the trade costs on all M-varieties) and falls in the peripheral one (since it pays the trade costs on all M-varieties). However, the emergence of regional imbalances is accompanied by faster growth in all regions (growth take-off). Of course, this is good also for the periphery and creates a tension between the static loss due to relocation and the dynamic gain due to faster growth. Thus, while the core is unambiguously better off, the take-off has ambiguous effects on the welfare of the periphery.

Intuition is served by Figure 7, which plots the long-run levels of welfare in the two regions as functions of trade freeness. In particular, it depicts a scenario in which lower trade costs drive all industry towards the North.

When trade is sufficiently closed, freer trade raises welfare in both regions because it lowers the price of imported manufactured goods. As trade freeness rises above the break point, North and South welfare levels diverge. The North benefits from agglomeration and faster growth. The South benefits only from the latter, while it is harmed by the former. This explains why the South's post-take-off welfare is always below the

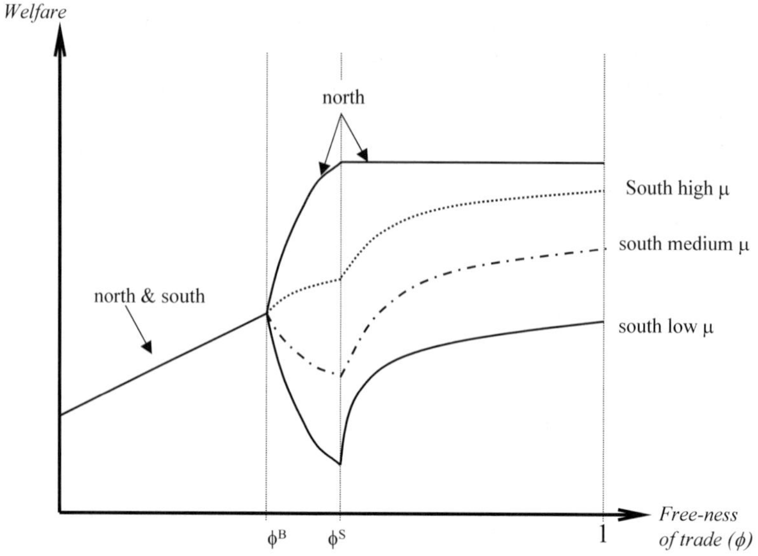

Figure 7. Agglomeration, growth and welfare.

North's. Once full agglomeration has been reached (i.e., freeness has risen above the sustain point), the North's welfare is constant.

The behavior of South's welfare is more complex. If the expenditures share of manufacturing goods μ is low enough, the increase in the growth rate has only a mild impact on welfare and the static loss dominates. In this case, the South loses from the take-off. This case is shown by the solid line (the lowest one in the diagram). On the contrary, if the share μ is sufficiently large, the dynamic gain dominates and the take-off benefits both regions, as shown by the dotted line. Finally, for intermediate values of μ, the South initially loses but eventually attains a welfare level that exceeds its pre-take-off situation. This is illustrated by the dashed curve.

Importantly, after the take-off lowering trade costs always improves welfare in the South because it decreases the price of goods imported from the North. Thus, even though the South may have been made worse off by agglomeration in the North, resisting further reductions in trade costs is not welfare improving.

4.4. The geography of goods and ideas: stabilizing and destabilizing integration

The main focus in the NEG literature has been on the consequence of falling transaction costs on trade in goods. We have shown that in a dynamic model with endogenous growth and localized spillovers, lower trade costs on goods have an effect on industry location but also on the growth rate. These effects can be "catastrophic" or not, depending on the mobility of capital.

Economic integration, however, is a multi-faceted phenomenon. Up to this point, we have look at two types of closer integration – lowering the cost of trade in goods, and making capital more mobility. There is another aspect of integration, however, which can also be important, namely integration that results in lower barriers to the spatial diffusion of learning knowledge spillovers. What might be called the cost of trading ideas. In the model introduced above (localised spillovers and immobile capital) we can study the impact of making trade in ideas freer by changing the 'learning spillover' parameter λ.[14]

4.4.1. Globalization and the newly industrialized countries

One exercise that illustrates the interactions focuses on the fact that both ϕ^{cat} and $\phi^{\mathrm{CP}'}$ are increasing in λ. The intuition is that as spillovers are becoming more global, an increase in the Northern share of capital does not decrease much the relative cost of innovation in the North (a destabilizing effect), so that the capital income effect (the stabilizing effect based on lower trade costs on goods) must be stronger. One important implication is that from a situation with full agglomeration in the North ($s_K = 1$) and fixed trade costs on goods, a gradual increase in λ (more globalized spillovers due for example to falling telecommunication costs) initially has no impact on Southern industry. However, because the cost of innovation in the South decreases with λ, Tobin's q in the South increases with λ. At some point, when λ is high enough, q^* becomes more than 1, and the South begins to innovate. The value of this threshold level which we call λ^{mir} (for "miracle") is

$$\lambda^{\mathrm{mir}} = \frac{\phi(2L+\rho)}{L(1+\phi^2)+\rho\phi^2}. \tag{30}$$

As in the case of falling trade costs on goods, there is a second critical value where the symmetric equilibrium becomes stable. This value, denoted as $\lambda^{\mathrm{mir}'}$ is the level of λ such that $\partial q/\partial s_K$ evaluated at the symmetric equilibrium becomes negative. As with the North take-off, the "miracle" in the South would appear as a virtuous circle: as it starts investing, its wealth and permanent income rise so that market size in the South and profits made by local firms increase. In turn, as the number of innovations made in the South increases, the cost of future innovations decreases. This "miracle" implies a jump in the investment rate, as Tobin's q in the South is more than 1, and rapid industrialization. Also incomes between the South and the North converge. Figure 8 describes the effect of an increase in λ on the model's stability properties in a diagram with λ and s_K on the axes.

[14] Keller (2002) shows that technology spillovers have indeed become considerably more global between 1970 and 1995.

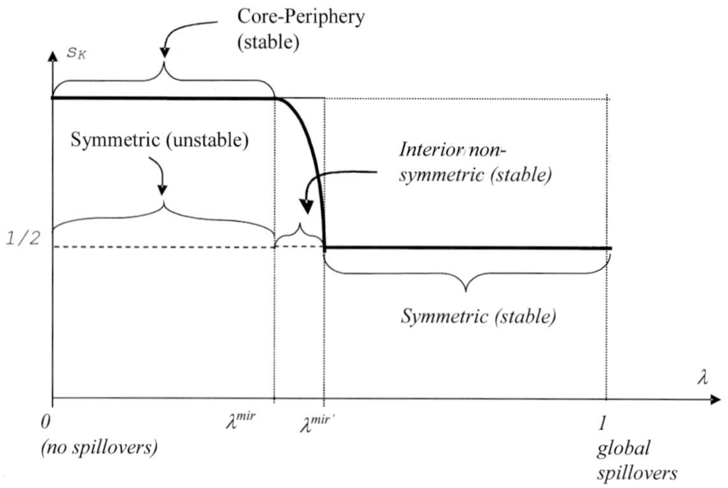

Figure 8. Falling transaction costs on ideas: stability properties of equilibria in the presence of localized spillovers.

4.4.2. *The learning-linked circular causality*

Another way to characterize the essential interplay between the cost of trading goods and ideas is to focus on the symmetric outcome rather than the fully-agglomerated outcome.

It is useful to point out that the localization of learning in the I-sector creates its own distinct agglomeration force. This new force, which is very much akin to a cost-linkage that operates in the I-sector, can be called learning-link circular causality. That is, if a region gets a slightly large amount of knowledge, it becomes a more attractive (cheaper) place to produce more knowledge, all else equal. Since a faster rate of knowledge creation sustains and deepens the region's advantage, an initial bit of 'knowledge shifting' leads to 'knowledge-creation shifting' which in turns leads to knowledge shifting.

Given this logic, it should be clear that *making it easier to trade ideas* (*i.e., raising* λ) *tends to stabilize the symmetric equilibrium*. We see therefore that there can be a tension between the de-stabilizing tendency that arises when goods become cheaper to trade and the stabilizing tendency that arises when ideas become easier to trade.

To investigate a scenario in which the cost of sharing ideas λ changes together with the cost of trading goods ϕ, Figure 9 depicts what Baldwin and Forslid (2000) call a "stability map". This shows how the model's stability properties vary with λ and ϕ. The diagram plots the break and sustain points against the various possible values of λ and ϕ. The dashed curve is the break point and the solid curve is the sustain point. The curves partition the map into three regions. When trade is not very free, and/or knowledge spillovers are very free, then the symmetric outcome is stable and the core–periphery outcomes does not exist. This is the Northwest region in the diagram. When

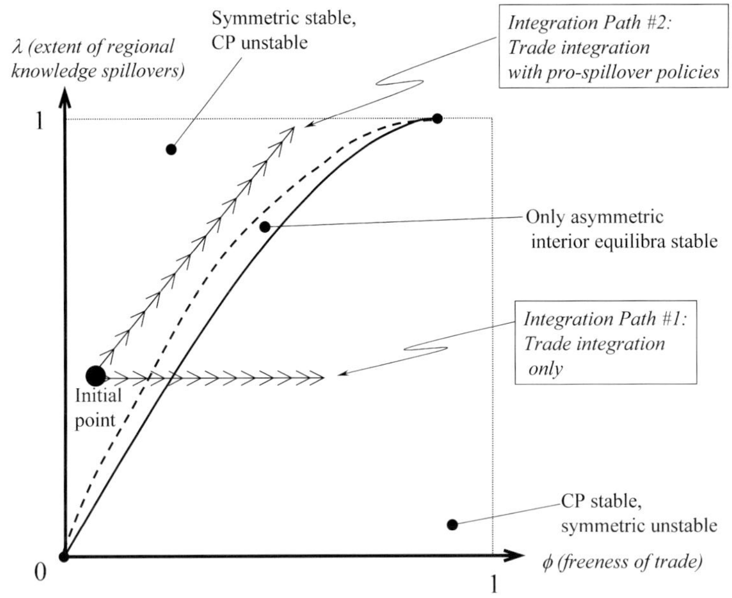

Figure 9. Stability map for LS model: stabilizing and destabilizing integration.

trade is quite free and/or knowledge flows are very restricted, only the core–periphery outcomes are stable. This is the Southeast region of the map. For a narrow range of ϕ's, two asymmetric interior equilibria are the only stable equilibria and this is shown as the area between the two curves.

The results also point out to a stark difference between lowering trade costs on goods and lowering transaction costs on ideas. *Lower trade costs on goods may foster divergence in incomes if it triggers an agglomeration process. However, lowering transaction costs on ideas has the opposite effect as it can make the core–periphery equilibrium unstable and trigger a sudden industrialization in the South which leads to convergence.* In our model, the distinction between trade costs on goods and transaction costs on ideas is an easy one. However, in reality trading goods often implies exchanging ideas in the process so that the processes that govern the evolution of the two types of transaction costs are certainly intertwined.

5. Other contributions

An early attempt to link growth and geography models was Walz (1996) who introduces endogenously expanding product variety in a model with vertical linkages and migration. His assumption of costless migration leads to a bang–bang migration behavior. Walz (1997) extends the model to a three-region setting.

Black and Henderson (1999) model the relation between urbanization and growth: there are localized knowledge spillovers so that urbanization affects the endogenous growth of the economy. Growth itself affects the size of cities. However, the assumption of a migration process that is determined by a city developer seems rather restrictive.

The models of growth and geography find their antecedents in models of endogenous growth and trade in particular Grossman and Helpman (1991). Some of the results on geography are already present as these authors show that with free trade and when knowledge spillovers are localized, the increasing returns activity concentrates in one location. Models of endogenous growth and trade do not however all imply that free trade leads to divergence if trade also involves capital goods as shown by Goh and Olivier (2002).

Fujita and Thisse (2002, Chapter 11) and (2003) combine a Krugman type core–periphery model and a Grossman–Helpman growth type model with horizontally differentiated products. As in the previous section and the earlier literature on growth and agglomeration, they use a set-up where the fixed cost of firms is a patent. They analyze the two cases of tradability and non tradability of the patents. The skilled workers who produce these patents are themselves mobile and they show that this is destabilizing factor. In the case of tradable patents, when trade costs are sufficiently low, a core–periphery pattern emerges with all the R&D sector as well as most of the manufacturing sector concentrated in one region. In this case, agglomeration takes place because of workers mobility and not because of growth but growth is influenced positively by spatial concentration because of the presence of localized spillovers. With non-tradability of patents, a third destabilizing force is added (the first being the mobility of skilled workers and the second being the localized spillovers) so that the core–periphery becomes sustainable at higher trade costs.

Baldwin (1999) presents a neoclassical growth model combined with an economic geography model. He shows that growth can affect the location industry since changes in regional capital stocks change the relative size of regional markets and this, via the home market effect, alters that spatial allocation of industry. The key to this is the fact that forces that encourage production in one region also tend to encourage capital accumulation in that region. To put it differently, capital accumulation is another way in which expenditure shifting can be tied to production shifting. Moreover, when this demand-linkage is neutralized by assuming that all capital earnings are repatriated, the linkage is broken.

When capital is immobile, the paper illustrates a second novel feature – geography can affect regional growth, at least in the medium run. In particular, the Perroux (1955) notion of 'growth poles and growth sinks' appears very clearly. Consider, for instance, initially symmetric regions facing trade costs that are high enough to ensure that the symmetric outcome is stable. When trade becomes free enough, symmetry becomes unstable. To be concrete, assume a small shock puts the North a little a bit ahead so the core will eventually end up in the North. The instability arises since the reward to capital rises in the North and falls in the South. This in turn would induce Northern residents to raise their investment rate above the rate necessary to sustain the initial capital stock. The consequence might be called agglomeration-induced, investment-led growth. The North's investment rate rises, boosting its capital–labor ratio, and thus its per capita income and output. This expansion of market size further favors investment in the region. In short, the North has become a growth pole. Circular causality has an interesting interpretation in this context. *Investment in the growing region is favored precisely because expenditure in the region is growing and expenditure is growing due to the high investment rate.*

The reverse process operates in the South. The lower rate of return induces Southern consumers/savers to stop investing, so depreciation erodes the Southern capital stock and Southern per capita income and output begin to drop. Given the particular depreciation process assumed, foreign firms shut down one by one. In the simple models we work with here, workers displaced by the downsizing of the South's industrial sector immediately find new jobs in the non-industrial sector. However, if finding a new job or expanding the non-industrial sector took time, the periphery's downward spiral would be associated with above-normal unemployment; the same labor market features would imply 'labor shortages' in the growing region. More colloquially, the declining region would resemble a 'rust belt' and the ascending region would resemble a 'boom belt'.

Allowing growth leads to another feature not commonly found in economic geography models that exclude considerations of growth. In the standard core–periphery economic geography model falling trade cost can produce asymmetries in initially symmetric regions. At intermediate trade costs, the two regions' also experience divergence of their real per capita incomes, but eventually, free trade re-equalizes incomes. This is illustrated in the left panel of Figure 10 with the heavy solid lines (CP model stands for

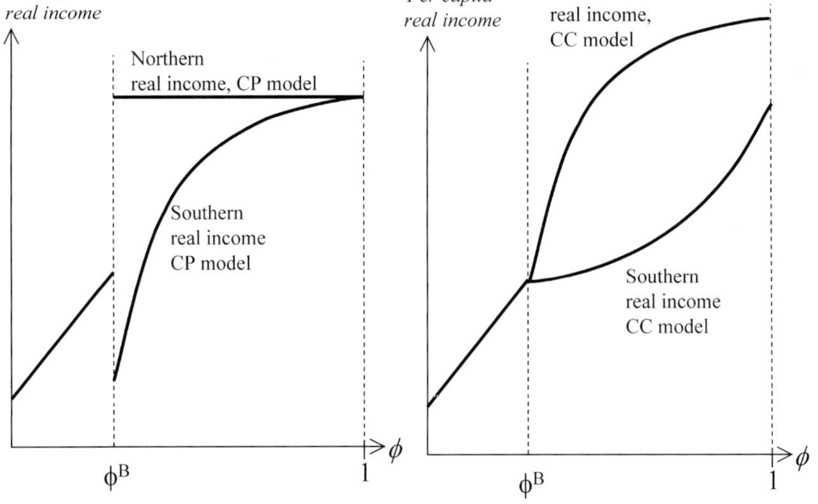

Figure 10. Real per capita income changes CP vs CC models.

core–periphery model). At the break point, all industry moves North (for convenience, the diagram assumes all H moves immediately) and this raises Northern per capita income.

In Baldwin (1999), which assumes capital is immobile, the core–periphery outcomes comes about as a result in a change in the two region's capital–labor ratios, with the North's rising and the South's falling. Thus even at free trade, the per capita incomes of the North are permanently higher than those of the South. This is shown in the right panel of Figure 10 with CC model standing for constructed capital model.

As an aside, we should also note that Baldwin (1999) also added a new element to the neoclassical growth literature. This literature typically predict convergence of regional income levels. In Baldwin (1999), however, progressive trade liberalization between symmetric nations eventually produces the core–periphery outcome. Thus, contrary to the standard assertion in the growth literature, in this neoclassical growth model, economic integration produces divergence in real per-capita income levels.

6. Concluding remarks

Introducing growth into economic geography models increases the degree of complexity of models that are already quite complex. Is it worth it? What insights do we gain from the marriage of growth and geography?

Geography and growth models display a number of features that do not appear in static economic geography models. These features are interesting since they help us organize our thinking about important real-world phenomenon and policies. Specifically:

(1) In these models growth affects geography by creating what could be called growth-linked circular causality; forces that foster the location of industry in a region also foster the investment, i.e., the accumulation of human, physical and/or knowledge capital in that region. Since these new factors earn incomes and spend part of these incomes locally, capital accumulation alters relative market size.

(2) The agglomeration process in these models would look like the appearance of growth poles and sinks – firms want to be in the growing region, people want to invest in that region since it is growing and this investment in turn makes the region grow faster. The opposite spiral would appear to be operating in the 'growth sink'.

(3) The simple geography models predict that everyone should be indifferent to agglomeration once trade became really free. In growth and geography models, region capital–labor ratio's 'endowments' are permanently altered by agglomeration. Thus regional, real per capital income differentials do not disappear as trade gets perfectly free.

(4) Economic integration is a multi-faceted phenomenon in the real world, yet the standard models focus almost exclusive in the cost of selling goods at a distance. Economic integration has a much richer meaning in geography and growth models. Geography and growth models show that the cost of moving capital across

borders (capital mobility) and the cost of moving ideas across borders (learning spillovers) are also important aspects of economic integration. In particular, these other policies can mitigate or extenuate the de-stabilizing aspects of freer trade.

(5) Perhaps the most important new feature of geography and growth models is the way in which they allow us to crystallize our thinking about the interplay between the location of economic activity and the growth rate of economic activity.

(6) One aspect of this interplay is important for policy analysis. Taking the standard economic geography models at face value produces higher protectionist policy implications [see Baldwin et al. (2003, Chapter 12)] since agglomeration of industry is always a win–lose situation. In the geography and growth models, the result is not so stark. The continual lowering of trade costs does produce uneven spatial development – real per-capita income rises in the core region and falls in the peripheral one. However, the emergence of regional imbalances is accompanied by faster growth in all regions. Of course, this is good also for the periphery and creates a tension between the static loss due to relocation and the dynamic gain due to faster growth. Thus, while the core is unambiguously better off, the take-off has ambiguous effects of peripheral welfare. A similar application is to realize that regional policies at the national level that seek to avoid geography concentration of industry may cost the country as a whole in growth terms. The introduction of growth in geography models thus adds a new dimension to the possible spatial equity-efficiency trade-off.

(7) Perhaps the most sweeping application of these models – and one that is not yet complete – concerns what might be called the grand unified theory of globalization and geography. Here are the stylized facts of globalization since the mid 19th century that the unified theory would have to explain. The world has seen two waves of globalization – one from roughly 1850 to 1914 and one from the 1960s to the present. At a high level of abstraction the key facts are:

Industrialization/de-industrialization. In the first wave, the 'North' (Western Europe and the U.S.) industrialized while South (especially India and China) de-industrialized. In the second wave, the South (East Asia) industrializes while the North de-industrializes.

Divergence. The first wave sees North and South incomes diverge massively, while the second wave witnesses a convergence, at least between the North and the industrializing South.

Trade. International trade in goods and factors (labor migration and long-term capital flows) exploded in the first wave. After being shut down by two world wars, a surge of protectionism and the Great Depression, the second wave was marked by a return of trade and capital flows to levels that have recently topped those seen in Victorian England. Mass international migration, however, remains small by the standards of the first wave.

Growth take-off. Sometime before the first globalization wave kicks in, the "Industrial Revolution" triggers modern growth in the North, but the South continues to stagnant in per capita terms. Modern growth, defined as a self-sustained growth process whereby output per hour worked rises steadily, begins in the UK and spreads to Western Europe and the U.S. around the middle of the 19th century. Of course, this it not independent of the income divergence since big differences in income levels come from sustained differences in growth rates – not from one-time shifts of the location of industry. Moreover, the limited income convergence in the second wave is linked to spectacular growth in the industrializing South and a moderate slowdown in the North.

Urbanization. While some of the largest cities in the world were in the South prior to the 19th century, the first globalization wave is accompanied by a rapid and historically unprecedented urbanization in the North. Northern urbanization continued during the second wave but cities grew even more rapidly in the South.

The closest the non-growth geography models have come to this is Krugman and Venables (1995), a paper that was known 'on the streets' as history-of-the-world-(part-I). This paper sews together the first three of the five facts as follows. In 1750 or so, the world's economic geography was quite homogeneous, i.e., poor and agrarian. With domestic and international trade costs nearly prohibitive, each village essentially had to make all its own goods; this meant manufactured goods were dear and the available range of varieties limited. As trade costs fell, both inside and between nations, specialization became feasible and this triggered a process of what Myrdal called cumulative causality. Modeling this circular-causality process is the heart of the NEG contribution, so an aside is in order. Migration of firms or workers de-homogenize the world, turning it into economically big and small regions (markets). When industries are imperfectly competitive and trade is costly, Krugman's 'home market effect' favors the location of industry in large regions, but since industries are marked by increasing returns, getting a disproportionate share of industry means a region's labor is disproportionately productive and this in turn results in higher real wages and/or a higher return to capital. The circle is closed by noting that capital and labor are attracted to the region with higher rewards and their migration makes the big region bigger and the small region smaller.

According to Krugman–Venables, advances in transport technology in the early 19th century triggered this de-homogenization of the world's economic geography, and, as history would have it, the North won at the South's expense. This single event is the root cause of the first three facts: Northern industrialization and Southern de-industrialization, the rapid expansion of international trade (England becomes the world's workshop providing cheap and varied manufactured goods in exchange for raw materials and this specialization both fosters trade and is fostered by it), and income divergence (due to increasing returns in industry and decreasing returns in other sectors, a high share of industry in GDP means high labor productivity and thus high incomes).

One problem with this story is that the magnitudes just do not fit. One-time concentrations of industry just cannot account for the observed income gaps. Here is the argument. Krugman–Venables ignore endogenous technological progress, assuming that physical technology is identical in the North and South. Thus in the Krugman–Venables story, the difference in incomes between the UK and India must be due to the difference in industry's share in the UK and Indian output mix and the productivity gap between industry and traditional sectors. If the UK's per capita income was 100 in 1850, India's was 23 according to Maddison (1995, Tables C16 & D1), so the income gap to be explained is 77. Moreover, Crafts (1989) tells us that in 1840, 47% of the UK workforce was in industry, and Bairoch (1989, Table 9) tells us that India was only 4.7% as industrialized as the UK in 1860, so (ignoring the mismatch in dates) we can conclude that the static allocation of industry can only account for the income difference if industrial workers are 171 times – i.e., 17,100% – more productive than workers in the traditional sector.

This just cannot be right. Plainly, the real story must lie elsewhere and growth is the obvious suspect. Indeed, since the headline story in the 19th century was the spread of modern growth, the Krugman–Venables story is a bit like Hamlet with the Prince. Clearly, one has to add endogenous growth to the Krugman–Venables story to account for the facts on income divergence/convergence as well as on growth take-offs.

As shown in this chapter, allowing for endogenous growth, localized spillovers and some capital immobility, we can get the fourth fact of globalization into a unified framework. The only facts left un-accounted for concerns urbanization. To get this into the story, one would have to allow internal geography in the regions considered, but once the technical difficulties were mastered, the economics would be straightforward. In the first wave of globalization, economic activity characterized by localized spillovers is concentrating in the North. It would not therefore be too surprising that urbanization proceeded faster in the North than in the South during this era. Likewise, in the second wave of globalization, the industrialization of the South (emergence of the Asian tigers, etc.) strengthens the forces that foster within South concentration of economic activity, i.e., urbanization, while the de-industrialization of the North does the opposite.

Acknowledgements

We are grateful to our discussant Jacques Olivier for helpful comments and especially to Jacques Thisse for detailed suggestions. This chapter is produced as part of a CEPR research network on 'The Economic Geography of Europe: Measurement, Testing and Policy Simulations', funded by the European Commission under the Research Training Network Programme (Contract No: HPRN-CT-2000-00069).

References

Audretsch, D., Feldman, M. (2004). "The geography of innovation and spillovers". In: Henderson, J.V., Thisse, J.-F. (Eds.), Handbook of Regional and Urban Economics, vol. 4. Elsevier, Amsterdam. This volume.

Bairoch, P. (1989). "European trade policy, 1815–1914". In: Mathias, P., Pllard, S. (Eds.). In: The Cambridge Economic History of Europe, vol. 8. Cambridge University Press, Cambridge.

Baldwin, R., Forslid, R. (1997). "Trade liberalization and endogenous growth: A q-theory approach". Journal of International Economics 50, 497–517.

Baldwin, R.E. (1999). "Agglomeration and endogenous capital". European Economic Review 43, 253–280.

Baldwin, R., Forslid, R. (2000). "The core–periphery model and endogenous growth: stabilising and destabilising integration". Economica 67, 307–324.

Baldwin, R., Forslid, R., Martin, P., Ottaviano, G., Robert-Nicoud, F. (2003). Economic Geography and Public Policy. Princeton University Press.

Baldwin, R., Martin, P., Ottaviano, G. (2001). "Global income divergence, trade and industrialization: The geography of growth take-off". Journal of Economic Growth 6, 5–37.

Barro, R.J., Sala-i-Martin, X. (1995). Economic Growth. McGraw–Hill, New York.

Basevi, G., Ottaviano, G. (2002). "The district goes global: Export vs FDI". Journal of Regional Science 42, 107–126.

Black, D., Henderson, J.V. (1999). "A theory of urban growth". Journal of Political Economy 107, 252–284.

Ciccone, A. (2002). "Agglomeration-effects in Europe". European Economic Review 46, 213–227.

Ciccone, A., Hall, R. (1996). "Productivity and the density of economic activity". American Economic Review 87, 54–70.

Coe, D., Helpman, E. (1995). "International R&D spillovers". European Economic Review 39, 859–887.

Coe, D., Helpman, E., Hoffmaister, A. (1997). "North–South R&D spillovers". The Economic Journal 107, 134–149.

Crafts, N. (1989). "British industrialization in an international context". Journal of Interdisciplinary History 19, 415–428.

De la Fuente, A., Vives, X. (1995). "Infrastructure and education as instruments of economic policy: evidence from Spain". Economic Policy 20 (April).

Duranton, G., Puga, D. (2001). "Nursery cities: Urban diversity, process innovation and the life cycle of products". American Economic Review 5, 1454–1477.

Esteban, J.M. (1994). "La desigualdad interregional en Europe y en España: descriptiŏn y análisis". In: Crecimento y Convergencia Regional en España y en Europa, vol. II. Instituto de Analsisi Economico, Barcelona.

Fujita, M., Krugman, P., Venables, A. (1999). The Spatial Economy, Cities, Regions and International Trade. MIT Press, Cambridge, MA.

Fujita, M., Thisse, J.-F. (2002). Economics of Agglomeration. Cambridge University Press.

Fujita, M., Thisse, J.-F. (2003). "Does geographical agglomeration foster economic growth? And who gains and looses from it?" Japanese Economic Review 54, 121–145.

Grossman, G., Helpman, E. (1991). Innovation and Growth in the World Economy. MIT Press, Cambridge MA.

Goh, A., Olivier, J. (2002). "Learning by doing, trade in capital goods and growth". Journal of International Economics 56, 411–444.

Henderson, J.V. (1988). Urban Development, Fact and Illusion. Oxford University Press, Oxford.

Hohenberg, P.M., Lees, L.H. (1985). The Making of Urban Europe (1000–1950). Harvard University Press, Cambridge, MA.

Jacobs, J. (1969). The Economy of Cities. Vintage, New York.

Jaffe, A., Trajtenberg, M., Henderson, R. (1993). "Geographic localization of knowledge spillovers as evidenced by patent citations". Quarterly Journal of Economics 108, 577–598.

Keller, W. (2002). "Geographic localization of international technology diffusion". American Economic Review 92, 120–142.

Krugman, P. (1991). "Increasing returns and economic geography". Journal of Political Economy 99, 483–499.

Krugman, P.R., Venables, A.J. (1995). "Globalization and the inequality of nations". Quarterly Journal of Economics 60, 857–880.

Lucas, R.E. (1988). "On the mechanics of economic development". Journal of Monetary Economics 22, 3–42.

Maddison, A. (1995). Explaining the Economic Growth of Nations: Essays in Time and Space. Elgar, Aldershot.
Manzocchi, S., Ottaviano, G. (2001). "Outsiders in economic integration: The case of a transition economy". Economics of Transition 9, 229–249.
Martin, P. (1999). "Public policies, regional inequalities and growth". Journal of Public Economics 73 (1), 85–105.
Martin, P., Ottaviano, G. (1999). "Growing locations: Industry location in a model of endogenous growth". European Economic Review 43, 281–302.
Martin, P., Ottaviano, G. (2001). "Growth and agglomeration". International Economic Review 42, 947–968.
Martin, P., Rogers, C.A. (1995). "Industrial location and public infrastructure". Journal of International Economics 39, 335–351.
Ottaviano, G.I.P. (1996). "The location effects of isolation". Swiss Journal of Statistics and Economics 132, 427–440.
Ottaviano, G.I.P., Tabuchi, T., Thisse, J.-F. (2002). "Agglomeration and trade revisited". International Economic Review 43, 409–436.
Ottaviano, G., Thisse, J.-F. (2004). "Agglomeration and economic geography". In: Henderson, J.V., Thisse, J.-F. (Eds.), Handbook of Regional and Urban Economics, vol. 4. Elsevier, Amsterdam, pp. 2563–2608. This volume.
Perroux, F. (1955). "Note sur la croissance". Économie Appliquée 1–2, 307–320.
Puga, D. (1999). "The rise and fall of regional inequalities". European Economic Review 43, 303–334.
Quah, D. (1996). "Regional cohesion from local isolated actions, 1: Historical outcomes". Mimeo. LSE.
Quah, D. (2002). "Spatial agglomeration dynamics". CEPR discussion paper No. 3208.
Romer, P. (1990). "Endogenous technological change". Journal of Political Economy 98 (5), S71–S102. part II.
Urban, D. (2002). "Neoclassical growth, manufacturing agglomeration and terms of trade". Mimeo. LSE.
Walz, U. (1996). "Transport costs, intermediate goods and localized growth". Regional Science and Urban Economics 26, 671–795.
Walz, U. (1997). "Growth and deeper regional integration in a three-country model". Review of International Economics 5, 492–507.
Williamson, J.G. (1988). "Migration and urbanization". In: Chenery, H., Srinivasan, T.N. (Eds.), Handbook of Development Economics, vol. 1. North-Holland, Amsterdam, pp. 425–465.
Yamamoto, K. (2003). "Agglomeration and growth with innovation in the intermediate goods sector". Mimeo. Graduate School of Economics, Kyoto University. Regional Science and Urban Economics. In press.

Chapter 61

KNOWLEDGE SPILLOVERS AND THE GEOGRAPHY OF INNOVATION

DAVID B. AUDRETSCH[1]

Max-Planck-Institut für die Erforschung von Wirtschaftssystemen, Germany
e-mail: audretsch@mpiew-jena.mpg.de

MARYANN P. FELDMAN

University of Toronto, Toronto, Canada
e-mail: maryann.feldman@rotman.utoronto.ca

Contents

[1] Also affiliated with CEPR.

Handbook of Regional and Urban Economics, Volume 4. Edited by J.V. Henderson and J.F. Thisse

DOI: 10.1016/S0169-7218(04)07061-3

Abstract

This chapter focuses on the geographic dimensions of knowledge spillovers. The starting point comes from the economics of innovation and technological change. This tradition focused on the innovation production function however it was aspatial or insensitive to issues involving location and geography. However, empirical results hinted that knowledge production had a spatial dimension. Armed with a new theoretical understanding about the role and significance of knowledge spillovers and the manner in which they are localized, scholars began to estimate the knowledge production function with a spatial dimension. Location and geographic space have become key factors in explaining the determinants of innovation and technological change. The chapter also identifies new insights that have sought to penetrate the black box of geographic space by addressing a limitation inherent in the model of the knowledge production. These insights come from a rich tradition of analyzing the role of both localization and urbanization economies, by extending the focus to the organization of economic activity within a spatial dimension and examine how different organizational aspects influence economic performance. While the endogenous growth theory emphasizes the importance of investments in research and development and human capital, a research agenda needs to be mapped out identifying the role that investments in spillover conduits can make in generating economic growth. It may be that a mapping of the process by which new knowledge is created, externalized and commercialized, hold the key to providing the microeconomic linkages to endogenous macroeconomic growth.

Keywords

spillovers, knowledge, clusters, entrepreneurship, innovation, technological change, regions

JEL classification: O3, R1

1. Introduction

In proposing a new theory of economic geography, Paul Krugman (1991, p. 55) asks: "What is the most striking feature of the geography of economic activity? The short answer is surely concentration... production is remarkably concentrated in space". Feldman (1994a) provided evidence that what Krugman observed to be true for production was even more pronounced for innovative activity. This finding helped trigger a new literature with the goal of *understanding the spatial dimension of innovative activity*, specifically the determinants and mechanisms that underlie the propensity of innovative activity to cluster spatially. Knowledge spillovers figure prominently in addressing these issues. This chapter introduces the reader to the path that scholars have taken to understand the geographic dimensions of knowledge spillovers.

The starting point on this intellectual journey is the literature that analyzes the economics of innovation and technological change. This tradition, reviewed in Section 2, focused on the innovation production function; however, it was *aspatial* or insensitive to issues involving location and geography. However, empirical results hinted that knowledge production had a spatial dimension. Armed with a new theoretical understanding about the role and significance of knowledge spillovers and the manner in which they are localized, scholars began to estimate the knowledge production function with a spatial dimension.

As Section 3 makes clear, *location and geographic space have become key factors in explaining the determinants of innovation and technological change*. There is a long and insightful literature that considers the spatial dimension of innovative activity and the factors that influence industrial clustering. A piece that had been missing in this older tradition was the role that knowledge spillovers play in providing access to new economic knowledge and increasing the productivity of economic actors.

Section 4 examines studies that have sought to penetrate the black box of geographic space by addressing a limitation inherent in the model of the knowledge production. These studies follow a rich tradition dating back at least to Hoover Jr. (1936) of analyzing the role of both localization and urbanization economies, by extending the focus to the organization of economic activity within a spatial dimension and examine how different organizational aspects influence economic performance.

While identifying the importance of geographic location in general, and agglomeration in particular, was a significant step in generating innovative activity, it provided little insight as to *how and why knowledge spills over*, nor did it illuminate the mechanisms that serve as conduits for the transmission of knowledge. Section 5 considers various potential spillover mechanisms and studies that examine these different mechanisms.

Section 6 examines one spillover mechanism which has generated a large body of research – entrepreneurship. Just as entrepreneurs have been found to originate in locations with strong knowledge assets, empirical evidence suggests that high rates of entrepreneurial activity contribute to higher growth performance. Finally, the last section provides a summary and conclusion.

2. The knowledge production function

The traditional starting point in the literature on innovation and technological change for most theories of innovation has been the firm [Baldwin and Scott (1987), Cohen and Levin (1989), Scherer (1984, 1991), Griliches (1979)]. In such theories firms are exogenous and their performance in generating technological change is endogenous [Scherer (1984, 1991), Cohen and Klepper (1991, 1992)]. For example, in the most prevalent model of technological change, the model of the knowledge production function [Griliches (1979)], incumbent firms engage in the pursuit of new economic knowledge as an input into the process of generating innovative activity. The most important input in this model is new economic knowledge. As Cohen and Klepper (1991, 1992) point out, the greatest source generating new economic knowledge is generally considered to be R&D. Other inputs in the knowledge production function have included measures of human capital, skilled labor, and educational levels. Thus, the model of the knowledge production function from the literature on innovation and technological change can be represented as

$$I_i = \alpha RD_i^{\beta} HK_i^{\gamma} \varepsilon_i, \tag{1}$$

where I stands for the degree of innovative activity, RD represents R&D inputs, and HK represents human capital inputs. The unit of observation for estimating the model of the knowledge production function, reflected by the subscript i, has been at the level of countries, industries and enterprises.

The logic of the production function held: innovative output was a function of innovative inputs. However, empirical estimation of the model of the knowledge production function, represented by Equation (1), was found to be stronger at broader levels of aggregation such as countries or industries. For example, at the unit of observation of countries, the empirical evidence [Griliches (1984)] clearly supported the existence of the knowledge production function. This is intuitively understandable, because the most innovative countries are those with the greatest investments to R&D. Less innovative output is associated with developing countries, which are characterized by a paucity of new economic knowledge. Similarly, the model of the knowledge production function was strong at the level of the industry [Scherer (1984), Griliches (1984)]. Again, this seems obvious as the most innovative industries also tend to be characterized by considerable investments in R&D and new economic knowledge. Not only are industries such as computers, pharmaceuticals and instruments high in R&D inputs that generate new economic knowledge, but also in terms of innovative outputs [Acs and Audretsch (1990)]. By contrast, industries with little R&D, such as wood products, textiles and paper, also tend to produce only a negligible amount of innovative output.

Where the relationship became less robust was at the disaggregated microeconomic level of the enterprise, establishment, or even line of business: there is no direct deterministic relationship between inputs and innovation.[2] Thus, the finding that the knowledge production model linking knowledge generating inputs to outputs holds at the more aggregated levels of economic activity suggests the presence of an externality.

The model of the knowledge production function also became less compelling in view of a wave of studies that found that small enterprises were an engine of innovative activity in certain industries. For example, Acs and Audretsch (1988, 1990) found that while large enterprises (defined as having at least 500 employees) generated a greater number of new product innovations than did small firms (defined as having fewer than 500 employees), once the measures were standardized by levels of employment, the innovative intensity of small enterprises was found to exceed that of large firms.[3] These results are startling, because as Scherer (1991) documented, the bulk of industrial R&D is undertaken in the largest corporations; and small enterprises account only for a minor share of R&D inputs. This raises the question of *how small firms obtained access to R&D inputs*. Either the model of the knowledge production did not hold, at least at the level of the enterprise (for a broad spectrum across the firm-size distribution), or else the appropriate unit of observation had to be reconsidered. In searching for a solution, scholars chose the second interpretation, leading them to move towards spatial units of observation as an important unit of analysis for the model of the knowledge production function.

3. Geography and the role of spillovers

As it became apparent that the firm was not completely adequate as a unit of analysis for estimating the model of the knowledge production function, scholars began to look for externalities. In refocusing the model of the knowledge production to a spatial unit of observation, scholars confronted two challenges. The first one was theoretical. What was the theoretical basis for knowledge to spill over yet, at the same time, be spatially within some geographic unit of observation? The second challenge involved measurement. How could knowledge spillovers be measured and identified? More than

[2] For example, while Acs and Audretsch (1988, 1990) found that the simple correlation between R&D inputs and innovative output was 0.84 for four-digit standard industrial classification (SIC) manufacturing industries in the United States, it was only about half, 0.40 among the largest U.S. corporations.

[3] The innovation rates, or the number of innovations per thousand employees, have the advantage of measuring large- and small-firm innovative activity relative to the presence of large and small firms in any given industry. That is, in making a direct comparison between large- and small-firm innovative activities, the absolute number of innovations contributed by large firms and small enterprises is somewhat misleading, since these measures are not standardized by the relative presence of large and small firms in each industry. When a direct comparison is made between the innovative activity of large and small firms, the innovation rates are presumably a more reliable measure of innovative intensity because they are weighted by the relative presence of small and large enterprises in any given industry. Thus, while large firms in manufacturing introduced 2445 innovations, and small firms contributed slightly fewer, 1954, small-firm employment was only half as great as large-firm employment, yielding an average small-firm innovation rate in manufacturing of 0.309, compared to a large-firm innovation rate of 0.202.

a few scholars heeded Krugman's warning (1991, p. 53) that empirical measurement of knowledge spillovers would prove to be impossible because "knowledge flows are invisible, they leave no paper trail by which they may be measured and tracked".[4]

In confronting the first challenge, which involved developing a theoretical basis for geographically bounded knowledge spillovers, scholars turned to the emerging literature of the new growth theory. In explaining the increased divergence in the distribution of economic activity between countries and regions, Krugman (1991) and Romer (1986) relied on models based on increasing returns to scale in production. By increasing returns, however, Krugman and Romer did not necessarily mean at the level of observation most familiar in the industrial organization literature – the plant, or at least the firm – but rather at the level of a spatially distinguishable unit. In fact, it was assumed that the externalities across firms and even industries would generate increasing returns in production. In particular, Krugman (1991), invoking Marshall (1920), focused on "external increasing returns" arising from spillovers from: (i) a pooled labor market; (ii) pecuniary externalities enabling the provision of non-traded inputs to an industry in a greater variety and at lower cost; and (iii) information or technological spillovers.

That knowledge spills over was barely disputed. Some thirty years earlier, Arrow (1962) identified externalities associated with knowledge due to its non-exclusive and non-rival use. However, what has been contested is the geographic range of knowledge spillovers: knowledge externalities are so important and forceful that there is no reason that knowledge should stop spilling over just because of borders, such as a city limit, state line, or national boundary. Krugman (1991), and others, did not question the existence or importance of such knowledge spillovers. In fact, they argue that such knowledge externalities are so important and forceful that there is no reason for a political boundary to limit the spatial extent of the spillover.

In applying the model of the knowledge production function to spatial units of observation, theories of why knowledge externalities are spatially bounded were needed. Thus, it took the development of localization theories explaining not only that knowledge spills over but also why those spillovers decay as they move across geographic space. An older but insightful literature addressed these concerns.

Jacobs (1969), writing about cities, suggests that *information*, such as the price of gold on the New York Stock Exchange, or the value of the Yen in London, has a familiar meaning and interpretation. By contrast, *knowledge* or what is sometimes referred to as *tacit knowledge*, is vague, difficult to codify and often only serendipitously recognized. While information is codified and can be formalized, written down, tacit knowledge, by definition, is non-codifiable and cannot be formalized and written down. Geographic proximity matters in transmitting knowledge, because tacit knowledge is inherently non-rival in nature, and knowledge developed for any particular application

[4] Lucas (2001) and Lucas and Rossi-Hansberg (2002) impose a spatial structure on production externalities in order to model the spatial structure of cities. The logic is that spatial gradients capture some of the externalities associated with localized human capital accumulation.

can easily spill over and have economic value in very different applications. Manski (2000) considers that many of the interactions in R&D and human capital formation that are important to endogenous growth theory occur in non-market environments and are influenced by the expectations, preferences and constraints of related economic agents. Moreover, social interactions have economic value in transmitting knowledge and ideas. Von Hipple (1994) explains that high context, uncertain knowledge, or what he terms *sticky knowledge*, is best transmitted via face-to-face interaction and through frequent and repeated contact. An implication of the distinction between information and tacit knowledge is that the marginal cost of transmitting information across geographic space has been rendered invariant by the revolution in telecommunications while *the marginal cost of transmitting knowledge, especially tacit knowledge, is lowest with frequent social interaction, observation and communication*. After all, geographic proximity matters in transmitting knowledge, because as Glaeser et al. (1992, p. 1126) observe, "intellectual breakthroughs must cross hallways and streets more easily than oceans and continents".

Feldman (1994a, 1994b) developed the theory that location mitigates the inherent uncertainty of innovative activity: *proximity enhances the ability of firms to exchange ideas and be cognizant of important incipient knowledge*, hence reducing uncertainty for firms that work in new fields. Innovation clusters spatially where knowledge externalities reduce the costs of scientific discovery and commercialization. In addition, Feldman (1994a) suggests that firms producing innovations tend to be located in areas where there are necessary resources: resources that have accumulated due to a region's past success with innovation. In this way, firms and resources are endogenous.

Studies identifying the extent of knowledge spillovers are based on the model of the knowledge production function applied at spatial units of observation. In what is generally to be considered to be the first important study re-focusing the knowledge production function, Jaffe (1989) modified the traditional approach to estimate a model specified for both spatial and product dimensions:

$$I_{si} = \alpha IRD^{\beta_1} * UR_{si}^{\beta_2} * \left(UR_{si} * GC_{si}^{\beta_3}\right) * \varepsilon_{si}, \tag{2}$$

where I is innovative output, *IRD* is private corporate expenditures on R&D, *UR* is the research expenditures undertaken at universities, and *GC* measures the geographic coincidence of university and corporate research. The unit of observation for estimation was at the spatial level, s, a state, and industry level, i. Estimation of Equation (2) essentially shifted the knowledge production function from the unit of observation of a firm to that of a geographic unit. Implicitly contained within the knowledge production function model is the assumption that innovative activity should take place in those regions, s, where the direct knowledge-generating inputs are the greatest, and where knowledge spillovers are the most prevalent. Jaffe (1989) dealt with the measurement problem raised by Krugman (1991) by linking the patent activity within technologies located within states to knowledge inputs located within the same spatial jurisdiction.

Estimation of Equation (1) essentially shifted the model of the knowledge production function from the unit of observation of a firm to that of a geographic unit. Jaffe (1989) found empirical evidence that $\beta_1 \geqslant 0$, $\beta_2 \geqslant 0$, $\beta_3 \geqslant 0$ supporting the notion knowledge spills over for third-party use from university research laboratories as well as industry R&D laboratories. Acs, Audretsch and Feldman (1992) confirmed that the knowledge production function represented by Equation (2) held at a spatial unit of observation using a direct measure of innovative activity, new product introductions in the market. Feldman (1994b) extended the model to consider other knowledge inputs to the commercialization of new products. The results confirmed that the knowledge production function was robust at the geographic level of analysis: the output of innovation is a function of the innovative inputs in that location.

Other studies concur that knowledge spillovers tend to be geographically bounded within the region where new economic knowledge was created [Agrawal (2002a, 2002b), Anselin, Acs and Varga (1997), Black (2003), Orlando (2000), Autant-Bernard (2001a, 2001b)]. Scholars have continued to work in this tradition adding new measures of innovative output and refining the measures of innovative inputs and outputs. For example, Black (2003) developed a measure of innovation based on awards made in the United States Small Business Innovation Research (SBIR) Program. In estimating a knowledge production function along the lines of Equation (2) for a variety of geographic units and using different measure of innovative output, the results concur that the logic of the knowledge production function is robust across geography. Autant-Bernard (2001a, 2001b) and Orlando (2000) model the interplay between geographic and technological proximity for inter-firm spillovers. Their results suggest the importance of geographic proximity for spillovers is dependent on the propensity of similar industrial activity to agglomerate geographically.

Estimation of the knowledge production function has typically varied the spatial unit from relatively broad geographic units of observations, such as states, to much more focused geographic units of observations such as cities, counties or even zip codes. Most scholars concur that states are probably too broad to represent an appropriate geographic unit of observation. Some have tried to estimate the geographic extent of knowledge spillovers in miles using the concept of distance decay [Adams and Jaffe (2002), Adams (2002), Wallsten (2001)]. Others contend that geography is more a platform for organizing economic activity and that "as the crow flies" measures of distance do not capture complex social relationships [Feldman (2002), Branstetter (2002)]. The role of social relationships will be explicitly discussed when we examine the literature on industrial districts.

There are also good reasons to believe that knowledge spillovers are not homogeneous across firms [Feldman (1993)]. In estimating Equation (1) for large and small enterprises separately, Acs, Audretsch and Feldman (1994) provide some insight into the puzzle about how small, and frequently new, firms able to generate innovative output while undertaking generally negligible amounts of investment into knowledge generating inputs, such as R&D. The answer appears to be through exploiting knowledge created by expenditures on research in universities and on R&D in large corporations. Their findings suggest that the innovative output of all firms rises along with an increase in the amount of R&D inputs, both in private corporations as well as in university laboratories.

However, R&D expenditures made by private companies play a particularly important role in providing knowledge inputs to the innovative activity of large firms, while expenditures on research made by universities serve as an especially key input for generating innovative activity in small enterprises. Apparently large firms are more adept at exploiting knowledge created in their own laboratories, while their smaller counterparts have a comparative advantage at exploiting spillovers from university laboratories.

Jaffe, Trajtenberg and Henderson (1993) and Jaffe and Trajtenberg (2002) analyze patent families – patents that reference or cite each other and indicate the flows of knowledge from one invention to another.[5] Specifically, they compare the probabilities of patents citing prior patents with inventors from the same city against a randomly drawn control sample of cited patents. Their results suggest that citations are significantly more localized than the control group. The same methodology has been applied by Almeida and Kogut (1997) to study patenting in the semiconductor industry. The basic results agree: patent citations are highly localized, indicating that location and proximity clearly matter in exploiting knowledge spillovers.

Audretsch and Feldman (1996) found that the propensity of innovative activity to cluster geographically tends to be greater in industries where new economic knowledge plays a more important role. This effect was found to hold even after holding the degree of production at that location constant. Audretsch and Feldman (1996) follow Krugman's (1991) example, and calculate Gini coefficients for the geographic concentration of innovative activity to test this relationship.[6] The results indicate that a key determinant of the extent to which the location of production is geographically concentrated is the relative importance of new economic knowledge in the industry. Even after controlling for the geographic concentration of production, the results suggest a greater propensity for innovative activity to cluster spatially in industries in which industry R&D, university research and skilled labor are important inputs. In this work, skilled labor is included as a mechanism by which knowledge spillovers may be realized as workers move between jobs in an industry taking their accumulated skills and know-how with them.

The spatial distribution of innovative output can be seen in Table 1. The measure of innovative output is new product innovations introduced to the U.S. market. The majority of new product innovations were located in cities indicating that innovation is an

[5] Griliches (1990) provides a survey of the uses and limitations of patent data.

[6] The Gini coefficients are weighted by the relative share of economic activity located in each state. Computation of weighted Gini coefficients enables us to control for size differences across states. The Gini coefficients are based on the share of activity in a state and industry relative to the state share of the national activity for the industry. The locational Gini coefficients for production are based on industry value-added. We calculate the amount of value added in an industry and a state divided by national value-added for the industry. This ratio is normalized by the state share of total manufacturing value-added in order to account for the overall distribution of manufacturing activity. An industry which is not geographically concentrated more than is reflected by the overall distribution of manufacturing value-added would have a coefficient of 0. The closer the industry coefficient is to 1, the more geographically concentrated the industry would be. Cases is which data are suppressed are omitted from the analysis. The Gini coefficients for innovation are based on counts of innovation in a state and industry are calculated in a similar way.

Table 1
Innovative activity in cities

Consolidated metropolitan statistical area	Innovations	Population (thousands)	Innovations per 100,000 population
San Francisco–Oakland	477	5368	8.886
Boston–Lawrence	345	3972	8.686
New York–Northern New Jersey	735	17,539	4.191
Philadelphia–Wilmington	205	5681	3.609
Dallas–Fort Worth	88	2931	3.002
Hartford	30	1014	2.959
Los Angeles–Anaheim	333	11,498	2.896
Buffalo–Niagara	35	1243	2.816
Cleveland–Akron	77	2834	2.717
Chicago–Gary	203	7937	2.558
Providence–Pawtucket	25	1083	2.308
Portland–Vancouver	25	1298	1.926
Cincinnati–Hamilton	30	1660	1.807
Seattle–Tacoma	37	2093	1.768
Pittsburgh	42	2423	1.733
Denver–Boulder	28	1618	1.731
Detroit–Ann Arbor	68	4753	1.431
Houston–Galveston	39	3101	1.258
Miami–Fort Lauderdale	13	2644	0.492

Source. Feldman and Audretsch (1999).

Table 2
The innovative advantage of U.S. cities (MSA and count)

	Industry	*N*	Most innovative MSA
3573	Electronic computing machinery	787	San Jose (166); Boston (48); Los Angeles (48); Anaheim (35)
3823	Process control instruments	464	Boston (45); Philadelphia (31); Chicago (26)
3662	Radio/TV equipment	311	San Jose (58); Boston (25); New York (17); Los Angeles (14)
3674	Semiconductors	168	San Jose (53; Boston (10); Dallas (10); Los Angeles (10)
3825	Instruments to measure electricity	114	San Jose (22); Boston (20)
2834	Pharmaceuticals	116	Newark (27); Philadelphia (11); New York (10)
3842	Surgical appliances	101	Newark (20); Nassau–Suffolk (10); Bergen–Passaic (8); Philadelphia (6)
3494	Values and pipe fittings	81	Anaheim (6); Los Angeles (6); Cleveland (6); Cincinnati (5)
3679	Electronic components	72	San Jose (19); Anaheim (7); Boston (6)
3561	Pumps and pumping equipment	68	Philadelphia (8); Aurora–Elgin (7)
3861	Photographic equipment	57	Rochester (8); Minneapolis (7)
3579	Office machines	54	New York (11); Philadelphia (7); Stamford (5)
3622	Industrial controls	51	San Jose (7); Cleveland (4)
3841	Surgical and medical instruments	51	Nassau–Suffolk (10); Bergen–Passaic (8)

Source. Feldman and Audretsch (1999).

urban activity. Table 2 shows that the propensity for innovative activity to cluster spatially is even greater for specific industries, such as computers and process control instruments, pharmaceuticals, etc. Even more mundane types of industrial activities such as industrial pumps and pumping equipment demonstrate a tendency to concentrate in certain locations.

In sum, *the empirical evidence suggests that location and proximity clearly matter in exploiting knowledge spillovers*. The geographic estimation of the knowledge production function, however, is limited because there is no understanding of the way in which spillovers occur and are realized at the geographic level. The pre-existing pattern of technology related activities makes it difficult to separate spillovers from the correlation of variables at the geographic level. Economic activity may be co-located, but the pattern of causality is difficult to decipher.

4. Penetrating the black box of geographic space

The contribution of the new wave of studies described in the previous section was simply to shift the unit of observation away from firms to a geographic region. But does it make a difference how economic activity is organized within the black box of geographic space? Geographers, political scientists and sociologists have long argued that the differences in the culture of a region and relationships between actors may contribute to differences in innovative performance across regions, even holding knowledge inputs such as R&D and human capital constant [see Malecki (1997) for a review of the literature]. For example, Saxenian (1994) argues that a culture of greater interdependence and exchange among individuals in the Silicon Valley region has contributed to a superior innovative performance than is found around Boston's Route 128, where firms and individuals tend to be more isolated and less interdependent.

Such observations suggest a limitation inherent to the general knowledge production function approach described in the previous section. While economists tend to avoid attributing differences in economic performance to cultural differences, there has been a series of theoretical arguments suggesting that differences in the underlying structure between regions may account for differences in rates of growth and technological change. In fact, a heated debate has emerged in the literature about the manner in which the underlying economic structure within a geographic unit of observation might shape economic performance [see Rosenthal and Strange (2004) in this volume]. In this section we review the debate that revolves around two key structural elements – the degree of diversity versus specialization and the degree of monopoly versus local competition.

One view, which Glaeser et al. (1992) attribute to the *Marshall–Arrow–Romer externality*, suggests that an increased concentration of a particular industry within a specific geographic region facilitates knowledge spillovers across firms. This model formalizes the insight that the concentration of an industry within a city promotes knowledge spillovers among firms and therefore facilitates innovative activity. To the degree that individuals in the population are identical and engaged in identical types of activities, the costs of communication and transactions are minimized. Lower costs of transaction in communication result in a higher probability of knowledge spilling over across individuals within the population. An important assumption of the model is that knowledge externalities with respect to firms exist, but only for firms within the same industry. Thus, the relevant unit of observation is extended from the firm to the region in the tradition of the Marshall–Arrow–Romer model, but the spillovers are limited to occur solely within the relevant industry.

By contrast, restricting knowledge externalities to occur only within the same industry may ignore an important source of new economic knowledge – inter-industry knowledge spillovers. After all, Griliches (1992, p. 29) defined knowledge spillovers as "working on similar things and hence benefiting much from each others research". Jacobs (1969) argues that the most important source of knowledge spillovers is external to the industry in which the firm operates and that cities are the source of considerable innovation because the diversity of these knowledge sources is greatest in cities. According to Jacobs, it is the exchange of complementary knowledge across diverse firms and economic agents which yield a greater return on new economic knowledge. She develops a theory that emphasizes that the variety of industries within a geographic region promotes knowledge externalities and ultimately innovative activity and economic growth.[7]

The extent of regional specialization versus regional diversity in promoting knowledge spillovers is not the only dimension over which there has been a theoretical debate. A second controversy involves the degree of competition prevalent in the region, or the extent of local monopoly. The Marshall–Arrow–Romer model predicts that local monopoly is superior to local competition because it maximizes the ability of firms to appropriate the economic value accruing from their investments in new knowledge. By contrast, Jacobs (1969) and Porter (1990) argue the opposite – that competition is more conducive to knowledge externalities than is local monopoly.[8] It should be emphasized that by local competition Jacobs does not mean competition within product markets as has traditionally been envisioned within the industrial organization literature. Rather, Jacobs is referring to the competition for the new ideas embodied in economic agents. Not only do an increased number of firms provide greater competition for new ideas, but in addition, greater competition across firms facilitates the entry of a new firm specializing in some particular new product niche. This is because the necessary complementary inputs and services are likely to be available from small specialist niche firms but not necessarily from large, vertically integrated producers.

A test of the specialization versus diversity debate measured economic performance in terms of employment growth. Glaeser et al. (1992) employ a data set on the growth

[7] For an extension, see Henderson (1997), Henderson, Shalizi and Venables (2001) and Rosenthal and Strange (2003).

[8] Porter (1990) provides examples of Italian ceramics and gold jewelry as industries in which numerous firms are located within a bounded geographic region and compete intensively for new ideas.

of large industries in 170 cities between 1956 and 1987 in order to identify the relative importance of the degree of regional specialization, diversity and local competition play in influencing industry growth rates. The authors find evidence that contradicts the Marshall–Arrow–Romer model but is consistent with the theories of Jacobs. However, their study provided no direct evidence as to whether diversity is more important than specialization in generating innovative activity.

Feldman and Audretsch (1999) identify the extent to which the organization of economic activity is either concentrated, or alternatively consists of diverse but complementary economic activities, and how the underlying structure of economic activity influences innovative output. They link the innovative output of product categories within a specific city to the extent to which the economic activity of that city is concentrated in that industry, or conversely, diversified in terms of complementary industries sharing a common science base. Feldman and Audretsch (1999) identify the extent to which the organization of economic activity is either concentrated, or alternatively consists of diverse but complementary economic activities, and how the underlying structure of

Table 3
Innovation in science-based industry clusters

Cluster	Prominent cities	Mean industry innovations per 100,000 workers
Agra-business	Atlanta	92.40
	Dallas	41.15
	Chicago	33.03
	St. Louis	91.74
Chemical engineering	Dallas	38.09
	Minneapolis	66.67
	San Francisco	43.89
	Wilmington	85.47
Office machinery	Anaheim–Santa Ana	92.59
	Minneapolis	31.86
	Rochester	72.20
	Stanford	68.40
Industrial machinery	Anaheim–Santa Ana	54.95
	Cincinnati	66.01
	Cleveland	141.51
	Passaic, NJ	90.90
High-tech computing	Boston	73.89
	Houston	62.08
	San Jose	44.88
	Minneapolis	181.74
Biomedical	Boston	38.71
	Cleveland	68.76
	Dallas	35.22
	New York	188.07

Source. Feldman and Audretsch (1999).

economic activity influences innovative output. They link the innovative output of product categories within a specific city to the extent to which the economic activity of that city is concentrated in that industry, or conversely, diversified in terms of complementary industries sharing a common science base.

Table 3 shows the innovative activity of cities sharing a common science base. Their results indicate that diversity across complementary economic activities sharing a common science base is more conducive to innovation than is specialization. In addition, their results indicate that the degree of local competition for new ideas within a city is more conducive to innovative activity than is local monopoly. Perhaps the most important conclusions from these two studies, however, is that more than simply an endowment of knowledge inputs is required to generate innovative activity. The underlying economic and institutional structure matters, as do the microeconomic linkages across agents and firms. These findings do not address the path that spillovers take or the mechanisms by which spillovers are realized. These have been examined by work reviewed in the following sections.

5. Spillover mechanisms

Romer (1986), Lucas (1988, 1993) and Grossman and Helpman (1991) established that knowledge spillovers are an important mechanism underlying endogenous growth. However, they shed little light on the actual mechanisms by which knowledge is transmitted across firms and individuals. By necessity, the knowledge production function focused on the quantifiable aspects of innovation. However, formal R&D data ignore the complex processes of technological accumulation whereby tacit knowledge is built up and accumulates meaning – complex transactions that involves local institutions, social convention and legal rights as well as economic interests [Feldman et al. (2002)]. Thus, *the literature on knowledge spillovers and the geography of innovation has begun to consider the mechanisms by which knowledge spills over and is put into economic use and the degree to which these process are geographically localized.* Understanding these issues are important because a policy implication commonly drawn from the new economic growth theory is that, as a result of convexities in knowledge and the resultant increasing returns, knowledge resources, such as R&D should be publicly supported. While this may be valid, it is also important to recognize that the mechanisms for spillover transmission may also play a key role and may also serve as a focus for public policy enhancing economic growth and development.

The concepts of localized knowledge spillovers and absorptive capacity – the ability of economic agents to recognize, assimilate and apply new scientific knowledge, are closely linked [Agrawal (2002a, 2002b)]. Cohen and Levinthal (1989, 1990) suggest that firms that invest in R&D develop the capacity to adapt knowledge developed in other firms and are therefore able to appropriate some of the returns accruing to external investments in new knowledge. Cockburn and Henderson (1998) build on this concept to suggest that firms that are connected to the community of open science are able to increase their investment in R&D by absorbing knowledge spillovers. Firms are able to acquire and benefit from external knowledge by cultivating relationships with universities, participating in research consortia and partnering with academics that do related scientific work.

Edwin Mansfield was perhaps the earliest to point out that research laboratories of universities provide one source of innovation-generating knowledge that is available to private enterprises for commercial exploitation [Mansfield (1995, 1998)]. The empirical work reviewed previously supported that finding. For example, Jaffe (1989) and Acs, Audretsch and Feldman (1992), Audretsch and Feldman (1996) and Feldman and Audretsch (1999) found that the knowledge created in university laboratories spills over to contribute to the generation of commercial innovations by private enterprises [Feldman and Desrochers (2003)]. Even after controlling for the location of industrial R&D, knowledge created at universities results in greater innovation. The ability of research universities to create benefits for their local economies has created a new mission for research universities and a developing literature examines the mechanism and the process of technology transfer from research universities [Mowery and Shane (2002)].

A different literature has emphasized the impact of networks and social capital found within a geographic region. Relational networks exist at multiple levels of analysis because they can link together individuals, groups, firms, industries, geographic regions, and nation-states. In addition, they can tie members of any one of these categories to members of another category. For example, Powell, Koput and Smith-Doerr (1996), Florida and Cohen (1999) and Feldman et al. (2002) demonstrate the ways in which research universities provide a link that facilitates knowledge spillovers in the form of recruiting talent to the region, transferring technology through local linkages and interactions, placing students in industry, and providing a platform for firms, individuals and government agencies to interact. Similarly, Florida and Kenney (1988) examine the connections and special access to talent and resources that venture capital firms provide to link their new high technology startups clients. Gompers and Lerner (1999) have shown how geography affects the location of venture capital. In particular, they show that the geographic distribution of venture capital is highly spatially skewed with California, New York, and New England as the major location of venture capital funds. Furthermore, Sorenson and Stuart (2001) show that location matters in obtaining venture capital. By analyzing the determinants of venture capital investment in the United States between 1986 and 1998, they find that the likelihood of a venture capitalist investing in a given target declines with geographical distance between the venture capitalist and the company.

Malecki (1997) was perhaps the first to note *the importance of skilled labor as a mechanism for knowledge transfer in technology based industrial clusters*. It is also the case that for certain science based industries that the location and preferences of scientists influence the geographical location of innovation. Zucker, Darby and Brewer (1998) and Prevenzer (1997) show that in biotechnology, an industry based almost exclusively on new knowledge and cutting edge scientific discoveries, firms tend to cluster together in just a handful of locations and find that this is due to the location of star scientists – those individuals with high amounts of human capital who are able to appropriate their knowledge through start-up firms. This finding is supported by Audretsch and Stephan (1996) who examine the geographic relationships of scientists working with biotechnology firms. The importance of geographic proximity is clearly shaped by the role played by the scientist. The scientist is more likely to be located in the same region as the firm when the relationship involves the transfer of new economic knowledge. However, when the scientist is providing a service to the company that does not involve knowledge transfer, local proximity becomes much less important.

6. Entrepreneurship as a spillover mechanism

The literature identifying mechanisms actually transmitting knowledge spillovers is sparse and remains underdeveloped. However, one important area where such transmission mechanisms have been identified is entrepreneurship. Entrepreneurship is concerned with the startup and growth of new enterprises.

Why should entrepreneurship serve as a mechanism for the spill over of knowledge from the source of origin? At least two major channels or mechanisms for knowledge spillovers have been identified in the literature. Both of these spillover mechanisms revolve around the issue of appropriability of new knowledge and absorptive capacity. This view of spillovers is consistent with the traditional model of the knowledge production function, where the firm exists exogenously and then undertakes (knowledge) investments to generate innovative output.

By contrast, Audretsch (1995) proposes shifting the unit of observation away from exogenously assumed firms to individuals, such as scientists, engineers or other knowledge workers – agents with endowments of new economic knowledge. When the lens is shifted away from the firm to the individual as the relevant unit of observation, the appropriability issue remains, but the question becomes: *How can economic agents with a given endowment of new knowledge best appropriate the returns from that knowledge?* If the scientist or engineer can pursue the new idea within the organizational structure of the firm developing the knowledge and appropriate roughly the expected value of that knowledge, he has no reason to leave the firm. On the other hand, if he places a greater value on his ideas than do the decision-making bureaucracy of the incumbent firm, he may choose to start a new firm to appropriate the value of his knowledge. Small enterprises can compensate for their lack of R&D is through spillovers and spin-offs. Typically an employee from an established large corporation, often a scientist or engineer working in a research laboratory, will have an idea for an invention and ultimately for an innovation. Accompanying this potential innovation is an expected net return from the new product. The inventor would expect to be compensated for his/her potential innovation accordingly. If the company has a different, presumably lower, valuation of the potential innovation, it may decide either not to pursue its development, or that it merits a lower level of compensation than that expected by the employee.

In either case, the employee will weigh the alternative of starting his/her own firm. If the gap in the expected return accruing from the potential innovation between the inventor and the corporate decision maker is sufficiently large, and if the cost of starting a new firm is sufficiently low, the employee may decide to leave the large corporation and establish a new enterprise. Since the knowledge was generated in the established corporation, the new start-up is considered to be a spin-off from the existing firm. Such start-ups typically do not have direct access to a large R&D laboratory. Rather, these small firms succeed in exploiting the knowledge and experience accrued from the R&D laboratories with their previous employers.

In the metaphor provided by Albert O. Hirschman (1970), if voice proves to be ineffective within incumbent organizations, and loyalty is sufficiently weak, a knowledge worker may resort to exit the firm or university where the knowledge was created in order to form a new company. In this spillover channel the knowledge production function is actually reversed. The knowledge is exogenous and embodied in a worker. The firm is created endogenously in the worker's effort to appropriate the value of his knowledge through innovative activity.

One group of studies has focused on how location has influenced the entrepreneurial decision, or the decision to start a new firm. Within the economics literature, the prevalent theoretical framework has been the general model of income choice. The model of entrepreneurial choice dates back at least to Knight (1921), but was more recently extended and updated by Lucas (1978), Kihlstrom and Laffont (1979), Holmes and Schmitz Jr. (1990) and Jovanovic (1994). In its most basic rendition, individuals are confronted with a choice of earning their income either from wages earned through employment in an incumbent enterprise or else from profits accrued by starting a new firm. The essence of the entrepreneurial choice model is made by comparing the wage an individual expects to earn through employment, W^*, with the profits that are expected to accrue from a new-firm startup, P^*. Thus, the probability of starting a new firm, $\Pr(s)$, can be represented as

$$\Pr(s) = f(P^* - W^*). \tag{3}$$

The model of entrepreneurial choice has been extended by Kihlstrom and Laffont (1979) to incorporate aversion to risk, and by Lucas (1978) and Jovanovic (1994) to explain why firms of varying size exist, and has served as the basis for empirical studies of the decision to start a new firm by Evans and Leighton (1989a, 1989b, 1990).

Geographic location should influence the entrepreneurial decision by altering the expected return from entrepreneurial activity, P^*. The theory of knowledge spillovers suggests that P^* will tend to be greater in agglomerations and spatial clusters, since access to tacit knowledge is greater. Geography and spatial location also influences entrepreneurship. The important role that geographic clusters and networks play as a determinant of entrepreneurial activity was identified in Europe and only recently has been discovered within the North American context [Porter (1990, 2000), Saxenian (1994)]. By contrast, there is a longer and richer tradition of research linking entrepreneurship to spatial clusters and networks in Europe. However, most of these studies have been in social science fields other than economics. For example, Becattini (1990) and Brusco (1990) identified the key role that spatial clusters and networks play in promoting SMEs in Italy. With the development of recent theoretical models by Soubeyran and Thisse (1999) and Soubeyran and Weber (2002), it became clear and accepted that spatial agglomerations were also important in the North American context.

An important distinction between the European literature and the emerging literature in North America was the emphasis on high technology and knowledge spillovers in the North American context. By contrast, the European tradition focused much more on the role of networks and clusters in fostering the viability of SMEs in traditional industries, such as textiles, apparel and metalworking. For example, seminal studies by Becattini (1990) and Brusco (1990) argue that small and new firms enjoy a high degree of stability when supported by networks in Italy. A rich literature has provided a body of case studies, spanning the textile industries of northern Italy to the metal working firms of Baden Wuerttenberg [Piore and Sabel (1984)], documenting the long-term viability and stability of small and new firms embedded in the so-called industrial districts of Europe. Pyke and Sengenberger (1990) argue that through the support of an industrial district, small firms in European spatial clusters have been able to compensate for what would otherwise be an inherent size disadvantage. According to Pyke and Sengenberger (1990), an industrial district is a geographically defined production system, involving a large number of enterprises engaging in production at a wide range of stages, and typically involved in the production of a well-defined but differentiated product. A particularly significant feature of Italian industrial districts is that almost all of the firms are small or even micro-enterprises. Examples of such industrial districts include Prato, Biella, Carpi and Castelgoffredo, which specialize in textile (coolants in Castelgoffredo); Vigevano, Montebellune and Montegranaro where shoes are manufactured (ski boots in Montebellune); Pesaro and Nogara which manufacture wooden furniture; Sassuolo where ceramic tiles are produced.

Brusco (1990) emphasizes the cooperation among network firms within an industrial district. Such cooperation presumably reduces any size-inherent disadvantages and improves the viability of small firms operating within the network. According to Pyke and Sengenberger (1990, p. 2), "A characteristic of the industrial district is that it should be conceived as a social and economic whole. That is to say, there are close inter-relationships between the different social, political and economic spheres, and the functioning of one, say the economic, is shaped by functioning and organization of the others." Grabher (1993) similarly argues that the social structure underlying industrial networks contributes to the viability of small firms that would otherwise be vulnerable if they were operating in an isolated context.

Feldman (2001) and Feldman and Francis (2002) examine the formation of innovative clusters and argue that entrepreneurs are key agents. Based on an analysis of the development of an Internet and biotechnology cluster around Washington, DC, Feldman (2001) provides evidence that clusters form not because resources are initially located in a particular region, but rather through the work of entrepreneurs. Entrepreneurship is a local phenomenon as most entrepreneurs were previously employed in the region.

Moreover, entrepreneurs are endogenous and organize resources and institutions to support their firms. An industry agglomeration is simply a collection of localized firms with a common focus and there are gains to collective action. As their businesses begin to thrive, resources such as money, networks, experts, and related services develop in, and are attracted to, the region. With this infrastructure in place, more entrepreneurial ventures locate and thrive in the region, which ultimately may create a thriving cluster where none previously existed. Feldman and Francis (2002) develop a conceptual model to formalize the process of cluster formation through entrepreneurism. Using simulations, Zhang (2002) demonstrates how a small number of successful entrepreneurs can generate a cluster.

A series of studies, spanning a broad spectrum of countries, has attempted to link entrepreneurial activity to characteristics specific to a geographic region, including measures of knowledge, such as R&D and human capital. Entrepreneurship activity has been typically measured as new-firm startups (rates), self-employment (rates), business ownership (rates), or a combination of startups and exits referred to as turbulence (rates). For example, the collection of European country studies included in the special issue of *Regional Studies* on "Regional Variations in New Firm Formation" [Reynolds, Storey and Westhead (1994)], along with the survey by Storey (1991) suggest that the empirical evidence has been generally unambiguous with respect to the findings for population density (a positive impact on startup rates), population growth (positive impact on startup rates), skill and human capital levels of the labor force (positive impact), and mean establishment size (negative impact on startup rates). By contrast, the empirical evidence about the impact of unemployment on startup rates is considerably more ambiguous. But an unambiguous positive relationship has emerged between measures of human capital and entrepreneurial activity at the regional level.[9]

Audretsch and Fritsch (1996) examined the impact that location plays on entrepreneurial activity in (West) Germany. Using a data base derived from the social insurance statistics, which covers about 90 percent of employment, they identify the birth rates of new startups for each of 75 distinct economic regions. These regions are distinguished on the basis of planning regions, or *Raumordungsregionen*. They find that, for the late 1980s, the birth rates of new firms are higher in regions experiencing low unemployment, which have a dense population, a high growth rate of population, a high share of skilled workers, and a strong presence of small businesses.

Similarly, Pfirrmann (1994) has found that the innovative activity of small- and medium-sized firms in West Germany is shaped by regional factors. He uses a database consisting of innovative small and medium-sized firms and finds that the innovative activity of small- and medium-sized enterprises tends to be greater in those regions where there is a strong presence of knowledge resources. However, his results also indicate

[9] The positive relationship between entrepreneurship activity and economic growth could also be at least partially explained by the fact that a large number of entrepreneurs implies a greater number of firms and a stronger accumulation of physical capital.

that factors internal to the firm are more important for the innovation efforts of a small firm than is the regional environment.

If entrepreneurship serves as a mechanism for knowledge spillovers, it should not only be reflected by the model of entrepreneurial choice, or the decision to start a new firm. Rather, measures of entrepreneurial activity should also be positively linked to the growth performance of regions. The view of entrepreneurship is based on its role as an agent of change in a knowledge-based economy implies that a positive economic performance should be linked to entrepreneurial activity. This hypothesis has raised two challenges to researchers: (1) what is meant by economic performance and how can it be measured and operationalized? and (2) over which units of analysis should such a positive relationship between entrepreneurship and economic performance be manifested? In fact, these two issues are not independent from each other. The answer to the second question, the appropriate unit of analysis, has influenced the first question, the performance criteria and measure.

The most prevalent measures of performance has been employment growth. The most common and most exclusive measure of performance is growth, typically measured in terms of employment growth. These studies have tried to link various measures of entrepreneurial activity, most typically startup rates, to economic growth. Other measures sometimes used include the relative share of SMEs, and self-employment rates.

For example, Audretsch and Fritsch (1996) analyzed a database identifying new business startups and exits from the social insurance statistics in Germany to examine whether a greater degree of turbulence leads to greater economic growth, as suggested by Schumpeter in his 1911 treatise, *A Theory of Economic Development*. These social insurance statistics are collected for individuals. Each record in the database identifies the establishment at which an individual is employed. The startup of a new firm is recorded when a new establishment identification appears in the database, which generally indicates the birth of a new enterprise. While there is some evidence for the United States linking a greater degree of turbulence at the regional level to higher rates of growth for regions [Reynolds (1999)], Audretsch and Fritsch (1996) find that the opposite was true for Germany during the 1980s. In both the manufacturing and the service sectors, a high rate of turbulence in a region tends to lead to a lower and not a higher rate of growth. They attribute this negative relationship to the fact that the underlying components – the startup and death rates – are both negatively related to subsequent economic growth. Those areas with higher startup rates tend to experience lower growth rates in subsequent years. Most strikingly, the same is also true for the death rates. The German regions experiencing higher death rates also tend to experience lower growth rates in subsequent years. Similar evidence for Germany is found by Fritsch (1997).

Audretsch and Fritsch (1996) conjectured that one possible explanation for the disparity in results between the United States and Germany may lie in the role that innovative activity, and therefore the ability of new firms to ultimately displace the incumbent enterprises, plays in new-firm startups. It may be that innovative activity did not play the same role for the German *Mittelstand* as it does for SMEs in the United States. To the degree that this was true, it may be hold that regional growth emanates from SMEs only when they serve as agents of change through innovative activity.

The empirical evidence suggested that the German model for growth provided a sharp contrast to that for the United States. While Reynolds (1999) had found that the degree of entrepreneurship was positively related to growth in the United States, a series of studies by Audretsch and Fritsch (1996) and Fritsch (1997) could not identify such a relationship for Germany. However, the results by Audretsch and Fritsch were based on data from the 1980s.

Divergent findings from the 1980s about the relationship between the degree of entrepreneurial activity and economic growth in the United States and Germany posed something of a puzzle. On the one hand, these different results suggested that the relationship between entrepreneurship and growth was fraught with ambiguities. No confirmation could be found for a general pattern across developed countries. On the other hand, it provided evidence for the existence of distinct and different national systems. The empirical evidence clearly suggested that there was more than one way to achieve growth, at least across different countries. *Convergence in growth rates seemed to be attainable by maintaining differences in underlying institutions and structures.*

However, in a more recent study, Audretsch and Fritsch (2002) find that different results emerge for the 1990s. Those regions with a higher startup rate exhibit higher growth rates. This would suggest that, in fact, Germany is changing over time, where the engine of growth is shifting towards entrepreneurship as a source of growth. The results of their 2002 paper suggest a somewhat different interpretation. Based on the empirical evidence that the source of growth in Germany has shifted away from the established incumbent firms during the 1980s to entrepreneurial firms in the 1990s, it would appear that a process of convergence is taking place between Germany and the United States, where entrepreneurship provides the engine of growth in both countries. Despite remaining institutional differences, the relationship between entrepreneurship and growth is apparently converging in both countries.

The positive relationship between entrepreneurship and growth at the regional level is not limited to Germany in the 1990. For example, Foelster (2000) examines not just the employment impact within new and small firms but on the overall link between increases in self-employment and total employment in Sweden between 1976–1995. By using a Layard–Nickell framework, he provides a link between micro behavior and macroeconomic performance, and shows that increases in self-employment rates have had a positive impact on regional employment rates in Sweden.

Hart and Hanvey (1995) examine measures of new and small firms start-ups to employment generation in the late 1980s for three regions in the United Kingdom. While they find that employment creation came largely from SMEs, they also identify that most of the job losses also came from SMEs.

Callejon and Segarra (2000) use a data set of Spanish manufacturing industries between 1980–1992 to link new-firm birth rates and death rates, which taken together constitute a measure of turbulence, to total factor productivity growth in industries and regions. They adopt a model based on a vintage capital framework in which new entrants embody the edge technologies available and exiting businesses represent marginal obsolete plants. Using a Hall type of production function, which controls for imperfect competition and the extent of scale economies, they find that both new-firm startup rates and exit rates contribute positively to the growth of total factor productivity in regions as well as industries.

The evidence linking entrepreneurship to growth at the regional level may actually be more convincing in the European context than in the North American context. Only a handful of studies have been undertaken for North America, while the evidence from Europe is considerably more robust and consistent.

In the U.S., a series of studies [Wilson (1996), Bates (1998)] have attempted to identify whether the determinants of entrepreneurial activity differ for different immigrant and ethnic minority groups. In one of the most important studies, Saxenian (2001) documents that the decision to become an entrepreneur is shaped by immigrant group status. In particular, she provides evidence that the fastest-growing groups of immigrant engineers in Silicon Valley are from Mainland China and India. Chinese, in particular, are increasingly visible in the computer science and engineering departments on university campuses located in the Silicon Valley region. Saxenian (2001) suggests that these immigrant entrepreneurs provide a mechanism for a two-way flow of ideas and knowledge between Silicon Valley and their home regions in Asia.

7. Conclusions

Perhaps the greatest development in the literature on the economics of innovation and technological change in the last decade has been the insight that geography matters. A long tradition of analyzing the innovative process within the boundaries of the firm and devoid of spatial context has given way to the incorporation of spatial context in models of innovation and technological change.

Incorporating spatial relationships into the model of the knowledge production function has redeemed the view that knowledge inputs are linked to innovative output. While the boundaries of the firm still matter, so do the boundaries of spatial agglomerations. Geography has been found to provide a platform upon which new economic knowledge can be produced, harnessed and commercialized into innovations. Thus, *the model of the knowledge production has been found to hold better for spatial units of observation than for enterprises in isolation of spatial context.*

This is not to say that the research agenda of the geography of innovation and knowledge spillovers is in any way complete. Rather, a broad spectrum of research issues and questions remain open and virtually unexplored. One important but relatively unchartered area for future research involves the life cycle of spatial units, such as agglomerations, clusters and regions. Due to data constraints, most of the research reported in the chapter is based on cross-sectional analyses. *While research has determined that geographic space matters for innovation, it has yet to unravel how agglomerations are formed, where they come from, how they are either sustained and strengthen, or else deteriorate over time*. With the prevalence of new longitudinal panel data, we look forward to answers to these questions being provided by a new generation of scholars researching the spatial dimensions of innovative activity.

As this chapter concludes, scholars have confirmed that knowledge spills over and that such knowledge spillovers matter in the formation of clusters and agglomerations. But to move beyond this insight much work remains to be done. The concept of knowledge spillovers has been generally treated as being homogeneous. Yet, surely not all knowledge is the same. We look for a greater taxonomy identifying the rich heterogeneity involved in knowledge and the process by which it spills over. Just as the Eskimos have names for the many different types of snow, scholars must begin the arduous task of identifying and distinguishing among the many types of knowledge spillovers.

Similarly, the mechanisms transmitting knowledge spillovers remain relatively unexplored and unknown. How and why does knowledge spill over is more than an academic question. Firms would like to know how spillovers can be accessed and places – cities, states, regions and countries – would like to know how strategically invest in the development of absorptive capacity to enhance the spillover of knowledge. Thus, while the endogenous growth theory emphasizes the importance of investments in research and development and human capital, a research agenda needs to be mapped out identifying the role that investments in spillover conduits can make in generating economic growth. It may be that a mapping of the process by which new knowledge is created, externalized and commercialized, hold the key to providing the microeconomic linkages to endogenous macroeconomic growth.

Acknowledgements

We acknowledge the comments of Vernon Henderson, Jacque Thisse, Will Strange and the participants at the CEPR Meetings in December 2002. We are also grateful to the comments and suggestions made by Luigi Guiso. Feldman acknowledges financial support of the Connaught Fund at the University of Toronto. Comments are welcome and appreciated.

References

Acs, Z.J., Audretsch, D.B. (1988). "Innovation in large and small firms: an empirical analysis". American Economic Review 78, 678–690.

Acs, Z.J., Audretsch, D.B. (1990). Innovation and Small Firms. MIT Press, Cambridge, MA.

Acs, Z.J., Audretsch, D.B., Feldman, M.P. (1992). "Real effects of academic research". American Economic Review 82, 363–367.

Acs, Z.J., Audretsch, D., Feldman, M.P. (1994). "R&D spillovers and recipient firm size". Review of Economics and Statistics 100 (1), 336–367.

Adams, J.D. (2002). "Comparative localization of academic and industrial spillovers". Journal of Economic Geography 2, 253–278.

Adams, J.D., Jaffe, A.B. (2002). "Bounding the effects of R&D: an investigation using matched firm and establishment data". RAND Journal of Economics 27, 700–721.

Agrawal, A. (2002a). "Importing scientific inventions: direct interaction, geography and economic performance". Mimeo. MIT.

Agrawal, A. (2002b). "Innovation, growth theory and the role of knowledge spillovers". Innovation Analysis Bulletin 4 (3), 3–6.

Almeida, P., Kogut, B. (1997). "The exploration of technological diversity and the geographic localization of innovation". Small Business Economics 9 (1), 21–31.

Anselin, L., Acs, Z.J., Varga, A. (1997). "Local geographic spillovers between university research and high technology innovations". Journal of Urban Economics 42, 422–448.

Arrow, K. (1962). "Economic welfare and the allocation of resources for invention". In: Nelson, R. (Ed.), The Rate and Direction of Inventive Activity. Princeton Univ. Press, Princeton, NJ.

Audretsch, D.B. (1995). Innovation and Industry Evolution. MIT Press, Cambridge, MA.

Audretsch, D.B., Feldman, M.P. (1996). "R&D spillovers and the geography of innovation and production". American Economic Review 86 (4), 253–273.

Audretsch, D.B., Fritsch, M. (1996). "Creative destruction: turbulence and economic growth". In: Helmstädter, E., Perlman, M. (Eds.), Behavioral Norms, Technological Progress, and Economic Dynamics: Studies in Schumpeterian Economics. Univ. of Michigan Press, Ann Arbor, pp. 137–150.

Audretsch, D.B., Fritsch, M. (2002). "Growth regimes over time and space". Regional Studies 36 (2), 113–124.

Audretsch, D.B., Stephan, P. (1996). "Company–scientist locational links: the case of biotechnology". American Economic Review 86 (4), 641–652.

Autant-Bernard, C. (2001a). "Science and knowledge flows: evidence from the French case". Research Policy 30 (7), 1069–1078.

Autant-Bernard, C. (2001b). "The geography of knowledge spillovers and technological proximity". Economics of Innovation and New Technology 10 (4), 237–254.

Baldwin, W.L., Scott, J.T. (1987). Market Structure and Technological Change. Harwood Academic, London.

Bates, T.M. (1998). Self-Employment and Upward Mobility: An Illusive American Dream. Johns Hopkins Univ. Press, Baltimore.

Becattini, G. (1990). "The Marshallian industrial district as a socio-economic notion". In: Becattini, G., Pyke, F., Sengenberger, W. (Eds.), Industrial Districts and Inter-Firm Co-operation in Italy. International Labor Studies, Geneva, pp. 37–51.

Black, G. (2003). The Geography of Small Firm Innovation. Kluwer Academic, Dordrecht.

Branstetter, L. (2002). "Measuring the link between academic science and innovation: the case of California research universities". Mimeo. University of California, Davis.

Brusco, S. (1990). "The idea of the industrial district, its genesis". In: Becattini, G., Pyke, F., Sengenberger, W. (Eds.), Industrial Districts and Inter-Firm Co-operation in Italy. International Labour Studies, Geneva, pp. 10–19.

Callejon, M., Segarra, A. (2000). "Business dynamics and efficiency in industries and regions: the case of Spain". Small Business Economics 13 (4), 253–271.

Cockburn, I.M., Henderson, R. (1998). "Absorptive capacity, coauthoring behavior and the organization of research in drug discovery". The Journal of Industrial Economics 66 (2), 157–182.

Cohen, W.M., Klepper, S. (1991). "Firm size versus diversity in the achievement of technological advance". In: Acs, Z.J., Audretsch, D.B. (Eds.), Innovation and Technological Change: An International Comparison. Univ. of Michigan Press, Ann Arbor, pp. 183–203.

Cohen, W.M., Klepper, S. (1992). "The tradeoff between firm size and diversity in the pursuit of technological progress". Small Business Economics 4 (1), 1–14.

Cohen, W.M., Levin, R.C. (1989). "Empirical studies of innovation and market structure". In: Schmalensee, R., Willig, R. (Eds.). North-Holland, Amsterdam, pp. 1059–1107.

Cohen, W.M., Levinthal, D.A. (1989). "Innovation and learning: the two faces of R&D". Economic Journal 99 (3), 569–596.

Cohen, W.M., Levinthal, D.A. (1990). "Absorptive capacity: a new perspective on innovation and learning". Administrative Sciences Quarterly 35, 128–152.
Evans, D.S., Leighton, L.S. (1989a). "Some empirical aspects of entrepreneurship". American Economic Review 79 (3), 519–535.
Evans, D.S., Leighton, L.S. (1989b). "The determinants of changes in U.S. self-employment". Small Business Economics 1 (2), 11–120.
Evans, D.S., Leighton, L.S. (1990). "Small business formation by unemployed and employed workers". Small Business Economics 2 (4), 319–330.
Feldman, M.P. (1993). "An examination of the geography of innovation". Industrial and Corporate Change 4, 451–470.
Feldman, M.P. (1994a). The Geography of Innovation. Kluwer Academic, Boston.
Feldman, M. (1994b). "Knowledge complementarity and innovation". Small Business Economics 6 (3), 363–372.
Feldman, M.P. (2001). "The entrepreneurial event revisited: firm formation in a regional context". Industrial and Corporate Change, 861–891.
Feldman, M.P. (2002). "The internet revolution and the geography of innovation". International Social Science Journal 54, 47–56.
Feldman, M.P., Audretsch, D. (1999). "Innovation in cities: science-based diversity, specialization and localized competition". European Economic Review 43, 409–429.
Feldman, M.P., Desrochers, P. (2003). "The evolving role of research universities in technology transfer: lessons from the history of Johns Hopkins University". Industry and Innovation 10, 5–24.
Feldman, M.P., Francis, J.L. (2002). "The entrepreneurial spark, individual agents and the formation of innovative clusters". In: Quadrio Curzio, A., Fortis, M. (Eds.), Complexity and Industrial Clusters. Springer-Verlag, Heidelberg.
Feldman, M.P., Feller, I., Bercovitz, J.E.L., Burton, R.M. (2002). "University-technology transfer and the system of innovation". In: Feldman, M.P., Massard, N. (Eds.), Institutions and Systems in the Geography of Innovation. Kluwer Academic, Boston, pp. 55–78.
Florida, R.L., Cohen, W.M. (1999). "Engine or infrastructure? The university role in economic development". In: Branscomb, L.M., Kodama, F., Florida, R. (Eds.), Industrializing Knowledge: University–Industry Linkages in Japan and the United States. MIT Press, Cambridge, MA, pp. 589–610.
Florida, R.L., Kenney, M. (1988). "Venture capital, high technology and regional development". Regional Studies 22 (1), 33–48.
Foelster, S. (2000). "Do entrepreneurs create jobs?" Small Business Economics 14 (2), 137–148.
Fritsch, M. (1997). "New firms and regional employment change". Small Business Economics 9 (5), 437–448.
Glaeser, E., Kallal, H., Scheinkman, J., Shleifer, A. (1992). "Growth of cities". Journal of Political Economy 100, 1126–1152.
Gompers, P., Lerner, J. (1999). The Venture Capital Cycle. MIT Press, Cambridge, MA.
Grabher, G. (Ed.) (1993). The Embedded Firm. On the Socio-Economics of Industrial Networks. Routlegde, London and New York.
Griliches, Z. (1979). "Issues in assessing the contribution of R&D to productivity growth". Bell Journal of Economics 10, 92–116.
Griliches, Z. (1984). R&D, Patents, and Productivity. Univ. of Chicago Press, Chicago.
Griliches, Z. (1990). "Patent statistics as economic indicators: a survey". Journal of Economic Literature 28 (4), 1661–1707.
Griliches, Z. (1992). "The search for R&D spill-overs". Scandinavian Journal of Economics 94, 29–47.
Grossman, G.M., Helpman, E. (1991). Innovation and Growth in the Global Economy. MIT Press, Cambridge, MA.
Hart, M., Hanvey, E. (1995). "Job generation and new and small firms: some evidence from the late 1980s". Small Business Economics 7, 97–109.
Henderson, J.V. (1997). "Externalities and industrial development". Journal of Urban Economics 42, 449–470.

Henderson, J.V., Shalizi, Z., Venables, A. (2001). "Geography and development". Journal of Economic Geography 1, 81–106.

Hirschman, A.O. (1970). Exit, Voice, and Loyalty. Harvard Univ. Press, Cambridge, MA.

Holmes, T.J., Schmitz Jr., J.A. (1990). "A theory of entrepreneurship and its application to the study of business transfers". Journal of Political Economy 98 (4), 265–294.

Hoover Jr., E.M. (1936). "The measurement of industrial localization". Review of Economics and Statistics 18 (4), 162–171.

Jacobs, J. (1969). The Economy of Cities. Random House, New York.

Jaffe, A.B. (1989). "Real effects of academic research". American Economic Review 79 (5), 957–970.

Jaffe, A.B., Trajtenberg, M. (2002). Patents, citations, and innovations: a window on the knowledge economy. MIT Press, Cambridge, MA.

Jaffe, A.B., Trajtenberg, M., Henderson, R. (1993). "Geographic localization of knowledge spillovers as evidenced by patent citations". Quarterly Journal of Economics 63, 577–598.

Jovanovic, B. (1994). "Entrepreneurial choice when people differ in their management and labor skills". Small Business Economics 6 (3), 185–192.

Kihlstrom, R.E., Laffont, J.J. (1979). "A general equilibrium entrepreneurial theory of firm formation based on risk aversion". Journal of Political Economy 87 (4), 719–748.

Knight, F.H. (1921). Risk, Uncertainty and Profit. Houghton Mifflin, New York.

Krugman, P. (1991). Geography and Trade. MIT Press, Cambridge, MA.

Lucas, R.E. (1978). "On the size distribution of business firms". Bell Journal of Economics 9, 508–523.

Lucas, R.E. (1988). "On the mechanics of economic development". Journal of Monetary Economic 22, 3–39.

Lucas, R.E. (1993). "Making a miracle". Econometrica 61, 251–272.

Lucas, R.E. (2001). "Externalities and cities". Review of Economic Studies 4, 245–274.

Lucas, R.E., Rossi-Hansberg, E. (2002). "On the internal structure of cities". Econometrica 70, 1445–1476.

Malecki, E. (1997). Technology and Economic Development: The Dynamics of Local, Regional and National Competitiveness, second ed. Addison–Wesley, Longman, London.

Mansfield, E. (1995). "Academic research underlying industrial innovations: sources, characteristics, and financing". Review of Economics and Statistics 77 (1), 55–65.

Mansfield, E. (1998). "Academic research and industrial innovation: an update of empirical finding". Research Policy 26, 773–776.

Manski, C.F. (2000). "Economic analysis of social interactions". Journal of Economic Perspectives 14, 115–136.

Marshall, A. (1920). Principles of Economics. Macmillan, London.

Mowery, D.C., Shane, S. (2002). "Introduction to the special issue on university entrepreneurship and technology transfer". Management Science 48 (1), 1–6.

Orlando, M.J. (2000). "On the importance of geographic and technological proximity for R&D spillovers: an empirical investigation". Federal Reserve Bank of Kansas City Research Working Paper.

Pfirrmann, O. (1994). "The geography of innovation in small and medium-sized firms in West Germany". Small Business Economics 6 (1), 27–41.

Piore, M.J., Sabel, C.F. (1984). The Second Industrial Divide: Possibilities for Prosperity. Basic Books, New York.

Porter, M.E. (1990). The Comparative Advantage of Nations. Free Press, New York.

Porter, M.E. (2000). "Locations, clusters, and company strategy". In: Clark, G.L., Feldman, M.P., Gertler, M.S. (Eds.), The Oxford Handbook of Economic Geography. Oxford Univ. Press, Oxford, pp. 253–274.

Powell, W., Koput, K.W., Smith-Doerr, L. (1996). "Interorganizational collaboration and the locus of innovation: networks of learning in biotechnology". Administrative Science Quarterly 42 (1), 116–145.

Prevenzer, M. (1997). "The dynamics of industrial clustering in biotechnology". Small Business Economics 9 (3), 255–271.

Pyke, F., Sengenberger, W. (1990). "Introduction". In: Pyke, F., Becattini, G., Sengenberger, W. (Eds.), Industrial Districts and Inter-Firm Co-Operation in Italy. International Institute for Labour Studies, Geneva, pp. 1–9.

Reynolds, P.D. (1999). "Creative destruction, source or symptom of economic growth?". In: Acs, Z.J., Carlsson, B., Karlsson, C. (Eds.), Entrepreneurship, Small and Medium-Sized Enterprises and the Macroeconomy. Cambridge Univ. Press, Cambridge, MA, pp. 97–136.
Reynolds, P., Storey, D.J., Westhead, P. (1994). "Cross-national comparisons of the variation in new firm formation rates". Regional Studies 28 (4), 443–456.
Romer, P.M. (1986). "Increasing returns and long-run growth". Journal of Political Economy 94 (5), 1002–1037.
Rosenthal, S.S., Strange, W. (2003). "Geography, industrial organization and agglomeration". The Review of Economics and Statistics 85 (2), 377–393.
Rosenthal, S.S., Strange, W. (2004). "Evidence on the nature and sources of agglomeration economies". In: Henderson, J.V., Thisse, J.-F. (Eds.), Handbook of Regional and Urban Economics, vol. 4. Elsevier, Amsterdam, pp. 2119–2171. This volume.
Saxenian, A. (1994). Regional Advantage: Culture and Competition in Silicon Valley and Route 128. Harvard Univ. Press, Cambridge, MA.
Saxenian, A. (2001). "The role of immigrant entrepreneurs in new venture creation". In: Schoonhoven, C.B., Romanelli, E. (Eds.), The Entrepreneurship Dynamic. Stanford Univ. Press, Palo Alto, pp. 40–67.
Scherer, F.M. (1984). Innovation and Growth: Schumpetrian Perspectives. MIT Press, Cambridge, MA.
Scherer, F.M. (1991). "Changing perspectives on the firm size problem". In: Acs, Z.J., Audretsch, D.B. (Eds.), Innovation and Technological Change. An International Comparison. University of Michigan Press, Ann Arbor, pp. 24–38.
Schumpeter, J.A. (1911). Theorie der wirtschaftlichen Entwicklung. Eine Untersuchung, ueber Unternehmergewinn, Kapital, Kredit, Zins und den Konjunkturzyklus. Duncker und Humbolt, Berlin.
Sorenson, O., Stuart, T. (2001). "Syndication networks and the spatial distribution of venture capital investments". American Journal of Sociology 106 (6), 1546–1588.
Soubeyran, A., Thisse, J.-F. (1999). "Learning-by-doing and the development of industrial districts". Journal of Urban Economics 45, 156–176.
Soubeyran, A., Weber, S. (2002). "District formation and local social capital: a (tacit) co-opetition approach". Journal of Urban Economics 52, 65–92.
Storey, D.J. (1991). "The birth of new firms – does unemployment matter? A review of the evidence". Small Business Economics 3 (3), 167–178.
Von Hipple, E. (1994). "Sticky information and the locus of problem solving: implications for innovation". Management Science 40, 429–439.
Wallsten, S.J. (2001). "An empirical test of geographic knowledge spillovers using geographic information systems and firm-level data". Regional Science and Urban Economic 31, 571–599.
Wilson, W.J. (1996). When Work Disappears: The World of the New Urban Poor. Knopf, New York.
Zhang, J. (2002). Growing Silicon Valley on a landscape: an agent-based approach to high technology industrial clusters. Public Policy Institute of California.
Zucker, L.G., Darby, M.R., Brewer, M.B. (1998). "Intellectual human capital and the birth of U.S. biotechnology enterprises". American Economic Review 88, 290–306.

Chapter 62

REGIONAL (DI)CONVERGENCE

STEFANO MAGRINI

University "Ca' Foscari" of Venice, Venice, Italy
e-mail: smagrini@unive.it

Contents

Handbook of Regional and Urban Economics, Volume 4. Edited by J.V. Henderson and J.F. Thisse

DOI: 10.1016/S0169-7218(04)07062-5

Abstract

Do regions converge? This essay provides an overview of the key developments in the study of regional convergence, discussing the methodological issues that have arisen since the first attempts to analyse convergence and critically surveying the results that have been obtained for different regional systems. Two underlying arguments will guide the attempt to reach an answer: (i) not all empirical approaches to the analysis of convergence appear equally reliable and not all results equally convincing; (ii) although most regional convergence studies make use of empirical methods originally developed to analyse cross-country convergence, regions and countries are far from interchangeable concepts. The picture that emerges from this particular perspective is one in which convergence is often confined to groups of geographically contiguous regions.

Keywords

regional income convergence, neoclassical growth, cross-section regression, time series, panel data, distribution dynamics, Markov chain processes, stochastic kernels, spatial adjustment, spatial dependence, spatial econometrics

JEL classification: C20, D30, E13, O18, O41, R11, R12, R15, R23

1. Introduction

The question whether incomes are converging across regional economies has long attracted the attention of economists and decision makers. On the one hand, there is a widespread perception that persistent disparities in aggregate growth rates have led to sizable differences in welfare not only across countries but within them as well. On the other hand, the ample body of empirical research on the subject has not yet reached a common answer as to whether, and under which conditions, convergence actually takes place.[1]

The present paper aims at providing an overview of the key developments in the study of regional convergence, discussing the methodological issues that have arisen since the first attempts to analyse convergence and critically surveying the results that have been obtained for different regional systems.

In general, two broad threads of analysis can be identified. Within the first thread, the *regression approach*, a variety of methods has been developed to test the convergence predictions of the traditional neoclassical model of growth. Initially, following the seminal contribution by Baumol (1986) later refined by Barro (1991) and Barro and Sala-i-Martin (1991, 1992), a large number of studies has made use of cross-sectional growth regressions to see whether regions are converging towards steady-state paths and, if so, at what speed. Later, in order to control for unobserved heterogeneities that bias conventional cross-sectional convergence regressions and to deal with endogeneity concerns, panel data methods have been adopted. Other researchers have instead chosen to implement the regression approach by means of time-series methods in which the definition of convergence relies on the notions of unit roots and cointegration. The first part of the chapter (Section 2) will therefore describe the main developments of this approach up to its most recent applications to regional datasets and discuss the many problems that still exist. A first underlying argument will be that the regression approach tends to concentrate on the behaviour of the representative economy. In other words, convergence analyses based on such an approach are, with few exceptions, uninformative: they can only shed light on the transition of this economy towards its own steady state whilst giving no information on the dynamics of the entire cross-sectional distribution of regional incomes. A second important point will be that most of the empirical work on regional convergence within the regression approach applies virtually the same empirical methods originally developed to analyse convergence across nations. However, regions and nations, being characterised by profoundly different degrees of openness, are far from being interchangeable concepts. Thus, by totally overlooking this important difference, these empirical methods fail to properly account for spatial interaction effects.

The remainder of the chapter will therefore deal with these two issues. Section 3 will start by considering the theoretical implications for convergence once openness is

[1] Interestingly, Williamson expressed similar concerns back in 1965 [Williamson (1965)] while introducing his empirical investigation into the relationship between regional inequalities and the process of national development.

introduced into the neoclassical model of growth. In particular, it will be shown that the open-economy version of the neoclassical model predicts a faster speed of convergence than its closed-economy counterpart. Moreover, the existing evidence on the role that interregional flows brought in by openness may play in the explanation of regional convergence will be considered. The second part of the section will instead concentrate on the consequences of spatial interaction effects on convergence analyses from an econometric perspective and, after presenting the different sources of misspecification problems that have been identified in the spatial econometric literature, it will describe the ways in which these problems have (or have not) been addressed in regional convergence studies.

Section 4 will instead focus on an alternative approach to the analysis of convergence, the *distribution dynamics approach*, that examines directly how the cross-sectional distribution of per capita output changes over time, putting emphasis on both the change in its external shape and the intra-distribution dynamics. Examples are Markov chain methodologies or, more generally, approaches using stochastic kernels to describe the law of motion of cross-sectional distributions. A fundamental point will be that the distributional approach to convergence is not without problems of its own. However, despite these problems, the distributional approach to convergence – particularly when based on nonparametric stochastic kernel estimations – appears to be generally more informative than convergence empirics within the regression approach, and therefore represents a more promising way forward. Thus, an application of this methodology to data on per capita income for European regions over the period 1980–1995 is carried out at the end of the chapter. In particular, this analysis makes it possible not only to characterise regional convergence dynamics in Europe but also, using a spatial conditioning scheme, to evaluate the role of spatial factors in these dynamics. Finally, the adoption of a set of functionally defined regions highlights the risks from the use of datasets on administrative regions such as European NUTS. The boundaries of these regions are in fact the result of political and historical factors which are country-specific so that not only do they bear no relationship to the socio-economic factors that form the basis of a functional region, but they also vary from country to country. As a result, data for administratively defined regions are likely to be characterised by significant nuisance spatial dependence that, if not taken into adequate consideration, runs the risk of concealing important features of regional distribution dynamics.

2. The 'regression approach'

2.1. *Theoretical foundations*

The traditional neoclassical model of growth, originally set out by Solow (1956) and Swan (1956), and, following the work of Ramsey (1928), subsequently refined by Cass (1965) and Koopmans (1965), has provided the theoretical background for a vast body of empirical analyses on income convergence. The standard model and its main empirical implications for the convergence debate are well known so just a brief recap is offered in what follows.

Consider an economic system in which physical capital, K, and labour, L, are used in order to produce a homogeneous consumption good:[2]

$$Y = F(K, \widetilde{L}),$$

where $\widetilde{L} \equiv L \cdot A(t)$ is the effective amount of labour input and $A(t)$, the labour-augmenting technical change, grows exponentially at the exogenously given rate μ: $A(t) = A(0)e^{\mu t}$. Defining quantities per unit of effective labour as $\tilde{y} \equiv Y/\widetilde{L}$ and $\tilde{k} \equiv K/\widetilde{L}$, the (twice differentiable, homogeneous of degree 1, increasing, jointly concave in all its arguments and strictly concave in each) production function becomes

$$\tilde{y} = f(\tilde{k}). \tag{1}$$

Two accumulation frameworks are possible. In the Solow–Swan approach, an exogenously given fraction of output is saved and invested in new physical capital while the rest of output is consumed. Alternatively, in the Cass–Koopmans approach, rational households with perfect foresight choose the consumption path, and thus the saving path, by maximising intertemporal utility subject to a flow budget constraint:

$$\dot{\tilde{k}} = f(\tilde{k}) - \tilde{c} - (\delta + n + \mu)\tilde{k}, \tag{2}$$

where δ is the rate of capital depreciation and n is the rate of population growth.

The system exhibits saddle-path stability under either accumulation frameworks [Barro and Sala-i-Martin (1995), Durlauf and Quah (1999)], so that the economy converges to a steady-state equilibrium in which the level of income per capita, consumption per capita and the capital–labour ratio all grow at the exogenous rate of technological progress while variables per unit of effective labour are constant. If the share of capital in total income is a constant, as in the case of Cobb–Douglas technology, it is easy to show that the growth rate experienced by the economy is negatively related to the level of the capital–labour ratio: the lower the capital–labour ratio and, therefore, the lower per capita output, the further the economy is from its balanced growth path, and the higher its growth rate.

Finally, we can turn to the cross-sectional dynamics which can be derived from the empirical implications of the neoclassical model of growth around the steady state. Considering observed per capita income $y = \tilde{y}A$, a Taylor series approximation of the system's dynamics around the deterministic steady state yields:

$$\log y(t) = \left[\log y(0) - \left(\log \tilde{y}^* + \log A(0)\right)\right]e^{-\beta t} + \left[\log \tilde{y}^* + \log A(0) + \mu t\right], \tag{3}$$

[2] Mankiw, Romer and Weil (1992) add human capital to the basic Solow–Swan framework; since this feature does not affect our main points it is largely ignored in what follows.

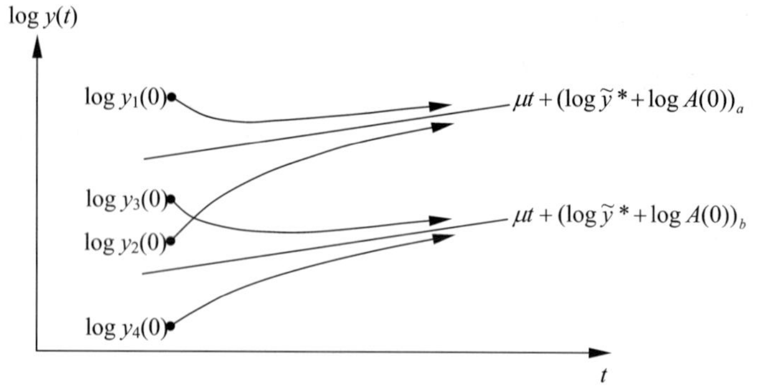

Figure 1. Possible steady-state paths in the neoclassical models.

where the coefficient β, describing the speed with which the economy converges towards the steady state, can be shown to be inversely related to capital's share in income so that as this coefficient approaches unity, the convergence rate tends to zero. According to Equation (3), the log of per capita income can hence be viewed as having two components: a convergence component (the first term of the right-hand side, involving $e^{-\beta t}$) and a levels component (the rest of the right-hand side). Figure 1, in which different steady-state paths corresponding to two possible values for the sum $\log \tilde{y}^* + \log A(0)$ have been exemplified, shows that as long as this sum remains unobserved or unrestricted, any pattern of cross-sectional growth and convergence is consistent with the model. While economies 2 and 3 diverge away from each other, the rich economy 1 stays rich and the poor economy 4 remains poor: if the number of economies exceeds that of the underlying time paths, then a clustering in the cross-sectional distribution (twin-peakedness or club convergence) could arise.

2.2. *Empirical implementation: cross-sectional method*

In a seminal study, Baumol (1986) implemented a method of testing the neoclassical prediction of convergence based on a simple cross-sectional regression:

$$\log\left[y(t)/y(0)\right] = a + b \log y(0),$$

where the left-hand side of the equation represents the growth rate over the period $(0, t)$. Obviously, the negative value for the coefficient b found by Baumol is interpreted as evidence of convergence, as this would mean that the economies with low initial levels of per capita GDP have experienced the fastest growth rates. Barro (1991) and Barro and Sala-i-Martin (1991, 1992) expanded and refined this approach. Firstly, they pointed out that the traditional neoclassical model predicts that the growth rate of an economy is inversely related to the distance from its steady state. Therefore, poor economies grow faster than rich ones only if they all share the same steady state. By contrast, if differences in technological levels and attitudes toward saving exist among economies, then these economies are characterised by different steady states and the negative relationship between the growth rate of per capita GDP and its initial level does not hold in a cross-sectional sample. Convergence towards the same steady state is then labelled by these authors as *absolute or unconditional convergence*, while the second type of convergence is labelled as *conditional convergence*.

The fundamental element of the empirical analyses carried out by Barro and Sala-i-Martin is derived from the logarithmic linearisation of the transitional dynamics of the traditional neoclassical model around the steady state considered above. Equation (3) implies that, starting from the initial time 0, the average growth rate over an interval of $t \geqslant 0$ time periods is given by

$$(1/t)\log\left[y(t)/y(0)\right] \\ = \mu + \left(1 - \mathrm{e}^{-\beta t}\right)/t \cdot \left[\log \tilde{y}^* + \log A(0)\right] - \left(1 - \mathrm{e}^{-\beta t}\right)/t \cdot \log y(0)$$

so that, other things being equal, the average growth rate of per capita income depends negatively on the initial level of per capita income, conditioned on the steady-state value of per capita income per effective worker, on the exogenous growth rate of technology and on the initial level of technology. Since the exact value of these is unknown, they suggested that they should test the following convergence equation:

$$(1/t)\log\left[y(t)/y(0)\right] = c - \left(1 - \mathrm{e}^{-\beta t}\right)/t \cdot \log y(0) + u(t), \tag{4}$$

where $u(t)$ is a random disturbance while the constant summarises the unobserved parameters. The key parameter to be empirically estimated in this approach is the speed of adjustment to the steady state, β, i.e., the rate at which the economies approach their steady-state growth paths. As already seen, within the theoretical framework adopted this parameter crucially depends on the capital-share coefficient; as this coefficient tends to one, so that if diminishing returns to capital no longer apply, the rate of convergence tends to zero.

To test the neoclassical prediction that the growth rate of an economy is inversely related to the distance from its steady state, or β-convergence as Barro and Sala-i-Martin label it, data sets have to be conditioned on the steady state. These authors suggest two possible ways of overcoming the problem. The first is to identify a group of homogenous economic systems characterised by similar technological levels and institutional environments, thus fulfilling the conditions assuring convergence towards the same level of steady-state income. In this case, unconditional (or absolute) convergence is expected and Equation (4) can be applied directly. In practice, however, the assumption of independence across economies for the error term implicit in Equation (4) is far from being realistic as disturbances tend to affect different groups of regional economies in different ways. If this is the case, $\log y(0)$ and $u(t)$ are not uncorrelated, and the least-squares estimations of β are biased. This problem is overcome by decomposing the error term u_t into two separate components. The equation describing the behaviour of an economic system around its steady state thus becomes:

$$(1/t)\log\left[y(t)/y(0)\right] = c - \left(1 - \mathrm{e}^{-\beta t}\right)/t \cdot \log y(0) + \varphi s(t) + v(t), \tag{5}$$

where $v(t)$ is an independent disturbance, $s(t)$ is an aggregate disturbance and φ measures its effect on the growth rate of the economy. Assuming that, cross-sectionally, φ is distributed independently of $v(t)$ and that $\mathrm{cov}[\log y(0), \varphi] = 0$, the composite error term is not correlated with $\log y(0)$ and the least-squares estimate of β is not biased.

In other cases, when the group of economies differ in their fundamentals, the group will show multiple steady states and the neoclassical model invokes the concept of conditional convergence. From an operational point of view, this requires the introduction of additional explanatory variables in the cross-sectional regression (5), which represent proxies for the different steady states.

Examples of analyses of this type are abundant within a regional context. Following Barro and Sala-i-Martin (1991, 1992, 1995) and Sala-i-Martin (1996), who reported the existence of unconditional convergence across U.S. states, Japanese prefectures and several European countries (Germany, UK, France, Italy and Spain) and conditional convergence across a group of European regions, a vast number of studies have reported unconditional or conditional β-convergence across groups of regional economies worldwide [see Sala-i-Martin (1996), Durlauf and Quah (1999), De la Fuente (2000), for reviews]. So, while Shioji (1996) confirms earlier results for Japan, Holtz-Eakin (1993), Garofalo and Yamarik (2002) and Vohra (1996), although using a human capital augmented version of the neoclassical growth model [Mankiw, Romer and Weil (1992)], report evidence of convergence within the U.S., and Cashin (1995) suggests that there exists β-convergence across the seven states of Australia. Similarly, several empirical studies, following comparable methodologies, confirm the original findings by Coulombe and Lee (1993) that unconditional convergence across Canadian provinces cannot be rejected [Coulombe and Lee (1995), Lee and Coulombe (1995), Coulombe and Day (1996), Coulombe and Tremblay (2001)]. It is also interesting to note that, together with the general support to β-convergence, another empirical regularity seems to emerge from this group of studies: the estimated value of β, the speed with which economies converge to their steady state, is rather small (around 2 percent per year) and fairly stable across different samples.

Moving now to European countries, studies of β-convergence have been carried out for regions in Austria [Hofer and Wörgötter (1997)], West Germany [Niebuhr (2001), Herz and Röger (1995), Funke and Strulik (1999)], Spain [De la Fuente and Vives (1995), De la Fuente (1996)], Italy [Fabiani and Pellegrini (1997), Paci and Pigliaru (1995)], UK [Chatterji and Dewhurst (1996)], and Greece [Siriopoulos and Asteriou (1998)], to cite just a few. It has to be noted, however, that while evidence of this type of convergence is reported in most cases, wide variations in the estimated values of the rate of convergence are found in different countries. When the attention is shifted to the whole of Europe, similar to Barro and Barro and Sala-i-Martin's analyses, member state dummy variables (as proxies for differences in countries' steady states) and other variables (to allow for industry structure differences between regions) are generally considered and conditional convergence across various groupings of European NUTS regions is again often found [Button and Pentecost (1995, 1999), Armstrong (1995a, 1995b, 1995c), Neven and Gouyette (1995), Martin (2001),

Cuadrado-Roura, Mancha-Navarro and Garrido-Yserte (2000b), Fagerberg and Verspagen (1996), Tondl (1999, 2001), Maurseth (2001)]. However, it is also generally emphasised that there have been profound changes in the pattern of convergence over time: while conditional β-convergence was rather strong up to the end of the 1970s, it came to a halt during most of the 1980s and then re-emerged, although at quite a slow pace. Moreover, the results are not only sensitive on the choice of countries being considered and the level of NUTS regions employed, but β-convergence estimates are also somewhat sensitive to the choice of the additional explanatory variables. Overall, the general impression is that β-convergence is much weaker in Europe than in other areas, and is governed by a considerable country-specific component.

Researchers have identified a number of problems with cross-sectional regression analyses [see, e.g., Durlauf and Quah (1999) and Temple (1999) for surveys], the most important of which can be briefly examined. The first limitation of the cross-sectional regression approach is that, despite the fact that it is directly derived from the traditional neoclassical model, it does not test the validity of this model against alternative and conflicting ones. As clearly pointed out by several authors [Romer (1993, 1994), Fagerberg (1994), Paci and Pigliaru (1997), Durlauf and Quah (1999), amongst many others], dynamics such as those illustrated in Figure 1 are implicit in widely different theoretical interpretations of the growth process. Specifically, these interpretations range from the closed-economy, human capital-augmented version of Solow's traditional neoclassical model [Mankiw, Romer and Weil (1992)] to theories of technological diffusion, either within the neoclassical tradition – as the endogenous growth models [Aghion and Howitt (1992, 1998), Barro and Sala-i-Martin (1995, 1997), Grossman and Helpman (1990, 1991), Helpman (1993), Lucas (1988), Rivera-Batiz and Romer (1991), and Romer (1986, 1990a, 1990b)] – or within the evolutionary tradition – as the literature on the technological gap [Gerschenkron (1962), Abramovitz (1979, 1986), Fagerberg (1988), Verspagen (1991); and, for an adaptation which allows for spatial proximity and localised technological spillovers; Caniëls (2000), Caniëls and Verspagen (2001)]. Moreover, a set of theoretical models explicitly develops cross-sectional dynamics which conform to the behaviour depicted in Figure 1. In the first of such models [Quah (1996d)] – in which ideas are an important engine of growth and specialisation in production makes it possible to exploit economies of scale – economies endogenously select themselves into coalitions or convergence clubs depending on the initial distribution of characteristics across economies. In the second group [Azariadis and Drazen (1990), Durlauf (1996), Galor and Zeira (1993), Murphy, Shleifer and Vishny (1989), Quah (1996a)], nonconvexities in the aggregate production function associated with threshold effects lead to long-run dependence from initial conditions and polarization effects. A first natural conclusion therefore is that, if the aim of a researcher is to provide evidence to discriminate between different growth theories, cross-sectional regressions are of limited use. The regression techniques so far discussed at best produce results which are not inconsistent with neoclassical growth theories. But since they are also consistent with other explanations, they do not constitute a test of traditional neoclassical theory in any scientific sense. Moreover, under the neoclassical model, the conventional cross-sectional growth equation is (approximately) linear. In contrast, in many endogenous growth models it is highly nonlinear and, as shown in Bernard and Durlauf (1996), a linear specification is unable to discriminate between these models.

A second important line of criticism has concentrated on the informative content of cross-sectional regressions. First of all, several researchers [Friedman (1992), Quah (1993b), amongst others] emphasise the analogy between regressions of growth rates over initial levels and Galton's fallacy of regression towards the mean. In other words, they demonstrate that a negative relationship between growth rates and initial values does not indicate a reduction in the cross-sectional variance and, moreover, that it is also possible to observe a diverging cross-sectional distribution even when such a negative relationship holds.[3] In other words, standard convergence empirics are, at best, uninformative as they concentrate on the behaviour of a representative economy. Even if the law of motion of an economy is actually independent of the behaviour of other economies, the best the traditional convergence approach can do is describe how this economy converges to its own steady state. However, this approach is completely silent on what happens to the entire cross-sectional distribution of economies. In contrast, in the presence of nonconvexities in the production function associated with threshold effects or interdependencies such as those described in coalition models, the traditional convergence approach is not only uninformative with regard to growth and convergence dynamics but can also be misleading. Within the standard neoclassical approach, dynamics such as those depicted in Figure 1 essentially depend on differences in one or more structural characteristics of each economy, regardless of the starting conditions. In contrast, within theoretical models with nonconvexities or models with club formation, these dynamics could be the result of differences in initial conditions across economies with similar structural characteristics. Thus, if a conditioning explanatory variable is not actually determining an economy's economic position as in the standard neoclassical approach but, rather, is evolving endogenously as a response to initial factors determining club membership, a traditional researcher would incorrectly attribute growth and convergence to the conditioning variable and never discover the true growth determinants.[4]

[3] The fact that a positive β coefficient is a necessary but not a sufficient condition for a reduction in the cross-sectional dispersion is acknowledged by the proponents of the cross-sectional regression approach. A positive value for β is thus interpreted as indicating the existence of forces reducing the cross-sectional distribution while ongoing disturbances are seen as forces pushing in the opposite direction. The practical value of this interpretation is however somewhat dubious since even if information about these shocks was used in a cross-sectional regression, still a positive value for β would not imply that the variance of the cross-sectional distribution is decreasing.

[4] A similar concern is expressed by De la Fuente (2000) who notes that in practice the difference between conditional and unconditional convergence is not totally transparent. If we find that a number of explanatory variables enter significantly in Equation (5) we would be tempted to conclude that convergence is only conditional since there are significant differences across economies in their underlying "fundamentals". However, if these variables change over time and tend to converge, it might well be that income is unconditionally converging in the long run.

2.3. Empirical implementation: panel data methods

A second tactic to implement the regression approach is to resort to panel data methods, thus combining cross-sectional and dynamic information. Proponents of this approach argue that it has a clear advantage over cross-sectional regressions. As previously noted, conditional cross-sectional convergence analyses must allow for steady-state income determinants in order to provide consistent estimates. Given that some of these determinants might be unknown or unmeasurable – and thus constitute nuisance parameters – it is argued that the only way to obtain consistent estimates is to use panel data methods.

The simplest fixed effects panel data model of the convergence process would then be

$$\log\left[y(t)/y(t-1)\right] = c_0 + c_1(t) - b \log y(t-1) + u(t), \tag{6}$$

showing that the original constant c is now decomposed into an unobservable economy-specific effect (which is constant over time and determines the region's steady state) c_0, and a time-specific effect, c_1, affecting all economies. For the estimation, the least squares dummy variable estimator [Hsiao (1986)] was initially applied. However, since this estimator is consistent only for a large number of observations over time [Nickell (1981)], the most widely adopted alternative is represented by the 2-step GMM estimator suggested by Arellano (1988) and Arellano and Bond (1991) and introduced into the growth literature by Caselli, Esquivel and Lefort (1996). Starting from an autoregressive model with unobserved individual-specific effects, the approach requires taking the first-differences of the regression equation to remove unobserved time-invariant country-specific effects, and using levels of the series lagged two periods or more as instruments for the equation in first-differences, thus alleviating measurement error and endogeneity biases.

The results from convergence analyses adopting these panel data methods are generally at odds with those from cross-sectional regression studies. For example, in contrast with Barro and Sala-i-Martin's findings, Lall and Yilmaz (2001) find no evidence of absolute convergence among U.S. states. Moreover, the estimated rate of mean reversion appears to be considerably higher than in previous estimates. When European regions are employed, De la Fuente (2000) finds annual convergence rates between 26 and 39% within the five largest EU countries, depending on the estimation procedure adopted. Similarly, Tondl (1999, 2001) reports a convergence rate of approximately 20%, and Cuadrado-Roura, Mancha-Navarro and Garrido-Yserte (2000a) a rate of 17%. Canova and Marcet (1995), via a Bayesian-motivated parameterisation of the individual effects, find a convergence rate of about 23%, with each European region converging to its own steady state. Moreover, they find that individual effects do differ across economies implying that poorer regions stay poor. As for individual EU countries, Funke and Strulik (1999) report an average convergence rate of about 10% among German *Länder* using a Bayesian approach, while De la Fuente (1996) estimates a convergence rate of 12.7% for Spain using a fixed effect model and subsequently confirms this estimate [De la Fuente (2002)] using a standard fixed effects model and a hybrid model with structural variables and fixed effects.

In general, therefore, estimates of the convergence rate via conventional panel data methods are substantially higher than cross-sectional estimates. However, it should be noted that Bond, Hoeffler and Temple (2001) have recently emphasised that the first-differenced GMM estimator may be subject to a large finite-sample bias when the time series are persistent – as is usually the case with output series – and short, so that lagged levels of the variables are weak instruments for subsequent first-differences. To overcome the problem they suggest using a system GMM estimator [Arellano and Bover (1995), Blundell and Bond (1998)], i.e., a system combining the usual equations in first-differences with equations in levels in which the instruments are lagged first-differences. Applying this estimator to the same data set employed by Caselli, Esquivel and Lefort (1996), Bond, Hoeffler and Temple (2001) find a convergence rate of approximately 2% for both the basic Solow model and its human capital-augmented version. In other words, they re-establish the low convergence rate common to cross-sectional regression studies, and interpret the considerably higher estimates commonly found using first-differenced GMM estimators as arising from the substantial finite-sample bias of this estimator in the presence of weak instruments.

The value of panel data methods appears controversial. From an econometric point of view, the advantages over cross-sectional regressions are apparent: unobserved heterogeneities that bias conventional cross-sectional convergence regressions can be controlled for, and lags of the regressors can be used as instruments to deal with endogeneity concerns. However, if conditioning out for individual heterogeneities might represent an improvement from an econometric point of view, it appears a disadvantage from a conceptual one: conditioning out economy-specific heterogeneities means giving up any attempt to uncover what happens to the entire cross-sectional distribution as it is exactly these heterogeneities that explain who is rich and who is poor and how this pattern evolves over time. In other words, both the problem of open-ended alternatives and, more importantly, the failure to reveal any insight into how the entire cross-sectional distribution of economies evolves already noted during the discussion of cross-sectional regressions remain unsolved.[5]

2.4. *Empirical implementation: time-series methods*

The last way to implement the regression approach is via time-series methods in which the definition of convergence relies on the notions of unit roots and cointegration.

One such method has been developed by Evans and Karras (1996a, 1996b) who use a panel data approach in which economies $1, 2, \dots, N$ are said to converge if deviations of $y_{1,t+k}, y_{2,t+k}, \dots, y_{N,t+k}$ from their cross-economy average $\bar{y}_t$ are expected, conditional on current information, to approach a constant value as k tends to infinity:

$$\lim_{k\to\infty} E(y_{i,t+k} - \bar{y}_{t+k} \mid I_t) = \mu_i, \tag{7}$$

[5] An exception is the analysis by Funke and Strulik (1999) who, using a Bayesian panel data technique similar to Canova and Marcet (1995), find evidence of persistence of inequality among West German *Länder* for the period 1970–1994.

which holds if, and only if, every $y_{i,t}$ is nonstationary but every $y_{i,t} - \bar{y}_t$ is stationary. Moreover, convergence is absolute if $\mu_i = 0$ for all i or conditional if $\mu_i \neq 0$ for some i, while divergence is found if, and only if, $y_{i,t} - \bar{y}_t$ is nonstationary for all i.

In operational terms, moving from Equation (5) and supposing that only cross-sectional data are available on the additional variables representing proxies for the different steady states, we can obtain

$$\Delta y_{i,t} = d_i - \eta_i (y_{i,t-1} - \tau_{t-1}) + \xi_{i,t}, \tag{8}$$

where $\Delta y_{i,t}$ is the first difference of $y_{i,t}$, d_i is a parameter that incorporates the proxies for the different steady states, τ_t is a common trend of steady-state per capita income level, and $\xi_{i,t}$ is a stationary error term with zero mean and finite variance. Moreover, by averaging across economies and subtracting each member of the resulting equation from the corresponding member of Equation (8) gives

$$\Delta(y_{i,t} - \bar{y}_t) = (d_i - \bar{d}) - \eta_i (y_{i,t-1} - \bar{y}_{t-1}) + (\xi_{i,t} - \bar{\xi}_t).$$

Finally, since the error term component $\xi_{i,t} - \bar{\xi}_t$ may be serially correlated, convergence is analysed running the augmented Dickey–Fuller (ADF) regression:

$$\Delta(y_{i,t} - \bar{y}_t) = \delta_i + \rho_i (y_{i,t-1} - \bar{y}_{t-1}) + \sum_{r=1}^{q} \phi_{i,r} \Delta(y_{i,t-r} - \bar{y}_{t-r}) + \upsilon_{i,t}, \tag{9}$$

where $\phi_{i,1}, \phi_{i,2}, \ldots, \phi_{i,q}$ are parameters arising from the serial correlation, υ_{it} is a serially uncorrelated error term with zero mean and finite variance, and ρ_i is negative if the economies converge and nonnegative if they do not converge. In particular, Evans and Karras (1996a) carry out an overall test of convergence by combining the information in the individual ADF statistics, on the grounds that this method, treating the data as a panel, is expected to have greater power than performing a separate unit root test for each economy [Levin, Lin and Chu (2002)], and find strong evidence in favour of rapid conditional convergence for the 48 contiguous U.S. states over the period 1929–1991. A similar procedure is also applied by Funke and Strulik (1999) who report evidence of conditional convergence among West German *Länder* between 1970 and 1994.

Using a similar framework, Carlino and Mills (1993, 1996a, 1996b) carry out individual ADF tests with a time trend as well as a constant to allow for time-invariant equilibrium differentials in relative per capita incomes (i.e., conditional convergence). They find no evidence of convergence in per capita income and per capita earnings among U.S. regions and U.S. states during the 1929–1990 period as they are not able to reject the null hypothesis of unit root for any of the regions and only for 18 states. However, after exogenously allowing for a break in the rate at which the regions were converging in 1946, they are able to reject the null of a unit root for 3 regions and 29 states when using per capita income, and for 1 region and 19 states when using per capita earnings. These results, together with evidence on the amount of persistence of shocks in the time series using parametric and nonparametric methods, are then interpreted as evidence for conditional convergence in per capita income and, to a much lesser extent, in per capita earnings. Moreover, Loewy and Papell (1996), incorporating endogenously determined break points, are able to reject the unit root hypothesis in seven regions, thus supporting Carlino and Mills' evidence on conditional convergence. On a similar vein, more recent evidence on convergence among U.S. regions is also found by Tomljanovich and Vogelsang (2001).

A different method, based on a pure time-series model, has instead been developed by Bernard and Durlauf (1995) who model an economy's output series as satisfying

$$a(L)y_{i,t} = \mu_i + \varepsilon_{i,t},$$

where $a(L)$ has one root on the unit circle and $\varepsilon_{i,t}$ is a mean-zero stationary process, thus allowing for both linear deterministic and stochastic trends. Convergence in output is then defined as the equality across economies of long-term forecasts of per capita income taken at a given fixed date. In particular, given the information I_t at time t, two economies i and j are said to exhibit stochastic convergence if the long-run forecasts of output are equal, that is

$$\lim_{k\to\infty} E(y_{i,t+k} - y_{j,t+k} \mid I_t) = 0. \tag{10}$$

Similarly, economies $p = 1, \ldots, N$ converge if the long-run forecasts of output for all economies are equal

$$\lim_{k\to\infty} E(y_{1,t+k} - y_{p,t+k} \mid I_t) = 0 \quad \forall p \neq 1, \tag{10$'$}$$

thus making it possible to distinguish between convergence between pairs of economies and convergence for all economies.

An important feature of this dynamic definition of convergence is that its existence also implies the definition of convergence as catching-up (i.e., β-convergence). Indeed, if convergence as catching up between t and $t+T$ is defined as entailing a decrease in the expected deviation in output between economies:

$$E(y_{i,t+T} - y_{j,t+T} \mid I_t) < y_{i,t} - y_{j,t} \quad \text{if } y_{i,t} > y_{j,t},$$

it can be shown that time-series forecast convergence implies β-convergence, when growth rates are measured between dates t and $t+T$ for some fixed T. In other words, time-series analyses based on Equations (10) and (10$'$) appear to resort to a stricter notion of convergence than cross-sectional analyses discussed above [Bernard and Durlauf (1996)].

Testing for convergence requires checking for the compatibility of $y_{i,t} - y_{j,t}$ with a time-invariant Wold representation of the form

$$y_{i,t} - y_{j,t} = \kappa_{i,j} + \sum_{r=0}^{\infty} \pi_{i,j,r}\varepsilon_{i,j,t-r},$$

such that $\kappa_{i,j} = 0$ and $\pi_{i,j,r}$ is square summable. According to Bernard and Durlauf, convergence, as defined by Equations (10) and (10$'$), thus requires that $y_{i,t} - y_{j,t}$ is a mean-zero stationary process, which again can be verified applying standard unit roots and cointegration procedures [Bernard and Durlauf (1995, 1996)]. Following this strategy, Tsionas (2001) finds strong evidence against the hypothesis that per capita income in U.S. regions has converged over the period 1929–1997.

Several authors have stressed the existing discrepancies in the results obtained from similar datasets using different approaches and methods. Bernard and Durlauf (1996) argue that the discrepancies between cross-sectional and time-series analyses could be partly explained by the fact that time-series tests are based on a stricter notion of convergence than cross-sectional tests. Moreover, they emphasise that the two approaches take a different view of the data: while time-series methods assume regions are close to limiting distributions and convergence is interpreted as meaning that initial conditions have no effect on the expected value of output differences, cross-sectional methods assume regions are in transition towards a limiting distribution and convergence is interpreted to mean that initial output differences dissipate over a fixed time period. This interpretation is however challenged by Carvalho and Harvey (2002), who note not only that, while some unit root tests are sensitive to initial conditions, the ADF test is robust to initial values different from zero but also that, when the constant is dropped, its power increases the further the initial conditions are from equilibrium.

In order to explain the discrepancies deriving from the application of different time-series methods, Nahar and Inder (2002) point to the inconsistencies in the links between the different definitions of convergence and the stationarity of output differences. In particular, as far as the method developed by Bernard and Durlauf is concerned, they note that certain nonstationary $y_{i,t} - y_{p,t}$ processes can meet their definition of convergence so that a test for stationarity of the process may fail to reject the null hypothesis of unit root and wrongly conclude that there is no convergence. A similar argument applies to the method developed by Evans and Karras, according to whom a necessary and sufficient condition for convergence, as defined by Equation (7), is that every $y_{i,t}$ is nonstationary while every $y_{i,t} - \bar{y}_t$ is stationary. However, also in this case Nahar and Inder show that a nonstationary $y_{i,t} - \bar{y}_t$ process can meet the definition given in Equation (7), thus implying that stationarity is not a necessary condition for convergence.

A different perspective is offered by Carvalho and Harvey (2002) who instead emphasise that while some unit root tests are sensitive to initial conditions, making them unsuitable when analysing whether regions are in the process of converging, the ADF t-test is the most robust and should be preferred. However, they note that even this test has virtually no power when a time trend is included, as in Carlino and Mills' studies. Moreover, they criticise the use of overall tests, as applied by Evans and Karras (1996a, 1996b) or Funke and Strulik (1999), as these tests do not take account of the cross-correlation between the series and remark that even individual tests, when based on equations such as (9), become uninformative when one region does not converge but all others do, so that $y_{i,t} - \bar{y}_t$ is nonstationary for all economies. As a consequence, fitting a model similar to (9), they run pairwise ADF tests to the differences between all the annual series for the eight U.S. census regions between 1950 and 1999, finding that convergence is confined to the six poorest regions while the two richest ones, New England and Mid East, diverged.

Generally, Carvalho and Harvey maintain that running unit root tests to decide whether convergence is taking place is at best of limited value and that a better strategy could entail fitting multivariate unobserved components (structural) time-series models so making it possible to gather information about both cycles and convergence [Carvalho and Harvey (2002), Harvey and Carvalho (2002)]. In particular, they develop a model combining unobserved components with a second-order error correction mechanism thus allowing a decomposition into trend, cycle and convergence components. Fitting this model to annual (1950–1999) and seasonally adjusted quarterly (1969:1–1999:4) data on per capita income of U.S. census regions, these authors show that absolute convergence is confined to the group of six poorest U.S. regions while the two richest ones have diverged, especially during the last two decades. Moreover, they show that the convergence processes characterising the group of poorest regions are neither monotonic across time nor homogenous across space, thus casting serious doubts against the results obtained via cross-sectional and panel data approaches to convergence.

3. Factor mobility and spatial interaction

In the previous section, we concentrated our attention on the theoretical foundations of the regression approach to convergence and on the different ways in which this approach has been developed and implemented. Before moving to an alternative approach to convergence that answers some of the critical issues already raised, it is however necessary to focus on an aspect that has been so far largely neglected, i.e., the role of spatial interaction effects.

The traditional neoclassical model of growth has been developed starting from the assumption that the economies are fundamentally closed. This comes from the fact that the model was originally intended to explain the evolution of a single economy's growth rate over time. Only later has the model been employed for explaining differences of per capita income growth across different economies; but despite this change of perspective, the original assumption has been retained and transferred to empirical analyses on international convergence.

Moreover, as documented in the previous section, virtually the same empirical methods originally developed to analyse convergence across nations have been widely used to test for convergence processes at a sub-national level. Unfortunately, this attention to regional growth and convergence appears to be fundamentally motivated by the fact that regions offer data sets which are new, larger and more homogenous [Blanchard (1991)] without a proper recognition of the fact that regions and countries are far from being interchangeable concepts. So, while the assumption of a closed economy may be defensible for countries, it is clearly implausible for the regions within a country, where barriers to trade and to factor flows are considerably less. As a consequence, among the many issues of interest, at least two need to be emphasised:

(i) What are the implications for convergence once openness is introduced into the theoretical framework?

(ii) Since interregional flows imply the existence of spatial dependence effects, how do these effects influence the empirical results?

3.1. Implications of interregional flows

The simplest way to start answering the first question is to consider the open-economy version of the traditional neoclassical model developed by Borts and Stein (1964) within the Solow–Swan framework. The basic hypotheses of this version are equivalent to those for a closed economic system. In addition, it is assumed that a factor's remuneration rate, determined by marginal productivities in perfectly competitive markets, can differ across regions, that factors can move freely in response to these differentials in rates of remuneration, and, finally, that agents of different regions have access to similar technologies and share roughly similar preferences.

In such a setting, Equation (2), which represents the fundamental differential equation of the model, becomes

$$\dot{\tilde{k}} = f(\tilde{k}) - \tilde{c} - (\delta + n + \mu)\tilde{k} + G_K(r - r^{\mathrm{o}}) - G_L(w - w^{\mathrm{o}}),$$

where r (w) and r^{o} (w^{o}) represent the rates of return to capital (labour) within and outside the region, while G describes the interregional flows of factors as a function of differential rates of return. In particular, G shows a positive, negative, or zero value according to whether there are positive, negative, or no interregional differentials in the rates of return.

Again, given the assumption of common technology and preferences, each regional economy converges to the common steady-state equilibrium in which variables per unit of effective labour are constant. Similar to the closed-economy case, off steady-state capital and labour rates of return may differ between regions only if the existing levels of capital–labour ratio differ. Moreover, the conventional neoclassical assumptions about the production function imply that the marginal product of capital is higher in regions with a lower capital–labour ratio, whereas the marginal product of labour is higher in regions with a higher capital–labour ratio. Since there are no constraints to interregional flows of capital and labour, capital will tend to flow from the regions with a higher capital–labour ratio to the regions with a lower level of capital per worker while labour will tend to flow in the opposite direction. As a consequence, regions with a higher capital–labour ratio will be characterised by a negative value for G_K and a positive value for G_L, thus reinforcing the convergence to the steady-state predictions of the closed-economy model. Finally, while transitions to the steady state are taking place, the regions with lower capital–labour ratios will show higher income per (effective) worker rates of growth. In such a setting, if reaction functions $G(\cdot)$ are such that adjustment in either capital or labour markets is instantaneous, the speed of convergence would be infinite. To alleviate this paradoxical implication, the original setting then has to be modified introducing adjustment costs for investment and migration, so that the rate of convergence to the steady state is higher than in the closed-economy case, but with a finite value. It should be noted, however, that this framework has a particularly unappealing feature in the present context: the capital market is not integrated in the sense that residents cannot borrow at a common, countrywide interest rate r. However, eliminating this feature leads to a further paradoxical result within the traditional neoclassical setting [Barro and Sala-i-Martin (1995)]: consumption per unit of effective labour tends to zero and assets become negative for all regions except the most patient one, i.e., the one in which the preference parameters are such that per capita consumption grows at the slowest rate. This region will asymptotically own everything and consume all the overall output. As argued by Barro and Sala-i-Martin (1995), eliminating such implications in an open-economy setting might require a model combining credit market imperfections, finite lifetimes, and adjustment costs for investment. Even leaving aside issues concerning the appropriateness of such a modification within a regional context, the predicted rate of convergence, albeit finite, would nevertheless be higher than the rate predicted within a closed-economy setting.

Convergence in interregional per capita income within the traditional neoclassical setting can also be reinforced by trade relations rather than factor mobility. Even in the absence of factor mobility, progressive equalization in commodity price and specialization of regional productive structures according to relative factor abundance result from interregional trade, thus leading to factor price equalization (the traditional Samuelson factor price trade equalization theorem). Moreover, in the presence of disparities in regional technological attainment, interregional trade can promote technological diffusion when technological progress is incorporated in traded goods, thus providing yet another possibility for poorer economies to converge with richer ones [Nelson and Phelps (1966), Grossman and Helpman (1991), Segerstrom (1991), Barro and Sala-i-Martin (1995)].

To sum up, the traditional neoclassical model describes an inherent tendency for the economic system to reach a situation of equilibrium not only for the regional markets but for the relationships between the region and the rest of the economic system as well. The regional economies that form the system described by the authors are populated by people sharing similar technological systems. The obvious implication is that these regional economies also share the same steady state. Within this context, therefore, any differences in regional economic growth are fundamentally the result of two combined sources: (i) the internally financed growth of the stock of capital per worker, and (ii) a progressive reduction of an initial interregional misallocation of resources, brought in by openness. As a combination of these two sources, speed of convergence to the steady state is faster than in the closed-economy case.

It is now tempting to see whether the open version of the neoclassical model can accommodate the outcomes of regression analyses. Obviously, this question might appear of limited relevance to those who share the belief that estimates from these analyses are severely biased either because of the reasons discussed in the previous section or, as will be explained below, because they are obtained starting from the implausible assumption that geographical units are fundamentally closed. However, even from such a radical perspective, this could still prove a valuable effort since it forces us to consider explicitly some mechanisms that, according to the neoclassical model, drive convergence across regions, other than the internally financed accumulation of capital.

As is widely recognised in the literature, convergence rate estimates from cross-sectional regressions are unenthusiastically low, even in international studies. As already mentioned, the coefficient describing the rate of convergence to the steady state is inversely related to capital's share in income. Indeed, the low speed of convergence usually found in cross-sectional regression studies, about 2 percent, requires capital's share in income to be close to 0.7 or 0.8, a value much higher than the conventional value of 0.4 given in national income accounts. To account for these findings, Mankiw, Romer and Weil (1992) suggest a modified version of the closed-economy traditional neoclassical model in which the usual production function is extended to allow for human capital. Indeed, by thinking of capital in a broad sense that includes human capital elements, the labour share is reduced to a value that thus is consistent with the cross-sectional evidence on the speed of convergence. However, as pointed out at the outset of this section, this way of reconciling theoretical predictions with cross-sectional empirical results appears inadequate in the present context.

At a first sight, more promising results are offered by estimates obtained from panel data approaches, which tend to be markedly higher than those found in cross-sectional analyses. In particular, these higher estimates have explicitly been interpreted by some authors [for example, Caselli, Esquivel and Lefort (1996)] as supporting the validity of the open-economy version of the neoclassical growth model versus its closed-economy counterpart. However, there appear to be at least a couple of reasons for being sceptical about such an interpretation. As previously pointed out, Bond, Hoeffler and Temple (2001) argue that the high estimated rates of convergence commonly found using first-differenced GMM estimators arise from the substantial finite-sample bias of this estimator in the presence of weak instruments. Using a system GMM estimator, they re-establish the low convergence rate common to cross-sectional regression studies. On the other hand, convergence rate estimates via panel data methods are quite similar across widely different regional data sets, which are known to be characterised by very different degrees of openness, and are not materially higher than those found in international studies.

Probably, a more productive way of dealing with the issue is to look for more explicit evidence on the role played by the different interregional flows on convergence. Unfortunately, though, this type of study is not abundant. Focussing on the role of migration, Barro and Sala-i-Martin (1991, 1995) include the net migration rate as an explanatory variable in the growth regressions for U.S. states, Japanese prefectures and the regions of five European countries. The expectation was that, holding migration rates constant, the estimates of the rate of convergence should be reduced, while the size of the reduction would provide a direct measure of the actual role played by migration on convergence. Contrary to these expectations, however, they found that the estimates of the rate of convergence were not significantly affected by the introduction of migration rates, even when instruments were employed in order to allow for the likely endogeneity of the net migration rates. These results, together with the findings that the rate of net migration tends to respond positively to the initial level of per capita income, are then interpreted as suggesting that migration plays a small part in the explanation of convergence, while the bulk of the explanation is left to the internally financed adjustment of capital–labour ratios.

Quite a different implication emerges from the studies of Blanchard (1991) and Blanchard and Katz (1992). Using a simple model of a system of small open economies producing different bundles of goods and characterised by high factor mobility, Blanchard (1991) shows not only that U.S. states per capita incomes tend to converge towards a stable stochastic steady-state distribution, but also that a crucial element of this convergence process is represented by labour mobility. Within a similar framework, the latter study tends to confirm the conclusion about the importance of migration over other forms of adjustment among U.S. states and further qualifies this conclusion suggesting that migration tends to be determined more by changes in unemployment than by changes in relative wages. Obviously, grounded as they are on the application of a VAR technique to very short samples, these strong conclusions are open to question on econometric grounds [Hall (1992)]. Keeping this in mind, it is nonetheless somewhat surprising that what seems to be the main message of this work, i.e., that mobility of factors is crucial to the understanding the dynamics of regional growth, has gained so little attention in the literature on regional convergence. Moreover, this message appears to have rather more force for all those regional systems which are known to be characterised by a much lower degree of labour mobility than the U.S. and Europe is obviously the first case that comes to mind. There is ample evidence supporting such concerns. While relative unemployment and wages affect interregional migration in Great Britain [Pissarides and McMaster (1990)], and in West Germany [Decressin (1994)], the resulting regional adjustment to shocks is very low. Barro and Sala-i-Martin (1991, 1995) find that the rate of net migration tends to respond positively to the initial level of per capita income in the case of U.S. states or Japanese prefectures but that this relation is much weaker for European regions. Moreover, Eichengreen (1993), comparing labour mobility in the U.S., Britain and Italy, finds that the elasticity of migration to unemployment differentials is twice as large in the U.S. than either European countries and even larger in the case of relative wages. A similar result is found by Bentivogli and Pagano (1999), who also note that, consequently, wage and unemployment differentials are generally greater and more persistent in the European Union than in the United States.

However, it should be noted that although labour migration could be rather imperfect as an adjustment mechanism within Europe, other mechanisms might substitute. For example, Eichengreen (1993) suggests these mechanisms could include interregional capital mobility and government policy, Decressin and Fatas (1995) point to changes in labour-force participation, while Cheshire and Magrini (2002) find evidence that, in those parts of the European Union where urbanisation is more dense, changes in commuting patterns can play a significant role as an alternative source of spatial adjustment.

3.2. Implications of spatial interaction effects

Having suggested that interregional flows brought in by openness may play an important role in the explanation of regional convergence, we can now move to the second question outlined at the outset of this section and see, from an econometric perspective, the consequences of spatial interaction effects on convergence analyses.

In general, two broad sources of misspecification problems have been identified in the spatial econometric literature: spatial dependence and spatial heterogeneity [Anselin (1988)]. Spatial dependence (or spatial autocorrelation) arises from a lack of independence across spatially organised observational units [Cliff and Ord (1973)]. In particular, Anselin and Rey (1991) distinguish between *substantive* and *nuisance* spatial dependence. Substantive spatial dependence reflects the existence of spatial interaction effects, such as technological spillovers or factor mobility, which are substantive components of the evolution of income disparities across regions. Nuisance spatial dependence, instead, may result from measurement problems such as a mismatch between the spatial pattern of the process under study and the boundaries of the observational units. The second source of misspecification problems, spatial heterogeneity, reflects a general instability of a behavioural relationship across observational units.

As emphasised by Rey and Montuori (1999), the literature on spatial econometrics offers a rich set of procedures for testing for the presence of spatial effects [Anselin (1988, 1995), Anselin and Bera (1998), Anselin and Florax (1995), Anselin and Rey (1991), Anselin et al. (1996), Getis and Ord (1992)]. Moreover, within the cross-sectional regression approach, there exists a number of estimators for models that treat spatial effects explicitly.

A first form of substantive dependence can be incorporated into the traditional cross-sectional specification through a spatial lag of the dependent variable, i.e., the spatial lag model. If W is a row-standardised matrix of spatial weights describing the structure and intensity of spatial effects, based on Equation (4), the spatial lag model would be

$$(1/t)\log\left[y(t)/y(0)\right] = c - \left(1 - \mathrm{e}^{-\beta t}\right)/t \cdot \log y(0) + \lambda_1 W \log\left[y(t)/y(0)\right] + u(t), \tag{11}$$

where λ_1 is a spatial autoregressive parameter of the spatially lagged dependent variable. This specification can be interpreted as a way of controlling for spatial dependence in regional growth due to the convergence mechanism operating on spatially autocorrelated initial incomes [Anselin and Bera (1998)], or to spatial interaction in the data generating process arising when a region's growth rate is related not only to its own starting level of income but, indirectly through the effect on income growth, to those in other regions as well following a distance decay pattern [Anselin, Varga and Acs (1998)]. Ordinary least squares to the spatial lag model are inconsistent and alternative estimators based on maximum likelihood and instrumental variables should be employed [Anselin (1988)]. A second form of substantive dependence reflects spatial autocorrelation in the starting levels of income and can be dealt with a spatial cross-regressive model in which a spatial lag of initial per capita incomes is added to the original specification:

$$(1/t)\log\left[y(t)/y(0)\right] = c - \left(1 - e^{-\beta t}\right)/t \cdot \log y(0) + \lambda_2 W \log y(0) + u(t). \quad (12)$$

Since both the initial levels and the spatial lag of per capita income are exogenous, estimation of a spatial cross-regressive model can be based on OLS.

As for nuisance dependence, in the presence of this form of spatial interaction, the error term in the cross-sectional regression models becomes nonspherical:

$$\varepsilon(t) = (I - \lambda_3 W)^{-1} u(t) \quad \text{with } \varepsilon(t) \sim N\left(0, \sigma^2 I\right),$$

where λ_3 is a scalar spatial error coefficient.[6] As a consequence, estimation via OLS will lead to unbiased estimates for the convergence parameter but biased estimates of its variance, thus generating potentially misleading inferences. In this case, inference should be based on the spatial error model

$$(1/t)\log\left[y(t)/y(0)\right] = c - \left(1 - e^{-\beta t}\right)/t \cdot \log y(0) + (I - \lambda_3 W)^{-1} \varepsilon(t), \quad (13)$$

estimated via maximum likelihood or general method of moments. From a spatial process perspective, another particularly interesting consequence of nuisance dependence is highlighted by Rey and Montuori (1999). In this instance, a random shock affecting a particular region affects the growth rates of all other regions through the spatial transformation $(I - \lambda_3 W)^{-1}$. Put it in a different way, movements away from a steady-state growth path may not be a function of region-specific shocks alone, but of shock spillovers from other parts of the system as well.

As we already noted, conventional cross-sectional regression analyses that allow for the role of spatial effects are exceptions rather than the norm. Perhaps, the most comprehensive study is that of Rey and Montuori (1999). Focussing on the experience of 48 coterminous U.S. states between 1929 and 1994, they find strong evidence of positive spatial dependence in both levels and growth rates of per capita income, i.e., spatial clusters of states which are homogenous in terms of income levels and growth rates. Moreover, they find that the rich clusters tend to grow more slowly than poor clusters, a pattern that could be explained by the clustering of initial income levels together with a process of unconditional convergence. However, the estimation results for the different spatial dependence models in Equations (11)–(13) make it possible to rule out such an explanation due to the presence of spatial error autocorrelation rather than the spatial lag. In addition, the analysis suggests that the traditional unconditional model suffers from misspecification due to omitted spatial dependence and that random shocks to individual states not only affect the state's dynamics toward the steady state but propagate throughout the system. Finally, they also find evidence that the indications of a structural change at the end of WWII in the rate of convergence of U.S. states [Carlino and Mills (1996a)] tend to vanish when spatial dependence is taken into account.

[6] Anselin (1982) shows that the matrix $(I - \lambda_3 W)$ is invertible when $-(1/\omega_{\max}) < \lambda < 1$, where $\omega_{\max}$ is the largest negative eigenvalue (in absolute value) of W.

In studying convergence among European NUTS regions, Armstrong (1995b), López-Bazo et al. (1999) and Rodríguez-Pose (1999) report the presence of significant spatial autocorrelation both for income levels and growth rates. These studies thus provide evidence for the European context also that traditional convergence analyses may suffer from a misspecification due to omitted spatial dependence. Following the standard convergence approach, Armstrong (1995b) adds national dummies as explanatory variables as in Barro and Sala-i-Martin (1991) but interprets them as a way to control for the influence of spatial factors. A similar route is followed by Rodríguez-Pose (1999), who, employing nationally weighted variables to eliminate the spatial autocorrelation of the error term, also reports a sharp reduction in the estimated rate of convergence. These specifications, however, despite being able to substantially reduce (or to eliminate) the presence of spatial autocorrelation in the error terms, appear debatable for two reasons: they are too restrictive, excluding spatial effects across borders, and they overlook the possibility of spatial structures within each member state.

A confirmation of the latter is indirectly provided by the study by López-Bazo et al. (1999), who, employing a more disaggregated regional data set, detect strong intra-national local spatial association in per capita income levels. Further evidence is provided by Niebuhr (2001), who, focussing on West German planning regions,[7] finds strong evidence of spatial dependence both in levels and growth rates of per capita Gross Value Added. This study, moreover, following an empirical strategy similar to Rey and Montuori (1999), confirms two of the findings of that study relating to U.S. states: (i) allowing for spatial effects results in a somewhat slower rate of convergence compared to that estimated following the traditional approach; (ii) spatial effects are not explained by a process of unconditional convergence coupled with the clustering of initial income levels. On the other hand, in contrast to the U.S. case where Rey and Montuori find evidence of nuisance spatial dependence, spatial dependence in West Germany appears to be of the substantive form. Niebuhr interprets this difference as a consequence of the different choice of observational units. As recalled above, nuisance spatial dependence may result from measurement problems such as a mismatch between the spatial pattern of the process under study and the boundaries of the observational units. Since U.S. states are large administrative areas while German planning regions are smaller functional regions which take commuting patterns into account, the author suggests the effects of an inadequate choice of the observational units might hide substantial dependence of income growth.

A similar call for greater attention to the issue of what spatial units are most appropriate for regional analysis has been recently made by other authors [Cheshire and Carbonaro (1995), Cheshire and Hay (1989), Cheshire and Magrini (2000), Magrini (1999)]. Due mainly to the availability of data, administratively defined regions are commonly used in empirical analyses. Within the European context, the typical example is represented by the Nomenclature of Territorial Units for Statistics (NUTS),

[7] German planning regions (Raumordnungsregionen) are functionally defined and contain several German NUTS3 regions linked by intensive commuting.

Table 1
Per capita GDP in selected NUTS-I and FURs

	1995		1980		% change	
	FUR	NUTS	FUR	NUTS	FUR	NUTS
Bremen	16,941	21,990	16,295	21,155	4.0	3.9
Hamburg	21,749	27,946	19,491	25,053	11.6	11.5
Île de France/Paris	23,675	25,901	21,701	21,889	9.1	18.3
Brussels/Bruxelles	16,002	24,366	14,742	23,414	8.5	4.1
Greater London/London	17,947	19,394	17,028	19,420	5.4	−0.1
EU12	14,603		13,472		8.4	

Note. Per capita GDP is measured in purchasing power parities at 1990 prices.
Sources. Eurostat and CRENOS for NUTS; estimates using Eurostat data and Cheshire and Hay (1989) definitions for FURs.

a multi-level classification characterised by a profound heterogeneity at every level, being the result of the unification of the regional systems already existing in EU member countries. Suffice to say that NUTS-I level (the highest tier in the classification underneath the national level) comprises a heterogenous set of regions which include both large metropolitan areas alongside even larger regions containing several metropolitan areas and other regions containing just parts of one metropolitan region. However, two fundamental problems arise from the use of administratively defined regions in the present context. On the one hand, since output is measured at workplaces while population at residences, unless the definition of a region has been selected to abstract from commuting patterns, the measured levels of per capita income will be highly misleading. In addition, processes of decentralisation or recentralisation of residences relative to workplaces is likely to affect per capita income growth rates for administratively defined regions. The extent of these problems is exemplified in Table 1 that reports per capita GDP levels and growth rates for five NUTS-I metropolitan regions and for the corresponding Functional Urban Regions[8] (FURs).

Overall, once it is recognised that regions are naturally open to a range of economic flows and that, as a consequence, substantial interaction exists between them, the need of an explicit treatment of spatial interaction effects in regional convergence studies becomes apparent. The literature on spatial econometrics offers a number of estimators for models that treat spatial dependence explicitly but techniques for handling spatial dependence appear to be essentially confined to cross-sectional studies. Within the panel data approach, Badinger, Müller and Tondl (2002), in the absence of a direct estimator for dynamic panels with spatial dependence, propose a two-step procedure in which a

[8] Functional Urban Regions have been derived by Hall and Hay (1980) and are broadly similar in concept to the (Standard) Metropolitan Statistical Areas used in the U.S. In particular, they are defined on the basis of core cities identified by concentrations of employment and hinterlands from which more commuters flow to the employment core than to any other subject to a minimum cut off. Cheshire and Hay (1989) provide a detailed description of their definition.

system GMM for dynamic panels is used after a spatial filtering technique proposed by Getis and Griffith (2002) is employed in order to remove existing spatial correlation. Applying this procedure to a set of European NUTS-II regions over the period 1985–1999, they obtain a convergence rate estimate of about 6 percent, hence substantially lower than estimates from previous panel data studies.

However, despite the obvious advantages of spatial econometric techniques in the present context, there remain reasons to be sceptical from a more conceptual standpoint. As we noted earlier, spatial dependence may arise from the existence of spatial interaction effects (substantive spatial dependence) or from measurement problems (nuisance spatial dependence). While filtering out the latter is clearly advisable, following a similar strategy for the former source of dependence appears somewhat more controversial. After all, substantive spatial dependence carries with it a lot of valuable information on the working of adjustment mechanisms within a system of open economies and filtering all this information out appears to be to abandon any attempt to explain the significant effect of the interaction across individual economies on convergence dynamics or throw light on spatial adjustment processes. In contrast, theoretical explanations of the working of a spatial economy are abundant and an alternative empirical strategy could be to look first at these theoretical explanations for guidance on how to define spatial variables capable of capturing adjustment mechanisms and, only at a later stage, turn to spatial filtering if tests point to the existence of further specification problems. Finally, it should be emphasised that the use of functionally defined regions could also prove useful as a strategy for minimising spatial nuisance dependence. This seems to be particularly important where the change in commuting patterns – rather than migration – represents an important source of spatial adjustment, as has been argued to be the case in densely urbanised areas of the European Union.

4. The distributional approach to convergence

One of the fundamental messages conveyed in the second section of this chapter was that the regression approach, given its attention to the concept of β-convergence, tends to concentrate on the behaviour of the representative economy. In other words, with few exceptions, convergence analyses based on such an approach can only shed light on the transition of this economy towards its own steady state whilst giving no information on the dynamics of the entire cross-sectional distribution of income. On this basis, several authors have argued that the concept of β-convergence is irrelevant. To address these concerns, proponents of the regression approach suggest combining the analysis of β-convergence with an analysis of the evolution of the unweighted cross-sectional standard deviation of the logarithm of per capita income [Barro and Sala-i-Martin (1991)]. A reduction over time of this measure of dispersion is then labelled σ-convergence. However, concentrating on the concept of σ-convergence does not appear to represent an effective solution: analysing the change of cross-sectional dispersion in per capita income levels gives no information on the intra-distribution dynamics. Moreover, as discussed above, a constant standard deviation is consistent with very different dynamics ranging from criss-crossing and leap-frogging to persistent inequality and poverty traps. Distinguishing between these dynamics is, however, of essential importance.

In what follows, we will therefore focus on an alternative approach for analysing income convergence, the distributional approach to convergence. The first part of the presentation will concentrate on its general features and the main methods proposed for its implementation. Later, given the discussion of the previous section, attention will be moved to the ways in which the role of space can be allowed for within this approach.

4.1. General features of the distributional approach to convergence

The distributional approach represents a radical departure from the regression approach: it examines directly how the cross-sectional distribution of per capita output changes over time, putting emphasis on both the change in its external shape and the intra-distribution dynamics. The approach, firstly suggested by Quah (1993a, 1993b, 1994, 1996a, 1996c, 1997a, 1997b) thus concentrates directly on cross-sectional distributions of per capita income, using stochastic kernels to describe their law of motion.

Let F_t denote the cross-sectional distribution at time t, and ϕ_t an associated probability measure. The simplest scheme for modelling the dynamics of $\{\phi_t\colon t \geqslant 0\}$ is a first order dependence specification:

$$\phi_t = T^*(\phi_{t-1}, u_t) = T^*_{u_t}(\phi_{t-1}), \tag{14}$$

where u_t is a sequence of disturbances, T^* an operator that maps the Cartesian product of probability measures at time $t-1$ and disturbances at time t, and $T^*_{u_t}$ absorbs the disturbance into the definition of the operator and encodes information of intra-distribution dynamics.

A first way to use Equation (14) for the study of income convergence is to make the income space discrete, as a result of which the measures ϕ_t can be represented by probability vectors and $T^*_{u_t}$ simplifies into a transition probability matrix M_t whose rows and columns are indexed by the elements of the discretisation, and where each row reports the fraction of economies beginning from that row element and ending up in the different column elements.

Assuming that the underlying transition mechanism is time-invariant, the model in Equation (14) thus becomes a time-homogeneous (finite) Markov chain. Then, iterations of (14) yield a predictor for future cross-sectional distributions

$$\phi_{t+s} = M'^s \phi_t, \tag{15}$$

since the matrix M'^s contains information about probability of moving between any two income classes in exactly s periods of time. Moreover, taking (15) to the limit as $s \to \infty$, enables us to characterise the likely long-run or ergodic cross-sectional distribution of incomes via the ergodic row vector satisfying

$$\phi_\infty = M' \phi_\infty.$$

Implications for the convergence debate are then drawn from the study of ϕ_{t+s} or ϕ_{∞}: if they display a tendency towards a point mass, then we can conclude that there is convergence towards equality. If, on the other hand, ϕ_{t+s} and ϕ_{∞} display a tendency towards a two-point or bimodal measure, one could interpret this as a manifestation of income polarization.

Different ways of partitioning the income space are obviously possible but very often subjectively chosen equi-sized cells or cells with variable upper endpoints (so as to get approximately the same number of occurrences in each class) are adopted. Applying this procedure to U.S. states, Quah (1996c) finds a high degree of mobility among classes and an ergodic distribution presenting no signs of bimodality. Different conclusions are reached for European NUTS regions by López-Bazo et al. (1999), who report evidence of a particularly high degree of persistence in lower-income classes, indicating the existence of a poverty trap. Fingleton (1997, 1999) partitions the cross-sectional income space into four large classes and adopts various Markov chain log-linear models to investigate convergence among European NUTS-II. The results suggest that European regions are converging towards a limiting distribution characterised by sizeable differentials in per capita income levels and consistent with the existence of multiple steady states from which economies are continuously displaced by shocks. There is also some evidence suggesting that the limiting distribution of the Markov process had been attained in 1975.

One general problem with Markov chain methods is that they impose quite restrictive assumptions on the data generating process [Bickenbach and Bode (2003)]. In their attention to future and ergodic cross-sectional distributions predicted by means of the transition probability matrix M_t, these approaches assume that the data generating process is time-invariant and satisfies the Markov property. Bickenbach and Bode (2003) therefore propose chi-square tests of the Markov property and, using five income classes, suggest that the evolution of the income distribution across the 48 coterminous U.S. states between 1929 and 2000 has not followed a Markov process.

In addition, another significant difficulty comes from discretisation. Indeed, as commonly recognised in the literature, discretising a continuous first-order Markov process is likely to remove the Markov property. While Quah (1996c) suggests that the distortion arising from partitioning into five large cells is not likely to conceal the most important features of the process, Magrini (1999) adopts a procedure aimed at reducing the degree of arbitrariness in the discretisation by concentrating on histograms as approximations to continuous distributions and choosing the income grid optimally so as to minimise the (mean-squared or integrated absolute) error of approximation. By applying this procedure to a set of 122 European functionally defined regions, he reports a strong tendency towards polarisation in the cross-sectional distribution. Bulli (2001) however argues that discretisation of a continuous state-space Markov chain concentrating on the distribution of the process at some point in time is misleading, and recommends adopting a regenerative discretisation method originally employed in the Markov chain Monte Carlo literature.

Given these critical remarks, a radical alternative is to get rid of discretisation altogether. In this case, the operator in Equation (14) can be interpreted as a stochastic kernel [Quah (1996a, 1997a] and convergence can be studied analysing directly the shape of a three-dimensional plot of the stochastic kernel, thus also avoiding to impose restrictive assumptions on the data generating process. Figure 2 shows the nonparametric estimate of the three-dimensional stochastic kernel for the transition dynamics across 110 European NUTS regions and, in the lower part, the corresponding two-dimensional contour plot.[9] In particular, these plots describe how the cross-sectional distribution of per capita income relative to EU12 has evolved over the 1980–1995 period. The 45-degree diagonal in both graphs highlights persistence properties: if most of the graph were concentrated along this diagonal, then elements in the cross-sectional distribution remain where they started. In contrast, a 90-degree counter-clockwise rotation from that 45-degree diagonal indicates that substantial overtaking occurs, thereby suggesting that poor and rich economies periodically exchange their relative positions over the 15-years horizon under analysis. Finally, a tendency towards convergence to equality over this 15-years horizon in the cross-sectional distribution of per capita income would be signalled by a concentration of most of the graph around the 1-value of the 1995 axis and parallel to the 1980 axis.

As is evident from the figure, in the case of the European NUTS regions, despite a (very) slight counter-clockwise rotation for middle-low income regions suggesting that some degree of overtaking might be present between middle- and low-income regions, the fact that most of the graph is concentrated along the 45-degree diagonal indicates that persistence is the most evident feature across European regions over the 1980–1995 period. A different outcome is apparent if this same method is applied to data on U.S. state income levels. Johnson (2000) finds evidence of convergence in the cross-sectional income distribution, confirming results obtained by Quah (1996c) by means of the time-homogeneous (finite) Markov chain methodology.

As emphasised at the outset, the distributional approach to convergence, studying both the shape and mobility dynamics of cross-sectional distributions of per capita income, appears to be generally more informative about the actual patterns of cross-sectional growth than convergence empirics within the regression approach. However, the work just described, while being able to formalise certain facts about the patterns of cross-sectional growth, does not provide an explanation for them. To address this issue, Quah (1996b, 1997a, 1997b) proposes the application of a conditioning scheme. In technical terms, given a set of economies S, a conditioning scheme Ψ is defined

[9] Following Paci (1997) and Paci and Pigliaru (1999), the set of regions includes different levels of NUTS regions on the grounds that the NUTS classification is not only quite heterogenous in socio-economic terms but also has, in some cases, no relationship with the administrative organisation of member countries. In particular, the set adopted combines: NUTS-0 for Denmark, Luxembourg and Ireland; NUTS-1 for Belgium, Germany, Netherlands and UK; NUTS-2 for Italy, France, Spain, Portugal, and Greece (see Appendix A for the list of regions). GDP (adjusted for purchasing power parities and at 1990 prices) and population are based on Eurostat data and refined by CRENOS.

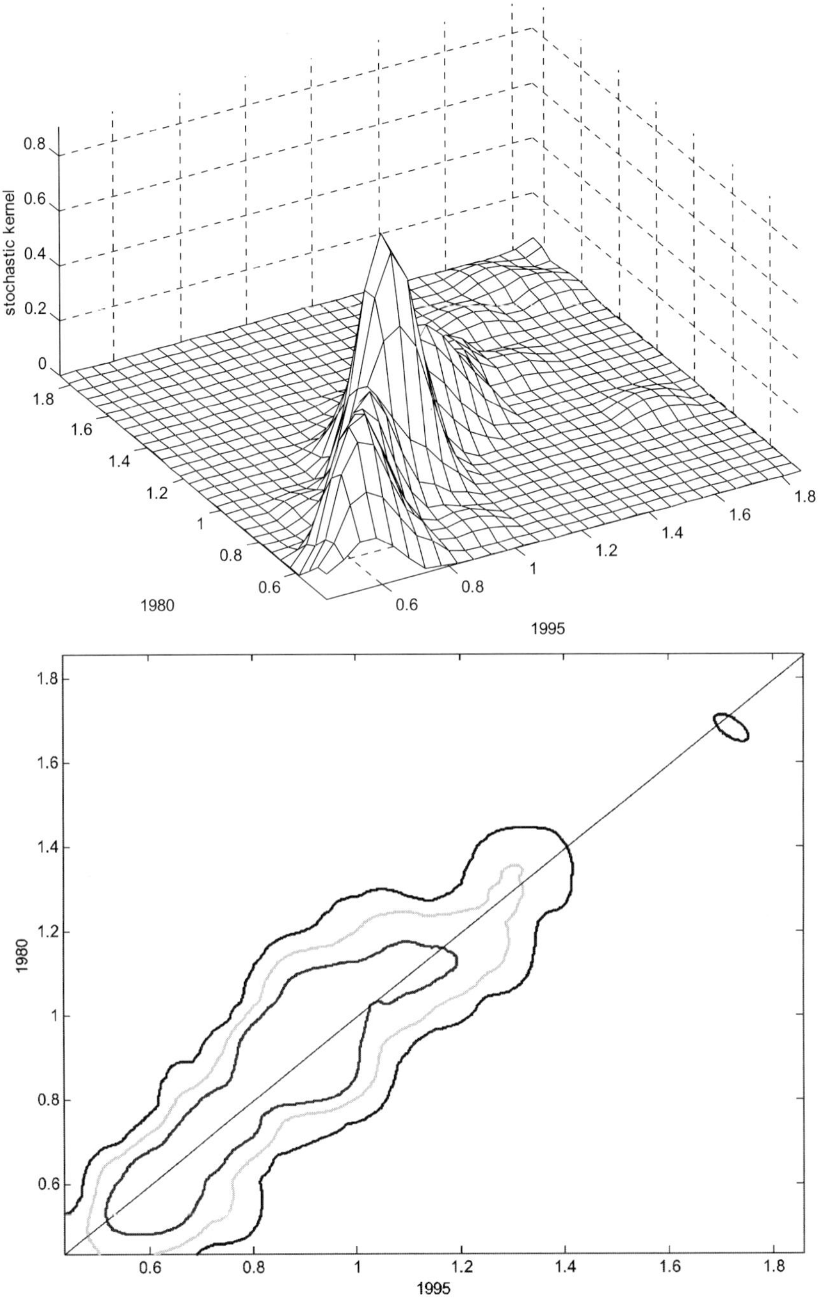

Figure 2. Relative (per capita) income dynamics across selected NUTS regions, 1980–1995. Epanechnikov kernel taken over a fifteen-year transition horizon. Contour plot at levels 0.05, 0.15, 0.3.

[Quah (1997a)] as a collection of triples, one for each economy i in S at time t, where each triple is made of:

(i) an integer lag $\tau_i(t)$;

(ii) a subset $C_i(t)$ of S;

(iii) a set of probability weights $\omega_i(t)$ on S, never positive outside $C_i(t)$.

Within this scheme, the subset $C_i(t)$ identifies the collection of economies which are in some form of functional association, based on a theoretically motivated set of factors, with economy i and hence influence its evolution. Moreover, the set of probability weights $\omega_i(t)$ describe the relative strength of each member of the subset in affecting the evolution of i, while $\tau_i(t)$ represents the delay with which economy i is affected by the development of the economies in $C_i(t)$. Finally, if original observations on per capita incomes are represented by $Y = \{Y_i(t)\colon\ i \in S \text{ and } t \geqslant 0\}$, the conditional version $Y|\Psi = \widetilde{Y}$ is defined as follows:

$$\widetilde{Y}_i(t) \equiv Y_i(t)/\widehat{Y}_i(t),$$

where, for $j \in C_i(t)$,

$$\widehat{Y}_i(t) \equiv \sum_j \omega_j(t) Y_i\big[t - \tau_i(t)\big].$$

In other words, observations in the conditional version $Y|\Psi = \widetilde{Y}$ are simply obtained normalising each region's observations by the weighted average of per capita income in functionally related regions.

Having defined the conditioning scheme, we can first of all see how a set of factors alters the cross-sectional distribution of income. For instance, suppose that inspection of kernel estimates of the cross-sectional distribution of per capita income at time t suggests the existence of bimodality, i.e., the presence of two convergence clubs. In this case, an interesting question would be whether this feature could be explained by a set of factors. In order to answer this question, the first step is to derive the conditioned version per capita income $Y|\Psi = \widetilde{Y}$, where conditioning is based on the chosen set of factors. At this point, to understand if this set of factors actually explains bimodality, all we need is an estimate of the stochastic kernel mapping the unconditional distribution to the conditioned one; then, if most of the graph is concentrated around the 1-value of the axis corresponding to conditioned data, and parallel to the unconditioned data axis, this indicates that the chosen set of factors are actually determining the observed bimodality.

In addition, conditioned income distributions can also give us information on dynamics. In this case, the effect of the set of factors on growth and convergence dynamics over a τ-year period starting at year t can be studied analysing directly the estimate of the stochastic kernel mapping the conditioned distribution at time t to the corresponding distribution at time $t + \tau$.

By means of this conditioning scheme, Quah (1997a) has emphasised the relevance of trade patterns and geographical spillovers for understanding cross-country patterns of economic growth and convergence. Moreover, in a different study [Quah (1996b)], he has also shown that while national macro factors and geographical spillovers must both be considered in order to explain observed distribution dynamics across European NUTS regions in the 1980s, the latter factor appears to play a particularly significant role. But before turning to spatial issues in more detail, it is important to conclude this general overview of the distribution analysis approach with a cautionary note on the use of kernel density estimates. If, as already mentioned, maintaining the income space continuous makes it possible to avoid the restrictive assumptions on the data generating process imposed by Markov chain methods, on the other hand, an important difficulty with the use of kernel density estimation is whether the observed features are actual features of the data as opposed to being artefacts of the natural sampling variability. While the main features of the data are unlikely to be affected by this problem, it must be said that a more rigorous solution has yet to be provided.

4.2. Spatial interaction issues within the distributional approach

To avoid misguided inferences, the role of spatial effects has to be properly accounted for in this approach as with others. For example, Bickenbach and Bode (2003) emphasise that, although the Markov chain approach requires spatial independence and spatial homogeneity, these assumptions are very rarely tested for.

Some evidence on the potential difficulties arising from the presence of spatial dependence is offered by Magrini (1999), who concentrates on the effects of nuisance spatial dependence, i.e., on spatial dependence arising from measurement problems such as a mismatch between the spatial pattern of the process under study and the boundaries of the observational units. In particular, modelling distribution dynamics as a time-homogeneous (finite) Markov chain but choosing to discretise the income space optimally so as to minimise the integrated absolute error of approximation, strong evidence of per capita income absolute convergence among 169 NUTS-II regions over the 1980s is found. In contrast, when attention is shifted to 122 European FURs, i.e., on regions defined so as to minimise the extent of nuisance spatial dependence problems, a clear tendency towards divergence is reported, with six rich regions – Düsseldorf, Hamburg, Stuttgart, München, Frankfurt and Paris – growing away from all the others.

Remaining within Markov chain methods, a decisive step towards integrating local spatial statistics into these methods is taken by Rey (2001). Building on the conditioning scheme developed by Quah and presented above, Rey suggests a number of new spatially explicit measures that can be applied to the study of regional income convergence. Central to these new developments is the spatial Markov matrix, i.e., a modified traditional Markov matrix that conditions a region's transition probabilities on the income class of the region's neighbours. It thus summarises the space–time evolution of income distributions. Parallel to Quah's (1996b) results for European NUTS regions, application of the spatial Markov chain method to U.S. state income data shows that flows across geographically contiguous regions do matter for the evolution of regional income distributions as the upward and downward mobility rates are sensitive to the relative position of adjacent regions. In particular, Rey shows that the probability of a low-income state moving upwards decreases as the income level of its neighbours also decreases; and mirroring this, the probability for a high-income region moving downward increases as the income of adjacent regions gets lower.

However, despite the fact that a spatial transition matrix, taking substantial spatial dependence into explicit consideration, makes it possible to eliminate one potential source of misspecification within Markov chain methods, it is still true that these approaches impose quite restrictive assumptions on the data generating process and that a continuous first-order Markov process need no longer be even Markov when inappropriately discretised. Once more, a solution to this is represented by stochastic kernel estimation. Moreover, combining stochastic kernel estimation with the conditioning scheme suggested by Quah, it is also possible to evaluate the role played by space on growth and convergence dynamics across open economies. In order to address this issue within the European context, let S be a set of European regions, $y_i(t)$ denote per capita income in region i at time t and $\bar{y}_S(t)$ the corresponding European average value. Moreover, define $Y_i(t)$ as per capita income in region i and a time t relative to the European average. As a result, $Y = \{Y_i(t)\colon\ i \text{ in } S \text{ and } t \geqslant 0\}$ denotes the observations on regional per capita income relative to the European average. At this point, we can consider the following particular conditioning scheme Ψ. Set the time lag $\tau_i(t)$ equal to zero; moreover, let the subset $C_i(t) = C_i(0)$ identify the set of the five closest[10] regions surrounding i but excluding the region itself, and define $\omega_i(t) = \{1/5 \cdot \bar{y}_S(t) \text{ on } C_i(0) \text{ and } 0 \text{ elsewhere}\}$. In other words, $\widehat{Y}$ is the average per capita income in the five closest regions to i, and $\widetilde{Y} = Y|\Psi$ is per capita income in i relative to that in surrounding regions.

Having defined the conditioning scheme, it is now possible to assess the role played by spatial interaction among contiguous regions. Note in fact that a stochastic kernel mapping the unconditional distribution in Y to the conditional $Y|\Psi$ allows to confront the original distribution of regional (per capita) income relative to the European average to the spatially conditioned distribution, i.e., the distribution of regional (per capita) income relative to the average in each region's geographical neighbours. As a result, if local spatial factors account for a substantial part of the distribution of incomes across regions, then the stochastic kernel mapping Y to $Y|\Psi$ would depart from the identity map. Indeed, Figure 3 conveys precisely this message. In particular, these graphs show the stochastic kernel mapping the unconditional (original) distribution for European NUTS regions in 1980 to the spatially conditioned distribution in the same year. The evident counterclockwise shift in mass to parallel the *original* axis on value 1 of the *spatially conditioned* axis (compared to Figure 2) indicates that local spatial interaction flows do account for a large part of income inequality across European regions, thus confirming earlier results by Quah (1996b).[11] Moreover, in order to get information

[10] These are identified on the basis of great circle distances, using the main administrative city as the region's centre.

[11] Note, however, that the conditioning scheme adopted here is slightly different from the scheme in Quah (1996b, 1997a). In particular, the subset $C_i(t)$ here identifies the five closest regions to i rather than those physically contiguous.

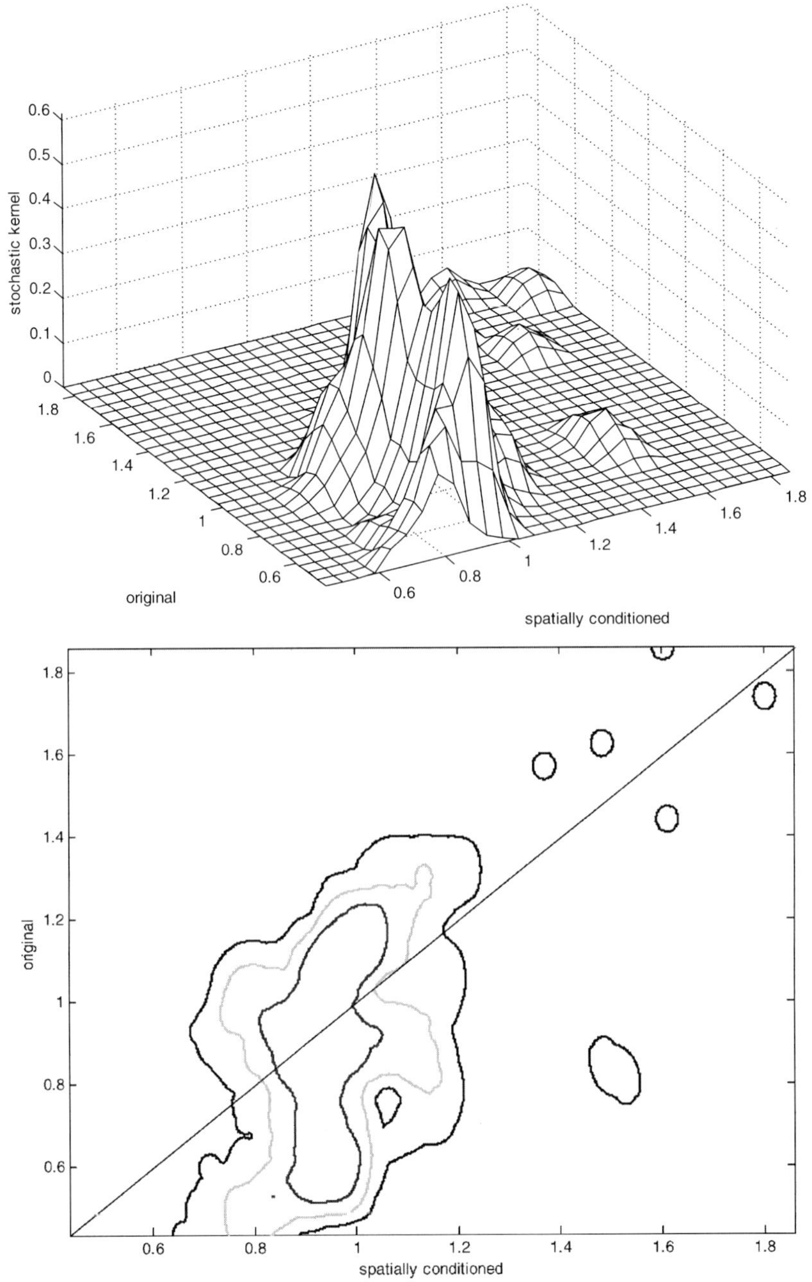

Figure 3. Relative (per capita) income dynamics across selected NUTS regions, 1980. Spatially conditioned. Epanechnikov kernel taken over original and spatially conditioned relative per capita income. Contour plot at levels 0.05, 0.15, 0.3.

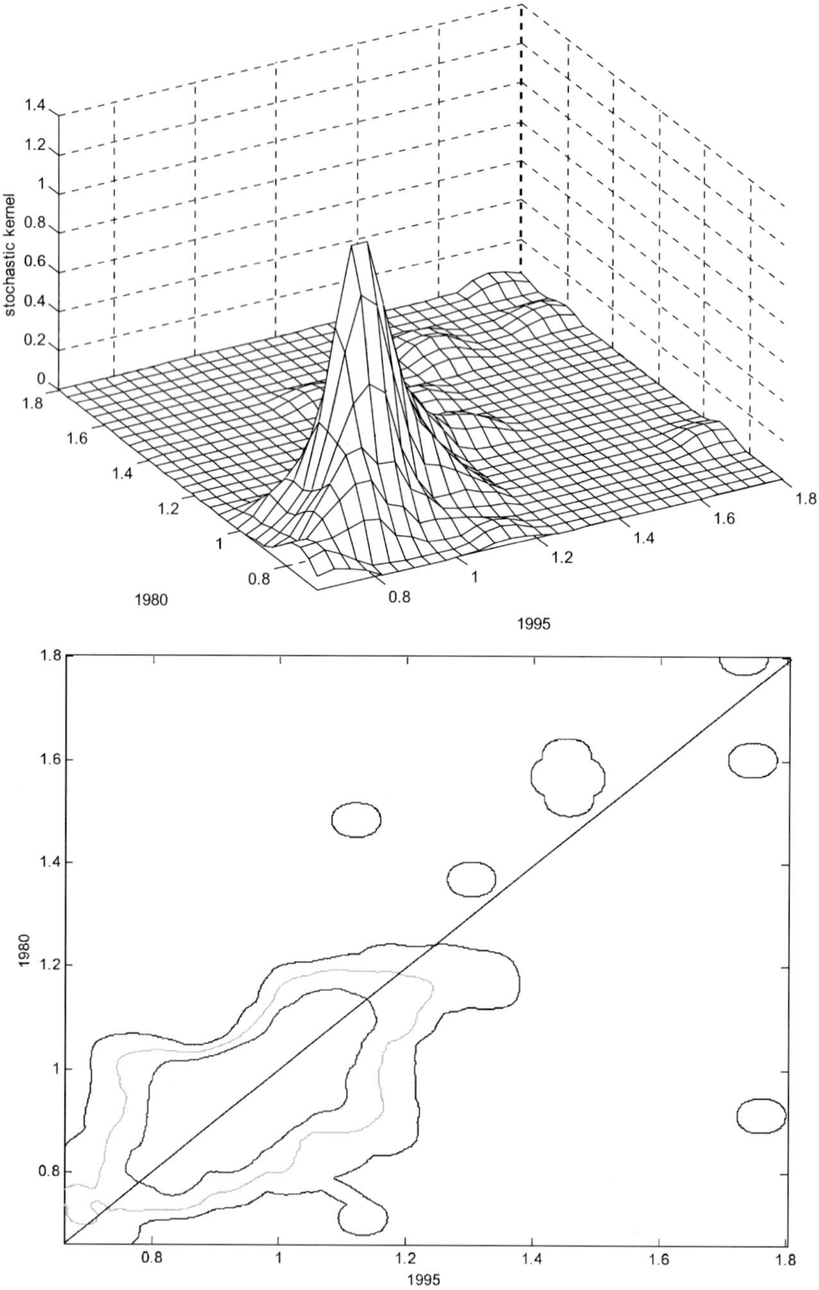

Figure 4. Relative (per capita) income dynamics across selected NUTS regions, 1980–1995. Spatially conditioned. Epanechnikov kernel taken over a fifteen-year transition horizon. Contour plot at levels 0.05, 0.15, 0.3.

on the dynamics, Figure 4 provides stochastic kernel representations on the 1980–1995 transition in spatially conditioned incomes. As with unconditioned income data (Figure 2), persistence seems to dominate. Overall, then, the picture that emerges from the estimates presented here is that of a substantial degree of persistence in (relative) per capita income across European regions. Moreover, the use of spatially conditioned income data suggested that a substantial part of this finding can be attributed to spatial factors: once the effect of proximity is allowed for, convergence clearly manifests itself.

But, are these findings robust to the presence of nuisance spatial dependence? As discussed earlier, administratively defined regions are likely to misrepresent both the actual level and the growth rate of per capita income of the underlying economies and muddle up truly spatial differences. In addition, as Table 1 bears witness, the incidence of nuisance spatial dependence appears to be particularly acute among European NUTS, mainly as a result of the profound degree of heterogeneity that characterises their definition. Further insights are provided in Appendices C and D which illustrate the growth dynamics of European NUTS and FURs over the period 1980–1995. In particular, Appendix C displays the growth rate of (annual average) per capita GDP for the 110 NUTS regions, grouping them into quintiles. Appendix D conveys the same sort of information for 122 European FURs.[12] The remarkably different dynamics that emerge thus suggest that, if we are to evaluate growth and convergence dynamics across regions correctly, the use of spatial units defined so as to abstract from commuting patterns is pretty much essential. Hence, Figure 5 provides stochastic kernel representations of transition dynamics across 122 Functional Urban Regions over the period 1980–1995. In general, the first thing to note is that the previous findings of high persistence across European regions are broadly confirmed as most of the mass is concentrated along the 45-degree diagonal. However, in contrast to the case of the NUTS regions, a twin-peak property now manifests itself for FURs, with a group of richer regions growing away from the rest of the cross-sectional distribution. Hence, as noted elsewhere [Magrini (1999)], the use of data for administratively defined regions effectively runs the risk of concealing important features, as well as changes in those features, of the European regional distribution of income.

The next step is to analyse whether this twin-peak feature can be explained by spatial factors. As before, this can be done by means of the spatial conditioning scheme defined above. Figure 6 thus reports the stochastic kernel mapping the original distribution to the spatially conditioned distribution in 1980. While there still is a pronounced counterclockwise shift in mass to parallel the *original* axis, this shift appears somewhat less pronounced than that observed in Figure 3. Moreover, the twin-peak property still manifests itself. In other words, while geographic proximity of regions with a similar level of per capita income still accounts for a large part of the distribution of income across NUTS regions, this appears to be true to a lesser extent for FURs, i.e., when (at least part of) nuisance spatial dependence is removed via a functional definition of the

[12] The full list of FURs is given in Appendix B.

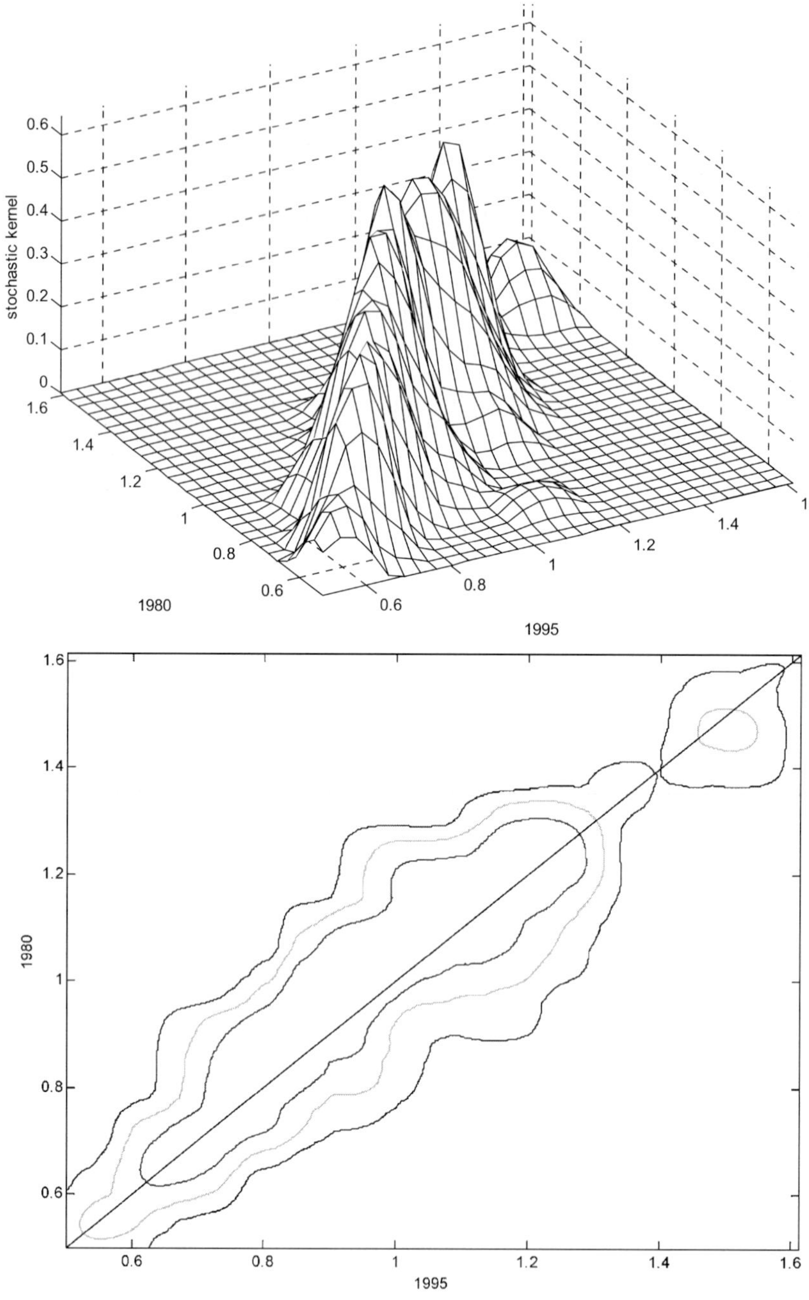

Figure 5. Relative (per capita) income dynamics across FURs, 1980–1995. Epanechnikov kernel taken over a fifteen-year transition horizon. Contour plot at levels 0.05, 0.15, 0.3.

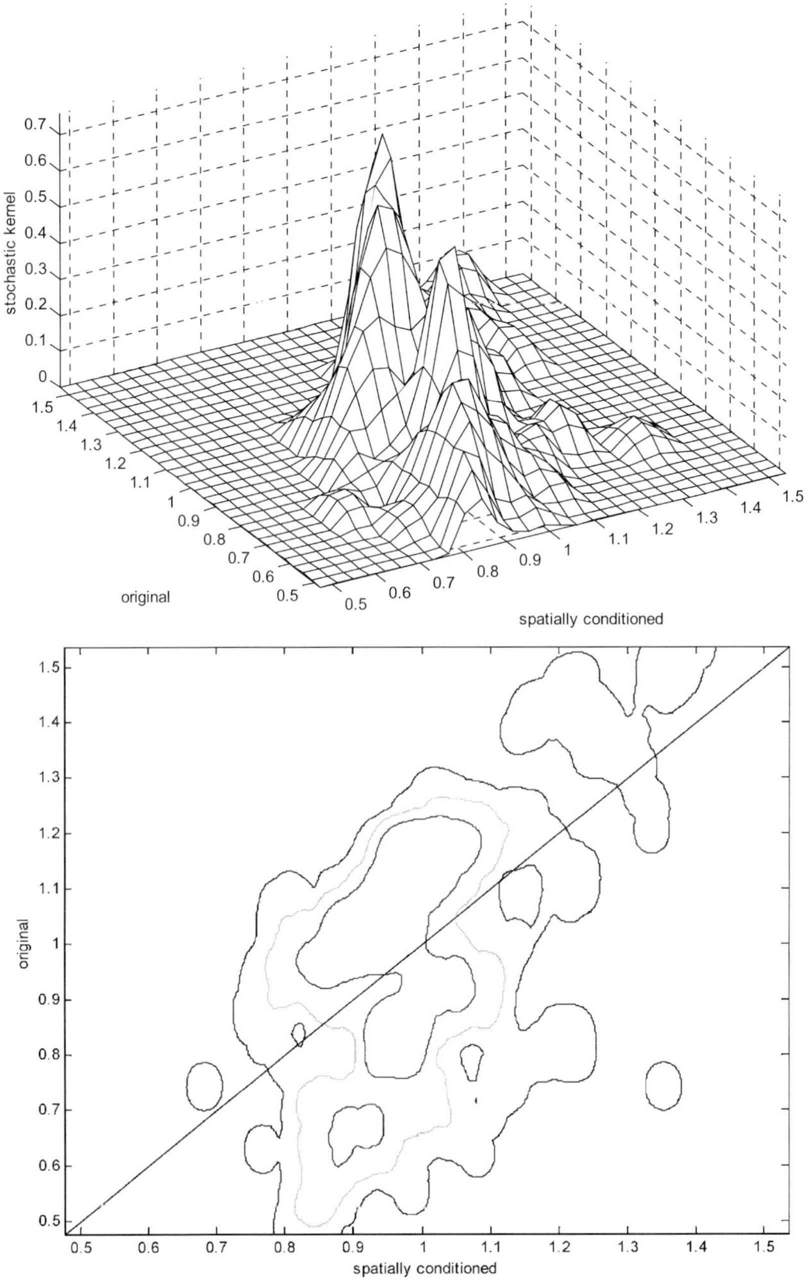

Figure 6. Relative (per capita) income dynamics across FURs, 1980. Spatially conditioned. Epanechnikov kernel taken over original and spatially conditioned relative per capita income. Contour plot at levels 0.05, 0.15, 0.3.

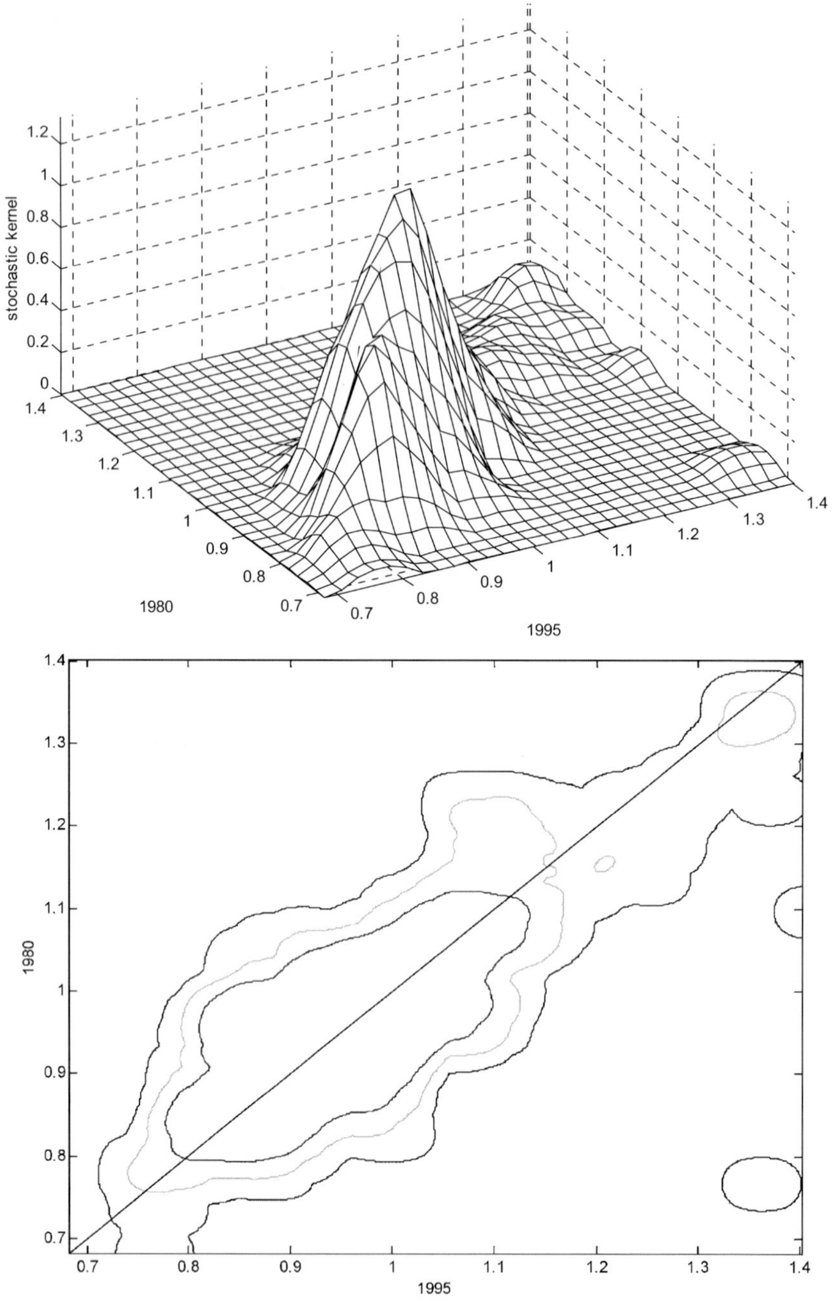

Figure 7. Relative (per capita) income dynamics across FURs, 1980–1995. Spatially conditioned. Epanechnikov kernel taken over a fifteen-year transition horizon. contour plot at levels 0.05, 0.15, 0.3.

regions. Finally, Figure 7 provides stochastic kernel representations on 15-year transitions in space-conditioned incomes for FURs. The message from unconditioned income (Figure 5) is somewhat amended but not overturned: clearly, high persistence manifests again, but the evidence of twin-peakedness becomes slightly weaker.

5. Conclusions

Do regions converge? At least on the face of it, the large body of empirical research on regional convergence overviewed in this chapter looks something of a disappointment when we try to formulate a decisive answer to this question. Indeed, profoundly different results are obtained from similar datasets using different approaches and methods and no obvious pattern seems to emerge even when attention is concentrated on a particular system of regions. However, not all approaches appear equally reliable and not all results equally convincing. Thus, while fully aware of the dangers from any generalisation, this last section will nonetheless make an effort to articulate a tentative answer by means of a personal interpretation of the main lessons that have so far emerged.

The first lesson is that typically the literature on regional convergence neglects the role of spatial interaction. The traditional neoclassical model of growth, that provides the theoretical framework for much of the empirical work on convergence, has been developed starting from the assumption that the economies are fundamentally closed. Moreover, virtually the same empirical methods originally developed to analyse convergence across nations, in which case the closed-economy assumption can questionably be retained, have been widely used to examine the existence of convergence processes at a sub-national level. However, regions and countries are far from being interchangeable concepts, and once this fact is recognised, two important consequences follow. From a theoretical point of view, convergence in an open-economy version of the neoclassical model of growth should be faster, and possibly more complete, than in the closed-economy case because the traditional source of convergence, the internally financed growth of the stock of capital per worker, is paralleled by interregional interaction that progressively reduces an initial misallocation of resources. Moreover, from an econometric point of view, the recognition that regions are naturally open to a range of economic flows and, consequently, that substantial interaction exists among them calls for an explicit treatment of spatial interaction effects in regional convergence studies. Regrettably, to date this call has gone largely unanswered.

The second lesson emerging from the examination of the different approaches developed for the analysis of income convergence is that empirical methodologies within what we have labelled the ‘regression approach’ suffer from substantial drawbacks, the most important of which relate to their informative content. Most applications of this approach in fact concentrate on the behaviour of the representative economy and are thus not only silent as to the cross-sectional distribution dynamics but can also be misleading as to the identification of the determinants of growth. There are nonetheless a few exceptions, particularly within time-series methods. However, the lack of adequately extended series of data at the regional level hampers the general application of these methodologies. A viable alternative is represented by the 'distributional approach to convergence' that, using stochastic kernels to describe the law of motion of cross-sectional distributions of per capita income, puts emphasis on both shape and mobility dynamics and thus appears to be generally more informative on the actual patterns of cross-sectional growth than convergence empirics within the regression approach. In particular, two directions of empirical research on distribution dynamics strike us as promising. The first is represented by methodologies that allow the income state-space to be continuous and use nonparametric estimates of the stochastic kernel. These avoid some important drawbacks that characterise Markov chain methodologies. The second is the development of conditioning schemes for cross-sectional distributions that, used jointly with stochastic kernel estimates, provide an explanation for the patterns of cross-sectional growth.

We can now return to the question that motivates the chapter and look at the body of empirical research on regional convergence from the particular, and admittedly subjective, angle suggested from these broad lessons. The picture that emerges appears to lend little support to the convergence predictions of the traditional neoclassical model of growth, particularly when we focus on the U.S. case. Here, the traditional tenet is that the substantial lack of legal, cultural, linguistic and institutional barriers to factor movements should favour a process of rapid (and absolute) convergence across regions. Recent work based both on time-series and distribution dynamics, however, strongly rejects the hypothesis of absolute convergence and suggests instead that the interregional distribution of per capita income is becoming polarised.

When we turn to the European case, a substantial lack of convergence emerges again but, compared to the U.S. case, this result is somewhat less controversial. Indeed, persistence in income disparities, rather than convergence, has been reported in many studies over a considerable period and the recognition of a European 'regional problem' has also meant that a substantial amount of resources have been spent in an attempt to mitigate its manifestations. Whether regional transfers taking place under structural and cohesion policies have proved to be an ineffective, misplaced or insufficient effort is obviously an important and intensely debated question, but a full account of the ongoing discussion on this issue would lead us way off the mark. Instead, returning to our original question, we can note that persistence is also confirmed by the inspection of the stochastic kernel estimates presented in Section 4, using data on two different sets of European regions.

However, the analysis presented in the latter section served two other purposes. First, it suggested that the use of administratively defined regions, such as the European NUTS, could lead to misleading inferences due to the presence of significant nuisance spatial dependence. In fact, the adoption of a set of functionally defined regions, i.e., of spatial units defined so as to reduce or eliminate nuisance spatial dependence, on the one hand confirms the high persistence across European regions but, on the other, suggests a process of polarisation, with a group of richer regions growing away from the rest of the cross-sectional distribution. Second, it revealed that a substantial part of the features of the cross-sectional (per capita) income distribution can actually be attributed to spatial factors. In particular, the use of a spatially conditioned distribution of income suggested that Europe is characterised by geographic clusters of regions with similar levels of per capita income and that once the effect of geographic proximity is allowed for, convergence tends to manifests itself. While valid in general, however, this finding is again sensitive to the presence of nuisance spatial dependence.

Acknowledgements

I am very grateful to Monica Billio, Donata Favaro, Dino Martellato, Raffaele Paci, Danny Quah and participants to the ESRC Workshop on "Cities and Geography" (Paris, December 2002) for helpful discussions. I especially thank Paul Cheshire, Vernon Henderson and Jacques-François Thisse for support and constructive comments that played a major role in shaping and improving the essay.

Appendix A: NUTS regions

Code	Name	Code	Name	Code	Name
be1	Région Bruxelles-cap. Brussels hoofdstad gewest	gr25	Peloponnisos	fr24	Centre
		gr3	Attiki	fr25	Basse–Normandie
be2	Vlaams Gewest	gr41	Voreio Aigaio	fr26	Bourgogne
be3	Région Wallonne	gr42	Notio Aigaio	fr3	Nord–Pas-de-Calais
de1	Baden–Württemberg	gr43	Kriti	fr41	Lorraine
de2	Bayern	es11	Galicia	fr42	Alsace
de3	Berlin	es12	Principado de Asturias	fr43	Franche–Comté
de5	Bremen	es13	Cantabria	fr51	Pays de la Loire
de6	Hamburg	es21	Pais Vasco	fr52	Bretagne
de7	Hessen	es22	Comun. Foral de Navarra	fr53	Poitou–Charentes
de9	Niedersachsen	es23	La Rioja	fr61	Aquitaine
dea	Nordrhein–Westfalen	es3	Comunidad de Madrid	fr62	Midi–Pyrénées
deb	Rheinland–Pfalz	es41	Castilla y León	fr63	Limousin
dec	Saarland	es42	Castilla–La Mancha	fr71	Rhône–Alpes
def	Schleswig–Holstein	es43	Extremadura	fr72	Auvergne
dk	Denmark	es51	Cataluña	fr81	Languedoc–Roussillon
gr11	Anatoliki Makedonia, Thraki	es52	Comunidad Valenciana	fr82	Provence–Alpes–Côte d'Azur
		es53	Baleares		
gr12	Kentriki Makedonia	es61	Andalucia	fr83	Corse
gr13	Dytiki Makedonia	es62	Murcia	ie	Ireland
gr14	Thessalia	es7	Canarias (ES)	it11	Piemonte
gr21	Ipeiros	fr1	Île de France	it12	Valle d'Aosta
gr22	Ionia Nisia	fr21	Champagne–Ardenne	it13	Liguria
gr23	Dytiki Ellada	fr22	Picardie	it2	Lombardia
gr24	Sterea Ellada	fr23	Haute–Normandie	it31	Trentino–Alto Adige

Code	Name	Code	Name	Code	Name
it32	Veneto	ita	Sicilia	ukc	North East
it33	Friuli–Venezia Giulia	itb	Sardegna	ukd	North West
it4	Emilia Romagna	lu	Luxembourg	uke	Yorkshire and The Humber
it51	Toscana	nl1	Noord-Nederland	ukf	East Midlands
it52	Umbria	nl2	Oost-Nederland	ukg	West Midlands
it53	Marche	nl3	West-Nederland	ukh	Eastern
it6	Lazio	nl4	Zuid-Nederland	uki	London
it71	Abruzzo	pt11	Norte	ukj	South East
it72	Molise	pt12	Centro (P)	ukk	South West
it8	Campania	pt13	Lisboa e Vale do Tejo	ukl	Wales
it91	Puglia	pt14	Alentejo	ukm	Scotland
it92	Basilicata	pt15	Algarve	ukn	Northern Ireland
it93	Calabria				

Appendix B: Functional urban regions

Code	Name	Code	Name	Code	Name	Code	Name
1	Antwerpen	32	Stuttgart	63	Nancy	93	Amsterdam
2	Bruxelles-Brussel	33	Wiesbaden	64	Nantes	94	Rotterdam
3	Charleroi	34	Wuppertal	65	Nice	95	S-Gravenhage
4	Liège	35	Athinai	66	Orléans	96	Utrecht
5	Århus	36	Saloniki	67	Paris	97	Lisboa
6	Københavns	37	Alicante	68	Rennes	98	Porto
7	Aachen	38	Barcelona	69	Rouen	99	Belfast
8	Augsburg	39	Bilbao	70	St. Etienne	100	Birmingham
9	Berlin	40	Cordoba	71	Strasbourg	101	Brighton
10	Bielefeld	41	Gijon/Aviles	72	Toulon	102	Bristol
11	Bochum	42	Granada	73	Toulouse	103	Cardiff
12	Bonn	43	La Coruna	74	Valenciennes	104	Coventry
13	Braunschweig	44	Madrid	75	Dublin	105	Derby
14	Bremen	45	Málaga	76	Bari	106	Edinburgh
15	Dortmund	46	Murcia	77	Bologna	107	Glasgow
16	Düsseldorf	47	Palma De Mallorca	78	Brescia	108	Hull
17	Duisburg	48	Sevilla	79	Cagliari	109	Leeds
18	Essen	49	Valencia	80	Catania	110	Leicester
19	Frankfurt	50	Valladolid	81	Firenze	111	Liverpool
20	Hamburg	51	Vigo	82	Genova	112	London
21	Hannover	52	Zaragoza	83	Messina	113	Manchester
22	Karlsruhe	53	Bordeaux	84	Milano	114	Newcastle
23	Kassel	54	Clermont-Ferrand	85	Napoli	115	Nottingham
24	Köln	55	Dijon	86	Padova	116	Plymouth
25	Krefeld	56	Grenoble	87	Palermo	117	Portsmouth
26	Mannheim	57	Le Havre	88	Roma	118	Sheffield
27	Mönchengladbach	58	Lille	89	Taranto	119	Southampton
28	München	59	Lyon	90	Torino	120	Stoke
29	Münster	60	Marseille	91	Venezia	121	Sunderland
30	Nürnberg	61	Montpellier	92	Verona	122	Teesside
31	Saarbruecken	62	Mulhouse				

Appendix C: NUTS – per capita GDP (annual average) growth 1980–1995*

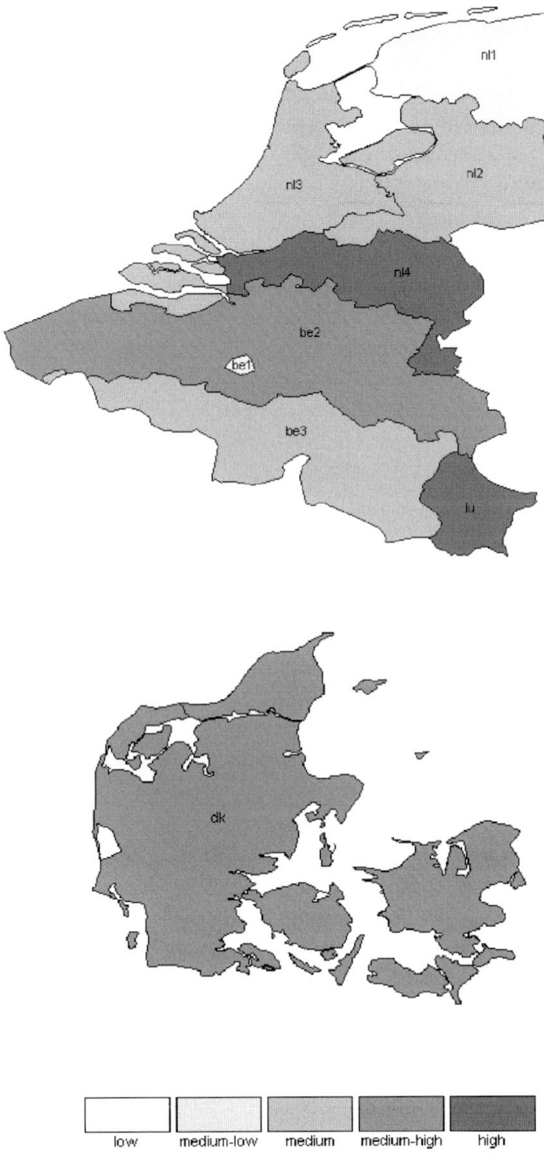

* For a colour reproduction of the figures in this appendix, see the colour figures section, pages 3055–3058.

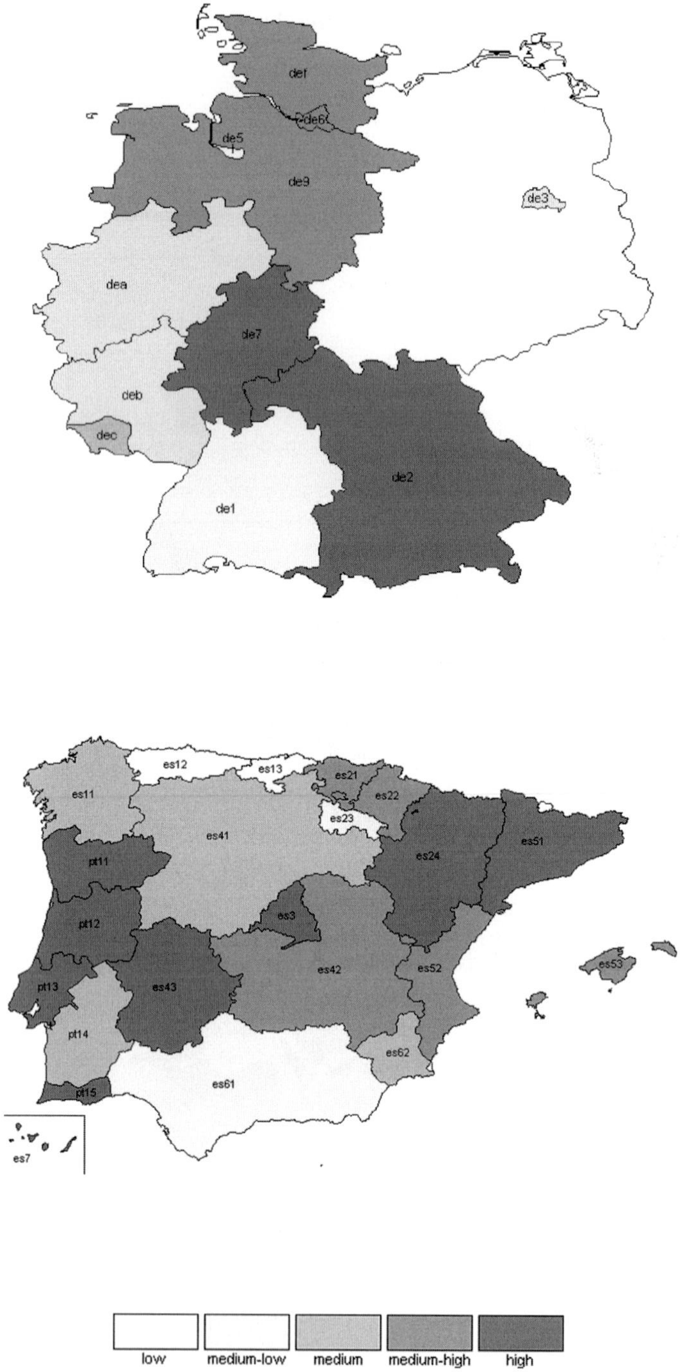
def
de6
de5
de9
de3
dea
de7
deb
dec
de2
de1
es12
es13
es21
es11
es22
es23
es41
es51
pt11
es24
es3
pt12
es42
es52
es53
pt13
es43
pt14
es62
es61
pt15
es7
low
medium-low
medium
medium-high
high

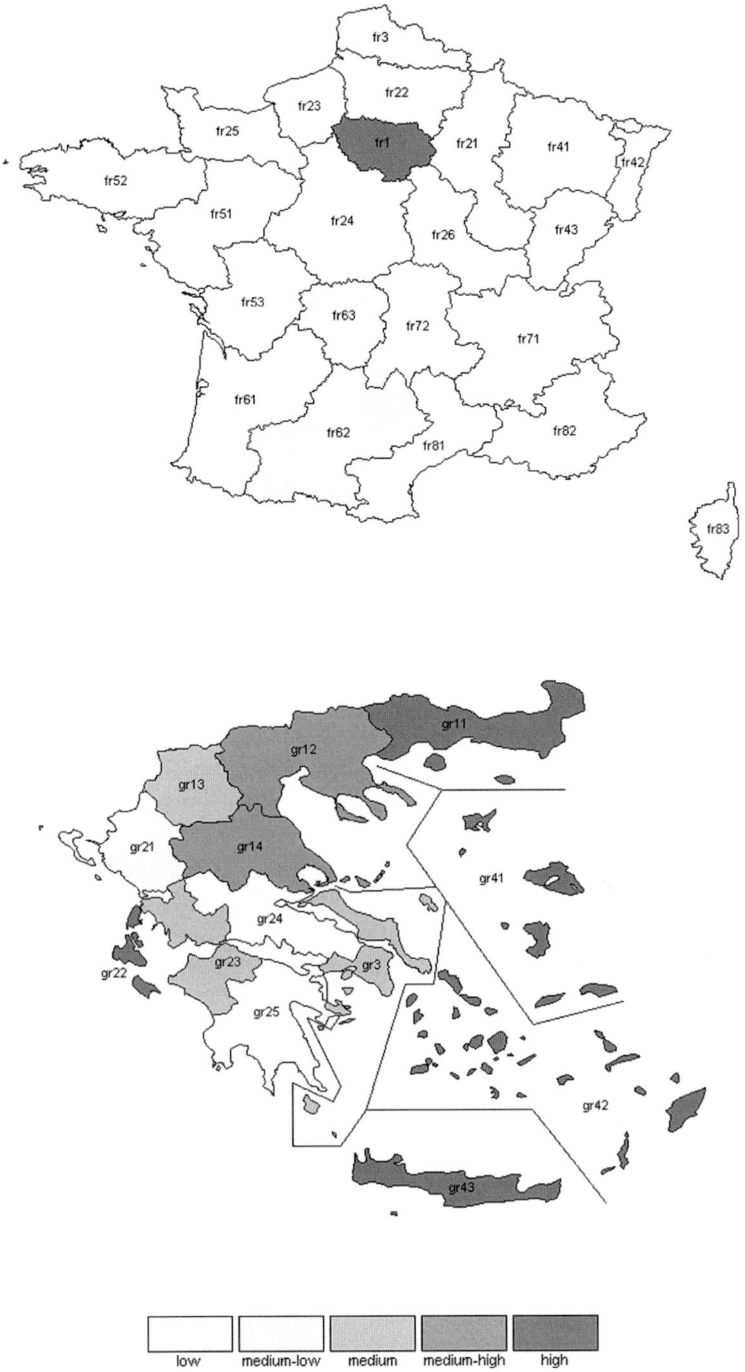
fr3
fr22
fr23
fr25
fr1
fr21
fr41
fr42
fr52
fr51
fr24
fr26
fr43
fr53
fr63
fr72
fr71
fr61
fr62
fr81
fr82
fr83
gr11
gr12
gr13
gr21
gr14
gr41
gr24
gr22
gr23
gr3
gr25
gr42
gr43
low
medium-low
medium
medium-high
high

it12
it11
it13
it2
it31
it32
it33
it4
it51
it52
it53
it6
it71
it72
it8
it91
it92
it93
itb
ita
ukm
ukn
ie
ukc
ukd
uke
ukf
ukg
ukl
ukh
uki
ukj
ukk
low
medium-low
medium
medium-high
high

Appendix D: FURs – per capita GDP (annual average) growth 1980–1995*

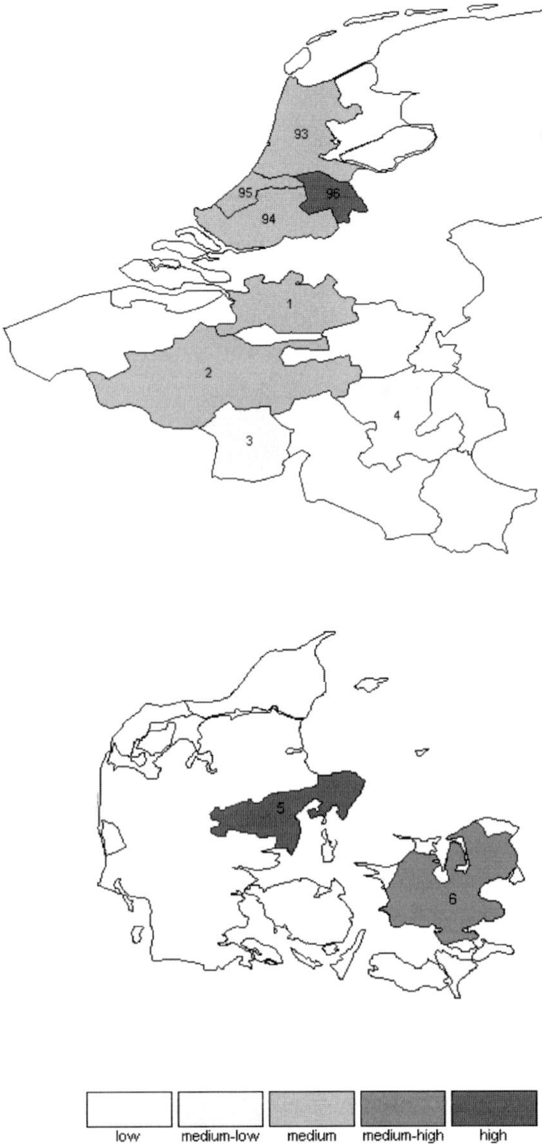

* For a colour reproduction of the figures in this appendix, see the colour figure section, pages 3059–3062.

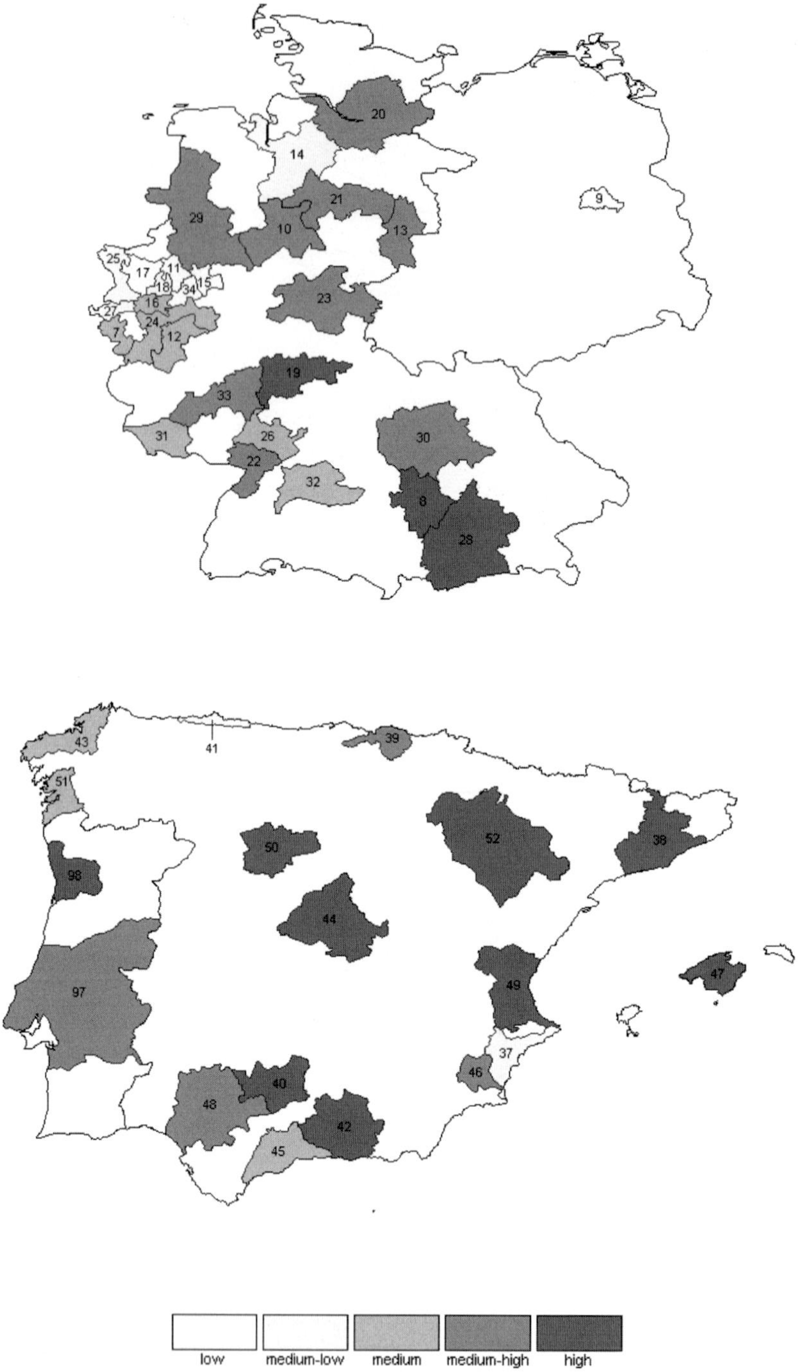
low
medium-low
medium
medium-high
high

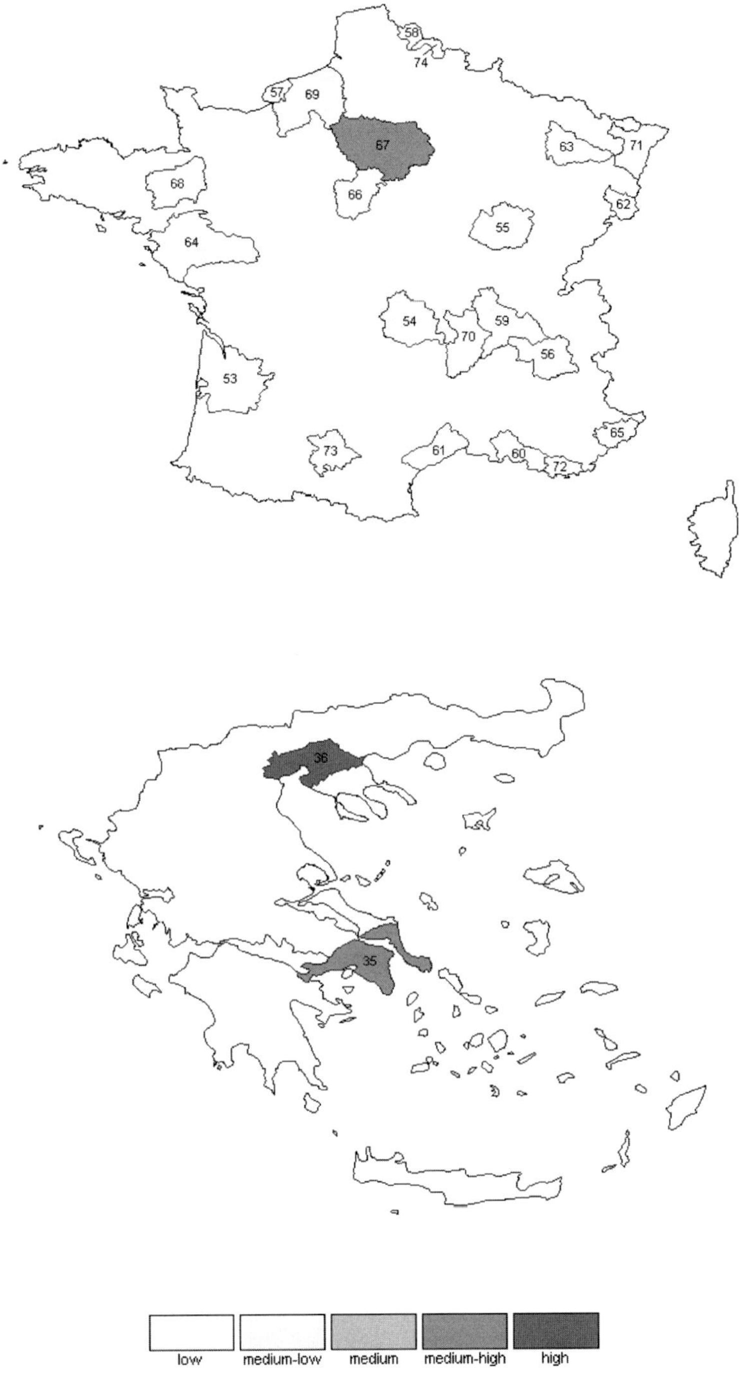
58
74
57
69
67
63
71
68
66
62
55
64
54
59
70
56
53
65
73
61
60
72
36
35
low
medium-low
medium
medium-high
high

107
106
114
121
122
99
75
109
108
111
113
118
120
105
115
110
100
104
112
103
102
119
117
101
116
84
78
92
91
86
90
82
77
81
88
85
76
89
79
83
87
80
low
medium-low
medium
medium-high
high

References

Abramovitz, M. (1979). "Rapid growth potential and its realisation: The experience of capitalist economics in the postwar period". In: Malinvaud, E. (Ed.), Economic Growth and Resources: vol. 1, The Major Issues. Macmillan, London.

Abramovitz, M. (1986). "Catching up, forging ahead, and falling behind". Journal of Economic History 46 (2), 385–406.

Aghion, P., Howitt, P. (1992). "A model of growth through creative destruction". Econometrica 60 (2), 323–351.

Aghion, P., Howitt, P. (1998). Endogenous Growth Theory. MIT Press, Cambridge, MA.

Anselin, L. (1982). "A note on small sample properties of estimators in a first order spatial autoregressive model". Environment and Planning A 14, 1023–1030.

Anselin, L. (1988). Spatial Econometrics: Methods and Models. Kluwer Academic, Boston.

Anselin, L. (1995). "Local indicators of spatial association – LISA". Geographical Analysis 27 (2), 93–115.

Anselin, L., Bera, A. (1998). "Spatial dependence in linear regression models". In: Ullah, A., Giles, D. (Eds.), Handbook of Applied Economic Statistics. Dekker, New York.

Anselin, L., Florax, R.J.G.M. (Eds.) (1995). New Directions in Spatial Econometrics. Springer-Verlag, Berlin.

Anselin, L., Rey, S.J. (1991). "Properties of tests for spatial dependence in linear regression models". Geographical Analysis 23 (2), 112–131.

Anselin, L., Bera, A., Florax, R.J.G.M., Yoon, M. (1996). "Simple diagnostic tests for spatial dependence". Regional Science and Urban Economics 26 (1), 77–104.

Anselin, L., Varga, A., Acs, Z.J. (1998). "Geographic and sectoral characteristics of academic knowledge externalities". Working Paper. Bruton Center for Development Studies, University of Texas.

Arellano, M. (1988). "An alternative transformation for fixed effects models with predetermined variables". Applied Economics Discussion Paper No. 57. Institute of Economics and Statistics, University of Oxford.

Arellano, M., Bond, S. (1991). "Some test specification for panel data: Monte Carlo evidence and an application to employment equations". Review of Economic Studies 58 (2), 577–597.

Arellano, M., Bover, O. (1995). "Another look at the instrumental variable estimation of error-components models". Journal of Econometrics 68 (1), 29–51.

Armstrong, H.W. (1995a). "Trends and disparities in regional GDP per capita in the European Union, United States and Austria". European Commission report 94/00/74/017, Brussels.

Armstrong, H.W. (1995b). "An appraisal of the evidence from cross-sectional analysis of the regional growth process within the European Union". In: Armstrong, H., Vickerman, R. (Eds.), Convergence and Divergence among European Regions. Pion, London.

Armstrong, H.W. (1995c). "Convergence among regions of the European Union, 1950–1990". Papers in Regional Science 74 (2), 143–152.

Azariadis, C., Drazen, A. (1990). "Threshold externalities in economic development". Quarterly Journal of Economics 105 (2), 501–526.

Badinger, H., Müller, W., Tondl, G. (2002). "Regional Convergence in the European Union (1985–1999): A spatial dynamic panel analysis". IEF Working Paper No. 47. Vienna University of Economics.

Barro, R.J. (1991). "Economic growth in a cross-section of countries". Quarterly Journal of Economics 106 (2), 407–443.

Barro, R.J., Sala-i-Martin, X. (1991). "Convergence across states and regions". Brooking Papers on Economic Activity 1, 107–182.

Barro, R.J., Sala-i-Martin, X. (1992). "Convergence". Journal of Political Economy 100 (2), 223–251.

Barro, R.J., Sala-i-Martin, X. (1995). Economic Growth. McGraw–Hill, New York.

Barro, R.J., Sala-i-Martin, X. (1997). "Technological diffusion, convergence, and growth". Journal of Economic Growth 2 (1), 1–26.

Baumol, W.J. (1986). "Productivity growth, convergence, and welfare: What the long-run data show". American Economic Review 76 (5), 1072–1085.

Bentivogli, C., Pagano, P. (1999). "Regional disparities and labour mobility: The EURO-11 versus the USA". Labour 13 (3), 737–760.

Bernard, A.B., Durlauf, S.N. (1995). "Convergence in international output". Journal of Applied Econometrics 10 (2), 97–108.

Bernard, A.B., Durlauf, S.N. (1996). "Interpreting tests of the convergence hypothesis". Journal of Econometrics 71 (1–2), 161–173.

Bickenbach, F., Bode, E. (2003). "Evaluating the Markov property in studies of economic convergence". International Regional Science Review 26 (3), 363–392.

Blanchard, O.J. (1991). "Comments on [Barro and Sala-i-Martin, 'Convergence across states and regions']". Brooking Papers on Economic Activity 1, 159–174.

Blanchard, O.J., Katz, L.F. (1992). "Regional evolutions". Brooking Papers on Economic Activity 1, 1–75.

Blundell, R., Bond, S. (1998). "Initial conditions and moment restrictions in dynamic panel data models". Journal of Econometrics 87 (1), 115–143.

Bond, S., Hoeffler, H., Temple, J. (2001). "GMM estimation of empirical growth models". CEPR Discussion Paper No. 3048. CEPR, London.

Borts, G.H., Stein, J.L. (1964). Economic Growth in a Free Market. Columbia Univ. Press, New York.

Bulli, S. (2001). "Distribution dynamics and cross-country convergence: A new approach". Scottish Journal of Political Economy 48 (2), 226–243.

Button, K., Pentecost, E.J. (1995). "Testing for convergence of the EU regional economies". Economic Enquiry 33 (4), 664–671.

Button, K., Pentecost, E.J. (1999). Regional Economic Performance within the European Union. Elgar, Cheltenham.

Caniëls, M.C.J. (2000). Knowledge Spillovers and Economic Growth. Elgar, Cheltenham.

Caniëls, M.C.J., Verspagen, B. (2001). "Barriers to knowledge spillovers and regional convergence in an evolutionary model". Journal of Evolutionary Economics 11 (3), 307–329.

Canova, F., Marcet, A. (1995). "The poor stay poor: Non-convergence across countries and regions". CEPR Discussion Paper No. 1265. CEPR, London.

Carlino, G., Mills, L. (1993). "Are U.S. regional incomes converging?" Journal of Monetary Economics 32 (2), 335–346.

Carlino, G., Mills, L. (1996a). "Testing neoclassical convergence in regional incomes and earnings". Regional Science and Urban Economics 26 (6), 565–590.

Carlino, G., Mills, L. (1996b). "Convergence and the U.S. states: a time-series analysis". Journal of Regional Science 36 (4), 587–616.

Carvalho, V.M., Harvey, A.C. (2002). "Growth, cycles and convergence in U.S. regional time series". Cambridge Working Papers in Economics No. 0221. Cambridge University.

Caselli, F., Esquivel, G., Lefort, F. (1996). "Reopening the convergence debate: A new look at cross-country growth empirics". Journal of Economic Growth 1 (3), 363–389.

Cashin, P. (1995). "Economic growth and convergence across the seven colonies of Australia: 1861–1991". Economic Record 71 (213), 132–144.

Cass, D. (1965). "Optimum growth in an aggregative model of capital accumulation". Review of Economic Studies 32, 233–240.

Chatterji, M., Dewhurst, J.H.L. (1996). "Convergence clubs and relative economic performance in Great Britain: 1977–1991". Regional Studies 30 (1), 31–40.

Cheshire, P.C., Carbonaro, G. (1995). "Convergence–divergence in regional growth rates: An empty black box?" In: Armstrong, H.W., Vickerman, R.W. (Eds.), Convergence and Divergence Among European Regions. Pion, London.

Cheshire, P.C., Hay, D.G. (1989). Urban Problems in Western Europe: An Economic Analysis. Unwin Hyman, London.

Cheshire, P.C., Magrini, S. (2000). "Endogenous processes in European regional growth: Convergence and policy". Growth and Change 31 (4), 455–479.

Cheshire, P.C., Magrini, S. (2002). "The distinctive determinants of European Urban growth: Does one size fit all?" Research Papers in Environmental and Spatial Analysis No. 73. London School of Economics.
Cliff, A., Ord, J. (1973). Spatial Autocorrelation. Pion, London.
Coulombe, S., Day, K. (1996). "β-convergence, σ-convergence, and the stationary-state level of regional disparities: the case of Canada". University of Ottawa Research Paper No. 9608E.
Coulombe, S., Lee, F. (1993). "Regional economic disparities in Canada". University of Ottawa Research Paper No. 9317E.
Coulombe, S., Lee, F. (1995). "Convergence across Canadian provinces, 1961 to 1991". Canadian Journal of Economics 28 (4a), 886–898.
Coulombe, S., Tremblay, J.-F. (2001). "Human capital and regional convergence in Canada". Journal of Economic Studies 28 (2–3), 154–180.
Cuadrado-Roura, J.R., Mancha-Navarro, T., Garrido-Yserte, R. (2000a). "Regional productivity patterns in Europe: An alternative approach". Annals of Regional Science 34 (3), 365–384.
Cuadrado-Roura, J.R., Mancha-Navarro, T., Garrido-Yserte, R. (2000b). "Convergence and regional mobility in the European Union". In: 40th Congress of the European Regional Science Association, Barcelona.
De la Fuente, A. (1996). "On the sources of growth and convergence: A closer look at the Spanish regions". CEPR Discussion Paper No. 1543. CEPR, London.
De la Fuente, A. (2000). "Convergence across countries and regions: Theory and empirics". CEPR Discussion Paper No. 2465. CEPR, London.
De la Fuente, A. (2002). "On the sources of convergence: A close look at the Spanish regions". European Economic Review 46 (3), 569–599.
De la Fuente, A., Vives, X. (1995). "Infrastructure and education as instruments of regional policy: Evidence from Spain". Economic Policy: A European Forum 0 (20), 11–51.
Decressin, J.W. (1994). "Internal migration in West Germany and implications for East–West salary convergence". Weltwirschaftliches Archiv 130 (2), 231–257.
Decressin, J.W., Fatas, A. (1995). "Regional labour market dynamics in Europe". European Economic Review 39 (9), 1627–1655.
Durlauf, S.N. (1996). "A theory of persistent income inequality". Journal of Economic Growth 1 (1), 75–93.
Durlauf, S.N., Quah, D.T. (1999). "The new empirics of economic growth". In: Taylor, J., Woodford, M. (Eds.), Handbook of Macroeconomics. North-Holland, Amsterdam.
Eichengreen, B. (1993). "Labour markets and European monetary unification". In: Masson, P.R., Taylor, M.P. (Eds.), Policy Issues in the Operation of Currency Unions. Cambridge Univ. Press, Cambridge, UK.
Evans, P., Karras, G. (1996a). "Convergence revisited". Journal of Monetary Economics 37 (2), 249–265.
Evans, P., Karras, G. (1996b). "Do economies converge? Evidence from a panel of US states". Review of Economics and Statistics 78 (3), 384–388.
Fabiani, S., Pellegrini, G. (1997). "Education, infrastructure, geography and growth: An empirical analysis of the development of Italian provinces". Temi di discussione No. 323. Banca d'Italia, Roma.
Fagerberg, J. (1988). "International competitiveness". Economic Journal 98 (391), 355–374.
Fagerberg, J. (1994). "Technology and international differences in growth rates". Journal of Economic Literature 32 (3), 1147–1175.
Fagerberg, J., Verspagen, B. (1996). "Heading for divergence? Regional growth in Europe reconsidered". Journal of Common Market Studies 34 (3), 431–448.
Fingleton, B. (1997). "Specification and testing of Markov chain models: An application to convergence in the European Union". Oxford Bulletin of Economics and Statistics 59 (3), 385–403.
Fingleton, B. (1999). "Estimates of time to convergence: An analysis of regions of the European Union". International Regional Science Review 22 (1), 5–34.
Friedman, M. (1992). "Do old fallacies ever die?" Journal of Economic Literature 30 (4), 2129–2132.
Funke, M., Strulik, H. (1999). "Regional growth in West Germany: Convergence or divergence?" Economic Modelling 16 (4), 489–502.
Galor, O., Zeira, J. (1993). "Income distribution and macroeconomics". Review of Economic Studies 60 (1), 35–52.

Garofalo, G.A., Yamarik, S. (2002). "Regional convergence: Evidence from a new state-by-state capital stock series". Review of Economics and Statistics 84 (2), 316–323.

Gerschenkron, A. (1962). Economic Backwardness in Historical Perspective. Belknap, Cambridge, MA.

Getis, A., Griffith, D.A. (2002). "Comparative spatial filtering in regression analysis". Geographical Analysis 34 (2), 130–140.

Getis, A., Ord, J.K. (1992). "The analysis of spatial association by the use of distance statistics". Geographical Analysis 24 (3), 189–206.

Grossman, G.M., Helpman, E. (1990). "Comparative advantage and long-run growth". American Economic Review 80 (4), 796–815.

Grossman, G.M., Helpman, E. (1991). Innovation and Growth in the Global Economy. MIT Press, Cambridge, MA.

Hall, P., Hay, D.G. (1980). Growth Centres in the European Urban System. Heinemann, London.

Hall, R.E. (1992). "Comments on [Blanchard and Katz, 'Regional Evolutions']". Brooking Papers on Economic Activity 1, 62–65.

Harvey, A., Carvalho, V.M. (2002). "Models for converging economies". Cambridge Working Papers in Economics No. 0216. Cambridge University.

Helpman, E. (1993). "Innovation, imitation, and intellectual property rights". Econometrica 61 (6), 1247–1280.

Herz, B., Röger, W. (1995). "Economic growth and convergence in Germany". Weltwirtschaftliches Archiv 131 (1), 133–143.

Hofer, H., Wörgötter, A. (1997). "Regional per capita income convergence in Austria". Regional Studies 31 (1), 1–12.

Holtz-Eakin, D. (1993). "Solow and the states: Capital accumulation, productivity, and economic growth". National Tax Journal 46 (4), 425–439.

Hsiao, C. (1986). In: Analysis of Panel Data. In: Econometric Society Monographs. Cambridge Univ. Press, Cambridge, UK.

Johnson, P. (2000). "A nonparametric analysis of income convergence across the U.S. states". Economic Letters 69 (2), 219–223.

Koopmans, T. (1965). "On the concept of optimal economic growth". In: The Econometric Approach to Development Planning. North-Holland, Amsterdam.

Lall, S., Yilmaz, S. (2001). "Regional economic convergence: Do policy instruments make a difference?" Annals of Regional Science 35 (1), 151–166.

Lee, F., Coulombe, S. (1995). "Regional productivity convergence in Canada". Canadian Journal of Regional Science 18 (1), 39–56.

Levin, A., Lin, C.-F., Chu, C.-S.J. (2002). "Unit root tests in panel data: Asymptotic and final-sample properties". Journal of Econometrics 108 (1), 1–24.

Loewy, M.B., Papell, D.H. (1996). "Are U.S. regional incomes converging? Some further evidence". Journal of Monetary Economics 38 (3), 587–598.

López-Bazo, E., Vayá, E., Mora, A.J., Suriñach, J. (1999). "Regional economic dynamics and convergence in the European Union". Annals of Regional Science 33 (3), 343–370.

Lucas, R.E. (1988). "On the mechanics of economic development". Journal of Monetary Economics 22 (1), 3–42.

Magrini, S. (1999). "The evolution of income disparities among the regions of the European Union". Regional Science and Urban Economics 29 (2), 257–281.

Mankiw, G.N., Romer, D., Weil, D.N. (1992). "A contribution to the empirics of economic growth". Quarterly Journal of Economics 107 (2), 407–437.

Martin, R. (2001). "EMU versus the regions? Regional convergence and divergence in Euroland". Journal of Economic Geography 1 (1), 51–80.

Maurseth, P.B. (2001). "Convergence, technology and geography". Structural Change and Economic Dynamics 12 (3), 247–276.

Murphy, K.M., Shleifer, A., Vishny, R.W. (1989). "Industrialization and the big push". Journal of Political Economy 97 (4), 1003–1026.
Nahar, S., Inder, B. (2002). "Testing convergence in economic growth for OECD countries". Applied Economics 34 (16), 2011–2022.
Nelson, R.R., Phelps, E.S. (1966). "Investment in humans, technological diffusion, and economic growth". American Economic Review 56 (2), 69–75.
Neven, D., Gouyette, C. (1995). "Regional convergence in the European Community". Journal of Common Market Studies 33 (1), 47–65.
Niebuhr, A. (2001). "Convergence and the effects of spatial interaction". Jahrbuch für Regionalwissenschaft 21 (2), 113–133.
Nickell, S. (1981). "Biases in dynamic models with fixed effects". Econometrica 49 (6), 1417–1426.
Paci, R. (1997). "More similar and less equal: Economic growth in the European regions". Weltwirtschaftliches Archiv 133 (4), 609–634.
Paci, R., Pigliaru, F. (1995). "Differenziali di crescita tra le regioni Italiane: un'analisi cross-section". Rivista di Politica Economica 85 (10), 3–34.
Paci, R., Pigliaru, F. (1997). "Structural change and convergence: an Italian regional perspective". Structural Change and Economic Dynamics 8 (3), 297–318.
Paci, R., Pigliaru, F. (1999). "European regional growth: Do sectors matter?" In: Adams, J., Pigliaru, F. (Eds.), Economic Growth and Change. National and Regional Patterns of Convergence and Divergence. Elgar, Cheltenham.
Pissarides, C.A., McMaster, I. (1990). "Regional migration, wages and unemployment: Empirical evidence and implications for policy". Oxford Economic Papers 42 (4), 812–831.
Quah, D.T. (1993a). "Empirical cross-section dynamics in economic growth". European Economic Review 37 (2–3), 426–434.
Quah, D.T. (1993b). "Galton's fallacy and tests of the convergence hypothesis". Scandinavian Journal of Economics 95 (4), 427–443.
Quah, D.T. (1994). "One business cycle and one trend from (many,) many disaggregates". European Economic Review 38 (3–4), 605–613.
Quah, D.T. (1996a). "Convergence empirics across economies with (some) capital mobility". Journal of Economic Growth 1 (1), 95–124.
Quah, D.T. (1996b). "Regional convergence clusters across Europe". European Economic Review 40 (3–5), 951–958.
Quah, D.T. (1996c). "Empirics for economic growth and convergence". European Economic Review 40 (6), 1353–1375.
Quah, D.T. (1996d). "Ideas determining convergence clubs". LSE Economics Department Working Paper. London School of Economics.
Quah, D.T. (1997a). "Empirics for growth and distribution: Stratification, polarization, and convergence clubs". Journal of Economic Growth 2 (1), 27–59.
Quah, D.T. (1997b). "Regional cohesion from local isolated actions: I. Historical outcomes". CEP Discussion Paper No. 378. CEP, London.
Ramsey, F. (1928). "A mathematical theory of saving". Economic Journal 38 (152), 543–559.
Rey, S.J. (2001). "Spatial empirics for economic growth and convergence". Geographical Analysis 33 (3), 194–214.
Rey, S.J., Montuori, B.D. (1999). "U.S. regional income convergence: A spatial econometric perspective". Regional Studies 33 (2), 143–156.
Rivera-Batiz, L.A., Romer, P. (1991). "International trade with endogenous technological change". European Economic Review 35 (4), 971–1004.
Rodríguez-Pose, A. (1999). "Convergence or divergence? Types of regional responses to socioeconomic change". Journal of Economic and Social Geography 90 (4), 363–378.
Romer, P. (1986). "Increasing returns and long-run growth". Journal of Political Economy 94 (5), 1002–1037.

Romer, P. (1990a). "Capital, labor and productivity". Brookings Papers on Economic Activity: Microeconomics, 337–367.
Romer, P. (1990b). "Endogenous technological change". Journal of Political Economy 98 (5), S71–S102.
Romer, P. (1993). "Idea gaps and object gaps in economic development". Journal of Monetary Economics 32 (3), 543–573.
Romer, P. (1994). "The origins of endogenous growth". Journal of Economic Perspectives 8 (1), 3–22.
Sala-i-Martin, X. (1996). "Regional cohesion: Evidence and theories of regional growth and convergence". European Economic Review 40 (6), 1325–1352.
Segerstrom, P.S. (1991). "Innovation, imitation, and economic growth". Journal of Political Economy 99 (4), 807–827.
Shioji, E. (1996). "Regional growth in Japan". CEPR Discussion Paper No. 1425. CEPR, London.
Siriopoulos, C., Asteriou, D. (1998). "Testing for convergence across Greek regions". Regional Studies 32 (6), 537–546.
Solow, R.M. (1956). "A contribution to the theory of economic growth". Quarterly Journal of Economics 70 (5), 65–94.
Swan, T.W. (1956). "Economic growth and capital accumulation". Economic Record 32 (63), 334–361.
Temple, J. (1999). "The new growth evidence". Journal of Economic Literature 37 (1), 112–156.
Tomljanovich, M., Vogelsang, T.J. (2001). "Are U.S. regions converging? Using new econometric methods to examine old issues". Empirical Economics 27 (1), 49–62.
Tondl, G. (1999). "The changing pattern of regional convergence in Europe". Jahrbuch fur Regionalwissenschaft 19 (1), 1–33.
Tondl, G. (2001). Convergence after Divergence? Regional Growth in Europe. Springer-Verlag, Wien.
Tsionas, E.G. (2001). "Regional convergence and common, stochastic long-run trends: A re-examination of the U.S. regional data". Regional Studies 35 (8), 689–696.
Verspagen, B. (1991). "A new theoretical approach to catching up and falling behind". Structural Change and Economic Dynamics 2 (2), 359–380.
Vohra, R. (1996). "How fast do we grow?" Growth and Change 27 (1), 47–54.
Williamson, J.G. (1965). "Regional inequality and the process of national development: A description of the patterns". Economic Development and Cultural Change 13 (4), 3–45.

Chapter 63

SPATIAL DISTRIBUTION OF ECONOMIC ACTIVITIES IN NORTH AMERICA

THOMAS J. HOLMES[1]

University of Minnesota, USA
e-mail: holmes@econ.umn.edu

JOHN J. STEVENS

Board of Governors of the Federal Reserve System, USA
e-mail: john.j.stevens@frb.gov

Contents

[1] Also affiliated with Federal Reserve Bank of Minneapolis and National Bureau of Economic Research.

Handbook of Regional and Urban Economics, Volume 4. Edited by J.V. Henderson and J.F. Thisse

DOI: 10.1016/S0169-7218(04)07063-7

to other chapters; in particular, see the chapter by Gabaix and Ioannides (2004) in this volume.] We define a location as *specializing* in a particular industry if that location's share of employment in the industry exceeds the national average. For example, Michigan specializes in automobile production because the share of Michigan's employment that is in automobile manufacturing is approximately seven times the national share. We focus on employment to measure specialization because excellent, publicly available data exist with information on employment at the establishment level. Information about other measures of activity, such as sales or value added, is not as readily available. We provide an in-depth discussion of the potential data sources in Section 2.

We document in Section 3 that, for industries producing nontradable goods or services like retail, there is little specialization, while for tradable goods like manufactures, mining output, and agricultural products, there is a substantial amount of specialization across regions. As late as the 1950s, manufacturing activity in the United States was heavily concentrated in the Northeast and Upper Midwest around the Great Lakes, in an area often called the *manufacturing belt*. In the ensuing decades, U.S. manufacturing moved out of this northern region and into other parts of the country. We show that as of 2000, the area once delineated as the manufacturing belt in fact no longer specializes in manufacturing. In contrast, certain areas of the South have become quite specialized in manufacturing, in effect fashioning a new manufacturing belt.

We also document in Section 3 the extent of specialization among narrowly defined industries. A problem with the narrow definition of industries is that the definition may encompass only a few establishments, even at the national level. (In some cases we have as few as 10!) In such cases, the "dartboard" effect of randomness emphasized by Ellison and Glaeser (1997) potentially plays a role; we therefore use their methodology to try to control for the dartboard effect.

The new economic geography literature places great emphasis on the relation between specialization and market size. In Section 4 we report that specialization varies to a substantial degree with a particular measure of market size – the concentration of population. Obviously, specialization in farming varies inversely with the concentration of population. But, less obviously, as of 2000, rural areas specialize in manufacturing, in contrast to earlier times when manufacturing was an urban activity. Even when we exclude rural areas and look only across urban areas, we find substantial variation in specialization based on market size.

An important goal of economic research in this area should be to determine the source of specialization patterns. We have made our job easy from the start by not setting this as the goal for the chapter; however, Sections 5 and 6 do move in this direction. Section 5 discusses facts about variables that are consistently found to be correlated with industry concentration. For example, one robust fact is that industries with larger plant sizes tend to have higher levels of geographic concentration. Another robust fact is that within an industry, areas of industrial concentration tend to have larger plants. Theories that try to explain concentration should be consistent with these facts. Section 6 briefly discusses several forces that are thought to determine the location of economic activity. We illustrate these forces using two familiar examples from the economic geography literature – the beverage industry (a classic "weight-gaining" industry) and the joint-location of sugar beet processing facilities and sugar beet farms (a classic "weight-losing" industry). Interpreting these classic examples through the lens of the new economic geography literature (i.e., scale economies) reveals new insights into these industries.

2. Data

We begin with a discussion of U.S. data and then turn to a brief discussion of Canadian data. The ability to conduct cross-country analysis with North American countries has recently been enhanced by the joint adoption of the North American Industry Classification System (NAICS) by the United States, Canada, and Mexico. Before the adoption of NAICS, cross-country analysis was difficult because each country had its own classification system. In addition to having greater harmonization across countries, NAICS has greater classification detail about new and emerging industries, such as services, compared with the Standard Industrial Classification (SIC) system that it replaced in the United States. Further details about the data are available in Appendix A.

2.1. United States

This subsection begins with a discussion of the County Business Patterns (CBP) data published by the U.S. Census Bureau. These data are the primary information that we use to summarize location patterns in the United States, but they do not include information about government employment, sole proprietorships, or agriculture (crops and farm animals), so we also discuss sources for this information. We conclude by mentioning other sources of data on location patterns.

The CBP data set contains information about the location of the approximately 7 million establishments with employment in the United States. The source of these data is the Census Bureau's "Business Register" (formally called the *Standard Statistical Establishment List*). The Census Bureau updates the Business Register by conducting an annual survey of multi-establishment firms, called the *Company Organization Survey*, and by incorporating various administrative data that it receives from other government agencies, including the Internal Revenue Service.

The raw, establishment-level micro data are released annually in the form of cell counts by employment-size class, industry, and location. The employment-size classes are relatively narrowly defined (Table 1). Large establishments, defined as those with 1000 or more employees, are broken up into four relatively narrow categories. Other Census Bureau programs have only one category for establishments in the 1000-plus category. The industry information is the six-digit NAICS code, which is the highest degree of detail for establishment classification. The location information is the county identifier.[2]

[2] There is also ZIP code information, but we focus on county data. Although ZIP codes present a finer level of geographic detail than counties (there are 40,000 ZIP codes compared to 3000 counties), they are not as

Table 1
Mean employment by size category

Employment-size range	Average employment	Number of establishments
1–4	1.7	3,807,810
5–9	6.6	1,365,401
10–19	13.5	895,312
20–49	30.2	613,540
50–99	68.8	212,293
100–249	150.1	123,924
250–499	340.7	32,691
500–999	681.3	12,170
1000–1499	1208.8	3,170
1500–2499	1892.9	2,188
2500–4999	3374.7	1,138
5000 or more	9592.0	411

Source. Authors' calculations using the 2000 County Business Patterns data. Mean employment estimates for categories above 1000 use authors' algorithm discussed in Appendix A.

Figure 1 illustrates the kind of information that is available with the CBP cell counts. It plots the location of the 19 brewery establishments (NAICS industry 31212) in the United States with 500 or more employees in the 1999 CBP. The mapping program randomly assigns an establishment in a given county to some point within the polygon defined by the county boundaries. The resulting figure is called a dot density graph. County boundaries encompass a much larger area in the western states.

The small dots denote plants with 500–999 employees; the large dots represent the three plants with more than 1000 employees. As mentioned, the CBP data break up the 1000-plus size class into more detailed groupings. Only one plant is in the 2500–4999 employment-size range, and it is located in Jefferson County, Colorado. Publicly available data sources can be used to establish that this is the Coors brewery in Golden.[3] Only one plant is in the 1500–2499 category, the Anheuser–Busch plant in St. Louis, Missouri. It is against the law for the Census Bureau to present data that would disclose the operations of an individual employer. However, the Bureau does not consider cell count information to be a disclosure and has published cell counts by employment-size class for many decades. According to Census Bureau documentation [Bureau of the Census (2002a, p. vii)], "The number of establishments in an industry classification and

clean a geographic unit as counties. Some locations have multiple ZIP codes, and the definitions change over time according to the U.S. Postal Service's administrative needs. Another issue with the ZIP code data is that the establishments with more than 1000 employees are aggregated into a single employment-size class rather than the four employment-size classes used for the county data.

[3] For example, the U.S. Environmental Protection Agency's Toxic Release Inventory (TRI) data provide address and industry information for manufacturing plants with toxic releases. (See Appendix A.) The Coors plant is the only brewery in this data set in Jefferson County.

Figure 1. Location of large breweries (CBP 1999). For a colour reproduction of this figure see the colour figures section, page 3063.

the distribution of these establishments by employment-size class are not considered to be disclosures, and so this information may be released even though other information is withheld".

Because of nondisclosure requirements, the Census Bureau routinely withholds data from the information it publishes regarding total employment and payroll aggregated across establishments in the same county or state and industry. The Census Bureau requires at least three establishments in an industry/county pair before it will report total employment, but it withholds data even for industry/county pairs with hundreds of establishments. Overall, approximately 20 percent of all establishments are in industry/county pairs with withheld data. The nondisclosure issue is a severe problem if one needs to know the exact employment at a particular location. For example, if a city planner were interested in the growth in brewery employment in St. Louis from 1998 to 1999, he or she would find two establishments in this industry/county pair and would find that total employment is not disclosed. Various means to try to extract the nondisclosed employment data have been proposed, including techniques that exploit the information in the published state-level totals and further aggregated industry totals [see Gardocki and Baj (1985)]. Despite these efforts, the CBP would be of limited value in determining the exact employment growth in St. Louis breweries from 1998 to 1999.

Our interest is in documenting and understanding the location patterns of industries, and for this purpose the complete disclosure of the raw micro data, in terms of cell counts, is of substantial value. To begin with, some exercises involve combining plants into size groupings anyway, so there is literally no loss from using the public-release micro data rather than the actual Business Register. [Figure 1 is an example; see also Dinlersoz (2004).] For other exercises one might need an estimate of industry employment at a particular location. With the public-release micro data, one can straightforwardly calculate an estimate of total employment across establishments by using the mean employment in the establishment's size class from Table 1 as an estimate of establishment employment and then aggregating [Holmes and Stevens (2002), Holmes (1998)].[4] We use this procedure here; further details are available in Appendix A.

To illustrate the usefulness of these estimates for our purposes, consider the Gini coefficient for the 33 three-digit NAICS industries for which employment information is completely disclosed in every state (there are 50 remaining three-digit NAICS industries that have some data withheld). In the first column of Table 2, the Gini coefficient (discussed below) is calculated at the state level. In the second column, the Gini is constructed using the publicly available establishment-level size class data to estimate establishment employment. The Gini calculated with the estimates is virtually the same as with the actual data, even though for some states and industries the error in the employment estimate is large, as high as 20 percent in some cases. The comparison in Table 2 shows that the establishment-level data provide an excellent approximation to the results we would obtain if we were to use the confidential Business Register data at a secure Census Bureau facility. We also note that a useful property of the CBP data is that they are available in computer readable files from 1974 to the present.[5]

Although the industry coverage of the CBP is broad, it does not include information about farm establishments, government establishments, or sole proprietorships (self-employment). If one is interested in these forms of economic activity, then other data sources are required. The U.S. Department of Commerce's Bureau of Economic Analysis publishes this information under the Regional Economic Information System at the county and detailed sector levels. Data-withholding issues exist in some cases, but we already have data on private-sector employers from CBP, so all we need is government employment, agriculture employment, and proprietorships. For these three sectors, disclosure is not an issue.

The CBP does not provide data on output measures such as sales or value added. This information is collected by the Economic Census, which is conducted every five years. Henderson (1988) is an example of a study on productivity that uses the published Economic Census data. A difficulty with these data is that information for certain location/industry combinations is withheld. For sectors other than manufacturing, a complete release of cell counts is available by sales-size categories for ZIP codes. However, the size categories and industries are highly aggregated, so the cell counts are not as useful as the CBP release.

[4] Some researchers use the midpoint of the cell's range. However, the size distribution is skewed, so the mean is preferred. The mean has to be estimated for size classes above 1000 (see Appendix A).

[5] Before 1974 the CBP data are available on paper; they are used by Glaeser et al. (1992). A change was made in 1974 regarding reporting units. The methodology since then has been the same (except for the switch from SIC to NAICS in 1998).

Table 2
Comparing actual and estimated CBP data

NAICS	Industry	Gini actual data	Gini estimated data
233	Building, developing and general contracting	0.119	0.115
234	Heavy construction	0.241	0.247
235	Special trade contractors	0.097	0.096
311	Food mfg	0.279	0.284
323	Printing and related support activities	0.198	0.198
327	Nonmetallic mineral product mfg	0.191	0.192
337	Furniture and related product mfg	0.348	0.346
339	Miscellaneous mfg	0.201	0.201
421	Wholesale trade, durable goods	0.085	0.085
422	Wholesale trade, nondurable goods	0.114	0.114
441	Motor vehicle and parts dealers	0.087	0.087
442	Furniture and home furnishing stores	0.073	0.076
443	Electronics and appliance stores	0.088	0.092
444	Bldg material and garden equip and supp dealers	0.091	0.088
445	Food and beverage stores	0.073	0.073
446	Health and personal care stores	0.091	0.091
447	Gasoline stations	0.191	0.193
448	Clothing and clothing accessories stores	0.089	0.089
451	Sporting goods, hobby, book and music stores	0.097	0.096
452	General merchandise stores	0.121	0.122
453	Miscellaneous store retailers	0.066	0.066
454	Nonstore retailers	0.163	0.158
484	Truck transportation	0.201	0.199
488	Transportation support activities	0.248	0.252
541	Professional, scientific and technical services	0.163	0.157
551	Management of companies and enterprises	0.173	0.177
611	Educational services	0.226	0.211
621	Ambulatory health care services	0.075	0.074
721	Accommodation	0.302	0.304
722	Food services and drinking places	0.060	0.060
811	Repair and maintenance	0.077	0.076
812	Personal and laundry services	0.057	0.055
813	Religious, grantmaking, civic, prof and like organizations	0.094	0.094

Source. Authors' calculations using the 2000 County Business Patterns.

An important development in recent years is the increased access by outside researchers to the confidential micro data via the Census Bureau's Center for Economic Studies (CES) and the related Resource Data Centers (RDCs). Access to these data means that it is now possible to study questions that are impossible to answer with the public-establishment-level CBP data. One can examine establishment-level productivity and the link with agglomeration [Henderson (2003)]. One can link different establishments over time and examine establishment growth [Dumais, Ellison and Glaeser (2002)]. Or one can link establishments of the same firm [Holmes (2002)]. The ability to conduct such studies makes the increased access to data through the CES and RDCs an important development.

The Census Bureau data have limitations. Although one can do some things only in the Census, the reverse is also true: Some things can be done outside the Census that cannot be done inside. For example, the Census Bureau is careful about disclosure. One cannot use the Business Register to make a map like that in Figure 1. Nor can one write a paper with access to the Business Register and mention anything about Coors or Anheuser–Busch. If one is interested in exploiting establishment links across time or within the firm, or if one wishes to study plant-level productivity, one must obtain access to the confidential data. If instead one is interested in studying the distribution of employment across counties, then given the disclosure issues, not to mention the substantial expense in time and money for the Census Bureau, the use of public CBP data is probably the preferred option.

The CBP and Economic Census data discussed so far are data collected at the *establishment* level. The Census Bureau also publishes detailed geographic data based on data collected at the *individual* level as part of the decennial census. We focus on data collected at the establishment level because industry definition is generally more detailed and more reliable than it is for data collected at the individual level. Furthermore, in part of our analysis we exploit the information on establishment size in the CBP data, information that is not available in the population data. We use the establishment-level data here, but the population data are also a rich source for information on the geographic distribution of economic activity.

In addition to the Census Bureau, private companies collect information about establishment location. Dun & Bradstreet is perhaps the best known of these firms. Its data have been used recently by Rosenthal and Strange (2001) and earlier by Evans (1987) and others. An advantage of the Dun & Bradstreet data is that they are more accessible than the confidential Census Bureau data. However, "The data are not collected or organized with scientific research in mind, and there are consequently a variety of potential problems" [MacDonald (1985, p. 173)]. In particular, small firms tend to be underrepresented. Moreover, there are problems with industry definitions.[6] If one is conducting a cross-section analysis of the location of employment across counties or ZIP codes, then the public, establishment-level CBP data are superior to the Dun & Bradstreet data because the CBP data are free of charge and are of higher quality. If, instead, one needs to link establishments across time (e.g., to look at firm births), and if access to the confidential micro data is unavailable, then the Dun & Bradstreet data are a useful alternative [Rosenthal and Strange (2001)].

[6] In the Dun & Bradstreet data, administrative offices of manufacturers, for example, clearly are counted as manufacturing establishments, whereas the Census Bureau treats them by their function, i.e., a sales office is in wholesaling. This distinction may explain why the Dun & Bradstreet data consist of 670,000 manufacturing establishments, almost twice as many as recognized by the Census Bureau.

2.2. Canada

StatCan, the Canadian statistical agency, conducts the Canadian Census every five years for both population and business. It creates a database similar to the U.S. CBP database known as the Canadian Business Patterns. The employment-size cell counts are not as fine; 500 and above is a single category. We use the data in a manner similar to that for the U.S. CBP data.

StatCan data are costly relative to the U.S. CBP data. The U.S. Census Bureau places its data in the public domain, where it can be reproduced free of charge. A compact disk (CD) containing the data sells for $50. In contrast, the Canadian data are protected as intellectual property. The Canadian CD costs $1000 with an academic discount.

3. Patterns of regional specialization

This section discusses patterns of regional specialization in three parts. The first part examines patterns for broad sectors and broad regions. Here we introduce some common measures of specialization, including the employment location quotient and the locational Gini coefficient. The second part examines specialization patterns for narrowly defined industry and geographic definitions. Here the dartboard issues raised by Ellison and Glaeser (1997) are relevant, and we use their measure of concentration to classify industries. The third part gives special attention to the specialization patterns of the manufacturing sector.

3.1. Broad sectors and broad regions

We begin by describing the location of economic activity for highly aggregated geographic industries and regions. The simplest measure of geographic concentration is the *location quotient*, or LQ. Suppose there are M locations indexed by i. Let s_i denote location i's share of industry employment, and let x_i denote its share of total employment. The LQ for location i is then defined as

$$\mathrm{LQ}(i) \equiv \frac{s_i}{x_i}.$$

The LQ is therefore a ratio of a location's share of industry employment to its share of aggregate employment. Values above one mean that the location is relatively specialized in the industry, while values below one indicate that the location has less industry employment than would be predicted based on its aggregate employment share. While we typically use employment when calculating LQs, in principle we could use sales, number of establishments, or any other measure comparable across industries and regions. Tables 3 and 4 display employment LQs for major sectors of the economy by census divisions for the United States and groupings of provinces for Canada.[7] U.S. census

[7] The nine U.S. Census divisions are New England (ME, NH, VT, MA, RI, CT), Middle Atlantic (NJ, NY, PA), East North Central (OH, IN, IL, MI, WI), West North Central (MN, IA, MO, ND, SD, NE, KS), South

Table 3
Employment location quotients for the United States

	Share of national employment (%)	West South Central	East North Central	East South Central	Middle Atlantic	Mountain	New England	Pacific	South Atlantic	West North Central
Crop and Animal Production	2.38	1.47	0.87	1.83	0.38	0.99	0.28	0.96	0.71	2.35
Agriculture, Forestry, Fishing and Hunting excluding Crop and Animal Production	0.15	1.13	0.41	1.78	0.34	0.90	0.69	2.09	1.18	0.50
Mining	0.39	3.66	0.42	1.28	0.34	2.74	0.12	0.50	0.60	0.69
Utilities	0.52	1.17	1.04	0.95	1.09	1.12	1.04	0.72	0.99	1.01
Construction	4.57	1.09	0.89	1.00	0.81	1.44	0.81	1.02	1.13	0.90
Manufacturing	12.88	0.86	1.36	1.34	0.85	0.65	1.06	0.94	0.88	1.03
Wholesale Trade	4.56	0.97	1.00	0.88	1.14	0.88	0.94	1.14	0.89	1.00
Retail Trade	10.97	0.99	1.01	1.05	0.94	1.04	1.01	0.92	1.06	1.01
Transportation and Warehousing	2.68	1.12	0.98	1.06	1.07	1.03	0.68	1.05	0.90	1.02
Information	2.41	0.89	0.79	0.67	1.16	1.03	1.18	1.26	0.95	1.04
Finance and Insurance	4.46	0.84	1.00	0.75	1.34	0.88	1.35	0.92	0.91	1.02
Real Estate and Rental and Leasing	1.43	1.00	0.85	0.73	1.04	1.14	0.86	1.27	1.07	0.77
Professional, Scientific, and Technical Services	4.73	0.88	0.86	0.62	1.19	1.01	1.06	1.21	1.10	0.75
Management of Companies and Enterprises	2.07	1.01	1.17	0.82	1.21	0.74	0.99	0.94	0.86	1.03
Administrative and Support and Waste Management and Remediation Services	6.01	1.11	0.92	0.81	0.90	1.09	0.88	1.06	1.21	0.74
Educational Services	1.73	0.66	0.87	0.69	1.64	0.62	2.02	0.90	0.88	0.92
Health Care and Social Assistance	10.63	0.98	0.99	0.98	1.19	0.83	1.25	0.86	0.95	1.06
Arts, Entertainment, and Recreation	1.24	0.76	0.84	0.72	0.94	1.29	1.17	1.29	1.07	0.94
Accommodation and Food Services	7.36	0.98	0.95	0.96	0.84	1.47	0.94	1.05	1.04	0.94
Other Services	3.90	1.03	1.02	0.97	1.01	0.93	0.89	0.95	1.07	1.00
Public Administration	14.95	1.06	0.91	1.02	0.99	1.06	0.87	1.02	1.06	0.99

Source. Authors' calculations based on agriculture employment data from the BEA's REIS for 1997; Public Administration data from the U.S. Census of Governments (1997); and the 1998 County Business Patterns.

Table 4
Employment location quotients for Canada

	Share of national employment (%)	Quebec	Ontario	East	West
Crop and Animal Production	2.68	0.71	0.67	0.77	1.69
Agriculture, Forestry, Fishing and Hunting excluding Crop and Animal Production	0.96	0.92	0.28	4.25	1.20
Mining and Oil and Gas Extraction	1.09	0.41	0.32	0.97	2.29
Utilities	0.76	0.93	1.01	1.05	1.02
Construction	5.64	0.82	0.98	1.12	1.13
Manufacturing	13.96	1.26	1.18	0.78	0.64
Wholesale Trade	4.41	1.04	1.06	0.78	0.95
Retail Trade	11.27	1.01	1.00	1.06	0.98
Transportation and Warehousing	4.97	0.95	0.94	0.98	1.12
Information and Cultural Industries	2.68	0.98	1.07	0.80	0.97
Finance and Insurance	4.08	0.93	1.20	0.68	0.89
Real Estate and Rental and Leasing	1.67	0.81	1.09	0.74	1.09
Professional, Scientific, and Technical Services	6.31	0.94	1.14	0.59	0.97
Management of Companies and Enterprises	0.10	0.83	1.34	0.61	0.80
Administrative and Support and Waste Management and Remediation Services	3.89	0.87	1.10	1.07	0.95
Educational Services	6.55	1.01	0.94	1.05	1.05
Health Care and Social Assistance	9.70	1.05	0.91	1.16	1.03
Arts, Entertainment, and Recreation	1.95	0.90	1.04	0.87	1.05
Accommodation and Food Services	6.72	0.91	0.94	1.02	1.13
Other Services (except Public Administration)	4.80	1.05	0.95	1.09	1.01
Public Administration	5.81	1.08	0.89	1.45	0.96

Source. Authors' calculations based on 2001 Census Bureau data. "East" includes New Brunswick, Nova Scotia, Prince Edward Island, Newfoundland, and Labrador. "West" includes Manitoba, Saskatchewan, Alberta, British Columbia, Yukon Territory, and Northwest Territories.

divisions are roughly on the same order of magnitude in terms of population size – the largest is only three times bigger than the smallest. For Canada we use four groups: Ontario, Quebec, the eastern provinces, and the western provinces including territories. Including Quebec with the eastern provinces would make for three groups with nearly identical populations, but this would mask the obviously different industrial profiles of Quebec and the eastern provinces.

The degree of geographic concentration exhibited by certain sectors in Tables 3 and 4 is striking. First consider manufacturing. The shares of employment in manufacturing in

Atlantic (DE, MD, DC, VA, WV, NC, SC, GA, FL), East South Central (KY, TN, AL, MS), West South Central (AR, LA, OK, TX), Mountain (MT, ID, WY, CO, NM, AZ, UT, NV), and Pacific (WA, OR, CA, AK, HI). The Canadian groupings are Quebec, Ontario, the eastern provinces (New Brunswick, Nova Scotia, Prince Edward Island, Newfoundland, and Labrador), and the western provinces (Manitoba, Saskatchewan, Alberta, British Columbia, Yukon Territory, and Northwest Territories).

the East South Central and East North Central regions of the United States are nearly 35 percent greater than in the nation as a whole. (These regions have LQs of 1.34 and 1.36.) In contrast, the Mountain region, with a manufacturing LQ of 0.65, has a manufacturing share of employment that is 35 percent lower than the national share. The variations in agriculture and mining are even more dramatic. New England's LQ for agriculture is only 0.28 and for mining is only 0.12 (which happens to be the lowest LQ in the entire table). Manufacturing, mining, and agriculture are obviously sectors with substantial possibilities for trade across regions. Tables 3 and 4 indicate that these possibilities for trade are being realized as regions specialize.

The possibilities for trade in sectors like retail are relatively limited. Accordingly, there is little specialization across regions in this sector. The LQ ranges from a high of 1.06 to a low of 0.92. The government sector is also fairly evenly distributed across census divisions, but perhaps less so than one might expect. At the state level, the government sector exhibits even more concentration; for example, the effect of federal employment in the District of Columbia and the surrounding states of Maryland and Virginia becomes apparent. The LQs for educational services in the Middle Atlantic and New England regions are high, reflecting the location of many colleges and private schools in these areas.

Canada is also characterized by a significant amount of concentration. Ontario is the business capital; it specializes in manufacturing, finance and insurance, real estate, and business service industries. Quebec is the most specialized region in manufacturing, but, excluding those industries closely tied to natural resources, it otherwise resembles the nation as a whole. The combined eastern and western provinces dominate the natural resource sectors – agriculture, fishing and trapping, logging and forestry, and mining – in terms of both relative and absolute employment.

The broad picture of concentration is unchanged if we drop the government and farm sectors (not shown); the U.S. LQs typically change by no more than 0.01. Therefore, in most of what follows, we will drop the government and farm sectors since they are not a part of the U.S. CBP data set.

LQs are useful for describing which locations specialize in an industry. But if all one wishes to know is whether geographic specialization is a characteristic of a particular industry, then a single statistic that summarizes the information contained in the industry's LQs would suffice. One such statistic is the *locational Gini coefficient*. Let i index the set of M locations ordered by decreasing values of LQ. Then this coefficient is defined as

$$\text{Gini} \equiv 1 - \sum_{i=1}^{M} x_i \left(s_i + 2 \sum_{j=i+1}^{M} s_j \right).$$

The Gini coefficient takes on values in [0, 1], where a value of zero denotes equal specialization across locations and a value of one denotes extreme inequality. Kim (1995) uses Gini coefficients to show the long-run trends within U.S. manufacturing concentration. He shows that concentration increased until the turn of the twentieth century,

Table 5
Gini coefficients for the United States

	1977	1997
Agriculture	0.21	0.13
Mining	0.47	0.50
Construction	0.15	0.10
Manufacturing	0.10	0.10
Transportation	0.06	0.05
Wholesale	0.05	0.05
Retail	0.04	0.03
FIRE	0.07	0.09
Services	0.05	0.03

Source. Authors' calculations using 1977 and 1997 County Business Patterns data for major SIC industries.

flattened out, and then declined continuously from the 1930s until the end of his panel in 1987. Table 5 shows that at the sector level, the Gini coefficients changed very little over the last part of the twentieth century.[8] Unsurprisingly, mining and agricultural services have the highest Gini coefficients, while retail and services have the lowest.

3.2. Narrow industries and more detailed geography

We now turn to more narrowly defined industries and locations. The examples of specialization of the auto industry in Detroit, of high-tech in Silicon Valley and Boston's Route 128, and of gambling in Las Vegas and Atlantic City are very familiar. Here we assess the quantitative significance of specialization in industries at this level of detail.

When we examine narrowly defined industries, naturally we will find some industries with a relatively small number of plants. In an important paper, Ellison and Glaeser (1997) argue that in industries with relatively few establishments, randomness alone can create the illusion of concentration even if the underlying process that allocates establishments to locations does so uniformly. They term this the dartboard problem, drawing an analogy between the clustering of establishments in space to the random clumping of darts on a dartboard. They create an index that measures the amount of clustering over and beyond that which we would expect to find based on randomness alone. In this subsection we first discuss the EG index and then apply it to the CBP data.

The EG index is defined as

$$\gamma \equiv \frac{G - (1 - \sum_i x_i^2)H}{(1 - \sum_i x_i^2)(1 - H)}, \tag{1}$$

[8] The NAICS data begin in 1998. To make the intertemporal comparison, we use SIC code data that are available for 1977 and 1997.

where

$$G \equiv \sum_{i=1}^{M} (s_i - x_i)^2$$

is a measure of raw geographic concentration, s_i denotes the share of an industry's employment in each of M locations, x_i denotes the share of aggregate employment in each location, and

$$H \equiv \sum_{j=1}^{N} z_j^2$$

is the plant Herfindahl for the industry. Ellison and Glaeser show that if plants are randomly distributed across locations with probabilities given by x_i, then the expected value of this measure is zero. Thus, a positive value of γ indicates a level of concentration over and above what one would expect by chance.

If we define an industry at a highly aggregated level, such as all of manufacturing, the plant-level Herfindahl is essentially zero. In this case, the Ellison and Glaeser (1997) measure of concentration [or related measures like that proposed by Maurel and Sédillot (1999)[9]] collapses down to a measure of raw geographic concentration obviating the need for the EG index. This justifies our use of the easy-to-interpret Gini coefficient in the previous subsection. In narrowly defined industries with few plants, the Herfindahl may be much greater than zero, so using the EG approach will make a difference.

We use the CBP [Bureau of the Census (2002b)] data to calculate the EG index. The fact that this data set has establishment-level employment estimates permits us to estimate H. Ellison and Glaeser calculated their index for each manufacturing industry, using states as their benchmark geographic unit. Following their lead, we use states as our geographic unit, but we expand their analysis by calculating the index for all 1082 six-digit NAICS industries in the CBP data.

Table 6 summarizes these calculations by major sector. The distributions are generally quite skewed as a comparison of the mean and median values of γ suggests. The median industry within manufacturing has an index of 0.020 while the mean is 0.041. With a maximum value over manufacturing industries of 0.585, it is clear that there are some highly concentrated industries. However, in about half of the major sectors, the minimum is negative. Out of the 1082 industries, 48 have negative values for γ.

[9] Maurel and Sédillot (1999) compute an EG-type index of the form

$$\gamma^{\mathrm{MS}} \equiv \frac{G^{\mathrm{MS}}/(1 - \sum_i x_i^2) - H}{1 - H} \quad \text{where } G^{\mathrm{MS}} \equiv \sum_{i=1}^{M} (s_i^2 - x_i^2).$$

Thus, γ^{MS} looks just like the EG index but with a different measure for raw geographic concentration as discussed in their paper.

Table 6
Summary of U.S. Ellison–Glaeser indices by major sector

	Median	Mean	Minimum	Maximum	Number of industries
Agriculture, Forestry, Fishing and Hunting excluding Crop and Animal Production	0.058	0.071	0.002	0.207	15
Mining	0.137	0.204	0.002	0.909	29
Utilities	0.013	0.022	0.001	0.091	10
Construction	0.004	0.009	0.001	0.120	28
Manufacturing	0.020	0.041	−0.203	0.585	473
Wholesale Trade	0.004	0.011	−0.005	0.108	69
Retail Trade	0.002	0.005	0.000	0.056	72
Transportation and Warehousing	0.017	0.035	−0.138	0.283	54
Information	0.029	0.052	−0.010	0.314	34
Finance and Insurance	0.009	0.040	−0.041	0.237	38
Real Estate and Rental and Leasing	0.006	0.008	0.000	0.029	24
Professional, Scientific, and Technical Services	0.005	0.016	0.000	0.229	46
Management of Companies and Enterprises	0.003	0.004	0.002	0.009	3
Administrative and Support and Waste Management and Remediation Services	0.004	0.006	−0.002	0.032	43
Educational Services	0.004	0.007	−0.006	0.038	17
Health Care and Social Assistance	0.004	0.006	−0.003	0.034	39
Arts, Entertainment, and Recreation	0.015	0.030	−0.003	0.180	25
Accommodation and Food Services	0.005	0.039	0.000	0.458	15
Other Services	0.003	0.006	−0.001	0.037	48

Source. Authors' calculations based on 1999 County Business Patterns data. Geographic aggregation was at the state level. Indices were computed for every six-digit NAICS industry and then summarized by major sector.

There is an open issue concerning how one should interpret a negative γ. One idea is to interpret it as indicating a less-than-random distribution of establishments. For example, suppose we throw capitol buildings at states like darts on a dartboard with a $1/50$ probability of landing in each state (so that $s_i = 0.02$). The probability that we will observe exactly one capitol building in each state is extremely low. It is far more likely that at least some states will get more than one capitol building. Given the observed realization of one capitol building in each state, it is straightforward to calculate that $G = 0$ in this case and that $\gamma = -1/49$. In this case the negative γ gets things right at least in terms of the sign. Capitol buildings are *more* geographically dispersed than we would get from a dartboard process. This example is symmetric to the positive γ case in which a particular industry is *less* geographically dispersed than in a dartboard process.

This idea is intuitive. Some of the industries with negative values for γ are those like radio networks that we expect to be dispersed. Nonetheless, we think this issue warrants additional work, because a negative γ has no structural interpretation. In the original Ellison and Glaeser setup, the limiting case of $\gamma = 0$ is the pure dartboard model. It would be useful to generalize this structural approach to explicitly incorporate a "more dispersed than random" portion of the parameter space. In Section 6 of this chapter we return to this issue.

Table 7 displays the most and least concentrated industries for our U.S. data. Several observations are in order. In both lists, the plant Herfindahls vary greatly. A large

Table 7
Most and least concentrated industries according to EG index

	Gamma	Geographic concentration	Plant Herfindahl	Number of plants
Most concentrated				
Anthracite mining	0.909	0.912	0.058	64
Sheer hosiery mills	0.585	0.579	0.031	139
Kaolin and ball clay mining	0.561	0.587	0.075	42
Copper ore and nickel ore mining	0.553	0.596	0.121	57
Iron ore mining	0.524	0.569	0.129	36
Wineries	0.498	0.491	0.028	788
Gold ore mining	0.492	0.502	0.060	307
Phosphate rock mining	0.467	0.569	0.196	16
Casino hotels	0.458	0.450	0.012	279
Tobacco stemming and redrying	0.415	0.455	0.085	27
Carpet and rug mills	0.408	0.401	0.172	478
Oil and gas field machinery and equipment	0.394	0.387	0.011	555
Petrochemical mfg	0.380	0.400	0.048	53
Other hosiery and sock mills	0.333	0.327	0.010	412
Motion picture and video distribution	0.314	0.433	0.201	706
Least concentrated				
Laminated aluminum foil mfg for flexible pkg	−0.008	0.049	0.058	47
Cyclic crude and intermediate mfg	−0.009	0.053	0.063	57
Scale and balance (except laboratory) mfg	−0.009	0.024	0.034	119
In-vitro diagnostic substance mfg	−0.009	0.089	0.101	223
Radio networks	−0.010	0.113	0.127	339
Explosives mfg	−0.019	0.036	0.055	95
Copper wire (except mechanical) drawing	−0.021	0.041	0.062	67
Cellulose organic fiber mfg	−0.026	0.259	0.279	10
Motor vehicle air-conditioning mfg	−0.026	0.149	0.176	70
House slipper mfg	−0.026	0.178	0.204	20
Cane sugar refining	−0.040	0.073	0.110	19
Monetary authorities – central bank	−0.041	0.020	0.059	46
Other ordnance and accessories mfg	−0.044	0.188	0.230	65
Other urban transit systems	−0.138	0.269	0.365	27
Engineered wood member (exc. truss) mfg	−0.203	0.244	0.376	8
Memo				
Median	0.011			

Source. Authors' calculations based on 1999 County Business Patterns data. Geographic aggregation was at the state level.

Herfindahl is neither necessary nor sufficient for a large γ. For example, both casino hotels and scale and balance manufacturers have small Herfindahls, but only casino hotels are concentrated due to their high degree of geographic concentration. Conversely, engineered wood member manufacturers and phosphate rock mining both have relatively large Herfindahls and a large degree of geographic concentration, but only the phosphate mining is concentrated according to the EG index. Engineered wood manufacturing is an example of an industry where concentration is driven by dartboard effects. The interaction between plant concentration and geographic concentration permits a rich array of possibilities.

In addition to the negative γ issue, we mention another issue that remains open. Duranton and Overman (2002) note that the EG index, and related indices, will be downwardly biased due to the "border effect". To see how this effect arises, suppose we are computing EG indices at the state level. Then any agglomeration of economic activity that crosses the state boundary will be chopped into two pieces. For example, Gary, Indiana, is separated from Chicago, Illinois; Kansas City, Missouri, is separated from Kansas City, Kansas; and so on. This problem increases as we move to finer geographic units such as counties. To address this issue, Duranton and Overman take a unique approach afforded them by a very detailed data set on the locations of establishments in the United Kingdom. They are able to compute, with a high degree of accuracy, the universe of pairwise distances between establishments. This allows them to look at the entire distribution of plant-to-plant distances and to measure cumulative agglomeration effects at any given distance. This same approach could be used with the CBP data or ZIP code data, which, as we have argued earlier, are a form of public release of the micro data. However, note that the plant distance measures here are only an approximation, as the county or ZIP code is known, but not the precise geographic coordinates. For studying certain issues in agglomeration, like that in the automobile parts industry where the distances involved are can be fairly large (on the order of 50 to 200 miles), plant distance measures constructed from the CBP will be satisfactory. But in other cases where we are interested in a very fine degree of geographic detail, such as where shops are located within a shopping mall, these distance measures will be unsatisfactory.

3.3. Regional specialization in manufacturing

In this subsection we give special focus to the location of manufacturing activity. As discussed in the first part of this section, there is substantial regional specialization in manufacturing. Here we examine how this specialization pattern has evolved over the postwar period.

We begin with a map of the location of large manufacturing plants in the United States in 1947. Each dot in Figure 2 represents the location of a single manufacturing plant with 250 or more employees. The location data are from the 1947 Census and are analogous to the CBP data. (See Appendix A for a discussion of the data.) There were 10,219 manufacturing plants with 250 or more employees in 1947, and they ac-

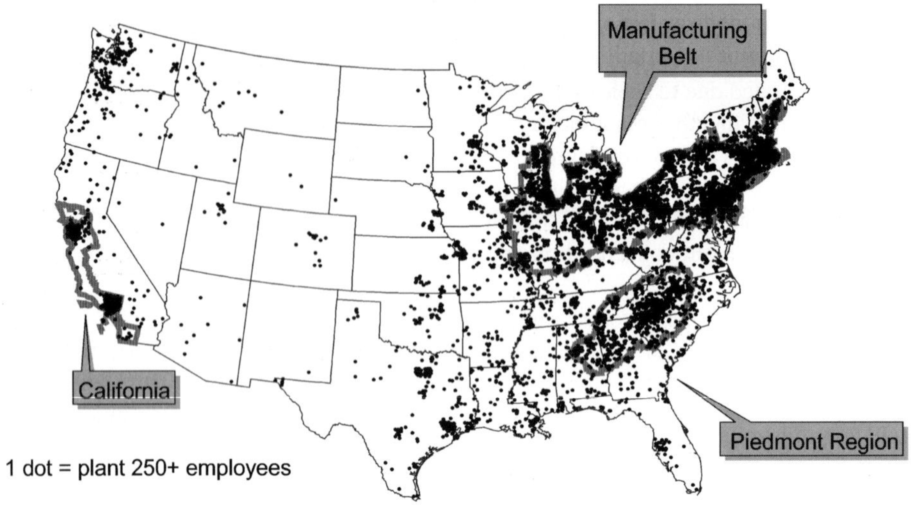

Figure 2. Location of large manufacturing plants (1947). For a colour reproduction of this figure see the colour figures section, page 3063.

counted for approximately 8.5 million employees, more than half of the 14.3 million manufacturing employees.

A striking feature of this map is the high concentration of large manufacturing plants around the Northeast and Great Lakes regions. Economic geographers have referred to this region as the *manufacturing belt*, and over the years various delineations of the boundary for this belt have been proposed. In Figure 2, we follow the definition of the manufacturing belt proposed by Fritz (1943) in the *Industrial Location and Natural Resources* volume referred to in the introduction to this chapter.[10] The same map in the Fritz work identifies two other manufacturing areas that we illustrate in Figure 2. One is the Piedmont manufacturing region in the Southeast. The other is the California manufacturing zone (which is essentially a box that connects the Bay area with Los Angeles).

Note that the three demarcated areas, while having much more manufacturing activity than the rest of the country, are not each uniformly covered with dots. In the Piedmont area, the area of heaviest concentration is well within the boundary. In the manufacturing belt, there is a large gap separating the Midwest from what geographers call *Megalopolis*, the area stretching from Washington, DC, to Boston. This gap contains the Appalachian Mountains and is part of what is designated *Appalachia*.

[10] We use county boundaries to delineate the manufacturing belt border; a county is either inside the belt or outside it. In Fritz (1943), the boundary is not based on counties. The boundary we illustrate here is the best approximation we can make using counties. A more recent alternative delineation that is very similar is in Pred (1965).

Table 8
Summary statistics for U.S. manufacturing belts in 1947 and 1999

	United States	Manufacturing belt	Piedmont	California Region	Rest of the continental U.S.
1947					
Man. emp.	14.304	10.049	0.965	0.602	2.689
Share	1.000	0.702	0.067	0.042	0.188
Est. 250+	10,217	7,152	862	378	1,825
Share	1.000	0.700	0.084	0.037	0.178
Total emp. 1950	56.148	27.675	3.098	3.302	22.072
Share	1.000	0.493	0.055	0.059	0.393
LQ man. emp.	1.000	1.425	1.222	0.715	0.427
LQ est. 250	1.000	1.420	1.529	0.629	0.454
1999					
Man. emp.	16.559	6.712	1.559	1.571	6.716
Share	1.000	0.405	0.094	0.095	0.406
Est. 250+	12,586	4780	1512	945	5349
Share	1.000	0.380	0.120	0.075	0.425
Total emp. 1950	110.088	41.920	7.540	10.620	50.008
Share	1.000	0.381	0.068	0.096	0.454
LQ man. emp.	1.000	1.064	1.375	0.983	0.892
LQ est. 250	1.000	0.997	1.753	0.778	0.936

Note. Employment in millions.

Outside of these three regions, there are a few cities with substantial manufacturing, like Minneapolis, Houston, and Dallas. But much of the rest of the country is essentially devoid of large manufacturing plants. North Dakota, Nevada, and Wyoming have only two such plants, and New Mexico has only one plant.

Of course, states like North Dakota also have extremely low populations and low overall employment. Table 8 presents information about the distribution of manufacturing plants, manufacturing employment, and total employment. In 1947, the manufacturing belt accounted for 70 percent of large manufacturing plants and 70 percent of overall manufacturing employment across all sizes of plants. But it accounted for 49 percent of total employment, so the LQ is 1.42 for each measure of manufacturing activity. The Piedmont region accounted for 8.4 percent of large plants and 6.7 percent of overall manufacturing employment. The LQ for the Piedmont region is 1.53 with activity measured by the number of large manufacturing plants and 1.22 for activity measured by total manufacturing employment. These numbers indicate that manufacturing employment in the Piedmont area in 1947 tended to be in larger plants compared with the nation as a whole. In contrast, the California region had a smaller share in large plants than its share of the total employment, and so it has an LQ of less than one.

Figure 3 presents the analogous map of the location of large manufacturing plants (250 or more employees) for 1999. For 1999 there are 12,586 plants, about 20 percent

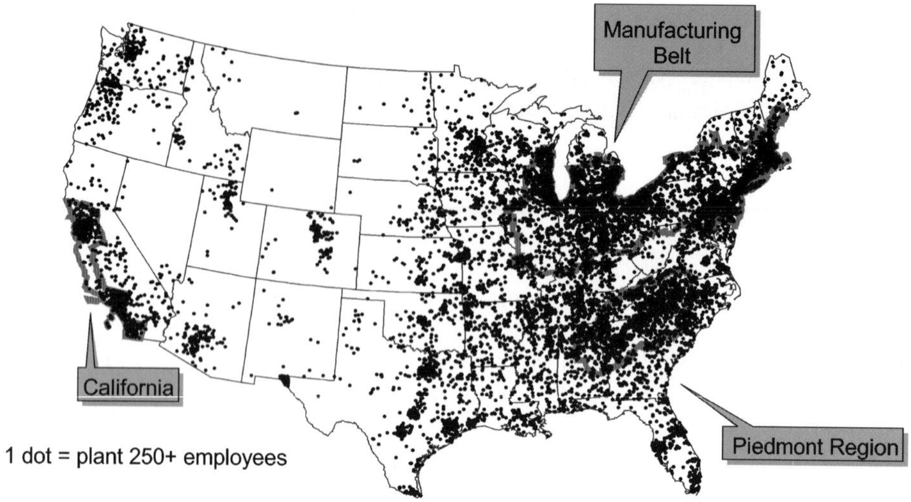

Figure 3. Location of large manufacturing plants (1999). For a colour reproduction of this figure see the colour figures section, page 3064.

more than the 10,217 in 1947.[11] The similarities are impressive. Concentration is still heavy in the Megalopolis and around the Great Lakes. The Piedmont region in the South remains an area of high concentration, and Appalachia is still devoid of manufacturing.

But the contrast is also impressive. Manufacturing is clearly much more dispersed. There are only approximately 2000 more plants, but it seems like many more because they are much more spread out. The big stories here are states like Tennessee, which had little manufacturing in 1947, but now has an extremely high manufacturing presence. Similar stories can be told for Arkansas and Mississippi. Prairie states like the Dakotas and Nebraska have also had substantial increases in manufacturing.

Table 8 presents the shares for the various regions. The decline in the manufacturing belt is striking. Notice that the manufacturing belt lost a third of its employment and a third of its large manufacturing establishments. This decline is masked in a comparison of Figures 2 and 3 as the spreading out of plants in the 1999 figure gives the illusion that there are more plants. It is notable that the manufacturing LQ for the manufacturing belt equals one in 1999. The term *manufacturing belt* is no longer appropriate for this area. Note that manufacturing remains concentrated in the Piedmont area. The LQs for this area, already bigger than one in 1947, increased further. Finally, note that the LQ for the residual region (in plants with 250 or more employees) rose from 0.45 in 1947 to more than 0.9 in 1999; the residual region now looks much more like the nation as a whole than it did in 1947.

[11] It is interesting to note that total employment is lower, so mean size conditional on being above 250 is lower.

We conclude that between 1947 and 1999, the manufacturing belt experienced a significant decrease in manufacturing, whereas areas with low manufacturing increased their level of manufacturing, and the southern area, which was already concentrated in 1947, further increased in concentration.

4. Specialization by urbanization

The composition of economic activity varies substantially across big cities, small cities, and rural areas. It is obvious that certain types of economic activities in big cities (e.g., Broadway plays, stock exchanges) are very different from the activities in rural areas (e.g., dairy farms). But there are also differences between medium-sized cities and small cities. In his classic work on central place theory, Christaller (1966) shows how the range and type of goods that can be found in the city differs systematically by the size of the city [see also Berry (1967)]. Another important reference that documents the strong specialization patterns with city size is Henderson (1988). This section follows in the tradition of this earlier work and lays out the specialization patterns by degree of urbanization in the United States and Canada at the turn of the 21st century.

4.1. A measure of urbanization

We begin by defining a county-based measure of urbanization used previously in Holmes (1999). For each county i and j, we determine the distance d_{ij} between the two in miles.[12] We define the neighborhood of county i to be

$$N_i = \{j \mid \text{such that } d_{ij} \leqslant 30\}.$$

This neighborhood includes counties within 30 miles of county i, including county i itself. Define the *neighboring population of i* to be the total population of all the counties in N_i. We use population as determined by the 2000 Census.

A more common method of classifying locations by city size is to use metropolitan statistical areas (MSAs) defined by the Census Bureau. The MSA classification system is convenient for many purposes, and we often use it in our own work. When we redo the analysis below with the MSA classification system, we obtain similar results. We choose to report the results with the neighboring population definition because we think it is preferable for the particular exercise we conduct. The MSA classification system treats all geographic points in a metropolitan area equally, even though they can be quite different. For example, the New York consolidated MSA includes high-density Manhattan as well as relatively low-density portions of northeastern Pennsylvania. In addition, definitional issues arise as to whether San Francisco and Oakland should be

[12] We use the longitude and latitude coordinates for each county provided in the 2000 Census. In most cases this is the geographic centroid, but in other cases it is just some point lying within the county.

considered a part of the same MSA. Ciccone and Hall (1996) raise these issues and argue that population density is the appropriate way to measure concentration of people. However, county boundaries can vary in arbitrary ways, and these boundaries can have a big influence on a measure of population density. Furthermore, density at a particular point may not be all that is relevant; population nearby this point may also matter. An ideal measure for our purposes is one that takes each geographic point and counts the exact number of people within a fixed distance from that point. Our county-based measures fall short of this ideal because county boundaries are arbitrary – the neighborhood N_i defined above does not form a perfect circle. However, for the purposes at hand the approximation is a reasonable one as discussed further in Holmes (1999).

The variation in neighboring population is quite dramatic. Using the data from the 2000 Census, the maximum value is 15.4 million and is attained in Hudson County, New Jersey. This is across the river from Manhattan (neighboring population 15.0 million). The lowest value, 67, is obtained for Loving County, Texas. Weighting by population, the median value is 1.2 million. Thus, half of the U.S. population lives in a county with neighboring population of 1.2 million or greater.

Our interest is in how city specialization varies by city size. As before, we use employment to measure economic activity. We divide the total U.S. employment of 165 million into quartiles based on the neighboring population of the location of employment. This partitions the United States into four parts each with 25 percent of total U.S. employment.[13] We henceforth refer to these groups as *urbanization quartiles*.

Table 9 presents summary statistics for the quartiles. While each quartile has 25 percent of total U.S. employment, the quartiles differ dramatically in land mass. The bottom quartile has approximately 87 percent of the U.S. land mass, and the top quartile

Table 9
Summary statistics for city size groups

	Quartile 1	Quartile 2	Quartile 3	Quartile 4
Maximum neighboring population (millions)	0.421	1.369	3.426	15.369
Number of counties	2432	468	151	59
Percent of land area	87.2	8.3	3.6	0.9
Percent of employment	25.0	25.0	24.8	25.2
Percent of population	27.7	25.3	23.6	23.5
Employment as a percent of population	53.0	58.0	61.8	62.9
Percent of population 65 or older	14.0	12.6	11.6	11.2
Percent college graduate of population 25–34 years old	18.5	25.6	31.0	34.6

Note. The data on land area, population, and population characteristics are all from the 2000 Decennial Census.

[13] Lumpiness in county employment size prevents an exactly equal division. The percentages for the four groups are 25.0, 25.0, 24.6, and 25.4.

has less than 1 percent. While the bottom quartile has a slightly higher share of population at 27.7 percent, the top quartile has a slightly lower share of population at 23.4 percent. This pattern reflects the fact that employment as a percentage of the population is higher in large cities than in rural areas, rising from 53 percent in the bottom quartile to 62.9 percent in the most urban quartile. In part, this difference is because the rural population is older and more likely to be retired. As shown in the table, 14 percent of the rural population is 65 or older while only 11 percent of the most urban population is 65 or older. The table also shows that individuals in urban areas tend to be much better educated than their counterparts in rural areas. From this we can anticipate that there will be relatively more white collar jobs in urban areas compared to rural areas.

4.2. Specialization

Table 10 presents LQs for the major sectors in each of the four urbanization quartiles.[14] Since each quartile has 25 percent of all employment by definition, the sum of the location quotients across the four quartiles must add up to four. In particular, if all of an industry's employment is in a given urbanization quartile, then the LQ in that quartile will be four and the rest will be zero. The final column shows the difference between LQ_4 and LQ_1. We define this difference as a summary measure of an industry's tendency to locate in more urban locations. The table is sorted in terms of increasing urbanization. Table 11 presents industries defined at the narrowest level possible (six-digit NAICS). In this table we present the ten narrowly defined industries that are least urbanized as well as the ten most urbanized. For these examples the degree of specialization is extreme. The six-digit industry iron ore mining has an LQ_1 of approximately four, meaning that virtually the entire industry is in the least urbanized quartile. At the other extreme the six-digit commodities exchange industry has an LQ_4 of approximately four, meaning that virtually the entire industry is in the top quartile.

Turning back to Table 10 for the major sectors, notice that there is a gap in the urbanness measure between −0.36 and −0.22 and again between 0.20 and 0.57. We use these gaps to define three groups of sectors. The sectors with urbanness below −0.36 we call *rural sectors*. The sectors above 0.57 we call *urban sectors*. The sectors in the intermediate range between −0.22 and 0.20 are *diffuse sectors*.

Consider first the rural sectors. Observe that with one exception, the LQ monotonically declines across the urbanization quartiles. The one exception is mining, where the LQ increases from 0.28 to 0.44 from quartile 3 to quartile 4; in both quartiles the LQ is quite small. It is no surprise to see agricultural sectors and mining classified as rural sectors. It may be more of a surprise to see manufacturing in this group. In earlier days manufacturing activity was associated with cities. In the U.S. economy today,

[14] This is the same set of sectors used in Section 3.1 with the addition of proprietorships as an additional sector of employment. This sector consists of self-employed individuals. Unfortunately, the data for proprietorships are not broken down by industry, or we would have allocated this employment to each of the various sectors.

Table 10
Distribution of employment across density quartiles (major sectors sorted by urbanness of industry)

NAICS	Description	Share of total employment	LQ_1	LQ_2	LQ_3	LQ_4	Sector urbanization (LQ_4–LQ_1)
Rural							
111–112	Crop and Animal Production	0.019	2.75	0.85	0.31	0.08	−2.67
113–115	Agriculture, Forestry, Fishing and Hunting excluding Crop and Animal Production	0.001	2.60	0.91	0.34	0.16	−2.43
21	Mining	0.002	2.50	0.78	0.28	0.44	−2.06
31	Manufacturing	0.100	1.18	1.13	0.93	0.76	−0.43
22	Utilities	0.004	1.22	1.04	0.90	0.84	−0.39
–	Government	0.138	1.22	1.04	0.89	0.86	−0.36
Diffuse							
44	Retail Trade	0.090	1.08	1.07	1.00	0.86	−0.22
–	Proprietorships	0.156	1.13	0.97	0.97	0.93	−0.21
72	Accommodation and Food Services	0.060	1.03	1.04	1.06	0.87	−0.16
62	Health Care and Social Assistance	0.085	1.04	1.01	0.96	0.99	−0.05
23	Construction	0.040	0.89	1.08	1.14	0.89	0.00
99	Unclassified Establishments	0.001	1.07	0.85	0.96	1.11	0.04
71	Arts, Entertainment and Recreation	0.011	0.84	0.97	1.17	1.03	0.19
81	Other Services (except Public Administration)	0.032	0.87	1.05	1.02	1.07	0.20
Urban							
48	Transportation and Warehousing	0.023	0.73	0.93	1.03	1.31	0.57
42	Wholesale Trade	0.037	0.66	0.93	1.14	1.26	0.61
53	Real Estate and Rental and Leasing	0.012	0.67	0.90	1.12	1.31	0.65
95	Auxiliaries (exc. Corporate, Subsidiary and Regional mgt)	0.006	0.61	0.89	1.20	1.30	0.69
56	Admin, Support, Waste mgt, Remediation Services	0.053	0.57	1.00	1.18	1.26	0.69
52	Finance and Insurance	0.036	0.62	0.92	1.13	1.33	0.71
61	Educational Services	0.015	0.68	0.94	0.98	1.40	0.72
51	Information	0.021	0.57	0.81	1.14	1.48	0.91
55	Management of Companies and Enterprises	0.017	0.35	0.90	1.27	1.48	1.13
54	Professional, Scientific and Technical Services	0.041	0.46	0.78	1.11	1.64	1.17

Table 11
Distribution of employment across density quartiles (top 10 and bottom 10 detailed industries sorted by urbanness of industry)

NAICS	Description	LQ_1	LQ_2	LQ_3	LQ_4	Industry urbanization (LQ_4–LQ_1)
Bottom ten						
212210	Iron ore mining	3.94	0.03	0.03	0.00	−3.93
212111	Bituminous coal and lignite surface mining	3.71	0.20	0.09	0.01	−3.70
212222	Silver ore mining	3.67	0.31	0.01	0.01	−3.66
321212	Softwood veneer and plywood mfg	3.65	0.28	0.08	0.00	−3.65
212324	Kaolin and ball clay mining	3.49	0.41	0.10	0.00	−3.49
325182	Carbon black mfg	3.60	0.17	0.06	0.17	−3.43
115111	Cotton ginning	3.43	0.47	0.09	0.01	−3.42
315291	Infants' cut and sew apparel mfg	3.47	0.40	0.05	0.08	−3.39
212112	Bituminous coal underground mining	3.36	0.49	0.14	0.01	−3.35
113310	Logging	3.37	0.48	0.13	0.02	−3.35
Top ten						
512199	Other motion picture and video industries	0.20	0.32	0.45	3.02	2.82
512191	Teleproduction and other postproduction services	0.09	0.29	0.66	2.95	2.86
523110	Investment banking and securities dealing	0.05	0.24	0.73	2.96	2.91
523130	Commodity contracts dealing	0.11	0.31	0.41	3.15	3.04
522293	International trade financing	0.09	0.10	0.54	3.25	3.16
512120	Motion picture and video distribution	0.07	0.30	0.29	3.31	3.24
483112	Deep sea passenger transportation	0.03	0.30	0.19	3.44	3.41
512220	Integrated record production, distribution	0.03	0.25	0.21	3.48	3.45
485112	Commuter rail systems	0.17	0.00	0.04	3.75	3.57
523210	Securities and commodity exchanges	0.00	0.00	0.06	3.90	3.90

rural areas are net exporters of manufactured goods, while large cities are net importers. For this sector, the LQ is 1.18 and 1.13 in the bottom quartiles and 0.93 and 0.76 in the top quartiles. Thus, both of the bottom quartiles tend to specialize in manufacturing in contrast to the agricultural sectors, where just the very bottom quartile has an LQ above one. Also among the rural sectors are utilities and government. The utility sector is a small sector (0.4 percent of the employment) and consists primarily of power plants, which tend to locate disproportionately in rural areas. Government employment is a large sector of the economy. The fact that government concentrates in rural areas initially came as a surprise to us. We suspect this might have something to do with the absence of economies of scale in rural areas for various government services such as education. Also, some government activity, such as military bases and national parks, tends to be in rural areas.

Next consider the diffuse sectors. These consist of the types of goods, such as retail and health care, that are generally regarded as nontraded goods. Even though the LQs for these sectors are fairly close to one in all urbanization quartiles, there are some patterns in the data. The LQ for retail is 1.08 in quartile 1 and monotonically declines to 0.86 in quartile 4. Analogously, the LQ for health care takes on its highest value of 1.04 in the most rural quartile. One factor contributing to this pattern is that less urbanized areas have a higher ratio of population to employment as noted above. (Retired people shop and require medical attention even if they do not work.) Furthermore, the inability to exploit economies of scale in rural areas also plays some role. (More employment is needed to provide a given service level.) Note that there is a slight tendency for proprietorship employment to be concentrated in rural areas, also presumably due to the absence of scale economies in rural areas, which tends to favor small-scale enterprises.

Finally, consider the urban sectors. Without exception, the LQ monotonically increases in urbanness for all of these sectors. This group of sectors includes service-type goods such as wholesale trade, finance, and business services. It also includes transportation, because major transportation hubs are concentrated in big cities. It is interesting that all of the new sectors of the economy added through NAICS, such as "Information and Professional Services", are urban industries.

In the top half of Table 12, we combine all the rural sectors and similarly all the diffuse and all the urban sectors. The total employment share of the rural industries is 0.26. By coincidence, the total employment of the urban sectors is also 0.26. The remaining diffuse group accounts for 0.48. The table reports the weighted average of the LQs for each group. For the rural sectors, on average the LQ falls from 1.33 in quartile 1 to 0.76 in quartile 4, a fall on the order of 50 percent. In the urban sectors, on average the LQ increases from 0.58 in quartile 1 to 1.38 in quartile 4, an increase of approximately 70 percent. These values indicate that for over half of the economy, there is substantial specialization by the degree of urbanization.

In the bottom half of Table 12, we conduct a similar exercise using narrow industries rather than broad sectors. We sorted narrow industries by the urbanization measure, and – to be comparable to what we did with the broad sectors – picked cutoffs to get approximately one quarter of employment classified in rural industries and one quarter

Table 12
Distribution of employment by groups and urbanness quartile

NAICS	Share of total employment	LQ_1	LQ_2	LQ_3	LQ_4	Industry urbanization (LQ_4–LQ_1)
Major sectors						
Rural	0.264	1.33	1.06	0.86	0.76	−0.57
Diffuse	0.474	1.05	1.02	1.01	0.93	−0.12
Urban	0.262	0.58	0.91	1.13	1.38	0.79
Narrow industries						
Rural	0.282	1.45	1.06	0.81	0.68	−0.78
Diffuse	0.451	1.02	1.04	1.02	0.93	−0.09
Urban	0.266	0.50	0.88	1.16	1.46	0.96

in urban industries.[15] The quantitative results with narrow industry definitions are fairly close to what we got with the broad definitions at the sector level. For example, using the broad sectors, and looking at the top quarter of industries, we see that the LQ increases from 0.58 in the bottom quartile of locations to 1.38 in the top quartile. This change is similar to the increase from 0.50 to 1.46 we get with the narrowly defined industries. We conclude that the main pattern of specialization occurs at the broad sector level.

This result may come as a bit of a surprise, because we know that in *some* of the most narrowly defined sectors we see the highest specialization. But there is an offsetting factor as well. Consider, for example, the major sector "Finance and Insurance". Its index of urbanization is 0.71, making it one of the most urbanized sectors. Within this sector are the narrow industries "Commodity Contracts Dealing" and "Commodity Exchanges" that are extremely concentrated in the largest cities with indices of 3.04 and 3.90. But this sector also has industries such as "Consumer Lending" and "Commercial Banking" that are relatively spread out, having indices of 0.10 and 0.14. We conclude that within a broad industry there are some narrow industries that provide retail-like services that are spread out and other industries that are tradable and specialized.

So far we have ignored the dartboard issues highlighted by Ellison and Glaeser (1997). These effects of chance are important when a small number of establishments are allocated across a large number of locations. Here we have only four locations, all of equal size. In the case where industries are defined at the sector level, all industries have a large number of establishments. If establishments in these sectors were randomly assigned to the locations with a 25 percent probability, the resulting location quotients would be close to one, as we have verified by simulation exercises. Thus, the specialization illustrated in Table 12 for major sectors has nothing to do with dartboard issues. In the case of narrowly defined industries, some industries have relatively few establishments, even as few as 10 or 11 in some instances. In such cases, the dartboard issues

[15] It is not exactly one quarter because of lumpiness in the industries.

emphasized by Ellison and Glaeser (1997) have a greater potential to play a role. Nevertheless, we have done some simulation analysis at the level of narrow industries and found that these dartboard issues are not quantitatively significant for our case. This should not be much of a surprise since the median industry has over 1000 establishments and these establishments are being allocated across only four locations. In such a situation we expect the law of large numbers to be in force, in which case the random factors average out.

4.3. *Canadian data*

Having examined the U.S. data, we now turn to the Canadian data. We classify the 288 Canadian census divisions in the same way that we classified the 3000 U.S. counties on the basis of neighboring population. (Here we use population from the 2001 Census.)[16] From Table 9, the cutoffs for neighboring population that define the quartiles are used to define the quartiles for the United States. In the United States, the median county, weighted by total employment, has 1.4 million in neighboring population. In Canada, the median census division has 1 million in neighboring population, again weighted by employment. The 75th percentile is 3.5 million for the United States and 3.5 million for Canada. Differences emerge at the 25th percentile; 0.4 million for the United States and 0.2 million for Canada.

Table 13 reports the LQs for Canada, sorting industries by the urbanization index LQ_4—LQ_1, as before. For the most part, the pattern of location for the Canadian industries is very similar to the pattern for the United States. With two exceptions, the urban sectors in the United States are urban sectors in Canada. The education sector is not an urban sector in Canada, but that is due to a discrepancy in data collection. In Canada, education includes public schools, and employment is disproportionately high in rural areas because of the lack of economies of scale. In the United States such employment is treated as government employment. So the education sector in the United States is largely university employment, which is concentrated in big cities. The other exception is " Transportation and Warehousing".

Turning to the industries that were classified as rural in the United States, the major exception in Canada is manufacturing. This is an urban industry in Canada. In Canada, the manufacturing base has been maintained in major urban areas (e.g., Toronto and Montreal) in a way that is different from that in the United States.

We can also compare the United States and Canada for more detailed industry definitions. The highest level of comparable detail is the four-digit NAICS. At this level of detail, there are approximately 300 industries.[17] We calculated the LQ for each ur-

[16] For locations in Canada near the U.S. border, we count as neighbors only Canadian locations. This is analogous to what we did when calculating neighboring population in the United States.

[17] The Canadian Business Patterns data include industries such as Crop Farming and Livestock Farming that are not in the U.S. County Business Patterns data. There are 321 four-digit NAICS industries in the Canadian Business Patterns and 290 in the U.S. CBP.

Table 13
Location quotients for Canada

NAICS	Description	Share of total employment	LQ_1	LQ_2	LQ_3	LQ_4	Sector urbanization (LQ_4–LQ_1)
113–115	Agriculture, Forestry, Fishing and Hunting excluding Crop and Animal Production	0.009	3.24	0.41	0.38	0.05	−3.19
21	Mining and Oil and Gas Extraction	0.012	2.07	0.64	1.38	0.09	−1.99
111–112	Crop and Animal Production	0.011	2.07	1.25	0.63	0.13	−1.94
61	Educational Services	0.046	1.77	1.02	0.76	0.50	−1.27
91	Public Administration	0.039	1.06	1.50	0.97	0.52	−0.54
62	Health Care and Social Assistance	0.093	1.26	1.09	0.93	0.75	−0.51
48–49	Transportation and Warehousing	0.039	1.13	1.06	1.07	0.78	−0.34
72	Accommodation and Food Services	0.084	1.14	1.03	1.04	0.82	−0.32
44–45	Retail Trade	0.117	1.10	1.02	1.03	0.87	−0.22
23	Construction	0.064	1.05	1.05	1.08	0.85	−0.21
71	Arts, Entertainment and Recreation	0.018	0.96	0.89	1.25	0.93	−0.03
81	Other Services (except Public Administration)	0.041	0.97	1.05	1.04	0.95	−0.02
22	Utilities	0.005	0.73	1.53	0.83	0.89	0.16
31–33	Manufacturing	0.145	0.90	1.07	0.85	1.14	0.24
53	Real Estate and Rental and Leasing	0.025	0.74	0.90	1.24	1.14	0.40
55	Management of Companies and Enterprises	0.016	0.60	0.89	1.11	1.36	0.75
52	Finance and Insurance	0.044	0.60	1.01	0.89	1.43	0.84
56	Administrative and Support, Waste Management and Remediation Services	0.043	0.59	0.83	1.05	1.47	0.88
41	Wholesale Trade	0.061	0.62	0.84	0.97	1.51	0.89
54	Professional, Scientific and Technical Services	0.065	0.40	0.73	1.34	1.50	1.10
51	Information and Cultural Industries	0.022	0.49	0.71	1.06	1.66	1.17

banization quartile for each industry for both Canada and the United States. The construction sector and the wholesaling sectors are apparently not harmonized yet so we can only directly link up 256 industries. For these industries, we compared the urbanization measure (i.e., LQ_4–LQ_1) in the two countries and found a correlation of 0.65. This indicates a strong tendency for the pattern of concentration to be the same in the two countries.

5. Some facts about specialized industries

The preceding two sections focused on characterizing the extent to which various industries are concentrated. In this section we present selected facts about concentrated industries. We make two kinds of comparisons. First, we look *across* industries. We compare the characteristics of industries that have high geographic concentration with those that have low geographic concentration. Second, we look *within* industries. Here we compare establishments in the same industry across locations. We compare these plants in areas of concentration with plants in the same industry in isolated locations.

5.1. Across industry comparisons

In this subsection we discuss two industry characteristics that have been found to be associated with high industry concentration. The two characteristics are *establishment size* and *materials intensity*. Using two-digit level manufacturing data for the United States over the period 1880–1987, Kim (1995) reports a positive correlation between geographic concentration and both establishment size and materials intensity. Table 14 uses the EG indices constructed in Section 3 to illustrate these tendencies.

The first set of figures reported in Panel A are calculated with the set of all 1082 NAICS six-digit level industries from the 1999 CBP. Each industry is classified by average establishment employment size. The 1082 industries are divided into four categories based on employment size so that the number of industries in each category is close to being the same as is feasible. The table reports that the average employment size in the bottom quartile of industries is 6.6 employees per establishment, and this rises to 167.2 in the top quartile of industries. The table also reports the mean EG index among the industries in each quartile. The mean rises from 0.027 in the bottom quartile to 0.062 in the top quartile, a sharp increase. This pattern has a fairly straightforward explanation. Industries with large establishments tend to be manufacturing industries while industries with small establishments tend to be retail and services. The industry with the largest average size (2400 employees), "Guided Missile Manufacturing", has a γ of 0.13. The industry with the smallest average size (2.4 employees), "Footwear Repair", has a γ of 0.005. As discussed in Section 3, manufacturing industries tend to have large EG indices, while the EG indices are close to zero for retail and services. This result reflects the fact that manufacturing industries tend to be industries with trade (and, hence, specialization) compared to retail and services.

Table 14
Variation in industry characteristics by degree of concentration

Panel A. Plant size (employment per plant)

	All industries		Manufacturing industries only	
Quartile	Average size	Mean EG	Average size	Mean EG
1	6.6	0.015	25.0	0.027
2	16.1	0.025	48.4	0.035
3	41.2	0.034	80.3	0.040
4	167.2	0.060	268.0	0.062

Panel B. Materials intensity (materials as a fraction of total sales)

	Manufacturing industries	
Quartile	Mean	Mean EG
1	0.35	0.027
2	0.45	0.032
3	0.52	0.040
4	0.66	0.065

Note. Panel B can be constructed only for manufacturing. "EG" refers to the Ellison–Glaeser (1997) index of geographic concentration.

The second set of figures in Panel A restricts attention to the 473 different six-digit NAICS manufacturing industries and defines quartiles in this subset as before. The average concentration index increases with average establishment size, just as it does when we consider the entire cross-section of all industries. The manufacturing industry with the smallest average size (5.3 employees), "Dental Laboratories", has a γ of 0.002. The next two on the list are "Retail Baking" ($\gamma = 0.007$) and "Quick Printing" ($\gamma = 0.001$). These manufacturing industries with very small establishment sizes are obviously "retail-like" in their nature, and so it is not surprising that they tend to be geographically dispersed.

We next consider materials intensity, which, following Kim (1995) and Holmes (1999, p. 314), we define to be purchased inputs as a percentage of total sales. This information is available only for manufacturing.[18] Panel B classifies manufacturing industries into quartiles by the materials ratio. The average value of the concentration index increases from 0.027 in the bottom quartile to 0.065 in the top. Industries with very high materials ratios tend to be first-stage processors of raw materials located near the source of these raw materials (and, hence, are geographically concentrated). For example, the industry with the highest share (0.88), "Soybean Processing", has $\gamma = 0.07$.

It is possible to make other cross-section comparisons. For example, if we classify the 1082 six-digit NAICS industries in the CBP data into quartiles by average pay per

[18] The data we use are from the 1997 Census of Manufactures.

employee, the resulting average γ increases from 0.015 in the bottom quartile to 0.060 in the top quartile. This result is not surprising, since manufacturing tends to be high-pay and concentrated, while retail is low-pay and dispersed. Interestingly, if we construct quartiles with just manufacturing, we get something of a U-shaped relationship with the quartiles defined by pay. At the top of the pay scale are industries like Petrochemical Manufacturing and Guided Missile Manufacturing that tend to be highly concentrated (γ equal to 0.38 and 0.13). But at the bottom of the pay scale are textile industries, and these also tend to be geographically concentrated.

5.2. *Within industry comparisons*

Within industries, establishment size, plant turnover, productivity, and plant specialization all vary across locations. These variations are related to the degree of local industry concentration. Holmes and Stevens (2002) find a positive correlation between an establishment's size and local industry concentration. This correlation persists in virtually every major sector of the economy and for various degrees of industry and geographic aggregation. Importantly, it remains even after controlling for an establishments's own effect on local concentration. In the manufacturing sector, for example, "plants in the highest quintile of the own-plant excluded measure of concentration are on average 64% larger than plants in the lowest quintile" [Holmes and Stevens (2002, p. 683)].

Dumais, Ellison and Glaeser (2002) examine the relationship between industry concentration and establishment turnover. Using plant-level data from the Census Bureau's Longitudinal Research Database, they find that plant births tend to disperse employment away from concentrated areas, whereas plant closures tend to reinforce existing concentrations. They also report that even though aggregate levels of concentration have remained constant, over time there is some shift in the centers of concentration. They suggest that small, young plants with high turnover that exist outside centers of concentration may serve as experimental draws in a search process for new centers of concentration.

There is a long-standing debate on the relative importance on productivity of localization (having many own-industry neighbors) versus urbanization (having many neighbors from any industry).[19] Early work, such as Sveikauskas (1975) and Segal (1976), reports evidence on the importance of urbanization. Later, Henderson (1986) reports evidence on the importance of localization. Using Census micro data, Henderson (2003) expands this work in a number of directions. In particular, he permits the relationship between productivity and city and industry size to differ by plant type (single plant firms or corporate plant), considers alternative sources of spillovers (employment, number of plants, and plant births), and introduces a time dimension to allow for what he calls "dynamic externalities". From this rich structure he finds that manufacturing externalities are very local and depend on the number of plants in the same industry and same

[19] External effects may also operate at the worker level. For example, Glaeser and Maré (2001) find that cities seem to speed the accumulation of human capital.

county. For static externalities, this result holds for both single plant firms and corporate plants, while for dynamic externalities it seems to matter more for single plant firms. Another approach is to look at density of employment rather than levels of employment. Ciccone and Hall (1996, p. 54) find that "a doubling of employment density increases average labor productivity by around 6 percent".

One potential benefit of agglomeration is that the greater concentration of similar firms may result in a local network of intermediate goods providers and more specialization among firms. Evidence from Holmes (1999) shows that purchased inputs as a percentage of the value of output is greater in locations where local industry concentration is higher: "a plant with anywhere from 10,000 to 25,000 in own-industry neighboring employment has a purchased-input intensity that, on average, is three percentage points higher than a plant with fewer than 500 in own-industry neighboring employment" [Holmes (1999, p. 314)]. Ono (2001) also reports a connection between outsourcing and concentration.

6. Understanding the location of industry

This chapter has focused on presenting basic facts about patterns of industry location; it leaves to other chapters the job of discussing theories of firm location and their empirical importance. Nonetheless, we think it is useful to include a section that reports some observations related to the issue of *why* industries concentrate. In this discussion, we focus on three factors that affect the location of industry: natural advantage, what we call the *concentrated market factor*, and government policy. We recognize that there are other factors at work, but again we are relying on other chapters for a more comprehensive discussion of these factors.

6.1. Natural advantage

Locations differ in innate physical attributes, such as climate, soil, minerals, and access to deep water ports. Differences in such natural advantages can lead to specialization. This follows from the standard analysis of Ricardian comparative advantage.

The natural advantage force is obviously of overwhelming importance in agriculture, an industry with a substantial degree of specialization. Figure 4 presents a dot density map for selected crops. (Each dot represents 50,000 tons of a particular crop.) Different colored dots represent different crops. Observe that for most of the crops, the colored dots demarcate areas with sharp boundaries. For example, the eastern part of Arkansas has heavy rice production; the western part has essentially zero.

While natural advantage is, of course, the primary factor leading to specialization, we think it is worth noting that scale economies may be playing a supporting role. The types of scale economies we have in mind include the usual ones that lead to industry agglomeration. Different crops have various specialized intermediate inputs, and, of course, transportation costs are important, so what we refer to below as the *concentrated*

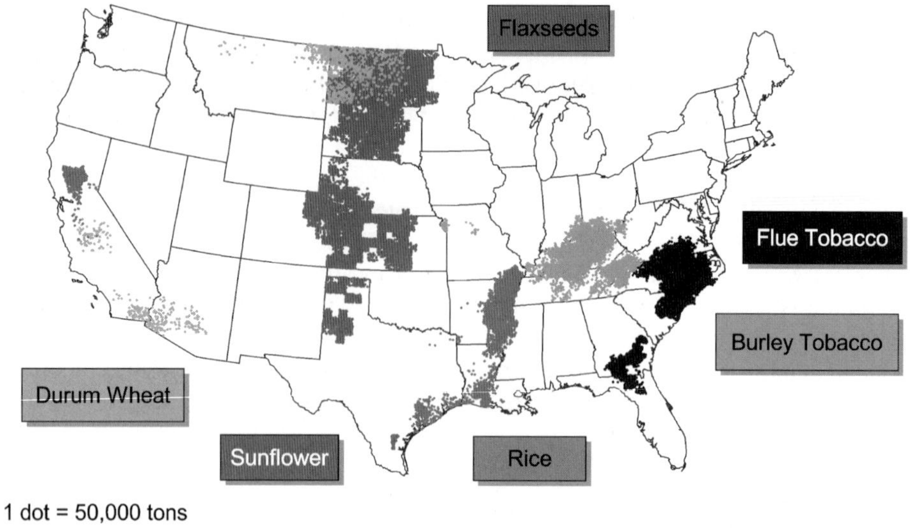

Figure 4. Location of Durum Wheat, Rice, Flue Tobacco, and Burley Tobacco. For a colour reproduction of this figure see the colour figures section, page 3064.

market factor should matter. We expect knowledge spillovers to matter as well. And there is the issue that custom hybrid seeds are developed for particular areas to exploit the climate; this is a fixed cost. [See Griliches (1957) for a classic study of the diffusion of hybrid corn.]

These issues can be illustrated nicely with the example of sugar beets. Hoover (1948, p. 33) presents a map of the joint location of sugar beet farms and processing plants as of 1939. Figure 5 uses recent data to update this earlier map, though the pattern has changed little. The largest area of beet production is in the Minnesota/North Dakota region, but there are several other regions of production. The locations of the 39 sugar beet processing plants (from the 1999 CBP data) are closely connected to the locations of beet production.

In the traditional classification of industries developed by Weber, some are *transportation-cost-oriented* and others are *production-cost-oriented*. Of the transportation-cost-oriented industries, some are materials-oriented and others are market-oriented. The sugar beet processing industry is a classic example of a *materials-oriented* industry. The sugar content of sugar beets is roughly 15 percent by weight, so seven tons of beets must be used to get one ton of sugar. The incentives to place processing facilities near field crops and vice versa are obvious. The EG index for the processing industry is 0.13, a very high number. It is clear that this high concentration of processing is being driven by the high geographic concentration of the upstream crops.

Sugar beet processing plants are relatively large. In 1999, the average plant size was 186 employees, more than four times the average plant size of 46 employees for manufacturing as a whole. This large plant size suggests that scale economies may be im-

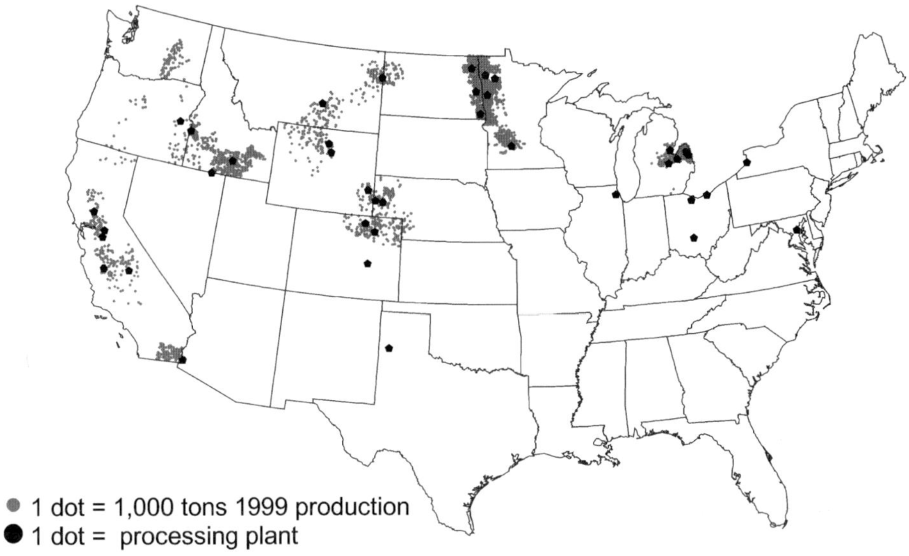

Figure 5. Location of Sugar Beet Plants and Sugar Beet Crops. For a colour reproduction of this figure see the colour figures section, page 3065.

portant. Note that there are several production regions on the map with access to only a single plant. This is true in southern California and in the eastern Montana/western North Dakota region. If scale economies in processing are important and if local beet farming does not reach a large enough scale to support the processing plant, the local beet farming activity may have to shut down. The industry's trade literature suggests that the issue of economies of scale is crucial. One reads about plants shutting down because they cannot contract for a sufficiently large number of acres or about farmers not planting crops because a plant has closed.

This last point can be clearly made with an example about a 4-H club in California.[20] (A 4-H club is a youth group that focuses, in part, on farming activities.) For 33 years this particular club had run a project in which the youth grew their own sugar beets and had them processed by the local plant. But no more. According to the article, "Imperial Sugar Co. decided to cease sugar production at its Woodland and Tracy processing plants by the end of the year… This impacts the Glenn County 4-H sugar beet project since it is too far to transport beets to other facilities." The 4-H club would like to continue the production and in that sense has a "natural advantage". But this small production will not keep a 200-employee factory busy, and so it does not happen.

[20] See "4-H project ends with closure of sugar beet processing plant", by Christine Souza, January 10, 2001, in *Crisis on the Farm: A Special Series from Ag Alert,* California Farm Bureau Federation, www.cfbf.com/agalert/2001/crisisstory3.htm.

The role of comparative advantage in contributing to regional specialization in the United States does not receive much research attention, in contrast to the trade literature where there is substantial research on the importance of both Ricardian comparative advantage and Hecksher–Ohlin factors. A few exceptions are Ellison and Glaeser (1999), Kim (1995), and Hanson and Slaughter (2002). Ellison and Glaeser attempted to control for natural advantage characteristics by, for example, controlling for the amount of nearby agricultural production. They found that the mean EG index declined by 20 percent after doing so, and they conjecture it might fall by half if they had better data. We think this is an interesting line of work that would be fruitful if pushed further. But we want to introduce a word of caution that even for agricultural industries, scale economies may be playing some role in determining location patterns. To the extent this is true, the EG procedure will overstate the importance of natural advantage.

6.2. Concentrated market factor

When scale economies and transportation costs both matter, there is an incentive to *concentrate* a market. With a large market in the same place, economies of scale can be enjoyed and transportation costs avoided. In the literature this factor is also called the *variety effect*, or the *Chamberlinian factor* [see Fujita and Thisse (2002)], or the *intermediate-inputs factor*. The last term seems limiting because the logic applies not just to intermediate inputs but also to final goods, as will be the case in the example we consider.

There has been a substantial amount of theoretical work on this issue [Fujita, Krugman and Venables (1999), Fujita and Thisse (2002)], but little empirical work. How much of this factor can account for the agglomeration of industry is a key question. Papers on this topic are starting to appear and include Holmes (2002) and papers cited in the chapter by Rosenthal and Strange (2004) in this volume.

In this subsection we illustrate the empirical importance of this factor by considering the example of the beverage industry. This is a classic example of a weight-gaining industry – water is added to other materials in the final stage of production. Here there is an incentive to place production near consumers. But there are economies of scale, so we do not expect to see production in every random rural hamlet.

We narrow things further by looking at the beer industry and, in particular, the plant location patterns of the largest brewer, Anheuser–Busch. Anheuser–Busch has 12 breweries, and these plants are quite large; the largest in St. Louis has over 1500 employees. With scale economies and high transportation costs, the concentrated market factor should matter here if it matters anywhere.

Figure 6 plots the location of this company's 12 breweries. The location of the breweries is from the TRI database (discussed in Appendix A), which provides the exact geographic coordinates of each factory. The black dots are the breweries; each red dot represents 10,000 people. There are two things to note about this graph. First, there are no plants in the extreme rural areas; i.e., plants tend to be close to population centers. Second, the plants appear to be spread out in a way that would be consistent with keep-

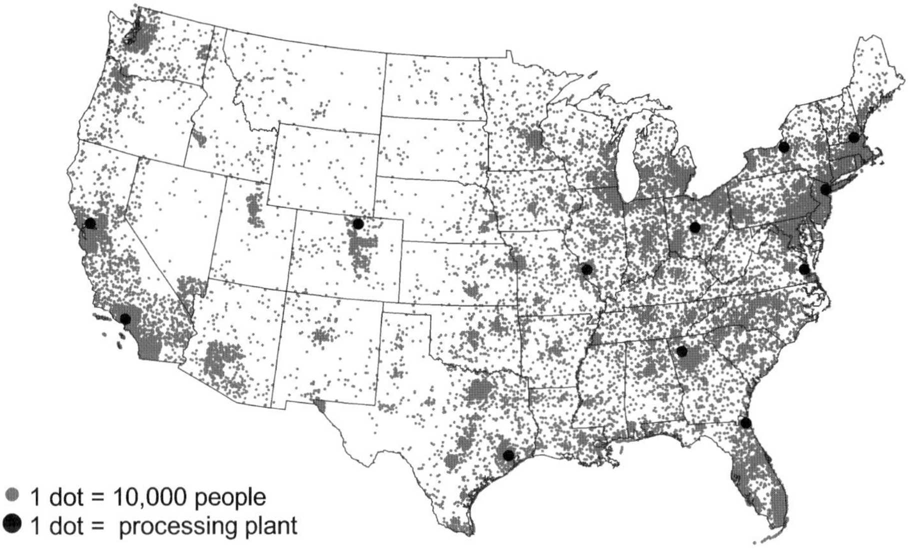

Figure 6. Location of Anheuser–Busch breweries and population (2000). For a colour reproduction of this figure see the colour figures section, page 3065.

Table 15
Location and market areas of Anheuser–Busch plants

Plant Location	Average distance of market	Estimated share of market	Neighboring population percentile of location
Fairfield, CA	285.8	0.084	0.551
Van Nuys, CA	125.8	0.099	0.952
Fort Collins, CO	319.4	0.050	0.282
Houston, TX	207.7	0.097	0.788
St. Louis, MO	270.7	0.143	0.667
Cartersville, GA	153.2	0.084	0.479
Columbus, OH	163.5	0.130	0.578
Jacksonville, FL	197.7	0.064	0.450
Williamsburg, VA	135.2	0.067	0.366
Baldwinsville, NY	93.3	0.021	0.391
Newark, NJ	50.1	0.115	0.979
Merrimack, NH	70.6	0.046	0.408

ing transportation costs low. For example, we do not see two plants in the same metro area. We now provide some more formal evidence of these two propositions.

For evidence that plants are not in rural areas, consider the last column of Table 15. This column reports for each plant the neighboring population percentile for the county where the plant is located. As before, we use a distance of 30 miles to define neighboring population. For example, the percentile for the Fairfield, California, plant is 55.1. This means that the neighboring population of the plant location is higher than 55.1 percent of other locations in the continental United States (weighting the other locations by population). The lowest percentile across the 12 plants is 28.2 percent. If the plants were randomly distributed on the basis of population, the probability that all plants would land in the 28.2 percentile or higher is only $(1 - 0.282)^{12} = 0.019$. Thus, plants tend to be located away from rural areas in a disproportionate sense. This is consistent with theories from the concentrated market literature, which find that plants will tend to be located in areas with large home markets.

We now turn to the second claim that plants are spread out to minimize transportation cost. Note that two plants located in the same metro area would duplicate fixed costs but contribute nothing to reducing transportation costs. To get some idea of the extent to which the selected locations minimize transportation costs, we consider the following calculation. Assume for this analysis that Anheuser–Busch's sales at each location are proportionate to the population at each location. (Here we use the county as the location unit.) For the purpose of discussion, suppose that Anheuser–Busch delivers a case of Budweiser to every person in the United States. Assume that each location is supplied by the closest brewery. Table 15 presents the market share of each of the 12 breweries based on this calculation. We sort the breweries going from west to east. We also report the average distance per consumer served per brewery. The weighted average transportation distance across all the breweries is 178. Put another way, the average person in the United States is 178 miles from the closest brewery.[21]

As a benchmark, we first compare this cost to what we would expect the cost to be if plants were allocated randomly, like in Ellison and Glaeser (1997). Suppose the 12 plants are randomly distributed across counties in proportion to population, each dartboard toss being independent and identically distributed. After throwing 12 darts, we then calculate the average distance. We repeat this 10,000 times. We find that the average distance across simulations is 246 miles and that the standard deviation is 50 miles. In a fraction of only 0.004 of the simulations is the average distance less than or equal to the average actual distance of 178 miles. We can therefore strongly reject this dartboard model. Observed transportation cost is much lower than what would happen with a random distribution of plants.

For the sake of argument, one might try to make a case that the plant location choices reflect some systematic natural advantage factor. For example, suppose (hypothetically) that beer produced in rural areas were to taste bad compared to beer produced near urban areas. To give this alternative explanation a chance, we have also considered various randomizations like those above that exclude rural areas. It turns out that this exclusion led to virtually no reduction in the expected cost of a randomly drawn configuration. Thus, even when rural locations are excluded, the random configuration does much

[21] This calculation excludes Alaska and Hawaii, but the populations of these states are quite small, so including them would have a little effect.

worse than the actual configuration. The proposed natural advantage theory can explain why plants are not in rural areas but cannot account for the configuration of plants across nonrural areas.

We conclude that the evidence suggests that the concentrated market factor is an important determinant of the plant location strategy of Anheuser–Busch. Obviously, it is not the only factor. We believe an important area of future research is to disentangle the importance of the concentrated market factor from other factors. We believe that work with micro data sets that consider multi-plant firm location problems, as discussed here and in Holmes (2002), will prove useful in getting to the bottom of this issue.

6.3. *Government policy*

One of the most important and controversial issues in location analysis is the role that policy plays in influencing location decisions. It is important because policies are something societies can change and economic analysis can provide guidance for these public choices. It is controversial because policy effects are difficult to pin down. Not only do researchers have to disentangle policy effects from other factors, but they also have to deal with complicated causality issues.

It is impossible in this brief section to survey this literature. Instead we make mention of a few contributions that illustrate recent progress on this issue. For references to the earlier literature, see Herzog and Schlottman (1991).

One issue that has attracted much attention is the effect of environmental regulations on the location of economic activity. While earlier research often found relatively small effects, the more recent research of Becker and Henderson (2000), Greenstone (2002), and Henderson (1996) finds relatively large impacts. A hallmark of this new research is the use of richer data compared with previous studies, making it possible to do a better job of measuring the incidence of policy and of controlling for confounding factors. While the earlier literature generally treated the regulatory policies as occurring at the state level, this new literature points out that much policy is administered at the county level. In particular, because of federal law, each county is classified as being either in attainment or not in attainment, and various restrictions are imposed in non-attainment counties. All three studies find that non-attainment status in a county leads to shifts in the location of polluting industries away from such counties.

A second issue that has attracted attention is the role that policy has played in regional shifts in manufacturing. As discussed in Cobb (1993), southern states have actively pursued a host of pro-business policies to attract manufacturing. These include policies hostile to labor unions like right-to-work laws as well as low taxes and subsidies. Progress in quantifying the effects of such pro-business policies has been hampered by the difficulty of distinguishing the effects of state policies from the effects of other state characteristics that are unrelated to policy. In a recent paper, Holmes (1998) uses a regression discontinuity design to try to control for these other factors. Specifically, he examines the differences in manufacturing levels and growth rates at state borders between "pro-business" and "anti-business" states. Near the border, other differences

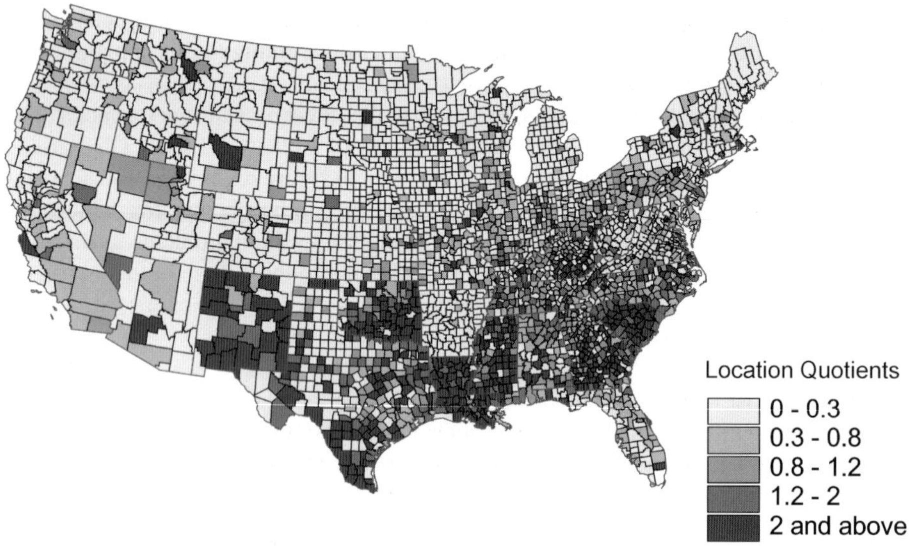

Figure 7. Location of Consumer Lending (NAICS 522291) (Location Quotient by County). For a colour reproduction of this figure see the colour figures section, page 3066.

unrelated to policy are likely to be very similar, and so the difference at the border identifies the effect of policy. Holmes finds relatively large effects of policy near these borders.

We illustrate the idea by looking at an example industry in which the policy effects are so overwhelming that the point is crystal clear. Figure 7 is a map of county-level LQs for the "Consumer Lending" industry NAICS 522291.[22] This industry is defined as "establishments primarily engaged in making unsecured cash loans to consumers". Included in this industry are establishments that make short-term loans with exorbitant interest rates. It is readily apparent that there is wide variation across the United States in the extent of this activity. The key thing to observe in this table is the sharp differences in state boundaries. Note in particular the state in the center close to the bottom that is very light but is surrounded on the left bottom and center by states that are completely dark. The state in question is Arkansas, and the surrounding states are Oklahoma, Louisiana, and Mississippi. The sharp difference at the border makes it obvious that there must be a policy difference between Arkansas and its neighboring states. One policy difference is the unusually strong anti-usury laws that exist in Arkansas and the absence of those laws in the neighboring states.[23]

Observe that in the region of southern states like Oklahoma, Texas, Louisiana, and Mississippi, activity in the consumer lending industry tends to be high. If we worked

[22] The LQs are based on County Business Patterns 2000 employment.

[23] See "The bad side of town", in the Economist, 11/28/98, pp. 30–31.

with just state-level data, we might not be able to distinguish a policy explanation from an argument that the South has a natural advantage in this industry. Indeed, it is obvious that if we regress state-level LQs on latitude we will get some explanatory power. It is only by looking at detailed geographic data near the border that we get a "smoking gun" effect of policy.

7. Conclusion

In this chapter, we reviewed data sources that are useful for studying the geographic specialization of industry in the United States and Canada. In particular, we emphasized the use of detailed data on establishment counts by employment-size categories and fine industry and geographic classifications. Basic facts about specialization were elicited from these data using standard measures, such as employment location quotients.

The chapter also touched on a classic, unresolved question: Why do specialization patterns emerge as they do? In recent years, a resurgence of work in economic geography has made theoretical inroads into this interesting and important question. However, many open issues remain, and empirical work continues to lag behind the theoretical frontier. Progress has been hampered by difficult identification problems, such as how to sort out the relative importance of natural advantage versus scale economy explanations for industry agglomerations [as explained by Ellison and Glaeser (1999)]. We are optimistic that strategies can be devised to overcome these hurdles [e.g., by looking at multi-location firms as in Holmes (2002) and in the Anheuser–Busch example of Section 7] and that much progress will be made in the coming years.

Acknowledgements

Holmes acknowledges support from the NSF through grant SES 0136842. The authors thank Edward Glaeser, Vernon Henderson, and Jacques-François Thisse for helpful comments. They also thank Alice Schoonbroodt and Brian Rowe for research assistance. The views expressed herein are those of the authors and not necessarily those of the Federal Reserve Bank of Minneapolis, the Board of Governors of the Federal Reserve System, or the Federal Reserve System.

Appendix A: Data sources

This appendix provides details about the various data sources discussed in the text.

A.1: Sources of the CBP data

The CBP data are available in computer readable files from 1974 to the present. The years 1974–1976 are distributed, for a small fee, on a custom-made CD-ROM by the U.S. National Archives and Records Administration (NARA at www.nara.gov); NARA does not distribute data on the Internet. Beginning in 1977, the CBP data are archived at the Inter-university Consortium for Political and Social Research (ICPSR at www.icpsr.umich.edu) and are freely available on the Internet to participating institutions; for example, the data for 1977 are in ICPSR file 8464. Beginning in 1986, the data are also distributed on CD-ROM by the Census Bureau. The Census Bureau also tabulates these data on a ZIP code basis in a publication called *ZIP Code Business Patterns* that is available on CD-ROM with data beginning in 1994.

Additional information about the CBP data and an establishment-level version of the 2000 CBP are available for download at www.econ.umn.edu/~holmes/data/CBP.

A.2: Mean employment by size class

Table 1 in the text reports average establishment employment in each establishment-size class based on the CBP data. For establishment-size classes with fewer than 1000 employees, this average is calculated by taking the total employment in the United States in each size class and dividing by the total number of establishments in the size class. Unfortunately, the aggregate data for the United States do not break down the 1000-plus category into the four narrow size classes for which we have establishment count data. Therefore, we estimate the mean sizes for these four categories using the following estimation procedure. We assume that a log normal distribution of employment holds for establishments in the 1000-plus and up class. We use a generalized method-of-moments to estimate the parameters of this distribution, using the following as moments: (1) total employment in the 1000-plus class and (2) establishment counts in the four component narrow size classes. The reported cell averages are for the estimated distribution.

A.3: Economic Census data

As discussed in the text, the Economic Census also releases establishment cell counts at the county level. The data on establishment counts with 250 or more employees used to construct Figure 2 are from the 1947 Census of Manufactures. These data were published in the *1949 County and City Data Book* (variable #42) and are available in computer readable files, along with all the data in the county and city data books for the period 1944–1977 [Bureau of the Census (1978)], from ICPSR study 7735.

The Census of Manufactures has published cell counts by detailed industry and county and size class since at least 1954. This publication is called *Location of Manufacturing Plants*. A computer file with this data is available for 1972 from NARA (www.nara.gov). The data for later Economic Census years are available from the Census Bureau on CD-ROM.

A.4: Canadian Business Patterns and Census data

Section 3 uses province-level census data on total employment by NAICS sector for 2001; these data are published by Statistics Canada (2001) (www.statcan.ca) and are available on the Internet. Two aggregates (shown in Table 4 in the text) were constructed from the eastern and western provinces to facilitate the regional comparisons.

Section 4 uses data from the Canadian Business Patterns CD-ROM. These data report cell counts at the four-digit NAICS level by Census Division (the analog of a U.S. county) and employment-size category. There is no information on total employment from which to calculate mean employment in the cell, so we used the U.S. average sizes as an estimate. The cells 1–4, 5–9, 10–19, 20–49, and 50–99 correspond to cells (or groups of cells) in the U.S. data and so we directly use the U.S. mean. The cells 100–199 and 200–499 are slightly different from their counterparts 100–249, 250–499, in the U.S. data. We adjust the estimates for Canada so that the mean relative to the range is the same as for the United States. For example, the mean employment in the U.S. data for the cell 100–249 is 150.1, which is a fraction 0.336 of the way between 100 and 249. We therefore set the cell average for the 100–199 range in Canada to 133.2, because this is a fraction 0.336 of the way between 100 and 199.

A.5: BEA data

We obtained data from the U.S. Department of Commerce's Bureau of Economic Analysis (BEA at www.bea.gov) on government employment and proprietorships (self-employment). BEA data are available on CD-ROM and on the Internet. The BEA aggregates certain counties that the Census Bureau treats separately; therefore, the BEA data have 3110 distinct counties compared to the 3131 counties that meet the Census Bureau's definition. For example, Virginia treats independent cities as counties and separates them from the surrounding area, while the BEA merges these cities with the surrounding areas. In Section 4 we use the BEA county definitions.

A.6: Other data

We used establishment-level data from the Toxic Release Inventory (TRI) collected by the U.S. Environmental Protection Agency to identify the locations of the Anheuser–Busch plants. These data are available on the Internet at www.epa.gov/tri/. These data provide the location (including exact geographic coordinates) of establishments required to file toxic release forms.

The data on agricultural crops were obtained from the Agricultural Statistics Data Base (www.nass.usda.gov) produced by the U.S. Department of Agriculture, National Agricultural Statistics Service.

References

Becker, R., Henderson, J.V. (2000). "Effects of air quality regulations on polluting industries". Journal of Political Economy 108, 379–421.

Berry, B.J.L. (1967). Geography of Market Centers and Retail Distribution. Prentice Hall, Englewood Cliffs.

Bureau of the Census (1978). County and City Data Book [United States] consolidated file: City Data, 1944–1977 [computer file]. U.S. Deptartment of Commerce, Bureau of the Census , Washington, DC [producer]. Inter-university Consortium for Political and Social Research, Ann Arbor, MI [distributor], 2000.

Bureau of the Census (1985). County Business Patterns, 1977 [United States]: U.S. Summary, State, and County Data [computer file]. U.S. Department of Commerce, Bureau of the Census, Washington, DC [producer]. Inter-university Consortium for Political and Social Research, Ann Arbor, MI [distributor], 1986.

Bureau of the Census (2002a). County Business Patterns 2000. U.S. Department of Commerce, Bureau of the Census, Washington, DC.

Bureau of the Census (2002b). County Business Patterns 1999–2000. U.S. Department of Commerce, Bureau of the Census, Washington, DC. CD-ROM C1-E00-CBPX-01-US1.

Bureau of Economic Analysis (2002). Regional Economic Information System (REIS), 1969–2000. U.S. Department of Commerce, Bureau of Economic Analysis, Washington, DC. CD-ROM RCN-0295.

Christaller, W. (1966). Central Places in Southern Germany. Prentice Hall, Englewood Cliffs. Translated by C.W. Baskin.

Ciccone, A., Hall, R.E. (1996). "Productivity and the density of economic activity". American Economic Review 86, 54–70.

Cobb, J.C. (1993). The Selling of the South: The Southern Crusade for Industrial Development, 1936–1990, 2nd ed. University of Illinois Press, Urbana, IL.

Combes, P.P., Overman, H.G. (2004). "The spatial distribution of economic activities in the European Union". In: Henderson, J.V., Thisse, J.-F. (Eds.), Handbook of Regional and Urban Economics, vol. 4. Elsevier, Amsterdam. This volume.

Dinlersoz, E.M. (2004). "Cities and the organization of manufacturing". Regional Science and Urban Economics 34, 71–100.

Dumais, G., Ellison, G., Glaeser, E.L. (2002). "Geographic concentration as a dynamic process". Review of Economics and Statistics 84, 193–204.

Duranton, G., Overman, H. (2002). "Testing for localisation using micro-geographic data". Centre for Economic Policy Research Discussion Paper 3379.

Duranton, G., Puga, D. (2004). "Micro-foundations of urban agglomeration economies". In: Henderson, J.V., Thisse, J.-F. (Eds.), Handbook of Regional and Urban Economics, vol. 4. Elsevier, Amsterdam, pp. 2063–2117. This volume.

Ellison, G., Glaeser, E.L. (1997). "Geographic concentration in U.S. manufacturing industries: A dartboard approach". Journal of Political Economy 105, 889–927.

Ellison, G., Glaeser, E.L. (1999). "The geographic concentration of industry: Does natural advantage explain agglomeration?" American Economic Review 89, 311–316.

Evans, D.S. (1987). "Tests of alternative theories of firm growth". Journal of Political Economy 95, 657–674.

Fritz, W.G. (1943). "Natural resource – minerals". In: Industrial Location and Natural Resources. U.S. Government Printing Office, Washington, DC.

Fujita, M., Kanemoto, Y., Henderson, J.V. (2004). "Spatial distribution of economic activities in East Asia". In: Henderson, J.V., Thisse, J.-F. (Eds.), Handbook of Regional and Urban Economics, vol. 4. Elsevier, Amsterdam. This volume.

Fujita, M., Krugman, P., Venables, A.J. (1999). The Spatial Economy: Cities, Regions, and International Trade. MIT Press, Cambridge, MA.

Fujita, M., Thisse, J.-F. (2002). Economics of Agglomeration: Cities, Industrial Location, and Regional Growth. Cambridge University Press, New York.

Gabaix, X., Ioannides, Y.M. (2004). "The evolution of city size distributions". In: Henderson, J.V., Thisse, J.-F. (Eds.), Handbook of Regional and Urban Economics, vol. 4. Elsevier, Amsterdam, pp. 2341–2378. This volume.

Gardocki Jr., B.C., Baj, J. (1985). "Methodology for estimating nondisclosure in county business patterns". Center for Governmental Studies, Northern Illinois University.

Glaeser, E.L., Kallal, H.D., Scheinkman, J.A., Shleifer, A. (1992). "Growth in cities". Journal of Political Economy 100, 1126–1152.
Glaeser, E.L., Maré, D.C. (2001). "Cities and skills". Journal of Labor Economics 19, 316–342.
Greenstone, M. (2002). "The impacts of environmental regulations on industrial activity: Evidence from the 1970 and 1977 Clean Air Act amendments and the Census of Manufactures". Journal of Political Economy 110, 1175–1219.
Griliches, Z. (1957). "Hybrid corn: An exploration in the economics of technological change". Econometrica 25, 501–522.
Hanson, G.H., Slaughter, M.J. (2002). "Labor-market adjustment in open economies: Evidence from U.S. states". Journal of International Economics 57, 3–29.
Henderson, J.V. (1986). "Efficiency of resource use and city size". Journal of Urban Economics 19, 47–70.
Henderson, J.V. (1988). Urban Development: Theory, Fact, and Illusion. Oxford University Press, New York.
Henderson, J.V. (1996). "Effects of air quality regulation". American Economic Review 86, 789–813.
Henderson, J.V. (2003). "Marshall's scale economies". Journal of Urban Economics 53, 1–28.
Herzog Jr., H.W., Schlottman, A.M. (1991). Industrial Location and Public Policy. University of Tennessee Press, Knoxville, TN.
Holmes, T.J. (1998). "The effects of state policies on the location of industry: Evidence from state borders". Journal of Political Economy 106, 667–705.
Holmes, T.J. (1999). "Localization of industry and vertical disintegration". Review of Economics and Statistics 81, 314–325.
Holmes, T.J. (2002). "The role of cities: Evidence from the placement of sales offices". Federal Reserve Bank of Minneapolis Staff Report 298.
Holmes, T.J., Stevens, J.J. (2002). "Geographic concentration and establishment scale". Review of Economics and Statistics 84, 682–690.
Hoover, E.M. (1948). The Location of Economic Activity. McGraw–Hill, New York.
Kim, S. (1995). "Expansion of markets and the geographic distribution of economic activities: The trends in U.S. regional manufacturing structure, 1860–1987". Quarterly Journal of Economics 110, 881–908.
MacDonald, J.M. (1985). "Dun and Bradstreet business microdata research applications, and the detection and correction of errors". Journal of Economic and Social Measurement 13, 173–185.
Maurel, F., Sédillot, B. (1999). "A measure of the geographic concentration of French manufacturing industries". Regional Science and Urban Economics 29, 575–604.
Ono, Y. (2001). "Outsourcing business service and the scope of local markets". Working Paper 01-15. U.S. Census Bureau, Center for Economic Studies.
Pred, A. (1965). "The concentration of high-value-added manufacturing". Economic Geography 41, 108–132.
Rosenthal, S.S., Strange, W.C. (2001). "The determinants of agglomeration". Journal of Urban Economics 50, 191–229.
Rosenthal, S.S., Strange, W. (2004). "Evidence on the nature and sources of agglomeration economies". In: Henderson, J.V., Thisse, J.-F. (Eds.), Handbook of Regional and Urban Economics, vol. 4. Elsevier, Amsterdam, pp. 2119–2171. This volume.
Segal, D. (1976). "Are there returns to scale in city size?" Review of Economics and Statistics 58, 339–350.
Statistics Canada (2001). Canadian Business Patterns. CD-ROM.
Sveikauskas, L.A. (1975). "The productivity of cities". Quarterly Journal of Economics 89, 393–413.

Chapter 64

THE SPATIAL DISTRIBUTION OF ECONOMIC ACTIVITIES IN THE EUROPEAN UNION

PIERRE-PHILIPPE COMBES[1]

CERAS, 48, bd Jourdan, 75014 Paris, France
e-mail: combes@enpc.fr
url: http://www.enpc.fr/ceras/combes

HENRY G. OVERMAN[2]

Department of Geography and Environment, London School of Economics, Houghton Street, London WC2A 2AE, United Kingdom
e-mail: h.overman@lse.ac.uk
url: http://cep.lse.ac.uk/~overman

Contents

[1] CNRS researcher also affiliated with the Centre for Economic Policy Research.
[2] Also affiliated with the Centre for Economic Policy Research, and the Centre for Economic Performance at the London School of Economics.

Handbook of Regional and Urban Economics, Volume 4. Edited by J.V. Henderson and J.F. Thisse

DOI: 10.1016/S0169-7218(04)07064-9

to doing two things. First, identifying exactly what they do tell us about the spatial distribution of economic activity in the EU. Second, arguing that they cannot tell us much about location theory more generally because data problems and methodological errors mean they are less informative about theory than papers published elsewhere. The second problem relates to a somewhat smaller body of literature and is in some ways the mirror image of the first. A number of papers use EU data in ways that do tell us things about location theory more generally, but then tend to be ignored because they get labelled as area based and are thus considered too specific for a broader audience. We also consider these papers here and try to spell out what a broader audience may learn from them. The reader should note that this focus tends to move us away from the more descriptive work in the two companion chapters and thus involves considerably more discussion of econometric issues than is found there.

Before outlining the structure of the paper, a comment on what we do not cover. We will not consider national or regional convergence in the EU, innovation, or FDI and trade as these literatures are considered elsewhere in this handbook, by Magrini (2004), Audretsch and Feldman (2004), and Head and Mayer (2004), respectively. In addition, we only cover the EU as it now stands, with no consideration of the economic geographies of the 10 countries that will join the EU in 2004.

Turning to what we do cover, the rest of the chapter is split into three parts. In the first, we consider the main sources of data for studying EU location patterns. This survey is brief and less helpful than it could be, reflecting the woeful state of pan-European national and sub-national data. The second part describes the location of economic activity in the EU. This focuses on three key aspects. First, the pattern of overall agglomeration as reflected in differences in regional GDP and GDP per capita. Next we consider the specialisation patterns of particular areas and the concentration patterns of particular activities at both the national and sub-national level. We also consider the characteristics of spatially concentrated industries. Finally, we show how micro-geographic data may be used to compare spatial patterns in the U.S. and the EU. The third part of our survey considers the literature that seeks to explain location patterns in the EU. After a very brief theoretical survey we focus, in turn, on spatial inequalities in terms of industrial localisation, labour productivity, wages, and growth.

1. Data for studying the spatial distribution of economic activity in the European Union

In this section, we consider the data that are available for studying the spatial distribution of economic activity in the EU. After reviewing the literature, and given our first-hand knowledge, the only conclusion that we are able to reach is that the European data are a mess. It is not clear where blame for this situation lies. It is clear that part of the problem stems from the institutional framework within which most EU governmental statistical agencies work. In particular, the fact that they often have no mandate to facilitate the reuse of data collected to fulfil their institution roles. Even where they do have a mandate, data are often expensive and incentives to ensure efficient delivery appear to be limited. It is clear that these barriers could be removed, but this would require political support across the EU. Even if this support were forthcoming, variations in collection policies, access and pricing conditions, confidentiality requirements and legal frameworks would still hamper unified data provision. These problems clearly present considerable barriers for Eurostat, the EU's statistical office, in delivering on its mission "to provide the European Union with a high quality statistical information service". However, it is probably fair to say that the delivery itself leaves something to be desired. Informal discussions suggest that two of the biggest frustrations for academic researchers are poor documentation and the inconsistency across different versions of the same datasets. For example, paper copies will have different coverage from the electronic copies and coverage will change over time (not necessarily expand). There is usually little or no discussion of why these differences occur. Even the names of data sets can change frequently over time, a problem that is clearly illustrated below. As this brief discussion makes clear, the pan-European data situation is not a happy one. In this section, we will discuss the major data sources, giving some idea of their coverage and the main problems associated with using them.

We start with data that allows us to assess overall agglomeration patterns. REGIO is Eurostat's regional database. It provides data on GDP and GDP per capita on a comparable basis for regions across the EU 15.[3] The coverage of regions is based on Eurostat's Nomenclature of Territorial Units for Statistics (NUTS). NUTS is a hierarchical classification dividing each country into a number of NUTS 1, with each NUTS 1 divided into a number of NUTS 2 and so on down to NUTS 5. There are 78 NUTS 1 regions, 210 NUTS 2 regions, 1092 NUTS 3 regions. NUTS 4 is only defined for a limited number of countries.[4] There are 98,433 NUTS 5 regions corresponding to communes or their equivalent. The classification is based primarily on existing institutional divisions and thus, to the extent national systems differ, meets no consistent requirements across the EU. Areas for instance may significantly differ for a given level of NUTS. REGIO usually provides data at the NUTS 2 or NUTS 3 level. Theoretically, data are available for GDP, population, employment and wages. In reality, a complete GDP series for the entire EU 15 at approximately NUTS 2 is only available from 1995 onwards. NUTS 2 GDP data for the EU 12 is generally available from 1980 onwards,[5] although the accounting system and the NUTS classification changed in 1996 and 1998, respectively. Population and employment data have slightly better coverage while wage data coverage is extremely variable and generally quite poor.

[3] The EU 15 is used to designate all 15 current member states: Austria, Belgium, Denmark, Finland, France, Germany, Greece, Ireland, Italy, Luxembourg, the Netherlands, Portugal, Spain, Sweden and the UK. The EU 12 consists of the EU 15 less the three 1990s entrants: Austria, Finland and Sweden.

[4] Finland, Greece, Ireland, Luxembourg, Portugal and the UK.

[5] Data for the UK, Denmark, Ireland and Luxembourg are at NUTS 1.

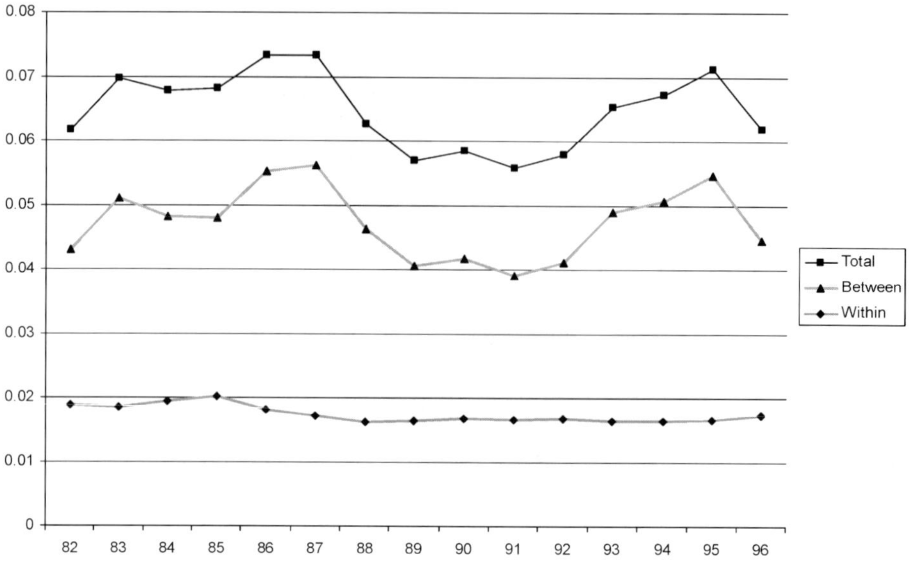

Figure 2. Theil Index for regional GDP per capita (EU 12).

The lower map also plots data for 1996, but now for total GDP rather than GDP per capita. Comparing these two maps we see that the core–periphery pattern is much less marked when it comes to total GDP. This comparison neatly demonstrates another key stylised fact about the spatial distribution of economic activity in the EU. Population (and hence aggregate activity) remains quite spread out in the EU, despite very large differences in GDP per capita across EU regions.

There is some evidence that this core–periphery pattern in GDP per capita may be weakening between countries, while stable within countries. To highlight this, Figure 2 plots a Theil index for regional inequalities in the EU 12 between 1982 and 1996. The figure also decomposes this Theil index into its between-country and within-country components. The overall Theil index rose until 1987, then fell until 1992 and has been increasing since. Over the whole period, inequalities are fairly stable. As is also clear from the figure, this pattern is driven mainly by between-country inequality. Within-country differences have remained stable.

Two key questions emerge. First, what drives this strong EU-wide core–periphery pattern and the changes that we are seeing over time? Second, are the changes that we are seeing related to deeper EU integration? Researchers seeking to address these two questions have turned to the idea of accessibility as a key driver of these patterns. It is to this issue that we now turn.

2.1.2. Accessibility

Since Harris (1954), researchers have used the idea of market potential to measure the accessibility of different locations to national markets. According to Harris, a region's market potential could be measured as a distance-weighted sum of economic activity in all other locations:

$$MP_i = \sum_j \frac{x_j}{d_{ij}},$$

where x_j is some measure of economic activity in location j and d_{ij} is the distance between location i and j. In the EU, the issue of market potential remains an area of interest to both academics and policy makers. This partly reflects the fact that people believe that accessibility explains the core–periphery pattern in terms of GDP per capita. That the two are correlated is plain to see from Figure 3 which plots basic market potential calculated on the same GDP per capita and total GDP data used above.[11] Again, darker colours signify higher values. The core–periphery pattern is clear for both market potentials, although the pattern is again stronger when considering GDP per capita.

The interest in market potential also reflects the impact of integration in encouraging particular dimensions of the EU area studies. Economic geography models tell us that accessibility can matter and integration explicitly changes accessibility. Hence the interest in describing what is happening to accessibility in the EU. The stylised fact that emerges from this literature, is that integration is associated with improving accessibility of all locations in the EU, but the accessibility of the core regions is improving relatively faster than regions in the periphery. This finding is reversed if we consider travel cost indicators rather, than market potential à la Harris (1954): In contrast to accessibility, travel cost indicators have actually fallen fastest in the periphery. A non-exhaustive list of articles with further discussion includes: Keeble et al. (1982, 1988), Lutter (1993), Spiekermann and Wegener (1994, 1996), Chatelus and Ulied (1995), Gutiérrez and Urbano (1996), Copus (1997), Vickerman et al. (1999), Schürmann and Talaat (2000), Schürmann, Spiekermann and Wegener (2001).[12]

The entire burgeoning literature revolves around a number of controversies relating to exactly how the formula should be applied. Many variants have been suggested as regards the way the centre of locations are defined; the way distance between the centres should be measured; the way distance within the region should be measured (and whether this component should be included); and how economic mass at each location should be measured. Different answers to these questions generally deliver different measures of regional accessibility. See Copus (1997), Head and Mayer (2002) and Combes and Lafourcade (2003) for discussion.

[11] For our calculations x_j is region j GDP or GDP per capita, d_{ij} is the distance between the geographic centres of region i and region j. The internal distance (of region i from itself) is computed as two-third of the square of the ratio of area over π.

[12] The list only includes cross European studies. There is a vast literature studying accessibility at the national level.

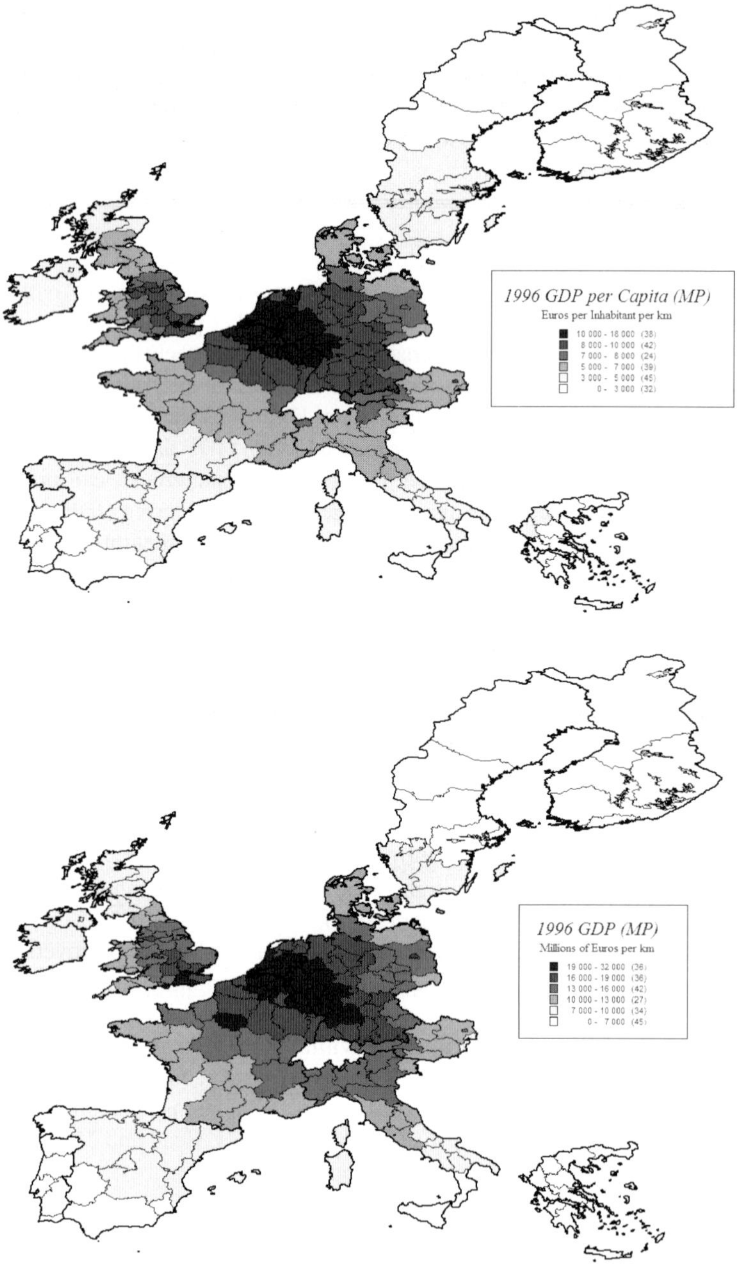

Figure 3. Market potential of per capita (top) and total (bottom) GDP in European NUTS2 regions. For a colour reproduction of this figure see the colour figures section, page 3068.

Economists coming back to this issue in light of the New Economic Geography often find this list of controversies somewhat puzzling because they fail to address two fundamental questions. What does theory tell us about why and how we should be calculating accessibility? These two questions are intimately linked and will determine how we then use accessibility to explain location patterns. Traditionally, geographers have limited themselves to fairly simple correlations between outcomes and accessibility. Economists have recently begun to take a very different approach using market potential estimated on the basis of functional forms that are clearly related to theory [see Hanson (2002) and Redding and Venables (2004)]. This literature has had very little impact on how the area-based literature has approached this issue for the EU.

2.2. *Concentration and specialisation in the EU*

In this section, we turn from the distribution of total production to the sectoral composition of economic activities. We document a number of stylised facts:

- Although production structures differ across EU countries, we can identify groups of countries with similar structures. Differences in structure have slowly increased between the 1970s and the 1990s, as EU countries became more specialised.
- EU regions show a much more mixed pattern. Between the 1980s and the 1990s, approximately 50% of EU regions have become more specialised, while the remaining 50% have become less specialised. Overall changes in specialisation are small however.
- The extent of industrial concentration varies widely by industry. Most studies find that high-tech, increasing returns to scale activities are more spatially concentrated. Results are less clear on resource intensive activities and activities that have strong linkages with other sectors. Changes over time show a mixed pattern. Between the 1970s and the 1990s, roughly one third of EU industries became more concentrated, while the rest became more dispersed.

The first two sets of facts consider what particular locations do and how this changes over time. The interest in *changes* clearly reflects the influence of EU integration in shaping the debate. Our major focus is the third set of facts on where particular activities locate. Again, the role of integration in motivating the literature is obvious. However, just because integration is the motivating factor, it does not mean that we necessarily have to learn nothing about location theory more generally from studying European data. We will return to this issue below.

2.2.1. *Standard methodology*

The literature uses a variety of measures to describe the spatial location of economic activity in the EU. Most papers also include a discussion of why some measures are better than others when it comes to examining location patterns. However, there has been no systematic attempt to outline the criteria by which we should be assessing these measures. Thus, it seems appropriate to begin our survey by the consideration of some baseline criteria. Our philosophy in developing these criteria has been to allow for the strong theoretical tradition in the location literature by incorporating theoretical considerations directly into the criteria rather than adopting the first principles (axiomatic) approach that has tended to form the basis of the income inequality literature.[13] We outline the criteria focusing on measures of concentration (i.e. for the geographical concentration of particular activities). It should be obvious how to develop very similar criteria for measuring industrial specialisation of given locations, an issue to which we return briefly below.

1. Measures should be comparable across activities. This criteria is important for two reasons. First, it allows us to make meaningful statements about whether (say) broad sectors are more concentrated than specific sub-sectors. Second, it allows us to consider the extent of concentration at (say) the three-digit level after controlling for the extent of concentration at the two-digit level. This second example actually implies a somewhat stronger criteria – that measures should be additive across spatial scales. Most standard measures do allow some comparisons across activities if correctly implemented. It turns out, however, that these indices may fail on this condition once we consider our third criteria.
2. Measures should be comparable across spatial scales. This is often assumed for existing indices but never explicitly discussed. It is the mirror image of the first criteria and matters for similar reasons. First, it allows us to make meaningful statements about whether (say) activity is more concentrated at the national than the regional level, or more concentrated in the U.S. than the EU. Second, it allows us to consider the extent of concentration at (say) the county level after controlling for the extent of concentration at the regional level. This second example again implies a somewhat stronger criteria – that measures should be additive across spatial scales.
3. The measure should take a unique (known) value under the 'null hypothesis' that there is no systematic component to the location of the activity. We may need to think of this from both a deterministic and stochastic perspective and allow for the fact that the systematic component will often be identified by theory. To give an example, Ellison and Glaeser (1997) point out that industrial concentration can lead to geographical concentration even when activities are randomly located due to the 'lumpiness' of individual establishments. They develop a measure of concentration by defining random location as the patterns that would emerge by throwing darts at a map. The darts differ in mass (to allow for industrial concentration), are thrown randomly (a stochastic component) and their probability of landing in any given region is proportional to the amount of overall activity in that region (a deterministic component). While data limitations rule out the use of the

[13] Kaplow (2002) argues for a far great role for theory in deriving useful descriptive measures of income inequality. This clearly goes against the idea of a-priori principles as emphasised in the existing literature. Our feeling is that location theorists should be pursuing the theory route in their descriptive work if they want to make anything but the most basic claims about theory.

Ellison and Glaeser index for EU-wide studies (calculating industrial concentration needs information on plant sizes), careful consideration of this criteria may still rule out some of the measures that have been used. Notice that much of the debate over absolute versus relative measures [see Haaland et al. (1999)] is basically about this issue, although the criteria itself is much broader than just that consideration.

4. The significance of the results should be reported where appropriate (i.e. when statements about concentration are probabilistic as a result of meeting criterion 3).
5. Measures should be unbiased with respect to arbitrary changes to the spatial classification. Nearly all existing measures take points on a map and allocate them to units in a box. The importance of this criterion comes from recognising that these boxes are then treated as separate units. As a result, bias with respect to spatial classification has two origins. First, clusters of industries may cut the boundaries of these boxes. Therefore, changing the boundaries changes the measure even for a given number and size of sub-units. Next, activity in neighbouring spatial units is treated in exactly the same way as activity at opposite ends of the country. In other words, the distance between sub-units is not taken into account and again, very different spatial configurations may end up with the same value. Duranton and Overman (2002) discuss the issues in some depth and propose a measure that satisfies the criteria by using data reported on continuous space. Again, data limitations prevent implementation of this measure for EU-wide studies, but that does not reduce the importance of the criterion for assessing the performance of existing measures.
6. Measures should be unbiased with respect to arbitrary changes to industrial classification. This is the mirror image of the fifth criteria. There the problems occurred because spatial classifications discretise continuous space into boxes. Here problems occur because industrial classification discretises the activities of firms into a given number of boxes and again, these boxes are then treated as separate units. Bias can occur for exactly the same reasons. This is a particular problem if the level of disaggregation varies systematically with activity types. For example, if sectoral disaggregation is finer for manufacturing than it is for services, then changes in the composition of output towards services may change measures of concentration even if the location patterns of firms remain unchanged.
7. If we want to make any statements about theory, then we should understand the way the measure behaves under the alternative hypothesis suggested by theory. That is, our choice of measure should reflect a consideration of both the null of random/non-systematic location and the alternative of what forces should drive systematic location patterns.

Applying these criteria to measuring specialisation involves straightforward extension, although some criteria have received more attention, and some criteria (not necessarily the same ones) are clearly more important than others. For example, criteria 2 and 5 (regarding issues of spatial scale), tend to be downplayed for specialisation indices, often because criterion 7 (theory) has played a strong role in deciding the spatial scale at which such measures should be imposed. Criteria 3 and 4 (on the null hypothesis and significance) have probably received less attention than they should have done. For example, it would be of interest to know how much specialisation remains to be explained after conditioning out the effects of industrial concentration. We have seen no consideration of this sort of issue.

No measure currently meets all of these criteria. The measure proposed by Ellison and Glaeser (1997) satisfies criteria 1, 3 and 4. That of Duranton and Overman (2002) satisfies criteria 1 to 5 but is demanding in terms of data. Little progress has been made in satisfying criterion 6 although Rosenthal and Strange (2004) discuss the issue in a different context (the measurement of location externalities) in their chapter in this volume. There has also been very little progress on criterion 7. This is an issue to which we return below when we consider the characteristics of spatially concentrated industries. We note in passing, that even once we have such a measure, taking it to real world data will involve resolving a number of issues. Presumably we are trying to pick up structural change rather than the business cycle, so we may need to time-average data, for example. We should also understand how the measure behaves when there are missing data. Finally, if the measure does satisfy criterion 7, then following Kim (1995), we presumably want the industrial classification to group activities that are similar in terms of the impact of location forces and define regions that are similar in terms of location attributes.

Although there are measures that meet most of the criteria, the measures that are applied when considering EU-wide location patterns tend not to. For our current purposes, spelling out these criteria is aimed at meeting two goals. First, they should be in the back of our mind as we review the existing evidence to avoid misinterpretations of empirical findings. Second, progress on meeting these criteria should be a key research goal if we want to take the descriptive literature forward. In this spirit, we use these criteria (referenced as C1 to C7) to help assess the descriptive work that we outline in the next section. Before doing this, we briefly consider the Gini coefficient and Krugman index, the two most common measures of concentration and specialisation used in descriptive work.

Start with a measurement of the activity level of industry k in location i, and call this x_i^k.[14] This measurement may be based on employment, value-added, gross output or any other activity measure. If results change according to the units of measurement, then we need to consider which measure best captures structural changes and whether theory tells us anything about which measure is preferable for distinguishing between the null and alternative (C3 and C7). All the measures we consider express activity as a share, either of total EU activity in the industry (s_i^k), or activity in a given location (v_i^k). That is

$$s_i^k = x_i^k / \bar{x}^k \quad \text{and} \quad v_i^k = x_i^k / \bar{x}_i,$$

[14] The exposition here closely follows Midelfart-Knarvik et al. (2002). For simplicity, we ignore time.

where $\bar{x}^k = \sum_i x_i^k$ is total EU activity in industry k and $\bar{x}_i = \sum_k x_i^k$ is total activity in location i. The most frequently used measures are the Gini coefficients of concentration and specialisation based on the 'Location Quotient', or 'Balassa Index':

$$LQ_i^k = s_i^k / \bar{s}_i = v_i^k / \bar{v}^k,$$

where $\bar{s}_i \equiv \sum_k x_i^k / \sum_i \sum_k x_i^k$ is the share of location i in overall EU activity and $\bar{v}^k \equiv \sum_i x_i^k / \sum_k \sum_i x_i^k$ is the share of the same industry in total EU activity.[15] The Lorenz curve associated with the Gini coefficient of concentration of industry k ranks LQ_i^k across regions in ascending order and plots cumulated values of s_i^k on the vertical axis against cumulated values of $\bar{s}_i$ on the horizontal. The Gini is equal to the area between the Lorenz curve and the 45° line. The Lorenz curve corresponding to the Gini coefficient of specialisation is calculated similarly for a given region by ranking LQ_i^k across industries and plotting cumulated values of v_i^k against cumulated values of $\bar{v}^k$. The implied null hypothesis for both indices is that each location should just be a scaled version of the average "representative" EU region. Comparisons across locations, industries or time can be problematic. For instance, calculations from Midelfart-Knarvik et al. (2003) suggested that the associated Lorenz curves cross for at least 50% of changes over time. This happens when industry shares are declining simultaneously in both low- and high-share regions. Clearly, the first change increases concentration, while the second decreases it making statements about global changes dependent on the dominating effect.

Haaland et al. (1999) have argued for the use of Gini coefficients based on absolute shares rather than relative shares. The Lorenz curve associated with this absolute Gini of concentration ranks s_i^k, instead of LQ_i^k, and then plots cumulated shares against cumulated values of $1/N$ where N is the number of locations. The implied null hypothesis is rather odd: Each location has an identical share in each industry independent of the locations' overall size. It is hard to think of a random location model that would produce such a distribution. Unfortunately, under the null that each location should just be a scaled version of the average "representative" EU region, the value of this index depends on the distribution of overall activity across locations, again making comparisons difficult. This index does have the distinct advantage, however, that the level of concentration for a particular industry does not depend on the size of the country in which the industry is concentrated.

Another frequently used index was proposed by Krugman (1991a) to measure specialisation:

$$KS_i = \sum_k \left| v_i^k - \bar{v}^k \right|.$$

[15] Midelfart-Knarvik et al. (2002) suggest making this share country specific by only considering the share of the same industry in all other countries (i.e. $\bar{v}^k \equiv \sum_{j \neq i} x_i^k / \sum_k \sum_{j \neq i} x_i^k$). This can help ensure the index is comparable across different locations (C1) if the locations differ greatly in size, but then it is not clear what is the null hypothesis (C3).

The index takes value zero if location i has an industrial structure identical to that of the rest of the EU and has an upper bound of 2.[16] A similar index can be constructed for concentration if we instead sum across locations relative to the share of each location in overall EU activity:

$$KC_k = \sum_i \left| s_i^k - \bar{s}_i \right|.$$

The implied null for both indices is that each location should just be a scaled version of the average "representative" EU region. The index can be difficult to interpret when some industries are growing faster than others because magnification of existing initial differences changes the value of the index. It does, however, have the nice property that it can be used for bilateral comparisons of locations or industries.

Applications of these indices to EU-wide data suffer from a number of generic problems. First, given the data available, the measures used can take no account of industrial concentration as a driver of location and hence concentration or specialisation (C3). If we think this is important then these measures are not strictly comparable across industries or locations (C1). Second, the significance of results is often not reported (C4), often because there has been no explicit consideration of what random location would look like (C3). Third, the indices are not comparable across spatial scales or unbiased with respect to spatial scale (C2 and C5) because they take no account of the relative position of locations after we divide the EU into a set of countries or regions. Fourth, as should be clear from our discussion in Section 1, the level of detail in the industrial classification varies systematically for EU data depending on whether the activity is classified as manufacturing or services (C6). Finally and importantly, theories of location actually tell us very little, if anything, about how any of these measures should change with trade and integration, so these descriptive statistics can tell us very little about theory (C7). In addition, to these problems with the measures used, most studies fail to time-average the data, meaning that we cannot distinguish between temporary and structural changes and many studies are based on data which does not cover all industries or all locations, but there is no discussion of how completing the data would affect the results.

Other descriptive measures have been proposed and used in the literature. For instance, Greenway and Hine (1991) use the mean of the Finger–Kreinin for production and export data. Brülhart and Traeger (2002) study the generic family of entropy indices. Herfindhal indices, based on the sum of squares of industry shares in local activity, have also been quite widely used. The reader can assess for themselves which criteria these measures fulfil, but problems are in general similar to those encountered with the Gini and Krugman indices.

[16] A point which seems to have gone unnoticed in the literature is that the maximum value for the Krugman localisation index is not known. To see why, consider a two-region, two-industry situation. For industry one to be completed concentrated (i.e. $KL = 2$) it would need to be located in a region which had no share in overall manufacturing. Clearly this is not possible. The upper bound for any given industry approaches two as the industry becomes infinitely small with respect to overall manufacturing.

2.2.2. Specialisation patterns across EU countries

In describing the specialisation patterns of EU countries, we will refer exclusively to the group of papers that consider overall patterns for a majority of the countries in the EU. Earlier studies for individual countries exist; see, for example, Henner (1976) for France or Hine (1989) for Spain. However, we feel that a focus on pan-European papers is warranted given our interest in location patterns across the EU as a whole. We come back to the role of individual country studies in Section 2.3.

Table 2, taken from Midelfart-Knarvik et al. (2002) reports Krugman specialisation coefficients for 14 EU countries based on data from the OECD STAN database for 36 industries covering the period 1970 to 1997. Minimum values for each country are highlighted in bold. From the table, it is clear that the UK and France are the least specialised of the EU 15 countries. For these two countries, only roughly 10% of industrial activity would have to switch industry to bring them into line with the rest of the EU.[17] Ireland and Greece are the most specialised. For Ireland, 39% of industrial activity would have to switch industry to bring it into line. We can roughly identify four groups of countries in terms of specialisation patterns. The big core countries (France, Germany, and the UK) tend to be the least specialised. Small core countries tend to be

Table 2
Specialisation patterns in the EU

Country	1970–1973	1980–1983	1988–1991	1994–1997
Austria	0.314	**0.275**	0.281	0.348
Belgium	**0.327**	0.353	0.380	0.451
Denmark	0.562	**0.553**	0.585	0.586
Spain	0.441	**0.289**	0.333	0.338
Finland	0.598	**0.510**	0.528	0.592
France	0.204	**0.188**	0.207	0.201
Germany	0.319	**0.309**	0.354	0.370
Greece	**0.531**	0.580	0.661	0.703
Ireland	0.701	**0.623**	0.659	0.779
Italy	**0.351**	0.353	0.357	0.442
Netherlands	**0.508**	0.567	0.547	0.517
Portugal	0.536	**0.478**	0.588	0.566
Sweden	0.424	**0.393**	0.402	0.497
UK	0.231	**0.190**	0.221	0.206
Weighted average	0.326	**0.302**	0.33	0.351

Note. Minimum values for each country in bold font. Calculations based on four-year averages at the dates indicated.

[17] The rest of the EU is calculated excluding the country in question. The amount of industry that would have to move is calculated as the Krugman index divided by 2, because the measure counts both positive and negative deviations.

slightly more specialised (Austria, Belgium, the Netherlands). Scandinavian countries are still more specialised (Sweden, Denmark, Finland). Finally cohesion countries tend to be the most specialised (Greece, Ireland and Portugal).[18] Of course, these groups have fuzzy boundaries and overlap somewhat. Spain and Italy are outliers from this classification. Italy is a big core country with specialisation patterns roughly similar to the smaller core countries. Spain is a cohesion country with remarkably low levels of specialisation.

Further results from Midelfart-Knarvik et al. (2003) on bilateral comparisons and the type of industries in which countries specialise helps understand these differences. The French and UK economies are very similar to one another and quite similar to Germany. All three countries tend to specialise in high-tech, high-skill industries. In contrast, France, the UK and Germany are most dissimilar to Greece and Ireland and fairly dissimilar to Portugal explaining the high specialisation of these three countries. The least specialised of the cohesion countries, Spain, is relatively similar to the big three. In terms of the types of industries in which the Cohesion four are specialising, Ireland is the clear outlier. Greece and Portugal are tending to specialise in low-tech, low-skill industries, Spain in medium-tech, medium-skill, while Ireland has focused on high-tech, high-skill industry. Patterns in terms of the other two groups are also mixed. Of the three small core countries, Austria and Belgium are fairly similar in terms of both production structure and the type of industry (medium-skill, medium-tech). The Netherlands is the outlier of that group, both in terms of production structure and the type of industry (higher-skill, but lower-tech). Amongst the Scandinavians, Finland and Sweden have similar production structures although Sweden's is slightly higher-tech. Denmark's production structure is quite different to both these countries focusing on industries that are medium-skill and medium-tech making it more similar to Austria and Belgium. The reader is referred to Midelfart-Knarvik et al. (2003) for more details.

Once we turn to changes in specialisation, we can draw on a wider literature. In an early paper, Helg et al. (1995) present specialisation figures for the EU 12 countries based on the OECD Indicators for Industrial Activity for eight, 1-digit ISIC industries. Their results suggest that all countries, except France, Portugal and Spain become more specialised between 1975 and 1995. Their results are hard to interpret, however, as they are purely based on the shares of output of each industry in each country. Changes in the composition of output that are common across EU countries (say a move from textiles into chemicals) will show up as increased specialisation. Thus, these numbers capture both the change in individual countries relative to the rest of the EU and the change in the EU relative to the rest of the world. More recent studies have tended to focus on shifts in countries specialisation patterns relative to the rest of the EU as the key

[18] The "Cohesion countries" is often used to describe the four poorest members of the EU 15: Greece, Ireland, Portugal and Spain. The name reflects the fact that all four receive Cohesion Fund money from the EU aimed at increasing economic convergence with the rest of the EU.

variable of interest. Amiti (1999), Brülhart (1998a, 1998b, 2001a, 2001b), Brülhart and Torstensson (1996), CEPII (1997), OECD (1999), WIFO (1999), Midelfart-Knarvik et al. (2002, 2003) and Storper et al. (2002) all present results on specialisation for EU nations. Some differences arise due to differences in data, time periods and measurement techniques. However, the results from Midelfart-Knarvik et al. (2002) reported in Table 2 tell the basic story. Most countries were least specialised at the beginning of the 1980s, although four countries had already reached their minimum in the 1970s. Subsequent changes led all countries to become more specialised. Findings from WIFO (1999) using the more detailed industrial classification available for the DAISIE database are similar (although the exact timings differ slightly). Midelfart-Knarvik et al. (2003) also report bilateral comparisons using the same data. Of 91 distinct pairs, 71 exhibit increasing difference between the early 1980s and the 1990s.

Our feeling is that this sort of study has now hit fairly rapidly decreasing returns. As outlined in Section 3.1 attempts to collapse the entire structure of industrial production down to one number that can be compared across time and across countries are fraught with many difficulties and these studies suffer from a number of problems. These descriptive pieces epitomise the area-based approach we discussed in the introduction. They are useful for generating some stylised facts about location and integration in the EU, but they can tell us very little about what is causing those patterns or about location theory more generally. To summarise, the key stylised finding that does emerge – the degree of specialisation varies substantially across the EU and the bulk of the evidence suggests that EU countries are slowly becoming more specialised.

2.2.3. *A mixed picture for regional specialisation*

Following our discussion in Section 1, it should be clear that data availability means that making statements about economic activity in the EU at the regional level is much more difficult than making comparisons at the country level. Again, individual country studies exist for example, Smith (1975) for the UK, or Paluzie et al. (2001) for Spain, but there are relatively few studies taking an EU-wide perspective.

Molle (1997) provides the longest historical perspective that we can find. He reports Krugman coefficients of specialisation for 96 EU regions providing figures every 10 years from 1950 to 1990. Data limitations mean that he considers NUTS 2 regions for France, Spain and Italy, NUTS 1 regions for the UK and Germany, and country data for Sweden, Finland, Denmark, Ireland, Portugal and Greece.[19] He identifies three groups of regions. The overwhelming majority saw specialisation fall continuously throughout the period. A much smaller number saw a small rise in the 1950s, but a fall since. Finally, another small group saw no change, but these regions tended to have low specialisation coefficients to begin with. This is hardly the mixed picture to which the title of this subsection alludes. However, on close inspection, the numbers turn out to be quite hard to interpret. The calculations are based on Eurostat's NACE 17 industrial

[19] It is not clear how the paper deals with the three Benelux countries.

classification dividing employment into 17 branches. As we saw in Section 1, six of these branches cover service sectors. Of these service branches, five are market service branches and the sixth one is non-market services. Between them, these service sectors account for nearly 70% of employment by 1990. Arguably, the composition effects from the growth in services,[20] the tendency for some of the services (such as catering) to closely mirror population, the non-market nature of non-market services, and the rather aggregate regional classification mean that any changes in specialisation patterns are likely to be obscured. More recent work suggests that all of these concerns may be relevant.

Hallet (2000) suggests that even small increases in the number of regions tend to give a more mixed picture. Using the same NACE 17 industrial classification, but 119 regions instead of 96, he finds that between 1980 and 1995, 34 regions became more specialised, while 85 regions became less specialised. In contrast to Molle (1997), Hallet (2000) does discuss the fact that the changing composition of output from industry (where the NACE 17 classification is finer) to services (where it is more aggregate) will artificially reduce measures of specialisation, but does not then present figures just for the nine industrial branches. Midelfart-Knarvik and Overman (2002) do just that. Just focusing on industrial branches, they find a much more mixed picture. Now, a majority of regions (53%) become more specialised, with the remainder showing either a decrease or no change. On average, however, increases in regional specialisation are small.

Given the problems with EU data at the regional level, it could be useful to look at individual country data to get a richer picture. Unfortunately, these papers usually suffer from all the same problems as the EU-wide papers and are nearly always written from a national perspective. To take a good example, Paluzie et al. (2001) consider specialisation for 50 Spanish provinces (NUTS 3) for 30 manufacturing sectors over the time period 1979–1992. They find that 16 out of the 50 provinces show very small increases in specialisation while the rest show moderate decreases in specialisation. However, results from Table 2 suggest that Spain became more specialised relative to other EU countries. So, the fact that Spanish regions did not change much with respect to one another does not mean that Spanish regions did not become more specialised relative to the rest of the EU. Of course, which of these questions is more interesting may well depend on the theoretical model that you have in mind (C7). This brief discussion also suggests decomposing changes into within- and between-nations although we do not know of any study that does this.

All of this suggests the need for considerable caution in reaching conclusions at the regional level. Problems with getting regional data, composition effects and the lack of good detailed disaggregate data makes it difficult to reach broad conclusions for the EU's regions. The pattern appears mixed, but it is clear that more careful analysis and

[20] The classification for industrial activity is much finer relative to the overall industrial employment than the classification for services (9 industrial classifications to cover 30% of employment versus 6 industrial classifications to cover 70%). Thus as activity switches from several manufacturing branches into fewer service branches, we get a statistical reduction in specialisation.

better data seem to be pushing us in the direction of finding slightly more regional specialisation than we initially thought.

2.2.4. A mixed pattern for industrial concentration

Overall manufacturing activity is concentrated in the four biggest countries of the EU. In the mid-1990s Germany accounted for roughly 30% of total output, France 15%, Italy 14.5% and the UK 14%. Patterns in terms of overall manufacturing share are remarkably stable between 1970 and the mid-1990s at the national level. France and the UK have been the biggest losers with roughly a 2 and 3 percentage point decline, respectively. Italy has been the biggest gainer, increasing its share from 12.5% to 14.5% [Midelfart-Knarvik et al. (2003)]. The picture is different at the regional level where overall concentration (as measured by the coefficient of variation) has increased considerably, at least from 1980 onwards.

As for regional specialisation, when we turn to looking at the distribution of individual industries across locations, the pattern is again mixed. There are marked differences across industries in the degree to which they are concentrated. In terms of changes over time, some industries are becoming increasingly geographically concentrated, others are becoming less concentrated. We first deal briefly with the changes over time, before considering the characteristics of spatially concentrated industries in some detail in Section 2.2.5.

Midelfart-Knarvik et al. (2003) use production data from the OECD STAN database to calculate absolute Gini coefficients of concentration for 36 manufacturing sectors based on four-year averages (1970–1973, 1980–1983, 1990–1993, and 1994–1997). They find that concentration is increasing for 12 industries and decreasing for the remaining 24 industries. There is considerable variation over time. In the 1970s, 11 industries became increasingly concentrated, while 25 became less so. This pattern was reversed in the 1980s, with increasing concentration the norm (23 industries relative to 13 industries) before reversing again in the 1990s (15 industries increasing relative to 21). Table 3 shows the Gini coefficients for the 1970s, the 1990s and the change between those two periods. The industries are sorted from most to least concentrated according to how concentrated they were in the 1990s. The results broadly agree with those of Amiti (1999) using UNIDO production data for 27 manufacturing sectors for 10 EU countries.[21]

Turning to the regional level, we are again hampered by data availability. As for specialisation, Molle (1997) provides the longest historical study we can find looking at changes in industrial concentration from 1950 to 1990. The paper uses the Krugman

[21] They differ somehow from Brülhart (2001a) who conducts a similar exercise using employment data for 12 of the EU 15 countries. Brülhart's results are hard to interpret, however. First, he excludes Belgium, Ireland and Luxembourg due to data availability. Second, he fails to time-average the data, instead presenting the change between 1996 and 1972. It is thus difficult to know whether his findings are driven by structural differences, or just differences in the business cycle across countries.

Table 3
Industrial concentration across EU countries

Industry	Gini	Change	Industry	Gini	Change
Motor vehicles	0.703	0.009	Furniture & fixtures	0.596	0.028
Pottery & China	0.695	0.071	Machinery & equipment nec	0.592	−0.071
Aircraft	0.693	0.016	Tobacco	0.592	−0.070
Leather & products	0.685	0.138	Railroad equipment	0.591	−0.048
Petroleum & coal products	0.682	0.009	Communication equipment	0.589	−0.065
Motorcycles & bicycles	0.671	0.029	Glass & products	0.569	−0.047
Footwear	0.669	0.075	Metal products	0.567	−0.009
Electrical apparatus nec	0.645	−0.023	Textiles	0.566	0.012
Transport equipment nec	0.628	0.077	Beverages	0.557	−0.090
Rubber products	0.624	0.005	Other manufacturing	0.552	−0.025
Non-ferrous metals	0.623	0.042	Industrial chemicals	0.546	−0.067
Chemical products nec	0.622	−0.036	Non-metallic minerals nec	0.542	−0.034
Petroleum refineries	0.621	−0.010	Pharmaceuticals	0.519	−0.078
Wearing apparel	0.613	0.038	Printing & publishing	0.515	−0.024
Iron & steel	0.611	−0.014	Wood products	0.498	−0.035
Office & computing machinery	0.608	−0.072	Paper & products	0.479	−0.025
Plastic products	0.600	−0.002	Food	0.460	−0.043
Professional instruments	0.597	−0.068	Shipbuilding & repairing	0.445	−0.022

index of concentration. The data and regional definition are the same as for his study of regional specialisation. The results show that most sectors experience a decrease in concentration. Only Agriculture and Textiles show an increase, while Mining, and Food, Beverages and Tobacco show no clear pattern. However, as for specialisation, the inclusion of service sectors makes the results very hard to interpret due to the compositional changes over the time period. To see the problem, consider one particular manufacturing sector such as Transport Equipment. Imagine that, relative to manufacturing, the concentration of Transport Equipment remained unchanged. What happens to the index will now be driven purely by the relationship between changes in regional manufacturing shares and changes in shares in other activities. Again, whether this makes sense will depend on the null hypothesis (C3) and theory (C7) one has in mind.

We have little additional evidence. In a recent paper, Brülhart and Traeger (2002) consider changes in regional specialisation using data for NUTS 2 regions disaggregating employment into eight sectors covering the full range of economic activities. They decompose concentration into what they call topographic and relative components. Topographic concentration considers the degree to which sectors are concentrated in geographical space, relative concentration considers the degree to which sectors are concentrated relative to overall activity. Although preliminary, their results suggest that the topographic distribution of total employment is stable. Broad sectors show conflicting movements, with agriculture becoming more topographically concentrated and manufacturing less. For individual sectors however, only Transport and Communication services and Non-market services show significant decreases, while the four remaining sectors remain unchanged. This overall stability is increasingly driven by between-country considerations rather than within-country considerations. Turning to relative concentration, they find that there has been a monotonic increase in the relative concentration of manufacturing. Further, their evidence suggests that these increases are significant. In contrast, Transport and Communications and Non-market services have seen significant reductions in their relative concentration.

2.2.5. The characteristics of spatially concentrated industries

In the introduction, we suggested that in an ideal world, this chapter would need to do two things. First, spend a lot of time describing the location of economic activity in the EU. Second, explain these patterns drawing widely on other chapters in the handbook, leaving us to consider in depth only material that helps us understand why things in the EU might be different. Obviously, this second stage would require us to clearly identify the differences between the EU and the U.S. Data quality and conceptual issues mean that this has proved difficult to do, so the literature has taken a different route. This area-based descriptive work has now spawned a new set of area-based explanatory pieces using methodologies that allow for the limited amount of data available in the EU.

In this section, we consider the characteristics of concentrated industries by looking at what we think of as this "first generation" of area-based studies. These follow Kim (1995) in examining the determinants of concentration by considering the correlation between spatial concentration and industry characteristics. We review this literature in depth here. We conclude that, for a number of reasons, this work often ends up telling us very little about what explains the economic geography of Europe. While the authors often claim that these papers represent tests of various economic geography models, we believe that they are purely descriptive in nature.

Two early papers, Brülhart and Torstensson (1996) and Brülhart (1998b) use employment data to compute rank correlations between Gini indices of spatial concentration and returns to scale and to consider whether concentrated industries are found in core or peripheral locations. They do this for two years, 1980 and 1990, for 11 countries (EU 12 minus Luxembourg) and 18 manufacturing industries. Data are from EUROSTAT and the OECD. Returns to scale are based on Pratten (1988). Core and peripheral locations are defined using a simple market potential based on GDP and geodesic distances. Brülhart (1998b) extends this work by further classifying industries according to their labour and resource intensity, whether they are science based, and whether goods are highly differentiated. His classification is taken from OECD (1987). Both papers also study the impact of these determinants on intra-industry trade using a Grubel–Lloyd index for six points between 1961 and 1990.

In contrast to Kim (1995), neither paper uses time-varying explanatory factors ruling out the use of industry fixed effects. This is unfortunate as industry fixed effects could control for some of the problems with both the concentration measure and the explanatory variables. In particular, in line with the discussion of C3 in Section 2.2.1, fixed effects can partly account for the fact that the Gini index does not control for the degree of industrial concentration. Note, however, that industry fixed effects cannot totally control for industrial concentration in the way suggested by Ellison and Glaeser (1997) because the Herfindahl enters their index non-linearly. Fixed effects also control for omitted variables, such as the nature of competition, if these characteristics are time-invariant. Interpretation of the intra-industry trade results is also difficult because as, Brülhart (1998a) himself notes, the link between intra-industry trade and spatial concentration is complex and non-monotonic. Cross-sectional differences in intra-industry trade tell us little about spatial concentration if we cannot control for all the other determinants of trade. Even for a given industry, more concentration does not necessarily imply less intra-industry trade if global volumes of trade have changed.

Amiti (1999) moves beyond simple correlations making her paper closest in spirit to Kim (1995). Using Eurostat data, she computes Gini indices of production and employment concentration across 5 EU countries for 65 manufacturing industries between 1976 and 1989. She captures Heckscher–Ohlin effects through the share of labour in value-added and uses the cost of intermediate inputs divided by value-added to proxy for demand and cost linkages arguing that high intermediate input usage should encourage concentration near intermediate suppliers. Plant size is used as a proxy for increasing returns. Results on these variables should be interpreted with caution, however. Labour intensity only considers one type of factor while inputs include raw materials, so the intermediate input variable actually confounds Heckscher–Ohlin and linkages effects. Average plant size is only a good proxy for increasing returns under strong conditions.[22] Some of these problems are mitigated by the fact that estimations allow for time and industry fixed effects.

Haaland et al. (1999) extend Amiti (1999) to consider more countries (EU 15 apart from Luxembourg and Ireland) at the cost of a more aggregated industrial classification (35 industries from STAN) and less time-series coverage (data is only available for 1985 and 1992, which prevents them from using fixed effects). As discussed in Section 3, they calculate both an absolute and relative Gini coefficient of concentration. Their explanatory variables capture labour intensity, human capital intensity, technology level, returns to scale, non-tariff trade barriers and concentration of final demand.[23]

This brief survey of papers is not exhaustive. Other studies providing simple correlations include Brülhart (2001a) and Brülhart (2001b) covering 32 manufacturing sectors

[22] It assumes that the industry is in long-run equilibrium so that firm numbers have adjusted to ensure zero profit. Further, if firms behave strategically or products are differentiated, firm size can differ across industries with the same degree of economies of scale unless strategic behaviour and the degree of product differentiation are identical across sectors. Other considerations can also break the link between plant size and returns to scale. In particular, in some models firm size is codetermined with spatial concentration meaning this variable may be endogenous as well as a bad proxy for returns to scale.

[23] Returns to scale are based on Cawley and Davenport (1988) which basically transforms Pratten's (1988) ordinal ranking into a continuous variable. Factor and input intensities are calculated from Eurostat input–output tables and the OECD (1994). The final demand variable is based on final expenditure data. This last variable is potentially endogenous and is instrumented using lagged values when necessary, although the suitability of lagged values as an instrument is not tested.

from 1972–1996. Midelfart-Knarvik et al. (2003) consider additional characteristics including capital intensity, within- and between-industry linkages, agricultural inputs, and final demand bias for 36 industries for 14 EU countries for 1970–1997 using data from OECD STAN.

If we take their results at face value, what do we learn about the spatial concentration of EU industries from this series of papers?

Labour, capital, and resource intensity. The papers find little evidence that labour, capital or resource intensive activities tend to be more concentrated. Amiti (1999) finds no correlation with labour intensity. Haaland et al. (1999) find a weak positive correlation with labour intensity in 1992, but not 1985, and the reverse for human capital intensity. This is supported by Midelfart-Knarvik et al. (2003) whose simple correlations suggest a positive effect of skill intensity only in the 1970s and no effect of capital intensity for any period. Brülhart (1998a) finds that both labour- and resource-intensive industries are more dispersed across space than the average. The high intra-industry trade observed in labour-intensive industries leads to a similar conclusion although these trade volumes are low for resource-intensive industries.

Technology. Technology-intensive and science-based industries are more concentrated than average according to both Brülhart (1998a) and Haaland et al. (1999) although both studies detect a decline of spatial concentration in these sectors.

Increasing returns to scale. All papers except Haaland et al. (1999) find a positive correlation between increasing returns to scale and spatial concentration.

Demand and cost linkages. Evidence on the role of demand and cost linkages are mixed. Brülhart (1998a) finds that concentration takes places in high market potential areas. Amiti (1999) finds a positive correlation for the intermediate input cost variable, while the own input variable of Haaland et al. (1999) is associated with increased absolute, but not relative, concentration. In contrast, Midelfart-Knarvik et al. (2003) find no significant correlation with intra- or inter-industry inputs. Nor do they find any correlation with final demand.

Trade barriers and trade liberalisation. Results on transactions costs are inconclusive and somewhat contradictory. Non-tariff barriers are not correlated with relative concentration [Haaland et al. (1999)], nor intra-industry trade [Brülhart (1998a)]. On the other hand, Haaland et al. (1999) show that absolute concentration is associated with high trade barriers.

For comparison, we briefly review what this approach tells us about the spatial concentration of activities in the U.S. Kim (1995) has data on employment for 20 industries across 9 regions at 5 points in time, 1880, 1914, 1947, 1967 and 1987. He uses this data to calculate a Gini index of employment concentration across regions. He assumes two variables which can explain variations across industries and time – the share of raw material in value-added and average plant size in the industry to capture differences in the degree of increasing returns to scale. As for the EU, Kim (1995) finds positive effects of increasing returns to scale, but in contrast to the EU, he also finds a positive significant effect for raw materials. Taken at face value, this suggests an important difference between EU countries and U.S. regions. In the EU, transaction costs have prevented countries from specialising according to their comparative advantage.

At first glance, the results presented in this section seem to paint a fairly rich picture, even if they are not always consistent with one another. Overall though, we feel that the methodological problems are such that despite the claims of the authors an acceptable *explanation* of EU location patterns cannot, and will not, be based on the kind of evidence that we have considered here. One can even question their validity as useful descriptions of the industry characteristics associated with spatial concentration.

From an econometric point of view, we can identify a number of serious problems with regressions based on indices and industry characteristics.

(i) Differences in spatial concentration are captured using summary measures of the kind we described in Section 2.2.1. As such, they suffer from all the problems that we outlined in detail there.

(ii) The number of explanatory variables in these studies is low (often less than three) compared to the complexity of the phenomenon that is studied, and it is sometimes difficult to link the way in which some variables are computed and the effects they are supposed to capture.

(iii) Dealing with omitted variable problems that we know are present requires at least introducing industry fixed effects, which in turn requires industry characteristics to vary over time. A similar observation can be made with regard to country fixed effects.

(iv) Explanatory variables may be endogenous and simultaneously determined in a complex way suggesting the need for instrumenting.

(v) We need to take account of spatial autocorrelation and other sources of heterogeneity.

Of course, many of these criticisms reflect data problems. However, there are two key conceptual issues here. First, given the state of the art, theory tells us nothing about the relationship between these indices and industry characteristics when the number of regions is larger than two. Second, as pointed out by Midelfart-Knarvik et al. (2000), working on concentration indices (and other summary statistics) wastes information on the location of industries across space. If concentration indices can be computed, then data on industry shares are available and can be used as dependent variable. Why not use this information instead of calculating one summary statistic? This is not just a question of throwing away information. Ellison and Glaeser (1999), Midelfart-Knarvik et al. (2000), Gaigné et al. (2002), and Combes and Lafourcade (2001) all develop theoretical models that make predictions about industry shares. We believe that understanding the determinants of economic location in the EU requires an approach which explicitly builds on theory and which uses the existing data in the most efficient way to assess these theories. We consider this issue further in Section 3.

Where does this leave us with respect to industrial concentration? First given the quality of available data, it is clear that making further progress at the national level will be difficult. Brülhart and Traeger (2002) suggest that some limited progress could be made at the regional level. However, our feeling is that without significant improvement in the quality of EU regional data, this sort of approach is also going to run into decreasing returns to scale very soon. We now turn to outline a more positive research agenda.

2.3. Comparing the EU and the U.S.: a role for micro-geographical data?

To avoid some of the problems underlined in the previous section, we also need to use the limited amount of data that we have more effectively. In Section 3, we outline some explanatory work that begins to do this. Before that, however, we want to outline how a different approach to descriptive work might also help. Krugman (1991a) introduced the idea that activity in the U.S. may be more concentrated than in the EU by comparing employment data for four U.S. regions (Northeast, Midwest, South and West) with four large European countries (Germany, France, the UK and Italy). The comparison is interesting if we can think of the U.S. as a large integrated economy that may act as a benchmark for where an integrating Europe might be heading. Of course, certain features of the economic geography literature argue caution in undertaking such an exercise. For example, in formal models, whether agglomeration occurs depends on the share of the increasing returns to scale, transport intensive good in consumption. This share may have changed over time. Coupled with the path-dependant nature of economic geography models, it is unclear to what extent the U.S. is a good benchmark for the future of the EU. With this caution in mind, we still believe that such a comparison would be useful.

Unfortunately, a more rigorous comparison has not been forthcoming. The key problem is that the U.S. and Europe are differently sized and shaped. This introduces problems if concentration measures are not comparable across spatial scales (C2) and are biased with respect to spatial scale (C5). Given that most existing measures do not meet these criteria, comparing levels of these concentration measures is non-informative (although comparing changes over time may be). As discussed in Section 2.2.1, this is not just a matter of having the same number of spatial units, or the same size spatial units, but a more fundamental one about making comparisons between geographical areas on the basis of discretising continuous space.[24] Midelfart-Knarvik et al. (2003) come the closest to addressing this issue by proposing a spatial separation index which takes into account the distance between spatial units (in their case countries). This allows them to distinguish between industries that may appear equally geographically concentrated using standard measures, while one is predominantly located in two neighbouring locations and the other split between (say) Finland and Portugal. To compare concentration in the EU and the U.S., they propose calculating a conditional spatial separation index

[24] This point is still misunderstood. For example, Aigenger and Leitner (2002) emphasise the importance of getting data for an approximately comparable number of regions in the U.S. and Europe. But this does not resolve the issue.

as the spatial separation index for each industry divided by that for manufacturing as a whole. This controls for the greater geographical size by making all statements conditional on the distribution of overall manufacturing. They calculate this conditional measure for 21 industries in the mid-1990s and compare EU countries with U.S. states. They find that in 15 out of 21 industries, the location of activity is less concentrated in the EU than the U.S. This finding is evocative, but we think that a more careful analysis is needed before a clear conclusion can be reached.

It seems to us that too little of the existing literature confronts this key question head on. In what ways does the EU differ from the U.S.? It should be clear from the discussion above that we have not reached a conclusion about this on the basis of studying pan-European data. Indeed, the quality of the EU data is the fundamental barrier to reaching such a conclusion. It is also clear that we are unlikely to see a significant improvement in this pan-European data in the near future. This is, of course, unfortunate, because we would like to know (say) if labour immobility in Europe leads to EU activity being more dispersed and we can probably only answer this question with better pan-European data. However, some key questions can be answered now using the micro-geographic data that is beginning to emerge in countries across the EU.[25]

These micro-geographic data sets allow us to calculate indices which come close to meeting the criteria that we outlined in Section 2.2.1. Further, they allow us to do this for fairly detailed industrial classifications. There are, of course, problems with making precise comparisons across countries due to the fact that industrial classifications differ. But the results do allow us to begin to identify some of the detailed differences between EU countries and the U.S.

To see what we can learn from this approach, we will compare three papers that apply the Ellison and Glaeser (1997) index of concentration to three different countries – Ellison and Glaeser (1997) for the U.S., Maurel and Sédillot (1999) for France and Devereux et al. (2002) for the UK. The Ellison and Glaeser methodology was discussed briefly when we considered criterion C3 and is outlined in depth by Rosenthal and Strange (2004) in this volume, so we do not describe it in detail here. The basic idea is to use micro-level firm data to assess whether or not industries are randomly located once we condition on the overall distribution of manufacturing and "lumpiness" due to industrial concentration.

Ellison and Glaeser (1997) consider 459 four-digit industries. Firms can be located in counties, regions or states. Maurel and Sédillot (1999) consider 273 four-digit industries. Firms can be located in 22 regions or 95 departments. Finally, Devereux et al. (2002) consider 214 industries for 124 postcode areas. Let us start by considering the comparison of the UK and the U.S. Table 4 presents the most concentrated industries in the UK that can be matched to a reasonable U.S. counterpart, while Table 5 presents

[25] At the time of writing, we are aware that researchers are being given access to these micro-geographic data sets in Belgium, France, Germany, Ireland, Italy, Portugal and the UK.

Table 4
Most concentrated industries in the UK and their U.S. counterpart

	Rank UK	Rank U.S.
Spinning and weaving	1	13 (Yarn and spinning), 20 (Throwing and winding), 21 (Thread mills)
Jute and polypropylene	3	17 (Broad woven fabric mills – man-made fibre and silk)
Lace	5	Top 60
Cutlery	6	Top 120
Other carpets	7	6 (Carpets and rugs)
Hosiery	9	3 (women's), 5 (men's)
Jewellery	11	8 (Costume jewellery), 10 (Jewellers material lapidary)
Weaving cotton	13	17 (Broad woven fabric mills – man-made fibre and silk) 28–32? (Broad woven fabric mills cotton)
Caravans	14	36–41 (Motor homes)
Woollen	15	Top 70 (Broad woven fabric mills – woollen)
Spirit distilling	16	2 (Wines, brandy, spirits)

Table 5
Most dispersed industries in the UK and their U.S. counterpart

	Rank UK	Rank U.S.
Sugar and its by products	1	14th most dispersed (Cane sugar refining)
Water supply	2	40th most dispersed (Manufactured ice)
Synthetic rubber	3	60th most concentrated (Synthetic rubber)
Rubber tyres	4	Median (Tires and inner tubes)
Tobacco	5	22nd most concentrated (Tobacco)
Adhesive film	6	40th most dispersed (Adhesives an sealants)
Ordnance small arms	7	6th most dispersed (Small arms ammunition), 70th most concentrated (Small arms)
Telegraph and telephone apparatus	8	30th most dispersed (Telegraph and telephone)
Musical instruments	9	40th most dispersed (Musical instruments)
Wheeled tractors	15	30th most dispersed (Industrial trucks and tractors)

the most dispersed industries.[26] The first column gives the name of the UK industry. The second gives the rank. For the concentrated industries this ranks from most concentrated, for the dispersed industries from most dispersed. As mentioned above, problems with the classifications mean that we cannot always find a match for an industry. Still, the results are fascinating. For the matched top 11 UK industries (i.e. top 5%), all of the U.S. industries are at least in the top 120 industries (i.e. the top 25%). For 10 of them, the U.S. industries are at least in the top 70 industries (i.e. top 15%). For 7 of them the corresponding U.S. industries are (roughly) in the top 20 industries (i.e. top 5%). The

[26] Calculating a more formal correlation is not possible given the problems of matching the classifications. However, a much more systematic attempt to match classifications should be possible.

Table 6
Most concentrated industries in France and their UK and U.S. counterparts

	Rank France	Rank U.S.	Rank UK
Steel pipe and tubes	2	Above median (Steel pipe and tubes)	76 (Steel tubes)
Combed wool spinning mills	3	Top 70 (Broad woven fabric mills – woollen)	15 (Woollen)
Wool preparation	5		
Periodicals	6	Top 80 (Periodicals)	14 (Periodicals)
Flat glass	8	Bottom 150 (Flat glass)	195 (Flat glass)
Carded wool weaving mills	11	Top 70 (Broad woven fabric mills – woollen)	15 (Woollen)
Carded wool spinning mills	15		
Book publishing	13	Top 80 (Book publishing)	26 (Books)
Cutlery	14	Top 120 (Cutlery)	6 (Cutlery)
Small arms	15	6 (Small arms ammunition), 60–70 concentrated (Small arms)	7th most dispersed (Small arms ordnance)

most remarkable thing to emerge from this table is the fact that concentrated industries in the UK also tend to be concentrated in the U.S. The story is more mixed when we turn to the dispersed industries. 6 of the most dispersed industries match with industries that are amongst the 40 most dispersed industries in the U.S. Ordnance small arms matches exactly for Small arms ammunition, but Small arms themselves are quite concentrated in the U.S. The Rubber industry appears quite dispersed in the UK, but quite concentrated in the U.S., and the same is true of Tobacco. Again, we would argue that one of the more remarkable things is the similarity between dispersed industries in the UK and the U.S. The overall picture that emerges is one of very similar concentration patterns. Of course, some differences need explanation, but the similarities are striking.

What about France? In Table 6 we compare the results from Maurel and Sédillot (1999) to both the U.S. and the UK. Again, the match between classifications is not perfect and we have systematically ignored the extraction industries which Maurel and Sédillot (1999) report, but Ellison and Glaeser (1997) do not. The match between rankings here is clearly not quite as tight as for the UK and the U.S. However, note that for 8 out of the 10 top ranked matched activities, similar industries are above average in both the U.S. and the UK. Only for Flat glass and Small arms does there seem to be some really different patterns across the three countries.

Rather than going through a similar exercise with dispersed industries, we can use the results in Maurel and Sédillot (1999) to ask what might happen if we could achieve a better ranking between industrial classifications. Table 7, taken from Maurel and Sédillot (1999) reports what happens when we calculate the Ellison and Glaeser (1997) index for 2-digit industries that are broadly comparable across the two countries.

The Spearman rank correlation between these rankings is 0.6. Maurel and Sédillot (1999) get the same number if they consider the correlation between the levels of the Ellison and Glaeser (1997) index for these 2-digit industries. Again, we are struck by the similarities. Further, if we could explain a small number of differences, for example, publishing and printing, the match between the concentration patterns would really start

Table 7
Two-digit industries rankings in France and the U.S.

	U.S.	France
Textile mill products	1	2
Leather and leather products	2	1
Furniture and fixtures	3	10
Lumber and wood products	4	8
Primary metal industries	5	9
Instruments and related products	6	5
Transportation equipment	7	17
Apparel and other textile products	8	4
Miscellaneous manufacturing ind	9	6
Chemicals and allied products	10	7
Paper and allied products	11	11
Electronic and other electrical equipment	12	13
Printing and publishing	13	3
Fabricated metal products	14	14
Rubber and misc plastics	15	12
Stone, clay and glass products	16	15
Industrial machinery and equipment	17	16

to look quite strong. Finally, results in Duranton and Overman (2002) suggest that we may need to consider alternatives to Ellison and Glaeser (1997) that are unbiased with respect to spatial scale. This also might help explain some of the differences that we see here.

We believe that our discussion here highlights the possibility for a much more constructive research agenda on the spatial distribution of economic activity in the EU. Using micro-geographical data sets at the national level we should be able to get a much more detailed picture of the similarities and differences between the EU and the U.S. We should also be able to compare the economic geographies of countries within the EU. Indeed, work in progress by Barrios et al. (2003) provides just such a comparison for Belgium, Ireland and Portugal. Their preliminary results suggest that there are marked similarities between industrial location patterns in Belgium and Portugal while Ireland's pattern of agglomeration differs significantly from the other two countries. However, their results do raise some questions about the applicability of the Ellison and Glaeser index to countries with such different internal geographies (C2 and C5). Our rather casual look at the micro-geographic descriptive evidence available for France, the UK and the U.S., suggests that similar industries are concentrated in all three countries. A much deeper understanding of the similarities would have profound implications for on going research. If concentration patterns are comparable across countries then we should be able understanding those patterns with reference to a large body of existing literature (mostly based on U.S. data). This is *not* what is happening at the moment. The mirror image argument also holds. Where similarities exist, we can learn about location theory more generally by considering the very good data that is available at the individual country level in the EU.

Of course, such comparisons cannot yet provide us with a direct comparison of the EU and the U.S. Indeed, similarities at the country level may point to the fact that inertia characterises most location decisions and that EU countries have built their economic spaces before the making of the EU could have a significant impact. Getting at this direct comparison calls for an even more ambitious project structured around the merging of plant level data sets from different EU countries. From our brief discussion, however, it should be clear that such an undertaking could have big payoffs in terms of our understandings of the differences between the EU and the U.S.

2.4. Where we stand

EU area studies presented in this section give us some ideas about broad spatial location patterns both in terms of individual activities and in terms of the core–periphery pattern for aggregate activity. We have some ideas about which types of economic activities are concentrated. We have less idea about whether this makes us different from other economic areas of the world. This is unfortunate, because area-based descriptive work that does not allow comparison with other economic areas cannot really tell us much about location theory more generally. In this section, we have suggested two areas where further descriptive work might deliver interesting insights. First, we would benefit from direct comparisons of EU location patterns with other economic areas, particularly the U.S. These direct comparisons will need to deal with most of the problems we raised in Section 2.2.1 if they are actually going to be informative about the similarities and differences. Second, given the appalling state of EU-wide data, we think that individual-level micro-geographic surveys could also be used to facilitate this sort of comparison. Indeed, our limited comparison above suggests that there are many similarities between UK, French and U.S. concentration patterns once we start considering detailed location patterns. This is interesting, because most European area-based studies start with the premise that there are fundamental differences between the EU and the U.S. in the nature and strength of agglomeration and dispersion forces. From the evidence we have so far, this argument receives only limited empirical support. Conditional on the location of overall manufacturing, EU industries do seem slightly more dispersed than their U.S. counterparts. However, within-country rankings of most to least concentrated industries appear to show a reasonable degree of correlation. We are struck as much by the similarities as the differences. The same will be true when we consider explanations of these patterns, an issue to which we now turn.

3. Explanations

Section 2 has considered what we know about concentration and specialisation in the EU. We now turn to those studies assessing the possible explanations of these patterns.

The empirical papers that try to explain the distribution of economic activities across space share the same global theoretical corpus. This corpus, however, is not unique, homogenous, or unified. Further, and in line with our earlier comments, the existence of an EU area-based approach to determinants of location is only truly justified if this body of theory suggests that the EU is somehow different from other economic entities. We consider this issue in Section 3.1. This section also helps when we turn to the interpretation of the empirical studies in the following sections.

3.1. A brief survey of location theory and its application to the EU

We start by considering the three main families of theory dealing with space and agglomeration – traditional trade theory, economic geography, and urban and spatial economics. We then present a classification of the different forces pushing towards more or less agglomeration. We emphasise that some of these forces are common to different theories. Finally, we study two critical determinants shaping these forces – transaction costs and labour mobility. We argue that justifications for an area-based study of EU location patterns requires not only that the EU is different with respect to these determinants, but also that this has significant implications for understanding the economic geography of the EU.

3.1.1. Theories of space and location

3.1.1.1. Trade theory under constant returns to scale and perfect competition. Theories of comparative advantage make clear predictions about location. Trade allows specialisation with each location specialising in the goods in which it has a comparative advantage. In Ricardian models, comparative advantage is a result of exogenous technology differences, in Heckscher–Ohlin a result of exogenous differences in endowments. We refer to this strand of literature as "traditional trade theory".

3.1.1.2. Economic geography. This set of models adopts assumptions polar to traditional trade theory. Technology is increasing returns to scale and identical across locations. Competition is imperfect. Endowments are identical, but factors may be mobile across locations so that incomes and factor prices can be endogenously driven by location choices. Increasing returns encourage firms to concentrate output in a limited number of plants. The location of these plants will depend on agglomeration and dispersion forces. Core locations give good access to suppliers and customers (cost and demand linkages). Peripheral locations avoid product and factor market competition. If agglomeration forces dominate dispersion forces, firms concentrate in a few places and export to other locations. We refer to this strand of literature as "economic geography". See Ottaviano and Thisse (2004) in this volume for a detailed review.

3.1.1.3. Urban and spatial economics. Economic geography models emphasise cost and demand linkages as the key agglomeration force. Urban and spatial economics considers additional agglomeration externalities arising from localised knowledge spillovers, labour market considerations and the provision of public goods. We refer to this strand of literature as "urban economics". See Duranton and Puga (2004) in this volume for a detailed review.

3.1.2. Agglomeration and dispersion forces

Each of these theories contains features that explain the forces driving location and thus allow us to assess how these might differ for the EU. Our strategy is not to consider all of these in details, but instead to consider the main forces that shape the distribution of economic activities and consider how these forces might differ between the EU and other areas.

3.1.2.1. Local endowments. In many models local endowments have a direct impact on location. Considered in their broadest sense, local endowments can capture the effects of factors, technology, physical geography (including natural resources), local public goods (including transport networks), cultural goods and local institutions or legislation. Although most theories take these endowments as given, physical geography is the only one which is clearly exogenous. Factor endowments are endogenous if factors are mobile while technology may depend on the composition and size of local industry. Local public goods are only exogenous if provision is independent of local economy composition and finance is not local (as for some public services in Europe). This suggests key ways in which the EU may differ from other areas. Either with respect to its physical geography or with respect to other endowments and their responsiveness to local economic conditions.

3.1.2.2. Within-industry interactions. In most theoretical models, a key factor shaping the distribution of spatial activity are interactions between local agents. Here we consider within-industry (or localisation) economies that arise because of interactions between agents in the same industry. Urban economics and economic geography consider within-industry demand and cost linkages as one source of localisation economies. These effects can also occur in traditional trade models. There is a key difference however – demand and cost linkages are magnified in economic geography models due to the presence of increasing returns to scale. Technological spillovers and labour market externalities can also work within-industry while localisation diseconomies are also possible when good and factor market competition depends on the number and size of local competitors in the same industry.

Do within-industry interactions provide a second source of differences between the EU and other areas? The answer is not clear and would involve EU industries "working" in different ways from the same industries in other areas. Different contractual settings might influence the degree of outsourcing and thus the nature of inter-firm input–output linkages. Different labour market institutions could change the way in which labour market externalities operate in the EU, while different intellectual property rights could change the nature of technological spillovers. Finally, different anti-trust regimes might change the nature of local competition. All of these are possibilities, but we know little about whether or not they are realities.

3.1.2.3. Between-industry interactions. Between-industry interactions (or urbanisation economies) depend on overall activity in an area. The impact may vary across activities. For example, access to final demand will depend on the overall population but will matter more for industries that sell a high proportion of their output to final consumers. Local public goods provision can also depend on overall size, as can cost linkages and technological spillovers. In some theories, where CES preferences (or technology) mean that variety increases utility (or efficiency), diversity matters rather than overall size. Jacobs (1969) also claims that many technology spillovers depend on diversity. Urbanisation diseconomies, including congestion effects, occur if firms compete for the same factors (e.g. land) or customers.

Do between-industry interactions provide a third source of differences between the EU and other areas? As before, contractual arrangements, labour market institutions, anti-trust laws and intellectual property rights could all play a role. Another more realistic possibility is that institutional differences concerning land use and local taxation may change the nature of urbanisation diseconomies. Again, we have little idea if these possibilities are realities.

3.1.3. The determinants of agglomeration and dispersion forces

It is clear from the discussion above that we do not have a clear idea how individual agglomeration and dispersion forces may differ between the EU and other areas. Here, we briefly consider the factors that can explain why the strength of these forces may be different in the EU.

3.1.3.1. Transaction costs. Transaction costs play a key role in determining the location of activity. For high transaction costs, economic activities are dispersed. The agglomeration gains that could emerge from concentration are more than offset by dispersion forces. As long as economic activities remain dispersed, lowering transaction costs increases the level of trade between locations. For a range of intermediate transaction costs firms have incentives to agglomerate despite competition and congestion. If transaction costs fall far enough, the process of concentration may be reversed due to congestion costs induced by spatial concentration. Whether this happens depends on the assumptions made on the nature of competition and the degree of product differentiation, increasing returns to scale, and factor mobility. As we know of no compelling evidence to suggest that these three factors should be modelled differently in the EU we do not consider this issue further. However, differences in factor mobility may matter and it is this issue we now turn to.

3.1.3.2. Factor mobility. To see the importance of labour mobility, note simply that if higher real wages in core regions encourage migration, this both increases demand linkages and mitigates product and factor market competition. Although this migration may increase congestion and land prices, these effects may be secondary and thus, in models where factors are mobile, activity should be at least as concentrated for any given level of transaction costs.

3.1.3.3. Location in the EU: two key differences? Casual observation suggests that the EU has higher transaction costs and lower labour mobility than the U.S. More formal analysis confirms this.[27] It is these two key differences which have been used to justify an area-based approach to explaining location in the EU. For the moment, we put aside whether this is a valid justification and turn to consider the explanatory literature in depth and assess what it tells us about the role of these differences.

3.2. *Industrial localisation in the EU*

In this section we consider explanations of the location patterns of particular industries. In the next section, we consider labour productivity and wages. In the final section we turn to consider the dynamics of localisation.

3.2.1. *Trade-based approaches*

Traditional trade theories emphasise supply considerations as the key determinant of the location of different industries. Two additional factors, the distribution of demand and the ease of trade, should also play a role. As we saw above, these two factors have a stronger impact in economic geography models with imperfect competition and increasing returns to scale. Both sets of models predict that the impact of explanatory factors will differ across industries.

Traditional trade models that explain location in terms of differences in technology or factors can be used to derive simple estimating equations by imposing few additional assumptions. For example, Harrigan (1997) assumes a translog functional form for the revenue function and technological differences that are Hicks neutral and industry specific to derive the following specification straight from theory:

$$s_i^k = \sum_{h=1}^{K} a_{kh} \ln \theta_i^h + \sum_{f=1}^{F} r_{kf} \ln v_i^f + \varepsilon_i^k.$$

where k indexes goods ($k = 1, \ldots, K$), f indexes factors ($f = 1, \ldots, F$), s_i^k is the share of good k value added in location i's GDP, θ_i^h is a scalar productivity parameter measuring the productivity in industry h of location i relative to productivity in a base

[27] A large number of studies in the run up to the single market showed that EU markets where significantly segmented for a wide range of goods. On labour mobility, to give just one example, Eichengreen (1993) shows that the elasticity of inter-regional migrations with respect to local wages is twenty-five times higher in the U.S. than in Great Britain.

country and v_i^f is location i's endowment of factor f. The a's and r's are parameters to be estimated. Harrigan (1997) estimates this specification industry by industry using a panel of OECD countries. Note that the a's and the r's are industry specific, so the way technology and factor supplies affect output is only constrained to be the same across locations not industries. In contrast, as we will see, economic-geography models that need to incorporate both supply and demand effects impose more structure on the differences across industries. These differences will usually be parameterised using observable industry characteristics so that the specification involves the interaction between industry *and* country characteristics. That is, both elements determine location, a point that is not taken into account in the papers we presented in Section 2.2.5.

Ellison and Glaeser (1999) develop one such estimating equation using the simple location model that they used to justify their dartboard approach in Ellison and Glaeser (1997). In their model, an industry consists of a number of plants that choose locations sequentially to maximise profits. Expected profits depend on both location specific costs and spillovers from other firms. Location specific costs, or natural advantages, are divided into observable and unobservable components. Choosing a particular probability distribution for the unobserved component allows the authors to solve for the expected share of employment in each industry and thus specify an index of geographic concentration beyond that accounted for by observed natural advantage. For their empirical work, they need to specify how observed natural advantage affects expected profit. When doing this, they "economize the number of parameters by assuming that the effect on industry profitability of the difference in the cost of a particular input [across locations] is proportional to the intensity with which the industry uses the input, rather than estimating a separate coefficient for each industry" [Ellison and Glaeser (1999, p. 313)]. These assumptions make expected shares, $\mathrm{E}(s_i^k)$, a non-linear function of $\sum_{f=1}^{F} \beta_f y_{kf} p_i^f$ where p_i^f is the price of natural endowment f in location i, y_{kf} the intensity with which industry k uses factor f and β_f are coefficients to be estimated. Comparing this to the expression derived by Harrigan (1997), we see that these intensities are common across industries. Thus parameterising the coefficients in this way reduces the number of coefficients on endowments from $K \times F$ to F. The resulting expression gives location shares as a function of the interaction between industry characteristics *and* location characteristics. Estimation involves pooling across industries and locations.

Although Ellison and Glaeser (1999) propose a simple firm location model to justify their estimating equation, the assumption that intensities can be used to parameterise responsiveness of profits to natural endowments is essentially *ad hoc*. Midelfart-Knarvik et al. (2000) develop a trade model which gives theoretical underpinnings to the estimation strategy proposed by Ellison and Glaeser (1999). The model allows for endowments, final demand effects, and demand and cost linkages on intermediate inputs. The model is based on a constant returns to scale production function with production using both primary factors and intermediate goods. Factors are immobile across countries but goods can be shipped by incurring a trade costs that is origin, destination and industry specific. Preferences are CES with an Armington assumption so that goods are also differentiated according to source. However, the model assumes perfect competition. Implicitly, each variety is produced by a large number of producers implying marginal cost pricing. Since the number of varieties is indeterminate in equilibrium due to constant returns to scale, the authors have to make the black-box assumption that the number of varieties is proportional to industry and country size. Using the same notation as above, linearising the model gives relative shares, s_i^k as a function of

$$\sum_{f=1}^{F} \beta_f y_{kf} p_i^f + \sum_{h=1}^{K} \beta_h y_{kh} mp_i^h$$

where mp_i^h is the elasticity of market potential in country i with respect to industry characteristic h.[28] That is, shares are predicted by the interaction between location characteristics and intensities, as in Ellison and Glaeser (1999). The two types of interactions reflect the fact that both input price variation and demand variation matter for output shares.

Midelfart-Knarvik et al. (2002) estimate the model using data from OECD STAN for 14 European countries and 33 manufacturing industries for four periods (1970–1973, 1980–1983, 1990–1993, 1994–1997). They allow for six interaction effects. Three capture Heckscher–Ohlin effects (agricultural, low/medium-skill and high-skill endowments) and three capture geography effects (cost linkages on intermediate inputs, final demand/transport costs interaction, and intermediate demand linkages). Taking the empirical specification to the data is not straightforward due to data availability. Factor prices have to be proxied using information on endowments. Capturing the geography effects involves estimating market potentials with all the problems we alluded to in Section 2.1.2. In addition, some explanatory variables are endogenous according to theory. Given the lack of suitable instruments, the results may be biased to the extent that these variables are in fact endogenous in practise.

The preferred specification, allowing coefficients on the interactions to vary over time, explains 14 to 18% of the country–industry variation. When country and industry fixed effects are introduced, the R^2 increases to between 17 and 24%. Introducing fixed effects controls for omitted variables, such as physical geography, and does not change the basic results. In contrast to the studies using concentration indices discussed in Section 2.2.5, Heckscher–Ohlin effects are present in all periods although there is some variation over time. The skilled labour endowment variable is always strongly significant and has the highest impact. Intermediate cost linkages, have a positive impact on

[28] The actual expression involves centring each interaction with respect to a reference industry and a reference country. These references reflect the general equilibrium nature of the model. They are not predetermined and must be estimated. This has the added attraction that the reference points make the explanatory variables comparable across both industries and countries and remove the need for fixed effects. Finally, the theoretical derivation suggests that some variables enter as levels and some as elasticities.

the relative industry share but are only significant in the final period. Intermediate demand linkages are significant in all time periods.[29] Changes across time suggest that the effect of cost linkages is increasing relative to demand linkages although these changes are not significant. Overall, results on the economic geography variables suggest that intermediate cost and demand linkages matter for location, while final demand does not. This approach has the appealing property that it gives a fairly simple functional form while allowing for a variety of agglomeration and dispersion forces. Differences in factor endowments and intensities induce specialisation, while trade costs mean that the location of intermediate and final demand matters. However, the model does not include any imperfect competition and increasing returns to scale effects. As underlined in Section 3.1, both of these may have an important impact on agglomeration since they magnify both demand and competition effects. Unfortunately, experience from theoretical modelling suggests that including these additional effects can lead to complex functional forms that are not analytically tractable. Taking these models to data is difficult and the complexity could lead to empirical exercises that are not easily interpretable.

3.2.2. Dixit–Stiglitz based approaches

Work by Gaigné et al. (2002) highlights the possible problems. They develop an R-region, S-industry location model based on increasing returns to scale production functions that use both intermediate inputs (a CES combination of output from all S industries) and I different types of skilled labour. Firms compete on a monopolistically competitive goods market [à la Dixit and Stiglitz (1977)]. Solving the model involves assuming that workers are sectorally mobile, but spatially immobile. More problematically, the empirical exercise considers only the firm labour demand equation, but no other equilibrium relationships. This ignores many critical endogenous effects, in particular, the endogeneity of demand and firm location choices. Linearising the model gives the number of plants in a region–industry as a complex non-linear function of demand and supply conditions.[30] Interestingly, many of the variables enter in the form of interactions suggesting that it may be possible to extend the approaches outlined above while maintaining the basic idea of the importance of interactions between industry and location characteristics.

Even with good data from France, the authors are not able to measure many of these variables precisely and are instead forced to approximate them or even ignore them.

[29] The final demand transport cost interaction has a negative sign, which contradicts theory, but results are only significant when pooling across all four time periods.

[30] Specifically: vertical linkages between all industries, the intensity with which each industry uses each type of labour, the wage of each type of labour in each location, the employment in each sector in each location, substitution elasticities, local demand for each final and intermediate good, final and intermediate goods prices, the share of household expenditures on the good, the fixed cost of each sector, the variable cost of each sector and the transport cost in each sector.

In the end, they estimate a reduced form model to explain the region–industry location coefficient as a linear function of local labour costs, local final demand, local vertical linkages, a labour productivity effect and a competition effect. Estimation is performed on a spatial panel of 67 sectors and 341 French labour market areas allowing for sector and region fixed effects. At this spatial scale, the authors find that vertical linkages induce firms to agglomerate but final demand has no effect. Industry by industry estimation suggests that local labour costs tend to encourage dispersion in roughly 50% of industries, but play no role in the location of the remaining 50%.

At a first pass, the paper by Gaigné et al. (2002) looks like it might justify the approach based on Kim (1995) that we discussed above. On closer inspection, however, it becomes clear that the theory is being used only to help in giving the functional form for the explanatory variables and does not help to determine how these variables should really affect the location coefficient. We feel this serves to strengthen the point that we made above. A fully specified economic-geography model does not deliver predictions on the relationship between industry characteristics and industrial concentration so simply, as those assumed by many authors (see Section 2.2.5) as soon as the number of regions exceeds two. On the other hand, estimating the fully structural model is not possible with the data that is available.

3.2.3. Cournot competition-based approaches

Work by Combes and Lafourcade (2001) shows that a more tractable structural model can be developed in a Cournot competition framework. They consider an R-region, S-industry model where single-plant firms produce for their local market and export to all other regions. Labour and all S goods are used as inputs. Technology is increasing returns to scale Cobb–Douglas and independent of region. Wages are assumed to be the same in all regions.[31] However, non-labour input prices are endogenous and determined by Cournot competition and thus depend on the number of plants located in each region and on inter-region transaction costs. The main agglomeration force in the model comes from intermediate and final demand linkages. Demand is larger in regions where more plants are located. In addition, imperfect competition and strategic interaction mean that input prices are lower in more central regions and this cost-linkage gives these regions an endogenous comparative advantage. Offsetting this is the fact that lower prices reduce mark-ups in large regions. Despite the similarities in terms of agglomeration and dispersion forces, these price and competition mechanisms are very different from those in monopolistic competition settings à la Dixit and Stiglitz (1977) where mark-ups are constant and independent of plant locations.

Combes and Lafourcade (2001) estimate the model using French data for 341 employment areas and 64 industries. Teixeira (2002) applies the same model to Portuguese

[31] This is the only assumption that does not make this model a full general equilibrium one. Labour is also assumed to be immobile across regions and unemployment is supposed to emerge in all regions.

data for 18 districts and 21 industries. In both cases, the only parameter in the model for which real data is not available is the industry-k-specific inter-regional transaction cost t_{ij}^k between region i and j. Given data on generalised road transport costs t_{ij},[32] both papers assume that industry specific transaction costs are given by

$$t_{ij}^k = \upsilon^k t_{ij},$$

where υ^k is an industry-specific parameter to be estimated. The υ^k parameters encompass all of the effects in the model and have no straightforward interpretation. However, they do serve for two purposes. First, a test of the model can be based on the fact that negative υ's are not consistent with the model. Second, given that the underlying model is structural, the estimated parameter values can be used to simulate the change in economic geography in response to changes in the economic environment.

In both France and Portugal, the model is clearly not rejected by the data. In France, only one out of 70 industries has a significantly negative coefficient. At a more aggregate level (10 industries), all 10 coefficients are positive, 9 significantly. For Portugal, the 21 coefficients estimated are all significantly positive, most of them at the 1% level. Region and industry fixed effects significantly improve the fit. These fixed effects may capture forces that are not present in the model, for instance, endowment effects, physical geography features, or good access to the rest of the world. Last, controlling for endogeneity by instrumenting leads to comparable results.

In addition to a test of the Cournot competition model, the results can be used to examine other spatial features of the two economies. As a first example, the model can be used to compute variables that are not directly observable. Figure 4 reproduces, for France, estimates of the average mark-up per unit sold and the variable profit per plant, on the upper and lower maps, respectively. The average mark-up presents an interesting spatial pattern simultaneously high around Île-de-France and in peripheral regions, while low in between. In central regions, marginal and transport costs are low, but competition is high with the costs effects dominating. In peripheral regions, marginal and transport costs are high, but competition is low and the competition effect dominates. Firms in intermediate regions benefit neither from low cost nor low competition. Despite these findings on mark-ups, production per plant and profit per plant show a marked core–periphery pattern decreasing from the centre to the periphery.

As a second example, the model can be used to calculate the degree of trade integration. France appears to be much more integrated than Portugal with transaction costs ten times higher in the latter than the former. Many other predictions of the model can be re-examined once the model is estimated. We cannot detail them here, but the above examples underline how fully structural estimations on detailed subnational data allow us to reach conclusions on general theoretical mechanisms and to provide precise comparisons across EU countries.

[32] See Combes and Lafourcade (2003) for a detailed description of the methodology used to calculate these costs.

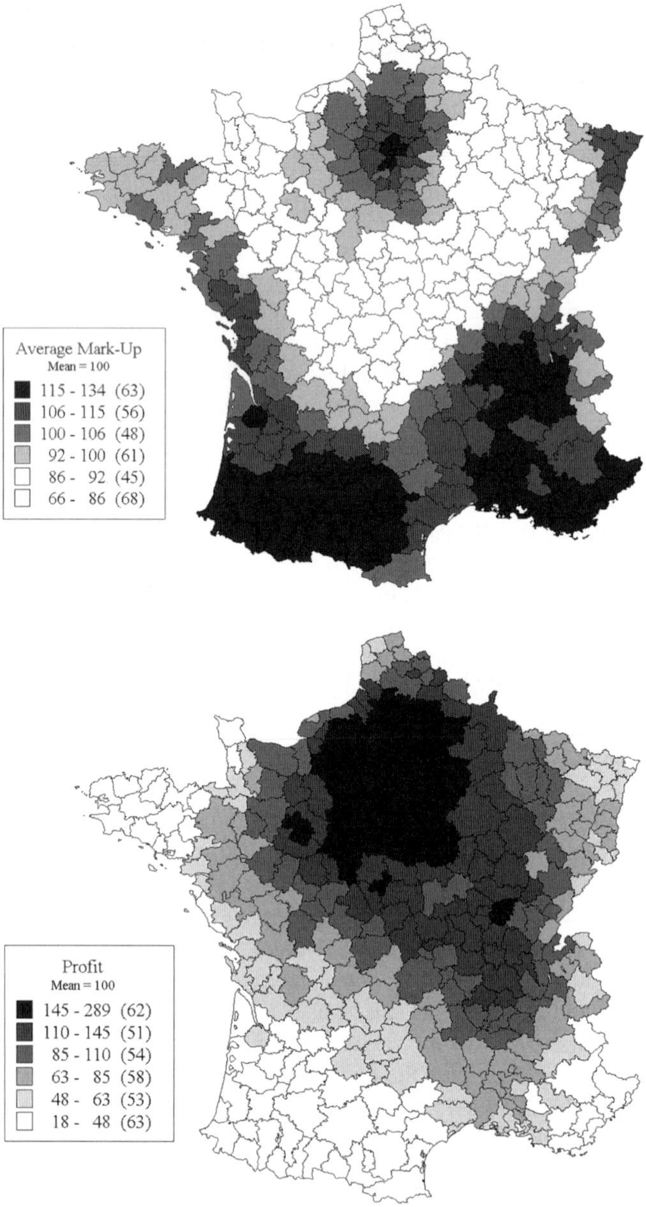

Figure 4. Average mark-up (top), variable profit per plant (bottom). For a colour reproduction of this figure see the colour figures section, page 3069.

3.2.4. Where do we go from here?

Two features separate the approaches presented in this section from those we outlined in Section 2.2.5. First they use all available information instead of working on summary statistics. The results suggest that this presents a much richer picture of the determinants of location in the EU. Moreover, the use of underlying models is crucial in both the specification and interpretation of results. Clearly considerable work is still needed on these models. In particular, we do not yet have a fully specified general equilibrium economic geography model which can be taken to the available data.

In addition, it is not yet explicit what these models tell us about the difference between the EU and the U.S. Precise comparisons between the Ellison and Glaeser (1999) results for the U.S. and those from Midelfart-Knarvik et al. (2002) for the EU are not possible because of the range of variables included in the U.S. study that do not fit into the theoretical specification used for the EU. However, it does appear that in the both cases natural endowments have a greater role to play in explaining industrial location than economic geography forces. This may be because of the assumption-intensive way that economic geography forces enter into the theoretical specification. It may also reflect the fact that the theoretical specification does not yet capture increasing returns to scale effects. Taking the comparison at face value, however, might help us understand some of the similarities that we uncovered in Sections 2.2 and 2.3. If natural endowments are important in explaining location patterns and trade acts as a substitute for factor mobility then we may find similar location patterns in the EU and the U.S. despite the fact that factors are less mobile in the EU.

The structural models suggest another route for making comparisons both across the EU and between the EU and the U.S. Here is not the place for an in-depth discussion of the pros and cons of structural estimation[33] but we do note that replications of this kind of methodology provide one way of comparing agglomeration mechanisms in different economies. Indeed, the comparison of the extent of integration in France and Portugal is a first step along these lines. Clearly, estimating the same model for the U.S. would also lead to comparisons between EU economies and the U.S. However, as in our discussion of the use of micro-level data, we note that considerable work may need to be done before this sort of approach can allow us to make comparisons between the EU as a whole and the U.S. This suggests that these comparisons may tell us more about the role of differences in labour mobility (which is relatively low even within EU countries) than they do about the role of transaction costs (where presumably the largest EU–U.S. differences occur because of high inter-country transaction costs).

As these papers stand, they tell us more about economic geography in general than they do about the specifics of the EU. That is, they are an example of the kind of work

[33] The interested reader is referred to Combes and Lafourcade (2001) for the arguments in favour and to Sutton (2000) for a more critical perspective.

on EU data that may end up being ignored as part of the area-based approach, but are really about fundamental aspects of economic geography. In particular, this work has provided theoretical foundations for some existing studies on U.S. data and has highlighted a number of methodological problems with existing studies.

3.3. Labour productivity and wage inequalities

The previous section considers the role of agglomeration forces in determining employment shares of particular locations. However, these agglomeration effects may actually impact directly on productivity and only indirectly on employment concentration via the differences in local productivity this generates. In some cases, in particular, when thinking about employment dynamics, this may be problematic if productivity advantage translates into employment savings rather than higher employment. Indeed, as argued in Combes et al. (2004), higher productivity implies larger employment only if the demand elasticity is sufficiently large and if the substitution of other inputs for labour is not too important. If we are primarily interested in these differences in productivity, then it makes sense to study the impact of agglomeration externalities directly, instead of considering indirect evidence via employment shares.

These regional differences in labour productivity may be large. For instance, Ciccone (2002) reports that the five most productive NUTS 3 regions in Germany are 140% more productive than the five least productive. The gap for France, Italy and Spain is 66% and 33% for the UK. We note in passing, that these figures are close to those obtained for the U.S. by Ciccone and Hall (1996) who find that output per worker in the most productive state is two thirds higher than in the least productive.

Given these large differences we now turn to consider the evidence on local productivity differences in the EU. Before we start, note that lack of data means these studies only work with differences in labour productivity, not total factor productivity. We begin by considering direct evidence on labour productivity, before turning to the literature that uses wages as an index of labour productivity. Once we do this, we have to deal with an extra complication – labour is not homogenous and so we need to account for local differences in skills. In contrast to the literature on localisation, these two types of studies have tended to focus on what kind of local economic structure most enhances productivity, without worrying too much about the underlying causes. However, these studies sometimes do try to distinguish between within and between interactions. While the objectives of the literature differ somehow, the issue of the role of theory in structuring empirical work is a common thread that connects the two literatures. We finish the section by considering a fully structural approach pioneered by Hanson (2002) on U.S. data that has been replicated for data from a few European countries. For all of the approaches we consider here, comparable studies exist for the U.S., allowing an interesting comparison with the European results.

3.3.1. Labour productivity

Based on a methodology close to Ciccone and Hall (1996), Ciccone (2002) studies the impact of employment density on labour productivity at the NUTS 3 regional level for a subset of the EU including France, Germany, Italy, Spain, and the UK. Even though the impact of only one factor is studied, the methodology that considers both fixed effects and instrumentation allows a rigorous comparison with the results obtained for the U.S.

Estimations are based on the specification of a local production function that includes three inputs, (labour, human and physical capital) and an externality arising only, by assumption, from local production density. Labour productivity is derived directly from this specification. Data on physical capital is not available. However, using the optimality condition for physical capital use, Ciccone argues that the total production level and the capital rental price can be substituted for this unobservable endowment. Assuming that capital markets clear at a geographical level higher than NUTS 3, these prices can be treated as supra-regional fixed effects. This leaves regional labour productivity as a function of supra-regional fixed effects, the share of different education levels in regional employment (proxies for human capital), and of the regional employment density. An extension allows externalities to arise from contiguous regions. In this case, labour productivity also depends on the contiguous regions employment densities.

Before presenting the results, we offer a few comments on this framework. First, only the net impact of density is estimated allowing for possible congestion effects and decreasing labour marginal productivity. Indeed, the framework can only be used to estimate these net effects as congestion and agglomeration effects cannot be identified separately. Second, fixed effects not only capture the role of physical capital, but also control for exogenous differences in labour productivity across regions due to differences in endowments or technology. As no time-series data is available, the supra-regional fixed effects assume that these exogenous differences are identical for all sub-regions. Last, and most importantly, note that it is crucial to instrument the main explanatory variable, density. Since the specification only relies on a production function, both traditional trade theory and economic geography tell us that labour productivity and employment density are simultaneously determined. Ciccone (2002) argues that regional total land areas is a proper instrument for density since NUTS 3 region borders have, in most cases, been established more than a century ago and thus have no reason to be correlated with current productivity shocks. Total land area is very well correlated with current employment density, however, making it a good instrument.

The data used to implement this methodology offer an excellent example of the problems one may encounter with EU-wide data, as detailed in Section 1. First, data are available only for five countries, consisting of 628 NUTS 3 regions. No capital endowments are available at this geographical level so only labour, and not total factor, productivity can be computed. This data restriction explains the choice of the dependent variable as well as the fixed-effect trick used to deal with the local capital endowment.

Because employment density may have different effects on agricultural productivity, the data needs to separate out manufacturing and services. Unfortunately, only total value-added is available at the NUTS 3 level in Italy and the UK, so the share of agriculture at the NUTS 2 level has to be used to estimate this share. For the human capital variables, the problem is that the number of education levels reported differs across countries. Finally, data are not available at exactly the same dates for the different countries, so data is used from the period 1986 to 1988. All of this clearly demonstrates that EU-wide studies can be performed only at the cost of this kind of imprecision with the data.

Turning to the results, a first regression with no instrumentation and only country fixed effects gives a precise estimate of elasticity of labour productivity with respect to employment density equal to 5.1%.[34] At the other extreme, when regressions are instrumented and include NUTS 2 fixed effects and neighbouring regions density effects, the lowest estimate of the impact of local density on productivity is equal to 4.4%, with a 1% standard error. The impact of neighbouring region density is 3.3%, which adds to the local effect. A somewhat lower estimate, 3.4%, is obtained when the share of agriculture in value-added is included in the regressions to account for within-region differences in terms of agriculture occupancy. This extra variable may be endogenous, however, and no instruments are found to tackle this problem. Employment density is shown to be moderately endogenous and thus require instrumentation. Differences across European countries appear to be rather small. Estimates for Germany, France, and Spain are close to 5%, are 3.2 percentage points higher for the UK and 2.5 percentage points lower for Italy. None of these differences are significant, however.

Interestingly, the impact of employment density on labour productivity is extremely close to the U.S. figure leading Ciccone (2002, in abstract) to conclude that his "empirical results suggest that agglomeration effects (in France, Germany, Italy, Spain and the UK) are only slightly smaller than agglomeration effects in the U.S.: the estimated elasticity of (average) labour productivity with respect to employment density is 4.5% compared to 5% in the U.S." Therefore, the robust methodology proposed in this study not only evaluates the elasticity of labour productivity with respect to density at the NUTS 3 level in Europe but also allows us to conclude that Europe and the U.S. share a very similar effect of global agglomeration on local labour productivity.

3.3.2. Wages

Ciccone (2002) represents the only EU-wide evidence we have on regional productivity differences. Slightly more evidence is available if we turn from EU-wide studies to national studies. Unfortunately, even for given countries, a time series of value-added often is not available at the regional level. However, if one is willing to assume that local labour markets are perfect, labour productivity should be equal to wage and wage

[34] White robust standard error is 0.42%.

data are more generally available. With this assumption in mind, we now turn to additional evidence on labour productivity differences that come from studies on wages inequalities in the EU. Once again, evidence from the U.S., presented in Glaeser and Maré (2001) acts as an interesting reference point even if the methodologies are not as closely comparable as in the previous section.

As a general point, failure to control for heterogeneous skill composition across regions may considerably limit the interpretations that can be given to regional differences in labour productivity or wages. Higher productivity or wages might not reflect local agglomeration externalities at all, but only differences in local labour composition. For this reason, Ciccone (2002) included education controls in his regressions. If one thinks that the composition of regional labour markets is relatively constant across time, regional fixed effects might also partly control for such problems.

Duranton and Monastiriotis (2002) highlight the main issues in their investigation of the role that such labour characteristics may have on the evolution of earnings across UK regions. Their work is based on a panel of the 12 UK NUTS 1 regions spanning from 1982 to 1997. Data is available on both earnings and local labour market characteristics including gender composition, education and experience levels. Without any controls, average earnings in the two richest regions, London and the South East were 121% and 103% higher than the national average in 1982. The gap increased to 137% and 109% by 1997. The coefficient of variation across regions has increased almost three-fold. All of this shows an important increase in inequalities across the UK regions during the period. Three phenomena explain this trend. First, educational attainment, already higher in London and in the South East, increased more rapidly there than anywhere else. As educated people are paid more, this magnified differences in regional earnings. Second, the national gap in earnings between skilled and unskilled worker simultaneously increased, which favoured more skilled regions. Third, London initially had lower returns to education, but the difference decreased during the period. Importantly, none of these explanations of the divergence of regional earnings in the UK refers to agglomeration externalities, even though more dense areas such as London appear to be favoured. The spatial sorting of skilled workers, not agglomeration effects appear to be the main explanation. These results highlight the importance of controlling for skills and labour sorting when explaining wages inequalities in the EU. This is true, despite the fact that inter-regional mobility is supposed to be low and falling in the UK.

As a comparison, consider results for the U.S. reported in Glaeser and Maré (2001), that try to evaluate the impact of skill composition on the wage premium, i.e. the fact that wages are higher in cities. Results from two sources of individual data, the Panel Study of Income Dynamics (PSID) and the National Longitudinal Survey of Youth (NLSY) are comparable. The wage premium in dense metropolitan areas is estimated to be 28.2% and 24.9%, in each panel respectively, falling to 25.9% and 24.5% once they allow for labour market, occupational, and education controls. One could therefore conclude that the skill bias is not so strong as for the UK. However, once individual fixed effects, controlling for any possible individual abilities, are included simultaneously with a tenure variable, the wage premium in dense metropolitan areas falls to 4.5% and

10.9%, respectively.[35] Individual abilities and tenure would divide the wage premium by between 2.3 and 6.3. Comparable magnitudes are obtained for the wage premium in non-dense metropolitan areas. Once again, controlling for skills and for individual fixed effects drastically changes the verdict on the impact of agglomeration economies.

A more direct comparison to Glaeser and Maré (2001) is provided by Combes et al. (2003) who extend these ideas and methodology to France and to determinants of local wages other than density. Their aim is to explain the impact on city industry wage inequalities of skills and individual abilities, natural endowments (geography features, but also possibly technology or public good endowment), within-industry and between-industry interactions. The data are an example of the excellent data that may exist at the country level in Europe. The panel they use follows individuals providing earnings information across time, locations and occupation. The data is annual covering 1976–1998 and may be disaggregated across 341 regions and 114 industries (including both manufacturing and services). Their sampling framework selects 1/20th of the data leaving them with 2,664,474 person–year observations.

Estimation results show that a very large proportion of regional wage inequalities are explained by individual abilities. Estimation using individual fixed effects alone gives an R^2 of 69%. This rises to 80% with all explanatory variables but falls to only 31% without individual fixed effects. As for the U.S., comparisons with aggregate regressions, suggest that observed individual characteristics, such as occupation, only capture individual abilities very imperfectly. Localisation and urbanisation economies remain significant but their magnitude is at the lower bound of those found in the literature [see Rosenthal and Strange (2004) in this volume]. For instance, the elasticity of wages with respect to density is around 6% on aggregate data, which is close to the estimates found on labour productivity both for the EU and the U.S. by Ciccone (2002) and Ciccone and Hall (1996). But this elasticity falls to around 3.5% when individual abilities are controlled for. Furthermore, density is endogenous and when instrumented by population density, its effects fall to 2.5%. Similarly, the impact of specialisation on wages, falls from 4.3% when estimated on aggregate data to 2.1% once individual abilities are taken into account. These results underline that workers sort across space, which significantly biases upward both localisation and urbanisation economies. This sorting is occurring in France and the UK much as it is in the U.S. Once again, we are struck by the similarity of the results. Despite measured differences in short-run labour mobility, the impact of sorting is broadly similar across these three economies.

3.3.3. Monopolistic competition-based approaches

Studies in the two previous sections provide interesting, and robust, descriptive results on local determinants of labour productivity and wage inequalities. As for much of the

[35] The wage premium disappears altogether once they control for urban costs (housing plus commuting). That is, there is no evidence of a *real* wage premium in metropolitan areas once we allow for individual effects.

localisation literature, links with theory remain rather fuzzy and distant. Estimations are based on the specification of a production function only. Hanson (2002) pioneered a fully structural approach to consider wages inequalities based on an economic geography model. While he implemented his methodology on U.S. data, his approach has been replicated on several European countries. Mion (2002) considers 103 provinces in Italy, Roos (2001) considers 327 districts for West Germany (327 districts), Brakman, Garretsen and Schramm (2004) consider 151 districts for East and West Germany and de De Bruyne (2003) considers 43 districts for Belgium.

These structural estimations allow for clear U.S./EU comparisons but there are two important drawbacks to this approach to wages inequalities. First, estimations cannot be performed at the industry level due to the lack of data. Second, use of one model restricts the agglomeration forces at play to those based on monopolistic competition and love of diversity in final consumption. However, as this framework is one of the most frequently used in theoretical economic geography, we consider these estimations as an important contribution to understanding the empirical economic geography of the EU.

These structural estimations are based on the Helpman (1998) economic geography model. Though very close in spirit to Krugman (1991b), a few key assumptions make it different in terms of economic implications. Instead of assuming that a constant returns to scale / perfectly competitive sector produces a homogenous good that can be freely exported ("agriculture"), this good is assumed to be non-tradable and its local endowment exogenously fixed ("housing"). As a result, its price differs across locations, and increases with the size of the local population. This creates an additional dispersion force absent from Krugman (1991b). An agglomeration force is also suppressed: The homogenous good income, higher in larger areas, is redistributed at the national level and not locally. While functional equilibrium relationships may look very similar in both models, they lead to opposing comparative statics in terms of one crucial parameter, the inter-regional transaction cost. While reducing transaction costs increases agglomeration in Krugman (1991b), it makes regions more similar in Helpman (1998). These results are not contradictory, however. Each model emphasises one side on the well-known bell shaped curve that links transaction costs and regional inequalities [see Puga (1999)]. It is important to keep in mind this difference when interpreting the estimation results. Finally, note that equilibria in the Helpman (1998) model are interior, while one region may end up with no manufacturing employment in Krugman (1991b), a problematic property when one deals with real data. Indeed, this is the main reason why Hanson (2002) chose to estimate the Helpman (1998) model. See Head and Mayer (2004) in this volume for more discussion of this issue.

The estimated specification is directly derived from the theoretical model. It links the wage in a given region to a market potential function of income, wage, and housing stock in all other regions, discounted by distance. More precisely, estimations are based on the following equation:

$$\log(w_i) = \alpha_0 + \frac{1}{\sigma}\log\left(\sum_k Y_k^{\frac{1}{\mu}(1-\sigma(1-\mu))} w_k^{\frac{1}{\mu}(\sigma-1)} H_k^{\frac{1}{\mu}(\sigma-1)(1-\mu)} \mathrm{e}^{-\tau(\sigma-1)d_{ik}}\right),$$

where w_k, Y_k, and H_k are the wage, total income, and housing stock in region k, respectively. d_{ik} is the distance between regions i and k. σ is the elasticity of substitution between varieties, μ is the share of non-housing goods in total final consumption, and τ reflects the impact of distance on inter-regional transaction costs.[36] The model is consistent only under the following constraints:

$$\sigma > 1, \qquad 0 \leqslant \mu \leqslant 1 \quad \text{and} \quad \tau \geqslant 0.$$

Two critical econometric issues characterise the estimation of this equation. One is the need to use non-linear estimation taking into account the constraints due to the links between the parameters. All the studies use non-linear constrained estimation procedures although Mion (2002) also proposes an appealing alternative approach based on linearisation. Second, endogeneity may clearly bias the parameter estimates. First, the dependent variable directly enters as an explanatory variable. Second, local income, which enters as an explanatory variable, is simultaneously determined with wages in the long-run equilibrium. Third, even if housing stocks are exogenous in the model, they are probably dependent on local incomes in the data. Notice also that including local fixed effects makes sense in this setting to control for all forces not considered in the theoretical model and constant across time. However, if important for the spatial distribution of economic activities, these fixed effects should again be correlated with the residuals. Hanson (2002) tackles this last endogeneity issue by first-differencing the series. In addition, he computes explanatory variables at a geographical level higher than the one of the dependent variable. County wages are regressed on the explanatory variables computed for sixteen ring areas surrounding the county. Following Hanson (2002), Roos (2001), De Bruyne (2003), and Mion (2002), also use a higher administrative level. While simplifying computations, it is doubtful, however, that such an estimation procedure controls for endogeneity: If explanatory variables are correlated with residuals at the lowest level, their sum should share the same property. Furthermore, as argued by Mion (2002), this is close in its spirit to an instrumental variable method, where instruments would be the aggregated explanatory variables, but it is much less efficient since a lot of information is lost. Hanson (2002) also presents regressions excluding the observations related to the largest counties, which does not change his results markedly, and finally proposes a non-linear instrument variable method, based on the county population levels lagged by more than 10 years, which seems to be the most reasonable approach.

The U.S. and EU results are easy to compare since the same model is estimated with the same non-linear estimation procedure. However, only Roos (2001) and Mion (2002) present results for first-differences and only the latter presents instrumented results for Europe.

Results for the elasticity of substitution, σ, are fairly consistent across studies. U.S. estimates vary between 4.9 and 7.6, equal 6.2 in West Germany, 5.5 in Belgium and

[36] α_0 is function of σ, μ, and of the fixed cost, but this cannot be identified in the first-differences estimations performed.

are between 5.9 and 6.7 in Italy. In all studies, σ is often not precisely estimated, and is not significantly different from 0 in West Germany and Belgium, possibly due to the aggregation procedure used for explanatory variables. When this aggregation procedure is not performed, σ is much more precisely estimated: equal to 3.9 in Germany and only 1.9 for Italy. These results suggest that EU consumers more strongly differentiate varieties implying higher mark-ups in Europe than in the U.S. Turning to the share of housing in consumption, it is estimated to be negative, although insignificant, in Germany and Belgium. In the other studies, it is significantly positive, taking the same value of around 0.1 in the U.S., in West Germany and Italy. This estimate is pretty low. Hanson (2002) argues that a reasonable value should be at least 0.2. The value of $\sigma(1-\mu)$ determines whether wages reflect only exogenous housing endowments, or are also determined by the model's endogenous agglomeration and dispersion forces. A value greater than 1 signifies the former.[37] For all countries, the value is less than one (although not always significantly) suggesting that endogenous economic geography forces matter in shaping the spatial wage distribution. Finally, distance is found to significantly increase transaction costs for all countries but West Germany where the effect is not significant. Unfortunately, the impact of distance is not comparable across countries since it depends on the way (e.g. geodesic vs real) and the units in which distance is measured (time vs distance for instance).

From a technical view point, the non-linear estimation results may be sensitive to the choice of starting point. Given this, one can question the validity of first differencing and instrumenting such estimations. Mion (2002) proposes an alternative approach, linearising the equilibrium equations of the Helpman (1998) model, as Combes and Lafourcade (2001) do for the structural estimation of their Cournot competition model (see Section 3.2.3). This is quite simple once a different specification for the impact of distance on transaction cost is assumed. Mion (2002) adopts a power function that is standard in empirical trade, θd_{ik}^{-1}, where θ is estimated. Mion (2002) also proposes using the Arellano and Bond (1991) procedure for dynamic panels to properly instrument the estimation and take endogeneity into account.[38] The reader is referred to Mion (2002) for further details. This procedure leads to very precisely estimated parameters. The elasticity of substitution is 3.4, which is reasonable when one considers that the manufacturing sector may cover a large spectrum of goods. The share of housing is 0.2. The two together give a value of $\sigma(1-\mu)$ significantly lower than 1. Hence, as estimated by Mion (2002), the Helpman (1998) model seems to explain spatial wage inequalities in Italy quite well. The explanatory power is actually higher than for the U.S., although the estimated values of underlying parameters are not so different.

As an example of the predictions that can be made on the basis of this structural estimation, Figure 5 presents the simulated wage changes induced by a 10% negative

[37] This is the no-black-hole condition. The interpretation of the condition is different in Krugman (1991b) and Helpman (1998) since it implies full agglomeration in the former and full dispersion in the latter.

[38] This methodology is close to the one adopted by Henderson (1997) and Combes et al. (2004) to study local employment short-run dynamics: see Section 3.4.2.

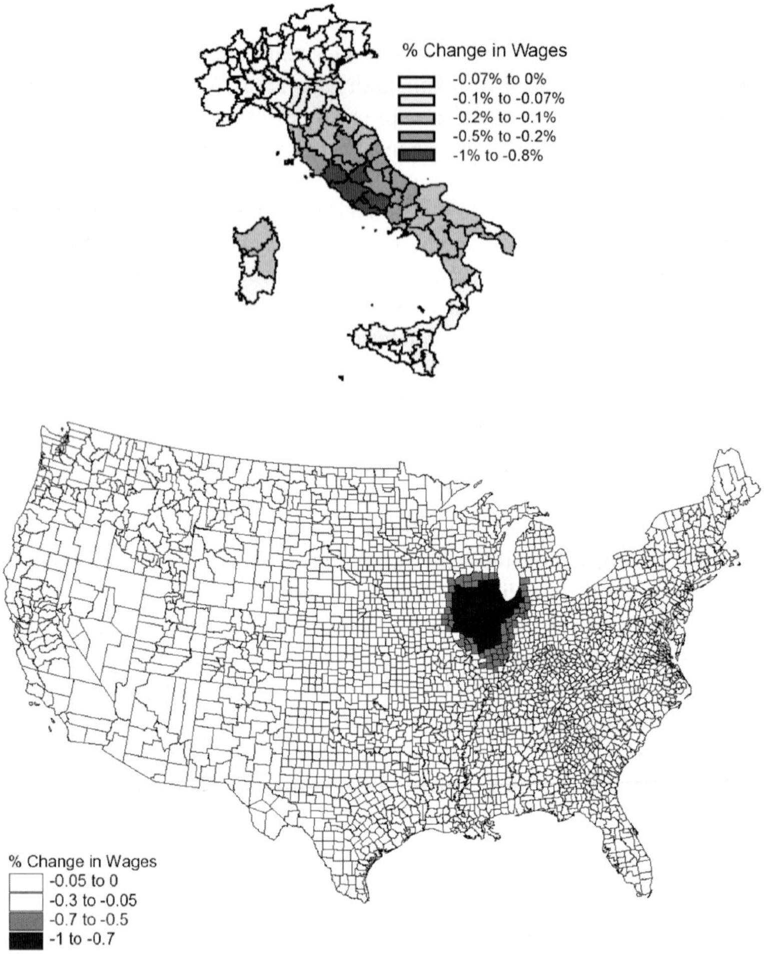

Figure 5. Simulated wages changes in Italy (top) and the U.S. (bottom). For a colour reproduction of this figure see the colour figures section, page 3070.

income shock in the five Latinium regions in Italy [Figure 5 (top), reproduced from Mion (2002)] and in Illinois in the U.S. [Figure 5 (bottom), reproduced from Hanson (2002)]. The role of distance appears to be quite important, the effect of the 10% shock being lower than 1% even in the closest areas, and lower than 0.1% for the farthest. The distance and magnitude of the shock impact are comparable, but, due to the different sizes of both countries, this implies that a much smaller share of the country is affected in the U.S. This may be due also to the fact that both estimations do not use the same specification of distance, Hanson's exponential choice converging faster towards zero.

3.3.4. Where do we go from here?

The structural estimations we have just presented allow for precise comparisons intra-EU and between EU countries and the U.S. Again, data availability means we are someway from being able to use these approaches for a comparison of the EU as a whole with the U.S.

The studies also provide interesting extensions, in terms of econometric methodology. If one believes in the role of skills and spatial labour sorting as underlined by the earlier wage inequalities studies, the Helpman–Hanson structural estimation should be extended along a number of lines. First, skills and ability should be controlled for. Hanson (2002) and Brakman, Garretsen and Schramm (2004) are the only two studies to do so using local education levels. One might think that the consideration of local fixed effects is enough to address this issue, due to the inertia of the local skill composition but this remains to be proved and our discussion of results on spatial sorting urge caution in drawing that conclusion. Second, this methodology has not been implemented for different industries. Again, one may think that differences across industries should be important. A multi-industry extension of the monopolistic competition economic geography model is surely worth considering. This would certainly also need to include a differentiated input setting, as found in Krugman and Venables (1995).

More generally, the two structural approaches we have considered dealing with employment and wage inequalities, are complementary in the sense that they are based on different theoretical models and therefore on different agglomeration and dispersion mechanisms. In both cases, the main agglomeration force relies on final demand linkages playing on increasing returns to scale while dispersion is fostered by some kind of increased competition in central places. However, the underlying mechanisms are quite different. The second approach, based on monopolistic competition à la Dixit and Stiglitz (1977), makes the role of love of diversity central, whereas imperfect competition mechanisms are rather soft. In the first approach, Cournot competition on homogenous goods ensures competition is stronger and that real strategic interactions take place. Results from both sets of estimations can thus be viewed as a first comparison of two competing settings. This remains rough, however, and should be made more precise. Indeed, European area-based studies have for the moment mainly tried to assess whether a given model explains the observed spatial patterns. There is obviously another use of structural estimations, which consists in testing given models against one another. This is often more difficult, since the same specification has to be consistent with both models, the value of the estimated parameters allowing us to select one of them. In trade theory, Davis and Weinstein (1999) take this approach for testing traditional trade theory against trade theory under increasing returns to scale [see Head and Mayer (2004) in this volume]. However, these kinds of tests have not yet been implemented in economic geography.

What should be clear from our brief survey is that this sort of approach may present yet another way to make general comparisons between the economic geographies of different areas. Again, we think that the results available so far point more towards similarities across the EU and the U.S. than differences. These similarities occur despite underlying differences in mobility and the extent of integration.

3.4. The dynamics of localisation in the EU

The studies presented in Sections 3.2 and 3.3 explain employment, labour productivity and wages as functions of local characteristics *at the same date*. We now turn to the analysis of local *growth* as a function of *past* determinants. This literature talks to an old debate on whether local externalities are mainly static or dynamic. The literature in this section assumes that local externalities affect local growth while effects were assumed to be instantaneous in the studies in the previous section.

The earlier literature sought to determine the impact on local growth of localisation economies (within-industry interactions) and urbanisation economies (between-industry interactions). This body of work also considered the role of other factors such as local competition or plant size. As a general point, notice that even if authors mainly interpret these variables as capturing technological spillovers, many other market based interpretations can be given as is clear from our theory survey in Section 3.1.

We begin by considering determinants of long-run growth before turning to the study of short-run dynamics, which allows us both to refine our conclusions and to tackle important endogeneity problems. In both cases, we argue that EU results are again not so dissimilar from results for the U.S.

3.4.1. Long-run growth

3.4.1.1. The methodology. Glaeser et al. (1992), followed by Henderson et al. (1995), first proposed regressing local employment growth over a longish period of time on initial economic characteristics. These papers regress city-industry employment growth on a specialisation index and on an industrial diversity index, both computed at the city level. The former should capture all within-industry interactions and the latter all between-industry ones. The specialisation index is the share of the industry in the city. To measure diversity, Glaeser et al. (1992) use the share of the five largest industries in the city excluding own industry, while Henderson et al. (1995) use a Herfindhal index computed on all industry shares in the city employment. Glaeser et al. (1992) also include the number of plants per employee [the inverse of plant average size as used by Kim (1995)] as a competition index, while Henderson et al. (1995) ignore this variable, but do include city employment in all other industries as an extra urbanisation variable. Both papers include a number of additional controls.

Results for the U.S. are not consistent across the two studies. Glaeser et al. (1992) find that local growth is positively influenced by diversity and negatively by plant size and specialisation. In contrast, localisation economies are at work in all five industries studied in Henderson et al. (1995), while urbanisation ones are observed in the high-technology sectors only. These discrepancies might be explained by appealing to data [the fact that the period considered is not the same – 1956–1987 versus 1970–1987 and that Glaeser et al. (1992) includes services, while Henderson et al. (1995) do not], estimation [Glaeser et al. (1992) regressions are pooled whereas Henderson et al. (1995) are run industry by industry] or problems with the overall methodology.

Combes (2000) identifies a number of problems with these two papers and the papers that replicate them for other city systems, especially in Europe. The first relates to the inclusion of city-industry employment level in addition to specialisation and total employment. In Henderson et al. (1995) both specialisation and total employment have positive impacts on employment growth, while industry employment has a negative effect. The positive coefficient on specialisation is interpreted as evidence of localisation economies. But, to increase specialisation either industry employment must rise or total city employment must fall and both of these other explanatory variables induce offsetting negative effects. Thus, if we include more than one city employment variable, we break the link between the specialisation index and localisation economies. A similar argument can be made for the link between total employment and urbanisation economies. A second source of problems relates to the need to include industry fixed effects when running pooled estimations. Glaeser et al. (1992) centre some but not all variables using national values of the variables. Clearly, centring all variables or including fixed effects would be preferable. Other pitfalls relate to the problems of interpreting plant size variables (as discussed in Section 2.2.5), the endogeneity of variables, potential selection problems if industries are not present in a city in the first period and the need to account for the fact that employment data might be censored.

3.4.1.2. Replications on EU countries. If we ignore these methodological points and take results from the EU at face value, the evidence appears to support the Glaeser et al. (1992) findings rather than those of Henderson et al. (1995). Paci and Usai (2002) consider Italian data for 1991–1996 at a very low geographical scale (784 local labour systems). They find evidence of a positive effect of local industrial diversity and a negative impact of specialisation. Contrary to Glaeser et al. (1992), they also find a positive impact of firm size. Further evidence from Italy, this time for 92 Provincias, is provided by Cainelli and Leoncini (1999). They also find a negative impact of specialisation, but effects are reversed for firm size and diversity. Now both impact negatively on local growth. When Italy is sub-divided into four large regions, the impact of diversity becomes positive for both North industrialised regions. Still in Italy, and again at the local labour system level, but for 1971–1991, Forni and Paba (2002) estimate a specification in which specialisation in all 88 industries is separately introduced in the explanatory variables. They find that both own specialisation and specialisation in related industries favour local growth. In the Netherlands in the 1990s and for two different geographical scales [57 cities at the country level (1991–1997) and 416 zip codes in South-Holland (1988–1997)], Van Soest et al. (2002) find a similar role for diversity and specialisation, and a negative role of plant size, as in Glaeser et al. (1992). Almeida (2001), using 1985–1994 data for the 275 Portuguese "concelhos", finds that the impact of local characteristics varies across activities. Services and most manufacturing sectors show a negative effect of specialisation and plant size, and a positive impact of diversity. There are a few industries, however, for which the opposite holds. These results are broadly consistent with those of Combes (2000) for the 341 French employment areas for 1984–1993. His estimations, taking account of the points that we raise above, find that diversity has a positive effect on service sectors and a negative effect on manufacturing. Specialisation has a negative effect in both cases. Again, for some industrial sectors specialisation has a positive impact. In addition, he distinguishes the effect of competition from that of plant size. Both appear to have a negative impact in most sectors.

3.4.1.3. Productivity growth. If our primary interest is productivity then, as before, working on employment growth might be problematic because positive productivity shocks could impact employment growth negatively if production is not expanded sufficiently. In addition, some agglomeration effects may directly impact on labour supply without affecting productivity. Both these effects make the employment growth interpretations difficult and suggest that determinants may be different for productivity growth. If data is available, it is clearly preferable to work on this variable directly.

de Lucio et al. (2002) assess the links between labour productivity and localisation and urbanisation economies in Spain. They find no effects of competition or diversity on labour productivity growth, and a U-shaped effect for specialisation. Low levels of specialisation reduce productivity growth, while high levels foster it. Studying 784 local labour systems in Italy, Cingano and Schivardi (2004) make two contributions. First, they use total factor productivity growth as the dependent variable. They show that both specialisation and city size have a positive impact. This positive impact is also observed on wage growth. In contrast, diversity, competition, and plant size variables are not significant. Second, using the same sample, they study the differences that are observed when working on local employment growth as dependent variable. They show that the effects of specialisation and city size are reversed, becoming negative, while the other local characteristics now have a significant impact on local employment growth. This appears to confirm that the local growth of employment and productivity may be fostered by different determinants.

3.4.2. Short-run dynamics and endogeneity controls

City employment is sometimes available for many consecutive years. In this case, it is possible to use the three dimensions of the panel (city, industry, and time) to improve the methodology. First, industry and city fixed effects may be included. Importantly, this controls for local effects that do not change across time. As a consequence, the identification of local externalities is only based on changes across time. The panel dimension also allows for a real test of whether externalities are static or dynamic. Indeed, including many lags and testing their significance qualifies the duration of the effects. Thus, fixed, static, and dynamic effects are properly distinguished in time-series approaches.

Endogeneity is a very important issue in this literature. Both fixed effects and other explanatory variables are likely to be correlated with unobserved shocks to city industry growth (the dependent variable). One can deal with the fixed effects endogeneity by simply first differencing the series. The remaining endogeneity, present in any theory dealing with agglomeration (see Section 3.1), must be controlled for using instrumental variable methods. This is rarely done in long-run estimations. de Lucio et al. (2002) is the exception on European data.

Henderson (1997) is the first implementation of this time-series methodology, using data on 742 urban U.S. counties between 1977 and 1990. He finds strong localisation economies that die out after six years. Note, however, that the simultaneous introduction of specialisation and lagged values of the dependent variable leads to the same interpretation problems as we discussed with respect to the long-run methodology. Urbanisation economies are smaller but also persist longer, at least till the end of the time horizon (eight or nine years back).

Combes et al. (2004) implement this methodology for 341 French metropolitan employment areas levels and for 36 manufacturing and services industries between 1984 and 1993. The Henderson (1997) methodology is extended by noticing that city-industry employment is the product of the average city-industry plant size times the city-industry number of plants. Therefore, local employment growth can be decomposed into internal growth (the growth of the size of existing plants), and external growth (the creation of new plants).[39] The determinants of the dynamics of both variables are simultaneously studied in a VAR setting and therefore linked to each others dynamics. Model selection techniques are used to determine the duration of local effects. Combes et al. (2004) prefer not to use the specification including the own industry employment. Localisation economies are captured only through the inclusion of the lagged dependent variable. They consider two alternative measures of diversity in addition to total employment as well as two indices of local competition. For France the selected model, an ARMA (1, 1), has an order that is low compared to the between six and nine order processes found by Henderson (1997). Hence, in France, static externalities appear to be prevalent while in the U.S., dynamic effects are more important. The approach proposed by Combes et al. (2004) allows for additional results. In France, on average, larger areas have both more plants and larger average plant size in all industries while a pool of industries of comparable size favours both internal and external growth, even if the total number of these industries does not need to be large. Hence, technological spillovers could work across selected industries but need not extend to all of them, as long-run regressions seem to imply. The impact of local competition is shown to be non-linear.

[39] This local growth decomposition leads to further policy issues. One can compare the impact of a given policy on each growth component or determine what is the optimal policy for each target. Indeed, Duranton and Puga (2001) show that the impact of urbanisation economies may differ from localisation ones depending on the product life cycle. Industrial diversity favours innovations and therefore fosters plant creation. Less urbanised but more specialised areas favour mass production. Actually, in France, 72% of plant relocations take place from an area with above median diversity to an area with above median specialisation in the corresponding sector. Moreover, the pattern is stronger for plants in more innovating and technology intensive sectors.

Plants appear to be larger in areas where they are more numerous, but of uneven size. This suggests that large leaders may encourage growth in smaller plants surrounding them. On the other hand, the number of plants grows faster in places where plants are less numerous and of even size. Replicating the methodology on other European countries could lead to potentially interesting pan-European comparisons.

3.4.3. What we learn and a comparison with the U.S.

Regressions in this local growth literature share some poor properties with the reduced form estimations of Section 2.2.5. First, precise theoretical foundations are lacking and no structural approach has been developed to formalise this work. Local productivity, or productivity growth, is assumed to depend on local economic characteristics in a black-box fashion. Most of the underlying models do not go further than the specification of a production function and the use of first-order conditions with respect to input choices. This also prevents us from testing one given theory against others and only determines the local economic structure that has the strongest impact on growth without identifying the channels through which this works. Second, the city-industry dependent variable is a function of own city characteristics only, and not on other cities. In static contexts, more structural approaches assuming trade between regions imply inter-city effects, which is almost never taken into account here. Some authors, such as Cingano and Schivardi (2004), include market potential variables as controls, but this remains crude.

Overall, the evidence suggests that localisation economies seem to be absent in the EU, as Glaeser et al. (1992) found for the U.S. One possible exception may be for high specialisation levels in Spanish provinces. More often, diversity has a positive impact on local labour growth, which is again consistent with the U.S. findings. Another common feature is that results vary considerably across industries. For instance, a common finding is that urbanisation economies appear to be stronger in high-tech and service industries than in manufacturing. Finally, local effects dissipate quicker in France than in the U.S. As well as these similarities in terms of findings, we again note that some of these EU studies have broader methodological implications for future empirical work.

4. Conclusions

This chapter set out to describe the economic geography of the EU and to consider what we know about the forces determining that geography. At times, our review has been fairly critical. European data is a mess and European researchers have often not used this data as efficiently as possible. But some positive lessons also emerge, and it is these that we want to focus on in this conclusion.

First, we do know much more about the economic geography of the EU as a whole than we did a decade ago. Many gaps remain to be filled, but we do now have some idea of the spatial structure of both aggregate activity and particular industries. One key gap in our knowledge remains. That is, how does the economic geography of the

EU compare to that of other large integrated economic areas? In practise, answering this question will involve identifying how the economic geography of the EU differs from that of the U.S. This question is of fundamental importance for a very simple reason. Empirical work suggests two key ways in which the EU is different from the U.S. Our product markets are less integrated and our labour is less mobile. Theory tells us that these two factors *could* be enough to leave the EU with a very different economic geography to the U.S. Current empirical evidence does not allow us to assess whether these two factors *do* mean that the economic geography of the EU and the U.S. are different. Resolving this issue is important, because it will be fundamental in deciding whether a separate European area-based literature is really needed, or whether empirical research on the EU is just about studying the same economic geography mechanisms with different data.

The evidence that we do have so far points to some marked similarities. Micro-level data suggests that the same kind of industries may be localised in both the EU and the U.S. Other work, suggests that there are similarities between the EU and the U.S. in the workings of the agglomeration and dispersion forces that determine economic geography. We have seen that similarities between the two areas exist in the relationship between wages and density, the determinants of wage differences and the spatial nature of these differences, and the dynamics of city growth in both the short and long run. Given the excellent data that is becoming available across the EU, making further significant progress on resolving these issues should be the main task for the coming decade.

Acknowledgements

We thank Gilles Duranton, Vernon Henderson, Thierry Mayer, Giovanni Peri, Diego Puga, Bertrand Schmitt, and Jacques-François Thisse for very useful discussions. We also thank seminar participants at NHH, a CEPR conference in Paris, and a CEPR Economic Geography Network meeting in Villars. This paper was produced as part of a CEPR research network on 'The Economic Geography of Europe: Measurement, Testing and Policy Simulations' funded by the European Commission under the Research Training Network Programme (Contract no: HPRN-CT-2000-00069). This paper was written while Combes was visiting Boston University. Hospitality from the Economics Department there is gratefully acknowledged.

References

Aiginger, K., Leitner, W. (2002). "Regional concentration in the United States and Europe: who follows whom?" Weltwirtschaftliches Archiv 138, 1–28.

Almeida, R. (2001). "Local characteristics and growth in Portuguese regions". Processed. Universitat Pompeu Frabra.

Amiti, M. (1999). "Specialization patterns in Europe". Weltwirtschaftliches Archiv 135, 1–21.

Arellano, M., Bond, S.R. (1991). "Some tests of specification for panel data: Monte Carlo evidence and an application to employment equations". Review of Economic Studies 58, 277–297.

Audretsch, D.B., Feldman, M.P. (2004). "Knowledge spillovers and the geography of innovation". In: Henderson, J.V., Thisse, J.-F. (Eds.), Handbook of Regional and Urban Economics, vol. 4. Elsevier, Amsterdam, pp. 2713–2739. This volume.

Barrios, S., Bertinelli, L., Strobl, E., Teixeira, A.-C. (2003). "Agglomeration economies and the location of industries: Evidence for three small European countries". Processed. CORE, Louvain La Neuve.

Brakman, S., Garretsen, H., Schramm, M. (2004). "The spatial distribution of wages and employment: estimating the Helpman–Hanson model". Journal of Regional Science. In press.

Brülhart, M. (1998a). "Economic geography, industry location, and trade: the evidence". The World Economy 21, 775–801.

Brülhart, M. (1998b). "Trading places: industrial specialization in the European Union". Journal of Common Market Studies 36, 319–346.

Brülhart, M. (2001a). "Evolving geographic concentration of European manufacturing industries". Weltwirtschaftliches Archiv 137, 215–243.

Brülhart, M. (2001b). "Growing alike or growing apart? Industrial specialisation of EU countries". In: Wyplosz, C. (Ed.), The Impact of EMU on Europe and the Developing Countries. Oxford University Press.

Brülhart, M., Torstensson, J. (1996). "Regional integration, scale economies and industry location in the European Union". CEPR discussion paper no. 1435.

Brülhart, M., Traeger, R. (2002). "An account of geographic concentration patterns in Europe". Processed. University of Lausanne.

Cainelli, G., Leoncini, R. (1999). "Externalities and long-term industrial development. Some empirical evidence from Italy". Revue d'Économie Industrielle 90, 25–39.

Cawley, R., Davenport, M. (1988). "Partial equilibrium calculations of the impact of internal market barriers in the European Community". In: Commission of the European Communities Research on the Cost of Non-Europe, vol. 2: Studies on the Economics of Integration. European Commission, Luxembourg.

CEPII (1997). "Trade patterns inside the single market". In: The Single Market Review, Subseries IV: Impact on Trade and Investment. Commission of the European Communities, Brussels.

Chatelus, G., Ulied, A. (1995). Final report on union territorial strategies linked to the Transeuropean Transportation Networks. Paris/Barcelona.

Christaller, W. (1933). Die zentralen Orte in Süddeutschland; eine ökonomisch-geographische Untersuchung über die Gesetzmäßigkeit der Verbreitung und Entwicklung der Siedlungen mit städtischen Funktionen. Gustav Fischer, Jena. Published in English as: The Central Places in Southern Germany. Prentice Hall, Englewood Cliffs, NJ, 1966.

Ciccone, A. (2002). "Agglomeration effects in Europe". European Economic Review 46, 213–227.

Ciccone, A., Hall, R. (1996). "Productivity, and the density of economic activity". American Economic Review 86, 54–70.

Cingano, F., Schivardi, F. (2004). "Identifying the sources of local productivity growth". Journal of the European Economic Association. In press.

Combes, P.-P. (2000). "Economic structure and local growth: France, 1984–1993". Journal of Urban Economics 47, 329–355.

Combes, P.-P., Duranton, G., Gobillon, L. (2003). "Wage differentials across French local labour markets: endowments, skills, and interactions". CEPR Discussion paper no. 4240.

Combes, P.-P., Lafourcade, M. (2001). "Transportation costs decline and regional inequalities: Evidence from France". CEPR discussion paper no. 2894.

Combes, P.-P., Lafourcade, M. (2003). "Core–periphery patterns of generalized transport costs: France, 1978–1998". CEPR discussion paper no. 3958.

Combes, P.-P., Magnac, T., Robin, J.-M. (2004). "The dynamics of local employment in France". Journal of Urban Economics. In press.

Copus, A. (1997). A new peripherality index for European NUTS II regions. Report for the Highlands and Islands European partnership.
Davis, D., Weinstein, D. (1999). "Economic geography and regional production structure: an empirical investigation". European Economic Review 43, 379–407.
De Bruyne, K. (2003). "The location of economic activity. Is there a spatial employment structure in Belgium?" Processed. CES-KU, Leuven.
de Lucio, J., Herce, J., Goicolea, A. (2002). "The effects of externalities on productivity growth in Spanish industry". Regional Science and Urban Economics 32, 241–258.
Devereux, M., Griffith, R., Simpson, H. (2002). "The geographic distribution of productive activity in the UK". Regional Science and Urban Economics. In press.
Dixit, A., Stiglitz, J. (1977). "Monopolistic competition and optimum product diversity". American Economic Review 67, 297–308.
Duranton, G., Overman, H.G. (2002). "Testing for localisation using micro-geographic data". CEPR discussion paper no. 3379.
Duranton, G., Monastiriotis, V. (2002). "Mind the gaps: The evolution of regional inequalities in the UK 1982–1997". Journal of Regional Science 42, 219–256.
Duranton, G., Puga, D. (2001). "Nursery cities". American Economic Review 91, 1454–1477.
Duranton, G., Puga, D. (2004). "Micro-foundations of urban agglomeration economies". In: Henderson, J.V., Thisse, J.-F. (Eds.), Handbook of Regional and Urban Economics, vol. 4. Elsevier, Amsterdam, pp. 2063–2117. This volume.
Ellison, G., Glaeser, E. (1997). "Geographic concentration in US manufacturing industries: A dartboard approach". Journal of Political Economy 105, 889–927.
Ellison, G., Glaeser, E. (1999). "The geographic concentration of industry: Does natural advantage explain agglomeration?" American Economic Review 89, 311–316.
Eichengreen, B. (1993). "Labour markets and European monetary unification". In: Masson, P., Taylor, M. (Eds.), Policy Issues in the Operation of Currency Unions. Cambridge University Press, Cambridge, pp. 130–162.
Engels, F. (1845). Die Lage der arbeitenden Klasse in England. Leipzig. Published in English as: The Condition of the Working Class in England. Stanford University Press, Standford, CA, 1958.
Forni, M., Paba, S. (2002). "Spillovers and the growth of local industries". Journal of Industrial Economics 50, 151–171.
Fujita, M., Henderson, J.V., Kanemoto, Y., Mori, T. (2004). "Spatial distribution of economic activities in Japan and China". In: Henderson, J.V., Thisse, J.-F. (Eds.), Handbook of Regional and Urban Economics, vol. 4. Elsevier, Amsterdam. This volume.
Gaigné, C., Huiban, J.-P., Schmitt, B. (2002). "Do labour costs and home market size matter for local industrial specialisation? Evidence for France". Processed. ENSEAD, Dijon.
Glaeser, E.L., Kallal, H.D., Scheinkman, J.A., Shleifer, A. (1992). "Growth in cities". Journal of Political Economy 100, 1126–1152.
Glaeser, E., Maré, D. (2001). "Cities and skills". Journal of Labor Economics 19, 316–342.
Greenway, D., Hine, R.C. (1991). "Intra-industry specialization, trade expansion and adjustment in the European economic space". Journal of Common Market Studies 29, 603–622.
Gutiérrez, J., Urbano, P. (1996). "Accessibility in the European Union: impact of the trans-European Road Network". Journal of Transport Geography 4, 15–25.
Haaland, J.I., Kind, H.J., Midelfart-Knarvik, K.H., Torstensson, J. (1999). "What determines the economic geography of Europe?" CEPR discussion paper no. 2072.
Hallet, M. (2000). "Regional specialisation and concentration in the EU". The European Commission, Directorate General for Economic for Economic and Financial Affairs Economic Papers no. 141.
Hanson, G. (2002). "Market potential, increasing returns, and geographic concentration". Processed. University of Michigan, November. Revised version of NBER working paper no. 6249. February 1998.
Harrigan, J. (1997). "Technology, factor supplies and international specialisation: Estimating the neo-classical model". American Economic Review 87, 475–494.

Harris, C.D. (1954). "The market as a factor in the localisation of industry in the United States". Annals of the Association of American Geographers 64, 315–348.

Head, K., Mayer, T. (2002). "Illusory border effects: How far is an economy from itself?" CEPII discussion paper no. 2002-01.

Head, K., Mayer, T. (2004). "The empirics of agglomeration and trade". In: Henderson, J.V., Thisse, J.-F. (Eds.), Handbook of Regional and Urban Economics, vol. 4. Elsevier, Amsterdam, pp. 2609–2669. This volume.

Helg, R., Manasse, P., Monacelii, P., Rovelli, R. (1995). "How much (a)symmetry in Europe? Evidence from industrial sectors". European Economic Review 39, 1017–1041.

Helpman, E. (1998). "The size of regions". In: Pines, D., Sadka, E., Zilcha, I. (Eds.), Topics in Public Economics. Cambridge University Press, Cambridge, pp. 33–54.

Henderson, J.V. (1997). "Externalities and industrial development". Journal of Urban Economics 42, 449–470.

Henderson, J.V., Kuncoro, A., Turner, M. (1995). "Industrial development in cities". Journal of Political Economy 103, 1067–1152.

Henner, H.F. (1976). "La specialisation internationale de l'économie française". Revue Économique 27, 31–53.

Hine, R.C. (1989). "Customs union enlargement and adjustment: Spain's accession to the European Community". Journal of Common Market Studies 28, 1–27.

Holmes, T.J., Stevens, J.J. (2004). "Spatial distribution of economic activities in North America". In: Henderson, J.V., Thisse, J.-F. (Eds.), Handbook of Regional and Urban Economics, vol. 4. Elsevier, Amsterdam, pp. 2797–2844. This volume.

Jacobs, J. (1969). The Economy of Cities. Random House, New York.

Kaplow, L. (2002). "Why measure inequality?" NBER working paper no. 9342.

Keeble, D., Owens, P.L., Thompson, C. (1982). "Regional accessibility and economic potential in the European Community". Regional Studies 16, 419–432.

Keeble, D., Offord, J., Walker, S. (1988), Peripheral regions in a community of twelve member states. Report for the European Commission, Brussels.

Kim, S. (1995). "Expansion of markets and the geographic distribution of economic activities: the trends in US regional manufacturing structure, 1860–1987". Quarterly Journal of Economics 110, 881–908.

Krugman, P. (1991a). Geography and Trade. MIT press, Cambridge, MA.

Krugman, P. (1991b). "Increasing returns and economic geography". Journal of Political Economy 99, 483–499.

Krugman, P., Venables, A.J. (1995). "Globalization and the inequality of nations". Quarterly Journal of Economics 110, 857–880.

Lutter, H. (1993). "Accessibility and regional development of European regions and the role of transport systems". European Regional Planning, Report no. 55. Council of Europe Press, Luxembourg.

Magrini, S. (2004). "Regional (di)convergence". In: Henderson, J.V., Thisse, J.-F. (Eds.), Handbook of Regional and Urban Economics, vol. 4. Elsevier, Amsterdam, pp. 2741–2796. This volume.

Marshall, A. (1890). Principles of Economics. Macmillan, London.

Maurel, F., Sédillot, B. (1999). "A measure of the geographic concentration in French manufacturing industries". Regional Science and Urban Economics 29, 575–604.

Midelfart-Knarvik, K.H., Overman, H.G. (2002). "Delocation and European integration: Is structural spending justified". Economic Policy 35, 323–359.

Midelfart-Knarvik, K.H., Overman, H.G., Redding, S.J., Venables, A.J. (2002). "Integration and industrial specialisation in the European Union". Revue Économique 53, 469–481.

Midelfart-Knarvik, K.H., Overman, H.G., Redding, S.J., Venables, A.J. (2003). "The location of European industry". In: European Integration and the Functioning of Product Markets. European Economy, Special report No. 2. European Commision Office for Official Publications, Luxembourg.

Midelfart-Knarvik, K.H., Overman, H.G., Venables, A.J. (2000). "Comparative advantage and economic geography: Estimating the location of production in the EU". CEPR discussion paper no. 2618.

Mion, G. (2002). "Spatial externalities and empirical analysis: The case of Italy". CORE discussion paper no. 2003/15.

Molle, W. (1997). "The regional economic structure of the European Union: an analysis of long term developments". In: Peschel, K. (Ed.), Regional Growth and Regional Policy within the Framework of European Integration. Physica-Verlag, Heidelberg, pp. 66–86.

OECD (1987). Structural Adjustments and Economic Performance. OECD, Paris.

OECD (1994). Manufacturing Performance: A Scoreboard of Indicators. OECD, Paris.

OECD (1999). EMU: Facts, Challenges and Policies. OECD, Paris.

OECD (2001). STAN Database. OECD, Paris.

Ottaviano, G., Thisse, J.-F. (2004). "Agglomeration and economic geography". In: Henderson, J.V., Thisse, J.-F. (Eds.), Handbook of Regional and Urban Economics, vol. 4. Elsevier, Amsterdam, pp. 2563–2608. This volume.

Overman, H.G., Puga, D. (2002). "Unemployment clusters across European countries and regions". Economic Policy 34, 117–147.

Paci, R., Usai, S. (2002). "Externalities and local economic growth in manufacturing industries". CRENOS working paper no. 01/13.

Paluzie, E., Pons, J., Tirado, D.A. (2001). "Regional integration and specialization patterns in Spain". Regional Studies 35, 286–296.

Pratten, C. (1988). "A survey of the economies of scale". In: Research on the "Cost of Non-Europe", vol. 2, Studies on the Economies of Integration. Commission of the European Communities, Luxembourg.

Puga, D. (1999). "The rise and fall of regional inequalities". European Economic Review 43, 303–334.

Redding, S.J., Venables, A.J. (2004). "Economic geography and international inequality". Journal of International Economics 62, 53–82.

Roos, M. (2001). "Wages and market potential in Germany". Jahrbuch für Regionalwissenschaft 21, 171–195.

Rosenthal, S.S., Strange, W. (2004). "Evidence on the nature and sources of agglomeration economies". In: Henderson, J.V., Thisse, J.-F. (Eds.), Handbook of Regional and Urban Economics, vol. 4. Elsevier, Amsterdam, pp. 2119–2171. This volume.

Schürmann, C., Talaat, A. (2000). Towards a European Peripherality Index. Final Report. Report for DG REGIO. Institut für Raumpanung, Dortmund.

Schürmann, C., Spiekermann, K., Wegener, M. (2001). "Regional economic impacts of trans-European transport networks". In: 2001 WCTR Proceedings. WCTR Society, Seoul.

Smith, B. (1975). "Regional specialisation and trade in the United Kingdom". Scottish Journal of Political Economy 22, 39–56.

Spiekermann, K., Wegener, M. (1994). "The shrinking continent: New time-space maps of Europe". Environment and Planning B 21, 653–673.

Spiekermann, K., Wegener, M. (1996). "Trans European Networks and unequal accessibility in Europe". European Journal of Regional Development 4, 35–42.

Storper, M., Chen, Y., De Paolis, F. (2002). "Trade and the location of industries in the OECD and European Union". Journal of Economic Geography 2, 73–107.

Sutton, J. (2000). Marshall's Tendencies: What Can Economists Know? MIT Press, Cambridge, MA.

Teixeira, A. (2002). "Transport policies in light of the New Economic Geography". Processed. CORE, Louvain La Neuve.

Vickerman, R., Spiekermann, K., Wegener, M. (1999). "Accessibility and economic development in Europe". Regional Studies 33, 1–15.

Van Soest, D., Gerking, S., van Oort, F. (2002), "Knowledge externalities, agglomeration economies, and employment growth in Dutch cities". CentER discussion paper no. 2002-41.

WIFO (1999), "Specialisation and (geographic) concentration of European manufacturing". Background paper for the competitiveness of European Industry; the 1999 report. Working paper no. 1. EC Enterprise Directorate-General, Brussels.

Chapter 65

SPATIAL DISTRIBUTION OF ECONOMIC ACTIVITIES IN JAPAN AND CHINA

MASAHISA FUJITA

Institute of Economic Research, Kyoto University, Japan

TOMOYA MORI

Institute of Economic Research, Kyoto University, Japan
e-mail: mori@kier.kyoto-u.ac.jp

J. VERNON HENDERSON

Department of Economics, Brown University, USA

YOSHITSUGU KANEMOTO

Department of Economics, Tokyo University, Japan

Contents

Handbook of Regional and Urban Economics, Volume 4. Edited by J.V. Henderson and J.F. Thisse

DOI: 10.1016/S0169-7218(04)07065-0

Abstract

In this chapter we look at the spatial distribution of economic activities in China and Japan. Japan has excellent data and relatively uniform institutions since World War II, which allow us to track its spatial evolution and detail its key features today. For Japan we show how structural shifts in the national economy involved major transformations of the regional structure of economic activity. We address a central policy issue, the high extent of urban agglomeration in Tokyo. Then we turn to the details of the spatial distribution of industrial activity across cities, to see what general patterns hold and what they imply for our understanding of the role of different cities in the urban hierarchy. For China the approach is different. With the radical institutional changes since 1978 moving China away from being a planned economy, there is little consistency in data definitions and coverage over time and less detailed data are available. We focus on the last decade and on policy issues. We observe that Chinese cities tend to be over-capitalized and undersized, with strong spatial biases to policies, concerning migration, capital allocations, infrastructure allocations and location of FDI.

Keywords

agglomeration economies, core–periphery pattern, Japan, convergence, globalization, Henry George Theorem, Hierarchy Principle, China, urbanization, urban agglomeration

JEL classification: F23, O18, O53, R11, R12, R14, R23, R58, O0, P3, R0

1. Introduction

In this chapter we look at the spatial distribution of economic activities in Japan and China. For Japan there are excellent data and relatively uniform institutions since World War II, which allow us to detail the evolution of the spatial economy and its key features today. In contrast, China moves from a closed, planned economy in 1978 towards a more market based economy that more fully emerges in the 1990s. With radical institutional change, definitions of spatial and economic units are not consistent over time and until the 1990s data quality is more suspect. So for China, discussion involving data analyses is more restricted to the 1990s. Moreover, given the radical institutional change in China, the focus is less on details of spatial evolution and more on the impact of policy and policy changes.

The material on Japan is divided into four sections, focusing on the impact of rapid economic growth in the 20th century on the tremendous changes in spatial structure of activities. In Section 2.1, we examine the regional transformations that arose in postwar Japan. Roughly speaking, after WW II the Japanese economy has experienced two phases of major structural changes. For our purpose, the interesting aspect is that *each phase of industrial shift has been accompanied with a major transformation in the nation-wide regional structure*. The Japanese economy now seems to be in the midst of a third one and we offer some conjectures about its possible evolution.

Perhaps the most important public policy issue concerning urban agglomeration in Japan is the Tokyo problem. Tokyo is the largest metropolitan area in the world with a population exceeding 30 million. The dominance of Tokyo has increased steadily over the 20th century, ultimately absorbing a quarter of the Japanese population in 2000. In Section 2.2, we discuss attempts to test empirically the hypothesis that Tokyo is too big.

In Section 2.3, we move to the spatial distribution of industries among cities. Some metro areas have attracted a disproportionately large number of industries, leading to great variations in industrial diversity among metro areas. The most diverse metro is obviously Tokyo, with positive employment in 122 industries out of the 125 manufacturing 3-digit sectors considered, while the least diverse is Iwamizawa with only 46 industries. In elaborating more on that point, we will report on the two main empirical regularities regarding industrial and population distributions across locations. First, there is a strong negative log-linear relation between the number of metro areas occupied by an industry and the average population size of the corresponding metro areas. This regularity has itself remained very stable in the period 1980–2000. Second, the industrial location patterns observed during this period are highly consistent with Christaller's *Hierarchy Principle* of industrial location behavior, which asserts that an industry found in any given metro area will also be found in all larger metro areas.

The section on China will argue that the history of policy in China has resulted in an urbanization process where these cities are significantly undersized and agglomeration economies not fully exploited (in strong contrast to Tokyo). Cities tend to be over-capitalized relative to the rural sector and there is nationally a high degree of individual and regional income inequality. Coastal cities and regions have been favored at the expense of the hinterlands. We will explore these and other key features of spatial development in China, the underlying policies, and the dimensions of the costs of particularly restrictive policies.

2. Distribution of economic activities in Japan

2.1. City size distribution and regional transformations in postwar Japan

2.1.1. Evolution of city size distribution in Japan

We start with a brief examination of the evolution of the city size distribution in Japan in the 20th century. To do so, we have to define urban areas. Here, we adopt a recently

Figure 1. Metropolitan employment areas. For a colour reproduction of this figure see the colour figures section, page 3071.

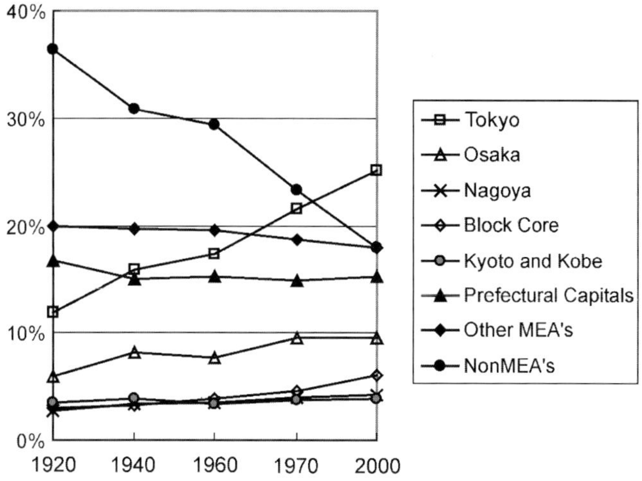

Figure 2. Long-term trends in Japanese metropolitan areas.

proposed version called Urban Employment Area (UEA).[1] The UEAs are divided into Metropolitan Employment Areas (MEAs) whose central cities have DID (Densely Inhabited District) populations exceeding 50,000 and Micropolitan Employment Areas (McEAs) with the DID populations between 10,000 and 50,000. In 1995 there are 118 MEAs and 160 McEAs. Figure 1 shows all MEAs except those in Okinawa Prefecture (see a colored map in the end of this volume for a more detailed version).

Figure 2 shows first the population shares of the three largest metropolitan areas, Tokyo, Osaka, and Nagoya, and other categories of MEAs from 1920 to 2000, using the 1995 MEA definition. After that metropolitan areas are grouped, with the block core in the graph consisting of Sapporo, Sendai, Hiroshima, and Fukuoka that are the regional centers of four regions, Hokkaido, Tohoku, Chugoku, and Kyushu. Prefectural capitals include 33 MEAs that are prefectural capitals (47 prefectures in Japan) and do not belong to other categories of MEAs.

From 1920 to 2000, the share of non-metropolitan areas decreased from 36.4 to 17.9%, most of which was captured by Tokyo that increased its share from 11.8 to 25.1%. Block core MEAs that grew from 3.0 to 6.1% in the same period constitute another high growth category. Osaka showed considerable growth between 1920 and 1970 (from 6.0 to 9.5%) but stagnated since then. Smaller size MEAs decreased their share

[1] The Japanese government provides statistics only for legal jurisdictions, i.e., cities and prefectures, and no official data are available for metropolitan areas. A number of researchers have developed their own definitions, however. Examples are the Standard Metropolitan Employment Area (SMEA) by Yamada and Tokuoka, the Functional Urban Core (FUC) by Kawashima, and the Integrated Metropolitan Area (IMA) by Suzuki and Takeuchi. Recently, Kanemoto and Tokuoka (2002) proposed a new version called Urban Employment Area (UEA) which we adopt in this chapter.

slightly from 20.0% in 1920 to 18.0% in 2000 while prefectural capitals kept their share from 1940 on after a 1.7% drop between 1920 and 1940.

In Japan, Tokyo is by far the largest metropolitan area with population exceeding 30 million in 2000. Over the 1970s, most of the major metropolitan areas experienced significant population growth. The Tokyo metropolitan area gained about 4.5 million in the 1970s, which is about the size of Nagoya that is the third largest metropolitan area. Sapporo, Fukuoka, and Sendai (which with Hiroshima constitute Block Cores in Figure 2) had higher rates of growth than Tokyo, however. These three cities experienced very high rates of growth also over the 1980s and 1990s, about 6–11% above the rate of national population growth, while Tokyo's growth rate decreased to just over 2% above the national population growth rate.

2.1.2. *Three cycles of regional transformation in postwar Japan*

In order to understand the basic trends in the regional transformation in postwar Japan, it is best to start with Figures 3 and 4.[2] First, Figure 3 shows the net migration to each of the three largest metropolitan areas (MAs), Tokyo, Osaka and Nagoya, over the period of 1955 to 2001. (For the Japanese map, see Figure 1.)

This figure indicates that Japan experienced two cycles of regional transformation since the mid-1950s, and now may be in the midst of a third. In the first cycle from the mid-1950s to the mid-1970s, each one of the three MAs experienced a high rate of

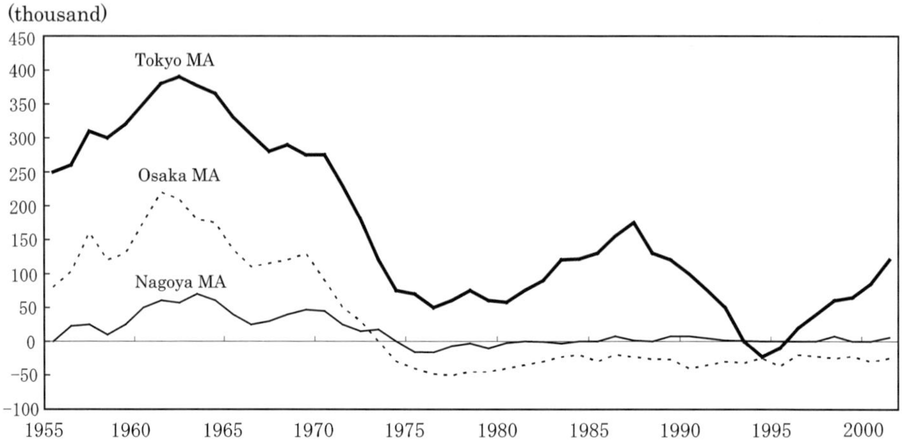

Figure 3. Net migration to the three largest metropolitan areas. *Note*. Tokyo MA: Tokyo, Kanagawa, Saitama, and Chiba prefectures; Osaka MA: Osaka, Hyogo, Kyoto and Nara prefectures; Nagoya MA: Aichi, Gifu and Mie prefectures. *Source*. Ministry of Home Affairs (Japan).

[2] This section is mainly based on Fujita and Tabuchi (1997).

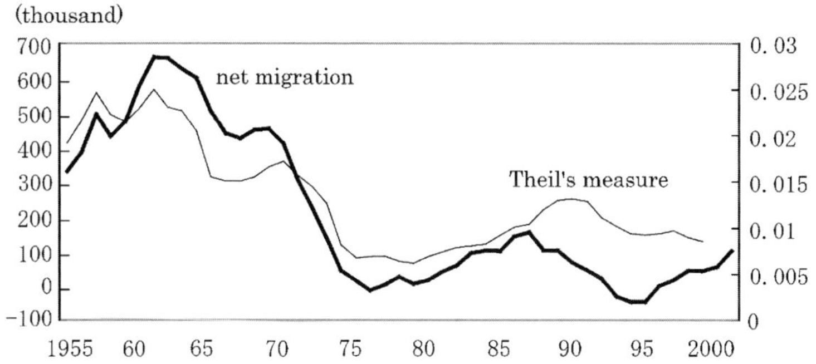

Figure 4. The net migration to the three largest MAs and the Theil's measure of the inter-regional per capita real income differential. *Source*. Economic Planning Agency and Tanioka (2002).

net migration until 1970 with the peak in the early 1960s, followed by a sharp drop. In this first cycle, the roughly inverse-U-shaped pattern of net migration was synchronized among the three MAs. However, in the second cycle from the mid-1970s to the mid-1990s, such synchronization among the three MAs was totally disrupted. That is, only the Tokyo MA exhibited the same characteristics of the net migration curve as in the first cycle (but with a lower volume than the first). In contrast, the Nagoya MA had a nearly zero rate of net migration, while the Osaka MA changed to a significantly negative rate of net migration. Finally, the third cycle that seems to have started in the mid-1990s exhibits, so far, a pattern similar to the first part of the second cycle.

Figure 4 depicts the sum of the net migration flows to the three MAs in Figure 3 and the inter-regional income differential represented by Theil's measure of the per capita real income differential across prefectures. This figure indicates a clear synchronization between the net migration to the three MAs and inter-regional income differentials, which again suggests the three cycles of regional transformation in Japan after WW II.

We examine each cycle of regional transformation in turn.

2.1.2.1. The first cycle (the mid-1950s to the mid-1970s): agglomeration into the three MAs, and then the expansion to the Pacific Industrial Belt. Soon after the war-shattered Japanese economy recovered to prewar levels in the mid-1950s, the Japanese economy started growing rapidly – a trend that continued until the early 1970s. (Over the period of 1956 to 1970, the average annual growth rate of real GNP was 9.7%.) During this period of rapid economic growth, as shown in Figure 5, Japanese industries experienced a major shift from the primary (mainly agriculture) to the secondary (mainly manufacturing) and the tertiary (mainly service) industries. In particular, the GDP share of the secondary industry increased significantly over the period of 1955 to 1970.

In order to examine the changes in the composition of the manufacturing sector, we show in Figure 6 the GDP shares by manufacturing industries. This figure indicates that the rapid growth of the manufacturing sector over the period of 1955–1970 was led by the high growth rates of electrical, transport, and general machineries, supported by

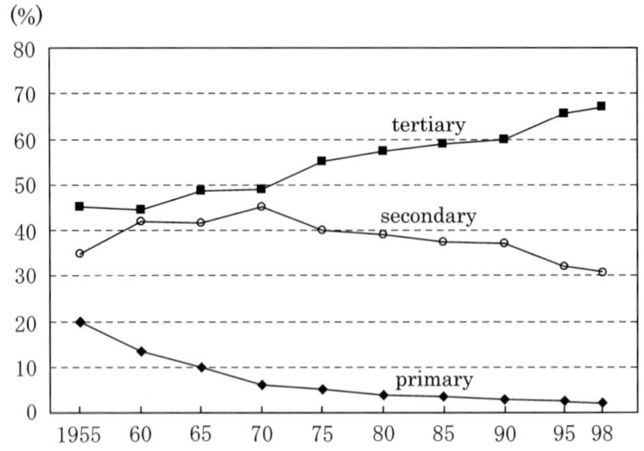

Figure 5. Industrial GDP shares. *Source*. Annual Report on National Accounts (Japan).

the corresponding growth of material industries, or ‘heavy industries’, such as iron and steel, fabricated metals and petrochemicals. Over the same period, the relative share of the textile industry (i.e., the most labor-intensive one) declined sharply.

Figures 3–6 suggest that the first cycle of regional transformation was led in part by linkage-based agglomeration economies, which conforms well with the basic result of the so-called new economic geography. [See the chapter by Ottaviano and Thisse (2004) in this volume]. But it is also the case that technological externalities such as localized information spillovers as emphasized in the traditional systems of cities literature played a role in certain manufacturing sectors, as well as the rapidly growing service sectors heavily concentrated in the largest metropolitan areas. [See the chapters by Duranton and Puga (2004) and by Abdel-Rahman and Anas (2004) in this volume.] More specifically, the factors that propelled the rapid concentration of many industries and workers into the three largest MAs are the following:

(i) decrease in the share of the primary (i.e., land-based) industries, which freed a large number of rural workers,
(ii) substitution of imported raw materials such as coal and iron ore for domestic ones, which made the availability of these raw materials freer of location constraints in Japan,
(iii) increase in the GDP shares of the secondary and tertiary (i.e., non-land-based) industries,
(iv) increase in the shares of manufacturing industries which have strong technological linkages (i.e., electrical, transport, general machineries and material industries), and
(v) improvement in the nation-wide transport networks (of railways, highways and ports).

These five factors together created circular causations, for the agglomeration of industries (covering most types of manufacturing and services) and workers (= consumers)

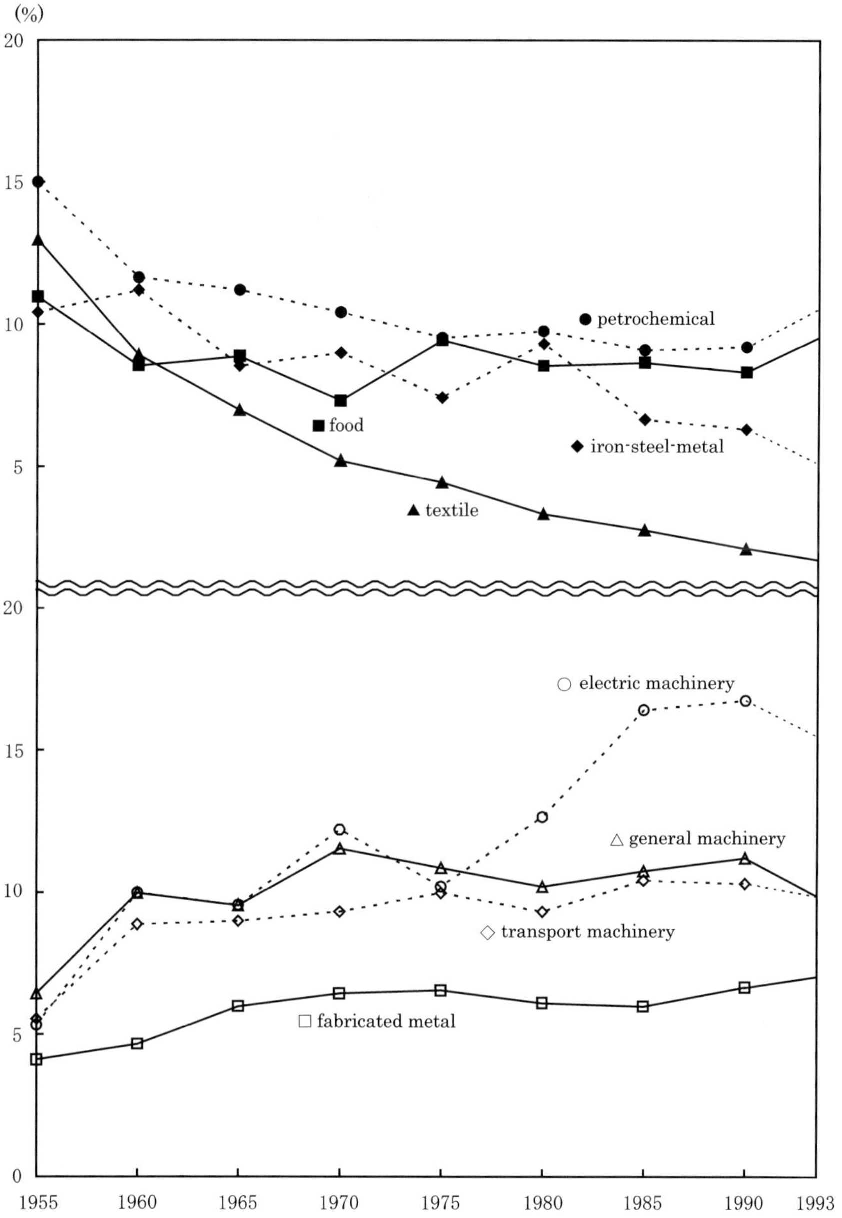

Figure 6. GDP shares by manufacturing industries. *Source*. Census of Manufactures (1955–1993).

into the three largest MAs, through the attraction of workers and firms to big cities due to good accessibility to a large variety of consumer/intermediate goods and the attraction of producers to big cities due to good accessibility to big markets, as well as externalities related to information spillovers, labor market pooling and the like, leading to a rapid growth of the three MAs. However, in the mid-1960s, the growth rate of the three MAs started decreasing gradually because of the rising land prices and wages (i.e., local factor prices). This in turn promoted the expansion of the industrial sites (in particular, of land-intensive industries) towards the surrounding areas of the three MAs, eventually resulting in the formation of the 'Pacific Industrial Belt' connecting the Tokyo MA to the northern part of Kyushu, by the late 1960s. This process of industrial dispersion from the agglomeration core to the surrounding areas due to factor price differentials also conforms well to both results of the new economic geography[3] and the product cycle model of traditional systems of cities [Duranton and Puga (2001)].

In Figure 4, over the period of 1955 to 75, the two curves are roughly bell-shaped and well-synchronized, supporting the inverse-U hypothesis of regional development by Williamson (1965) and Alonso (1980). Using Sim's test of causality, Tabuchi (1987) demonstrated that inter-regional migration in Japan over that period is a consequence of the income differential. That is, the rural–urban income differential statistically preceded the rural–urban migration by a few years.

2.1.2.2. The second cycle (the mid-1970s to the mid-1990s): development of the Tokyo monopolar regional system. During the second cycle of regional transformation in Japan over the period of the mid-1970s to the mid-1990s, only the Tokyo MA (among the three largest MAs) exhibited a significantly positive flow of net migration, leading to the development of the so-called 'Tokyo monopolar regional system'. Such a radical departure from the past trend of migration patterns reflected major structural changes in the Japanese economy which were, in turn, brought about through profound changes in the macro-environment of the world economy since the early 1970s.[4]

A fundamental cause of such changes in both the world economy and Japanese economy is the marked reduction in the (broadly defined) 'transport costs' for the international and inter-regional movement of information, goods, services, capital and people, which has been on-going since the early 1970s. Part of the reduction in transport or trade costs is due to the political progress towards détente in East–West relations and the liberalization of global trade in goods, services and capital. But the more fundamental part involves the revolutionary technological development in computers, information

[3] It should be noted that several national comprehensive plans played a role in facilitating the relocation of industrial complexes, although their true economic impacts are uncertain and are difficult to measure. We may also note that the government policies usually follow, rather than precede, the actual transformation in the structure of industries, so we do not enter into details here.

[4] Cochrane and Vining (1988) reports that the renewed trend of the positive net migration to the core regions of an economy was observed in several developed countries starting around 1980. The international nature of this trend called 'population turnaround' indicates that such a trend reflects the structural changes in the world economy.

processing and networking, and telecommunications, which opened the new age of the so-called information technology (IT) revolution.

In particular, the rapid progress in telecommunications technologies vastly improved the speed, reliability and capacity of communications; furthermore, the costs of such communications are less sensitive to distance. In addition, the advancement of computer integrated manufacturing (CIM) methods enabled the complex production technologies to be embodied in machines, reducing the skill-requirements of workers in standard production operations. Therefore, by effectively combining CIM methods and modern telecommunications technologies, large firms (which have a sufficient capital and accumulation of know-how together with R&D capability) can more freely organize the location of the various units of their entire operations, encouraging the formation of multi-location or multinational firms (MNFs).

Furthermore, the rapid technological progress in ICs and IT contributed not only to the vast technological progress in production and transportation (of goods and passengers), but also to the creation of a wide range of new industries such as the global financial industries, computer-soft and game-soft industries. These developments are related to the vast expansion of the overall service sector, which is highly concentrated in large cities. Meanwhile, the globalization of the world economy due to the successive reduction in 'transport costs' has been accompanied by intensifying competition among the U.S., Japan, EC countries and the NIEs of East Asia, making innovations (for both products and processes) a key strategy for survival and growth of large MNFs.

In addition, several major changes occurred in the Japanese economy. First, the Japanese yen appreciated about 50% immediately after the start of the floating exchange rate system in 1970 (Nixon shock); it appreciated further about 100% after the Plaza Accord of 1985. Furthermore, through two oil shocks in 1973 and 1979, oil prices in Japan increased about eight times. Finally, the rapid growth of 'heavy industries' during 1960s caused severe environmental problems in Japan.

These profound changes in the macro-environment brought about the following major structural changes in the Japanese economy since the mid-1970s.

(i) Given intensifying competition in global markets together with the high valued yen, high wage rates, high energy costs, and severe environmental problems, Japanese manufacturing shifted from the traditional commodity production (which gradually moved to the Asian NIES and other developing countries) to 'high-tech' products based on the newest technologies. In particular, as shown in Figure 6, a rapid growth of the electric machinery industry occurred since the mid-1970s, reflecting the growth of high-tech electronics products related to ICs and IT machinery.

(ii) Given the high valued yen and the high wage rate in Japan, as well as the successive reduction in 'transport costs', many large manufacturing firms moved an increasing share of their labor-intensive operations to low-wage countries (in particular, those in East Asia). Furthermore, the intensifying trade frictions with the U.S. and EC countries and the growing markets there induced many Japanese manufacturing firms to establish their new production plants in these countries.

Both movements expanded rapidly the number of Japanese MNFs as well as the extent of their overseas operations (see Section 2.4.2 for further details).

(iii) As noted previously, the intensifying competition in the global markets together with the successive expansion of the scientific knowledge base of society made technological innovations a key strategy for survival and growth of these MNFs. This induced firms to allocate an increasing proportion of their financial and human resources to R&D activities, while moving their labor-intensive operations to low-wage countries. In addition, global expansion of their operations required these MNFs to strengthen the management functions at their headquarters (HQs) located in Japan.

(iv) The liberalization of global financial and capital markets and the rapidly expanding global operations of MNFs made financial industries (in particular, international finance) grow in Japan. In addition, the growth of high-tech industries and MNFs (focused on R&D and HQ operations in Japan) induced a notable growth of advanced producer services and business services in Japan. Such an expansion of financial industries, producer services and business services partly explain the significant increase (decrease) in the relative GDP-share of the tertiary sector (the secondary sector) in Japan since the mid-1970s, as shown in Figure 5.

(v) In addition to the growth of these advanced services, the technological development related to ICs and IT created new industries also in Japan such as computer software, animation and game development, as well as new types of information and communication services, all of which heavily involve knowledge-intensive activities.

(vi) Finally, the development of the nation-wide high-speed transportation networks of railways (i.e., the Shinkansen), highways and airways mostly centered around Tokyo accelerated in the early 1970s.

All these factors worked together for the development of the Tokyo monopolar regional system. One interpretation is that the marked decrease in 'transport cost' within Japan led, in effect, to the notable contraction of the 'economic space' of Japan, which, in turn, made *unstable* the previous regional system centered around Tokyo, Osaka, and Nagoya. Thus, in the process of reestablishing a new *stable* regional system of Japan, one of the three cities was destined to become the unparalleled top-ranked city, with the remaining two demoted to second-ranked cities. In this process of determining the top-ranked city of Japan, a number of factors favored Tokyo.

First, although Osaka was traditionally the economic center of the western half of Japan until the 1960s, Tokyo, the seat of the central government, was significantly larger than Osaka. Furthermore, Nagoya, situated in the middle of Tokyo and Osaka, was always much smaller than the two others. Second, the expansion of the Shinkansen and airway networks since the early 1970s, which set most major cities in Japan within a one-day-trip business area, were mostly centered around Tokyo. Furthermore, only Tokyo had the first-class international airport until Osaka built one in 1994.

Meanwhile, as noted previously, since the mid-1970s, the leading economic activities of Japan steadily shifted from the traditional commodity production (based on established technologies) to knowledge-intensive activities including the R&D of high-tech products, HQ operations of MNFs and other large firms, advanced business services, and IT-related new industries. For the productivity of such knowledge-intensive activities, the most crucial factor is knowledge externalities which are created and accumulated locally through the exchange of tacit knowledge and information, mostly via face-to-face communications among knowledge-workers. In contrast, using modern information technologies, explicit knowledge and information can be transferred with little obstacle of distance, which can actually lead to greater demand for spatial proximity. And, in the early 1970s, Tokyo had already the biggest concentration of such knowledge-intensive activities. Based on Gaspar and Glaeser (1998), the revolution in telecommunications may enhance the demand for face-to-face communications. Enhanced telecommunications enlarges the menu or array of contacts, but face-to-face interactions are required to sort through and make fertile these contacts.

Therefore, being attracted by the synergy of Tokyo's centrality in transportation and information networks and the highest level of knowledge externalities there, a dominant share of growing knowledge-intensive activities started locating in Tokyo in the mid-1970s. In turn, this strengthened further Tokyo's centrality in transportation and information networks and knowledge externalities there, creating a snowball effect that reinforced Tokyo's dominance. On the other hand, Osaka (more precisely, the Osaka MA) unable to regain its prominence in present-day Japan, has been the biggest loser. In contrast, the Nagoya MA (having Toyota's HQs and mother plants) succeeded in keeping its relative strength by becoming the center of Japanese manufacturing in advanced transportation and general machineries. As shown in Figure 4, Theil's measure of the inter-regional per capital real income differential increased from the mid-1970s until 1990, indicating that the disparity between the core and non-core regions of Japan as well as the disparity among the three MAs increased over that period [see Fujita and Tabuchi (1997), for the decomposition of Theil's measure into various components].

2.1.2.3. The third cycle (the mid-1990s to the present): renewed trend towards the dominance of the Tokyo MA. In the early 1990s the severe and prolonged recession enhanced by structural problems in the traditional financial and land market sectors, curtailed in-migration to Tokyo as illustrated in Figure 3. The net migration to the Tokyo MA, however, turned positive again in 1996. And, it has been steadily climbing up since then, indicating a renewed trend towards the dominance of the Tokyo MA. We consider, tentatively, the period since the mid-1990s the beginning of 'the third cycle' of regional transformation in Japan.

One may suspect that 'the third cycle' may actually be the continuation of the second cycle which was suspended in the mid-1990s because of the severe recession. There is, however, a significant difference between the past two cycles and 'the third cycle'. That is, although there was always a strong correlation between the rate of net migration to the Tokyo MA and the growth rate of national GDP during the past two cycles, there is little such correlation in the third cycle. In particular, although the GDP growth rate was almost zero over the past several years (especially, −2.5% in 1998), the net migration to the Tokyo MA has been steadily climbing.

In closing this section, it must be noted that the results presented in this section are not inconsistent with the comprehensive study of Japanese regional economy by Barro and Sala-i-Martin (1992, 1995) which reports, among others, the (absolute β) convergence of personal income across Japanese prefectures over the period of 1930 to 1990. That is, the convergence of personal income across prefectures which Japan experienced in the very long run proceeded with a cyclical transformation of nation-wide economic landscape discussed earlier in this section.

2.1.3. The evolution of the core–periphery pattern of regional system in Japan

The New Economic Geography predicts the formation of a core–periphery structure (CP-structure) in manufacturing at various scales of the spatial economy.[5] In this section, first we consider the Japanese regional economy as a whole, and show that the economic growth of Japan was accompanied with the formation of a typical CP-structure at the nation-wide scale, and that a systematic transition of industries occurred among macro-regions of Japan. Then, we take the Tokyo MA as an example of a sub-economy, and show that a typical CP-structure was developed also within the Tokyo MA.

First, we device Japan into the following three macro-regions by aggregating 47 prefectures:

- Japanese Core (J-Core) = Tokyo and Kanagawa (the core of Tokyo MA) + Aichi (containing Nagoya MA) + Osaka and Hyogo (the core of Osaka MA);
- Japanese Semi-Core (J-Semi-Core) = Pacific Belt zone excluding the J-Core;[6]
- Japanese Periphery (J-Periphery) = the rest of Japan.

Figure 7 shows the national shares of each region in regional GDP, employment (EMP), manufacturing GDP (M-GDP), and manufacturing employment (M-EMP) over the period of 1955 to 1995.

As the figure indicates, in 1955 (when Japan just recovered from WW II), each of the three regions had almost the same GDP-share and EMP-share in the national economy. This means that in 1955, the average labor productivity was almost the same in the three regions. However, we can see from the top part of the figure that the ratio of GDP-share over EMP-share, i.e., the average labor productivity, in the J-Core increased rapidly from 1955 to 1970, and it continued to increase slowly over the most period since 1975. In contrast, in the bottom part of the figure, from the GDP-share and EMP-share curves for the J-Periphery, we can see that almost the opposite trend occurred in

[5] This section is based mainly on Fujita and Hisatake (1999).

[6] More precisely, J-Semi-Core consists of the following 18 prefectures: Ibaraki, Saitama, Chiba, Shizuoka, Gifu, Mie, Kyoto, Nara, Wakayama, Okayama, Hiroshima, Yamaguchi, Kagawa, Ehime, Fukuoka, Oita, Saga, Nagasaki.

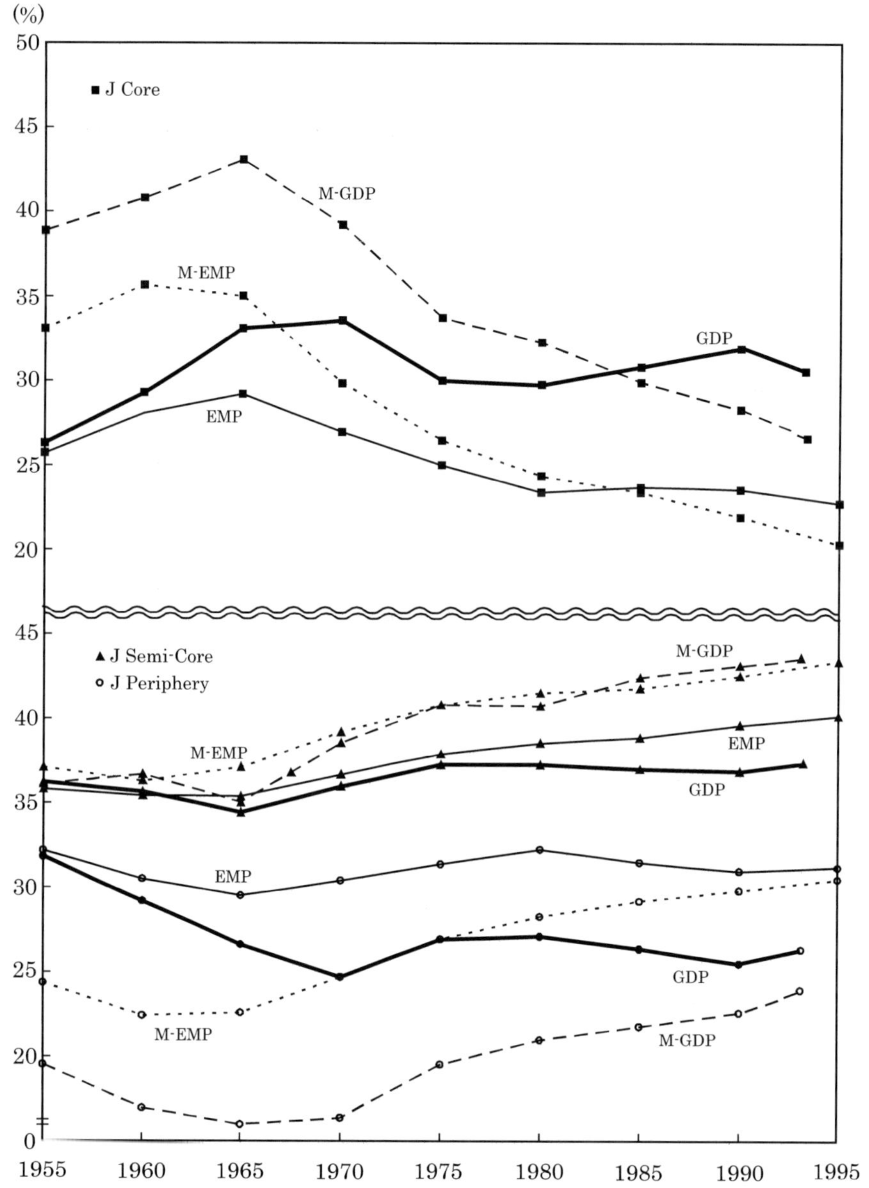

Figure 7. Regional shares of GDP, Employment, M-GDP and M-Employment. *Source*. Annual Report on Prefectural Accounts and Population Census of Japan.

the J-Periphery. Meanwhile, in the middle part of the figure, the ratio of GDP-share over EMP-share remains almost constant.

We can conclude, therefore, that after 1955, Japanese regional economy developed a typical core–periphery structure (having a semi-core region in the middle), which essentially remains the same today. This also indicates that the J-Core rapidly developed strong agglomeration economies after 1955 which are still retained today. That core–periphery structure is not specific to manufacturing.

Focusing on manufacturing industries, we can see from Figure 7 that the manufacturing sector in the J-Core had a relatively high labor productively already in 1955, whereas the opposite holds for the J-Periphery. Furthermore, the rapid growth of the M-GDP share in the J-Core indicates that the rapid growth of the J-Core in the initial period (since 1955) was led by the concentration of manufacturing industries there, which suppressed the growth of the J-Periphery (in relative terms). However, since the mid-1960s, both the M-GDP share and M-EMP share of the J-Core have been declining steadily until recently, while the GDP share of the J-Core remains high since the mid-1960s (although there was a slight decline in the mid-1970s). This means that in the J-Core, while the 'hollowing-out' of manufacturing continued since the mid-1960s, its growth since then has been led mainly by the growth of service industries having high labor productivity. It must be noted, however, that the labor productivity of manufacturing in the J-Core has continued to increase (relative to the national average) even after the mid-1960s because its shares of M-GDP and M-EMP have been declining in parallel while the former is always higher.

In contrast, in the J-Semi-Core, both the shares of M-GDP and M-EMP have been steadily increasing since the mid-1960s. That the two share curves are almost the same means that the labor productivity of manufacturing in this area coincides with the average of Japan. We can also see from Figure 7 that since the mid-1960s, the J-Semi-Core has been (slightly more) specialized in manufacturing (than in services). Finally, in the J-Periphery, both the share of M-GDP and M-EMP has been steadily increasing since the late 1960s. That the two curves are parallel while the M-GDP share is always much lower than the M-EMP share means that the labor productivity of manufacturing in the J-Periphery has been always much lower than the national average.

Summarizing the observations above, we can conclude that a sort of 'flying geese pattern' of inter-regional manufacturing relocation occurred within Japan.[7] That is, manufacturing first grew rapidly in the J-Core, then a little later it grew fast in the J-Semi-Core, and then a bit later in the J-Periphery. However, the labor productivity in manufacturing has been always the highest (the lowest) in the J-Core (in the J-Periphery). The maintained high nominal productivity in the core is consistent with product cycle analysis [Duranton and Puga (2001)]. As we will see in Section 2.4, standardized manufacturing decentralized while more experimental manufacturing remained in the core.

[7] We discuss in further detail the 'flying geese pattern' of manufacturing relocation in East Asia, in Section 2.4.

2.2. Urban agglomeration and city size

2.2.1. Productivity and city size: statistical tendencies

Productivity tends to be higher in larger cities because of agglomeration economies. This higher productivity in turn compensates for the much higher living costs in larger cities due to higher commuting and housing costs. Figure 8 depicts the relationship between production (GDP) per worker and city size (in natural logarithm) for MEAs in 1995.[8] Although the two variables appear to have a modest positive correlation, there are wide variations in labor productivity among MEAs and the correlation is partly driven by outliers in the graph. GDP per worker ought to net out economies and diseconomies, to offer roughly equal "real" GDP per worker across cities. One reason for inter-city variation in GDP per worker is differences in capital stocks. Figure 9 shows that private capital per worker varies widely among cities of similar sizes. It also shows that correlation between private capital per worker and city size is very small. The social overhead capital also has wide variations but it has fairly strong negative correlation with city size, as shown in Figure 10. This reflects a strong tendency to use public investment for

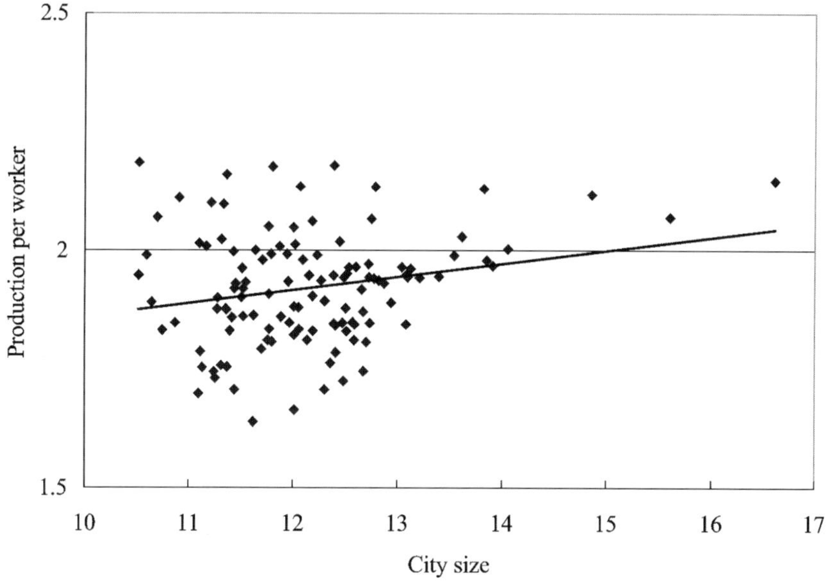

Figure 8. GDP per worker and city size in natural logarithm.

[8] In this diagram, both variables are in natural logarithms. The city size is represented by the number of workers who work in the MEA.

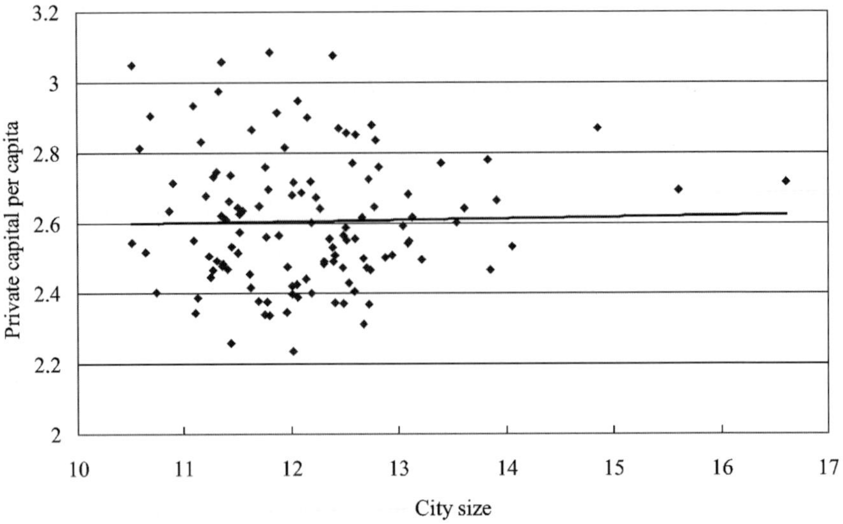

Figure 9. Private capital per worker and city size in natural logarithm.

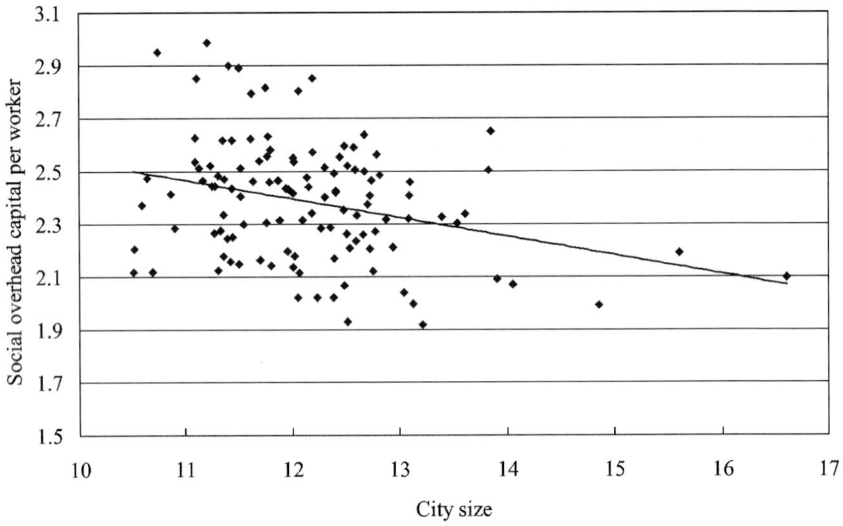

Figure 10. Production and private capital per worker in natural logarithm.

income redistribution between regions: more public investment has been allocated to regions with lower income levels. Figures 11 and 12 show that private capital and social overhead capital have completely opposite relationships with GDP per worker.

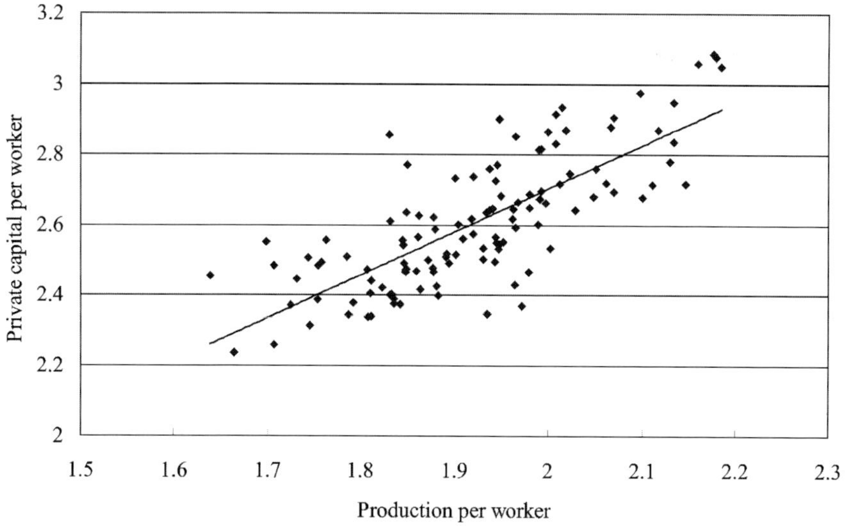

Figure 11. Social overhead capital per worker and city size in natural logarithm.

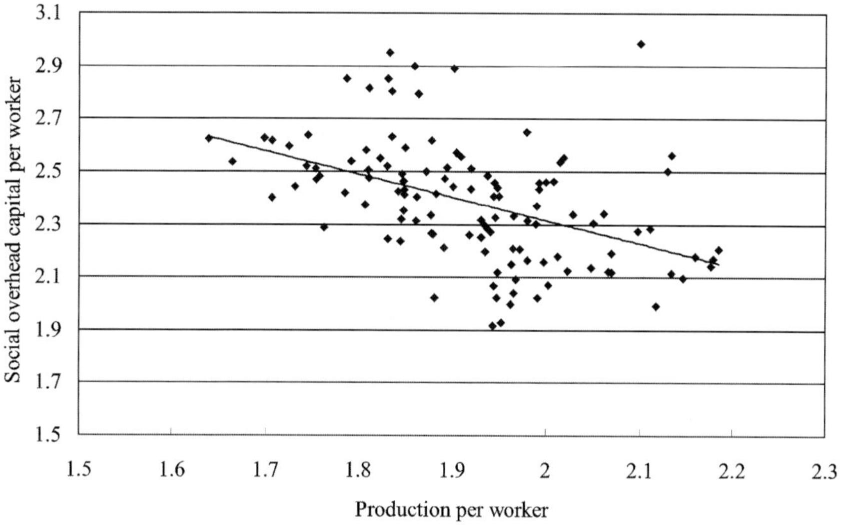

Figure 12. Production and social overhead capital per worker in natural logarithm.

2.2.2. The Tokyo problem

An obvious policy question concerning urban agglomeration is whether or not actual city size is close to the optimum and, if not, what can be done. In Japan, many people argue that the concentration of economic activities in Tokyo is excessive. The population of the Tokyo metropolitan area exceeds 30 million and congestion in commuter railways is almost unbearable. However, it is also true that Tokyo is very convenient for business interactions and trade in intermediate and final outputs. In order to examine whether Tokyo is too large or not, we would have to compare agglomeration economies with a variety of diseconomies such as longer commuting time and congestion externalities.

The issue has direct policy relevance. The proposed relocation of the capital away from Tokyo is a hot issue in Japan. The House of Representatives adopted the resolution on the Relocation of the Diet and Other Organizations in 2000 and the selection process of the new city has been under way since then. At the moment however there is no sign that actual relocation will occur in the near future. In order to evaluate the impacts of the relocation of the capital and the potential de-emphasis of Tokyo, we need to have a good understanding of the magnitude of inefficiencies that are caused by the current city size distribution. Here we present a conceptual framework and some preliminary illustrative results.

2.2.2.1. The Henry George Theorem and a test for optimal city size. Any policy discussion in economics must start with the identification of the sources of market failure. An optimal sized city balances urban agglomeration economies with diseconomy forces, and the first task is to check if these two forces involve significant market failure. On the agglomeration economy side, a variety of micro-foundations are possible for agglomeration economies, including Marshallian externality models [see Duranton and Puga (2004) in this volume] and new economic geography (NEG) models [see Ottaviano and Thisse (2004) in this volume]. Although the NEG type models do not have any technological externalities, agglomeration economies that they produce involve market failure similar to them. That is, urban agglomeration economies are external to each individual or firm and a subsidy to increase agglomeration may improve resource allocation. This suggests that agglomeration economies are almost always accompanied by significant market failure.

Kanemoto (1990) illustrates this point by reinterpreting the non-monocentric city model developed by Imai (1982) and Fujita and Ogawa (1982). Imai (1982) and Fujita and Ogawa (1982) interpret spatial interactions among firms as technological externalities, but they can be reinterpreted as the market transactions of intermediate inputs. The reinterpreted model does not have any technological externalities, but they yield locational externalities. These locational externalities do not arise if there are no scale economies in production, since without them all commodities can be produced in the backyard of each house. When scale economies exist, the locational decision of a firm changes transportation and communication costs of its trading partners, resulting in locational externalities. Although NEG models do not have explicit spatial structure within a CBD, they also yield externalities.

In addition to these problems, the determination of city size involves market failure due to incomplete markets in the face of lumpiness in city formation. A city must be large enough to enjoy benefits of agglomeration, but it is difficult to create a new city of a large size, due to problems of land assembly, constraints on the operation of large scale land developers, and insufficient fiscal autonomy of local governments. If we have too few cities, individual cities tend to be too big. In order to make individual cities closer to the optimum, a new city must be added. It may be difficult, however, to create a new city of large enough size that can compete with the existing cities. A constrained, decentralized market mechanism may fail to yield the optimum number of cities.

These two types of market failure are concerned with two different 'margins'. The first type represents divergence between the social and private benefits of adding one person to a city, whereas the second type involves the benefits of adding another city to the economy. In order to test the first aspect, we have to estimate the sizes of external benefits and costs. We have not seen any serious empirical work on this for Japan. The second aspect can be tested by invoking the so-called Henry George Theorem. In the simplest case where the only agglomeration forces are externalities among firms in a city and the only diseconomy forces are commuting costs of workers who work at the center of the city, then the optimal city size is achieved when the total Pigouvian subsidy for the agglomeration externalities equals the total differential urban rent.

2.2.2.2. Empirical tests. Kanemoto, Ohkawara and Suzuki (1996) and Kanemoto and Saito (1998) attempt to test the Henry George Theorem. A direct test of the Henry George Theorem is very difficult because good land rent data are not available and we have to rely on land price data instead. The conversion of land prices into land rents is bound to be inaccurate in Japan where the price/rent ratio is extremely high and has fluctuated enormously. Roughly speaking the relationship between land price and land rent is

$$\text{land price} = \text{land rent}/(\text{interest rate} - \text{rate of increase of land rent}).$$

In a rapidly growing economy, the denominator tends to be very small and its small change results in a big change in land price. The total real land value of Japan tripled from about 600 trillion yen in 1980 to about 1800 trillion yen in 1990, and then fell to about 1000 trillion yen in 2000.

Given possibly inflated and fluctuating land price estimates and the inability to get good land rent data, instead of testing the Henry George Theorem directly, the authors compute the ratio between the *total* land value and the total Pigouvian subsidy for each metropolitan area, to see if there is a significant difference in the ratio between cities at different levels of the urban hierarchy. Their hypothesis is that cities form a hierarchical structure where Tokyo is the only city at the top. Equilibrium city sizes tend to be too large at each level of hierarchy. But the divergence from the optimal size may differ across levels of hierarchy. At a low level of hierarchy, the divergence tends to be small because it is relatively easy to add a new city. For example, moving a headquarter or a factory of a large corporation can easily result in a city of 20 thousand people. In fact, the Tsukuba science city that was created by moving national research laboratories and a university to a middle of nowhere now has a population of more than 500 thousand. At a higher level, it becomes more difficult to create a new city because larger agglomerations are more difficult to form. For example, the population size difference between Osaka and Tokyo is close to 20 million and making Osaka into another center of Japan would be very difficult. Kanemoto, Ohkawara and Suzuki (1996) therefore test whether the divergence from the optimum is larger for larger cities, in particular if the ratio between the total land value and the total Pigouvian subsidy is significantly larger for Tokyo than for other cities.

The total Pigouvian subsidy is computed by estimating an aggregate production function for the Integrated Metropolitan Areas.[9] The estimated equation has a simple Cobb–Douglas form:

$$\ln(Y/N) = A_0 + a_1 \ln(K/N) + a_2 \ln N + a_3 \ln(G/N),$$

where Y, K, N, and G are the total production, the private capital stock, the labor force, and the social overhead capital in a metropolitan area. The estimates of coefficient a_3 for the social overhead capital turn out to be negative in both studies although they are not statistically significant for larger metropolitan areas. As discussed later, this result reflects the tendency that infrastructure investment is more heavily allocated to low-income regions.

The coefficient a_2 indicates the degree of increasing returns to scale in urban production. Under the assumption that without urban agglomeration economies the production function is homogeneous of degree one with respect to capital and labor, this coefficient represents the elasticity of urban agglomeration, i.e., the percentage increase in urban production due to 1% increase in labor force in an urban area. The estimates of a_2 range between 0.01 and 0.07, where it tends to be higher for larger urban areas.

The total Pigouvian subsidy in a city is computed as $PS = a_2 Y$, and this is compared with the total land value. A number of heroic assumptions are necessary for this formulation. Most important among them are the following two. First, production requires only labor and private capital so that in the absence of agglomeration economies $a_2 = 0$. Second, no agglomeration economies exist on the consumption side.

Kanemoto, Ohkawara and Suzuki (1996) find that total land values are very high compared with the total Pigouvian subsidies in all cities, but the ratio for Tokyo is slightly below the average for 17 largest cities in Japan. Kanemoto and Saito (1998) changed the metropolitan area definition to SMEA and used a different land price data to obtain the opposite result. The ratio between the aggregate land price and the total Pigouvian subsidy for the Tokyo metropolitan area is 68.9, which is much higher than the average of largest twenty metropolitan areas, 40.9. While this says nothing about whether cities in general are over-sized, since to assess that we would need to compare land rents, not prices, with the Pigouvian subsidy, it may indicate that Tokyo is over-sized relative to other Japanese cities.

[9] See Footnote 1 in Section 2.1 for various definitions of metropolitan areas in Japan.

2.2.2.3. Directions for future research. These two studies are very preliminary and face problems. First, the estimation of the aggregate urban production function is rather crude in a number of respects. OLS estimates involve simultaneous equation biases, and they do not estimate the magnitudes of agglomeration economies on the consumption side. A significant number of articles have estimated urban agglomeration economies in Japan, using different sets of data and estimation techniques. These studies indicate directions for future research.

For example, Tabuchi (1986) and Tabuchi and Yoshida (2000) explicitly deal with simultaneous equation bias, either by adding a supply side equation or by using instrument variables. Dekle and Eaton (1999) introduce jurisdictional (prefecture) dummies in a panel data estimation to reduce simultaneous equation bias. Nakamura (1985) augments a translog production function with a cost-share equations and estimates by three stage least squares. Some of these studies find higher agglomeration economies, especially for specific industries. These studies suggest that the use of instrument variables, panel data estimation techniques, cost share equations and examination of specific industries should be considered in the next step.

As another example, Tabuchi and Yoshida (2000) estimate agglomeration economies on the consumption side, using a dual approach. They find that urban agglomeration economies are significant on the consumption side as well as on the production side. Production-side agglomeration economies are about 10% and those on the consumption side are about 7 to 12%. Both of these estimates are high compared with those of other studies.[10]

Following the pioneering work of Mera (1973), many studies try to estimate the productivity of social overhead capital. Examples are Asako et al. (1984), Yoshino and Nakano (1996), Mitsui, Takezawa and Kochi (1995), Kanemoto, Ohkawara and Suzuki (1996), Iwamoto et al. (1996), Kanemoto and Saito (1998), Yoshino and Nakajima (1999), and Shioji (2001). Most of these studies [exceptions are Kanemoto, Ohkawara and Suzuki (1996), Kanemoto and Saito (1998), Yoshino and Nakano (1996), and Yoshino and Nakajima (1999)] ignore urban agglomeration economies. Introducing both social overhead capital and agglomeration economies is obviously necessary. As noted above, however, a simple OLS tends to produce negative coefficients for social overhead capital, reflecting the fact that public investment is used for income redistribution among regions.[11]

[10] In their work there is a question about their choice of land price variables, in the dual approach. They use average land prices in commercial areas for land prices for both office and housing use. Commercial land prices tend to be extremely high in large metropolitan areas. It is of interest to know how sensitive the estimates are to the choice of land price data.

[11] This is another simultanesous equation bias problem. Iwamoto et al. (1996) points out the importance of simultaneous equation bias caused by the government policy of allocating more infrastructure investment to low-income regions. They propose three approaches to avoid the simultaneous equation bias. The first is to use the fixed effect approach in the estimation of panel data. The second approach is to aggregate samples to several groups according to income levels. The third approach disaggregates regional output into primary, secondary and tertiary sectors although input variables other than labor are not disaggregated.

Finally, we note that Karato (2000) and Hatta and Karato (2001) propose a novel approach that looks at variations in office rents within a single city. Their hypothesis is that higher employment density raises the productivity of firms in central cities, which is reflected in higher land rents. Hatta and Karato compute the percentage increase in total production in the Tokyo CBD caused by a percentage increase in employment in five subareas. According to their estimates, the elasticity is 0.01 for Marunouchi area (which is the center of the Tokyo CBD) and 0.0064 for Shinjuku (which is one of the largest subcenters within the CBD). These figures are much lower than those estimated using aggregate data for cities. The relationship between micro-level and macro-level estimates has not been studied yet, and this is one of the fruitful directions for future research.

In addition to the estimation of urban agglomeration economies, there are a number of issues that have to be examined. For example, the magnitudes of congestion externalities such as traffic congestion must be estimated. There is also a theoretical problem that the Henry George Theorem may not hold in a second best situation. This is a serious issue because the main part of urban agglomeration economies arises from locational externalities in an NEG type spatial economy. A market equilibrium in a model of this type is not in general Pareto optimal. As far as we know, Abdel-Rahman and Fujita (1990) is the only one that explicitly examines whether or not the Henry George Theorem holds in an NEG type model. Their result is that, in a model where the Dixit–Stiglitz type structure is assumed for intermediate products, the Henry George Theorem holds even in the second best. We do not yet know if this result is general, but it is possible that the theorem holds either exactly or approximately in a more general setting.

2.3. *Spatial distribution of economic activities*

In this section, we look at the location patterns of industries and of population in 1980/1981 and 1999/2000 (where population data is available for 1980 and 2000, while industrial data for 1981 and 1999). Our discussion draws from Mori, Nishikimi and Smith (2003).[12]

We begin with the description of data. The geographic unit we consider is the metro area. The definition of a metro area adopted here is the Metropolitan Employment Area (MEA) (refer to Section 2.1.1). We identified 105 MEAs in 1980 and 113 in 2000. Both the definition of counties and the county population data employed are based on the Population Census of Japan in 1980 and 2000.[13] The employment data used are classified

[12] While very few attempts have been made to characterize the overall patterns of economic location in Japan, many case studies of location patterns of population and individual industries in Japan have been accumulated by geographers. Kitamura and Yada (1977) reported detailed historical industrial geography of Japan since 19th century, and in particular, concerning the formation of industrial belt along the Pacific coast connecting Tokyo through Fukuoka during the high-growth period in the 1960s. Inoue and Ito (1989) and Yada and Imamura (1991) focus on Kyushu region, while Itakura (1988) puts emphasis on Tohoku region. See also Kosugi and Tsuji (1997), Seki and Fukuda (1998), and Shimohirao (1996) for case studies of the localization of specific industries.

[13] The county here is equivalent to the shi-cho-son in the Japanese Census.

according to the three-digit Japanese Standard Industry Classification (JSIC) taken from the Establishment and Enterprise Census of Japan in 1981 and 1999, and applied to the respective population data in 1980 and 2000. Since industrial classifications have been disaggregated for most sectors during this 20-year period, we have attempted to reconcile the two classifications by aggregating the 1999 classification. Among the three-digit JSIC-industries, we focus here on three broad sectors, namely, manufacturing, services, wholesale and retail, which together include 264 industries.[14]

To establish the regularities discussed in the introduction of this section, it is essential to identify for each industry the set of MEAs in which that industry operates (i.e., employment is positive), defined as the *industry-choice MEAs* for that industry. Industry-choice MEAs for a given industry can be considered as the viable locations for that industry. Indeed, the literature suggests that there is a persistence of industrial locations: once an industry has successfully located in an area, the size of this industrial presence may grow over time even in the presence of high turnover rates of establishments.[15] This is also supported by our own data which indicate that between 1981 and 1999, the number of industries in operation in more than 90% of MEAs has increased. The number of industry-choice MEAs for a given industry can then be considered as reflecting the *degree of localization* for that industry. For instance, Spearman's rank correlation between the number of industry-choice MEAs and the raw measure of geographic concentration G of Ellison and Glaeser (1997) calculated at the county level is about -0.9.

2.3.1. Number–average size (NAS) rule

Figure 13 shows the relationship between the number and average (population) size of industry-choice MEAs for each three-digit industry in 1980/1981 and 1999/2000.[16]

Except for three outliers in 1999/2000,[17] the relationship is clear: *average size* ($\overline{\text{SIZE}}$) *is strongly log-linearly related to the number of industry-choice MEAs* (#MEA). The

[14] The set of sectors includes 125 manufacturing, 90 services, and 49 wholesale and retail industries, for which data are publicly available. It is also to be noted that industries (such as tobacco) which belong to public sector are excluded. See Mori, Nishikimi and Smith (2003) for more details.

[15] Henderson, Kuncoro and Turner (1995) argue that one-standard deviation increase in the proportion of 1970 local employment in a specific industry results in 30% increase in 1987 employment controlling for urban size, current labor market conditions, etc. See also Henderson (1997) for a related discussion. Dumais, Ellison and Glaeser (2002) report for the case of the U.S. that nearly three-fourths of plants existing in 1972 were closed by 1992, and more than a half of all manufacturing employees in 1992 did not exist in 1972.

[16] The plots by sectors (manufacturing, service, wholesale and retail) are available in Mori, Nishikimi and Smith (2003). Manufacturing is the most diverse in terms of the number of industry-choice MEAs, while wholesale and retail are the most ubiquitous, locating in more than 78% of MEAs. Note that each plot is independent from the others.

[17] One of the three outliers is coke manufacturing, while the other two are arms-related industries. The latter two outliers may be attributable to the fact that while arms-related industries are technically in the private sector, location decisions in these industries are heavily influenced by government policies in Japan. In addition, it should be mentioned that tobacco manufacturing has been excluded from the analysis, because it was

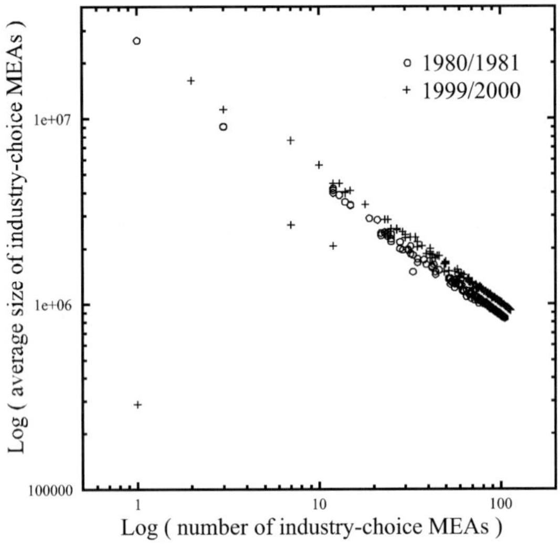

Figure 13. Size and number of industry-choice MEAs.

OLS estimation gives the following result:

$$\text{1980/1981:}\quad \log(\overline{\text{SIZE}}) = \underset{(0.005193)}{7.376^{**}} - \underset{(0.002750)}{0.7204^{**}} \log(\#\text{MEA}),$$

$$R^2 = 0.9962; \tag{2.1}$$

$$\text{1999/2000:}\quad \log(\overline{\text{SIZE}}) = \underset{(0.004232)}{7.427^{**}} - \underset{(0.002750)}{0.7124^{**}} \log(\#\text{MEA}),$$

$$R^2 = 0.9975, \tag{2.2}$$

where the values in parentheses are standard errors, and ** indicates the coefficient to be significant at 1% level. While the significance levels appear high estimates of standard errors may be biased downwards, given correlated error terms created by the ordering of the data [see Gabaix and Ioannides (2004) in this volume]. The equations indicate a strong, tight relationship, over and above what might be explained by dartboard considerations (an association in a model with just random location patterns, where more individual industries are likely to be found in larger metro areas per se, because they are a "bigger" target [see Ellison and Glaeser (1997)]. This relationship is also seen to remain quite stable over time [see Mori, Nishikimi and Smith (2003), for more details]. The results of this analysis show that only the intercepts are significantly different (at

classified in the public sector in 1981. By 1999 tobacco was privatized. Hence it is of interest to note that this industry is also an outlier in 1999, and that this again may be attributable to government policies before privatization.

5% level) between the two periods, while the slope, i.e., the elasticity between the number and average size of industry-choice MEAs, has been invariant overtime (with a 1% increase in the number of MEAs chosen by an industry corresponding approximately to an expected decrease of 0.7% in the average sizes of these MEAs).

However the intercept change does reflect a significant effect, namely a differential shift between the numbers of industry-choice MEAs and the average size of those MEAs. On the one hand, there has been a dispersion of industries, as reflected by a 12.4% average increase in the numbers of industry-choice MEAs. On the other hand, the average size of industry-choice MEAs has increased by only 10.4%. Given that the number and average population size of MEAs increased by 7.6% and 16.7%, respectively, one would have expected to see a smaller increase in the number of industry-choice MEAs and a larger increase in the average size of industry-choice MEAs. Clearly, there has been *a trickling down of industries from bigger MEAs to a larger number of smaller MEAs*,[18] tending to lessen the effect of population growth.

Despite the similarity of the slopes of these two log-linear regressions, it is worth noting that this trickling down effect is very significant. While both MEA sizes and numbers of industry-choice MEAs have increased, they have done so in a manner that leaves their elasticity invariant. In other words, the percent change in average industry-choice MEA sizes relative to percent change in numbers of industry-choice MEAs has remained essentially constant. Hence this empirical regularity appears to be much stronger, and suggests the presence of a fundamental invariance relation governing the location of industries. As a parallel to the well-known rank–size rule for city size distributions [see the chapter by Gabaix and Ioannides (2004) in this volume], this new relation could be designated as *the number–average size* (*NAS*) *Rule* for industrial location patterns.[19]

The rank–size rule shows a strong negative relationship between city size and rank. For the Japanese MEAs, we have obtained the estimated values for the rank–size coefficient of -0.95 ($R^2 = 0.95$) for 1980 and -1.00 ($R^2 = 0.95$) for 2000. Takahashi (1982) reports a coefficient of -0.93 ($R^2 = 0.99$) in as early as 1875. Similarly the NAS shows a strong negative relationship between the average size of industry choice MEAs and the number of industry-choice MEAs. Mori, Nishikimi and Smith (2003) explore the theoretical relationship among the NAS rule, the Hierarchy Principle discussed next and the rank–size rule, finding a strong connection among them and establishing inter-connections among the empirical regularities.

2.3.2. *The Hierarchy Principle*

The basic mechanism behind the Hierarchy Principle described in the introduction is related to one of the most distinctive features of industrial location behavior observed in a

[18] This trickling down effect is reported also by Mano and Otsuka (2000). They conclude that the main factor leading this effect is considered to be the congestion costs.

[19] For different geographic units such as counties and prefectures, the relationship is less clear. See Mori, Nishikimi and Smith (2003) for more details.

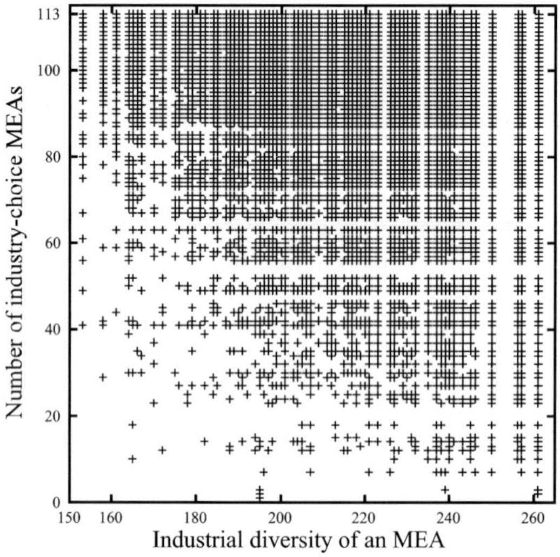

Figure 14. Hierarchy Principle (1999/2000).

domestic economy. Since inter-regional migration is generally less costly (than international one), firms are attracted mainly by the absolute advantage of locations. As a result, certain advantageous locations are seen to attract a disproportionately large number of industries, leading to greater variation in industrial diversity among locations. Hence, a smaller city can attract only a subset of industries located in larger cities. Recent theoretical developments suggest a far-reaching principal, focused mainly on production and demand externalities. In the context of new economic geography, such externalities can be shown to lead to the formation of industrial agglomeration consistent with the Hierarchy Principle [Fujita, Krugman and Mori (1999)].

The presence of an industrial hierarchy for MEAs in Japan has been shown by Mori, Nishikimi and Smith (2003) as in Figure 14.[20] Here MEAs are ordered on the horizontal axis by their industrial diversities (i.e., numbers of industries they contain), and industries are ordered on the vertical axis by their numbers of industry-choice MEAs. Hence each point "+" in the figure represents the event that the MEA in that column contains the industry in that row.

Notice that the points are sparser near the southwest corner, thus meaning that the industries with a smaller number of locations are found mainly in MEAs with large industrial diversity. On the other hand, MEAs with small industrial diversity tend to have more ubiquitous industries (i.e., those locating in a large number of MEAs). Mori, Nishikimi and Smith (2003) have shown that the actual location pattern shown in the

[20] See Takahara (1999) for a related case study for the case of Japanese cities.

figure is highly consistent with the Hierarchy Principle (i.e., the actual industrial hierarchy is highly non-random) even after controlling for the relative industrial diversities among MEAs.[21]

Now, let us discuss on the relationship between the Hierarchy Principle and the specialization of MEAs. Though the Hierarchy Principle makes no assertion about the relative employment sizes of industries in each MEA, *under this principle, it is natural to expect that the employment within any given industry should be greater in larger MEAs.* To check this, Mori, Nishikimi and Smith (2003) calculated Spearman's rank correlations between the employment size of each industry in an MEA and the population size as well as diversity of an MEA. This correlation only fails to be significant (at the 5% level) for population size and/or diversity in 33 (respectively, 18) of the 264 industries in 1980/1981 (respectively, 1999/2000). The average rank correlations are 0.61 and 0.50 (respectively, 0.62 and 0.61) with population size and diversity, respectively, in 1980/1981 (respectively, 1999/2000). Thus, the above claim does hold approximately, though it is by no means universal.

One possible reason for the imperfect correlation between size/diversity and industry employment in MEAs is that the Hierarchy Principle itself has other explanations and must accommodate other facts. Some medium size MEAs are highly specialized in a few industries, and correspond more closely to Henderson's (1988) "specialized cities". Henderson emphasizes industry-specific localization economies as a source of city formation. In addition, Henderson (1997) notes that medium/small size cities (with population size smaller than 500,000) tend to exhibit the strongest specialization. In 1999/2000, more than 10% of total employment was concentrated in a single MEA for 48 industries, among which 17 are in small/medium MEAs. Typically, the specialization of these MEAs is based on immobile resources (e.g., wood material and liquor manufacturing), historical background (e.g., explosive assembling), or plant-level scale economies (e.g., steel manufacturing, metal and alloy rolling). Specialization and the Hierarchy Principle may have an intersection, based on differences in exactly what varieties of a product are produced in different cities. So for example standardized steel products are produced in a few, smaller specialized cities and no where else at the lower levels of the hierarchy; but steel production may occur also in most cities at the higher levels of the hierarchy. However Tokyo steel products may be small scale, special order, tailored products, that can only be produced and marketed in a large local consumer market, given consumer–producer interaction costs in design.

[21] It is to be noted that for the testing purpose, Mori, Nishikimi and Smith (2003) redefined the principle as follows. *An industrial location pattern is said to satisfy the Hierarchy Principle if industries found in a given MEA are also found in all MEAs with diversities at least as large.* The Christaller's definition of the principle (i.e., with respect to the population size of MEAs), any attempt to relocate population along with industries will necessarily change the population distribution, and hence, create certain ambiguities in the interpretation of the principle itself. Moreover, there is close agreement between the rankings of MEAs in terms of diversity (i.e., the number of industries in operation) and population size (Speaman's rank correlation is greater than 0.9). See Mori, Nishikimi and Smith (2003) for a further discussion.

2.3.3. Implications for regional development

The empirical regularity observed in the relationship between industrial and population location presented above appears to have some important implications for regional development policies. A main regional policy objective is to identify those industries that are potentially sustainable in a given region (MEA). The results so far presented suggest that *such sustainability* depends not only on region-specific factors, but *also on the global structure of the regional system*. Such global considerations are often ignored in regional industrial policy decisions. In fact, there may be little freedom in the location pattern of industries, as there is a stable relationship between the number and size of MEAs in which a given industry can successfully locate. In particular, with respect to size, the Hierarchy Principle suggests that there is a *critical MEA size* for each industry, and that only MEAs with sizes greater than this level can provide viable locations for that industry. Hence to attract such high-order industries, it would appear that MEAs should focus first on attracting the lower-order (feasible) industries that will most help to stimulate regional growth. More generally, knowledge of prevailing global industrial location patterns should enhance the efficiency of regional industrial development policies.

2.3.4. Concluding remarks

As a final remark, we would like to comment on the more fundamental issue regarding the geographic scale at which the regularity emerges in the space-economy. Like most of the literature on Zipf's law or the rank–size rule, the present analysis has focused on global industrial location patterns at the national level. But, in the same way that "administrative cities" can be questioned as the relevant geographic unit, one may ask whether countries are indeed the relevant geographic collection of units. While there is no question that national boundaries are generally sharp barriers in terms of both population and industrial location, it nevertheless may often be true that certain groups of regions within a given country represent more meaningful spatial economic systems than the entire country itself. For example, in the same way that commuting patterns are used to defined MEAs, one may take the patterns of inter-regional travel behavior to define relatively coherent subsystems of regions within national economies. [For example, in Japan, it appears that there is a natural nesting of three regional systems based on inter-regional travel flows: Tokyo–Osaka–Nagoya, as discussed in Mori, Nishikimi and Smith (2003)]. From this viewpoint, it is then natural to ask whether empirical regularities of industrial location patterns are more readily identified at these subsystem levels. In particular, are these regularities the same as those at the national level, or are they qualitatively different? This seems to be an exciting topic for future research.

2.4. Globalization in East Asia

2.4.1. Introduction

Thus far, we have examined the spatial distribution of economic activities in Japan and in the next section we will look at China. In the increasingly borderless world economy, however, it is intuitive that the changes in the spatial distribution of economic activities in one country are closely related with those in the rest of the world, in particular, with those in the neighboring countries. In this section, while still focusing on Japan, we present some empirical data that support this conjecture. First, in Section 2.4.2, we examine the relationship between the changes in the location of manufacturing industries within Japan and those in the rest of East Asia. Then, in order to supplement the "macro-analyses" of industrial location in the previous section, in Section 2.4.3 we focus on the nine largest electronics MNFs of Japan, and study the transformation of their global production system. Section 2.4.2 is based mainly on Fujita and Hisatake (1999), and Section 2.4.3 on Fujita and Ishii (1999).

2.4.2. Regional structure of manufacturing industries in East Asia and Japan

The rapid growth of many countries in East Asia, or the so-called "Asia's Miracle", during the last few decades demonstrates that the economic growth tends to be highly concentrated also internationally. In particular, the spectacular collapse of financial markets in these countries in the late 1990s, following that of Japan, indicates how strongly the entire economy of East Asia is integrated.

The growth process of East Asia's economy has been likened to the "formation of flying geese". Although there seems to exist no clear definition of the flying geese pattern of economic development, here we loosely interpret it as follows.[22] A group of countries located in geographical proximity (in the present case, East Asia) achieves a rapid economic growth, mainly through market mechanisms, by deepening the international division of labor in industrial production such that the most developed country (Japan), or the "lead goose", becomes more and more specialized in technologically advanced industries by successively shedding industries in which she no longer holds a comparative advantage; these industries, in turn, locate in the nearby, less developed countries (Asian NIEs), or the "following geese": in turn, over time, these developing countries upgrade their own industrial structures by themselves shedding outdated industries to the neighboring, less developed countries (ASEAN and China), and so on.

[22] As is well known, the term of "flying geese" originates in the "flying geese theory" of economic development proposed by Akamatsu (1937). Here, our interpretation essentially follows that of Hatch and Yamamura (1996, p. 27). The flying geese theory is closely related to the "product cycle theory" introduced by Vernon (1966). The former observes the same phenomena from the view point of a developing country, while the latter from the view point of a developed country.

Table 1
Concentration of economic activity within Japan and East Asia in 1990

	Japan share in East Asia	J-Core share within Japan	J-Core share in East Asia
Area	3.5%	5.2%	0.18%
Population	7.9	33	2.5
GDP	72	40	29
M-GDP	67	44	29

Source. National Economic Statistics (Japanese EPA) and Key Indicators of Developing Asian Pacific Countries (Asian Development Bank).

To explain "Asia's Miracle", a variety of hypotheses have been proposed, ranging from cultural explanations to a statism approach. Not denying the valuable insights offered by these hypotheses, we provide below empirical data that suggest that linkage-based agglomeration economies and knowledge externalities have been at work in such a process of economic development in East Asia.

We focus on Japan, and nine other countries in Asia (Asia-9): NIES 4 (Republic of Korea, Taiwan, Hong Kong and Singapore), ASEAN 4 (Philippines, Thailand, Malaysia and Indonesia), and China. We call Japan and Asia-9 countries together East Asia, of which the total population in 2000 is approximately 1.6 billion. Given that the distance between Tokyo and Singapore is about the same as that between New York and San Francisco, East Asia has roughly the same geographical extent as that of the U.S.

The first column of Table 1 shows the extent of Japan's economic dominance in this region. That is, in 1990, Japan, having only a 3.5% area and 7.9% population of East Asia, accounted for the 72% GDP, and 67% manufacturing GDP.[23] The second column, in turn, shows the extent of the dominance of Japanese economy itself by its core region (J-Core). Here the J-Core, defined in Section 2.1.2, represents the five prefectures that contain the core parts of the three major metropolitan areas of Japan. As shown in the table, the J-Core with just a 5.2% area accounted for the 33% population, 40% GDP and 44% M-GDP of Japan in 1990. This leads to the third column, indicating that for the entire East Asia, the J-Core with a mere 0.18% of total area accounted for 29% of both GDP and M-GDP.

Given that the (financial) capital became rather freely movable internationally by the early 1980s and that both labor and capital are almost perfectly mobile within Japan, these high concentrations of economic activity in both Japan and the J-Core would be hard to explain without taking account of some kind of agglomeration economies.

To investigate the nature of such agglomeration economies, here we focus on manufacturing, and present in Figure 15 the regional structure of manufacturing industries in Japan and East Asia in 1985.

[23] International GDP-related figures in Table 1 and Figure 15 are based on exchange rates of corresponding years reported in the *International Financial Statistics Yearbook* (IMF).

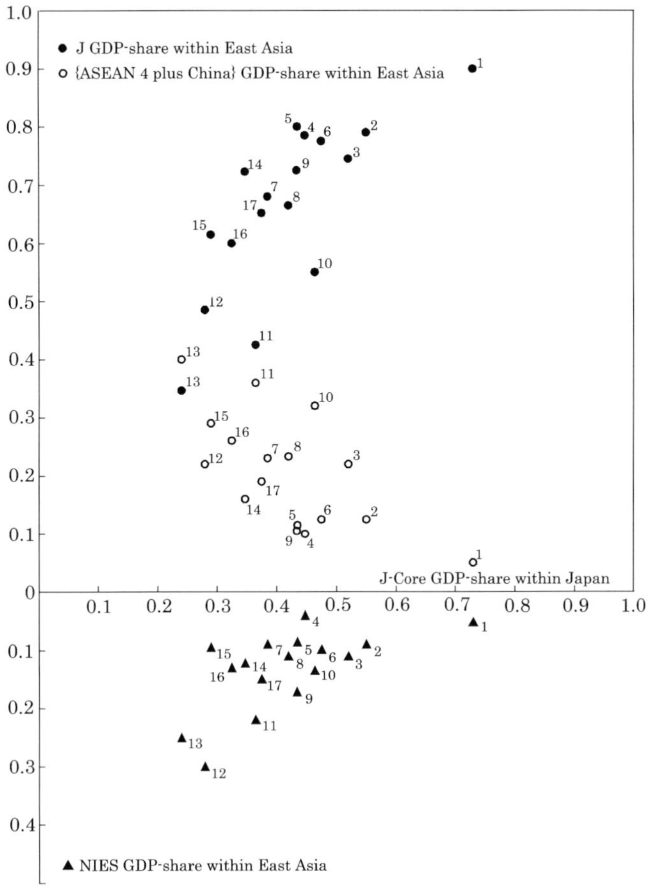

1. Publishing and printing, 2. Transport equipment, 3. Machinery (non-electrical), 4. Electrical machinery, 5. Precision instruments, 6. Fabricated metal products, 7. Basic metal, 8. Chemical and chemical products, 9. Plastic products, 10. Rubber products, 11. Textile, 12. Wearing apparel, 13. Petroleum and coal products, 14. Paper and paper products, 15. Non-metallic mineral products, 16. Food, beverage and Tobacco, 17. Others

Figure 15. Regional structure of manufacturing industries in Japan and East Asia in 1985. *Source*. Census of Manufactures (Japan) and Industrial Statistics Yearbook (United Nations).

The entire manufacturing is divided into 17 industries as denoted in the bottom of the figure. The horizontal axis in the figure represents for each industry the GDP share of the J-Core region within Japan. The vertical axis for black dots shows for each industry the GDP share of Japan within East Asia; the vertical axis for white circles shows (for each industry) the GDP share of {ASEAN 4 plus China} within East Asia.

We can see an apparent positive correlation between the two indices for Japan, indicating that *the more highly Japanese industries concentrate in the J-Core, the more strongly they dominate in East Asia*. In contrast, the set of white circles for the {ASEAN 4 plus China} looks almost the mirror image of the set of black dots for Japan, implying that *these countries are stronger in those industries that are less agglomerated in the J-Core.*[24]

In particular, two groups of industries in the figure present interesting and contrasting cases for Japan. One is the machinery-metal group, consisting of industries 2–7, which locate together in the upper-middle (next to industry 1) of the figure. The position of this group of Japanese industries in the figure suggests another strong case of linkage-based agglomeration economies at work. In fact, Michael Porter (1990) discusses extensively how such linkage-based agglomeration economies have been realized by this group of industries in Japan.

The contrasting case is presented by the textile–apparel group (industries 11 and 12). Until the late 1950s, this textile–apparel group constituted a major part of manufacturing activity in both Japan and J-Core. In 1955, for example, this group accounted for the 15% of the total manufacturing GDP in Japan, of which 45% was concentrated in the J-Core. As shown in the figure, however, in 1985 Japan was among the weakest in these industries (within East Asia), and they are among the least agglomerated in the J-Core.

Although Figure 15 is about 1985, these patterns persist to a lesser extent into the 1990s, with agglomeration economies of the J-Core relative to the rest of Japan and East Asia weakening over time.

2.4.3. Globalization of Japanese multinational firms

In Section 2.1.2, we discussed briefly the rapid expansion of the overseas operations of Japanese multinational firms (MNFs) during the second cycle (the mid-1970s to the mid-1990s) of the regional transformation in Japan that led to the Tokyo monopolar system observed today. In order to present additional empirical data supporting previous discussions on MNFs, in this section we focus on the nine largest electronics firms in Japan, and study the transformation of their global production system over the period of 1975 to 1994. In particular, we investigate how their global location behavior affected the transformation of the Japanese regional system. The firms considered are Hitachi, Matsushita Electric, Toshiba, NEC, Mitsubishi Electric, Fujitsu, Sony, Sanyo Electric and Sharp, of which total sales in 1990 were almost 200 billion dollars. As we have seen in Figure 6, the electronics industry is the largest and most rapidly growing among all manufacturing industries in Japan since the mid-1970s, which is dominated by the nine MNFs above.[25]

[24] Given that Asian NIES 4 are relatively specialized in industries 9–13, no clear correlation exists between the two indices for this group of countries. Notice also that industry 10 is rather exceptional in Figure 15 because this industry includes both synthetic rubber and crude rubber, the former (the latter) is relatively strong in Japan (in ASEAN).

[25] Our discussion below includes the activities of the world-wide subsidiaries of these nine firms. Furthermore, throughout this section, the term 'electronics' should be understood broadly to include both electric and electronic products.

In Figure 16 (respectively, Figure 17), we present the changes in the global distribution of the production plants and in 17 the same for R&D facilities for these nine firms between 1975 and 1994.

As can be seen from Figure 16, over the 19-year period from 1975 to 1994, the number of world-wide manufacturing plants owned by the nine Japanese firms increased more than twice from 285 to 689. In particular, while the number of domestic plants increased about 70% (from 211 to 354), that of overseas plants jumped 4.5 times (from 74 to 335). As a consequence, in 1994 the nine firms had roughly the same number of plants in Japan and overseas. Their overseas plants are mostly concentrated in East Asia, North America and the EU. The number of plants in East Asia increased greatly from 40 to 163, most of which have been serving as exporting platforms to the global markets while taking advantage of low wages elsewhere in the region. The number of plants in North America and the EU also increased greatly from 7 to 80 and from 7 to 64 respectively, to serve the big markets in these countries.

Next, Figure 17 indicates that over the same 19-year period, the nine firms greatly expanded their R&D capacity in Japan (from 24 to 115 laboratories) and in the U.S. (from 1 to 18, mostly located in California State and the Northeast Coast). Several R&D laboratories were also established in the EU. The number of overseas R&D laboratories (of the nine firms) in East Asia is very small in comparison with that of their manufacturing plants, which indicates the spatial division of labor among global regions being developed by the firms.

By the mid-1990s, each of the nine firms developed a very advanced global network for the integrated operation of its entire value-chain including the management, R&D, production, procurement, distribution, sales operations world-wide. Figure 18 summarizes the locational tendencies of organizational units of the nine firms in 1994. As can be seen from the figure, each unit has a different locational tendency. (In these figures, MA refers to the Tokyo and Osaka MAs, while Non-MA represents the rest of Japan.)

As shown in the top box in Figure 18, all HQs are located in the two primary MAs in Japan (i.e., six in the Tokyo MA and three in the Osaka MA), and are mostly in the CBDs. The figure also indicates that all their basic R&D laboratories (R&D controlled by HQs) are located in the two MAs, where 95% are situated in their suburbs. Furthermore, 65% of development R&D laboratories are located in the suburbs of the two MAs and 30% of them in non-metropolitan areas mostly together with mother plants). The middle two boxes in Figure 18 indicate that trial-production plants, which are closely related to their HQs and R&D laboratories in terms of information exchange, are mostly located in the two MAs (24% of them in the CBDs and 67% in their suburbs). In contrast, domestic mass-production plants are much more dispersed: 40% of them located in the suburbs of the two MAs, while 57% in non-metropolitan areas of Japan. Next, as indicated in the bottom three boxes of Figure 18, overseas regional HQs are located either in North America (7 in the U.S.), the EU (3 in the UK and 1 in Germany), or East Asia (2 in Singapore). Fifty-six per cent of overseas R&D laboratories are located in the U.S., while 22% of them are in the EU, and 12% in East Asia. Finally, overseas production plants are dispersed throughout the world: specifically, in North America

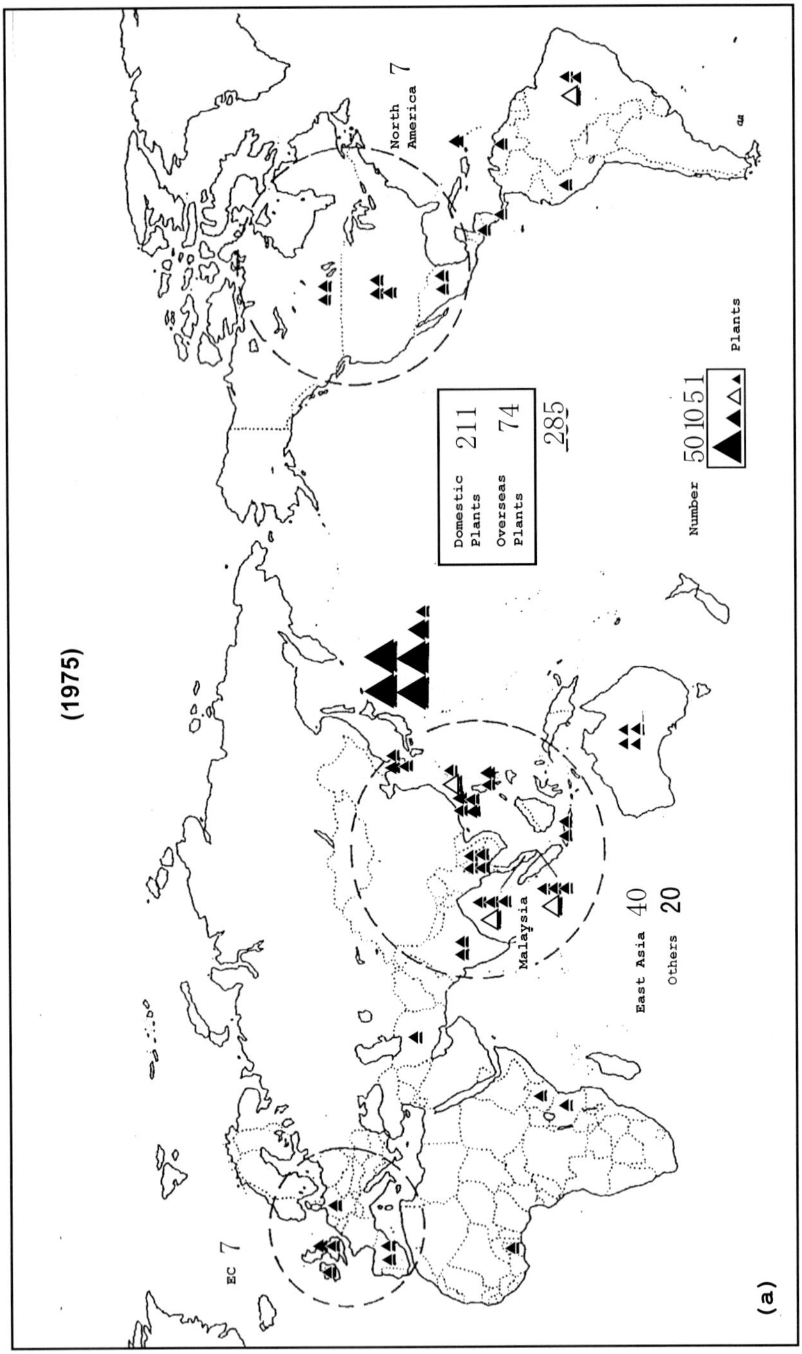
(1975)
North America 7
Domestic Plants 211
Overseas Plants 74
285
Number 50 10 5 1 Plants
Malaysia
East Asia 40
Others 20
EC 7
(a)

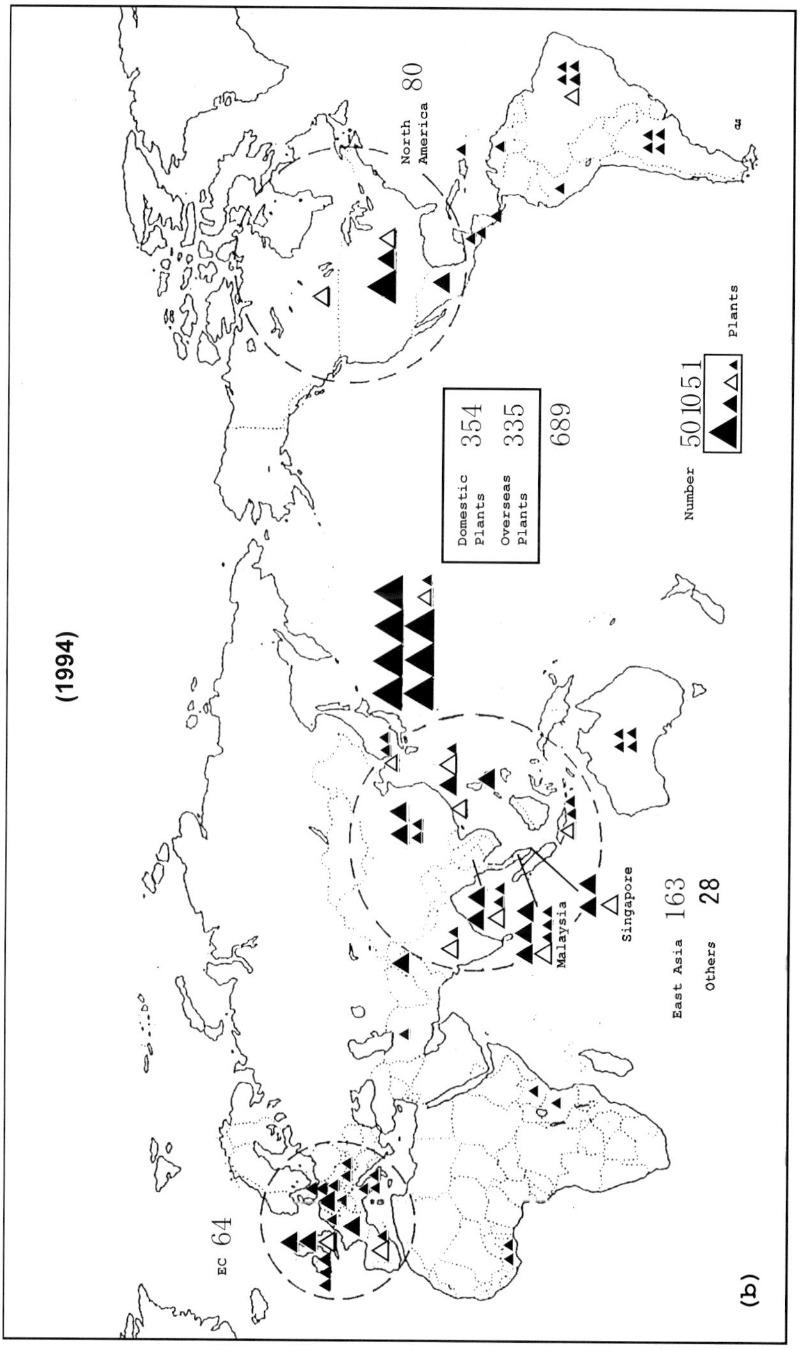

Figure 16. Location of the production plants of nine Japanese electronics firms in 1975 and 1994. *Source*. Fujita and Ishii (1999).

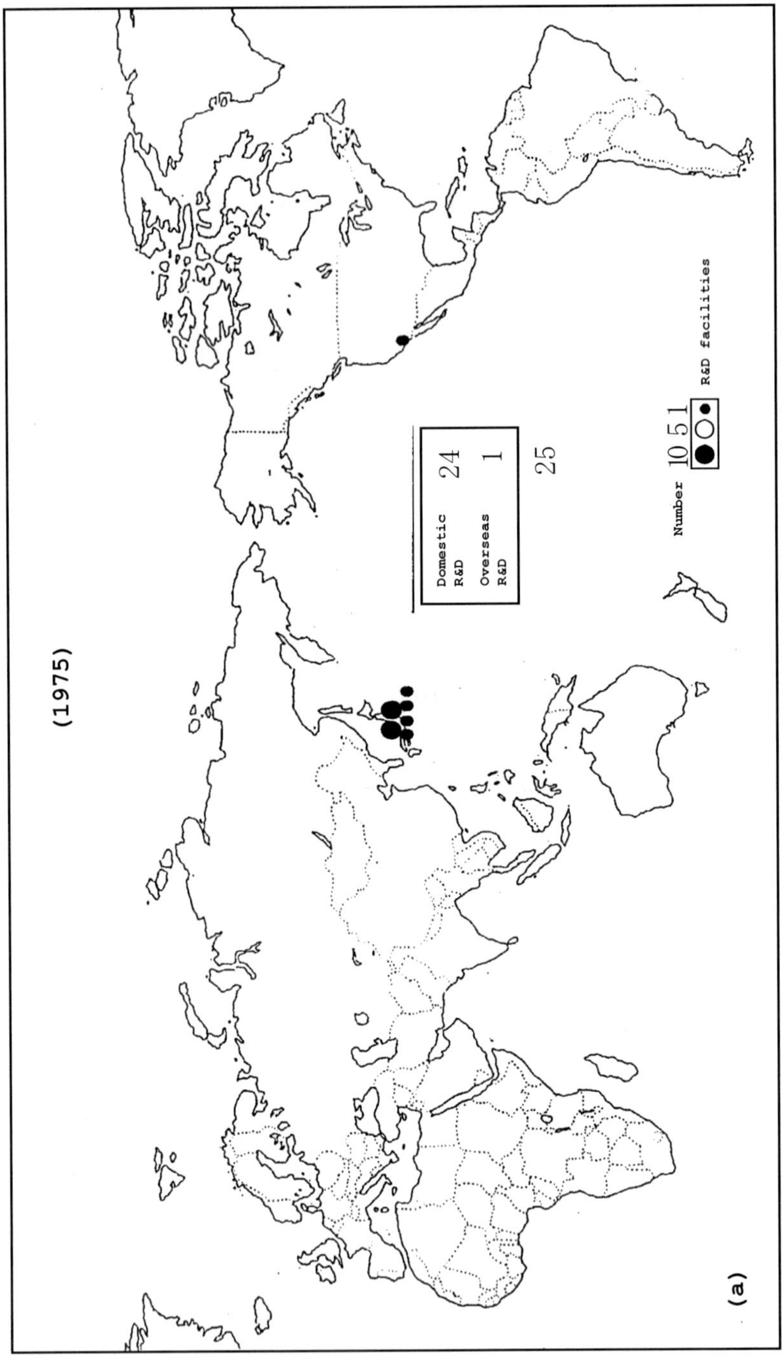
(1975)
Domestic R&D 24
Overseas R&D 1
25
Number 10 5 1
R&D facilities
(a)

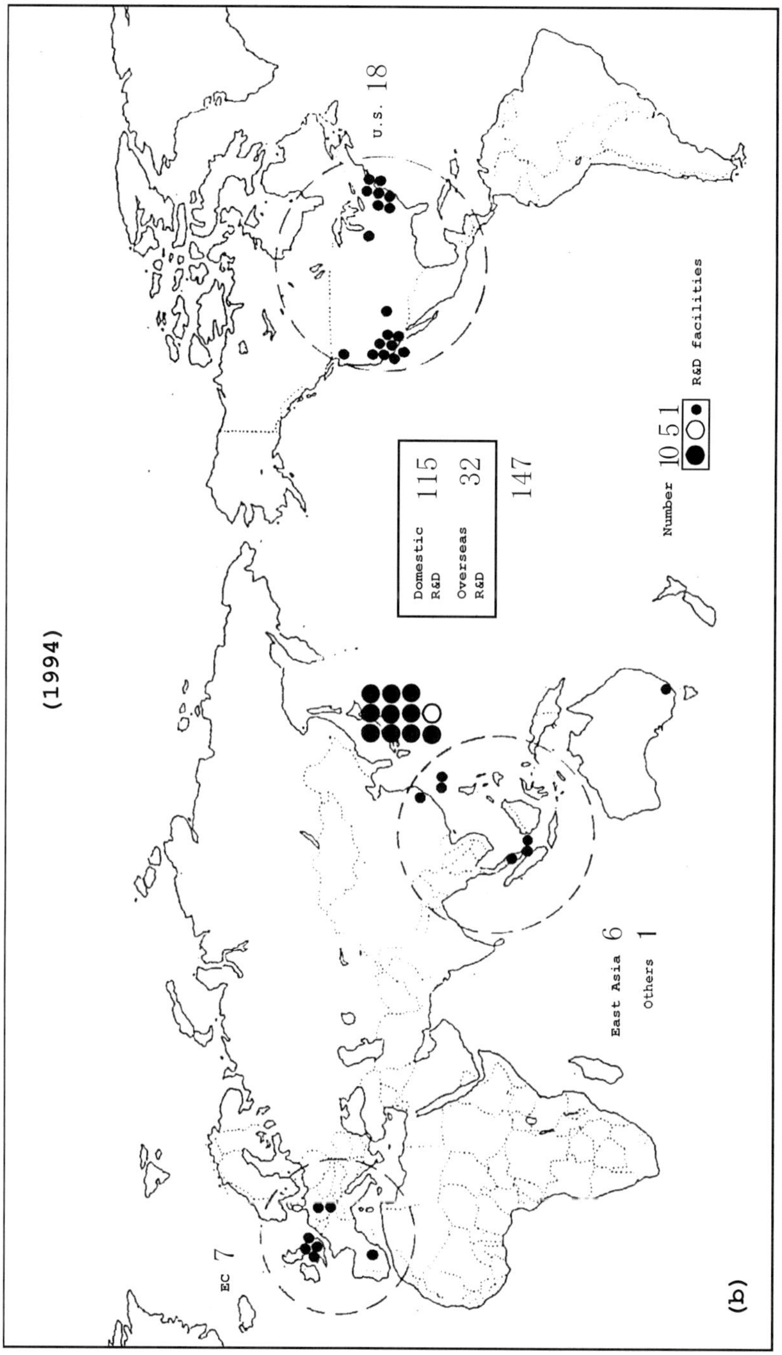

Figure 17. Location of R&D facilities of nine Japanese electronics firms in 1975 and 1994. *Source*. Fujita and Ishii (1999).

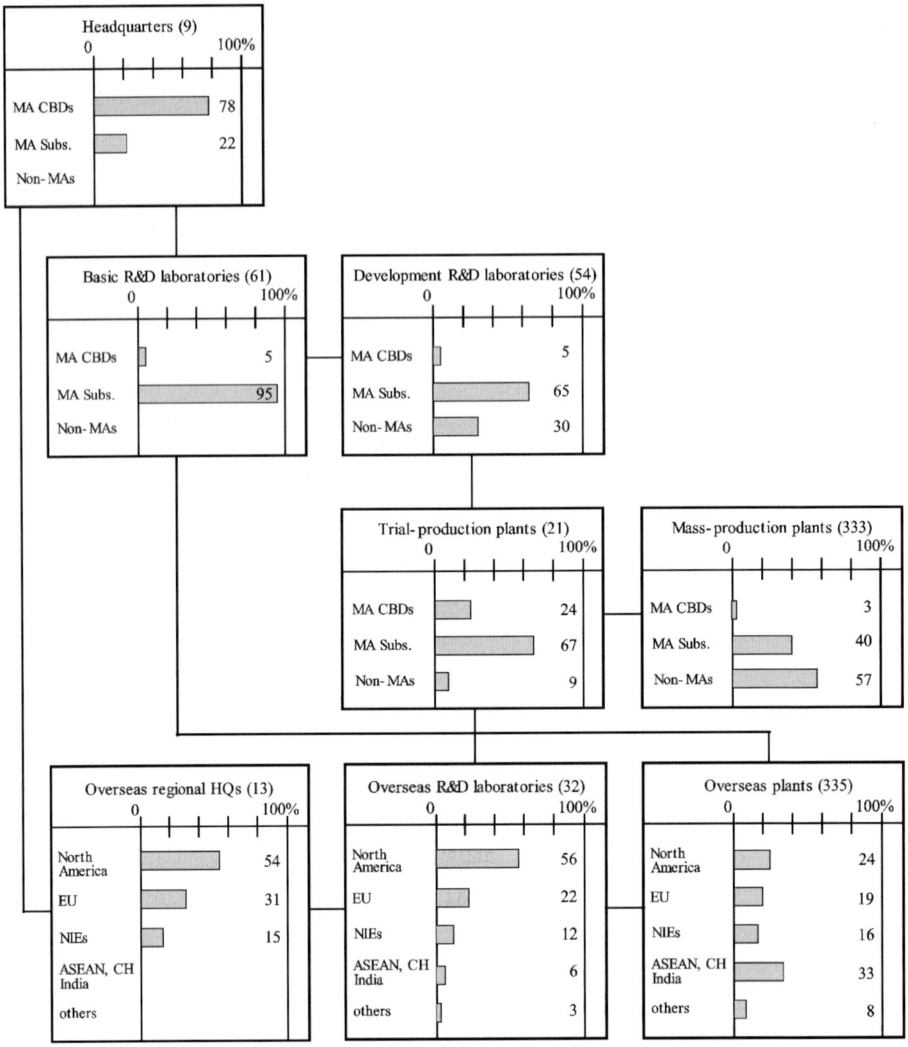

Figure 18. Locational tendencies of organizational units of the nine Japanese electronics firms in 1994. *Source*. Fujita and Ishii (1999).

(24%), the EU (19%), NIEs (16%), ASEAN together with China and India (33%), and the rest of the world (8%).

From Figure 18, we can conclude that the knowledge-intensive activities (such as HQs, R&D laboratories and trial-production plants) of the nine Japanese electronics firms are mostly concentrated in the Tokyo and Osaka MAs, while their mass-production plants are dispersed throughout Japan and overseas countries. In fact, this phenomenon is common to almost all MNFs based in Japan (regardless of their industrial types). It is interesting to note that this dual spatial trend (i.e., the increasing agglomeration of knowledge-intensive activities into the primary cities and the global dispersion of mass-production plants) emerged from the dual nature of recent developments in communications technologies and transportation networks, as discussed above. New mass-production plants do not follow the urban hierarchy, but tend to disperse themselves to non-metropolitan areas in Japan and even overseas. The location of mass-production plants follows basic local (non-agglomeration) factors such as availability of disciplined workers, basic infrastructure, low wage rates and low land prices, following more the product cycle hypothesis. In contrast knowledge-intensive or information-oriented activities favor close clustering in the primary cities due partly to the convenience of face-to-face communications and more generally to enjoy the agglomeration economies which are generated by accumulated knowledge and information there.

The fact that the leading activities of the Japanese economy are changing from material-production to information oriented or knowledge-intensive activities may be enhancing the major transformation of the traditional Japanese regional system centered around Tokyo, Osaka and Nagoya to a system dominated by Tokyo, i.e., the *Tokyo monopolar system*, as has been explained in Section 2.1.2. The establishment of most new mass-production plants overseas, by skipping the peripheral regions of Japan, may partly explain the recent renewed trend in the increasing income differential between the core and peripheral regions of Japan, as shown in Figure 4.

3. Urbanization in China

China with a de facto urban population of about 500 million has the largest urban population and system of cities in the world.[26] In 1996, there were over 650 cities, defined as agglomerations of over 100,000 urban residents. To have some sense of the geography of urban China and vocabulary of the urban sector, we examine key city definitions and maps. Cities have an administrative hierarchy. At the top are cities with the administrative powers of a province: Beijing, Tianjin and Shanghai, with the recent addition of Chongqing (originally part of Sichuan) – followed by prefecture-level cities of which in any year there are about 225. Provincial and prefecture-level cities administer large land areas, comprised of urban districts forming the city proper and huge ex-urban areas, or rural counties. The definitions of city proper are updated regularly to roughly comprise the contiguous urbanized area of the prefecture, surrounding the nuclear city – a good definition of the metropolitan area, by international standards. Below prefecture-level cities are county-level cities – either traditional county cities or townships that have

[26] China's definition of urban has varied over the last 10 years with the stated percent urban ranging from about 30% up to 43% (SSB in 1996). Based on international standards, most observers ascribe an urbanization level nearer the 40–45% range. See Ebanks and Cheng (1990) and Chang (1994, 2000).

Figure 19. Provinces of China.

evolved into cities. These county-level cities can also administer large rural areas, but there is generally no breakdown between the urban and ex-urban portions, making it difficult to count de facto urban populations.

In Figure 19, we show provinces for reference in the text. In Figure 20, we show by city size category all cities in 1996 based on city proper populations for prefecture-level cities and total populations for county-level cities. We name the cities over 3 million population for reference. Given prefecture-level cities contain large non-urban populations, as explained below we often track population movements by looking at non-agricultural employment. Accordingly, Figure 21 shows growth categories in terms of non-agricultural employment for 1990–96, for cities present in 1990. As we will detail later in Table 2, the number of cities grew by 6% a year from 1990–1996 and non-agriculture employment in 1990 cities by 4.3% a year, creating and reflecting enormous urban-economic change in China. Data are from the annual volumes of the *Urban Sta-*

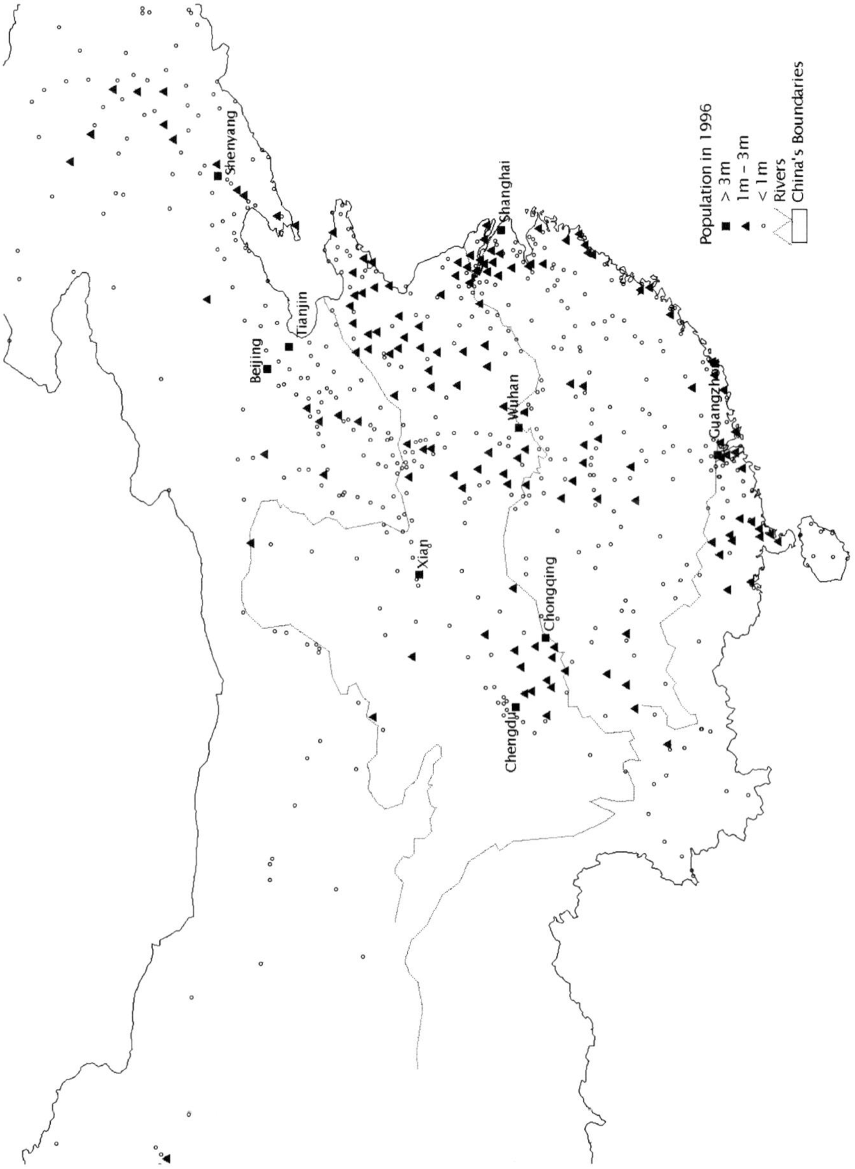

Figure 20. Population of all cities (1996).

Figure 21. Growth of non-agricultural labor force (1990–1996).

tistical Yearbook of China and *Cities China 1949–1998*, augmented by discussion in Chan (1994).

The maps reveal particular spatial features of China. There are huge coastal concentrations of population around Shanghai and Guanzhou in Figure 20, the two southern river delta areas. However there are also huge hinterland populations, with a swath of large cities in the central region and near western region, many of which are experiencing rapid employment growth. Sichuan province in the (south-) west has over 100 m people (including Chongqing), more than almost all other countries in the world. But the far western minority areas of Tibet, Xinjiang, Qinghai and Gansu contain vast tracks of mostly arid land and low population, and are outside most of the discussion in this paper and cut-off in Figures 20–22.

Besides this basic layout of cities, China has a number of key features to its urban system that we note in Section 3.1. Then in Section 3.2, we turn to a discussion of urban policy from 1950 on, which has led to these features and the geographic layout in the maps. Finally in Section 3.3, we review empirical evidence on some of the key issues facing the urban system in China.

3.1. *Some key features of the urban system*

3.1.1. *Low urban concentration*

Chinese cities are relatively small and equal sized, compared to most countries. The UN puts the population of Shanghai metro area, the largest city, at 12.3 million in 2000, although its city proper is only listed at 10.7 million in 1998 (with little growth). In either case this is well below the populations of the 10 largest metro areas in the world. More critically, China only has 9 metro areas with populations over 3 million (Figure 20) while it has another 125 or so metro areas with populations from 1–3 million; – a ratio of 0.072, compared to world-wide ratio for the same size categories of 0.27 [Henderson and Wang (2003)]. To give a more common frame of reference for comparisons, we examine spatial Gini's.

For 1657 metro areas with populations over 200,000 in 2000 for the world, the spatial Gini is 0.564.[27] The Gini is the usual one: rank cities from smallest to largest and plot the Lorenz curve of their accumulated share of total population for the sample (world cities in this case). The Gini is the share of area below the 45° line that lies between the 45° line and the Lorenz curve. China's Gini is 0.43 in 2000, way below the world, and compares to 0.65, 0.65, 0.61, 0.60, 0.60, 0.60, 0.59, 0.58, 0.56, 0.54 and 0.52 for other large countries respectively of Brazil, Japan, Indonesia, UK, Mexico, Nigeria, France, India, Germany, U.S. and Spain. Only former Soviet bloc countries have similarly low Gini's, Russia with 0.45 and Ukraine with 0.40.

[27] Calculated from a World city data set prepared by Rupa Ranganathan, Hyoung Wang, and J.V. Henderson, for 1960–2000.

In Section 3.3, we will argue that Chinese cities in general are too small, leading to significant efficiency losses. In fact we will argue more generally that there is insufficient spatial agglomeration throughout, in both the urban and rural sector.

3.1.2. Regional income inequality

Spatial equality in the size distribution of cities does not translate into income equality. Another key feature of China is the high degree of income inequality, deriving traditionally mostly from inequality across geographic units, rather than within units. China's income Gini of 0.42 in 1995 far exceeds South Asian countries such as India, Bangladesh and Pakistan[28] (with Gini's around 0.3), not to mention high equality countries of Japan and Korea. Income differences tend to be across geographic units and are increasing. Lin, Cai and Li (1996) calculate the ratio of urban to rural incomes at 2.4 and 2.6 in 1978 and 1994, respectively, with greater consumption gaps: 2.9 and 3.6 in 1978 and 1994, respectively [see also Johnson (2001)]. Regional gaps are also large. For the coast versus the west region (for a three region division: coast (= east), central, west), in 1994 the per capita income ratios were 1.8 overall, 1.4 for urban residents and 2.0 for rural residents, with much higher rural resident ratios between individual richest coastal and poorest western provinces. Fujita and Hu (2001) argue that intra-regional disparities have improved somewhat in recent years but inter-regional inequality is growing and there is no convergence in regional per capita income.

3.1.3. Restricted migration: the hukou system

In China, the geographic-urban dispersion of population and the high spatial inequality is maintained by strong migration restrictions, under the *hukou system*. Migration restrictions play such a strong role in the society and economy that it is critical to describe them. The hukou system in China is similar to an internal passport system [see Chan (1994) for a detailed description]. A person's local "citizenship" and residence is initially defined for a child as a birth right, traditionally by the mother's place of legal residence. The entitlements and details of the system differ for urban and rural residents. Legal residence in a city entitles one to local access to permanent jobs, regular housing, public schooling, and public health care (where almost all health care is public) in that city. Until the early 1990s, it also entitled urban people to "grain rations" – rations of essentials such as grain and kerosene.

Legal residence in a village or rural township entitles residents to land for farming, township housing, job opportunities in rural industrial enterprises, and access to local health and schooling facilities in their town. Residents also have some degree of "ownership" in local enterprises; although distributed profits all go to the local public budget, which may be used to finance township housing and infrastructure. Again, until recent

[28] From World Development Indicators, World Bank (1998).

years, legal residence in a township also entitled a "peasant" to some share in locally produced (or allocated from the outside) grain and other essentials.

How does a person change their local citizenship? There are several common mechanisms. First is education. A smart rural youth may persist through the competitive county system to get a spot in a college. Upon college graduation, the rural youth will be hired into an urban job, with an urban hukou. Second, the state at times can open the gates, permitting factories to hire permanent workers from rural areas, permitting family reunification, or permitting legal migration from rural areas to nearby small cities. However the official changes in residence or hukou status average about 18 million (in under 1.3% of the population) a year over the last 20 years with little annual variation [Chan (2000)].

People can migrate to an areas without local hukou, or an official change of residence/"citizenship", either illegally ("unregistered") or legally as a temporary worker or as a "permanent resident" on a long-term permit. For example, a rural person may be hired as a "contract worker" in industry or services, for a term of three years. Or a rural person may get permission to work temporarily in another local rural area in construction, food services, domestic services and the like. People may move illegally, without registering in the new location, and work in the informal sector for low pay, under poor conditions, with risk of deportation. Despite these possibilities and despite some recent relaxations of restrictions in particular provinces, the restrictions in migration remain tight.

Temporary migrants to larger cities typically have no, or very high priced access to health care and schooling facilities and regular, "legal" housing. In fact cities have strict national guidelines on conversion of agriculture to urban land; and institutional difficulties in housing markets in expanding supply makes it particularly difficult for migrants to find decent housing. All this means living and social conditions for migrants and their families are extremely difficult, since children face no or very high priced access to schooling and health care. But there are other restrictions. Legal temporary migration requires getting a permit from the city of in-migration and cities can impose various hurdles to getting a permit – permission from the home location, proof of a guaranteed job and specific housing, and the like. Cities also publish job lists, citing jobs for which migrants are not eligible; in 2000, Beijing listed over 100 occupations as non-eligible ones. Migrants may still have to pay taxes to their rural home village for services they do not consume and on land left fallow. Finally migrants face direct fees [Cai (2000)]. There is a license fee to work outside the home township paid to the township that can be equivalent to several months' wages. At the destination, there can be fees for city management, for being a "foreign" worker, for city construction, for crime fighting, for temporary residence, and even for family planning if the migrant is female. All these restrictions sharply reduce the benefits and raise the costs of migration, particularly into large cities. Migration is limited and most migration is short-term, or "return" migration, as we will detail with data below. Overall the hukou system holds hundreds of millions of people in locations where they are not exploiting their earning potential, as again we will detail below.

3.1.4. *Transformation of the urban system*

The urban system since 1950 has faced repeated system-wide political and economic shocks, inducing enormous transformations. In the next section we will briefly review some of the early episodes; here we focus on the 1990s. Tables 2 and 3 present some details, starting with the overall urban system in Table 2. Columns in Table 2 give figures for all cities present in 1990, for prefecture-level cities (including provincial cities) present in 1990, for county-level cities present in 1990, and for county-level cities after 1990. The first four rows show high overall non-agricultural employment growth from 1990 to 1996, over 4.3% per year for all cities, but much slower population growth, about 1.9% per year. The differential reflects two things. In some cases in 1990, cities contained significant rural-agricultural populations that during the decade moved into non-agricultural employment. This is urbanization from within, although overall local absolute agricultural employment in cities grew modestly from 1990 to 1996. Second and more critically, population numbers may exclude certain types of immigrants while employment figures better reflect them. In particular are shorter-term or longer-term migrants working in the city, who either live in the city but are not counted in population enumeration or who can't obtain housing within the city and reside just beyond the boundaries of urban districts (in often "illegal" rural housing). As a result, it is often better to measure size in terms of non-agricultural employment.

Table 2 also shows that real output per worker grew at an incredible rate during the period; for all cities, the average annual rate was about 7.8% a year. Second, over time the manufacturing to service ratio declines. The decline involves some redefinition of manufacturing activity as service activity around 1993–1994. In the data, over the 1990–1993 period the ratio declines modestly in total by 4%; between 1993 and 1994 it declines by 24% with redefinitions; and from 1994 on it declines by 4–5% a year, as restrictions on

Table 2
The Chinese urban system

Cities	Present in 1990			New
Level	All	Prefecture	County	County
Avg. population 1996 (thousands)	811	1050	589	706
Pop. growth 1990–96	12%	15%	7.9%	n.a.
Avg. non-agri. employ. 1996 (thousands)	327	511	158	183
Non-agri. employ. growth 1990–96	29%	26%	40%	n.a.
% population (over age 6) completing high school in 1990	14.6%	21.7%	12.8%	8.8%
Distance to coast	7.1	6.3	9.4	5.4
Avg. output per worker in 1996 (1990 yuan)	8942	10198	7802	9229
Growth in real output per worker 1990–96	57%	53%	62%	n.a.
Avg. manu. service ratio 1996	1.52	1.59	1.47	1.59
Change in manu. serv. ratio	−25%	−32%	−8.2%	n.a.
N	459	220	240	193

Table 3
Transition matrices (all 669 cities ever present)

		not present	first quartile	second quartile	third quartile	fourth quartile
				A. Output per worker (1996)		
	not present	6	46	47	51	55
1990	first quartile	1	**58**	35	10	12
	second quartile	1	46	**33**	28	8
	third quartile	3	13	33	**39**	28
	fourth quartile	0	2	16	37	**61**
				B. Employment (1996)		
	not present	5	56	65	51	28
1990	first quartile	1	**91**	21	4	0
	second quartile	2	17	**65**	24	7
	third quartile	2	0	13	**79**	22
	fourth quartile	0	1	1	7	**107**

private service sector development are loosened. Later we will note the rapid growth of business services in particular.

Looking across the urban system, prefecture- and higher-level cities are larger and have much greater human capital. Among county-level cities, there are many new cities, which are larger than traditional county cities, have more industry, and are nearer the coast. These cities reflect rapid urbanization and industrialization of former rural towns and townships.

The period 1990–1996 is one of rapid industrial reforms, removing some of the props under state-owned industry and exposing them to increasing competition. Mostly heavily hit were interior and northern heavy industry cities, especially under the reforms in 1993–1994. These reforms moved most planning functions to a market basis and represent a break point in terms of how outputs are evaluated. Along with the rapid growth of business and financial service activity, the result, in this very short period of time, is to dramatically shake up the urban system. To get a sense of the overturning of the old industrial order, we look at transition matrices, as a tool to display mobility. In Table 3A, is the transition matrix for real output per worker. The first row shows into what 1996 quartile new cities, or entrants from 1990 to 1996, would enter. Interestingly, new cities would enter fairly evenly, across states. The second through fifth rows show transitions for 1900 cities. So of the 116 cities in the lowest quartile in 1990, 58 remain in the lowest quartile, while 35 move to the second and 12 to the fourth. In addition 1 city in the first quartile in 1990 disappears from the data set by 1996.

What is stunning about Table 3A is the incredible mobility. The diagonal measuring the propensity for a city to stay in its original quartile is small, as indicated by the bold numbers. The average probability across states of remaining in the own state is only 0.41.[29] As noted, 12 of 116 cities jump from the lowest to highest state in just 6 years,

[29] For prefecture-level cities alone, the transition matrices are very similar to those in Table 3.

while 18 of 116 fall from the highest state to one of the two lowest states. Consistent with the picture of turmoil is the notion of lack of persistence. The correlation between growth in output per worker from 1990 to 1991 and growth between 1995 and 1996 is zero. A city's features that gave it a comparative advantage in 1990 may not do so in 1996.

The transition matrix for total employment in Table 3B is more "regular". The average probability of staying in the own state is 0.74; and cities in the top state in 1990 have a very high probability of staying there – 0.92. Although there is more motion in terms of relative size changes than in a developed country, cities tend only to move to adjacent states and big cities persist in remaining big, just as one would find in other countries [Eaton and Eckstein (1997) and Black and Henderson (2003)].

3.1.5. Urban specialization and manufacturing agglomeration

The urban economics literature suggests that efficiency in urban production particularly for medium size cities involves relative and even absolute local specialization in production. For many standardized manufacturing activities, localized external economies within the own industry are prevalent. Industry-specific agglomeration and hence local specialization are key to industrial efficiency [see Duranton and Puga (2004) in this volume for a review of theory and evidence]. For China an issue is whether local scale externalities are not being fully exploited both because local industrial bases are too diffuse and producers within a city are too spatially dispersed, reducing inter-firm information spillovers.

Under the "planning" regime under Mao which remained in force up to 1978, there was no coherent national economic plan, based on national input–output tables [World Bank (1981)]. In fact no national input–output table used by Chinese planners existed until the mid-1980s. *Planning was done at the provincial level, with provinces tending to autarky*, apart from national ministries governing mining, energy, and transportation. As a result inter-provincial and even inter-prefecture trade was low. Bigger cities tended to try to produce the entire range of manufactured products. By the mid-1980s, after the economic reforms starting in 1978, Henderson (1988, Chapter 11) presents a picture of bigger cities with extremely diversified industrial bases but some degree of relative specialization, but nothing like the specialization seen in cities in countries like U.S., Brazil, or India. That pattern appears to persist well into the 1990s. For example, Ningbo, a city of only 1.2 million people in coastal Zhejiang, based on international 3-digit SIC classifications, still produces in 68 or 70 possible manufacturing categories in textiles, apparel, leather, chemical, plastics, machinery, electronics and instruments sectors, as well as most food, wood, and metals products (from 1998 Ningho Statistical Yearbook). There is some degree of concentration in textiles, apparel, petroleum and electrical equipment (each over 10% of local manufacturing GDP), but that itself is diffuse. Such detailed city data are hard to get on a widespread basis, so it is hard to say how the degree of specialization at the city level has been increasing over time. But more aggregate data suggest increasing specialization.

Fujita and Hu (2001) in examining provincial-level data, find strong evidence of increasing agglomeration from 1985–1994 at the provincial level in textiles, apparel, machinery, electrical machinery, electronics, metal products, and rubber and plastic – key sectors where localized intra-industry scale economies may dominate and where agglomeration is highest. In general the increased agglomeration reflects relative gains by coastal provinces, with the four dominant provinces (out of 30 provinces) having shares of 50–60% of national gross output value in chemical fibers, rubber and plastics, textiles, garments, electrical machinery and equipment, and electronics by 1994. However in many cases, the province with the highest share in an industry changes from 1985 to 1994. Fujita and Hu interpret this growth in agglomeration as "self-agglomeration" or clustering promoted by FDI and trade policies (see below) that favored industrialization in certain coastal enclaves. Guangdong province around Guangzhou (Canton) with its more freewheeling economy has been the biggest gainer. By 1994 Guangdong commanded market shares in electronic products such as recorders and cameras of over 85%.

3.1.6. Governance

The final key aspect of the urban system is governance. In general, especially in economic plans formulated in the 1980s, spatial hierarchy is a strong notion in China. Big (prefecture-level) cities "lead" smaller (county-level) cities, and both lead rural counties. Politically large cities have some authority over nearby township and county city governments. High-level units are favored in terms of tax policy, redistribution, and degree of autonomy. Planning of product lines favored higher-level units, granting state enterprises monopoly rights over product lines that rural enterprises were starting to encroach on. This hierarchy notion is also played out in other dimensions – the spatial allocation of revenue and investment of FDI and trade initiatives, and of transport infrastructure investment.

In the next two sections, we focus on key aspects of spatial bias in current economic policy. In Section 3.2, we start with an explicit consideration of urban policy in China from 1950 to the present and of the impact of reforms in the post-Mao period since 1978.

3.2. A brief review of urbanization and urban policy in China since 1950

In the period 1950 to 1978, urbanization in China was driven by volatile central government economic and social policy. Table 4 shows the annual rate of urban population growth for China under different socio-economic regimes from 1950–1990, based on Chan (1994, Table 2.4). Discussions of official versus de facto urban policy may be found in Kwok (1982), Paine (1981), O (1993), Chan (1994) and Kojima (1996), with further references in Chan. The period 1950–1961 was one of massive capital investment in mostly heavy manufacturing, with an accompanying recruitment of rural labor by urban state-owned enterprises. Although migration restrictions were enacted in 1957,

Table 4
Urbanization in China (1950–1990)

Years	Rate nationally of urban population growth (%)	Notes
1950–57	7.2	Russian influence; establish industrial centers
1958–61	9.1	Great Leap Forward "production first; living second"
1961–65	−2.1	Famine
1966–77	2.0	Cultural Revolution: % urban declines
1978–90	4.5	Post-Mao: the four modernizations and beyond

on-going migration to cities up to 1961 was enormous as column 2 of Table 4 indicates. While the Great Leap "forward" from 1958–1961 is often associated with backyard rural steel production, in fact the story is one of massive urban emphasis.

Starting in 1961, a combination of weather calamities, chaos in the rural commune sector created by the Great Leap, and poor grain distribution policy led to the famines of the early 1960s in which millions died. Migration reversed, as an attempt to deal with food shortage problems and upheaval in the commune sector. 1966–1977 marks the period of the trauma of the Cultural Revolution. Rustification of youth and other social-cleansing policies led to an urban population growth rate below the national population growth rate.

Overall from 1950–1977, China's urban has several consistent features, despite the turmoil and time varying patterns of rural–urban migration. Official policy was distinctly anti-urbanization, with cities viewed as potential centers of Western "spiritual" pollution and counter-revolutionary forces. The rhetoric emphasized rural industrialization and uplifting of the masses. De facto policy differs in key ways. Throughout, capital investment favors heavy urban industries; and rural industrialization is minimal. In 1978 non-farm activity in the rural sector is negligible and even by 1984 in the post-Mao period only 11% of rural labor is engaged in non-farm activity, compared to 20–40% in the rest of the world [Perkins (1994) and Henderson (1988)]. While official policy post-1960 does emphasize relative rural population growth, at the expense of urban population growth, cities remain the recipients of capital investment and income distribution. As noted earlier, in 1978 urban incomes are 2.4 higher than rural incomes; and China's overall degree of income inequality equals or exceeds India's [World Bank (1981)].

3.2.1. Post-Mao reforms

The "four modernizations" in 1978 started to introduce market forces into China. Productivity growth in agriculture under Mao was negative and consumer goods, including housing, had been de-emphasized under the "production first ... living second" policy. Reforms are discussed in many places and a nice review is in Perkins (1994), as well as Lin, Cai and Li (1996). Here we note four key elements, before turning to items with specific spatial-urban features. The personal responsibility system was introduced into agriculture, moving agriculture away from a commune system to a quasi-market system where increasingly individual farmers chose their own crops and inputs, and sold increasing portions of output at free market prices. Compared to an annual growth rate of agricultural GDP of 1.4% from 1957–1978 (far less than the rural population growth rate), the annual growth rate for 1978–1984 is 7.3%, which then levels off at 3.7% for 1984–1992 [Perkins (1994)]. Further productivity advances in agriculture are limited by two items relevant to the urban sector – continued restraints on rural–urban migration and continued diversion of capital away from the rural sector, as well as failure to enact full property right reforms in the rural sector.[30]

While urban state-owned enterprises (SOE) were subject to reforms attempting to introduce incentives for workers and managers, SOEs still faced soft budget constraints, rigid employment, wage, and compensation policies, and constraints on production choices [Jefferson and Singhe (1999)]. Industrial reform really came through first the vast expansion of the collective, mostly rural, industrial sector (see below) and then the expansion of private industry in the 1990s, with the state-owned sector increasingly withering away.

Reforms also altered the composition of national output, away from heavy industry towards first lighter, consumer-oriented manufacturing and then services, with both playing a role discussed below in urban policy. Nationally China's service sector accounted for 15–23% of GDP in 1978 (with the percent depending on whether domestic/historic (15%) or international 1990 (23%) prices are used). Today the share has risen past 30%. But it is still far short of the $42^{+}\%$ found in low-income countries or the $52^{+}\%$ found in low-middle income countries.

The final background element we note is that economic reforms were constrained by a lack of political reform. The effective rule of law and transparency in accounting and fiscal rules and procedures have been very slow to develop, with the Party and personal relationships substituting. Later we will note some key urban components that emerge.

3.2.2. Urban policy since 1978

There are implicit and explicit urban policies, and our discussion is a mixture of the two. The key implicit policy is that the hukou system remains in place, so free migration with a permanent change of residence is still not a feature of China. The details and implications of this are discussed in the next section. However China's urban population growth rate as seen in Table 5 is 4.5% for 1978–1990 versus 2% in the previous 11 years. So migration policy as part of urban policy has changed.

As defined in part by the 1982 Sixth 5-Year Plan, as well as the Seventh 5-Year Plan, the post-Mao period has a set of initially defined urbanization policies that persist today. Good sources on aspects of these policies include Chan (1994), Kojima (1996),

[30] In particular, the maximum lease length in agriculture remains at 15 years inhibiting the incentive of farmers to undertake long term investments in, for example, irrigation and local transport projects.

Table 5
Aspects of urban change

A. Ex-urbanization of manufacturing
Share of city proper in prefecture secondary sector employment

Industry	1990	1997/98
Tianjin	81	81
Shanghai*	70	68
Chengda	59	43
Changsha	54	39
Hangzhou	37	33
Zhuzhou	47	42
Xiangtan	66	51

B. Percent growth in GDP of business services and trade† (1987–1997)

	Industry	Trade	Business services	1997 Share of Business Services in local GDP
Beijing, Tianjin, Shanghai	−14.7	55.9	70.4	7.5
Coast	15.7	85.0	48.7	2.6
Center	15.6	86.2	94.7	3.0
West	9.4	68.1	56.4	2.3

*The figure under 1990 for Shanghai is for 1994. The area of the city proper in Shanghai was tripled in 1993.
†Trade is wholesale and retail. Business services here include Chinese sectors labeled as real estate, leasing, public facilities, hotel, tourism, recreation, computer services, and information and consultancy (e.g., advertising).

O (1993), Lin, Cai and Li (1996), Ebanks and Cheng (1990), Fujita and Hu (2001), Wei and Wu (2001), Shixun and Xian (1992), and Henderson (1988). First urban population was to expand, but through the rapid growth of smaller cities relaxing hukou transfers at that level, while containing the sizes of larger cities. Table 2 and the spatial Gini's cited earlier show the impact of that policy. The 1990s witnessed the rapid growth in number of cities, as many places were recognized as having passed 100,000 urban population mark. However, China's spatial Gini and degree of urban concentration remains very low by world standards and even lower in 2000 than in 1960 (0.42 versus 0.47). General urban population expansion has also been fueled by rapid growth, particularly in coastal towns, of township populations, always pushing these towns towards (or past) the 100,000 mark to be a city [Ma and Fan (1994)].

In the Sixth and Seventh 5-year plans there is a sense of hierarchy, played out both in governance structures and in economic policy. Larger cities are to lead smaller ones and rural areas; the coast is to lead the center and west. "Leading" has many dimensions. Larger cities focus on newer production – initially high-tech and light industry and then business service development in recent years. Large cities receive new technologies and hand-down traditional activities to their hinterlands, in particular contracting-out parts and components production to small cities, towns, and rural areas, and relocating heavy, polluting production to their peri- or ex-urban areas. Tables 5A and 5B illustrate aspects of this. This is not to say these changes are the consequence of planning. Rather planning may have been consistent with natural market forces, and helped ignite them. Table 5A shows the move of industry from the urbanized city proper in specific prefecture-level cities to the ex-urban rural hinterland areas of these prefectures in the 1990–1997 time period. Note in Table 5A, the already high degree of suburbanization of industry in some cities by 1990. Suburbanization of manufacturing to lower wage cost ex-urban or fringe areas with potentially more readily available land is part of market driven urban spatial development. Mature manufacturing firms in core cities typically suburbanize once their need for core city information spillovers declines.

Table 5B shows the expansion of the business service sector. The table shows the rapid growth of business services in all regions and shows their relatively high level in the three traditional provincial cities – roughly a 3-fold higher level than in the rest of the country in terms of share of local GDP. More generally among prefecture-level cities, as in other countries, a negative correlation between city size and the ratio of secondary to tertiary sector activity has developed. By 1997 most major cities in China, such as Beijing, Shanghai, Chengdu, and Changsha proudly reported that they had passed the 50% mark – over 50% of local GDP from the tertiary sector. Again given China's low service production, expansion of this sector in response to market forces is not surprising.

Another aspect of urbanization policy, implicit and as part of big cities leading the rest, is played out in the development of rural industry – the town and village enterprise sector (TVE). The rapid productivity growth in agriculture after 1978, coupled with prior restrained urbanization, meant a vast surplus of labor in agriculture. Given the desire to continue to restrain urbanization (although at a much higher rate after the 15 or so years before 1978), a policy of "leave the land but not the village" was crafted. The rural sector was to industrialize, but generally not spatially agglomerate. TVE development was constrained by under-capitalization, an inability to spatially agglomerate, and in the 1980s policies restraining its competition with SOE's (followers are not supposed to out-compete leaders!).[31] However, TVE growth by 1997 VA in the TVE sector was twice that in remaining SOE's (independent accounting units). TVEs had hard budget constraints, fewer regulations, and greater ability to respond to input (hiring and promotion, choice of sellers of intermediate inputs) and output (product demand) market conditions. By the early 1990s, Jefferson and Singhe (1999) document how TVE total factor productivity exceeded SOEs, ascribing that to the greater operational freedom and hard budget constraint of TVE's, illustrated by Murakami, Liu and Otsuka (1996) in terms of buying and contracting-out decisions.

Still TVE sector development was constrained by the under-capitalization of the rural sector that has been a feature of modern China. Based on micro data, Jefferson and

[31] Shifting restrictions on products that could be produced by TVEs was the competition restraint. Success by a TVE could lead to its product line being terminated [Henderson (1988)].

Singhe show that the rate of return on capital in the TVE sector in 1997 exceeded that of SOEs by 25%. Similarly Au and Henderson (2002) calculate that, while the social marginal product of labor in prefecture-level cities is only 7% higher than in the TVE sector, the marginal product of capital in the TVE sector in 1997 is 40% higher than in prefecture-level cities. In calculating social marginal products of labor in the urban versus rural sector another aspect of "leading", or bias in the urban-rural allocation of resources concerns education. The higher wage and compensation returns to labor in the urban sector combined with college education being the key to permanent migration from rural to urban areas, means the more educated population is funneled into cities. An area of investigation is the very high social returns to education in the rural sector, improving township allocation decisions of resources between agricultural, animal husbandry and TVE activities [Yang and An (1997)]; also [Au and Henderson (2002)].

In addition to these policies governing rural–urban (and big city–small city) allocation of capital and labor there are other much more explicit policies with a spatial bias [Chan (1994), Yang (1997), Naughton (2002), Fujita and Hu (2001)]. While they have some big city–small city/town flavor, they also have a coastal versus rest of the country flavor. Arguably the key element is initial policies that directed FDI and trade to certain coastal cities. In the early (1979) reforms, 4 coastal special economic zones, centered on 4 prefecture-level cities were created to encourage free market experimentation, an inflow of FDI, and development of international trade. In the mid-1980s, 14 more coastal cities were declared as open cities to foreign investors, with 2 more coastal cities added by 1990. In addition 10 cities (half overlapping with open status) were given separately listed status – economic decision making powers equal to the provincial cities of Beijing, Tianjin, and Shanghai.

Fujita and Hu (2001) show that 14 open cities and 4 spatial economic zones accounted for 42% of national FDI from 1984–1994. The 24 "special status" cities (special economic zones, open, and separately listed) plus Beijing accounted for 65% of all FDI in prefecture-level cities, while accounting for only 36% of value-added in nonagricultural production of prefecture-level cities. This initial advantage persists, despite opening of the entire economy. These 25 cities account for 63% of all FDI accumulated from 1990–1997 in all prefecture (or provincial) level cities. Figure 22 illustrates. It takes the upper quartile of all cities in terms of their ratio of accumulated FDI from 1990–1996 (in dollars) divided by their 1996 GDP (in RMB), and then divides that upper quartile into four quartiles in terms of ranking of relative accumulated FDI. The cities in the top group (0.0568 – 0.443, for the upper 1/16 overall) are heavily concentrated along the coast, except for a few inland special cities.

Fujita and Hu (2001) argue persuasively that the agglomeration of electronics and light manufacturing in coastal areas such as the region around Guangzhou is due to these initial policies promoting FDI and trade in these favored coastal areas. The effect is reflected in the ratio of investment occurring in coastal versus interior regions: in 1984 the ratio is 1.12 while 10 years later it is 1.93 [see also Naughton (2002)]. These policies and their impacts are deliberate spatial policies of the Sixth and Seventh 5-year plans, favoring development in a spatial hierarchy of the coastal region. On a more positive

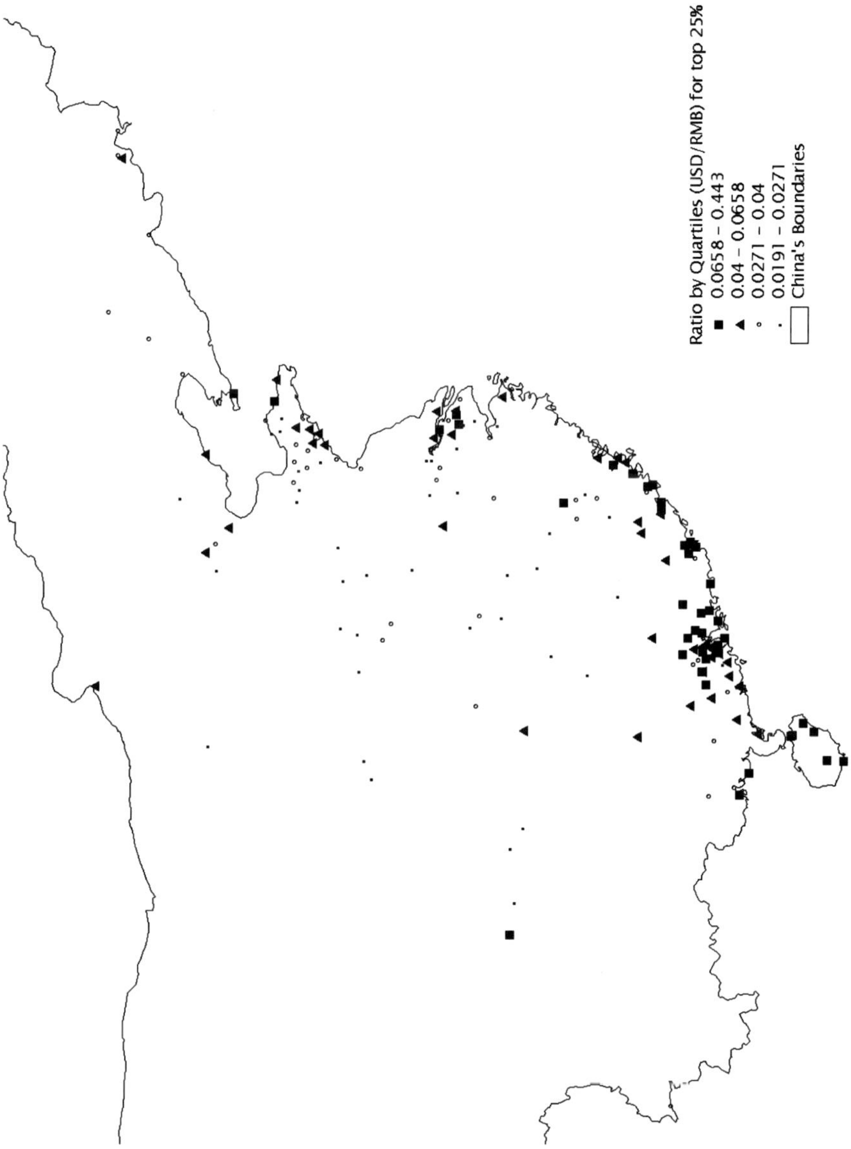

Figure 22. Ratio of accumulated FDI to value-added in 1996, for major receiving cities.

note, Wei and Wu (2001) do show the expanding trade within these favored regions, tended to reduce rural–urban income inequality, because trade helped the TVE sector in the urban fringe (rural) areas.

An entirely different aspect of this spatial policy bias involves transportation. On a world scale, China has an anemic road system. Its ratios of national roads to land, roads to population, or paved roads to land or to population in 1995 are very low by international standards. For example, its normalized ratio of roads to population in 1995 is 1.2, to be compared to 2.1 for India, 1.5 for Pakistan, 1.9 for Indonesia, or 2.7 for Mexico. Half of these roads are paved in India but only 15% in China. For a country with far-flung populations, this places hinterlands at great disadvantage in their ability to secure inputs and truck products to coastal and international markets. Only now is a highway being built to link Chengdu, Sichuan's capital, and the 100 million people in the Sichuan region to the coast.

The final aspect of spatial bias involves governance and fiscal relations. Fiscal rules and inter-governmental relations in China are not well defined and transparent. Revenue redistribution contracts send monies coming from the center back to provinces and cities; up to the mid-1990s these appeared to favor bigger and richer cities. But much official public expenditure is extra-budgetary – local revenues retained within localities [Jin and Zou (2002)]. What is retained and the specifics of a city's fiscal allocations from above, whatever the rules, are in part the result of bargaining. And in the hierarchy of big city versus small or coast versus interior, the bigger and the coastal have greater bargaining power. Actual results depend on the personalities and power of local leaders, with an interesting literature on China documenting this [Cheung, Chung and Lin (1998)]. Bigger cities have more effective fiscal autonomy and more control over key appointments (e.g., heads of local state-owned banks which become a source of funds and subsidies of local industries). Cities compared to rural areas are favored with the ability to offer lower tax rates on FDI firms. The issue is a difficult one and there has emerged no clear way to quantify the fiscal advantage of one city or set of cities over others. But the spatial bias and lack of transparency is a key feature of China's urban sector.

3.3. *Some evidence on key issues*

In this section, we focus on agglomeration economies and city sizes in China – the extent to which cities in China may be too small and the welfare losses from that, the extent of rural–urban migration that is actually occurring, and how one could model the process of city population growth in China. At the end we will turn to the issue of spatial bias and history of pro-coastal policies.

3.3.1. *Under-agglomeration in cities*

Using data for 1996 and 1997, Au and Henderson (2002) estimate city production functions for 212 prefecture- or higher-level cities. Output is value-added per worker in the non-agricultural sector of the city proper. Determinants include the capital stock to labor ratio, share of accumulated FDI in capital stock, distance to the coast, education and scale measures. These city-level figures on GDP, investment, and other economic data are considered to be reliable and consistent in collection and accounting methods across cities. The city statistical bureaus which collect these data have traditionally been responsible de facto for the nationa-level urban economic data. National figures were simply aggregates of provincial figures, which in turn were aggregates of the city reported numbers. Given this institutional "accident", these are the only reliable GDP numbers at the city level (i.e, at the level of the city proper, or the de facto urbanized area) that we are aware of internationally.

Following traditional systems of cities analysis [see the chapters by Duranton and Puga (2004) and by Abdel-Rahman and Anas (2004) in this volume], real output per worker is postulated to be an inverted U-shape function of local scale, as measured by total local non-agricultural employment. In this analysis, cities are in an economic "hierarchy" where cities relatively or absolutely specialize in different products. In general, the manufacturing to service ratio of cities declines as city scale rises, or cities move up the hierarchy. To capture this, Au and Henderson (2002) postulate that the inverted U-shape shifts right as the manufacturing to service ratio drops. They estimate a relationship for city i where

$$\ln(VA_i/L_i) = \beta X_i + \alpha_1 L_i + \alpha_2 L_i^2 + \alpha_3 L_i \cdot MS_i. \tag{3.1}$$

In (3.1), X_i are controls on technology, capital-labor ratio, access and the like. VA_i is value-added; L_i is total (non-agricultural) employment, and MS_i is the manufacturing to service VA ratio (secondary to tertiary sector VA). In Equation (3.1) output per worker peaks where

$$L_i^* = \frac{\alpha_1 + \alpha_3 MS_i}{-2\alpha_2} \tag{3.2}$$

where $\alpha_2 < 0$, $\alpha_1 > 0$, $\alpha_1 + \alpha_3 MS_i > 0$ and $\alpha_3 < 0$. The last reflects the economic hierarchy idea: bigger cities are more service oriented, so L_i^* declines as MS_i rises.

Estimation of (3.1) in Au and Henderson (2002) is by instrumental variables using 1990 (planning period) variables as instruments. Estimation produces a tight fit with excellent specification test results. Table 6A shows relevant manufacturing to service ratios, the peak points (L_i^*) where value-added per workers is maximized and the 95% confidence interval for peak scale. Note scale is in thousands of workers. Most Chinese cities (85%) lie to the left of their peak points and 43% are below the 95% confidence interval on L_i^*. That is, 43% of cities are significantly to the left of L_i^*, or significantly undersized. Table 6B shows the percent gain in VA per worker from moving below the peak to the peak.

For county-level cities, Au and Henderson are unable to quantify an inverted-U, instead finding unbounded scale effects (for these smaller city sizes). Similarly for TVEs across provinces, local scale economies (average township TVE employment by province over three years) are unbounded and very large – a 10% increase in local scale

Table 7
A city growth equation [change in ln(employment) from 1990 to 1997]

1990 variables	3SLS
ln(capital/labor)	0.104
	(0.074)
% pop. (over age 6) with high school	0.00832†
	(0.00374)
FDI/labor	0.000592†
	(0.000253)
ln(market potential)	0.244†
	(0.106)
manufacturing/service (VA)	−0.0476*
	(0.0267)
ln(city employment)	−0.219†
	(0.0367)
favored city dummy variable	0.266†
	(0.0829)
distance to coast	0.00848*
	(0.00453)
adj R^2	0.171
N	210

Notes. The primary effect of instrumenting is to double the coefficients for ln(capital/labor) and % pop. with high school and raise the employment coefficient by 30%. Instruments are: distance to coast, favored city, west region, center region, land area, 1990 FDI or not, 1990 FDI, manufacturing/service ratio, ln(market potential), ln(capital stock), ln(capital stock) $*$ manufacturing/service ratio, ln(SOE VA/city VA), doctors per person, telephones per person, books per person, roads per person.
*significant at 10% level
†significant at 5% level

From 1990–1997, prefecture-level cities average from Table 2 about a 25% increase in employment. As Table 7 shows, these cities grow as variables which enhance urban worker productivity grow. A one standard deviation increase in the capital to labor ratio, FDI per worker, and education raise city growth points (in percent) by 3.7, 6.1, and 7.2. Special status cities are the 25 cities noted earlier which have special, open, or separately listed status (plus Beijing) in 1990. As results in Table 7 show, even after accounting for greater FDI and better educated populations, these cities grow much more quickly than other cities – about 27 percent points, presumably reflecting their greater freedom and ability to recruit contract workers (as temporary migrants). Access to the coast per se has a weakly significant impact, while market potential is significant. Market potential of a city is the sum of populations in all other prefecture and county-level cities discounted by distance from the city to all others. Market potential represents a source of demand for a city's products. A one standard deviation increase in ln(MP) raises growth by 5.8. Finely bigger cities grow more slowly. Larger cities are nearer their peak and also have smaller urban–rural utility gaps. If a city is larger to begin with, ceteris paribus, it has a smaller urban–rural gap and has significantly lower growth.

3.3.4. Spatial discrimination and the coast versus the hinterlands

China has subsidized FDI (through tax breaks) in prefecture-level cities and encouraged FDI and trade development in certain coastal cities, as part of a general program emphasizing coastal development, over hinterland development. The question is whether the FDI policy is efficient. On the subsidization question, the argument is that FDI brings in technology transfer, as well as creating job opportunities for low cost Chinese labor. The counter-argument is that FDI is not particularly high tech, compared even to more sophisticated domestic production, and FDI may discourage, or divert funds from local R&D. The evidence is not conclusive. For example Au and Henderson (2002) find that, ceteris paribus (same total capital to labor ratio) that cities with a one-standard deviation higher FDI/capital ratio have 8% higher output per worker. As noted above, FDI also enhances city growth rates. And in Fujita and Hu (2001) as noted earlier, FDI is associated with coastal agglomeration.

Assessing the issue of the efficiency of coastal versus hinterland development is less straightforward. On FDI, in Au and Henderson (2002), there is no evidence that FDI interacts with distance to the coast or city size – returns to FDI occur in the same degree for all cities regardless of size or location. But there is a more general question of coastal versus hinterland development. The Gallup, Sachs and Mellinger (1999) story is that hinterlands are inherently inferior locations for economic development, compared to coastal locations. Démurger et al. (2001) amend the story for China to argue that favored provinces tend to be coastal provinces so that the faster growth of coastal provinces is explained by a combination of policy-bias and inherent advantage.

A flaw in the analysis of coastal advantage is the failure to control for market potential of cities, a control fundamental in the analysis of economic geography [see the chapter by Head and Mayer (2004) in this volume]. Statistically the issue is that in many countries (e.g., U.S.), historically populations have agglomerated on coasts. So access to the coast captures both greater domestic market potential effects, and pure coast effects. In Au and Henderson (2002), distance to the coast on its own in Equation (3.1) significantly reduces productivity. However introduction of market potential eliminates the effect of access to the coast, and produces large significant effects for market potential. Similarly in the Section 3.3.3 regression, access to the coast is only weakly associated with higher growth per se, once FDI and market potential differentials are accounted for. For example, if we consider Sichuan in Western China, its 100 million residents have enormous market potential. With proper modern highway links to the coast, it in some sense will become "coast", with easier access to the coast. While coastal provinces still have better access to international markets, Sichuan may be domestically competitive, relatively specializing in domestic products. Its "disadvantage" may reflect policy disadvantage in terms of transport development, FDI, and loosening of planning constraints, more than an inherent disadvantage of hinterland location.

References

Abdel-Rahman, H.M., Anas, A. (2004). "Theories of systems of cities". In: Henderson, J.V., Thisse, J.-F. (Eds.), Handbook of Regional and Urban Economics, vol. 4. Elsevier, Amsterdam, pp. 2293–2339. This volume.

Abdel-Rahman, H.M., Fujita, M. (1990). "Product variety, Marshallian externalities and city sizes". Journal of Regional Science 30, 165–185.

Akamatsu, K. (1937). "Shinkoku Kogyo no sangyo hatten" ("The industrial development of newly emerging industrial nation"). Ueda Teijiro Hakushi Kinen Ronbunshu 4.

Alonso, W. (1980). "Five bell shapes in development". Papers of Regional Science Association 45, 5–16.

Asako, K., Tsuneki, A., Fukuda, S., Teruyama, H., Tsukamoto, T., Sugiura, M. (1984). "Shakai shihonno seisanryoku koka to kokyo toshi no keizai kosei hyoka" (Productivity of government capital and the welfare evaluation of government investment policy). Economic Analysis 135, 1–90.

Au, C.C., Henderson, J.V. (2002). "How migration restrictions limit agglomeration and productivity in China". NBER Working Paper #8707 and Brown University April 15 mimeo.

Barro, R.J., Sala-i-Martin, X. (1995). Economic Growth. McGraw–Hill, New York.

Barro, R.J., Sala-i-Martin, X. (1992). "Regional growth and migration: a Japan–U.S. comparison". Journal of the Japanese International Economies 6, 312–346.

Black, D., Henderson, J.V. (2003). "Urban evolution in the USA". Journal of Economic Geography 3, 343–372.

Cai, Fang (2000). Zongguo Liudong Renkou Wenti (The Mobile Population Problem in China). Henan People's Publishing House, Zhengzhou.

Chan, K.W. (1994). Cities with Invisible Walls. Oxford University Press, Hong Kong.

Chan, K.W. (2000). "Internal migration in China: trends, determination, and scenarios". Report prepared for World Bank. University of Washington (April).

Cheung, P.T.Y., Chung, J.H., Lin, Z. (Eds.) (1998). Provincial Strategies of Economic Reform in Post-Mao China: Leadership, Politics, and Implementation. M.E. Sharpe, Armonk, NY.

Cochrane, S.G., Vining, D.R. (1988). "Recent trends in migration between core and peripheral regions in developed and developing countries". International Regional Science Review 11, 215–243.

Dekle, R., Eaton, J. (1999). "Agglomeration and land rents: evidence from the prefectures". Journal of Urban Economics 46, 200–214.

Démurger, S., Sachs, J.D., Woo, W.T., Bao, S., Chang, G., Mellinger, A. (2001). "Geography, economic policy and regional development". Asian Economic Papers 1. In press.

Dumais, G., Ellison, G., Glaeser, E.L. (2002). "Geographic concentration as a dynamic process". Review of Economics and Statistics 84 (2), 193–204.

Duranton, G., Puga, D. (2001). "Nursery cities, urban diversity, process innovation, and the life-cycle of products". American Economic Review 91, 1454–1463.

Duranton, G., Puga, D. (2004). "Micro-foundations of urban agglomeration economies". In: Henderson, J.V., Thisse, J.-F. (Eds.), Handbook of Regional and Urban Economics, vol. 4. Elsevier, Amsterdam, pp. 2063–2117. This volume.

Eaton, J., Eckstein, Z. (1997). "Cities and growth: evidence from France and Japan". Regional Science and Urban Economics 27, 443–474.

Ebanks, G.E., Cheng, C. (1990). "China: a unique urbanization model". Asia–Pacific Population Journal 5 (3), 29–50.

Ellison, G., Glaeser, E.L. (1997). "Geographic concentration in U.S. manufacturing industries: a dartboard approach". Journal of Political Economy 105, 889–927.

Fujita, M., Hisatake, M. (1999). "Development of regional economic system in Japan and East Asia: an empirical study based on new geographical economics". Review of MITI Studies 13, 40–101. In Japanese.

Fujita, M., Ishii, R. (1999). "Global location behavior and organizational dynamics of Japanese Electronics firms and their impact on regional economies". In: Chandler Jr, A.D, Hagstrom, P., Solvell, Orjan (Eds.),

The Dynamic Firm: The Role of Technology, Strategy, Organization, and Regions. Oxford University Press, Oxford, pp. 344–383.

Fujita, M., Krugman, P., Mori, T. (1999). "On the evolution of hierarchical urban systems". European Economic Review 43, 209–251.

Fujita, M., Ogawa, H. (1982). "Multiple equilibria and structural transition of non-monocentric urban configurations". Regional Science and Urban Economics 12, 161–196.

Fujita, M., Tabuchi, T. (1997). "Regional growth in postwar Japan". Regional Science and Urban Economics 27, 643–670.

Fujita, M., Hu, D. (2001). "Regional disparity in China 1995–1994: the effects of globalization and economic liberalization". The Annals of Regional Science 35, 3–37.

Gabaix, X., Ioannides, Y.M. (2004). "The evolution of city size distributions". "Theories of systems of cities". In: Henderson, J.V., Thisse, J.-F. (Eds.), Handbook of Regional and Urban Economics, vol. 4. Elsevier, Amsterdam, pp. 2341–2378. This volume.

Gallup, J.L., Sachs, J.D., Mellinger, A.D. (1999). "Geography and economic development". International Regional Science Review 22, 179–232.

Gaspar, J., Glaeser, E. (1998). "Information technology and the future of cities". Journal of Urban Economics 42, 136–156.

Hatch, W., Yamamura, K. (1996). Economics of Agglomeration: Cities, Industrial Location and Regional Growth. Cambridge University Press.

Hatta, T., Karato, K. (2001). "Toshin ni okeru yosekiritu kanwa no rodo seisansei josho koka" ("The labor productivity enhancement effects of raising the limits on floor air ratios in central cities"). Housing and Land Economics 41 (Jutaku Tochi Keizai), 20–27. In Japanese.

Head, K., Mayer, T. (2004). "The empirics of agglomeration and trade". In: Henderson, J.V., Thisse, J.-F. (Eds.), Handbook of Regional and Urban Economics, vol. 4. Elsevier, Amsterdam, pp. 2609–2669. This volume.

Henderson, J.V. (1988). Urban Development: Theory, Fact and Illusion. Oxford University Press.

Henderson, J.V. (1997). "Medium size cities". Regional Science and Urban Economics 27, 583–612.

Henderson, J.V., Kuncoro, A., Turner, M. (1995). "Industrial development in cities". Journal of Public Economy 103, 1067–1090.

Henderson, J.V., Wang, H.-G. (2003). "Urbanization and city growth". Brown University mimeo.

Imai, H. (1982). "CBD Hypothesis and Economies of Agglomeation". Journal of Economic Theory 29, 275–299.

Inoue, Y., Ito, M. (1989). Sentan-Sangyo To Chiiki-Keizai. Minerva Shobou, Tokyo. In Japanese.

Itakura, M. (1988). Nippon-Kougyou No Chiiki-System. Daimeidou, Tokyo.

Iwamoto, Y., Ouchi, S., Takeshita, S., Bessho, T. (1996). "Shakai shihon no seisansei to kokyo toshino chiikikan haibun" ("Productivity of social overhead capital and the regional allocation of public investment"). Financial Review 41, 27–52. In Japanese.

Jefferson, G., Singhe, I. (1999). Enterprise Reform in China: Ownership Transition and Performance. Oxford University Press, New York.

Jin, J., Zou, H.-F. (2002). "Soft budget constraint on local governments in China". World Bank mimeo.

Johnson, D.G. (2001). "Have the urban–rural disparities increased since 1978 in China?" University of Chicago mimeo.

Kanemoto, Y., Tokuoka, K. (2002). "Nihon no toshiken settei kijun" ("Proposal for the standards of metropolitan areas of Japan"). Journal of Applied Regional Science 7, 1–15. In Japanese.

Kanemoto, Y., Saito, H. (1998). "Tokyo wa kadai ka: Henry George teiri ni yoru kensho" ("Is Tokyo too large? A test of the Henry George Theorem"). Housing and Land Economics 29 (Jutaku Tochi Keizai), 9–17. In Japanese.

Kanemoto, Y., Ohkawara, T., Suzuki, T. (1996). "Agglomeration economies and a test for optimal city sizes in Japan". Journal of the Japanese and International Economies 10, 379–398.

Kanemoto, Y. (1990). "Optimal cities with indivisibility in production and interactions between firms". Journal of Urban Economics 27, 46–59.

Karato, K. (2000). "Tokyo-to ni okeru shuyo gyomu chiku eno kinsetsusei no rieki to shuseki no keizai" ("The benefit of accessibility for main business districts and agglomeration economy in Tokyo metropolitan area"). Journal of Applied Regional Science 5, 41–52.

Kitamura, Y., Yada, T. (1977). Nippon-Kougyo No Chiiki-Kouzou. Daimeido-Hakkou, Tokyo. In Japanese.

Kojima, R. (1996). "Breakdown of China's policy of restricting population movement". The Developing Economies 34, 370–401.

Kosugi, T., Tsuji, G. (1997). Nippon no sangyo kozo to chiiki keizai. Daimeido-Hakkou, Tokyo. In Japanese.

Kwok, W.Y. (1982). "The role of small cities in chinese urban development". International Journal of Urban and Regional Research 6, 549–564.

Lin, J.Y., Cai, F., Li, Z. (1996). The China Miracle: Development Strategy and Economic Reform. The Hong Kong Centre for Economic Research and The International Center for Economic Growth, The Chinese University Press.

Ma, L., Fan, M. (1994). "Urbanization from below: the growth of towns in Jiangsu, China". Urban Studies 31, 1625–1645.

Mano, Y., Otsuka, K. (2000). "Agglomeration economies and geographical concentration of industries: a case study of manufacturing sectors in postwar Japan". Journal of the Japanese and International Economies 14, 189–203.

Mera, K. (1973). "Regional production function and social overhead capital: an analysis of Japanese case". Regional and Urban Economics 3, 157–186.

Mitsui, K., Takezawa, Y., Kochi, S. (1995). "Shakai shihon no chiikikan haibun, seisan kansu to hiyo kansu ni yoru suitei" ("Interregional distribution of social capital: estimates based on production function and cost function"). IPTP (Institute for Posts and Telecommunication Policy) Review 6, 205–261. In Japanese.

Mori, T., Nishikimi, K., Smith, T.E. (2003). "Some empirical regularities in spatial economies: a relationship between industrial location and city size". Discussion Paper No. 551. Institute of Economic Research, Kyoto University.

Murakami, N., Liu, D., Otsuka, K. (1996). "Market reform, division of labor, and increasing advantage of small-scale enterprises: the case of the machine tool industry in China". Journal of Comparative Economics 23 (3), 256–277.

Nakamura, R. (1985). "Agglomeration economies in urban manufacturing industries". Journal of Urban Economics 17, 108–124.

Naughton, G. (2002). "Provincial economic growth in China: causes and consequences of regional differentiation". University of California, San Diego mimeo.

O, J.C. (1993). "Reform and urban bias in China". Journal of Development Studies 29, 129–148. 4.

Ottaviano, G., Thisse, J.-F. (2004). "Agglomeration and economic geography". In: Henderson, J.V., Thisse, J.-F. (Eds.), Handbook of Regional and Urban Economics, vol. 4. Elsevier, Amsterdam, pp. 2563–2608. This volume.

Paine, S. (1981). "Spatial aspects of Chinese development: issues, outcomes, and policies 1949–1979". Journal of Development Studies 17, 132–195.

Perkins, D. (1994). "Completing China's move to the market". Journal of Economic Perspectives 8 (2), 23–46.

Porter, M.E. (1990). The Competitive Advantage of Nations. Free Press, New York.

Rappaport, J. (2000). "Why are population flows so persistent?" Federal Reserve Bank of Kansas City mimeo.

Seki, M., Fukuda, J. (Eds.) (1998). Henbousuru Jiba Sangyo. Shinhyoron, Tokyo. In Japanese.

Shimohirao, K. (1996). Jiba Sangyo. Shinhyoron, Tokyo. In Japanese.

Shioji, E. (2001). "Public capital and economic growth: a convergence approach". Journal of Economic Growth 6 (3), 205–227.

Shixun, G., Xian, L. (1992). "Urban migration in Shanghai 1950–88: trends and characteristics". Population and Development Review 18, 533–548.

Tabuchi, T. (1986). "Urban agglomeration, capital augmenting technology, and labor market equilibrium". Journal of Urban Economics 20, 211–228.

Tabuchi, T. (1987). "Interregional income differentials and migration: their inter-relationships". Regional Studies 22, 1–10.

Tabuchi, T., Yoshida, A. (2000). "Separating urban agglomeration economies in consumption and production". Journal of Urban Economics 48, 70–84.

Takahara, K. (1999). Chiiki System To Sangyo-Network. Horitsu-Bunka-Sha, Tokyo. In Japanese.

Takahashi, J. (1982). "Toshika-katei to toshi-shisutem". In: Tanabe, K. (Ed.), Nihon No Toshi Shisutem. Kokon Shoin, Tokyo, pp. 58–70.

Tanioka, K. (2002). "A time series analysis of inter-regional income disparities in Japan". PhD Thesis. Osaka Commerce University, Japan.

Vernon, R. (1966). "International investment and international trade in product cycle". Quarterly Journal of Economics 80, 190–207.

Wei, S.-J., Wu, Y. (2001). "Globalization and inequality: evidence from China". CEPR discussion paper No. 3088.

Williamson, J. (1965). "Regional inequality and the process of national development, a description of the patterns". Economic Development and Cultural Change 13, 3–45.

World Bank (1981). "China, socialist economic development". Report No. 3391 – CHA, Main Report and Annex C.

Yada, T., Imamura, A. (1991). Seinan-Keizai-Ken Bunseki. Minerva Shobou, Tokyo. In Japanese.

Yang, D.T., An, M.Y. (1997). "Human, capital entrepreneurship, and farm household earnings". Duke University mimeo.

Yang, D.L. (1997). Beyond Beijing: Liberalization and the Regions in China. Routledge, London.

Yoshino, N., Nakajima, T. (1999). Kokyo Toshi no Keizai Koka (Economic Effects of Public Investment). Nihon Hyoron Sha, Tokyo, Japan. In Japanese.

Yoshino, N., Nakano, T. (1996). "Kokyo toshi no chiikikan haibun to seisan koka" ("Regional allocation of public investment and production effects"). Financial Review 41, 16–26. In Japanese.

PART 4

THE LONG-RUN VIEW ON CITIES AND GEOGRAPHY

Chapter 66

HISTORICAL PERSPECTIVES ON U.S. ECONOMIC GEOGRAPHY

SUKKOO KIM

Department of Economics, Washington University, USA

ROBERT A. MARGO

Department of Economics, Vanderbilt University, USA
e-mail: robert.a.margo@vanderbilt.edu

Contents

Handbook of Regional and Urban Economics, Volume 4. Edited by J.V. Henderson and J.F. Thisse

DOI: 10.1016/S0169-7218(04)07066-2

Abstract

We review historical patterns of economic geography for the United States from the colonial period to the present day. The analysis is framed in terms of two geographic scales: regions and cities. The compelling reason for studying geographic area of two different scales is that models that explain location of economic activities at one scale may not apply to other scales. We consider the process of settling the frontier; the development of national markets in goods and factors and, more generally, the convergence (and divergence) of regional economies; the growth of cities and the relationship between urbanization and trends in aggregate economic structure, such as industrialization; and changes in the internal structure of cities.

Keywords

economic integration, regional specialization, regional economic growth, urban development

JEL classification: R0

1. Introduction

Economic geography is central to economic development. As economies develop, the initial allocation of resources across locations rarely remains fixed. New industries develop and, for technological or other reasons, find it profitable to situate in different locations than old industries. Transportation networks emerge, linking far-flung markets, within and across countries, again potentially altering the spatial distribution of resources. Equally as or even more importantly, the density of economic activity changes with development. In low income societies, much economic activity is concentrated in low-density activities, such as agriculture or cottage industries. As per capita income rises, capital and labor migrate to cities, and average density rises. But within cities, density may also change over time, as people and firms find it to their advantage to spread out over a wider "metropolitan" area.

We explore the economic geography of the U.S. from a historical perspective in two geographic scales: regions and urban areas. The most compelling reason for studying geographic areas of differing scales is that models which explain the location of economic activities at one scale, such as the region, may not apply to smaller scales such as urban areas, or even finer ones like financial and industrial districts.[1] Further, the examination of these two geographic units of observation, regions and urban areas, presents a more coherent understanding of the historical geography of the U.S., than treating each geographic dimension separately.

We have three major goals: to systematically present historical data on U.S. regions and urban areas, to survey the existing literature on the historical geography of the U.S., and to direct scholars to promising avenues of research. Because this subject is a vast one that touches on many disciplines, our review of the literature is necessarily selective and highly incomplete. However, even an incomplete review, we believe, can offer important insights on the fundamental role of geography in American economic development. It is impossible, in our opinion, to understand long-term development of the U.S. divorced from its geography. Surprisingly, however, many important areas remain relatively unexplored and we try to highlight the most significant of these in our review.

2. U.S. regional development

One of the most distinctive characteristics of America is space.[2] In 1800, the United States was already one of the largest nations in the world. In the nineteenth century, the

[1] Fujita and Thisse (2002) note that geographers have long known that geographic scale matters. According to Fujita and Thisse, to ascribe what is true at one spatial scale to another is to commit ecological fallacy.

[2] "North and South, East and West, city and country, from the 1790s to the 1850s, the most powerful influence in shaping of American society was space. The ideas about space, the uses of space, the projects across space, and the accommodations to space, above all else, charted the basic changes that occurred between these years". Robert H. Wiebe as quoted in Meinig (1993, p. 219).

U.S. became a continental nation of enormous proportions from sea to sea. Moreover, the Americans faced unprecedented challenges in integrating vast unpopulated territories politically and economically. The Northwest Ordinance provided an orderly procedure for incorporating unsettled territories into states, but sectional differences over slavery led to divergence and disunion. However, by the early twentieth century, the states of the union emerged as a unified nation. This section addresses three of the most significant developments in U.S. economic geography from a regional perspective: the westward migration of Americans, the rise of a national economy, and the divergence and convergence of U.S. regional economies.

2.1. Settlement of the U.S. continent

In the colonial period, most Americans of European and African descent lived along the eastern seaboard. With the Treaty of Versailles in 1783, Americans gained independence and vast stretches of land through the mid-Western U.S. Between 1783 and 1898, through purchase, conquest, or treaty, Americans acquired a continental area of 3 million square miles. Moreover, Americans migrated westward in waves. During the first half of the nineteenth century, people from the Northeast migrated to the East North Central region, and those from the Southeast migrated to the East South Central region. In the second half of the nineteenth century, migration continued westward to the West North Central and, to a lesser extent, the West South Central region. Finally, in the twentieth century, population migrated further west and south to the Mountain, Pacific and West South Central regions (see Figure 1).

Most migrants moved west along the latitude. Meinig (1993) documents the geographic patterns of westward migration and the establishment of western settlements in the nineteenth century. Since most people involved in the westward migration were farmers, people may have migrated along the latitude because they acquired latitude-specific skills in agriculture [see Steckel (1983)]. However, the westward migration is not without puzzles. Normally, economists argue that individuals migrate from low to

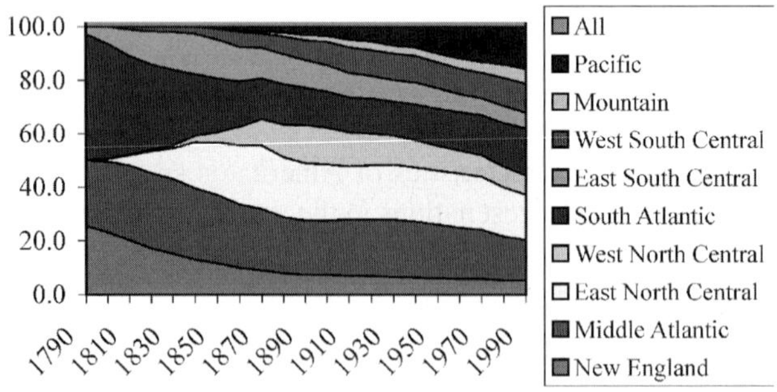

Figure 1. U.S. population distribution, 1790–1990 (percent). For a colour reproduction of this figure see the colour figures section, page 3072.

high per capita income areas, all other things equal. In the case of the South, this appears to be consistent with the gradient of per capita incomes (higher in the West than in the East). But in the North, the gradient ran in the opposite direction – incomes were higher in the East than in the West.

Why did people go West? The most famous explanation is the safety valve hypothesis proposed by the historian Frederick Jackson Turner; the economically dispossessed Easterners migrated to the West where land was cheap. However, most economic historians dismiss the safety valve hypothesis on the grounds that migration to the West was costly, both in terms of opportunity costs and resources. In particular, farm-making on the western frontier was very costly, well beyond the means of unemployed industrial workers in eastern cities. Nevertheless, using sophisticated econometric methods, Ferrie (1997) finds some evidence that migration was indeed selective in the sense required by the safety valve hypothesis. In addition, the safety valve hypothesis is consistent with Fogel and Rutner's (1972) analysis that the sale of large tracts of western lands by the federal government induced the westward movement.

The safety valve hypothesis is consistent with the East–West gradient of per capita income distribution in the North, but many scholars believe that income per capita does not always accurately measure gains to migration. It is well known that fertility was high on the western frontier. Adjusting for the higher dependency ratio (children to economically active adults) narrows the difference in per capita incomes between the Midwest and the Northeast [Fogel (1989)]. More recently, Margo (1999, 2000) has provided real wage indices that are corrected for regional differences in cost of living. Margo (1999, 2000) finds considerable evidence for the hypothesis, initially proposed by Coehlo and Shepherd (1976), that westward migration was prompted by higher marginal product of labor on the frontier than in the East. According to Margo's estimates, real wages of unskilled labor were about 30% higher in the Midwest than in the Northeast ca. 1830. However, as East–West migration began in earnest, the real wage gap in the North diminished to about 15% or so on the eve of the Civil War. By the end of the nineteenth century, a gap remained, but it was smaller (about 10%) than the gap that existed just prior to the War. Margo also shows that the real wage gap for skilled labor was initially much higher, but also converged before the Civil War.

Finally, migration to the antebellum frontier may not be explained by current income, but by future returns – that is, by capital gains. There is evidence that "getting there first" had economic value on the frontier. Early migrants got the best land and, if and when the railroad came through, got the most capital gains [Galenson and Pope (1992), Craig, Palmquist and Weiss (1998), Coffman and Gregson (1998)].

2.2. Economic integration and the rise of a national economy

In the seventeenth and the eighteenth centuries, the colonial economies were integrated with Europe and the West Indies. Beginning in the early nineteenth century, greater investments in internal transportation began to integrate the domestic economy intra-regionally and inter-regionally. Initially, private construction of turnpike roads increased the mileage of roads in New England and Middle Atlantic regions from 4684 to 11,662 miles between 1810 and 1830.[3] However, most of these investments were not profitable. In the following decades, the construction of canals and the use of steamboats on navigable waters lowered the costs of trade markedly. However, the integration of U.S. regional economies really began in earnest with the emergence of the railroads in the 1850s. The growth in the mileage of railroads and telegraphs between the late nineteenth and the turn of the twentieth centuries was spectacular. For example, between 1860 and 1890, the mileage of operation in railroads increased sharply from 30,626 to 166,703 miles whereas that of telegraphs increased from 50,000 to 19,382,000 miles.[4] These advances in transportation led to dramatic declines in domestic freight rates [see North (1965)].

Regional convergence in prices suggests that integration occurred at different rates for goods and factor markets. Goods market integration seems to have been realized by the latter half of the nineteenth century, capital markets by the early twentieth century, and labor markets by the mid-twentieth century. North (1961) and Harley (1980) find rapid convergence in the prices of goods such as lard, pork, flour, and wheat across regions between 1820 and 1860. Davis (1965) finds marked convergence in interest rates by the early 1900s.[5] Finally, while there is convergence of wages and earnings by the mid-twentieth century, labor markets seem to have remained segmented for a longer period between the North and the South [Rosenbloom (1990), Margo and Villaflor (1987), Goldin and Margo (1992), Margo (2003)].

Over the past two centuries or so, the United States has become, in effect, a national market in goods and factors of production. Incomes are now less tied to place than they are to skills, and regions are more homogenous with respect to economic activity than they once were. Nonetheless, it would be a mistake to conclude that region no longer "matters" in the United States. Regions are still subject to economic shocks, and the evidence is that such shocks have consequences for incomes and employment, at least for the medium run, if not for the very long run [Blanchard and Katz (1992)].

2.3. Divergence and convergence of U.S. regional economies

The most significant long-run trend in U.S. regional economies is the divergence and convergence of U.S. regional economies. In the colonial period, regional differences in industrial structures and incomes were relatively slight. The U.S. regional economies

[3] See Fishlow (2000) for a summary of developments in internal transportation during the nineteenth and the early twentieth centuries.

[4] Despite the growing importance of the railroads, Fogel (1964) argues that the direct benefits from lower transportation costs due to the railroads were about two percent of GNP in 1890.

[5] However, Bodenhorn and Rockoff (1992) suggest that the integration of capital markets occurred much earlier. They find that regional interest rates were well integrated in the antebellum period, but that the disruptions of the Civil War caused the dis-integration of capital markets in the postbellum period, especially in the South and the Pacific Coast regions.

diverged between the nineteenth and the early twentieth centuries. The divergence was first seen in industrial structures as the Northeast region industrialized during the first half of the nineteenth century. In the late nineteenth century, industrial divergence deepened with the formation of the manufacturing belt in the North and the continued specialization of agriculture in the South. The divergence in income per capita, especially between the North and the South, emerged strongly in the postbellum period. Southern income per capita fell relatively and absolutely. However, in the second half of the twentieth century, regional industrial structures as well as regional income per capita converged dramatically.

2.3.1. *Trends in U.S. regional economic structures*

The colonial economy was dominated by agriculture, extractive industries and fisheries and was motivated by trade with Europe and the West Indies. Data on exports constructed by Shepherd and Walton (1972) suggest that the American colonies were highly specialized in their export staples.[6] The New England colonies were specialized in fish, meat, wood products, whales, potash and grain; the Middle Colonies in grain, and to a smaller extent in flaxseed, wood, iron, meat and potash; the Upper South colonies in tobacco, and to a lesser extent in grain, iron and wood products; the Lower South colonies primarily in rice and indigo as well as deerskin, naval store, wood, grain and meat products. Most scholars believe that these patterns of colonial regional economic specialization can be explained by regional comparative advantage based on soil, climate and geography [McCusker and Menard (1985)].

The early industrialization of the U.S. economy led to the first divergence of U.S. regional economies. Prior to industrialization, domestic manufactured goods were produced by artisans in urban areas. As the U.S. economy industrialized in the first half of the nineteenth century, manufacturing moved out of artisan shops into non-mechanized and mechanized factories. Sokoloff (1984, 1986) documents that the rise of factory production in a variety of industries such as boots and shoes, coaches and wagons, furniture, hats, paper, leather tanning, and textiles was associated with significant increases in labor and total factor productivity. The early industrialization led to regional divergence as manufacturing became increasingly concentrated in the Northeast region. In 1840, the share of the labor force in New England and Middle Atlantic regions in non-agricultural activities was 38 and 32%, respectively, whereas, for the remaining regions, the figure ranged from 10 to 18%.

Why did industrialization begin in New England? Historians like Hunter (1979) have emphasized the abundance of waterpower sites in New England. However, it is also well known that women and children played an important role in the early industrialization

[6] The New England colonies consist of Massachusetts, New Hampshire, Connecticut, and Rhode Island; the Middle colonies consist of New York, New Jersey, Pennsylvania, and Delaware; the Upper South colonies consist of Maryland and Virginia; and Lower South consists of North Carolina, South Carolina, Georgia, and Florida.

of the U.S. Goldin and Sokoloff (1984) propose that early industrialization proceeded in New England because of the opportunity costs of women and children relative to men in farming were lower in that region than in others. Goldin and Sokoloff find that the relative wages of women and children compared to men were lower in New England than in other regions. Moreover, the relative wage of females rose sharply with industrialization.

Sokoloff (1984) documents that the extension of markets due to the construction of canals led to the re-organization of production from one based on artisanal shops to non-mechanized and mechanized factories in the Northeast. Sokoloff suggests that initial advantages of factory production came from firm reorganization. The greater division of labor caused by the extension of markets in non-mechanized factories led to significant increases in productivity. However, increased inventive activity caused by extension of markets, also documented by Sokoloff (1988), may have contributed to the second phase where increases in productivity are associated with mechanized factories that adopted new methods of production, power sources, and new machinery. Lindstrom (1978) proposes a slightly different hypothesis for the concentration of manufacturing in the Northeast based on demand. Lindstrom argues that the increase in intra-regional demand brought on by falling transportation costs in the Northeast led to the concentration of manufacturing in that region. Overtime, however, supply-side factors may have become more important.[7]

The rise of a mature industrial economy in the U.S. between the late nineteenth and the early twentieth century was accompanied by a significant divergence in U.S. regional economies, especially between the North and South. Manufacturing spread from the Northeast to the East North Central region to form the manufacturing belt whereas the South remained entrenched in agriculture. In the second half of the twentieth century, as manufacturing spread South and West, U.S. regional economies converged significantly.

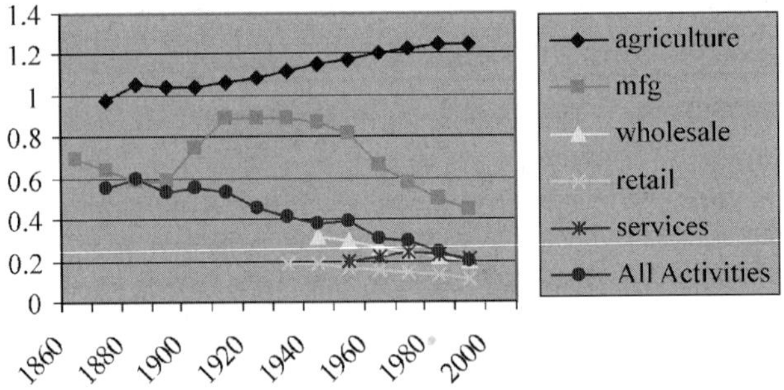

Figure 2. U.S. regional specialization, 1860–1990. *Source*. Kim (1995, 1998). Index of regional specialization is based on Krugman (1991). For a colour reproduction of this figure see the colour figures section, page 3072.

[7] See Rosenberg (1963).

The divergence and convergence of U.S. regional economies are documented by Kim (1995, 1998). Kim finds that the patterns of U.S. regional specialization differed considerably by sector (see Figure 2). In agriculture, regions continued to become more specialized over time in various crops such as wheat, barley, corn, oats, rye, cotton, tobacco and vegetables. In manufacturing, data at the two-digit industry level indicate that regions became more specialized between the late nineteenth and the early twentieth centuries; however, since the mid-twentieth century, regions became substantially more similar in industrial structure.[8] Regional specialization in the service industries, wholesale trade, retail trade, and other services were low for the second half of the twentieth century when data were available.[9]

Kim (1998) finds that regions became more specialized at the 1-digit sectoral level between 1870 and 1880, fell slightly between 1880 and 1910, and then fell significantly over the twentieth century.[10] However, the data indicate that differences in regional industrial structures between the North and South were particularly high until the second half of the twentieth century. Between the late nineteenth and the early twentieth centuries, regional industrial structures between the North and South differed by more than 50% from that of the overall average. This difference was caused by the concentration of manufacturing in the North and the concentration of agriculture in the South. In the twentieth century, regional industrial structures converged significantly. The convergence was caused by the dispersal of agriculture and the shift in economic structure into services.

For most regional and urban economists, the emergence of the manufacturing belt during the second half of the nineteenth century marked a major turning point in the U.S. economic geography.[11] The manufacturing belt, composed mostly of the New England, Middle Atlantic and East North Central regions, contained the majority of manufacturing employment between the late nineteenth and the first half of the twentieth centuries. Krugman (1991) proposes that the U.S. manufacturing belt emerged when economies of scale in production rose and transportation costs fell. To minimize transportation costs, firms chose to locate in one region – the manufacturing belt. The concentration of firms

[8] The two-digit industries in manufacturing are food, tobacco, apparel, lumber and wood, furniture and fixtures, paper, printing and publishing, chemicals, petroleum and coal, rubber and plastics, leather, stone, clay and glass, primary metal, fabricated metal, machinery, electrical machinery, transportation, instruments, and miscellaneous.

[9] The wholesale industries match the two-digit industries in manufacturing; the retail industries consist of food and general stores, general merchandise, apparel, furniture, automotive, filling stations, eating, drug stores, and other; services industries consist of hotel and lodging, personal, business, auto repair, garages, miscellaneous repair, motion pictures, amusement and recreational, health, legal, educational, social, museum and botanical zoological gardens, membership organizations, and miscellaneous.

[10] For 1870 and 1950, the one-digit industries consist of agriculture, mining, forestry, fishing, manufacturing and services. For the years between 1939 and 1987, construction, transportation, wholesale trade, retail trade, and government industries were also included.

[11] See Holmes and Stevens (2004) for an informative map of the manufacturing belt and the location of large manufacturing plants in 1947 and 1999.

further increased local demand and locked in the initial advantage. Krugman suggests that the manufacturing belt also benefitted from a denser population and a transportation network that provided a substantially larger local market.

Meyer (1983, 1989) presents a slightly different interpretation of the rise of the manufacturing belt. For Meyer, the manufacturing belt arose as series of regional industrial systems in the antebellum period that merged to form the manufacturing belt in the late nineteenth century. Meyer, in an analysis similar to that of Lindstrom (1978) for early industrialization, argues that local regional demand triggered industrialization in a series of regions stretching from the East to the Midwest over time. Although regions like the Midwest industrialized later than those in the Northeast, Meyer argues that high interregional transportation costs enabled Midwestern manufacturers to develop their own manufacturing sector during the antebellum period. When transportation costs fell in the late nineteenth century, Midwestern manufacturers were able to effectively compete with Eastern producers.

Kim (1999) presents alternative evidence for the rise of the manufacturing belt based on natural advantages. Since data on interregional trade are not available to test the Heckscher–Ohlin model, Kim exploits the Rybczynski theorem that provides a linear relationship between factor endowments and production. Kim finds that a relatively small number of factor endowments is able to explain significant variations in U.S. state production for twenty 2-digit manufacturing industries for 1880 and 1900 as well as later periods in the twentieth century. While these results do not rule out the importance of increasing returns, they suggest that natural advantages may have played a significant role in the rise of the manufacturing belt.

The emergence and persistence of the manufacturing belt was a significant phenomenon in U.S. economic history. It justly deserves greater attention by scholars. However, the declining importance of the manufacturing belt and the rapid convergence of regional industrial structures during the second half of the twentieth century should receive equal attention. Kim (1995) argues that the rise and decline of regional specialization, or the divergence and convergence of regional industrial structures, can be accounted for by changes in the factor mobility of factors and goods. As transportation costs of final goods relative to inputs fell between the nineteenth and early twentieth centuries, regions became more specialized in order to exploit their comparative advantage. During the second half of the twentieth century, as factors became increasingly more mobile relative to goods, and as new technologies such as electricity reduced the importance of regional differences in resources, regional industrial structures converged.

An alternative interpretation of the convergence of U.S. regional industrial structures is the core–periphery reversal [Krugman and Venables (1995), Puga (1999), Tabuchi (1998), Helpman (1998)] or the bell-shaped relationship discussed in Ottaviano and Thisse (2004). Assuming labor mobility throughout, as transportation costs fall low enough with any type of congestion in the core (or with limited mobility throughout), the core–periphery structure will reverse with industrial diffusion. However, at this point, we do not know of any empirical studies based on this theory.

2.3.2. Trends in U.S. regional incomes

In the colonial period, differences in regional income per capita seem to have been slight. While we do not have estimates of regional income per capita, we have estimates of regional wealth per capita. Using probate records, Jones (1980) finds that differences in wealth per capita were very small. In 1774, wealth estimates in pounds sterling for New England, Middle Colonies and the Southern colonies were £36.4, £40.2 and £35.4, respectively. However, the wealth per capita for the free population was significantly higher for the Southern colonies.

In the early nineteenth century, regional incomes diverged somewhat. Yet the divergence was not along North and South. Although income per capita in the Northeast was higher than the national average, it was highest in the West South Central region in 1840 and 1860 [see Table 1 and Fogel (1989)]. In the second half of the nineteenth century, Figure 3 shows that regional incomes diverged significantly, especially between the North and the South. Income per capita in the South fell sharply during the Civil War decade, absolutely and relative to other regions. Although there was some recovery after the initial decline, the pace was slow. By 1900, the income per capita of the South was barely half of the national average. However, during the second half of the twentieth century, regional incomes converged substantially [Easterlin (1960, 1961), Mitchener and McLean (1999)]. Although there are still regional differences, these are much smaller than before World War II, particularly in the case of the South.

Barro and Sala-i-Martin (1991) find that the convergence of U.S. regional income per capita in the twentieth century is consistent with the predictions of the neoclassical growth model. As predicted by the model, growth in income per capita was inversely correlated with initial incomes in 1880. However, there is no work in the growth literature that examines the divergence of U.S. regional income per capita in the late nineteenth century. While this divergence may be consistent with models of growth based

Table 1
Per capita income by region, 1840 and 1860 (in 1860 prices)

	Total population			Free population	
	1840	1860	1880	1840	1860
National average	$96	$128	$173	$109	$144
North	109	141	205	110	142
Northeast	129	181	244	130	183
North Central	65	89	170	66	90
South	74	103	88	105	150
South Atlantic	66	84	78	96	124
East South Central	69	89	88	92	124
West South Central	151	184	104	238	274

Source. Fogel (1989).

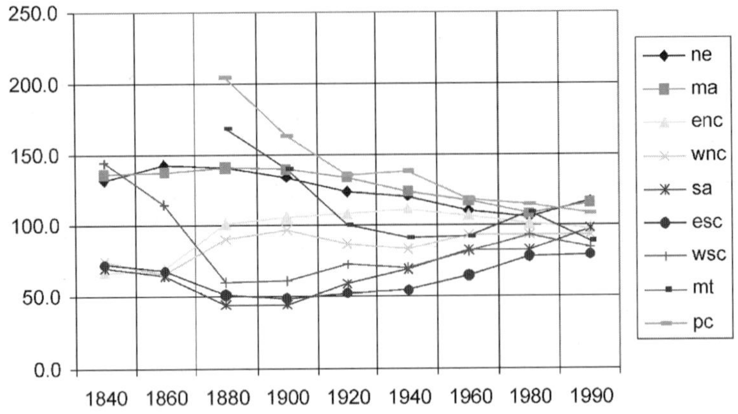

Figure 3. Regional income per capita, 1840–1990 (U.S. = 100). *Sources.* Easterlin (1960, 1961), Statistical Abstract of the U.S., various years. For a colour reproduction of this figure see the colour figures section, page 3072.

on increasing returns, scholars have not examined regional income per capita between 1860 and 1900 using this framework.

The divergence and convergence of regional industrial structures can potentially cause divergence and convergence of regional income per capita. To the extent that wages differ across industries, regional specialization in different industries may cause aggregate incomes to differ. Using a simple decomposition procedure, Kim (1998) finds that, while the level of importance varies with regions and time, the divergence and convergence of regional industrial structures are highly correlated with that of regional income per capita. Caselli and Coleman (2001) report similar findings with a more sophisticated decomposition procedure. In addition, these studies also show that differences in regional wages in identical industries also contributed to the divergence and convergence of regional incomes. However, this latter component is better explained by models of economic growth rather than economic geography.

For Krugman, the divergence and convergence of regional incomes are accounted for by transportation costs and increasing returns. When transportation costs fell, increasing returns in manufacturing led to the rise of the manufacturing belt where high-wage jobs were concentrated. However, Krugman and Venables (1995) show that when transportation costs fall even further, then regions eventually converge even when increasing returns are present. On the other hand, Kim (1998) and Caselli and Coleman (2001) present explanations for the divergence and convergence of regional incomes based on comparative advantage.[12] Caselli and Coleman suggest that the shift out of

[12] Kim's (1998) argument is outlined above. Caselli and Coleman (2001) present an interesting model based on the following assumptions: less than unit income elasticity of farm good demand, faster factor productivity growth in agriculture, and declining costs of acquiring non-farming skills.

agriculture in the South was aided by the declining costs of acquiring non-agricultural skills.[13]

However, most economic historians argue that the institution of slavery had a major impact on U.S. regional development over time. Slavery and its dissolution greatly influenced the productivity of agriculture in the South before and after the Civil War and, consequently on U.S. regional per capita incomes. The legacy of slavery and the Civil War led to an isolated labor market in the South and it contributed to poor educational infrastructure. Economic historians interpret the Civil War as a major negative shock that took many years to work through. Many economic historians also believe that the federal government played an important role in the integration of thc South into the national economy [Wright (1986)].

The causes of the decline in per capita incomes in the South have been extensively studied by economic historians. There is general agreement that the economic dislocation caused by the Civil War was responsible for at least some of the initial decline. Fogel and Engerman (1974, 1977) argue that slave labor was relatively efficient compared with free labor in the South, due to the use of the so-called "gang system" by slave owners. With the end of the War came emancipation and the end of slavery, and a once-and-for-all loss in productivity in southern agriculture [Fogel and Engerman (1974, 1977), Moen (1992)]. Other potential causes of the relative decline in southern income per capita incomes include a reduction in the rate of growth of the demand for southern cotton [Temin (1976)], as well as the possibility that per capita incomes in the South in 1860 may have been above their long-run trend [Wright (1979)].

Recent work by Margo (2003) has examined this issue from the perspective of regional wage gaps. Wright (1986) points out that, at the turn of the twentieth century, the South – particularly the South Atlantic – was a low-wage region in a high-wage country. The South ca. 1900 could have been low wage due to recent economic shocks. Or it could have been low-wage for some time – that is, predating the Civil War. Margo presents a variety of data on wages in the South relative to the North, before and after the Civil War. His results show that all three explanations have merit. Wages in the South Atlantic regions were below those in the North before the Civil War, although not in the South Central regions. Wages in the South also declined relative to the North in the 1890s, possibly due to a short-run decline in agricultural productivity. However, the data clearly show that the war left an imprint on the regional wage structure – as was true of per capita incomes, wages in the South declined sharply relative to the North between 1860 and 1870.

Why was convergence delayed so long? Economic historians have suggested several answers to this question. One answer emphasizes the "flawed" economic institutions

[13] Caselli and Coleman (2001) argue that the costs of acquiring education fell as reductions in transportation costs in rural areas allowed schools to exploit economies of scale, as school curricula was transformed in the early twentieth century, as life expectancy rose over time, and as desegregation improved the access to education for Blacks.

23% of the population was employed in mercantile or commercial activities, 24% in manufacturing, 50% in services and 4% in government.[14] Thus, despite the reputation of port cities as centers of mercantile activity, the industrial and service sectors were responsible for the majority of the labor force.

The cities in the colonial period arose along the eastern seaboard. Urban economists believe that port cities arise because of increasing returns and because geography bestowed on them lower transport costs.[15] However, few mainstream urban economists have examined the rise of port cities in the colonial period. Most of what is known about cities in this period derives from the work of historians. While these works are rarely guided by explicit economic theory, most scholars seem to believe that merchants became concentrated in cities to benefit from information spillovers. Merchants gathered regularly in coffee shops and exchanges to discuss market conditions in Europe and the West Indies.[16]

Most historians believe that port cities arose in places endowed with excellent harbors and access to a rich hinterland.[17] Due to high interregional transportation and communications costs, the size of the hinterland determined the size of a city's mercantile activity and the quality of the port determined the costs of transportation overseas Yet, while this thesis may explain the rise of cities like New York and Philadelphia in the Middle Colonies or even Boston in New England, it does not easily explain why there were no major cities in the Upper South, and why cities in New England were so numerous. The Chesapeake region had excellent navigable waters and a rich hinterland; on the other hand, New England's hinterland was relatively small.

Historians have proposed a variety of theories to explain the absence of cities in the Upper South, but the most attractive theory is based on colonial regulation of trade.[18] According to Price (1974), the lack of cities in the Chesapeake is accounted for by British regulation of tobacco trade. The Navigation Acts restricted exports of tobacco to England whereas similar restrictions did not apply for fish, wheat, corn, pork, beef, etc. In addition, regulations and high customs duties greatly restricted entry into the tobacco

[14] Also see Warner (1968).

[15] Fujita and Mori (1996) and Konishi (2000).

[16] See Albion (1939); also see Burrows and Wallace (1999).

[17] Boston, the largest port city in the U.S. until the mid-seventeenth century, possessed an excellent, deep, sheltered harbor, and a hinterland composed of coastal settlements from Cape Cod to Maine; Philadelphia, the premier city between the mid- to the end of the seventeenth century, possessed an excellent agricultural hinterland but a harbor subject to freezing in winter; New York, the foremost city from the early eighteenth century, possessed a harbor unparalleled as well as a rich agricultural hinterland [see Price (1974)].

[18] Two of the more prominent explanations for the lack of cities in the Upper South are the abundance of navigable waters in the Chesapeake and that tobacco required little processing [see Middleton (1953), Carville (1992)]. Neither of these explanations seem satisfactory. First, if mercantile activity in tobacco is subject to spillovers, then lower transportation costs should foster rather than deter the concentration of merchants in cities. Second, it is not clear that the processing of wheat or other crops was any more extensive than that of tobacco. In any case, forward linkages associated with wheat processing seems an unlikely explanation for significant agglomeration economies in Philadelphia or New York.

trade. For both of these reasons, a handful of merchants coordinated the tobacco trade from London and Glasgow rather than from cities in the Chesapeake.[19] By contrast, merchants in New York or Philadelphia exported their products to many markets, and entry into the business was relatively open. For these merchants, regular meetings in coffee houses provided valuable information spillovers on local and overseas market conditions as well as information on trustworthy contacts and potential partners.[20] Thus, when Baltimore and Alexandria and other cities arose in the Upper South in the mid-eighteenth century, their activity was based on wheat rather than on tobacco.[21]

Despite the fact that most scholars believe that port cities arose for mercantile reasons, the occupation structures of cities indicate that the number of merchants were equaled by artisans and surpassed by service workers. Urban artisans, working alone or with an apprentice, produced a wide variety of products such as barrels, kegs, bread, candles, soaps, etc. Why did artisans locate in cities? Historians and economists seem to rarely ask this question. The most likely answer is transportation costs. Due to high transportation costs, except for trade in export staples, most cities produced goods for local consumption. As local demand for manufactures grew, artisans emerged in cities to satisfy this demand. Services in cities, such as tavern and inn keeping, can be explained in a similar manner. Thus, the concentration of artisans and service workers added greatly to an urban economy, but these activities alone did not sustain an urban area during this period.

3.2. Urbanization and industrialization

In the United States, there was a strong correlation between industrialization and urbanization. While cities existed in the pre-industrial era, the rapid growth in the number and size of cities coincided with the development of a manufacturing economy. Moreover,

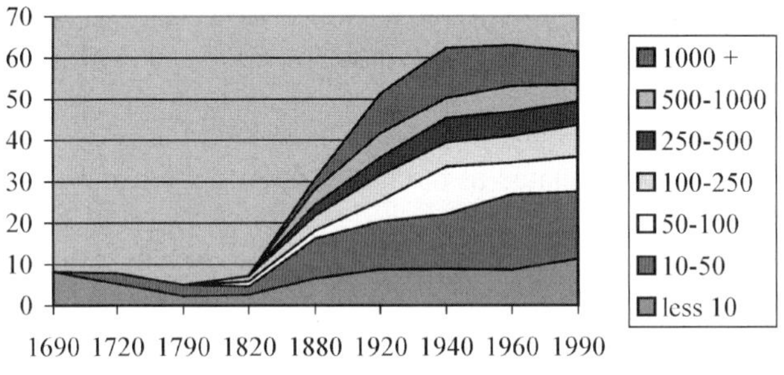

Figure 4. U.S. urban population by size, 1690–1990 (percent). *Sources*: see Table 2. City size is in thousands. For a colour reproduction of this figure see the colour figures section, page 3073.

[19] See Price and Clemens (1987).

[20] See Doerflinger (1986).

[21] See Klingaman (1969).

cities were concentrated in regions where industrialization began. Table 2 and Figure 4 show that in the early phase of industrialization, urban population grew from 7% in 1820 to 20% in 1860. Between 1820 and 1860, urban population grew by an average of 57% per decade. Moreover, the cities became significantly larger. In 1820, there was only one city with a population above 100,000; in 1860, there were 9. Throughout this period, New York remained the largest city with its population increasing from 123,706 to 805,651. The urban population in the first half of the nineteenth century was concentrated in the Northeast region where industrialization began. For these Northeastern cities, Williamson and Swanson (1966) find that manufacturing accounted for approximately 60% of the labor force during this period.

Did industrialization cause urbanization in the U.S.? The accepted view in the development literature is that urbanization and industrialization go hand in hand. Labor saving technological change combined with innovation and development of new manufactured and service products spur the growth of urban areas where products are most efficiently produced. However, did industrialization lead urbanization or vice versa?

While few studies examine this question directly, the existing literature hints at the possibility that industrialization led urbanization. First, the Goldin–Sokoloff hypothesis on U.S. early industrialization argues that industrialization first began in rural areas where the opportunity cost of women and children relative to men were low. Although the Goldin–Sokoloff model does not address the issue of industrialization and urbanization, the fact that industrialization is seen to arise in rural areas suggests that industrialization preceded urbanization. Thus, in the Northeast rural regions, cities arose as manufacturing developed in these areas.

Williamson's (1965) work on urban growth during early industrialization seems to confirm the view that industrialization led urbanization. If urbanization caused industrialization, then industrialization should take place in large urban areas which formed prior to industrialization. Moreover, larger cities rather than smaller cities or rural areas should industrialize and grow faster over time. However, contrary to expectations, Williamson (1965) finds that rates of urbanization converged rather than diverged between 1790 and 1890. During this period, rural areas urbanized more rapidly than the developed urban areas. In addition, according to Williamson and Swanson, urban growth was consistently unrelated to the initial size of cities and younger cities grew faster than older cities.

The U.S. became a mature industrial economy between the second half of the nineteenth and the early twentieth centuries. America also became an urban nation during this period. By 1920, more than half of the population lived in cities. In this period, based on a sample of cities, Weiss (1972) finds that slightly less than 50% of the labor force was engaged in manufacturing, 50% in services, and a tiny fraction in agriculture. The rise of an industrial economy was accompanied by the rise of the manufacturing belt as industrialization moved westward but not southward. Once again, as with early industrialization, there was high geographic correlation between later industrialization and urbanization as the urban population was highly concentrated in the industrial belt. In addition, the cities in this region were significantly more oriented toward manufacturing than those in other regions. The cities in the New England, Middle Atlantic and East North Central regions had twice the labor force allocated to manufacturing than that of cities in other regions.[22]

Despite the historical importance of urbanization during this period, the topic has received limited attention from economists and economic historians in recent years. The most widely shared interpretation of the rise of cities in this period is based on pecuniary and Marshallian externalities. Meyer (1983, 1988) emphasizes pecuniary externalities; for Meyer, the manufacturing belt is really an agglomeration of regional urban city systems. Ades and Glaeser (1999) find that initial development proxied by urbanization in 1850 was significantly correlated with later urban development. Thus, increasing returns led to divergent urban development. However, Ades and Glaeser find openness or the extension of markets was negatively correlated with urban growth.

Kim (2000) argues that the location of cities was largely driven by superior access to resources and that cities arose to take advantage of economies in local public goods and in transportation. A variety of factors suggest that the concentration of manufacturing cities in the industrial belt resulted from that region's comparative advantage in resources. First, the cities in the industrial belt were specialized in manufacturing. They had a significantly higher proportion of the labor force engaged in manufacturing than cities in other regions. Second, within the manufacturing sector, the cities were highly specialized in one or two industries and cities within a region tended to specialize in the same set of industries. City specialization in a few industries might signal the importance of localization economies, but it cannot explain why cities within regions tended to specialize in the same set of industries. Third, the rise of the Midwestern cities in the industrial belt was correlated with the growing importance of primary metals, machinery, and transportation industries.

3.3. Urbanization in the twentieth century

The pattern of urban development in the second half of the twentieth century differed in nature and scope from the industrial period (see Table 2 and Figure 4). First, the pace of urbanization slowed. The share of population in cities rose modestly from 51.2 to 61.6% between 1920 and 1990. Second, Table 3 and Figure 5 show that the urban population became increasingly more suburbanized in metropolitan areas; in 1940, there were 138 metropolitan areas in the U.S. which contained 51% of the U.S. population. However, in 1990, the number of metropolitan areas in the U.S. rose to 335 as did the share of population in these areas to 77.5%. In this period, the industrial structure of cities shifted dramatically into services. By the end of the twentieth century, the percentage of employment in services reached almost three times that of manufacturing [see Kolko (1999)].

The patterns of urbanization in the second half of the twentieth century exhibited marked regional convergence. The regional distribution of cities became more even as

[22] See Kim (2000).

Table 3
Number and population of metropolitan areas in the United States, 1940–1990

Size categories	1940	1960	1990
		Number of cities	
50,000–100,000	15	24	26
100,000–250,000	69	91	143
250,000–500,000	30	52	75
500,000–1,000,000	13	31	45
1,000,000+	11	24	46
Number	138	222	335
		Distribution of population (percent)	
50,000–100,000	1.0	1.1	0.9
100,000–250,000	16.9	8.2	9.1
250,000–500,000	8.3	9.7	10.6
500,000–1,000,000	6.9	12.0	13.1
1,000,000+	26.2	34.3	43.9
Total metropolitan	51.0	65.3	77.5
		Size of population (millions)	
Metropolitan population	67.1	116.6	192.9
U.S. population	131.7	178.5	248.7

Note. In general, the metropolitan area is a county or a group of contiguous counties (except in New England) which contains at least one central city of 50,000 inhabitants or more or "twin cities" with a combined population of at least 50,000. In New England, towns and cities are used in defining metropolitan areas.
Sources. County Data Book, 1947; Statistical Abstract of the U.S., 1965; Census of Population, 1990.

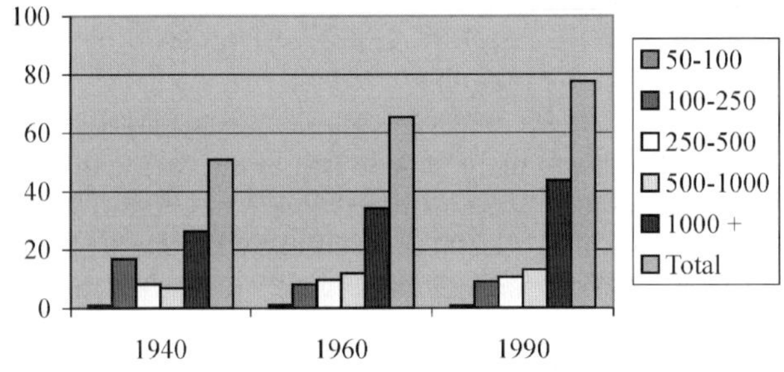

Figure 5. U.S. metropolitan population by size, 1940–1990 (percent). *Sources*: see Table 3. Metropolitan size is in thousands.

the shares fell in the Northeast and the Midwest and rose in the West. While economic structures of cities continued to differ by size, they converged rapidly across regions. Kim (1995, 2000) suggests that these trends, like those of regions, are roughly consistent with diminished differences in regional comparative advantage. During this period, regional input supplies became more similar as factors became more mobile and as technical advances reduced regional differences in inputs. The shift in industrial structure toward services further reduced the importance of differences in resources. Thus, the convergence of geographic differences in resources accounts for the convergence of city industrial structure as well as the convergence of the geographic distribution of cities across regions.

It is beyond the scope of this section to summarize the literature on modern twentieth century data. For excellent reviews, we refer the reader to Duranton and Puga (2004) and Rosenthal and Strange (2004). Since some kind of agglomeration economies are needed to generate cities, the literature on cities attempts to identify which sources of agglomeration economies are most important for urban development. Here, we highlight a few papers that possess long-run historical dimension. Two of these studies emphasize the role of Marshallian externalities. Simon and Nardinelli (2002) find that cities with higher levels of human capital in 1880 grew faster over the next one hundred years, suggesting the importance of knowledge spillovers. Beeson, DeJong and Troesken (2001) find that initial advantages have persistent results for a much longer period in U.S. history. However, Rappaport and Sachs (2001) argues that geography, especially access to coasts of both oceans and Great Lakes play an important role in explaining population distribution and density. Mitchener and McLean (2003) find that states with navigable waterways, large mineral endowment, and no slaves in 1860 had higher labor productivity levels between 1880 and 1980.

3.4. *Spatial structures of cities and metropolitan areas*

The land use patterns of U.S. urban areas have changed dramatically over time. In the colonial period, cities were small, compact and densely organized near the waterfront. Between the nineteenth and the mid-twentieth centuries, urban boundaries increased as outlying areas were annexed. However, cities generally became more dense as population migrated to cities and building density in downtowns rose. The land-use patterns of urban areas changed dramatically in the second half of the twentieth century. As population moved further away from city centers, outside traditional municipal boundaries, a new definition of urban areas emerged based on the metropolitan area. In this period, urban densities declined dramatically as density in city centers fell and as urban boundaries increased ever more outwards. In this section, we use the density gradient, which measures changes in density as one moves further away from the city center, and average density, defined simply as persons per square mile, to study the historical trends in urban spatial structures.

3.4.1. *Density gradients*

Due to data limitations, it is difficult to construct data on spatial structures of cities until the late nineteenth century. However, using federal census documents, tax records and the city directory for Philadelphia in 1790, Schweitzer (1993) was able to identify the locations of residence and occupation of a majority of inhabitants in Philadelphia in

1790. Schweitzer finds that the population density gradient was very steep and population densities were significantly lower just a few city blocks away from the waterfront on the Delaware River. Schweitzer also finds that there was significant spatial differentiation by socioeconomic groups. Most merchants lived near the waterfront, artisans were distributed throughout the city, the wealthy were clustered in an area known as the New Society Hill, and the poor were found everywhere but disproportionately present in the outskirts of the city.

One of the most striking empirical regularities in urban economics is the consistent decline in density gradients of cities over time. Mills (1972) finds that density gradients of four metropolitan areas, Baltimore, Milwaukee, Philadelphia, and Rochester, declined more or less monotonically over time between 1880 and 1963.[23] Macauley (1985) estimates that, for a sample of 18 metropolitan areas, density gradients in population and employment for manufacturing, retailing, wholesaling and services all tended to decline over the twentieth century. Similar trends are found by Edmonston (1975) for a larger sample of metropolitan areas as well as for the same sample of cities as Mills.

The Alonso–Muth–Mills monocentric city model provides a number of possible explanations as to why urban population or employment might eventually decentralize or why the density gradient might fall. According to this model, households choose where to reside within an urban area, given their tastes for housing versus other goods. To make this concrete, imagine that households maximize a utility function $U(h, x, t)$ where $h =$ housing services, $x =$ a composite commodity, and $t =$ leisure. The budget constraint is $p(r)h + x = A + w(T - cr - t)$, where $p(r)$ is the price of housing at distance r from the central business district (CBD), A is non-labor income, T is the household's time endowment, w is the wage per unit of time, and c is time spent commuting per unit of distance r from the CBD. Employment in this model is concentrated in the CBD but households may choose to live at various points r from the CBD. The model can readily accommodate fixed or variable monetary costs of commuting but for our purposes it is not necessary to include these.

In this model the variable r serves as the indicator of "suburbanization" because higher values of r correspond to distances further from the urban "core" (the CBD). The first order condition for r is $p'h = -wc$. This equation will hold at non-zero values of r because the slope of the pricing function, p', is negative – housing price declines as distance r from the CBD increases. In choosing its optimal location, each household trades off a lower price of housing versus higher commuting costs.

If housing is a normal good – and all empirical studies suggest that it is – it is straightforward to demonstrate that $\mathrm{d}r/\mathrm{d}A > 0$. That is, an increase in non-labor income will cause the household to live further away from the CBD – to suburbanize. The demand for housing increases (because A has increased), and the household chooses optimally

[23] Mills' (1972) estimate of Philadelphia's density gradient for the late nineteenth century is considerably lower than that of the other three cities. However, Mills believes that the low estimate may have been due to problems with data construction associated with Philadelphia.

to locate further away where housing price is lower. However, an increase in w has off-setting income and substitution effects. The income effect of an increase in w is the same as the effect of an increase in A, as long as housing is a normal good. But the substitution effect goes in the opposite direction because a higher wage means a higher time cost of commuting. If the income effect outweighs the substitution effect, an increase in w will imply an increase in r, that is, a distance further from the CBD.

In the Alonso–Muth–Mills model, higher income households choose to suburbanize because they demand more housing relative to other goods, and the relative price of housing of land is cheaper at locations that are distant from the CBD than at locations that are close in. Of course, there may be other reasons why higher income households choose to live in the suburbs. It is possible, for example, that suburban local governments might be more efficient at providing local public goods, such as education, and these goods could be income-elastic. Models of jurisdictional "sorting" – the archetype being the Tiebout model – imply that households sort across local governments on the basis of their demands for local public goods. Such sorting may be reinforced by "peer group" effects – the quality of the local public schools, for example, may be affected by socioeconomic backgrounds of the students that attend them.

The existence of a density gradient for Philadelphia in 1790 presents a puzzle for the monocentric city model. In that model, the density gradient is generated by the commuting choice of households. However, in this period, very few people commuted to work. Most people worked where they lived. Thus, it is more likely that the density gradient was caused by the fact that businesses found it desirable to locate near the waterfront on the Delaware River [see Fujita and Ogawa (1982), Berliant, Peng and Wang (2002), Lucas and Rossi-Hansberg (2002), and Rossi-Hansberg (2002) for possible explanations].

The decline in the density gradient or the decentralization of employment and population, especially in the second half of the twentieth century, is often attributed to developments in transportation and rising incomes. Glaeser and Kahn (2004) argue that the adoption of automobiles and trucks fundamentally transformed how Americans live and work in the latter half of the twentieth century. Automobiles and trucks lowered transportation costs and, just as importantly, eliminated fixed costs associated with rail depots and ports. The decline in agglomeration economies associated with these fixed costs enabled firms and households to decentralize and organize their activities around a more dispersed environment.

Margo (1992) finds that rising incomes also played an important role in suburbanization. Margo uses the public use sample of the 1950 census, which provides information on household and personal characteristics, including whether households living in metropolitan areas reside in central cities or suburban rings. Margo estimates a cross-sectional logistic regression of the probability of suburban residence as a function of household characteristics, including household income, which is instrumented. The model is identified by assuming that education and industry of employment affect income, but do not otherwise (that is, independently) affect the likelihood of a suburban residence. The estimated coefficient on income in this regression is positive and highly significant.

Using this coefficient in conjunction with the mean growth of real household income between 1950 and 1980, Margo predicts that the percent suburbanized should have increased by 7.4 percentage points. The actual increase was 17.5 percentage points (from 42.7 to 60.2 percent). Thus, according to Margo's calculation, changes in income account for about 43 percent of suburbanization over the 1950 to 1980 period. It is likely that this estimate is biased upwards, for several reasons. First, education and industry may not be proper instruments. For example, education may have a direct impact on the likelihood of a suburban residence, if better-educated parents value their children's schooling, and suburban schools, as most studies indicate, are superior in quality to urban schools. Similarly, industry may have a direct effect on the likelihood of suburban residence, if industries differ in their ability to substitute land for other inputs. As a result, some industries locate further away from the CBD than others, and their workers follow suit.

Second, as Margo (1992, p. 308) notes, some central cities expanded their boundaries by annexing suburban areas after 1950. Had jurisdictional boundaries remained constant between 1950 and 1980, the increase in the proportion suburbanizing after 1950 would have greater than 17.5 percentage points. Third, Margo's calculation is partial equilibrium. In particular, it does not take into account induced effects on price of housing in the suburbs relative to central cities. These effects are positive – house values should [and did, see Collins and Margo (2002)] rise in the suburbs relative to the central cities, dampening the incentive to suburbanize due to rising incomes.

It is important to recognize that Margo's calculation does not identify precisely why higher income households suburbanize. This could be because of the causal mechanism identified by the Alonso–Muth–Mills model, or it could be for some other reason. Glaeser, Kolko and Saiz (2001) argue, in fact, that the reason emphasized in the Alonso–Mills model – land prices – is not the reason why "[t]he poor live in cities". Rich people, Glaeser et al., agree, do have a higher demand for land than poor people, but the income elasticity of the demand for land is not high enough to explain the positive association between income and suburban residence. Poor people, their argument continues, live in cities because the poor place a high value on public transportation. In Glaeser et al.'s modification of the Alonso–Mill's model, the marginal monetary cost of public transportation is cheap, but the fixed and time costs are large relative to automobile transport.

3.4.2. *Urban densities*

While the density gradient and other measures of decentralization are informative, we believe that a study of simple average density of cities provides a fuller picture of urban spatial structures. Shammas (2000) finds that colonial cities were compact and dense. In 1800, data on sample of four cities (Philadelphia, New York, Baltimore and Boston) indicate that each city consisted of less than 2 square miles of area. Population densities of these cities ranged from Boston's 20,781 to Philadelphia's 45,800 persons per square mile. The differences in population densities in these cities reflected their differences in housing lot sizes. It appears that Philadelphia's high density relative to other cities was due to its relatively small house lot sizes. While Philadelphians averaged 7.1 compared to Boston's 8.7 persons per dwelling, Philadelphia's house lot sizes only averaged 1392 square feet as compared to Boston's 3441.

Unfortunately, systematic information on urban land areas is available only from 1890 onwards with the publication of the *Social Statistics of Cities*. Kim (2002) finds that urban densities rose and fell between the late nineteenth and the twentieth centuries. Between 1890 and 1950, average population density rose from 7230 to 8876 persons per square mile for a consistent sample of cities whose population was greater than 25,000

Table 4
Population and employment densities of cities, 1890–1990

	Number of cities	Average population (sq. miles)	Average area	Average population density
1890	122	113,835	16.7	7648
1900	160	123,243	20.2	7377
1910*	184	148,442	23.1	7176
1920*	252	145,966	20.9	7597
1930*	310	152,890	21.9	7366
1940	412	128,051	19.2	6742
1950	481	128,811	19.5	6536
1960	673	112,400	22.8	5340
1970	835	104,785	28.5	4673
1980	944	97,756	32.8	3998
1990	1068	98,108	34.9	3783

Note. The data, except for years 1910–1930, are for cities with population over 25,000. In 1890, two cities were omitted due to lack of data on land area. Cities in Alaska and Hawaii are excluded.
Sources. Social Statistics of Cities, 1890; Census of Population, 1900; Financial Statistics of Cities, 1910, 1920, 1930; County and City Data Book, 1949, 1952, 1962, 1972, 1982, 1988, 1994.
*Data for 1910–1930 are for cities with population over 30,000.

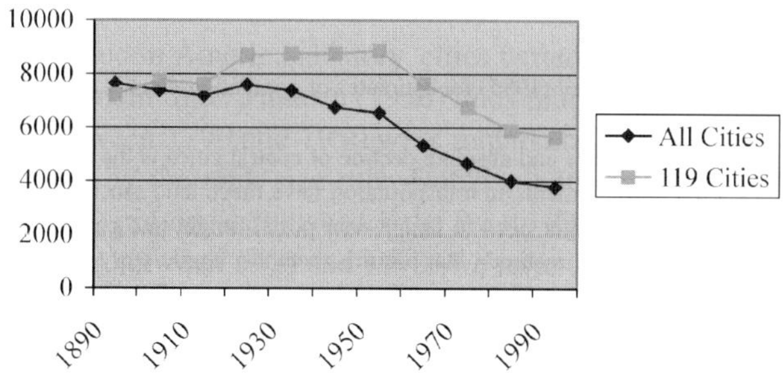

Figure 6. Population density of cities, 1890–1990 (persons per square mile). *Sources*: see Kim (2002). For a colour reproduction of this figure see the colour figures section, page 3073.

transportation nodes.[26] Weiman (1988) argues that the initial growth of Atlanta was due to its strategic location at the intersection of three railroads, but that its emergence as a regional metropolis was accounted for its development as a mercantile and financial center that cleared regional transactions. Odell and Weiman (1988) suggest that the founding of the Federal Reserve Banks in Dallas and Atlanta was due to their positions as regional centers of commerce and finance in the Lower South.

Why do cities lower the costs of trade? Every trade must overcome two types of costs: transportation and information. Since goods are traded over space, they must incur transportation costs. In addition, specialization reduces the information set of agents. As compared to a more self-sufficient economy, information on demand and supply are geographically more dispersed. Specialization also exacerbates the problems of asymmetric information where sellers are more informed about the quality of their product than the buyers. The concentration of merchants, exchanges, insurance firms, lawyers, judges, etc. in larger cities lowers the costs of trade by providing better market information on supply and demand for goods and by solving the asymmetric information problem.[27] Kim (2000) finds that the size distribution of cities is partly explained by the concentration of transaction services in the larger cities.

William Cronon's (1991) *Nature's Metropolis* provides an excellent illustration on the role of markets in causing the rise of Chicago. While Cronon's work is loosely based on Christaller's (1966) central place theory, scholars find his distinction between "first nature" (natural landscape) and "second nature" (human actions) particularly useful. Cronon argues that the growth of Chicago was due as much to "second nature" than to "first nature".[28] Although Cronon's definition of "second nature" is rather all encompassing, many urban scholars like Krugman (1996) have interpreted "second nature" as indicating the importance of increasing returns that is often self-reinforcing. Cronon's various case studies of wheat, lumber, meat, capital and reapers provide us with a good sense of what he means by "second nature".

While each case study is somewhat idiosyncratic, the case of wheat is illustrative. There is no doubt that Chicago was endowed with a rich hinterland west of the Great

[26] See Cain (1985).

[27] Ogawa and Fujita (1980) and Imai (1980) provide models of agglomeration based on the exchange of information. In their model, firms own bits of information and due to its public goods nature, the benefits of face to face communications rise with the number of firms. In their model, communication is costly as the exchange of information requires organization and time [see Fujita and Thisse (2002)].

[28] Cronon (1991, pp. 56–57) writes: "A kind of 'second nature', designed by people and 'improved' toward human ends, gradually emerged atop the original landscape that nature – 'first nature' – had created such an inconvenient jumble. Despite the subtly differing logic that lay behind each, the geography of second nature was in its own way as compelling as the geography of first nature, so boosters and others often forgot the distinction between them. Both seemed quite 'natural'. Nowhere was this more true than in the new artificial transportation technologies that changed the ways people and commodities moved back and forth between city and country... Second nature defined the corridors of commerce at least as much as first nature."

Lakes for growing wheat. Without first nature, no wheat would flow to Chicago.[29] However, St. Louis, not Chicago, was the major destination of wheat when transportation was based on water. The "second nature" advantages of Chicago were tied to the coming of the railroads. The railroads and the steam-powered grain elevator fundamentally changed how wheat was transported. Under the water-based marketing system, wheat was transported as sacks of grain; under the railroad-based system, grain was shipped freely in carloads. The railroad, as compared to water transportation, enjoyed significant economies of scale and labor-saving benefits.[30]

Yet, while the increase in productivity of transportation and storage may explain why grain was shipped to Chicago rather than to St. Louis, it does not explain why grain was shipped to these cities in the first place. Why did farmers not simply sell their products to merchants or consumers in the cities of final destination? Why did wheat move through Chicago or St. Louis?

Cronon's answer is "second nature". "By imposing their own order and vocabulary on the world of first nature, the city's traders invented a world of second nature in which they could buy and sell grain as commodity almost independently from grain as crop" [Cronon (1991, p. 146)]. Once quality was assured with the adoption of a standard grading system by the Chicago Board of Trade, buyers and sellers across the country could trade grain without sampling it in advance. In addition, the concentration of grain exchanges in Chicago meant that the posted trading prices provided instant information on grain market conditions of the entire nation.

3.6. Urbanization and inventive activity

The industrialization of the U.S. economy was accompanied by a significant increase in inventive activity. Sokoloff (1988) finds that the expansion of markets brought on by canals in the early nineteenth century significantly increased inventive activity. Sokoloff and Kahn (1990) show that the growth of inventive activity in this period was due to inventions of ordinary citizens with common skills and knowledge. However, Kahn and Sokoloff and Lamoreaux and Sokoloff (1999) find that, over time, more and more inventors became career specialists who produced patents that were sold or leased. Thus, unlike during the second half of the twentieth century when research and development was mostly done by firms in-house, Lamoreaux and Sokoloff find that most patented inventions in the late nineteenth and the early twentieth centuries were traded in the marketplace.

[29] Lumber illustrates the primacy of first nature. When the supply of white pines from its hinterland diminished, Chicago's wholesale market in lumber declined as well. In addition, unlike grain, Chicago's advantages in the lumber trade were linked to transporting timber via the Great Lakes rather than railroads.

[30] Cronon (1991, pp. 113–114) writes: "The economic benefits of such efficient handling were so great that moving a bushel of grain from railroad car to lake vessel cost only half a cent, giving Chicago a more than tenfold advantage over St. Louis." According to Cronon, St. Louis did not construct grain elevators until the end of the Civil War because, unlike the railroad owners, river interests faced high coordination costs and because the changing height of the Mississippi River made it impractical to build one on the levee.

Inventive activity was concentrated in urban areas. In the early nineteenth century, Pred (1973) finds that the three largest cities, New York, Philadelphia, and Boston were responsible for over 20% of all patents granted [also see Feller (1971)]. However, while Sokoloff (1988) also finds that per capita patenting rates were significantly higher in urban areas during this period, he also notes that patenting was concentrated in the Southern New England and New York regions, and that both urban and rural places in these regions had disproportionately higher rates of patenting than elsewhere. In the late nineteenth and the early twentieth centuries, Lamoreaux and Sokoloff (1999) show that patents were concentrated in the New England, Middle Atlantic and the East North Central regions and that per capita patenting rates were positively correlated with city size.

The concentration of inventive and innovative activities in urban areas is often interpreted as providing evidence for the importance of information spillovers in generating new ideas. Lamoreaux and Sokoloff (1999) write that the concentration of patent agents and attorneys and the availability of a wide array of publications such as the Scientific American promoted the diffusion of technological knowledge in the Northeast and in urban centers. However, an alternative explanation is also possible. Patent agents and patent attorneys were intermediaries who facilitated trade in inventions, and like other intermediaries, it is not surprising that they were concentrated in urban areas. However, why should inventors reside in cities if not for information spillovers? Lamoreaux and Sokoloff note that it was not a simple matter for inventors to obtain property rights to their inventions. Potential ideas had to be shepherded through the Patent Office application process and then protected in court in cases of infringement. Thus, inventors may have chosen to locate near patent agents and lawyers because access to these intermediaries lowered the costs of securing property rights to their inventions as well as lowering the transactions costs of marketing their inventions.

3.7. *Urbanization and productivity*

Direct historical information linking urban locations to productivity are minimal. In his study of economies of scale in antebellum manufacturing, Sokoloff (1984) finds that firms located in more urbanized counties had higher levels of total factor productivity. Using a sample of manufacturing firms from the 1880 census, Atack, Bateman and Margo (2003) find that urban establishments were more productive, all other factors held constant, than rural establishments.

There is a considerable body of evidence showing that, throughout most of U.S. history, urban wages were higher – sometimes markedly so – in nominal terms than rural wages. Sokoloff and Villaflor (1992) find that in the New England and Middle Atlantic regions, wages were higher in urban than rural areas for various years between 1820 and 1860. However, the urban–rural wage gap declined over this period. In 1820 and 1842, nominal wages were 15–20% higher in urban rather than in rural counties. In 1850, the urban–rural wage gap declined to 10% and, by 1860, the gap was insignificant. Furthermore, Goldin and Sokoloff (1984) find that in the early nineteenth century male wages were positively correlated with urbanization but that female wages were negatively correlated. It appears that female workers who were employed in large textile mills near waterpower sites earned relatively higher wages. For the late nineteenth century, Atack, Bateman and Margo (2000) find that nominal urban wages, based on data from samples from the decennial census manuscripts of manufacturing, were significantly higher than non-urban areas in 1850 and 1880. Moreover, the data indicate that the urban–rural wage gap increased over this period.

For the twentieth century, using data on a sample of cities from every decade between 1900 and 1990, Dobkins and Ioannides (2000) find that population size was significantly correlated with nominal wages. More specifically, they find that after controlling for individual, time and regional effects, a 10% increase in population was associated with a 1% increase in wages. Glaeser and Maré (2001) find that wages in large cities are 33% higher than outside metropolitan areas in 1990.

While economic historians have documented the urban–rural wage gap, few have attempted to explain the causes of this gap for the nineteenth and the early twentieth centuries. While most scholars believe that the urban wage premium is due to the higher productivity of urban workers, it is important to establish the sources of these productivity gains. It is also important to rule out the alternative hypothesis that the urban–rural wage gap is simply caused by the fact the more able workers choose to live in cities. In the early nineteenth century, Sokoloff (1984) finds that employees in urban firms may have been more productive because larger markets led to greater division of labor. In the twentieth century, Glaeser and Maré (2001) suggest that urban workers were more productive because cities enabled workers to accumulate more human capital.

3.8. Urbanization and health

The industrialization and urbanization of the U.S. economy between the early nineteenth and turn of the twentieth centuries were associated with significant increases in productivity and real wages. Yet, despite the fact that income per capita rose over this period, the average quality of health for Americans declined markedly over this period. The heights of native-born males, as well as life expectancy, fell between 1830 and 1890 and recovered to 1830 levels only by 1930.[31] Since health is an important component of human welfare, Costa and Steckel (1995) estimate that the overall welfare of Americans may have stagnated or fallen between 1830 and 1890.

Economic historians suspect that much of the decline in health was associated with urbanization. Unfortunately, the U.S. economy industrialized and urbanized prior to the invention of modern medicine and public health. People living in high density areas were subject to greater exposure to infectious and parasitic diseases, both respiratory (air-borne) and gastrointestinal (water-borne). Consequently, the health of urban Americans was much worse than their rural counterparts. In 1900, Haines (2001) finds that

[31] See Fogel (1986) and Costa and Steckel (1995).

life expectancy of urban Americans was 10 years less than rural Americans. In 1880, Higgs (1979) finds that the urban mortality rate was 50% higher than rural mortality; in 1890 and 1900, Condran and Crimmins (1980) finds that the urban–rural differential was 27 and 18%, respectively. The urban–rural mortality differential was even more significant for infants and young children. For infants, excess urban mortality was 63 and 49% in 1890 and 1900, respectively, and for young children aged one to four, the figures were 107 and 97%, respectively. Furthermore, Costa (2000) finds that exposure to diseases at early ages may have had long-term health consequences. Costa finds that Union Army veterans who grew up in large cities faced much higher mortality rates at older ages.

The urban–rural differentials in health and mortality began to decline and reverse over the twentieth century. By around 1940, it was sometimes healthier to reside in urban rather than in rural areas. Scholars attribute the decline and elimination of excess urban mortality to improved public works such as sewers and water systems and advances in public health and medicine [Haines (2001)]. However, the transition to a healthier urban environment did not occur without complications. In 1897, half of all municipalities installed lead pipes to deliver water. Troesken (2003) finds that municipalities which used lead water pipe systems experienced higher rates of infant mortality and stillbirths by 25 and 50%, respectively.

3.9. Immigration and urbanization

Since the early nineteenth century, immigrants have been concentrated in cities, especially in the North [Ward (1971)]. By 1890, Easterlin (1972) shows that 53% of the urban population was foreign born and the presence of foreign born seems to be positively correlated with city sizes [see Thompson and Whelpton (1933)]. In contrast, 75% of native Whites lived in rural areas in 1890. Moreover, within cities, immigrants tended to live in close geographic proximity, forming distinctive ethnic neighborhoods, especially in the larger cities.

Why are the foreign born more attracted to urban areas than natives? Why do immigrants form ethnic enclaves? Borjas (1995) argues that ethnic neighborhoods in cities arise because of ethnic specific externalities that are captured by residents who live in close proximity. While the process by which ethnic externalities are transmitted is not well understood, Borjas suggests that ethnic spillovers foster the accumulation of human capital that raises the productivity of workers.

4. Conclusion

The most important lesson that emerges from this review of U.S. economic geography from a historical perspective is that economic geography is fundamentally linked to the process of economic development. While no overwhelming consensus emerges on the causal relationship between economic geography and development, the review highlights the enormous advances made on this subject by economic historians in recent decades.

From a regional perspective, while there is continued debate on the exact causes, it is now widely believed that the westward migration was caused by higher productivity of labor in the West. Moreover, the work on early industrialization and slavery enhance our understanding of when and why U.S. regions diverged and converged. It appears that regional divergence began in the early nineteenth century as the Northeast began to industrialize. Yet, in the antebellum period, due to the relatively high productivity of Southern agriculture under slavery, the divergence was not fully reflected in the regional income per capita. In the postbellum period, regional divergence was felt even more keenly due to the elimination of slavery in the South. However, despite the important impact of slavery on regional incomes, the root cause of the divergence and convergence of U.S. regional economies is likely to be related to the development of an industrial and post-industrial society.

From an urban perspective, the review indicates that cities have come full circle. In the colonial period, as is today, urban activities are largely based on services. However, the rise of an urban society was due to the rise of industrial cities. Urbanization was significantly correlated with industrialization over time and across space. The number and size of cities rose with industrialization and cities were geographically concentrated in areas where industrialization began and spread. The spatial structures of cities changed markedly over time. Scholars find that the changes in land-use patterns are explained by falling commuting costs and rising incomes. We also have a much better understanding of what factors differentiate urban from rural areas. Inventive activity, productivity, nominal wages, immigrants, government, and entertainment all favor urban areas. However, urbanization was not always associated with positive developments. Because urbanization occurred prior to advances in modern medicine, urbanization was associated with a significant decline in the health of Americans.

The review also highlights a number of interesting puzzles and many important areas that remain relatively unexplored. In the colonial period, even prior to industrialization, why were cities and towns more abundant in New England and relatively absent in the Chesapeake? Why is there a rent gradient in 1790 Philadelphia when people did not commute to work? If industrialization and urbanization were associated with a significant deterioration of health, why did rural Americans migrate to urban areas in significant numbers? What are the causal relationships between industrialization and urbanization? If industrialization preceded urbanization, what kinds of agglomeration economies in manufacturing led to urbanization? In later industrialization, what forces led to the rise of the manufacturing belt and why did its importance decline in the twentieth century? Additionally, are cities, as argued by Glaeser, Kolko and Saiz (2001), becoming consumer cities?

Finally, we point to two neglected areas of research. First, few works have systematically examined the relationship between demography and economic geography [see Costa and Kahn (2000)]. The long-run changes in population, fertility, mortality, life expectancy, family size and income are likely to have major impact on how Americans organize their spatial environment. Second, the role of political economy on the location of economic activities is not well understood. Recent work by Holmes (1998) suggests that state policies have an important impact on the location of industries. However, we know very little how the long-run changes in the political economy of the federal, state and local governments influenced the evolution of the economic geography of the United States.

Acknowledgements

We thank Vernon Henderson and participants at the North American Regional Science Association meetings in Puerto Rico for their comments.

References

Ades, A., Glaeser, E. (1999). "Evidence on growth, increasing returns, and the extent of the market". Quarterly Journal of Economics, 1025–1045.

Albion, R. (1939). The Rise of New York Port, 1815–1860. Scribner's, New York.

Atack, J., Margo, R. (1998). " 'Location, location, location!' The price gradient for vacant urban land: New York, 1835 to 1900". Journal of Real Estate Finance and Economics 16, 151–172.

Atack, J., Bateman, F., Margo, R. (2000). "Rising wage dispersion across American manufacturing establishments, 1850–1880". NBER Working Paper No. 7932.

Atack, J., Bateman, F., Margo, R. (2003). "Productivity in manufacturing and the length of the working day: Evidence from the 1880 Census of Manufactures". Explorations in Economic History. In press.

Barro, R., Sala-i-Martin, X. (1991). "Convergence across states and regions". Brookings Papers in Economic Activities 1, 107–182.

Beeson, P., DeJong, D., Troesken, W. (2001). "Population growth in U.S. counties, 1840–1990". Regional Science and Urban Economics 31, 669–699.

Berliant, M., Peng, S.-K., Wang, P. (2002). "Production externalities and urban configurations". Journal of Economic Theory. In press.

Black, D., Henderson, J.V. (2002). "Urban evolution in the USA". Mimeo.

Blanchard, O., Katz, L. (1992). "Regional evolutions". Brookings Papers on Economic Activity 1, 1–75.

Bodenhorn, H., Rockoff, H. (1992). "Regional interest rates in antebellum America". In: Goldin, C., Rockoff, H. (Eds.), Strategic Factors in Nineteenth Century American Economic Growth. Cambridge Univ. Press, Cambridge, UK.

Borjas, G. (1995). "Ethnicity, neighborhoods, and human-capital externalities". American Economic Review, 365–390.

Bridenbaugh, C. (1938). Cities in the Wilderness. The Ronald Press.

Burrows, E., Wallace, M. (1999). Gotham: A History of New York City to 1898. Oxford Univ. Press, London.

Cain, L. (1985). "William Dean's theory of urban growth: Chicago's commerce and industry, 1854–1871". Journal of Economic History 45.

Carville, E. (1992). Geographical Inquiry and American Historical Problems. Stanford Univ. Press, Stanford, CA.

Caselli, F., Coleman, W.J. (2001). "The U.S. structural transformation and regional convergence: A reinterpretation". Journal of Political Economy 109, 584–616.

Chatterjee, S., Carlino, G.A. (2001). "Aggregate metropolitan employment growth and the deconcentration of metropolitan employment". Journal of Monetary Economics 48, 549–583.

Christaller, W. (1966). The Central Places of Southern Germany. Prentice Hall, New York.

Coehlo, P., Shepherd, J. (1976). "Regional differences in real wages: The United States, 1851–1880". Explorations in Economic History 13, 203–230.

Coffman, C., Gregson, M.E. (1998). "Railroad development and land values". The Journal of Real Estate Finance and Economics 16, 191–204.

Collins, W.J. (1997). "When the Tide turned: immigration and the delay of the Great Black Migration". Journal of Economic History 57, 607–632.

Collins, W.J., Margo, R.A. (2002). "Race and the value of owner-occupied housing, 1940–1990". Regional Science and Urban Economics 33, 255–286.

Condran, G., Crimmins, E. (1980). "Mortality differentials between rural and urban areas of states in Northeastern United States, 1890–1900". Journal of Historical Geography 6, 179–202.

Costa, D. (2000). "Understanding mid-life and older age mortality declines: Evidence from Union Army veterans". NBER Working Paper No. 8000.

Costa, D., Kahn, M. (2000). "Power couples: Changes in the locational choice of the college educated 1940–1990". Quarterly Journal of Economics 115, 1287–1315.

Costa, D., Steckel, R. (1995). "Long-term trends in health, welfare, and economic growth in the United States". NBER Historical Paper No. 76.

Craig, L.A., Palmquist, R.B., Weiss, T. (1998). "Transportation improvements and land values in the antebellum United States: A hedonic approach". The Journal of Real Estate Finance and Economics 16, 173–189.

Cronon, W. (1991). Nature's Metropolis. Norton, New York.

Davis, L. (1965). "The investment market, 1870–1914: The emergence of a national market". Journal of Economic History 25, 355–393.

Dobkins, L., Ioannides, Y. (2000). "Dynamic evolution of the size distribution of U.S. cities". In: Huriot, J.-M., Thisse, J.-F. (Eds.), Economics of Cities. Cambridge Univ. Press, Cambridge, UK.

Doerflinger, T. (1986). A Vigorous Spirit of Enterprise: Merchants and Economic Development in Revolutionary Philadelphia. Univ. of North Carolina Press, Chapel Hill.

Duranton, G., Puga, D. (2004). "Micro-foundations of urban agglomeration economies". In: Henderson, J.V., Thisse, J.-F. (Eds.), Handbook of Regional and Urban Economics, vol. 4. Elsevier, Amsterdam, pp. 2063–2117. This volume.

Easterlin, R. (1960). "Interregional differences in per capita income, population, and total income, 1840–1950". In: Parker, W. (Ed.), Trends in the American Economy in the Nineteenth Century. Princeton Univ. Press, Princeton, NJ.

Easterlin, R. (1961). "Regional income trends, 1840–1950". In: Harris, S. (Ed.), American Economic History. McGraw–Hill, New York.

Easterlin, R. (1972). "Population". In: Davis, L., et al. (Eds.), American Economic Growth. Harper & Row, New York.

Edel, M., Sclar, E. (1979). "The distribution of real estate value changes: Metro Boston, 1870–1970". Journal of Urban Economics 2, 366–387.

Edmonston, B. (1975). Population Distribution in American Cities. Lexington Books.

Feller, I. (1971). "The urban location of United States invention, 1860–1910". Explorations in Economic History 8, 285–304.

Ferrie, J. (1997). "Migration to the frontier in mid-nineteenth century America: A re-examination of Turner's 'safety-valve' ". Department of Economics, Northwestern University Manuscript.

Fishlow, A. (2000). "Internal transportation in the nineteenth and early twentieth centuries". In: Engerman, S., Gallman, R. (Eds.), Cambridge Economic History of the United States, vol. II. (Cambridge Univ. Press, Cambridge, UK.

Fogel, R. (1964). Railroads and American Economic Growth. Johns Hopkins Univ. Press.

Fogel, R. (1986). "Nutrition and the decline in mortality since 1700: Some preliminary findings". In: Engerman, S., Gallman, R. (Eds.), Long-Term Factors in American Economic Growth. Univ. of Chicago Press, Chicago.

Fogel, R. (1989). Without Consent or Contract. Norton, New York.

Fogel, R., Engerman, S. (1974). Time on the Cross. Little, Brown, Boston.

Fogel, R., Engerman, S. (1977). "Explaining the relative efficiency of slave agriculture in the Antebellum South". American Economic Review 67 (3), 275–296.

Fogel, R., Rutner, J. (1972). "Efficiency effects of federal land policy, 1850–1900". In: Aydelotte, W., et al. (Eds.), Dimensions of Quantitative Research in Economic History. Princeton Univ. Press, Princeton, NJ.

Fujita, M., Mori, T. (1996). "The role of port in the making of major cities: Self-organization and hub-effects". Journal of Development Economics 49, 93–120.

Fujita, M., Ogawa, H. (1982). "Multiple equilibria and structural transition of non-monocentric urban configurations". Regional Science and Urban Economics 12, 161–196.

Fujita, M., Thisse, J.-F. (2002). Economics of Agglomeration. Cambridge Univ. Press, Cambridge, UK.

Gabaix, X., Ioannides, Y. (2004). "Evolution of city size distribution". In: Henderson, J.V., Thisse, J.-F. (Eds.), Handbook of Regional and Urban Economics, vol. 4. Elsevier, Amsterdam, pp. 2341–2378. This volume.

Galenson, D.W., Pope, C. (1992). "Precedence and wealth: Evidence from nineteenth-century Utah". In: Goldin, C., Rockoff, H. (Eds.), Strategic Factors in Nineteenth Century American Economic History. Univ. of Chicago Press, Chicago.

Gin, A., Sonstelie, J. (1992). "The streetcar and residential location in nineteenth-century Philadelphia". Journal of Urban Economics 22, 92–107.

Glaeser, E., Kahn, M. (2004). "Sprawl and urban growth". In: Henderson, J.V., Thisse, J.-F. (Eds.), Handbook of Regional and Urban Economics, vol. 4. Elsevier, Amsterdam, pp. 2481–2527. This volume.

Glaeser, E., Kolko, J., Saiz, A. (2001). "Consumer city". Journal of Economic Geography 1, 27–50.

Glaeser, E., Maré, D. (2001). "Cities and skills". Journal of Labor Economics 19, 316–342.

Goldin, C., Margo, R.A. (1992). "Wages, prices, and labor markets before the Civil War". In: Goldin, C., Rockoff, H. (Eds.), Strategic Factors in Nineteenth Century American Economic Growth. Cambridge Univ. Press, Cambridge, UK.

Goldin, C., Sokoloff, K. (1984). "The relative productivity hypothesis of industrialization: The American case, 1820–1850". Quarterly Journal of Economics 99, 461–488.

Haines, M. (2001). "The urban mortality transition in the United States, 1800–1940". NBER Historical Paper No. 134.

Harley, C.K. (1980). "Transportation, the world wheat trade, and the Kuznets cycle 1850–1913". Explorations in Economic History 17, 218–250.

Helpman, E. (1998). "The size of regions". In: Pines, D., Sadka, E., Zilcha, I. (Eds.), Topics in Public Economics. Cambridge Univ. Press, Cambridge, UK.

Higgs, R. (1979). "Cycles and trends of mortality in 18 large American cities, 1871–1900". Explorations in Economic History 16, 381–408.

Holmes, T. (1998). "The effect of state policies on the location of manufacturing: Evidence from state borders". Journal of Political Economy 106, 667–705.

Holmes, T., Stevens, J. (2004). "Spatial distribution of economic activities in North America". In: Henderson, J.V., Thisse, J.-F. (Eds.), Handbook of Regional and Urban Economics, vol. 4. Elsevier, Amsterdam, pp. 2797–2843. This volume.

Hunter, L. (1979). "History of Industrial Power in the United States, 1780–1930". In: Water Power in the Century of the Steam Engine, vol. 1. Univ. Press of Virginia, Charlottesville.

Imai, H. (1980). "CBD hypothesis and economics of agglomeration". Journal of Economic Theory 28, 275–299.

Jones, A.H. (1980). Wealth of a Nation to Be. Columbia Univ. Press, New York.

Kain, J. (1968). "The distribution and movement of jobs and industry". In: Wilson, J. (Ed.), Metropolitan Enigma. Harvard Univ. Press, Cambridge, MA.

Kau, J.B., Sirmans, C.F. (1979). "Urban land value functions and the price elasticity of demand for housing". Journal of Urban Economics 6, 112–121.

Kau, J.B., Lee, C.F., Sirmans, C.F. (1986). "Urban econometrics". Research in Urban Economics 6, 388–406.

Kim, S. (1995). "Expansion of markets and the geographic distribution of economic activities: The trends in U.S. regional manufacturing structure, 1860–1987". Quarterly Journal of Economics, 881–908.

Kim, S. (1998). "Economic integration and convergence: U.S. regions, 1840–1987". Journal of Economic History, 659–683.

Kim, S. (1999). "Regions, resources, and economic geography: Sources of U.S. regional comparative advantage, 1880–1987". Regional Science and Urban Economics 29, 1–32.

Kim, S. (2000). "Urban development in the United States". Southern Economic Journal 66, 855–880.

Kim, S. (2002). "The reconstruction of the American urban landscape in the twentieth century". NBER Working Paper No. 8857.

Klingaman, D. (1969). "The significance of grain in the development of the tobacco colonies". Journal of Economic History 24, 268–278.

Kolko, J. (1999). "Can I get some service here? Information technology, service industries, and the future of cities". Mimeo.

Konishi, H. (2000). "Hub cities". Journal of Urban Economics.

Krugman, P. (1991). Geography and Trade. MIT Press, Cambridge, MA.

Krugman, P. (1996). The Self Organizing Economy. Blackwell, Oxford.

Krugman, P., Venables, A. (1995). "Globalization and the inequality of nations". Quarterly Journal of Economics 110, 857–880.

Lamoreaux, N., Sokoloff, K. (1999). "Inventive activity and the market for technology in the United States, 1840–1920". NBER Working Paper No. 7107.

Lindstrom, D. (1978). Economic Development in the Philadelphia Region, 1810–1850. Columbia Univ. Press, New York.

Lucas, R.E., Rossi-Hansberg, E. (2002). "On the internal structure of cities". Econometrica 70 (4), 1445–1476.

Macauley, M. (1985). "Estimation and recent behavior of urban population and employment density gradients". Journal of Urban Economics 18, 251–260.

Madden, C. (1956). "On some indicators of stability in the growth of cities in the United States". Economic Development and Cultural Change.

Margo, R.A. (1990). Race and Schooling in the South, 1880–1950: An Economic History. Univ. of Chicago Press, Chicago.

Margo, R.A. (1992). "Explaining the postwar suburbanization of population in the United States: The role of income". Journal of Urban Economics 31, 301–310.

Margo, R.A. (1996). "The rental price of housing in New York City, 1830–1860". Journal of Economic History 56, 605–625.

Margo, R.A. (1999). "Regional wage gaps and the settlement of the Midwest". Explorations in Economic History 36, 128–143.

Margo, R.A. (2000). Wages and Labor Markets in the United States, 1820–1860. Univ. of Chicago Press, Chicago.

Margo, R.A. (2003). "The North–South wage gap: Before and after the Civil War". In: Eltis, D., Lewis, F., Sokoloff, K., (Eds.), Slavery in the Development of the Americas. Cambridge Univ. Press, Cambridge, UK. In press.

Margo, R.A., Villaflor, G. (1987). "The growth of wages in antebellum America: New evidence". Journal of Economic History 47, 873–896.

McDonald, J., Bowman, H.W. (1979). "Land value functions: A re-evaluation". Journal of Urban Economics 6, 25–41.

McCusker, J., Menard, R. (1985). The Economy of British America, 1606–1789. Univ. of North Carolina Press, Chapel Hill.

McMillen, D.P., Jarmin, R., Thorsnes, P. (1992). "Selection bias and land development in the monocentric model". Journal of Urban Economics 22, 273–284.

Meinig, D.W. (1993). The Shaping of America, vol. 2. Yale Univ. Press, New Haven, CT.

Meyer, D. (1983). "Emergence of the American manufacturing belt: An interpretation". Journal of Historical Geography 9, 145–174.
Meyer, D. (1988). "Industrial retardation of southern cities, 1860–1880". Explorations in Economic History 25, 366–386.
Meyer, D. (1989). "Midwestern industrialization and the American manufacturing belt in the nineteenth century". Journal of Economic History 49, 921–937.
Middleton, A. (1953). Tobacco Coast. Johns Hopkins Univ. Press.
Mills, E. (1969). "The Value of Urban Land". In: Perloff, H. (Ed.), The Quality of the Urban Environment. Johns Hopkins Press, Baltimore, pp. 231–253.
Mills, E. (1972). Studies in the Structure of the Urban Economy. Johns Hopkins Press, Baltimore.
Mitchener, K., McLean, I. (1999). "U.S. regional growth and convergence, 1880–1980". Journal of Economic History 59, 1016–1042.
Mitchener, K., McLean, I. (2003). "The productivity of U.S. states since 1880". NBER Working Paper No. 9445.
Moen, J. (1992). "Changes in the productivity of southern agriculture between 1860 and 1880". In: Fogel, R.W., Engerman, S.L. (Eds.), Without Consent or Contract: Markets and Production, Technical Papers, Vol. 1. Norton.
North, D. (1961). The Economic Growth of the United States 1790–1860. Prentice Hall, New York.
North, D. (1965). "The role of transportation in the economic development of North America". In: Les Grandes Vois dans le Monde, XV–XIX Siècles. SEVPEN, Paris.
Odell, K., Weiman, D. (1988). "Metropolitan development, regional financial centers, and the founding of the fed in the Lower South". Journal of Economic History 58, 103–125.
Ogawa, H., Fujita, M. (1980). "Equilibrium land use patterns in a non-monocentric city". Journal of Regional Science 20, 455–475.
Ottaviano, G., Thisse, J.-F. (2004). "Agglomeration and economic geography". In: Henderson, J.V., Thisse, J.-F. (Eds.), Handbook of Regional and Urban Economics, vol. 4. Elsevier, Amsterdam, pp. 2563–2608. This volume.
Pred, A. (1973). Urban Growth and the Circulation of Information: The United States System of Cities, 1790–1840. Harvard Univ. Press, Cambridge, MA.
Price, J. (1974). "Economic function of the growth of American port towns in the eighteenth century". Perspectives in American History 8, 121–186.
Price, J., Clemens, P. (1987). "A revolution of scale in overseas trade: British firms in the Chesapeake trade, 1675–1775". Journal of Economic History 47, 1–43.
Puga, D. (1999). "The rise and fall of regional inequalities". European Economic Review 43, 303–334.
Ransom, R., Sutch, R. (1975). One Kind of Freedom: The Economics of Emancipation. Cambridge Univ. Press, Cambridge, UK.
Rappaport, J., Sachs, J. (2001). "The U.S. as a coastal nation". Mimeo.
Rosenberg, N. (1963). "Technological change in the machine tool industry, 1840–1910". Journal of Economic History.
Rosenbloom, J. (1990). "One market or many? Labor market integration in the nineteenth century United States". Journal of Economic History 50, 85–108.
Rosenthal, S., Strange, W. (2004). "Evidence on the nature and sources of agglomeration economies". In: Henderson, J.V., Thisse, J.-F. (Eds.), Handbook of Regional and Urban Economics, vol. 4. Elsevier, Amsterdam, pp. 2119–2171. This volume.
Rossi-Hansberg, E. (2002). "Optimal urban land use and zoning". Mimeo.
Schweitzer, M. (1993). "The spatial organization of federalist Philadelphia, 1790". Journal of Interdisciplinary History 24, 31–57.
Shammas, C. (2000). "The space problem in early United States cities". William and Mary Quarterly 57, 505–542.
Shepherd, J., Walton, G. (1972). Shipping, Maritime Trade, and the Economic Development of North America. Cambridge Univ. Press, Cambridge, UK.

Simon, C., Nardinelli, C. (2002). "Human capital and the rise of American cities, 1900–1990". Regional Science and Urban Economics.

Smith, F.H. (2001). "Real estate values and the location of economic activity: A case study of the urban form of Cleveland, 1915–1960". PhD dissertation. Department of Economics, Vanderbilt University.

Sokoloff, K. (1984). "Was the transition from the artisanal shop to the non-mechanized factory associated with gains in efficiency? Evidence from the U.S. manufactures censuses of 1820 and 1850". Explorations in Economic History 21, 351–382.

Sokoloff, K. (1986). "Productivity growth in manufacturing during early industrialization: Evidence from the American Northeast, 1820–1860". In: Engerman, S., Gallman, R. (Eds.), Long-Term Factors in American Economic Growth. In: Studies in Income and Wealth, vol. 51. Univ. of Chicago Press, NBER, Chicago.

Sokoloff, K. (1988). "Inventive activity in early industrial America: Evidence from patent records, 1790–1846". Journal of Economic History 48, 813–850.

Sokoloff, K., Kahn, Z. (1990). "The democratization of invention during early industrialization: Evidence from the United States, 1790–1846". Journal of Economic History 50, 363–378.

Sokoloff, K., Villaflor, G. (1992). "The market for manufacturing workers during early industrialization: The American Northeast, 1820 to 1860". In: Goldin, C., Rockoff, H. (Eds.), Strategic Factors in Nineteenth Century American Economic Growth. Cambridge Univ. Press, Cambridge, UK.

Steckel, R. (1983). "The economic foundations of East–West migration during the nineteenth century". Explorations in Economic History 20, 14–36.

Tabuchi, T. (1998). "Agglomeration and dispersion: A synthesis of Alonso and Krugman". Journal of Urban Economics 44, 333–351.

Temin, P. (1976). "The Post-Bellum recovery of the South and the cost of the Civil War". Journal of Economic History 36, 898–907.

Thompson, W., Whelpton, P.K. (1933). Population Trends in the United States. McGraw–Hill, New York.

Troesken, W. (2003). "Lead water pipes and infant mortality in turn-of-the-century Massachusetts". NBER Working Paper No. 9549.

Ward, D. (1971). Cities and Immigrants. Oxford Univ. Press, London.

Warner, S. (1968). The Private City: Philadelphia in Three Periods of its Growth. Univ. of Pennsylvania, Philadelphia.

Weiman, D. (1988). "Urban growth on the periphery of the antebellum cotton belt: Atlanta, 1847–1860". Journal of Economic History 48, 259–272.

Weiss, T. (1972). "The industrial distribution of the urban and rural workforces: Estimates for the United States, 1870–1910". Journal of Economic History 32, 919–937.

Williamson, J. (1965). "Antebellum urbanization in the American Northeast". Journal of Economic History, 592–608.

Williamson, J., Swanson, J. (1966). "The growth of cities in the American Northeast, 1820–1870". Explorations in Entrepreneurial History, 3–101.

Wright, G. (1979). "The efficiency of slavery: another interpretation". American Economic Review 69, 219–226.

Wright, G. (1986). Old South, New South. Basic Books, New York.

Chapter 67

THE HISTORICAL GEOGRAPHY OF EUROPEAN CITIES: AN INTERPRETIVE ESSAY

PAUL M. HOHENBERG (PROF. EMERITUS)

Rensselaer Polytechnic Institute, Troy, NY, USA
e-mail: hohenp@rpi.edu

Contents

Handbook of Regional and Urban Economics, Volume 4. Edited by J.V. Henderson and J.F. Thisse

DOI: 10.1016/S0169-7218(04)07067-4

Permanence. Despite the enormous increase in the urban population – absolute and relative – since medieval and early modern times, Europe's urban map has in many ways remained remarkably stable, to say nothing of the many places that date back earlier, notably to Roman times. The big cities of the past have more or less kept their place in the hierarchy or at least remained significant. Other present-day large centers are less ancient, owing their existence or importance to early modern absolutism or to 18th–19th century industrialization, whereas only a few date from the 20th century. Finally, while towns, indeed large cities, can today be found in all parts of Europe, the urban grid reflects the past, in that the areas longest urbanized, constituting the urban core of Western Europe, retain the highest density of urban places.

Evolution. Although the larger historical context in which Europe's cities have developed is rich in revolutions, economic as well as social and political, the urban system has – with important exceptions – changed mostly by increments. While the general direction is clear and the overall growth has been enormous, change has at times been slow and its rhythm and incidence, spatial as well as functional, uneven and complex. Indeed, an important theme of this paper is that ongoing urbanization does not preclude a re-emergence of earlier patterns, *mutatis mutandis.* Just as radical social movements born in the nineteenth century have been pretty well abandoned as bases for organizing European societies, so some aspects of nineteenth-century urbanization, which gave enormous weight to factory industry, inter-urban rail transport, and the centralized nation state as agglomerative forces, are being partially rolled back. The rollback, largely spontaneous and unforeseen, has allowed older urban traditions to re-emerge. To express the matter more broadly, Europe's cities and its urban system exhibit considerable *path dependence*, but also decidedly non-linear behavior involving punctuated equilibrium, with spurts of change and with reversals as well as declines and stagnation [Arthur (1988)].

Context. Finally, it is important to set the story within the large-scale social processes and transformations that mark Europe's history: the rise of *capitalism* – a multi-dimensional concept if it is to retain meaning – and of territorial sovereign *states*, empire or nation; the more recent reaction to the hegemonic nation-state represented by European *integration* and *regional autonomy* (or separation); the *demographic transition*; *global ties*, ancient and modern; and successive *technological regimes*, to name a few. Clearly, the present chapter will not try to summarize these, let alone offer original interpretations, but they must be kept in mind.

Two points deserve a brief initial mention, both having to do with the relative role of states and markets. One concerns the relation of the city to the growth of a market economy. Cities have been the cradle of commerce and of the market economy, the first places created for exchange and totally dependent on it for their subsistence. Yet they have also housed both strong forces of resistance vis-a-vis unfettered markets and institutions to regulate them, and they embody the sources of market failure that microeconomic theory and a mixed market economy must wrestle with.

The second point relates specifically to the pre-industrial period and the long run-up to sustained economic growth, understood in the sense of increasing per capita income. The prevailing wisdom has been that Malthusian limits on resources constrained the system, with population growth acting as a brake on economic growth, and then slowing itself, notably in the 14th and 17th centuries. Improvements in technology, as well as the opening up of overseas sources of "land", then allowed Europe to overcome the ceiling on output per head. This view has been challenged by new work that stresses early institutional barriers to efficient use and full development of available resources. Some focus on the beneficial effects of limits to political power that safeguard private property [North (1990)], whereas others stress the ability of the strong central state to pacify and integrate large territories with positive effects on market activity [Epstein (2000)].

2. A systems perspective

Europe's array of cities and towns can be approached along a number of dimensions: spatial, numerical/functional (to distinguish and classify the units), and, in the present chapter, temporal. Yet accounting for how large each city is, where it is situated, its principal activities, and how it came to be what it is, even if it were possible, would yield little understanding. Cities are both pointless and inviable in isolation. Thus it is the relations of the city with what is outside itself that matter most. Urban places are elements in an interacting set, in other words, in a *system*.

A great deal has been written about urban systems, much of it using the term to mean little more than an array, an ensemble. Somewhat more analytic is the idea of an urban system as a hierarchy, with population size, political function, and spatial centrality as possible metrics. Unfortunately, much of a city's activity, notably commercial, financial, and more broadly "informational", is at best crudely grasped by these criteria.[2] But the real difficulty is that even an ordered set of cities offers only a synchronic view, whereas the concept of system also needs to explicate the processes by which an array or hierarchy comes into being and evolves over time. Thus the approach followed here, and developed in earlier work, proceeds from the logic of urban systems rather than from certain manifestations of that logic in particular times and places [Hohenberg and Lees (1995)]. The argument is that the systemic logic antedates the full development of Europe's urban array, and transcends particular numerical properties, such as a rank–size distribution, that may develop and that some have viewed as defining the urban system. As envisaged here, that logic is dual, in that two types of system effectively model urban Europe.

From the origin of cities onward, two sets of forces have driven the process of urban development, expressed respectively in *central places* and *networks*. The arrays of cen-

[2] It should be noted that W. Christaller, who defined central place systems in 1933, used the intensity of telephone traffic as a measure of centrality.

tral places that service and administer a(n) (agricultural) territory build toward a pyramidal structure, with many small centers and (numerically diminishing) tiers of larger, higher-order centers culminating in a single capital. These arrays show great spatial and rank stability over time. The system may develop from the top, with small centers as outposts of an initial center or gateway, or emerge by selection of high-order centers from among an array of small ones, or experience a mixture of the two processes. Cities that participate strongly in network relations, on the other hand, form a spatially fluid system where distance as such counts for little, thanks to long-standing reliance on water (more rarely caravan) transport. Being in competition with other cities, network cities can seldom preserve a high order of "nodality" or dominance for very long. For certain periods the dichotomy of prince's cities and merchant cities [De Long and Shleifer (1993)] captures the dual systems perspective pretty well. Figure 1 sketches the spatial relationships in the two systems.

Functionally, central places tend to house diverse service activities, whose range and "level" matches the size of the center, so that high-order places serve as centers of (smaller) centers. Their services are typically administrative and cultural as well as

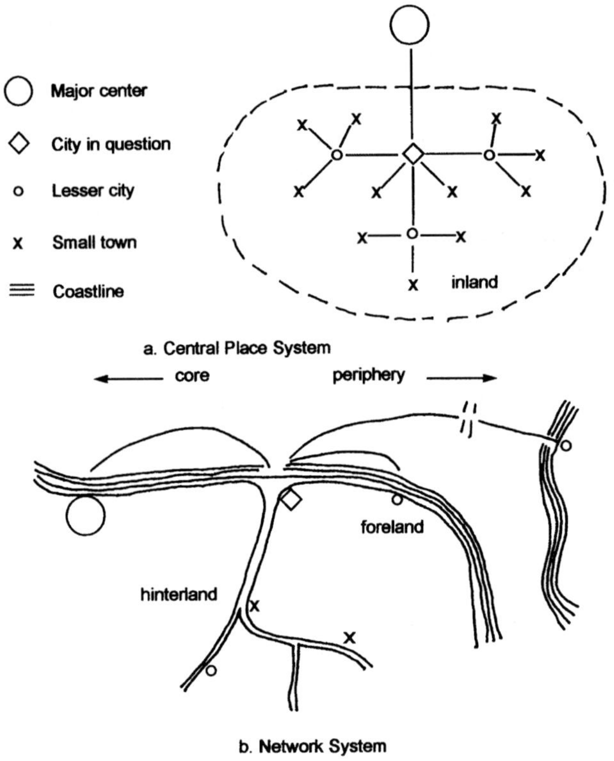

Figure 1. Spatial relationships in the dual urban systems model.

market-oriented. Networks, on the other hand, link specialized cities and zones of production (mines, plantations) in an inter-urban, often international, division of labor, and thus typically feature a limited range of activities in a single place. The political role even of a major network city may be informal and subordinate to commerce. (Population) size is an imperfect indicator of role, or importance, in networks, and its growth can be quite irregular, by contrast with central places whose size generally follows their degree of centrality. Dominance or subordination in network cities thus depends on function more than on size, with finance and headquarters functions considered privileged. Given cities can find a place in either or both types of system. While one system or the other may clearly dominate, we shall argue that a balanced role – regional or national capital plus cosmopolitan node – can prove a particularly vital basis. While this is clearly true, to take one example, for London from the 17th century on, it also applies to cities of less than metropolitan size. In our time, such places as Munich, Bordeaux, Barcelona, and Florence offer examples.

The growth of cities in each system follows a distinctive pattern. Central places tend to show a bias toward more rapid growth of larger cities, with a frequent tendency to *primacy* or gigantism in the principal city, usually a political capital. Small centers may grow or may fail to grow and in time shrink as they lose all central-place functions. Large ones, on the other hand, resist decline, except relative to those above them, counting on the state to supply facilities and subsistence when needed. In the network system, by contrast, growth can be very rapid, as for example in a mining district or when a new trade or industry opens up. Yet booms may well be followed by busts, while the most brilliant mercantile cities have resisted letting their numbers exceed their employment opportunities. As a result, the relation of growth rate to initial size is somewhat negative among network cities whereas it is positive for the array of central places. The whole may be summed up in a model derived from Robson (1977) (Figure 2). It will be noted that the overall relationship between growth and initial size is nearly neutral, with only a

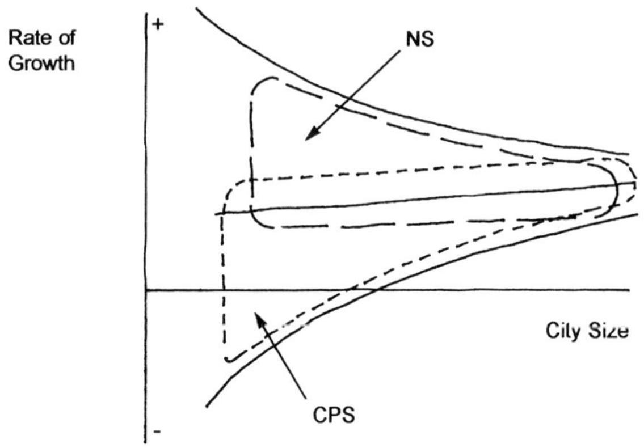

Figure 2. Growth of cities relative to size in Central Place (CPS) and Network Systems (NS).

slight tendency to favor the large cities, but the underlying dynamics bring out the more complex set of system-based relationships.

In terms of the long-term changes in European urban systems, network system logic is behind most structural transformations, whereas the central place system has shown much greater stability over time. Political changes have given rise to new capitals, and more rarely demoted others, most notably in the period of absolute monarchy (early modern times), also in later eras of nationalism and break-up of empires, including most recently the Soviet. These aside, the high-order central places have tended to hold their position for a very long time. Network logic, on the other hand, is behind the rise and fall of great city-states such as Venice, and later the sometimes explosive rise of industrial settlements that sometimes coalesced into great conurbations. Other specialized cities, some achieving considerable size, also derive their dynamics from network system logic. What is most telling, perhaps, is that industry has on its own spawned so few cities that have achieved a high order of either centrality or nodality, the UK offering partial exceptions (Manchester, Leeds, Glasgow, ...). Mere size does not automatically confer important leadership functions. Finally, network relations are behind the macro transformations of the European urban system, such as the shift from the Mediterranean to the northwest in early modern times and the more recent rustbelt-to-sunbelt move from regions of heavy industry to ones with a better climate and a more nearly unspoilt landscape.

Much of the work on economic models of cities and urban systems focuses on forces of agglomeration in production, and within that on material production or manufacturing. Yet in the historical context, these represent only a part of the basis for urban agglomeration. Indeed, where large-scale manufacturing coupled with strong specialization has been the driving force, the resulting agglomerations have often proved especially limited in their capacity to renew their economic base or to engender a strong urban identity. Thus, history indicates that long-lived agglomerative forces come largely from services – not least trade, finance, and informational pursuits – and small-scale material production on the one hand, and from consumption and administration on the other. At the same time, the absolute level of material production and associated employment in particular cities, especially large ones typed as non-industrial, has often been underestimated. Early modern and nineteenth-century capitals and ports (Naples and Bordeaux before 1800, London and Vienna after) are historical examples.

The systems approach is also relevant to the debate, mentioned earlier, regarding institutional forces that freed Europe for economic growth in the early modern period. Those who stress the weakening of political constraints on markets, with competition between states curbing the arbitrary power of the sovereign over persons and property, would consider network cities key incubators for modern growth. Europe's overtaking of China can, in this view, be ascribed to the relative fragmentation of political units in the former [Jones (1981), Diamond (1997)]. On the other hand, those who view the integration of states as the key process that allowed markets to put resources to best and full use will put the accent on the role of central places in the administration, unification, and structuring of the territory [Epstein (2000)].

A systems view, finally, casts a skeptical light on two quantitative constructs that economists have applied to arrays of cities: the rank–size rule and optimum city size. As regards the size distribution, central place systems should ideally feature certain favored size ranges corresponding to the order of centers. There would thus be one largest city, n cities ($n = 3$–7) of the next lower order and size, n^2 of the next, and so on. The size–rank distribution would feature steps rather than a smooth log-linear decay. Network cities or those with significant network ties complicate the picture, their population being at any rate imperfectly related to their network role. While the end result, factoring in noise (historical contingency), may well approximate a rank–size array, it is difficult to derive strong conclusions from the fact, beyond the simple idea that a number of forces have contributed to the distribution of population among cities.

As regards optimum city size, the systems model not only recognizes different types of cities, from diverse service centers to places specialized in one or a few activities, but also hierarchic relationships. Without small centers as relays, for example, large ones cannot carry out their high-order functions. Thus no one size will work for all types. Small places will feature lower (congestion) costs in exchange for limited amenities in consumption and weak urbanization economies in production. Large ones will require massive infrastructural investments, justified, one hopes, by the unique functions their size makes viable. Cities can only be efficient or inefficient in size for the role they play. Of course, the question persists as to whether market forces, and particularly migration, the dominant source of change in city size, will yield a reasonably efficient size array of places. The confidence of economists that individual choices tend to provide positive guidance to the system as a whole seems fraught with problems in this case. Rural-to-urban migrations can often take on siphon-like characteristics, further emptying regions that have lost any excess population and adding to urban congestion at their destination. Ireland in the late 19th century is a case in point, with the migrants ending up in the most crowded cities of Great Britain and North America. Of course, many migratory streams originate in stark necessity or coercion rather than in free choice by maximizing agents, while potential movements are often hampered by administrative and political barriers at either end of the journey.

This is not the place to re-open the discussion of the origins, really the rebirth, of cities in medieval Europe. Specialists ponder and debate the scrappy evidence, archeological and numismatic more often than documentary. Suffice it to say that economic motives are hard to find in the origins, though they come into their own in explaining later relative growth and functional characteristics. Prototypically, the seed of an urban formation was a fortified center of power, royal, noble, or religious, perhaps within the remains of a Roman city that had acquired and retained ecclesiastical functions (episcopal see). An abbey (monastery) sited nearby often served as the kernel of a civil settlement, as in the case of the Cité and St. Germain-des-Prés, separated by a few hundred meters in the heart of today's Paris. The earliest trade may well have involved servants of the local lord, entrusted with transforming rents/taxes/tithes collected (in kind) from the manors into more exotic and finer goods from elsewhere. Did these men begin a merchant settlement between castle and abbey while still dependent, or had they become autonomous merchants before starting the settlement process that would transform their successors into burghers or bourgeois, inhabitants of the burg or town [Verhulst (1999)]? By specializing and attaining some scale, towns also presumably gained an advantage over rural manors in the production of craft goods.

The systemic dualism we introduced earlier was at work even in the earliest stages. While the proto-towns depended on local rents and those who appropriated them, and housed local periodic markets, services, and specialized craft workers, the more active places were sited on routes that served for long-distance trade, offering the wandering traders shelter, provisions, and an occasion to trade. In this case, the periodic market might eventually rise to the status of a fair, purchasing protection from the local lord for the duration of the event. We are speaking here of the period, the 9th and 10th centuries C.E., which scholars no longer dismiss as the Dark Ages, despite the depredations of foreign raiders (who also proved to be active traders). While the Vikings came from the North, others originated in areas south and east that had a higher level of economic development and urban life. Europe itself was at that time a periphery of the Byzantine and Muslim empires in the Near East. Byzantium and Cordoba were, in fact, much the largest cities in what we today call Europe.

3. Pre-industrial spatial patterns

After the millennium, the pace of urban formation and growth accelerated in Western Europe. But while many towns were founded and grew, their distribution was far from uniform. By the 13th century, a clear pattern had emerged, with two cores near the coasts of the inland seas: the Mediterranean/Adriatic and North/Baltic. Linking the Northern Italian and Low Country centered concentrations were a number of towns and urban-studded routes, from Paris in the west to central Germany in the east. Periodic fairs added to the opportunities for intermediation. Trade would flow in one or another of these network channels depending on the vagaries of war, the greed of robber-barons who controlled rivers and passes, the daring of bandits, and other market and non-market circumstances. At the external margin, a number of ports on the coasts of the inland seas funneled the products of the interior for shipping to the core areas. Elsewhere, urban density tailed off as one moved east or west away from the core, and arable agriculture gave way to pasture, in a sort of macro-von Thünen pattern. In general, the South was more urban, more intensively settled, than the North, and the Italian core more developed than the Netherlandic one.

However active, most of the towns in medieval Europe were small. Florence topped out at 90,000 before the famines and plagues of the 14th century.[3] But the bulk of places could count their numbers with four and even three digits, falling well short of

[3] Its greatest cultural flowering took place after the population had been reduced by half.

what today can be called a town. In addition to offering commercial and administrative services, towns carried on craft production for markets, local or distant. Cloth was the dominant commodity – wool, silk, linen, and some mixtures – but metal, leather, wood, and glass/ceramic wares abounded. The town exchanged these with its environs for the food, materials, and also the wood it needed for fuel and so many other uses. Strong urbanization co-located with intensive and advanced agriculture, though the direction of causation is hard to establish. Financial institutions – the early bankers, credit instruments, high-value coins, bourses, and systems of accounts – were also to be found in the urban cores.

The fourteenth century witnessed a crisis, leading to a general cessation of urban growth except in the East where the process was just under way (Poland). Diminishing returns to agriculture on densely populated land farmed with poorly sustainable techniques (fallow) were largely responsible, most scholars agree. Dearths (worst around 1315) were followed by the bubonic plague at mid-century, with recurrences. Although the 15th century flowering of the arts in the urban cores disguises the fact, recovery was slow, and it was marred by an upsurge in armed conflicts.

Medieval Europeans were far from immobile as the flowering of towns attests. Urban settlements were founded and sustained by migrants, without whom few could maintain their numbers, let alone grow. High urban mortality was part of the problem, but celibacy among servants and clergy, and late marriage for female commoners, also contributed. While the drift of rustics to town often represented a search for opportunity, other movements were generally motivated by fear and necessity rather than hope and opportunity. Towns offered possible refuge from violence and, paradoxically, from dearth, but, despite having all the doctors, not from infectious disease. In more quiet times, travelers as well as migrants dotted the roads and waterways. Pilgrims, pedlars, carters, and craft workers – aptly named journeymen – joined agents of the Church and of secular lords moving from one town to another.

Physically, towns grew by accretion rather than plan. The exceptions that have come down to us usually reveal the failure of growth to overrun an initial scheme. The planned towns tended to be outposts (*bastides*) for clearing or holding territory, or inhabited fortresses. Within the town, inhabitants congregated by profession, area of origin, or "clan". Prestige attached to a more central location, a forerunner of choices that still distinguish European cities, at least Continental ones, from the American norm. Most urban plots were narrow and deep, as frontage counted for more than total area. Public spaces, though important for markets, festivities, and other gatherings, were typically limited in size and hard to expand. Masters of each craft clustered, e.g., on the butchers' street or in the weavers' quarter, testifying to the regulatory power of the guilds as well as to economies of agglomeration. Areal expansion was discontinuous, since a new wall generally had to be built, so crowding was frequent. Settlements outside the walls, along the roads or at bridgeheads, enjoyed no prestige. Finally, whether it was a sweeping shoreline or a sluggish and small stream, scarcely a town did not boast some body of water running through or lying by it. The need for an adequate supply as well as the advantages of water transport, even on small or difficult rivers, were compelling.

The political and institutional context of urban growth and commerce must be evoked, though it deserves a treatise rather than a paragraph. A legend of free, enterprising, and even democratic towns amidst a society that remained rural, feudal, and Church-ridden has come down to us, one which, as usual, mixes gross oversimplification and idealization with kernels of truth. Cities often achieved political autonomy, with remaining obligations to a nominal lord exercised collectively, and they did allow citizens to participate in governance, but with property and other restrictions on full citizenship and office-holding. While ways were found around the more commerce-inhibiting rules of the Church, towns imposed plenty of regulations of their own, typified by guild rules restricting entry into craft and other trades and prescribing product as well as process. On the larger political scene, urban oligarchies, which might in fact entrust effective power to an outsider, contended with and against rulers, powerful nobles, and the secular power of the Church and its bishops, in an unending series of struggles and alliances. Urban leagues such as the Germanic Hansa were only one manifestation of a struggle that inexorably saw power pass over time to unified kingdoms over much of Europe. Only the Northern Netherlands, the Swiss Alpine cantons, and some Italian and German cities – all within the old core – managed to remain outside the monarchic framework much past the 16th century.

4. The early-modern period (1500–1800)

The era of absolutism and European expansion was marked by relatively modest changes in overall urbanization, and indeed in population. The beginning and end of the period saw growth, in the first case representing recovery from the late-medieval crisis, in the second the forerunners of mass urbanization and accelerated population growth in the centuries to come. In between, the 17th century shows up as another difficult period in most places. Two large-scale processes dominated urban change during this period: the formation of centralized and powerful states, notably in the areas where the feudal system had been strongest (the edges or semi-periphery of the urban core), and the expansion of European trade, settlement, and control to territories overseas and to the East. We must drastically summarize the changes these forces and processes wrought on the urban map of Europe.

- *The North gained on the South*, with the Northwest of Europe overtaking the Mediterranean. Antwerp, Amsterdam, and London were successive financial and commercial centers, while Genoa, Venice, and Florence gradually slipped into relative somnolence. Yet the South remained more urbanized overall, in fact until the 19th century.
- *The fringes of the urban core gained* on its heartland, especially in terms of where the fastest-growing cities were located.
- *The fast growers were mainly territorial capitals*, from Madrid and Lisbon to Berlin and St. Petersburg. Already large, London, Paris, and Naples attained a size (one half million or more) not seen in the Christian West since the great days of

Rome. On a smaller scale, court cities in Germany outpaced the free Imperial cities [François (1978)]. Dynastic power also gave rise to new cities that were not capitals but served that power as ports, fortresses, or garrison towns.

- *Growth was generally concentrated in large cities*, particularly in the 17th century, when many smaller ones declined [De Vries (1984)]. This is why, despite the spectacular cases of growth, the best data suggest little or no overall increase in the urban percentage. While some declines reflected the loss of pretension to urban status in very small towns, the difficulties of the core areas in Flanders and Northern Italy also led to a decline in their precociously high urban percentages. It needs to be mentioned that most scholars have, for data reasons, had to use a threshold city size of at least 5000. This leaves out a significant – and secularly declining – fraction of the population that would at the time have been reckoned as urban, and thus overstates the gradual increase in urban share.
- *Absolutism worked against a high urban share*, despite the fast growth of capital and court cities [De Long and Shleifer (1993)]. To be sure, the fact that strong rulers prevailed in areas of previously modest urban share, outside the old urban cores, biases the results. Path dependence again plays a role. This result holds despite the fact that capitals, but not ports, tended toward gigantism, as detailed below. The particular failure of cities located near capitals to grow suggests that the latter cast a strong shadow [Hohenberg and Lees (1996)].
- *Ports stand out among cities that grew for economic reasons*, particularly those on the Atlantic coast, from Cadiz to Glasgow. By contrast, interior market centers fared less well. Of course, the ports, conforming to network system logic, tended not to grow excessively in population, unlike certain much less economically active capital cities (Madrid versus Cadiz, Brussels overtaking Antwerp, Naples' ever greater primacy in Southern Italy).

The early modern period saw little clear-cut or rapid growth in income per capita (or even total product and income, since population generally rose more slowly than it did earlier or later). But the changes that did take place take on added importance in view of the massive transformation that first took hold in England after 1750. What is noteworthy is that developments which anticipated the future were not typically urban, though cities had a part in mediating them. Again, a brief summary must suffice.

- *Agriculture* underwent a gradual and slowly-diffusing process of intensification and commercialization that resulted in a more sustainable system as well as a more productive one. Modern scholars emphasize the role of markets, transport, and communication – and thus of cities – in the diffusion process [Hoffman (1996)], and we previously noted that intensively urbanized (core) areas also developed the most sophisticated agriculture.
- *Mobility*, of persons, capital, and information increased. Cities clearly played the major role here, not only drawing immigrants – and large cities were particularly hungry for human fodder, owing to the large natural deficit they typically ran – but housing the institutions that mobilized and transmitted both tangible and intangible capital, from early banks to schools and printers.

- *Individual property rights* were better safeguarded despite fiscal and judicial systems that added absolutist and mercantilist demands to stubborn feudal exactions. Institutionalists have stressed the importance of secure property and freedom of contract, practices that were developed in and defended by cities long before they were generally accepted by rulers [North (1990)].
- *Long-distance trade*, though significant in Europe from far earlier than is often realized, expanded during the period, notably overseas. Moreover, trade policy became an integral part of power politics, leading to overseas settlement and conquest and to aggressive policies concerning shipping, trade, and monetary matters (mercantilism). Some cities and nations thrived, while others stagnated or lost their commerce as a result. Not until 1815, with the end of Napoleon's attempt to control the shores of Europe (and thus break commerce-dependent England) did central governments begin to loosen their grip on trade, retaining mostly tariffs as instruments of control. In the major maritime countries, the great trading companies acted as surrogate governments with respect to the colonial areas and trades they controlled.
- *Manufacturing* expanded, though technical change was limited. However, large-scale production was mostly confined to what were called "manufactures", royally sponsored producers of luxuries or military goods, which appear to have played little part in the industrial revolution to come. Some coal was used as fuel, but wood remained dominant, along with other "organic" and natural sources of energy – animal, wind, and water. Cottage or domestic, and other small-scale industry, on the other hand, with large numbers of small producers typically coordinated by putting-out merchants, had more impact. The connection of this activity to cities, its geography, and its relation to the mechanized manufacturing to come raise complex and problematic issues and require separate treatment.

5. Proto-industrialization and towns

The late F. Mendels coined the term *proto-industrialization* to draw attention to development and change in manufacturing during the early modern period [Mendels (1971), Leboutte (1996), Glennie (1998)]. He asserted that rural manufacturing, notably of cloth but also of other wares, for sale outside local markets, broke the near-monopoly of urban craft production, and had significant impact on agriculture, trade, and demography as well. It thus represented, in his words, the "first stage of industrialization". While the movement may have begun almost surreptitiously (since towns tried hard to enforce their long-standing hold), using labor from peasant families with seasonal or other surpluses, it gradually took over the economy in a number of regions. Full-time or near full-time workers could marry earlier than peasants, who had to wait for a tenancy or inheritance of land. The increased population came to depend for food on nearby commercial agricultural areas. Thus, a series of markets, for food, mass-quality manufactures, and labor, came into being or were stimulated and extended.

The success of proto-industrial production carried the seeds of its own destruction, once mechanization and factory organization began to push costs lower. Full-time workers were not so cheap as peasant by-labor, nor could they so easily be treated by merchant-entrepreneurs as a reserve to be employed or released to farming according to fluctuations in product demand. Such workers had moved halfway to the status of an industrial proletariat, and so were ripe for the transition to the factory and the town. Also, the use of low-skill rural labor required that industrial processes be broken down into simpler steps, anticipating later mechanization. Finally, markets for manufactures of ordinary quality, which developed in the proto-industrial period, built demand and so reduced the subsequent risk of fixed capital investment in machinery and factory buildings.

The proto-industrial model elaborated by Mendels and others soon came under attack, although the research it stimulated is a tribute to its persuasiveness and elegance. Historians, it must be said, have a visceral distrust of models, and fiercely defend the uniqueness of the particular situation. This bias aside, it proved difficult in many regions to document the neat juxtaposition of proto-industry and commercial agriculture, or the acceleration of nuptiality and fertility, that the model specified. Eventually, many historians focused on institutions, which they identified with "power", as the main explanatory variable in the study of why proto-industrialization took hold in some regions and not others. Why institutions should be exogenous and unresponsive to economic incentives is a question usually not asked, let alone answered.

More to the point here, the view of proto-industry as a dynamic rural counter to hide-bound, rent-seeking urban craft guilds proved much too simple and categorical [Hohenberg (1991)]. Not only did the commercial aspects of this activity continue to involve towns and town-dwelling merchants, but stages of production requiring fixed capital, skill, or close control also remained urban. Many towns, with or without guilds, embraced domestic and small-scale workshop industry wholeheartedly, so that even simple manufactures by no means became entirely rural. Finally, luxury sectors that remained urban throughout also saw expansion; for example, the making of clocks, fine furniture and clothing, porcelain, and other decorative objects profited from the domestication of aristocrats by the monarchies, as well as from imitation of their lifestyles by rich burghers.

The geography of proto-industrialization is not simple to summarize, nor is it all that well known. An important point is that, by contrast with the iron and coal-based industry of the next century, proto-industry has left very few physical traces in town or country. A very rough summary indicates that it first took hold in and around the urbanized core, from the West of England to Northern Italy, with a few patches in Iberia and central Europe [Glennie (1998, p. 263)]. By the 18th century, when the movement peaked, larger areas were involved, including Southern Spain, Northwestern France, Eastern Sweden and Ireland, and much of central Germany, while some Alpine territories had faded. However, the map from which these indications are drawn is rightly offered with warnings and cautions by its author. At any rate, the areas active in this form of production would have the most varied destiny in the industrial age to come, ranging from complete de-industrialization through flexible adaptation to full participation.

6. The early modern city: an appraisal

From the point of view of spatial arrangements, early modern cities also conspicuously juxtaposed continuity and change. Those whose growth was sponsored by political leaders saw expansion, not only to house larger numbers but for the palaces and "hotels" of nobles required to attend the court, as well as for monuments and perspectives to celebrate power. Aside from the very privileged, however, big-city dwellers tended to experience mostly increased crowding. Commercial centers, on the other hand, showed a general disinclination to invest large sums in expansion or beautification, nor was population growth there as rapid as in capitals even in prosperous times. Of course, cities such as Amsterdam and St. Petersburg, built in swamps, required major infrastructural investment. While the Great Fire of London, in 1666, stimulated rebuilding and some major architectural works in Wren's churches, the opportunity to recast the city in the Versailles style (see Washington, DC) was passed up.

To summarize, the early modern period witnessed significant changes in urban development without much overall increase in the urban share of the population, with an exception for 18th century England's head start on the industrial age. In the logic of central places, growth favored mostly the largest centers, those exercising political control of a high order. Urban networks saw fierce competition, favoring ports over inland towns and the West and North of Europe over the Mediterranean. Within the winning region, leadership passed successively from Bruges to Antwerp, to Amsterdam, and to London. Capital of a long-stabilized monarchy and a major port in the most active 18th century economy, London became Europe's largest city, nearing a million inhabitants by 1800. But population grew only modestly in more purely commercial centers. For example, Vienna, Moscow, Madrid, and Naples grew larger than Amsterdam, Nantes, or Bristol, despite the contrary contrast in their economic vitality.

7. Cities and industrialization

A good deal of what follows is concerned with the effects on cities, and urban growth generally, of industrialization, or modern economic growth, as it appeared in, and spread from, England between 1750 and 1914. Then and later, successive technological regimes stimulated the concentration of a growing population in urban places, creating many, favoring some pre-existing ones while bypassing others, and generally exercising a major influence on the structure of the urban fabric. A much more difficult although equally compelling question is what role cities, namely those that antedate industrialization, played in the growth/development process itself. The a priori case for the Industrial

Revolution as an urban phenomenon seems compelling, but the evidence is elusive and contradictory.

As we have already seen, in the age of domestic industry a shift of production to rural sites formed an integral part of the expansion, and it was precisely those aspects that distinguished proto-industrial production from the traditional urban crafts (division of labor, production for non-local markets, loss of control over materials by producers) that pointed the way to the mechanized factory. Within the latter, water power dominated in the early stages, so that this was a major locational factor and often dictated a rural or suburban site. On the other hand, many cities were leery of industry, not only because of the dangers and disamenities that crude machinery and processes entailed, but also because the prospect of masses of landless, rootless workers raised fears of unrest and disorder, civil and political. Many cities relegated industry, and the worker housing that had to remain near it, to the suburbs, although this would eventually pose serious problems as the city expanded. A final point is that the new factory labor was not often recruited from established town dwellers, if only because other aspects of urban economies provided adequate growth in employment.

When it comes to the technological developments that have caused the Industrial Revolution to be labeled by some a "wave of gadgets", the picture is equally murky [Mokyr (1995)]. Some cities witnessed episodes of clustered technological or entrepreneurial creativity, for example Birmingham, Basle, and Lyon, but other important beginnings have no obvious urban ties. Three things may be said with some confidence:

- All the forces that economists identify as centripetal, and thus agglomerative, strengthened greatly in the period of industrialization: economies of scale, inter-industry linkages, knowledge spillovers, and reduced transport costs. Not only did transport become cheaper, but the reduction was concentrated until the 1890s on inter-urban routes or lines served by steam-powered trains and ships.
- The institutions that turned technological change from a series of individual inventions to a regular process of search, trial, application, and diffusion of knowledge, and management of intellectual property, developed and found their home in cities. Patent offices, scientific societies, laboratories, libraries, and schools of all levels grew in importance as the 19th century wore on.
- With the 19th century emphasis, even in technological development, on nation states, the central place system drew these knowledge institutions increasingly toward the largest cities, and in particular the capitals. Case in point, the old universities outside large cities, as in Germany and England, played only a minor role in advancing technology; exception, a few firms, e.g., in the German chemical industry, sited their laboratories with their plants outside major centers.

8. Urban formations of the industrial age

Overall, the period of industrialization saw great acceleration in Europe's population and in the share of that population living in urban places. The first of these trends is not so obviously linked to industrialization, since it can be found in parts of Europe, from Russia and Italy to pre-famine Ireland, decades before they experienced any real industrial development. The second, however, does follow the spread of industry pretty closely. The demography of urbanization is another complicated subject that we must slide over, save to say that accelerating population growth allowed the cities to expand even when the countryside was also growing. Only in a second phase would "rural exodus" become general, pushed by a combination of labor-saving agricultural technology and the loss of non-agricultural rural employment, pulled to overseas as well as urban destinations.

For the most part, then, urban growth was fed by rural migrants, while the enormous increases in the population of metropolitan cities drew also on movement out of other, usually smaller, towns, up the central place hierarchy. When migrants came from regions of high human fertility, as of course many did, they in time adopted the much more restrained fertility behavior of city dwellers. By the time improvements in public health and sanitary infrastructure ended excess urban mortality, diminished fertility would keep "natural" population growth in cities modest or even negative.

In the interests of clarity and economy, we may schematize the most common urban types that industrialization produced or advanced.

- *Local and regional centers* often expanded, at least in early stages. It is too often forgotten that the rural population, farming or not, increased almost everywhere until modern growth was well along, or until a demographic trigger, foreign or urban-bound emigration, relieved the pressure on the land.[4] Agriculture intensified with the spread of better rotations, convertible husbandry, and other yield-increasing techniques, while labor-saving mechanization only came along gradually. Increased commercialization and better communications, however slow and uneven their progress before the generalization of rail, stimulated the development of urban centers, from the smallest upward. So did the increasing activities of the centralized state, with Napoleonic administrative structures, for example, outliving French occupation. It is likely that many services we think of as traditional in small towns – shops, apothecary, solicitor/notary, carriage maker, tailor, publican – often go back no farther than the 19th century (or the mid-eighteenth in England). Still, provincial towns did not match the new industrial centers for activity, and many gradually became reservoirs of labor to be exploited for such routine products as boots and shoes. This phenomenon of industrial deconcentration is characteristic of mature industrialism and prefigures the 20th century policies of deliberate decentralization, whether for strategic, cost-minimizing, or developmental purposes.
- *Industrial city regions* developed in several variants. Some grew around natural resource points, such as coal or metal ore mines, or emerged from a proto-industrial

[4] France is the exception, the one country with substantial regions of low rural fertility as early as the 18th century.

concentration around a city. Such places as Sheffield and Birmingham, for example, gave the name of the principal city to an industry (and its wares) that spread over a much wider area. The city-region could also arise with no prior urban center, out of a series of settlements that coalesced with growth. Examples are Staffordshire (The Potteries), Le Creusot, and, of course, the Ruhr. The largest came to be known as *conurbations*. Finally, industrial regions could constitute a more structured urban system, as was the case in Lancashire. Manchester was its center, with Liverpool as the port of entry and exit, but the bulk of cotton mills were actually situated in a ring, or double ring, of towns around Manchester. St. Helens, also some distance from Manchester, furnished the chemicals vital to the textile industry.

- *"Alpine" industrial concentrations* denote a form of settlement that even today is insufficiently appreciated. In the upland valleys of many regions of Europe, but most notably in the Alps, proto-industrial production gradually modernized, adopting the factory mode of organization and power-using machinery, etc. The continuing pattern of small and medium firm and establishment scale has been compensated by other advantages, giving rise to a system described as one of "flexible specialization" [Piore and Sabel (1984)]. Swiss watchmaking is a long-standing example, but familiar products range from quality textiles to pipes and even cuckoo clocks. The workers tend to live in small places strung out in the valleys, while the principal centers have comparatively unfamiliar names such as St. Gallen, Roanne, Elberfeld-Barmen (later Wuppertal), Prato, or Verviers.
- *Industry in large cities* also developed, though it tended not to be so dominant or visible as in the sort of places sketched above. Within established cities, much of the activity took place in small establishments, externally little different from the domestic and workshop crafts of proto-industrial times. In fact, the coming of electricity gave new impetus to small-scale production, since it made possible compact and flexible equipment such as sewing machines and power tools for working wood, metal, or leather. Heavy industry, on the other hand, located on the outskirts, in the "red belts" or in satellite towns. Entire suburbs could be dominated by a single firm, as with Siemensstadt in Berlin and the Renault works in Boulogne outside Paris. Within the city itself, factories and workshops in working-class districts were overshadowed by the more central and showy temples of finance and commerce.

Given the costs of carrying on industrial production in large cities, affecting everything from materials transport to labor and land rent, there had to be compensating advantages. As in earlier times, the critical property was the information embodied in the product. Old criteria of labor skill, fashion, and uniqueness (one-off or custom-made articles) were joined by considerations of technical complexity and innovation. Prototypes would be made in the big city, whereas routine mass production could be located in some lower-cost site. This suggests a product cycle, with "new work", in Jane Jacobs' phrase, characteristically metropolitan [Jacobs (1969), Gaillard (1977)]. In a more recent context, [Aydalot and Keeble (1988)] contrast the early stages of an industry, characterized by spatial concentration of small firms, with the later (presumably less innovative) stages, where the firms are larger but production is spatially distributed.

One urban formation is noteworthy by its absence from the list. Except for Britain, it is hard to find genuinely new cities with important central-place functions, or even a leading role in networks, that emerge as a result of industrial urbanization. Manchester is an exception, and one can perhaps add Düsseldorf (previously a minor court city), Leeds and Bradford, and Bilbao to the list, but not many more. Some ports, Liverpool, Glasgow, Le Havre, and Bremerhaven being a few examples, were founded or came to prominence. As for the rest, fast as they might grow and large as they might become, industrial settlements seldom matured into high-order centers. This typifies network logic, where even populous places can maintain a high degree of specialization and depend for many functions on imports and ties to other places. Of course, the industrial settlements gradually added amenities, from shops to cultural, educational, and sanitary institutions, but usually with a lag and for local consumption only. Thus, industrialization had an enormous urbanizing impact if one looks at population, but much less restructuring force in terms of urban systems, especially the central place hierarchy and its metropolitan cities. In the main, the pre-existing big and important places merely became larger and more important, whether one looks at political, cultural, or financial and commercial leadership. Some, but not all, countries saw a fusion between the two urban systems at the top, with the national capital acquiring a leading role in global finance and commerce. Elsewhere dual "capitals" persisted.

9. Migration

As pointed out earlier, urban growth was fed by migration, either directly from rural areas or by successive moves up the central place system from smaller to larger centers. There was, of course, a great deal of inter-urban movement and some return flow to rural areas, and it is not always easy to distinguish temporary movements from migration, but the net flows are pretty clear cut. The move to the cities was driven by both pull and push factors, again not always easy to distinguish clearly [Williamson (1994)], and it mingled very short moves, from neighboring villages or farms, with quite distant migrations across regional, cultural, and national boundaries. Of course, Europe's rural dwellers also peopled the great cities and lesser towns of the Americas and of the Antipodes, including South Africa.

Our image of the 19th century industrial city is dominated by crowding, squalor, and pollution. The image is largely accurate, though one should remember that the migrants kept coming and for the most part remained town dwellers once settled. A number of factors contributed to bad conditions: the irregular nature of migration, which tended to come in waves; the primitive industrial technology, introduced as quickly as possible and only gradually refined and perfected in use; the long hours of work and the poor, relatively expensive, transport that forced workers to reside near their place of work.

We can also add weak urban governance and administration, in all cities but especially in nascent ones, justified by the triumphant liberal ideology, but due also to competing claims for capital; the revealed preference of worker families, which spent discretionary income on other things and often let some of their exiguous space to lodgers; finally, the competition for land in and near the center for public and commercial uses chiefly, also for wider and straighter streets on the model Haussmann applied to Paris. The perverse impact of "urban renewal" on the poor goes back a long way. Scandal and catastrophe compel notice, so it must be noted that millions lived under better conditions, however drab the urban landscape of industrialism might generally be, and that matters tended to improve with time, civic betterment, and rising incomes and as the influx of newcomers slowed.

10. Metropolitan areas and their transformations in the industrial age

Whereas even large or fast-growing industrial areas were often left to shift for themselves, national governments paid a good deal more attention to the capital. Not only did elites of wealth as well as of culture and caste reside there, so did political unrest and the "dangerous classes". Yet economic forces also played an important part in transforming the metropolis. Along with a share of industry, old and new, these cities saw enormous growth in commercial and financial activity. Banking, securities trading, and insurance represent sectors that centralized strongly. More generally, information-rich activities, from product development and fashion to publishing and communications, sought out the big city. Purveyors of high and popular culture and those who aspired to careers in these fields also gravitated to the capital. Many large firms, as well as once-regional banks, moved at least their headquarters to the big city, although a few industrial firms, typically with a secure market position and close inside control, chose to remain in their place of origin, perhaps turning it into a company town. These offer an interesting contrast to the typical industrial city, offering the workers better physical amenities in exchange for closer corporate control outside the workplace.

Two big changes in land use clearly observable in metropolitan cities were the separation of workplace and residence and, once people were no longer closely tied to the place of work, the generalization of socially homogeneous neighborhoods. Ironically, European factory workers in their peripheral locations were among the last to win some choice in where to live. The old patterns, such as living above the shop, or a vertical social gradient with "noble" and "servile" floors in a single multi-story building, gradually (though not fully) gave way to the more homogeneous blocks of flats, row houses, or detached villas. Progress in transport, successively omnibus, rail, tram, underground, bus, and motor car, with falling cost and improving quality, was key to the process. While each city has its own story, two features stand out in the new social geography. One is that European elites were not nearly so quick to abandon the center as their American counterparts, Britain, in this respect, being somewhat intermediate. The other is that expansion out from the center followed a sectoral spatial pattern, often with the West bourgeois and the East popular.

We have mentioned the hardships caused by land clearances and land-use succession generally. In the big cities, these projects could take on special scope, for example to accommodate rail terminals and freight yards, or government buildings and showplace plazas. The edge of the city, which traditionally housed the lowest and most noxious functions, and the most marginal people, also posed problems that had to be addressed as the built-up area pressed outward. In Paris and Vienna, for example, fortifications were demolished late (after 1920 in the former case!), yielding great opportunities but also posing problems. Finally, if urban development usually lacked adequate planning and infrastructure provision – though massive and impressive investments to provide transport, sanitation, and water, were eventually made – the situation was often far worse with regard to suburbs. For every planned "garden city", many straggling and unplanned settlements remained practically devoid of services.

11. Laggards and losers

Not every city and town gained in the general wave of urbanization. Certain regions lost their (proto-) industrial role, and this affected their centers. Agriculture began to shed labor, as we noted, in England as early as the mid-19th century (sooner in industrial regions), on the European fringes much later. Gradually, very small rural centers gave up their urban functions to larger ones, a trend that would greatly strengthen with the coming of the automobile. Also, despite the spread of secondary, light rail networks, the fortunes of smaller towns depended on whether or not they were served by a line. Regions of precocious high urban density, the old cores of Mediterranean and Low Country Europe, lagged behind industrially and experienced little urban growth. Finally, old network nodes, many with a glorious past as centers of finance and commerce, were by-passed. Lübeck, Venice, Bruges, Leiden, La Rochelle, and many others, could only aspire to the role of living museum. In the second half of the 20th century, the very absence of industrial development during the "paleotechnic" phase [Mumford (1961)] could prove a major asset in attracting new activities and residents.

12. Urban growth and urban systems in the industrial age

In the aggregate, industrial-age urbanization left the size distribution of European cities not very much changed in shape, although, of course, greatly shifted toward larger size. A system perspective brings out a somewhat richer story. The hierarchy of central places showed more rapid growth in the higher ranks, although some of this represented the incorporation of satellite towns into a metropolis and can thus be considered in part a statistical artifact. In general, the clear-cut boundary of each city, whether walled or not, gave way to a fuzzier notion of "urban area", posing definitional problems of arbitrary inclusion or exclusion of suburban and satellite settlements. On the other hand, the network system engendered a host of specialized, often but not always industrial, agglomerations, whose growth might well be explosive from the start. Non-industrial places included rail junctions, garrison towns, ports for war, commercial fishery, or commerce, and spas or other resorts. Here again, the growing together of nearby settlements into a conurbation gives an upward bias to the measure of growth relative to start-of-period size.

Overall, the combination of biases regarding the relationship of growth rate to initial size yielded the almost neutral result of proportional growth. Within the countries of Europe, therefore, the distribution tended toward a log-linear rank–size relationship, or the rank–size rule ($P = P^0/r$), where P is the population of a given city, P^0 that of the largest city, and r the given city's rank in the hierarchy. Exaggerated growth of the capital or *primate* city characterized some countries (Austria, France, Sweden, even England) while others developed an oligarchy of major towns with no one city dominant (Netherlands, Switzerland). However, these departures from the rank–size order to an extent cancel one another out if one looks at the whole of Europe.

In systemic terms, the single greatest change was a fusion at the top. National capitals tended to add network leadership to their central place functions, including international finance and cosmopolitan exchanges of information and persons. Vienna and Berlin, though not so much Madrid, The Hague, or Rome, followed the lead set by London and Paris. A telling indicator is that banks bearing their provincial origin in their name – Dresden, Lyon – moved their headquarters to the capital. Of course, colonial empires blurred the distinction between national and international links.

13. The first twentieth century

In the first half of the 20th century, a number of factors caused urban growth to slow down and the systems to stabilize. Wars and depression slowed and sometimes even reversed rural-to-urban migration, while emigration for political reasons affected urban dwellers more than rural folk (unlike earlier currents). Until World War II, destruction was confined to Belgium and Northern France, and to Spain, with Liege, Lille, and Madrid the only large cities with much experience of it.

The economic slowdown and its crises, particularly in the 1920s (England, Germany) and 1930s (France), affected most strongly the industrial conurbations that specialized in a limited range of industries such as mining/metallurgy/metal-working or textiles. Although periods of war, re-armament, and reconstruction reversed the trend, it prefigured the definitive decline of these incipient "rust belts". New industries, many making and transforming light metals and petrochemicals to make plastics, appliances, vehicles, and the like, sought out other locations. Ports and metropolitan areas received their full share, but nothing like the massive concentrations of the previous century developed. Of course, late-Imperial Russia and the Soviet Union, rushing to make up for industrial retardation, did develop coal/iron/engineering complexes in the Ukraine and Urals, along with factories in old and new cities.

While economic growth faltered, the quality of life in cities underwent great improvements. Much of it was a matter of the infrastructure catching up with earlier growth, but there was more to it. The technology of the "second industrial revolution", centered on advances in electricity, chemistry, and biology, proved urban-friendly. Sanitation and security improved, pollution diminished, and intra-urban transport was revolutionized. Progress in administration and public health, and the gradual extension of voting rights (at first only among men) also gave impetus to civic improvement. Most visible is the development of social housing, increasing supply and improving the standard in the large cities where crowding was most severe. Elsewhere, increased firm scale made possible more employer-provided housing.

One feature that distinguishes European from American cities is the absence of skyscrapers in the former. Even in the heady days of the Belle Epoque, before the outbreak of war in 1914, Central Business Districts did not grow upward to take advantage of the electric elevator and structural steel construction as they did in New York and Chicago. Yet if one widens the view to the built-up area as a whole, Europe's cities show greater, not lesser density. Except in the North, where row houses predominate, the prevailing form of housing in large cities was and is the apartment block, 4–7 stories high. They can be found from Naples to Edinburgh and from Madrid to Moscow.

14. The second twentieth century

World War II posed a challenge for Europe's cities not seen since the Great Plague of the 14th century, with aerial bombing, artillery battles, sieges, and house-to-house combat, to say nothing of willful destruction, wreaking havoc.[5] In addition, masses of refugees fled cities, during the war and in its aftermath, often with little idea of where to go. Economic life came to a near-halt in many places, confiscation adding to the miseries wrought by occupation or fighting. While much has been written of economic miracles in postwar Europe, the fact that most cities were up and running within a decade is certainly as remarkable as the "30 glorious years" of growth.

What is equally surprising is how little change reconstruction wrought in terms of the urban fabric and "build" in the first postwar decade. Very little realignment of streets or radical innovation in design and land use took place. Even where blocks had been flattened, invisible constraints remained: the underground infrastructure of sewer and water lines, sometimes also gas, electricity, and telephone conduits, and the intangible pattern of property rights. Reconstruction was too urgent for either to be reworked. So old urban

[5] It should be noted that massive bombing raids on cities had little impact on the war, in terms of either material production or morale. If anything, they increased British determination and German mobilization for war production.

cores retained their crooked and narrow streets, which soon became prized pedestrian zones. As for new construction, the general quality was quite poor in the first phase, but the need was desperate. A few of the most heavily damaged centers were singled out for special care, usually building in a pastiche of the former style (Caen, Warsaw) or one that purported to be modern (Rotterdam, East Berlin). Yet these failings must not be allowed to overshadow the quantitative achievement of urban reconstruction, which had to compete for resources with rail, road, and factory investments, to say nothing of a consumption-starved population. Baby booms also soon mandated investment in child care and school facilities.

While technological catching-up helped Europe launch and sustain a great economic boom, from the narrow point of view of cities the actual technological developments of the last half century have proved a mixed blessing. The enormous increase in human capital formation and use has proved a strong centripetal force, the manipulation and communication of symbols replacing the handling of materials in the work of more and more persons. On the other hand, many industries have become footloose, with the drop in transport costs turning industrial location into a complex game, with public policymakers as one, sometimes more than one, player. As for information technology, one can only say that its full impact has yet to make itself clear, let alone to play out.

Of course, the single most influential technology of the period is the internal combustion engine, where Europe incurred, and then largely made up, an enormous quantitative lag relative to the United States. Once hailed as the savior of cities, when horses and their by-products (not least carcasses left where they fell) threatened to choke the streets completely, the motor car has become an ecological monster, almost literally eating the urban fabric. While European cities have devoted far more effort and resources to taming the beast than their more spread-out American counterparts, it remains true that the limits to traffic on both sides of the ocean are set by congestion and not by the supply of alternative modes.[6]

Changes in the structure of output and employment have been profound in the past half century, with strong implications for cities. The old industries have faded badly, their decline fueled by gains in labor productivity and by competition from newly industrialized countries. Service employment, on the other hand, has grown, though in ways that defy easy generalizations about either job quality or locational impacts. It may be true that the largest cities tend toward a polarization between high-skill, high status jobs in information-rich occupations and menial service jobs, but it is easy to exaggerate that trend and forget the myriad of occupations in between [Sassen (1991)]. Those concerned with economic development often argue that services alone – even if they are "basic" in the sense that tourism, entertainment, or higher education are when they serve non-residents – cannot sustain prosperity, that manufacturing is needed. The result has been an intense effort to attract or grow "hi-tech" industries: high growth potential, high value-added, clean. The Holy Grail of regional and national development

[6] It would seem that improving public transport and commuting fares to passes good for a period of time results in greater use, notably at off-peak hours, but not in much modal substitution.

efforts has been to breed new Silicon Valleys, whether in the glens of Scotland, on the Riviera, or in Bavaria. While concentrations have indeed developed, trying to implant this sort of self-organizing and -replicating cluster or complex has proved about as difficult as growing the equally prized truffle.

Economists debate the merits – for both static efficiency and endogenous growth – of diversified versus specialized cities. In our terminology, the distinction is akin to that between central place and network cities. One thesis that harkens back to earlier work by Chinitz (1961) and Jacobs (1969) has recently been modeled by Duranton and Puga (2001). It argues that innovation, the key to growth, thrives in diverse cities, whereas routine production gets shifted toward more specialized agglomerations. The argument raises two points of doubt. The first is that it is difficult to separate diversity from size, since large cities are inherently more diverse than small ones. In fact, as production gets shifted from large to small places, while establishment size typically becomes large as a technology matures (see pp. 3039–3040), specialization will increase at the destination. The second point is that innovation is today the principal "product" of high-tech clusters or complexes of the Silicon Valley type. These specialized breeding grounds of new technology complement their intense internal exchanges of information and people with far-flung ties to universities, linked industries, and clients. These connections embody network relations at their most characteristic. Of course, in such a system many cities specialize away from organized innovation. We conclude that diversity is conducive to innovation in one system (central place), whereas innovation is highly consistent with specialization in the other (network).

Tourism and travel, for leisure and business, have become enormous sectors in Europe, since almost everyone now travels, including the young and old, as well as "guest workers" returning to their native region on paid vacations. Mass seasonal migrations to the seaside and the ski slopes, tours to the high spots of culture, gastronomy, fashion, sport, or art, meetings of all kinds, and weekend jaunts to second residences keep a variety of travel and leisure, as well as home improvement, industries busy. The wonder is that the prime destinations do not succumb, or at least lose their attraction, under the weight of so much popularity. By contrast, urban entertainment, from cinema and theater to street festivals, is caught between the competing forces of more exotic destinations, TV at home, and weekend absences, and has stagnated. Shopping and eating out have clearly overtaken other urban leisure pursuits.

While the general growth of service employment has been a factor of agglomeration, within other-than-leisure services, as with residence and manufacturing location, one can observe areas of decentralization. According to Klodt (1995), who looked at the case of the Federal Republic of Germany, only "disembodied" services, generally referred to as FIRE (finance, insurance, real estate), show large economies of scale (and agglomeration?) and a preference for city centers. Others are either footloose, which means they follow residents to the suburbs, or tied to their customers in peripheral locations. The issue in evaluating European developments would seem to be whether one looks at absolute change or uses the North American (U.S.) pattern as a norm, in which case one continues to see relatively slow decentralization. But this could represent a lag rather than a lasting difference.

15. Urban growth and migration

Housing shortages apart, barriers to mobility have been sharply reduced in postwar Europe. People can move as family, career, life-cycle stage and sometimes just taste dictate. The once-elite notion of dual (or several-fold) residences has spread to the middle class, and a vacation house may turn into a retirement residence. In fact, many city dwellers had always had a second home in the village or small town from which they or their forebears had come. Daily or weekly commuting over considerable distances has also become common, helped by massive investment and favorable pricing strategies in inter-urban transport. European integration, affluence, and globalization have extended mobility well beyond national boundaries and even Europe itself.

Despite the quickening of gross flows, population growth in urban areas – in some cases their decline – still depends on net flows or migration. After about 1960–1970, earlier or later in given areas, the bulk of the new urban dwellers came from abroad rather than from the own countryside. Some countries, such as Britain, France, and Germany, had a long experience of foreign immigration, but not on the scale they experienced now; others were used to seeing their people leave and needed to adjust to the reversal of direction. Spain, Italy, and Ireland are examples. For all the stresses they brought (and experienced), foreign migrants have provided much of the labor supply on which growth has drawn and changed the look and life of Europe's cities.

The origins and motivations of migrants to Europe and its cities (only a few, such as some Europeans repatriated from North Africa to France or Spain took up farming or settled in villages) are varied. Many came from colonial and former colonial possessions overseas, taking advantage of the legacy that gave them a shared language and culture and, though with complications, a nationality. Others were brought in from Southern Europe to the richer countries, in principle strictly to work for a limited time and return. However, many eventually brought families and settled, and the host countries proved unwilling or unable to enforce their return. Political refugees have followed in the aftermath of periods of war, persecution, or unrest, while the opening up of Eastern Europe brought still others.

Not only did international migrants overwhelmingly choose urban residence, but they showed a preference for large cities and industrial conurbations, depressed as the latter's lead industries might be. As may be expected, they clustered strongly. Algerians, Turks, Sumatrans, Jamaicans, Pakistanis, and many other groups make up neighborhoods in and around the large cities, and people the housing estates where miners and steelworkers once lived. The social problems raised by the clash of cultures and the difficulties of employment have become more acute with the generation born in Europe, among whom many are not so much bi-cultural as a-cultural. Resistance to immigration has become the rallying cry of the political Right in Europe, just as the environment has energized the Left, taking over the roles once played by nationalism and worker solidarity, respectively.

16. Recent urban formations

Just as the industrial zones of the nineteenth century tended to coalesce into a single conurbation, new urban entities have come into being, with or without gaining name recognition. Most studied, perhaps is the Dutch "horseshoe" of towns running north from Dordrecht and Rotterdam to Amsterdam in the west and back down past Utrecht in the east. While the identification of Randstad by planners is tied to concerns for inter-urban linkages within the complex, it is equally about preserving green space inside the horseshoe. Europeans are clearly much concerned with sprawl, and prepared to fight it, however aware that they are engaged in a defensive struggle.

A term that characterizes recent change in Europe, and is construed as both criticism and recognition, is *counter-urbanization*, the move out of larger cities to previously rural areas (or to heretofore sleepy local centers and by-passed regions). Leisure activities fuel it, from ski or beach resorts to vacation houses in once nearly abandoned villages, as does the preference of business for greenfield over brownfield locations. Mediterranean Europe has been the recipient of much of this attention, and one can now define a second "banana" of intensive urban and economic development reaching from Ljubljana to Cadiz, that cuts across the traditional core (stretching roughly from Newcastle to Rome).

Within this old core, and outside it too, in central France, Southern Poland, and South Wales, to name a few, are the old industrial areas, or rust belts. Their cities have never freed themselves of dependence on the fading industries that engendered them, and efforts from outside to renew the economic base face almost insuperable odds. In Belgium, for example, the Borinage (Meuse Valley) cannot compete with the Antwerp to Brussels corridor as a location for new ventures. A side effect, peculiar to the case of this bi-community nation, is that the once-subordinate Flemish North has now leapt ahead of the Walloon South. (Urban sprawl also means that suburban residents of the once-francophone Brussels agglomeration increasingly find themselves in Flemish territory.) England too has reversed the pattern that gave rise to the proverb, "where there's muck, there's brass", associating heavy industry with prosperity. The once-bucolic South has greatly overtaken the gritty North, while Germany and France have similar, perhaps less dramatic stories to tell.

In a system perspective, one can grasp that underneath the apparent stability of the urban structures and national identities a sea change has actually taken place. Its centerpiece is a certain weakening of the hierarchic national systems with their over-development of the national capital at the expense of both regional centers and network cities. An exception so far, at least concerns the new nations formed by the breakup of the Soviet Union and some of its satellites, where fresh nationalism also enhances the capital city. The factors behind this change are pretty clear: trade liberalization, leading to European integration and globalization, and political decentralization fueled by concerns for equity and by demands for autonomy at the regional level. At the policy level, what began as efforts to prop up backward areas and prevent exodus has become a positive policy of devolution and regional autonomy in many countries.

Decentralizing forces respond to and in turn strengthen a marked revival of regional identity, in some cases very strong (Catalonia), elsewhere a bit forced and artificial, that has given a corresponding boost to provincial or regional capitals. Cities with cosmopolitan identity and network ties, often of long standing, have also benefited from the loosening of ties to the center. They were long stifled by the territorial states to which they belong and thus subordinated to the capital. Germany (the Federal Republic) offers the best example, having profited from the half-century isolation of once-dominant Berlin to develop at least five moderately-sized but genuinely world-class cities: Hamburg, Frankfurt, Munich, Stuttgart, and Düsseldorf. However, France, Britain, Italy, and Spain offer examples as well. Most telling are cases, such as Barcelona, Florence, and Strasbourg, where a city has both a strong regional role and a real cosmopolitan reach. Swiss and Dutch cities, never subordinated to a primate capital, also display this positive local/global mix.

17. Urban spatial structure in post-industrial Europe

After a relatively quiescent period following reconstruction, many large cities became the object of plans rivaling the most ambitious of any earlier period. Vast renewal projects have transformed parts of Paris, London, Vienna, Barcelona, and, most recently and dramatically, Berlin. While each is distinctive, and the focus of critical comment and contestation, one can say that recent projects at least pay lip service to modern ideas of participation, ecological and cultural sensitivity, and the need to sustain and preserve the historic urban fabric. To be sure, balancing the demands of the automobile with a livable townscape calls for expensive investments in below-ground roads, rail lines, and parking structures. But they have often been made.

Planners also seek to retain a socio-economic mix within the city, despite housing costs that promote gentrification. This objective applies equally to places of business, the fear being that small independent firms, whether workshops or retail establishments, will be squeezed out. Gentrification does have the advantage that the upper-income targets show a clear-cut preference for rehabilitated old buildings and distinctive products and services. This counters the "urban removal" reflex of planners, bureaucrats, and developers, who like to wipe the ground clean, start afresh, and avoid risk with big tenants. For a time, housing shortages all over Europe enforced social mixing by not allowing people to be too choosy about the neighborhood where they settled. There are still urban areas with a real mix, but one consequence of large-scale foreign immigration is to discourage such integration. To be fair, issues of schooling may play a greater role in this issue than unvarnished racism or xenophobia. Of course, relegating working-class and migrant families to the periphery does not mean that social problems are reduced or even excluded from the city center.

While city centers are more lively and better preserved in Europe than in the United States, the peripheral patterns typical of the latter are present as well. Sprawl, complete with villa estates, large malls, commercial strip development, reliance on automobiles, etc., can be found at the edge of every city, but so can pedestrian zones in old village and town centers, clustered dwellings, green spaces, and other anti-sprawl measures. Perhaps the most telling difference from one side of the Atlantic to the other, at least to one observer, is the provision in Europe of paths for foot and bicycle traffic in many sub- and ex-urban areas. The sorry sight, so frequent in the U.S., of joggers or walkers having to fight traffic in lightly built-up places is much less common in Europe. But road congestion, whether of commuters and trucks or on weekends and at holiday times, is certainly no less serious.

One phenomenon that we have so far not evoked, although it has occasioned enormous study, is New Towns. One theme of this chapter is that the creation of vital urban entities or cities is something of an art, perhaps a lost art. Cities born in the 19th century have a poor record of standing on their own, in terms of renewing their economic base and sustaining their attraction to outsiders and natives. The 20th century has fared no better in this respect. This is not for want of attempts to generate true cities, as opposed to suburbs or renamed clusters of pre-existing settlements. New Towns have been touted as the answer to sprawl and to congestion in capitals. In fact, they have turned out to be reasonably successful suburbs, more safe and comfortable than vital and exciting. Even where a reasonable balance of housing and employment was achieved, most workers commuted in or out, contrary to the goal of the planners. Commuting is the present-day equivalent of residential crowding in the industrial era: consumer behavior refuses to conform to the preferences and patterns planners think they should embrace.

Finally, the secular process of *triage* among very small centers continues. Many lose their urban character, while the remaining ones extend their reach and the range of their services. Enhanced mobility, along with greatly increased demands for goods and services, drive the process. With everyone attending secondary school, visiting doctors, and indulging in shopping and other social leisure pursuits, only services of a relatively high standard are viable, and they require a sizeable market. The historic process of urbanization, at least in the central place system, seems akin to the "Big Bang" model of cosmology. All centers were created very early, and their subsequent evolution is principally a structuring and selection to form an orderly hierarchic system. On the other hand, the formation of new centers, of concern to economic geographers and location theorists, responds to the logic of the network system.

18. Conclusion

Although cities are human artifacts, perhaps the most impressive tangible achievements of what is aptly called *civ*ilization, a historical examination reveals that, once established, they take on a life of their own. In particular, public policy can do only so much to stimulate or contain growth, to renew the economic base, or to instill a spirit of enterprise and creativity. On the other hand, cities show remarkable resilience. Very few decline much or disappear if they once reach a reasonable threshold, and they have time and again demonstrated the ability to recover from grave difficulties. This applies in the short and medium term to traumatic events – visitations from the four horsemen of the apocalypse – but also to a longer-term eclipse caused by political or other factors. With changes in technology, industrial structure, openness to movement of goods, capital, and persons, and political regimes, long-dormant places can thrive once more, drawing new strengths from very old traditions. The obverse is that cities, especially those whose activity operates through networks, are apt to stay at the top for only a limited time before competition, technological obsolescence, or the stifling effects of politically imposed controls drive high-level activity elsewhere.

Taking both the resistance and the resilience of cities together, it is perhaps not so surprising that the European system should rest so heavily on places many centuries old, despite the enormous increase in the urban population and the transformations in urban economies. Models of economic location, like policies for local development, while not naively or passively extrapolating from the past, must take path dependence into account. And admirers of cities can take heart from the past. Cities seem to have fared better than a cold calculation of costs and benefits, as well as risks, would suggest. Perhaps they will also show greater staying power in a time when advances in communication and transport appear (threaten?) to render agglomeration obsolete.

References

Arthur, W.B. (1988). "Urban systems and historical path dependence". In: Ausubel, J.H., Herman, R. (Eds.), Cities and Their Vital Systems: Infrastructure, Past, Present, and Future. National Academy Press, Washington, DC, pp. 85–97.

Aydalot, P., Keeble, D. (Eds.) (1988). High Technology Industry and Innovative Environments: The European Experience. Routledge, London.

Chinitz, B. (1961). "Contrasts in agglomeration: New York and Pittsburgh". American Economic Review 51, 279–289.

De Long, B., Shleifer, A. (1993). "Princes and merchants: European city growth before the industrial revolution". Journal of Law and Economics 36, 671–702.

De Vries, J. (1984). European Urbanization, 1500–1800. Harvard Univ. Press, Cambridge, MA.

Dematteis, G. (1999). "Introduction: cities as nodes of urban networks". In: Bonavero, P., Dematteis, G., Sforzi, F. (Eds.), The Italian Urban System: Towards European Integration. Ashgate, London.

Diamond, J. (1997). Guns, Germs, and Steel: The Fates of Human Societies. Norton, New York.

Duranton, G., Puga, D. (2001). "Nursery cities: urban diversity, process innovation, and the life-cycle of product". American Economic Review 91, 1454–1477.

Epstein, S.R. (2000). Freedom and Growth: The Rise of States and Markets in Europe, 1300–1750. Routledge, London.

François, E. (1978). "Des Républiques marchandes aux capitales politiques: Remarques sur la hiérarchie urbaine du Saint-Empire à l'époque moderne". Revue d'Histoire Moderne et Contemporaine 25, 587–603.

Gaillard, J. (1977). Paris la ville, 1852–1870. Champion, Paris.

Glennie, P. (1998). "Industrial change, 1500–1740, and the problem of proto-industrialization". In: Butlin, R.A., Dodgshon, R.A. (Eds.), An Historical Geography of Europe. Clarendon, Oxford, pp. 259–279.
Hoffman, P. (1996). Growth in a Traditional Society: The French Countryside, 1450–1815. Princeton Univ. Press, Princeton, NJ.
Hohenberg, P.M. (1991). "Urban manufactures in the proto-industrial economy: culture versus commerce?" In: Berg, M. (Ed.), Markets and Manufacturers in Early Industrial Europe. Routledge, London, pp. 159–172.
Hohenberg, P.M., Lees, L.H. (1995). The Making of Urban Europe, 1000–1994. Harvard Univ. Press, Cambridge, MA.
Hohenberg, P.M., Lees, L.H. (1996). "Urban systems and economic growth: town populations in metropolitan hinterlands, 1600–1850". In: Clark, P., Lepetit, B. (Eds.), Capital Cities and their Hinterlands in Early Modern Europe. Scolar Press, Aldershot.
INSEE-IGN (2002). Territoires vécus: organisation territoriale de l'emploi et des services. Map prepared by INRA for the French government.
Jacobs, J. (1969). The Economy of Cities. Random House, New York.
Jones, E.L. (1981). The European Miracle. Cambridge Univ. Press, Cambridge, UK.
Klodt, H. (1995). "Structural change in urban growth". In: Giersch, H. (Ed.), Urban Agglomeration and Economic Growth. Springer-Verlag, Berlin, pp. 157–182.
Leboutte, R. (Ed.) (1996). Proto-industrialization: Recent Research and New Perspectives. Droz, Geneva.
Mendels, F. (1971). "Proto-industrialization: the first phase of the industrialization process". Journal of Economic History 32, 241–261.
Mokyr, J. (1995). "Urbanization, technological progress, and economic growth". In: Giersch, H. (Ed.), Urban Agglomeration and Economic Growth. Springer-Verlag, Berlin, pp. 3–37.
Mumford, L. (1961). The City in History. Harcourt Brace, New York.
North, D.C. (1990). Institutions, Institutional Change, and Economic Performance. Cambridge Univ. Press, Cambridge, UK.
Piore, M.J., Sabel, C.F. (1984). The Second Industrial Divide. Basic Books, New York.
Robson, B.T. (1977). Urban Growth: An Approach. Methuen, London.
Sassen, S. (1991). The Global City. Princeton Univ. Press, Princeton, NJ.
Verhulst, A. (1999). The Rise of Cities in North-West Europe. Cambridge Univ. Press, Cambridge, UK.
Williamson, J. (1994). "Leaving the farm to go to the city: Did they leave soon enough?" In: James, J., Thomas, M. (Eds.), Capitalism in Context: Essays in Economic Development and Cultural Change. Univ. of Chicago Press, Chicago.

COLOUR FIGURES

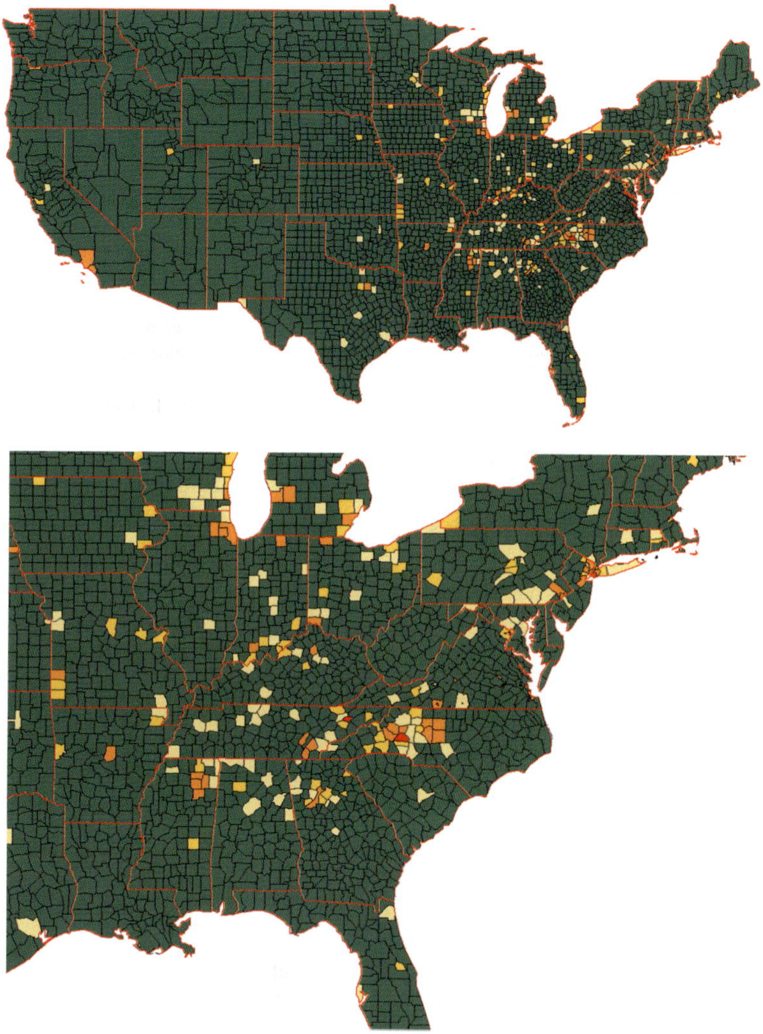

Chapter 49, Fig. 1, p. 2122. Furniture employment (SIC 25) per square mile. Fourth quarter 2002; source: Dun and Bradstreet. Red: greater than 10; orange: 4 to 10; dark yellow: 2 to 3; light yellow: 1 to 2; green: 0.

Handbook of Regional and Urban Economics, Volume 4. Edited by J.V. Henderson and J.F. Thisse

DOI: 10.1016/S0169-7218(04)07401-5

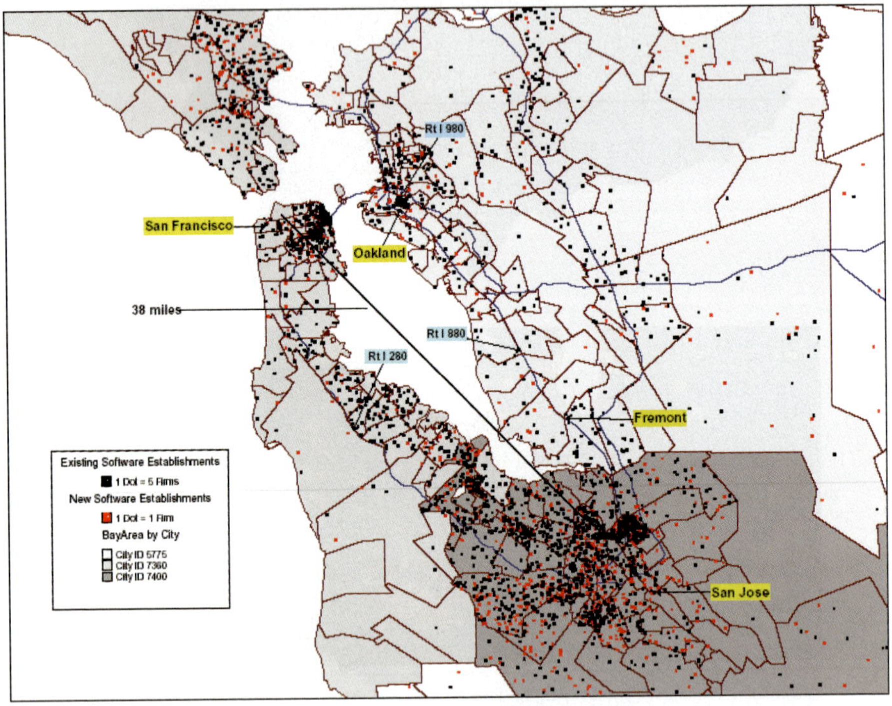

Chapter 49, Fig. 2, p. 2123. Existing and new software establishments in Silicon Valley. Fourth quarter 1997; source: Dun and Bradstreet.

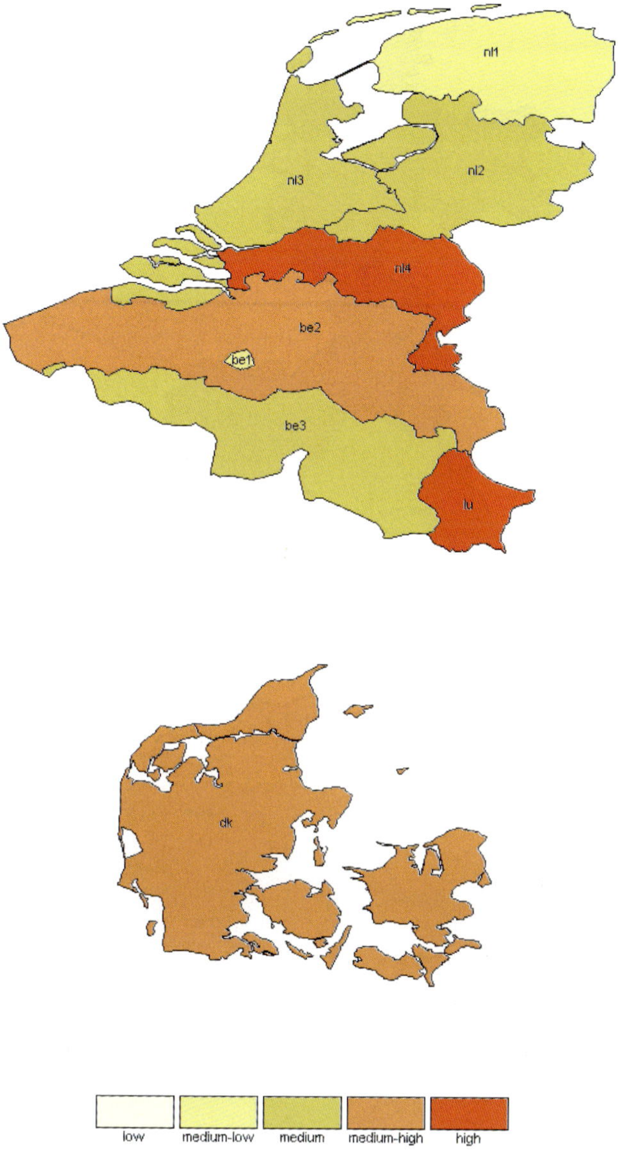

Chapter 62, p. 2783

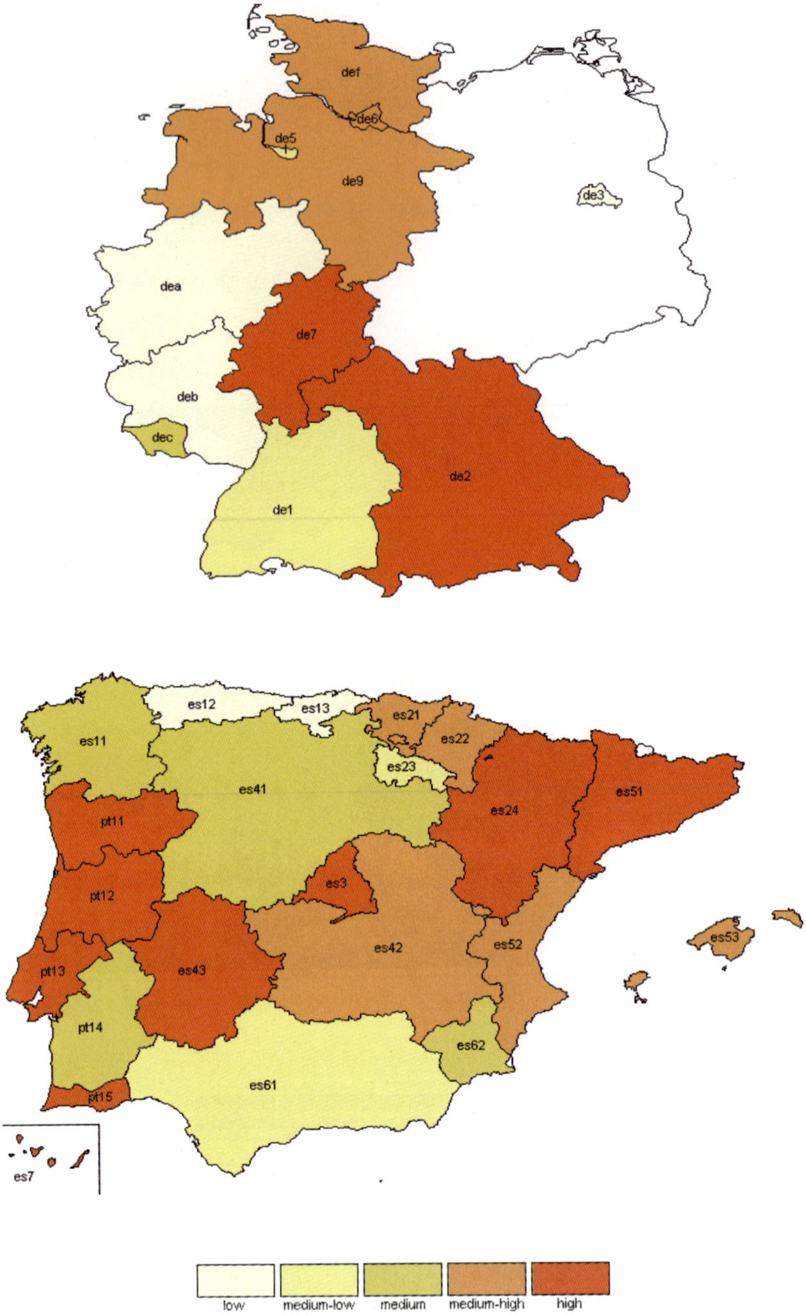

Chapter 62, p. 2784

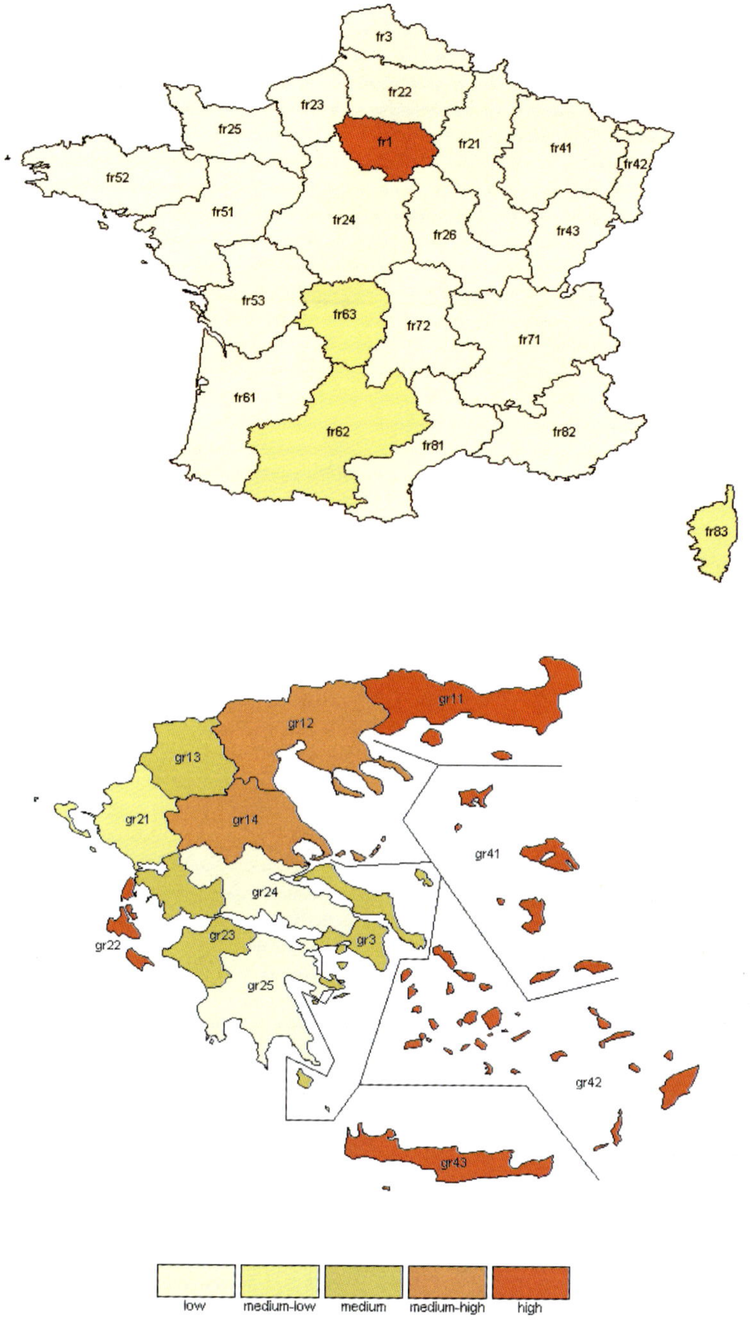

Chapter 62, p. 2785

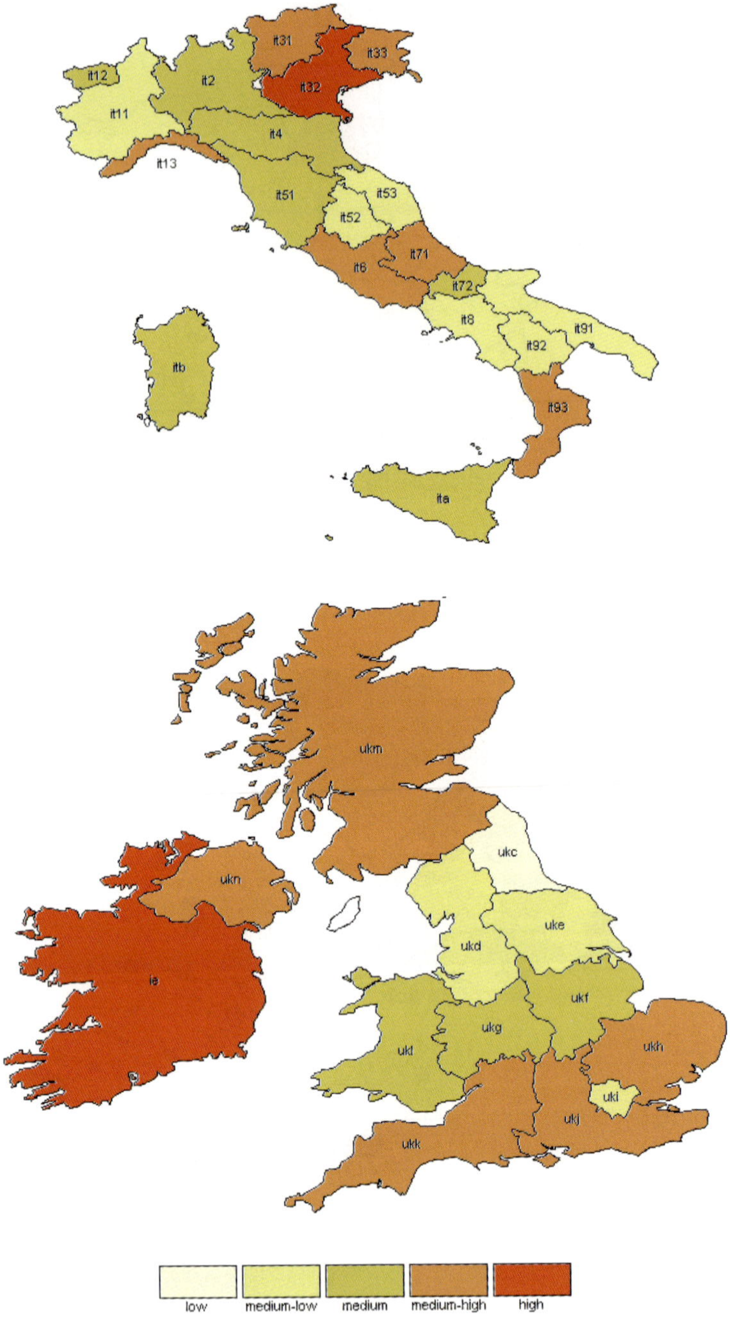

Chapter 62, p. 2786

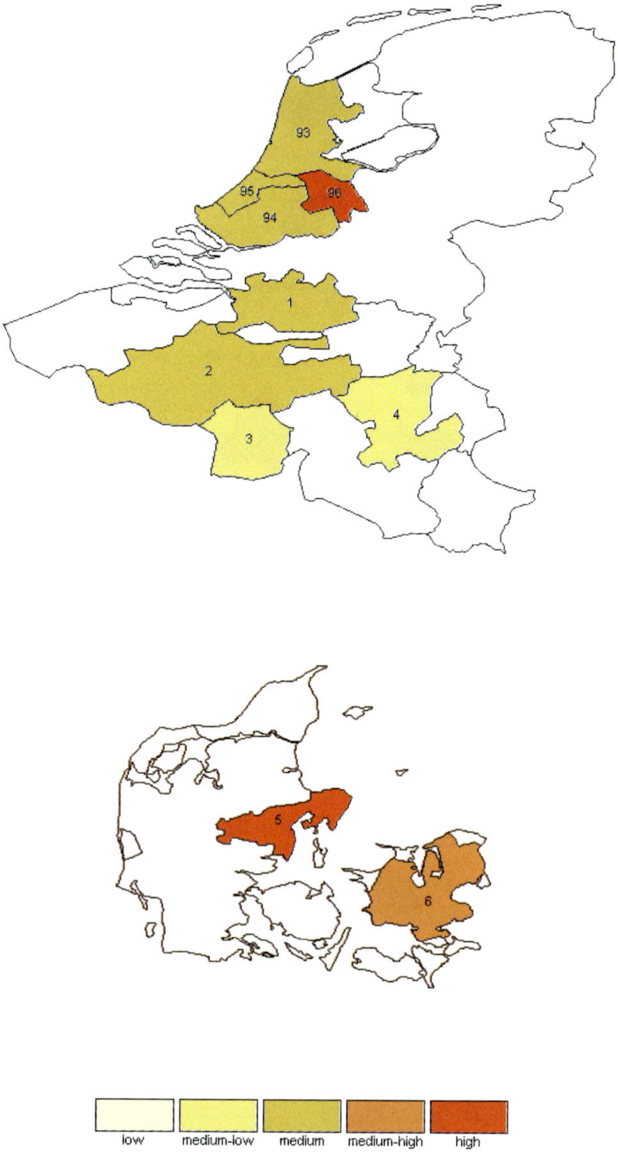

Chapter 62, p. 2787

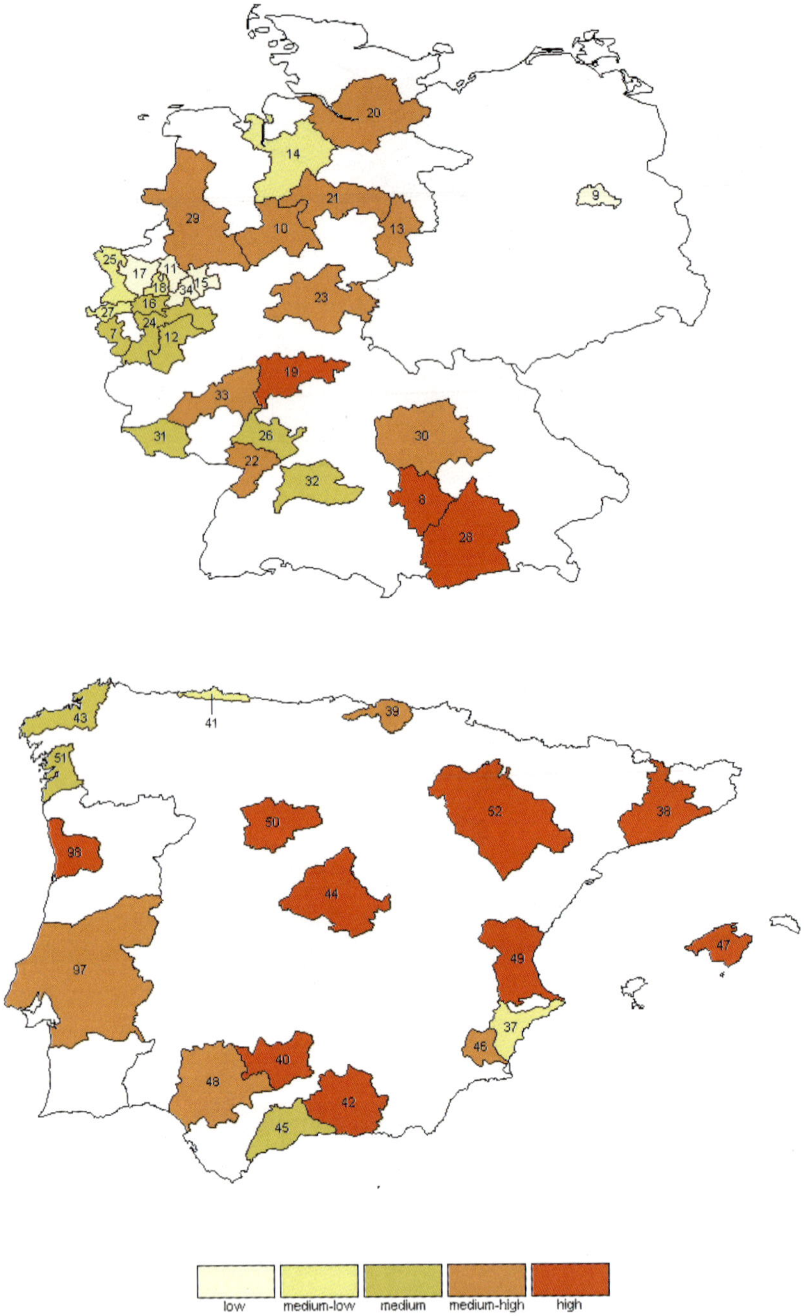

Chapter 62, p. 2788

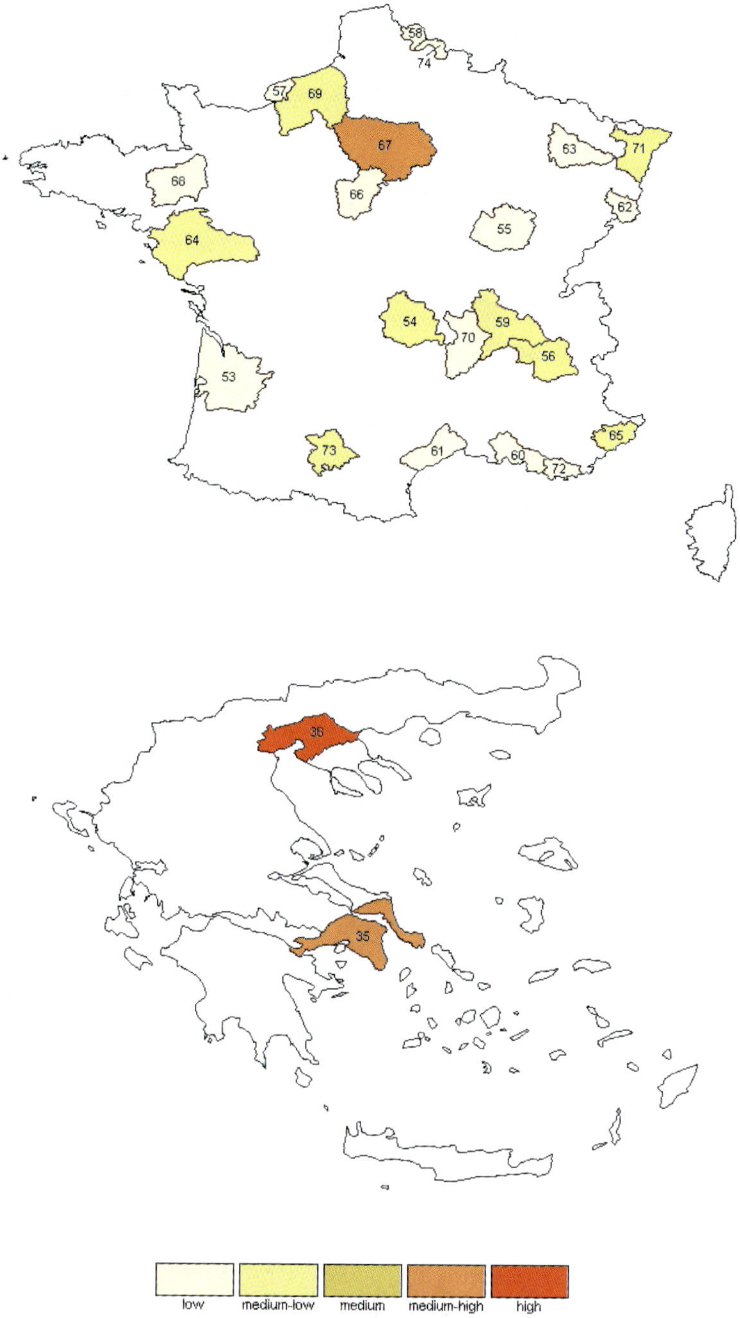

Chapter 62, p. 2789

Chapter 62, p. 2790

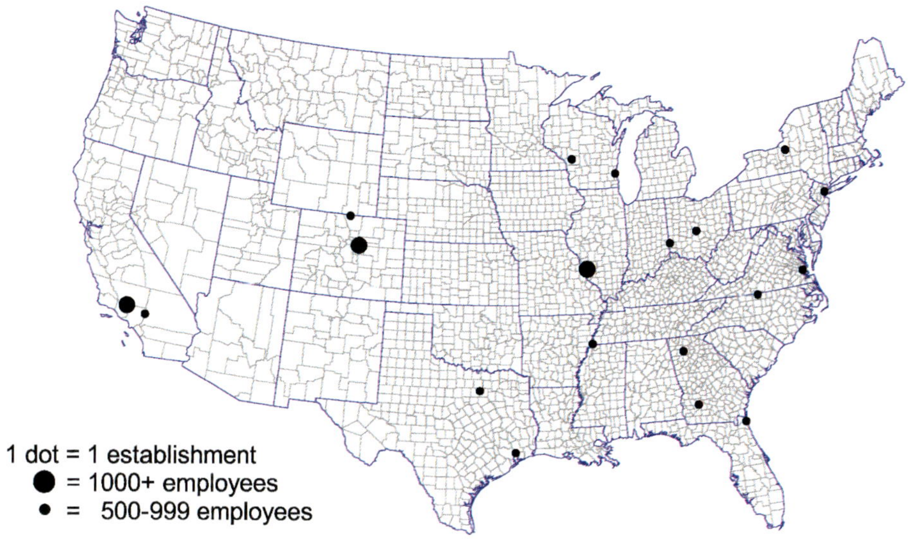

Chapter 63, Fig. 1, p. 2803. Location of large breweries (CBP 1999).

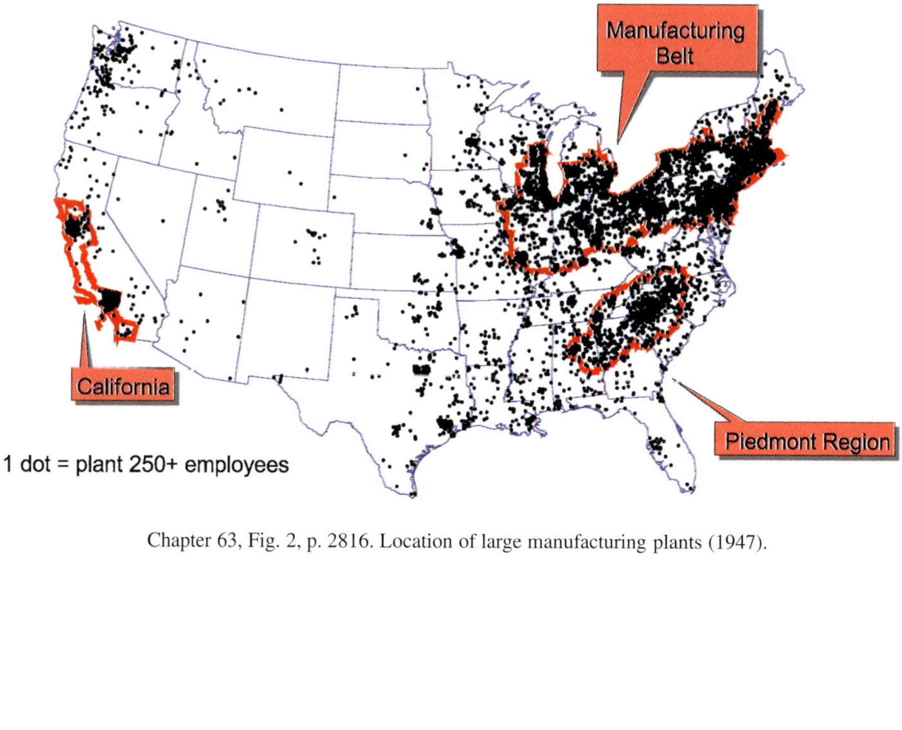

Chapter 63, Fig. 2, p. 2816. Location of large manufacturing plants (1947).

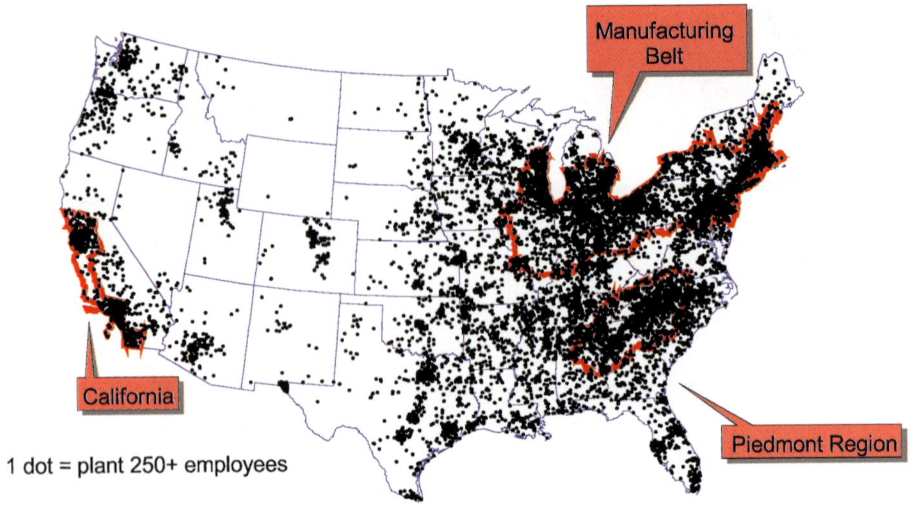

Chapter 63, Fig. 3, p. 2818. Location of large manufacturing plants (1999).

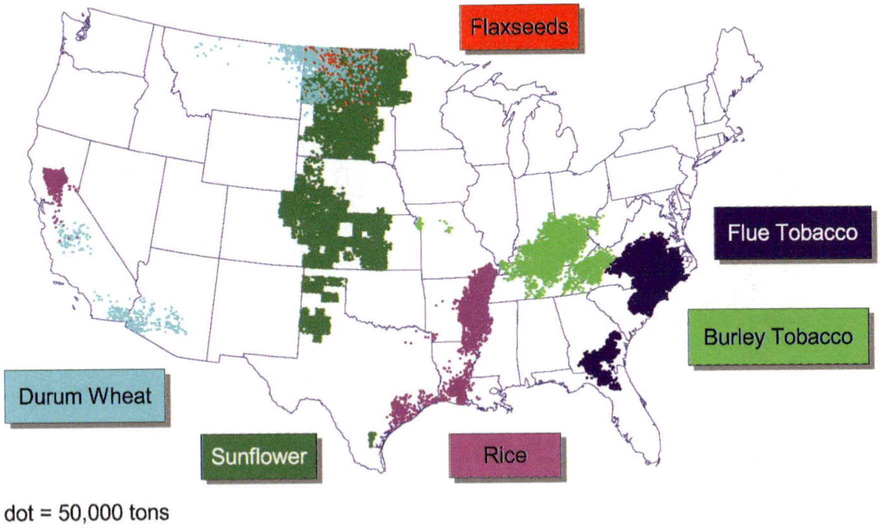

Chapter 63, Fig. 4, p. 2832. Location of Durum Wheat, Rice, Flue Tobaco, and Burley Tobaco.

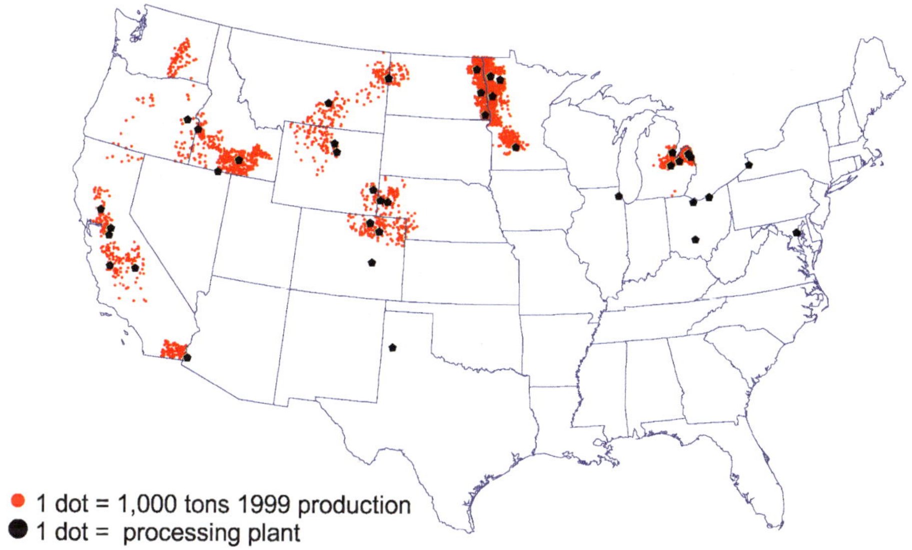

Chapter 63, Fig. 5, p. 2833. Location of Sugar Beet Plants and Sugar Beet Crops.

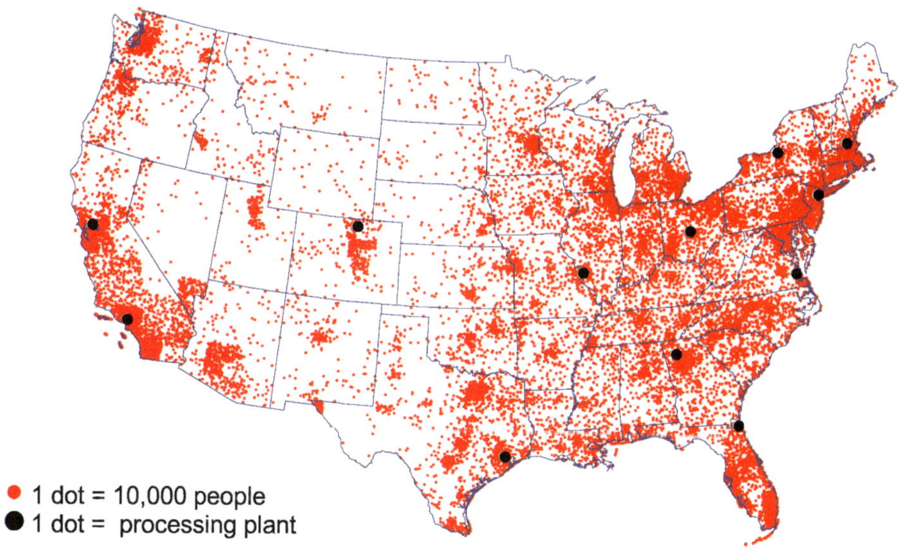

Chapter 63, Fig. 6, p. 2835. Location of Anheuser–Busch breweries and population (2000).

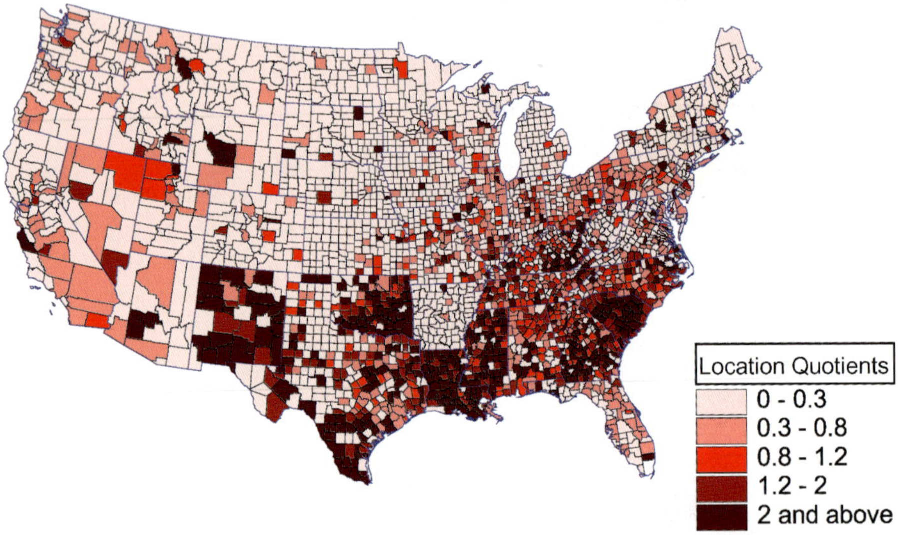

Chapter 63, Fig. 7, p. 2838. Location of consumer lending (NAICS 522291) (location quotient by county).

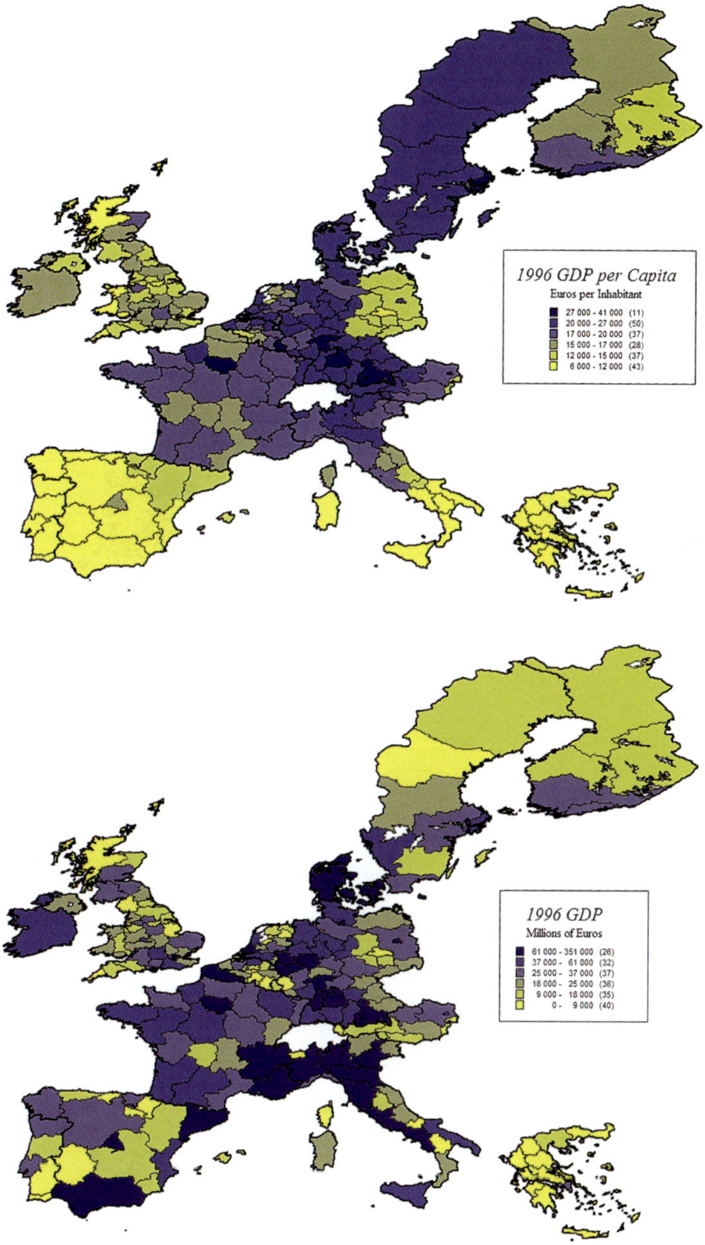

Chapter 64, Fig. 1, p. 2853. Per capita (top) and total (bottom) GDP in European NUTS 2 regions.

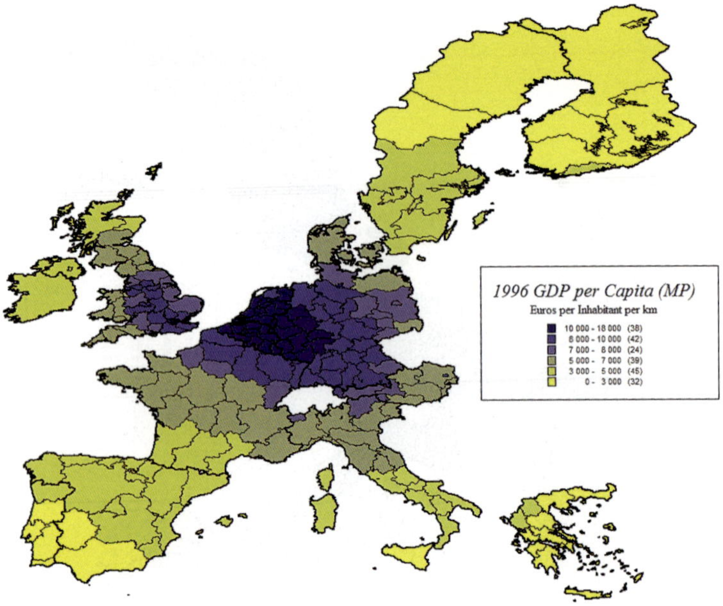

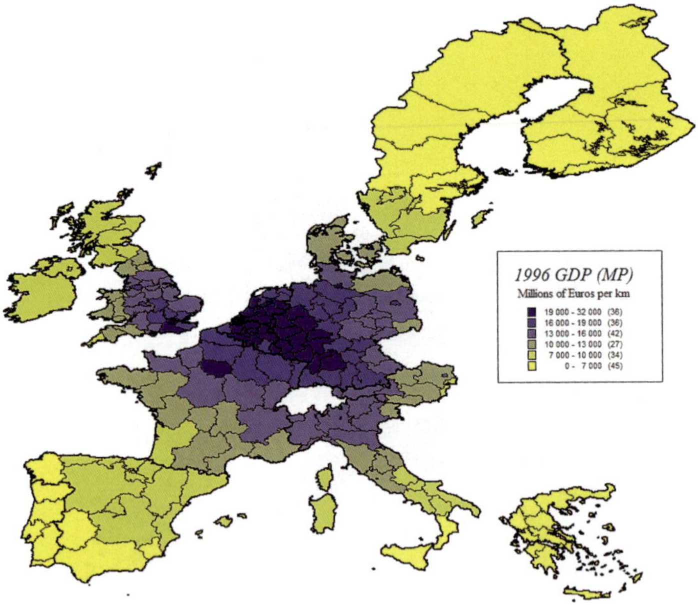

Chapter 64, Fig. 3, p. 2856. Market potential of per capita (top) and total (bottom) GDP in European NUTS2 regions.

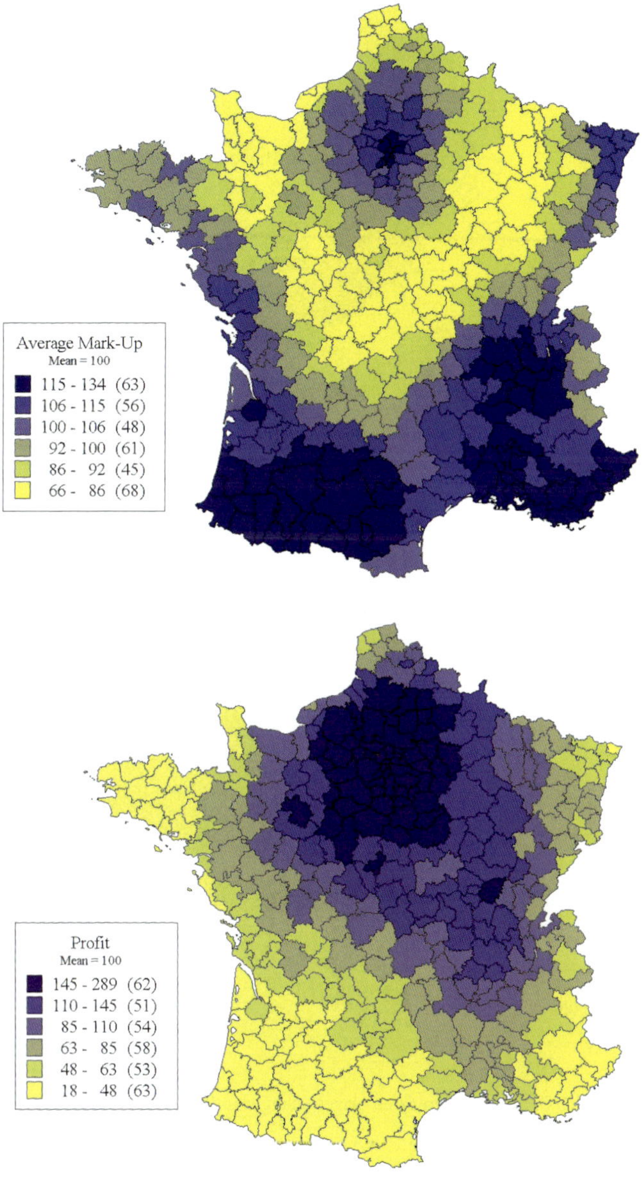

Chapter 64, Fig. 4, p. 2888. Average mark-up (top), variable profit per plant (bottom).

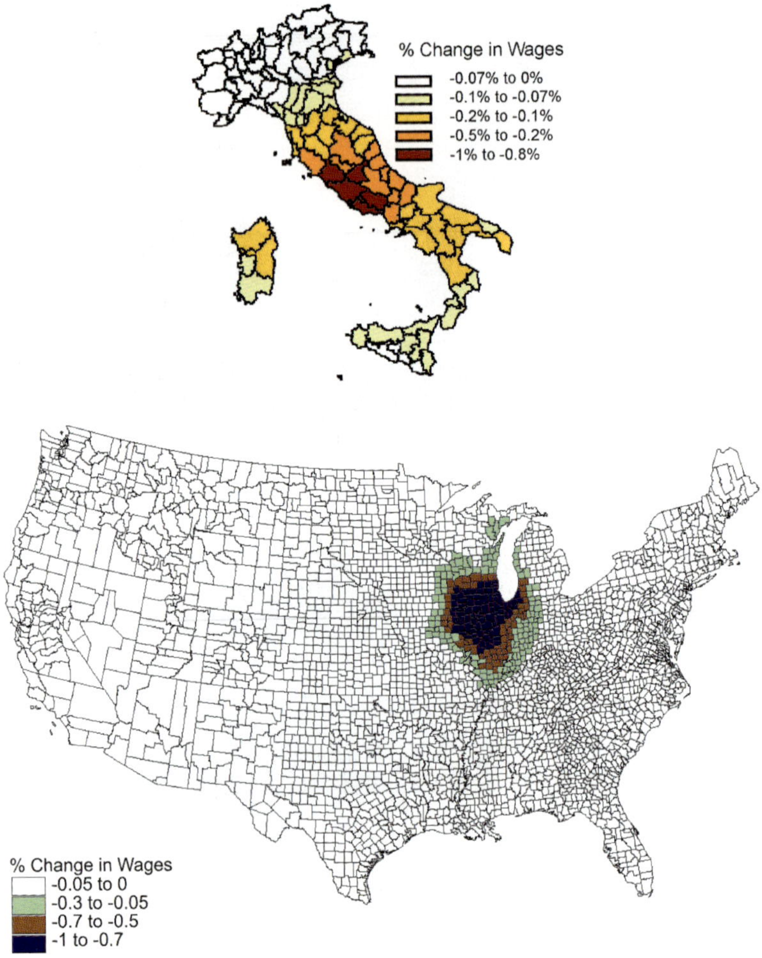

Chapter 64, Fig. 5, p. 2898. Simulated wages changes in Italy (top) and the U.S. (bottom).

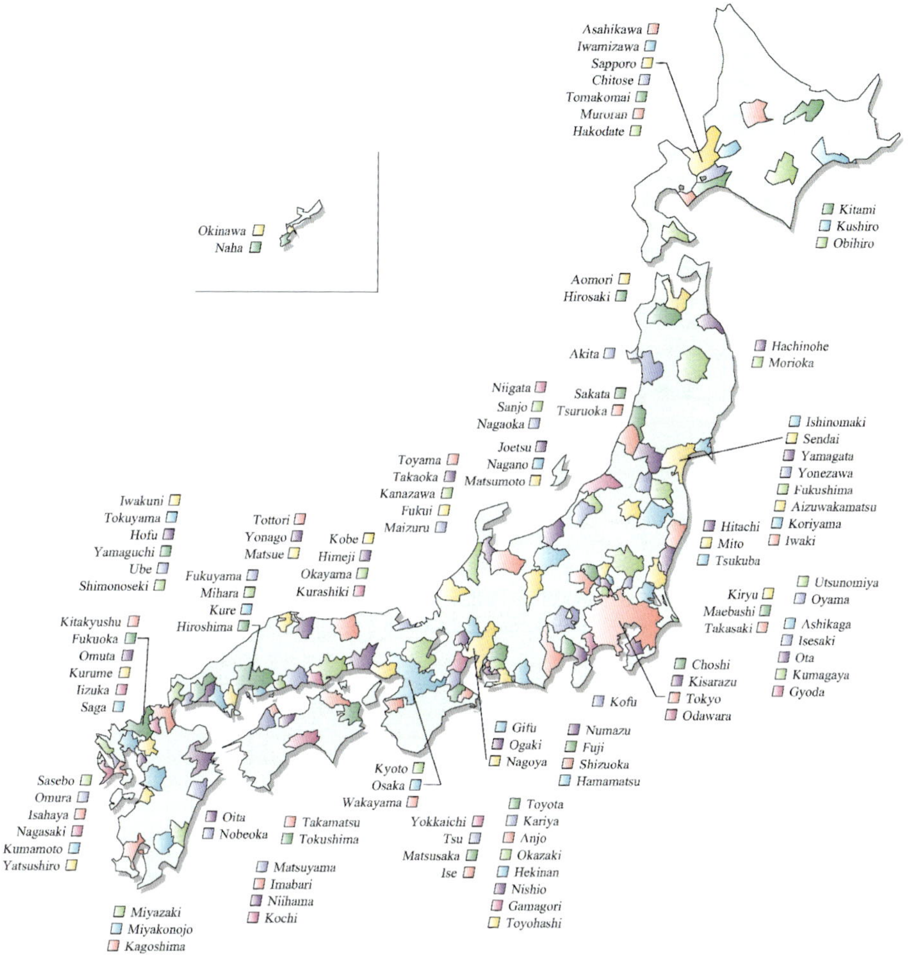

Chapter 65, Fig. 1, p. 2914. Metropolitan employment areas.

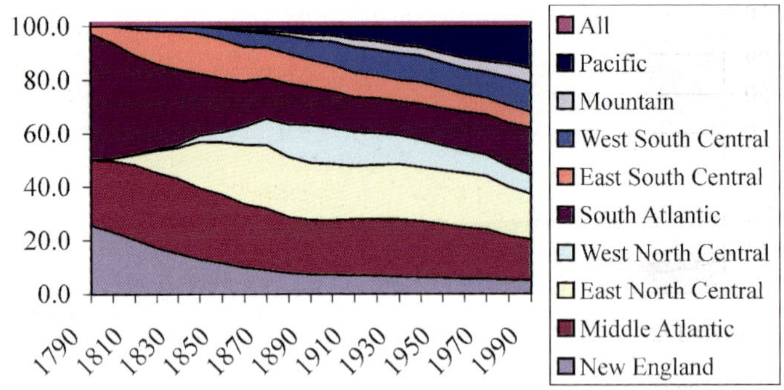

Chapter 66, Fig. 1, p. 2984. U.S. population distribution, 1790–1990 (percent).

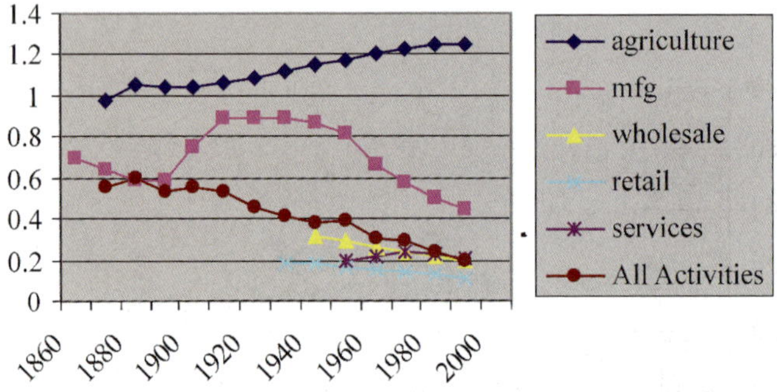

Chapter 66, Fig. 2, p. 2988. U.S. regional specialization, 1860–1990. *Source*. Kim (1995, 1998). Index of regional specialization is based on Krugman (1991).

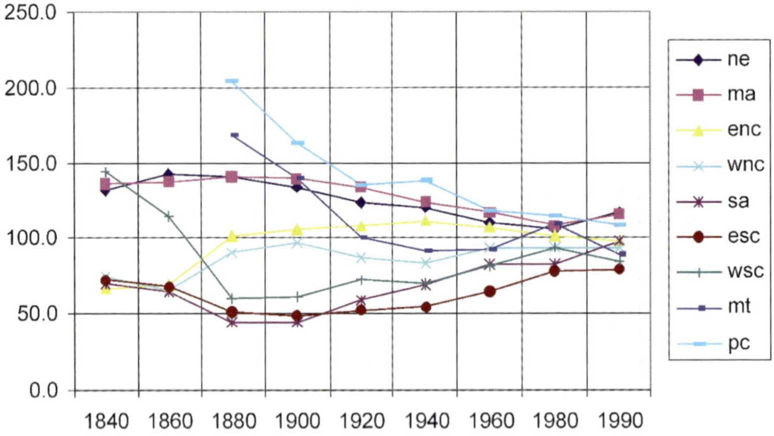

Chapter 66, Fig. 3, p. 2992. Regional income per capita, 1840–1990 (U.S. = 100). *Sources*. Easterlin (1960, 1961), Statistical Abstract of the U.S., various years.

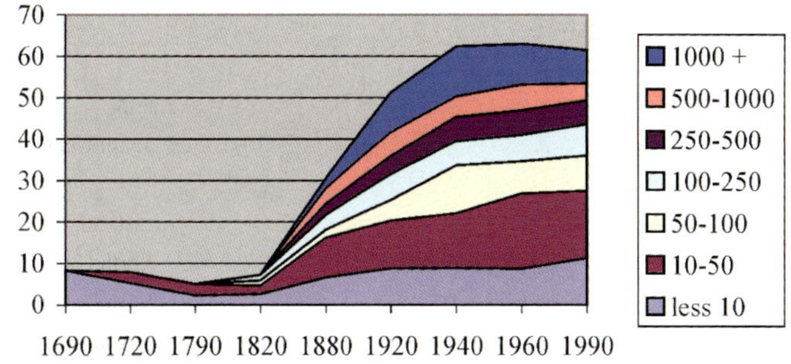

Chapter 66, Fig. 4, p. 2997. U.S. urban population by size, 1690–1990 (percent). *Sources*: see Table 2. City size is in thousands.

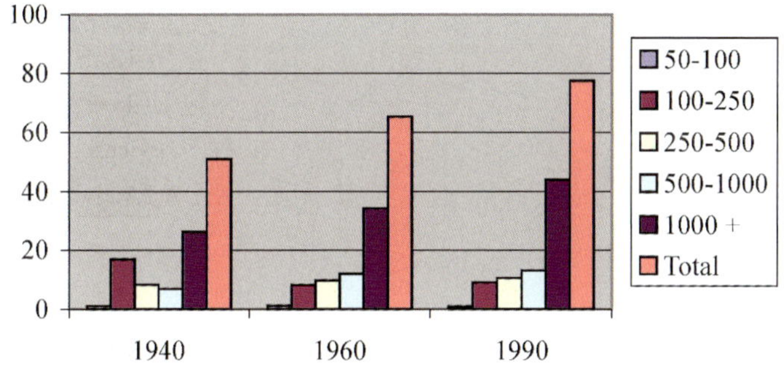

Chapter 66, Fig. 5, p. 3000. U.S. metropolitan population by size, 1940–1990 (percent). *Sources*: see Table 3. Metropolitan size is in thousands.

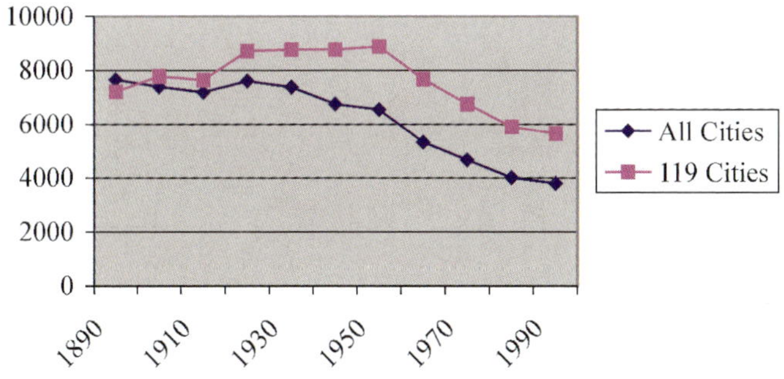

Chapter 66, Fig. 6, p. 3005. Population density of cities, 1890–1990 (persons per square mile). *Sources*: see Kim (2002).

AUTHOR INDEX

n indicates citation in a footnote.

SUBJECT INDEX

HANDBOOKS IN ECONOMICS

1. HANDBOOK OF MATHEMATICAL ECONOMICS (in 4 volumes)
   Volumes 1, 2 and 3 edited by Kenneth J. Arrow and Michael D. Intriligator
   Volume 4 edited by Werner Hildenbrand and Hugo Sonnenschein
2. HANDBOOK OF ECONOMETRICS (in 6 volumes)
   Volumes 1, 2 and 3 edited by Zvi Griliches and Michael D. Intriligator
   Volume 4 edited by Robert F. Engle and Daniel L. McFadden
   Volume 5 edited by James J. Heckman and Edward Leamer
   Volume 6 is in preparation (editors James J. Heckman and Edward Leamer)
3. HANDBOOK OF INTERNATIONAL ECONOMICS (in 3 volumes)
   Volumes 1 and 2 edited by Ronald W. Jones and Peter B. Kenen
   Volume 3 edited by Gene M. Grossman and Kenneth Rogoff
4. HANDBOOK OF PUBLIC ECONOMICS (in 4 volumes)
   Edited by Alan J. Auerbach and Martin Feldstein
5. HANDBOOK OF LABOR ECONOMICS (in 5 volumes)
   Volumes 1 and 2 edited by Orley C. Ashenfelter and Richard Layard
   Volumes 3A, 3B and 3C edited by Orley C. Ashenfelter and David Card
6. HANDBOOK OF NATURAL RESOURCE AND ENERGY ECONOMICS
   (in 3 volumes). Edited by Allen V. Kneese and James L. Sweeney
7. HANDBOOK OF REGIONAL AND URBAN ECONOMICS (in 4 volumes)
   Volume 1 edited by Peter Nijkamp
   Volume 2 edited by Edwin S. Mills
   Volume 3 edited by Paul C. Cheshire and Edwin S. Mills
   Volume 4 edited by J. Vernon Henderson and Jacques-François Thisse
8. HANDBOOK OF MONETARY ECONOMICS (in 2 volumes)
   Edited by Benjamin Friedman and Frank Hahn
9. HANDBOOK OF DEVELOPMENT ECONOMICS (in 4 volumes)
   Volumes 1 and 2 edited by Hollis B. Chenery and T.N. Srinivasan
   Volumes 3A and 3B edited by Jere Behrman and T.N. Srinivasan
10. HANDBOOK OF INDUSTRIAL ORGANIZATION (in 3 volumes)
    Volumes 1 and 2 edited by Richard Schmalensee and Robert R. Willig
    Volume 3 is in preparation (editors Mark Armstrong and Robert H. Porter)

11. HANDBOOK OF GAME THEORY with Economic Applications (in 3 volumes)
Edited by Robert J. Aumann and Sergiu Hart

12. HANDBOOK OF DEFENSE ECONOMICS (in 1 volume)
Edited by Keith Hartley and Todd Sandler

13. HANDBOOK OF COMPUTATIONAL ECONOMICS (in 2 volumes)
Volume 1 edited by Hans M. Amman, David A. Kendrick and John Rust
Volume 2 is in preparation (editors Kenneth L. Judd and Leigh Tesfatsion)

14. HANDBOOK OF POPULATION AND FAMILY ECONOMICS (in 2 volumes)
Edited by Mark R. Rosenzweig and Oded Stark

15. HANDBOOK OF MACROECONOMICS (in 3 volumes)
Edited by John B. Taylor and Michael Woodford

16. HANDBOOK OF INCOME DISTRIBUTION (in 1 volume)
Edited by Anthony B. Atkinson and François Bourguignon

17. HANDBOOK OF HEALTH ECONOMICS (in 2 volumes)
Edited by Anthony J. Culyer and Joseph P. Newhouse

18. HANDBOOK OF AGRICULTURAL ECONOMICS (in 4 volumes)
Edited by Bruce L. Gardner and Gordon C. Rausser

19. HANDBOOK OF SOCIAL CHOICE AND WELFARE (in 2 volumes)
Volume 1 edited by Kenneth J. Arrow, Amartya K. Sen and Kotaro Suzumura
Volume 2 is in preparation (editors Kenneth J. Arrow, Amartya K. Sen and Kotaro Suzumura)

20. HANDBOOK OF ENVIRONMENTAL ECONOMICS (in 3 volumes)
Volume 1 is edited by Karl-Göran Mäler and Jeffrey R. Vincent
Volumes 2 and 3 are in preparation (editors Karl-Göran Mäler and Jeffrey R. Vincent)

21. HANDBOOK OF THE ECONOMICS OF FINANCE (in 2 volumes)
Edited by George M. Constantinides, Milton Harris and René M. Stulz

All published volumes available

FORTHCOMING TITLES

HANDBOOK OF EXPERIMENTAL ECONOMICS RESULTS
Editors Charles Plott and Vernon L. Smith

HANDBOOK ON THE ECONOMICS OF GIVING, RECIPROCITY AND ALTRUISM
Editors Serge-Christophe Kolm and Jean Mercier Ythier

HANDBOOK ON THE ECONOMICS OF ART AND CULTURE
Editors Victor Ginsburgh and David Throsby

HANDBOOK OF ECONOMIC GROWTH
Editors Philippe Aghion and Steven N. Durlauf

HANDBOOK OF LAW AND ECONOMICS
Editors A. Mitchell Polinsky and Steven Shavell

HANDBOOK OF ECONOMIC FORECASTING
Editors Graham Elliott, Clive W.J. Granger and Allan Timmermann

HANDBOOK OF THE ECONOMICS OF EDUCATION
Editors Eric Hanushek and Finis Welch